Conscience in Ac...

Kim Dae-jung

Conscience in Action

The Autobiography of Kim Dae-jung

Foreword by Lee Hee-ho

Kim Dae-jung

Translated by Jeon Seung-hee

ISBN 978-981-10-7622-0   ISBN 978-981-10-7623-7   (eBook)
https://doi.org/10.1007/978-981-10-7623-7

Library of Congress Control Number: 2018932369

This Palgrave Macmillan imprint is published by the registered company Springer Nature Singapore Pte Ltd. part of Springer Nature.
The registered company address is: 152 Beach Road, #21-01/04 Gateway East, Singapore 189721, Singapore

This book is a translation of the two-volume Kim Dae-jung Jaseojeon ("Autobiography of Kim Dae-jung"), Seoul: Samin, 2010. The translator has tried to be faithful to the original, but also wishes to clarify that it is not a verbatim translation. In translating Korean proper names and nouns, I have tried to apply individual preferences, as well as customary practices, which include the official South Korean transcribing system for South Korean names and the North Korean system for North Korean names. The final version was proofread by Nikki Van Noy.

Foreword: To My Dear Husband

It has already been almost a year since you passed away. My heart aches when I envision your smile. Our house remains the same. I planted our favorite safinias, crape myrtles, globe amaranths, and pansies in the garden. How much you would have enjoyed seeing these beautiful flowers!

We often enjoyed drinking coffee and looking at the garden from our living room together. Feeding the sparrows that visited our house was your only leisure activity. These days, even more sparrows visit our house, waiting to be fed. Whenever I hear them chirp, I am reminded of you and I cannot help tearing up.

When you began writing your autobiography, you said, "I'll write everything truthfully and dedicate it to history and our descendants." Reading your finished work, I am reminded in rapid succession of the various periods we spent together. It makes me feel as if you're alive and here with me. In retrospect, I really did not know that such a difficult life lay ahead of us.

You lived a truly eventful life filled with adversity. In *Romans*, there is a phrase that reads: "Our present sufferings are not worth comparing with the glory that will be revealed in us." As if to illustrate this point, your dramatic life was a continuation of unimaginable hardships. You survived several life-or-death crises. You did not give up your beliefs despite all the hardships you endured through exiles, house arrests, and imprisonment. You resolutely refused to compromise with the forces that oppressed you, and you even forgave them. Through this, you made major contributions to bringing democracy to our country.

After being elected president, you worked tirelessly from dawn until midnight in order to save our country, which had just been thrown into a precipitous financial crisis. You overcame it and established South Korea as an IT powerhouse. You forged inter-Korean reconciliation in order to achieve national reunification, your lifelong dream. You achieved the historic inter-Korean summit, where the South and North Korean Accord was announced.

I believe that your dream of building a nation where democracy, freedom, and peace bloom is still being carried out. All of this is thanks to the fact that you never despaired, and continued to move forward toward a future of hope, no matter what your circumstances.

We will continue to strive to achieve those goals you worked so hard for. We will never rest until the day when the South and North demolish the wall dividing them and are reunited as one. I pray for the day when the reunification that you so wished for—no, that we *all* wish for—is achieved.

We will act as *conscience in action*, help our neighbors in plight, and live peacefully, as you so sincerely hoped. We will work hard to achieve peace in the world. I hope that our descendants will continue to work to fulfill your wishes.

Many people have worked diligently to publish your autobiography, which documents your life of overcoming hardships. Your respected friends, former president of the United States Bill Clinton, former president of Germany Richard Von Weizsäcker, and former president of the Soviet Union Mikhail Gorbachev also sent warm remarks in honor of the publication of your autobiography.

I still cannot believe that you are no longer here with us. Although I spend my days missing you, I feel comforted to think that God has granted you a crown of triumph.

I think of the forty-seven-year life that we lived together every day. I always admired and loved you. I will pray for and love you until my last breath.

I trust that God will respond to our prayers with His endless love. May you rest in peace in His embrace.

Seoul, South Korea   Lee Hee-ho
Summer 2010

A DEFENDER OF HUMAN RIGHTS AND EQUALITY

President Kim Dae-jung was a wise and courageous leader who served South Korea well and inspired people who love peace and freedom all over the world. He lived his life with a vision for peace, and I continue to be inspired by the bravery he demonstrated in defending democracy, and pursuing reconciliation with North Korea. I will also be forever grateful for his friendship and unfailing kindness to me.

President Kim led his people into a new century with a careful eye on the future. He worked tirelessly to realize the potential of his nation, and to help create a world with more partners and fewer adversaries. He saw the immense opportunity in forging relationships rather than abandoning them. He possessed a rare understanding of the modern, interdependent world, and recognized that South Korea's fate was bound to the international community.

In the midst of the Asian Financial Crisis, President Kim advanced business privatization and the development of global economic partnerships, and his financial strategies did more to open world markets to South Koreans than those of any previous administration. In the process, he ushered in a new era of business engagement and prosperity for the South Korean people—an age of growth they continue to enjoy today.

I met President Kim in 1992, and had the privilege to work with him in strengthening the ties and deepening the friendship between the US and South Korea. In the years we served together, I witnessed how committed he was to promoting peace and intercultural understanding. To this day, I still believe that one of his most profound moments in office was his visit to Pyongyang—the first summit meeting between the leaders of

North and South Korea since before the War. His "Sunshine Policy" solidified his strong commitment to advancing diplomacy and cooperation on the Korean Peninsula, and it showed he believed that working in partnership rather than in isolation would lead to a brighter tomorrow for Koreans in both nations. The "Sunshine Policy" was a profound gesture of solidarity that gave more hope for lasting peace and reconciliation between North and South Korea than ever before. Had President Kim been able to achieve the partnership he dreamed of, we would be living in a more secure and equitable world today.

President Kim bravely championed democracy, defended human rights and equality, brought his country back from economic crisis, and enhanced national security. His Nobel Prize was richly deserved.

As we continue into the twenty-first century, our pervasive interdependence makes President Kim's legacy more relevant than ever. If we want to build a world that is more equal, more stable, and more sustainable, leaders should bear in mind President Kim's faith in the power of partnership: we can only move forward together, and because of this inescapable reality, we must lead with the same courage and dedication that President Kim Dae-jung exhibited throughout his life.

New York, USA
May 12, 2010

William Jefferson Clinton

Outstanding Statesman and a Man of Extraordinary Destiny

I was deeply honored and moved to be invited by Madam Lee Hee-ho to write a short preface for President Kim Dae-jung's autobiography.

For more than two decades, President Kim and I were united in a collaborative relationship, based on a deep mutual understanding and close friendship. Throughout the course of our relationship, I had multiple opportunities to confirm that President Kim Dae-jung was an extraordinary statesman, a thinker devoted to the cause of democracy, and a man of special destiny.

There is no one who would not admire President Kim's role in modern Korean history and his courage as manifested in his resistance to dictatorship for the sake of the democratic development of Korea. Even various forms of imprisonment and threats to his life could not break his belief and will.

Entrusted with the presidency at the turn of the century and the beginning of a new millennium, President Kim rescued Korea from a serious financial crisis and carried out fundamental reform that can be dubbed the "Korean *perestroika*." Above all, the Sunshine Policy that President Kim declared and carried out clearly showed his outstanding leadership. His leadership enabled the unprecedented (and still unparalleled) inter-Korean summit and the development of inter-Korean humanitarian and economic cooperation. In addition, the six-party talks to solve the problems on the Korean Peninsula began under his leadership. There have been disputes on the Korean Peninsula since then, but they have only proved the importance of the Kim Dae-jung initiative.

International society regarded President Kim Dae-jung's policies with high esteem. His Nobel Peace Prize in recognition of his contribution to inter-Korean reconciliation and his efforts for democracy and human rights served as proof of this. President Kim continued to passionately work on those areas even after his presidency ended. In fact, his efforts continued until the very last moment of his life.

I remember the 2006 Forum of Democratic Leaders in the Asia-Pacific that President Kim and I co-hosted and held with other Nobel Peace Prize laureates in Gwangju. We held this forum in honor of the Gwangju Uprising against General Chun Doo-hwan's violence and dictatorship in 1980, as well as the sixth anniversary of the 2000 inter-Korean summit. During that event, I was deeply moved by President Kim Dae-jung's profound thoughts and sincere remarks about his regional and global plans, both while listening to his speeches and in the course of conversations with him.

President Kim Dae-jung passionately supported the development of a comprehensive Korea-Russia relationship. He visited Moscow many times and actively interacted with the Soviet and Russian people and political and academic leaders. He also received a PhD in political science from the Diplomatic Academy of the Ministry of Foreign Affairs of the Russian Federation and became an honorary professor of Moscow State University.

I firmly believe that readers not only from Korea, but also from around the world, will welcome and be excited about the publication of this autobiography, which President Kim Dae-jung completed through tremendous effort and his wife Madam Lee Hee-ho prepared.

Moscow, Russia   Mikhail Gorbachev
May 31, 2010

THE ROAD TO A PEACEFUL AND JUST WORLD

Through President Kim Dae-jung's autobiography, we are given a look into the life of a most extraordinary and moving person of great character. This book contains stories of an amazing life, tremendous challenges, and the marvelous triumphs of a person who overcame all manner of adversity and suffering with tireless courage.

In spite of falsehood, hatred, violence, imprisonment, and house arrests, he tried to safeguard his country, painstakingly working toward bringing more freedom, democracy, livelier unity, and détente to South Korea. He triumphed and succeeded. Moreover, he neither resented nor sought revenge on his former enemies and opponents.

As the president of South Korea, he pursued the Sunshine Policy toward North Korea. President Kim worked hard to reduce suffering in his cruelly divided country and to establish a solid foundation for peaceful reunification.

I was deeply moved by him throughout our long period of wonderful friendship, and continue to be even after his passing. Although the distance between Germany and Korea is great, our opinions on politics were close. Through his life, President Kim Dae-jung taught us that the only way to break the vicious cycle of countering violence with violence is to establish a system based on truth and peace. His life shows his infinitely firm belief that the road toward a more peaceful and just world is a worthy one that we should never give up on.

Berlin, Germany   Richard von Weizsäcker
April 2010

At the End of My Life: Author's Preface

The sun has set and it's quiet all around me. I would like to leave the story of my life behind. I would like to piously show the past years of my life, as I consider it my last rite of respect for history. Now that I face my last task, I wonder if mine was a life without regrets. Although my life was full of suffering, I don't for a minute consider it an unhappy one. Not because I achieved something, but because I tried my best to live a just life.

There are many people in history whom I admire. Although I was nurtured by the sympathy and inspiration I felt for them, I would not want to exchange my life for any of theirs. I love my life. Were I to be reborn and relive it ten times over, I would gladly repeat my life over and over again. I stand here today after pushing through many twists and turns in turbulent times. Looking back, I don't know where I got this kind of courage.

I have lived through the periods of violent Japanese occupation, national liberation, war, and division. Was there any period that was harsher than those in Korean history? It was a time of violent waves, radical changes, and passionate engagement. I faced the gusty wind of the world head on. I tried not to run away from reality. I did not hesitate to collide with anything if I considered it right to do so. I did not yield to any coercion or bribe. This is why my life has been neither affluent nor elegant.

I confess that I have been tempted by evil whispers numerous times. But I could never betray the Korean people, or God, who is in charge of justice and knows the truth behind history. I could not discourage my wife, who firmly stood by me. I could not teach lies to my children. I also believed that history would appreciate my efforts, even if my contemporaries did not.

Occasionally, I asked myself why I entered politics. The answer is, I did so in order to change the world. Observing the political crisis in Busan during the Korean War, I dreamt of a new world. I neither hated politics nor disparaged politicians. A politician should work together with people to eliminate the structural evils that harass them. Isn't politics that is built upon the respect of its people and that considers the people its lords perhaps one of the holiest things? I wanted to become the president who changed the world. Some people disparaged me for this dream of mine, calling me a "president-complex" patient. It did not bother me.

To me, politics is not a pure lily in a remote valley, but a lotus flower blooming out of muddy water. Seclusion and silence in the face of evil is self-deception and hypocrisy. I do not claim to have been an outstanding politician, but I do not regret my life as a politician. It was a difficult life as I was always on the road, but I did not compromise, and I watched out for my own laziness. I hoped not to be a philosopher, but a person who loved his neighbors and dedicated himself to humanity.

Upon reflection, it was a truly eventful life. It took me nine years after I entered politics to sit inside the National Assembly Building. It took me no less than twenty-seven years after first being nominated as a presidential candidate in 1970 to become president. I survived five life-or-death crises, was imprisoned for six years, and had to endure decades of exile and house imprisonment. Whenever turmoil struck our country, I stood at its center and my title would change from presidential candidate to the opposition party president, from a rebellious ringleader to a political exile, or to a procommunist element.

My political enemies called me "pro-communist." Regional antagonism followed me wherever I went. The more I tried to get out of the mire, the more deeply I was dragged into it. I grew angry and frustrated on countless occasions, but every time I invariably found patience and rose again. I believed that the day would come when my enemies would feel ashamed. But, at some point, I also realized that that day might *not* come during my lifetime. So what? Don't we have history, which is fair to us all? Despite the sadness that came with this thought, I decided to persevere and wait.

I continued to study throughout my life. In the midst of countless suffering and failures, I prepared for the future. I did not despair, even when I fell into the valley of death. Even as I cried with fear, I planned for the future. I waited for the day when I would dedicate myself to the Korean people and nation. A condemned criminal and president—that juxtaposition summarizes my life. It was a miracle for a condemned criminal to become president. This miracle was not only mine, but also the miracle of modern history that the Korean people nurtured and achieved.

Looking back on my life at its very end, there were too many crises. Numerous friends and comrades stood by my side during every crisis. Some passed away before me, but others still breathe the contemporary air with me. I am truly grateful to them all. How many people suffered, were hurt, or died because of me! I made so many people cry. Even so, I could not wipe away all of their tears. I would sincerely like to ask for their forgiveness.

There might be people who feel hurt because of this autobiography, but I wanted to write it truthfully and frankly. Things happened during my life that should never be repeated. And perhaps my footprints will be helpful in building our national road.

I did my best. In retrospect, the past looks beautiful. My autobiography is my farewell to the heroes and heroines of the future, and my prayer for their happiness. I wish that you all live in peace in a world where people are lords.

Seoul, South Korea   Kim Dae-jung
Spring, 2009

CONTENTS

List of Figures

LIST OF PHOTOS

PART I

Conscience in Action

CHAPTER 1

1924–1959

A Remote Island Boy (1924–1936)

I was born in Hugwang-ri, Haui-myeon, Muan-gun (now known as Sinan-gun), Jeollanam-do, on January 6, 1924. I suspect that Mother was particularly attached to me because mine was a very difficult birth. Her labor lasted for more than a day, and even Father was exhausted by the end of it from simply standing next to her. When I was born, the umbilical cord was wrapped around my shoulders, and I was neither breathing nor crying. Mother asked Father to hold me upside down and slap my bottom, and when he did as he was told I finally began to breathe. Later, Mother told me about a dream she had during her pregnancy. In her dream she was holding a tiger in her arms, a sign that she would give birth to a child who would grow up to become a great man. She also told me never to roll about in the muck because I came from a "higher place."

My father had two wives; my mother, Chang Su-geum, was his second. He had a son and three daughters with his first wife, and three sons and a daughter with my mother. I was my mother's first and my father's second son. Mother lived in a separate house from the main house, and I went back and forth between the two houses.

Throughout my long political career, I never talked about this facet of my family history despite various insulting accusations. It wasn't unusual for a man to have two or three wives at that time. Still, I wanted to protect

© The Author(s) 2019
Kim Dae-jung, *Conscience in Action*,
https://doi.org/10.1007/978-981-10-7623-7_1

Mother from slander. It wasn't an easy decision to write about this topic here, but I believe no one has the right to defile Mother's honor—not when she raised me well despite all of her difficult circumstances. I love her dearly. I believe she reconciled with all her earthly fates before she went to Heaven.

Hauido Island is located 34 kilometers away from Mokpo, the Korean Peninsula's southwestern most tip. When I was growing up, the islanders were all tenant farmers of a Japanese landlord, Tokuda Yashichi. Yashichi owned the entire island, and our land was dubbed "Tokuda Farm." Hauido Island eventually fell into the hands of a Japanese owner when the Joseon dynasty's King Injo married his daughter, Princess Jeongmyeong, to this island's Hong family. King Injo granted the family the right to collect a rice tax for a span of four generations; however, the Hong family did not return this right for eight generations, and eventually secretly sold the land to the Japanese around the time of the coercive annexation of Korea by Japan. Naturally, the tenant farmers organized an uprising, a lengthy struggle later called the Hauido Island Peasant Movement. Although the same peasants farmed the land for decades, its official ownership changed hands nine times. Meanwhile, the peasants' continued protests were ignored, and it took a considerable length of time for their voices to be heard in the peninsula at all. Fraud and violence were rampant. In spite of all our sorrow and frustration, Hauido Island was beautiful, and the islanders were always generous toward one another.

During my childhood on Hauido Island, Japan staged the Manchurian Incident, announcing its intention to trample China and subject them to Japanese rule. Previously, during the Emperor Taisho period (1912–1926), Japan actively experimented with a party-based political system called the Taisho Democracy. The first party-based cabinet was launched in 1918. Japan introduced the Cultural Rule policy in Korea after the 1919 Independence Movement. During the ensuing Emperor Showa era (1926–1989), however, this atmosphere changed radically. Although apparently still grounded on party-based governance, the military took power by force and carried out a bloody coup. After that, the military turned its ambitions toward the rest of Asia.

In the Korean Peninsula, the Singanhoe Association—an independence movement organization based on the coalition between nationalists and socialists—dissolved in 1931 under violent Japanese oppression. Independence movement activists had to either go into exile or go underground. Japan blocked all information from reaching the Korean people. It was a dark age during which Koreans couldn't see an inch beyond their faces, let alone into the country's distant future.

The only useful land in Hauido Island was mostly reclaimed. Upon this land people built their houses and farmed rice, vegetables, and salt. Salt produced from Hauido Island was popular and sold not only in Mokpo and Yeongsanpo, but also as far north as Ganggyeong in Chungcheongnam-do. Some of the islanders had to skip meals from time to time, but most did not experience too much destitution. They harvested grains from their mort-gaged farms and high-quality salt from their own salt fields, and gathered or caught marine products. Although it was an island, most residents were farmers rather than fishermen. My family were farmers, but my father owned the only boat in the village equipped with a fishing reel. During the agricul-tural off-season, villagers went out to sea in their boats to fish. All kinds of fish bit the bait hanging from those fishing lines. All of the villagers shared the catch—everything from *buseos* to eels to soft shell clams was piled up in my father's backyard. My home village of Hugwang, which I later adopted as my pen name, meant "large backyard" because of the large expanse of reclaimed land behind the original village, Dae-ri.

Because Hugwang-ri was reclaimed land, there wasn't a fountain in the village. We had to fetch water from another village located under a hill approximately 8 kilometers away. Men carried water jars on A-frame carriers and women carried them on their heads. Perhaps because of this childhood experience, to this day I feel very anxious whenever I see a leaky faucet. No matter how hurried I am, I have to turn off the faucet before anything else.

My father, Kim Un-sik, was a farmer and the village chief. It was a low-key, unpaid position. Still, the Korean daily newspaper and the organ of the Japanese Governor-General, *Maeil Sinbo*, was delivered to him in a bundle every few days because of his position. I was able to read this Chinese char-acter-studded newspaper from early on thanks to my village school educa-tion. The newspaper brought me news from the outside world—I read about the Manchurian Incident, Japanese cabinet changes, personnel changes in the Japanese Governor-General administration, domestic agricultural news, trade with Japan, and cultural news. I was particularly interested in the poli-tics section, which I always read through from top to bottom.

Father was a gentle man, affectionate toward his children and generous to others. Once, he saw me fiddling with a toy boat as he was headed out. Noticing I needed help, he took off his coat and sat down on the floor to saw. After he finished sawing off several large pieces, he shaved them down with a sickle. He finally hurried out after two hours of hard, sweaty work, but only after making sure the rattan boat could stay afloat.

What I really wanted was a *real* boat, not a toy one. As I watched Japanese battleships lie at anchor near Okdo Island in front of Hauido Island, I dreamt of someday making a real battleship. Grown-ups said they saw the Japanese fleet mooring in wait for the Russian fleet during the Russo-Japanese War. The Japanese battleships looked so enormous and impressive that I can still picture them as if they were right in front of my eyes. Over and over again I thought, *How powerful Japan is!*

Father had great musical talent. He was a great *pansori* singer. He danced well, too. I loved to listen to him sing the "Ssukdaemeori," a segment in *Chunhyanga*. It is thanks to him that I can insert encouraging phrases in appropriate places during *pansori* performance and play various traditional drums. If he had learned *pansori* from the masters in the city, he might have become an expert singer.

Thanks to Father's love of music, our family had the only record player on Hauido Island. Songs by the master singers Im Bang-ul and Ihwajungseon continued to flow out of our house. Father often introduced the music and explained the characteristics of each master singer to the villagers who crowded into our house to listen. I remember when Father first bought the record player, villagers crowded our house and marveled, asking, "How can a man sit and sing in such a small box?" It was a big event in our village.

Like most artistic people, Father was a very affectionate person—except when it came to Japan, Korea's violent occupier. Although Emperor Hirohito was supposed to be called "Arahitogami," a living god, Father called him "Yuin," the Korean pronunciation of his name. It was a daring act that could land him in prison. Whenever Father poured out his thoughts, condemning Japan for its violent annexation of Korea, listeners always worried about his safety.

Despite my father's antipathy toward Japan, he welcomed modernization, believing that Koreans should learn from others to make their own country stronger. Once, Father slipped behind a neighbor who insisted on keeping his traditional topknot, and suddenly lopped it off. Father was a man in tune with the tides of the times.

Father also occasionally took out his Joseon dynasty chart, which was considered a seditious document, from its secret hiding place and taught his children about it. We learned all about the different kings and the events that occurred during their reign. Father wanted us to know that Korea had its own independent history and kings.

Thus, my interest in politics was piqued. When I was in the third and fourth grades, I even copied facts about the cabinet shift in Japan and carried the paper with me. I don't know why but, at the time, I thought that I would someday become a king. It might have been because of the legend that a descendent of my family, Kim from Kimhae, would rise to a high position because of our propitious family gravesite. In that site between Unggok-ri and Hugwang-ri there were about twenty ancestral graves. I remember that I got angry once because of a rumor that a fortuneteller had predicted a newborn in a neighboring village would become king.

My mother had great hopes for her children, and she had an especially deep love for me. I still can't help tearing up whenever I think about her. The harder her life was, the stronger she became. Whether her children were considered "illegitimate" or not, she inspired us to become great. It was thanks to Mother that I was able to receive my education at the village school early on, rather than just learning to work in the field or the sea like most children on the island at that time. Mother was always busy with farming or housework. It was thanks to my strong mother that our family was able to rise up in the world. It was because of her work, too, that our family became relatively well off on Hauido Island.

Despite Mother's special devotion to me, she did not favor me above my siblings. She loved us all dearly, but she also disciplined us severely. When I was four or five, I found a peddler sleeping on the street one day as I was playing with the neighborhood children. Next to him was a bag full of not only taffy, but also cosmetics, combs, and tobacco pipes. We all took his goods home. I took a pipe for Father, not knowing I was doing anything wrong. When I handed the pipe to Mother, I expected praise. But she just stared at me for a while and then asked, "Where did you get this?"

I told her proudly how I had obtained the pipe, only to see her face change color as she flew into a rage. She hit my calves until they bled with a bush clover whip. "You! Still wet behind ears and you're learning to steal?"

Her furious voice hurt me more than her whip. After this punishment she took me, still crying, to the peddler who was still sleeping by the road. She woke him up and scolded him too. "I don't know how much money you have, but why do you turn young children into thieves?"

I returned the pipe and asked him for forgiveness. I can still remember Mother's face, red and furious, and I miss her so much that it hurts me.

I began attending the village school at age six. This traditional school was the only school on Hauido Island. My teacher's name was Kim Yeon; he was also known as Choam. The school was called Deokbong Seodang because it was located under Mt. Deokbongsan, but people often called it Choam Seodang after the teacher's pen name. Master Choam was a renowned scholar of Chinese classics. From him I learned *Cheonjamun* [Thousand Character Classic], *Sajasohak* [Four-Character Elementary Learning], and *Dongmongseonseup* [Advanced Youth Reader], texts that were equivalent to today's elementary school textbooks. Students came from all over to learn from him, including from much larger nearby places like Jindo Island, Muan, Haenam, and Heuksando Island. There was even a young man from the inland city of Naju, about 60 kilometers away from Haiudo Island. I remember him always wearing a straw hat. *Choam Munjip* [A Collection of Choam's Writings] is kept in the Deokbong Gangdang, a building his students later built to commemorate his teaching career. Master Choam loved me. I heard later that he often told people that Kim Dae-jung would become a great man.

We went to the village school with a cloth bundle, in which we placed our books, brushes, and paper. Master Choam was quiet and benevolent, but very strict when it came to learning. We were occasionally given tests during which we would recite what we'd learned and explain its meaning. It was a sort of practice civil service examination for students. I scored the highest on the first test, called the *gang*, and Master Choam gave me a first-place award certificate, upon which he wrote praises about me. I ran back home to brag about the news.

Mother and Father were extremely happy about my award and hung the certificate on the wall. Then Mother cooked all kinds of food for my teacher and the other students, including rice cakes and meat, and brought them to school, carrying them on her head; there was so much food that our servant additionally carried an A-frame on his back. This treat was Mother's way of celebrating my academic achievement. "Study hard," she told me. "I'll support your studies no matter what."

Mother was a great cook whose skill was known throughout the entire village. People would even come from afar to taste her *dongchimi*. Even when all of us had to starve because of food shortages, Mother often took me to a back room and gave me a rice cake. I will never forget the taste of those cakes; I've cherished the taste of her food throughout my entire life.

When I entered the newly established modern elementary school Haui Elementary School by chance when I was nine, Master Choam was very disappointed. My father took me along to "look around" at the new school when he dropped off my younger brother, Dae-ui, on his first day there. Father returned from inside the classroom to where I was waiting outside. His face all smiles, he said, "Dae-jung, you can enter as a second grader. Why not give it a try?" I started right away.

I loved to study. There were many things to memorize, but I was good at memorization. I was especially good at liberal arts, and I loved history.

I had many friends. I have memories of wrestling matches in the school playground, though I don't remember having fights with anyone. It was about 3 kilometers both ways from my house to school. Village children walked to and from school together. In winter, we frequently had severe snowstorms and had to wear ski mask-like headgears. I believe those travels to and from school supported my entire life and, especially, my ability to go canvassing during elections.

Since I grew up on an island, I looked at the sea to my heart's content. And yet, I have never grown tired of the sea. A dear wish of mine is to build a beautiful traditional-style house and live there for the rest of my days. I even have a specific place in mind—a rather high hill behind Mt. Yudalsan in Mokpo, where you can look down in the direction where Daebandong Beach used to be. The seascape from there is beautiful and reminds me of one I used to look down at from the hill behind the Hugwang-ri village. From far away, the sea in front of Daebandong Beach looks like a lake because of the row of small islands in front of it. Top it off with ships floating on the sea, and the scenery looked like a painting. I miss it very much.

The sea always excited me, and I wondered what the world beyond it was like. The beach was our playground. My friends and I swam naked in summer. We dug a hole in the beach and caught an octopus, which we ate alive (this required special skills because their tentacles could enter into and block our nose). We fished for gobies and ate them raw after removing their innards.

Sometimes village children took the cows to low hills, where we would leave them alone to graze while we played on the grass. I once followed our cow and it kicked me with its hind legs. I caught wild ducklings from the marsh and tried to raise them a few times, but they always quickly died or flew away. When village adults cooked our family dog, I threw a huge tantrum, crying and kicking. I still ate its meat when it was offered to me.

We also poached barley in early summer and beans in the fall, but we often got caught by adults and ran away.

My siblings and I got along very well. We bathed in the brook and wrestled on the beach. I was the most easily scared among us. After I heard a goblin folktale, I was so afraid of the dark that I couldn't even go to the toilet across the yard. On windy winter nights, it was even more frightening. Upon realizing that everyone dies, I remember crying alone at night over the possibility of Mother's death. Always weakhearted, I was very anxious before important meetings, even as a child. I still am to this day.

When I was young, I was embarrassed that I belonged to a generation older than most other clansmen, who all lived collectively in the nearby Dae-ri. Even the elderly called me uncle. Gi-bae, the *myeon* chief, called me Uncle Dae-jung when he visited my house. I was so embarrassed that I ran away.

When I was a fourth grader, my family finally moved to Mokpo. I had been pestering my parents, asking them to send me to the peninsula or Japan to study, saying that I was willing to earn my way as a newspaper boy. At first, Mother wouldn't listen to me so I waged a hunger strike. Eventually, though, it seemed that my parents couldn't completely ignore my wish. It was also Mother's wish to educate her children in the outside world. One night I overheard her telling Father, "Dae-jung is a smart kid. Let's take him to Mokpo. If we sell our estate, we can start a business."

That was the kind of woman Mother was. During the 1930s, when so much of our world looked bleak both politically and socially, it was an audacious thing to give up a relatively secure life on the island and move to Mokpo, a city unfamiliar to all of us villagers. Even from today's perspective, she deserves respect and admiration. Without her keen foresight I would not be here today.

We were sad to leave, but the future was beckoning and we were excited. We boarded a ship to Mokpo in the fall of 1936.

PEOPLE WHO LOVED ME AND WHOM I LOVED
(1936–1945)

In the 1930s, Mokpo was one of the seven largest cities in Korea, a port city that was expanding by the day. Passenger ships, fishing boats, and freighters frequented it incessantly. An important international port between Nagasaki, Japan, and Shanghai, China, Mokpo was where the Japanese shipped home the rice, cotton, and marine products they had plundered from across the entire Korean Peninsula and transported on the Honam train line that opened in 1914.

Our family arrived in Mokpo after a three-hour voyage from Hauido Island aboard the Ganggyeong. I can still vividly remember how amazed I was. Flags fluttered on every ship and boat whistles rang everywhere. Everything was alive and kicking, and I felt alive, too. It was another world. Everything was new and amazing.

A ferryman's song flickeringly seeps into the waves around Samhakdo Island/A bride's skirt is dampening on the wharf—perhaps because of tears from sorrowful separation? Oh, Mokpo's sorrow!
     Below stacked grain harboring three hundred years of grudge, clear is his trace—oh, how sorrowful!/Even Mt. Yudalsan wind embraces River Yeongsan—oh, how he is missed—Mokpo's song!

These are lyrics from the 1935 song "Mokpo's Tears," sung by Yi Nan-yeong, the daughter of Mokpo. Its mournful tune conveys a meaningful message. "Stacked grain harboring three hundred years of grudge" clearly refers to the local legend of Admiral Yi Sun-sin vanquishing the second Japanese Invasion about 300 years ago by covering rocks with straws so they would look like stacks of rice. Thus, this song was not just a pop song, but the song of a nation grieving the loss of their country and wishing for its independence.

Speaking of Yi Sun-sin, I remember a day during my Mokpo Commercial High School years when I saw the spoons and bowls that the Joseon naval forces must have used excavated from the old fortress site near my house. I was deeply moved, realizing that Admiral Yi's navy must have been stationed and fought right there. During that Japanese colonial period, Admiral Yi was naturally not only my, but also *all* of the Korean people's, hero.

I transferred to Mokpo Public First Normal School, a six-year elementary school, as a fourth grader. My parents bought and ran an inn called Yeongsin Inn, located at 1 Mokpodae, Hang-dong, Mokpo. Although my parents were quite wealthy on the island, they could afford only a small inn atop a hill in Mokpo. Also, since it didn't have a spring on site, I often had to carry water from a well up many flights of stairs. Still, from up there on the hill we could enjoy a spectacular view and see all sorts of ships come and go.

I was taller than most of the other children in my class, but they, nonetheless, made fun of me. They called me country bumpkin, and some of the larger boys even beat me up. I became a loner, spending recesses alone in a corner next to the restroom. But it was there that I soon met another transfer student, a boy named Jeong Jin-tae. We became friends immediately and later went to Mokpo Commercial High School together. We learned to play the guitar and sang popular songs together.

My fourth-grade teacher Mr. Song Chi-gang praised me often, which gave me confidence when I was anxious about studying with the city students. Soon after I transferred, I won a writing contest on traffic order. It was a pretty big competition sponsored by a local newspaper company, so our Japanese principal Mr. Saito presented the award to me in front of the entire school. As a result, I attracted attention from both inside and outside of the school. Girls began to notice me, and my classmates treated me differently. I finished my fourth-grade year second out of seventy-three in my class.

When I was a sixth grader, Korean class was abolished and we were allowed to speak only Japanese at school. I was still a child, but I had never been so sad. One day I saw my father in the schoolyard and went to him. After a long, sad silence, I whispered to him, "Let's talk at home, Father." It was stifling to live in that sort of environment.

That same year, the Sino-Japanese War broke out. The Japanese seemed to believe that they would be able to occupy China overnight. I can still remember the principal's enthusiastic speech, when he declared, "It's now time we punish that tyrant Chiang Kai-shek."

Mr. Inoue was my sixth-grade teacher. He favored me, even taking me to his home, where he gave me cookies and praised me in front of his wife. I was first in the class at the end of that graduation year; however, I won the award for second in class because, for no apparent reason, my teacher did not give me the top mark for my conduct during my fifth-grade year. In order to be awarded first in class, you also had to get the top mark in conduct every school year. Because the school principal knew me well, he was surprised that I wasn't able to get the top award, and he even summoned my fifth-grade teacher to suggest he consider a grade change. In the end, though, they decided it would set a bad precedent, so I graduated with the second-place award, the *Mokpo Sinbo* Newspaper President Award. That was an interesting coincidence (I would even go so far as to say some sort of premonition of my future) because I later became the president of that same newspaper company. Also, interestingly, that fifth-grade teacher who gave me an unreasonable B for my conduct later asked a favor of me. I didn't hold any grudges against him and I helped as best as I could. It did teach me, though, to always avoid treating people in a manner I would regret were I to meet them later on.

Japanese teachers generally didn't discriminate against Korean students at random. Still, their salaries were twice as much as that of Korean teachers. I once asked a Japanese teacher about the fairness of this arrangement; he was so upset that I regretted even asking him. "We came all the way here away from our home in Japan," he replied. "We deserve it. Why else would anyone want to work away from home?"

In the sixth grade, I developed a crush on a girl who was a grade below me. She was small with bright eyes and, in my estimation, beautiful. She had assisted at the award ceremonies, an honor given only to students with excellent grades and conduct. It was love at first sight for me. Still, I felt ashamed about my feelings because boys and girls weren't supposed to hang out together then. She didn't know I had crush on her.

When I was a student at Mokpo Commercial High School and she entered Mokpo Public Girl's High School, I would see her on the way to our respective schools. It just so happened that I went to school by traveling from the south to the north side of the city, while she traveled from the north to the south side. In order to see her every morning, I took a little detour, but I was so happy just to see her that it was worth it. Eventually, she found out I had a crush on her. We dated just once, going to the theater together after we graduated from high school. I might have married her if I hadn't met my first wife, Cha Yong-ae. This girl with the bright eyes was my impossible first love. To this day, I can still see the road I took only to see her, and I still haven't forgotten her face.

I entered Mokpo Public Commercial School (later, Mokpo Commercial High School, and, today, Jeonnam First High School) as its top student. Renowned throughout the country, this five-year high school was the only boys' high school in Mokpo at the time. One hundred sixty-four students entered; half of them were Japanese and half were Korean. I was the president of the vocational class.

My second-year homeroom teacher Isaburo Mukumoto had a keen interest in politics. One day he told us to discuss current affairs. After I stood up and spoke for a bit, he praised me, saying, "Kim Dae-jung's speech was as good as a Japanese representative's speech." I learned a great deal from him, and had the good fortune of meeting him again at a hotel in Tokyo when I was the president of Korea, and he a retired Japanese diplomat. Mr. Mukumoto went back to Japan, graduated from college, became a diplomat, and worked as ambassador to Ethiopia and Uruguay. He was the envoy to Turkey when the Kidnapping of Kim Dae-jung Incident occurred. He told me that he sent me a letter to inquire about my state and to see if there was anything he could do to help me after I was rescued in the nick of time. That letter, however, was never delivered to me.

I also remember a drill instructor, a first lieutenant in active service, who offered a monthly current affairs lecture. Once, during a Q&A session, I asked him about the current European situation, specifically in connection with the Dardanelles Strait in Turkey. He didn't even know where the Dardanelles Strait was, which drew the attention of others to me.

One of the most pivotal experiences of my high school years occurred during my second year, when Koreans were forced to adopt Japanese names. Koreans believe our last names originate in Heaven and are passed down from there through our ancestors; with this in mind, we consider them as precious as our lives. In the Confucian tradition, changing one's last name is considered the greatest betrayal one can commit against his or her ancestors. To express one's dedication to something, a Japanese individual will say he would "sacrifice his life" for it; however, a Korean will say he would "change his last name." Therefore, the edict requiring Koreans to adopt Japanese names was truly an act of brutal violence. This order was related to the Japanese Imperialization Policy, under which they also introduced their conscription system. Previously, this system had been compulsory only for Japanese men, but it now included Korean men as well.

Throughout the entire country, Koreans lamented the loss of their names. It is very difficult for me to even remember my adopted Japanese name. Occasionally, the Japanese ask me what my Japanese name was out of pure curiosity, but I can never answer that question. It was one of the most humiliating experiences I have ever had.

I learned a lot from my third-year homeroom teacher Noguchi Jinroku, who also taught Japanese and judo. While emphasizing that we should be faithful to our principles, he also advised us that success mandated we be flexible in applying those principles in action. According to him, in this matter of balancing principles and flexibility, human life was similar to judo. I was deeply impressed by his words and tried to apply them throughout my entire life. What I learned from him about being flexible in applying principles to practical situations was similar to the late Joseon reformist Confucianist philosophy about Seeking Truth Grounded on Concrete Evidence.

Most of my high school teachers liked me. My history teacher said I knew Japanese history better than the Japanese students. My math teacher also favored me—almost too much. Since I wasn't great in math, I'm still not sure why he praised me so much, but he frequently commended my honest face, bright eyes, and wise character.

I often climbed Mt. Yudalsan during my high school days, but, in fact, I frequently didn't make it to the top because of my fear of heights. Most of the time, I climbed only as far as the Opodae (a place from where people once shot cannonballs to indicate it was noontime), and looked down at the sea from there. Samhakdo Island was beautiful. Mt. Yudalsan wasn't very high, but it was very rocky. To this day, I still feel dizzy when I remember myself on the top of it. I begin to feel scared just imagining myself looking down from that mountaintop, even when I think of it from the safety of my own home.

Fear of heights notwithstanding, I was generally persistent and responsible. I once participated in a 7-kilometer running competition from school to Mt. Yudalsan. I ran in full gear, carrying a rifle, sword, and backpack full of books. I finished the race first, even though I carried an additional rifle for another student who was struggling.

One summer we all boarded at school instead of sleeping in our own homes. It was here that I took part in a "Courage-testing Competition" during a summertime volunteer project. The test involved walking to the public cemetery and back in the dead of night if a teacher woke you up. Contrary to my deepest hopes and desires, a teacher woke me up and gave me a note, ordering me to hang it at a certain place in the cemetery. Although I was easily scared, I didn't avoid the task. After I'd hung the note—my whole body trembling all the while—I was showered with rocks and frightening noises. I was scared, but I threw the rocks back in the general direction of the noise and yelled, "You dirty beast! Take a look at my rocks!" A few moments later, a teacher hastily replied, "Hey, Kim Dae-jung, it's me!"

In my third year of high school, I transferred to a college prep class. Korea's situation was becoming increasingly complicated, and I wanted to learn about the outside world. My plan was to go to Geonguk University in Manchuria, a school that all students entered on scholarship. But that winter (December 1941, to be precise), Japan declared war on the US. It was difficult to get to Manchuria during the war and all of the news was depressing. I lost interest in my studies. I was sorry that I couldn't study more, but now I'm glad I didn't go to Manchuria; had I been there at that time, I might not have been able to return to South Korea because of the country's later division.

It was during this period that I had my first taste of Japanese student violence. One day while a few students were cleaning the classroom after school, a student named Nagai began making a lot of noise. When I scolded him and ordered him to stop, he suddenly lunged at me and smacked me across my face. I was surprised, but I stood up and protested. He struck me again, but I took his fist and pinned him down on the floor. I knew how to handle the situation because I was a member of the school sumo team. I wanted to trample his face and I raised my military boot (which all students had to wear), before realizing I shouldn't. I stood him up and sent him away, asking, "How can you act like this when I was just talking?"

A couple of days later, several upper-class Japanese students dragged me to the back corner of the school and beat me brutally, even using their belts. They made accusations, such as "We heard that you harbor dangerous ideas." "You're against the Japanese, aren't you?" From that point on, I was often spoken ill of at school, and amid these insults were always accusations that I harbored dangerous ideas. The Japanese students were openly antagonistic toward me. Still, I tended to be persistent and wasn't easily disheartened by the bullying. In addition to this pressure, we were also subject to the draft system during this time. I was worried and, as a result, didn't do well academically.

I graduated from high school in an expedited wartime graduation in December 1943, finishing thirty-ninth out of 164 students in my class. Soon, I got a job at the Jeonnam Steamship Company, a Japanese-owned merchant ship company. It was easy to get a job then because of the wartime shortage of people everywhere. I worked hard and was solely in charge of the company's accounting.

Once, during a conversation about dogs with the Japanese branch director of a bank our company was borrowing from, I happened to recite an English sentence I learned in school: "A dog is attached to a man, while a cat is attached to a place." I uttered these words during a time when it was risky to speak or learn English; however, the branch director's face suddenly lit up and he was eager to do me a favor. It turned out he had experience working in San Francisco and was so pro-America that he wore a tie to work, despite wartime regulations.

Around that time, Japan was conscripting more and more young men—including many Korean men—to send to the front lines. Like so many Korean parents who would do anything to free their sons from conscription, my father officially changed my birth date to December 3, 1925. While most people tried to raise their sons' ages to avoid conscription, my father lowered my age, pushing my conscription period back from the first to the third period. My father's application was the only one accepted by the office, and I was safe and whole when we welcomed Korea's liberation.

When I was finally conscripted, an unforgettable incident occurred. While training at the elementary school in my hometown of Hauido Island, a Japanese teacher in charge of the training beat me out of the blue. He probably wanted to dampen my spirits, as I was well known as a promising young man on the island. My mother, who had accompanied me, just stood there, looking on helplessly and overwrought. Interestingly, though, the war was over fairly soon, and word got to me in Mokpo that this Japanese teacher couldn't leave Hauido Island for fear of my retaliation against his violence. Of course, I didn't retaliate, and the teacher returned to Japan safely.

In the summer of 1944, a woman passed by my office building while I happened to be standing outside. She had tidy hair and wore a white dress. She seemed even brighter than the brilliant summer sun. I had never seen such an elegant and beautiful woman—it was a love at first sight. I asked around and found out she was Cha Yong-ae, my high school classmate Cha Won-sik's younger sister. Summoned by her father, who was worried about her safety amid the intensifying US bombings in Japan, she was home from her studies at Ina Girls High School in Nagano Prefecture, Japan. Ultimately, most of her classmates perished in the military supply factory in Nagoya during the bombing.

Because she was my friend's sister, I visited their house often under the pretense of seeing my friend … but, really, just to see her. I was able to approach her through her younger siblings, who liked me because of the stories I told and the candy I brought. My friend approved of our relationship, too. He even joked, "Yong-ae, you should marry Dae-jung." She smiled at the thought. Her mother also liked me and said that she wanted me as her son-in-law. In the end, we confessed our love for each other and promised to marry. It was thanks to her that I was able to live through that bleak wartime period. She was not only beautiful, but also very wise.

Unfortunately, her father Cha Bo-ryun (who was the owner of the second or third largest print shop in Mokpo) was against our marriage because I could be called to the front lines at any time. He tried to force Yong-ae to marry a man of his choice, despite all his family members' opposition. As the atmosphere in their house grew more and more tense by the day, Yong-ae's mother called me in to see her. In front of everyone, she insisted that the decision should be up to her daughter. Everyone looked at her closed lips, and I felt like I was suffocating from anxiety. Although she was ordinarily gentle and shy, Yong-ae spoke clearly this time. "I will marry Dae-jung. If I can't, I'd rather die."

That was it. Her father approved our marriage and began to favor me completely. We were married on April 9, 1945, in the middle of a blooming spring shortly before the liberation. Because our marriage occurred during the later phases of wartime, we weren't able to go on a honeymoon.

Instead, we lived in fear of the call-up papers that could arrive any day. As the situation on the front lines grew worse, the Mokpo port that shuttled military supplies back and forth became more and more depressing.

We lived close to the port, and so our house was demolished in anticipation of bombing. We had to move.

The Japanese government published only victorious news about the war, so many people believed Japan was winning and would soon rule all of Asia. Still, some things didn't make sense and there were rumors. As the major battleground moved from the South Pacific to the Solomon Islands, then to Okinawa, it seemed clear to me that Japan was losing. Still, when we sat around the radio to listen to the emperor's major announcements on August 15, 1945, we didn't really expect to hear him speak the words "unconditional surrender."

My wife and I cheered, crying and laughing at the same time. We ran out into the street and shouted, "Joseon's independent! Joseon's independent!" We took paper from my father-in-law's print shop and wrote, "Japan Unconditional Surrender," then pasted our homemade signs on walls bordering the streets.

In retrospect, it was a pretty dangerous thing to do because the Japanese police and military were still in power. In one alley, I encountered a friend who was a revenue office clerk. He got off his bicycle and saluted me, saying, "Thank you for all of your help. I'm on my way into the army today." When I said, "Goodness, the war is over. They lost," he responded, "America lost?" He didn't believe me at first when I informed him it was Japan that lost. It was understandable, due to the censored information we had been receiving all this time.

BEATING HEART, DIFFICULT WORLD (1945–1950)

With Korea's liberation at hand, my wife and I were overjoyed to be free of the fear of my conscription. All of Jeonnam Steamship Company's managerial staff returned to Japan, like most of the Japanese who returned without any confrontation from Koreans.

After a brief period of quietude, downtown Mokpo became crowded and lively again. Twenty Korean employees took charge of the Jeonnam Steamship Company's management. Elected as the chairman of its managerial committee, I ran the company for a while until a powerful man from Seoul with a connection to the US military government took away our managerial rights. Many people tried to snatch formerly Japanese-owned companies around that time. I went to Seoul and negotiated to regain my managerial rights. Perhaps because of this incident, the other employees trusted me. Also, probably because of this affair, the employees of Daeyang

Shipbuilding Company, the largest shipbuilding company in Mokpo, requested that I manage their company as well.

I also participated in the Mokpo branch of the Preparatory Committee for National Construction (PCNC), one of 145 branches of the PCNC. I was excited to participate in this branch where leftists and rightists collaborated. Although the Mokpo branch was originally organized around Reverend Yi Nam-gyu, it gradually fell under the control of communists. Because communists led the independence movement during the colonial period and many released political prisoners were also communists, most young people like me did not have any enmity toward communists; some even favored them.

I, too, didn't particularly dislike communists. Frankly speaking, after having undergone the dark ages of colonialism I really did not know much at all about democracy or communism. I was just excited to be part of the process of building a new country. As the propaganda department head, I felt nothing could be more exciting and rewarding than dedicating my youth to rebuilding my country.

PCNC president Yeo Un-hyeong convened a nationwide people's representative assembly on September 6, 1945. At the assembly he declared our country's name to be the People's Republic of Joseon. The assembly elected central people's committee members, who were mostly former independence fighters. On September 14, the assembly announced a cabinet under the leadership of Chairman Rhee Syngman and Vice Chairman Yeo Un-hyeong. This cabinet included Kim Koo and Cho Man-sik, although none of these leaders had agreed to join the cabinet. The leftists attempted to control the new government in this way, but, at the time, Kim Koo was in China, Rhee Syngman in the US, and Cho Man-sik in Pyongyang. Their attempt was not successful.

On September 8, major US forces entered Incheon and the US military government was established south of the 38th Parallel, while the USSR controlled the north. Still, people did not worry about the division, believing it was only temporary. Ideological division seemed like an even more urgent problem than territorial division. The US military government did not acknowledge Yeo Un-hyeong's People's Republic of Joseon as they were wary of entrusting a suspicious leftist-leaning group with governing the country. After the assembly, the PCNC changed its name to the People's Committee. Reverend Yi Nam-gyu left the Mokpo branch in protest of what he perceived as a violation of its original mission. I remained, though, and made posters and fliers as well as press conference materials.

In December 1945, a critical development in the destiny of Korea occurred. At the Moscow Conference of Foreign Ministers of the US, the UK, and Soviet Union, it was decided that a four-power trusteeship was necessary for as long as five years before Korea could attain its own independence. Koreans—regardless of their political affiliations—opposed this, staging rallies and other protests. The next year, Yeo Un-hyeong's Central People's Committee and Pak Heon-yeong's Communist Party suddenly decided to support the decision, dividing public opinion along ideological lines. Although exiled national leaders returned home one after another, no one came up with a more satisfactory solution.

I was also against the trusteeship at first, but came to rethink the matter as time went on. I noticed that, although the US and USSR opposed each other in other matters, they were in agreement about Korea's trusteeship. Also, the military governor of South Korea, General John R. Hodge, argued that Koreans should accept the trusteeship temporarily. It seemed to me that being united as one country under the trusteeship of four countries was preferable to being divided into two countries sponsored by the US and USSR, respectively. If this division were reinforced through the establishment of two separate governments, it would be much harder for the two countries to be reunited. I thought General Hodge's words also implied these concerns. I was extremely disheartened and angry to see Korean leaders divided and fighting among their different groups. Hoping they would reconcile soon, I waited in vain in the marginal city of Mokpo for better news from Seoul.

On June 3, 1946, the rightist leader Rhee Syngman suddenly suggested that the South should form a separate government. Kim Koo was still against both the trusteeship and the establishment of a separate government. Leftist Pak Heon-yeong was also against the establishment of a separate government. The country was sharply divided.

I joined the Sinmin Party, which was established by those who had returned from participating in the Independence Alliance in Yanan, China, proclaiming the benefits of a left–right collaboration. With Kim Du-bong and Choi Chang-ik in the foreground, the Independence Alliance, which was headquartered in Pyongyang, established the Joseon Sinmin Party in February 1946.

Although I joined the Sinmin Party because of its support of the left–right collaboration, it soon became clear that several of our members were communists. At the time, I was not really well versed in all of the political parties that seemed to sprout up all over the country overnight. It was a confusing time, and it seemed like I could never get to know the real color of the political party I joined until the day an incident made the character of that party very clear. During that period, there was a rumor circulating that Korean communists were calling the USSR their fatherland and the red flag "our" flag. I confronted my fellow party members, telling them, "Whoever calls the USSR 'their fatherland' and the red flag 'our flag' deserves to be stoned to death." In retrospect, it was too extreme a statement. My party members' reaction was vehement: "How could you say that about the USSR, our benefactor?" "Our benefactor is one thing, but our nation is another," I replied. "Is there really something wrong with what I just said?"

I immediately left the party office after this incident, and that was the end of my Sinmin Party career. I also made a clean break from the Communist Party. My father-in-law, who was vice chairman of the rightist Hanmin (Korean Democratic) Party Mokpo branch, influenced me considerably in these decisions. He had always been a wealthy man and was always critical of communists. According to him, he had gotten to know the communists better while working with them during the independence movement in 1927. He seemed to have many dark memories from that time and always warned me about the party. When I witnessed their attitudes toward the USSR and the red flag, my tiniest illusions about communists were completely shattered.

As expected, on September 5, 1946, the Sinmin Party merged with a faction of the People's Party of Korea and the Communist Party. The Sinmin Party in the North had already merged with the Communist Party to form the North Workers' Party of Korea in August the same year. Of course, Kim Il-sung seized power.

Meanwhile, tension between the leftists and the rightists in the South increased. Stirred up by the railway worker union, publishing company union, and electronic communication labor union strikes in Seoul, a much larger-scale strike occurred in Daegu on October 1, 1946. Although poor working conditions and the need for improved laborer treatment were the apparent causes of the strike, their demands included canceling the arrest warrant for all Communist Party leaders issued by the US military government, which had already adopted a hardline approach toward the Communist Party.

During this Daegu October 1st Incident, leftists rallied in various places in the Jeolla and Gyeonggi provinces. There was an incident where a police office branch in Mokpo was attacked as well. Incredibly, I became involved in it, even though it was the same day my wife gave birth to our first daughter, leaving our family thrilled and overjoyed, not to mention unaware of what was happening in the outside world. The very next day, though, rightist organization members dragged me to an unknown place and interrogated me. They told me that someone had already reported me so I had no reason not to confess. I found out later that person was Hong Ik-seon, who considered me his rival.

I was beaten black and blue. It drove me mad because I had nothing to confess. Although I told them that my in-laws could vouch for me, they beat me over the course of several days before handing me to the police. My father-in-law was finally able to visit me at the police station and have me released. Still, they didn't apologize, but, rather, warned me against future misconduct. It was a very confusing time, and many people were dragged away only to vanish without any legal recourse. It was probably thanks to this experience that I formed a firm belief in building a world of and for the people. Hong Ik-seon continued his attempts to entrap me, accusing me of being a leftist when I ran for the National Assembly in Inje, Gangwon-do. However, he eventually got to know me better and helped me when I ran for the National Assembly in Mokpo in 1963. Since then, he's helped me a lot. Ours was a strange karma.

While all of this was happening politically, personal tragedy struck. Our first son, Hong Il, was born. Like my own birth, my son's, too, was extremely difficult, as he entered the world legs first. My wife, the mid-wife, and I were all exhausted by the end of his birth. After this difficult birth, my adorable and beautiful daughter So-hui suddenly died. We were all absolutely devastated. While we were grieving and couldn't muster the courage to bury So-hui, my friend Kim Moon-soo, a member of the US Counter Intelligence Corps (USCIC), heard the news and visited us. He told us to stay behind, took So-hui to the cemetery in a tiny casket, and buried her for us. It still hurts to think of So-hui.

After the October 1st Daegu Incident, I bought a small boat and established the Mokpo Marine Transport Company. As time went by, it had become more and more difficult to run the Jeonnam Steamship Company. The employees expected and demanded a lot from me, and its collective management system lacked efficiency during the turbulent period immediately following the liberation. All of this made me want to have my own business. After discussing it with my father-in-law, I launched a merchant ship company that transported cargo between Mokpo and Busan, Gunsan, and Incheon. Gradually, the company began to flourish. I added two more 70-ton ships and bought a two-story house in Sangrak-dong after years of living in a rental. Everyone in my family was happy and I felt rewarded. The business sailed smoothly and my youthful days flourished.

Yeo Un-hyeong, one of the central figures in Korea's early left-right collaboration, was assassinated in the middle of the street midday on July 19, 1947. He was an outstanding leader who gave everything he had to save our nation during that difficult liberation period. The assassin was a nineteen-year-old anti-communist, probably deeply indoctrinated; people have often said Yeo was sacrificed to ideology. But, strictly speaking, he was sacrificed for the greed of power-grubbers who used ideology as an excuse. It was a truly deplorable event that frustrated the left-right collaboration effort for good.

Kim Koo and Rhee Syngman were the only remaining leaders. While Rhee argued for independence through separate elections in the South, Kim Koo opposed it. As time passed, the UN Temporary Commission on Korea was more inclined toward Rhee's proposal. Together with Kim Gyu-sik, however, Kim Koo proposed a Joint South-North Representative Meeting in order to prevent the country's division. Koreans (including myself) watched the results of Kim Koo's proposal intently as we thought this might be the last opportunity for our country to unify. The North accepted Kim Koo's proposal and the joint meeting occurred in Pyongyang from April 18 through 30, 1948. On April 26, Kim Koo and Kim Gyu-sik from the South and Kim Il-sung and Kim Du-bong from the North participated in a four-way meeting that ended without any concrete results. Kim Koo returned to Seoul only five days before the South's general election on May 10.

The South was heated with election fever. Through this election, a power was to be born in a liberated space. Returning empty-handed, Kim Koo looked too shabby to be a legitimate candidate, and his report on the joint meeting was buried in the flurry of election frenzy. The first National Assembly elected Rhee Syngman as our country's first president. The results were expected as Kim Koo and his Handok Party refused to participate in the election following Kim Koo's resolution not to participate in any activity if the country was divided. At last, the Republic of Korea was born on August 15, 1948. In the North, the Democratic People's Republic of Korea was established twenty-five days later, on September 9. The division between South and North was complete. Just four days after the May 10 general election, the North cut off the South's electricity supply, which it had provided since the liberation.

During this period, I deeply admired Dr. Seo Jae-pil (Philip Jaisohn) because of his virtuous actions during Japanese colonialism. He was the earliest enlightened intellectual and seemed to be continuing along a righteous course. He established the Independence Association and published *The Independence* newspaper. Even more impressive was his decision to adopt *hangul* (Korean script) for *The Independence* instead of Chinese, a more commonly used language among intellectuals at that time. This was a remarkable move, even from today's perspective. The fact that he argued for women's liberation, the equality of all people, and instituted the All People's Congress was further proof of his prescience. He thought not only of the immediate causes of independence, but also of the future course of democracy.

Dr. Seo was also a great example of the "Seeking Truth Grounded on Concrete Evidence" philosophy. He remained separate from the power struggle between Rhee Syngman and Ahn Changho and their followers, simply becoming a doctor and donating his earnings to the independence movement. I admired his practical yet consistent belief system and upright life, so on May 25, 1948, I added my signature to the appeal letter for Dr. Seo's candidacy for presidency.

On June 26, 1949, at the age of seventy-four, Mr. Kim Koo was assassinated in his house by Ahn Doo-hee, a second lieutenant in the active service. Rumor had it that Ahn was part of a broad Rhee Syngman regime conspiracy. Some believed that Rhee himself was involved. With Kim's death, the window for dialogue between the South and North disappeared. As we buried one of the most trusted leaders in all of Korea, the Korean people also buried their desperate hopes for unification. Leaderless, we grieved dearly, commemorating Kim's achievements and crying through his funeral procession.

If I may dare to evaluate Mr. Kim Koo's political activities, I feel he might not have been the most skillful politician, although he was a historically notable independence fighter and a matchless patriot. I believe he should have more actively participated in left-right collaborative activities if he wanted to block the country's division. He also shouldn't have opposed the trusteeship unconditionally but, rather, accepted it first and then found a way to achieve independence within the three- to five-year period. Also, when the decision to establish a separate South Korean government was made, I believe he should have participated in the general election. If he campaigned actively for his party, it could have secured more than half the seats, cornering Rhee Syngman and his Hanmin Party. I don't believe I am alone in this opinion; it is how quite a few people felt at that time. After his return home, Mr. Kim Koo's activities seemed to drop off dramatically. His attempt to foster a South-North dialogue did not yield any major achievements; all he did was oppose the trusteeship.

Although I know it's foolish to apply *what ifs* to history, I still believe that if Mr. Kim Koo had participated in the May 10 general election, Rhee Syngman would not have been elected president and the dictatorship of pro-Japanese collaborators would not have taken root in Korea through the pretense of anti-communism. The election of President Rhee Syngman marked the beginning of Korea's tragic modern history. Under Rhee's regime, pro-Japanese collaborators took power and their descendants were able to flourish thanks to their wealthy background and education. Meanwhile, independence fighters lived abject lives, starving and out in the cold. Their descendants are still suffering without any hope of a quality education. How many died under Rhee Syngman's dictatorship! If Mr. Kim Koo and his followers had assumed power, we would not have atrocities like the Geochang Civilian Massacre Incident or the National Guard Incident.

I believe that in a scenario where the best option is not available, a politician should choose the second best option in order to avoid the absolute worst one. It is my opinion that a politician needs to seek forward-thinking truths based on reality, never ignoring reality for the sake of truth. Although all our people, including me, admired Mr. Kim Koo, I invariably feel sad about his political career. He might have been too passionate to handle the cold reality of our situation.

After leaving the Sinmin Party, I registered with the right-wing camp; however, I didn't actively participate in that one, either. Instead, I tried to expand my businesses. After entering into a contract with the Joseon Merchant Ship Company, my company began to ship grains from all over the Mokpo area and I thus became a man of influence in Mokpo.

Around this time, I was asked to participate in the National Guidance Alliance, an anti-communist organization led by former leftist defectors. Like most other businessmen, I sponsored it financially but did not get personally involved. When the Korean War erupted, the government had the police and military massacre its members during the early stages of the Southern retreat.

The situation around the Korean Peninsula was becoming grave. On April 3, 1948, the April 3rd Incident occurred under the US military government. The US military government ruthlessly suppressed the Jeju people's uprising against the separate South Korean election by mobilizing not only the police, but also the National Guard. Tens of thousands of people were massacred all across Jeju Island. In addition, the newly inaugurated Rhee Syngman government ordered the dispatch of the 14th Regiment from Yeosu to Jeju. Many soldiers rebelled on October 20, incited by the leftists and with the belief that they could not kill their own people. These rebels occupied not only Yeosu, but also Suncheon. Rhee Syngman's regime suppressed them ruthlessly as well, massacring many innocent civilians who were accused of having communist ties. Jeju Island and southern regions of Korea were dyed in blood. Additionally, all along the 38th Parallel, large- and small-scale military confrontations occurred more and more frequently.

It was an ominous time. Blood stained the liberation space across the peninsula. The April 3rd Incident ignited the Yeosu-Suncheon Incident, which, in turn, led to the tides of the Korean War. Unbeknownst to us, Bloody Sunday was approaching.

DEATH NEXT TO ME (1950)

I encountered the beginning of the Korean War on my tenth day in Seoul. I was staying at the Lim Inn near Gwanghwamun while taking care of business matters. As I was walking with a navy officer friend after a lunch in Myeong-dong, a military truck suddenly appeared with its loudspeaker blaring, "All military personnel, return to your units immediately! All military personnel, return to your units!"

We, of course, didn't know what to make of it. At any rate, my friend hurried back to his unit and I tried to return to the inn amid the confused, scattered crowd. I could tell that something serious had happened, so I dropped by an acquaintance's house nearby. The radio was now repeating the news: "The North Korean puppets provoked an all-out war!"

I wasn't too worried, though, because there had been skirmishes along the 38th Parallel for a while now. Also, the South Korean government always boasted about its military might; they threw around proud declarations of their victories, such as: "We shot our enemies to death." "We vanquished all of them immediately after they provoked the fight!" I still vividly remember our Defense Minister Shin Seong-mo's words: "If Mr. President orders it, our military can reach Pyongyang in three days and the Amnok River in a week. We'll bring back Amnok River water to Mr. President."

In addition, President Rhee advocated for the Unification by Armed Conquest of the North policy every opportunity he got. Many people thought the news of the armed struggle between the two Koreas meant that President Rhee had put his unification plan into action. It was a collective illusion.

Like many other people, I listened to news of everything that was happening on the radio, believing that the South would defeat the North in no time at all. Newspaper and radio news confirmed our belief: "Our military has counterattacked and is currently advancing northward." Two days after the war broke out, President Rhee announced: "We will defend Seoul at all costs. Please rest assured."

It was all a lie. Even as the radio broadcast his announcement, President Rhee was in Daejeon and our government had already moved to Suwon. It poured cats and dogs that night. I went out the next morning and discovered that the North Korean People's Army had already occupied Seoul. The streets were filled with refugees. It was more ludicrous than terrifying. The enemies had managed to occupy Seoul a day after our president promised to defend it at all costs ... and yet the entire government fled, leaving its citizens hostages! Soon after, another piece of upsetting news arrived: Our military had destroyed the Han River Iron Bridge to prevent North Korean advance. Since there was no warning, scores of cars fell into the water and hundreds of refugees and soldiers were also cruelly sacrificed.

I had no choice but to remain in Seoul, where North Korean flags now fluttered everywhere. The biggest problem was learning how to survive. I had no money since I had given all I had with me to my relatives and friends, who left for Mokpo as soon as the war broke out. I kept a large stash of cash that I had received from the Joseon Merchant Ship Company in a safe at the company, but when I went to retrieve it, I discovered that the People's Army had locked the safe. I barely scraped by, selling my watch and suits.

One day, I happened to witness the so-called people's court on some school grounds near the Russian Embassy. From my hiding place, I could see a man kneeling in front of a large crowd. A man with an armband listed all of the kneeling man's crimes and asked the congregants present, "What should we do with this reactionary element?" "Kill him!" they cried in response.

That was it. The man was then dragged away to the execution grounds. It was chilling. I confirmed once again that I could never accept communism. Food was getting harder to obtain and young men were being forced to volunteer for the North Korean Army. I was also worried about my mother and other family members in the South. My wife was in her last month of pregnancy. I had to escape Seoul.

I gathered everyone who wanted to come with me—my brother-in-law, a friend from Boryeong named Cho Jang-won, a Joseon Merchant Ship Company clerk named Han To-won, and a person who wanted to go to

Gunsan. We secretly hired a ferryman to cross the Han River. We met at Mapo Ferry and boarded near Sogang Station. From there, we could see a US bombing under way nearby. Amid a blaze that reddened the river, we stared at each other, wondering if we would survive, if we would arrive at our homes again.

It's about 400 kilometers from Seoul to Mokpo. Once on the other side of the river, we began to walk southward. Luckily, it was summer, so we could sleep anywhere. Once a farmer caught us eating melons on his farm near Byeongjeom. I offered him money, but he frowned and refused to take it.

Near Cheonan, we saw an exhausted woman trudging along with a baby on her back. Both of them were covered with dust. We took turns carrying the baby and supporting the mother. Since we thought it would be dangerous to go straight to Daejeon, we decided to go through Dangjin and Boryeong. In Dangjin, we went to the largest house in the area and asked them to let us sleep there. The owner not only offered us lodging, but also fed us both dinner and breakfast. When we offered to pay him, the mute owner waved his hand, making a *woo-woo* sound to indicate he didn't want our money.

We had to climb a steep mountain path in Hongseong. We were extremely thirsty, and found a house on the mountain road where we hoped to quench our thirst. The owner immediately pointed to a jar he had filled with barley tea in order to prevent refugees from drinking unboiled water and getting sick. In Boryeong, I stayed at my friend Cho Jang-won's house for two days before resuming my journey to Mokpo.

There were refugees everywhere. People carried their household items in wrapping cloths either on their heads or in their arms. Occasionally, there were oxcarts, but most people walked. They were all wearing either work clothes or traditional white cotton clothes. Women were carrying not only bundles on their heads and in their arms, but also crying babies on their backs. The world outside was luxuriant with summer green, but people on the street were expressionless, as if their hearts had been burnt out. The present was nothing but hardship and the future was unknown. Everyone just walked. *Who is this war for?* I was overwhelmed by sadness and anger. Bombs fell and bullets poured down all around us like rain. We were hungry, had a long way to go, and death was near.

Around Mangyeong Field in Gimje, a fighter jet suddenly appeared and began bombing the other end of a bridge I was about to cross. After it finished, I dashed across the bridge, but my straw hat fell off in the middle of my mad run. I don't know why I stopped to pick it up in such a danger-ous situation, but I did. When I was almost at the other end of the bridge, the fighter jet appeared again, this time bombing the spot where I had crouched to avoid the previous bombing. I could have died if I hadn't run across. The distance between life and death was only a few steps.

I kept on walking. I could not see a single South Korean soldier. I had heard that the People's Army had already gained control of Mokpo. It might not have been safe to return to Mokpo, but I couldn't return to Seoul, either. I had to leave everything to fate. When I arrived in Iro-myeon near Mokpo, I ran into a crowded fair. Suddenly, a US fighter jet appeared and rained machine-gun fire down on us. The fair field was soaked with blood. Although we ran toward a nearby hill, the fighter jet followed us and showered us with bullets. We ran, fell, and ran. By the time the fighter jet finally disappeared again, I did not have the strength to stand. I was scraped all over and my clothes were dyed red with blood. Most of the fair-goers were wearing white cotton clothes and they, too, had all been dyed red—I can still vividly remember those red spots on the white clothes. Everyone was either wounded or dead. It was absurd.

I arrived in Mokpo twenty days after I escaped Seoul. My house was near the pier and one of the biggest houses in the neighborhood because of the offices attached to it. The closer I got to home, the more impatient I became, worrying about my parents, siblings, and wife, who could have already given birth to our baby. Once I neared the house, I could see my mother sitting on a small chair in front of it. She had been waiting for me like that every day. She was so thin and haggard that she looked like a mummy. Within less than two months, she had grown too old and too small, almost like a child. When I hugged her, she began to sob. When I tried to take her into the house, she wailed. She explained that my house had been designated the property of a traitor and we could not enter it. They called me a right-wing reactionary element, and took everything from the house. They also arrested Dae-ui, my younger brother, for being a civilian worker for the South Korean military. My wife had given birth to our second son, Hong Up, in a bomb shelter the Japanese had Koreans build during World War II because she couldn't even step foot inside our house, let alone a hospital.

Captain Pak Dong-ryeon, who worked for my company, took care of my family the entire time I was gone. During that time, a lot of employees treated their employers cruelly, but Captain Pak embraced my family warmly and let me stay in his house as well. I didn't know what to do or who to meet, but I felt relieved that my family was safe. After two nights of rest, I went out to see what was going on outside. Soon, a stranger called me out of the blue and asked me to accompany him for a short while. That's how I was detained at the Mokpo police station, which had been commandeered by the People's Committee. Kim Seong-su, a former guerrilla and then-People's Committee political defense department officer, interrogated me. He asked me how many of his comrades I snitched on and smacked me across my face when I denied ever doing so.

"Do you know how worried we were that you might rat out our fellow patriots (communists)? You still lie! You must have no regrets for what you did!" Then he ordered, "Lock him up right now!"

I was sent to Mokpo Prison. There were no more interrogations. They tried to recruit other prisoners to become their collaborators or volunteers for their army, but they left me alone, most likely because they considered me irredeemable.

The most difficult thing to contend with in prison was the hunger. They gave me a tiny barley ball served with seaweed soup twice a day, which I drank up until I saw the dirt underneath it. All I could think about there was not my family, but food. Memories of eating fish with someone or meat somewhere danced through my head. I was absolutely drained to the point where it was hard to even sit up. In the afternoon, I lay face down and breathed quietly to minimize my energy consumption.

On September 28, 1950, all the prisoners were rounded up in an auditorium. We couldn't wash our faces, so we all looked terrible. My brief hopes of a release were soon shattered. We were paired up and our arms were tied together with either handcuffs or wire. I was tied with wire to a man named Han Wal-su.

More and more prisoners were brought to the auditorium. Latecomers sat near the entrance. They wore regular clothes so they must have been taken straight from the police station. I was sitting inside. While we wondered about the situation, the People's Army soldiers began dragging away people who were sitting near the entrance. We all instinctively knew that we were about to be executed.

People began to cry and struggle against being taken. When a soldier asked, "Who told you you're going to be killed?" the answer to that apparent rhetorical question seemed clear: "You."

The auditorium turned into hell, with people shrieking and begging for their lives. "What crime did I commit to deserve execution?" "I'm a communist guerrilla's family. What crime have I committed?" Soldiers aimed their rifles at people's chests or randomly struck people with their rifle stocks.

People were taken out by the twenties. Their cries pierced the hearts of those that remained like a dagger. Others silently accepted their fate. I began to feel dizzy thinking that I would be executed soon and wondering how little time I had left.

Suddenly, there was complete silence outside. No one else was taken out. We just waited, not knowing what was happening. Those who have not experienced a period of time waiting for their own death cannot understand what it feels like. The silence was oppressive, absolute.

Toward the evening, commotion began again. The People's Army soldiers had all disappeared, and the local communists took us back to the prison. About eighty of us prisoners remained. About a hundred people had been taken out—life and death divided us.

I later heard that the People's Army wanted to kill us all off before they made their retreat upon hearing news of the September 28 UN Incheon Landing. They were unable to complete their plan, though, because a truck transporting prisoners broke down on the road. Some said that the truck driver intentionally caused it. At any rate, the North Koreans had no choice but to retreat after ordering the local communists to burn us in prison. The local communists couldn't burn their neighbors, though— some of those neighbors were actually family members and relatives.

We were imprisoned and began to feel hungry again. In every prison cell, people were making noises, asking for food. The communists gave us food—a lot more than usual because they had to feed a lot fewer prisoners than before the execution. I played the role of chief among my cellmates and distributed the food evenly. I've never devoured food like I did then. Although my stomach looked like a frog's, it kept on clamoring for more food. Other people might have died, but we had to eat and survive.

After satisfying my hunger, I tried to find out what was going on outside. I watched the tiny opening in the door intently and caught and tugged the pant leg of a passing prison guard. He squatted down instead of kicking me, as he would have done before. He was a local communist.

"Hello. What on earth is happening to us? Are we going to live or die?" I asked.
"How can a Southerner kill another Southerner?" he replied.
"Did the North Koreans retreat?" I asked again.
"No, not really, but ..."

I realized something had happened. As I crouched by the door and clung to hope, someone passed by and called out, "Im-chul! Im-chul!" Im-chul was my fellow Mokpo Commercial High School alumnus. Realizing that Im-chul must have been a prisoner, too, I said, "Hey, here I am," pretending I was Im-chul. When the man came outside, I asked him to open the door, saying that Im-chul was sick. I could hear him breaking the lock outside and then prisoners kicked the iron door down from inside. My prison mates flooded out and I ran around the prison to tell the other prisoners, "The People's Army have run away! Break out! I'll try to break the lock here. All of you, be brave!"

Pretty soon, all the prisoners had escaped their cells. Although it was night, the prison yard was fairly bright because of a fuller moon. It was the seventeenth day of the eighth lunar month, two days after the Chuseok. The moon, beautiful and bright, shone over me, a dirty-faced prisoner with a frog belly.

In order to avoid recapture by People's Army soldiers who might still be lingering nearby, we tried to get our private clothes back. It was impossible to reclaim your own clothes, though. You just had to wear whatever fit you. In the midst of all this confusion, I heard a voice saying, "This is not mine. It's not." It was my brother Dae-ui.

I rushed over to him. "Are you really looking for your own clothes now? Just put anything on!" Dae-ui was shocked to see me, and we were both overjoyed. Still, we didn't have time to linger.

After hiding in a neighborhood near Mokpo Prison for a while, we headed toward our house early in the morning. A woman with a baby on her back was lingering on the street and crying. It was my wife. She'd been crying all night long because of a rumor that all of the prisoners had been executed. I had survived, but she couldn't stop sobbing.

Dae-ui said that only three out of his nine cellmates survived. As soon as we were arrested, our youngest brother, Dae-hyeon, had volunteered for the People's Army in order to rescue us. He escaped in the dark around Jeollabuk-do while the People's Army was retreating. Incredibly, all three of us siblings had survived right on the threshold of death.

You might say that my father-in-law's survival was a miracle. He was among those who had been taken to the execution grounds. When they fired, he fainted. Although he had been shot at twice more, the bullets simply scraped his ears. After the enemies left, he waited till dawn and then escaped, his hands still tied behind him. He was the only survivor out of more than a hundred prisoners who had been taken to that valley of death.

Prison escapees like my brother and I had to hide because communist guerrillas were still hunting for us. As they continued to chase and kill prison escapees, only thirty out of us eighty escapees survived in the end. My brother and I hid in the house of a sister of another marine transport company owner near the wharf. Because the US fighter jets frequently bombed the wharf area, we thought it was safer there. On our fifth day of hiding in the ceiling area, using bedpans to conceal us, the South Korean Marine Corps finally arrived to occupy Mokpo.

My family and I were extremely lucky to have survived that period, but the meaning of the Korean War had become clear. *Why fight and die?* The fratricidal massacres would never end. When the communists retreated, the leftists would have to die, and vice versa. *What is ideology? Why should ideology turn human beings into beasts? Should ideology reign over individual and national happiness?* I clearly saw what war was, and what the world ruled by communists would look like—how that world was uninhabitable. I have dreamt of national reconciliation and a world without war my entire life.

Success, Frustration, and Challenge During the War (1950–1953)

Of course, we had to make a living, even during the war. The sun rose and the flowers bloomed amid the bombs and billowing gunpowder smoke. Mokpo port still bustled with boat whistles, and savory smells wafted out of the taverns. Children continued to be born. As time marched on, war became a part of our everyday life.

I resumed my business with a single remaining ship, one ship having been commandeered and the other vanished after a bombing. I worked hard and my business began to thrive again. I was a young businessman going about Mokpo in a jeep. At the time, only a few dignitaries, like the mayor, naval commander, and provost marshal, drove around in jeeps.

I was able to succeed even in the midst of war because of three principles I had learned throughout my business career. These principles were— First, to understand and ride the overall economic trends. Second, not to fear an appropriate level of risk-taking. Third, to maintain a good relationship with your employees.

I always tried to evaluate overall circumstances and take on new challenges. Also, a good relationship with my employees was always my priority. After all, it was an employee who protected my family and me during the difficult wartime period. Also, all my employees had petitioned for me while I was detained in the police station and prison. I still feel happy that they defended me in that utterly terrifying and contentious wartime. I'm both grateful for them and proud of myself.

The military used my commandeered ship to transport military supplies. In order to assist the military, I also participated in the establishment of the Coast Guard Jeonnam Headquarter toward the end of 1950. Mr. O Jae-gyun served as its captain and I the first mate. We transported food and other military supplies. The Coast Guard didn't engage in the combat itself—our main duty was to help the military with their local battles, like guerrilla mop-up operations. Once the Jeonnam Headquarter was established, young men crowded to volunteer. After their brief experience living under communist rule, they were eager to defend us from the communists.

As a branch officer of the Coast Guard, I got to know naval officers stationed in Mokpo. The most memorable among them were Mr. O Se-dong and Mr. Park Sung-chul. Mr. Park later became a rear admiral in the Marine Corps, and he also worked as the head of my security guard office until the 1980 military coup. When I was imprisoned after the May 17th Incident, he was also detained and suffered greatly. His rank was stripped from him and he was denied a military burial in the National Cemetery following his death. It was so unjust that I petitioned for the recovery of his honor and he was finally moved to the National Cemetery. I also met Mr. Yang Soon-jik, a troop information and education officer (a lieutenant) at the Coast Guard Mokpo branch. He later worked with me in the Pyeongmin Party. At the time, I had no idea that our meeting at sea would later continue on land.

In October 1950, I took over the Mokpo Newspaper Company, the largest local newspaper in Korea during the Japanese colonial period. As the war progressed, the newspaper ran into financial troubles. The employees of the newspaper company contacted me to see if I wanted to take it over. I had always been interested in the news media so I didn't hesitate to accept the invitation.

I asked that all reporters adhere to fair reporting standards—my managing principle was to not hurt anyone because of unfair reporting. Once, the vice president of the Bank of Korea and the bank's Mokpo branch president visited the company during the former's visit to Mokpo. He asked me, "Where's the president?"

The Bank of Korea Mokpo branch president responded in utter embarrassment, "He's the president."

The vice president said he didn't expect to meet such a young president and we shook hands. That evening at a local businessmen's social gathering, I described point by point how difficult it was to do local business to the vice president of the Bank of Korea. I also detailed the discrimination against certain regions and how businesses in similar conditions but from different regions were treated very differently. A business in Busan, for example, would receive a loan, but its Mokpo equivalent wouldn't.

When I finished, the vice president stood up and praised me. "I am really surprised today. President Kim Dae-jung's understanding of the current financial situation is accurate and beneficial to everyone. He is an asset to this region. You should all encourage the growth of a talent like him."

I felt flattered. After he finished speaking, the vice president handed me a note that read:

Dear Bank of Korea Mokpo Branch Chief,
    Please approve Mr. Kim Dae-jung's loan application. The main branch will co-sign the loan.

Although I simply expressed my thoughts, my words probably carried more weight because I was the newspaper company president. During my presidency, I never tried to influence anybody inappropriately. I just focused on business management so that reporters could focus on their job of fair reporting. Two years later, I decided to move to Busan and returned management to the reporters. Mr. Kim Mun-ok, singer Nam Jin's father, served as its president for a long time after that. He was a man of influence in the area, and later served as a national assemblyman as well.

Seoul was occupied again on January 4 and the government temporarily moved to Busan. All offices and organizations gathered in Busan, so I had to move my business there as well. I established the Heungguk Marine Transport Company and transported grain, fertilizer, and straw ropes and sacks for the Financial Cooperative Federation (later called the National Agricultural Cooperative Federation). Although I owned only five ships, I managed more than ten ships by renting others. My family lived behind Namhangdong Market in the Yeongdo district of Busan.

During this period, I learned a great deal more about the world. In a way, I opened my eyes for the first time. I met many people from Busan. I visited Mr. Cho Bong-am in Yeongdo, and met Mr. Park Ik-soo, Ms. Kim Jung-re, and Mr. Kang Yong-hun. I met Mr. Kim Il-nam from Mokpo almost every day and talked about current affairs.

I met Ms. Kim Jung-re under rather strange circumstances. I traveled to Incheon with a ship fully loaded with rice immediately before the January 4th Retreat. Just as I finished selling all the rice, the January 4th Retreat refugees crowded the Incheon port like the inflow of the tide. I had to rush back to Mokpo. When I arrived at my ship, I found a young woman directing people to my ship at random. When I asked her who she was, she politely greeted me and asked me to help her send some refugees south. She seemed like an honest and affable person, so I allowed them onboard. I later ran into her again in Busan.

In Busan, I hung out with members of a group called Myeonuhoi, although I was not a member myself. Myeonuhoi was composed of college students from Seoul and we discussed life, philosophy, and our country's future. Our conversations were lively and helpful, despite the fact that our reality was depressing. We became so close that, as time went on, we talked about personal matters as well.

I got to know my current wife, Lee Hee-ho, in that group, though we had briefly met at a YWCA dinner with Ms. Kim Jung-re before becoming good friends at the Myeonuhoi gatherings. Although she later became my colleague and companion, then we were just two young people eager to learn about the world and life. She often appeared in a dyed military uniform, but she looked even more feminine that way. Her beautiful, bright smile revealed brilliant white teeth.

During our conversations, we understood each other uncannily well. One day, we took a walk together in the Gamcheon area near the Busan Station. I picked wild flowers for her. We talked about current affairs and, especially, politics. We were both enraged over Rhee Syngman's scheme for permanent rule. She had clear opinions about things and was thoughtful. She said she was planning to study abroad when things became better, both for her personally and for our country. She was simultaneously strong and warm.

Events continued to occur that made me despair even more than the war did. War ravaged the country, and people's hearts were ripped and torn in the process. In regions where guerrillas were active, people lived in fear of the South Korean military during the day and the

People's Army at night. After the January 4th Retreat, guerrillas waged uprisings on the home front. At last, the Geochang Civilian Massacre occurred in February of 1951. The South Korean military ruthlessly massacred hundreds of civilians based on accusations of aiding the enemy. Using heavy artillery, they randomly massacred 136 young and middle-aged men in a valley in Naetan Village on February 10, and 527 people in Baksan Valley on February 11.

Shin Jung-mok, a national assemblyman from Geochang, first revealed the details of the tragic events. When the National Assembly fact-finding mission arrived, though, the Gyeongnam Marshall Law Enforcement Headquarters Civilian Matters Department Chief Colonel Kim Jeong-won tried to block their investigation by stationing a platoon-sized troop disguised as guerrillas to shoot the mission. This incident could have been covered up but for the national assemblyman's exposure.

It was clear that similar incidents were happening in many places. Tales of similar bloodbaths were being inscribed all over the country, and mountains and fields were becoming gravesites. After South Korean soldiers came and killed scores of civilians and opposing troops, the guerrillas retaliated. This vicious cycle repeated itself over and over again.

Soon after this, we heard news of the National Guard Incident. After China declared its participation in the war, the South Korean government hastened to organize a National Guard of men aged seventeen to forty. But the National Guard's chief officers, including its highest commander, embezzled government money and supplies and, as a result, tens of thousands of National Guard troops died of hunger and cold on the road. Meanwhile, National Guard leaders transported the embezzled money in their jeeps every night and squandered it on drinking and sex in Daegu.

Defense Minister Shin Seong-mo resigned because of this incident and the National Assembly decided to dismantle the National Guard on April 30. After this decision went into effect on May 12, the surviving National Guard troops were left destitute and homeless, wandering around the streets of Daegu. We were all outraged. The Coast Guard, of which I was a member, was also dismantled. Our country was in such disarray that it didn't deserve the name "country."

Then, on May 26, 1952, the Busan Political Crisis occurred. While North Koreans occupied Seoul and fresh young men sacrificed their lives to defend their country on the front lines, independents claimed more than 60 percent of the National Assembly after the second general election on May 30, 1952. It was clear then that President Rhee could not be reelected president for a second term, which would begin in August 1952. In order to reverse these prospects, President Rhee established the Liberal Party and tried to amend the Constitution to introduce a direct presidential election, while the opposition wanted to replace the presidential system with a parliamentary government system.

Supporters of President Rhee held a rally urging for a direct presidential election, mobilizing bands of thugs and right-wing organizations in the process. Additionally, thugs besieged National Assembly Hall and the government declared martial law and arrested opposition members, accusing them of being international communist organization members. In the end, Prime Minister Chang Taek-sang proposed a compromise bill that included a direct presidential election and a two-house system. This bill was passed only after national assemblymen, even those in prison, were taken to the assembly hall by force, surrounded by policemen and thugs.

I could clearly see how former pro-Japanese collaborators and their supporters were abusing anti-communism to satisfy their own greed. I was shocked to see representatives betraying the people's will and yielding so easily to dictatorship. Events like these led me to think more earnestly about politics and politicians. I decided to devote myself to politics after witnessing and experiencing two disasters—the war and this Busan Political Crisis.

During the Korean War, I saw our leaders lie, the country driven into crisis, and the people into despair. It was clear that unjust politics trampled on human rights and would do nothing to protect people's lives or property. Also, the Busan Political Crisis showed me how a dictatorial regime could debilitate the National Assembly and change the Constitution at random, all in the name of the people's will. These experiences taught me that only true democracy could guarantee people's happiness, that only proper politics would guarantee proper places for us all. I jumped into politics, an exciting move that also marked the beginning of my hardships.

Loss After Loss (1954–1959)

In 1954, I ran as an independent for the third House of Representatives election in Mokpo. I didn't want to go near the ruling Liberal Party, nor did I seek to join the opposition Democratic People's Party, despite their invitations. I made this decision because I received firm support from the labor union's Mokpo branch. At that time, support from the labor union guaranteed a win, as was the case with the previous election.

Labor union leaders liked my fair approach to their positions and my effort to improve my employees' conditions. In exchange for their support of me, they requested that I run as an independent, which I agreed to. My high school alumni helped my campaign, and my win seemed guaranteed until the unexpected arrest of the labor leaders.

The police summoned them one by one and demanded that as "members of official organizations," they support the Liberal Party candidate rather than an independent. They had them write a memorandum promising their support to the ruling party candidate. Labor leaders, under strict surveillance, were mobilized to support rallies for the ruling party candidate. Although they showed my number with their fingers while making a speech in support of the ruling party candidate, it was of no use.

When the results came in, I came in fifth out of ten candidates. Although I'd lost, I learned a great deal about the political process. Above all, I realized that it was extremely difficult to run a campaign without the backing of a party organization. I also learned that it was very expensive to run a campaign. Labor leaders, including Kim Jin-hae, the Labor Union Confederation secretary and a progressive northern region native, cried with me after the election.

The next year, I left Mokpo—an attractive and dynamic city that had captured the heart of a boy from the remote Hauido Island, the nest for my love and my family, the city where I had acquired my world perspective and so much wisdom, my second home. My life there was rich because I engaged in business in a commercial city after graduating from a commercial high school. I owned a business that was built from my sweat and passion. When I decided to leave Mokpo, memories of my life there through colonial periods, liberation, and war passed through my mind. Still, I decided that in order to become a politician I had to leave Mokpo for Seoul, just as I had left Hauido for Mokpo. My wife packed without a word of objection. How grateful I was, and what a reliable partner she was! We left Mokpo with our young children, but Mokpo continued to give me so much more. I am always moved and overwhelmed when I think of Mokpo.

I liquidated my businesses one by one. We found a house in Namyeong-dong in the Yongsan area and my wife began to run a beauty salon. I took a position as the editor-in-chief at the Korea Labor Issue Research Institute near Samgakji, where my friend Cha Guk-chan was the director. I wrote articles about labor issues. At that time, corporations bribed or oppressed labor unions and labor unions were being mobilized for the Liberal Party during elections. I pointed out this situation and explored an alternative, a way for both employers and employees to live together. In order to study Japanese examples of similar cases, I searched bookstores in the Myeong-dong alleyway. My articles were published in *Donga Ilbo* and *Sasanggye*. In particular, I contributed a lead article, "Korean Labor Movement's Path," to *Sasanggye*, the leading current affairs magazine.

I also served as the editor-in-chief of the monthly publication, *Sinsegye*. Yoon Hyung-doo, who later became the president of a successful publishing company (Beomu Publisher), worked with me as a reporter. *Sinsegye* opposed dictatorship and advocated economic freedom and social reform. As this aligned with what the government perceived as opposition party lines, the government oppressed us. We were unable to procure advertisers or bank loans and, in the end, had to abandon it.

I also established a public speech training school called the Asian Public Speech Institute. I'd shown talent in delivering public speeches since high school; at the time, public speeches were a politician's most valuable weapon. I taught about fifty students, including professional public speech coaches, office workers, and would-be politicians. I met Kim Sang-hyun and Kim Chang-kon, my future political colleagues and national assemblymen, there. I taught skills to convey one's ambition through speech—including honing pitch, gesture, and content.

I also participated in the establishment of the Republican Party in March 1956. Bae Eun-hui, Chang Taek-sang, and Yi Beom-seok were among its supreme council members. In recognition of my activities in document-creation and public relations, I was chosen to be the party's spokesperson, although I wasn't a known personality. Mr. Chang Taek-sang helped me a great deal. He also referred me to the *Hankook Ilbo* newspaper's president Chang Ki-young as an editorialist. However, due to conflicts between Chang Taek-sang and Yi Beom-seok, the majority of party members (including myself) left, and the Republican Party collapsed in less than a year.

In May 1956, the presidential election's major conflict was between President Rhee Syngman and the Democratic Party's candidate Shin Ik-hui. The vice presidential candidates were Lee Ki-poong and Chang Myon. Although I hadn't joined the Democratic Party, I supported Shin Ik-hui and Chang Myon. The Korean people and the opposition coalition who wished for regime change enthusiastically supported Mr. Shin. As Election Day approached, the election results seemed fairly obvious. Even governmental officials secretly visited Mr. Shin's camp, and there were rumors that local police chiefs had vouched loyalty to opposition camp leaders. Nobody doubted Mr. Shin's landslide victory. The ruling Liberal Party's election fraud tactics were too obviously dishonorable, and public opinion favored a regime change.

The hope for a peaceful regime change was shattered only ten days before the election, when Mr. Shin suddenly died of stroke while on his campaign train to Jeollabuk-do. Many of his supporters voted for Cho Bong-am or didn't vote at all. There were also allegations that the votes for Cho Bong-am had mysteriously shifted to votes for Rhee Syngman. Despite the will of the majority, Rhee Syngman was elected for a third term. The historical current was going against people's wishes. One silver lining was the election of Chang Myon as vice president. Due to the notorious Round-up Constitutional Amendment, the vice president was to succeed presidency for the remainder of the president's term should it become necessary. Because President Rhee was eighty-one years old, the ruling party had waged an all-out campaign to elect Lee Ki-poong; however, the safety valve the ruling party prepared became a ticking time bomb. This was the people's judgment. The ruling party tried to amend the Constitution once again, this time to eliminate the article regarding the vice president's succession. The Democratic Party tried to block these efforts with all of their might. The matter of succession for presidency became the eye of a typhoon.

In June 1956, I was baptized into the Catholic Church with Vice President Chang as my godfather. My choice to become Catholic was the result of many influences. My wife's family was deeply Catholic, and my friend Choi So-myeon, the Catholic Seoul Parish chief, had also actively urged me to convert. I was also deeply moved by Dr. Chang Myon's sincere actions and words. Additionally, I admired the dedication of those Catholic fathers and nuns who pledged celibacy. How hard it would be to lead a life of celibacy—I certainly couldn't do it! I also liked the way the Catholic Church was unified.

Father Kim Cheol-gyu led the baptismal ceremony in Archbishop Paul Ro Ki-nam's office at Myeongdong Cathedral. My baptismal name was Thomas More; of this Father Kim said: "Thomas More is an English thinker and politician. He became a martyr instead of obeying King Henry VIII's separation of the Anglican Church from Catholicism. He chose to be guillotined rather than accepting the despot's demand to acknowledge divorce. Receive this name with a resolution to dedicate your life to the church like him."

I found the ceremony chilling, because my belief was not deep enough then. I wondered why he chose the name of an executed person for me instead of someone like Thomas Aquinas, the great theological scholar. However, as I got to know more about Thomas More, I felt blessed to have been given his name. When he was in prison, many people visited him in an attempt to save his life, but he refused to betray his beliefs. Although he could have enjoyed power and wealth, he instead chose a clean conscience and his religious beliefs. I also liked that he was not a biblical character, but a real, breathing, historical person. Over the years, I have wondered if perhaps my political career has involved so many life and death crises because of my baptized name. But I accept it as God's will and am grateful that God has guarded my will.

Just a few months later, on September 25, I pledged myself to another affiliation—the Democratic Party. I made this decision based on my respect for Vice President Chang. The party was formed just a year earlier by Cho Byong-ok, Chang Myon, Kwak Sang-hun, and Baek Nam-hun. The Democratic Party fought against the Rhee regime's dictatorship as well as a government-controlled economy. It also worked for peaceful reunification. Because I agreed to these principles, I chose to join. There were two schools within the Democratic Party: the Old School was composed mostly of former Hanmin Party members, and the New School was composed of Catholics, Young Korean Academy members, and former officials. Culturally, the Old School was more political, while the New School was more policy-oriented. Naturally, the Old School was more conciliatory toward the government and the ruling party, whereas the New School was more confrontational.

I belonged to the New School, because it was more progressive and included people I respected, such as Dr. Chang Myon and Dr. Jeong Il-hyeong, one of my lifelong supporters. As I was keenly interested in labor issues, I worked at the party's labor division and soon became its vice chief.

A few days after I joined the party, an assassination attempt was made against Vice President Chang's life. A veteran jumped up and shot at the vice president as he was leaving the podium following his speech at the party's convention. There was no doubt that the ruling power was behind the assassination attempt. Luckily, only Dr. Chang's left hand was hurt. When I visited him at the hospital, I could not help crying over our depressing political reality. Seeing him lying there on the hospital bed, I thought about the future of our democracy.

Around that time, I visited Mr. Cho Bong-am, a progressive politician, at his residence in Dojeonggung, Sajik-dong, to hear his opinions about current political affairs. I'd met him in Busan during the war. Although a former Communist Party member, Mr. Cho attracted attention because of his complete and open severance from it. He had been the first Minister of Agriculture and Forestry. He had done pretty well during the presidential election as well—people viewed his progressive socialism favorably.

I suggested to him, "You have experience in the Communist Party and now you're working in the Democratic camp. I think you're the best person to let citizens know why the Communist Party is wrong. If you tell them why you denounced it in a fair manner, they'll learn about their true identity and support you more."

Mr. Cho's answer was not what I expected, though. "I agree with you, Comrade Kim," he said, "but some people worry that such actions could alienate my supporters."

I was disappointed. I felt a great leader like Cho Bong-am should show people his resolution at the right moment, no matter how it translated into votes. Instead, he hesitated, and was later executed for being a spy. It was a truly tragic event. The Cho Bong-am I knew was a charming, affable man. He just lacked the skills to break through more difficult situations.

The general election season returned in the spring of 1958, but I couldn't run in Mokpo because the current assemblyman Mr. Chung Jung-sup was from the Democratic Party. After much thought and discussion with party leaders, I decided to run for the seat in Inje, Gangwon-do. Inje previously belonged to North Korea, but become part of South Korea following the war. I was a carpetbagger without any acquaintances in the region. But, luckily, more than 80 percent of the voters were soldiers, military personnel, or families thereof. Because we didn't have an absentee voter system then, all of them voted where they worked and lived. Because military personnel knew very well that the system was corrupt, they tended to favor opposition parties and change. Soldiers were sent out for work unrelated to military needs. They had to cut trees and produce and sell charcoal. Unjust treatment and abuse of power were rampant. Young people supported opposition parties during this time when there was no such term as "regional tension."

By the time I registered, the ruling party candidate had also already registered. Because election fraud attempts by the ruling party were rampant—and becoming bolder and craftier as each election went by—I had to be extremely cautious. In order to register, I needed one hundred voter signatures and seals. Since duplicate signatures meant cancellation of the later signatures, I gathered 130 signatures. Even then, I received three sets of these signature forms and two of my staff members each kept a precautionary copy in addition to my own.

In an effort to prevent any foul play, when I registered at the Election Administration Committee at the Inje district office, I requested the officer give me the list of voters who signed for the ruling party candidate. The officer said he would do so the next day, and locked up my registration documents in a safe. Although suspicious, I had no choice but to leave and begin campaigning, hanging placards and pasting posters everywhere I went. The next day, my worries proved well founded. The Election Administration Committee announced that my registration was vacated because more than seventy of my signatures had already appeared on the other candidate's registration documents.

I later found out that the district office interior department chief and the police had conspired overnight to work this out. They checked the signatures on my registration form and then visited signers to have them add signatures to the other candidate's registration form. I had no choice but to get new signatures within a day of the deadline. It was difficult because I didn't know many people and the Liberal Party's presence was threatening. I had to visit people door to door and appeal to them with my cause. No one had their registered seals because village headmen had collected them under the pretext that they needed them to distribute fertilizers to them. As a stopgap measure, I made a form that said, "Although I do not have my registered seal with me now, I hereby permit Candidate Kim to make my seal and use it for this document." In this way we gathered their thumbprints on the documents.

When we went to seal shops, though, we encountered another problem. No one would agree to make seals for us. Clearly, the police had already pressured them. As the deadline approached, we had to make seals in whatever way possible, and quickly. Someone came up with the idea of using pumpkin stems. We gathered pumpkin stems and made seals out of them. Thus, the famous "pumpkin stem seals" were born.

When we submitted the registration form with all the signatures, the Liberal Party camp was duly surprised. Election Administration Committee members again made an issue out of the documents, although the committee chair Kim Chang-yun, the head of local registry and an upright man, said they looked legitimate. The registry belonged to the judiciary, so he was probably more independent from the administration than other members. Other committee members, however, insisted that I bring the seals of all the signers. When I protested this and the committee chair sided with me, the other members, in turn, moved against the chair until he yielded to their decision that my registration be canceled if I didn't bring the signers' seals.

I protested with the following statement: "The Election Administration Committee's decision to judge the legitimacy of my registration form based on seals is clearly an arrogation. This power belongs to the judiciary alone. The Election Administration Committee's job is to grant registration if the form is appropriate. Whether the seals are effective or not should be judged only in court. This is not a matter for a district Election Administration Committee to decide on." The Supreme Court later judged that this cancellation of registration was wrong for the same reason.

After another contentious, loud argument, the decision was delayed until the next day. I was so dejected and angry I couldn't sleep. My wife watched me silently. I told her that I would never yield to such injustice, to which she responded, "Fight for the right cause and your belief till the end. If anything happens to you, I'll take care of our two children. So don't worry about us. Do as you believe right!"

I wanted to comfort her, but I didn't know what to say. Inje was an unfamiliar place, not only to me, but also to her. Nevertheless, she was calm and encouraging. The spring night was getting deeper and we could occasionally hear birds chirping. In our rented room in this remote place, we could not fall asleep.

The next day, the Inje District Election Administration Committee approved my registration. I breathed a sigh of relief and headed to Seoul to prepare for the campaign. But, soon, news that the registration was canceled reached me. I immediately boarded a jeep to leave. It took eight hours to travel from Seoul to Inje, and my jeep was overturned twice on that rocky road. Although its roof was disfigured, the engine was okay. I arrived at the district office later that afternoon when they were about to decide on the number for each candidate by a lottery. Although I was bruised all over because of the accidents, I rushed into the office and yelled as loudly as I could. Nobody responded at first, overpowered by my appearance and spirit. But soon, Na Sang-geun, the Liberal Party candidate, called a policeman over. "Hey, you, why don't you get him out of here? Hurry! Now!"

The police jumped at me, but I felt I couldn't yield against this unjust and barbaric group. I held onto a desk leg tight, but was thrown out in the end. The ruling party was an omnipotent power. Only when I was thrown out did I feel any pain in my body. The registration was vacated and my dreams were dashed. I felt heartbroken, furious, and helpless. Although it happened in a remote place, the media paid attention to the incident. I visited the Army Division Commander Park Chung-hee's official residence near the district office, hoping the military might understand this incident's injustice. I was told he was not in. Most likely, he was avoiding me.

Although I was thrown out of the election as a candidate, I couldn't just give up. I decided to work for the campaign of Shin Hyeong-gyu, an independent candidate. During the ballot counting, I worked as a witness. As expected, Shin lost.

I also made speeches in support of Candidate Lee Tae-young in Jecheon and Candidate Gye Gwang-sun in Chuncheon. During my speeches, the audience paid close attention to my words even though they lasted a few hours. Because we didn't have TV yet, an election campaign was a sort of performance and entertainment. The audience cheered my speeches criticizing the Liberal Party's dictatorship and inability, encouraging me greatly. Candidate Gye called me "Lime," because the audience wouldn't get off me once they stuck to me. I don't know how much my speeches contributed to their success, but both candidates won. The Liberal Party candidate Hong Chang-sup said that he lost not to Gye Gwang-sun, but to Kim Dae-jung. Hong was soon appointed governor of Gangwon-do, and campaigned hard against me in the next election. The election was a Liberal Party landslide.

I instituted a lawsuit over the registration-blocking incident as soon as the election was over. I won in March 1959 and the election results in Inje were vacated. That day, they said that Na Sang-geun heard the news while hooting at the podium, without any knowledge of the decision. Another assemblyman approached him and let him know the news; he had to leave the Assembly Hall in front of more than 200 fellow assemblymen, reporters, and the audience.

When I registered for the special election, I faced a storm of malicious propaganda. My opponent was Jeon Hyeong-san, a former police chief. In a region like Inje, the police chief and division commander were like kings. The ruling party first agitated people, saying, "Why vote for a carpetbagger like Kim Dae-jung?" But, that was just the beginning. They brought two people from my home region—Hong Ik-seon and Lee Do-sun from Gwangyang—and had them attack me relentlessly, accusing me of being a communist. Hong said, "Kim Dae-jung is clearly a Communist Party member. I know very well because I was in Mokpo when he led the Namgyo-dong Police Station Attack Incident."

I had never even met Yi, but he claimed, "I grew up with Kim Dae-jung. We were close enough to bathe together. I know he's a Communist Party member. Why else would I come all the way here to let you know this? Don't be fooled!" He was even crying by the end.

In Inje, where civilians were mostly refugees from the North, "anti-communism" was the most critical agenda for both civilians and the military. Voters believed—or, to be more precise, they were *deceived* by—this malicious propaganda. They didn't know me very well, so they believed the two Jeolla-dialect-speaking orators. It was an impossible fight to win.

One particular episode during that campaign illustrates well how low they would go to procure a win. One evening, a military goods supplier and supporter of the opposition party from Masan named Jeong Yeong-geuk treated me to a meal at a high-end restaurant to wish me good luck in the election. Female servers sat next to us. I left the restaurant at the height of festivity and returned to my residence to prepare for the next day's campaign. When I lay down, my party's branch vice chair abruptly opened my door, pushed in a young woman, and immediately ran off saying, "Chairman, I brought a beautiful woman for you. Please spend the night with her."

Utterly shocked, I called to him, but he had disappeared. I then sent the woman back, after explaining to her that I couldn't do such a thing. After a half hour or so, my room door abruptly opened again; this time it was a policeman who came to search my room. "I'm sorry, sir. I'm just making my rounds," he apologized before disappearing into the darkness.

It was clear the policeman had come to capture me with the woman. Although Jeong Yeong-geuk wasn't involved, one of the informants in the high-end restaurant must have cooked up the plot.

The Liberal Party's election fraud attempts reached the military as well. We could not distribute any election material to soldiers. We couldn't paste posters within the base and soldiers weren't allowed a leave during the election period. In an effort to reach them, I made a speech, aiming a megaphone toward the base. Only plainclothes detectives and military intelligence personnel came to my rally. Still, I tried to speak loudly enough that voters could hear from their homes.

Fraud continued until election day. Each military unit officer checked the ballots one by one, and put ballots for the ruling party candidate into the box after tearing up the ballots for me. You couldn't call it an election at all. Although the majority of the military at that time was for the opposition party, ordinary soldiers couldn't dare protest. The results showed that I had won only in the main military headquarters. It turned out that was the only place where they hadn't checked each ballot.

As most soldiers who made up the voting contingent cast an open ballot, I couldn't win, no matter what. It was a fraudulent election rehearsal for the presidential election. I lost. I had to lose. And I had nothing left.

I lost in the 1954 Mokpo election and the 1958 and 1959 Inje elections. Running a campaign meant spending money. People even said running for election just once was enough to uproot a family's foundation. After the second Inje election I again had nothing left. There was no food at home. I felt embarrassed to be home, so I boarded a bus to avoid it, but I had no place to get off. I wanted to see people, but I couldn't. I wanted to hide, but there was nowhere to hide.

While I was whiling away my days like this, the Liberal Party offered me money and certain positions in exchange for joining their party. At that time, many assemblymen were changing party affiliation under pressure and because of financial hardships. Frankly speaking, it wasn't easy for me to resist that seductive offer. They even specified the actual salary amount, saying they'd treat me on a level equivalent to a national assemblyman.

"Do you mean to throw your talent away? Join the ruling party and really take full advantage of it. You've too much talent to waste." Their secret whispers were sweet, but I resisted.

In order to resolve the issue of livelihood, I decided to go into business again. I was going to partner with a friend and I borrowed money from a secondhand dealer in Masan, who would be our investor. Unfortunately, my partner ran away with the money. I blamed my poor judgment of character, and honestly explained to the investor what had happened, including the fact that I had already used some of that money personally. If he had gone to the police, I could have been punished for embezzlement. But he trusted me and said, "You're not an embezzler. I don't want to ruin your future over a matter like this. I don't need that money."

I was grateful. If I had been prosecuted for embezzlement then, the politician Kim Dae-jung may never have existed. Much later, when I became a national assemblyman, I inquired about the secondhand dealer and visited his home. He had already passed away, and his wife and son were having a difficult time. I found a job for his son.

My wife, Cha Yong-ae, left this world toward the end of that luxuriant summer. I received so much from her and she left without getting anything back from me. She suffered from pyrosis often. The day she passed, she took medicine for severe pyrosis, and somehow lapsed into a coma. I happened to be home and rushed to the doctor. When the doctor and I arrived home, she was already gone. The daughter of a wealthy family, she married me and had a difficult life. When she became ill, she didn't even have a chance to see a doctor. I sobbed and sobbed. In the midst of this tragedy, a rumor took hold that she had committed suicide because of the shock from my continual losses and poverty. People knew she'd experienced hard times since the beginning of my political career. I feel sorry to her, even to this day. I am also grateful. She truly loved me and gave her all to me. When we were having hard times, she never complained. Since coming to Seoul for my political career, we moved eight times, each time reducing the size of our rental home. We envied people who owned their own houses.

She worked as a hairdresser to help with our household. When she could no longer pay for the shop, she received customers at home. She wasn't afraid of any hardship faced for the sake of her family. I remember one day when I helplessly watched her scold our second son for complaining that one of his shoes that had a hole in it. My wife who said she'd rather die than not marry me. My wife who gave birth to a baby in a bomb shelter while waiting for me during the war. My wife who encouraged me and my political career, telling me never to worry about my family. Cha Yong-ae. During the Rhee Syngman government, she hadn't missed any of the rallies against the controversial Amendment of the National Security Law.

I have always been grateful for and will always cherish her memory. I am truly happy to have been blessed with such a wife. When I see our two sons and my grandchildren, I feel moved. I tell her, "Look, they are your offspring. You didn't die. You'll live through them forever. Because you were such a good and beautiful person, their lives will be beautiful and their families will be happy."

After I buried my wife, I climbed Mt. Namsan with my two sons. We looked down at downtown Seoul from the Palgakjeong Octagonal Pavilion. I said to them, "You shouldn't despair because you don't have a mother. You have to be good people. That's what your mother wanted. She was a good person. I know you know that. You shouldn't forget what a good person your mother was. She looks down at you from the other world."

My young sons were quiet. I turned around and cried again. It was a bitter time.

CHAPTER 2

1959–1970

THE COLLAPSE OF THE RHEE SYNGMAN REGIME (1959–APRIL 19, 1960)

The Liberal Party regime abruptly announced that it would hold the fourth presidential election on March 15, 1960, thus violating the customary May election mandate that had been in place since the founding of the Republic of Korea. Behind this decision was cold political calculation; the Liberal Party intended to take advantage of the conflict over the party presidential candidate selection between the Old and New Schools of the Democratic Party. The ruling party sought to deny the Democratic Party a favorable opportunity to sort out its factional differences.

In November 1959, Democratic Party chair Mr. Cho Byung-ok (of the Old School) was nominated as the Democratic presidential candidate at the party primary, defeating Dr. Chang Myon by only three votes. In the supreme committee member election the next day, however, Dr. Chang won by an overwhelming majority. As the party's Gangwon-do chief, I'd campaigned hard for Dr. Chang.

During the vice presidential campaign, I'd made campaign speeches on a truck with a loudspeaker in hand. One day, when my truck passed a military base in Gangwon-do, soldiers crowded behind the wire fence and shouted for our fliers. Although the Liberal Party truck, which was following our truck, also offered theirs, the soldiers refused to take them. It was stark proof that public sentiment had abandoned the ruling party.

© The Author(s) 2019
Kim Dae-jung, *Conscience in Action,*
https://doi.org/10.1007/978-981-10-7623-7_2

Then, the nightmare of the previous election struck again. Just like four years ago, Democratic Party candidate Cho Byung-ok collapsed during the presidential election. It was ominous. Mr. Cho was rushed to the US for treatment on January 29 the next year, but he was too far gone. I don't think highly of Mr. Cho's career as police chief under the US military government, but he was an outstanding politician who continued to fight against dictatorship. He was a highly talented, generous, brave leader—one who'd given up his candidacy to Mr. Shin Ik-hui during the 1956 election for the united front of the opposition.

Because the candidacy registration deadline had already elapsed, the Democratic Party was unable to register Dr. Cho's replacement. President Rhee's win was all but predetermined. Naturally, the vice presidential election became more critical as President Rhee was now even older than he had been four years before. Unfortunately, however, the Democratic Party's Old School put forth a fairly passive campaign.

The same could not be said of the Liberal Party. Rhee was old and frail and his successor Lee Ki-poong was also sickly, which worried Rhee's sycophants. Although they should have been driven out of power for their irresponsible conduct during the war, the two had, in fact, consolidated their power thanks to this tumultuous period. A thick human wall of ex-pro-Japanese sycophants surrounded the president.

Meanwhile, scandals continued without end: the Second National Guard Incident, the Geochang Civilian Massacre Incident, the 1952 Political Crisis, the Ministry of Agriculture and Forestry Corruption Incident, the Round-up Constitutional Amendment Crisis, the Kyunghyang Sinmun Discontinuance Incident, the Seditious Documents Delivery Incident ... the list goes on. The children of those with power and money could get exemption from compulsory military service. All manner of aid finances were ending up in the pockets of the corrupt. President Rhee was obstinate, but unprincipled. It was inevitable that sycophants would surround a leader without any beliefs or principles.

Maintaining a government that lacked popular support required increasing brutality. It constantly had to manipulate or distort popular sentiment during the election period. Before the March 15 elections, popular anger became about as open and flagrant as the regime's tyranny. Despite media warnings, election fraud methodically proceeded. National assemblymen Koo Chul-hoi, Kim Gyu-man, Kim Sak, Song Young Joo, and Heo Yun-su left the Democratic Party to join the Liberal Party for cash incentives. Rhee Syngman campaigned all over the country for Lee Ki-poong. In Yeosu and Gwangsan, Jeollanam-do, Democratic Party members died in suspicious attacks. Thugs belonging to Shin Do-hwann's Anti-communist Youth Group, Im Hwa-su's Anti-communist Artists Group, and Lee Jung-jae's Dongdaemun Gang raged at the loyal dogs guarding the Liberal Party.

By March 15, the entire country had become a sort of Wild, Wild West. The police and Anti-communist Youth Group members surrounded polling booths all over the country. Opposition party observers were bribed, beaten, or dragged out of office. In Gimpo, a rash of mobster stabbings was reported by opposition party observers who tried to stand their ground. Because of rampant preelection voting and ballot box stuffing, more votes were cast for the ruling party candidates than the number of actual existing registered voters in many polling booths. Embarrassed, the National Election Commission temporarily stopped the vote counting and tried to reduce the number of votes for the ruling party candidates.

Citizens poured into the streets of Masan. In almost all polling booths, opposition party observers were kicked out, voters were told to fold their ballots inside out, and ballots were taken away from likely opposition party voters. Citizens of Masan gathered around the Democratic Party office, where we disclosed examples of election fraud. Around 3:00 p.m., citizens and Democratic Party members began to protest. Although the police dispersed these crowds, more than a 1000 people gathered in front of the Democratic Party office again at 7:00 p.m. Together with students, they marched toward the municipal office. People joined from one alley after another, chanting: "Fair election now! Cancel the rigged election!"

In the end, the furious crowd and the police confronted one another. A fire engine charged toward the demonstrators and fired water at them. Citizens and students threw rocks in response. The fire engine driver abruptly tore back and struck an electric pole, which crashed. Instantly, silence reigned as the entire city fell into darkness. Suddenly, shots tore through the silence and mayhem overtook downtown Masan as it was filled with the sound of gunshots and shrieks. Groups of protesters tried their best to avoid the police, who pursued them in jeeps and fire engines. The police randomly shot protesters until around midnight.

A beautiful flower of the April 19th Revolution, Kim Ju-yeol, fell and died at the age of seventeen. The Masan Commercial High School freshman was killed when a teargas bullet was fired through his eye. The police tied a stone around his corpse to weigh it down and threw him into the sea. His body floated back up to the surface twenty-seven days later.

Hectic days followed. I was the vice chief of the Democratic Party public relations department. Assemblyman Cho Jae-cheon, a famous former spokesperson and rising star of our party, was the department chief. (He later became the minister of justice during the Democratic government after the April 19th Revolution.) Although Dr. Chang Myon lost miserably in the vice presidential election, the people's wrath over election fraud was still extremely high. News of bloody confrontations between protesters and the police bred extreme tension over the political situation. Citizens petitioned the Democratic Party to lead a demonstration all over the country, and the Democratic Party decided to hold a street rally on April 6.

We decided that Kim Hong-ju and I would be in charge of megaphones. I was to lead the slogan, chanting either in front of or behind the protesters. If the police violently suppressed us, a slogan-chanting leader would surely become their priority target. The interior minister had already proclaimed they would violently suppress street demonstrations. I suddenly felt dizzy as I left my house to lead the protest rally. I was about to leave my life in the hands of a dictatorial regime. My wife was dead and my family had no food at home. It was suffocating to watch my two sons see me off with a bow while my mother looked silently on. I felt tremendously sad and guilty. But I had to go. I turned around and looked up at the sky. I just had to leave everything to God. I said to myself, "Someone has to take this job on. I could have died during the war. My life since then has been a free gift, so I shouldn't begrudge losing it. I must do what I can."

We gathered at the Seoul City Hall Plaza. The crowd started as a few hundred participants, but soon grew to a few thousand. Tens of thousands of additional people looked on from both sides of the street. When we began chanting slogans, the police immediately surrounded us; they didn't actively suppress the rally, but blocked off the road to prevent onlookers from joining. We began marching in the direction of Euljiro. More and more people gathered by the side of the road. After we passed Euljiro and turned toward Tapgol Park, the protest became heated and onlookers began to cheer excitedly.

The protesters now numbered more than 10,000. We continued chanting, and at some point the slogan changed to "Down with the Rhee Syngman regime!"

Mr. Kwak Sang-hun, our party supreme committee member, hurried over to me. Clearly disconcerted, he yelled, "Are you out of your mind?"

A few moments later, the students who had joined us around Tapgol Park steered us toward the Central Government Building via Gwanghwamun. They, too, began chanting, "Down with the Rhee Syngman regime!"

After this rally, high school students began to march across the country. On April 18, approximately 1000 Korea University students scrummed out onto the street and gathered in front of the National Assembly Building. When they returned after a sit-in demonstration, high school students and citizens followed them. Around 7:00 p.m., armed thugs jumped students gathered in front of the Cheonil Department Store on Cheonggye-4-ga. The thugs wielded iron hammers, clubs, wooden bars, and hooks. Scores of demonstrators fell on the spot. Someone shouted, "Hoodlums!"

By the time the students eventually struggled back onto their feet, the thugs had disappeared. Later, we learned they were members of the Anti-communist Youth Group Jong-no branch. This was not to be the last of the clashes between hired thugs and students. Blood was shed in Seoul as well.

The fated day, April 19, arrived. The morning paper smelled of blood. After reading articles about the attack on Korea University students, people were not only nervous about the political situation, but they were also nearly overwhelmed with anger. Seoul National University students took to the streets around 9:20 a.m., and students from Korea University, Konkuk University, Dongguk University, and Sungkyunkwan University followed. Around noon, the participants—almost all college students, including those from Yonsei University, Hongik University, Kyonggi University, the Hankuk University of Foreign Studies, Dankook University, Kukhak University, Kookmin University, and Sorabol College of Art—began chanting and marching toward the Central Government Building.

One after another, students broke through the police barricades. All the streets within and around Sinchon, Dongdaemun, Seoul Station, and the Central Government Building flooded with protesters. Around 1:30 p.m., some students captured a fire engine and drove it to Gyeongmudae (later called the Blue House) with other protesters. When the protestors approached the last police barricade, the police immediately began shooting. About ten or so students fell and the blood began to run—Bloody Tuesday. The blood of South Korea's youth pooled in the streets.

Protesters immediately gathered again and stood face to face with the police. When they approached Gyeongmudae again, bullets poured like rain and students fell again. By then, protesters and the police were fighting all over downtown Seoul. The more shots were fired, the louder the chants became: "Down with Rhee Syngman!"

Around 3:00 p.m., emergency martial law was declared in Seoul and a fire erupted in the ruling party-controlled *Seoul Sinmun* Building. Fairly soon after that, the headquarters of the party's terror organization, the Anti-communism Association Building, lit up in flames. Demonstrations spread to Busan, Daegu, Incheon, Gwangju, Jeonju, and more. Emergency martial law was expanded to the entire country at 5:00 p.m. In reaction to this, the US Embassy issued a statement advising the Korean government to attend to the demonstrators' justifiable complaints and for the demonstrators and the police to cooperate to regain order.

US Ambassador to Korea Walter P. McConaughy visited the Gyeongmudae and his presence had an immediate effect on the country's political climate. Demonstrators opened the road for his car and cheered. McConaughy must have made the seriousness of the situation clear to President Rhee. The demonstrators present that day had been very careful not to provoke the US. When they attacked Lee Ki-poong's house, for example, they left the American flag in his house untouched. In fact, a demonstrator actually returned it to the American reporter on-site. Amazingly, everyone seemed to be aware that they should neither underestimate US influence nor antagonize it for the sake of our own national interests.

There was neither violence nor any pro-communist slogans during the April 19th Demonstration. This kind of mature demonstration induced support from the ordinary citizens of the country, especially middle-class white-collar workers—something that would be a critical element in the success of the April 19th Revolution.

For several days after the April 19th Demonstration, the situation was extremely confusing. The Liberal Party feigned listening to demonstrator demands, although their actual policies remained unchanged. A series of statements and decrees confirmed the regime's unchanged authoritarian approach. In response, this time the professors took to the streets. Two hundred and fifty-eight professors from various universities gathered at the Seoul National University Faculty Club on the afternoon of April 25 and left the university gates at 5:45 p.m. They marched the streets with a placard that read: "Recompense for Fallen Students' Blood for the Noble April 19th Uprising!"

This was the first ever professor-led demonstration in Korean history. They threw their bodies into the fray to make clear their rejection of the martial law mandate, which forbade assembly and demonstration. They marched through Jong-no and Sejong-no, finally arriving at the National Assembly Building. Students and citizens surrounded them there as well. The participating professors read a prepared statement: "In order to take responsibility for the March 15th Fraudulent Election and the April 19th Incident, the president, national assemblymen, and Supreme Court judges should all resign, and a recall election should be implemented."

The crowd cheered. I was present, too. I had been working around the clock on my party's PR work as well as participating in demonstrations and chanting. The professors shouted "Hurrah!" three times and dispersed, but the crowd remained. The number of citizens and students grew larger as the sun began to set. After the 7:00 p.m. curfew passed, two tanks approached demonstrators with a roar. Soldiers arrived with fixed bayonets. Someone in the crowd shouted, "Brother, we're the same people!"

Others began to shout as well: "Hurrah, Korean soldiers! Hurrah, Korean soldiers!" The crowd burst into tears. Demonstrators and soldiers hugged each other and cried. Students and citizens climbed the tanks and cheered. The demonstrators attacked government-hired thugs Im Hwa-su's and Lee Jung-jae's houses that night.

On April 26, the day broke with the demonstrators' roar. Citizens gathered on the streets of Sejong-no around 8:00 a.m., as if they had planned it beforehand. Soon afterward, the crowd increased to 30,000; by 10:00 a.m., there were over 100,000 people. Around that time, demonstrators attacked Lee Ki-poong's house. Downtown Seoul was in utter chaos. As the crowd increased and time went by, the soldiers were soon rendered helpless. Extremely excited at this point, the people proposed a march to the Gyeongmudae.

Upon assessing the situation, Lieutenant General Song Yo-chan quickly understood its gravity. Together with fourteen demonstrator representatives consisting of college students, high school students, and ordinary citizens, Lieutenant General Song visited the Gyeongmudae and requested an interview with the president. The representatives delivered the public sentiment to President Rhee and demanded his resignation.

The president responded, "A country where the young do not rise up against injustice will collapse. If there really has been election fraud, then a students' uprising was truly just. If this really happened, I must resign."

At 10:20 a.m., news of President Rhee's resignation rang out to demonstrators from the martial law enforcement force's speakers. The street was awash in cheers. It was truly a people's victory. Almost immediately afterward, President Rhee's resignation statement came through the radio: "Since returning to my home country after its liberation, I have lived well with my fellow patriotic citizens. If I leave this world now, I have no regrets. I will always follow the people's will and that has always been what I wanted ... If the people want it, I will resign."

President Rhee submitted his resignation to the National Assembly the morning of April 27, and it was accepted the same day. President Rhee clearly hadn't known election fraud was being so openly and meticulously enacted. He was eighty-five years old when his twelve-year dictatorship ended; the next day, Dr. Rhee moved to his private house in Ihwajang. Although he wanted to walk, he had no choice but to take a car. Many citizens sent him away with applause. Some of them wiped tears from their eyes.

When Rhee Syngman returned home following the liberation, the Korean people welcomed him as an independence fighter and intellectual leader who had once been able to guide the country to its future. With his blue-eyed wife, he seemed like a mythical character. His greatest mistake was enjoying the flattery of a large number of pro-Japanese collaborators and appointing them to important posts, which I find hard to understand. The world had been unable to change when the police—who also oppressed patriots during the colonial period—remained at the same posts. Likewise, Rhee completely ignored the independence fighters who braved their own lives in China and Primorsky Krai. The military was given to former Japanese and Manchurian military members.

Intellectuals who had urged people to be loyal to the Japanese emperor, to die as Japanese soldiers, to volunteer for the military and forced labor, and to serve as comfort women continued to maintain their status and enjoy power. Pro-Japanese collaborators trampled on the people's hopes for a new world, ignoring the people, scorning democracy, and continuing to enjoy wealth and power. Meanwhile, patriots and their families starved to death in slums. This failure to eliminate pro-Japanese collaborators—and Rhee's shameless defense of them—was at the heart of all of contemporary Korea's tragedies.

Also, by pushing the establishment of a separate South Korean government, Rhee contributed to the consolidation of our country's division. He changed the Constitution simply to extend his term. He hid the country's frail national defense capabilities with the exaggerated slogan: "Unification by the Armed Conquest of the North," while ruthlessly suppressing his political rivals. History would not forgive his dictatorship under the pretext of anti-communist and national security defense. Ultimately, his presidency was an extended attempt at permanent rule.

Innumerable people died under Rhee's government. The majority of them died unjustly and without knowing why they were being executed. His opponents were all accused of being communists. If only he had established an admirable model during his first presidency, if only he weren't so corrupt that he needed to be expelled by his own people, our political history would not have been stained with so much blood later on. If only he had taken the straight and narrow road, a path deserving of the title "Father of Korea." If only, then we could have prevented a tragic turn in our contemporary history. To a considerable degree, later military coups and dictatorship merely followed in Rhee's footsteps.

People have called Rhee an "elder patriot" because he resigned like a defeated gentleman. Of course, the US influenced his decision, but he still made the right choice when he resigned without any more bloodshed. It was an unusually brave action for him to allow an interview with the demonstrators' representatives and to praise their courage.

The April 19th Revolution was immediately made known to the entire world. This kind of complete victory from a student-led revolution was unprecedented in world history. We should not forget the background factors that enabled it.

First, I would like to emphasize that we must remember the opposition Democratic Party was at the center of the nationwide demonstrations. Although the Democratic Party lost its presidential candidate abruptly, it fought hard for the vice presidential election. This fight was the focal point of the people's hope for democracy. In Masan, the first rally against election fraud—the key event leading up to the April 19th Revolution—occurred in front of the Democratic Party branch office on March 15. The Democratic Party offered a space for citizens to complain, make indictments, and appeal decisions. There is no doubt that the students' noble spirit and pure-hearted courage enabled the success of the April 19th Revolution, but we should also remember the anguish and tears of us politicians as well.

Second, we should remember that the middle class actively participated in demonstrations. Their participation was a critical element that enabled the US to support its cause. The middle class participated in the April 19 demonstrations because they were non-violent, they weren't pro-communist, and they weren't anti-US. Peaceful demonstrations drew the middle class to their side, which, in turn, moved the US to action.

Third, the military maintained its neutrality. Rather than continuing to antagonize citizens, the military eventually ended up siding with them.

The April 19th Revolution influenced me a great deal. Above all, I was a direct witness to the awe-inspiring power of the people's will. I learned that radical positions and violence could not win the people's support. These are ordinary, but constant truths. Since then, I have often pondered what it means to win the people's hearts, remembering my experiences of the April 19th Revolution.

PASSIONATE SPOKESPERSON FOR THE VIRTUOUS PRIME MINISTER (APRIL 1960–MAY 1961)

After the revolution, we had neither a president nor a vice president. A transitional cabinet led by Minister of Foreign Affairs Huh Jung was formed. On June 15, 1960, an amendment that introduced the bicameral system passed in the National Assembly. Although the National Assembly would elect the president, the president would only be the symbolic head of the nation. The Korean people welcomed this change.

The general election for the fifth-term Congress and the first-term Senate was scheduled for July 29, 1960. I ran as the Democratic Party candidate in Inje. Support for the Democratic Party was strong, and this was a great opportunity for me to join the National Assembly; however, my misfortunes continued.

Despite Dr. Chang Myon's New School opposition, the Old School (headed by Yun Po-sun and Yu Jin-san) passed the absentee voting system in the National Assembly after a secret deal with the ruling Liberal Party. This was a heavy blow to me because 80 percent of military voters from Inje—that is, young voters passionate for change, the Democratic Party, and me—were unable to vote in Inje. Their votes were dispersed all over the country. Only members of the New School ran for the election in the front region, including Cheorwon, Goseong, Inje, and Yanggu. I campaigned hard, but lost again. Although I won in five out of six administrative divisions by a slim margin, I lost in one by a large margin. The win went to a regional native who successfully campaigned by emphasizing his roots in the area. All in all, I lost by 1000 votes.

Despite my loss, the Democratic Party won a landslide victory in both the Congress and the Senate, winning 175 out of 233 seats in the Congress and 31 out of 58 seats in the Senate. Mr. Yun Po-sun of the Old School won the fourth presidential election in the joint National Assembly election.

An agreement was in place between the Old and New Schools to divide the offices of president and prime minister between themselves. This was the general expectation among the people, too. But President Yun betrayed this agreement by nominating Mr. Kim Doh-yeon of the Old School as prime minister. However, the National Assembly frustrated this scheme. Mr. Kim won 111 votes, 3 votes less than the majority. President Yun had no choice but to nominate Dr. Chang Myon as promised, and Dr. Chang was elected prime minister by winning three more votes than the majority.

Prime Minster Chang then nominated me as the party's spokesperson. Since the Democratic Party members took up more than half of the National Assembly, this was an unusual decision. When Congressman Cho Jae-cheon, the previous spokesperson, joined the cabinet as the attorney general, he recommended that I succeed his post. Additionally, most of the other party officials, including newly appointed Defense Minister Hyon Sok-ho, also actively supported me. I was deeply moved. I also realized that who was working at what position and how were always carefully observed. There were a few young congressmen who didn't like this decision, but Prime Minister Chang's support of me was firm.

The Chang Myon cabinet was shaky from the beginning. As the major players of the revolution, college students had returned to school and turned away from the world of politics, and politicians were now under heavy pressure to execute the spirit of their revolution. All policies needed to be fundamentally examined, and their legitimacy was always controversial. In addition, the Old School attacked the cabinet even more severely than the opposition party.

The Old School had always been rather conciliatory toward the Liberal Party, always willing to make secret deals behind closed doors. It was the New School that led the April 6th Demonstration that sparked the April 19th Revolution. As a result, although the Old School could claim strong opposition party roots, in fact they had a very weak connection with post-revolutionary realities. The New School, on the other hand, was proud of their role in the revolution.

Eighty-six national assemblymen belonging to the Old School formed their own separate parliamentary negotiation body called the Democratic Party Old School Fellowship Association. They also demanded their share of cabinet seats, successfully entering five members of the Old School into the cabinet. The Democratic Party formed a coalition cabinet between the Old and New Schools. Even then, the Old School continued to quarrel with the New School, eventually naming its own spokesperson and criticizing the government harshly, thus signaling a party separation. Prime Minister Chang tried very hard to embrace the Old School but to no avail. The Old School members left the Democratic Party en masse by late 1960 and established a new party called the Sinmin Party on February 20, 1961.

In addition, President Yun, supposedly the symbolic head of the nation beyond political factionalism, was becoming actively involved in the politics of these power struggles and began to shake the cabinet at random. As the ruling party spokesperson, I was strongly critical of his behavior, but it was all in vain. Eventually, Yun even held the Sinmin Party's official meetings at the presidential office. The Sinmin Party's only concern was to take power away from the Democratic Party.

Although he should have been the nation's arbiter and fine-tuner of political disputes, President Yun ultimately failed to show any maturity as a political leader. Instead, his office became a source of political strife and dispute. Naturally, the political situation became chaotic. Politicians engaged in dogfights even as the blood of so many students remained fresh. People began to say that the Chang cabinet would collapse because of the three *sins*: the *Sin*min Party, the *sin*mun (newspapers), and the Hyeok*sin*gye (Reform School).

Meanwhile, the media was enjoying the freedom they had long yearned for under the dictatorship. Unfortunately, they poured all of their pent-up frustration into criticizing the government. Media outlets treated the new democratic government in the same way as it would a dictatorial, corrupt government. Virtually every newspaper—including those that were government-owned—ganged up on the government like never before. Newspaper editors openly professed, "If you don't criticize the government, you're not a newspaper."

Although the Reform School finally acquired freedom under the Chang cabinet, they antagonized the cabinet. About two months before the military coup, I strongly warned them: "Under Liberal Party rule, Mr. Cho Bong-am of the Progressive Party was executed after being unfairly charged with being a communist spy. All of you Reform School members have been imprisoned or undergone other great difficulties. Have you all forgotten? Which government gave you the freedom you enjoy now? If you destroy this government, the next government is going to be a military one. And then another period of trouble will come. Why are you tearing at the lips that protect your teeth?"

Newspapers reported this warning to the Reform School but, in the end, the leaders didn't listen. Instead, they put forward irresponsible arguments that were nearly impossible to accept. Some of their slogans included: "Unification via Internationally Guaranteed Permanent Neutrality," "Neutrality after Unification," and "Disarmament of Both Koreas and Withdrawal of Foreign Troops." They tried to agitate people through a midnight torchlight demonstration. Their extreme arguments and demonstrations made people nervous; Korea wanted stability and feared communism. Divided into the Tongilsahoe (Unification Socialist) Party and Sahoedaejung (Socialist People's) Party, the reformists competed to see who could swing the ax harder at the Democratic Party.

The Democratic Party's Sinpung Association, which consisted of younger generation activists, also continued to criticize the government. In exchange for their votes for Prime Minister Chang's appointment, they demanded their share in the cabinet. The Chang cabinet ignored this demand and the Sinpung Association continued to make trouble in every possible way. The Tungsten Export Contract Incident—the biggest, most groundless scandal during Democratic Party rule—was one of their greatest fabrications.

Tungsten, a strategic material used to manufacture rockets and spacecraft, was Korea's most important export item at the time. As the existing contract with the US was set to expire in 1961, the next deal was a matter of urgent interest. There was a report that the Korea Tungsten Company president would sell the company's 400-ton inventory to the Japanese-owned Tokyo Foods at a bargain price to create political funds. The previous Rhee government did something similar. Because of this precedent, Koreans were quick to be alarmed and outraged, overturning the political arena. At the same time, a national assemblyman belonging to the Sinpung Association of the ruling Democratic Party came forward with the claim that the Chang cabinet was behind it all and that it was set to receive a $1 million kickback.

A National Assembly fact-finding mission was hurriedly formed, but no matter how deeply they dug, no evidence of corruption surfaced. Despite the results of this fact-finding mission, the Democratic Party would never recover from this image of an ethically corrupt party. Although this incident later provided the biggest excuse for the May 16th Coup, investigators weren't able to find any evidence of corruption during the Park regime, either.

I recall one instance when Prime Minister Chang and I discussed how to handle Sinpung Association members. I suggested that it would probably be advisable to offer a cabinet position to their leader Congressman Lee Chul-seung. It seemed to me that stability would be greatly improved if the administration wasn't being constantly rocked from within. I thought that once given some responsibility, they might not behave so irresponsibly. Prime Minister Chang responded with silence.

Prime Minister Chang could neither embrace nor expel the Sinpung Association. In my opinion, the Democratic Party regime's dramatically short life and failure to guide the country's hopeful vision for the future was in large part because of the pincer attack of the *four sins*: the *Sin*pung Association, along with the aforementioned three *sins*.

As a result of this barrage of attacks, the Chang administration was practically a minority one. Governance was never stably managed. No matter how well formulated a policy was, it, nonetheless, became an excuse for petty squabbling. People began to complain that the Democratic Party regime was no different than the Liberal Party regime. These complaints were also accompanied by rumors of an impending military coup.

There were demonstrations in front of the National Assembly Hall every day. All manner of desires that had been suppressed during the dictatorship—feelings about unification plans, governmental reparations for wounded veterans, labor treatment reform, subsidies for various organizations—gushed out nearly simultaneously. Koreans would joke that any Korean who hadn't participated in demonstrations once didn't deserve to be called a human, or that we needed a demonstration to demand a stop to demonstrations.

As the party's spokesperson, I met with Prime Minister Chang every day. He would frequently say: "My greatest mission is not to become a prime minister again, but to peacefully hand over the administration to the opposition party in the next election, to build a history of peaceful administration change. I believe that's my mission."

I thought he was too weak and sometimes too pitiable. I wondered if he was already thinking about the end of his administration. Although a very noble person, Prime Minister Chang was not decisive, which made him unfit to lead a confused society. Still, he had a long-term view. He knew our democratic soil was still barren. The fact that it took our country thirty-seven years to experience a peaceful regime change proved this.

Prime Minister Chang was a moderate democrat and a resolute anti-communist. Once I complained about the excessive actions by opposition parties and the media and he calmly responded, "Don't think like that. Being patient and tolerant of such behaviors is democracy. Democracy grows through this."

As the spokesperson of the ruling party, I went to various rallies and forums to explain government policies. I prepared diligently, spoke sincerely, and always tried to maintain my dignity. People listened to me, and I became recognized as a popular and well-prepared spokesperson. Because I was the ruling party spokesperson, I could more easily secure data that weren't available to the opposition party and could deliver the essence of policies or incidents based on detailed and accurate analyses. The media paid attention to my briefings and interviews. I fought against the spokespersons of the opposition party, the reformists, and the independents almost every day. It was always a one-on-three fight, but I looked forward to it because I was confident in my ability to persuade.

Once, during a debate about the Korea-US Trade Agreement Amendment at the Seoul City Public Auditorium, the opposition party and reformist leaders attacked the ruling party and government for selling Korea off to the US. Representatives of the Sinmin Party, the reformists, and the independents came forward one after another and led the discussion against the amendment. From the Sinmin Party, Representative Park Jyun-kyu claimed that the government had sold off our country. Yoon Giel-joong, the reformist leader, also attacked the government: "Who's benefitting from the April 19th Revolution? Power moved from Rhee Syngman to Chang Myon, and from the Liberal Party to the Democratic Party. The wounded are left only with their injuries. The Korea-US Trade Agreement is simply a betrayal of our country."

The atmosphere in the auditorium was tense. Minister of Recovery Tae Wan-son's attempt to further explain the situation and potential agreement was drowned out by jeers. When I took to the podium, it was chaos. I held up the opinion page of that morning's *Chosun Ilbo*. The essence of its op-ed piece was that this amendment was a progression from the previous agreement. "As you well know, the *Chosun Ilbo* is an opposition paper," I said. "But, according to the editorial, this is what they believe: The government is to blame if people oppose an agreement even an opposition newspaper appreciates. I do think it's our government's fault that we have brought about such a misunderstanding. It's because it failed to fully explain the agreement's content."

Surprised to hear me attack the government, the audience began to listen. I then saw a person in the audience who must have been embarrassed by this change of attitude. He tried to interfere with my speech. I changed my passive tone, pounded the platform, and roared: "There. You! Stand up, please! Do you know why the April 19th Revolution was so important? Didn't we protest against the Rhee Syngman regime because we were deprived of our right to speech? Now we live in a time when everyone has the right to speech, so why are you preventing me from talking, and why are you monopolizing the right to speak? Isn't this like you've all returned to Rhee Syngman regime? You're practicing dictatorship. If all those students sacrificed their lives for your brand of dictatorship, what could be more unjust than that? If you had a chance to speak, then shouldn't you listen?"

In response, I could hear people throughout the assembly begin to cry out:

"Be quiet!"
"Go on—speak, please!"
"Let's listen!"

Order was reestablished in the auditorium.

I then emphatically detailed how important the Korea-US relationship was and why the amendment was not selling off our country. The audience hushed and gradually began to listen. When my speech ended, they enthusiastically cheered and applauded. I later heard that a Catholic priest present in that room visited Prime Minister Chang and heaped praises on me. "Kim Dae-jung is the only person who's working hard for you," he said. I received high praise from Dr. Chang. From that day on, the reformists withdrew their planned rally against the amended agreement. My speech had indeed moved people. It was clear to me that the greatest virtue is courage, and that speech based on truth is the best weapon. I also acquired the firm belief that people would understand when you told them honestly what you believed to be true.

In the spring of 1961, society was regaining order and, above all, the political arena was becoming more stable. The number of demonstrations was significantly reduced and people began to pay less attention to them.

Instead of applauding demonstrators, they began to refute them. We finally seemed to be coming out of a very long tunnel.

The Chang Myon cabinet and ruling party established the Comprehensive National Land Development Plan. The government systematically employed college graduates and established various scholarships to help lower-income students fund their studies. These various policies were introduced not only to help students, those agents of our past democratic revolution, find the means to study, but also to invest in our country's future. We also established the Economic Development Plan in order to elevate our economy. Later, Park Chung-hee coup d'état forces emulated this plan and announced it publically as if it was their own creation. The Park regime intercepted the fruit of the Chang administration's plan.

The Chang administration established the National Land Building Headquarters and appointed Mr. Chang Chun-ha, the publisher of *Sasanggye*, a monthly magazine trusted and preferred by intellectuals of that time, as its head. Eager building began here and there throughout the country. We also quickly introduced local autonomous government systems and had people elect local administrative officers, right down to administrative division chiefs. The Chang administration worked diligently, but it was invisible work, buried under the heat of demonstrations.

As the ruling party regained the people's trust, prospects everywhere were hopeful. The economy began to stabilize as well. Prime Minister Chang was looking forward to his visit to the US and the Korea-US summit conference scheduled in June. President Kennedy favorably viewed our democratic government and its leader Dr. Chang. They might have related to each other better because they were both Catholic. It was a great opportunity to receive large-scale aid from the US, which was necessary for building a new country. Everything was progressing well, and we were hopeful about the future of Korean democracy.

Warm spring winds blew on me as well. The congressman from Inje who had beaten me by 1000 votes was found to have been involved in election fraud. A special election was held on May 13, 1961; I ran again as a Democratic Party candidate and finally won. This was my first victory after four losses in the seven years since my 1954 Mokpo campaign. When I received the certificate from the Election Administration Committee office on May 14, my heart was too full for words. I remember wondering, "Were all my troubles so that I could finally have this moment?"

My deceased wife Cha Yong-ae came to mind first, and I burst into tears. I would be receiving a golden badge in Seoul. I wanted to visit my wife's grave wearing it.

On May 14 and 15, I visited Inje to thank its citizens for my victory. The residents of Inje congratulated me sincerely. Their faces looked apologetic for not electing me before, and they held my hands warmly. I was deeply moved and remembered my resolution when I'd decided to jump into politics: "I'll dedicate myself to just politics. I'll devote everything to the people."

The day and night of victory went by and May 16 dawned.

May 16: Dark Times (May 1961–May 1962)

At 3:00 a.m. on May 16, 1951, the military coup d'état began. The second marine company led the coup by entering downtown Seoul across the Han River Bridge and taking over all of the major buildings in the area: the Capitol, the army headquarters, the Korea Broadcasting Company, the Korea Power Plant, and more.

Major General Park Chung-hee led the coup and proclaimed that the military group had to come forward because they believed "that the fate of our nation and people cannot be entrusted to the corrupt and incompetent regime and its politicians." At the same time, they proclaimed Six Revolutionary Pledges, which stated in part: "We will establish anti-communism as our foremost priority and reorganize and reinforce an anti-communist system, which has existed only as a formal slogan."

A party member woke me up from my sweet and exhausted sleep after a late night of thank-you visits to inform me of the news. I immediately got up and thought about it, but decided it wasn't serious. Still, I had to go to Seoul as soon as possible. Voters in the region, including Gangwon-do Governor Park Young-rok, had congratulated and wanted to see me, but Prime Minister Chang asked me to hurry back.

When I was passing by the corps headquarters in Sinnam-myeon, Inje-gun, on my way to Seoul, a military vehicle approached my car. A lieutenant colonel greeted me and told me the commander sent him. "We don't know what exactly happened in Seoul, but we'll work closely with the police to maintain order in this region," he told me. "Will that be okay?"

"Of course, please proceed," I replied.

To this the lieutenant colonel responded, "The commander ordered me to take you to Seoul by helicopter."

After an intensive campaign season in the mountainous regions of Inje, my car had practically fallen apart. Their offer seemed to imply they wanted to treat me in proportion to my position as an elected congressman; however, I refused because I didn't feel that I should be going to Seoul by military helicopter when there was a military coup in progress.

Around Yangpyeong, I saw a large-scale military troop head toward Seoul on military trucks decorated with hundreds of flags. I later discovered they belonged to the corps participating in the coup. At the same time, I heard a joint statement by Minister Marshall Green, Charge d'Affaires, American Embassy, and General Carter B. Magruder, commander-in-chief of the United Nations Command (UNC), on the radio: "We wish to make it emphatically clear that the US supports the constitutional government of the ROK as elected by the people of the Republic last July, and as constituted by the election of a prime minister last August. We expect that the chiefs of the Korean Armed Forces will use their authority and influence to see that control is immediately returned to the government authorities and that order is restored in the armed forces."

I felt relieved and optimistic about the stabilization of the situation; however, when I arrived in Seoul, tightly guarded by the military, I immediately sensed that something was wrong. The next day, I asked my brother Dae-ui to register my election at the National Assembly. Immediately after my registration, the Military Revolutionary Committee dispersed the National Assembly. I had no chance to wear the golden badge or to sit on the seat at the National Assembly Hall.

The May 16th Coup was an attack on the US military, which controlled the Korean military, as well. In the US, public sentiment was largely against the South Korean military coup. It was known that President Kennedy was angry at the report and had immediately looked for Prime Minister Chang. Unfortunately, he had gone missing.

By the time the coup forces arrived at room 808 in the Bando Hotel (later the location of the Lotte Hotel) near the City Hall Plaza in Seoul, Prime Minister Chang had already gone into hiding. He tried first to hide in the US Embassy near his residence, but it was locked at that early hour. I later heard he had lost his glasses on his way to the car. As the Democratic Party government had lost its metaphorical eyes upon his disappearance, that incident might have foreshadowed the second republic's demise. Dr. Chang hid in the Carmel Convent behind the Hyehwa-dong Catholic Church and spent the next fifty-five hours in prayer and anguish.

During those fifty-five hours, the Republic of Korea was moving in the opposite direction of democracy. Incredible incidents were waiting for me; I would have to fight against military dictatorship for decades, although I didn't know it then.

If Prime Minister Chang had escaped to the US Embassy, our government could have easily suppressed that "clumsy coup d'état" by a meager 3600 troops. I wonder even now why he didn't simply climb over the embassy wall, even if the door was locked. Also, when he was in the convent, he could have tried to communicate with the UN or the US Embassy. The event could have taken a dramatically different turn. In retrospect, this must have been our nation's fate.

General Magruder desperately attempted to find Dr. Chang, to no avail. In the end, together with Minister Green, he visited President Yun Po-sun and requested that he order the mobilization of the entire military to suppress the coup. Strangely, President Yun turned down this request, saying his request constituted intervention in the domestic affairs of another country.

Later, President Yun said he acknowledged the coup for the sake of national security. His logic here was very strange. I believe he should have deferred to General Magruder had he really been concerned about national security since the US military had much more accurate information on the matter at hand than Koreans did. Although President Yun was the commander-in-chief of the Korean military and head of the country, in the end he did nothing to defend the legitimate government. Instead, he chose to defend his personal political interests as the head of the Sinmin Party. At that time, there was a rumor that President Yun also had a backdoor deal with the coup forces.

It is well known that when he met the coup leaders President Yun said, "This had to come." It was an extremely political statement, mindful only of his party's interest. What he wanted to gain by acknowledging the failure of the government he headed is very clear based on his later actions. Not only did he ignore the US request, but he also actively supported the coup by sending a signed letter that ordered First Army Commander Lee Han-lim (who was in charge of a field army) not to mobilize.

Yun must have believed what Park Chung-hee said during their visit. "We rose up for Mr. President's sake." He must have been planning a political restructure, with himself at the center. The president, who should have defended the Constitution with all his might, accepted the military coup and stayed in office for ten more months, practically handing over legitimate, legalized control to the coup forces. Because the president accepted the coup and the prime minister disappeared, there was nothing the US could have done. Several critical days passed when it was still possible to salvage the country's democracy.

Army Chief of Staff Chang Do-yeong's actions were also questionable. Prime Minister Chang Myon trusted Chief Chang Do-yeong, appointing him to the post after firing his predecessor Chief Choi Gyeong-rok. The prime minister did this despite cabinet members' opposition based on Chief Chang's loyalty to Lee Ki-poong during the previous regime. Prime Minister Chang asked Chief Chang several times in front of me, "Are there any grounds to the rumor about a possible coup by Major General Park Chung-hee?"

Every time Chief Chang answered, "That rumor is completely groundless, sir. Some people have even accused me of participating in Major General Park's coup." Every time he claimed he was in complete charge of the military.

When the coup occurred, Chief Chang did nothing to suppress it. On the contrary, he remained in communication with Major General Park to buy time for the coup forces. In my opinion, if Chief Choe had still been in office, the coup could have been halted. Later, I joked to my friends, "Mr. Park Chung-hee must have been born with great fortune considering his clumsy coup attempt succeeded. It's like he dug under his own front porch and found a treasure."

After betraying Lee Ki-poong for Chang Myon, Chang Do-yeong then assisted and supported "the revolutionary forces." Based on his actions, it's clear that he tried to balance the demands of both the coup forces and the Democratic Party government. Ultimately, his career ended miserably after he was elevated to the position of the supreme leader of the military government. He was arrested for being an "anti-revolutionary" and banished abroad. Park Chung-hee's coup forces used and discarded him.

Three days after the coup, on May 18, Prime Minister Chang appeared and held the last cabinet meeting at 12:30 p.m., ratifying the martial law. That afternoon, Military Academy students marched through the main streets of Seoul, leading troops wearing Revolutionary Army armbands. The second republic vanished into history.

The police came to my house to arrest me after the dispersion of the National Assembly. The coup forces, which emphasized a Political Party Corruption Cleanup policy, appeared to think that I, as the ruling party spokesperson and a critical official to all proceedings, was naturally connected to the alleged corruption.

As the ruling party spokesperson, I had campaigned across the country and, together with college students, attended various meetings to stabilize the political situation. I was assigned "public relations expenses," which I distributed to students for their travel-related costs. Believing that I must have embezzled this money, they included these allegations when they branded the Democratic Party corrupt.

After escaping military tribunal, I was sent to civilian court. I explained in detail to the prosecutor how I had distributed the money to students and their organizations. The prosecutor summoned and interrogated the students in question and discovered that they'd actually received more money from me than was first assigned. This was natural, though, as I'd contributed my own money to their funds when necessary. The prosecutor eventually dropped all charges. I still clearly remember the anger in his voice when he said, "Fabricating bastards!" I was released after two months of these ordeals. During that martial law period, an unusual amount of courage was required for the prosecutor to do that.

Besides me, a significant number of leaders and officials—including government officials, Democratic Party officials, and more than a 1000 reformist leaders—were also imprisoned. *Minjok Ilbo* Newspaper Company president Cho Yong-su and many others were sentenced to death or severe prison terms. They were treated like communists. After the reformists attacked the Chang Myon cabinet so passionately, the final fruit of their efforts was the destruction of their own right to action and freedom of thought.

The military government claimed it would make anti-communist defense its most important national policy. This was a ridiculous claim. What if communism were to disband? Would they, then, disband our country based on its anti-communist stance? Anti-communist defense should be a means of defending democracy, not a goal in and of itself.

Nevertheless, one could describe the way the coup forces carried out their business as solving a knotty problem once and for all. Under martial law, the military appeared to take care of all matters clearly, efficiently, and based on clear principles. They did this all while accusing the Chang Myon cabinet of corruption and incompetence. As citizens had indeed grown tired of the continual political strife since the launch of the Chang cabinet, some favored the military, although many were angry and hurt that our democracy had been trampled on again.

The coup leaders claimed that they had to come forward to prevent our country from collapsing because of the pro-communist, incompetent, and corrupt Chang cabinet. This was clearly false, though. According to their own later publication of the *Korean Military Revolution Trial History*, revolutionary leaders—including Kim Jong-pil, Kim Hyong-uk, O Chi-song, and Kil Chae-ho—discussed a possible coup on September 10, 1960, at a high-end restaurant called Chungmujang in Chungmuro, Seoul. As the Chang Myon cabinet was formed on August 23, this implied that they were always prepared for the possibility of a coup, predicting the cabinet's pro-communist incompetence and corrupt future within only eighteen days of its formation—an entirely absurd argument! While the entire nation was congratulating the new cabinet and the Democratic Party government was planning the future of a nation, the coup leaders were conspiring to overthrow it. When I later resumed my political career, I exposed this fact to the consternation of all.

The military government's all-out effort to label the Chang cabinet corrupt proved fruitless, despite mobilizing not only the police but also the media. The only conviction they were able to make was Secretary of Treasury Kim Young-sun's acceptance of a used refrigerator during his stay in the US. Their accusation of the Chang cabinet's corruption was pure fabrication, designed to conceal the ambitions of a few political soldiers. In fact, the second republic tried very hard to remain a clean government. Prime Minister Chang even carried his own homemade lunch to the office. We have to acknowledge these efforts to stay faithful to the pure spirit of the April 19th Revolution.

The Korean Central Intelligence Administration (KCIA) establishment law was proclaimed on June 10, with Mr. Kim Jong-pil appointed as its first chief. All political conspiracy and surveillance would be born there. It was the beginning of the frightening world of intelligence politics. The KCIA controlled all political activities in the country.

The KCIA was the centerpiece that safeguarded the eighteen-year Park Chung-hee regime, the headquarters for organized corruption and the annihilation of human rights and democracy, the control tower for successive fraudulent elections. It was the omnipotent institution that guarded the military regime, sacrificing countless politicians and democracy movement leaders. It was the sword and the barrel for military presidents whose line continued to Chun Doo-hwan and Roh Tae-woo. The barrel of that gun was aimed straight at me and pursued me to the end of the time; my life was always the candlelight before the wind. In a historical twist, its creator Kim Jong-pil later became its victim. He was ultimately exiled himself, pushed out by the appeasing, threatening actions of the KCIA.

Judging from the Revolutionary Pledges (or the later infighting between political leaders throughout the Park regime), the May 16th Incident clearly didn't have a solid ideology or firm policies already in place. No matter how hard one tries to beautify it, the events of the May 16th Incident do not deserve the title of "revolution." It was no more and no less than a violent power grab. It nipped democracy in the bud and trampled party politics and parliamentary democracy for years to come. The military became a privileged group that controlled political supremacy entirely. Political soldiers gained power unchecked. As a result of this military coup, Korean history stepped back thirty years.

May Bride, My Eternal Companion (May 1962– October 1963)

I married Lee Hee-ho on May 10, 1962. When I met her in Busan, I was a successful young businessman and she was the International Relations Department Chief of YWCA and a graduate of the Seoul National University College of Education. After the war, she went to the US to study for four years, and then worked as the manager of the YWCA Seoul headquarters. Although I met her when I was at the most affluent point in my life, I married her when I was at my lowest.

We ran into each other on the Jong-no Street of Seoul toward the end of summer in 1959. Very glad for this chance encounter, we had tea together. She looked the same as I remembered. After catching up with one another, we went our separate ways. Since I was an active politician and she a women's movement activist, we each knew what the other had been doing for a while now.

Some time after the military coup, I frequented Myeong-dong and the nearby YWCA building to meet Lee Hee-ho after work. Gradually, we met more frequently at parks and restaurants. Because my finances were in poor shape then, she paid for our dates most of the time. During this period, I had nothing else to do during the day but watch movies on the fifth floor of the Hwashin department store in Jong-no. In that shabby theater you could watch double features. I whiled my days away, watching them with friends or by myself. Sometimes I didn't even have bus fare. At one point during that period, I once borrowed money from my younger friend's college tuition to pay for my basic costs of livelihood. He had to go on leave because of me and I have felt indebted to him my entire life. I could not engage in political activities because of the Political Purge Act, and my future was utterly unclear. Nevertheless, Lee Hee-ho understood me deeply and comforted me with warm words, worrying about my poverty-stricken life as though it were her own.

Lee Hee-ho's attractiveness was in her gentleness, which captivated me more and more. She was intelligent and active, but never arrogant. She grew up in an affluent family and was a promising female leader, but modest. She was outspoken, but open-minded. She was progressive, and her view of the world was accurate.

When we met, we talked mostly about society and, especially, politics. I don't have many memories of us talking about our affections. Perhaps because we met when we were older, we felt more like companions than lovers. We understood each other deeply. It wasn't a heated love, but we could see one another's innermost thoughts and feelings. I felt extremely at ease with her, and I gradually felt like living my dream with her. I realized *that* was love.

Although our love deepened, I could not help being passive because I didn't have anything great to offer her. In contrast, she was active in everything. Although I could clearly see her love for me in her eyes, I hesitated. In the end, though, I proposed to her at Tapgol Park on a somewhat chilly March evening.

When we announced our engagement, people around Lee Hee-ho—not only her family, but also her friends, colleagues, and fellow women's movement activists—tried to dissuade her. She didn't budge, though. On the contrary, her resolve grew firmer. My family situation was very hard at that time. I was living in rented housing with my sickly old mother, a sister with heart disease, and two sons. It was probably natural that Lee Hee-ho's friends and family were against her marrying me. Still, she remained steadfast, saying, "He is an excellent person who needs my assistance."

She was the first daughter of eight siblings—six sons and two daughters—between father Lee Yong-gi, a doctor and graduate of Severance Union Medical School, and mother Lee Sun-yi, who passed away when Lee Hee-ho was nineteen.

In the end, we married at her maternal uncle's traditional Korean home in Chebu-dong. Her uncle's name was Lee Won-soon. Reverend Cho Hyang-rok officiated our wedding. We promised to love and respect each other in a large living room in front of about a hundred guests, including family, friends, and women's movement leaders. Lee Hee-ho, my May bride, became the woman in my life. She has loved, understood, and cared about me more than anyone else in the world.

Our honeymoon was shattered only ten days later, on May 20, when the KCIA showed up and dragged me to their secret location. They alleged Democratic Party officials had tried to overthrow the "revolution." It was an absurd investigation. It was impossible for us to even think about meeting together for that kind of discussion because of the stifling intelligence activity of the period. They knew it, too. It was simply their way of threatening us so that we wouldn't even dream of any "anti-revolutionary" actions. I was released after a month's detainment.

My tumultuous relationship with the KCIA began even before my wedding. After the KCIA was established, an intelligence officer and my acquaintance from Mokpo visited me with a box of taffy, a rarity because of the sugar shortage. Before long, he abruptly began to spit harsh criticisms against the military government. I didn't chime in because it felt somewhat suspicious, claiming that I was no longer interested in politics. I later confirmed that KCIA agents had begun to visit politicians with hidden recorders. If I had chimed in then, I may have suffered greatly. Mr. Kim Sang-don, a former mayor of Seoul, received a similar visit from an acquaintance and vehemently criticized the military. He ended up in prison for years.

While I was idling away my days following my release from prison, another misfortune visited my family. My sister, an Ewha Womans University student, died of a valvular disease of the heart. A Korean literature student, she was a talented would-be poet who I thought had a bright future as a writer. I wonder why a terrible disease like that had to visit such a beautiful and noble soul. At that time, surgery had not developed much, and, even if it had, we couldn't afford it. Whenever I visited her in the hospital, she tried to smile, even as she labored just to breathe. The image of her trying to smile is still so vivid in my mind. All I could do was cry as I watched her die at Seoul Red Cross Hospital. I regretted that I had chosen a political career. As the impoverished head of the household, there was nothing I could do for her. I could barely manage to take care of myself, and deplored my depressing political reality. I still can't help but cry when I visit her grave.

If I remember correctly, in February 1963 a KCIA high official contacted me to meet him at Bando Hotel, then the secret headquarters of the KCIA. There, he asked me to participate in the Republican Party if I wanted to continue my political career. The Supreme Council had lifted the ban on political activities for 171 politicians, but I was excluded from that list. After resigning as KCIA head, Kim Jong-pil was working to establish the Republican Party. They needed a good cause and some talent for this new party. They tried to entice me, saying, "We know very well about your ability and talent. They're all proven. We know you deserve to become more than just an assemblyman. Please join us, and then we'll treat you according to your abilities. There's a right time for everyone. Now's the time for you to exercise your talents. If you reject our proposal now, you should forget about politics for the next eight years."

It was a very enticing proposal with a veiled threat at the core. At that time, forgetting politics for eight years was like a death sentence to any politician. I still refused. "I was the spokesperson of the Democratic Party that you overthrew. You claim you had to come forward because the Chang Myon cabinet was corrupt and inept. I appealed to the people for their support for that very same administration, claiming that it was historically the best administration. If I now tell people that you're the best, what will they think of me? If I change my tune, wouldn't people call me a traitor? What good would it do for you to welcome a traitor into your party? It would only be detrimental to you."

General elections were approaching, and every politician was anxious. Many politicians had given up hope, as had I. Kim Jong-pil was waiting in the adjacent room. The official asked me to meet him before I made my final decision, but I stood up, saying, "Don't think about changing my thoughts any more. I said what I had to say, so I'd like to leave now."

Suddenly, he cursed me from behind. "You fucking son-of-a-bitch! Just wagging your tongue at me, aren't you?"

I simply walked out. What an outrageous man! I suppressed my anger. They never tried to approach me again. I was excluded from the second political activity ban lift, too. I remained banned until the last restitution of political activity rights.

Our family moved to Donggyo-dong, Mapo-gu, Seoul, in April 1963. This was my eighth move within Seoul in nine years. We moved into a small house built for low-income families, based on a national bank's investment, which received aid from US International Cooperation Administration (USICA). We rented first, and later bought the house when I became an assemblyman. Eventually, we bought a house adjacent to it and hung a nameplate with both my and my wife's names on it. For us, at least, it was always home, sweet home; I had lived in it until very recently. When we bought the house, Donggyo-dong was an outskirt of

Seoul, surrounded by zucchini farms. Whenever it rained, the road became slick with mud and we had to wear rain boots.

As time went by, it became clearer that the coup power's pledges were hastily put-together makeshift promises, rather than a well-thought-out plan. Among their pledges, their promise of agrarian improvement was the most widely favored by people, 70 to 80 percent of which were farmers. At first they seemed to follow through on this, attempting to reform the farmers' usurious credits. But that was it in terms of any reform agenda for agriculture or farmers.

As mentioned before, the military regime's five-year Economic Development Plan was a carbon copy of the plan the Democratic Party had prepared. However, they were never really able to understand or enforce the plan's true spirit through their military order system and arm-chair governance. Ignoring plans for farmers, they only pushed through policies that benefited large enterprises and cities. The gap between cities and the countryside inevitably widened. The countryside became alien-ated and farmers' lives grew more difficult by the day.

While rice production rapidly decreased, the import of excess US prod-ucts was delayed. By 1962, the food shortage had become a serious prob-lem. As their policies continued to fail, inflation grew out of control. The economy plunged irredeemably. They had to revise their five-year Economic Development Plan only a year later.

What people found truly unforgivable, though, was the corruption committed by the coup forces themselves. Their excuse for overturning the Democratic Party leadership was "cleansing of corruption." People expected that the military was clean, if nothing else; however, they turned rotten as rapidly as any other regime—and to an unthinkable degree.

While the coup forces were devising a law that punished the accumula-tion of wealth by illicit means, they demanded political contributions from conglomerates in exchange for tolerating their illicit activities behind closed doors. Eventually, Four Suspicious Incidents and Three Powder Incidents occurred. The Four Suspicious Incidents were KCIA-created incidents to secure political funds for the Republican Party, including the Stock Crisis, the Walker Hill Incident, the Saenara Automobile Incident, and the Pachinko Incident.

The Stock Crisis involved the KCIA garnering undue profits by first controlling the Korea Exchange, then manipulating stock prices. About 5300 investors lost tremendous amounts of money, and many of them committed suicide. In order to generate political funds, the insurgent forces did not hesitate at all in actions that would drive innocent investors to their death.

The Walker Hill Incident involved the building of Walker Hill Hotel—an entertainment facility in Gwangjang-dong, Seoul, designed for US military stationed in Korea—under the pretext of generating foreign income. The government lent the builders money and received a considerable portion of it as a kickback. They also pressured the Transportation Ministry and military troops to mobilize their facilities and personnel for this private enterprise. When the US military received wind of this, they banned their troops from using the hotel.

As for the Saenara Automobile Incident, the KCIA illegally imported Nissan automobiles from Japan and sold them for more than twice their price. They established Saenara Automobile Manufacturing Company under the pretext of nurturing the national automobile industry and awarded it the monopoly for automobile import and sales rights. In reality, Saenara Automobile was a front for illegally peddling automobiles imported from Japan tax-free.

With the Pachinko Incident, the government permitted 800 pachinko machines to be imported from Japan tax-free and to be operated in Seoul. They brought the machines into the country illegally by disguising them as the personal goods of a Korean ex-pat in Japan. When pachinko gambling became rampant under martial law, people had to wonder about the military government's true identity. The government rushed to cancel the permit. There was no doubt that the KCIA was behind it all.

These four incidents revealed the coup forces' true colors. All of them—tax evasion, embezzlement, budget misappropriation, and stock fraud—were as ugly and corrupt as anything the nation had ever seen. Public opinion worsened.

People began to wonder, "What on earth is better about this government than the previous one?" They criticized it, saying, "This new evil is worse than the old evil." Eventually, someone had to take responsibility. Kim Jong-pil resigned from his post as head of the KCIA ("half-heartedly," to use his own words) and was banished overseas.

As if all of this wasn't enough, three incidents involving the illicit production of three powders—cement, flour, and sugar—occurred toward the end of the military government's reign. Although the companies that produced them made undue profits through illicit means, the military looked the other way in exchange for enormous political contributions. Due to price fixing, the cost of these three materials soared to two or three times their original value overnight, once again bringing a great deal of pain and suffering to innocent people.

In the aftermath of these scandals, Head of the Supreme Council Park Chung-hee's position became extremely shaky. Before these developments, Park laid out plans to relinquish power to a civilian government. On March 19, 1962, Park announced that he would hand over his power to a civilian government the next year. On November 17, he announced that the coup leaders would participate in civilian politics. Then, on December 27, he announced his intention to run for the presidency. Finally, despite this escalating series of politically related announcements, on February 18, 1963, he abruptly announced that he would not participate in civilian politics.

Less than a month after that announcement, on March 15, eighty military officers belonging to the Capital Defense Command waged a scandalous demonstration in front of the Supreme Council building. They demanded that Head of the Supreme Council Park withdraw his decision not to participate in the civilian election and that he extend the military government. Their intentions were crystal clear. The idea of a military officer demonstration was absolutely grotesque.

As expected, Park Chung-hee immediately responded with the announcement that he would, indeed, extend military rule for four years, and that he would ultimately decide it via referendum. Naturally, a political furor ensued. Every political force in the country opposed Park's decision. The US immediately responded as well. Ambassador to Korea Samuel Berger and the State Department expressed their regrets. President Kennedy sent a letter of protest directly to the military government and suspended aid to the five-year Economic Development Plan. Embarrassed, Park was forced to surrender the idea of extending a military government. On July 27, he announced that he would hand over power to a civilian government before the year's end. The date for the presidential election was set for mid-October.

Park Chung-hee, who'd already usurped power as a major general, repeatedly broke his promises. He clearly had no intention of relinquishing power. From the outset, he'd never intended to keep his promise to return to the military. After an unofficial decision to accept the position of president of the Republican Party and its presidential candidacy, he resigned from his military position just one day before the primary.

On August 30, the day of his discharge, Park stated: "I hope there will never be a soldier as unhappy as I am."

I wonder why he called himself an unhappy soldier. One thing, however, was clear: Park made the history of modern Korea an extremely unhappy one. A number of soldiers followed in his footsteps. Our political scene has seen an unhappy state of affairs for a very long time.

PRESIDENT PARK CHUNG-HEE, ELECTED THANKS TO HONAM (1963–1964)

I resumed my political career after the ban on my political activities was lifted on February 27, 1963, and participated in rebuilding the Democratic Party with a number of old colleagues. We elected Madam Pak Sun-cheon, who was well trusted and respected among opposition party members, as our party president during the party-founding event on July 18, 1963. Once again, I was elected spokesperson. Before our party's establishment, on May 14, members of the former Sinmin and Liberal Parties, as well as some independents, established the Minjeong Party and elected Mr. Kim Byeong-ro as their Supreme Council president. On September 5, the Gugminui Party was established around Mr. Huh Jung.

At first, we former Democratic Party members tried to embrace Mr. Huh Jung; however, he chose to associate only with former Liberal Party members. He was also too self-righteous to work in the same party. The Republican Party (officially known as the Democratic Republican Party) had already been established on February 26. They elected Cheong Ku-yeong as their party president and Kim Chung-yul as their party chairman.

The political situation was hectic. The opposition camp had to nominate a unified presidential candidate before the October 15 election. Feeling responsible for its loss of power to the military coup, the Democratic Party decided not to elect its own candidate. At first, we were hesitant about supporting Yun Po-sun because of his questionable collusion with the coup forces, but Mr. Huh Jung was collaborating with former Liberal Party forces. Yun was the second-worst alternative; we also took the fact that he was a known personality into consideration. Candidate Huh eventually yielded his candidacy to Candidate Yun so the opposition camp could unite behind a single candidate. Although Park had become a civilian, he was "a soldier in plainclothes." We had to form a unified front to end his military rule.

I attacked the military government's corruption and the Park Chung-hee dictatorship's problems before the election campaign could get heated.

At that time, Park was the chairman of the Supreme Council as well as an army general as a result of his rapid promotion since the military coup. Although he had become a member of the Republican Party immediately after his discharge, I discovered that this sequence was in violation of the Emergency Measure Law for National Reconstruction, the law that the coup forces instituted after the coup, and that was supposedly above the Constitution. I made this fact public and maintained that his Republican Party membership was invalid. Embarrassed, they attempted to solve the situation by amending the Emergency Measure Law for National Reconstruction. This all-out attack rocked the political world. I wonder if this laid the foundation for Park's lifelong hatred of me. If nothing else, he began paying attention to me because of that incident.

The likely outcome of the election was unclear but, despite all the confusion, people predicted Park Chung-hee would lose because of the many failures of his military government. The public had come to believe that the military was incompetent in handling politics. During the thirty-one-month military regime, the country had fallen into chaos again and the economy had become extremely depressed.

Nevertheless, Candidate Yun Po-sun also had many weaknesses. Above all, he acknowledged the coup as a legitimate regime. Instead of defending the Constitution, he prioritized his and his party's interests over it. He slept in the same bed with the military that had destroyed the Constitution. It was only after they dumped him that he began to criticize the military. The public never approved of this. Still, Yun Po-sun was an extremely well-known politician with many secured supporters because of his long political career.

It was a tight race. In the beginning, Candidate Yun appeared to be on top for his just causes; however, he made the critical mistake of accusing Park of being communist, which proved to be a supremely unwise tactic. Although he didn't name names, he noted, "One of the presidential candidates was involved in the Yeosu-Suncheon Rebellion Incident."

Clearly, this attack was aimed at Park, who had been indicted for that very allegation when he was a major. Still, the critique had no effect on a candidate who proclaimed anti-communism and defense of the nation against communism as his primary national policy. Moreover, this sort of red-bashing reminded people of the dark times dominated by the Hanmin Party, which had ruthlessly cleansed all opposition, including Mr. Kim Koo, by accusing them of being communists under US military rule. Yun's accusation reminded voters of the kind of terror politics that had long dominated during the US military and Rhee Syngman's regimes. In a tight race, Yun's mistake was costly.

Park won the election by a meager 156,000-vote margin. It was incredibly close. Of course, there was a great deal of fraud during the election. The military generously spread the money the KCIA had secured through various illegal and corrupt means, including the Four Suspicious Incidents and the Three Powder Incidents. Still, I believe the opposition could have won had it not been for Candidate Yun's mistake. It was Park's good fortune that he could continue wielding power by taking advantage of his opponent's tactical error.

Park lost in Seoul, Gyeonggi-do, Gangwon-do, and Chungcheong-do, and won only in Gyeongsang-do, his home province, and Jeolla-do, with which he had no connection. He won Jeolla-do by a particularly wide margin of 350,000 votes. In other words, he won the election thanks to the Jeolla votes. Jeolla-do residents voted for him mostly because of the pro-communist accusation Yun directed at Park.

And yet, Park alienated Jeolla-do as soon as he was sworn in as president. His regional discrimination policy was the origin of the regional antagonism that has plagued our country ever since. The biggest political and ethical fault of his eighteen-year regime was his policy of regional discrimination. That was a historical sin.

Immediately after the presidential election, a general election for the sixth National Assembly was held across 131 precincts. I ran for the Mokpo precinct as a Democratic Party candidate. The people of Mokpo recommended that I run based on my reputation and political career, including my position as the ruling party spokesman. Although it was in Mokpo that I lost my first election, this time it welcomed me.

My opponent was Mr. Cha Mun-seok, a Republican Party candidate. His father, one of the richest men in Mokpo, served as a *chamui* (a Japanese-appointed senator) at the Jungchuwon during the Japanese colonial period. Although I didn't have an election chest as large as Mr. Cha's, I was confident about my campaign. My successive previous losses had made me stronger. I appealed to the people: "Although I am the son of Mokpo, I have had to wander around strange places. I ran in Inje, the farthest possible point from Mokpo, and won after indescribable hardships. I have also worked as the ruling party spokesman. Gangwon-do and Seoul recognize my ability; would it be just for Mokpo citizens to ignore me? If I lose in my hometown, I will have nowhere else to go. Please raise me! I'll repay you by becoming a great man."

In the middle of this campaign, US President John F. Kennedy was assassinated during a parade in Dallas on November 22. I was utterly shocked to hear the news. President Kennedy, the youngest president in US history, was my idol. His televised debate with Nixon during the presidential campaign was a great event that radically changed election culture. During the Cuban Missile Crisis, he had skillfully handled the situation against Khrushchev, managing to be both flexible and firm, and achieving the great compromise that resulted in the USSR's withdrawal of missiles from Cuba in exchange for the US suspension of their invasion of Cuba. He also used it as an opportunity to create the Comprehensive Nuclear Test Ban Treaty and contributed to the lightening of the tension between the two blocs.

Kennedy was a mythic character who embodied true courage. He was young and full of energy to change the world. By pursuing change, he offered people hope. Although I had never even met him, I felt it so unjust that he no longer existed in this world. I could see his face before me during my campaign. Although he was the president of another, faraway country, his actions gave me power and courage. Like him, I, too, wanted to present the hopeful road to our people by dedicating my youth to the betterment of Korea. I wanted to change the rotten world—that's why I entered politics.

The general election was becoming more and more murky as Election Day drew near. This was true in Mokpo as well. The Republican Party had mobilized the police and local government officials to interfere with the opposition party campaign. Still, there were good, virtuous people everywhere. The Mokpo Police Station Intelligence Department Chief Police Sergeant Na Seung-won rolled out a secret directive involving election fraud called the "National Assemblymen Election Measure." Police Sergeant Na held a press conference at the Minjeong Party office and disclosed the thirteen secret orders for election frauds, all of which clearly targeted my defeat. This document became the prime example of the ongoing election fraud that all opposition parties condemned. We pressured the government, demanding the dismissal of the minister of internal affairs and police commissioner, and threatening an election boycott. In Mokpo, the situation became overwhelmingly favorable to me. Since the revelation by Police Sergeant Na, the Republican Party didn't dare attempt fraud. I won by a landslide.

Kwon Rho-kap, who helped me during the Inje election, helped me in Mokpo as well. A junior alumnus of Mokpo Commercial High School, Kwon resigned from his position teaching English to help me run my campaign.

He knew people from all walks of life. Eom Chang-rok, another assistant during the Inje election, also worked very hard for me.

Nevertheless, the Republican Party won by a landslide overall, taking 110 out of 175 seats, including members elected from the national constituency. The Liberal Democratic Party added nine seats to the side of the ruling party. In the opposition camp, the Minjeong Party won forty-one seats, and the Democratic Party, to which I belonged, won thirteen seats.

On November 12, fifteen days before Election Day, I heard the news that my third and last son, Hong Gul, was born. I grieved that I couldn't be with my wife in Seoul when she gave birth. I held Hong Gul in my arms as a presumptive national assemblyman. I was forty and my wife was forty-two years old. I was overjoyed.

After the elections, the civilian regime headed by Park Chung-hee was born. Through popular vote, the amended Constitution went into effect, and the third republic was launched. The Park regime's first project was to normalize diplomatic relations between Korea and Japan. The national economy was in the worst shape—rice prices leapt drastically due to poor harvests, and they had to execute the five-year Economic Development Plan they had pledged during the election campaign. Economic aid from Japan was necessary.

The Park regime had already reached an agreement with Japan on Korea's property claims against Japan during the military period. Through negotiations between Japanese Foreign Secretary Ohira Masayoshi and KCIA Chief Kim Jong-pil over the course of two meetings in October and November 1961, they produced the so-called Kim-Ohira Memorandum. The essence of this agreement was that Japan would provide Korea with $300 million worth of free economic cooperation, a $200 million governmental loan, and a $100 million commercial loan. Because this agreement was made through secret negotiations, the opposition parties were against it.

The opposition camp immediately responded. Minjeong Party Chairman Yun Po-sun declared that his party was "against the proposed Korea-Japan Agreement to the death." He claimed that Korea should not discharge Japan from responsibility for its past aggressions and sell off the Rhee Syngman Line (aka, the Peace Line, a sovereignty boundary line established unilaterally by Rhee Syngman in his declaration in 1952) at the cost of only $300 million. Yun also strongly condemned the agreement as an unpatriotic act that positioned Korea as an economic colony of Japan. A fierce opposition movement unfolded. On March 9, 1964, three days before the sixth Korea-Japan Main Conference, about 200 opposition party leaders and notables representing various facets of society gathered and formed the Nationwide Struggle Committee Against Disgraceful Diplomacy with Japan.

Nevertheless, I didn't agree with Yun's Unconditional Opposition to the Korea-Japan Conference. Both Madam Pak Sun-cheon and I objected to Yun labeling government officials as unpatriotic, too. To me, it seemed that normalizing our relationship with Japan was necessary for our national interests. I also noticed that all former colony countries around the globe were normalizing their relationships with their former colonizing countries. In international society, there can be neither permanent friends nor permanent enemies. Besides, Japan had already become our close neighbor through various other exchanges.

At that time, Japan was a rapidly growing economic powerhouse. Rather than simply envying them, we had to know and use Japan's potential to our advantage. I was worried that we could become isolated from global trends if we delayed normalizing our relations with Japan.

At that time, the US was also actively supporting the normalizing of Korea-Japan relations behind the scenes. In order to stabilize East Asia, the US needed a US-Japan-Korea security system. During the Cold War period, Korea could not ignore the US. Also, all the countries in the world (except for Taiwan, vis-à-vis leader Chiang Kai-shek) were supporting Korea-Japan relation normalization. Surrounded by North Korea, China, and the Soviet Union, South Korea did not have the option of antagonizing Japan. I argued to that effect in an opposition party meeting, saying: "We must pursue the normalization of Korea-Japan relations. Countries that were once colonies of the UK and France normalized their relationship with their former colonizers. I don't believe they did it because they weren't proud enough. It was for the sake of their national interests. One thing we need to be careful about is securing our interests in the negotiations. Opposition parties should present an appropriate alternative to our government's plan. We cannot simply oppose a deal that would guarantee mutual interests."

However, the hardliners, including Yun, remained adamant in their position. "The normalization of Korea-Japan relations is anti-patriotic and the only alternative to an anti-patriotic act is to oppose it," detractors claimed.

One day I discovered a strange rumor circulating within the opposition camp: I was the ruling party's spy, a *sakura* (an opposition politician bribed by the ruling party), and a king *sakura* at that. At the time, a politician's life would be all but over once labeled a *sakura*. Another rumor was circulating that I had received a whopping 30 million won check issued at the Namdaemun branch of the Chohung Bank. It was as if someone had really witnessed it. Even the check's number was mentioned.

Nevertheless, I went to Mokpo to hold my assembly activity report-back meeting. Almost 10,000 people attended. Before the event, I told my friends and party members that I would use the opportunity to clarify my position on the Korea-Japan talks. Everyone told me to avoid the topic; it was too sensitive a subject, they said. I didn't follow their advice, though. As I told them, "I have to be honest about what I believe. I believe it's my duty as a politician to speak my honest opinion for the sake of our country."

At the event, I indeed voiced my honest opinions. Surprisingly, the audience applauded at the end. At the time, the public was largely swayed by their feelings, rather than reason, which the Yun-led opposition had been using to their advantage up until that point. But I could not bend my beliefs just because of popular sentiment; in my opinion, this is something a politician should never do. I hoped that the Korean public would eventually come around as the audience had that day.

When I finished my speech, our party Mokpo branch officer rushed up to me and asked what I had been thinking by making such a dangerous speech. What would I do in the next election? Had I decided I was done with my political career?

"If my arguments turn out to be wrong, I won't run for the election," I answered calmly. "I won't trouble you. But, I believe my opinion is correct. I don't think people are against normalizing relations with Japan. What matters is the terms of the agreement, and what's important is to monitor it to make sure we are not left at a disadvantage."

Around this time, I went to a discussion meeting with a group of Ewha Womans University students, prepared by Madam Lee Tai-young. There, I calmly sought to persuade the students who seemed to consider politicians to be generally spineless. I said, "We cannot live forever without normalizing our relationship with Japan. If we are to ever collaborate with Japan, this is the right time. What matters is how to maximize our interests. It is because the opposition camp unconditionally opposes it that the Japanese government and Park regime have completely ignored the opposition and made illicit deals behind closed doors. We can secure our interests only when we oppose it with our demands.

"I'm not supporting normalizing relations with Japan in order to help the Park regime. I'm supporting it for the future of our nation. When many people think this is the right time to form a friendly relationship with Japan, we have to think about what we can gain from it instead of opposing it absolutely. We have to resolve the matter of Dokdo and demand an apology for Japanese aggression. If we simply oppose it, all these issues will be buried. What if the Japanese government and the Park regime sign an agreement with terms, disadvantageous to us and rush the bill through the Assembly by surprise? It's only going to be our people's loss. I came forward because we cannot throw out our national interests because of our feelings."

Students who had appeared antagonistic toward me in the beginning nodded their heads when I finished my speech. I continued to argue for "conditional opposition" in party assemblies and other speech events. The opinion in the party gradually favored my proposal.

Nevertheless, it remained a very difficult time of my life. Many public and private voices didn't even bother trying to understand my arguments. Rumors begot rumors. Bad rumors even crossed the sea to Hauido. Father sent me a letter, scolding me. "What's going on?" he wrote. "I heard that my son who once had such a bright future is now being called a *sakura*. Why are you doing things that only bring contempt on yourself?"

Father then came to Seoul to scold me in person. My wife also had to hear people sneer and protest: "Is it true that your husband's become the tool of the ruling party? How did he end up like that?" Even my two sons' classmates sneered, sending them home crying. It was all extremely difficult. The difficulty of holding on to my belief and not being understood made me feel as though my heart and body were being stabbed.

Around that time, I happened to read President Kennedy's *Profiles in Courage*, which discussed many American politicians who worked hard to overcome their friends' and the public's misunderstandings of their ideas. Their efforts drove them to near collapse, but they eventually persuaded the people of what they'd long argued for their nation's sake. Even from heaven, Kennedy gave me a great present. After I finished that book, I hardened my resolution and felt more at peace.

University students demonstrated on the streets of Seoul in protest of the disgraceful agreement with Japan. A lecture meeting held by the Nationwide Struggle Committee Against Disgraceful Diplomacy with Japan and led by opposition party hardliners ignited the rally. Approximately 40,000 people attended the meeting and, although it dispersed peacefully, struggles spread all across the country.

At noon on June 3, about 50,000 students and citizens gathered in Gwanghwamun for a sit-down demonstration. In this anti-government demonstration, later dubbed the June 3rd Incident, students also waged a sit-down strike on the main thoroughfare that connected the downtown Sejong-no Government Building with the Blue House. The police showered them with tear gas so indiscriminately and severely that the sky grew dark. The crowd attacked police and fire stations and commandeered police vehicles.

The government summoned a National Security Council and emergency cabinet meeting and declared emergency martial law in Seoul. The Park regime issued arrest warrants for about 400 people, including student leaders and journalists.

The opposition camp had a meeting at the Minjeong Party office to discuss how to handle the situation. Minjeong Party president Yun Po-sun proposed, "Let's rise up with students. Hundreds of thousands of people will join. I will lead the crowd."

Worried about the hardline tactic's results, I disagreed. "The government will be sure to declare nationwide martial law." However, the hardliners wouldn't listen. They argued that even if martial law was declared, people would follow their lead; the situation would be to our advantage. However, when the martial law was, indeed, declared, hardliners failed to show up in their party offices. Everyone went into hiding. They had no excuse to protest if they were accused of engaging in irresponsible demagogy.

The US was on the Park regime's side in this matter. The normalization of Korea-Japan relations was at the heart of US policy in Asia. According to what I later heard, when President Park considered resigning because of escalating demonstrations and protestors blocking all exits, the US strongly urged him to remain in position by sending in the Korean UN commander via helicopter. The commander delivered the message to President Park to stand his ground in the Blue House's garden. I don't believe the US did this because they liked him personally, but because they could not rely on the opposition, which was adamantly against normalizing Korea-Japan relations.

In retrospect, the opposition party hardliners invited their own international isolation. They made a critical mistake in not paying attention to world opinions and our country's future interests. Although the public was opposed to normalization for emotional reasons, they would have understood if our government had engaged in more tactful diplomacy that wasn't to Korea's disadvantage. Above all, we needed to become friends with Japan for national security and for our economy. The opposition camp engaged in an anti-government struggle that was supported by neither power nor cause and ended up obstructing its own agenda. At that point, on June 3, the opposition camp completely lost its spirit. The military thoroughly suppressed demonstrations under martial law and the newspapers' critical tone toward the Park regime weakened.

In the end, the hardline tactics of the opposition camp completely failed. They had not accurately read the people's thoughts and sentiments. And when the Korean people— especially the middle class—began to look away, all hope of success in any struggle vanished. The hardline tactics by the opposition camp only offered an excuse to reinforce and strengthen the dictatorship of the Park regime.

Fight Against Self-righteousness, Inability, and Falsehood (1964–1967)

On April 21, 1964, the Republican Party proposed a bill ratifying the arrest of Assemblyman Kim Jun-yeon before the National Assembly after he alleged that the ruling party had secretly received $130 million during its secret Ohira-Kim Jong-pil meetings. Whether the content of this allegation was true or not has never been clarified but, regardless, the country was thrown into turmoil.

Although the government had the authority to arrest him without National Assembly approval the very next day (when the National Assembly would not be in session), the ruling party wanted to make a point of punishing him at the risk of the regime's honor. They charged him for spreading false information and committing libel. Because of time constraints, the ruling party was rushing to pass the bill. When I returned to Assembly Hall after lunch, Han Kun-soo, the leader of the Samminhoe (a negotiation body our party had formed together with other assembly members), rushed over to me.

> "Representative Kim, the ruling party is pushing to ratify a bill allowing the arrest of Master Nangsan (Mr. Kim Jun-yeon's alias). You have to come forward. Please delay the bill from passing until midnight."
> "My! How can I do that?"
> "Stay on the floor and deliver a speech regarding a point of order."
> "It's not easy to speak for an hour on a regular matter. How am I supposed to stay on the floor that long giving a speech on a point of order?"
> "That's why we're asking *you*. Even the leaders all agree that only *you* can do this. Please."

Back then, there was no time limit on speeches in the National Assembly, so I decided to give it a try. After obtaining the floor, I first raised the point that the bill had not been fully examined. I pointed out that there were likely political intentions behind this rushed effort, considering the representatives didn't even understand the full scale and details of this matter.

I then proceeded to explain how Representative Kim Jun-yeon's actions were based on his love of country and people. I talked about his patriotic eight-year imprisonment and nine-year house arrest as a result of his anti-Japanese activities. I also read passages from his memoir, *Independence Course*. Finally, I said, "We, his fellow assemblymen, should not support the criminalization of this patriot who has devoted his entire life to his country and people, should we? By the way, Mr. Chairman, may I continue after a bathroom break? I'm in a hurry to go."

The audience burst into laughter. The chairman also laughed and allowed me to have a bathroom break, after which I continued my speech. Unbeknownst to me, DongA Broadcasting Station was airing my speech to people across the entire country, using a microphone hidden beside the podium and under a newspaper. I later heard that people had crowded in front of downtown electronics stores to listen. The ruling party representatives proposed to the party leadership that they come up with a way of frustrating my filibuster. However, the floor leader of the Republican Party Kim Yong-tae ignored this suggestion. "Leave him alone," he told them. "How much longer can he go on? He'll get tired. I'm sure he won't last longer than an hour."

The sun set and darkness overshadowed Assembly Hall. I continued to talk. It was clear that if I talked about anything unrelated to the bill in question, the audience would begin to hoot and the chairman would stop me. I had to be very careful not to wander. Suddenly, the chairman interrupted me, "Representative Kim! Representative Kim! Please stop your speech for a moment! How much longer are you planning to talk?"

"I shall continue until Mr. Chairman declares that we will not vote on this matter."

"Fine. That won't happen, so continue."

Our party members handed me eggs and beverages from time to time. The audience encouraged me often, shouting, "Cheer up!"

In the end, the chairman stopped me and declared an adjournment. The media reported that my speech lasted five hours and nineteen minutes. This speech was later recorded in the *Guinness Book of World Records* as the longest speech in a national assembly. I was, of course, not interested in setting any records, but I still feel proud of that speech because I was able to block the Park regime's plot to criminalize a fellow national assemblyman without due investigation and examination. Of course, Representative Kim Jun-yeon was still arrested the next day, but without his fellow assemblymen's consent. I garnered attention because of this incident and members of the opposition parties treated me like a hero. President Park must have been furious.

Around this time, I founded the Hanguk Nae-oe Munje Yeonguso (Korean Domestic and Foreign Affairs Research Institute) in order to develop policies on domestic and foreign affairs and to fortify my organization. It was rare for a national assemblyman to establish a private institute at that time. Its office was located behind the Gamnihoegwan (Methodist Hall) in Gwanghwamun. Professor Nam Duck-woo of Sogang University and Professor Park Hyun-chae of Chosun University did research and led discussions. Later, leading national assemblymen also participated in its activities, turning it into the cradle of new policies. The institute was active until my first exile to Japan.

The Korea-Japan Basic Treaty was initialed at the Capitol building in Seoul on February 20, 1965. This was the first treaty between the two countries since Korea's liberation from Japan. The five basic articles of this treaty included: (1) the establishment of diplomatic relations between the two countries; (2) confirmation that previous treaties and agreements were null and void; (3) recognition that the government of the Republic of Korea was the only lawful government in Korea; (4) respect for the principles of the charter of the UN; (5) negotiations for the conclusion of treaties or agreements to place both countries' trading, maritime, and other commercial relations on a stable and friendly basis. This treaty was subject to ratification by both countries' national assemblies.

I participated in the National Assembly Special Committee for the Korea-Japan Treaty, where we argued with the government every day. I pointed out the injustice in the basic treaty articles, Korea's waiver of its property claims against Japan, and its approach to maritime relations. I also criticized the Korean government's disgraceful and humiliating approach to this treaty and urged them to devise a better alternative. I later heard that President Park listened in on our committee sessions through an interphone and was furious with Prime Minister Chung Il-kwon and Minister of Foreign Affairs Lee Dong-won for not handling me better. From the government's perspective, it was easier to deal with unconditional opposition, such as that of the opposition party president,

Mr. Yun Po-sun. Indeed, the ruling party leaders confessed, "Mr. Yun Po-sun's criticism that we are selling our country is anachronistic, so we can simply ignore it. But it's far more difficult to deal with a demand like Kim Dae-jung's because he agrees with us about the necessity for the Korea-Japan Treaty but demands better alternatives."

During this period of deliberation, Minister of Foreign Affairs Lee Dong-won attended the special committee and made a surprising announcement at the end of his speech. "I have some special news. I'm proud to tell you that Japan officially acknowledged that Dokdo is a Korean territory."

Dokdo was a very sensitive diplomatic issue between Korea and Japan because Japan maintained that Dokdo was Japanese territory, calling it Takeshima. Everyone was surprised to hear this news, which signaled a major victory for Korea. But something didn't sound right. The Japanese government wouldn't have given up on the matter because of Japanese public opinion. Assemblyman Kim Seong-yong responded that this was hard to believe and we needed proof that it was true. Mr. Lee answered, smiling, "Sir, Dokdo is ours, so why do we need proof? That's like a bum asking you to bring proof that your wife, with whom you already live, is indeed your wife. If you live with that woman, then she's yours." The ruling party members burst into triumphant laughter. The committee adjourned after that.

The next day, I won the floor and spoke up. "Mr. Minister of Foreign Affairs, you talked yesterday about a bum and a man's wife. I don't think it becoming for a minister of foreign affairs to use a word like 'bum,' but since you used it, I'll use it, too. You don't have to worry about such matters if the bum doesn't complain about your wife. But this bum isn't doing that. He visits you every day and complains loudly, 'She's not your wife, but mine, so return her. If you don't, I'm going to court!' Isn't he? That's what Japan is doing about Dokdo. Japan will deny what you said soon."

We didn't have to wait long for that denial. Japan made a statement the next day, flatly denying Minister Lee's statement.

During a standing committee session, I gave the minister a series of questions that needed to be answered immediately. At that time, it was customary practice for the assemblymen to ask an entire series of questions together, and for the minister to read his staff-prepared manuscript briskly and all at once. This practice made the question and answer session a mere formality. But for an assemblyman to ask a series of questions that required immediate individual answers, the assemblyman needed to know the issue at hand inside and out. The same was true of his respondents. When our committee introduced this style of Q&A session according to my proposal, the atmosphere became consistently tense; however, this system didn't last long due to opposition from the ruling party.

I thoroughly prepared for my speeches at the Assembly. During my preparation, I always very carefully considered the possible public responses. When it was my turn to deliver my speech, the assemblymen playing *baduk* in the lounge would crowd the conference hall. I was always thorough in pointing out the problems with the various issues under discussion, grilling the prime minister and other cabinet members not only in the standing committee meetings, but also in the plenary sessions. I once heard that President Park scolded his cabinet members for their inability to handle me. "How could all of you not handle Kim Dae-jung, just one person? Not just once, but over and over again?"

When the government planned a new policy, I always pointed to the government policy's problems and offered a better alternative. During the sixth-term National Assembly, I prepared and pressed my position hard. The librarians at the National Assembly remembered me as the assemblyman who used the library most often. I studied not only for pending questions, but also for the future of the Korean Peninsula and the human race. For example, I asked the following question about the state of affairs surrounding Korea in an October 26, 1964, assembly: "Due to the success of PRC's nuclear test, its influence on the Third World is expanding and there is an increased possibility of Japanese rearmament. What are our government's measures for addressing this situation? Due to the US' preferential policy toward Japan, there's the worrisome possibility of increasing Japanese influence in Korea. Does our government have any plans to tackle this possibility?"

I also worked hard to implement autonomous local governments based on my belief that democracy could be materialized only when local autonomy was guaranteed. During my questioning session at the Budget and Finance Committee, I persisted in asking hard questions about the introduction of the autonomous local government. Prime Minister Chung Il-kwon and Interior Minister Lee Ho had a difficult time answering my questions on several occasions. For example, on November 28, 1966, I made this vigorous attack on Interior Minister Lee Ho during a budget deliberation session: "It goes without saying that, together with the National Assembly, local autonomy is one of two pillars of democracy. Democracy means 'No vote, no tax.' This is an ironbound rule of democracy. Nevertheless, the current government avoids the implementation of autonomous local governments. People pay taxes and do their part, but they don't have votes in the local government. Therefore, they don't know how their tax money is being used, how the local government is doing their business. There is no way for them to check what kind of administration is carried out for their wellbeing. There isn't any other country in the world that claims to be democratic but avoids autonomous local governments. Are you going to implement autonomous local governments or not? Please answer me, Mr. Minister."

"We will."

"You said the same thing a while ago, and now you're giving me the same answer again?"

"We are not ready yet."

"Then please tell me what you have done so far to get us ready."

To them my question might have seemed harsh, but as a representative of the Korean people I had no other choice but to ask these sorts of hard questions. Besides, the local autonomy question was just too important. I had to question and interrogate them to see if they really did have the will to implement it. Ministers could not simply dance around my questions. They had to answer them. I thought how it was impossible to block election fraud on the local level and, therefore, to change regimes without the implementation of autonomous local governments. Of course, it was also impossible to expect the improvement of local well-being. Later, I won on the issue of autonomous local government implementation by committing myself to a thirteen-day hunger strike.

On June 22, 1965, Korean and Japanese leaders signed the Korea-Japan Basic Treaty at the official residence of the prime minister in Tokyo. This treaty addressed all initialed articles except for the Dokdo islets. The Korean media criticized this treaty as a second Eulsa Protectorate Treaty, accusing the negotiator of being a second Lee Wan-yong, a pro-Japanese minister of Korea, who signed the Japan-Korea Annexation Treaty, which placed Korea under Japanese rule in 1910. Student-led demonstrations against the treaty began to pick up steam once again.

Opposition parties also joined forces to effectively carry out the struggle before the treaty was signed, forming the Minjung Party [People Party] on June 14. Ms. Pak Sun-cheon was elected chairwoman of the supreme council and Mr. Yun Po-sun became a member of the advisory committee after unexpectedly losing the chairman election. His loss indicated that many new party members were worried about Mr. Yun's hardline tactics. Hardliners proposed that all of our party assembly members resign from the National Assembly as a protest against the Korea-Japan Basic Treaty. Along with myself, Chairwoman Pak disagreed. There were only 65 opposition party members out of 175 seats in the assembly. Despite the party leaders' dissuasion, seven assemblymen from the Yun faction and one assemblyman from the Pak faction resigned.

The situation wasn't much different in Japan. The leaders of Japan's Democratic Socialist Party, which opposed the Korea-Japan Basic Treaty, visited Korea and had dinner with our party leaders, including Mr. Hong Ik-pyo. I also attended that dinner meeting, and explained to them our party's position: Although we were for the normalization of diplomatic relations between the two countries, we were against its humiliating terms. Japan's Democratic Socialist Party leaders found this conditional approval from a Korean opposition party surprising. They also seemed impressed by our alternative proposals. After their visit, Japan's Democratic Socialist Party switched their position from *against* to *for* the treaty. I believe my explanation contributed to their change in position.

On August 14, 1965, the National Assembly passed the Korea–Japan Basic Treaty and all additional agreements; all opposition party members boycotted. The most critical issue in this treaty (problems regarding property and claims between Japan and Korea) was settled with a $300 million grant and economic cooperation, a $200 million governmental loan, and a $300 million civilian loan. The treaty also made the settlement between the two countries final: "By this Agreement, problems in regard to property and claims between Japan and Korea have been settled completely and finally." In terms of the fisheries, the agreement decided that each party "has the right to establish a sea zone … extending no more than twelve nautical miles from its respective coastal base line, over which it will have exclusive jurisdiction with respect to fisheries." This nullified the Rhee Syngman Line.

I felt more ashamed than angry with the contents of the treaty and agreements. Above all, the $300 million grant was the lowest among the proposed demands made by the various South Korean regimes. The Rhee Syngman regime had demanded $2 billion and the Chang Myon regime $2.85 billion; comparatively, $300 million was an absurdly small amount. No one could think this sum was enough to compensate for thirty-five years of exploitation and plundering. At the next National Assembly I argued: "Let's not accept any money at all. Although we're not rich, we get by. It'd be better to flatly refuse claims, rather than accepting such a shameful amount. Instead, it's more important to receive a true apology from Japan. We can settle past scores better that way. The Korean people would prefer such an honorable approach."

I also argued that we had to improve the trade deficit situation with Japan rather than merely accepting these sorts of dishonorable grants and loans. "Instead of receiving any money, if we propose a 1:1 fair trade, I don't doubt that the Japanese would approach our proposal seriously. Reversing the trade deficit will benefit Korea substantially, enabling us to revive domestic industries through active trade. Let's first look at our trade deficit with Japan, which has already risen to more than $300 million. Let's also take a look at the $300 million grant. According to the agreement, this amount will be equally divided and paid over a 10-year period, with $30 million distributed annually; however, our trade deficit during the next ten years will be more than $3 billion. It simply does not make sense to accept a tenth of $3 billion to settle the past."

The Korea-Japan Basic Treaty unconditionally erased the history between Korea and Japan. It was a solemn and grave matter. Koreans ended up giving up their legal right to claim for so many tragic issues, including the Korean Hiroshima victims, compulsory drafts, the so-called comfort women, and the repatriation of Koreans in Sakhalin. To me, it was clear that the ratification of the Korea-Japan Basic Treaty was a blatant crime against the Korean people and history.

After the ratification of the treaty and agreements, 10,000 college and high school students took to the streets to protest, demanding the treaty be declared null and void. The government announced a garrison decree and mobilized the military to suppress all demonstrators. Demonstrations could not spread to the Korean population in general, though, due to the opposition party's unjustifiable hardline opposition to the treaty itself. As a result, the opposition party could neither defend Korean national interests nor strengthen its domestic position. The opposition party continued to fall.

After the treaty, the Park regime and Japan grew close rapidly. The Park regime acquired aid for economic development from Japan and won absolute support from the US (which still frowned upon the opposition party's hardline approach). Despite fierce resistance from the opposition party, the US and the world began to trust the Park regime for its reconciliatory abilities as illustrated through the Korea-Japan Basic Treaty.

The relationship between the Park regime and the US became closer with the Korean government's dispatch of Korean troops to Vietnam.

Korea had been sending only medical military personnel to Vietnam, but in 1965 the US government officially demanded Korea send combat troops. The US pressured the Korean government by circulating rumors that the US would withdraw its military forces from Korea if we refused to send troops to Vietnam. The Park regime, which desperately needed stability, took advantage of this to shift the entire political situation in its favor. Korea dispatched the 2nd Marine Division (Blue Dragon Division) first, followed by the Capital Mechanized Infantry Division (Tiger Division), and the 9th Infantry Division (White Horse Division).

The US was mired in the Vietnam War, and poured an enormous amount of money and resources into it; however, their prospects were gloomy. Young people were dying in strange, far-off jungles. The economic programs for President Johnson's Great Society were halted or came to an outright end. Public anti-war sentiment in the US was rising. The American people's pride had been wounded. In this context, for President Johnson, the news of Korea's decision to dispatch troops must have been like rain after a long drought. Both the Johnson regime and the American people were grateful for Korea's increased involvement.

The opposition party fundamentally opposed this dispatch of troops. I also very strongly opposed the military's actions. I was worried that it might heighten tensions in the Korean Peninsula and that Korean military activities might provoke North Korea to reignite fighting. I also thought that a defeat in this already seemingly doomed war would mean a futile sacrifice of Korea's young men. Nonetheless, the Park regime forced a dispatch of troops despite the disadvantageous and humiliating conditions of the war. Although the Park regime used such high-flown rhetoric as "Troop dispatch keeps faith with our ally, and vigorous Korean youth protects the peace," the Korean troops were treated much worse than troops sent from other countries. These more aggressive military actions also turned the gentle image of Korea's youth into images of a horde of belligerent, mercenaries. The youth of Korea gave their lives to their country only to receive blame and condemnation from the international community. It was a tragedy.

Our party proposed that if we had to yield to US demands, we send a volunteer army instead of troops in active service. The Park regime ignored our proposal. The hardliners in our party opposed the launch of Korean troops fiercely, calling our troops mercenary soldiers of the US, and the policy an act of "selling blood for money." This kind of extreme rhetoric did nothing to garner public support, though, and distanced our party further from the US. The dispatch of troops to Vietnam was sanctioned at the National Assembly.

After our troops were sent to Vietnam, the Korean and US presidents exchanged visits. President Park was welcomed enthusiastically in the US and was given the opportunity to speak at the National Press Club. President Johnson gave a firm promise to support the Park regime. In October 1966, President Johnson visited Korea as well. Mobilized by the authorities, people crowded the streets to welcome President Johnson on a scale unseen in other parts of the world.

I witnessed an interesting incident during President Johnson's visit to Korea. Both presidents held a joint reception at the Walker Hill Hotel. I was also there as an invitee. Immediately after the reception began, a minute-long blackout unexpectedly occurred. I was worried about President Johnson's safety during that very long minute. When the lights came on again, we found only President Park and President Johnson had disappeared. My own fear was mirrored in the utter alarm on participants' faces. But President Johnson was safe. As soon as the light went out, bodyguards led him away to a safe place through a pivoted window, which they had prepared ahead of time. I was impressed by their skillful protection of the president.

Although I opposed sending our troops, I felt I had to visit the field where our youth were sent—we had to boost their morale as they were sent in the name of our country. On September 1, 1966, I visited Vietnam with Chairwoman Pak and National Assemblyman Ko Heung-mun. Assemblyman Kim Sang-hyun later joined us as well. The commanding officer of ROK forces in Vietnam welcomed us sincerely and the US commander was also grateful. The Americans told us, "Korea is a truly democratic country. The opposition party members, who opposed sending troops, have come to console the troops. In what other country would such a thing be possible? We sincerely admire you."

At that time, President Nguyen Van Thieu was the symbolic head of Vietnam, while Prime Minister Nguyen Cao Ky held the actual power. They also received and welcomed us, and the prime minister invited us to a dinner reception. Many cabinet members came with their wives, who wore gem-studded necklaces and bracelets. Assemblyman Ko Heung-mun said, "Look at them! Their hands are covered with diamonds."

Surprised, I tried to stop him; I was afraid the Vietnamese would understand the word "diamond" and his critical tone.

The next day I saw South Vietnamese troops move to the front on an Landing Ship, Tank (LST), an oceangoing military ship, used by amphibious forces for landing troops and heavy equipment on beaches. Soldiers took not only their families, but also their poultry livestock, believing that no one other than themselves could guarantee their families' safety. I could not help noticing the contrast between the previous evening's splendid dinner and the ordinary soldiers' hard conditions. It was also known that high officials routinely sent their children away to Hong Kong and the US. It seemed absurd that our youth had to risk their lives for a country like this.

Vietnam was not the only devastating event during this period. Just a few months before my visit to Vietnam, on June 4, 1966, my godfather Dr. Chang Myon passed away. After retiring from political life, Dr. Chang devoted himself to religion. His last years were truly desolate. I visited him often when he was bedridden with hepatitis. His wife told me, "Friends in need are friends indeed. Thank you, Assemblyman Kim. People treat us differently. We know very well how you feel, so please don't visit us too often. Instead, visit other people more."

Dr. Chang's passing was truly somber. He was my godfather not only in religion but also in politics. He was given a national funeral. Later, I took charge of the events commemorating him. Dr. Chang's wife had prayed for me every morning at a Catholic church when I was imprisoned by the new militarists in 1980. His children visited my house and gave my family precious articles left by Dr. Chang. He was a gentle leader of democracy—and a tragic one.

Between 1965 and 1969, the Park regime was able to stabilize the Korean economy and lay the foundation for massive economic growth thanks to strong US support, Japanese loans and grants, Korean military pay sent home from Vietnam, and the boom in the military industry. One might call this period the heyday of the Park regime. Korea's annual economic growth rate averaged an excess of 10 percent, and Korea was touted as a model for developing countries. As we built highways and towering skyscrapers and expanded the Ulsan Industrial Complex, our apparent growth seemed brilliant.

I visited the US for the first time on February 21, 1966, at the invitation of the US State Department. I toured Washington, DC, New York City, Denver, and New Orleans with Assemblymen Choi Yeong-geun and Park Young-rok. The forests of apartment buildings in city downtowns and the flood of cars on the roads were impressive, but I was most impressed by their long, straight highways. To me, they delivered a sense of the country's power and massive, underlying energy.

After my visit to the US, I traveled to Europe and visited France, England, Germany, Italy, and, later, India, as well. I liked the freedom in advanced countries. The people were kind and modest.

In 1967, Korea held another presidential election. On February 7, the Minjung and Sinhan Parties merged to form the Sinmin Party. This merger was necessary to fight against the Park regime. It was also what the people wanted.

The process of nominating our party presidential candidate was torturous. We commissioned full power to a conference composed of Yu Chin-o, Yun Po-sun, Paik Lak-geoon, and Lee Bum-suk. Although they sat down and discussed the matter extensively, they could not agree on a candidate. In the end, their choice came down to Yu Chin-o and Yun Po-sun. The Minjung Party diligently tried to recruit Dr. Yu Chin-o, whom many considered a safe choice. But he seemed a bit too gentle for a politician, as was the case with many scholars-turned-politicians.

Many people also thought that Yun Po-sun, who had lost to Park Chung-hee in the previous election, was sure to lose again. But his followers passionately pushed for him, arguing that the margin of 150,000 in the previous election was very slim. Mr. Yun had a very strong desire to become president and there was no way he was going to give up on his candidacy. This stubbornness on his part threw our party into a divisive crisis yet again. In the end, Mr. Yun became our candidate due to his obstinacy … and that obstinacy would ruin the election again.

As expected, when the campaign started, the public's response to Candidate Yun was not terribly enthusiastic. Over the four-year period of the Park regime, the opposition party's power had weakened following the Korea-Japan Basic Treaty ratification; meanwhile, the Park regime had only gained confidence thanks to the full support it received from the US and Japan. Although opposition forces rallied behind Candidate Yun, he was no longer popular among the people. His hardline policies during the Korea-Japan Basic Treaty fight and Vietnam War troop dispatch struggle had alienated the general public.

WAR IN MOKPO (1967)

My heart still pounds at the thought of the seventh-term National Assembly election, held on June 8, 1967. It was a heated and fierce event. I'm still moved at the thought of the Mokpo citizens' support. I dare call it the election where the united power of the citizens vanquished injustice. During that time, I cried and laughed together with the citizens of Mokpo. I still wonder how I was able to muster the courage, make the speeches, and come up with the strategies I did.

I planned to stand again as a candidate for Mokpo. As the spokesperson of the opposition party, I was already popular. I thought it would be an easy election for me, but sinister rumors began circulating even before my candidacy registration. Rumor had it that the regime was planning to defeat me in the election and that President Park was spearheading this campaign.

Since I attacked the failures of Park's military regime head-on and drove President Park into a plight many times, anyone would expect that President Park wanted to get rid of me. But I did not expect (and couldn't believe!) this particular sort of targeting. I learned that President Park summoned the KCIA and Interior Ministry officials to the Blue House and instructed them: "You have to defeat Kim Dae-jung this time, no matter what. I don't care if that means ten or twenty other candidates in our party lose. Still, you must not let him win."

Since this occurred before the introduction of autonomous local governments, every government official was under the president's direct control, and the president's words could make or break the election. Throughout all of the previous elections, no president had ever ordered a particular person's defeat. His loyal subordinates immediately began to carry out Operation Defeat Kim Dae-jung. Many worried for me. Our party leader of the National Assembly cautioned: "You'd better be careful because you're President Park's target. I think one plan for you might be to avoid a reckless fight. How about giving up Mokpo and moving to the national constituency or a district in Seoul? It's harder to commit election fraud in Seoul. It might be worth the fight."

I seriously considered this proposal. It was not an easy decision. Frankly speaking, I was terrified. My family, associates, and I could all be harmed. Still, I couldn't back down without fighting. I decided to fight even if I would eventually lose to a dictatorial regime. I calmed myself, thinking, "A national assemblyman becomes a former national assemblyman whether he serves one, two, or three terms. Whatever the result, what matters is fighting with all your might."

It seemed impossible for me to win against an opponent who would mobilize all kinds of corrupt tactics, including voter fraud, illegal balloting, fraudulent ballot counting, bribery, and intimidation. I realized that I could win only when the citizens of Mokpo were determined to prevent election fraud, even if that meant mobilizing for a second March 15th Masan Uprising. To push forward, I literally had to put my life on the line.

Out of 135 election districts, Mokpo drew the most heated media attention, both domestically and abroad, and even before the full campaign season began. The media was releasing news almost immediately as it occurred.

My apparent opponent was Mr. Kim Byung-sam, a former army major general who had also worked as the minister of communication, but my real opponent was President Park. Mr. Kim Byung-sam was from Jindo, where he could have been elected without campaigning at all. It was President Park who insisted that he change his election district. When Mr. Kim Byung-sam hesitated, it was rumored that President Park said, "You just need to declare yourself a candidate. I'll make you win."

I suppose Mr. Kim Byung-sam really must not have wanted to run for election in Mokpo, where I was an overwhelming constituent favorite. Because he needed an excuse not to run, he shot his own leg; however, his injury was not considered serious and he had to run anyway.

Mr. Kim Byung-sam campaigned by relying entirely on the powerful support of the regime. His argument for election rested on Mokpo's development: as Kim Dae-jung was an opposition party member, he could not mobilize the kind of resources that he could as a ruling party candidate. He showered people with a slew of rosy development promises: harbor repair, airport construction, industrial complex invitation, and more. The public's favor rapidly shifted toward him.

President Park also came down to Mokpo to support Mr. Kim Byung-sam, promising his full support for all of Mr. Kim Byung-sam's promises for the development of Mokpo. Although it was legally forbidden for a government official to make a public speech in support of a candidate, President Park continued to deliver speeches at large-scale rallies. One of his speeches was made to an audience of 10,000 in front of Mokpo Station.

Mokpo had been severely discriminated against since the beginning of the Park regime, and had lost its former grandeur and vitality as a city that was once counted as one of ten greatest in Korea. Citizens could not help but be swayed in their convictions given the rosy blueprints and development plans presented by the president himself. Additionally, President Park even held a cabinet meeting in Mokpo. All cabinet members came down to Mokpo, turning Mt. Yudalsan into the Blue House.

The theme of this cabinet meeting was "The Development of Mokpo." Economic Planning Board Minister Chang Ki-young announced a dreamlike plan to invite numerous factories to Mokpo. This news was reported with banner headlines in the *Mokpo Ilbo* newspaper, and the newspaper was dropped into every household in Mokpo. I could barely stand seeing this in a newspaper I had so passionately worked to grow for so many years.

The Park regime's pandering continued endlessly. Honeypots dropped every day in Mokpo—there were gifts and money for everyone. People joked that Mokpo was being flooded with *makgolli*, and that they could soon build bridges with noodles. It was a fierce battle. Government employees and merchants couldn't vote for me.

From the way the election was going early on, it was clear that I would lose without putting up a good fight. We needed an unusual strategy to counteract the pandering and cajoling of the powerful. We decided to concentrate on moon villages, where poor voters were densely populated. These poor people had such hard lives that they didn't pay much attention to the election. Some of them simply voted for the candidate the head of their neighborhood association recommended.

We entered their communities. Some of our campaigners began to live with them and spread rumors, pretending to be day laborers. "Park Chung-hee wants to get rid of Kim Dae-jung because he's afraid of Kim getting elected for president in the next election. Let's elect Kim Dae-jung so he'll become president. Let's have a president from Mokpo—then we'll really begin to get benefits."

The rumor spread. Of course, at that point, I didn't really intend to run for president during the next election. Yu Chin-o was our party's potential presidential candidate.

As the election fight became more and more fierce, more newspaper and broadcasting reporters stationed themselves in Mokpo. A secretary at the US Embassy seemed to almost live there, too. National newspapers featured the Mokpo campaign every day. People's interest also focused on Mokpo. The campaign was dubbed "The War in Mokpo."

I campaigned around, making speeches, while my wife did door-to-door visits. She also organized a housewives' association. She worked extremely hard and never avoided difficult jobs. She had a very friendly manner, which gave people a positive impression of our platform. She would also prepare meals from our house in Bukgyo-dong and have them delivered to our campaign headquarters. She always remained calm. She never bragged about me, neither. She just helped me however she could from near or far. Her care and advice were always encouraging. I trusted her calm, thoughtful assistance.

Mokpo and its population of 170,000 were thrown into the whirlwind of election campaigning. The regime poured an astronomical amount of money into their campaign against me. From behind the scenes, a Mokpo-based brewing company called Samhak actively supported Mr. Kim Byung-sam—even if they wanted to support me, they couldn't have. The KCIA and police had me under constant surveillance; they made sure to prevent businessmen and businesses from approaching my campaign. Samhak went bankrupt soon after the election, and, as the general public did not know what had gone on behind the scenes, there was a rumor that it was because Samhak had contributed to my campaign, but that was not true at all.

My campaign lacked money and manpower. Not only small business owners, but even merchants shunned me because they were afraid of retaliation. They had no choice but to support me only morally. However, the poor helped me anonymously. They handed me crumpled notes, smiled, and ran off before anyone could notice them.

A high government official also visited me once before the campaign became heated. He handed me an envelope and said, "If Mr. President learns of this, I'm a dead man. Please accept this as my contribution to your campaign. I won't be able to give you anything later." It wasn't a lot of money, but I was really grateful. There were people like him everywhere who supported me in secret. The people's will was powerful.

The Republican Party had a hard time distributing its excessive money to voters. Target recipients had to be approached secretly and with precision. To accomplish this, campaigners for Mr. Kim Byung-sam first marked every house in Mokpo according to their leanings: O for ruling party households, Δ for neutral homes, and X for opposition party households. With the help of local police branch officers and district office clerks, they distributed money to households marked with O and Δ immediately before Election Day.

Our campaigners found out about this scheme, and used the information to confuse the regime, revisiting many of the houses already marked and changing Os to Xs and Xs to Os under the dark cloak of night. The next day, there was nothing but confusion. Those who'd waited overnight didn't receive any money, whereas those in favor of me did. We protested these corrupt practices, and ruling party supporters were upset they hadn't received any of the money that the opposition party supporters had.

The ruling party's dishonest tactics were pervasive and never-ending. They ignored our protests. Mobsters hired by the ruling party threatened citizens and police officers and government officials ran wild. I confronted them head-on. This was truly a life-or-death conflict. The citizens of Mokpo were moved by my courage and positive momentum spread like wildfire. The mayor of Mokpo spearheaded the regime's campaign to defeat me, and rumors openly circulated that he would become the governor of Jeollanam-do if they defeated me. The citizens of Mokpo grew angrier and angrier.

The citizens of Mokpo began to wonder what the real reason was for President Park's tenacious desire to defeat me. It began to make sense that the president wanted to nip me in the bud as a potential presidential candidate, so the election became a sort of primary for the presidential election. The regime devoted itself wholeheartedly to defending President Park's pride.

Toward the end of the election campaign, Kim Byung-sam's camp came up with a new tactic and tried to persuade people with a new line of reasoning. "Kim Dae-jung is certainly an excellent national assemblyman. We acknowledge this, too. But we can't keep electing an opposition party candidate if we want to develop Mokpo. Let's elect the ruling party candidate this time, and entrust the ruling party with the task of Mokpo's revival. And let's support Kim Dae-jung during the next election. Just this once, Kim Dae-jung should yield. Let's revive Mokpo, and then raise Kim Dae-jung. If we elect him this time, Mokpo will collapse." It was a pretty effective strategy. The election campaign centered around the opposition between the regional development argument and the great figure argument.

Around this time, people began to gather en masse at my speeches.

"Let's go see Kim Dae-jung!"

"Let's support Kim Dae-jung, Mokpo's son!"

I cried out to the audience: "I don't know how to thank all of you patriotic citizens who have been terrorized, fired from your jobs, spent your own money for the sake of my campaign, and prayed for me in churches and temples. I tell you that I am determined to defeat my opponent in this evil, dirty, and unprecedentedly fraudulent election, and be elected a member of the seventh-term National Assembly to repay all your hard work.

"Ladies and gentlemen, I will protect democracy at the risk of my life. If I die during this fight, please, before you lay flowers over my grave, proceed over my body and overthrow the second Choe In-gyu, the chief instigator of the fraudulent April 19 election. Please continue your fierce struggle to uproot election fraud in our country. If not, I won't be able to die with my eyes closed.

"Ladies and gentlemen, I stand now in front of the poisonous blade of the Park regime's knife. They assault me, just one fragile man, with daggers, knives, axes, and scythes. I own neither power nor money nor a newspaper nor a broadcasting station. You are my only hope. Although I have neither power nor money, I have you. You can save me.

"I ask Mt. Yudalsan, Yeongsan River, and Samhak Island: Mt. Yudalsan, if you have a soul; Samhak Island, if you have a spirit; Yeongsan River, if you have a will, I'd like to appeal to you, together with all the citizens of Mokpo, please protect me from a government that is trying to kill Kim Dae-jung, a man raised in Mokpo, who would like to devote himself to his country!

"Ladies and gentlemen, let's condemn this fraudulent election! Let's oppose this fraudulent election! Let's win glory in Mokpo through citizen power, our power, our will!"

The speech was almost tragic. Even *I* trembled during it. The audience looked just as indignant at the injustice of it all as I felt, and began to cry. They refused to leave even after I finished. They waited for hours just to shake my hand or obtain my signature. I couldn't satisfy all their needs. Girls asked for my signature on their blouses and went to school wearing them. Some people asked me to sign their handkerchiefs and hats. I signed children's notebooks and many of them pasted them on the walls over their desks. Usually I wrote, "Together with Kim Dae-jung." Shaking hands and handing out signatures was harder than I expected. My hand began to grow numb, then hurt, and by the end, I couldn't feel a thing in it. I was happy, nevertheless.

There was great excitement everywhere I went to deliver a speech. Women who sold clams and fish in stalls on the pier followed me around and cheered wherever I went to make a speech. I was grateful, but sorry as well. When my wife tried to dissuade them from coming, their answer was that she need not worry for them: "We'll survive even if we don't make any money today. Don't you worry!"

My campaign headquarters was located on the second floor of a Japanese-style house in front of Mokpo Station; every day, people gathered around the building and chanted my name.

Mokpo was boiling. Crowds seemed ready to explode at the slightest touch. If the regime continued to push through their farce of an election, it looked as though the people would rise up against the authorities as they had in Masan after the 1960 election, which had given rise to the April 19th Revolution. A tidal wave of popular sentiment clearly favored us.

The most worrisome sort of fraud we were expecting was voter fraud. After checking the 100,000 names on the voter registration list one by one, we found that, under the leadership of the Mokpo mayor, 3700 false names had been added. We raised this as a deeply troubling inconsistency, and pressed authorities hard, saying we would rise up with Mokpo citizens if they didn't correct this wrong. Eventually, a KCIA agent in charge of Mokpo visited us. He asked what we wanted, and hinted that the government was changing its attitude because of alarming popular sentiment. I demanded that they remove the names of the ghost voters and implement fair voting and vote counting. In the end, the names of ghost voters were removed.

I later found out that KCIA Director Kim Hyung-wook had come down to Gwangju to check on the state of the election campaign. He reported to the president that Mokpo could turn into a second Masan. President Park had no choice but to agree to halt their election schemes, despite fierce opposition from the Mokpo mayor.

We learned through various sources that the Kim Byung-sam campaign planned to implement voting and ballot-counting fraud, and came up with a new tactic to beat their attempts to bribe witnesses. The day before Election Day we summoned our witnesses and offered them an orientation seminar regarding their roles; however, this was a high-level disguise tactic. The witnesses we summoned for orientation were not our real witnesses, although even those summoned were unaware of this. As expected, the Kim Byung-sam campaign tried to bribe each one of the attendees that night. But when Election Day arrived, our real witnesses showed up first and took up their seats. We explained our strategy to the "false" witnesses who arrived later, and asked for their understanding. The final overnight scheme of my opponent's campaign came to a grinding halt.

Voting went smoothly. All of the ballot boxes were gathered and ballot counting began in a hall at Yudal Elementary School late that rainy night. The authorities dispatched the police, and I stayed at the ballot-counting hall with my campaigners. We thought we would win if we got through that night without foul play. About 15,000 citizens crowded around the school. Most of them came to make sure the ballot counting went smoothly, without any foul play. From the darkness, all eyes were glued to the brightly illuminated ballot-counting hall. The atmosphere was tense.

Our witnesses had prepared flashlights and candles in preparation for a blackout, which suddenly occurred only a few minutes into the ballot counting. The people began shouting, "Turn on the light! Turn on the light!"

Immediately, the filming lights of several TV stations—including two Korean stations, MBC and KBS, and stations from Japan and other foreign countries—blazed on at the same time. Witnesses flipped their flashlights on as well. Some people lit candles. Despite the blackout, it wasn't too dark inside. Fifteen thousand citizens cheered outside; those of us inside could hear their grand, majestic cheers and shouts. There were two more blackouts that night but each time, lights from other sources flared up immediately and the crowd outside cheered.

Their cheers spread into the night sky like thunder. The dark forces that had tried to commit fraud under the cloak of darkness again and again were forced to supply electricity themselves. The results of the counting revealed the truth: I'd won, with a count of 29,279 votes to Kim Byung-sam's 22,738 votes; a total of 52,017 valid votes were cast. It was a great victory of people over government power.

I toured all over Mokpo on the back of a truck to thank the citizens. Both the citizens and I were moved, and we cheered for each other, celebrating our victory. I cried out to the crowds, "My dear Mokpo citizens, I won this election thanks to your support. Your heroic struggle enabled this victory. You gave life not only to Mokpo, but also to Korea's democracy. To repay you, I'll run for the presidency later. I'll become Kim Dae-jung of Korea and Kim Dae-jung of the world."

I boarded the Honam Line train alive, holding the election victory certificate high in my hand.

After the election ended, I lodged a complaint against the Mokpo mayor for violation of election laws. Everyone knew about his activities encouraging election fraud. Upon hearing he was in danger of being arrested, he visited my house, falling to his knees before me and pleading, "Please help me." Then he began to criticize the ruling party candidate. "I was used, too. As soon as he lost, he didn't care about me at all. He even embezzled some of the election funds sent by the president. The president asked me how much money we needed to win the election and he sent the amount I reported." Was this how the human mind worked? I felt quite disillusioned. I withdrew my complaint and forgave him.

When President Park came to Mokpo to support his party candidate, I asked him publicly, "If President Park was spearheading the election fraud, does this mean he intends to introduce a 3-term presidency constitutional amendment? I can't think of any other explanation for his reckless actions. The president has to clarify his intention responsibly."

The next day, President Park retorted, "I have absolutely no intention to introduce a 3-term presidency constitutional amendment. I don't even know what such a term might mean. This accusation is politically motivated, malicious slander."

Although President Park denied any accusations, I did not believe him. The ruling party won this election by an overwhelming margin, winning more than two-thirds of the seats. This meant they could amend the Constitution whenever they wished. After the election, opposition party assemblymen boycotted the following National Assembly session because of widespread election fraud. People supported the opposition party, and public opinion was about to explode. Student demonstrations spread across the country. The ruling party yielded to public opinion and proposed to voluntarily give up fifteen to twenty seats. This meant the ruling party would not be able to achieve a constitutional amendment on its own.

I strongly proposed that our party president Dr. Yu Chin-o accept this proposal. I also argued that we should demand autonomous local government as well. We could block election fraud and win the election only when autonomous local government was in place. We could turn this crisis into an opportunity. Dr. Yu agreed with me and, as our party's spokesperson, I announced that we were accepting this proposal from the ruling party. News of this agreement made every headline.

The next day, however, hardliners within the party demanded the entire election be nullified and a reelection held. Surprisingly, Dr. Yu joined forces with these dissenting voices. "Why did you break our promise? Why don't you believe me? This will only bring about the constitutional amendment and we won't be able to even mention a word about autonomous local governments. We're courting the worst possible situation here."

My worries turned into reality. As conflicts continued indefinitely, people began to criticize the irresponsibility of the National Assembly. These confrontations could not go on any longer; it was becoming burdensome to both the ruling and the opposition parties. In the end, the opposition party had to accept the ruling party's compromise proposal, which replaced the president's apology for election fraud with an expression of regret. It also proposed a special investigative committee within the National Assembly to handle the matter of reelections in precincts where fraud was suspected. It was a pathetic result for our party.

Our party finished its five-month-long boycott on November 19. We had gained nothing and lost people's trust. Although the hardline can seem clear, sometimes it is irresponsible.

I'd conditionally supported even the Korea-Japan Basic Treaty, risking severe criticism. This time, as well, I argued that we should compromise to block their sinister plans for a three-term presidency constitutional amendment. If we had accepted their initial proposal and taken twenty seats away from the ruling party, the tragic three-term presidency constitutional amendment wouldn't have been possible.

As mentioned previously, KCIA Director Kim Hyung-wook had been fairly respectful toward me, as illustrated by an episode at a National Assembly session. In July 1967, the KCIA announced the East Berlin Incident, a major spy organization case involving Korean students and diaspora in Germany and France who had allegedly worked as North Korean spies. This list of spies included world-famous composer Yoon I-sang and renowned painter Lee Ung-no. The incident clearly appeared to be fabricated. Additionally, some overseas Koreans and students had been kidnapped and repatriated by KCIA agents, causing diplomatic friction between the Korean and German governments. Assemblyman Chough Yoon-hyung offered a scathing but respectful critique of the incident: "Our country lost its face because of this incident." This infuriated Director Kim. He yelled back at Assemblyman Chough: "Is arresting communists a crime? Which country does this National Assembly belong to?" He stamped his feet, hammered the table with his fist, and glared at every assemblyman present.

Ruling party members defended Director Kim, and some opposition party leaders even chimed in. This was understandable considering KCIA directors wielded near-unchallenged power then. Nevertheless, I thought this point should not be overlooked. So I won the floor and asked, "As far as I've heard, Assemblyman Chough didn't oppose arresting communists. He recommended our government arrest them legally and without causing diplomatic incident by arresting them in a manner that would appear to be a kidnapping. Did I misunderstand something? Director Kim Hyung-wook, you heard the same thing I did, and I think what I heard was correct. What do you think?"

Director Kim said nothing, so I continued: "Fellow assemblymen! Are you really assemblymen? Are you so afraid of the KCIA director that you would condemn your fellow assemblyman's speech like that? Are you not ashamed of yourselves? And, you, Director Kim! What are you? You're in the National Assembly building and we represent the Korean people. The Republic of Korea is a democratic country and we represent the sovereign people. So how dare you admonish us?"

The room was dead silent. I was tense, too. After a long silence, Director Kim came forward and bowed deeply. "My dear, respectable Assemblyman Kim Dae-jung," he said. "I apologize. I apologize to you, my assemblymen, as well. It seems I was rash."

I heard from a number of people that Director Kim Hyung-wook praised me often. He was later deserted by President Park and exiled to the US. When he gave testimony about me at the US congressional hearings, he spoke well of me. It was unusual that the head of an intelligence agency that had oppressed so many democratic leaders would speak highly of someone like me—a political enemy of the president.

A Presidential Candidate in His Forties (1968–1970)

On January 21, 1968, thirty-one North Korean guerrillas appeared near Segeomjeong in Seoul. After crossing the military demarcation line over the frozen Imjin River, they arrived in front of the Jahamun police station in Segeomjeong, on a hill directly behind the Blue House. After a hail of bullets was exchanged by both sides, all but one guerrilla were shot to death. Without hesitation, the survivor Kim Sin-jo declared on TV: "We came to cut Park Chung-hee's throat."

It was a shocking and ludicrous incident, particularly because the Park regime had justified its military coup and dictatorship for reasons of national security.

North Korean military provocation continued into 1969. In April of that year, a North Korean fighter jet shot down US reconnaissance plane EC-121 on the East Sea shore. It was not clear why North Koreans continued to provoke us. My guess is that they felt threatened by the strengthening Korea-US relationship after the dispatch of Korean troops to Vietnam and the revived Korea-Japan relationship following the normalization of diplomatic relations between the two countries.

Meanwhile, North Korean provocation was affecting the South Korean people's psyche, which the Park regime was taking advantage of to bolster its dictatorial hold. National Assembly was beginning to discuss a three-term presidency constitutional amendment under the pretext that the current national emergency situation necessitated it. While the president didn't directly broach this topic, the ruling party leaders led this discussion.

When Assemblyman Kim Sang-hyun visited President Park at the Blue House in 1968, President Park had the following to say: "I don't know why the opposition party opposes everything we do. It really doesn't make sense for you to oppose governmental economic policies. I am carrying out those policies because the Korean people have entrusted me with the task. I have the obligation and the right. If they find my policies wrong, then they can replace me with someone else during the election. But it's not acceptable for you to oppose every single policy matter while the government carries it out. If, on the other hand, I attempt a three-term presidency constitutional amendment, then please attack me with a dagger, Assemblyman Kim! You'll naturally have the right to do so."

Although I heard all about this from Assemblyman Kim Sang-hyun, I didn't believe President Park's assertion. If President Park didn't intend to amend the Constitution, he wouldn't have attempted such large-scale election fraud. From the way he was risking popular resistance to secure two-thirds of the assembly seats, it was clear he was planning a three-term presidency constitutional amendment. As time passed, the ruling party members mentioned the notion itself more openly and frequently. The political situation turned tense with arguments and debates about this issue. This was the result of the ruling party's clever tactics.

On June 5, the Nationwide Struggle Committee Against Three-term Presidency Constitutional Amendment formed, spearheaded by the Sinmin Party. Out-of-office politicians, religious leaders, scholars, and retired generals participated as well. Reverend Kim Jae-joon, founder of the Presbyterian Church of the Republic of Korea, willingly took the position of committee chair. He was a courageous and thoughtful leader with excellent political sensibilities, as fine as any politician's. I worked with him on the committee, and he and I were often of the same opinion. Reverend Kim didn't waver in front of the conservative Christian elders' criticisms. He embodied the spirit of a true clergyman. Much later, during the Seoul Spring, he sent me a lengthy letter from Canada. His letter, written with a brush and as elegantly as a calligraphy piece, expressed his sincere hope for democratization. When the martial law enforcement forces later detained me, they confiscated that letter, which I'd so carefully preserved. I still remember very clearly, though, a phrase included in it: "I support you, comrade Kim Dae-jung. Please use my name whenever and wherever you need it."

The Sinmin Party was far more united in this struggle than any other. Mostly, Mr. Kim Young-sam, Mr. Lee Chul-seung, and I—the three candidates who later competed for our party's presidential nomination—

made speeches at the rallies. Many people still remember the rally at the Hyochang Field. The Korean people needed a breakthrough. The situation was grave and the future looked gray. I wanted my speech to contribute to a true change of momentum. I had to expose the ruling party's base tricks and appeal to the people to become fighters, to prevent a three-term presidency constitutional amendment. I wrote my speech with brave resolve (Photo 2.1).

On July 19, the audience packed Hyochang Field, where we held our Grand Rally Against the Three-term Presidency Constitutional Amendment. The authorities mobilized all manner of tactics to interfere with this rally. For example, they rushed to move up the reserve force training date, originally scheduled for July 22, to July 18. This mobilized more than 400,000 people. They also pressured tradesmen's associations to hold social gatherings that day. Nevertheless, the public, angry at the general state of affairs, crowded the field. When I stood on the podium, it felt like I was floating on a sea of people. I began my speech entitled "The Three-term Presidency Constitutional Amendment Is a National Polity Reform" with the story of an ox, the symbol of the Republican Party. "According to an article from this morning's newspaper, in Anseong,

Photo 2.1   Kim Dae-jung at the presidential campaign rally at Hyochang Park in Seoul in 1969

Geyonggi-do, a mad ox butted its owners with its horns and badly hurt them. Although the villagers tried to catch the ox with clubs, they failed to do so. In the end, a policeman had to come and shoot it five times. When I read this story I thought, 'Heaven really isn't indifferent!' Why? The Republican Party's symbol is an ox, and it has now gone mad, plotting a 3-term presidency constitutional amendment to hurt the Korean people's sovereignty. And, so, now even an ox has chimed in and has attacked its owner.

"Before the summer vacation could even begin, demonstrations protesting the 3-term presidency constitutional amendment have already spread across the country. Where have these demonstrations been the fiercest? Not in Seoul, but in Gyeongsang-do, the home of this regime. In particular, Gyeongsangbuk-do is Mr. Park Chung-hee's home. In Daegu, not only college students, but also high school students have taken to the streets to protest. I thought one of the slogans the students of Yeungnam University—a university President Park is later supposed to assume presidency of—was particularly funny: 'The Only Place a Mad Ox Should Go Is to a Slaughter House.'"

The audience burst into laughter and clapped and cheered. I asserted that the reason the Park regime wanted a three-term presidency constitutional amendment was because Mr. Park wanted to stay in power forever and build a one-man dictatorship. I also decried the KCIA's control of the media, and even the judiciary branch becoming no more than the regime's maid. I roared, "Universities are prisons without prison bars, and professors are prisoners without prisoner numbers." I promised that I wouldn't hesitate to put my life—not just political, but also physical—on the line to fight against Park's three-term presidency constitutional amendment conspiracy; it would lead our country only to collapse and unhappiness.

"Last, but not the least, I would like to sincerely and resolutely advise and appeal to Mr. Park Chung-hee. Dear Mr. Park Chung-hee, if you have even a shred of conscience about our country's democracy, if you have any fear of your people and our history, if you feel responsible for the spirits of the fallen patriots during the April 19th Revolution and the Korean War, please don't try a 3-term presidency constitutional amendment. If you are still willing to force a constitutional amendment, I warn you more clearly than the fact of tomorrow morning's sunrise that you'll not only face our country's and people's resistance, but also you yourself will become the second Rhee Syngman and the Republican Party will become the second Liberal Party."

President Park finally broke his silence and provided a statement on July 25, 1969, six days after the rally at the Hyochang Field. "The opposition party's attack on me is absurd. I cannot resign from the presidency under such circumstances. Therefore, I have no choice but to pursue a 3-term presidency constitutional amendment."

He then declared that he would hold a referendum on the three-term presidency constitutional amendment and, if he failed in this referendum, he would consider that as a no-confidence vote for himself and his cabinet and resign. His term would end in 1971. His intention to call a referendum on the people's confidence was crystal clear. It was a base plot to force a three-term presidency constitutional amendment by connecting it to the people's confidence in him. It was a clear intimidation tactic against the Korean people. Although we had anticipated it, the state of affairs in the country was thrown into turmoil, as soon as the president himself made the issue of the constitutional amendment public.

I heard the news in Kuala Lumpur, Malaysia. I had been on a tour that began in Southeast Asia and was to go on through Europe, America, and South America, but I canceled my remaining schedule and returned home immediately. As the ruling party had more than two-thirds of the assembly seats, they could easily pass the constitutional amendment if they had a consensus about it within their party; however, Mr. Kim Jong-pil was against it because he was waiting as a second in line to succeed President Park. Also, there were many—more than thirty, according to media analysis—ruling party assemblymen who were against the constitutional amendment.

Nevertheless, President Park pushed the constitutional amendment through, backed by KCIA Director Kim Hyung-wook and the Blue House Chief of Staff Lee Hu-rak, and led by Assemblymen Baek Nam-eok, Kim Seong-gon, and Kil Chae-ho. In the end, the assemblymen belonging to the Republican Party began to favor the constitutional amendment one after another, yielding to conciliation and intimidation tactics. Mr. Kim Jong-pil also had a change of heart and began a speaking tour in support of it.

The regime also bribed some opposition party members. Still, they couldn't be confident that the constitutional amendment would pass since the voting would be done by a secret ballot. There were rumors that it would be impossible to pass it. Opposition party members were quite determined to oppose and were strongly united on this issue. While opposition party members occupied the main hall of the National Assembly, however, 122 ruling party members and independents secretly gathered at the 3rd Annex

Building and rushed the bill through, deceiving the public and reversing history at 2:00 a.m. on September 14, 1969. That was almost the same time of day the May 16th Military Coup occurred. The rushing through of this amendment was also a coup of sorts, this time a constitutional one. I later heard that the chairman had used a water kettle lid instead of a gavel. The Sinmin Party members who arrived late discovered that the Republican Party members had run through the back door. We cried until dawn.

Their handling of the bill was in clear violation of National Assembly law because they hadn't notified the opposition party assemblymen. By this act, the regime practically announced to the whole world that they were a dictatorial regime. They hadn't hesitated to commit illegal and unjust acts for their purposes.

The regime then held a referendum on the three-term presidency constitutional amendment. Voters supported the amendment overwhelmingly, which was expected because of the all-out fraud committed by all levels of the government. Since there was no autonomous local government system in place, there was no way to prevent this.

That October, I went with my family to see British pop singer Cliff Richard's concert at Ewha Womans University Auditorium. The audience went absolutely wild during the concert, to the point where I couldn't hear any music. I looked around and realized that most of the screaming audience members were middle and high school students. The college students' response was entirely different: "*Tsk, tsk*, they are all crazy!"

I was surprised to see the great gap between college and high school students. I also thought that young people were so excited because they didn't have proper channels through which they could work off their youthful energy. The military regime's repression was getting harsher by the day, and the fierce confrontation between the South and North was spreading a bloodthirsty mood into all areas of society. The future was murky and dark. I worried that our children would lose heart and hope in this sort of atmosphere.

The gate opened for President Park's third term. We had to fight again and win the election to block him. All of us believed the Sinmin Party's best potential candidate was party president Yu Chin-o; however, closer observation ultimately led me to believe he was not quite qualified in terms of his political insights and leadership. He wasn't able to take advantage of the Republican Party's all-out election fraud to change the political atmosphere. Unable to control his own party, he was being dragged around by hardliners. It seemed to me that he was kicking his own fortune to the curb.

While I was deeply troubled by this situation, it was Lee Yong-hee who suggested, "We cannot depend on President Yu. He will not do. You'll have to run for the presidency."

I felt inspired by what he said, but I didn't mention it to people. I worked hard to fight for Dr. Yu. We first formed our staff and toured our party's local branches all across the country to strengthen our party's organizational basis.

In the middle of this, President Yu collapsed from a stroke; he traveled to Japan in November and expressed his wish to resign from the party president post. All of us were tense; we remembered our past misfortunes when opposition party candidates or presidents had collapsed from illness. Everything seemed to be repeating once again. Dark clouds hung over the Sinmin Party.

In early January 1970, a Sinmin Party provisional national convention was held and Mr. Yu Jin-san was elected president. Nicknamed "Sakura," Mr. Yu Jin-san was not trusted by the people. He might have held the position of the party president, but he could not become our party's presidential candidate. Mr. Kim Young-sam, the Sinmin Party assembly leader, had already called for a generation shift, which was dubbed "Standard-bearers in Their Forties." I agreed with his argument.

We needed to settle on our party's presidential candidate as soon as possible to fight against an opponent as formidable as President Park. However, President Yu Jin-san unilaterally decided to postpone our party's candidate nomination, which was originally scheduled for January. Clearly, he was weighing whether or not he should run as the party's candidate, but even his closest associates failed to show any support for him. The people's voice, demanding a candidate in his forties, was becoming stronger by the day.

Within the party, there were three leaders in their forties: Kim Young-sam, Lee Chul-seung, and me. President Yu launched a hit on us, saying, "They're still only political minors. They still smell of milk." But the public opinion of him was cold.

On September 25, just four days before the convention for the nomination—by which point it was clear that he had no chance of being nominated—President Yu called the three of us to his house in Sangdo-dong and proposed that he be given the authority to nominate one of us. At that time, the Jin-san circle was the mainstream within the Sinmin Party, while I belonged to a non-mainstream circle along with Jeong Il-hyeong and Lee Jae-hyeong. Despite the fact that we belonged to the same party,

President Yu Jin-san and I didn't share the same political ideas. Both Mr. Kim Young-sam and Mr. Lee Chul-seung accepted President Yu's proposal, while I resolutely refused it; it was clear that he wouldn't nominate me. Also, this sort of process was against democratic principles and our party members' general opinion. A presidential candidate needed the nomination of each and every party member from all over the country, of their own volition.

In the end, President Yu decided to nominate Kim Young-sam, leaving Lee Chul-seung furious. Lee's followers, who, like me, belonged to the New Faction, turned to me. Party leaders like Jeong Il-hyeong, Jeong Heon-ju, Yoon Giel-joong, Kim Eung-joo, and Kim Won-man supported me as well.

The nomination had to be decided through party delegates' vote. The Jin-san circle was confident of Mr. Kim Young-sam's victory. The media also reported that the nomination was a matter of formality. Even the people closest to me advised me to resign voluntarily. Nevertheless, I was confident. I toured the country and talked with the ordinary people. As a result, ordinary party members asked their delegates to vote for me. People also liked my resolute refusal to recognize the party president's authoritative nomination proposal.

After declaring my candidacy at the party convention in September, I began an eight-month tour of the country to meet local party members. Party members everywhere welcomed me. Their enthusiasm was palpable, especially in Gyeongsang-do. My wife also worked passionately for me. She visited delegates at their homes—many of which were located in moon villages. She moved delegates' wives and families, who then moved delegates. In this way I calmly accumulated my votes. The night before the convention, I visited delegates at their lodgings and shook hands with them. I did my best until the very end.

The day of the Sinmin Party presidential nomination convention arrived on September 29, 1970. My supporters floated advertisement balloons across the sky. Hundreds of party members wearing sashes across their chests surrounded the Civic Center (now the Sejong Center) and chanted my name: "Kim Dae-jung, Kim Dae-jung, President Kim Dae-jung!" Dr. Jeong Il-hyeong (a party supreme committee member and supporter of mine) and I stood in front of the building, holding pickets.

I was deeply moved. It was overwhelming. I felt good about the upcoming results. My posters were all over the walls near the convention center. Picketing crowds in support of me covered the floor of the convention center. I couldn't see Mr. Kim Young-sam's crowd. It was an unprecedented show of enthusiasm for modern Korean party history. My staff created a festive atmosphere by imitating the American presidential nomination convention. Convention Chairman Kim Hong-il announced the convention was open. Mr. Lee Chul-seung declared his resignation and left. Amid this tense atmosphere, the first round of voting results was announced: 421 for Kim Young-sam, 382 for Kim Dae-jung, and 82 invalid votes out of 885 total.

The delegates and reporters who had expected a landslide victory for Mr. Kim Young-sam were restless. Unbelievably, some evening newspapers had already printed newspapers with headlines blaring "Kim Young-sam Nominated" and distributed them throughout the convention center. For this first round of voting, Lee Chul-seung's followers had cast blank votes. As soon as the results were announced, I went to the front and shouted, "Now, I'm the presidential candidate nominee!"

All eyes were onto me. The hall became quiet instantly.

Before the runoff voting began, I again predicted to the reporters that I would win the nomination. I had reason to be confident. As I mentioned earlier, Lee Chul-seung's followers belonged mostly to the New Faction. I had asked them to vote for me if Mr. Lee Chul-seung resigned. Also, before the runoff voting, Mr. Kim Jun-sub, a Lee Chul-seung circle member, asked me to write a memorandum promising to support Mr. Lee Chul-seung at the next party president election, saying he would vote for me if I did so. I gladly wrote a memorandum on one of my name cards. I needed to win this nomination, and I didn't think then that Mr. Lee Chul-seung was unworthy of the position. Unfortunately, Mr. Lee Chul-seung never ran for the party president position, so I didn't have a chance to keep my promise. At any rate, I worked hard to accumulate votes, hedging against any worst-case scenarios. While the runoff voting continued, I examined the number of votes I was likely to win and realized that I couldn't lose the nomination. The results arrived: 458 for Kim Dae-jung, 410 for Kim Young-sam, and 16 invalid votes out of 884.

President Kim Hong-il struck the gavel. By winning the majority vote, I'd been nominated as the Sinmin Party presidential candidate. The delegates' applause went on and on. It was a dramatic reversal that would long be remembered in Korean political history. The Kim Young-sam camp had been supremely confident of a victory; now they seemed stupefied.

In my acceptance speech, I said: "A new age begins this very moment. I will block the long-term seizure of power by the Park Chung-hee regime and achieve the democratic regime change the Korean people have yearned for since the founding of our nation, standing at the forefront of the fight for Korean people's freedom and happiness in this new age."

A candidate in his forties signaled a new political wind. More than anyone else, my nomination victory surprised the Park regime. The KCIA director had been mistaken in his prediction that there was no chance I could possibly win. And, perhaps because of this mistake, he was replaced before the next presidential election season.

The generation shift in the opposition party was a prelude to a new kind of politics. I was to face President Park in a fateful confrontation. Although President Park had battled for my defeat in the previous election, I appeared to be leading him as a presidential candidate. Perhaps he instinctively saw a threat in me and was thus trying to eliminate a future political enemy.

I resolved to put my life on the line in the fight to finish off the Park regime. I resolved to repay the support of every party member and every civilian voter by getting our party out of its eternal opposition party chain. A great storm was brewing in Korean politics, and I had just walked right into the eye of it.

CHAPTER 3

1970–1972

Breaking a Taboo in a Barrack-like Nation (1970–1971)

On October 16, 1970, I held my first press conference as a presidential candidate, wherein I outlined the policies our party had prepared. In the past, the opposition party couldn't gain the people's trust because it focused more on attacking the regime's government mishandling and corruption than on presenting its own policies and visions. I decided we had to present ourselves as a party worthy of governing the country through a showdown of policies. It was not an easy task to present policies that everyone could relate to.

I never personally attacked Republican Party candidate Park Chung-hee or any other leaders. We had plenty of personal evidence to use against them, but I wanted to make this election a policy fight. I felt confident that I could take charge of this election's focus only by presenting our policies and visions. I researched our policy stances thoroughly and polished my ideas.

The policies I proposed included abolishing the Homeland Reserve Army; pursuing a mass-participatory economy system; securing war deterrence by allying with the four powers of the US, China, the USSR, and Japan (Security by Four Powerful Countries); reconciling and pursuing free exchange between the South and the North; pursuing improved relations and trade with communist countries; abolishing school supporting fees at elementary and middle schools; establishing a luxury tax; abolishing

© The Author(s) 2019
Kim Dae-jung, *Conscience in Action*,
https://doi.org/10.1007/978-981-10-7623-7_3

academic cliquism; and introducing a double grain price system. Each item had a far-reaching influence. The public showed a particularly fiery interest in my proposals to abolish the Homeland Reserve Army, to establish national security through a Security by Four Powerful Countries policy, to promote free exchange between the South and the North (as well as peaceful unification of the two countries), and to introduce a mass-participatory economic system.

The Homeland Reserve Army was founded with 2 million reserve forces on April 1, 1968, soon after the North Korean Guerrilla Incident. In this system, reserve forces would ordinarily work civilian jobs until war called upon them to resume their lives as soldiers. The Homeland Reserve Army was the equivalent of the North Korean Workers and Farmers Red Guards. According to the precepts of this system, the military could summon these reserve forces for training at any time. This often involved being called to the police substation chief's house to take care of his children and gather firewood for his family. Not surprisingly, some people chose to bribe superiors or to send a proxy in order to avoid training.

Although the purpose of the reserve army was to defend our country against North Korean invasion, the Park regime was using it to control the South Korean people. National security was being used as an excuse to manage the entire population like a military organization. As the regime could turn civilians into soldiers at a moment's notice, it could mobilize them for unjust purposes any time. The public vehemently resented and complained about this.

People responded enthusiastically to my policy of abolishing the Homeland Reserve Army. President Park had Defense Minister Jung Nae-hiuk hold a meeting as a countermeasure to this proposal. He also instigated defense-related organizations to attack me: "The abolition of the Homeland Reserve Army is a serious threat to our country's existence. As it induces North Korean invasion, we request that you withdraw your proposal immediately!"

I refused to withdraw my pledge. Despite the regime's critiques and attacks, the absolute majority of the Korean people were in favor of abolishing the Homeland Reserve Army. Nonetheless, there were some people in my party who thought this promise had been too hastily made. They argued that I should have presented this pledge toward the end of the presidential campaign, therefore not allowing time for the regime to counterattack.

It was certainly true that I now had to face an enormous counterattack. The regime mobilized the newspapers, party publications, and public broadcasting stations. They presented me as dangerous and irresponsible, someone with a complete lack of national security awareness. However, it was also true that I needed explosive issues that could unite my party members and draw in powerful popular interest. I also needed to change the social atmosphere in which the anti-communism slogan made it impossible for people to even breathe. I needed a detonator that would shatter the Park regime's anti-communist dictatorship framework. Still, it's hard to say how different the outcome of the election would have been had I presented my proposal for abolishing the Homeland Reserve Army immediately before the election, after gaining the people's trust with other promises.

My promise to create Security by Four Powerful Countries and establish an interchange between the South and the North to peacefully unite the countries shocked the regime. Prior to my pronouncements, they had been steadily elevating tensions in the Korean Peninsula to maintain power. Naturally, they immediately claimed that the Security by Four Powerful Countries was entirely unrealistic, nothing more than an illusion. Considering security personnel checked your background for even mentioning the word "reunification," this was not surprising. They went so far as to call it madness and obvious pandering. Mr. Park Chung-hee spearheaded the attack: "He proposes entrusting our security with the USSR and China, our enemies. What does he mean by that? This proposal violates our firmest anti-communist beliefs, our country's foremost national policy stance."

They distorted my argument. The Security by Four Powerful Countries didn't mean that our security would rely entirely on foreign nations, but that we would demand promises from the four countries to encourage neither the North nor the South to invade the other. My argument was well received by intellectuals and garnered international attention as well. Weren't the current Six-party Talks (which included the four great international powers and both Koreas) based on the same idea? I knew then about the constant power dynamics among influential countries surrounding the Korean Peninsula and the conditions for true peace in it. In retrospect, I feel proud that I judged correctly and acted justly.

The Republican Party attacked my promises of a peaceful reunification and interchange between the South and the North. They argued: How can we reconcile with them while the North is plotting reunification by force? President Park and Mr. Kim Jong-pil vilified me daily, constantly accusing me of being pro-communist: "When Kim Dae-jung plays a pipe, Kim Il-sung dances, and when Kim Il-sung beats a drum, Kim Dae-jung beats time with it."

It was only a year later that the Park regime pursued the same reunification policy. Upon the South Korean government's proposal, the two nations held the South-North Red Cross Conference, and on July 4, 1972, both sides adopted the famous South-North Joint Communiqué. Although they ultimately adopted my policies, their intentions were quite different from mine. The Park regime's goal was not reconciliation and collaboration between the South and the North, but the regime's own security and appeasement of the popular wish for reunification.

Through my mass-participatory economy policy, I aimed to run an economy by the people, for the people, and of the people on both institutional and policy levels. Since the Rhee Syngman regime, the Korean economy had been operating based on the actions and priorities of a privileged class. It was an economy originating from authoritarianism. This tendency had only intensified during the Park regime. Ordinary citizens were facing a growing sense of hardship and long-standing problems were accumulating. Korea desperately needed a theory and strategy that countered the Park regime's developmental dictatorship framework. I decided to publicize a new blueprint for a far more democratic economy in Korea.

My mass-participatory economy policy was born of my observation and experiences with the Korean post-liberation economy, as well as my activities in the Finance and Economy Committee at the National Assembly. I tried to publicize this through various media outlets long before my presidential election campaign. My 1969 article "Advocacy for Mass-participatory Economic Policy," published in a 1969 issue of *Shindonga*, contained the essence of my argument. In that article I'd defined it as a policy that developed an economic system that encouraged the working people's wisdom and ability to their fullest extent, while also systematically guaranteeing their well-being. This economic policy was possible only when the democratic system was complete. Popular will was its essential element.

In this article, I proposed implementing a Fair Economy Operation Commission. This commission would work to promote the fair and transparent management of national economy and strengthen the social responsibility of businesses. This institution would provide measures to guarantee fair trade and consumer protection in all industries, as well as fair income redistribution for the working people. I also argued for the privatization of state-owned enterprises and an employee stock ownership system, both of which were very unfamiliar concepts at that time.

I summarized these arguments in a book published in 1971, *Mr. Kim Dae-jung's Mass-participatory Economy Policy: 100 Questions and 100 Answers*. It was prepared as election campaign PR material for ordinary voters after many discussions with scholars and professionals such as Professors Kim Byeong-tae, Jeong Yun-hyeong, Park Hyun-chae, Choi Ho-jin, as well as my staff members, including Bang Dae-yeop and Kim Gyeong-gwang. The intelligence agency's interference during the preparation of this book was beyond imagination. We had to check into inn after inn to avoid intelligence surveillance, and often communicated in secrecy. It was not easy to secure a printer for the book, either. A few related people were taken to secret intelligence offices and underwent some rather rough periods.

At any rate, this work contributed to turning the presidential election campaign into a policy debate. My argument that ordinary citizens should participate in the economy was like a breath of fresh air at the height of the military regime's government-controlled economy. At the time, the Park regime was interested only in export increase and economic growth. They did not care who the principal economic agents were or how the matter of wealth distribution was approached.

The Park regime gave an astronomical level of preferential treatment to a small privileged class. Under the Park regime, the government paid attention only to economic growth by completely controlling general market functions, including price decision making, loan distribution, and relations between labor and capital. This government control drove the Korean economy into extreme imbalance—there were imbalances between manufacturing and farming; between large, mid-sized, and small companies; and between cities and countries. These imbalances were intensifying every day. In short, the Park regime economy's essence guaranteed the privileges of large enterprises on the basis of the sacrifices of farmers and laborers. In this privilege-based economy, the working masses suffered from low grain prices and low wages. It was hard to imagine the formation of a middle class. I'd formed my particular brand of mass-participatory economy theory as a counterargument to this devastating economic policy.

Fundamentally, the mass-participatory economy theory served as a blueprint for economic democracy through rational mediation in economic development, equitable income distribution, and price stabilization.

The Wa-u Apartment Collapse Incident in April 1970 (in which thirty-three individuals died in a sudden apartment cave-in) served as a symbolic incident revealing the accumulated economic and social evils in our society. The tragedy was the result of an employee of the Seoul city government accepting bribes to overlook the builder's substandard construction. Although it reflected a materialistic and corrupt social atmosphere, the tragedy also served as a dire warning against an economic policy that blindly pursued economic growth without mass participation and supervision. This was the beginning of a series of events that all proved to be the side effects of the nation's accelerated and condensed growth. Since then, Koreans have had to live in fear of such large-scale catastrophes. Policies focusing on growth necessarily beget governmental control and interference, distort market functions, and corrupt government officials and employees.

In my mass-participatory economy, I pursued the fair distribution of economic growth among people and between current and later generations. For the same reason, I argued for the double grain price system, wherein the government would buy rice and barley at higher prices from farmers and sell them at lower prices to consumers. Japan had successfully implemented this system, satisfying both producers and consumers in the process—farmers enjoyed a comfortable life and there were no longer mass food shortages in Japan. When farmers have high purchasing power, city industries also flourish. The Park regime later adopted this system. In fact, although the Park regime criticized and oppressed me, it later adopted *most* of my promises as its policies.

In my mass-participatory economy theory I emphasized that the core of the market economy is the existence of truly creative and free entrepreneurs and enterprises. The world's economic history has recorded the crumbling of the Marxist illusion and the limits of the Keynesian economy. The state cannot replace the market and so it follows that politicians and bureaucrats cannot replace entrepreneurs. However, the market, when left alone, repeats certain failures as well. The only state that can monitor the market justly is a democratic state, and only middle-class participation and careful political maintenance can protect democracy. In Korea, the market economy would not settle for a long while yet. It was much too barren an environment for creative entrepreneurs to emerge. During that period when politicians and businessmen enjoyed a fairly cozy relationship and the government-controlled loans, businessmen needed to regularly conduct underhanded deals with politicians and government employees. This practice had continued since the Rhee Syngman regime, and I felt sorry for the businessmen.

Businessmen require complete trust in the free market and need to feel some pride and mission for its protection and development. Likewise, they also need to contribute to the free market system with their creativity and adventurous spirit. It's nothing but hypocrisy, however, to support the free market economy only when it's favorable for you and to ask for governmental interference and protection when market competition becomes more challenging.

In the economic environment of Korea then, how could the economy develop and the fruits of that development be distributed fairly? Businessmen also needed to change their basic attitudes and to resist accepting their continuing privileges. They needed to lead the market economy with creativity and a competitive spirit. The only institutional alternative that could enable this is democracy, the essence of both this mass-participatory economy theory and the philosophical basis for my later theory of parallel development of democracy and market economy.

After many revisions, my theory of mass-participatory economy was reborn as a book entitled *Mass-participatory Economy*, which Rutgers University Professor of Economics You Jong-keun helped me to prepare. I was able to write the book thanks to the Korean people's support for my ideas. The public read my book despite the constant, terrifying presence of government surveillance and oppression. Without them, there could never be a *Mass-participatory Economy*, which remained on the censored book list throughout the neo-military regime period of the 1980s. In 1985, the book was translated into English and published under the title *Mass-participatory Economy: A Democratic Alternative for Korea* by Harvard University Press. I hear that it has been used as a supplementary textbook in various college classes in America.

At the beginning of my presidential term decades later, I couldn't quite contextualize the matter of distribution I'd emphasized in my mass-participatory economy theory. However, after successfully easing the foreign currency crisis, I devoted myself to distribution policies and presented my productive welfare plan. During my administration, I'd already proposed reforms in the four prime economic areas of finance, entrepreneurship, government, and relations between labor and capital. My mass-participatory economy theory had matured by the time it was adopted as a foundation for my administration's official policies.

The policies I proposed became large social issues, while the ruling party's policies consistently failed to attract any attention. It was a curious phenomenon. Whenever I announced my policy plans, the government and the ruling party were united in coming forward to find fault with them, but the people responded enthusiastically. In the outpost action before the full-scale presidential campaign I could get ahead of the ruling party when it came to policy conflicts.

The Sinmin Party didn't have the organization to systematically establish policies. My policy ideas were the result of my work, a crystallization of my sweat, and consisted of my own far-reaching plans for our nation's future. Although the Republican Party could utilize vast administrative organizations, and the party itself had a heavily funded policy research organization, it never presented any meaningful policy ideas. My reform ideas left the public excited for the election. A policy confrontation was one of the most effective election campaign tools for an opposition party with inferior funds and organization.

Not coincidentally, the government and the ruling party also criticized my policies for not considering an appropriate budget. I responded by offering concrete budget figures for each policy initiative and an explanation for how I would procure these funds. The people came to trust me more after that. I also proposed to President Park that we hold joint election speech rallies and TV debates. President Park never responded.

POPULAR SENTIMENT REBELLION: FROM WHIRLWIND TO TYPHOON (1971)

I visited the US with my wife in late January 1971, three months before Election Day. By then, Korea's allies were paying attention to the Korean election. US political leaders conveyed their wish to see me through US. Ambassador to Korea William J. Porter. I gathered they wanted to see the opposition party candidate raising a whirlwind. Likewise, I wanted to meet and network with American leaders; it could only be helpful for me to discuss current affairs with US leaders the most influential to Korean military and economy—both for the election and for my future political activities.

The US officials and leaders welcomed me warmly. I met with Secretary of State William P. Rogers, Assistant Secretary Marshall Green, and Director of Korean Affairs Donald L. Ranard for an official conference. I also met a number of US Senate leaders, including Senator Edward

M. Kennedy and Senate Foreign Relations Committee Chair James William Fulbright. Secretary of State Rogers made encouraging remarks about my fight for democracy: "The U.S. supports democracy and will never forget leaders who fight for democracy."

Senator Kennedy's remarks were thoughtful and warm, too. "I notice they called you the 'Korean Kennedy.' We Kennedys haven't lost an election so far. You must win, too. The current US administration supports the military regime in Korea. But there are those of us who worry about it and pay close attention to the situation in Korea. So, please don't worry about us, and do your best to win the election. Please call me from Korea if there's anything I can do to help you." Senator Kennedy listened very carefully to my policy ideas as well. He was especially supportive of my South-North reconciliation policy.

My conversation with Senator Fulbright was useful, too. When I visited him, he was in a meeting, but adjourned it to speak with me. As soon as we entered the Senate Foreign Relations Committee chair's room together, he asked rather sarcastically, "Are you running for presidency with the thought that it's possible to change the regime in Korea, a military dictatorship country?"

I answered, "Your ancestors fought for independence and freedom against England two hundred years ago. Americans then didn't fight with any guarantee that they'd win. They fought only because they desperately wanted to achieve freedom, didn't they? One of your founding fathers, Thomas Jefferson, said that the tree of liberty must be refreshed from time to time with the blood of patriots and tyrants. I don't know whether I will succeed in my effort, but I believe it's just work that I am obliged to do. As Jefferson said, 'If I fought with blood and tears, I'm confident that there will be days when we accomplish liberty and democracy. We will keep on fighting.'"

Senator Fulbright listened to me very carefully and sincerely said, "I understand you completely. I wish you success." I also brought up another matter, risking impoliteness. Although I opposed the dispatch of Korean troops to Vietnam, I couldn't overlook the fact that he called the Korean troops mercenaries. Korea hadn't wanted to send its troops. We had to yield to American pressure, partially because of the threat that the US would withdraw its troops from Korea, and partially because Korea wanted to repay the sacrifice of so many young US soldiers during the Korean War. Knowing these were the sentiments of most Koreans, the Park regime forced sending Korean troops and proceeded to take advantage of it for regime security and financial gain.

The young Korean men fighting and dying in foreign jungles believed they were defending democracy in Vietnam. The entire world might criticize the Korean troops, but the US had no right to criticize us; they should have been grateful to our young people. I told Senator Fulbright, "I can understand your criticizing the Korean or American governments. But I think it an insult to call Korean troops—who are risking their lives for an ally and for democracy in Vietnam—mercenaries. Americans, if no one else, should at least appreciate the sacrifice of the Korean youth."

Senator Fulbright was as generous as (and more flexible than) I'd heard. Wearing an apologetic expression, he immediately responded, "I'm sorry if the Korean people felt hurt by what I said. But my intention was to condemn US governmental policy and a Korean government that's long been too servile to the US government. I had no intention whatsoever of criticizing the Korean people."

Senator Fulbright introduced me to other senators encouragingly, always prefacing his introduction with, "Senator, here's a young Korean democracy fighter." Senator Fulbright had been critical of Korea's dictatorial regimes. Considering his steadfast refusal to interview Korean politicians, his attitude toward me was exceptional.

I gave a speech at the National Press Club in Washington, DC, and explained my policies. I also talked about the Korean people's enthusiastic desire for democracy and my belief that one day we would achieve it. The Q&A session was very lively. It seemed that American leaders were impressed by my speech. I couldn't meet with President Nixon for "political" reasons (I was an opposition party presidential candidate), but I attended a breakfast prayer meeting he sponsored. My wife met First Lady Pat Nixon at the White House. The *Washington Post* ran an article about my visit to the effect that Kim Dae-jung was the most serious challenge to Park Chung-hee since the May 16 coup d'état.

After my visit to the US, I dropped by Japan, where I met with political leaders Tanaka Kakuei and Hashimoto Tomisaburo of the Liberal Democratic Party, Nishimura Eiichi of the Democratic Socialist Party, and Takeiri Yoshikatsu and Yano Junya of the New Komeito Party. At that time, the Liberal Democratic Party, the ruling party in Japan, was still in its honeymoon stage with the Park regime. Thus, they weren't particularly interested in me. When the Park regime passed its three-term presidency constitutional amendment bill, president of the Liberal Democratic Party

Kawashima even made a comment to the effect that "Korea needs a stable long-term regime." Whenever I met Japanese politicians, I told them, "Koreans won't like the Japanese supporting a dictatorial regime in Korea. The upcoming election is a fight between dictatorship and democracy, and I will win. Please pay attention so that it will be a fair and clean election."

I also gave a speech at the Foreign Correspondents' Club of Japan. My speech was unexpectedly well received. I was able to convince the audience that I was a powerful leader fighting against dictatorship, a practitioner of liberal democracy, and an ally to the US and Japan.

On the third day of my visit to the US, I heard that there had been an explosion in the front yard of my home in Donggyo-dong, Seoul. I immediately realized that it was most likely the regime conspiring to force me to stop my visit and meetings with American leaders. Since no one had been hurt, I continued my tour and returned on the originally planned day. Once home, I discovered this incident had made front-page headlines every day for the past twenty days. In the end, the National Assembly dispatched an investigation committee.

The incident had occurred the night of the lunar New Year's Day, on January 27. While watching TV in the living room, my family heard the explosion and ran out to the yard. Although it was loud, not even a single window had been broken, and no one was hurt. Nonetheless, the police promptly came running. They said that the explosive consisted of popgun powder. So, who was the perpetrator?

Everyone thought the Korean Central Intelligence Administration (KCIA) must be responsible for the explosion, but the police carried out their investigation under the assumption that people in my camp had staged it to attract attention and sympathy. They interviewed only people around my family and myself—scores of them, including my secretary, driver, guard, and housekeeper—in an attempt to fabricate perpetrators and pry into my personal life. They also took seven of my campaign staff members—Cha Yeong-ju in charge of Gangwon-do; Kim Won-sik, Hahn Hwa-kap, Park Dae-shik, and Kim Song-sik, all my Sinmin Party Seoul delegates; Kim Jang-kon, director of the Chungcheong-do organization and the Sinmin Party Fishermen Department; and Eom Chang-rok, my assistant and director of organization—and interrogated them about my election campaign organization.

They also tried to bribe my driver. The police asked him, "You're from Gyeongsang-do. Why should you be loyal to Kim Dae-jung, a Jeolla-do native?" They offered him a whopping 30 million won in cash on the spot in exchange for offering false testimony of my camp fabricating the incident.

They also tried to buy my secretary (who hadn't gone to college) off. "We'll send you to study abroad in the US right now," they said. "We'll arrange your meeting with high government officials and you'll receive tens of millions of won in cash. Testify that the Kim Dae-jung camp fabricated this incident." Later, they beat him as well.

All of these things that shouldn't have happened were revealed by the National Assembly Investigation Committee. But no one around me yielded to the violence, intimidation, and bribes, and everyone revealed the truth under oath. In the end, they arrested my eighth-grade nephew Kim Hong-jun, my brother Dae-ui's son. They mobilized 120 police officers to arrest this frightened, innocent young boy. My nephew was visiting my house to give the ceremonial New Year's bow to his grandmother, who lived with my family, when he was thrown into this incredible ordeal. As 120 police officers blocked the arrest scene, even reporters couldn't get through to him. Two reporters who tried to pass through this line were injured, and broadcasting station cars were broken into and left nonfunctional. The police tortured my nephew in order to extract a confession. They even forced his head into dirty water, which later led him to contract typhoid; he was feverish and in critical condition for weeks.

They also took my housekeeper, a teenage girl, and tried to extract false testimony from her at the police station. "You have to testify that you saw Mr. Kim's nephew do it," they informed her. "Then we'll release both of you. Just one word, that's it. If you don't want to rot in prison all your life, you have to." Terrified, she yielded to the threat. But when they didn't release my nephew, she realized she had been duped, and revealed how she had falsely testified under duress.

As there were fragments of explosives outside my house, it was clear to everyone that someone outside of my house had done it. Still, the police insisted it was the work of an insider. Although they couldn't catch the culprit, everyone knew who was behind all of it.

Another strange incident happened in the midst of this turmoil: Sinmin Party Presidential Campaign Chair Dr. Jeong Il-hyeong's house in Bongwon-dong in Seoul was burned down to the ground on February 5, 1971. The Sinmin Party's presidential campaign plans, all of our secret party documents, and documents on every party organization perished in the fire. The police announced that three cats had brought paper from a nearby trashcan into Dr. Jeong Il-hyeong's fireplace, and that while the cats played with the paper, it caught fire from a burning briquette. But why on earth would the three house cats have gone out to an empty lot and brought paper into the house? People dubbed this the Cat Arson Incident, and laughed at the police explanation. I commented on this event at the Jangchungdan rally, saying: "After setting fire to my campaign chair Dr. Jeong Il-hyeong's home, they claimed a bunch of cats did it because they couldn't come up with a false culprit. So, according to the police, Dr. Jeong's two cats called over a neighbor's cat and discussed their plan to set fire to their own house. Then they gathered the stray paper and started the fire by lighting it with a lit briquette. How did the police find out about these cats' conversation? Truly, the Korean police force does possess exceptional skills, unparalleled to any other country's police."

The police constantly harassed me and my camp during the campaign season. Once, when I was giving a speech at a theater in Gimpo-eup near Seoul, the police secretly recorded my speech in the projection room. They hid a microphone in a wall in order to record it without noise. My guards mistook it for a gun and entered the projection room by kicking in the door. Not only were the police unapologetic for their actions, but they also arrested my guards and attendants on the charge of interference with a public official in the execution of his duty.

Also, during the commotion, someone took a police gun and placed it in our car. Although my attendants immediately reported it to the police, they were arrested. More than a dozen of my staff members were unjustly imprisoned; they were not released until almost a year after the election.

There's one more example of unjust harassment activities by the police and the KCIA. As mentioned earlier, my wife had photos taken with First Lady Pat Nixon during our visit to the US. We had two rolls of pictures, one of which was developed at a photo studio. The police went to the photo studio and searched the premises under the pretext of searching for smuggled goods. Upon returning, photo studio employees found that both the photo printout and film had disappeared.

When the Sinmin Party spokesman condemned this, the Republican Party president and spokesperson held a press conference and counterattacked. "Mrs. Kim Dae-jung has never met with First Lady Pat Nixon. Kim Dae-jung fabricated this story to use to his advantage for the election."

They must have thought we had only one film of that picture, which is why they were able to attack us so comfortably. We invited a photographer to our home and had him develop the other roll of film. The next morning, every newspaper ran the photo of Mrs. Nixon and my wife shaking hands. The ruling party couldn't protest—or even comment—on this.

All of these corrupt practices could have been expected. Election fraud had been carefully planned and executed. President Park could use the government budget at his will. As the election approached, public works were launched everywhere in the country. Groundbreaking ceremonies for a building or a bridge occurred every day. Residents were invited to these ceremonies and showered with propaganda about the president's special interest in the region. Government employees, including the president's personal employees, were mobilized, and the state coffer was used like Park's personal purse.

The newspaper was under strict government control, with the KCIA behind it all. If a newspaper didn't follow governmental directives, retaliation followed. They not only oppressed the newspaper companies, but also corrupted them by employing journalists to governmental posts and granting these companies great favors. The government also pressured public hygiene and environment-related businesses like barbershops, bathhouses, and inns, for which the government had power to give or take away licenses. Even before the election began, the government and the ruling party had finished their preparations to implement election fraud.

The first stage of their election fraud scheme was to delete the names of those who were leaning toward voting for the opposition party from the registered voter list, while listing the names of voters who supported the ruling party multiple times. According to a later revelation, between 3000 and 5000 voter names were listed multiple times per precinct. Since there were 153 precincts in total, this means they were able to secure about 500,000 additional votes for the ruling party through this strategy.

They also made sure to block all campaign funds from flowing into the Sinmin Party. KCIA agents took businessmen who had no relation to me to their offices and scolded them for contributing to my campaign. Absolutely terrified, these businessmen were released only after they wrote notes promising never to fund my campaign. As a result, not only were all those who'd been threatened too frightened to contribute to my campaign, but also anyone who heard about these incidents. Businessmen couldn't really contribute because the KCIA agents tortured those who knew nothing about me at all, merely because their competitors reported they'd contributed to my campaign. Unlike today, back then there was no governmental assistance for candidates. It became extremely difficult to raise campaign funds.

According to the Campaign Fund Purification Act, businesses could deposit political funds to the Election Administration Committee, which would then distribute funds to each party based on the number of their National Assembly seats. However, at that time, no one would dare deposit political funds. It was well known that the ruling party utilized 3 billion won in addition to its official budget. The Sinmin Party's election fund was less than 1 percent of that. The situation was utterly pathetic. It was nearly impossible for the opposition party to win.

Amid all of this scheming and machination, my main advisor Eom Chang-rok defected, giving in to the ruling party's intimidation and conciliation. It was a tragic and heavy loss because Eom was an election campaign wizard. He'd helped me since the special election in Inje, Gangwon-do. His superb political ingenuity had disabled my opponent's governmental all-out election mobilization during the 1967 Mokpo election. He had the ability to read the state of affairs accurately and had exceptional insight into the public's psychology. Above all, he was a master of organization.

Under KCIA Director Lee Hu-rak's direct orders, intelligence agents intimidated his wife. "We cannot guarantee your husband's life. You decide what's best." Physically infirm, Eom yielded to money and intimidation. He left my campaign and disappeared amid rumors that intelligence agents had taken him to Hong Kong. If Eom Chang-rok had been in my camp, we could have at least prevented a great deal of the election fraud, and my campaign might have taken a different turn.

Also difficult for me was the fact that my competition within the party offered little to no aid. The only aid I did end up receiving was from party president Yu Jin-san, who went on his soapbox to bolster my campaign. Mr. Ko Heung-mun helped me with campaign fundraising as well.

The election campaign began to heat up, despite ominous signs and treacherous schemes. Popular will favored me—I could sense it during my canvassing tour. Although the Park regime was in its tenth year (including its military regime period), the ordinary person's life hadn't improved at all. Whenever I entered a rally, I could sense the burning desire for a true regime change. Together we chanted: "Ten full years of corrupt power— we can't stand it any longer. Let's change this regime!"

In both Gyeongsang-do and Jeolla-do, the audience gathered like clouds. Rally locations were completely packed several hours before my arrival. In large cities, hundreds of thousands of voters—and, in small towns, tens of thousands of people—were waiting for me. Five hundred thousand gathered in Busan and 300,000 in Daegu.

I was sad to see the audience's tired faces and shabby clothing. But when I saw their faces lighten up while listening to my speech, I felt something hot soaring inside my chest. I thought I wouldn't regret losing my life working for people who'd tirelessly worked for free will, people who kept on rising no matter how many times they were trampled upon.

I prayed to God to protect me and help me win for their sake. I prayed in the car, in bed, and at rallies. I gave more than ten speeches a day, each lasting about an hour. I traveled 400 to 500 kilometers a day, from early in the morning until ten at night or, sometimes, past midnight. The people called me Iron Man. Wherever I went, the audience crowded. When the crowd was in sight, I moved to a roofless car and entered the rally place, waving my hand. I ate rice, bread, and fruit in the car, always staying on the move. I fell asleep as soon as I closed my eyes. When I approached the next location, my guard woke me up. I moved to the roofless car, waved my hand, spoke, moved back to the car, ate, slept, and then delivered another speech. This went on all day long, day after day.

Believe it or not, the most difficult task was finding time to go to the bathroom. There were no bathroom facilities at the rally sites, and I couldn't just go anywhere in the field with all the cars around me. I had to carry a chamber pot in the car.

On November 13, 1970, twenty-two-year-old Jeon Tae-il, a worker at the Cheonggye Clothing Complex, committed suicide by setting himself on fire. I was utterly shocked by the incident, and heartbroken that he had to chant slogans such as "Enforce the labor code!" and "We are not machines!" even as his body was engulfed by flames. The poor labor conditions that had driven Jeon Tae-il to his death were not the problem of the Cheonggye Clothing Complex alone. All of Korea was a dark corner of human rights violations and laborer jeopardy. Jeon Tae-il had appealed to the crowds with his last words: "Don't let me die in vain!" I made a promise to myself that I *wouldn't* let him die in vain.

The Park regime had spent the past ten years suppressing laborers' needs in the name of economic development and modernization of the fatherland. Although the regime proclaimed the slogan "Construction First, Distribution Next," nothing was distributed to laborers in the end. Behind these grand slogans were the wretched lives of ordinary people. Although economic development in the 1960s was fueled by the blood and sweat of the working class, the fruits of their labor went only to a privileged few. Even the labor standard law, inept from today's perspective, was widely violated.

The Park regime's urban industry-centered economic policy drove young people out of their hometowns. In Seoul, the only jobs available were manual labor and factory work. Girls worked like slaves as maids. In the countryside, "so-and-so got a job in such-and-such a factory" was a source of pride, but the good children of the countryside could barely get by as factory workers. They still had to go to cities because the countryside was a land of despair.

In cities, the young floated on the outskirts of the city, driven out of the brilliant downtowns. They slept in illegal shacks in moon villages. The louder the slogan of economic development grew, the harder ordinary people's lives were. The propaganda tower of high growth, built on the backs of laborers, was doomed to collapse. Economic development was possible thanks only to wage exploitation; tragedy was inevitable. Jeon Tae-il condemned the tragic reality of laborer life by immolating his own body, and this event became the torchlight for the labor movement. It was hard to believe that the daily wages of a worker who labored sixteen hours a day in a windowless sweatshop was only 50 won, the price of a cup of tea. Although unspeakably sad, I thought his martyrdom would bloom as a sublime flower of the labor movement. It was an event of enormous significance in labor history.

I visited Jeon Tae-il's mother Madam Lee So-sun at her shack near Suyuri. I provided a house near Dongdaemun, where Jeon Tae-il's family, including his mother, could live. From that point on, Madam Lee So-sun worked hard and proudly for the improvement of labor conditions and Korean democracy. Mother carried out her son's wishes. Behind the great son there was an equally great mother.

THE AGE OF GENERALISSIMO TO COME (1971)

About ten days before Election Day, on April 18, 1971, a pivotal speaking event took place at Jangchungdan Park—one that may well be long memorialized in Korean history and, perhaps, even in world election campaign history. Roughly 1 million audience members were in attendance.

Although the event was scheduled to begin at 3:00 p.m., voters began to gather around 9:00 in the morning. By noon, not only the park, but also the roads—both the sidewalks and roadways—leading up to Jangchungdan Park from Toegye-ro, Yaksu-dong, and Hannam-dong were flooded with people. I left the Sinmin Party office around 2:00 p.m., and got in a roofless car near Anguk-dong Crossroads. Tens of thousands of people marched with my car from Jong-no to Jangchungdan Park. Every road was crowded with people. It took me more than an hour to walk from the car to the podium. Behind me, my wife's hair began to grow disheveled as she was jostled by the crowds on all sides. All of this told me how desperately people wanted a regime change and liberal democracy. It was a scene I'll never forget until the day I die.

The government and ruling party took various measures to prevent people from gathering at Jangchungdan Park. Government and public institution employees were required to attend group picnics with their family members. Those who did not attend were considered absent from work. Every theater and ancient palace in Seoul offered free admission. At 1:00 p.m., Changgyeong Palace hosted a Spring-welcoming Cherry Blossom Festival Show with performances by popular singers and comedians. According to police accounts, 360,000 people gathered to see the show. Although it was a Sunday, the Homeland Reserve Army was called out for an emergency training. The message was clear: Please do not go to Jangchungdan Park.

Nevertheless, the park overflowed with people. It was like a miracle. When I finally stood before the podium, all I could see was a sea of faces. I began my speech as passionately as I could: "My dear fellow citizens of Seoul! I respect and love you. Before I begin my address, I'd like to express a best wish to my opponent, Republican Party candidate Park Chung-hee, in front of you here. Citizens of Seoul! I have toured all over the country. The Korean people all across this country have risen to action for a definite regime change this time! From Gyeongsang-do, from Jeolla-do, from Chungcheong-do, and from Gangwon-do, the Korean people have risen up. Although I trusted that I'd definitely win this election after touring this country, I'm now even more confident telling you, after seeing more than a million audience members here—an unprecedented number not only in Korea, but also in the world—all gathered here in Jangchungdan Park, after hearing your roar, citizens of Seoul, I believe our victory is decisive.

"Ladies and gentlemen, if we fail to change the regime this time, our country will face the age of a generalissimo, the permanent Mr. Park Chung-hee regime. Although the Republican Party has tried to pursue Mr. Park Chung-hee's rule until our country's unification, they could not openly bring it up only because of the opposition from inside their party, the opposition party, and the Korean people. I have firm evidence that the Republican Party has plotted this scheme, and that the age of generalissimo, of permanent dictatorship without election, will come if Mr. Park Chung-hee wins this election."

The audience and I became one. A giant wave rose in the sea of people's will, as we all yearned for change together. I promised to abolish the KCIA, implement autonomous local governments, abolish the Homeland Reserve Army and military drills at schools, abolish school supporting fees, cleanse corruption, and implement a mass-participatory economic system. Whenever I raised my voice, the audience cheered. Their roars seemed on the verge of destroying Mt. Namsan, which loomed from behind the podium.

I finished my speech, saying, "The April 19th Revolution was a student-initiated revolution. May 16 was a military coup. Let us accomplish a great democratic revolution on April 27, neither by students nor by military, but by the united power of the people! Let us accomplish a peaceful regime change for the first time in our 5000-year history! Please, clap your hands and raise your voices to show your will to rise up with me.

"Thank you, ladies and gentlemen! I will win this election. You will win this election with me. Ladies and gentlemen, July 1 will be the day when a new president will be sworn in at the inauguration ceremony. To the 5,500,000 citizens of Seoul I say, 'Let us meet at the Blue House on July first!'"

Everywhere around Jangchungdan Park was pure excitement. It was a grand festival that showed that the people's will to oppose dictatorship was alive. It was an overwhelmingly moving experience for me, one I will never forget. The event ended around 6:30 p.m. When I got on the roofless car and waved, the audience surrounded me. The swarm of people marched through Dongdaemun and Jong-no to Gwanghwamun. The aftereffects lasted for a long time. Although I went in the direction of Sinseol-dong, the audience turned into demonstrators and marched on. Their chants shook downtown Seoul:

"Kim Dae-jung, Kim Dae-jung!"
"Regime change, regime change!"
"Number two won, Kim Dae-jung won!"
"Clean election, no third term!"

Pedestrians also joined in the chanting and procession. By the time they reached Danseongsa Theatre in Jong-no-3-ga, a crowd of more than 10,000 was present. They dispersed in Gwanghwamun well past 9:00 p.m., only after the riot police showered them with tear gas and pepper fog. It was the first demonstration to chant the words "regime change," "no third term," and "Kim Dae-jung" in downtown Seoul.

Candidate Park Chung-hee held a rally near Suseongcheon Brook in Daegu the same day. I heard that Candidate Park and the ruling party leaders were in utter shock after hearing the report about my event at Jangchungdan Park.

As the campaign season drew near its end, illegal, manipulative activities ran wild. The word "clean" had completely vanished. In the end, about sixty leaders of our society, including Kim Jae-joon, Lee Byung-rin, Cheon Gwan-u, and Nam Jung-hyun, formed the People's Council to Defend Democracy and made a statement on April 19:

1. We urge all people to look squarely at the destroyed basic democratic order of today and rise up to restore it.
2. We know that the upcoming election is a watershed moment in Korean democratic constitutional history, and we condemn all anti-democratic illegal and fraudulent actions as a historical crime in the name of Korean people.
3. We urge all people to solemnly exercise their sacred sovereignty, and flatly refuse to give in to political oppression and financial and other temptations.
4. We feel righteous indignation about the authorities' cruel suppression of students' peaceful demonstration and sternly protest it.

On the same day, the Nationwide Youth and Student Association to Defend Democracy issued a statement for clean election and freedom of the press. Two days later, on April 21, both the Youth Council to Defend Democracy and the Korean Branch of PEN international issued statements, also calling for a clean election and freedom of the press.

The regime's vile propaganda about me also ran wild. They condemned me for my promises to abolish the Homeland Reserve Army and to pursue peaceful reunification with the North, accusing me of being "a commie." They also tried to scare off my supporters by accusing them of being pro-communist.

Some newspapers also promoted regional antagonism by running articles about the "fateful antagonism" between Gyeongsang-do and Jeolla-do going back to the Three Kingdoms Period. This was an utter distortion of the situation. Before the Park regime, there was no regional antagonism whatsoever—citizens from Jeolla-do would live and be elected national assemblymen in Gyeongsang-do and vice versa. During the Park regime, however, they appointed only Gyeongsang-do natives to important governmental posts and invited enterprises to build factories and roads only in Gyeongsang-do, while neglecting Jeolla-do. The people from Jeolla-do had to move to Gyeongsang-do to get a job.

Television and radio stations and other mass media outlets were also mobilized to spread favorable images of Gyeongsang-do and negative images for Jeolla-do. Even regional dialects were discriminated. It was a frightening display of cultural discrimination, and a nation-dividing, nation-ruining plot. National Assembly Speaker Lee Hyo-sang openly urged, "Let us establish the Geyongsang-do regime by re-electing Candidate Park Chung-hee, a millennial leader since Silla."

Lee Hyo-sang also tried to instill regional antagonism in Daegu citizens. "An unhulled grain of rice will ruin cooked rice. If Jeolla-do-supporting votes mix with Gyeongsang-do votes, it's like mixing rice with foxtail millet. You mustn't vote for Kim Dae-jung."

The sentiment of Daegu's citizens was extremely negative after such base and extreme promotion of regional antagonism. Lee Hyo-sang lost in the National Assembly election a month after the presidential election. The people of Daegu punished his reckless remarks and actions.

The KCIA systematically distributed malicious propaganda fliers that read "Let us unite, fellow Jeolla-do residents!" all over Gyeongsang-do in order to provoke regional antagonism among the people of Gyeongsang-do. They coolly committed the crime of dividing Korea into east and west, when Korea was already divided into north and south.

Candidate Park Chung-hee also held a rally at Jangchungdan Park two days before Election Day. Naturally, the country paid attention to the audience size. The regime mobilized the audience, and so there were parades of cars headed toward Jangchungdan Park. The public said: "The audience *walked* to the opposition party event and *was carried* to the ruling party event." As expected, the audience was much smaller. Nevertheless, the media falsely reported that Candidate Park's audience was larger than mine.

At the Republican Party's rallying event, Candidate Park refuted my claim that he was plotting permanent dictatorship through a generalissimo system. "The opposition party is making false accusations that I would keep on assuming the reins of the government through a generalissimo system or something like it. The people haven't supported me to continue on and on as president through the 3-term constitutional amendment referendum, but to serve one more term. If you re-elect me this time, this will be my last political speech."

People might have heard the phrase "last political speech" and interpreted it to mean that he intended to retire after his third term. Media featured it that way. However, the plot to continue the regime's power without election and through emergency measures had been brewing within the regime ever since the three-term constitutional amendment. That was why Candidate Park didn't say he wouldn't continue to serve as president. In retrospect, this was a hint of the soon-to-come Yusin regime, where the president was indirectly elected.

That same day, I held a rally in Daegu, the home of President Park. Although Daegu was supposed to be a Republican Party stronghold, the citizens crowded Suseongcheon Brook. An audience of 300,000 attendees responded thunderously when I said, "If we don't complete this regime change, we'll be on the road to perpetual downfall and the age of Generalissimo Park Chung-hee will have arrived. I have evidence. The Republican Party has sent their associates to other countries to study the generalissimo system. There's a research institute that studies this very system on the eighth floor of the old Korean Air building in front of the Seoul Capitol building."

I was deeply encouraged by the enthusiastic audience response, especially because Daegu was Candidate Park's hometown. A government official visited me after the event and told me, "It looks like you'll win this time. Although there are many acquaintances of President Park in Daegu, 90 percent of my fellow employees support you, Mr. Kim."

April 27: Election Day arrived. I tried my best. The only remaining task was to prevent fraud during and after the voting. I knew the Sinmin Party alone couldn't prevent fraud. We absolutely lacked ballot-counting witnesses. Just in time, society leaders like Kim Jae-joon, Lee Byung-rin, and Cheon Gwan-u initiated a civilian ballot-counting witness movement. I ordered my Chief of Staff Kim Sang-hyun to aid in this. About 10,000 people, from groups of students to religious leaders to lawyers to writers, bravely volunteered to act as ballot-counting witnesses.

When the ballot-counting witnesses arrived in the Gyeongsang-do countryside, village leaders spoke through village speakers: "The cronies of that Jeolla-do fella have come. This election is a fight between Jeolla-do and Gyeongsang-do. If Kim Dae-jung is elected, the government employees and officials from Gyeongsang-do will all be fired. Kim Dae-jung's supporters are traitors. They must leave Gyeongsang-do."

It was incredible, and there was nothing we could do about it. In some places, they tried to bribe the witnesses, and if the witnesses refused to take the money, they met with mishaps; if they took the money, they had to look the other way at the fraud. The government employees in Daegu couldn't cast their votes freely; they received ballots with President Park's name already marked for them. They had to put those ballots in the ballot box and return their own ballots to the ruling party headquarters. Village chiefs failed to give ballots to opposition party supporters, preventing them from voting at all. Nobody knew where those missing ballots went.

Voting fraud continued to occur during ballot counting as well—even in my precinct. My wife and I voted at the Donggyo-dong 1st Precinct near our house a little after 7:00 a.m., amid domestic and foreign media attention. Believe it or not, 2700 ballots, including ours, were voided because they were missing the National Election Commission director's seal. Various forms of election fraud that the Sinmin Party and I had warned about—lost ballots, multiple and proxy voting—occurred systematically all across the nation.

Ballot-counting results seesawed in different regions until the tally's completion. The final tally was 6,342,828 votes for Park Chung-hee and 5,395,900 votes for Kim Dae-jung. Although I won the election virtually, I lost through voting and ballot counting. Professionals commented that I would have won by roughly a 1 million vote margin if the election were carried out cleanly. Nevertheless, I lost to the KCIA's election fraud operation and its instigation of regional antagonism. Although I fought my best fight, I was even more heartbroken because of the events that transpired. I pictured the simple and ardent faces of all those voters who had cheered and chanted my name wherever I went. *What if I had fought harder? What if we had fought to prevent election fraud better? What if the Sinmin Party had been more united? What if? What if?*

Still, I decided to let it go because the people's ardent desire for democracy was not in the past tense. I told myself that I would become calmer and stronger. I issued a statement that read:

"I thank you all. Everyone who supported me despite the Park regime's fundamental and comprehensive level of fraud, bribery, and terror. And I thank those intellectuals, religious leaders, journalists, and students who have voluntarily worked so hard to defend the people's rights and for a clean election.

"Personally, I feel extremely calm. But I cannot overlook the result of this illegal and corrupt election, in comparison to which the March 15th Fraudulent Election was nothing. At this point we can no longer expect regime change through election, not when the Korean people's ardent desire for a peaceful regime change has been so ruthlessly trampled upon. I will discuss my future actions with my party, but I can tell you one thing very clearly, and that is this: I have already devoted my life entirely to my country and people. I promise you, resolutely, that I will do my best to fulfill my responsibility according to my beliefs until the very end."

So many cried at the news of my defeat. Although I'd lost the election on a surface level, I won it because I'd won the people's minds and hearts. After the election, not only domestic but also foreign newspapers provided full reports of my good fight and speculated that I had been the real winner. The May 1 *Dong-A Ilbo* newspaper inspired great courage in me by publishing a column wherein the writer condemned the ruling party's instigation of regional antagonism:

Who's attempting national division in a country that is, as it was once said, smaller than a grasshopper's forehead?

No matter how he may like politics and covet the presidency, does he have to enjoy his personal wealth, honor, and distinction by dividing the nation? We must recriminate and punish this rash behavior in the name of our nation. If these actions are not properly handled, the future of our nation is hopeless. The Korean people need to broaden their perspective. When his nation and state faced crisis, didn't Napoleon of Corsican Island save France, and didn't Disraeli, a Jew, elevate the Privy Seal of Great Britain?

At any rate, Candidate Kim Dae-jung fought a great fight during this presidential election. He fully exhibited his God-given political abilities—his open-mindedness, his knowledge, and his honesty. He is now shining an expansive light over our nation like a comet. I cannot help asking him to act as a great tonic to our country's politics, so mired in muddy waters. There's a saying that winning or losing is an ordinary event for a man of arms. Therefore, some fights are won when they are lost, and others are lost when they're actually won. This is true of Candidate Kim Dae-jung and his battle.

Although he might be overwhelmed right now, Heaven might have given him this hardship only to entrust him with greater responsibility and hope.

As the saying goes, every cloud has a silver lining. We should not forget that human history has eventually always been on the side of the apostles of justice, who win even when they lose. The last chapter is the most important chapter in a person's biography. If our descendants read Candidate Kim's biography, they won't be able to suppress an even greater excitement and admiration because of middle chapters with these setbacks and disappointments during his bold fight against injustice and corruption that eat away the foundation of our country.

It was a generous evaluation. Still, it urged me to take on a greater responsibility. Since I'd lost the election I'd actually won, didn't this also mean that I'd won the election I'd lost? Still, as I expected, Park Chung-hee pursued a permanent dictatorship and the cruel time of Yusin regime was unfolding in front of us. Our nation and history might have entrusted me with great deal of responsibility, but my suffering was to be long and deep.

LONG CAMPAIGN MARCH (1971)

The government announced it would hold the National Assembly election on May 25, less than a month after the presidential election. After succeeding in the third-term presidential election, the Park regime wanted to use their momentum to take complete control over the National Assembly. It was a very difficult fight for the opposition party. There was really no time to take a breath—it was a surprise attack.

The day the regime made this announcement, the Sinmin Party issued a statement in which we wrote: "The April 27 election was a perfect crime plotted by the KCIA. It was an assassination of the opposition party by mobilizing every resource of our country." The statement condemned the ruling party for defrauding 3 million votes and openly instigating regional antagonism.

Unfortunately, at the same time this condemnation was under way, Sinmin Party President Yu Jin-san committed an act advantageous to the ruling party by giving up his Yeongdeungpo-gap precinct in Seoul to Park Chung-hoon, an unknown young man, and registering as the prime candidate from the national constituency. As this was the last day of registration, this incident, dubbed the Jin-san Crisis, was irrevocable. It was a thunderbolt from a clear blue sky. If he ran from his original precinct, he could have won without even campaigning. His abrupt betrayal begot many rumors. We all thought there had been some sort of backdoor deal between him and the ruling party as the ruling party candidate was Chang Deok-jin, President Park's relative by marriage.

Party nomination was supposed to have been decided through a discussion between President Yu and me, the party's presidential candidate. But, as soon as I lost the presidential election, my power and influence diminished rapidly. During our discussion of the national constituency the morning he gave up his precinct, President Yu didn't mention his intention to me. That afternoon, he dropped the bombshell. It was crystal clear that it was going to be a severe blow, not only to President Yu, but also to the entire party.

After hearing this news, young party members rushed to the National Election Commission. They surrounded President Yu and demanded he show them the national constituency document. Mr. Yu was unable to submit the document to the committee, and escaped to the National Election Commission director's office where he registered our party's national constituency nominees behind locked doors. His name topped the list. There was no dignity in his actions and I still wonder how he was corrupted to that degree.

President Yu remained locked in the National Election Commission director's office for an hour. After he returned home, the party members of Yeongdeungpo-gap precinct, his current precinct, surrounded his house and railed on him for his betrayal. Within just a few minutes, hundreds of citizens gathered around his home, shouting: "Jin-san is the number one national constituency candidate!" or "Jin-san sold our precinct!"

During this protest, about one hundred upset party members broke into his house while party headquarter members supporting President Yu tried to block them. Doors and windows were broken and many of those involved were injured. It was a tragedy inevitable for an opposition party led by a wrong leader.

The next day, every newspaper condemned this grotesque and unprecedented event. People everywhere cursed President Yu and our party. Our party's soaring popularity sank overnight. Public opinion toward us was cold, and our party was in despair.

On May 7, party leaders and elders gathered at my house to discuss how to rescue our party from this crisis. Although they asked me to

ing. My injuries from the accident were compounded by the fact that I kept on my stump schedule until midnight without getting proper treatment.

Despite the Jin-san Crisis at the beginning of the campaign, our party did well. The public's sense of crisis and belief that democracy would be annihilated the way things stood now had been revived. I believe my long campaign march also contributed to this. It helped that the Republican Party could no longer commit systematic election fraud like before thanks to the condemnation of their actions during the presidential election. They couldn't ignore it and publicly announced toward the end of the campaign that they'd cancel the results if any signs of election fraud were found.

Our party made rapid progress, winning 89 out of 204 seats. Fringe parties won only two seats. The margin was very slim, with the Republican Party winning 48.7 percent and the Sinmin Party winning 44.3 percent. The public chose two parties, thus consolidating the two-party system.

The election results in Seoul particularly stood out. The Sinmin Party won all precincts except for Yeongdeungpo-gap. Our party could have won every precinct if President Yu hadn't acted in such a strange manner.

In Busan, the opposition party won six out of eight seats. In Daegu— President Park's so-called stronghold—the opposition party won four out of five seats. In particular, young, lesser-known opposition party candidates defeated the heavyweight ruling party leaders. The loss of Assembly Speaker Lee Hyo-sang, who fanned regional antagonism by arguing for the Gyeongsang-do regime, was the talk of the town for a while.

The opposition party wind was a typhoon in the cities. Republican Party strongholds collapsed everywhere. To the ruling party leaders, the wind was "the wintry north wind in May." From the national constituency, the opposition party won twenty-four seats, well beyond the expected eighteen, while the ruling party won only twenty-seven seats out of fifty-one. The Sinmin Party had assumed a dignified status as a national party, which many had not expected in the early phases of the election campaign. The people's judgments were severe.

KIM DAE-JUNG VANISHED FROM MEDIA (1971)

In July 1971, I ran for party president. The public hoped I would lead the way toward building a strong opposition party. However, the actual state of the party at the time was another matter. As time passed, Mr. Yu Jin-san began to dream of a comeback. Although he knew he couldn't step forward because of adverse public opinion, he supported Mr. Kim Hong-il, someone with no party basis. Other young leaders who had argued for forties leadership and competed for the presidential candidacy with me also supported Mr. Yu Jin-san's proposal as a means of checking my rise to power. Mr. Yang El-dong also ran for the position, so I had to fight against two opponents.

In the aftermath of the accident, my physical condition deteriorated significantly. Despite treatment, my leg was getting worse; the doctors said my left hip joint was in bad shape. I was mentally tired as well. I couldn't fully devote myself to the election campaign.

As if all of this wasn't enough, once again the KCIA systematically interfered with this election within our party. Their goal was, of course, to make me lose the election. Intimidation and bribery were openly carried out against my supporters. During the first round of voting at the temporary party convention at the Seoul National Hall on July 20, no one won a majority. The second round of voting that immediately followed didn't produce a clear winner, either. I lost the third round of voting the following day. The public's wishes and the party's decisions were two different things.

Thousands of supporters who had gathered from all over the country stood in the rain chanting my name. These supporters wanted our party rebuilt; they wanted it to become an entity deserving of the title "opposition party." They cheered me, but cursed the party leaders who opposed me. Nevertheless, I could not become party president. The Jin-san faction was alive and well, despite scandals and suspicions of corruption. Although the Korean people wanted President Kim Dae-jung, our party was ruled by factionalism. It was a tragedy.

When I lost the party election, my supporters were so upset some of them became violent. They collided with the other faction supporters in the conference hall and, in the process, some people were hurt and a few facilities were broken. Assuming I was behind it all, the police fabricated a premeditated incident, planned by myself and my staff; however, the subsequent investigation cleared our name.

Although I lost, the Korean people continued to support me, which surprised even me. I believe that this kind of explosive interest in the party election was unprecedented in Korean political history. I still lost.

The aftermath of the presidential election and traffic accident left me ill in bed from the exhaustion of non-stop campaigning. It was painful not only physically, but also psychologically. I'd worked so hard, canvassing the country day and night, risking my own life, and now where was I? What had I gained? It all seemed so perfectly futile.

Even at this, the regime tried to bury me, to cripple me politically so that I could never dream of becoming President Park's opponent. The people knew it. Wherever I went, KCIA agents followed me. Our house phone was tapped day and night. They rented a few houses around mine and staked out my whereabouts without pause, often taking pictures of my visitors. The atmosphere in the alley of my house—the house the media called "Donggyo-dong"—was brutal.

After the election, more than a hundred businessmen were dragged to KCIA offices to be investigated about whether they had contributed to my campaign. They were then forced to promise in writing that they would never contribute to my campaign. My secretaries and bodyguards were also under surveillance. Sometimes, the KCIA offered a small carrot to win them over.

My name disappeared from the media, including newspapers, TV, and radio broadcasts. The KCIA agents censored everything every day. They even blocked me from running any advertisements. Announcements of any of my upcoming speeches published in the first print of a newspaper disappeared in subsequent printings.

It became exceedingly difficult to rent space for my speeches. When I did manage to rent a space, I received a call to cancel the contract immediately after booking. Agents were in charge of censoring and destroying my letters at the post office. Sometimes they took my letters out of their original envelopes and, instead, stuffed the envelopes with a ghost organization's handouts that condemned me. The KCIA's oppression was cruel and persistent.

Demands for democracy exploded. Accumulated complaints about a ten-year dictatorship began to ripple across the country. Due to the regime's dictatorship and a failed economic policy that discriminated against small businesses and adopted unprincipled tax systems, the grass roots suffered greatly. It's no wonder they rose up.

The Judicial Branch Crisis occurred on July 28. It originated from Judge Lee Bum-lyul's conscientious dismissal of National Security Law and Anti-communism Law violation cases and consistent practice of finding those indicted innocent. The dictatorial regime found him impertinent and sought an arrest warrant for his acceptance of a bribe from relevant parties that treated him during a business trip to Jeju Island.

It was clear this was retaliation. The prosecutor repeatedly sought an arrest warrant for him to no avail. In protest of this outrage, 37 fellow Seoul District Criminal Court judges resigned, and 153 judges in other districts joined in sympathy. The judges resolutely declared the judicial branch independent and demanded the elimination of outside pressure. They pierced the rampant power with the blade of law.

The Great Gwangju (later, Seongnam) Complex Incident followed in August. Before the elections, the city of Seoul evacuated about 140,000 urban poor to a 2-million-pyeong land in Gwangju-gun, Gyeonggi-do, with promises that they would build a new city in its place. However, it was a plan with no budget, and as soon as the elections ended, the Gwangju residents were left alone in a wasteland. The residents of Gwangju organized a committee to handle their situation and sent petitions to relevant offices to no avail. The residents then changed their committee to a more aggressive one and requested an interview with the mayor of Seoul. He did not respond. Riots erupted as angry residents set fire to police branch offices and other facilities.

The next serious incident, the Silmido Incident, occurred on August 23 when Special Forces troops, who had been trained to travel secretly to North Korea, appeared in the Daebang-dong thoroughfare in Yeongdeungpo-gu, Seoul. They had escaped Silmido Island near Incheon after killing a number of guards. In the end, all escapees were killed following a fierce gunfight with the military and police.

I was very surprised, but I also thought these runaway troops were victims of a political situation where the Cold War and détente intersected. Although they'd been trained to be sent to North Korea as spies, the plan was halted because of the détente current the US was riding. After losing their purpose and goal, they were practically abandoned on an isolated island. As each pointless day went by, they ended up throwing themselves to their own deaths. They were victims, discarded by the state.

On September 15, Hanjin Company workers broke into the Korean Air Building, demanding their back pay be cleared for disbursement. Although the company was flourishing with special demands because of the Vietnam War, the workers who'd been working in Vietnam were not being paid on time. Frustrated and furious, laborers set fire to the office and held out against the police for more than four hours until the police violently suppressed them, eventually arresting sixty-six workers in all.

Korea's entire society was rotting and seething from the inside. Every morning, we woke up to new incidents and crises. Even the Dongdaemun Market merchants organized themselves and protested against the government for a tax system favoring large businesses. Seoul National University Hospital interns demanded better treatment, while college professors protested against KCIA interference and pressure in schools.

The political and social situation in the country was extremely unstable. Our party demanded that cabinet members in charge of public security—Interior Minister O Chi-seong, Minister of Justice Shin Chik-soo, and Vice Prime Minister and Minister of the Economic Planning Board Kim Hak-nyeol—step down. The government did not accept this demand, though, so we proposed a vote of non-confidence at the National Assembly on September 29.

A subtle political current was underlying the Republican Party at that time. The Gang of Four (Party Chairman Baek Nam-eok, Policy Planning Committee Chair Kil Chae-ho, Central Committee Chair Kim Seong-gon, and Finance Committee Chair Kim Chin-man) sought to remove Interior Minister O Chi-seong. O had dismissed followers from the Gang of Four from the posts of police officials, mayors, and *gun*-magistrates through a large-scale personnel shake-up.

On October 2, the Gang of Four mobilized their followers at the National Assembly and petitioned a vote for the dismissal of the cabinet members. Out of a total of 203 votes, the result was 107 for the motion, 90 against it, and the rest invalid. Park Chung-hee was furious, and ordered a search for the leaders of this mutiny. KCIA agents dragged the Gang of Four to their Namsan safe house, where they were stripped naked and beaten like dogs. Assemblyman Kim Seong-gon's characteristic long, upturned moustache was pulled off and Assemblyman Kil Chae-ho was left all but dead. In the end, Kim Seong-gon and Kil Chae-ho had to withdraw from the Republican Party and automatically lost their status as assemblymen.

The Gang of Four, which had challenged Park Chung-hee's authority, was made to suffer all manner of insults and indignity before its collapse. Their stronghold was left weaker than a sand castle. Authority other than or successive to President Park could never grow within the Republican Party. No one even dared to dream of it. A direct government system by the king-like President Park was complete.

Although the state of affairs was troubling, the Sinmin Party wasn't behaving like an opposition party. Instead, it was rapidly drifting apart. While the four assemblymen were illegally detained and tortured, I argued for our party assemblymen to march into KCIA headquarters and condemn this brutality. I believed the ruling party members wanted this desperately, too. It wasn't something we should just sit by and look on at. After all, their immoral and illegal clubbing could direct itself at us at any time. It was a clear disturbance of our national order. "Let's all march to

Namsan," I argued. "If there are any laws and conscience in this country, they can't do this to national assemblymen. Let's say that we'll be glad to endure the same treatment if they aren't released immediately. These illegal actions are not just a matter for the ruling party."

Despite my earnest appeals, the Sinmin Party took no action. My words were often ignored because I belonged to the non-mainstream group. In the end, we lost a great chance to put a halt to KCIA violence and reprove the Park regime for its tyranny. On October 23, I condemned the KCIA's absurd and evil actions directly during the plenary session interpellation. "Currently, the KCIA is an omnipotent tyrant in this country. There is nothing they cannot do. During the election, they created a false new party, planned and executed election fraud, interfered with the ruling party nomination, plotted to divide the opposition party … the KCIA, whose responsibility should be to protect us from communists, has complete control over our domestic politics. The media's ability to report and criticize freely is greatly restricted because of KCIA pressure. KCIA agents frequent media companies and harass them in many various ways.

"Nobody, including artists and educators, can survive if they offend the KCIA. The KCIA even interferes with the Actors Association presidential election. In our country, the people might be able to criticize our prime minister or president, but they can't criticize the KCIA. The power the KCIA currently wields is absolute, reigning over the three branches of the government.

"As for the National Assembly, the KCIA clubbed and threatened assembly members who opposed the 3-term constitutional amendment. And the KCIA is now repeating the same behavior. It is now completely trampling on the National Assembly. By the way things are going these days, we'll all be the KCIA's slaves soon enough.

"I'm very sorry to say this to Prime Minister Kim Jong-pil, who's here now, but currently, no department in the administration can oppose the KCIA's orders and demand. Furthermore, officials are trembling with fear, worried that they might be summoned and interrogated by the KCIA. Those of you, prime minister, cabinet members, and assemblymen here: Is there even a single person whose phone has not been tapped by the KCIA? We now don't have the freedom of a private life. Even if I lose my life condemning the KCIA for their tyranny, even if I'm sacrificed to intelligence politics, I cannot be silent about what I believe in."

Around this time, college students found themselves being harassed as well. When active military officers were sent to college campuses to assume charge of the students' military drills, the students responded by collectively protesting the Park regime's clear attempt at militarizing college campuses. As a former presidential candidate who'd promised to abolish student military drills, I was very interested in their response.

On October 15, 1971, the Park regime implemented the Garrison Decree, using students' demonstrations against campus military drills as an excuse. The Garrison Decree was an executive order that enabled military troops to station themselves in certain areas to guard and protect people and key structures. Armed soldiers and armored vehicles began taking residence all over the nation's campuses; from afar, the college campuses looked like military bases. Armed military forces fired teargas randomly. As demonstrations intensified, the attorney general declared that arresting students without warrants was inevitable. Shortly after, the police arrested thousands of students.

Despite all of this, the opposition party remained inactive. In fact, contrary to expectations, the Sinmin Party published a statement suggesting that some student demonstration appeared excessive. The Sinmin Party was no different from the administration. Thanks to the tepid attitude of the opposition party, the ruling party felt no hesitation in pushing through their agenda. The Sinmin Party was inept at deliberating the budget. They passed the bill without opposition when the president threatened grave measures if the assembly wouldn't pass it by November 2.

Later that month, I traveled to Japan's Keiko University Hospital to treat my intensifying hip joint pain. While there, I met Minister of Commerce and Industry Tanaka Kakuei and Minister of Foreign Affairs Fukuda Takeo to discuss the state of current affairs in Korea. On December 6, I heard the news that President Park had declared the nation to be in a state of national emergency under the pretext of imminent North Korean invasion. "In order to protect our country from the communist invasion, we must restrict the people's freedom for a while. We are restricting the freedom of the press and freedom of assembly. Additionally, the president will have the privilege of using a part of the government budget freely as needed." This Declaration of National Emergency gave President Park authority above the law. I realized that President Park was finally beginning to show the tip of his bloodthirsty desire for long-term reign. Although my treatments had not ended, I rushed home on December 16.

I was away for less than a month, but a sea of change had swept through Korea. The Park regime had created a sense of crisis in the country, as if the North Korean invasion was imminent. Media outlets constantly broadcast images of North Korean military marches and drills as if they were live images. The Korean people were thrown into confusion; some believed the regime's propaganda and prepared for evacuation.

To me, the Park regime's intentions were crystal clear: The people's demand for democratization could not be oppressed anymore, so they must have realized they could no longer maintain their power without resorting to emergency measures. Park's last resort for permanent reign was to create tension by using North Korea.

The world, however, was beginning to emerge from the Cold War. In January of 1971, the phone line between East and West Berlin was reconnected. In April, China invited America's national table tennis team over as part of their "ping pong diplomacy." I made statements exposing the Park regime's hardline measures as flying against the détente trends of the world and concealing the regime's ultimate plans. "The latest series of hardline measures are nothing other than false propaganda aimed at strengthening this dictatorial regime. It is realistically impossible for North Korea to invade. Also, there have been no signs or ground movements detected whatsoever. All of their allegations are groundless."

I made statements despite the risk of bodily harm, but my appeals fell on deaf ears. Although I made these statements at live press conferences, not a single word I said was reported in the newspapers. Critiques of the regime were no longer newsworthy. So I tried to organize a speaking tour, but any assembly—and *especially* one where I was scheduled to speak—was thoroughly blocked.

I decided to visit the US and Europe to directly observe the rapidly changing state of world affairs. Honestly, I also hoped I could get a breath of fresh air for a little bit, away from the bloodthirsty atmosphere of the dictatorial regime I was now living in. I toured the US, England, Sweden, Denmark, West Germany, and France. I met various leaders in each of these countries and exchanged opinions. They all encouraged me, supporting my ideas about increased inter-Korean dialogues and interchanges and peaceful reunification. It was encouraging to confirm that people in many other countries were in support of my ideas; that they believed the promises I'd made during my presidential campaign were timely and appropriate.

But when I looked back at Korea, my home, from the vantage point of these advanced countries, I felt even more miserable. The Park regime's attempts to draw a stream of Cold War anxieties to bolster its dictatorship were truly pitiable and ridiculous. But when I thought of the Korean people, suffering and frustrated, my heart was truly in pain.

Even Japan—let alone America—refused to pay attention to the North Korean invasion theory that President Park repeated every opportunity he had. Countries all over the world condemned him, both directly and indirectly. Korea was isolated from the world. The Korean people were coming to realize President Park's claims were false as well.

THREE-STEP UNIFICATION PROPOSAL (1972)

On July 3, the administration announced it would publish a very important statement the next day. The Korean people weren't very anxious since they had heard too many so-called very important statements. The Park regime had declared too many emergencies. Also, because the regime announced oppressive policies to shift phases whenever it confronted a regime crisis, the Korean people had developed negative assumptions about the administration's trumpeted announcements.

But things were different this time. At a press conference, KCIA Director Lee Hu-rak announced that there would be a South-North Joint Communiqué on July 4. For a while, the public was so stunned that no one knew what to say. The media flooded outlets with special reports and extras. The country was on the edge of its seat. Reunification seemed imminent.

Before I go on, though, I'll provide a little background about this statement where the South and the North were seemingly ready to agree on grand principles of independent and peaceful reunification. Since the beginning of the 1970s, international politics rode the wave of détente. US President Nixon announced the White Paper, dubbed the Nixon Doctrine, on February 18, 1970. He declared that the US would no longer send ground troops to Asia, and that it would adopt a more flexible approach to communist countries. The US suggested it might withdraw from Vietnam and reduce troops from South Korea as well.

In April 1971, the fifteen-member US table tennis team, which attended the World Table Tennis Championships in Nagoya, Japan, along with four reporters, abruptly decided to visit China as well. The US team toured a number of major Chinese cities, including Beijing, Shanghai, and

Guangzhou, and played a series of friendly matches. This ping pong diplomacy was a historical event that proceeded to open the Bamboo Curtain. In July of 1971, Nixon sent Henry Kissinger, a superb secret envoy, to China. In February 1972, President Nixon himself visited China.

The Cold War system that had lasted almost a quarter century was beginning to collapse. Having already removed 20,000 troops from Korea, Nixon was also expecting a détente in the Korean Peninsula.

During the last election, the Park regime had also clearly seen that people no longer favored it; they needed a new strategy to shift phases. On May 2, 1972, President Park sent Lee Hu-rak to Pyongyang as his secret envoy. On May 29, North Korea's Second Vice-Premier Pak Sung-chul secretly visited Seoul. Following these clandestine meetings, they announced the July 4 South-North Joint Communique simultaneously signed by Lee Hu-rak and Kim Young-ju in Seoul and Pyongyang, respectively. They essentially agreed on central matters: they sought to achieve independent and peaceful reunification; to refrain from vilifying each other; to implement multifaceted exchange; and to establish direct phone contacts between Seoul and Pyongyang. The solemn statement the two sides made at the end was quite moving: "The parties solemnly swear to faithfully abide by the agreement, as desired by all of our countrymen."

The entire country welcomed this announcement. It was, above all, great news, but, frankly, it was also very confusing to me. I'd known of KCIA Director Lee Hu-rak traveling to and from North Korea, but I didn't expect this kind of sudden agreement. Just ten days earlier, on June 25, President Park declared the country to be in a state of national emergency against the communist threat, and made harsh attacks against North Korea in his address on the twenty-second anniversary of the Korean War. He claimed, "You cannot trust communists. They are unreliable. Twenty-two years ago, North Korea suddenly invaded South Korea after they proposed an exchange between Mr. Cho Man-sik, a Korean patriot detained in the North, and imprisoned communists in South Korea. We should not be deceived by North Korean peace offensive."

It was incredible and inexcusable to say this and then to deceive his people while receiving reports from his secret envoy and signing a joint agreement behind their backs.

The regime that had dragged so many to prison for arguing for détente in the Korean Peninsula, the regime that had accused so many ordinary citizens of being pro-communist for merely mentioning North Korea—that very same regime was now suddenly promising to establish a South-North dialogue and achieve peaceful reunification. How many of us—including me—were frustrated because of this violent oppression? It was a crime to argue for reunification, but it was acceptable for an administration to change its policies without asking the people's will?

How much of this is true? Why did North Korea agree to this? Does President Park really intend to pursue détente with the North? My head was full of questions, but I decided to accept it all at face value. After all, détente in the Korean Peninsula and peaceful reunification was what *I* had proposed. I had to support a statement that reflected my policies, so I welcomed it conditionally. On July 13, I issued a statement entitled "The South-North Joint Communiqué and My Arguments" at a foreigners' gathering in Seoul: "In principle, I support and welcome The South-North Joint Communiqué. However, I argue that President Park is not qualified to pursue this policy, and I seriously wonder if he isn't abusing this sacred and important national task as tool to cement his permanent rule.

"It is true that this joint statement is a great breakthrough in a 27-year period of complete severance and absolute hatred and confrontation for our nation. It will also contribute significantly to peace and the easing of tensions in Asia. It agrees to the contemporary worldwide trend of peace while recognizing the status quo. Above all, this joint statement corresponds with what I have argued so far.

"I have continued to oppose President Park's belligerent and unfriendly policy toward North Korea and have argued for a peaceful and open policy. In particular, during the last year's presidential election, I proposed to pursue South-North relations and diplomacy toward the communist bloc, as well as peace and security on the Korean Peninsula backed by the four powerful countries of the US, Japan, the USSR, and China. Recently, I also presented a three-step reunification proposal, the essence of which was peaceful coexistence of the South and North Koreas, expansion of various forms of dialogue between the two, and eventual peaceful reunification.

"President Park not only viciously condemned my proposal during the election campaign, but also declared a national emergency, claiming that North Korean invasion was imminent. I welcome the fact that President Park has since given up on those unwise policies, though belatedly, and has shifted his policy completely."

I then listed three reasons why President Park was not qualified to pursue this new policy.

"First, he deceived voters who supported him, and ridiculed all Koreans. During the last election, President Park thoroughly excluded any possibility of contact between the South and the North. Since the May 16 military coup d'état, he not only severely punished anyone who discussed reunification, but also consistently banned all reunification discussions, accusing them of being pro-communist.

"Second, the way President Park pursued the current measure was extremely anti-democratic and dangerous. While plotting this fundamental policy shift from his election promise, he neither asked for Korean people's understanding beforehand nor even went so far as to announce his intentions to the National Assembly and opposition party.

"Third, it's become obvious that President Park intends to take advantage of this joint statement and use it to strengthen his dictatorial regime and permanent reign."

Then, I presented three demands to President Park.

"First, President Park should withdraw the national emergency decree which now lost any cause for existence, and he should immediately abolish the National Security Law.

"Second, he should eliminate the unhappy shadow covering today's Republic of Korea. He should eliminate all dictatorial practices, guarantee maximum freedom of the people, guarantee people a decent living by discarding privilege-based economic policies that only widen the gap between the wealthy and the poor, implement a mass-participatory economic policy, and resolutely reform domestic administration by cleansing corruption and irrationality so that we would be guaranteed our 'conscience.'

"Third, President Park should govern with more honesty and humility as the president of a democratic country with the sovereignty of the people. Above all, he should clearly tell the people if he really intends to hand over the regime according to the people's will, and if he intends to run for the presidency again in 1975."

Before this press conference, I also proposed that both the South and the North simultaneously join the UN. It was an unconventional proposal. Not only did the ruling party oppose it, but so too did the Sinmin Party. They argued that North Korea was a puppet government so we could not acknowledge it. Only eleven months later, though, President

Park made the June 23rd Statement, which included a proposal that was exactly the same as mine.

In the end, the July 4th South-North Joint Communiqué, which excited the entire peninsula, ended up being quietly dropped by both Korean administrations after a few inter-Korean meetings wherein both parties pretended to explore one another's intentions. The statement only helped both regimes consolidate their power bases. Only three months after the joint statement, President Park enforced the October Yusin and began his reign of terror. Based on the fact that the regime had prepared for the Yusin system long before the July 4th South-North Joint Communiqué, we could not help but conclude they had planned to draw the curtain of dictatorship after seducing people with rosy reunification plans. On December 27 of that same year, when President Park was elected a permanent president through indirect election at the so-called National Council for Reunification, North Korea announced an amended Supreme People's Assembly Law establishing the state chairman position.

The July 4th South-North Joint Communiqué was a temporary rainbow that rose to the top of the clouds amid an international current of détente. But it was just an illusion—it disappeared before people could even stop cheering for it.

Before I go on, I'd like to talk a little about my vision of reunification. I have long firmly believed there cannot be true peace and prosperity in our nation without reunification. We have maintained a unified nation for more than a 1000 years since the Unified Silla. Therefore, this phase of division is but a brief moment in our long history; however, reunification cannot occur just by having sentimental hopes for it. We need to have a concrete, realistic plan.

The Park regime presented a plan to reunify through a general election under the supervision of the UN. However, this plan had many conditions attached to it that North Korea could never accept. I'd criticized this reunification plan throughout the sixth- and seventh-term National Assembly, and tried to prepare an alternative. I arrived at the conclusion that, under the current circumstances, it would be best to phase in the steps for reunification. Considering the twenty years of consolidated division, this was the only realistic plan for accomplishing peaceful reunification through the process of reconciliation and cooperation. I announced this plan in front of domestic and foreign reporters at the National Press Club during my visit to the US in February 1971. "I'd like to lay the foundation for reunification through three steps: easing tension through promises to give up armed reunification attempts; establishing non-military interchanges of reporters, letters, and sports; and laying down a political and economic dialogue."

I thought long and hard about how to prepare these statements. Even now, I feel that my three-step reunification plan was quite innovative under the circumstances, especially considering the Park regime's anti-communism and their argument for the eradication of communism. Although I was subject to all kinds of accusations and oppression because of this proposal, I am proud that the Korean people and the whole world later supported and sympathized with my proposal as the most reasonable and peaceful plan. I discussed it with domestic and overseas specialists and analyzed the international situation. My three-step reunification proposal can be summarized as follows.

The first step was for both parties to promise not to provoke war and to agree to peacefully coexist. Both parties need to acknowledge one another's presence, stop insulting each other, and curb any aggressive military outbreaks like the Sino-Japanese War or the Russo-Japanese War. For this, I explained that it was best for us to induce the four powerful countries to a cease-fire agreement, and then for both South and North Koreas to together receive recognition in international society. At the same time, I proposed that the four powerful countries guarantee security on the Korean Peninsula, that North Korea attend the UN, and that both Koreas simultaneously become members of the UN. At the same time, I urged that South Korea establish an embassy in Beijing and Moscow, while North Korea send its envoys to Tokyo and Washington, DC.

The second stage of my plan was to expand peaceful interchange—between reporters, and in the fields of culture, arts, and sports—and also to freely listen to one another's broadcasts. It was also important to pursue practical economic collaboration item by item.

After accomplishing these inter-Korean dialogues and recovering trust between South and North Korea—and, thus, successfully obtaining national consensus for the complete reunification—we could achieve peaceful reunification by the third stage. Over and over, I argued: "The Korean people have had no voice in discussions for reunification. Reunification needs to occur for all Korean people, both South and North, not just for both regimes."

I also thought we needed a reunification model that guaranteed mutual coexistence. It was obvious that reunification where one side would conquer the other would have enormous aftereffects. I thought we needed to recognize each nation's independence before reunification, and that we needed to decide on a system according to the people's free will only after complete reunification. For this, we needed to maintain two systems under one nation.

Although currently unified, Germany was then divided. Germany chose the "one nation, two states" approach. West and East Germany didn't develop a relationship with one another for the sake of reunification, but, rather, for coexistence. Not only the USSR, but also most of Western Europe, did not want a German reunification.

In the case of the Koreas, however, no other country would interfere with our reunification because there was no reason for it. The powerful nations surrounding Korea had no reason to fear our reunification. What worried them was that one nearby power would take advantage of a unified Korea. If we could calm this concern through certain guarantees, then there was no reason why any country would not want a Korean reunification.

Also, because Germany had been defeated even though they were the aggressor, they did not have much say on the matter of their reunification. Korea, on the other hand, was neither a defeated country nor an occupied one. Korea was divided because of the influence of foreign powers. Thus, there was no reason for them to not cooperate and there was no reason to interfere with reunification plans. We were radically different from Germany in this aspect. If we had the will, reunification was closer at hand to us than to Germany.

The Park regime ruthlessly attacked my three-step reunification proposal, making thousands of cuts to it. Park Chung-hee, the Republican Party, and several media outlets distorted my proposal and attacked me, claiming I was pro-communist and a commie. My proposal for peaceful reunification was leveraged as a major excuse for my persecution by the Park regime, subjecting me to kidnapping, house arrest, and imprisonment. Still, I have never wavered in my belief in peaceful reunification.

My three-step reunification proposal has continuously evolved. This evolution was due not only to a change of circumstance in the Korean Peninsula, but also to my constant research for a better solution to the reunification problem.

In the mid-1980s, I announced the Federal Republic Reunification Proposal, which consisted of three stages: (1) establishing peaceful coexistence and interchange, (2) creating a federal republic, and (3) complete reunification.

In the first stage, the South and the North would coexist and exchange dialogue under the umbrella of a symbolic federal organization, which is one stage of union. Independent governments in the South and the North would maintain autonomy in matters of diplomacy, domestic politics, and the military, while the federal government would remain in charge of peaceful coexistence and dialogue as a symbolic institution.

In the second stage, the federal government would assume responsibility for diplomacy, national defense, and major internal politics, while autonomous local governments would exist in the South and the North. In the third stage, the country would achieve reunification on the foundation established through peaceful coexistence and dialogue.

The big change in this version of my proposal was the idea of introducing a symbolic federal institution consisting of representatives of each government while leaving each government to maintain its existing authority. Over my long years of imprisonment, exile, and house arrest, I'd never stopped thinking about reunification. I visited professionals and scholars wherever I went. I looked and looked and asked and asked.

I compiled thirty years' worth of thoughts about the issue in *Kim Dae-jung's Three-step Reunification Proposal*, published in August 1995. Here, I presented my grand ideas in the form of concrete plans and thoughts. One could summarize the progression of my plans as establishing a confederacy that grows into a federation and ultimately results in a reunification, all stages of which are based on the principles of independence, peace, and democracy.

In the first stage of confederacy, we would establish collaborative institutions such as the Confederacy Summit, the Confederacy Council, and the Confederacy Cabinet Meeting, all the while maintaining separate sovereign and authoritative governments in the South and the North. These confederacy institutions would be in charge of carrying out programs to further the three principles: peaceful coexistence, peaceful interchange, and peaceful reunification.

In the second stage of federation, the federal government would assume charge of diplomacy, national security, and major domestic politics, and institute a federal president and assembly, all the while maintaining autonomous local governments in the South and the North. In the final stage of complete reunification, we would establish either a central government or a more refined federal government. The ideology and regime of the unified country would naturally base itself on democracy, market economy, an ethically advanced country, and pacifism.

On May 10, Mother passed away at my house in Donggyo-dong. She'd converted to Catholicism right before her death. Without Mother I could not have been who I am today. Without her warm love and teachings, how could I have dreamed of becoming a light in this world? If I have tried hard to live a righteous and just life, it is because of Mother's gift to me. If she didn't persuade Father to move to Mokpo, I might have lived on that remote island all my life. She died before I could properly fulfill my filial duties.

Throughout my mother's life, I kept on losing elections. I was imprisoned and twice survived death by the skin of my teeth. Whatever my intentions, it was unfilial. Mother always had to worry; nevertheless, she never showed her worry and bravely faced all hardships. In retrospect, her presence was a huge source of power and courage. Many people, including the vice prime minister and the leaders of ruling and opposition parties, paid their respects at her funeral. I feel now it was fortunate that she passed away when she did because my life had even worse turns in store after her death. If she were to experience them all, how anxious she would have been! How sad to think that she would have seen me wander around foreign lands in exile only five months later.

Still, the empty space she left behind was wide and deep.

THE OCTOBER YUSIN AND EXILE (1972)

I went to Japan again on October 11, 1972, so that Professor Koto Yuichiro could treat my leg. After the treatment, I was able to walk much better. Two days before I was to return home, my friend Choe Seo-myeon called me from Seoul around 5:00 p.m.

"Do you know there will be an important presidential announcement?" he asked.

"I haven't heard about it. Do you know what it's about?"

"Based on rumors, the situation seems pretty grave. It appears he's planning to dissolve the National Assembly and declare martial law."

It was inauspicious. I was deep in thought when a Japanese reporter visited me at a preexisting appointed time. He told me the same news.

I knew how much pain the Park regime had taken to maintain its dictatorial system after the election. Although I continued to warn people of the possibility of martial law since the election, I was still scared to realize it would become a reality. As expected, the announcement was made at 7:00 p.m. I watched it on TV with Kim Jong-chung, an elementary school friend who took care of me whenever I went to Japan, as if my matters were his own. President Park looked somehow unfamiliar on TV. As always, he read the prepared statement without expression. "My dear Koreans! I hereby declare my solemn resolution for the honorable exploration of our national history's fortune. I do this in support of your sincere wish for our fatherland's peace, reunification, and prosperity."

Park Chung-hee dissolved the National Assembly and declared emergency martial law over the entire nation. It was truly odious. Words cannot express the absurdity of his argument for dissolving the National Assembly and declaring martial law for the sake of peace and reunification. This was another coup d'état in the name of peaceful reunification and Korean democracy. What a disgrace!

The Park regime changed the Constitution yet again, calling it the Yusin Constitution. According to the Yusin Constitution, an electoral college called the Tongil Juche Gugminhoeui [the National Council for Reunification] would elect the president, who could then appoint one-third of the National Assembly members. The Yusin Constitution also allowed the president to declare emergency measures, thus enabling the president to reign over all three governmental branches. Furthermore, the elections were to be held every six years, with no presidential term limit provisions, which guaranteed Park's permanent power. It was a court coup d'état, based on Park's realization that he could no longer prolong his regime through legitimate means.

I closed my eyes. Kim Jong-chung was silent as well. Remembering the declaration of emergency about a year ago, I wondered why they committed such crimes whenever I was abroad.

I called home first. My wife told me not to worry about our family, but she expressed her own worries about me. She said, "It's very grave. It'd be better if you didn't return to Seoul right now."

Things progressed very quickly and in the worst possible direction. The first thing that came to my mind after the presidential declaration was my supporters—those people who yearned for regime change, people who'd been passionately hopeful for this change since the 1975 election. I couldn't fall asleep alone in a foreign land, remembering the people's faces cheering for me during my last presidential election campaign. How would those people receive this news? How disappointed and enraged they must feel! I could feel something hot choking up in my throat—sadness and anger.

I decided to fight against the Park regime even if I had to risk my life. I felt it was my duty and responsibility to the Korean people. The only thing in question was where and how.

I pondered the situation. No one in Korea could speak his or her opinion under this fierce dictatorship. There wouldn't be many leaders brave enough to even try. Luckily, I was abroad, so I could freely speak my mind. I should try to appeal to world opinion in other countries like the US and Japan. I should try to block the Park regime's relationship with other countries by publicizing the dictatorship's evils. That might encourage people within Korea in their fight against the Yusin. I had to fight abroad for Koreans who yearned for democracy. I would build an international organization for democratic struggle and fight with Koreans from abroad.

I was deciding if I should choose exile. Since I hadn't thought about exile at all until then I was at a loss. I didn't have much money and it was unclear when I could return home, how Americans and Japanese would treat me, if Koreans abroad would help me, what kind of evil schemes the KCIA might plot, and so much more.

I was also worried about my family, friends, and colleagues. In my absence, they were like hostages. How severely oppressive would the KCIA be to them? I pondered the two possibilities of exile and homecoming until dawn, at which point I felt newly encouraged. I chose exile.

I contacted my fellow assemblymen from the Sinmin Party who also happened to be visiting Japan at the time, including Kim Young-sam, Lee Chul-seung, Song Won-young, and Yang El-dong. I proposed we fight against the Park regime in Japan as all hope for democracy had vanished with the Park regime's violent coup. No one responded, though.

I made my first public statement against the Yusin coup d'état. A few media outlets showed interest because I'd been President Park's greatest political enemy during the previous election. However, domestic media sources ran nothing. After explaining to reporters how President Park's special statement was a scheme for permanent reign, I read the following statement entitled "On the Declaration of Martial Law": "Although seemingly speaking of reunification, President Park's current measures are alarmingly anti-democratic ones aiming at a permanent dictatorial reign. They violate the Korean Constitution and cruelly trample upon the Korean people's sincere wish for the speedy reunification of our country by the development of Korean democratic abilities against North Korea.

"I am confident that President Park's measure will be sternly criticized by the world community and that it will surely fail in the hands of the great

Korean people who overthrew the Rhee Syngman dictatorial regime out of their profound desire for democratic freedom."

I later heard that military investigators raided my and my fellow assemblymen's houses. The assemblymen who were detained included Kim Sang-hyun, Chough Yoon-hyung, Lee Jong-nam, Kim Nok-yeong, Cho Yeon-ha, Kim Gyeong-in, Park Jong-yul, Kang Keun-ho, Lee Se-kyu, Kim Han-su, and Na Sok-ho. Other people who suffered included Kwon Rho-kap, Hahn Hwa-kap, Eom Yeong-dal, Kim Ok-du, Bang Dae-yeop, Yi Su-dong, and my secretary Lee Yoon-soo. Of course, they hadn't brought any warrants. Military investigators tortured them brutally to get information about me. They employed unimaginable torture tactics, which included stripping them naked, depriving them of sleep, beating them with clubs and square bars, having them lie down and pouring water into their noses, beating them after hanging them like skewed chickens, and poking at the soles of their feet with awls.

After only one emergency cabinet meeting, the Park regime announced the new Yusin Constitution, a Constitution tailor-made for Park Chung-hee's dictatorship alone. I immediately made a statement entitled "On the Constitutional Amendment." It read in part:

1. Simply put, the current constitutional amendment practically introduces the generalissimo system, which aims to guarantee President Park's permanent re-election, a re-election he would have no chance of winning through legitimate direct election. He is doing this all in an attempt to fulfill his ambition for dictatorship and permanent reign. This constitutional amendment nullifies his own promise to Koreans and the world during his third-term presidency campaign last year that "this would be his last." Unfortunately, my repeated warnings during that election campaign that "if we don't change regime peacefully this time, there won't be any further opportunities to change the Park regime and a terrifying age of generalissimo would come" have come true.

2. President Park has continued to argue that democracy is superior to communism and that we would eventually prevail in the current competitive coexistence. However, the current constitutional amendment negates parliamentary democracy and the separation of the three governmental branches, along with the life of democracy, and closely approaches the North's uniform communist system. This goes entirely against his past argument and flies in the face of

the cause and belief in the Korean fight for freedom, which has been suffering from the division of our country, and the fratricidal war of the past twenty-seven years.

3. Although President Park mentioned reunification as the cause for his constitutional amendment, the result of this amendment has nothing to do with reunification and everything to do with the perpetuation and consolidation of his power. I solemnly promise here that I will continue to fight against President Park's brutal violation of our country's democratic foundational ideology and Constitution and his violation of his own promise with Koreans, and I firmly trust that the freedom-loving Korean people's stern judgment will be delivered unto him.

I exposed the Park regime's conspiracy and beastly ambition through Japanese newspapers, journals, TV, and attendance at various meetings. I also emphasized that the Korean people would never give up a liberal democracy. I contributed an article entitled "Straight Talk About the Korean Martial Law in Effect" to the *Asahi Weekly*. I wanted to ensure the Japanese and Koreans in Japan knew that there were democratic forces fighting against the dictatorial regime in Korea. They were all quite surprised at the news. My other contributions through articles and interviews in Japan included: "I am Enraged by the Korean Martial Law" (*Sunday Mainichi*, November 5, 1972), "Mr. Kim Dae-jung Appeals About Korean Crisis" (*Weekly Post*, November 17, 1972), "Enraged Appeal About Current Korean Situation" (*Sekai*, January 1973), "Agonizing Reality in Fatherland Korea" (*Chuokoron*, January 1973), "People Won't be Silent" (*Asahi Journal*, February 2, 1973), and "Democracy is Exactly What is Needed for Reunification" (*Economist*, February 6, 1973).

Shortly after this, I traveled from Japan to the US because Washington, DC seemed like it would be a more productive place than Tokyo to let the world know about Korea's dictatorial reality. The US could exercise an enormous influence on the Park regime.

As soon as I arrived, I met with my acquaintances to discuss my future activities in the US, including Yi Geun-pal, Im Byeong-gyu, Channing Liem, Yoo Ki-hong, and my brother-in-law Lee Sung-ho. I told them about my intention to fight for democracy and against the dictatorship. They told me many Korean-Americans were interested in Korean democracy, and it was likely they would find a way for me to collaborate with them.

I met with anyone—American or Korean—who was interested in my fight. Among them, I often met with a Professor Edwin O. Reischauer, the Japan Institute director at Harvard University, whom I had known for some time. He thought highly of me as a politician and proponent of democracy, a Christian, and as a man with strong convictions. Professor Reischauer introduced me to both Democratic and Republican Party leaders and other congressmen. The Speaker of the House at the time was Mike Mansfield of the Democratic Party, who later became the US ambassador to Japan; the House minority leader was Hugh Scott of the Republican Party. I explained Korea's dictatorial regime to them and asked for their help. I met with Senator Edward M. Kennedy in DC as well. He told me he trusted me and that I should come to see him whenever I ran into problems during my exile.

My activities in the US centered around university campuses. I held my first public speech at Columbia University in New York on December 14, 1972. We expected about 100 people to be in attendance, but approximately 500 people turned up. It was quite successful. I made an impassioned speech and the audience responded enthusiastically. I felt confident that I could succeed in my pro-democracy movement if I harnessed such enthusiasm. I embarked upon a speaking tour in America, making a case for the democratization of Korea to Americans and Korean-Americans at Missouri State University, Westminster University, Washington University, University of Chicago, and the Civic Auditorium in San Francisco.

Around that time, I received a letter from my wife, which was sent through acquaintances. Although most reporters couldn't approach my house, reporter Miyoshi from the Japanese broadcasting company TBC and reporter Han Yeong-do from the American broadcasting company CBS managed to visit my family. The two reporters told them how I was doing and offered to deliver my wife's letter to me. My wife and I corresponded with one another through the two reporters and Ms. U-sun, my wife's Ewha High School alumna. We were occasionally able to talk on phones other than our own, which we could only do after shaking off the forces that seemed to shadow us. It was as if we were committing espionage. The news my wife relayed to me in her letters was chilling.

She wrote that those who were detained were tortured and black-and-blue upon their release. Even their minds were black-and-blue. All of our secretaries, friends, and even our driver were dragged out and tortured, then released only after they'd written notes promising never to come to Donggyo-dong.

These detainees discovered that the KCIA agents knew even those things I said to my secretary when we were alone and to my wife in our bedroom; they even had a copy of the list of guests who visited and contributed to my mother's funeral. I was told they'd seen piles and piles of documents from the KCIA's detailed investigation of me.

"Perhaps you're the only person who can represent Korea at present?" my wife wondered in her writing. "People are so frustrated here because no one can speak their minds. I hear that the regime is most afraid of your statements made overseas and of other international opinions. Mr. Park Chung-hee is the only person who is really alive in this country, and his orders are the only laws. Everyone is afraid of even breathing aloud lest they're punished for making a noise. Please know that he hates you the most, and be stronger in your fight. Please don't be impatient about returning home, because you have to work to release the Korean people from this oppression and to let them breathe freely. Please don't go out alone, whether in America or in Japan, and be careful with your food. Please don't forget that someone is shadowing you, always and everywhere. Please take good care of yourself."

The Park regime's brutality sent shudders down my spine.

According to the Yusin Constitution, Park Chung-hee was elected as the eighth president at the Tongil Juche Gugminhoeui on December 23. It took no more than seventy days from the declaration of the Yusin Constitution to the presidential inauguration. I continued to criticize and condemn it from abroad.

Although Park Chung-hee was consolidating his dictatorial regime and arresting, torturing, and confining leaders of the democracy movement in their homes, North Korea had agreed to the establishment of the South-North Red Cross Conference and the South-North Joint Commission. North Korea also amended its Constitution in line with South Korean constitutional amendments. It was bizarre.

This attitude from North Korea misled some intellectuals in America and Japan to believe that both regimes really wanted reunification. Accepting the pretext of stability and security, the US and Japan looked the other way on a series of measures the Park regime took to strengthen its dictatorial grip. However, both Korean regimes' gestures toward reconciliation were nothing more than an attempt to consolidate their power bases by deceiving people with the illusory dream of reunification.

A series of gestures toward reunification could silence the condemnation of the dictatorial regime, albeit temporarily. It was a dark time for me and others who pursued democracy. We were completely isolated.

On January 5, 1973, I returned to Japan. I was in Tokyo when I heard the results of the Korean assembly election. The opposition party had done fairly well; however, the results were already guaranteed by the new format of the election. The ruling party had no problem securing a majority in the Assembly since one-third of the seats were recommended by the president. The ruling party nominated only one candidate to each precinct, which had been altered to send two members to the assembly, unlike the one before. As a result, a ruling party candidate and an opposition party candidate or an independent were elected as pairs in each precinct. The opposition party was only able to exist thanks to this generous arrangement by the ruling party.

A silver lining in this whole miserable business was that the rate of votes the ruling party candidates received was less than 40 percent, although they were able to procure more than half the seats. These results were a clear indication of the people's will and a great comfort to all who cared about Korean democracy.

I continued to fight against the dictatorship in Japan. It was a very lonely fight, but I couldn't stop. I explained to everyone I met how the dictatorial regime had abused its power and how harmful this would be to the common interests of Korea, the US, and Japan. Even many ruling Liberal Democratic Party members began to sympathize with what I said, despite the fact that the Japanese ruling party at that time consistently supported President Park. Mr. Kimura Takeo, a former cabinet member, was especially shocked to hear what I had to say. "I haven't been that interested in Korea, but this seems to be a situation that requires attention," he said in response. "Unimaginable things must be happening there."

Former Agriculture and Forestry Minister Akagi Munenori also expressed uncommon interest: "Although we try very hard to keep the promises made at the Korea-Japan Basic Treaty, the Park regime seems careless, using our loans for unrelated purposes. All our efforts could turn into nothing."

The Tokyo branch chair of *Time* magazine S. Chang introduced me to parliamentary member Mr. Utsunomiya Tokuma. Mr. Chang, who was

Korean-Japanese, had been to Korea to report about me. Mr. Utsunomiya, who was in charge of the Asia and Africa Research Association, to which scores of Japanese parliamentary members belonged, was almost as progressive as the Socialist Party members, although he was a ruling Liberal Democratic Party member. When he heard the truth about Japanese support for the Korean dictatorship and the close relationship between the Korean and Japanese economies, he was extremely upset, and arranged my speech event for the Asia and Africa Research Association members. I condemned Japan's indifference to Korean dictatorship, saying: "I hope Japan does not adopt the mistaken US policy of supporting dictatorial regimes if they adopt anti-communist stances. In fact, the US also did not support dictatorship in Korea unconditionally. During the last phase of the Rhee Syngman regime, the US supported the people's efforts to recover democracy. When the military coup d'état occurred, the US immediately condemned it. US pressure influenced the military hand-over of power to a civilian government. The US tried to stop the 3-term presidency constitutional amendment as well. It made a statement against the Declaration of National Emergency. It expressed its dissatisfaction with the Yusin regime officially and unofficially. The senate foreign relations committee report calls the Park regime 'the worst dictatorship since the Rhee Syng-man regime.'

"However, the Japanese government's attitude has been quite different from its US counterpart. It has consistently supported the Park regime, for example, sending economic aid in time for the 1971 presidential election. The Seoul subway is the symbolic example of this. Japan has shown no interest in the development of a Korean democracy."

"I, of course, know that there are many intellectuals and opposition party parliamentary members in Japan who care deeply about the future of both countries. What's troubling is the policy the Japanese government has consistently adopted toward Korea so far. Together with China, Japan is growing more and more powerful in Asia. Therefore, Japan's rightful policies toward Asia can enable competitive coexistence between communist and democratic systems and guarantee true happiness for Asia."

I ran around quite a bit in order to correct the false ideas the Japanese had about Korea. No one in Japan seemed much interested in the Korean political situation, though. Most were extremely surprised to hear of our dictatorial reality. I urged Japanese intellectuals to act. I pointed out how the Korean people were suffering as a result of the close ties between "pro-Korean" Japanese and the dictatorial Park regime.

I met a number of parliamentary members, including the Socialist Party Secretary Ishbashi Masashi. As I had done with Korean-Americans, I also appealed to Koreans in Japan to pay attention to the recovery of democracy in their home country.

I wrote *Dictatorship and My Fights* during this period. It was my story, but I wrote it to let the Japanese know the reality of the dictatorship crisis in Korea. This book was later translated into Korean and published under the title *Conscience in Action* by the Geummun Publishing Company, owned by Mr. Kim Hyeong-mun.

I went to the US again on March 25. After a speech in Chicago on April 28, I gave a speech at the International Hall in San Francisco on May 18. When I stepped to the podium after the former citizen-elected Seoul Mayor Kim Sang-don's introduction, about fifteen or so well-known Korean-American thugs in the front row began to make a fuss, throwing eggs and ketchup, and yelling at me. A very brave man named Mr. Song Sun-keon came forward and scolded them. Although the police had to be brought in, I was still able to finish my speech. Considering the vice consul had led them in, it was clear that the KCIA was behind this incident. I knew that they would follow me to the end of the world, but it was still chilling to see their violent actions firsthand.

Once, I was invited to give a speech at a Christian scholars' gathering, which I gladly accepted. But once the news was out, a KCIA agent in the US called the scholar in charge, threatening that there would be consequences if he didn't cancel the event. The Korean-American community was upset when the scholar bravely exposed this matter. In the end, the Department of State got wind of this and sent a strong warning to the Korean Consular Office: "Mr. Kim Dae-jung is legally in the US. Interfering with his activities is a clear intervention into the domestic affairs of the US. We will not tolerate another incident like this."

The US Department of State was quick and resolute. This must have been why the KCIA agents didn't harm me even when they surrounded me. I was really grateful for the US Department of State for their intervention.

While I was actively expanding my activity radius, on June 23, President Park announced a "Special Statement Regarding Foreign Policy for Peace and Reunification." This seven-article statement laid out the basic direction of Korean foreign policies. What stood out among the seven articles was the fourth ("We do not oppose North Korean participation in international organizations") and the fifth ("We do not oppose joint membership in the United Nations with North Korea"). The Korean government acknowledging the North Korean government and adopting a "one nation, two states" policy instead of the previous "one nation, one state" policy represented a major policy change. The Korean National Assembly supported this unilaterally, and the US and Japan supported it as well. This was the exact same policy I had argued for, and for which the regime had condemned me.

As I continued making speeches and lectures in the US, more and more people sympathized with my arguments. I was very encouraged and thought it would make sense to form an organization that would harness this energy and lead to an effective anti-dictatorship struggle. Luckily, Korean-Americans received this idea of mine enthusiastically and formed the National Congress of Democracy and Unification of Korea (NCDUK).

On July 6, 1973, we held a meeting of promoters at Mayflower Hotel in Washington, DC, with Kim Sang-don, Yi Geun-pal, Moon Myong-ja, and former Ambassador to the US Channing Liem. We succeeded in forming a major vehicle to carry Korean enthusiasm forward to democracy.

I was very clear about two things in that meeting: one was that we should support South Korea absolutely and the other was that we should adopt the principle of democracy before reunification. Some Americans argued that we should work for reunification first since the dictatorial government was using reunification. I opposed their argument, though, because we could be implicated in the Park regime's schemes. Even though they were trampling on democracy under the banner of reunification, they could also accuse reunification activists of pro-communism at any time. People eventually agreed to my democracy before reunification policy.

I contributed an article to the *New York Times* around that time. My two main points were that I supported the US troops stationed in Korea and that the US government should exercise its influence in Korea to end the dictatorship. It was the forum where I publicly announced my democracy before reunification policy in the US.

While establishing the NCDUK, some even argued that we should establish a Korean government in exile. In particular, Mr. Choe Seok-nam, a former general in the Korean Army, spearheaded this argument.

He thought very highly of my struggle for democracy. Although he seemed certain that I'd agree with him, I resolutely disagreed. "That won't do. You and I are both fighting to overthrow Park Chung-hee's Yusin system and to recover democracy in Korea. Korea is not a colony, but an independent country to which we should bring democracy. I believe the Korean dictatorial group wants us to establish a separate government in exile. If we do, what Koreans will follow and support us? The Park regime will maliciously advertise that we're North Korean tools. How disappointed and frustrated do you think the Korean people and my colleagues will be? I understand your sincere intentions, but please give up this idea."

Mr. Choe soon understood. No matter how spiteful Park Chung-hee was, and no matter how difficult and destitute our wandering exiled lives were, we had our own country to return to and we had an obligation to make democracy bloom there.

I went back to Japan on July 10 to organize NCDUK's Japanese headquarters. In Japan, I led a relatively peaceful life, preparing for the NCDUK organization and interviewing with Japanese reporters. Among the interviews I had then, my conversation with Mr. Yasue Ryosuke, editor-in-chief of the monthly magazine *Sekai*, stands out in my memory. When he asked what my beliefs were, I answered: "Even in the dead of night, we cannot doubt that the sun rises the next morning. I believe that there is God even in Hell where Satan reigns. And I believe in history. I believe that justice never fails in history. My only hero is the people. The people will win in the end, and they are the source of our conscience. I live by these beliefs.

"My family—my wife, my children, my siblings, and my 81-year-old father—all live in Korea. Although my big brother died in February this year, I wasn't able to attend his funeral. I accept this, though, as something inevitable.

"I believe that it is because our ancestors didn't have courage—except for a few independence fighters during the annexation of Korea by Japan—that Koreans still suffer one hundred years later. If Korea hadn't been annexed by Japan, Korea wouldn't have been divided. In the same way we blame our ancestors for their lack of courage, why wouldn't our descendants blame us for our actions now? I am working now so that our descendants will hold nothing against us; that is one of my consolations in this harsh reality. That's what I believe."

On July 13, I met a group of Koreans in Japan, including Bae Dong-ho, Kim Jae-hwa, Cho Hwal-jun, and Kim Jong-chung, at Keio Plaza Hotel. After explaining how I was involved in organizing the NCDUK in the US, I appealed for Koreans in Japan to similarly organize to work toward over-throwing President Park's dictatorial regime and recovering democracy. Everyone enthusiastically agreed.

In addition to the two principles of absolute support for South Korea and democracy before reunification, I also argued that the NCDUK should clearly sever its ties to the Pro-North Korean Residents' League in Japan. I also put a stop to the independence celebration event jointly held with the Pro-North Korean Residents' League in Japan on August 15. Some members protested this decision strongly, believing it shouldn't matter when South Korea was conferring with North Korea.

It was a violation of current Korean law for a South Korean to confer with North Koreans, however, so the Park regime could abuse this at any time. I left the conference room, saying I couldn't join them if they didn't agree with me on this point. In this manner, I got them to agree.

The final five-member meeting for the establishment of the NCDUK in Japan was held at Ikenohata Inn in Ueno. We checked and confirmed our preparations. First, we decided to have the inauguration assembly at Hibiya Public Hall on August 15. We informally decided to elect Kim Jae-hwa, Cheong Chae-joon, and Kim Yong-won as vice presidents; Bae Dong-ho as a standing advisor; Yang San-gi, Kim Jae-sul, and Yu Seok-jun as advisors; Cho Hwal-jun as Secretary General; and Kim Jong-chung as organizing division chief. After we adopted a platform, the five of us—Korean Residents Union in Japan Advisor Kim Jae-hwa, Korean Residents Union in Japan Tokyo Headquarters Director Cheong Chae-joon, National Reunification Council Chairman Bae Dong-ho, National Reunification Council SecretaryGeneral Cho Hwal-jun, and myself—signed the document. I was deeply moved by the establishment of this precious organization for the recovery of democracy in Korea in exile.

I planned to expand the NCDUK as a worldwide organization after first establishing branches in the US, Japan, and Canada. We tentatively decided on the branch presidents in three countries—Reverend An Byeong-guk in the US, Mr. Kim Jae-hwa in Japan, and Reverend Lee Sang-chul in Canada. I planned to travel to Canada immediately after establishing the NCDUK's Japanese branch; however, it turns out I was not to step on Canadian land due to the unexpected incident about to happen in only a few weeks that I will talk about in the next chapter.

My activities during my exile roused the democratic yearning of overseas Koreans. They saw their home country through me and became aware of Korea's current state. While Koreans in Japan and the US previously received Korean news as news from a faraway country, I could tell them in vivid detail what was really going on there—how the people suffered under dictatorship and how eagerly they wanted democracy. I also explained to them why we needed democracy before reunification and drew their sympathy for this argument. Intellectuals quickly understood my arguments. The seeds of democratization were sown in overseas Korean communities.

Although I lived an extremely active life during my time in exile, I was very lonely. Wandering without family, I faced my own loneliness every night. It was terribly difficult to endure this state. It was also scary to think that someone was always targeting me. Fortunately, my secretary, Yi Geun-pal, and my friend Kim Jong-chung stayed close to me in the US and Japan, respectively. Yi Geun-pal was a former diplomat, and worked extremely hard for me. Both of them were very bright and clear-thinking individuals.

When the Park regime failed in their efforts to stop my anti-dictatorship and pro-democracy struggles, they tried to appease me. In March of that year, a Liberal Democratic Party officer close to President Park asked me if I had any intention of compromising with the Park regime. He said that President Park wanted to work with me and intended to appoint me to the post of vice president. Although extremely offended, I politely refused. "I don't fight to rise up in the political ranks, but to achieve democracy. It's not important if I'm appointed to a high position or not."

Although I replied courteously, what I said about democracy must have stung the dictator. Perhaps this was when President Park decided to do away with me entirely.

In Korea, the KCIA's sixth division director visited my wife to urge me to return. "Tell your husband to return quickly. You don't know what will happen to him if he continues his anti-government activities. He may experience serious bodily harm."

Although I heard this threat from my wife, I trusted the abilities of the Japanese and American police. I probably had no other choice than to trust them, anyway. I could not avoid harm if a governmental organization like the KCIA mobilized their intricate intelligence network at a helpless exile like me. I knew it.

CHAPTER 4

1973–1980

I Saw Jesus (1973)

Politically, things seemed disquieting and threatening. People around me were getting more and more worried about my safety. When I quietly traveled from the US to Japan, my colleagues who came to welcome me at the airport said cautiously, "Korean-Japanese Yakuza's movements appear suspicious. They must be conspiring about something. Be careful during your stay here."

It was clear that someone was targeting me. We could feel some organizational movements. From Korea, my wife also wrote often in the letters delivered by friends and acquaintances about her sense of imminent threat.

I'm not sure what the KCIA is up to. Not only do they pay extremely vigilant attention to your activities abroad, but they also look like they're trying to prevent your continuing activities in whatever means is within their power. They might attempt to send your acquaintances to you to dissuade you from your activities. Please be very careful.

It is true that you're their headache. All the more reason why you should not return home yet. Even if they guarantee your safety, we cannot trust them.

They will target you and our family the more renowned you become and the more recognition you receive abroad. Please be very careful. Please don't return home, no matter what.

Kim Dae-jung, *Conscience in Action*,
https://doi.org/10.1007/978-981-10-7623-7_4

From her letters, I could sense my wife's growing worries. Perhaps one's partner instinctively knows what is about to happen.

In Tokyo, I couldn't keep on staying at a hotel. Not only was it expensive, but also I needed an office space from which to work to carry out anti-dictatorship activities. My comrades found an apartment in Harada Mansion, a twelve-story building near the Takadanobaba subway station. The building was located on a rather busy street. We rented room seven on the eleventh floor, and used it as my residence and office. We hung a small plate with the inscription "Korean Democratic System and Reunification Question Research Institute, Tokyo Branch Office." Comrade Cho Hwal-jun, who had worked as my chief of staff, served as the office manager.

My comrades tried first and foremost to find me a bodyguard. They recruited from the Korean Youth Association, a Korean-Japanese youth organization. A few people, including Kim Jong-chung, encouraged them, saying, "Let's protect Mr. Kim Dae-jung, the standard-bearer of the anti-dictatorship struggle." A young man named Kim Gun-bu volunteered as a bodyguard and secretary.

A young man named Kim Gang-su soon joined in the same capacity. He was very skilled in martial arts. Despite being an only son who supported his parents, he took charge of this dangerous task, which was exacerbated by the fact that we couldn't really provide him with any professional arms or equipment. I was grateful.

To remain safe, I followed my comrades' advice and changed my location every two or three days, staying not just in my residence, but also in downtown hotels.

On July 23, about a week after I moved into Harada Mansion, Kim Jong-chung found someone observing us around the building. On his way out, he saw a taxi standing halfway over the curb. When he asked the building guard about it, the guard told him it had been there for a long time. When Kim Jong-chung passed by the taxi, he saw a man making a phone call at a corner store while watching the entrance of the building. Kim immediately realized the man was watching our activities and called to let me know.

Something felt strange. My Chief of Staff Cho Hwal-jun proposed increasing the number of bodyguards, lest they attempt an assassination. Though chilling, I couldn't show my fear because my comrades were even more alarmed than I was.

Although peaceful on the surface, every day felt tense. On July 29, I met with Democratic Reunification Party President Yang El-dong. I was glad to see Mr. Yang, who used to call me his younger brother, in that foreign land. He was staying in Tokyo to treat his diabetes. He had left the Sinmin Party and founded the Democratic Reunification Party together with other anti-Yu Jin-san forces. When we parted, we promised to meet again before he returned to Korea.

On the night of August 4, Chief of Staff Cho Hwal-jun was tipped off by a source at the Korean Embassy that they were going to kidnap me. It seemed like reliable information and, if true, it would most likely be a Korean Central Intelligence Administration (KCIA) operation. We moved my residence almost every day. I stayed at the Harada Mansion on August 1, Okura Hotel on August 2 and 3, Pacific Hotel on August 4, Harada Mansion on August 5, Pacific Hotel on August 6, and Hilton Hotel on August 7. Despite these efforts, the fated day came.

August 8, 1973 was a very hot and muggy day. I began my day at the Hilton Hotel in Tokyo. Around 10:30 a.m., I left my room to attend a meeting with Democratic Reunification Party President Yang El-dong. Both my bodyguards Kim Gun-bu and Kim Gang-su accompanied me. I took a taxi in front of the hotel, leaving Kim Gun-bu at the hotel. As I got in the taxi, Kim Gun-bu asked with his eyes if I would be okay.

I arrived at Grand Palace Hotel a little past 11:00 a.m., and took the elevator to the twenty-second floor with Kim Gang-su. Since there was no place to wait in the corridor, I told Kim Gang-su to go down and wait for me in the lobby.

I knocked the door of room 2211, where President Yang was staying. He greeted me warmly. After we talked about the Korean political situation, he suggested I return to Korea. I said, "I do want to return; however, what can I do there when opposition party members are all controlled by the ruling party?" I then asked him to help me fund my overseas activities. President Yang didn't respond. Soon, there was a knock at the door and Assemblyman Kim Gyeong-in, my distant relative and a Democratic Reunification Party member, entered. Although unexpected, I was glad to see him.

This encounter with Assemblyman Kim was possible because he returned earlier than expected from his outing to get a book. After the three of us had lunch together, I left for my next appointment with the Japanese Congressman Kimura Toshio in the Akasaka district. Assemblyman

Kim saw me off, but as soon as I came out of the room, five or six big men jumped me, two of whom seized me by the neck.

"What are you doing? Who are you?" I thundered in surprise. Assemblyman Kim also shouted. The men quickly gagged me and I was dragged into the adjacent room, which they must have already checked in to. When I resisted, they kicked my knees and hit my jaw. They seemed like technicians who specialized in beating up people. I was quickly subdued without much chance of resistance. After throwing me down on to the bed, they covered my nose with a handkerchief. As soon as I thought, *This must be an anesthetic*, I lost consciousness. I woke up soon, though, perhaps because the anesthetic was not strong enough. Or, maybe, my constitution is resistant to anesthetic.

"Be quiet. You're a dead man if you don't," someone said in fluent Korean. I thought, *This is serious. I might die.* Red lights flashed in my head. Although I was semiconscious, I stayed prostrate as if I were unconscious. After a while—I still wonder how long it was—the men opened the door and checked the corridor. They surrounded me on both sides and dragged me into the elevator. They were really strong.

When the elevator stopped on the seventeenth or eighteenth floor, two young men entered. I began shouting in Japanese, "They are murderers! Help me! They are murderers! Please help me!" But, probably scared, the two men abruptly got off the elevator on the seventh floor. The kidnappers tightened their grip on my arms and beat me.

They took me to the basement, where a sedan was waiting. They pushed me into the backseat, and then sat on either side of me; another two were in the front seat. The two next to me sat me down on the floor and pushed my head with their legs. The car slipped out of the basement parking lot. Although I couldn't see outside, I could feel that the car was on the ground. I felt as if I had suddenly dropped underground from the twenty-second floor of the hotel. I seemed to be able to still hear President Yang's laughter that I had heard just a few minutes ago, but where was I now? This is how I was kidnapped.

The men covered my face with their clothes. My mouth was still gagged with cloth. As soon as I wiggled, I was kicked. From the way the car was driving, we seemed to be on the highway. After a while, the car stopped. It seemed as if the road was blocked. I thought maybe checkpoints had been established to find me. One of the kidnappers got out of the car and seemed to be asking for directions. I heard someone respond in Japanese, "This way is for Osaka, and that for Kyoto."

I wanted to shout, but I couldn't. I just hoped the police would look in the car, but only the kidnapper returned and the car began to drive again. After about an hour, the car slowed down. They seemed to be driving in a city now, but I couldn't guess where. One of the men said, "Let's go to An (安)'s house." Then, the driver said he didn't know where it was. Annoyed, the same man responded, "Yaskawa (安川)" in Japanese. We stopped somewhere and then drove again. It seemed we were going to a place different than they had originally planned. Finally, they stopped the car somewhere that seemed like a building's parking lot and took me out of the car. When I looked up I could see a ceiling with steel frames. Although there was a roof, it seemed we were outdoors.

They took me into the building, then pushed me into an elevator. Then I found myself in a *tatami* room. I could hear a young woman's voice, but I couldn't understand what she was saying. The men untied and ungagged me and took off my clothes. They took my watch, my wallet with all of my money in it, ID card, name cards, and everything else. They changed me into shabby clothes and sneakers, then tied my body up again. They wrapped my entire body (except for my face) with strong packaging tape. I was imprisoned in the room like that for about two hours. It was getting dark outside.

The men dragged me outside again. I was loaded into a car, with my arms and legs tied. Again, they pushed me down from both sides. After driving for about thirty minutes, I could hear waves. Clearly, we were at a beach. I was then taken to a motorboat. I could see other boats mooring nearby.

On the boat, the men covered my head with some cloth. Suddenly, there was darkness. It seemed I was about to die. I made the sign of the cross with my tied hand. Perhaps seeing me move my hand, a man kicked my belly and cursed at me. After about an hour of sailing, I was moved to a bigger ship. I could hear someone say it was 12:50 when asked the time. They were silent most of the time, saying only what was necessary. It seemed that they were well-trained professionals. They beat me again on the ship.

I said to them, "Stop it. You don't have to beat me. I am ready to die. You don't have to beat up someone who is about to die."

The beating stopped. It seemed the kidnappers who had brought me from Tokyo were handing me over to another set. They exchanged greetings. Because I had owned and run a marine transportation business, I could determine the size and capacity of a ship by its movement alone.

This ship was not rocking, which meant it was about 500 tons and more than 1000 horsepower.

I was dragged to the cabin under the deck and told to lie there. I dozed off; when I woke up the men came back. They first took the tape off of my face, then untied the ropes from my body. As soon as I felt freer, however, they began to tie again, even more tightly than before.

They tied my hands and feet together, then laid me down on a board like a mortuary plank, and tied me to it in three places—head, body, and feet—like a corpse. After making me bite a piece of wood, they wrapped my face with a bandage. It was like my body was being prepared for a burial. They attached something heavy that weighed about 30 or 40 kilograms—rocks or lumps of metal, I suppose—to each of my wrists.

They didn't say a thing and acted in such a manner that I couldn't anticipate their next movement. Five or six men tied my entire body very tightly with a rope. After finishing, they began to speak in undertones. I could decipher Gyeongsang, Jeolla, and Chungcheong dialects. From their manner of speech, it was clear they were Koreans.

"This looks secure enough not to unravel in the sea, right?"

"I heard a body won't float if you wrap it in a comforter. The cotton soaks up the water."

However, they didn't wrap me in a comforter. I heard the word "shark" in their conversation. It seemed clear they intended to throw me into the sea. *I could become food for a shark,* I thought. It seemed like the end of my life. As a Christian, I prayed every day, but I didn't feel like praying at this moment. Instead, the image of my last moment in the sea flickered in front of my eyes.

Can I take off the lumps of metal? Probably not. Since it's the sea, all will be over within a few minutes. The pain will disappear. And my hard life will be over, too. Whatever. I had a decent life, I thought. But immediately, I reconsidered. *No. I want to live. I must live! I have so much work to do. Even if I lose my lower body to sharks, I still want to live with my upper body.*

I strained my wrists, but the ropes tied around them wouldn't budge at all. There was nothing I could do. Things went black behind my eyes, and then Jesus appeared in front of me as I trembled in fear of death without even the courage to pray. Oh, Jesus! He looked exactly the same as the images I saw in the church. I held on to his sleeves and said, "Please let me live. I have a lot of work to do. I have work to do for Korean people. Please help me."

That was the first time since my baptism I begged Jesus to help me. At that very moment, I saw a red flash pass in front of my eyes. Suddenly, the engine made a roaring sound and the ship began shaking and dashing. In the cabin, men shouted, "An airplane!" and ran out to the deck. I heard the engine roar and could feel the ship sail at full speed. Something tense was happening, but I couldn't know what it was. After thirty or forty minutes, the ship slowed down and all became quiet, as if nothing had happened.

"Aren't you Mr. Kim Dae-jung?" I heard spoken in a Gyeongsang dialect. I barely managed to turn toward the sound and nodded. "I voted for you during the last presidential election in Busan," the voice continued.

That remark gave me hope. It became bright in front of my eyes. I felt like I was listening to the gospel. "You're now saved," the man whispered. After unwrapping the bandage from around my mouth, he gave me a lit cigarette and untied my hands and feet.

I am alive and smoking, I thought.

The man brought me a glass of juice.

I asked, "Where on earth are we?"

"We're on the sea near Tokushima."

"Then, this ship will definitely drop by a port. Please go to the police immediately when we stop at the port. The Japanese police will help me."

He said he would. It seemed to be around dawn then, but I couldn't know exactly what time it was.

The ship did not stop at a Japanese port.

Instead, it stayed on the sea for two days. Unlike before, they were kind when they gave me food and water. It seemed I had passed through a crisis, but I was still in the dark as to what was to come. My fate was floating on the sea. I wasn't sure when death would overtake me like waves. I spent the two days repeatedly dozing and waking. As my eyes were covered, I still couldn't see anything.

Around dawn on the eleventh, it got noisy and I could hear people speaking Korean. It seemed that the ship had entered a Korean port. A doctor came to the cabin and examined me. He treated wounds on my hands and feet. He also gave me an injection without telling me what it was. Scared, I wondered what it was for; the doctor later told me it was glucose. I felt upset that he hadn't given me that information beforehand.

I spent all day in the cabin and was dragged out of the ship at night. The kidnappers didn't tie me up any more, but my mouth was still gagged and my eyes were covered. They pushed me onto a car that seemed to have been waiting—most likely it was a three-quarter that the American military used widely then. They made me lie on a board in the car. The car stopped after a few hours of driving and then I was transferred to what seemed like an ambulance because there was a bed.

After driving for quite a while, I was taken out. I told them I wanted to use the bathroom. The toilet was made from half a cannon ball, which was frequently used in farmhouses at the time; this made me think we must be staying in a farmhouse. The leader told me to bear with them even though it was uncomfortable because the house was small. Then, he gave me two small pills, saying they were nutrients. When I took them, I felt uncontrollably sleepy. They must have been sleeping pills.

When I woke up the morning of August 12, I could see a little because the bandage around my eyes had loosened. I was not in the same farmhouse I had fallen asleep the night before; I was on the second floor of a Western-style two-story building. They must have transported me while I was sleeping. Men with hair cropped like soldiers were watching me. They were using a field telephone, so they could have been part of a military unit. The house looked like a KCIA safe house or an attachment to an institution. I spent another day in that building.

On August 13, the sixth day of my kidnapping, a man approached me and said, "Mr. Kim Dae-jung, let's talk." After a long pause, he asked, "Why are you waging a war against your country abroad?"

"That's not what I am doing. It's true that I am against the Park Chung-hee regime, but I have never denied or opposed liberal democracy and anti-communism. I never opposed the Republic of Korea. It is not our country, but the dictatorial regime that I oppose," I answered.

"The country is the regime. What difference is there between the two?" he bluntly responded.

I didn't answer. He changed the subject abruptly and said, "Mr. Kim Dae-jung, let's negotiate."

"Go on."

"I will drive you to your neighborhood. That's what I was ordered to do. You may return home, but please urinate where I drop you off. You may not unwrap your bandage, and you should not make any sound. After you urinate, you may go home. What do you say?"

I nodded.

They got me in a car and drove for a couple of hours. I talked with them occasionally. They called themselves the National Salvation Alliance Action Group. When I asked what kind of organization that was, they said they could not tell me. Then, after a while, they said, "It's an organization that defends liberal democracy and promotes anti-communism." After passing through a place that seemed like a highway tollgate, they returned my ID card and name cards and said they would return my wallet and money later. I never received them or my watch.

The car finally stopped and they let me out. As promised, I urinated where I got out. Then, I unwrapped the bandage covering my eyes. After a while, I was able to see things. There was the familiar gas station signboard in my neighborhood.

I stood in an alley near my house in Donggyo-dong. The moon was full and bright in the night sky. The alley was quiet. I had returned alive. I remembered that the moon was bright like that when I escaped the prison after surviving the communist massacre. Why was the moon always shining on my harsh fate?

I survived my third deadly crisis, returning home ten months after I left on October 11, 1972. The turbulent time when I worked passionately traveling back and forth between Japan and the US felt far away. It faded away behind my memories.

I could see people lingering outside in order to avoid the heat trapped indoors. *What on earth has happened to me?* I walked toward my house. It looked as familiar as if I were returning home after having left that very morning. I felt almost as if I was coming from an evening stroll.

The night was deep. I stood in front of the gate and looked up at the nameplate. "Kim Dae-jung Lee Hee-ho." The alley was quiet. I could see light through the windows. The Republic of Korea. Midsummer night. I rang the bell like the head of the household who had just returned home from work.

Cozy Relationship Between Korea and Japan After the Kidnapping Incident (1973–1974)

"Who is it?" a voice on the interphone asked.

"It's me. It's me."

Of course, my family hadn't even dreamt of me standing in front of the house. It was only a while later that someone inside shouted, "Mr. Representative is home!" My family rushed out of the door. I could see my wife and my youngest son, Hong Gul. They were all barefoot. I was thirsty. I entered the living room and asked for water. My family and assistants surrounded me.

"I experienced God's existence," I told them. "I am alive only by the grace of God. Let's pray."

We all kneeled together and prayed our thanks to God. Only after the prayer did I see the wounds all over my body. There was pus on my lower lip, and my wrists and ankles were purple and swollen. There was a black and blue tear over my left eyebrow. My face was covered with facial hair.

The phone rang. My secretary Mr. Kim Ok-du answered, then hung up almost as soon as he picked up. He said, "Someone called himself a member of the Patriotic Youth National Salvation Alliance asked if you returned home."

My eldest son, Hong Il, came and neighbors gathered too. They said they heard about my return from the DongA Broadcasting Station newsflash. A little later, more than fifty reporters from domestic and foreign media crowded my living room. I calmly detailed what had happened in the six days between the kidnapping and when I returned home. Interestingly, the kidnapping details I gave then from my memories were almost identical to the results of the later Japanese police investigation.

Although there were so many people, it was solemn and serious. The press conference lasted from 11:00 p.m. to 2:30 a.m. I choked as I said, "When I was about to be thrown off of a large ship and into the sea by kidnappers, I prayed to Jesus to save me." I ended up crying in front of the reporters (Photo 4.1).

After the incident, many people speculated on the role the Democratic Reunification Party president Yang El-dong and Representative Kim Gyeong-in might have played in the kidnapping. Based on testimonies and investigation results, the moment of kidnapping could be reconstructed as follows: When I came out of Mr. Yang's room with Mr. Kim, there were two men in front of the adjacent room 2210 and three men in front of the room across the hall, 2215. Three of them dragged me into room 2210, and the remaining two men pushed Mr. Kim, who was shouting and protesting, into Mr. Yang's room. Surprised, Mr. Yang yelled, "What are you doing? Where are you from?"

A man replied in fluent Korean, "Mr. Yang El-dong, we came from Seoul. This is a domestic matter. Let's take care of it quietly. It will be over soon, so please wait a little."

Because they looked like Koreans and claimed it was a "domestic matter," Mr. Yang and Mr. Kim decided to wait. Besides, the two men were practically pinning them down. Although Mr. Kim was held only by his wrist, he had a bruise that didn't go away until he returned to Korea. After

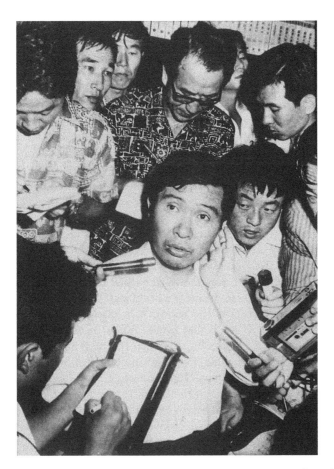

Photo 4.1　Kim Dae-jung at a press conference at his Donggyo-dong home in Seoul in August 1973, after the KCIA Kim Dae-jung Japan Kidnapping Incident

a while, Mr. Kim was worried, so he went to the room I had been dragged into earlier. Every time he went, though, two guards told him things hadn't settled quite yet. "It's going to be over soon," they told him. "If you make a fuss here, it will bring shame to Koreans. This could become a difficult international problem. Please be patient."

He couldn't hear a sound from the room. He went back to Mr. Yang's room again. Of course, it would have been best if he had opened the door to room 2210 and confirmed what was happening, but he could not because of the men. Mr. Kim checked the corridor every few minutes.

Around 1:20 p.m., my bodyguard and secretary Kim Gang-su, who had been waiting in the hotel lobby on the first floor, became worried and called room 2211 from the hotel phone. On the other end of the line, someone said something he couldn't understand, then hung up. Because Kim Gang-su had grown up in Japan, he didn't understand Korean very well. What he was told was "Come upstairs immediately."

When Representative Kim went to the corridor again, he found that the guards in front of room 2210 had disappeared. One of two men guarding Representative Kim also went away after saying he wanted to check the car waiting in the basement of the hotel. After a phone call, the last suspicious man went away too.

Kim Gang-su went up to the twenty-second floor at 2:00 p.m. When he knocked on room 2211, he found Mr. Yang and Mr. Kim. Kim Gang-su introduced himself as my bodyguard and secretary, and they told him to go to the adjacent room. Kim Gang-su rushed to room 2210 and tried in vain to open the door. He found the hotel staff and had them open it.

As soon as they entered the room, Kim Gang-su smelled something strange—some sort of medicinal smell. When he found that I was not there and discovered a paper bag between the beds and a bottle and gun magazine on the corner table, he called my Chief of Staff Cho Hwal-jun and let him know the situation. That was when the news of my disappearance was first known outside of the hotel. It was 2:05 p.m.

Around the same time, President Yang also notified the Korean Embassy and Representative Utsunomiya Tokuma, a Japanese Liberal Democratic Party member, of the incident. About twenty minutes later, my secretary Kim Gun-bu rushed to the hotel and carefully searched room 2210, but he could not find anything special. The medicinal smell still lingered in the room.

When they came out of the room, they found the door across the corridor was ajar. They would later learn that KCIA personnel had been waiting in that room. When they entered the room, they found nothing unusual ... just a tidy room. In room 2211, they found President Yang sitting on a sofa, stupefied. Soon, Kim Jae-gwon came from the Korean Embassy. My secretaries lost their temper and demanded that he find me.

My Chief of Staff Cho Hwal-jun reported this incident to the police around 2:40 p.m. The police and reporters arrived at the crime scene in Grand Palace Hotel at almost the same time.

A serious investigation began. There were two large empty backpacks, one small empty backpack, and a 13-meter-long rope between the two beds. On the corner table was a German pistol with seven bullets; a magazine; a small medicine bottle, which appeared to have contained anesthetic; a large brown envelope; and two North Korean cigarettes. On the floor were tissue paper and my pipe, which I bought a few days earlier at a Korean shop in Ueno.

It was difficult to guess who the kidnappers were based on those objects. It looked as if they were carefully calculated to confuse the investigators. Although the gun was German, three of the bullets were English and the other four were Swiss. Of those seven bullets, three were very old ones, often used by Japanese gangs at that time. The medicine bottle was filled with about one-third of a narcotic. Based on these objects, they must have planned to make the kidnapping look like the work of North Korean operatives or *yakuza*.

Judging by the empty backpacks, the original plan could have been to kill me on the spot, chop my body up, and carry my body parts in the backpacks. They must have had to change their plan because Representative Kim Gyeong-in unexpectedly returned early and joined us. If it was only me out in the corridor, they might have carried out their original plan. It could be because Representative Kim saw me off that they had to change their plan and decided to drown me in the sea. Representative Kim might have saved my life.

Japanese police were able to collect fingerprints from the bathtub. One of them was confirmed to be that of Kim Dong-un, a first secretary at the Korean Embassy in Japan. That fingerprint was decisive evidence that showed this kidnapping was staged by the KCIA. Japanese police also discovered that Kim Dong-un bought backpacks from a mountain-climbing equipment store near Grand Palace Hotel on the afternoon of August 6, two days before the incident. There was no doubt that the KCIA was behind this incident.

How, then, did the KCIA know about my planned visit to President Yang El-dong? It turned out that a diplomatic minister in charge of information at the Korean Embassy in Japan had visited President Yang El-dong when he was briefly hospitalized. He asked President Yang how he could meet me, and President Yang told him that he was going to see me soon. With this information, they must have watched President Yang's movement in the rooms adjacent to and across from his hotel room. In this sense, President Yang offered them a clue, but, clearly, it was not intentional. Even if I hadn't been kidnapped then and there, they must have targeted me continuously.

My kidnapping was known to the world through the NHK newsflash around 3:50 p.m., while I was being pushed down by the legs of kidnappers in a car driving on a highway.

My dramatic survival was possible thanks to American intervention. The American Embassy in Korea received news of my kidnapping at 3:00 p.m. on August 8. The CIA first informed Ambassador Philip Habib, who then summoned almost all information team members in Korea, including a political counselor, a military officer, and the US Information Agency head. Donald Gregg, who had come to Korea as the CIA station chief about a month before, was also included. Ambassador Habib urgently ordered, "Mr. Kim Dae-jung was kidnapped. It appears the KCIA is involved in it. Gather information quickly. We have to rescue him."

After gathering and analyzing information, Habib delivered news of the kidnapping and the US' concern about it to high-ranking Korean government officials. According to Donald Gregg's later testimony, Ambassador Habib had been expecting this kind of incident, since he already had detailed information about a series of Korean government operations interfering with my lectures in America and Japan. It was probably because of this knowledge and securing enough evidence that Ambassador Habib was able to calmly, resolutely, and immediately respond to my kidnapping when it occurred. Ambassador Habib rescued me from the threshold of death.

The airplane that appeared at that critical moment in the sea seemed to be a Japanese airplane. The US had quickly informed Japan about the kidnapping and requested subsequent action. The Korean government must have been embarrassed when its plan to murder me was revealed, so they had no choice but to let the Japanese government know the location of the operative ship.

Professor Jerome A. Cohen was told about the incident by Professor Channing Liem, who happened to be staying in Japan at the time; Professor Cohen, in turn, informed Secretary of State Kissinger. Secretary Kissinger, who was attending the UN General Assembly at the time, ordered all organizations under his directorship to find out the truth. Korean democratization movement activists in Japan played an important role in my rescue. Bae Dong-ho, Kim Jae-hwa, Cheong Chae-joon, Kim Jong-chung, Kwak Dong-ui, and Cho Hwal-jun held a press conference immediately after the kidnapping on August 8 and condemned the KCIA as the criminal mastermind behind this incident. This press conference played a decisive role in leading public opinion about the incident and drove the Park Chung-hee regime into a corner.

Later, it was discovered through testimonies and documents that under the directorship of KCIA Chief Lee Hu-rak, forty-six people in nine groups spent months planning the Kim Dae-jung Kidnapping Incident.

On June 10, 1998, a secret US document was unsealed. According to this document, under the leadership of KCIA Chief Lee Hu-rak, KCIA staff members carried out this kidnapping. It was most likely that President Park approved it either plainly or by implication.

It was clear to me, however, that President Park *ordered* this incident. KCIA Chief Lee Hu-rak, who took charge of the entire kidnapping operation, gave a very interesting testimony during the Seoul Spring in 1980. He told his hometown friend Representative Choe Yeong-geun that he carried out the operation under President Park's order. According to him, President Park summoned him one day and ordered him to "get rid of Kim Dae-jung." Lee was so surprised that he delayed the operation, but he was summoned again a month later. "Why are you not executing my order?" President Park yelled. "I've already discussed the matter with the prime minister. Hurry up."

Lee said that, although he didn't want to, he had to follow President Park's order despite all his subordinates' protests. I do believe what he said. Lee must have felt the need to confess when the new world seemed to emerge during the Seoul Spring. They tried to kill me. Therefore, "kidnapping incident" is actually a misnomer. The correct name should be the Kim Dae-jung Attempted Murder Incident.

I don't want to specify the names and actions of all those involved in this incident in this autobiography. I forgave them, and I know that they opposed this unjust order. Also, all the people in the world already know the truth of this incident, because it was already fully investigated and proven. I am still angry, however, about the low-grade behavior of the Korean and Japanese politicians who tried to cover up the truth through political collusion even after it was fully revealed.

The morning after my return, Madam Pak Sun-cheon, Representative Jeong Il-hyeong, and Madam Lee Tai-young visited my house. Soon after, the chief of the Mapo police station and detective division chief of the Seoul police station came and made a fuss, saying they should take my statement. I cooperated with them by presenting bandages and the blindfold as evidence. They conducted on-the-spot investigation where I was released in the alley near my house. The police established the Alleged

Kidnapping and Captivity Incident Investigation Headquarters at the Mapo Police Station. The Attorney General and the Culture and Public Relations Minister raised their voices: "We'll mobilize all possible investigative forces and we are determined to find the identity of these kidnappers."

But, a few days later, something strange happened. The chief of the Mapo police station came to my house and abruptly ordered everyone other than me, my wife, my driver, and our housemaid to leave. He declared that my secretaries couldn't enter the house, either. Both domestic and foreign journalists were blocked from approaching, too. They also blocked all alleys leading to my house with barricades, cutting our family off from the outside world completely. The imprisonment of my family and myself began like this. A policeman even accompanied Hong Gul, my youngest son who was then a third grader, on his way to and from school.

From that day on, the police occupied a room in our house. Weirdly, the direction of the investigation changed, too. They didn't seem to be interested in how I was kidnapped and how they would capture the kidnappers. Instead, they began to investigate my overseas activities. The prosecution, the police, and the KCIA colluded in questioning me closely for a week.

After that, Korean newspapers did not cover the Kim Dae-jung Kidnapping Incident at all. The authorities also shut down the Seoul branch of the Japanese newspaper *Yomiuri* because it reported: "The fingerprint of Kim Dong-un, a first secretary at the Korean Embassy in Japan, was discovered at the scene of the kidnapping in the Grand Palace Hotel in Japan, which indicates that the Korean government must be involved in this incident." The authorities expelled three Japanese correspondents, including the branch chief.

The kidnapping incident had enormous repercussions. It was obvious to everyone that the Park Chung-hee military regime committed this brutal political terror. It was an uncommon atrocity that astonished the entire civilized society of the world. Assemblymen debated this incident every day. The ruling party claimed that I staged the incident. They also attacked me personally, falsely accusing me of buying luxurious houses in the US and Japan and living lavishly. Although this was a complete lie, the newspapers featured the story.

Opposition party members were an even bigger problem than the ruling party members. Even the Sinmin Party members sided with the ruling party members by agreeing to their false claim that I had staged the kidnapping incident myself. It was incredible, and I felt really miserable about the way in which the ruling party controlled even the Sinmin Party. Nevertheless, Assemblyman Jeong Il-hyeong indirectly but justly pointed out that it was the regime that committed this incident. "It is obvious that the sun is in the sky. Everyone can know what really happened, as there is the sun in the sky. To deny it is like blocking the sun out with your hand and claiming that there is no sun. Isn't it obvious? The ruling party is lying."

The National Assembly was in an uproar. Assemblyman Jeong was the only one who dared to be principled in that bloodthirsty society. He was a very brave elder.

On September 5, Japanese investigation headquarters announced the result of their investigation. They officially confirmed that they found the fingerprint of Kim Dong-un, a first secretary at the Korean Embassy, and summoned him to the police station. However, the Korean Embassy refused to cooperate, using the excuse of diplomatic immunity. Korea-Japan relations quickly froze. As it became obvious that the Korean governmental agency was involved in the kidnapping, the Korean government went on the defensive. Japan demanded that the Korean government clarify the truth, return me to Japan, and offer an official apology.

Japanese investigation headquarters confirmed various facts, based on my statements to the media. The person who said, "This way is for Osaka, and that for Kyoto," turned out to be toll collector at the Otsu IC of the Meishin Highway.

On September 7, 1973, the *Chosun Ilbo* newspaper ran a noteworthy editorial entitled "On Fall Outing Season," written by Editor-in-Chief Sunwoo Hwi. It was the first editorial about my kidnapping. The very moderate piece was written in such a manner as to reassure KCIA agents stationed in the office; however, Sunwoo Hwi swapped the text they read with another version at the last minute. This piece that dealt with the Kim Dae-jung Kidnapping Incident was entitled "Our Sincerest Wish for the Authorities: The Sooner Your Resolution the Better."

These days, it is depressing and stifling because we don't know what we want to know and we can't say what we want to say. If asked what it is that we want to know and say so much about, I would immediately answer that it is the Kim Dae-jung Incident. If told that the incident is under investigation now and so we just have to wait for the result of the investigation, there is nothing we can do and this makes us more stifled. In this sense, this incident must be thoroughly investigated not because we have to consider the sentiments of or measures by our allies the US and Japan toward Korea, but because it is most important in the recovery of dignity of the Korean people and the elevation of our moral pride.

Therefore, what we sincerely hope for at this critical juncture is decisive high-level resolution by the authorities. Today, our mountains and rivers, handed down to us from our ancestors, are verdant and ripening. Birds sing high in the sky, and calves' cries softly cross the fields. If we drive through the mountains and fields, the roads are wide open and villages are full of energy unlike before. Why should our people feel anxious and why should these innocent and good people be worried so much today when we are about to make rice cakes out of new crops and offer them before the spirit of our ancestors?

Dear God, may you forgive and bless this people!

This editorial, published thanks to Editor-in-Chief Sunwoo's witty tactic, moved the minds of many people who remained in fearful silence. In fact, all people wanted to know the truth and full picture of the kidnapping incident. However, the KCIA's watchful eyes were everywhere in society. Those who knew couldn't say and those who didn't know couldn't ask.

Summer vacation was over and students returned to school. On October 2, approximately 300 Seoul National University College of Arts and Sciences students gathered to read a statement and staged a protest, declaring, "We can no longer overlook the cruel reality which threatens Korean people's right to live. We rise up resolutely in answer to the order of our conscience."

Students demanded "Investigation on the Truth of the Kim Dae-jung Incident," "Dissolution of KCIA," and "Stop Fascist Politics." It was the first student demonstration since the launch of the Yusin regime. Under the Yusin regime, assembly and demonstration were illegal. Students were taken into police custody, but people were gathering their will to overthrow the Yusin dictatorship.

The Japanese government indefinitely postponed the Korea-Japan Minister-level Conference, originally scheduled in the fall, in protest of the kidnapping incident. The honeymoon between the two governments was over. This was the first and biggest difficulty they had run into since the Korea-Japan Normalization Treaty. They exchanged secret envoys to address this strained relationship. On November 1, Foreign Minister Kim Yong-shik published agreements with Japan, known as the "November 1 Measures."

First, the first secretary Kim Dong-un at the Korean Embassy, who it is strongly suspected was involved in the incident, will be dismissed from his post. Second, the Korean government will not further investigate Mr. Kim Dae-jung's words and actions in Japan and the US before the incident, unless he is engaged in anti-national actions in the future. Third, Prime Minister Kim Jong-pil will visit Japan and deliver President Park's personal letter and express regrets.

Prime Minister Kim visited Japan the next day, delivered President Park's personal letter to Japanese Prime Minister Tanaka Kakuei, and expressed regret. That was a base attempt to recover from the ugly staging of the kidnapping incident.

The personal letter from President Park was released thirty-three years later in February 2006.

It is a joyful development that the friendship between Koreans and Japanese become stronger and the mutually beneficial collaborative relationship between two governments is expanding daily in all areas including politics, economy, society, and culture through new and persistent efforts after the two neighbors, Korea and Japan, cleanse all unhappy past history. It is highly unfortunate that the Kim Dae-jung Incident unexpectedly occurred and caused temporary trouble between the two countries. I express my regrets to Your Excellency and your people. No friction due to this incident should be allowed to impede the basic and traditional good-neighbor friendship between the two peoples. I would like to contribute further to the increased mutual trust and friendship by making my utmost effort to prevent any similar incident from happening between the two countries.

Prime Minister Tanaka replied:

It was really regrettable that a dispute occurred between Japan and Korea and disrupted our friendly relations because of the Mr. Kim Dae-jung Incident. Japanese government has wanted to resolve this incident in a reasonable manner that could be acceptable domestically and abroad. We are grateful that Mr. President dispatched Prime Minister Kim Jong-pil and had him deliver your personal letter of regrets, whereby contributing to the increased friendly relationship. I hope that this will be a diplomatic conclusion to the Kim Dae-jung Incident and I pray that both peoples' common wish for the fair and smooth development of Japan-Korea relations will be achieved.

This was the action that came out of a politically congenial spirit on the summit level between the two countries. It was, however, not a solution, but a stitching over. I was really disappointed at Japan's political climate. I was hearing that the Japanese political power had been continuously blocking Japanese investigative authorities in their efforts to thoroughly investigate the incident. Even worse, there was a rumor that Prime Minister Tanaka requested of Koreans, "It's troublesome to have Kim Dae-jung here, so please don't let him come to Japan."

There was also a rumor about monetary exchange between the two political powers. I couldn't believe it in the beginning, but I cannot help believing it today because of many reliable testimonies since then. The US State Department Korea Country Chief James Leonard testified in the congressional hearing that he believed the Korean government had delivered 300 million *yen* to Prime Minister Tanaka. Also, according to the report by Moon Myong-ja, a journalist based in the US, and the confession by Kimura Hiroyasu, who worked as Prime Minister Tanaka's secretary then, there seems to have been no doubt that President Park gave an enormous sum of money to Prime Minister Tanaka. It was the culmination of the bribery diplomacy, the result of collusion between the Korean dictatorial regime and Japanese plutocracy.

This kind of political corruption was harmful not only to me but also to both the Korean and Japanese people. Although Japanese sovereignty was violated within Japan, the Japanese government ignored international law and politically sutured it, deceiving both Koreans and the Japanese. Because of this political collusion, discovery of truth through thorough investigation and restoration of the original state before the kidnapping—which the Japanese government had promised—became a hopeless goal. I have also had to suffer greatly because of it since then.

House arrest continued. I heard from Professor Reischauer that he visited Seoul to deliver Harvard University's invitation to me and to arrange for my trip to the US. I was able to go to the airport with my wife, perhaps because of Professor Reischauer's reputation and influence.

That day, the day when the first frost of the season descended on Seoul, reporters crowded the airport despite rough weather. I couldn't have a good conversation with Professor Reischauer in the airport because we were being pushed around by reporters who didn't want to miss a word and by the police, who tried to block them with all their might. We could finally talk on the car ride from Kimpo Airport to downtown Seoul. Once we arrived at my house, we talked over the loud noise of the radio in an effort to counter the wiretapping. I felt really sorry for Professor Reischauer.

Professor Reischauer wrote a letter where he stated that he would guarantee my status in the US. However, the Ministry of Foreign Affairs official in charge of this matter did not show up, despite his earlier promise. My house arrest continued.

The police surrounded my house in many layers. Someone joked, "Your house is the safest house in the world." To be imprisoned in one's own house is pain itself. It was a house-sized grave and hell. It was hard for me to keep track of the day and the time.

On December 3, President Park dismissed Lee Hu-rak from the KCIA directorship as someone responsible for the kidnapping incident. Prime Minister Kim Jong-pil kept his post. However, changing a few cabinet members could not appease popular opinion. On December 24, thirty opposition party politicians, including former president Yun Po-sun, organized the Constitutional Amendment Petition Movement Headquarters and launched a signature-gathering campaign. Their goal was to gather a million signatures.

I had to greet the New Year gloomily at home. I could neither visit anyone, nor welcome visitors according to Korean New Year's Day custom. I missed people. At that time, demands for democratization were rising like the New Year's sun in all walks of our society. President Park declared Emergency Measures #1 and #2 according to the Yusin Constitution on January 8, 1974, as a response to an alarming anti-regime movement development under way. He banned the discussion and reporting of the constitutional amendment entirely, and arrested leaders of the constitutional amendment petition movement. Intellectuals, religious leaders, and politicians continued to be arrested. Mr. Chang Chun-ha and Mr. Baek Gi-wan were tried at the emergency military court and sentenced to fifteen years in prison. I listened to this news helplessly from home.

In February 1974, sad news came from my hometown in Hauido. My father passed away. Even though I knew that he was in critical condition, I could not visit him because the police blocked it. I could not even be there on his way to the other world because the Park regime blocked my attendance to my father's funeral. I wonder how they could be so cruel. I guess they were afraid crowds would gather if I attended the funeral, lest that led to an uprising. At any rate, I ended up becoming an unfilial son, who couldn't attend even his father's funeral. It is a matter of great regret to me. Even today, I look back at it with a heavy heart. How anxiously would my father have been waiting for me before he passed away?

EMERGENCY MEASURE #9 (1974–1975)

By the beginning of 1974, a rumor was already circulating about an impending crisis in March or April. College students were unusually active. In fact, Emergency Measures #1 and #2 had the effect of encouraging organized actions among the collegiate set. Students were the only ones who tried to fight against the military dictatorship, and they were exploring the possibility of a nationwide fight. Although they tried to organize secretly, there was no way the intelligence authorities were unaware of an attempt of this size. The National League of Democratic Youth and Students' (NLDYS) plan to rise up all across the country was easily detected.

On April 3, approximately seventy students gathered for a demonstration at the Seoul National University College of Arts and Sciences. About 200 plainclothes operatives—three times as many authorities as students—were watching them. All of the students were detained while chanting slogans like "Down with the Yusin!" However, ultimately, this was not the end, but the beginning. The Park regime took advantage of this event as an opportunity to declare Emergency Measure #4 at 10:00 p.m. on that very same day.

According to this measure, all activities related to NLDYS were banned; violators of this measure would be arrested and imprisoned without warrants and tried at the emergency military tribunal. The sentence was also prescribed as capital punishment or anywhere from five years to life in prison. Not only that, but the college of the violating student could also be closed. The measure contained frightful, unheard of contents.

On May 27, the prosecutorial department of the emergency military tribunal published a statement explaining that they viewed the NLDYS Incident as an attempted uprising to overthrow the state. They maintained that the underground communist forces belonging to the People's Revolutionary Party, such as Suh Do-won and Do Ye-jong, joined forces with the pro-North Korean residents' league in Japan, a small minority of religious leaders, and domestic anti-government forces in an attempt to overthrow the Korean government through a violent and bloody revolution and to establish a communist regime. There was no material evidence to this allegation.

Those related to the People's Revolutionary Party were ruthlessly tortured. Rumor had it that their intestines were slipping out of their bodies. This torture was to brand them as communists who instigated the establishment of NLDYS.

The result of the NLDYS trial was even more shocking. Altogether, 1024 people were investigated and 253 were sent to the military tribunal. The military tribunal sentenced capital punishment to eight alleged People's Revolutionary Party members, and six NLDYS leaders, including Yoo Ihn-tae, Lee Chul, and Kim Byeong-gon. Many other NLDYS leaders were sentenced to anywhere from ten years to life in prison. Poet Kim Chi-ha was sentenced to imprisonment for life, and Professor Kim Dong-kil, Bishop Tji Hak-soon, and Reverend Pak Hyeong-gyu received harsh sentences for aiding and abetting NLDYS. Completely taken aback, their attorney Kang Sin-ok said in court, "I would feel more comfortable to be tried with the defendants." He was arrested on the spot. This kind of arrest was unprecedented in judicial history.

On June 1, the Seoul District Court suddenly summoned me to appear in court on suspicion of violation of election law during my stump for Candidate Yun Po-sun in the 1967 presidential election. It was a ridiculous attempt to use something that happened seven years before to prevent me from traveling outside of the country. My defense counsel comprised attorneys Hahn Seung-hun, Park Se-kyung, Yu Taek-hyeong, and Lee Taek-don. Attorney Han has remained my comrade since then, and throughout my journey toward Korean democracy.

The judiciary was pitiable, too. It was admirable that the government even found those tattered old documents. Whenever the Japanese government requested my return to recover my pre-kidnapping state, the authorities claimed, "We cannot allow him to leave the country during trial. We cannot issue his passport." The Japanese government retreated. Although the Japanese and Korean governments squabbled with one another over this matter, they each continued to yield at critical moments. Leaving the country was out of the question for me because of the collusion between the two governments. I had to helplessly go to and from the court.

August 15, the twenty-ninth Independence Day of Korea, was a very personally meaningful day—it was the day my eldest son, Hong Il, got married. It was also the day First Lady Yuk Young-soo was assassinated at the Seoul National Theater of Korea during the Independence Day ceremony. While I was in my study, I heard from my secretaries that shots were fired at the ceremony. I quickly went to the living room to watch the

TV. The first lady had already been carried away to the hospital, and the theater was chaotic. I could see the president hide quickly behind the table. The first lady passed away around 7:00 p.m. This was the so-called Mun Se-gwang Incident.

Madam Yuk's assassination was a shocking event. I had a very good impression of her. When I went to the Blue House to attend the 1968 New Year's Day ceremony, she greeted me with a gentle smile and asked me about my wife. Koreans loved her as "the opposition party in the Blue House." Her death made us worry more about the future of the Park regime.

Mun was arrested on the spot. The Park regime soon published the result of their investigation: The second-generation Korean in Japan, Mun Se-gwang, used a US-made gun he had stolen from a Japanese police station under the order of a pro-North Korean organization in Japan. The Park regime demanded that the Japanese government issue an official apology for the assassination. It also wanted harsh measures instated against the pro-North Korean organization, which it understood as having ordered the assassination from behind the scenes. However, the Japanese government dismissed these demands, saying that Mun Se-gwang was Korean and there was no legal foundation for cracking down on the organization. The Korea-Japan relationship was strained again, and my kidnapping incident was pushed aside.

Hong Il's wedding was held in the garden of my eldest brother-in-law in Pil-dong, not very far from the Seoul National Theater of Korea. Hong Il insisted that he didn't want to have a large wedding ceremony while his father was imprisoned at home. As it rained, the ceremony happened in the living room, with Dr. Jeong Il-hyeong officiating. Only immediate families of the bride and groom gathered. Hong Il's new father-in-law Mr. Yun Gyeong-bin had worked as the chief security guard for Chairman Kim Koo at the provisional Korean government in Shanghai during the Japanese colonial period (he later worked as the president of the Korean Liberation Association under the democratic government). Hong Il, a twenty-seven-year-old first lieutenant in the air force, was manly, and his bride Hye-ra was more beautiful than a flower. I was very grateful to his in-laws for allowing their marriage during this time when people were reluctant to have anything to do with my family.

In April 1974, Sinmin Party president Yu Jin-san passed away from cancer. Although doctors forbade visitors, I visited President Yu during his hospitalization based on his special request. Looking at him lying and suffering in the hospital, I forgot all about past bad feelings and just felt sorry for him. I sincerely wished for his fast recovery. President Yu said to me, "You and I are the only people who think about the future of this country. Let's work together from now on." But he couldn't recover. I was relieved that we reconciled during his last days, despite confrontations during our political careers.

On August 23, the Sinmin Party held a party convention to elect the new president in the wake of Mr. Yu's passing. The KCIA's continuing interference with the opposition party's inside matters extended to the party presidential election. Through bribery and intimidation, they encouraged and supported a candidate who suited their taste. Since I couldn't really be involved in the election due to my house imprisonment, I encouraged colleagues belonging to the so-called Donggyo-dong faction to vote for Assemblyman Kim Young-sam, as he was one of our party's most powerful enemies of the Park regime.

The Sangdo-dong faction, led by Mr. Kim Young-sam, and the Donggyo-dong faction, which I led, were the two mountain ranges of the Sinmin Party at the time. At some point, Kim Young-sam, who belonged to the old Yu Jin-san faction, and I, belonging to the new Chang Myon faction, became rivals. However, factions could not matter in the face of the task of overthrowing the dictatorial regime. I believed Assemblyman Kim Young-sam thought along the same lines.

After being elected as the Sinmin Party president, Assemblyman Kim Young-sam presented three major political tasks: first, the amendment of the Yusin Constitution; second, the release of political prisoners; third, the guarantee of my leaving the country. Assemblyman Kim Young-sam proposed establishing the Special Committee for the Basic Discussion of Constitutional Amendment at the regular September session of the National Assembly. Finally, on November 27, the National Congress for the Recovery of Democracy was established as the central organization for those who yearned for democracy. I participated despite the fact that I was still imprisoned at home. Slogans like "Amendment of the Yusin Constitution," "Guarantee Freedom of the Press," and "Release the Arrested" reverberated far and wide.

The *DongA Ilbo* Advertisement Oppression Incident happened toward the end of that year. As reporters of the *DongA Ilbo* decided to exercise their freedom of the press and reported on anti-regime demonstrations, the regime put pressure on its advertisers. Around December 15, large corporations simultaneously canceled their advertisements, as if they had decided on it together. This was, of course, based on President Park's order.

Advertisers and their PR executives had been summoned to the KCIA. The *DongA Ilbo* had no choice but to publish the newspaper without advertisements. This was the well-known Blank Advertisement Incident.

There was a surprising turn of events that neither the regime nor the *DongA Ilbo* expected. Citizens and students rushed to run advertisements encouraging the reporters and newspaper. It was grassroots resistance to the power's oppression of the press that publicized the barbaric act of the dictatorial regime. Slogans encouraging the resistance appeared in those blank spaces: "Long Live Free Press!" "The Dawn of the Nation Will Come," "We Know the Meaning of Blank Advertisement," "We Will Not Ignore Your Suffering," and more.

The advertisement space of the *DongA Ilbo* then became a large open space for the people's hope and yearning for democracy. Readers read the advertisements before the regular articles. Through the advertisements, they confirmed each other's will for democracy.

I immediately ran an advertisement encouraging them, too. I also called my friends and acquaintance to encourage them to place their own advertisements. I wrote the advertisement in my own handwriting and sent it to the newspaper. This advertisement ran on the eighth page of the newspaper's New Year's Day issue with the signature "a citizen who wants to defend the freedom of the press." In order to prevent harsher oppression of both the newspaper and myself, I had to hide my name. Following is a passage from my advertisement entitled "Let's Defend the Freedom of the Press."

> The freedom of the press is our life. Without it, there are no human rights or social justice or freedom of scholarship and religion or national security based on the people's voluntary participation. Freedom of the press is the soul of the democratic people and the origin of all wishes. The blank advertisement space in the *DongA Ilbo* is the direct evidence of the regime's conspiracy and arrogance and a direct affront to the people's right to know. It is not just a matter for *DongA Ilbo*, but also a matter of all our life and death.
>
> As a citizen who passionately desires the freedom of the press and the recovery of democracy, I pay for this advertisement in order to protect the candlelight of the freedom of the press that had just begun to burn.

I then urged all of our people to participate in this defense of the freedom of the press against the regime's oppression of the media. Many years later, in 2006, I heard from Mr. Kim In-ho, the advertisement department chief of the *DongA Ilbo* at that time, that mine was the first advertisement of encouragement. I remember sending quite a lot of money for that advertisement despite my deplorable financial situation.

Extremely surprised by this turn of events, the Park regime met with the management of the *DongA Ilbo* to find a compromise. They agreed that the regime would stop the advertisement oppression in exchange for the newspaper company's dismissal of conscientious reporters. It was an ugly backdoor deal wherein money and the freedom of the press changed hands. The newspaper company dismissed eighteen reporters with the excuse of a worsening financial situation. In response, reporters held an emergency assembly and decided to wage a strike. They denounced the company's collusion with the power. Editor-in-Chief Song Kun-ho left the newspaper saying, "The *DongA* will be judged by history later." I was really disappointed, too.

Reporters were kicked out on to the street five days later. Citizens gathered in front of the newspaper company building and condemned it. Some demanded that the company refund their advertisement fee. The advertisements of encouragement completely disappeared from the *DongA Ilbo* after May 8 and the newspaper dismissed about one hundred reporters through a series of seven dismissals. It was an unprecedented journalist massacre.

This incident has been remembered as a momentous historical event, which became a precious seed for the freedom of the press. The dismissed journalists contributed greatly to the later democracy movement. I still admire their courage and sense of justice.

I feel sorry for one thing related to this incident, though. Before the mass dismissal of the journalists, I requested Kim Sang-hyun and Lee Tai-young meet with the CEO of the *DongA Ilbo* because I wanted to prevent these job losses. Through negotiations, they got the company to promise they would reinstate all reporters except for a few, who would be reinstated in a few months. I let this fact be known to the dismissed journalists. Unfortunately, they were angry and argued for the immediate reinstatement of all dismissed journalists, saying, "Who asked Kim Dae-jung to help us? It's all or nothing."

I sent people to persuade them otherwise, saying: "A pen is a journalist's weapon. What are you going to do without a pen? Since they promised to eventually reinstate all of you, couldn't those who are reinstated first help the few unreinstated for a few months?" They didn't agree, though. In the end, the police entered the building and stopped the strike, and the journalists all lost their jobs. I understand their righteous anger, but I was sad about their choice.

An incredible thing was happening in East Asia. North Vietnam won the Vietnam War by taking Saigon on April 30, 1975. This news reminded me of what I had seen when I visited Vietnam to comfort Korean soldiers. The sumptuous dinner of high officials and the luxurious clothing of their wives already suggested South Vietnam's defeat. How could a government that drove its people into war while enjoying luxury earn its people's trust? No matter how strong, a military cannot defend a government that does not win its people's hearts and minds.

South Vietnam's defeat was a great disaster for the Park regime. South Vietnam was our ally—a country that was under the protective umbrella of the US like us—and a cause to which we invested more than 300,000 troops. Both governments were similar in that they both lost their people's trust. Although apparently calm, it was clear that the Park regime was shocked and nervous about it.

President Park issued the "Special Statement Concerning the Defeat of Vietnam," in which he emphasized an all-out national security. He said he would defend Seoul and its population of 6.5 million to the end if war broke out. The Park regime had nowhere to turn when the US, which it relied upon completely, lost the war and the world left the Cold War behind. Wherever Koreans went, we saw the "All-out National Security" slogan. During this time, North Korean President Kim Il-sung went on a diplomatic tour of China and Eastern European countries. The Park regime was busy with propaganda, claiming there was a high possibility of an all-out North Korean invasion.

On May 13, 1975, President Park declared Emergency Measure #9. It included fourteen bloodthirsty articles. It banned all acts of arguing, petitioning, and instigating for the negation, opposition, slandering, amendment, and abolishment of the Yusin Constitution, as well as reporting on any of them. Violators would be arrested without warrant. It also banned students' assembly, demonstration, and political struggle, as well as rumor-mongering, rumor distribution, and distortion of facts.

If these articles should be strictly applied, it would have been hard for the press to even exist. The assemblymen's privilege of exemption from liability was also stripped. Therefore, if they said something in violation of Emergency Measure #9 in the National Assembly, they should be punished. Newspaper reporters worked in the office where the contents of Emergency Measure #9 were posted. There was even an exclusive desk in charge of censoring articles according to Emergency Measure #9. It was a rare, bizarre sight. There was no freedom of speech.

Although the Korea-Japan relationship had been stressed since the Mun Se-gwang Incident, the Park regime changed its position on my kidnapping incident. On July 22, 1975, the Korean government sent a verbal message to the Japanese government. "Regarding Kim Dong-un, we dismissed and investigated him, but did not indict him because we could not secure evidence. However, his words and actions in Tokyo degraded the government official's dignity, so we dismissed him." After receiving this message, Minister of Foreign Affairs Miyazawa Kiichi said, "I understand this concludes the Kim Dong-un problem that has been in the way of Korea-Japan relations." He then came to Seoul to meet Minister of Foreign Affairs Kim Dong-jo and President Park. After this conference with the president, he said, "This concludes the problem regarding Mr. Kim Dae-jung." This was the second political collusion between the two countries.

I expected that the Japanese government would approach my kidnapping incident from a human rights perspective. In fact, I had no doubt about it, as Japan was supposed to be an advanced country that respected human rights. But even after finding the fingerprints of KCIA personnel at the crime scene, the Japanese government chose not to handle it according to principle. It was really hard to understand. In the end, the rift between Korea and Japan caused by the Mun Se-gwang Incident was sutured through political collusion between the two countries regarding the kidnapping incident.

On October 24, 2007, the National Intelligence Service (NIS) Committee for Development Through Truth Examination of Past Incidents announced the result of the official government investigation of the kidnapping incident for the first time since its occurrence thirty-four years before. I was disappointed at the result of this investigation, though. The focus of the investigation was who ordered it and what its purpose had been, but their investigation result was unsatisfactory on both accounts.

Regarding who ordered the kidnapping, the NIS committee concluded: "It cannot be ruled out that the former president Park directly ordered it, and there was at least his tacit approval of the plan." It also stated: "If President Park was really unrelated to this incident, he should have naturally punished KCIA Director Lee Hu-rak. But the fact that he didn't and that he ordered to cover up the incident shows that President Park was either an accessary to or the principal of this incident." On the whole, based on these conclusions, the NIS committee should have clearly concluded that the kidnapping incident was a murder operation carried out by President Park's order. There can be no doubt as to this conclusion, based on the testimonies of the people involved in it. Therefore, it is hard to accept its vague conclusion.

It is truly regrettable that both the Korean and Japanese governments have yet to fulfill their obligation of clarifying the truth of the incident. The essence of the kidnapping incident was that the Korean government had its operatives sent to another country to kidnap its citizen. Although Japan's sovereignty was violated and Japan had a duty to protect me, its government neglected the whole incident and allowed my human rights to be violated.

In 1967, when the East Berlin Incident—in which KCIA operatives kidnapped a number of Koreans in West Germany and France and took them to South Korea—occurred, both French and the West German governments strongly protested it. As a result, the South Korean government returned all of its kidnapping victims to France and Germany. As there was this precedent, I expected Japan to do the same thing.

Much later, during my presidency, I was invited to visit Japan as a state guest. Should I, the victim of the incident, have brought this matter up? I did not think that would be right. The Japanese government should have volunteered to take proper measures about it—which, unfortunately, it didn't—before I, the victim of that incident, became president and was about to visit Japan again.

I really wanted to investigate this incident during my presidency, but refrained from doing so. I do not think it right that an incident in which the power was involved should be investigated by another power. I know that the government intelligence agency rushed to destroy documents related to me as soon as I was elected president.

I was kidnapped by the order of the president to "get rid of" me. I will continue to wait for the revelation of the truth. I would also like to receive true apologies from both the Korean and Japanese governments. This may not happen during my lifetime. But I believe that someone will reveal the truth someday. I will continue to wait because I believe that the truth should become history.

Into the Bloodthirstiness of Yusin Again
(1975–1977)

President Park proposed a referendum for the Yusin Constitution in connection with the people's confidence in him. It was a deceitful scheme to deprive people of their freedom to object to the Yusin regime, a scheme to avoid domestic and overseas condemnation of the Yusin system.

Democratic forces rejected the referendum. I urgently met with Sinmin Party President Kim Young-sam. Together, we announced the Code of Conduct for Referendum Rejection at a joint press conference. Former president Yun Po-sun added his signature to it. In it, we declared: "The Park regime is staging a political show named referendum in order to maintain its oppressive regime by spending an enormous sum of taxes paid by the sweat of Korean people. We declare the twelfth, the day of referendum, as Referendum Rejection Day."

I arrived at the Myeongdong Cathedral at 7:00 a.m. that day with my wife and prayed while fasting. Catholics and Protestants named that day the Day of National Salvation Prayer; we reported the death of democracy and prayed to God for its recovery. Three bells for the death of democracy, three bells for the overthrow of dictatorship, and then thirty-three bells rang. I published the following statement:

> The regime carries out today's referendum under the pressure of domestic and overseas criticism of its military dictatorship. As the regime will publish an already-prepared result, I cannot acknowledge it. Korean people, who have witnessed unjust and illegal activities throughout the entire process of referendum, would not accept the result, and world opinion will support us.

I had interviews with Japanese and Western media reporters, including reporters of the French newspaper *Le Monde*; American newspapers the *Washington Post*, the *New York Times*, and the *LA Times*; and German TV stations.

The next day, the regime published the referendum result that 79.8 percent of the Korean electorate participated and 73.1 percent approved the Yusin. President Park claimed that this was the Korean people's will, and then released social leaders and students who had been imprisoned for their violation of the Emergency Measures.

On February 15, Professor Paik Nak-chung, Reverend Ham Sok-hon, Mr. Kim Gwan-seok, Poet Ko Un, Mr. Kim Sang-hyun, and Ms. Kim Jung-re were released, and I went to greet them. Poet Kim Chi-ha, who had been imprisoned because of the NLDYS Incident, was released, too. Mr. Kim visited me at my house and I comforted him for his sufferings.

The Park regime did not allow released professors and students to return to school. College campuses were heating up again. Finally, slogans criticizing the current state of political affairs such as "Stop the Oppression of the Press!" and "Down with the Yusin!" appeared. The authorities immediately ordered the closure of the schools where student rallies occurred.

On April 7 and 8, Korea University students held fierce demonstrations demanding the resignation of the dictatorial regime and the abolishment of the Yusin Constitution. The Park regime immediately declared Emergency Measure #7 and closed Korea University. At the same time, military troops occupied the campus. On May 13, the Park regime declared Emergency Measure #9.

On August 17, Mr. Chang Chun-ha, a former independence fighter and current democracy fighter, died under suspicious circumstances. Mr. Chang had revealed Park Chung-hee's pro-Japanese career early on, and fiercely condemned his hypocritical political career. Mr. Chang was busy with activities to end the dictatorial regime.

Mr. Chang urged all pro-democracy forces to be united for an effective democracy struggle. Accepting his suggestion, Yun Po-sun, Yang El-dong, Kim Young-sam, and I met for a four-way conference on March 31. However, this effort was cut short because Sinmin Party President Kim Young-sam proposed President Park have an exclusive conference. After his visit to the Blue House, President Kim did not reveal what was discussed in the conference at all. He also postponed the constitutional amendment struggle. It was natural that people were suspicious of a back-door deal.

Disappointed at President Kim's change of position and the status of things, Mr. Chang visited my house at the end of July. There had been an uncomfortable feeling between us because Mr. Chang, who belonged to another camp, attacked me during the 1971 presidential election. Mr. Chang told me the purpose of his visit was to remove that discomfort between us. He said, "I'll actively support you from now on. I'd like to end the Yusin regime and accomplish democratic society with you."

I contributed to the magazine *Sasanggye*, which Mr. Chang ran both financially and as an editorial contributor. *Sasanggye* was a precious magazine that did not hesitate to defy the menacing dictatorship. The authorities forced the magazine to shut down in 1970 for publishing Poet Kim Chi-ha's political satire, "Five Bandits."

Mr. Chang and I had a very warm and friendly lunch together. He talked about how he enjoyed hiking and used it as a tool to regain his health, listing all the mountains he had traversed. Worried about his safety, I asked, "Is it okay for you to go about like that?"

"Would they possibly try to do anything to me?" he responded.

"Nevertheless, please don't go alone," I replied. "The state of affairs is too harsh."

That was our last conversation. Even as Mr. Chang's warm smiles and back leaving my house were still vivid in my eyes, I heard that his body was found in the Yaksabong Valley in Pocheon-gun, Gyeonggi-do. I regretted that I hadn't done more to dissuade him from hiking alone.

Strangely, there were no wounds on his body when he was found—wounds that *should* have been there if he had fallen from a mountaintop. Many people thought of murder when they heard the tragic news. Despite the many unanswered questions about his death, Mr. Chang's body remained silent. Although he had a hard life, his fights against Japanese colonialism and the Rhee Syngman and Park Chung-hee dictatorial regimes shine on. Firmly believing that it was a murder at the hands of the dictatorial regime, Mr. Ham Sok-hon said, "Chang Chun-ha's reconciliation with Kim Dae-jung brought his death to him. Those bastards knew what to expect from your collaboration. They had to get rid of at least one of you." There's no way of knowing whether or not this is true, but Mr. Chang Chun-ha left this world in such an absurd way. He had to close his eyes without seeing the free sky that he had so wanted to see.

The dictatorship was getting harsher and more murderous by the day. The Emergency Measures took away all our desires and hope from all walks of our lives. People kept silent. Realizing that they were exercising self-censorship, intellectuals trembled with shame. All kinds of humiliation accompanied the people's silence during that time.

Nihilism spread among the young people. Deprecatingly calling themselves "the Emergency Measure generation," they felt anguished over the dictatorial net that entrapped them. Police officers guarded every alley. Men with long hair were dragged to the police station and had their hair torn out. Women were taken into police custody because they wore short skirts. A lot of songs were banned for their lyrics, which, according to the random judgment of authorities, could be interpreted as critical of the regime. People could neither speak nor sing to their hearts' content.

Under Emergency Measures, participation in the anti-regime demonstration was a matter of weighty decision, which required one to risk his or her life. Students suffered from a nightmare and lost their sense of direction. Enormous violence stared people straight in the face.

I decided I had to do something. I visited Cardinal Kim Sou-hwan at Myeongdong Cathedral, feeling as though I was visiting him to deliver my last will. I said, "This can't do. I have to go to the prison. I'm telling you ahead of time." Cardinal Kim remained silent for a while, then held my hand tightly. It must have been very painful for him to see my resolution during such a harsh time.

Together with other democracy movement leaders, I prepared a statement that I planned to publish on the March 1st Independence Movement Day, a day when Koreans would think of our country the most deeply. I thought it would resonate most deeply among Koreans if I attacked the Yusin regime head-on that day. My expectation proved accurate. Although I, a former presidential candidate, ended up in prison with former president Mr. Yun Po-sun, our righteous rebellion drew attention from Koreans and foreigners alike. In particular, it had huge impact in the US and Japan.

The March 1st National Salvation Declaration originated from the same thought democracy movement leaders all shared. While I was preparing a statement with Dr. Jeong Il-hyeong and former president Yun Po-sun, I came to know that other democracy movement leaders were preparing a similar kind of declaration. I secretly sent my draft statement to Dr. Jeong Il-hyeong and Ms. Lee Tai-young. That draft was then sent to Reverend Moon Ik-hwan, while Reverend Moon's draft was sent to me. Reverend Moon's draft had many harsh expressions. We finished the statement through mutual revisions.

On March 1, about 700 Catholics gathered at Myeongdong Cathedral in Seoul. I attended the mass with my wife. After mass, there was a prayer meeting, which both Catholics and Protestants attended. Reverend Moon Ik-hwan's younger brother, Reverend Moon Dong-hwan, delivered a sermon, during which he said the following: "Moses, who had led Israelites out of Egypt, handed over the national leadership to Joshua before he entered Canaan. That is why he has been praised for a long time as the greatest leader. Therefore, if Park Chung-hee resigned at this point, he will become highly regarded in Korean history."

The congregants' faces turned pale. A short woman stepped forward. It was Professor Lee Oo-chung. In a clear and calm voice, she read the statement we had prepared, entitled "Democratic National Salvation Declaration."

> Today, we greet the fifty-seventh anniversary of the March 1st Independence Movement Day. As the loud outcry for self-reliance and independence that had reverberated all over the world on March 1, 1919 is still ringing in our ears, we believe that our non-action would be a crime that would bury our

ancestors' blood underground. Thus we gather our will and state the Democratic National Salvation Declaration today.

Although the tragedy of division of Korea that shattered Korean hopes after the August 15th Liberation continued to bring suffering to our nation, we have never lost our hope. We rose above the ruins of the Korean War and overthrew the Rhee Syng-man dictatorial regime through the April 19th Students Righteous Uprising, reviving hopes of liberal democracy in the hearts of our people.

That period of hope lasted only briefly, however, and Korean people were chained to a dictatorial regime again. The separation of three branches of government remained in appearance only. Under the pretext of national security, freedom of religion and conscience is decreasing every day, and the freedom of press and the independence of academe are crushed.

At this time when the Korean people should be advancing toward national reunification, which is our earnest wish, by growing and gathering democratic forces domestically and overseas, human rights are being trampled down and freedom is deprived under one-man dictatorship.

Thus, the Korean nation has lost its sense of goal and direction as well as its belief in democracy. Instead, it is approaching a total catastrophe. As we cannot simply look on this idly, we state this Democratic National Salvation Declaration despite our political differences and while looking ahead to the future of our country.

We then made the following three arguments:

- First, our country should be grounded on democracy.
- Second, the plan for and approach to national economic establishment should be fundamentally reexamined.
- Third, national reunification is the foremost task for our people today.

We ended this statement with "Long Live Democracy!" Altogether, ten people—Ham Sok-hon, Yun Po-sun, Jeong Il-hyeong, Kim Dae-jung, Yun Ban-ung, Lee Oo-chung, Moon Dong-hwan, Ahn Byung Mu, Seo Nam-dong, and Lee Moon-young—signed the statement. Reverend Moon Dong-hwan decided not to join it to finish his work of translating the Bible. During this reading, it was so quiet you could hear a pin drop. After the mass, we held a candlelight vigil.

I did not know when they would come to arrest me, but I felt comfortable in my heart. Then the expected happened. The minister of culture and public relations called our statement an "illegal activity that destroys constitutional order," and the prosecutor's office called it the Government Overthrow Incitement Incident. Those who participated in the mass—Catholic priests Ham Sei-ung, Shin Hyeon-bong, Mun Jeong-hyeon, Kim Seung-hoon, Chang Deok-pil, Kim Taek-am, and An Jung-seok; Ms. Kong Deok-gwi and Ms. Lee Tai-young; and Reverends Moon Ik-hwan and Yi Hae-dong—were all indicted. All people involved in it were arrested one after another. I was dragged to the police station in the wee hours of March 8. Altogether, eleven people—Reverends Moon Ik-hwan, Moon Dong-hwan, Yun Ban-ung, Seo Nam-dong, and Yi Hae-dong; Catholic priests Mun Jeong-hyeon, Shin Hyeon-bong, and Ham Sei-ung; Professor Lee Moon-young, Dr. Ahn Byung Mu, and I—were detained. Yun Po-sun was released because he was former president; Ham Sok-hon because of old age; Jeong Il-hyeong because he was the incumbent assemblyman; and Lee Tai-young and Lee Oo-chung because they were women.

Domestic newspapers could not publish a single line about this incident of mass detention of democracy movement leaders; however, it was broadcast in the global media through the intervention of foreign missionaries and Reverend Pak Dae-in (Edward Poitras).

I was imprisoned in the Seoul Prison. Moon Ik-hwan, Moon Dong-hwan, Lee Moon-young, Ham Sei-ung, and I were imprisoned in solitary cells after changing into blue prisoner clothes. It was very cold in the prison cell. Because of my distorted hip joint, it was extremely uncomfortable for me to sit on the floor. I could not fall asleep in whatever position I tried. Some nights I stayed up all night because of severe pain. On those nights I prayed to God to heal me quickly and I felt as if the pain alleviated. Because I couldn't bend my knees, it was painful to even eat. I asked for a chair and a table, but they did not listen.

Our families were proud of us. It wasn't until fifty-four days after our arrests that they were allowed to visit us in prison. Families of the imprisoned held an overnight prayer meeting on April 17, the eve of Easter. I heard they went to the hill behind the Seoul Prison at dawn and sang Easter hymns in the direction of the prison as loudly as they could, weeping as they sang, but their tearful early morning hymn didn't reach our cells.

The first court day was May 4. The Seoul District Court announced that they were limiting the number of admission tickets. Our families demanded an open trial, but this demand was rejected. Our families taped black crosses over their mouths in front of the court to protest this rejection.

Through this, they were expressing the crucifixion of democracy and freedom of the press. It also conveyed their belief in resurrection.

On the second court day, families burnt their admission tickets on the street because they weren't given enough admission tickets, while the courtroom was filled with intelligence operatives. From the next court day on, we all wore light violet traditional Korean clothes made of nylon and a ribbon on which "Open Trial" and "Democracy Recovery" were written. We could hear our families sing hymns and chant slogans from inside the prison bus, but we could not see them.

On another day, we carried white fans upon which we wrote "Open Trial" and "Release Democracy Movement Leaders!" On another occasion, we entered the court wearing large purple crosses attached to our clothes. Surprised, judges and prosecutors hastily declared adjournment.

Whenever our trial was in session, our families held demonstrations around the court. The authorities trembled with fear because they didn't know how their demonstration would develop. In the end, they pushed our families into a bus and dropped them off in suburbs like Children's Grand Park and Taeneung. Madam Kong Deok-gwi, Ms. Lee Tai-young, and my wife were all unloaded in remote places.

Those of us under trial met in the prison bus every Saturday when there was a trial. We were so glad to see each other. We asked how one another was doing and comforted each another. It was exciting on the prison bus. Being together gave us courage and strength.

Whenever our trial was in session, all other trials were cleared. The general public was not allowed into the courthouse, and the area was tightly guarded. The court turned into the lecture room for democracy, where people tried to awaken the conscience of the times. Well-ordered logic adopted by Catholic and Protestant priests seemed to try the Yusin dictatorship. Mr. Ham Sok-hon, indicted but not detained, attended the trial in funeral garments. Father Mun Jeong-hyeon went right up under the prosecutor and scolded him when a question directed to him was unjust. Father Shin Hyeon-bong wailed while going to the defendant's seat when the judge called him. When the judge asked him why, he calmly answered, "I'm mourning the death of Korean human rights and democracy."

Reverend Moon Ik-hwan said, "I am grateful for the privilege of being imprisoned with many comrades of the democracy movement."

I requested President Park be one of my expert witnesses about the Emergency Measures. Prosecutors and judges looked at one another's faces, embarrassed. Judges and prosecutors were diffident, while we alleged criminals were proud.

The court rushed the trial. In his closing statement Professor Lee Moon-young said, "I am happy to be in prison because I think of it as sharing in Jesus' suffering. I worried that the judge might release me because I am innocent."

On December 20, I made my closing statement at the appeals court. Domestic media did not report on this 20,000-letter statement, but foreign media showed keen interest, with the Japanese *Asahi* newspaper going so far as to run the entire statement on two pages. Following is an excerpt.

> It has been twenty years since I became Catholic. However, I have never felt as happy and as grateful about becoming a Christian as during the past 10-month imprisonment period. I have never prayed to and had conversations with God every day as I have during this period. I am grateful that God sent me to prison. Based on my experience and conscience, I know I am where I should be. I am still suffering from my illness. I still wake up three or four times every night to take medicine. But, I am overjoyed because I am liberated. If I hadn't participated in this March 1st Democratic National Salvation Declaration, or if I stood here as someone unarrested, how uneasy I must have felt. I am grateful that I am in prison.
>
> I am not interested in the judgment. I am sorry to say, but I am not concerned about the prosecutor. I hate nobody, because my God forbids it. When my wife visited me at prison she showed me "The Epistle to the Romans" 12:14, which goes: "Bless those who persecute you; bless and do not curse them." I pray every day for the recovery of democracy, for the liberation of the oppressed, for the churches, and for all those who currently hold power from the president down to correct the current regime according to democratic principle, their conscience, and justice.
>
> I know that the current regime clearly not only arrested me, but also tried to take my life from me. I don't think their intention has changed. They can always murder me. However, no matter what they do to me, they cannot change my loyalty to the Korean people and my sense of obligation toward our descendants. I am someone whose resolution cannot change.
>
> Ladies and gentlemen in this courtroom, and Korean people outside of this courtroom—I believe that we can achieve political freedom that can guarantee people's human rights regardless of our positions, a new economic order that guarantees egalitarian economic environment, and a just society where those who are honest, diligent, and conscientious succeed and there is freedom of conscience, scholarship, and religion. I would like to finish this closing statement of mine by holding each of your hands and sincerely appealing to you for the achievement of such a society.

I was sentenced to eight years in prison (prosecutorial demand was a ten-year imprisonment) in the first trial and five years (prosecutorial demand was a ten-year imprisonment) in the appeals trial. On March 22, 1977, the Supreme Court dismissed my final appeal, confirming the five-year sentence. The Supreme Court dismissed the final appeal of all eighteen defendants.

I got to know the true face of religious and intellectual leaders. I was deeply moved by their pure-hearted passion. Most of them hadn't known me at all. That incident was my first connection with them. This relationship has revived as comradeship during every crisis of the democracy movement since then. They were disadvantaged just because they were my acquaintances. Later, when the new military junta fabricated an incident involving me, they were dragged into it and suffered a great deal. They were truly brave and they sincerely loved Korean people. That's why they were proud.

SPECIAL HOSPITAL ROOM, SPECIAL PRISON (1977–1978)

I was transferred to Jinju Prison—the prison located furthest away from Seoul—on April 14, 1977. I was imprisoned in a solitary cell, with empty rooms to the left and right of me, and several prison guards watching me day and night. The guards trampled on my human rights, even interfering with my lawyer interview. In protest, I waged a six-day hunger strike—my only weapon to fight them—about two months after my transfer. Upon learning about my hunger strike, many people, including my family, protested and appealed the prison. Cardinal Kim Sou-hwan came forward and urged the authorities to implement humanitarian measures.

Although the Park regime tried to isolate me by sending me to Jinju, democracy movement leaders visited me. Of course, they weren't allowed to meet me, but they exchanged news about me and shared their indignation. In particular, many people came to visit me from Busan, Gimhae, and Hadong, and were greeted by my secretaries Kim Ok-du and Kim Hyeong-guk, who alternately stayed in Jinju. People also sent lots of letters of encouragement. I *was* allowed to meet with my attorneys, and met attorneys Hong Nam-sun, Lee Ki-hong, Yun Cheol-ha, Kim Gwang-il, Park Se-kyung, Lee Taek-don, Yu Taek-hyeong, Kim In-gi, and Kim Gi-su.

Scores of people came and sang hymns, shouted slogans, and prayed right under the walls of the prison every day. I could sometimes hear their voices. Whenever I heard someone shout, "We're here for you. Don't you worry!" it gave me great comfort. The prison was always on guard because of me. I later heard they begged the higher-ups to please transfer me to another place as soon as possible.

The only thing I could send to the outside world was letters. I earnestly wrote about things from my heart. The prison thoroughly censored my letters and didn't send those in which I mentioned anything remotely related to political or social situations. I acquired two very precious things in prison: deep faith and the knowledge and wisdom that can be gleaned from reading.

I could feel the warmth of Jesus in my cold prison cell. I came to understand the true Jesus, who had come not to be served but to serve. I wrote about it in a letter to my wife.

> Today's Jesus is Jesus the servant, and this is his true identity: Jesus who came not to be served, but to serve; Jesus who lifted up the lowly; Jesus who was recorded in Luke 1:51–53; Jesus who came to save and liberate sinners and the oppressed; and Jesus who was crucified while dedicating himself to sinners and fighting for them.

My wife always understood and encouraged me. Her letter always gave me courage.

> I picture your holy image, you who accept suffering gratefully and spend your days with prayer and patience. As human beings, how can we express the agony of not being treated for unbearable pains and not getting enough nutrients?
>
> However, like a miracle, your mind is stronger for it and you overcome your physical pain. This makes me think of God's grace.
>
> Enduring the hardship of prison life without getting proper treatment for the illness that is not visible to the naked eye or measured by your pulse or blood pressure—that is a double or triple hardship. To me, the way you bear your current suffering on behalf of Koreans, learn anew humility at the lowest and the basest place, and lead a deeply religious life looks only sublime.
>
> As my life becomes more precious and significant thanks to you, and especially thanks to your suffering, I feel happy that I can love many people more truly and follow a thorny path, looking ahead at tomorrow's new light with pride and hope.

Reading in prison was very helpful. Although reading generally offers us an indirect experience, those books I read in prison gave me much more than that. Because I paid full attention to the book, sometimes I felt as if I was speaking directly to the author. I avidly read books on history, religion, economy, philosophy, and literature. I set the goal of reading twenty or thirty pages of each book per day, and read various books simultaneously.

In particular, Arnold J. Toynbee's twelve-volume *A Study of History* inspired me greatly and gave me faith in the future. Toynbee's view that human beings grow and develop through God-given ordeals and that civilization is the product of our response to challenges offered great insight. I learned that we should not understand the rise and fall of civilization as fate, and that only those groups that successfully respond to challenges from their environment can achieve development as a society. This idea not only seemed to enlighten the future of our nation, but also put the hardships in my life into perspective.

My wife slept without heat, even in winter. She told me she could not sleep in warmth, thinking of me, who was especially sensitive to coldness, trembling in prison.

I was allowed to meet only my wife and only once a month. Nevertheless, she stayed in Jinju many days, thinking I would feel better if she was nearby. She lingered with bread and cookies outside of the prison wall in case she ran into a kind prison guard who would deliver them to me. She sent wool sweaters and mittens that she had knitted. She ironed underwear and sprayed perfume on it. I didn't feel like wearing the underwear because it felt so precious. I hugged it lest the scent disappeared. It was the fragrance of her love.

I missed *kimchi* and coffee the most in prison. Although we offered to pay for them, the prison did not allow it. I didn't mind the rice mixed with beans or barley, but the side dishes smelled so nasty that I couldn't eat them. The guards might have wanted to allow me to receive private food, but they were never free from the KCIA operatives' watchful eyes.

One day I saw a spider web in my prison cell toilet area. I stared as the spider waited for food to come its way. I wondered if there were any insects for that spider to eat in that dark cell with little sunlight. I wondered if it was visiting me on purpose. The more I looked at it, the more pity I felt for it. I caught a fly and I hung it on the spider web; however, the spider didn't at all care about the dead fly. So I trained myself to catch flies without killing them. Then I practiced hanging the fly without breaking the spider web. The spider was very cautious, so it wouldn't appear while I was watching. Only after I hid myself in a corner of the cell for a long time could I observe the spider eating the fly. After slowly descending upon the fly, the spider pushed a web out from its bottom and wrapped the fly in it. Then, it carried the fly to the ceiling, stuck a needle onto the fly's belly, and sucked it. Afterward, the spider dropped the empty shell of a fly onto the floor.

On the last day of October, Cardinal Kim Sou-hwan visited me to prison. I was deeply moved by his visit to such a faraway place. He prayed for me, holding my and my wife's hands. Although it was a short visit, it didn't feel that way—I felt blessed.

On December 19, 1977, I was transferred to Seoul National University Hospital. The authorities pretended this was to treat me humanely. Since my wife had requested treatment for my hip and leg pain many times, I also thought this was the case at first; however, it turned out the transfer was their way of avoiding domestic and international pressure for my release. Although all prisoners related to the March 1st Incident were released soon after their incarceration (on Christmas), I was left in room 201, the prison cell in Seoul National University Hospital. There, they guarded me even more strictly than they had in prison, with about twenty people—including prison guards, KCIA operatives, and police officers—watching over me at all hours. They blocked all contact from the outside world. In Jinju Prison, I could go outside, walk around, and look up at the sky for an hour every day. In the hospital, everything was banned. This special prison cell in the hospital was really a special hell.

In prison, I could read the Bible aloud and sing hymns. I could hum *pansori* and folk songs. In the hospital, guards watched my every move from right behind a thin board and listened to even the sound of the page of a book turning. Because the windows were all blocked, there was no sunlight, but the artificial light inside my room stayed on for twenty-four hours a day. I could not know whether the sun rose or set. It looked like a hospital room, but it was, in fact, a torture chamber.

The only good thing was that I could see my wife every day. Because I wasn't allowed to read the newspaper or listen to the radio, my only pleasure was hearing my wife talk about the outside world. Her dedication to me during that time was truly moving. She prepared my lunch in the morning and brought it around noon. After spending about two hours with me, she went back home, where she read the evening newspaper and took notes. She then prepared dinner and brought it to me around 5:00 p.m. She left the hospital around 7:00 p.m. to meet with other prisoners' families.

By the time my wife finished praying and discussing how to handle the current situation with other prisoners' families, it was very late. After continuing this schedule for quite some time, one day her legs swelled. She went to see the doctor and was told that she had arthritis due to malnutrition. While taking care of me day and night, she didn't take care of herself.

It was extremely hard to pass each day. I felt so exhausted, both physically and psychologically, that I didn't know what I was going to do. I requested that the attorney general and Seoul prison chief send me back to the prison, but didn't receive a response.

On New Year's Day 1978, my secretaries and friends came to the hospital to see me and offer a traditional big bow, but the guards and KCIA operatives blocked them. My two secretaries Hahn Hwa-kap and Kim Ok-du asked to be allowed to do the big bow from afar. The guards told them to wait. My secretaries waited, but never received an answer. Finally, they protested and were arrested for alleged interference with a government official in the execution of his duties. It was absurd.

They forbade me not only from exercising, but also from writing letters. Although I wanted to send messages to the outside world, I wasn't allowed even a stubby pencil. Understanding the situation, my wife brought a small nail and secretly handed it to me. This was not an easy feat because the guards watched over and listened to our visits.

I wrote letters by pressing the nail down hard on a chewing gum wrapper or the paper my wife used to wrap my meals. I hid them inside the empty space of the bathroom tissue roll. When I secretively blinked my eyes at my wife, she dropped by the bathroom, took my letters, and hid them in her pockets, socks, or the empty rice bowl with a lid. Once outside, she transcribed and delivered the letters to my acquaintances. In this way, I was able to deliver my thoughts to democracy movement leaders and help with their struggles. To be cautious, I used initials instead of people's names. My wife also secretly handed me newspaper scraps so that I could know what was happening in the outside world.

After sending a second request to the attorney general to return me to the prison, I began a hunger strike on September 9. You can imagine how miserable I was if I was begging to be sent back to prison. Being in that hospital room was like being trapped alive in one's casket. I could no longer stand their base trick. Although they claimed it to be a humane treatment, I was dying in the hospital. I was not really being treated for my illness; the hospital staff was simply measuring my temperature and superficially checking my health every day. Nobody showed any interest whatsoever in my illness.

As the news of my hunger strike spread, rallies were held in front of the hospital every day. Those who had been imprisoned and released for the March 1 Declaration for Democracy and National Salvation Event gathered along with their families, holding placards and chanting: "Release Mr. Kim Dae-jung immediately! If not, arrest us instead!" Comrades issued statements and participated in hunger or sit-in strikes, demanding my release. Reverend Yun Ban-ung and Moon Ik-hwan were arrested again.

Protests came from overseas, too. From Japan, the Korea-Japan Solidarity Committee leaders visited their Ministry of Foreign Affairs and officially requested that it protect me. I stopped my hunger strike on September 22. As my health deteriorated and I experienced enterohemorrhage, my lawyers and family tried hard to persuade me to stop. I had to listen to them.

One night in December, a guard woke me up and said, "You're released today." It felt like a dream. On the occasion of President Park's new term inauguration, I received the stay of execution of the sentence. Heavily guarded, I was transported to my house in Donggyo-dong. I returned home on December 27, 1978, after spending two years and ten months in prison. I issued the following statement:

> As I was just released by way of the parsimonious stay of execution of the sentence, I feel so sad that I left Poet Kim Chi-ha, Professor Lee Young-hee, Reverends Yun Ban-ung, Moon Ik-hwan, Pak Hyeong-gyu, Ko Yong-gun, Cho Hwa-sun, Kang Hui-nam, and all the other political prisoners who are priests, professors, journalists, students, laborers, and democracy movement activists behind in prison.
>
> I cannot help becoming angry about the regime's narrow-minded and anti-democratic attitude.
>
> During these days when the national policy of democracy is suffering and numerous civilian leaders and students are imprisoned, it was a natural obligation and honor for me, who participated in the national politics and received enormous popular support as the 1971 presidential candidate, to have been imprisoned for three years. I cannot help feeling happy about that honor.

President Park was elected as the ninth president from the National Council for Reunification on July 6, 1978. There was not a single "no" vote and only one invalid vote out of 2578. The twelfth National Assembly election was held on December 12. Out of 154 seats, the Republican Party won 68, and the Sinmin Party won 61, thus marking a huge stride. In terms of percentages, the Sinmin Party actually surpassed the Republican Party with 32.8 and 31.7 percent of the votes, respectively. The Unified Democratic Party won three seats and the independents won twenty-two. It was clear that even with corrupt election that mobilized government power and poured out illegal money, public opinion was leaving the regime.

Also, the relationship between the Park regime and the US was rapidly worsening. The Park Tongsun Lobby Scandal (also known as Korea Gate), which headlined the *Washington Post* in October 1976, caused diplomatic friction between the two countries. The fact that Korean businessman Park Tongsun and KCIA operatives bribed US congressmen to induce their support for the Park regime shocked the world.

Altogether, 115 congressmen and senators were involved in this scandal and the Korean government poured between $500,000 and $1 million per year into paying off US politicians. It was an ugly incident wherein a dictatorial regime bribed representatives of its ally nation in order to buy their support for its dictatorship.

Park Tongsun returned to Korea immediately. The two countries agreed that he would testify at the US House and court in exchange for dropping his charges. Korea Gate lasted for two and half years, ending with a joint statement issued by the US and Korea in mid-1979. This incident critically injured the trust between the two countries.

On June 22, 1977, former KCIA director Kim Hyung-wook testified about the Kim Dae-jung Kidnapping Incident in the US House of Representatives. The hall was completely packed two hours before opening. Mr. Kim Hyung-wook was sworn in, testified, and read the following statement.

> What President Park feared the most were Mr. Kim Dae-jung, his opponent in the 1971 presidential election, and the US Congress, which decides on the US foreign policy. President Park tried to solve the problem of Mr. Kim Dae-jung … through the Kim Dae-jung Kidnapping Incident. He also tried to solve the problem of the US Congress … through the Park Tongsun Bribery Operation.

He openly mentioned the relationship between President Park and myself.

I believe that there was more possibility that Mr. Kim Dae-jung was elected during the 1971 presidential election but for the unprecedented level of systemic election fraud. Mr. Park Chung-hee's feelings about Mr. Kim Dae-jung are not simply about his political opponent, but close to hatred, based on a deep inferiority complex.

He testified that the kidnapping incident could not have happened without President Park's sanction and submitted the list of people involved in it to the House subcommittee. He also testified that about twenty-five KCIA operatives were involved in Korea Gate, and that many Korean-Americans collaborated with them as well. In an interview with Japanese media, he revealed that the ship used during the kidnapping was called Yonggeumho, and it was a spy ship that the KCIA purchased for its North Korea operation during his tenure as director.

Kim Hyung-wook published his memoirs during his exile and disclosed President Park's wrongdoings and disgraceful acts in detail. Although the Park regime tried to appease and threaten him through various channels, all these attempts failed. On October 1, 1979, Kim suddenly went to Paris alone, and suspiciously disappeared on October 7.

There are many suppositions and theories about the Kim Hyung-wook Disappearance Incident, but no real evidence has been disclosed thus far. There is a strong possibility that this incident will forever remain a mystery. He served the longest term of any KCIA director. After wielding almost omnipotent power as one of the major players in creating Park's power, he was discarded by that very power. Ultimately, Kim ruthlessly condemned Park Chung-hee, whom he once served as though Park were a god. Although he was merely a tool of the dictatorship, Kim was probably an ordinary human being who wanted to live his remaining life comfortably.

During his campaign, President Jimmy Carter (who was inaugurated in January 1977) pledged to withdraw US troops from Korea. The Park regime was alarmed. Dictator Park Chung-hee could never mix peacefully with President Carter, who set forth "Moral Politics" and "Respect for Human Rights." As soon as Carter became president, he adopted two policies about Korea—human rights diplomacy and troop withdrawal—and sent a letter mentioning these two issues to President Park. President Park replied, "There are no political prisoners in Korea."

President Carter was scheduled to visit Korea in June 1979. Korean democracy movement leaders and students had high hopes for President Carter because of his human rights advocacy. However, his planned visit to Korea worried us because it could be interpreted as US tolerance of or support for the Park regime's dictatorship. Because our hopes were high, our worries were deep.

A movement against President Carter's visit to Korea began. Almost all democracy movement organizations issued statements against his visit. Families of the imprisoned and other democracy movement activists organized demonstrations in front of the US Embassy and its surrounding streets. Some set fire to the welcome arch and, as a result, President Carter's portrait on it burned. Despite this fierce opposition, a Korea-US summit occurred on June 29. The US requested human rights improvements in Korea and an increased Korean share of the cost for the US armed forces in Korea in exchange for revocation of its policy of US troop withdrawal. Park Chung-hee and Carter quarreled about both matters during their summit. It was the worst Korea-US summit ever.

President Carter wanted to meet me during his visit to Korea, but the Park regime completely blocked it from happening. Although we could not meet then, we later became friends and worked together for peace in the Korean Peninsula.

The Park regime was mistrusted by the US, which they had heavily relied on. Its diplomacy with the US was humiliating. Allies gradually turned their faces away, as the reality of the dictatorship became known. The Park regime was becoming isolated in the international world and it continued to face diplomatic disasters. However, even bigger problems were brewing domestically.

The Shriek of the Yusin (1978–1979)

I was imprisoned in my home again after I returned to Donggyo-dong. My name disappeared completely from the press according to KCIA orders. The media referred to me by covert descriptions: "a certain leader who is a non-Assembly member and was released for the stay of execution of the sentence," "a leader outside of the Assembly," or "an unnamed person in Donggyo-dong."

I was summoned to the prosecutor's office and investigated three times. The prosecutor asked me why I continued to violate the Emergency Measures.

"What have I violated?" I asked.

The prosecutor showed me major US and Japanese newspapers with articles that harshly criticized the Yusin regime.

The prosecutor said, "If you keep doing this, we have to resend you to prison. I remind you that you are currently released only because of the stay of execution of the sentence. You have to obey the law."

"I don't think I violate the law. The person who violates our country's law is President Park Chung-hee. Think about it. Where in the old Constitution are there articles that allow the president to dissolve the National Assembly, invalidate the Constitution, and adopt the Yusin Constitution unilaterally, through unilateral agreement and PR under the martial law?"

The prosecutor abruptly changed the subject. Rather than arresting me again, they tried to intimidate me and limit my activities. However, I was already above that.

On March 1, 1979, democracy movement leaders—including participants in the March 1 Declaration for Democracy and National Salvation Event (like former president Yun Po-sun, Mr. Ham Sok-hon, and Reverend Moon Ik-hwan)—established the National Coalition for Democracy and Reunification. I was honored to become its co-president. We planned to publish another national salvation declaration on March 1, but Mr. Ham Sok-hon and I were under house arrest. In the end, former president Yun Po-sun held a press conference in front of his house alone, during which he announced the organization's launch and read our declaration.

This time, however, nobody was imprisoned. International opinion had worsened, and the regime must have known that arresting us couldn't block the heat of pro-democracy fights.

Sinmin Party President Lee Chul-seung's collaboration with the Yusin regime completely alienated the people who passionately desired democracy. President Lee Chul-seung argued for "consolidation in the middle" and "reform during participation." Riding the bandwagon of the Yusin regime, the Sinmin Party could get sympathy from no one.

The Sinmin Party National Convention (where the party president was to be elected) was scheduled for May 30, 1979. President Park Chung-hee's Chief Bodyguard Cha Ji-chul, who had yielded unbridled power during this period, almost openly waged an operation to destroy the Sinmin Party by bribing and intimidating the Sinmin Party delegates to maintain the status quo by voting for Lee Chul-seung.

I decided to support Mr. Kim Young-sam, who threw his gauntlet down under the slogan of "A Clear-cut Opposition Party." Although I was imprisoned at my house, I had to work to support Mr. Kim Young-sam. I invited Candidates Mr. Park Young-rok, Chough Yoon-hyung, and Kim

Jae-gwang, and sincerely asked them to resign from candidacy. Although they had worked hard to gather votes, I was able to convince them.

A day before the convention, I was able to visit the Chinese restaurant Aseowon, where party delegates gathered. When I showed up unexpectedly, they welcomed me passionately, confirming that I lived in my comrades' hearts even though my name had disappeared from the media. I appealed the vote for Mr. Kim Young-sam despite his previous mistakes for the sake of waging a strong fight against the ruling party and the regime.

I also strongly condemned Mr. Lee Chul-seung's consolidation in the middle argument. "What is the consolidation in the middle theory?" I asked. "There is such a thing as compromise in politics. If two sides share the same principle, then we can compromise. However, if two sides have different principles, if they are headed in different directions, there cannot be a compromise. There is no consolidation in the middle of good and evil. How can we consolidate Confucius and a thief in the middle? If one side wants to save a person and the other side wants to kill him, how can we consolidate them in the middle? Half-kill him? There cannot be a compromise between democracy and dictatorship."

Because Mr. Kim Young-sam and I were rivals within the party, I had to convince party members that my support of him was sincere. Another candidate told me that I would definitely regret it if I helped Mr. Kim Young-sam's election. Still, I told him that the task of ending the Yusin took precedence over my personal interests.

I said to the delegates, "Please don't look at Mr. Kim and me only as rivals. For a country to do well, we need many leaders. Where is there a guarantee that either of us will survive to see the day when democracy is revived? No, we need the second and third Kim Dae-jung and Kim Young-sam. Then, even if one of us falls down and another gets ill, someone else can pick up the fight. Once democracy is recovered, we don't have to worry about rivalry. We can decide who'll be the leader according to the people's will and your opinion. We don't have to fight about the name of the baby before the baby is born. We need Mr. Kim Young-sam not just for today, but for the future of our country."

Delegates cheered and applauded. They seemed moved to see the face that had completely disappeared from the media. Shaking hands with them, I was moved, too.

Voting occurred the next day. No candidate won the majority in the first round of voting. Delegates had to decide among Kim Young-sam, Lee Chul-seung, and Lee Ki-taek by a second vote. If the votes were dispersed among the three of them, it was absolutely advantageous to Mr. Lee Chul-seung, the current power-holder. It looked as if Mr. Kim Young-sam could win if Mr. Lee Ki-taek resigned and supported him. I rushed to write a note to Mr. Lee Ki-taek, then delivered it to his wife, who took it to Mr. Lee quietly under the pretext of bringing him medicine. I wrote, "If you support democracy, please support Mr. Kim Young-sam. If not, we'll all be defeated. Because you work for democracy, I trust that you'll do the right thing."

After reading the note, Candidate Lee went up onto the podium. He declared his support for Mr. Kim Young-sam and resigned. I was really grateful. Even with that kind of effort and sacrifice, Candidate Kim won by only eleven votes. Despite the regime's open operation to destroy the Sinmin Party, we grabbed a precious victory.

Large incidents continued to shake the Park regime. President Park did not have a strategy or vision for the governance of our country. His only concern was his greed for power. Although the regime was collapsing due to its lack of public support, it pushed everything with power. During this turmoil, the YH Labor Union's Sit-down Strike at the Sinmin Party Headquarters Incident and the Busan-Masan Uprising occurred.

The YH Industry, which manufactured and exported wigs, was a typical export-oriented company that grew under the special favor of the developmentalist dictatorship. In 1970 it had 4000 employees. However, its management deteriorated rapidly due to the CEO's embezzlement of funds and diversion of foreign currency. Then the company's founder sold the company. The debt-saddled operation continued to be sold and resold. When the company was on the verge of bankruptcy, its employees tried very hard to normalize it, but management, nonetheless, announced its closing. Laborers—all women, who were then called by the pejorative nickname *gongsuni*—organized a union and fought to prevent the closure.

After losing their workplace, they visited all relevant offices, including the Ministry of Labor, where they begged, appealed, and protested in vain. In a last-ditch effort, they visited the Sinmin Party headquarters. It was their last battleground and refuge. They waged a sit-down strike, demanding: "Give us normalization of the company or death!"

At 2:00 a.m. on August 11, 1979, police raided the Sinmin Party Headquarters in Mapo. They randomly wielded clubs and dragged workers out of the building. Labor Union Executive Committee Chair Kim Gyeong-suk died during this excessively violent suppression operation.

The police did not stop at suppressing the strike, though. They raided the party president's office and the conference room on the second floor as well. In the conference room were President Kim Young-sam, about a dozen assemblymen, reporters, and party members. The police randomly beat everyone except President Kim. Minority leader of the assembly Hwang Nak-ju fell on the floor under their kicking boots, and party spokesman Park Kwon-hum's face was soaked in blood. Reporters and party members were all showered with beatings and cursing. The entire operation ended in twenty-three minutes. The Republic of Korea's opposition party headquarters was in ruins—it looked as if it had just been bombed.

This violent raid of the opposition party headquarters proved that the Yusin regime could no longer exist without wielding violence. Our good daughters—most of whom had come to Seoul at a tender age to work in factories so they could send money for their parents' medicine and younger sibling's education—were trampled upon by the mad violence of the Yusin. The police arrested not only the labor union leaders, but also eight democracy movement leaders, including Reverends In Myung-jin, Moon Dong-hwan, and Seo Gyeong-seok; Professor Lee Moon-young; and Poet Ko Un as their wirepullers.

Although the largest opposition party was trampled upon wretchedly, the only way to fight against the madness of the Park regime was to strike. The Park regime didn't care. Instead, it came up with another political scheme. They had three Sinmin Party local branch chairmen apply for an injunction for the suspension of execution of their duty against President Kim Young-sam. Their excuse was that a few delegates who had participated in the party convention were not properly qualified. The court accepted the application on September 8.

The Park regime's oppression didn't stop there. The Republican Party brought forward a motion for the punishment of President Kim Young-sam for his conduct—specifically, his remark during an interview with the foreign press that the "Carter Administration should stop its support of the Park regime." They argued that his remark harmed the dignity of national assemblymen since it was beneficial to our enemy and that he requested foreign interference in our domestic affairs. On October 4, assemblymen belonging to the Republican Party and Yujeonghoe (Yusin Political Friendship Association) passed this motion not in the main Assembly Hall, but in room 146. The opposition party president was ousted from the National Assembly. Assemblymen who were members of the Sinmin Party submitted their letters of resignation in protest.

On October 16, 1979, a large-scale college student demonstration was staged in Busan. The next day, citizens of Busan joined it in droves. President Park declared emergency martial law and sent airborne troops to the area. Then, the flame of democracy caught fire in Masan, a neighboring city. Laborers and high school students took to the streets. Demonstrators destroyed the Republican Party branch offices, police stations, and broadcasting stations. President Park declared the Garrison Decree in Masan and Changwon. This was the so-called Busan-Masan Rebellion.

When I heard this news, I thought of the April 19th Uprising. I believe everyone else did, too. The National Coalition for Democracy and Reunification, of which I was the co-chair, issued a statement about the Busan-Masan Rebellion, demanding that the regime seriously examine itself and cancel the emergency martial law, that the regime not mobilize the national army for its own security, and that it amend the Constitution.

The flame of democracy was catching fire all across the country. Large-scale demonstrations were scheduled in major cities, including Gwangju and Seoul. The people's resistance was moving to the north as it had during the April 19th Uprising.

The Yusin dictatorship was alive only in the Blue House and a few of their safe houses. Separated from people's minds and hearts, the Park regime was gasping for breath; however, the worse their alienation became, the more fiercely the regime shrieked. There was madness in the blood-shot eyes of the Yusin protagonists. Now they were being chased. They began to tremble. They were anxious today and nervous tomorrow. They were thirsty, so they gathered to drink.

One night, shots were heard in Gungjeong-dong, Seoul.

Shots in Gungjeong-dong (1979)

The phone rang around 4:00 a.m. It was a call from an acquaintance in Los Angeles. His voice was sharp as he said, "I heard President Park was assassinated."

It was news as chilly as the dawn. Dictator Park Chung-hee's life ended from a shot fired by one of his most trusted subordinates on the night of October 26, 1979. Like the end of all dictators, his end was also wretched. I felt seriously uneasy about this incident. I thought the end should have come from the power of the people, as was the case in the April 19th Uprising. As large-scale demonstrations were scheduled in Gwangju and

Seoul after Busan and Masan, it was very likely that a situation similar to the April 19th Uprising would develop.

It was known that President Park lived his life drunk after the assassination of his wife Madam Yuk. On October 26, two young women accompanied him as he drank together with the chief presidential secretary, chief bodyguard, and KCIA director. When they talked about the Busan-Masan Rebellion, KCIA Director Kim Jae-gyu reported that the situation was grave. Chief Bodyguard Cha Ji-chul said ruthlessly, "If they keep acting cheeky, let's mow them down with tanks." Director Kim pulled out his gun and said, "Mr. President, how can you do politics right when you use a bug like him?"

A shot tore through the darkness. Blood sprouted from Cha Ji-chul's body. The gun was then aimed at the president. Another shot was fired. Kim Jae-gyu later explained that he shot "the heart of the Yusin" with "a heart of a wild beast." The eighteen-year-long dictatorship, which had begun with the coup d'état in 1961, finally came to an end.

The power was coldhearted. Chief Bodyguard Cha ran to the bathroom, leaving the bleeding president—to whom he had seemed so loyal—alone. Park Chung-hee's disciples all dispersed. The eighteen-year ironfisted regime disappeared like a mirage. That's how empty dictatorship is: nothing is left after the death of the dictator. All those politicians, scholars, and high officials who had praised the Yusin system, calling it a "wise decision for national salvation," disappeared. The Yusin system was thrown out on the street and trampled upon.

I met President Park only once. On New Year's Day of 1968, immediately after my election to the National Assembly in Mokpo, I went to the Blue House for the New Year's greeting. I talked with him for about five minutes, standing the entire time. He was very kind to me then and tried to answer my questions earnestly.

A few months before the assassination, I could sense the regime's end was near. I decided to try to meet with him to discuss current affairs. There were loads of work to do domestically, and international affairs were complicated. The Yusin regime was completely separate from the people and heading toward a precipice. There was no emergency exit to be found. I wanted to know President Park's thoughts about this situation and to let him know how serious the crisis was.

In the middle of summer, I requested that Mr. Ye Choon-ho, Yang Soon-jik, and Park Jong-tae visit the Blue House, meet Chief Bodyguard Cha Ji-chul, and ask him to broker my meeting with the president. My message to Cha, then considered number two in the regime, was:

I don't have any conditions. I just want to be given an opportunity to tell him all the things I want to say. I will listen to any kind of criticism from him. I'd like to say everything I want. I would like to talk about my patriotism. It would be great if we could find an agreement, but I don't mind if we don't. Then we will at least know why we have different opinions and why we don't like each other, won't we?

Mr. President and I have opposed each other for almost twenty years. But we have never had a face-to-face conversation. I think we are beyond the stage of keeping distance or competing. I believe it is important to have an eye-to-eye, voice-to-voice conversation. We are at the point where it is critical for both of us and for the nation that we have a conversation. Our country is facing a grave crisis. To avoid it is a shameful act and committing a sin against our nation and history.

My request to have a conversation with President Park was rejected a while later. I don't know if Chief Bodyguard Cha delivered my message to President Park, or if Cha decided to reject it on his own. I'm sad that I didn't have a chance to talk with President Park Chung-hee.

Dictator Park Chung-hee.

There was no justifiable cause for the military coup d'état he led. This coup destroyed the sacred democracy students won by their blood. It was a crime. Park Chung-hee did not keep his promises to the Korean people—his promise to return to his work as a soldier after cleansing corruption; his promise that his third term would be his last.

I acknowledge that the Park regime contributed to economic development. He also inspired Korean people with his can-do spirit. However, I cannot agree that only a dictatorial regime can bring about economic development. The Korean economy was already moving from an aid-based economy to an independent one before the coup. Although the speed of economic development was slow at that time, it was moving forward and upward. Park Chung-hee took credit for the Five-year Economic Development Plan, but the plan was a carbon copy of the economic development plan the Chang Myon government had prepared.

As I mentioned earlier, Prime Minister Chang Myon was planning to visit the US to secure funding for his plan before announcing the Five-year Economic Development Plan. The US government had already promised to support it. Society was settling down, and people were beginning to trust the new government. Right in the midst of this development, immediately before Prime Minister Chang's visit to the US, the May 16th Coup d'État occurred.

What would have happened if the Prime Minister Chang regime, which trusted democracy, carried out the economic development plan? Although it is hard to say for sure, I would guess that we might have had a more effective economic development, thanks to the people's voluntary participation and support. Military dictatorship might have actually delayed the development. One thing that is clear is that a democratic government would have pushed forward a sounder economic development without giving privilege to a small minority of individuals or groups. If a democratic government gave special privileges to a *chaebol* and focused only on the development of cities, it would have faced people's resistance. How could a democratic government have ignored it?

The Park regime distorted the Five-year Economic Development Plan that the Chang Myon government had prepared. It pushed only for the growth of large corporations and urban development. Preferential treatment grew in the farm of dictatorship. *Chaebols* grew on that preferential treatment and offered a portion of the profit to the regime.

Under the Park regime, the gap between the haves and the have-nots grew wider and wider. As large corporations grew larger through low crop prices and low wages, small and mid-size businesses became dependent on large corporations. In this structure, the middle class could not grow. It is only when we have a thick layer of the middle class that we can achieve an ideal diamond-shaped economic structure. If the poverty class increases, the middle class necessarily collapses. Early on, I had warned about this kind of economic structure, which I called the *janggu* (hourglass-shaped drum) type.

The Park regime also carried out a large-scale rural area development plan called the Saemaeul (New Village) Movement. Every morning, the "Song of the Saemaeul" rang through villages, but the rural area was seriously worsening. Although thatched roofs were stripped off to give way to slate roofs, that was about the only change the Saemaeul Movement brought about. Everything focused on cities, and farmers had to leave their home. The Saemaeul Movement was pure deceit that created the illusion of a developed rural area. In reality, the rural area declined rapidly.

The greatest ill Park Chung-hee brought was his promotion of regional antagonism. This fault was comparable to President Rhee Syngman's patronage of pro-Japanese collaborators. Park Chung-hee openly embraced and developed the Gyeongsang-do province, while thoroughly discriminating against the Jeolla-do province.

President Park's discrimination against development in the Jeolla-do province occurred in three areas: cultural discrimination, discrimination in economic development, and discrimination in the selection of persons for higher positions. These discriminations were persistent and systematic. All kinds of tools were mobilized. In television and radio dramas, films, and songs, most thieves and crooks spoke the Jeolla dialect, while youths from Gyeongsang-do were depicted as brave and manly. Those images slowly and unconsciously influenced Korean sentiment. It was a scary cultural indoctrination.

Regional antagonism did not exist before the Park era. Gyeongsang-do and Jeolla-do worked together to overthrow the Rhee Syngman regime; however, the Park regime promoted regional antagonism at every election. It was during the Park regime that people from specific regions began to vote for a specific party en masse. The Daegu and Gyeongsangbuk-do area, where Park Chung-hee was born and raised, was called TK and all of the regime elites were from this region. A TK politician could automatically become a top-level elite just because of his place of birth.

Park Chung-hee liked Japan all his life, feeling something close to patriotism for it. He was born seven years before me as the fifth son of a poor family in Daegu. After graduating from Daegu Teachers College, he taught at elementary schools until he entered the new Military Academy Japan established in Manchuria. He was an honor student, and received a short sword from the Manchurian Emperor as a prize. After graduating from the Japanese Military Academy as a specially transferred student, he served as a first lieutenant with the Japanese collaborationist Manchukuo Imperial Army.

To me, Park Chung-hee seemed almost to wait on Japan after taking power. He tried to follow the Japanese model in every area of governance. Although he contributed to Korea–Japan relations to a degree, he failed to establish a mutually beneficial relationship between the two countries.

Whereas the Chang Myon administration proudly requested compensation for the damages done during the violent Japanese occupation of Korea, the illegitimate coup d'état forces led by Park almost begged for it. The result of this begging was pathetic. In addition, whenever difficult issues arose between the two countries, the Park regime opted for collusion with Japan for the sake of its own regime's security rather than Korea's national interest. This resulted in the Korean economy's dependence on Japan.

Park Chung-hee harassed me throughout his reign. As the coup happened only three days after my first election victory in Inje, I could not even enter the National Assembly Hall before it was closed down. Since that day, he and I continued to stand at opposite poles. I fought against the dictatorship, risking my life. It was also a fight against Park Chung-hee. The KCIA, his brainchild, watched and threatened me wherever I went. They tried to kill me twice. Both times, I miraculously survived.

Time passed and Park Chung-hee's eldest daughter Park Geun-hye visited me at the Kim Dae-jung Presidential Library and Museum on August 12, 2004, twenty-five years after her father's death. She was the president of the Grand National Party, the large opposition party. Unexpectedly, President Park Geun-hye apologized on behalf of her father. "I apologize to you as his daughter for your suffering and hardships during my father's times."

I was so grateful to hear that. *This can happen*, I thought. I felt as if Park Chung-hee came alive to offer me his hand to seek reconciliation. Although it was the dictator's daughter who apologized, I felt as if I was the one who was saved.

Grand National Party president Park Geun-hye expressed gratitude to me for my decision to build the Park Chung-hee Memorial Hall during my presidency. In fact, it was not an easy decision to build his memorial hall due to popular sentiment; however, I thought I would be the best person to allow its construction, as I was his direct victim. Although he was no doubt my worst political enemy, I thought his memorial hall could be a space where both his achievements and faults were clearly judged, which could pave the way toward historical progress.

I asked President Park Geun-hye to lead efforts to remove regional antagonism and promote harmony among the Korean people. Because her father divided Koreans, it would be meaningful if she led the effort to correct that wrong.

Prime Minister Choi Kyu-ha became the acting president according to the Constitution. The situation moved urgently. Many felt sympathy for Kim Jae-gyu, and some even called him a martyr. During my interview with *Newsweek* at that time, I was asked: "Many people call Kim Jae-gyu a hero of democracy. What's your opinion about it?"

I said, "You cannot bring democracy through coup d'état or assassination. True democracy is what the people's power brings."

My remark was rather different from general sentiment of the time. Public opinion was favorable toward Kim Jae-gyu, who claimed that he "shot the heart of the Yusin." However, I said what I believed. I thought it was not beneficial to Korean democracy that the dictator's assassination by a subordinate intercepted people's punishment of the dictatorship and achievement of democracy, which was ripening then. There could be various evaluations about Kim Jae-gyu. Although I pity him as a person, I don't want to value his action.

On November 10, acting president Choi stated that the new president would be elected at the National Council for Reunification according to the Yusin Constitution and that he would then pursue a constitutional amendment after gathering public opinion. Although this decision seemed harmless, it was the polar opposite of what people wanted. It was very ominous.

The Minju Cheongnyeon Hyeobuihoe (Democratic Youth Council), a democracy movement organization led by college students removed from school for their anti-dictatorship activities, held an emergency steering committee meeting. They decided that they should try to prevent another pseudo-presidential election. It was impossible to hold a rally under martial law, so they decided to host a fake wedding ceremony.

On November 24, the YWCA Fake Wedding Incident occurred. Democracy movement leaders and activists pretended to attend a wedding, but really gathered to protest the election of President Choi Kyu-ha at the National Council for Reunification. Immediately after they read their statement, the police raided the building and arrested the 150 participants. Fourteen were taken to the military security headquarters and brutally tortured. It turned out the KCIA was involved in this incident. By spreading news of this event among activists, the KCIA could gather democracy movement leaders and activists and effectively intimidate them. The KCIA hadn't changed at all.

I remained under house imprisonment as well. People paid close attention to the movement of the military. Chief Martial Law Administrator Jeong Seung-hoa held a press conference on November 28. Reporters asked him when I would be released from house imprisonment. His answer was strange. "I don't know. It's a matter for the administration. When a war breaks out, a soldier should defend his country. As a soldier who was once a communist even by mistake cannot become an officer, a suspicious character cannot be entrusted with the job of head of the state."

He was clearly implying me as that person to be avoided. He also invited executives of the press to the army headquarters three times and openly expressed his antipathy toward me. The state of affairs was very ominous. Under martial law, the chief martial law administrator held absolute power. At this juncture, US Ambassador to Korea William Gleysteen volunteered to defend me. He stated through his spokesperson, "The U.S. Embassy in Korea has a different opinion about Mr. Kim Dae-jung from that of

Korean martial law headquarters. We believe that Mr. Kim Dae-jung is a reliable democracy believer and anti-communist. If Korean military authorities publicize such distorted views, we will also publicize the U.S. opinion."

After this, the martial law headquarters did not mention me anymore. Even in this situation, and even when my house imprisonment continued, the Sinmin Party did not protest it at all. They did not issue even a single statement.

Despite the people's wish to amend the Constitution, acting president Choi Kyu-ha was elected president according to the Yusin Constitution and inaugurated as the tenth president on December 6. After the cabinet decision the following day, President Choi lifted Emergency Measure #9, effective at midnight on December 8. It had lasted four and a half long years. I was finally released from my 226-day house imprisonment. I issued a statement from home (Photo 4.2).

Photo 4.2 Kim Dae-jung with his wife Lee Hee-ho at their Donggyo-dong home after his release from house arrest in December 1979. The X marks in the calendar indicate the days when he was detained at home

I welcome the lifting of the Emergency Measure and the release of many democracy movement leaders today, although this came much too late. However, I also find it extremely regrettable that their rights were not recovered and many other leaders are still imprisoned for various other criminal charges.

I believe in liberal democracy and free economy, and I ardently wish for the establishment of a welfare society. I have a firm belief in the goal of quick establishment of democratic government. But I also believe that this process should be peaceful and that it should be pursued through dialogue, patience, and order.

We are at the crossroads of an unprecedented level of danger and importance. It is time when Koreans need to show our extraordinary wisdom and strength by overcoming this difficult situation through the spirit of self-reflection on the part of those who committed mistakes and the spirit of generosity on the part of those who suffered. Although I suffered a bit under the Park regime, I wish, based on my belief and conscience, that the kind of suffering I underwent should never happen again.

In that statement, I also presented five urgent measures for President Choi Kyu-ha.

- First, the release and restoration of rights of all political prisoners who were imprisoned under different criminal convictions than violation of the Emergency Measures.
- Second, presentation of a clear blueprint for the process of establishing a democratic government, including constitutional amendment and an election before the end of 1979.
- Third, the establishment of a neutral cabinet supported by the whole nation.
- Fourth, a quick lifting of martial law.
- Fifth, the establishment of a council to gather public opinion within the transitional government.

SEOUL SPRING (DECEMBER 12, 1979–MAY 1980)

Chief Martial Law Administrator Jeong Seung-hoa was arrested out of the blue. How could the chief martial law administrator be arrested under martial law? It was a rebellion. On December 12, 1979, a gun battle occurred in Seoul. The military police sent by Joint Investigation Headquarters Chief Chun Doo-hwan overpowered guards at the army chief of staff's official residence and arrested the chief martial law administrator. This arrest was made illegally and without authorization from President Choi. General Chun Doo-hwan emerged as a new power-holder during the power vacuum that followed President Park's assassination.

When Army Chief of Staff Jeong Seung-hoa was inaugurated as chief martial law administrator, strong voices inside the military argued for the expulsion of politically oriented soldiers. Chief Jeong planned to transfer Joint Investigation Headquarters Chief Chun to another post. When Chun found out about this ahead of time, he conspired with other Hanahoe members and arrested Chief Jeong.

The Hanahoe was a secret military club predominantly composed of Chun Doo-hwan's fellow graduates from the eleventh class of the Korea Military Academy. Every year, they added a few new members, mostly graduates from the Gyeongsang-do province. They enjoyed all kinds of privileges under Park Chung-hee's special guardianship. Following in Park Chung-hee's footsteps, these politically oriented soldiers carried out a rebellion, taking advantage of the power vacuum. They were successors of politically minded soldiers and children of dictatorship.

The December 12th Incident was a very ominous event. Chief Chun turned his muzzle toward his immediate superior Chief Martial Law Administrator Jeong Seung-hoa. It was unimaginable. Through this incident, I could vaguely sense the power of Chun Doo-hwan and his fellow politically minded soldiers. They were getting stronger, and Chun's ambition was visible.

Chun Doo-hwan and his faction's command of military power was a grave development that only political power could check. The most effective way to handle the situation was for the political power to unite and lift martial law in the National Assembly. Because I had not recovered my rights, I could not participate in political activities. So I reached out to Mr. Kim Jong-pil, who led the Republican Party, and Mr. Kim Young-sam, who led the Sinmin Party. I said, "This is a crisis of democracy. Chief Chun Doo-hwan has all the power and the martial law is his weapon. If you lift martial law, it is as if you remove the molars from a tiger."

Unfortunately, they did not listen to me. They responded as though I were making a fuss about nothing. Some even thought it was my tactic to restart my political life. All of the politicians were interested only in the constitutional amendment—their attention was devoted entirely to that end. The press was busy reporting on this, and did not report on my remark that the road to democracy would not be smooth.

When New Year's Day 1980 arrived, the state of affairs was insecure and disorganized. It was not clear who held the power. Politicians were wandering through a maze. People called it the Foggy Phase. President Choi was acting more and more strangely. People wanted a direct presidential election system. However, President Choi organized a Constitution Study Team emphasizing, "The current government is not a transitional government but a crisis management government." In other words, he made it clear that his government was different from the post-April 19th Uprising transitional government of Huh Jung. Although he declared during the New Year's press conference, "I will move for the constitutional amendment and hold a referendum about it," he frequently changed his words in the time that followed.

Around mid-January, the idea of a dual executive system began floating around; it was unclear where that idea originated. The essence of this system was that the president would be in charge of diplomacy and national security while the prime minister, elected by the National Assembly, would take charge of domestic affairs like the economy and police. Those around President Choi were also moving to reelect him by popular vote. The president's indecisiveness and greed, combined with the politicians' optimism, invited later misfortune.

Around the end of January, I heard that General Chun wanted to meet me. I went to meet him at the Joint Investigation headquarters safe house in a back alley in Anguk-dong, Seoul. General Chun did not show up, though. Instead, his two subordinates, Kwon Jung-dal and Lee Hak-bong, waited for me. They—especially Lee Hak-bong—ordered me to write a memorandum that stated: "I will not leave the country. I will be cautious in my political activities. I will cooperate with the government." They said that only then would they return my civil rights.

I pushed the paper away resolutely and said, "If so, then you don't have to return my civil rights. It is not for you to limit my civil rights to begin with. I don't have to write a memorandum to right this wrong. I don't want to get my rights back by such means."

It seemed that getting my rights back was out of the question. At the same time, it suddenly occurred to me that it was extremely alarming that the military was interfering with a matter that should concern the president. *Aren't they preparing the soil to capture the power?* I realized then why the transitional government chose to elect the president according to the Yusin Constitution. President Choi must have gradually been losing power.

I asked Mr. Han Wan-sang to broker a meeting with Capital Defense Commander Roh Tae-woo. I wanted to tell him not to think of usurping power because Koreans would not accept another dictatorship; however, the meeting did not happen and the military waged a coup d'état. They usurped power by sacrificing numerous people and, in the end, went down in history as criminals.

On February 29, a special pardon and restoration of civil rights was issued to 678 political prisoners, including myself. Seven years after the establishment of the Yusin regime, I could finally stand in front of the Korean people. In a long statement, I expressed the many things I had wanted to tell them for so long. "I cannot help being moved and over-whelmed as I can finally see you, whom I have missed so much during our bitter 7-year separation," I began.

"I believe that there have emerged two clear consensus points among Korean people since the October 26th Incident. One is the establishment of democracy that Koreans have passionately desired, and the other is that the current President Choi Kyu-ha government should literally be a tran-sitional government that wisely manages this transitional period for the birth of a new democratic government wherein Korean people will be the masters of the country, rather than a modified Yusin government follow-ing in the footsteps of the previous regime. Koreans feel anxious because the current government maintains martial law without clear causes, limits the freedom of the press, and delays the release of all prisoners imprisoned for their democracy movement activities.

"What causes Koreans—including myself—the most regret is that the leaders of the Yusin regime show no remorse or humility in the face of Korean people and history. I do not argue for revenge against those who made errors. If they really wish to participate in new democratic politics, they should con-vince the Korean people of their remorse and will to change."

That day, the Seoul Spring began.

The Sinmin Party wanted me to quickly join it. I had solo meetings with party president Kim Young-sam on March 6 and April 4. We dis-cussed how to work toward restoring democracy. President Kim contin-ued to urge me to join the party; however, I could not make that decision by myself. I had to discuss it with the other democracy movement leaders with whom I had shared life and death, suffering and enjoyment, during the last seven long and difficult years. It made sense that I work together with my comrades who resisted dictatorship and shouted for freedom, risking their own lives when the politicians kept silent.

The Sinmin Party wanted to absorb us out-of-office leaders. The party leaders leaked remarks like "There aren't many who could be accepted to our party." Those who stood idly by the dictatorial regime said they would judge who could join the party among us out-of-office leaders who had to suffer because we fought against the dictatorial regime for democracy. I really could not accept that kind of attitude.

When Emergency Measure #9 swallowed freedom from our land, democracy movement leaders rose up against the dictatorship at the risk of their own lives and their fight gave Korean people hope and courage. I believed that such belief and philosophy should flow into the political arena in order for the new government to have legitimacy in democracy.

I gave a lecture for the first time since the restoration of my civil rights on March 26 at the YWCA lecture hall. Entitled "Nation's Soul," it was my first public lecture in eight years. The audience responded enthusiastically. "We failed democracy twice," I said. "The US brought us democracy after the August 15 liberation, but Dr. Rhee Syngman trampled upon it because we did not gain that democracy by our own hands. Students, and not the entire people, were the leaders of the April 19th Uprising, and as students returned to school, General Park Chung-hee could easily take our democracy away from us. Under the Yusin regime, the Korean people finally realized: 'Democracy acquired not by our own hands is not true democracy. Democracy acquired not by our blood, sweat, and tears is not true democracy.' That's why, led by priests, so many people chose prison; fought with prayer outside of the prison; and, when they could not fight in person, offered support for them from their hearts. The Busan-Masan Incident was the explosion of that congealed energy. I can confidently say that the October 26th Incident occurred as a continuation of this 7-year persistent anti-Yusin and anti-dictatorship struggle."

In terms of the question of whether or not out-of-office leaders including myself would join the Sinmin Party, a war of nerves was being waged in the political arena. In the end, after confirming that the Sinmin Party did not have an active will to welcome us, I issued a statement that I had decided not to join the Sinmin Party.

Religious, academic, and cultural leaders who had been imprisoned for their fights against the Yusin regime quickly gathered to support my decision. They included Mr. Lee Moon-young, Pak Hyeong-gyu, Seo Nam-dong, Ms. Lee Oo-chung, Mr. Keh Hoon-je, Ko Un, Kim Yun-seek, Kim Jong-wan, Kim Seung-hoon, Ham Sei-ung, and Ye Choon-ho. Most of the out-of-office leaders then thought that I should become president.

They wanted to do their best for my sake. Moon Dong-hwan, Lee Moon-young, Han Wan-sang, Park Jong-tae, and Ye Choon-ho were especially enthusiastic. They worked together to help me become president. Ye Choon-ho was a patriot who had once been Secretary General of the Republican Party, but had been so disillusioned at the regime's dictatorship that he left the party. I admired his talent and planned to give him an important position.

On April 14, Joint Investigation Headquarters Chief and Defense Security Commander Chun Doo-hwan added another title to his resume—acting director of the KCIA. As a result, General Chun commanded all intelligence agencies in Korea. I warned again that this concentration of power and intelligence in one person is worrisome and that a crisis could come to democracy again. However, politicians were still optimistic and at ease. I realized that I had to suppress the military conspiracy by mobilizing the power of the people, so I went on a public lecture tour.

Sponsors of my lectures included the Korean Catholic Farmers Association (on April 11), Korean Theological University (now Hanshin University, on April 16), Dongguk University (on April 18), and the Kwanhun Club (on April 25). I also delivered a lecture celebrating the forty-eighth Anniversary of Patriot Yun Bong-gil's Noble Undertaking in Yesan, Chungcheongnam-do on April 29, as well as a lecture at the Donghak Commemorative Festival in Jeongeup on May 11. Audiences responded explosively. The general public outnumbered students at my lecture at Dongguk University. On April 18, 1971, I had delivered a stump speech as a presidential candidate in front of a million people at the Jangchungdan Park. On the ninth anniversary of that event, I gave a lecture at the same place. I had survived to deliver it.

I argued that our democratic government should be organized around those who fought against the dictatorial regime and who were imprisoned and stripped of their civil rights as a result. Only they should form a legitimate democratic government, together with the Korean people who supported them and those who showed remorse.

That is why we should work as well and carefully as possible. If we became hastily involved with things that could cause disorder, we should know that not only could our country become disorganized, but we also played into the hands of those who wanted that to happen.

Students took to the streets. Until then, they had demonstrated inside their college campuses, demanding only the democratization of academia and the resignation of regime-patronized professors. However, around

May 7, they began to go off campus because they could not trust the process of democratization currently under way, including the constitutional amendment. Tens of thousands of students demonstrated on the street, condemning the suspicious state of affairs. Their slogans included: "Lift Martial Law!" "Resignation of Chun Doo-hwan!" and "Punishment of Chun Doo-hwan!"

Demonstrations spread every day, even under martial law. Strangely, the military left demonstrators alone. Students' rallies and demonstrations were moving toward open opposition of the government. To me, this seemed dangerous. Whenever I had an opportunity, I tried to dissuade students from aggressive demonstrations, saying, "If demonstrations intensify, that can give the anti-democratic forces an excuse to obstruct democracy. The Korean people are concerned." The new military junta was looking for a cause to separate democracy movement forces from the general public. Social disorder could be that cause, so aggressive student demonstration was exactly what they were waiting for.

On May 13, I held a press conference from my home. I proposed a five-way conference with Choi Kyu-ha, Kim Young-sam, Kim Jong-pil, Chun Doo-hwan, and myself. This press conference was not reported in the media at all. That night, demonstrators filled the public plaza in front of Seoul Station and around nearby Namdaemun. Student council presidents of universities nationwide gathered at the Korea University Student Union Building and decided to lead student street demonstrations against the government.

On the afternoon of May 14, students carried out street demonstrations in major cities, including Seoul, Daegu, and Gwangju. Tens of thousands of people participated in them, chanting: "Lift the martial law! Chun Doo-hwan should step down! Down with the Yusin remnants! Guarantee the freedom of the press! Stop the government-led constitutional amendment!"

Student demonstrators headed toward Gwanghwamun from Cheongnyangni, Sinchon, and Chungmuro. Demonstrators collided violently with the police. About 600 demonstrators were taken to the police station. Many people were injured; however, the general public didn't seem sympathetic toward demonstrators.

US Ambassador to Korea Gleysteen visited me at my house. At the time, he was like President Carter's alter ego in Korea. His opinion was that a coup d'état was unacceptable, and no excuse for it should be given to the military. He was very concerned about the intensifying student demonstrations and violent confrontation between demonstrators and the police. "It is a grave situation," he said to me. "Your role is important. Please actively try to keep it under control."

I was of the same opinion, so I immediately held a press conference. I said, "The convocation of the National Assembly will occur on May 20. The lifting of the martial law will be discussed there. Please wait until then." However, this statement was reported as only a one-line article in a tiny corner of newspaper. The Martial Law Administration was censoring the press.

After the press conference, a reporter from *DongA Ilbo* newspaper asked me to write an article, saying I was the only person who could persuade students. He said he would ensure it made the headlines. It was a great offer, but I did not think it would pass military censorship. He confidently responded, "Why would it not pass censorship if you urge orderly conduct and stopping demonstration?" So I wrote a 1600-letter article but, as expected, it wasn't published.

Many things happened on May 14. Around 2:00 p.m., out-of-office leaders Moon Ik-hwan, Lee Moon-young, Ye Choon-ho, and Yi Hae-dong visited me. They seemed very excited and encouraged by the large-scale rally in front of Seoul Station the previous night. They appeared to believe the world would change right away. Reverend Moon presented me with a statement and asked me to add my signature to it. Former President Yun Po-sun had already signed it. The statement contained massive content: "All soldiers, take down your weapons and leave your bases! All workers, take down your hammers and leave your factories! All merchants, close your stores! All people, wear a black ribbon on your chest and gather in Jangchungdan Park!"

I was utterly surprised. I couldn't say a word for a while. My guests were looking at me, curious. "Do you want to end your lives? How many lives do you have?" I asked.

They seemed to understand what I was thinking and replied, "Former President Yun Po-sun signed."

"Whatever Former President Yun Po-sun does, they won't arrest him. But we are different. If you demand soldiers take down their guns and leave the bases, you can be summarily and legally executed. Who are you trying to help now? Do you think the Korean people want this? Do you think they want workers to strike and stores to be closed? People don't want disorder. That's why the military wants disorder the most. My goodness, they are looking out for social disorder so that they can present themselves! This is like pushing your head into a tiger's muzzle," I said.

Due to my opposition, they rewrote the statement so that it contained only demands that people would generally agree on—they called for the immediate lifting of martial law and the resignation of Chun Doo-hwan and Shin Hyun-hwak. I later confirmed that if we had issued the original statement, we wouldn't have survived, no matter how many lives we had. The detective who investigated me when I was later dragged in by the new military junta knew all about the initial statement. He told me that since they knew every movement of ours through tight surveillance, they were all disappointed that we didn't use the original draft.

On May 15, there was another large-scale rally and demonstration in the public plaza in front of Seoul Station. More than 100,000 people gathered. The situation was similar in major cities with colleges, including Daegu, Gwangju, Busan, Incheon, Mokpo, Cheongju, Chuncheon, and Cheonan. That night, student leaders suddenly decided to stop demonstrating and return to their colleges. This decision, dubbed the Seoul Station Retreat, was made because they thought it would be unwise to confront the military junta when there was no support from the general public. They said they would watch the process because they made their opinions fully known. They also checked themselves because of unusual military movements. Troops were dispatched to the outskirts of major cities. I was relieved by this change in direction. I held a press conference at home, welcoming their decision. On May 16, university campuses were incredibly peaceful. It appeared that the students' street demonstrations worked to put a check on the government's Yusin restoration conspiracy and vitalized the democracy movement camp. But the new military junta led by Chun Doo-hwan was plotting an elaborate and atrocious conspiracy at that very moment.

Everything seemed ominous. I contacted Sinmin Party president Kim Young-sam early in the morning. He came to my house. We agreed on and published Six Articles on the State of Affairs Control. The Six Articles included the immediate lifting of martial law; the release, pardon, and restitution of all political prisoners; and the abandonment of the government-led constitutional amendment. We also requested that students check demonstrations. I persuaded them by saying, "A situation where we won't be able to vote might come. We have to join forces to prevent it." That afternoon, I met with about thirty Sinmin Party national assemblymen and committee members at the Pugak Park Hotel. "The situation is quite grave," I said. "What we have worried about seems about to materialize. Let's pay close attention to it and handle it wisely."

Nevertheless, the new military junta took out their knives that night. After waiting for the intensification of demonstrations and the amplification of disorder, they took a decisive action to seize power. As soon as President Choi Kyu-ha returned from his Middle East tour, they held a midnight emergency meeting to handle public security. Prime Minister Shin Hyun-hwak, Chief Martial Law Administrator Lee Hui-sung, Minister of National Defense Choo Young-bock, and Minister of Home Affairs Kim Jong-hwan attended the meeting. Chun Doo-hwan had Shin Hyun-hwak reported to the president that the entire military commander conference would convene in order to expand martial law the next day.

Chun Doo-hwan made his move. On May 17, the bill for the expansion of the Emergency Martial Law that the minister of national defense had submitted before the entire military commander conference passed the cabinet meeting at 9:50 p.m. It was the May 17th Coup d'État, a successor of Park Chung-hee's May 16th Coup d'État.

CHAPTER 5

1980–1986

MAY GWANGJU, A CITY OF PURITY (1980)

It was 8:00 p.m. on May 17, 1980—a Saturday night. I was in my living room when my secretary Kim Ok-du hurriedly came in. "I just received information that a catastrophic event is underway, so you'd better escape, sir," he warned me. About ten minutes later, Assemblyman Cho Se-hyung called to tell me he had received a call advising him that we'd better take care of our personal safety. This news was not unexpected.

The doorbell rang a little after 10:00 p.m. My bodyguard, Chung Seung-hee, cautiously opened the door. Dark shadows pushed the door open and poured into the house. Someone hit Jeong on the head with the butt plate of an M16, and he fell. When another bodyguard, Yi Se-ung, tried to block the shadowed figures, they once again wielded butt plates. All of the rifles had their attached knives out. Utterly surprised, my secretaries rushed out to the hallway.

"You fuckers. We'll kill you all if you try anything stupid!" a voice shouted, just as approximately forty soldiers crowded into the living room. A few of them were holding guns. Two officers and six or seven soldiers aimed their rifles at my chest. The knives were more chilling than the muzzles. Ferociously, an officer said, "We're from the Joint Investigation Headquarters. You must come with us."

"Where to?" I asked.

"The Martial Law Enforcement Headquarters."

© The Author(s) 2019
Kim Dae-jung, *Conscience in Action*,
https://doi.org/10.1007/978-981-10-7623-7_5

I entered my bedroom to get my jacket. As soon as I returned, soldiers dragged me by my arms. I shook them off, saying, "I'll voluntarily go with you, so don't worry and leave me alone."

I picked up a pack of cigarettes from the table and put it in my pocket. Soldiers followed with their guns still pointed at me. My wife yelled, "He'd go if you just ask! Why are you aiming guns at him?"

To me, she said, "God will be with you."

They pushed me into a sedan. My secretaries and bodyguards were taken as well. Besides myself, secretaries Hahn Hwa-kap and Kim Ok-du, Chief Bodyguard Park Sung-chul, bodyguards Ham Yun-sik and Yi Se-ung, my younger brother Dae-hyeon, and my eldest son, Hong Il, were also dragged along. The Martial Law Enforcement Headquarters officially announced that they "arrested Kim Dae-jung."

I was imprisoned in the basement of the Korean Central Intelligence Administration (KCIA) building in Mt. Namsan in Seoul. It was outrageous to be arrested and investigated out of the blue like that. They asked me to write down in detail everything I had done from my birth until that moment. They accused me of plotting to overthrow the government and tried to find evidence to support the claim. They pushed documents from fifty years before under my nose, but they couldn't find any evidence.

Taking pity on them, I said, "You know very well that I appealed to students and citizens to refrain from waging violent demonstrations and to restore stability. I even wrote an op-ed piece about it for *DongA Ilbo*. It was you who prevented them from printing it. Still, you accuse me of plotting to overthrow the government—that is really outrageous."

They forced me not to sleep, and repeated the same questions over and over again. I couldn't keep on refusing to answer their questions so, after a while, I reluctantly provided answers. They asked me the same questions again. Since I am a human being, my answers weren't always the same. They latched on to those discrepancies. Interrogators rotated in and out, asking me the same questions twenty or thirty times a day. It was crueler than torture.

There were many interrogation rooms in the basement. Screams attacked my ears at all hours. I didn't know where they were coming from at first, but I later came to know they were from the mouths of all my acquaintances. All of them were implicated in the so-called Kim Dae-jung Conspiracy of Rebellion Incident.

I later heard that my comrades were in so much pain they wished for death. Poet Ko Un told me that he was intent on committing suicide when his mother appeared in a dream and dissuaded him. The Kim Dae-jung Conspiracy of Rebellion Incident was fabricated through torture in a dungeon at Mt. Namsan.

One day the interrogator asked me out of the blue, "Do you know that a huge incident happened in Gwangju?"

"I don't."

"Do you know Jung Dong-yun, a reinstated Chonnam National University student?"

"I don't know who he is."

"You gave him 5 million *won* and ordered him to lead an anti-government movement, didn't you? Confess."

Since I didn't know the student, I had nothing to confess. When I said that, though, the interrogator threatened to torture me.

"Please torture me," I said. "I feel uncomfortable not getting the same treatment as the others who are all being tortured. Please torture me."

Investigators took off all of my clothes and had me wear a military uniform. As soon as I was done putting on the uniform, someone entered the room. After whispering among themselves, they changed my clothes again. It seemed they received an order to stop the plan to torture me. I believe the new military leaders were receiving live reports about me.

Although I didn't know it at the time, the incident the interrogator referred to was the May 18th Gwangju Uprising. It occurred as a result of my confinement, the day after the new junta arrested me.

The military junta expected that citizens of Gwangju and Mokpo would rise up if the news of my arrest became known. The fact that they dispatched the elite airborne troops—Ranger Commando Force 7th, Airborne Brigade 33rd, and 35th Squadrons—to the outskirts of Gwangju *before* the uprising is a testament to this.

In retrospect, it was clear that the new junta aimed at Gwangju and me from the beginning. I had continued to be on the lookout for the possibility of military involvement in politics since the October 26th Assassination Incident. The new junta must have been incensed by this. What they feared most was solidarity between out-of-office politicians and civilian movement leaders. I was at the center of this solidarity.

The new junta abetted campus demonstrations and exaggerated the North Korean threat, using them as excuses for their involvement in politics. In order to weaken the popular and democracy movement camps, which were their last huddles, and smooth the road to political power, they waged the May 17th Coup d'État. They aimed straight at me.

The events in Gwangju in the ten days between May 18 and May 27 were too gruesome and horrifying to fathom. Airborne troops in full armament ruthlessly wielded iron-spiked clubs and butt plates upon unarmed civilians, regardless of their age or gender. It did not matter whether it was a grandfather protesting military brutality or a young girl running away from them. Bloodthirsty troops took the blood-soaked bodies and the injured to God knows where. The hospitals were full of injured people.

The government neither did nor said anything about these brutal atrocities that occurred in broad daylight. The press did not report on them either. Citizens of Gwangju united and rose up to rescue their families, friends, and colleagues. They confronted the airborne troops with whatever arms they could get their hands on—steel pipes, wooden bars, pickaxes, and kitchen knives.

Four days into the Gwangju Uprising, the Joint Investigation Headquarters provided a brief on the progress of their investigation of the Kim Dae-jung Conspiracy of Rebellion Incident. They said: "Recognizing the October 26th Incident as a great opportunity for his power capture, but realizing that he could not achieve this goal through normal party activities and legal procedures, Kim Dae-jung incited people's distrust in the government and created an irregular revolutionary situation. Setting the goal of creating an environment in which he could seize power with one strike, he devoted himself to a tactic that would mobilize all his followers and private organizations. He attempted to lead a student riot to popular rebellion by incorporating reinstated professors and students into his personal organizations in order to concretely carry out overthrowing the government by popular incitement."

This makeshift investigation progress report rang false to everyone. Citizens of Gwangju became even more infuriated than before. They chanted "Release Mr. Kim Dae-jung!" and "Away with Chun Doo-hwan!"

Soon, the airborne troops were given live cartridges, which they used to indiscriminately shoot people in front of the provincial government building. Citizens continued to be injured and killed. The airborne troops were no longer the people's soldiers. Citizens raided the Homeland Reserve Army armory to arm themselves. More bloodshed happened in front of the provincial government building when a gun battle broke out between citizen militia and airborne troops versed in special training. Even so, the citizen militia wasn't being pushed around. In the end, the Martial Law Enforcement Army had to retreat while firing at random. After the citizen militia drove out the Martial Law Enforcement Army on their own, the defeated army blockaded all of the roads leading to Gwangju with tanks and armored vehicles. Citizens stationed themselves at the provincial government building and kept order and public safety on their own. Their foremost principle was to never use violence.

About twenty social leaders—Catholic and Protestant priests, lawyers, professors, and politicians—formed the May 18th Committee to Control and Resolve the Situation. The committee made six demands to the government, including:

- They not send the troops into Gwangju before the situation was controlled.
- They release all detainees.
- They publicly acknowledgment the excessive suppression of demonstrators by the military.

Instead of listening to these demands, the prime minister issued a statement, claiming that "although a small minority of impure elements attacked government buildings, seized weapons, and fired at the military, the military did not shoot civilians according to government orders." Soon afterward, the Martial Law Enforcement Army issued an ultimatum to citizens that they return their weapons. Citizens marched, chanting slogans like "Let's defend Gwangju," "Let's fight to the last," and "Withdraw the Martial Law Enforcement Army!"

The last day of the siege, the Martial Law Enforcement Army disconnected telephone lines in the entire Jeollanam-do province, including Gwangju. At 4:00 a.m., commandos raided the provincial government building, indiscriminately shooting as they went. The civilian militia couldn't match them. The Martial Law Enforcement Army record shows "5:22 a.m.: Completion of removal of rebels hiding out in the provincial government building." That was the end of the Gwangju People's Uprising.

The government announced that 174 people—including 148 civilians and 26 military and police personnel—died during the Gwangju Uprising; however, this number was unreliable. The actual number was estimated to be much larger. We don't know where all those people loaded on military trucks were taken or how they died. Since the dead cannot tell us, we are only left with grief.

The Gwangju Uprising will leave its shiny mark on history. Although the citizens of Gwangju were armed, they demanded a dialogue. Although they were looking at unjustly killed bodies, they did not seek revenge. They kept order, and they neither stole nor looted. Envelopes with checks that civil servants had left in their desks in the provincial government building prior to the uprising were later found intact. Banks and stores remained open as usual.

Citizens were consistently non-violent, non-pro-communist, and non-anti-American. This kind of democratic revolution was unprecedented in world history. Although tragic, it was clearly a great revolution that will go down in the books. I infinitely admire and love the citizens of Gwangju, who not only confronted injustice, but who also remained realistic throughout the ordeal.

Later, during my second exile, many friends and acquaintances, including Mr. Kim Eung-tae, sent me documentaries about the Gwangju Uprising. Although I could not muster the courage to watch them at first, a little later I finally viewed them with other people who gathered as a group to study the event. I could not see the images through my tears.

Twenty years later, in August 2007, I saw the Gwangju Uprising once again, as depicted in the movie *May 18*. Literally translated, the movie's Korean title means "splendid vacation," which was the code name for the operation the new junta gave to their atrocious suppression of the Gwangju demonstration. While watching the movie, I could feel the day's pain all over again. How could I ever forget Gwangju? I tried not to cry in front of others, but both my wife and I wet our handkerchiefs. When reporters asked me about the movie, I answered, "I am truly proud to live with the citizens of Gwangju."

Gentle people, people who truly wanted peace, people who are like Mt. Mudeungsan in the middle of Gwangju—these are the people of Gwangju, and I will never forget them until the day I die. No, even after I die, I won't forget. It is a city that eventually vanquished the madness of dictatorship with its pure blood; Gwangju will eternally be the home of democracy.

On July 10, the same day I learned about the Gwangju Uprising, the chief of the joint investigation team, Colonel Lee Hak-bong (a powerful man behind the scenes), came to see me. He demanded that I cooperate with the new junta. "If you cooperate with us, we'll give you any position you want except for the presidency," he said bluntly. "If you refuse our demand, we cannot let you live. We'll kill you no matter what. A trial is just a matter of formal appearance. If you cooperate, you'll live. If you refuse, you'll die."

I was extremely exhausted after the fifty-day interrogation. Because the proposal was utterly unexpected, I went blank for a while. Colonel Yi left after saying, "Think hard about it. I'll be back in a few days."

After he left, an investigator threw a bundle of newspapers at me, filled with articles about the Gwangju Incident. They must have wanted me to know what was going on outside as a bid for my cooperation. Black bold-font headlines on white paper were all about the uprising—the newspaper felt like a giant obituary for Gwangju. The facts contained in the articles were shocking. As I soaked in the horrific details, I began to feel dizzy and everything went blank. I fainted.

When I came to, I found myself connected to the Ringer's solution, with a doctor standing next to me. I wanted to die. What could I do for the citizens of Gwangju who died for me, who died during their struggle for democracy? I'd rather die. How dare those who wielded rifles and knives against and trampled on righteous citizens demand that I cooperate with them? It was revolting.

How could I live to face the victims of Gwangju? I had to fight even in prison—even if I died during my fight. Three days later, Colonel Yi came again. I said to him, "I cannot cooperate. If you kill me, what can I do?" Colonel Yi looked clearly embarrassed. He came again two days later. I refused even more firmly.

"KIM DAE-JUNG, CAPITAL PUNISHMENT" (1980)

On July 15, 1980, I was transferred to the army prison in Seongnam. I saw the outside world for the first time since I had been imprisoned in the basement of the KCIA building sixty days before. The prison warden, a colonel, came to see me in my cell a few times. Without saying a word, he just looked at my facial expressions. It was clear that he wanted to check if I had changed my mind. "I know why you are here," I told him. "I haven't changed my mind, so please deliver that message to your superior."

"That's really admirable. I admire you," the warden politely responded. He then allowed me books, coffee, and cigarettes as I requested.

On August 8, the army prison authorities called my home and announced that my family could interview me in prison. In order to come see me, my wife left home for the first time since my detainment. I sat face to face with her, a table between us. On the table was a tape recorder. Although there were mountains of things to tell her, I could say nothing. Looking at my face, now half the size it used to be, she also seemed to forget words. She stammered and said that my son Hong Up was a wanted man.

On the morning of August 14, the first military tribunal about the Kim Dae-jung Conspiracy of Rebellion Incident was held under martial law. The atmosphere in the courtroom of the army headquarters was tense and warlike. Despite that, the twenty-four of us entrapped in this fabricated incident were glad to see each other for the first time. Others, too, were imprisoned in the army prison, including Moon Ik-hwan, Ye Choon-ho, Lee Moon-young, and Ko Un—all on the charge of conspiracy of a rebellion. Others were imprisoned at the Seodaemun Prison in Seoul on the charge of violation of martial law.

They indicted me on charges of conspiracy of a rebellion, sedition of a rebellion, violation of martial law, instigation of violation of martial law, violation of the National Security Law, violation of the Anti-communism Law, and the Foreign Exchange Control Law. The written arraignment on the conspiracy of a rebellion read:

> When Jung Dong-yun, a reinstated Chonnam National University student, visited him on April 12, Kim Dae-jung discussed with him the situation of student demonstrations in the Gwangju area, encouraged him to continue to fight for the restoration of democracy, and gave him a ballpoint pen as a souvenir. When Jung Dong-yun visited him again with Kim Sang-hyun on May 5 and asked for 5 million won in support of student demonstrations in Gwangju area, he gave 3 million won then, and 2 million won on May 8. Handing 5 million won over to Jung Dong-yun, Kim Dae-jung ordered him to distribute his books, propaganda pamphlets, agitation drafts, and "The List of the Kim Dae-jung Kidnapping Incident Perpetrators." He also instigated Jung to lead student demonstrations to focus on the lifting of the martial law, the opposition to the constitutional amendment for the introduction of a dual executive system, the shortening of political process, and stirred up sedition. Jung Dong-yun went to Gwangju according to Kim Dae-jung's order and gave 2.7 million won to Chonnam National University Student Council President Pak Gwan-hyeon and 1.7 million won to Chosun University demonstration leader Yun Han-bong as their student demonstration funds. Kim Dae-jung maneuvered the street demonstration by Chonnam National University students, which became the origin of the Gwangju Incident, from behind the scenes. He then had Chosun University students join Chonnam National University students' street demonstration and touched off the Gwangju Incident.

I did not know Jung Dong-yun. I had no memory of ever meeting him. I had been asked if I gave 5 million won to a student from Gwangju during the interrogation in the KCIA dungeon, but I did not even know about the Gwangju Incident then.

It turned out that the investigators found the name Jung Dong-yun on the list of visitors to my house; however, I was not home when he visited, so he did not see me. The claim of a 5 million won demonstration fund was all fabrication. It was later found that the investigator first suggested 10 million won to Jung Dong-yun as the number he received, and then proposed to change it to 5 million won, saying that 10 million won was too extravagant for students. Although Jung Dong-yun had to cooperate with their lies under brutal torture, he was so tormented by his false confession that he attempted suicide twice in prison. Later, after I returned home from my exile in the US, I met Jung for the first time. Jung said that he felt sincerely sorry for making that false confession under duress. We were all victims of the dictatorship. When I joked, "Return the leftover money from that 5 million won," he replied, "Since you did not give me 5 million won, please give it to me now." We laughed together.

It was only at the trial that I realized how many of my colleagues, comrades, secretaries, and family members were arrested just because they were related to me in some way. I met Sul Hoon, a Korea University student then, for the first time there. He would work as my aide and party spokesperson years later.

We were deprived of our right to appoint our own lawyers; instead, all of us were assigned court-appointed lawyers. We were all separately interrogated. The military prosecutor attempted to impose the crime of rebellion, but, realizing that it was too far-fetched, changed it to conspiracy of a rebellion. The most severe sentence they could give me, based on Jung Dong-yun's alleged "confession," was life in prison. I was relieved that I was not going to be killed.

The final written arraignment charged me with violating Clause 1 of Article 1 of the National Security Law as "the ringleader of an anti-national organization." They needed another crime in order to legally kill me. They defined the Korean Democracy Restoration and Unification Promotion National Congress as an anti-national organization and alleged that I was its president.

Although I was involved in the organization stage of the Korean Democracy Restoration and Unification Promotion National Congress, I was kidnapped before it even launched. Even after I returned to Seoul, I clarified my position to its officers. I sent letters to Kim Jong-chung twice (on June 21 and 26, 1975), in which I emphasized, first, the Congress' Japan branch should be clear about their support of South Korea; second, they should be faithful to the principle of "democracy before reunification"; and, third, they should draw a line against communism. Also, in my letter dated December 21, I informed them of the Korean atmosphere, which tended to define Congress as pro-communist and urged them to be cautious in their editing of *Minjok Sibo* [National Bulletin].

I did not have any intention of becoming the president of the Congress' Japan branch, nor was I in a situation to be that. My original plan was to become the president of the central headquarters of all branches of the Congress after establishing branches in the US, Canada, and Japan. Therefore, it was completely false that I had become the president of its Japan branch before I was kidnapped. Also, during my two trials since the kidnapping—one for the alleged violation of the Election Law and the other in relation to the March 1 Declaration for Democracy and National Salvation Event—my relationship with Congress never came up. As Colonel Lee Hak-bong warned me, they must have fabricated this incident simply to kill me.

They thoroughly traced my activities in Japan in violation of the Korean government's agreement with the Japanese government to not take issue with my overseas activities. I expected that the Japanese government would protest it with the new junta. However, the Japanese government did nothing about it except express its "concern." I was discouraged and angry that Japan, a supposedly democratic country, was so insensible about human rights and government-level promises. I wondered if this was because of the fact that Japan had not attained its human rights through bloody fights.

The trial went on toward the predetermined goal according to the script. Defense lawyers either pretended to defend or said something similar to the prosecutor's argument. I felt it would have been better if we hadn't had any lawyers at all. However, there was one brave attorney named So Jong-pal. He pointed out the absurdity of the prosecutor's argument, saying, "Although the prosecutor argues that the defendants conspired for a rebellion, there is no evidence of them carrying even a poker or a Bacchus drink bottle, let alone a wooden bar or a Molotov cocktail. The arraignment does not mention anything like that. What on earth are you accusing them of plotting to use for this rebellion?"

Attorney So was expelled during the trial, and there was no way of reaching him. It was a travesty of a trial. After that incident, other defense lawyers' remarks were pretty embarrassing to even listen to. At one point, novelist Song Gi-won couldn't take it anymore, and yelled: "Hey, are you an attorney? It's impossible to hear what you say, so stop it! Don't defend us! Although this is fabrication, what you chatter on about is worse than pulp fiction."

Song stood up to protest the defense attorney, but was pushed down by the military police. Family members in the audience also shouted, "Leave it!" Nevertheless, the trial went on. Defense lawyers continued to argue for the prosecutor rather than defendants. At one point, Kim Jong-wan shouted, "Hey, you! Shut up. Why do you keep chattering? Why do you talk nonsense when the defendants tell you to shut up?"

The court became noisy again. It was no trial. Reverend Moon Ik-hwan stood up and said, "We'll request the judges to be recused. We don't want this kind of trial." As soon as he finished speaking, I stood up and left the court. Others followed me.

Our families had an incredibly hard time as well. They didn't receive any sort of official notice after we were dragged away by the military out of the blue. Their fear was compounded by the Gwangju Incident. Our families were extremely worried and went everywhere to find their loved ones—they even went to the Joint Investigation Headquarters to find out whether we were alive or dead. Nobody told them where we were. Everyone avoided them. How scary and lonely it must have been for them to fight against this invisible enemy! Additionally, our wives were under constant surveillance by two or three intelligence officers. They were allowed to interview us only after we had been transferred from the KCIA building to the prison, two months after our detainment. That period was a living hell not only for us, but also for our families.

I later heard that one day some of the detainees' wives gathered together after giving their shadows the slip. They quickly got on a chartered bus and went to Gyeongpodae Beach in Gangneung. There on the beach, they began shouting their husbands' names one after another. They shouted that they loved their husbands and cursed the responsible parties. Some just screamed. In the end, they all huddled together and wept in the bus all the way back home. My wife could not join even in that gathering.

My family members were imprisoned in the house. Nobody told them where I was or how I was doing. After the Gwangju Uprising, my wife heard news about me through the Voice of America radio nightly broadcast. The news said I could be sentenced to death because of the Kim Dae-jung Conspiracy of Rebellion Incident. She remembers feeling as though "my internal organs were shrinking because of extreme worries."

On July 12, a notice was delivered to my home alerting my family that I had been transferred to a military prison, sent to trial, and that we should appoint a defense lawyer. My wife immediately asked the police to allow her to leave home to find a lawyer for me; her request was refused.

On August 16, President Choi Kyu-ha suddenly resigned after issuing a special statement wherein he offered his resignation based on his responsibility for the incompetent response to social disorder, including the Gwangju Incident. He also said that he supported the National Security Emergency Measures Committee Chair Chun Doo-hwan's presidential inauguration. On August 27, the National Council for Reunification elected Chun Doo-hwan as the eleventh president of Korea.

On September 8, ten defendants, including my eldest son, Hong Il, and my younger brother Dae-hyeon, were sentenced to three- to four-year prison terms. The press did not report on it at all.

On September 11, the prosecutor recommended sentences for twenty-four defendants accused of participating in the conspiracy of a rebellion. The prosecutor demanded capital punishment for me for violation of the National Security Law, arguing that I organized the anti-national Korean Democracy Restoration and Unification Promotion National Congress and acted as its ringleader.

That day, twenty-three defendants (all except for me) made their final statements. Defendants remembered the torture they had received, and their family members felt their pain. Reverend Lee Hae-dong revealed the torture he had suffered in the KCIA building dungeon. He said his flesh was torn off from the beatings. Defendants and their family members wept. Reverend Lee also made a declaration of conscience, saying, "It was under those circumstances that I made a statement against my will. A priest made a false statement. I am a coward and traitor who wrote a false statement and gave my thumbprint on it. I feel anguish about it."

In retrospect, all of the defendants were incredibly dignified despite the brutal torture and conciliation temptations they were subject to. Their only crime was that they knew me and shared my belief in democracy. Nobody I trusted betrayed me or lied about me. They did not blame others for their sufferings. They were worried about me even while they were themselves beaten and insulted.

Although we hadn't conspired together for a rebellion, we became united in prison; all of us would go down in history together as figures involved in the Kim Dae-jung Conspiracy of Rebellion Incident. I am sorry that the name of the crime included my name, but they did not blame me for anything and continued to support me throughout my journey toward democracy. I am still moved by and grateful for them. I call their names here quietly: Moon Ik-hwan, Lee Moon-young, Ye Choon-ho, Ko Un (Ko Eun-tae), Kim Sang-hyun, Seo Nam-dong, Kim Jong-wan, Han Sung-hon, Lee Hae-dong, Kim Yun-seek, Han Wan-sang, Yu In-ho, Song Kun-ho, Lee Ho-chul, Lee Taek-don, Kim Nok-yeong, Cho Seong-u, Lee Hae-chan, Lee Shin-bom, Song Gi-won, Yi Seok-pyo, and Sul Hoon.

Two days later, the defense attorneys presented their closing statements. The gist of my lawyer's argument was that it was impossible and out of question for defendant Kim Dae-jung to attempt a rebellion through a student uprising under the martial law and that he objected to the prosecutor's argument that I encouraged an anti-government demonstration in Gwangju area by giving 5 million won to a student.

When the time came for me to issue my final statement I pointed out the falsehood of the hollow Kim Dae-jung Conspiracy of Rebellion Incident item by item: "Standing here for my final statement, I remember one thing. I watched the state funeral of late president Park at home without missing a moment on November 5 last year. I still remember Cardinal Kim Sou-hwan's remark: 'Dear God, please help us all realize the meaning of President Park's death.' President Park's death, although personally extremely tragic, was the historical momentum that signaled the passing of the Yusin and the approach of a new democratic era. However, due to the expansion of the martial law to the entire country on May 17, our democracy encountered a serious trial (Fig. 5.1).

"Since the October 26th Incident, I have thought that national security, economic stability, and democracy restoration were the most important tasks and that I should cooperate with the transitional Choi Kyu-ha government for these causes. I have consistently argued for national reconciliation without retribution. In order to practice this, I requested a conference with President Choi and declared that I would forgive those who were involved in my kidnapping. In our country, the Yusin forces are gathered around President Chun, but the majority of people are in favor of democracy. I firmly believe that neither one of them could lead this

Fig. 5.1 Kim Dae-jung at a trial at the military tribunal after the Chun Doo-hwan-led military coup in 1980

country by oppressing the other force. Korean people want democracy and they do have the ability to carry it out.

"The authorities call this current incident the Kim Dae-jung Conspiracy of Rebellion Incident. But if they thought I, an individual, could incite and mobilize the majority of students and people, why did they censor my statement requesting self-control from students and my op-ed piece for the *DongA Ilbo*—which I wrote according to the newspaper's request—and ban it from being reported by the press? It wouldn't be impossible for the authorities to carry out my sentence, but please think carefully about whether doing so is lawful and appropriate in a democratic country. I hope for generosity more for other defendants than for myself because I am responsible for the charges brought against them …

"I will most likely be sentenced to capital punishment and am sure to be executed, but I have been ready for it since the beginning. I would like to say my last words to my fellow defendants: In my opinion, democracy will be recovered not too far in the future, during the 1980s. I firmly believe it. When that day comes, I would like to ask you to do me a favor and never to engage in political retaliation—not for me nor for anybody else.

"This is my last wish and my last words in the name of God."

The audience, which had been sobbing here and there, stood up as soon as I finished my statement. Although the judge urged silence, it was of no use. They began to sing our national anthem. Military police tried to stop them from singing by pushing their hands over the mouths of the audience, but people continued anyway. Some even bit the hands that covered their mouths. After the national anthem, they sang "We Shall Overcome," translated into Korean. Our families were dragged out one by one and loaded onto a bus. They struggled not to be taken; their shoes tumbled all over the courtroom. "Long live democracy! Long live Mr. Kim Dae-jung!" they shouted.

Defendants sobbed as well. Professor Han Wan-sang later remembered that moment as follows:

> The moment we twenty-four co-defendants cannot forget most would be perhaps the occasion of DJ's final statement. We sang our national anthem. Although it was a crime to make noise like that, I sang our national anthem from my belly for the first time, unable to suppress indignation. No, I might say that our national anthem just burst out of our bodies. DJ made his statement in a dignified manner for an hour and forty minutes. I was surprised to see how calm he was. Without being on the level of a so-called saint, a defendant who had just been recommended for capital punishment by the prosecutor could not state his thoughts that calmly.

> We realized that we had been crying continuously without being aware. Although we were helplessly bound, we were already winning morally and spiritually. Those hot tears were also coming from being moved by our higher-level victory. Although a short spring had passed and a long winter came upon us, we were anticipating a longer spring that would come after this long winter in those hot tears.

The sentencing was held on September 17. I entered the court wearing traditional Korean clothes, supported by military police on either side of me. One of my co-defendants, Reverend Moon, was already in the court. After a judge advocate read the summary of the causes of the sentences and the reasons for the weighing of the offenses, Judge Moon Eung-sik stood up.

I was waiting for the sentence, standing up with support on both sides. About forty family members, staff members of the American and Japanese

Embassies, and correspondents from foreign media, including the *Washington Post*, were watching the procedure. The trial at the court of first instance was drawing to a close after thirty-four days. My family members could not be in the audience because the authorities forbade them from attending. Later, even when my wife was allowed to attend, she could not come; she said she could not bear to see me enter the court in handcuffs.

Who would want to die? I wanted to live, too. I sincerely hoped that I would not be sentenced to capital punishment. I prayed in my heart even in the court. I stared at the shape of the judge's mouth. If his lips widened sideways, that would mean that I was sentenced to *sahyeong* (capital punishment). If his lips protruded to the front, it would mean that I was sentenced to *mugijingyeok* (life imprisonment). Depending on the shape of his lips, I would either die or live.

The judge's lips widened sideways. "Kim Dae-jung, capital punishment."

The World Shouts: "Save Kim Dae-jung!" (1980–1982)

I will be executed. What will it be like to die as a condemned criminal? If I say just one thing—that is, "I'll cooperate"—then I can live. Still, I must die. Perhaps my death is my life. If I die now, history books will record that I died fighting for democracy. Kim Dae-jung will be remembered to have lived a just life. People die all the time from traffic accidents, from illnesses, from falling, even in their sleep. I have lived pretty long, so I'll die honorably. How lucky that I have walked a straight line without being distracted. These are the thoughts that ran through my head after I was sentenced to death.

News about my sentencing instantly spread around the globe. World leaders expressed their concern. US Secretary of State Edmund Muskie issued a statement that the US was seriously concerned about the sentence of capital punishment for Mr. Kim Dae-jung. West Germany's Foreign Minister Hans-Dietrich Genscher proposed that all EC member countries protest to the Korean government. Even East German, Russian, and Chinese state news agencies criticized the Korean military regime. Only the Korean press mechanically reported that I was sentenced to capital punishment. They could not run a single comment.

My co-defendants and I immediately decided to appeal. The appeal had to be submitted to a general court martial within a week. We asked our attorneys to submit the appeal at the last hour of the last day in order to extend my life for as long as possible, but our lawyers broke their promise and submitted the appeal immediately. The defense lawyers had been subject to all kinds of pressure during the trial. It must have been hard for them to confront threats on them. The review trial occurred at the Army Grand Bench of the Supreme Court on November 3. The judge confirmed my capital punishment sentence.

An even more discouraging event happened two days later. US Democrat President Carter lost to Republican Party candidate Ronald Reagan in the US presidential election. Nobody told me about this news. Unable to suppress my curiosity, I asked a janitor. When he told me that Reagan had been elected the sky fell. I had hoped that the reelection of President Carter, who emphasized ethics and human rights, could change my destiny. The last levee of hope broke. I was extremely distraught. I cried out loud. I could not have any hope about Reagan, a conservative.

Am I really going to be executed? I wondered. *Did God really forsake me?* I was not the only one awaiting the results of the American presidential election. The military regime was also watching it very carefully. They wanted Reagan's victory and were using their connections to lobby hard on his side. I later heard that they cheered at the election results. They must have thought that the largest stumbling block in the way to eliminating me was lifted. Although hopeless, I submitted a statement of grounds for the final appeal to the Supreme Court.

I lived hopelessly as a condemned convict. I could not accept my title "Kim Dae-jung, condemned criminal." I suddenly began to doubt the existence of God. I felt very confused. If there wasn't a God, what would happen, not only to me, but also to all my efforts? My entire life would lose its meaning and be futile.

It was a time of spiritual crisis. In order to get answers to my questions, I read writings by philosophers such as Plato, Aristotle, St. Augustine, Anselmus, Descartes, and Kant; however, none of them helped alleviate my doubts about God. This doubt could be dissolved only through religious resolution. Jesus Christ held the key to this question. If Jesus was God's son, then God existed. Whether Jesus was God or not depended on his resurrection. So, I thought hard about how to believe in his resurrection.

I wrote about this spiritual quest of mine in a letter to my wife—it was the first letter I wrote after being imprisoned by the military. It reads like an earnest prayer.

I have thought so far that I had some faith. But facing death, I experience every day upon how weak a foundation my faith stands.

But, after many conflicts and wanderings, I came to the conclusion that faith is not based on feeling or knowledge, but it is acquired through our free will and resolution, that this resolution should be voluntary and conscious, and that our joy and gratitude and praise should first be processed through our will and then followed by our senses. Now I pray to the Holy Spirit that I may fix my unwavering eyes only on our Lord.

The greatest basis for the resolution of my will is the Lord's Gospel, and the most important in this resolution was my faith in Jesus' resurrection. If I could believe in Jesus' resurrection, I thought I could believe in everything, including God's existence, our binding by our sin, the existence and guidance of the Holy Spirit, God's ever-caring love, and the eternal life in Heaven.

I believe that Jesus' resurrection, although mysterious, has substantial and objective historical grounds as well. Without the experience of Jesus' resurrection, it would have been impossible for his disciples, who ran away for their dear lives during his passion, to devote their lives to preaching the gospel, risking their lives and enduring all kinds of hardships, after Jesus had died so helplessly and miserably. Besides, we cannot explain Paul's conversion and his superhuman and desperate missionary work without his experience of resurrected Jesus, given his background that he hadn't met Jesus while he was alive and that he persecuted Christians passionately and with a missionary zeal after Jesus' death.

To firmly believe in Jesus' resurrection is the biggest basis that supports my faith. I am trying my best to fix my eyes on him and not to let go of his sleeves. I am always praying, "I believe that God always loves me. Lord gave me my present circumstances. Lord would not have allowed it unless He thought this was best for me." As I cannot know the Lord's will and design, I will only believe in the Lord's love and obey and praise Him.

I wrote this letter on November 21. A few days later, I received a letter from my wife, written on the same day I wrote to her. My wife and I thought of God and death at the same time.

I ask, "Why, dear God?" Why this to you, whom I have always admired for your good nature and your conscientious effort to live honestly? I think that if you had a violent nature, or if you hadn't so earnestly wanted democracy, then we wouldn't have to feel this bone-chilling pain like now.

Please know that numerous brothers and sisters we don't even know are now praying for you overnight, in mountains, in attics, and even while fasting. How thankful we should be. Who would pray so hard for you, if you didn't face this enormous hardship? Please be hopeful about the future. As God, who saved you in the middle of the sea, is still near you, please believe that He will definitely save you this time as well and pray.

It was still hard to shake off the fear of death. I could not know when suddenly they would take me to execution. I was scared every time I heard the sound of footsteps outside my cell.

On January 18, 1981, an intelligence officer took me to his office. He asked me to write a note to the president to petition the commutation of my sentence. Naturally, I refused. But, he kept on asking. "Mr. Kim," he said, "you're a condemned criminal. To commute your sentence, we need a cabinet decision. We need a letter that says you feel responsible for what you have done so far and you will no longer engage in political activities. It is true that there are people within the government who oppose the commutation of your sentence. We need an excuse to persuade them. And we will not reveal your note."

In a way, I thought what he said made sense. They probably needed an excuse to persuade hawkish forces within their group. Also, he swore to God that, as a Catholic himself, he would not reveal the letter. So I wrote a note that read: "I will be cautious in my words and actions from now on and I promise never to participate in political activities again. And I am determined to actively cooperate with anyone for the sake of our fatherland's democratic development and national security."

After writing the note, I thought about it again and felt uneasy about the whole business. It was clear that it was the product of the situation in which the president threatened me after standing me on the gallows. Also, even if I wouldn't engage in politics, it should go without saying that I wanted to cooperate with anyone for our country's democratic development. I said to the person that I wanted to withdraw the note. He told me four times that he withdrew it.

When I was being transferred from their office to the army prison, I asked him to return the appeal note. He said casually, "I forgot it on my desk. It's all dealt with fine, so please don't worry about it. Let's go."

However, they broke their promise and later revealed the note. I confirmed once again that the Chun regime was unreliable. They must have judged that they needed to hurt me for their regime maintenance. Their intention must have been to show me as begging for my life. Nevertheless, I felt it better that they revealed it rather than trying to threaten or win me over by hiding it. I felt relieved. One thing that felt unjust to me was that I had no opportunity to tell anyone about how the whole thing went down. The only person I could tell about it was my wife, who came to see me in prison.

The hearing of the final appeal at the Supreme Court occurred on January 23. They didn't allow me to attend it. My wife came to see me in the afternoon. She said tearfully, "The final appeal was dismissed. I entrust God with everything."

I was ready to face it. While I was listening to her words, my wife kneeled on the cold cement floor with Hong Il's wife, Hong Up, and Hong Gul. She began to pray while crying. Her prayer ended with "God's will be done." I could not admire my wife more than I did then. Without my family's trust and love, I could have never overcome my more than twenty-year-long suffering. In the center of my family's trust and love was my dear wife, whom I admire and love.

Unexpectedly, my sentence was commuted to life imprisonment that afternoon. This was possible only thanks to world media, leaders of democratic countries, and the dedicated efforts of conscientious social leaders. The Blue House was swamped with letters that pleaded for anything but capital punishment for Kim Dae-jung; by then I was widely known throughout the world as an opposition party and anti-regime leader.

The Carter administration issued a statement that all accusations about me were fabricated. Donald Gregg, then the Asia policy and intelligence matters specialist for the US National Security Council, came to Korea with Secretary of State Harold Brown and met with President Chun Doo-hwan. He tried to persuade President Chun by saying, "If you execute Kim Dae-jung, it will have enormous repercussions throughout the world." However, President Chun did not give a definite answer. He was probably waiting for the result of the US presidential election. Although Cater lost the election, he strongly urged Reagan to save my life by including it as an important transfer item.

As a regime that took power by violence, the Chun regime desperately needed international recognition. For this recognition, a summit with President Reagan was crucial to them. The Reagan administration included the commutation of my sentence as one of their prerequisites for the summit. President Carter wrote in his memoir:

We talked about what was being done to save opposition leader Kim Dae Jung's [*sic*] life in South Korea, and I thanked him for sending a message to President Chun Doo Hwan urging that Kim's life be spared.[1]

In addition, president of West Germany's Socialist International Willy Brandt passed a motion to save Kim Dae-jung in its general assembly. West German President Richard von Weizäcker also participated in this movement to save me. Former Austrian Prime Minister Bruno Kreisky awarded me the Bruno Kreisky Peace Prize in prison. American leaders, including Senator Edward M. Kennedy and various organizations, urged my release. The Japanese government put a hold on their loans to Korea and their largest labor union organization, the Japanese Labor Union General Council, refused to load and unload Korean merchandises. In addition, overseas Koreans organized events for Korea's democratization. In fact, all around the world movements were under way to save me through assemblies, demonstrations, and press releases.

While I was in prison, the new junta founded the Democratic Justice Party with President Chun Doo-hwan as its president. Three more parties were successively established: the *Hangukgungmindang* (Korean National Party; headed by President Kim Jong-cheol), the *Minjuhanguktang* (Democratic Korean Party; led by President Lee Ji-song), and the *Mingwondang* (Democratic Rights Party; led by President Kim Euy-taek). At first glance, there seemed to be two conservative-leaning and two progressive-leaning parties. However, they were all government-controlled parties, established by the intervention of the Defense Security Command.

The regime devised a new Constitution, which centered on the seven-year single-term presidency and indirect election through the Electoral College. It also legislated the Basic Press Law, according to which newspapers and broadcasting stations were either merged or abolished. The Chun regime thoroughly controlled the press, which had to breathe more quietly than it had during any other period. They manipulated public opinion, covered up the truth, and glossed over current affairs.

The Chun Doo-hwan regime dismissed civil servants en masse and created the Samcheong Education Camp, where they committed inhumane brutalities toward 60,000 civilians under the pretext of reeducating mobsters. After this series of ugly measures, martial law was lifted and the presi-

---

[1] Jimmy Carter, Keeping Faith: Memoirs of a President (New York: Bantam Books, 1982), 578.

dential election was conducted. On March 3, 1981, Chun Doo-hwan was inaugurated as the twelfth president and launched the fifth republic.

In March 1982, the Busan United States Information Service (USIS) Arson Incident occurred when an arsonist lit the USIS building in Busan on fire, and a college student died in its library. Fliers entitled "Let us Continue to Fight Against the U.S." were scattered in the theater and department store in front of the USIS building. Catholic priests offered refuge to those responsible for this incident. The Chun regime waged a large-scale war against Catholics.

At first, the Catholic Priests Association did not get involved. But, as the fact that the police brutally tortured the arrested and distorted facts about the incident became known, religious leaders confronted the regime head-on. On April 15, the Church Council for Social Mission issued a statement in which they listed the US approval of the Gwangju massacre, insulting remarks about Koreans by Commanding US Officer General John A. Wickham Jr. and by US Ambassador to Korea Richard Walker, and the unequal relationship between Korea and the US as the background of the Busan USIS Arson Incident.

Indeed, General Wickham said in support of Chun Doo-hwan's coup d'état: "Koreans are like field mice, they just follow whoever becomes their leader. Democracy is not an adequate system for Koreans." Also, Ambassador to Korea Richard Walker called students and intellectuals working for democracy "spoiled brats." We proud Koreans simply could not accept these insulting remarks.

At first, the prosecutor's office summoned religious leaders and appeared to harshly suppress them, but ultimately released them all because the investigation inevitably led them to the Gwangju Uprising. However, this incident had lasting repercussions. Above all, Catholics came out of the long silence they had been under since the Gwangju Uprising. This awakening of the Catholics encouraged other democratic forces as well. They shed their fear of the military and their frustration about the 1980 Seoul Spring; this development offered the impetus for the long journey toward overthrowing the dictatorship and achieving democracy.

PRISON: A SMALL, YET BIG COLLEGE (1981–1982)

After my sentence was commuted from capital punishment to life imprisonment, I was transferred to a prison in Cheongju. The day of my transfer, January 31, 1981, I had my head shaved not as a condemned criminal, but as a regular criminal. I teared up, not because I was mortified, but because I was happy to have just escaped death. It was scary to think of death. I lost twenty-two pounds from the sheer stress of it all during the few months I spent waiting for judgment. When I met with my wife as a condemned criminal at the army prison neither of us shed a single tear; when I met my wife in Cheongju, I couldn't hold back my tears. Even though I refused to cooperate with the regime to save my life, I had, nonetheless, yearned to live. Still, I thanked the Lord for all my sufferings as I saw them as a sign of His love. I am grateful that the Lord had me share in His disgrace and solitude of the cross.

As soon as I arrived at the prison in Cheongju, I requested an electric stove. Although I thought there was no way they would comply with my request, it was too unbearably cold not to try. I barely ate dinner before going under the covers. There I wept, calling out, "Dear Father." After crying for a long time, I fell asleep. I was suddenly awoken by a noise that seemed to be due to construction. Surprisingly, they were installing an electric stove. The guards and workers looked like angels to me. I realized God was with me. Nevertheless, an electric stove was not a match for the bitter winter weather. Even with the stove, water still froze in the cell.

There were three compartments in my cell. I stayed in the middle compartment, and there was a small bathtub in another. My cell was completely blocked away from all of the other cells. The corridor was blocked with a concrete wall, and they built another wall around my cell. It was a prison within a prison.

Five guards were assigned solely to me—three during the day and two at night. There was a thick door in front and a tiny window at the back of my cell. I could see only little bits of sky through that window, as a finely latticed grate covered it. Neither the sky nor the moon looked whole. The lattice made it seem as though there were many moons when I looked at it through the window; I comforted myself with the thought that I was a rich man who had many moons.

I could not sit on the floor because of my injured hip and legs. The prison provided a chair, a desk, and a wooden bed, but they were very coarse. The food was worse. It was either too salty or too spicy, and frequently even rotten. Outside of the prison, I would not have eaten food like that, no matter how hungry I was. I could not eat much in prison, either.

A few days after my arrival in Cheongju, I had a dream. Workmen carried me to a suburb in a large wagon. There was a wasteland on the right side of the road, and they were going to dump me there to let me die. But a sudden change of plans led them to dump me right next to the road. Then they put me back on the wagon. Since it was a bitterly cold day and I was almost naked, I would have frozen to death even in the wagon. At that moment, God suddenly sent down two strands of red light from above the clouds. The light landed on the wagon and surrounded me in thin cloud-shaped strips that formed an oval cocoon. I felt heat run through my entire body; the wagoners were happy too, saying they were warm. My dream ended when the wagon stopped in front of a traditional Korean-tile-roofed house that looked like a public hall. It was only a dream, but I felt happy and honored. Thinking that my wife and children would like that dream, I wrote about it in a letter to them.

One day in April, I received a letter from my eldest son, Hong Il, who was currently being held in Daejeon Prison. The mere sight of that letter—the first I had received from him since our May 17 arrest almost a year before—was heart-wrenching. Tears streamed down my face and I just stroked the letter for hours. Only that night under the covers did I actually read the letter. I had to wipe my tears frequently.

> My eyes are moistening even at the thought of writing a letter to you, Father, whom I so want to see even in my dreams. I am above all grateful for the Lord's great blessing that saved your life, listening to our family's and many others' prayers. I believed that God was with you and knew that He gave you such hardship in order to use you for a noble purpose as shown in Isaiah 48:10: "See, I have refined you, though not as silver; I have tested you in the furnace of affliction." Nevertheless, as a weak human being, how worried I was! When I think of those times, I still feel a chill down my spine.

> As I missed you so much, I remembered various occasions when you have shown your love for us, like when you took Hong Up and me to the Palgakjeong Pavilion in Mt. Namsan and had a picture taken of us with you, us holding your hands on both sides of you. I hear from Mother, Hong Up, Hong Gul, and my wife how you have been during interviews and what you wrote in your letters. My heart aches to know that you are not well. I pray with all my heart for your health, trusting the Lord's care. Please cheer up and do take care of yourself.

> There was an appeals decision for my case at the Supreme Court today. I don't know what the decision was, but I don't have high hopes. However, perhaps because I am a weak human being, I pray for the good news of "meeting" and "freedom" for our family and all your co-dependents under God's great grace.

I heard that my children pray for their grandfather's and daddy's health and speedy return every meal and before they go to bed. I sincerely hope that their prayers will be heard.

I read the letter over and over again. We were worried about each other in prison. We were calling each other from Daejeon and Cheongju. Thinking of Hong Il who had to spend his youth in prison because of his father made me feel infinitely sad and extremely sorry. He wrote a post-script at the end that read: "Dear Sirs who handle this letter: Please be kind and make sure that my father receives this letter." I lay with the letter in my arms, but I couldn't fall asleep. It was a sad and painful spring night.

I thought a lot about God in prison. If God is good and omnipotent, why is there evil in this world? I could not understand why unjust people like Park Chung-hee and Chun Doo-hwan took power and people who tried to live justly were persecuted. I asked advice from people through my wife and I read books, too. Although their answers were not always the same, they mostly said: "God allowed evil in this world to test the free will that He gave only to human beings."

I really could not accept that answer, though. It seemed to me that God could have achieved His goal with only good. For example, if God divided the good into ten different levels and let people choose whether they wanted to go up the ladder of goodness or not of their own free will, that could have served the same purpose. There really did not seem any reason to have evil. Where would God's refinement or test of our free will be for people who were born disabled, died in a capsized ship, or were victimized during the nuclear bombing?

After much agonized searching, I finally found the clue to solve my question from Father Pierre Teilhard de Chardin's ideas, based on evolutionism. I may summarize them as follows:

It is true that God created the world. But God created not a perfect, but an imperfect one. The world is on its way to perfection, and there is friction in this work for perfection, such as illness, crime, and injustice. Jesus stands in the middle of this world and leads us to that day of perfection and His second coming.

For this perfection, Jesus needs our participation and cooperation. In fact, it is only through human cooperation that this world has brilliantly developed. Human freedom and justice have improved and many diseases including smallpox have been eradicated or can be treated. Slavery was abolished, and the rights of women and children improved.

Human beings are born into this world, invited by God to participate in His work of perfecting the world. If we try to realize God's justice, then we are participating in Jesus' construction work, no matter what we do. After living like this, we can die believing that God will save us. Those who were born disabled, or victimized by war, disease, or bad politics will all be saved when Jesus comes again, thanks to God's omnipotent power.

This is what I recognized as the answer to the question I asked when I was sentenced to capital punishment: "How can evil win and good lose? Where is God?"

Human beings have an amazing adaptive ability. No matter how miserable our situation is, we eventually learn how to cope with it. That is our survival instinct and wisdom. At first, it was impossible for me to accept the fact that I was completely isolated from the outside world. It was harder to accept because I had done nothing wrong.

However, thinking freed me. My feelings about unjustified hardship led me to theology and history. As I could control my feelings, gradually peace came over me, too. Later, I even came to enjoy my monotonous prison life. One might wonder what there was to enjoy in prison, a place where yesterday was like today, and today is like tomorrow. But there were indeed things to enjoy in prison.

My first source of enjoyment was reading. Like my time in prison in Jinju, I was entirely absorbed in reading during my two years in Cheongju Prison. I read books from various fields—philosophy, theology, politics, economy, history, and literature. I carefully reread Toynbee's *A Study of History*. The books I enjoyed included Bertrand Russell's *History of Western Philosophy*, Plato's *Republic*, Augustine's *The City of God*, Teilhard de Chardin's various books, theological books by Reinhold Niebuhr and Harvey Cox, and literature dating back to the time of ancient Greece.

Among the literature I read, I was especially moved and inspired by Russian literature, works by Pushkin, Lermontov, Dostoevsky, Tolstoy, and Turgenev. I also read Eastern classics like *Confucius, Mencius,* and *Records of the Grand Historian,* books on Silla monk Wonhyo and Joseon Confucian scholar Yulgok, as well as books by the Practical Learning School in the late Joseon period. My time in prison was a great time of learning. It was a time of fullness and spiritual happiness. Prison was my college.

My wife found all of the books that I wanted to read, whatever it took. She supplied me with a total of about 600 books. She also recommended books that she thought would be helpful to me. One of them was Alvin Toffler's *The Third Wave*. Although I had not heard of the book before, I was completely absorbed in it as soon as I began to read. It was a sort of guidebook for the future. Toffler claimed that while capital, labor, and land are essential elements for contemporary economy, information, knowledge, and creativity would be essential in the future. My dream of Korea as an information powerhouse began then.

I could not read quickly. After reading each book slowly and carefully, I always took notes about the essential elements and what I wanted to remember. On average, I read for about ten hours a day. So that I would not get bored, I read three or four books from different fields simultaneously. Although there was a ten-book per cell limit at a time, I requested that this number be increased and earned a thirty-book limit.

While reading all of these books, I often thought of all the things I wouldn't have learned had I not been in prison. I even felt lucky to be imprisoned because I acquired so much knowledge during those two years. After I was released, I sometimes missed having time to read. At those times, I even missed the prison—I almost felt the impulse to return.

My second source of enjoyment was meeting with my family. At first, I was allowed only a ten-minute interview with them once a month. That was twenty minutes shorter than what was legally allowed. I protested many times and was finally allowed two twenty-minute interviews per month. How I waited for that time! As soon as the interview was over, I began counting down to the next interview day. I counted dozens of times every day.

Although it was called an interview, I was never allowed to see their faces clearly. They specially renovated an interview room and installed a very thick glass between my visitors and me. Naturally, our conversations were recorded and transcribed. I talked with my family through an interphone. When our time was up, the phone was automatically disconnected. Often, we couldn't even finish what we were saying, and had to turn around without saying goodbye (Fig. 5.2).

Although I couldn't even touch their hands, meeting with my family was an extremely happy event. I missed and loved them so much. Sharing feelings with my family gave me the courage to survive within that extremely confined space.

My third source of enjoyment was receiving letters. Only letters from my wife, sons, siblings, and nephews and nieces were delivered. My sons, siblings, nephews, and nieces sent me around **600** letters.

Fig. 5.2 Kim Dae-jung when his family visited him in prison in Cheongju in 1981

My wife Lee Hee-ho wrote a letter every day as I was in prison as though it were a diary. I counted her letters later, and found that she sent me 649 total. She was always concerned about my health and encouraged me not to lose my courage. She wrote not only about how my family was doing, but also about my acquaintances and even the plants and a puppy I loved. On a spring day, she pasted lilac petals she had picked from our garden on a letter so that I could smell their fragrance. Sometimes she pasted a cute puppy picture or a piece of paper with a flower design on the letter. While reading her letters, I felt as though she was right in front of me. She also wrote about domestic and foreign current affairs, including her own analyses. The letters that began with "My Most Respected Dear" were a spring of information that delivered outside news to me. It was a joy to read them. Following are some excerpts.

> I love and admire you even more because your life is not easy. The way you believe in God in order to conquer all kinds of hardships, and pray to Jesus, holding on to his sleeves rather than enjoying wealth and status looks rather

pious and solemn. You have always worked hard with all your might, shedding blood and sweat. You have struggled to listen to the voice of conscience and live justly. You have a particularly strong love of your country and people. That's why you won this prize of hardship. (December 5, 1980)

Although you know me as someone without tears, I am actually a person with lots of tears. I try very hard not to show and just swallow my tears in front of others. Also, I did not want to show tears in front of you lest you'd be pained. And yet, I cried unaware. These days, often when I sing hymns in the church, I cannot help crying. (February 26, 1981)

I was happy to see garlic on the prison purchase list today. Please make sure to eat it. Consider it your medicine. In the same category, there are also two kinds of garlic pickles—jangajji and rakkyo. Remember them. After eating dishes mixed with vinegar, eating yogurt is useful to kill the aftertaste. You have to stay healthy, no matter what. (May 18, 1981)

I began knitting your socks today. I thought that your old socks might be less warm now that they must be worn out. While knitting your socks, I pray that everything including your health would be fine and our prayers will be heard. (October 28, 1981)

I also felt my sons' love for and pride in me through their letters.

In times of difficulty and anguish, I am reminded of what you said to me: "Nothing is entirely good or bad," and "Dear God! Give me courage to change and wisdom to accept what I cannot change!" As Mother says, this hardship gives us precious time for our family to unite with a firm belief in God. (Excerpted from my second son Hong Up's letter)

I try to remember and practice what you said last time I visited you. Also, I am proud of you because I know very well that you have worked only for God and people without coveting power or wealth. (Excerpted from my youngest son Hong Gul's letter)

I also sent letters to my family. I was allowed to write only one letter per month, and the length of the letter was limited to a letter card. This restriction had no legal basis. My request for more letter cards was denied so I had to write in a tiny font the size of sesame seeds. Once, I was able to squeeze 14,000 letters on a single letter card. This meant I squeezed in twenty-two letters in a one-letter box written on manuscript paper. The receiver of the letter could not decipher it without a magnifying glass.

It was very hard to write letters like that. However, I tried my best, thinking that my words might help my wife and children. In particular, I wanted to impart what I learned from my reading to my children. I began planning a letter two weeks before I could send it. As I wasn't allowed even a sheet of paper, I could not write a draft. I had to send a letter even if I wanted to edit awkward sentences.

I sent a total of twenty-nine letters between November 21, 1980 and December 15, 1982, the day before I was transferred to Seoul National University Hospital. A collection of these letters was first published in Korean in the book *Embracing People's Sorrow* (US, 1983). Soon after, the book was translated into Japanese by various Japanese scholars, including Professor Wada Haruki, and published in Japan. It was also translated into English by Professors Choi Sung-il and David McCann and published under the title *Prison Writings* in the US. In Korea, it was published under the title *Kim Dae-jung's Prison Writings*.

The book became a bestseller. Readers even began to read the books I mentioned in my letters. Then, the police raided bookstores and confiscated my books. They also pressured publishing organizations not to include it in their bestseller lists. The president of the publishing house was detained.

My fourth source of enjoyment in prison was growing flowers. I did this during about an hour of exercise time after lunch every day. The flowerbed I was in charge of was about 2 meters wide and 30 centimeters long. There were petunias, azaleas, dandelions, daisies, and salvias. In the fall, there were cosmoses and chrysanthemums. I liked azaleas and chrysanthemums the most.

I watered and weeded them carefully. Flowers are straightforward. They grow as they are taken care of, and flowered as prettily as anticipated. I often pictured the scenes in Saint-Exupery's book *The Little Prince*, where the little prince watered roses in his star. I seemed to be able to understand why that scene of the story was so important. Like that little prince, I also talked to the flowers.

In fact, the flowers were my only conversation partners in prison. Once, I whispered to a flower that didn't grow well despite my earnest care, "I'm disappointed in you. You don't respond to my care even though I have worked so hard. Why? Do you think my care is not enough? I really try my best." After our conversation, that flower grew strikingly better.

When I trimmed the branches, I apologized to them. "Does it hurt? Don't worry. I do this for your sake. You have to endure this much pain to grow beautifully."

Prison guards helped me take care of the flowerbed. At first, they just stood by and watched me work, but gradually they began to join. Even when the sun was hot and made them sweat, they did not leave the flowerbed. Taking care of the flowers allowed me to shed my sadness and worries. That was the reward flowers gave me.

The flowers I took care of lasted about a month longer than the flowers in other sections of the flowerbed. They brightened up the prison until late fall. The saying about flowers and children becoming more beautiful the more you take care of them is true.

In late fall 1982, I could not grow flowers outside any more because of the weather. I transplanted an azalea into a pot and took it into my cell. I moved it around in the room, following the sunlight. It grew flower buds during November and December and bloomed on December 16. I was so happy that I showed it to the prison guards. I wished I could have shown it to the entire world. I murmured to a prison guard, "Perhaps there will be good news as this azalea blooms in winter."

Indeed, good news came that very same afternoon: I was transferred to Seoul National University Hospital. It seemed the azalea, knowing I would be transferred, tried to bloom before I left.

Almost a year before that transfer, on January 6, 1982 (my birthday), my sons came and gave me a ceremonial kowtow on the other side of the window. I felt something hot inside my chest. After returning to my cell, I wrote a thirty-six-line *sijo* poem. Following are the first four stanzas.

> My three sons gave me a big bow on the floor of the interview room.
> My heart aches to see this celebration of the New Year's Day and my birthday.
> My dear wife, don't be so despondent; don't we have these great children?

> If someone asks me the meaning of my life, I'd answer:
> I just don't want to hand down to our descendants
> The kind of sorrowful life we ourselves had to endure.

> Lying alone in a prison cell on a long winter night
> I cannot fall asleep, worrying about the fate of our country.
> How bright the moon is, and how heavy my heart is!

> Dear clouds, please let me borrow you and wander around.
> I would like to see nature and look for my fellow countrymen.
> If not while I'm awake, then, how about in my dream?

I wanted to send this *sijo* poem to my wife in a letter, but the prison censors demanded I remove it. They must have feared the repercussions the publication of this poem might have.

My wife tried very hard to keep me warm in prison. She continued to knit and send wool gloves, pants, socks, and hats. In particular, she made my gloves so that I could take the tip of my index finger out to flip books. I marveled at her ingenuity and caring thoughts.

There is a common saying among prisoners that you get released if you see a clock in your dream. I came to lodge my hope on that saying even though I was imprisoned indefinitely. I wished to see a clock in my dream every night I went to sleep. One night, I finally saw clocks in my dream. There wasn't just one clock, but a room full of them. I was excited about this dream and, day after day, waited for the news of my release. Disappointed, I smiled bitterly to myself.

Time went by, even in prison. Although knowledge accumulated in the storeroom of my mind thanks to reading and thinking, life in a solitary cell was physically challenging. I developed neuropathy and my left ear rang. I experienced severe pain in my hip joint, and my legs often swelled and cramped. It was really hard to endure that life. My wife petitioned the attorney general to allow me outside treatments many times in vain. The prison food was of such poor quality that I couldn't eat well. Since I was constantly hungry, I purchased and ate a lot of candy. As a result, I gained weight, which put more pressure on my hip joint. Surprised to see me so chubby, my wife half-jokingly and half-seriously said, "You've grown so fat that nobody would believe you're having a hard time in prison, would they?"

One day in February 1982, my wife came to see me and told me that she had met President Chun Doo-hwan. Although she went to see him with great expectations, he didn't say much. A little later, on the occasion of the March 1st Special Amnesty, my sentence was commuted to a twenty-year term.

On April 25, 1982, Dr. Jeong Il-hyeong passed away. I knew it only from my wife's letter. Dr. Jeong was my political teacher and like a father to me. How cold-hearted the world is where I couldn't see him off with a big bow!

I heard that Dr. Jeong Il-hyeong was extremely shocked at the news of my capital punishment sentence. According to Reverend Kang Won-yong, when he visited Dr. Jeong on his sick bed, he held Reverend Kang's hands and pled while crying, "Please save Dae-jung. Save him!"

When I heard this, I, too, cried. During the 1970 presidential election, Dr. Jeong shouted my name on the street, holding a picket for a young man about his son's age. Age and hierarchy didn't matter to him. Scenes from the past flitted by in front of my eyes. Tears continued to stream down my face.

On December 10, 1982, a KCIA officer visited me. Abruptly, he asked if I wanted to go to the US. "I heard you're not well," he said. "Why don't you go to the US and get treatment there?"

Although I wasn't well, I did not want to leave my country. My comrades were still suffering in prison because of me. Also, how many students were suffering in prison due to their participation in the democratization struggle? Besides, I could not leave behind the citizens of Gwangju who were in prison due to the democracy movement. I politely refused and said, "If you really care about my health, please let me be treated within our country."

After he left, I realized a change in my situation might be afoot. A few days later, my wife came to see me. Unlike other times, nobody watched us. My wife told me she had met with KCIA director Roh Sin-young and he said, "I'd like to resolve the Kim Dae-jung question. Please encourage your husband to go to the US for medical treatment. I'll recommend to the president that he be sent to America with his family. This is my personal opinion, so please keep it a secret. I don't know if this is possible yet."

My wife urged me to accept their request. She said she discussed this option with Hong Il and Hong Up, as well as Mr. Ahn Byung Mu and Mr. Ye Choon-ho (who had already been released from prison), and that they all recommended I accept it. I did not want to go to the US, and did not think I needed to. I also told her I could not leave the country when my comrades were still unjustly imprisoned. My wife left the room helplessly.

Soon, my wife returned with a KCIA official and began to persuade me, stubbornly saying, "You can do nothing here in prison. Everyone says that you are the only person who can arouse international public opinion overseas. And, more importantly, they say it is only after we leave for the US that they can release your co-defendants."

I looked at my wife's face again. This was a valid point. After I confirmed this promise, I accepted their suggestion and asked them to release all other political prisoners. The KCIA official told me he needed my clear promise before anything else. He then handed me a piece of paper and asked me to write: *I'll concentrate only on my treatment and won't participate in any political activities.*

I refused, saying, "Even if I go to the US, I cannot help talking about human rights. Think about it. If I don't engage in such activities, people will think the current government bribed me. Besides, I cannot engage in political activities to begin with because of the Political Activities Renovation Law."

Nevertheless, the KCIA official insisted I needed to write this statement as a prerequisite for leaving the country. I felt I had no choice but to do so.

My wife went to Seoul with that petition. I later heard that she showed it to my eldest son, Hong Il, who was concerned that it did not include mention of the release of political prisoners. My wife met KCIA Director Roh the next day and asked him to allow her another special interview with me so that I could change the petition.

However, Director Roh responded casually, "This petition is for the president's eyes only. It's not a document to be published. Don't worry about it at all. If necessary, I'll testify to that condition."

"I will trust your character," my wife responded. Nonetheless, they revealed the petition. In order to prevent my political activities, they shackled me in both visible and invisible chains.

On December 16, I was transferred to Seoul National University Hospital and hospitalized in a special VIP room (room 21 in Ward 1 on the twelfth floor). The difference between this room and the room where I was previously imprisoned was like the difference between heaven and hell; however, I was still tightly guarded. Ten prison guards from Cheongju and ten police officers from the Seodaemun police station blocked the entrance and corridor. Hundreds of policemen surrounded the hospital. They announced to us that we should leave the country on the twenty-third. I was surprised our departure date was so soon.

That day, the culture and public relations minister held a press conference where he announced: "Kim Dae-jung was transferred to a hospital based on humanitarian grounds according to his family's request, and will go to America soon. The decision about this generous measure, including granting permission to be treated in the US according to Kim Dae-jung's and his family's wishes, was made based on the fifth republic's will to cleanse the remnants of the old era and to accomplish unity among all people, as well as President Chun's special humanitarian consideration."

This announcement was unacceptable because I was not going to the US "according to [my] and [my] family's wishes." There were indeed other reasons that the Chun regime hurried me out of the country. First of all, the regime's ironfisted politics based on the persecution of politicians and eradication of democratic forces met with serious opposition both domestically and overseas. There was also the Chang Yong-ja and Lee Chul-Hee Fraud Incident, a high profile scandal that involved President Chun's close relative. In addition, international communities were pressuring the regime to release me.

I felt it was wrong for them to take credit for sending me to the US. I also did not want to hurry out of my country while other prisoners had yet to be released—it seemed as if I was running away. I asked my wife to stop the process of leaving the country. The government volunteered a promise to release all prisoners related to my incident the day after I left the country. My wife also urged me to leave for the US. My doctor chimed in as well. "Your hip joint is in a very serious condition. Without proper treatment, it can deteriorate too much to fix, and you might end up not being able to walk." After much anguish, I decided to leave. My eldest son, Hong Il, decided to remain in Korea.

A little after 4:00 p.m. on December 23, my wife, Hong Il, Hong Up, and Hong Gul came to my hospital room. My brother Dae-hyeon also came, but he was not allowed to enter my room. A little after 6:00 p.m., the four of us left the room. Dae-hyeon and Hong Il were told to meet us at the airport. The corridor was quiet; the only sound was our footsteps. Plainclothes policemen were stationed on both sides of the corridor. We followed their lead and got on a large elevator. As it was the day after the winter solstice, it was very dark outside. I could not tell where we were when we got out of the elevator. We were immediately taken into an ambulance with the curtains drawn. The ambulance seemed not to go straight to the airport, but to make a detour. The KCIA agents spoke into their devices, using codes like "toad" and "owl."

Finally, we were told to get off the ambulance. The streetlamps were all turned off near Gimpo Airport. As we got off, the airplane stood right before us. After embarking, we found out we were on board a Northwest plane rather than the Korean Air plane on which we had purchased our tickets. Our luggage had already been sent to Korean Air. It was their tactic to shake off reporters who might be on board the same plane to interview me. While we were settling into our seats, the vice warden of Cheongju Prison appeared in front of us. He took a piece of paper from his pocket and read it: "I release you on suspension of execution of your prison term."

After he left, another person gave us our passports and airplane tickets. We could not meet anybody—not even my brother Dae-hyeon and my son Hong Il. The airplane took off in pitch dark as my wife wiped away her tears.

Second Exile, a Passionate Time (1982–1984)

We arrived at Washington National Airport at 10:45 p.m. on December 23. About 300 Korean-Americans were waiting for us at this late hour. The crowd included Reverend Moon Dong-hwan, Dr. Choi Sung-il, Dr. Han Wan-sang, my secretary Yi Geun-pal, Reverend Pharis J. Harvey, and Senator Edward M. Kennedy's chief of staff. They chanted my name while holding picket signs displaying my picture and the phrase "Conscience in Action."

Reverend Moon Dong-hwan made a welcoming remark. He said, "God, who saved Daniel from the lion's den, saved Mr. Kim Dae-jung from the hand of the ferocious dictator, Chun Doo-hwan." His kind-hearted eyes were teary. Reporters from all over the world surrounded me. Cameras continued to flash.

I had to make an impromptu speech at the crowd's request. I said, "I am grateful to God for saving my life. I thank President Reagan, Senator Edward M. Kennedy, and Representative Stephen Solarz. I thank people all over the world who have supported the restoration of my freedom. I'd like to return to my fatherland Korea as soon as my treatment is finished and continue my fight."

I thanked everyone. My wife was moved to tears. Reverend Moon recommended Hobart and William Smith Colleges Professor Dr. Choi Sung-il as my interpreter. He had an amazing linguistic talent, speaking not only English, but also German, French, Japanese, and Chinese. The next day, news came from Korea that all other prisoners related to my incident were released.

My family spent Christmas Eve at a hotel in DC. I prayed for God's grace upon my family and me, our nation, and my life in exile. Despite many people's warm welcome, I felt vaguely uneasy. I tried to muster courage. Although I achieved freedom, there were many conditions attached to it. I was able to stay strong thanks to God's presence next to me.

The New Year dawned and 1983 began. I spent my first day in the US with Korean-Americans. I met Reverend Moon Dong-hwan, Mr. Yi Geun-pal, Mr. An Byeong-guk, and Mr. Kim Dong-hyeon. I also met my wife's brother Lee Sung-ho and my wife's nephew Dr. Lee Yeong-jak. They gave our family courage. Their well wishes gave us hope. On January 3, Representative Solarz held a welcome dinner for us. On January 8, we found a place for my family to rent on the sixteenth floor of the Watergate Landmark Apartment in Alexandria, Virginia, near Washington, DC. This was, of course, the infamous complex known for the Watergate scandal. Guards checked people in and out, and there were meeting rooms that could be used for a small fee. I grew various plants in the apartment with the skills I had acquired in prison. The plants were always fresh and bloomed beautiful flowers.

On February 15, Senator Edward M. Kennedy held a welcome event for me at the Mansfield Room of the US Senate building. Hundreds of people, including former Secretary of State Muskie and National Security Advisor Richard Allen, attended and congratulated me on my release. They warmly embraced me, an exile in their country who had escaped his beloved fatherland, which was the jaw of death for me. Yet, I was sad that I had to be welcomed not in my country but as an exile in a foreign land. In my address there, I said: "We don't want US involvement in Korean domestic politics. We do not demand that the US work for the recovery of democracy in our stead. But we hope for the following two things from the US: first, to extend moral support for our aspiration for democracy; second, for the US government not to justify or encourage dictatorship under the pretext of stability and security."

The US was the best place to put pressure on the Korean dictator. I decided that informing their congressional leaders about the true state of the Korean dictatorship was the most effective method to achieving this goal. I also decided to emphasize that their support for the dictator would not benefit US interests, either. In addition, I requested that journalists, scholars, and religious leaders put indirect pressure on the Korean dictatorial regime and support democratic forces in Korea.

Soon after my arrival in the US, I took part in a press conference where a Japanese reporter asked me, "Do you know that Georgetown University proposed giving you a free operation about a year ago?"

It turned out that while I was still in prison, the Catholic-affiliated Georgetown University offered to operate on my hip joint for free; I hadn't heard about their proposal. I was planning to get treatment at a US army hospital, but was worried about the cost, so I was thankful for the news.

I immediately verified this offer with Georgetown University Hospital, which confirmed it. A doctor greeted me warmly. After the examination, he said it would take about six months to operate on and treat my hip, but that the treatment most likely wouldn't improve my pain and inconvenience. In fact, my health had improved greatly since I was released from prison. The doctor recommended that I not try operation right away, but decide later, after observing how it progressed.

I went to the US to take care of my health, but that purpose was ultimately eliminated. I could not idle away my time. Around this time, an outrageous rumor was circulating that I had received $200,000 from the Korean government. There was no doubt that the KCIA was behind this base fabrication. I announced to the Korean Embassy in Washington, DC: "I came to the US for the treatment of my illness, but found out that I didn't need it. I cannot spend my time idly. Many people are fighting for democracy in Korea now. I cannot stay silent in good conscience. I am going to fight for democracy here. I do not care if you call it political activity. If I have to, then I'll take responsibility. I, of course, do not mean to dishonor Korea. However, I will proudly argue against the Chun Doohwan regime. I believe that will honor the name of my country in the end. If I do something wrong, I will be judged legally after I return home."

In March, I gave a lecture entitled "Korean Christianity and Human Rights" at Emory University in Atlanta, Georgia. After the lecture, I visited former president Carter with Emory University president James T. Laney and went to the Carter Center. President Carter was as warm as a good neighbor. I sincerely thanked him for his role in saving my life. "I am deeply grateful for your hard work to save me when I was a condemned criminal. In fact, when you lost the election, I thought I was going to die and wept out loud."

I became tearful, which made the atmosphere solemn. President Carter said in a low voice, "I admire your courage and patience in front of dictators' threats and appeasement tactics. Please keep me posted. We are comrades."

That night Emory University president Laney held a dinner party for my family. Soon after, I received an Honorary Doctorate in Law from Emory University. President Laney held a congratulatory luncheon, to which Atlanta Mayor Andrew Young, Korean-American residents in the area, and human rights organization members were also invited. At other attendants' request, I calmly delivered a speech about my journey through the democracy movement in my awkward English.

In the two years and three months I stayed in the US I gave more than 150 lectures at churches and human rights organizations and associations. I talked mainly about Korean democracy and human rights and tried to inform the US government and Congress members, as well as religious communities, Korean-Americans, and world media, about the Korean reality. More than twenty universities invited me to visit. Wherever I went, regional broadcasting stations and newspapers requested interviews with me. I talked about the situation in Korea and appealed for their support of our democracy movement every time.

I was always on the road. I went wherever people called me. I spent more time in the car than in my house. I was always tired. Although many people applauded at my lectures and life and encouraged me, I felt lonely afterward. I sometimes cried by myself, not letting even my wife know.

From far away, the Korean situation looked hopeless. The freedom of the press was thoroughly infringed upon and human rights were trampled on. The opposition party was invisible, though it still existed. Democracy fighters were either in prison or imprisoned in their homes. In June 1983, I established the Korean Human Rights Question Research Institute in the US and officially registered it as a nonprofit organization. I planned to spread Korea's passion for democracy all across the US, and then to Korea from there. I was its president and there was a ten-member board of directors, including Lee Yeong-jak, Yi Geun-pal, Kim Kyung-jae, Yi Jae-hyeon, Choi Sung-il, and Reverend Harvey. We published a newsletter entitled *Conscience in Action*; the publication's editors included Sim Ki-sup and Chung Dong-chea.

It cost quite a bit to manage the institute and publish the newsletter. Although I contributed the profit from my calligraphy exhibition and lecture fees, my contribution was not nearly enough. I held calligraphy exhibitions in major cities like New York, Washington, DC, and Los Angeles. I wrote Chinese phrases like "Worship Heaven, love people," "Treat people like Heaven," "People are Heaven," and "Seeking truth grounded on concrete evidence." Although I don't think I am a great calligrapher, people gladly bought them. My wife contributed her calligraphy, too, and our works sold out everywhere. I believe people bought them to contribute to the Korean democracy movement and, for that, I am really grateful.

We could operate the institute only thanks to the help of Korean-Americans. In particular, Mr. Jeong Hyeong-gi, a jeweler in New York, contributed greatly. In retrospect, I received so much help from so many

Korean-Americans during my stay in the US. They must have gladly contributed just based on their sincere wishes for their fatherland's democratization. I'd like to extend my deepest thanks again here. Without their help, my exile in the US could have been really hard. I have never forgotten their passionate support.

During my stay in the US, I also paid attention to Korean-Americans' human rights. I emphasized the importance of their participation in American politics: "The most important thing is human rights, for which you need democracy. And for democracy you have to participate in the American democratic process." By participating in American democracy, they could move American public opinion, which could, in turn, move the American Congress and administration.

On the third anniversary of the Gwangju Uprising, former president of the Sinmin Party Kim Young-sam went on a hunger strike. He had been under house imprisonment after being banned from all political activities. A hunger strike is an extreme form of struggle and a last-ditch effort. I was deeply moved and felt a very strong sense of solidarity with him. President Kim made five demands:

- first, to release all detainees—students, religious leaders, intellectuals, and laborers;
- second, to allow political activities for all politicians and democratic citizens banned from them according to the Political Activities Regulation Law;
- third, to reinstate professors, students, and laborers expelled from schools and workplaces for political reasons;
- fourth, to nullify press mergers and abolition and reinstate dismissed journalists; and
- fifth, to amend or abolish all anti-democratic laws and recover the direct presidential election system.

I thought Mr. Kim Young-sam's hunger strike had a very significant political implication. First of all, it was the first resistance by the opposition party politician against the Chun regime. It could work to unite all democratic forces. However, President Kim's hunger strike was not reported in domestic media due to control and censorship of the press. On May 25, the eighth day of his hunger strike, the authorities forced him to be hospitalized at Seoul National University Hospital, and this news was delivered around the world through foreign media like AP, Reuters, and Kyoto.

I contributed a supportive column entitled "Kim's Hunger Strike" to the *New York Times* on June 9, 1983 and requested that Professor Jerome Cohen copyedit it for me. Professor Cohen, who knew Mr. Kim Young-sam very well, said, "I know he is your political rival. I'm surprised that you wrote a column like this. This is a beautiful thing. I am moved." Following is an excerpt from the column.

> All we ask is that the United States now make clear its support for the restoration of democracy in South Korea, a country that has been a staunch ally for three-and-a-half decades. Some of our American friends may say that dictatorship in South Korea, while objectionable, ought to be tolerated because of security needs and stability. I disagree. Without democracy there is neither lasting security nor stability. The best evidence is the current political instability in South Korea. Would American citizens accept a dictatorial form of government for themselves because of the threat from the Soviet Union? I think not. Why, then, should it be different for South Koreans because of the threat from North Korea? Some may even argue that South Koreans are not ready for democracy. I believe that this argument is untenable in view of the fact that the educational, cultural and economic standards of the South Korean people far surpass those of Americans 200 years ago, when American democracy was established. It is time for the United States Government to reaffirm the importance of freedom in South Korea. Without the restoration of democratic government and institutions, there will be neither stability nor security in my country. Kim Young Sam's fast and its political impact seriously challenge the United States Government to reconsider its policy.

I also participated in demonstrations with Korean-Americans on the streets of Washington, DC and New York City in support of Mr. Kim Young-sam's hunger strike. On June 4, we marched in DC's Dupont Circle, holding picket signs that said "Save Kim Young-sam!" We also demonstrated in front of the Korean Embassy building, the State Department building, and the White House. Mr. Kim Young-sam finished his hunger strike after twenty-three days (Fig. 5.3).

Since that time, Mr. Kim Young-sam and I have cooperated closely on current affairs. On August 25 that year, on the anniversary of Korea's liberation, Mr. Kim Young-sam and I issued a joint statement entitled "The Struggle for Democratization Is a Struggle for Independence and Liberation of Our People" in Seoul and Washington, DC. The statement ended with the following:

Fig. 5.3   Kim Dae-jung participating in a demonstration in support of Korean democratization movement during his exile in the US in 1983

> We cannot avoid our responsibility in our inability to stop the worsening situation in the spring of 1980 by failing to unite as opposition party politicians and, as a result, to prevent the massacre of hundreds and thousands of Koreans. As an expression of our self-blame and repentance, and in front of all Korean people's aspiration for democratization, we promise to cooperate toward the most important goal in the Korean people's history without seeking any titles.

We declared to people in and outside of Korea that we would fight together for democracy.

In early June, the editor-in-chief of the Japanese magazine *Sekai* Yasue Ryosuke visited me at Washington, DC for an interview. I had an interview with him a little before my kidnapping in Japan ten years before. The article was published on August 8, the day I was kidnapped. He began the interview by saying, "There were times when I thought I would never see you again. It is hard for me to talk because of so many thoughts intersecting in my mind. The past ten years were turbulent and difficult for Koreans."

He seemed deeply moved to see me. We talked for a long time. He asked what I saw as the essence of the Gwangju Uprising. Following is a part of my answer, as published:

> The event in Gwangju epitomizes the three aspirations that Korean people have cherished for the past hundred years: populism, democracy, and nationalism. When the 1894 Donghak Revolution occurred, Japan intervened, which led to the Sino-Japanese War, and this resulted in the suppression of the Donghak Revolution. Although it was frustrated, the Donghak Peasant Revolution was a truly remarkable and historically just struggle for modern rights, people's liberation, and anti-imperialism for which 100,000 peasants rose up. Some scholars argue that this self-liberating peasant revolution was a far more ideologically and historically justifiable struggle than, say, the Roman Spartacus Rebellion against slavery or the 1517 German Peasant War led by Anabaptist Müntzer.

> During the Donghak Revolution, peasants won against the royal forces, but lost to the Japanese. The March 1st Independence Movement of 1919 was also defeated by Japanese forces. The April 19th Revolution, wherein people rose up against dictator Mr. Rhee Syng-man, who took advantage of anti-communism and national security for his permanent reign, was also defeated by the military coup led by Mr. Park Chung-hee the next year. These three revolutions were all defeated in the end. However, after Mr. Park Chung-hee's assassination, Koreans were intent on carrying out the concerns from those three historical revolutions—populism from the Donghak Revolution, nationalism from the March 1st Independence Movement, and democracy from the April 19th Revolution. During the time when all people sincerely wanted to establish a democratic government of the people that would carry out freedom, justice, and human dignity and have this government pursue reconciliation between the South and the North and the unification of the country, Mr. Chun Doo-hwan led a coup d'état against the people's wishes and aspirations and turned back the historical clock.

> Citizens of Gwangju rose up against it. Of course, people did not rise up just in Gwangju, but all over the Jeolla-do province. In Mokpo, my hometown, people occupied the police stations for three days. However, Gwangju made the biggest sacrifice and waged the hardest fight.

Mr. Yasue thought very highly of the Korean democratization struggle in the 1970s. He wrote:

Koreans had been subject to enormous sacrifice and pain throughout the 1970s. Innumerable people were arrested and tortured. Some were driven to insanity during torture. Young people immolated themselves in protest. Remarkable people had to die because they were remarkable. And yet, excellent people rose up again and they tried a new unity. Many think that you are at the center of this new movement. That's why the Japanese are carefully watching for your return to Korea.

To this, I replied:

Throughout the painful struggle of the 1970s, Korean people advanced greatly in every field. I believe there are many leaders who can contribute to our nation. As they are like precious stones buried underground, I don't know them all. I only know a few. Therefore, I am bothered when I am the only one getting the world's attention and being evaluated as if I am the only one who has suffered in Korea. I always feel sorry because it feels as if I intercept all their sacrifice and achievement.

I think that I should belong to a generation that does not fear sacrifice. I believe that Korea will regain democracy in the 1980s. Although this is not a prediction, I am pretty confident that it will happen. I consider it my role to run in front and open up the road. I hope to open the road for the people's age, for a truly democratic regime, for Japan and the US, for the democratized and unified Korea to become a good collaborator of the Third World. I know that will be a road of suffering.

However, a road of suffering does not necessarily mean unhappiness. In some sense, I think General Chun Doo-hwan is a very unhappy person. Sometimes, I wonder, *How uneasy would he be? Why does he spend his only precious life in this way? Does he know what people think of his actions and how future history will evaluate him?*

I do not think of myself as a martyr. I do not believe myself to be an idealist. I am a realist. I think of martyrdom and ideals only when they coincide with realistic improvement. I want to try my best to really recover freedom and truly bring reunification for Korean people.

When this interview was published in *Sekai* it had great repercussions in Japan. The *Asahi Shimbun* newspaper chose it among five great articles of the year, and the *Yomiuri Simbun* newspaper counted it as one of three great articles of the year.

Incredibly, on August 21, I heard the news that Senator Benigno Aquino of the Philippines was assassinated during a return trip to his country. Dr. Choi Sung-il introduced me to Senator Aquino for the first time early that year. We had breakfast together afterward. He was informal and large-minded. He was also very optimistic. In contrast, his wife Mrs. Corazon Aquino was very calm. Senator Aquino and I were comrades because we were both in exile and participating in democratization movements. We talked about building a center for the Asian democratization movement—an Asian Democratic Front. At that time, I could see that he really wanted to return to the Philippines soon. I wished him a safe return home to lead his country to democracy.

The world was paying close attention to his return. Dictator and President Ferdinand Marcos openly threatened him about his return home. As a result, a lot of people accompanied Senator Aquino on his return trip. Nevertheless, he was shot dead as he disembarked his airplane at the Manila International Airport. It was shocking to see him lying lifeless in a pool of blood. Major television stations showed that shocking image all day long. It was hard to believe.

I issued a statement about Senator Aquino's assassination. I expressed my grief at the death of my comrade in the democratization movement and condemned the Philippine government. As this had to do with the US support of the dictatorial regime, I urged President Reagan to cancel his scheduled visit to the Philippines.

Although Philippine authorities declared that the perpetrator was a professional contract killer, people did not believe it. Aquino did not die in vain. After his assassination, the struggle for democracy blossomed in the Philippines and his calm and modest wife Mrs. Corazon Aquino became a democracy fighter. In February 1986, Mrs. Aquino was inaugurated as the first female Philippine president after overthrowing the twenty-year-long dictatorship. I admire her courage and resolution to transform herself into a politician according to the people's will. Mrs. Aquino encouraged and supported me during difficult crises, and she and I remain comrades in the democracy movement to this day. A few years after I returned to Korea, I received Mr. Aquino's old-fashioned typewriter and photos from a close friend of his. Picturing him in my mind, I felt sad again. The typewriter is currently on exhibition at the Kim Dae-jung Presidential Library and Museum.

That September, I began studying as a visiting scholar at Harvard University's Center for International Affairs. Although I had been invited to Harvard University by Professor Edwin Reischauer in 1973, I couldn't accept the offer due to various forms of imprisonment and political situations. When the opportunity for me to study finally came I met with Professors Ezra Vogel, Jerome Cohen, Ed Baker, Benjamin Brown, and Richard Cooper to discuss various topics.

Even while studying at Harvard, I remained very busy giving lectures at the various places to which I was invited; I also gave lectures at several institutes within Harvard. The topics of my lectures were mostly about the future of Korean democracy, the relationship between Korea and Japan, and my experience in prison. Once, following a lecture at the Asian Legal Center, someone asked me: "You have been fighting for Korean democracy in exile, but is democracy really possible in Korea? Democracy is the product of Western society. There is no democratic tradition in Korea, is there? Besides, I think the chance for democracy there is slim because of the strong Confucian tradition in Korea. What's your opinion about that?"

In fact, I had received similar questions many times during my lecture tours. I emphasized that Korean history included many democratic elements.

First, the Korean foundation myths, including the Dangun myth, contain a fundamentally democratic idea. The idea of *hongik ingan* (universal benefit for all human beings) assumes that people are the most important foundation of a country. In the foundation myths of Silla and Gaya, people gather to select their king. You very rarely find this kind of foundation myth. Donghak's (Eastern learning) idea of *innaecheon* (human beings are the heaven) is also based on the idea of *sainyeocheon* (to serve people like they are the heaven).

Second, the recent century of Korean history centers around the people's struggle against authoritarianism. During the March 1st Movement, only nine years after the collapse of the Joseon Dynasty, hardly anyone wanted restoration of the dynasty. This is remarkable when you consider that during the 200-year period following the French Revolution, restoration movements continued. The April 19th Revolution in 1960, the 1979 Busan-Masan Uprising, and the 1980 Gwangju Uprising were all struggles based on the democratic spirit.

Third, the fundamental philosophy of Confucianism that guided the 500-year Joseon Dynasty was democratic. Therefore, the common assumption that countries with a Confucian tradition are not familiar with democracy is a misconception. It may be surprising to know that Mencius actually declared that the people have the right to overthrow a ruler who does not provide for their needs.

During the 500-year history of the Joseon Dynasty, freedom of the press was respected as the highest value to uphold. *Saheonbu* (the Office of the Inspector General) and *Saganwon* (the Office of the Censor-General) existed within the court. Their tasks were to point out, condemn, and demand the correction of wrongs committed by the king and high officials. Even the king could not see official historians' records.

Fourth, Korean education is at the top level internationally. Democracy is based on people's level of education. Only educated people can protect and maintain democracy through their sense of sovereignty and responsibility.

All these facts prove that the Korean people are closely related to democracy. There *has* been a democratic tradition in Korean history. I talked about this everywhere I went.

Once I attended a Harvard fellows meeting with Harvard president Derek Bok. I asked him, "Many students from the Third World, including Korea, return home after graduating from renowned American universities and become the minions of dictators and a small minority of conglomerates. Wouldn't this be related to flaws in American education?" President Bok replied, "That's not a matter of university education, but a personal character."

I could not agree with his answer. If he was right, why did so many Korean students who didn't go to Harvard University gladly fight for democracy and go to prison, unafraid of oppression? They gave up the prospect of the good jobs guaranteed to them and fought without fearing imprisonment. It seemed to me that his answer couldn't explain that phenomenon. I expressed my opinion in a letter I wrote a few days later. A few days after that, I had the chance to meet one-on-one with President Bok. He told me that he had suggested the establishment of a special institution at Harvard Law School to study the question of human rights in the Third World. He and I became good friends after that. When I was about to return to Korea, he contributed an article to the *New York Times*, in which he urged the Korean government to make an effort to guarantee my safe return. He also added his signature to that of about 150 other world leaders on a petition to President Chun Doo-hwan.

I once had the opportunity to have a breakfast with Swedish Prime Minister Olof Palme, who visited the Harvard Kennedy School to give a lecture. I thanked him for his contribution to the movement to save me when I was sentenced to capital punishment. He had continued to support me since the kidnapping incident. He said that he had done what he had to, and told me to please make sure to visit Sweden when I had time.

At the end of the year-long visiting scholarship, I submitted a thesis on the Korean economy. Of course, I was not obligated to submit a thesis, but I wanted to have my economic theories tested. Dr. You Jong-keun, who worked for the New Jersey State government, helped me finish it. Harvard University professors thought highly of my thesis and arranged for Harvard University Press to publish it. They also assigned it as supplementary reading in their classes. This was the book I mentioned before, entitled *Mass-Participatory Economy: A Democratic Alternative for Korea*.

President Reagan was scheduled to visit Korea in October 1983. The American public was critical of this visit because people worried it could bolster Korean dictatorship when its violation of human rights was egregious. Many congressmen delivered their opinion against this visit to the White House. I also participated in the protest in front of the White House.

I was invited to appear on ABC's *Nightline* to discuss the issue. I hesitated because I was not confident about my English. Guests on this program had to be very careful as anchor Ted Koppel was a sharp interviewer who asked pointed questions. I had many discussions about whether or not I should accept the invitation. Surprisingly, those I spoke with strongly urged me to accept. They encouraged me, saying what I actually said was more important than fluency. I bravely accepted the invitation in support of Korea's democratization.

Four guests—two Americans and two Koreans—were scheduled to be on the program. An American and Korean pair was in favor of democratic forces and the other pair was in favor of the Korean government. Right before the scheduled date, the American in favor of the democracy movement announced that he could not attend. I, the person whose English was not so fluent, had to debate against two opponents. In addition, my Korean counterpart, National Assembly Foreign Affairs Committee Chair Pong Tu-wan, spoke fluent English. I tried to encourage myself, thinking, *That's fine. What I lack is not logic, but English.*

Ted Koppel must have been worried too. He asked me to see him before the broadcast. It seemed that he wanted to test me before the show. After talking with me, he encouraged me. "You should be fine," he said. "A foreigner doesn't have to speak fluent English. Take it easy. I know how hard you have been fighting for Korean democracy."

I later found out that at the end of his program on Christmas Eve in 1981 Ted Koppel said of me: "There are heroes suffering at this very moment when we are enjoying Christmas Eve with our family. They are fighting for human rights and democracy in prison or under surveillance. Numerous people like Kim Dae-jung of Korea, Andrei Sakharov of the Soviet Union, and Lech Walesa of Poland are fighting and suffering all over the world. We should not forget these heroes."

After meeting with him, I felt relieved and encouraged. On the program, I first explained the status of Korean human rights. Then, Koppel asked my opponents if what I said was true. Mr. Pong did not directly answer the question, but made a lengthy speech about the South-North confrontation and national security crisis. He probably did not want to lie. Koppel wouldn't let it go, though. He stopped Mr. Pong's speech and asked him to specifically express his opinion about my remark. Mr. Pong repeated what he had said before. Koppel then simply stopped him from speaking.

I was again given opportunity to speak. I argued, "If President Reagan visits Korea now, when the Korean human rights condition is this weak, it will encourage the dictatorial regime and approve its human rights oppression. His visit to Korea will disappoint the majority of Koreans and turn them against America. This is not a desirable development for either the US or Korea. Therefore, I urge strongly President Reagan to reconsider his plan to visit Korea."

The debate went on to my advantage, not because I spoke well, but because I spoke the truth. However, toward the end, my opponent lied. Although it was a lie, it was very effective in the debate. He said, "The human rights violation Mr. Kim Dae-jung has mentioned so far occurred during the Park Chung-hee regime. Nothing like that happens under the current regime. The Chun Doo-hwan regime guarantees human rights fully."

When I was about to refute this, Koppel wrapped up the debate. I hurriedly said, "Wait! Wait!"

Koppel reluctantly gave me a chance to refute my opponent, saying I should be brief. I said quickly, "What I said so far about the Korean human rights situation is not my personal opinion. I quoted from the 1982 Amnesty International Report. The 1982 US State Department Human Rights Report also confirms that. The American government proved that what I said is not a lie."

That was a decisive blow. As soon as I returned home, I was showered with phone calls from all over the US. Everyone said they were surprised at how well I handled the debate in English. In fact, it turned out that the Korean Embassy encouraged Korean-Americans to watch *Nightline*, expecting that I would have a hard time with my awkward English. It's true that I couldn't speak English well—if I moved the viewers, it's because I spoke the truth. Truth is always the most eloquent language.

One thing I should add is that the degree of English I *could* use for the purpose of this debate was thanks to my study of English in prison. Throughout my six-year imprisonment, I diligently studied the language. I read English grammar textbooks including the popular *The Trinity* many times. How would I have dared to study English in my fifties if I hadn't been in prison?

A STORMY HOMECOMING (1984–1985)

As 1984 dawned I contemplated whether or not I should return home. Above all, I wondered if I was putting my safety before everything else by staying in the US. I knew that the Korean democratization movement was not very lively, and that my attempts to influence the US administration and Congress did not show any immediate success in the way of changing the attitude of influencers. Not to mention the fact that it was a financial burden.

I discussed my next move with many colleagues, including Reverend Moon Dong-hwan. Opinions varied. As a last resort, I also sent questionnaires about my return home to various important people in the US. More than 60 percent of respondents replied that I shouldn't set a specific date for my return but, rather, make a decision based upon how the situation developed. They reasoned that the relationship between Korea and other nations—including the US—was in constant flux, that I would put myself in danger, and that inducing strategic change in American politics and government remained important.

I decided to continue to work to influence public opinion by contacting personalities in politics, journalism, religion, and academia. I frequently met with US congressmen from both sides of the aisle, including Jim Leach, Barney Frank, Paul Simon, William Gray, Tony Hall, Stephen Solarz, and Thomas Foglietta, to discuss the state of dictatorship in Korea. I emphasized the US role in Korean democracy. Even conservative politicians did not support the dictatorship, and I wanted to take advantage of this.

I argued that the American people believed in democracy. By supporting the dictatorial regime in South Korea, the US was creating enemies there. I encouraged them to think about how much those Koreans who believed in democracy just as Americans did suffered from dictatorship.

"You should not think of the Korean situation in terms of the conflict between the ruling and opposition parties," I urged them, "but in terms of democracy versus dictatorship."

My arguments were persuasive. Although there were many dictatorial countries in the world then, not many people went to the US to fight for their countries' democracy. I gave interviews to American media outlets whenever the opportunity presented itself.

One of the questions I received most often in the US was whether or not Korea had enough of a foundation for democracy. I was always eager to answer this question affirmatively. "During the April 19 Revolution, President Rhee Syngman resigned voluntarily," I explained. "People resisted peacefully, rather than violently, for democracy. This is also true of the Gwangju Uprising. Although victimized, the Korean people did not seek revenge until the very end. Koreans deserve democracy."

During my exile, groundless rumors about me were constantly fabricated and circulated in Korea, reaching all the way across the sea to America. According to some, I lived a luxurious life in a high-end apartment and wore a large ruby ring. There was no doubt that those groundless rumors were manufactured and leaked by the intelligence agency. The reality was that I lived in a $900 per month rental apartment and my "ruby ring" was an ordinary ring made for Harvard students.

The military regime tried to harm and dishonor me by manufacturing endless rumors, labeling me as a "radical" and "pro-communist" liar. I was more afraid of and pained by the Korean people's misunderstanding of me than the military regime's oppression of me. Although all of the rumors were false, people tend to believe something if they hear it often enough. It was very painful to see false rumors about me circulating like truth. I could not defend myself against them. I just had to suffer through what was essentially a dirty act of terror against my character.

The US published a human rights report every year, and I always made a point of checking on the state of Korea. In 1984, the report listed only some improvements in my country's situation. To protest, I requested an interview with the assistant undersecretary of the state in charge of human rights. My request was granted, and I met with Assistant Undersecretary Eliott Abrams at his office. I told him that true improvement in Korean human rights would be possible only through fundamental legal and institutional changes—not just through releasing students or allowing them to return to university campuses. I also emphasized that the US should change its overall policy toward Korea.

On my way out of our meeting I noticed that the office across from Assistant Undersecretary Abrams' was that of Assistant Undersecretary of State in charge of East Asia, who was in charge of supporting and pursuing policy collaboration with the current Korean government. Two offices engaging in works of an opposite nature were facing one another across the corridor. It was as if the idealist and actual versions of the US were facing off. As someone who risked my life for democracy, America disappointed me, but I never gave up despite the fact that the US administration supported the Korean regime. My ultimate goal was for America to criticize and check the Korean dictatorial regime and its human rights violation; at a minimum, I wanted to prevent the US from actively supporting Korea's dictatorial regime. I knew very well how unfavorable the US attitude toward Korean democracy was.

To my delight, my second son, Hong Up, married on March 10 despite an uphill battle. He and his bride Shin Seon-ryeon had been together in Korea before our family rushed to the US. Although I did not openly express my concern, I wondered how they could cope with such a difficult situation. My wife told me that they exchanged phone calls and letters every day. "It hurts me to see them miss each other so much," my wife sighed sadly.

I wanted to see their love to fruition—it would be too cruel if my son had to sacrifice love because of my situation. I decided I should help Seon-ryeon in her efforts to join Hong Up. Luckily, she was admitted to Hobart and William Smith Colleges. I met with former Ambassador to Korea Gleysteen and asked for his help in attaining a visa for Seon-ryeon. When she arrived in New York the year before marrying my son, our entire family welcomed her at the airport. On the bride's side, no guests were able to attend the wedding, so Reverend Moon Dong-hwan led her down the aisle on behalf of her father. A few days after the wedding, her parents unexpectedly came to the US, at which point they met their new son-in-law for the first time. Luckily, they liked him a lot.

Mr. Shin Hyeon-su, the father of the bride, was the chairman of the Board of Audit and Inspection. Based on his daughter's marriage to Hong Up, the Blue House staff in charge of audit and inspection advised him to resign from his post. Because Mr. Shin anticipated this, he willingly submitted his resignation letter to the president. Upon receiving the letter, President Chun called to ask Mr. Shin why he had resigned. Upon hearing his explanation, the president surprisingly returned the resignation letter commenting that "you can't control your children." Instead, President Chun congratulated

Mr. Shin on the nuptials, allowed him a vacation, and encouraged him to use this time to visit the newlyweds.

Upon the request of President Chun, Mr. Shin came to meet me again much later to dissuade my return home. It was a very difficult situation for both of us. I had no choice but to send Mr. Shin back unsuccessful in his mission. I was unhappy that they took advantage of our personal relationship for political purposes, and I felt sorry for Mr. Shin.

Back in Korea, the Council for the Promotion of Democratization (CPD) was founded on May 18, 1984, and its inaugural meeting was held on June 14. The Donggyo-dong and Sangdo-dong factions evenly split the officer positions. Mr. Kim Young-sam (Sangdo-dong) served as co-president with Mr. Kim Sang-hyun as acting co-president on my behalf. Being in exile, I assumed the position of advisory committee member. The birth of CPD served as a fresh wind in the land of dictatorship.

My passport, issued by the Korean government, acted as a shackle, limiting my travels to the US. I could not travel abroad at all. Although the Canadian Ministry of Foreign Affairs twice invited me to join my colleagues at the Harvard Center for International Affairs, I could not go because the Korean Consulate in New York would not even consider my request to remove my passport's destination limitation. In 1984, German President Richard von Weizsäcker and former Chancellor Willy Brandt invited me to Bochum University in West Germany, but, again, I could not go.

In July, Charles Manatt, the chairman of the Democratic National Committee, invited me to attend the Democratic Party National Convention in San Francisco as a VIP guest. I attended with my wife for four days, from July 16 to 20. Watching this grand political festival reminded me of the 1970 Sinmin Party National Convention, during which we nominated our party presidential candidate. The festival was beloved by the Korean people and I was sad to think that it had become a relic of the past. At the Democratic Party National Convention, I was most impressed by the pride exhibited by minorities, such as women, African-Americans, Hispanics, Asians, and the disabled. I could feel their improved rights situation and imminent emergence onto the center stage of history. I was also able to witness true democracy in action, where there occurred fair competition, free voting, and clean acceptance of the results. I could feel the underlying strength of the US as a nation. Although the country was losing its ethical reputation internationally, domestically it was a country of democracy and ethical politics. That year, Walter Mondale was nominated as the party's presidential candidate.

In early August, my eldest son, Hong Il, visited me in the US. This was the first time we had freely met since the May 17, 1980 arrests, and I was deeply moved and extremely happy. Since my departure for the US, Hong Il had been living in my house in Donggyo-dong and leading a difficult life, managing a restaurant. He brought me a photo of my third grand-daughter Hwa-yeong, who was born in February.

In the summer of 1984, I decided to return to Korea. The longer I stayed abroad, the more I missed my country. I felt as if I would not even mind a life in prison if it meant I could return home. I wanted to give everything I had to the Korean people. My only sorrow was that I didn't have much to give. But I could not stay in the US indefinitely. I had to return.

In early September, I sent a letter to Secretary of State George P. Shultz, letting him know my plan to return to Korea by the end of the year and requesting that he put his best efforts forth for Korean democratization. A few days later, I sent a registered letter to President Chun Doo-hwan, letting him know about my plan to return. I also issued a statement in which I explained my reasons for returning home. I had finished taking care of my health, which was the initial purpose of my visit to America, and now felt a moral obligation to return home to support the democratiza-tion movement leaders who were suffering in Korea. The political situa-tion there was in dire straits and there was much to be done for the reunification of the country. I felt the time had come to have a direct dialogue with the Chun Doo-hwan regime. Many journalists expressed interest in my plan and requested interviews with me.

I also let the Korean Embassy know that I was planning to return to my home country. Upon hearing this, Mr. Jeon, an intelligence agent from Seoul, came to visit me. He told me that he could not guarantee my safety if I returned home. It was a very clear threat. Still, I couldn't give up on my plan; however, I told him that I could delay my return if he helped me get a passport that would allow me to travel to Europe. As I had an invita-tion from German President von Weizsäcker, issuing this passport could be easily justified. Mr. Jeon eagerly agreed to try, asking me to give him my passport. I easily saw through his attempt to take away my passport. "If you disappear with my passport, what can I do?" I asked him. "I can-not even return to Korea, right? I cannot hand over my passport to you— it's like entrusting a cat with fish." In the end, Mr. Jeon returned to Seoul without my passport. I later heard from another source that he told an envoy sent from the KCIA at the Korean Embassy, "I wished to kill him if I had a silencer-equipped pistol."

After this incident, the assistant secretaries of state for East Asian affairs and human rights requested an interview with me and asked that I delay my return home. I told them I would think about it and discussed the matter with trusted sources. I thought long and hard about it, but no matter how many different angles I viewed the situation from, it was clear that I had to return. I made up my mind that I'd fight with all my body and heart, no matter how difficult it was. I wrote a letter stating my decision and sent it to the US State Department.

One day, a reporter from the *New York Times* called me on the phone. "The assistant secretary of the Blue House for state affairs stated today that they would imprison you if you return home. Do you still plan to go?" "Yes," I replied. My decision was reported in the media and public opinion formed around the desire that I not become "the second Aquino." I was inundated with interview requests, and the US government changed its position. Instead of trying to dissuade me from returning, they urged the Korean government to guarantee my safe return. The Korean Embassy also issued a statement declaring: "The assistant secretary of the Blue House for state affairs expressed his personal opinion, not the official position of Korean government."

This Korean government's retreat on its position was probably because it was aware of public opinion in the US. While all these events were happening, I was asked to deliver a lecture at the US Department of State, where I made a speech entitled "The United States and Third World Democracy" in front of 200 Department of State staff members. I pointed out that America was blinded by its pursuit of the anti-communist agenda and thus neglecting the right-wing dictatorial regimes' destructive basic principles of liberal democracy in the Third World. I also emphasized that the US needed to face the anti-American movement spreading around the world as the result of its faulty foreign policies and to fundamentally change those policies. Additionally, I explained the essence and reality of Korea's problems, and the US role in them. This lecture was beneficial to both parties. The officers of the Department of State learned about Korean current affairs and it also served as a tool for pressuring the Korean government because it signified the US government's support of me. I could not hate the US, which gave me such support. The audience rained down encouragement upon me and cheered at my speech, which I delivered in English.

Korea's twelfth general election was approaching. That November, the focus was on removing the ban on some politicians' participation in political activities. Since the new military junta's power capture, the Special Measure Act for the Reform of Political Climate banned 567 individuals from political activities. Since the initial ban, a considerable number had been allowed to participate in the political activities due to two measures lifting the ban, but there were still ninety-nine remaining. On November 30, the ban was lifted for a third time, but eleven people—myself included—were still banned even after that.

Nevertheless, a new movement was emerging from the lifting of the ban. The establishment of a new party was discussed, as existing opposition parties like the Minhan and Kukmin parties were government-fabricated opposition parties. The establishment of a new party, based on the CPD, was decided on. The founding members issued an official statement on December 11, in which the acting co-chairman Kim Sang-hyun and co-chairmen Kim Young-sam and I declared that the CPD would found a new party, which would participate in the general election. A large number of national assemblymen left the Minhan Party in order to join our new party.

Finally, the Sinhan Democratic Party (Sinmin Party) was founded at the Ambassador Hotel on January 18, 1985. We selected Mr. Lee Min-woo as the party president. The general election on February 12 was less than a month away. Journalists and professionals predicted that our party was in an inferior position and would most likely win less than twenty seats. The Chun Doo-hwan regime intentionally chose the Election Day in the middle of a severely cold winter to induce voter abstention. They must have thought that the cold weather would favor the ruling Minjeong Party, which was systematically managing pro-ruling party voters. They also lifted the ban on the political activities of politicians only seventy days before Election Day in order to block the storm from the new opposition party foundation. Their intentions were obvious, and the situation was absolutely unfavorable to our party, but, nonetheless, we had to participate in the election.

My colleagues were worried about my safety, but they also thought that my return to Korea itself would be beneficial to the election. Based on their advice, I decided to return to Korea before the election, on February 8.

Leaving is always sad. Although I had missed my home, it was sad to leave the US, all of my colleagues, and the Korean and American political leaders who had encouraged and supported me during my stay. I attended a few farewell gatherings before my departure, including a farewell lecture in Los Angeles on the evening of January 19. Approximately 5000 people gathered in the Grand Olympic Stadium. More than eighty journalists from foreign news media and major broadcasting stations such as ABC, NBC, and CBS covered the event. Former Foreign Minister of the Philippines Raul Manglapus, Executive Director of Amnesty International USA John Healy, Director of Physicians for Human Rights Jonathan Fine, Executive Director of International Human Rights Group Amy Young, and retired Rear Admiral of the US Navy Gene LaRocque attended as VIP guests. Former president of the United States Jimmy Carter, German president von Weizsäcker, former German chancellor Willy Brandt, president of the Japanese Socialist Party Ishibashi, and US senator Arlen Specter sent telegrams expressing their congratulations.

I shouted for the audience and it cheered for me. They were touching and grave cries that encouraged me and mitigate my fears. I hoped that our cries would be heard all the way to Korea. "If the Korean government imprisons me again, the whole world's public opinion, conscience of humanity, and the Korean people will never accept it. If they turn me into a second Aquino, they will have to face the same kind of fate as the Philippines," I said. My wife bade the crowd goodbye too, imploring them to remember all of the others who were suffering just like us.

A few thousand people gathered at the Farewell Rally at Madison Square Garden on February 3. I implored Koreans in the US to move American society. "It is important for us to gather and participate in the democratization movement, but we have to move American politics as well. You must always participate in elections and exercise your rights. Please participate in candidates' fundraising events and express your interests while making contributions to their campaigns by donating even just a dollar. Please continue to send your letters and make phone calls to the media and let your presence be known to them. If you read only Korean newspapers, listen only to Korean radio stations, watch only Korean television shows, go to only Korean churches, shop only at Korean grocery stores, and speak only Korean, the meaning of your life in America will be reduced. For both your sake and for Korea's, you have to advance in American society. Even if it's hard work, you should not avoid it. Democracy will definitely materialize in Korea. What can the people who enabled the April 19 Revolution and the Gwangju Democratic Uprising not do? You should trust them. I will take your encouragement back to my homeland in my arms and fight with your strength and courage."

The world media counted down the days as my return approached. For fear of my safety, thirty-seven people volunteered to accompany me as human shields on my trip to Korea. This included Congressmen Edward Feighan and Thomas Foglietta, former Assistant Secretary of State for Human Rights Patricia Derian, former Ambassador Thomas White, a retired navy admiral, the CEO of American Express, a female singer, Reverend Pharis J. Harvey, Professor Bruce Cumings, and other human rights activists. Also included were scores of journalists, as well as my colleagues in the US such as Yi Geun-pal, Kim Eung-tae, Choe Chang-hak, and Song Sun-keon.

It's true that anything could have happened upon my return. I began my perilous journey. The whole world was watching me, concerned that I could become the second Aquino. I myself could not help imagining this worst-case scenario.

The Northwest airplane carrying me and my colleagues finally left Washington International Airport at 10:15 a.m. on February 6. Hong Up and Hong Gul remained in the US. My family had left Korea with me under the cloak of night, but I returned with many colleagues and journalists in broad daylight. I felt secure, but also sorry for their troubles. I wrote calligraphy pieces while on the airplane and gave one to each of them as an expression of my gratitude.

We arrived at Japan's Narita Airport on February 7. When we arrived at the Holiday Inn near the airport, scores of journalists were waiting for me. I had never seen so many cameras in one place—it was like a mountain of cameras on either side of the hotel entrance. I heard that the Japanese police guarding the hotel was the largest ever. They followed the same plan they had prepared for the anticipated visit of American President Eisenhower (which was eventually canceled because opposition to him was gauged to be too strong).

Editor-in-chief Ryosuke of the Iwanami Bunko and Professor Wada Haruki of University of Tokyo were waiting for me at the press conference site. I initially conducted the press conference in Korean, English, and Japanese, but the questions were too many and answering in three languages took too long. I finally asked Korean journalists to forgive me and resumed the Q&A in Japanese and English.

The questions varied, but they all involved my potential fate. Although I could not know my fate, I resolutely declared, "Democracy is the only way to save our country. No matter what fate is waiting for me for tomorrow, I need to return home. It's a very significant event. Although I do not mean to stir up a large event, I also don't want to act cowardly."

A French reporter asked, "Some people say that your political career in Korea is over. What do you say about that?" I answered that I did not know, but would find out once I arrived in Korea.

At 11:40 a.m. on February 8, 1985, I landed on my home country's soil that I had so yearned for, even in my dreams. I told those who accompanied me, "Aquino was killed while he was guided by government agents after landing. I will refuse any special treatment. I will go to the same arrival gate as the general public. Please help me not be dragged away to another place by strangers."

As soon as the plane landed, a man wearing a gold-trimmed hat approached and saluted me. Introducing himself as the chief of the airport immigration office, he offered to guide me. I rejected his offer. Silently, he turned around. My party waited to disembark the plane until all of the other passengers got off.

As we entered the airport building, plainclothes policemen suddenly rushed toward me. Our party surrounded me, but the policemen jumped toward me and my wife. My human shield desperately tried to protect me as the policemen began using violence despite the presence of current American congressmen and former high government officials. Former Assistant Secretary of State for Human Rights Patricia Derian shrieked. I can still hear her frightened voice. Reporters took pictures of the scenes and disseminated the images out to the entire world.

After the police successfully separated our party from the general passengers, they again surrounded my wife and me. In the end, we were violently detached from our party and forced to get on an elevator. A white van was waiting outside of the first floor of the airport building. Although we resisted, they forced us in it.

They demanded that we present our passports for immigration, but I insisted that we would present them only when we passed through the regular immigration desk. In the end, we were taken out of the airport without proper immigration procedures. Curtains hung in front of the van windows, so we could not see outside. I could not see the hundreds of thousands of people waiting to welcome me. I did not even have a chance to issue the statement I had prepared.

My eldest son, Hong Il, my younger brother Dae-hyeon, and President Lee Min-woo of the Sinhan Party Lee Min-woo had been waiting for me at the airport, but, of course, we could not meet them there either. Mr. Kim Young-sam tried to come to the airport, but was put under house arrest. Crowds at the airport confronted the police, holding placards that read: "Welcome, Mr. Kim Dae-jung!" and "Conscience in Action Finally Back to Us!" Angry that I was taken away, the crowd demonstrated, and teargas and rocks were shot and thrown. Although I wasn't at the airport, those who accompanied me from the US were welcomed enthusiastically. I didn't find out about all of this until later.

When we arrived home in Donggyo-dong, high tents were hung around our house. We could not see outside at all. Again, hundreds and thousands of people were awaiting our arrival at the corner of the alley leading up to our house, but I could not see them (Figs. 5.4 and 5.5).

I returned in a storm. *Newsweek* reported my return in detail in a feature article entitled "A Stormy Homecoming":

> Thousands of South Koreans lined the long gray boulevard outside Seoul's Kimpo International Airport last week, waving banners and chanting: "Kim Dae Jung! Kim Dae Jung!" South Korea's leading dissident touched down aboard Northwest Orient Flight 191. He expected to greet the crowd.

Fig. 5.4 Kim Dae-jung and Lee Hee-ho in a photo in *People Magazine* in 1984

Fig. 5.5 *Newsweek* cover featuring Kim Dae-jung on his return to Korea after his second exile in the US in 1985

Instead, government authorities hustled him, his wife, and a group of US dignitaries into a sealed-off section of the terminal. There, more than fifty plainclothesmen moved in to separate the opposition leader from his escorts. They punched and kicked several of the Americans, knocking them to the ground. Then they manhandled Kim into an elevator. Kim and his wife were put on a white microbus and driven along back roads to their home. Once inside, Kim was immediately placed under house arrest.

55 Times of Imprisonment: Donggyo-dong Prison (1985–1986)

The police closely guarded my house in Donggyo-dong, turning it into a fortress no one could approach. They rented or bought houses nearby for special agents and policemen to live in. Hundreds of policemen surrounded my house in multiple layers. Our phone was tapped and our mail was censored. They interfered with my interviews with reporters and banned my books from bookstores. They blocked my speeches at rallies or meetings. They even made it impossible for me to make a confession of faith.

My return was a storm that set in four days before the election, transforming it into a fierce and unpredictable battle. It turned out that my house imprisonment was as powerful as my stump speeches could have been. Korean voters were moved that I returned home for the sake of Korean democratization, even at the risk of my life. During stump speeches for the Sinmin Party candidates, my name was mentioned without exception; it was shouted in the Chungcheong-do and Gyeongsang-do provinces. Some candidates exaggerated their relationship with me, claiming that we met individually to discuss the state of affairs.

When the results came in on February 12, voters cheered at the election revolution they had brought. The Sinmin Party won by a total of sixty-seven seats, fifty from local districts, and seventeen national seats. The Minhan Party, previously the first opposition party, won only thirty-five seats, twenty-six of which were from local districts and nine national. This was less than half of its eighty-one seats from the previous general election.

Nobody—including the Korean people, the ruling party, and even the Sinmin Party members—could believe this wonderful result. It told us how enthusiastically Koreans wanted a true opposition party and democratization. The election showed that people wanted to amend the

Constitution and elect their president directly. In the end, risking my life to return home awakened the Korean people's desire for democracy and an opposition party. Political commentators said, "Kim Dae-jung's return home before the general election was like the game-reversing, grand-slam homer at the bottom of the ninth inning."

As a result of this twelfth general election, the Minhan Party simply collapsed. Within two months of Election Day twenty-nine of the thirty-five newly elected Minhan Party assemblymen left their party for the Sinmin Party, following the public demand expressed in the election. The Minhan Party sank in the middle of the sea of public opinion and the Sinmin Party became the biggest opposition party with 103 seats.

On the fourth anniversary of President Chun Doo-hwan's presidency, the final political activities ban was lifted from the remaining sixteen politicians (including myself). I was, however, the only one still excluded from amnesty and reinstatement.

On March 15, I had an official meeting with CPD Co-chairman Kim Young-sam at Acting Chairman Kim Sang-hyun's house. Mr. Kim Young-sam requested that I accept the position of CPD co-chairman and I agreed, thus stepping forward to the front stage of Korean politics for the first time since the almost five-year ban was instated. The issue of the release of prisoners of conscience and suspension of my amnesty and reinstatement was a political detonator together. As the largest opposition party, the Sinmin Party negotiated with the ruling Minjeong Party about this matter, but could not find any common ground. The national assembly was to be held in May.

Although the ban on my political activities was lifted, my house imprisonment continued, making it impossible for me to be fully active. They sometimes allowed me to leave my house, but their standards for doing so were completely unclear.

The political situation was tense around the issue of constitutional amendment. The fate of Korea's political forces depended upon the structure of the power. The ruling party argued for the parliamentary government system while the Sinmin Party argued for direct election of the president. The ruling Minjeong Party didn't show any desire to negotiate or compromise.

I frequently met with Co-chair Kim Young-sam and party president Lee Min-woo to discuss current affairs. One day, Mr. Kim Young-sam requested that we meet secretly in a hotel room. He looked serious when he saw me, and said, "Since they won't seem to budge, how about accepting their proposal for constitutional amendment based on the parliamentary government system?"

I could not believe my ears. What he was proposing was utterly unimaginable. I resolutely rejected his proposal, saying, "The constitutional amendment for direct presidential election was our party's promise to the Korean people. Because our party overwhelmingly won the election with this promise, it is now our mandate from the people. Because the people support direct presidential election, isn't it our obligation to follow their will?" Mr. Kim Young-sam nodded.

The argument for the parliamentary government system often originated from the Sangdo-dong faction, and there were also assemblymen within our party who preferred that system. I thought our party needed to be united under the banner of direct presidential election as pledged during the election campaign, and rearranged as a powerful opposition party through a national convention.

I thought of a role division plan wherein Mr. Kim Young-sam would become the presidential candidate and I his running mate in the next presidential election. Before publicizing this plan, I thought long and hard about it. Considering the evil hands of intelligence agency-based politics, distorted reporting by the established media, and the conflict among internal forces with differing interests, it was obvious that I would get attacked and hurt. However, this was a matter that could not be avoided in order for the Sinmin Party to recover democracy. If the Sinmin Party accepted the parliamentary system, it would not only violate our campaign pledge, but it would also mean giving up on the next election. Unless I succeeded in collaborating with Mr. Kim Young-sam and unifying the Sinmin Party as a strong opposition party, voter expectation during the February election could go up in smoke. After much thought, I decided to discuss my thoughts with our party president Lee Min-woo in order to resolve the issue of the parliamentary government system and to accomplish a firm collaboration with Co-chair Kim Young-sam.

I met with both of them less than a month before the Sinmin Party Convention. I argued that Co-chair Kim Young-sam should become the party president in the upcoming convention. It felt awkward to argue this in front of President Lee, but I could speak my thoughts frankly because President Lee belonged to Mr. Kim Young-sam's Sangdo-dong faction. To effectively fight the ruling party it was essential we have strong leadership in anticipation of the crucial fights for the constitutional amendment that would come in autumn.

I suggested we announce our party's presidential candidate and running mate at the party convention. If I paired up with Mr. Kim Young-sam, both the Korean people and the out-of-office democratization movement activists would be relieved. This would also confirm our party's will for constitutional amendment. Both men listened carefully and did not raise any objections.

Despite this, I discovered an enormously false and slanderous allegation in the newspaper the following morning. According to the news, I had proposed that Mr. Kim Young-sam became the party president and I the presidential candidate. All of the newspapers attacked me for being greedy, accusing me of hastily and shamelessly volunteering to become our party's presidential candidate. It was absurd and shocking. I immediately publicly explained the result of our three-way conference. Mr. Kim Young-sam also issued a denial, but it was barely reported.

Enormous and unbearable criticism and accusations were directed at me; I was even called "president-obsessed." Condemning phone calls poured into both the party office and my house. I know that there are people who still believe that I made this proposal. For a long time, that incident remained a critical trauma for me.

On August 2, I attended our party convention. Both Mr. Kim Young-sam and I were elevated to standing advisors of our party. On August 15, President Chun Doo-hwan and our party president Lee Min-woo had a conference. President Chun was opposed to the direct presidential election favored by the Sinmin Party. At the time, the ruling party favored a dual executive system. Under this system, the president and prime minister would ostensibly share power, but, in reality, the president would be the sole power-holder because it was he who would appoint the prime minister. President Chun could not avoid the suspicion that he was planning to hold onto his power indefinitely.

The relationship between the South and North heated up the political arena from the summer to fall of 1985. After a successful bid to host the Olympics in Seoul, our government held the South-North Sports Conference, and tried very hard to focus people's interest solely on the Olympics and reunification. As a result, fifty South Koreans who were natives of the North had four days to visit their hometowns across the Demilitarized Zone (DMZ) for the first time since the division of the country forty years earlier.

On December 29, I went to the funeral of Reverend Moon Chae-rin, the well-known father of Reverends Moon Ik-hwan and Moon Dong-hwan. Although Reverend Moon Chae-rin was a modest and gentle person, he was a fierce fighter against injustice. This was shown through how righteously his children led their lives. The year was setting as I descended down from the hill where he was buried.

On January 16, 1986, President Chun poured cold water over the constitutional amendment discussion. In his State of the Nation speech, he proposed postponing the discussion, saying, "The matter of amending the presidential election method should be discussed in 1989 after we have achieved two urgent national tasks: establishing the precedent of a peaceful regime change and a successful hosting of the Seoul Olympics."

He was clearly taking advantage of the Olympics, using it as an excuse for a political ceasefire. The Sinmin Party flatly refused. On February 12, the anniversary of the general election, we launched the 10 million signature-gathering campaign, urging constitutional amendment in favor of the direct presidential election. President Lee Min-woo announced the campaign at a press conference at our party office. "On this first anniversary of the general election," he spoke, "we launch the signature-gathering campaign for the constitutional amendment for direct presidential election. Our advisors Mr. Kim Dae-jung and Mr. Young-sam, myself, the vice presidents, and constitutional amendment-promotion headquarters local branch chiefs will begin the signing." During the welcoming remarks I said, "We can achieve the restoration of democracy only through courage, unity, and sacrifice. It might be hard for us to gather like this again for a while."

My suspicions that I might be more harshly oppressed because of this movement were proven correct. The following day the police blocked the area surrounding my house completely, mobilizing about 300 people from two companies in addition to numerous automobiles. They also blocked two phone lines. My colleagues rushed to the scene and protested to no avail. I was imprisoned for twelve days. My secretaries, including Kim Ok-du, Bae Ki-sun, Sul Hoon, Lee Seok-hyun, Park Ho-duk, Bang Keung-nae, and Kong Eun-hye, stayed with me.

The signature-gathering movement spread throughout the entire country, and the regime responded harshly. They blocked the Sinmin Party office by mobilizing the police and raided the party and CPD offices. It was an attempt to violently suppress the constitutional amendment movement.

Around this time, a significant revolution occurred in the Philippines, which had been suffering from a dictatorial regime of its own. On February 25, long-time dictator Marcos was ousted from his position by the people.

Following this incident, Mrs. Corazon Aquino, the widow of Benigno Aquino, succeeded in capturing power. This news was like gospel to Koreans. When I examined the Philippines' case, however, I realized that their freedoms were quite different from those of our country. Filipinos enjoyed autonomous local government, and freedom of press, assembly, and demonstration. Compared to the Philippines, Korea's situation was much harsher.

Still, the ousting of the Philippine dictator was a spring breeze to us. On March 11, an event celebrating the launch of the Seoul branch of the Constitutional Amendment Promotion Committee was held at the Heungsadan office. I tried to attend the event, but the police locked me up at home. "Please send me to prison, instead!" I yelled at them. I gave interviews to US and West German media outlets that evening, pointing out the unjust actions of the Korean authorities.

Early on the morning of March 30, the day the Gwangju branch of the Constitutional Amendment Promotion Committee was scheduled to launch, the police disconnected my home's electricity from 2:00 to 6:30 a.m. This meant I couldn't leave for the airport because the automatic door of my garage did not work. After my secretaries' strong protest, the electricity supply resumed and I left for the airport; however, once on the road, we found about 200 police officers blocking the way, so I had to return home. They also blocked my path as I was en route to the Daegu branch opening. Nevertheless, both ceremonies were successful. While this was happening, US Congressman Stephen Solarz and his wife were visiting my home. Mr. Solarz comforted me, saying that he would testify to this situation upon his return home.

It was truly like the news of flowers moving northward that spring. About 40,000 people in Busan, 100,000 in Gwangju, and 20,000 in Daegu gathered for branch launching ceremonies. Because of my virtual imprisonment, I sent taped addresses to the events. Despite the fact that I was not there, the audience still chanted my name. The audience cheered and applauded particularly enthusiastically in Busan and Daegu, regions that were supposedly pro-government. College students also organized rallies on campuses. All these events and rallies proved to be more exciting than expected.

Then, President Chun invited Minjeong Party leader Roh Tae-woo and Sinmin Party president Lee Min-woo in for a meeting, the result of which was encouraging. It was summarized with the following statement: "The president is willing to pursue constitutional amendment if the ruling and opposition parties agree."

The Sinmin Party Constitutional Amendment Promotion Committee's Gyeonggi-Incheon branch launch event was scheduled for May 3, 1986. An hour before the event, students and the police collided. The Minjeong Party Incheon branch building and some cars were burnt, and fierce stone-missile fights erupted. As a result, the event could not happen. This radical protest resulted in many negative effects. Ordinary people who had supported the branch launching events in the three previous cities responded negatively to the radical demonstration in Incheon. Also, the US grew tense due to anti-American slogans that appeared during this protest.

This was exactly what the Chun Doo-hwan regime wanted. The authorities responded immediately and harshly. The public security authorities called this May 3 Incheon Demonstration "violent seditious acts by left-leaning procommunist forces." They clamped down harshly on out-of-office democracy movement forces. This was a strategy to break the solidarity between the Sinmin Party and out-of-office activists and students. In reality, the police fired teargas into the hall before the launching event even began, thus creating chaos. Ultimately, the police arrested thirty-two individuals on suspicion of instigation and other such charges, including National Coalition for Democracy and Reunification officials and students. Reverend Moon Ik-hwan, president of the National Coalition for Democracy and Reunification, was also arrested.

Watching this event evolve confirmed to me once again that the people's support was crucial to successful movements. No matter how desperate rally participants feel, it is of no use if people do not support their actions. Radical demonstration cannot expect the support of the people, which is precisely why the May 3 Demonstration failed.

On August 23, 1986, my family took our first vacation in a long while in Gucheondong in Muju, Jeollabuk-do. Most impressive about Gucheondong was the valley. The water, clear as jade, flowed down the seemingly endless valley. Although there weren't any fantastic rocks or cliffs, the entire valley looked beautiful. It was natural, ordinary, and eternally gorgeous. About one hundred people from the police, KCIA, and Defense Security Command monitored my family during that vacation. As I watched Gucheondong, they watched me. When we stopped by Daejeon and Yuseong, the police almost jumped at me, threatening to arrest me. On our way back home on August 26, we looked around the Folk Village in Yongin, which reminded me of my childhood days. Shortly thereafter, I received a phone call from Hong Up in the US. He told me that my grandson Jong-dae had been born. It was a week after the twenty-seventh anniversary of my late first wife Cha Yong-ae's death. Although she was gone, she was reborn through her descendants.

On October 28, 1986, about 2000 students from twenty-six colleges nationwide gathered at the Democracy Square in Konkuk University for the inaugural event of the Nationwide Anti-foreign Forces and Anti-Dictatorship Patriotic Students Struggle Association. Before long, police entered the campus firing teargas bombs. Students confronted them with rocks and Molotov cocktails, but, in the end, they were driven inside a building, which was surrounded by the police. With nowhere to go, the students began a sit-down demonstration.

The school demanded that the police forces withdraw. The school authorities tried to persuade the police that they would voluntarily disperse the students once they were guaranteed a safe return home. The Chun Doo-hwan regime ignored the school's arbitration efforts and accused the students of being "pro-North communist revolutionary elements." The media reported the government's accusation as if it were truth. On the fourth day of the sit-down demonstration the police carried out a ruthless suppression operation, mobilizing no less than 3000 troops. They took 1525 students to the police station, of which 1274 were arrested. This arrest number set the world record for the most arrests in a single incident.

While this Konkuk University Incident was happening, the Mt. Kumgang Dam Incident simultaneously occurred. According to the authorities, North Korea was building a dam in Mt. Kumgang in order to attack Seoul by flooding. The media sent out fearsome daily newsflashes that screamed headlines such as "Half of the 63 Building Will be Submerged," "Damages Expected to be Larger than from Atomic Bomb," "Sea of Water up to the Foot of Mt. Namsan," and "100-Meter High Water Column Strikes." The government announced its plan to respond by building the Peace Dam, which was followed by a nationwide fundraising campaign. Broadcasting stations reported all of this live, thus turning themselves into clowns in a fraudulent theater. They took microphones to the streets, schools, churches, and workplaces, pushing them under the noses of young children, white-haired senior citizens, Koreans abroad, and even prisoners.

Later, the Mt. Kumgang Dam Incident was revealed to be a total fabrication, which was an unforgivable sin. The intention behind this fabrication, which was publicized a day before the police raided Konkuk

University, was clear: It was a drama of terror produced by the KCIA, which had the monopoly on military information. The Department of National Defense and other relevant offices were in charge of props. The Chun Doo-hwan regime would stoop to any base trickery to divert the people's desire for constitutional amendment. At the time, their most useful tools were national security threats and the Olympics.

The serious political situation reminded me of how it was in 1980. The military could strike with extreme measure again, creating a crisis of the Konkuk University and the Mt. Kumgang Dam Incidents. In fact, there were signs indicating the Chun Doo-hwan regime was preparing for a second coup d'état. In early October, rumors about my arrest circulated, and reporters and citizens frequently called my house to find out the truth. I felt the need to create some momentum to break through the crisis. After thinking hard for days, I decided that I needed to declare that I would not run for the presidency in order to resolve the difficult political situation. I had to finish the military dictatorship even if I could not become president. I also wanted to see to it that the arrested students were released. It was truly a difficult decision. On November 5, I read a statement in front of domestic and foreign reporters at the CPD office: "Recently a cold wave, raised by the mad power, has thrown all of the Korean people into extreme turmoil and tension," I spoke. "This might be the last hardship on our way to democracy, but I've been watching this situation anxiously and regretfully, as I am helpless to break through this difficult situation due to my variously confined circumstances.

"In particular, I feel heart-wrenching pain that our young people, who did not do anything to bring about today's reality, were sacrificed en masse in the recent Konkuk University Incident. I think that this kind of incident could happen again.

"The only way to solve the current situation is quick democratization through constitutional amendment in favor of the direct presidential election. That is what the absolute majority of Korean people want. But the Chun Doo-hwan regime does not appear to listen to this national wish.

"Therefore, I declare my resolution that I will not run for the presidency even if I receive amnesty and reinstatement, if the Chun Doo-hwan regime accepts the constitutional amendment for direct presidential election."

After this declaration, Mr. Kim Young-sam, who was visiting West Germany, said at a press conference: "Once we achieve democratization through the direct presidential election system and Mr. Kim Dae-jung is pardoned and reinstated, we can think of his running for the presidency." I was very happy to hear this. When I returned home from exile, Mr. Kim Young-sam told me that, since I was older, he would support me as the presidential candidate once I was pardoned and reinstated. I took his remark at the press conference to mean that he still had the same intention.

The Chun regime ignored my statement and demand for constitutional amendment for direct presidential election. They neither accepted my proposal nor released students from prison. On the contrary, they escalated their harsh tactics. Minjeong Party Executive Director Lee Choon-koo immediately rejected my proposal, condemning the condition of direct presidential election. He declared that his party's pursuance of the parliamentary government system remained unchanged. Thus, the ruling party rejected the conditions for me waiving a future run for presidency.

Our party president Lee Min-woo also gradually began to demonstrate behaviors that deviated from our party's goal to achieve direct presidential election. Sometimes he even said things that sounded as if he were agreeing with the government and ruling party. In the end, Mr. Kim Young-sam and I had to pursue the establishment of a new party. With this development, my house arrest and monitoring intensified.

Between the time of my return to Korea and the June 29, 1987 Declaration that provided me amnesty and reinstatement, I had been imprisoned in my house no less than fifty-five times. I wasn't sure who made such decisions, but I was always notified of it at random. Sometimes it lasted only one day, but other times it lasted as long as two months. "House arrest" was, of course, a euphemism for illegal imprisonment.

On April 10, 1987, the Mapo police chief visited me late at night. I was scheduled to participate in a breakfast meeting of the Preparation Committee for the establishment of a new party at the Diplomatic Club in Mt. Namsan, but could not attend because of police interference. They were afraid of the storm I could raise and the establishment of a new political party. The police chief read a statement of warning to me. "A criminal whose sentence was suspended cannot participate in political party activities according to the Article 42, Clause 2 of the Political Party Act," he recited. "Therefore, from now on, you cannot go to the CPD or the Mingeonhoe offices, let alone being banned from any political party activities. Furthermore, you should not contact any politician."

He went on to announce that, beginning that day, with the exception of my family, drivers, maids, and domestic and foreign reporters, no outsider could visit my house. My secretaries and visitors, who happened to be at my house at the time, were all angered. I protested in vain, pointing out that the lifting of the political activities ban two years before had given me the freedom of political activity, and that their interference with foreign guests' visits and my house arrest were both illegal. I realized again that it was hard to live under bad laws, but it was even harder to live under a regime that did not follow even those bad laws.

As the police chief read the statement, layers of police officers surrounded my house. About 600 officers from four companies were deployed. Both sides of the front entrance of the house were barricaded to block people's approach. Even my neighbors had to go through checkpoints. My colleagues and secretaries, including Kim Young-bae and Heo Gyeong-nam, rushed to my house upon hearing the news, but they were no match for the police force, despite their loud protests and physical resistance. Although they screamed, they could not progress as much as a step.

Mr. Kim Young-sam visited me the next day. We shook hands over the fence because the police officers blocked his way.

This house arrest lasted much longer than previous ones—seventy-eight days altogether. During this period, my secretaries called my house "Donggyo-dong Prison House." I hung a calendar in the living room and marked every day I was imprisoned with a red X.

Every day, I walked from my bedroom to the library in the basement of my house, where I would work. I always wore a suit and a tie to work, feeling that I should not crumble under the circumstances. The authorities even prevented me from attending mass. Every Saturday and Sunday I protested to no avail. Their reply was always the same: "You cannot go because we did not receive an order from above."

On Easter Sunday, more than ten priests and about one hundred Christians gathered near my house and attempted to hold a street mass. They were all thrown into a police bus and dumped at random in suburban areas like Seongnam and Munsan. I heard that many of them protested, only to be beaten by the police. It was dismal.

In the end, the police blocked even my family and journalists from coming to my house. My home was an island in the middle of a metropolitan city and you could feel bloodthirstiness in the alleys leading to it. Citizens and students waged surprise demonstrations near my house, shouting: "Lift the house imprisonment of Mr. Kim Dae-jung!" and

"Reinstate Kim Dae-jung!" When this happened, the police officers beat them, threw them into a bus, and dumped them off at random places like the refuse disposal site, Nanjido Island. Inside the house, my family suffered through frequent threatening phone calls, where the person on the other end of the line threatened to do things like blow up our home or kill us.

I maintained a sense of normalcy by doing small things like taking care of our flower garden, which consisted of about forty different species of flowers, every day. I switched the flowerpots back and forth between the sun and the shade. When I talked to the flowers, they answered me. Although I sighed about my state of imprisonment, they smiled, satisfied to live in the world of my small garden. The flowers penetrated my heart and gently comforted me.

An event celebrating the founding of the Tongil Minju (Unification Democratic) Party was held on May 1. It was busy around my house, and the number of dispatched police officers increased to 1500. After the event, about 1000 party members marched toward my house from the Sinchon and Donggyo-dong rotaries. They chanted: "Immediately lift the illegal imprisonment of Kim Dae-jung!" and "Down with dictatorship!" Citizens gathered in every alleyway, cheering and chanting. My two secretaries, Kim Ok-du and Namkung Jin, climbed up to the rooftop of my home and spread out a placard made of bed sheets that read: "Lift the Illegal Imprisonment of Mr. Kim Dae-jung!" They remained on the roof in the hot May sun with sweat pouring off of them like rain, chanting for my freedom. This protest from the top of the Donggyo-dong Prison House attracted attention from all over the world after an AP reporter took a photograph of the surprise rooftop demonstration and wired it out to the corners of the earth. I had no choice but to watch the dangerous scene.

My only means of communication with the outside world was the telephone. Although occasionally disconnected by the authorities, it still worked most of the time. Of course, it was wiretapped all day long, but it was still a very useful fight tool. I completed telephone interviews with about forty media from twenty different countries. It was also through the phone that I received encouragement from foreigners and Korean citizens alike. It was my only source of communication with the outside world, and I was grateful to have it.

CHAPTER 6

1986–1997

June Uprising (1986–1987)

On Christmas Eve 1986, Sinmin Party president Lee Min-woo held a surprise press conference and announced his plan, which involved focusing on the idea of negotiating on the parliamentary government system following democratization. The main slant of this plan was that the opposition party would be willing to negotiate on the constitutional amendment in favor of a parliamentary government system if the Chun doo-hwan regime accepted seven prerequisite democratization measures, including introducing a local autonomy system; guaranteeing freedom of the press; political neutrality of government employees; and the release, amnesty, and reinstatement of political prisoners. This plan stood in contrast with the official party position that insisted on constitutional amendment in favor of direct presidential election. Also, although he was required to confer with Mr. Kim Young-sam and me about important matters like this, President Lee announced this plan without any discussion at all.

Minjeong Party leader Roh Tae-woo responded positively to the plan at a year-end meeting two days later. "I believe that President Lee Min-woo's plan suggests the possibility of the Sinmin Party's negotiation about the parliamentary government system," he said. "I think this is progress toward achieving the Korean people's wish of constitutional amendment and solving the current political impasse. If this plan indeed expresses the opposition party's willingness to negotiate on the parlia-

© The Author(s) 2019
Kim Dae-jung, *Conscience in Action*,
https://doi.org/10.1007/978-981-10-7623-7_6

mentary government system, then I am also willing to discuss it with them."

Things were regressing. Arguments erupted within and outside of our party. I received a flood of phone calls condemning President Lee; many people also warned me of Mr. Kim Young-sam. I decided I should point out the rashness of President Lee's plan to end the arguments and openly criticized President Lee's plan. "It's nonsense to assume that the seven prerequisites would guarantee democratization without a constitutional amendment in favor of direct presidential election," I pointed out. "Linking direct presidential election struggle with the seven prerequisites should be revoked. Democratization is a universal value that should be achieved at any time and by any regime. It should not be used as a negotiation tool in the current constitutional amendment talk."

Nevertheless, President Lee openly acted against the party's position. The media supported President Lee's plan and put pressure on Mr. Kim Young-sam and me. I could feel the evil hand of intelligence-agency-driven politics reaching out to strangle us.

While the political arena was in turmoil over this, Reverend Kim Jae-joon, the father of Korean *minjung* theology and the pioneer of active Christians, passed away. I had experienced many unforgettable memories with him: his support of me during the 1971 presidential election; the letter he sent me from Canada after the October 26, 1976 Incident; and his continued support and love for me in the time since then. He was a pure-hearted and true friend. Approximately 1000 people gathered for his funeral. I could feel the power of his virtue emanating throughout the ceremony. Reverend Kim used to wear old suits with patches, but he always carried a clean handkerchief. He lived his entire life without concerning himself about financial matters. He deserved the respect not only of Christians, but of all Koreans. Reverend Kim Jae-joon lived righteously in front of the eyes of God and his people, and he dedicated everything he had to his neighbors. He passed away after giving so much.

A few days later, I heard the unexpected but happy news that I had been nominated for the Nobel Peace Prize. A German reporter in Seoul called me to let me know that seventy-three German congressmen from the Social Democratic Party had nominated me for my "struggle for human rights and efforts for peaceful reunification." I was deeply moved. The following morning the newspaper ran a short article about my nomination and I received a flood of congratulatory phone calls.

Of course, the Lee Min-woo Plan was still bubbling away in the background. I frequently met and discussed the matter with Mr. Kim Young-sam. He told me that he regretted that the plan resulted in the misunderstanding that we could negotiate with the ruling party over the parliamentary government system and believed that we needed to eradicate this misunderstanding from public opinion.

President Lee Min-woo counterattacked by going to Onyang in Chungcheongnam-do after declaring that he could no longer lead the party. As President Lee was a member of the Sangdo-dong faction, Mr. Kim must have been shocked. Although President Lee ostensibly agreed on constitutional amendment in favor of direct presidential election, he reversed his position at every possible turn. Some time later, nine assemblymen from our party established the Democratic Association in support of the Lee Min-woo Plan. The members of this association included Lee Chul-seung, Kim Jae-gwang, Shin Do-hwann, Park Han-sang, Park Hae-chung, Cho Yeon-ha, Kim Ok-sun, Lee Taeck-hee, and Lee Taek-don. Before the party convention in May, I argued that Mr. Kim Young-sam should become our party president, but President Lee rejected this idea, proposing a competition for the party presidency and a collective leadership system.

On March 6, US Secretary of State George P. Schultz visited Seoul. Although he emphasized the importance of a dialogue and compromise between the ruling and opposition parties, he seemed to side with President Lee's democratization first argument. The Lee Min-woo Plan was revived and our party was internally divided. Mr. Kim Young-sam and I decided that collaboration with President Lee in our fight for direct presidential election would be impossible and declared our decision to officially divide our party.

On April 8, 1987, seventy-four out of the ninety assemblymen from the Sinmin Party broke away from the party. I don't know why President Lee never gave up his position. Only a small minority of the party supported it, but he might also have been encouraged by the US high officials' remarks in support of it. Assistant Secretary of State for East Asian and Pacific Affairs William Clark, Jr., who visited Korea before Secretary of State Schultz, expressed his deep interest in President Lee's democratization first position, while also emphasizing how important it was that President Chun follow through on his promise of a single-term presidency.

Assistant Secretary of State William Clark also visited me at my house to seek my opinion. I explained why people preferred direct presidential election, but he did not seem to understand my position. I felt that he had different interests at heart. Additionally, there was a pretty convincing rumor that President Lee's proposal was related to a Korean Central Intelligence Administration (KCIA) operation.

In the end, the Sinmin Party was divided, and Mr. Kim Young-sam and I devoted ourselves to establishing a new party. We named it the Tongil Minju Party (also known as the Democratic Party), and scheduled a promotion event on April 13. We decided to select Mr. Kim Young-sam as the party president.

The day before this event, President Chun issued a special statement, wherein he declared: "I judged that the constitutional amendment would be impossible during my term. I declare that I will hand over the government to my successor elected according to the current Constitution on February 25 next year, when my term comes to an end. I urge everyone to cease the divisive debate over the constitutional amendment until the 1988 Olympics are over." This was the so-called April 13 Constitution Protection Measure. Around the same time, 101 US congressmen requested that Secretary of State Schultz make a diplomatic effort to guarantee my amnesty and reinstatement.

The Chun regime's constitutional protection measure was a mistake that came from misreading public opinion. People could not forgive it, as it broke the last defense line. Professors of major universities issued statements demanding the measure be withdrawn, and priests and pastors began fasting prayers. Writers also issued statements in protest of the Constitution protection measure and began a sit-down strike.

The April 13 Constitution Protection Measure fanned the flames of our work establishing the Democratic Party, scheduled for May 1. While this was going on, a few non-mainstream Sinmin Party members mobilized thugs to prevent our party foundation work. Armed with steel pipes and thin square bars, these paid thugs raided our event site in the so-called Yongpari Incident. There was no doubt that the authorities, including the KCIA, were behind this disturbance, which happened in broad daylight. It was the product of operation politics using corrupt politicians. Despite this persistent interference operation, we successfully founded our party. Mr. Kim Young-sam was selected as president by consensus, and leaders of the Donggyo-dong faction (Lee Choong-jae, Yang Soon-jik, Roh Sung-hwan, and Lee Yong-hee) as well as those of the Sangdo-dong faction (Choi Hyung-woo, Park Yong-man, and Kim Dong-young) were elected as vice presidents. We adopted a party Constitution based on a one-man leadership system and our party policies contained the goal of direct presidential election.

The political situation was extremely confusing. Earlier that year, the Pak Jong-cheol Torture Death Incident occurred, during which Seoul National University student Pak Jong-cheol died from being tortured at the National Police Headquarters Anti-communism Annex. I could not help but feel anger and sadness about this outrageous incident. Pak Jong-cheol's father supported his education with a monthly income of only 200,000 won. *How long will this evil regime continue?* I wondered. There was a saying that the evil government was scarier than a tiger. Indeed, an evil government could cause its people far more harm than a tiger ever could. I resolved to fight with all my might.

The police reported that Mr. Pak died of a shock, but Dr. Oh Yeon-sang, the doctor who performed the autopsy, said that he suspected water-boarding. As all eyes and ears in the country were turned toward Mr. Pak's death the authorities rushed to cremate his remains. His father spread his ashes into the Imjingang River, but buried his son in his heart.

As the pressure of public opinion mounted, the authorities acknowledged the practice of waterboarding and arrested two police officers. They confessed that they had tied Mr. Pak's hands and legs, then repeatedly pushed his head into water. As a result, the government changed its interior minister and the head of the National Police Headquarters. The incident seemed to be set aside with this turn of events, but it emerged above again four months later.

On May 18, tens of thousands of students gathered at sixty-two college campuses nationwide to commemorate the seventh anniversary of the death of the victims of the Gwangju Uprising. That night, a mass was held at Myeongdong Cathedral. Cardinal Kim Sou-hwan preached, saying, "Gwangju's sorrow is our people's sorrow and the sorrow of history. Those absurd people who pushed knives into the hearts of our people and deeply hurt and bled them should come forward and confess their sins in order to be redeemed. I think that is probably the only way to relieve the sorrows of our people and to heal Gwangju's wounds. And that is the only way for them to save themselves and to save our country."

Cardinal Kim was directly condemning the Chun regime. After the mass, Father Kim Seung-hoon read a statement entitled "The Truth of Mr. Pak Jong-cheol's Torture Death Incident Was Fabricated" in a trembling voice. The statement, composed of more than 3000 characters, was concrete and solemn. Accusing the current regime of responsibility for the incident and the fabrication of the culprits, it demanded the punishment of those involved. The statement, issued under the name of the Catholic

Priests' Association for Justice, ended with the following: "Whether the ethicality of Korean authorities will be recovered or not will depend on whether the truth of culprit fabrication of this incident will be clearly revealed together with the truth of the homicide of Mr. Pak Jong-cheol through torture. In addition, the important question of whether Korean society will be able to take the road of truth and conscience as well as humanization and democratization or not depends on the solution of this incident."

This statement threw the political situation into turmoil once again. Three days later, the director of the Seoul branch prosecutor's office acknowledged the presence of three more culprits at the press conference. The prosecutors began a new investigation and arrested three more police officers. They also arrested the senior superintendent general for his involvement in the culprit reduction fabrication. Nevertheless, angry public opinion did not die down. On the contrary, people grew angrier by the day. As the situation became graver, President Chun Doo-hwan reshuffled the cabinet. Prime Minister Lho Shin-yong, KCIA director Chang Se-dong, Interior Minister Chung Ho-yong, and Attorney General Seo Dong-kown were dismissed based on their role in the incident, changing the power topography of the Chun regime.

Antipathy toward the April 13 Constitution Protection Measure spread rapidly. People couldn't accept violence by the authorities toward their citizens. A nationwide solidarity organization in support of this public sentiment was necessary.

On May 27, leaders of various civilian organizations including National Coalition for Democracy and Reunification (NCDR), the Council for the Promotion of Democratization (CPD), and Democratic Professors Association, together with religious and women leaders, gathered at Hyangrin Church and held a promotion event for the National Movement Headquarters for the Abolition of Constitution Protection and the Winning of Democratic Constitution (also known as National Headquarters). Because of an unclear future under the tight surveillance of the authorities, this promotion event was followed by an event for the founding of the organization on the very same day. Altogether 2191 people participated. Ham Sok-hon, Kim Young-sam, Moon Ik-hwan, Kim Chi-kil, Yun Gong-hoe, Hong Nam-sun, and I were selected as advisory committee members. The National Headquarters stood tall in the midst of the epoch-making June Uprising. Unfortunately, I could not attend the event because of my continued house imprisonment.

Popular anger continued into June. The National Headquarters decided to hold the People's Event for the Condemnation of Torture Homicide Cover-up and Fabrication, the Abolition of Constitution Protection, and the Winning of Democratic Constitution on June 10.

At noon on June 10, the Minjeong Party held a national convention and presidential candidate nomination event at the Jamsil Arena in Seoul. Mr. Roh Tae-woo was nominated as the presidential candidate. Their intention to elect a "gymnasium president" through indirect election was obvious. The Jamsil Arena was filled with cheers, while an orchestra, women's chorus, peasant band, famous singers and comedians, and cheerleaders entertained the audience. A singer sang "Bessame Mucho," Mr. Roh Tae-woo's favorite song, and Chun Doo-hwan raised nominee Mr. Roh's hand high in the air. Colorful flower petals poured down from the ceiling as about 10,000 attendees cheered.

Around the same time, the People's Event for the Abolition of Constitution Protection was held in the large auditorium of the Anglican Church. About twenty leaders from National Headquarters were already in the auditorium. The bell in the bell tower of the Anglican Church next to Deoksugung Palace rang forty-two times, asking the Korean people to wake up and drive out the dictatorial regime that still ruled even forty-two years after the country's liberation. At the same time, speakers blared out their condemnation of the Minjeong Party's conspiracy to hold power indefinitely. "We declare in the name of all Koreans passionately desiring democracy that the presidential candidate nomination occurring right at this moment at the Minjeong Party convention is null and void."

Similar broadcasting was under way in several other locations at the same time: the National Headquarters' office, Room 312 in the Christian Association Building, and the CPD office at the Pyeongchang Building in Mugyo-dong. The broadcasts shook downtown Seoul.

Mr. Yi Han-yeol, a Yonsei University student, had collapsed the day before the June 10 Event. During the rally for participation in the June 10 Event, students waged a fierce fight against riot police and plainclothes riot police (called "Skeleton Troops") at the college gate. Teargas powder heaped like snow in front of the gate. A teargas bomb struck the back of Mr. Yi's head. Although he was immediately rushed to the Severance Hospital Emergency Room, Mr. Yi was pronounced brain dead.

People were shocked when they saw the photo of Mr. Yi Han-yeol bleeding from the teargas bomb and supported by another student. Students printed the photo on handkerchiefs and scarves and distributed them to raise awareness. This photo became the symbol of the June Uprising. People foresaw the end of the regime from the news of Mr. Yi's cerebral death.

At 6:00 p.m. on June 10, cars on the street honked simultaneously as planned. Immediately afterward, demonstrators crowded downtown. White-collar office workers, dubbed "Necktie Troops," flooded the streets and joined demonstrators. As the evening grew darker, demonstrators increased. Throughout downtown, people chanted: "Abolish Constitution protection!" "Down with dictatorship!"

About 300,000 people participated in the demonstration at 514 locations across twenty-two cities nationwide. The police shot teargas bombs randomly. It was like street fighting. The police dispatched arrest units to arrest demonstrators. Nationwide, nearly 4000 people were taken into police custody in a single day. To avoid ruthless suppression by the police, demonstrators in Seoul escaped into Myeongdong Cathedral, their only sanctuary. That night the confrontation between those in the Myeongdong Cathedral and the authorities began.

It was deeply significant that the middle class participated in this demonstration. Citizens who had been critical of violent demonstrations acted in concert with or supported the demonstrators. It was a surprising change. Major news media outlets throughout the world—particularly in America—tried to analyze the cause of the Necktie Troop's participation. Because of my house imprisonment, I could not participate in that historical scene, but I was frequently updated throughout the day by my Head Secretary Kwon Rho-kap and Secretaries Hahn Hwa-kap and Lee Hyup.

As public opinion shifted, the US sent Ambassador to Korea James Lilley to visit Korean Foreign Minister Choi Kwang-soo and requested the Korean government cease violent suppression. Ambassador Lilley also stated that the US was against a violent raid of Myeongdong Cathedral. The US's attitude change was due to the support for democratization by ordinary citizens and the middle class. I continued to argue for a nonviolent, non-pro-communist, non-anti-American stance, despite objections from some. In retrospect, the US must have checked on these three items until the very end. It must have been only after the US verified the middle class' attitude that they applied pressure for constitutional amendment in favor of direct presidential election and my amnesty and reinstatement to the Chun regime. The Chun regime was being driven to the cliff.

As all of this was happening, hundreds of demonstrators, including citizens, students, and workers, were locked up in the Myeongdong Cathedral after being driven into it by police during the June 10 Event. National security authorities accused them of being subversive and breaching the national foundation. Tired of this old rhetoric, citizens delivered money and goods to support the demonstrators inside the cathedral. Still, the authorities could raid the cathedral at any moment. Catholic priests came forward and forty priests belonging to the Seoul Parish issued a statement, which read: "The fight against the current government, which has lost its ethics and legitimacy, is a just action and we will protect the sit-in demonstrators with our priestly conscience until the end." Cardinal Kim Souhwan also chimed in: "If they enter this building, they will see me first. They will see priests only after they throw me down, and they will see nuns only after they throw the priests down. It is only after they throw down the nuns that they will see the students."

In the end, the authorities had to yield to the priests. Cardinal Kim shook hands with every demonstrator in the cathedral before sending them out. The demonstrators left the cathedral, those in the front row carrying a large national flag of Korea together.

The demonstration was growing stronger. Many were wounded during demonstrations, particularly by teargas bombs. Mr. Yi Han-yeol remained cerebrally dead despite the Korean people's passionate wishes. National Headquarters organized the Committee for Measures for Teargas Bomb Victims and scheduled the Teargas Bomb Expulsion Day event on June 18. Over 1.5 million people in major Korean cities including Seoul, Busan, Daegu, and Gwangju participated in this rally. This rally brought an imminent sense of crisis to the Chun regime. At 10:30 a.m. the next morning, President Chun held a meeting with military leaders and the Agency for National Security Planning (ANSP) director to discuss how to cope with the developing situation. They decided to send military troops. The military was given specific deployment maps and dispatch plans. It was a hair-trigger crisis, but this plan was canceled at 4:00 p.m. the same day.

Although I don't know the details about the development of this plan, I believe that the US government must have expressed very strong opposition to it. Also, the regime probably couldn't commit such atrocities right before the Seoul Olympics as IOC president Juan Antonio Samaranch said that they would change the Olympic venue if there were disturbances in Seoul. The Olympics was the trump card that the Chun regime used to seduce the Korean people, but that Olympics shackled the regime. It was a giant boomerang.

US Assistant Secretary of State for East Asian and Pacific Affairs Gaston J. Sigur came to Korea on June 23. While here, he said, "We believe that the power will be peacefully handed over in February next year, and that democratic principles will be applied to this process." This was a great change from Secretary of State Schultz's March position, which emphasized just dialogue and compromise. By this point, Mr. Schultz had already clearly stated that he hoped strong demonstrations would not be used as an excuse for military involvement.

I was released from my latest house arrest that had lasted for seventy-eight days at midnight on June 25. I issued a statement demanding the withdrawal of the April 13 Constitution Protection, direct presidential election—or, at least, selective referendum—and a national independent cabinet. I also appealed to all democratization forces, imploring them to refrain from using any violent means. I met reporters for the first time in a long while.

A reporter asked me how I felt about having my house arrest lifted. "During my house arrest," I responded, "I was most moved by the great ability that the Korean people showed, which was confirmed during the June 10 Event, among others. It is this power of the Korean people that is changing American policy toward our government."

When asked about my seventy-eight-day imprisonment, I responded, "People say that you marry twice in your life, once when young, and again during the empty-nest period. For me, the period of house imprisonment was when I enjoyed my second honeymoon with my wife."

We all laughed, but the truth is that it was painful to be imprisoned in my own home every day. I was especially flooded with sadness when our students and young people perished during their struggle against dictatorship. I could not sleep well. The only thing I could do then was to kneel and pray. I felt so sorry for those just youth.

More than 1.8 million people nationwide participated in the People's Peaceful Grand March to Win a Democratic Constitution on June 26. The demonstrators often overpowered the police. Every day, the Chun regime barely managed to subsist on teargas bombs. In this life-or-death crisis, the June 29 Declaration occurred when Minjeong Party Chief Committee Member Roh Tae-woo held a press conference to declare his acceptance of the opposition party's demand for constitutional amendment for direct presidential election, as well as my amnesty and reinstatement. He also recommended eight articles to the president: the release of political prisoners; amendment of presidential election law; improvement of people's basic rights; advancement in the freedom of the press; and the introduction of a local autonomy system. This kind of declaration was, of course, impossible without prior discussion with the Blue House. The Minjeong Party followed up by holding a general assembly, during which they ratified this recommendation as the party's official position. President Chun issued a special statement declaring his acceptance of the entire June 29 recommendation.

The long and short of it is that President Chun had to give all of the credit to the Minjeong Party candidate when hardliner tactics were no longer effective. The recommendation was prepackaged merchandise of sorts, every detail of which the Blue House took care of and delivered to Mr. Roh. It was a movie produced and directed by President Chun where Mr. Roh starred. Although this was an elaborate scenario by the Chun regime, it was also a precious result of the June Uprising.

Two years and four months after the lifting of the political activities ban, the Chun regime awarded me amnesty and reinstatement as promised. A swarm of reporters asked me how I felt. "As I did not commit any crime that caused me to deserve amnesty and reinstatement, I have mixed feelings," I responded. "However, it is clear that this recovery of my rights is the result of the Korean people's sacrifice and support for me. I express my deepest gratitude to Korean people who have been constantly supporting me."

The direct presidential election was scheduled for the end of the year, just five months later. My wife and I visited the Severance Hospital where Mr. Yi Han-yeol was hospitalized. As expected, he was silent, so I expressed my sympathy to his father. "I hope that Mr. Yi miraculously revives just like democracy demonstrated the miraculous ability to revive yesterday."

Mr. Yi Han-yeol died five days later, almost a month after the teargas bomb hit him. In the meantime, the world had changed … but not before Mr. Yi witnessed that entire process from beginning to end. Even in the state of cerebral death, his strength added to the democratization of his homeland. As I visited the mortuary and prayed for his happiness in the other world, I wondered, *What can I do to repay these young people's pure-hearted sacrifices?*

At 7:00 a.m. on July 9, Mr. Yi's funeral service was held on the Yonsei University campus. The guests were innumerable, and the funeral streamers formed a forest. The ceremony was magnificent and the procession was solemn. It was a nationwide memorial that deserves entry in historical records. Mourners filled the roads and sidewalks all the way from

Yonsei University through Sinchon to Seoul City Hall. The grand ceremony ushering Mr. Yi to the next world served as a symbol of the last
phase of the June Uprising.

Together with the April 19, 1960, Student Revolution and the May 18,
1980, Gwangju Uprising, the June 1987 Uprising was a monumental
event in the Korean democratization movement; it signaled the people's
victory over dictatorship. History will forever remember that passionate
month.

LOST AGAIN IN THE PRESIDENTIAL ELECTION (1987–1988)

The constitutional amendment process that began in July 1987 gradually showed its contours. Both the ruling and opposition parties agreed
that the president would serve only a single five-year term. They also
eliminated the president's authority to implement emergency measures
and dissolve the National Assembly. Workers were guaranteed the rights
of organization and collective bargaining. This amended Constitution
was ratified at the national referendum with 93.1 percent support on
October 27.

At first, I argued for the president and vice president running mate
system and two four-year terms for the team; however, the ruling party
was vehemently against it. They were worried that Mr. Kim Young-sam
and I would pair up as running mates. We had to yield to their life-or-
death opposition.

I thought the opposition party would have no problem coming up with
a unified presidential candidate. I believed Mr. Kim Young-sam's frequent
public promises that he would yield to me as presidential candidate once I
was pardoned and reinstated. I was shocked when I found out through a
messenger that Mr. Kim Young-sam had changed his previous position,
and said that he wanted to run for the presidency himself.

A unified candidate from the opposition party became the biggest
political issue. Mr. Kim argued that I should not run for the presidency as
I had promised the previous November; I responded that my declaration
was null because of the Chun regime's April 13 Constitution Protection
measures. I also argued that Mr. Kim should keep his promise to yield to
me once I was pardoned and reinstated.

Unfortunately, the media continued to distort my declaration that I
would not run for president as if it were still valid. I wouldn't have objected
to a demand that I show greater ethics than my opponent, but I could not

accept reporting that was distorted. It was a base tactic designed to stab the "conscience in action" that I had worked so hard to preserve.

I visited Gwangju, Mokpo, and Hauido Island in early September. There were many purposes for my visit, but, most of all, I wanted to gauge public opinion there. I arrived in Gwangju on September 8 for the first time since my stump speeches for other national assembly candidates in May 1971.

My visit to Gwangju couldn't be all joy. To stand in front of great Gwangju citizens was an awe-inspiring event. I got on the train to Gwangju with a group of people. Around the time when we passed Daejeon, I saw crowds gathered on the platforms of each station, waving our national flag and chanting my name. They welcomed me with cheers and waving placards and pickets.

When I arrived in Gwangju, crowds filled not only the train station, but also the public square in front of it and all of the streets downtown. I gave a brief speech before heading directly to the May 18 graveyard. Placards hung along the streets with messages like "Let Democracy Revive!" and "Please Wipe Away Our Tears!" Tens of thousands of people were waiting for me when I arrived at the graveyard. All I could do was cry as I embraced the wounded victims and the families of the dead. I cried so much that I cannot even remember the details of the scene. I tore up as I dedicated my memorial address to freedom and the victims' spirits. "Dear spirits!" I spoke. "Mt. Mudeungsan is watching us with eyes as generous and merciful as our mothers' embrace. I understand the depth of pain felt by the poet who cried that he would not sing about our loving hometown Gwangju yet. It is because Gwangju continues today. And it is impossible to justly advance our national history if we detour Gwangju. On that day when the hymn of peace, freedom, and democracy rang from Halla to Paektu, Gwangju will lead our nation to the future as a symbol of redemption and eternal starlight."

A car parade ran from the entrance of Geumnamno Street to the provincial government building. It was estimated that 700,000 people filled the six-lane street to welcome me. They came right up to my car with pickets that read: "National Leader Kim Dae-jung" and "Down with Regional Antagonism, Dictatorship's Legacy!" We had to stop my car in front of the crowds chanting my name. I shouted right back to them, the patriotic citizens of Gwangju, the holy city of democracy, "It is you, Korean people, citizens of Gwangju, and the spirits in Mangwoldong graveyard that have beaten the dictatorship!"

We ran into welcoming crowds endlessly flooding the streets of Mokpo as well. Once we reached the square and Mokpo Station, we could not advance at all because of them. I was moved to see that the citizens of Mokpo still embraced me as their son. It was so intense that I got on the boat to Hauido Island two hours later than scheduled.

This trip marked the first time I had set foot on Hauido Island in twenty-eight years. The first place I went upon arriving was my family's graveyard. Although it had been thirteen years since my father passed away, this marked my first visit to his grave. Much to my sorrow, the *yusin* dictatorship had imprisoned me in my house and blocked my attendance at my own father's funeral.

The residents of Hauido Island also gathered around my family's graveyard. I gave an address promising them that I would not disappoint my hometown and its people. After the speech, I visited my relatives. My elder sister, grown older, welcomed me warmly.

I visited Daejeon two days later. Around 50,000 people were waiting for me at the Daejeon Station Square. After I gave an address, a car parade delivered me to the hotel where I was staying. I then visited various places like Incheon, Gyeonggi, and Cheongju. I could affirm the Korean people's constant support for me in those places and felt it was my duty not to ignore it. However, in order to achieve power change, the opposition party needed to be united under a single candidate.

The Sangdo-dong faction, which had unilaterally decided that Kim Young-sam should be the unified candidate, urged me to give up my candidacy. Without any other alternative, I requested that I'd be given the authority to appoint chief organizers for the thirty-six yet-to-be-founded district party chapters. Although I was appointed Democratic Party advisor, my foundation within the party was very weak. I proposed that we elect our party candidate through a vote to be held at the national convention. It seemed to me that we needed at least the appearance of fair competition. Nevertheless, the Sangdo-dong faction rejected my proposal.

As a last resort, I proposed that both of us participate in televised debates and joint canvassing tours, from there selecting the candidate who received the most support from the people. This proposal was also rejected.

One day, Kim Byung-kwan, the chairman of *Donga Ilbo* newspaper, invited me to a meeting at a Korean restaurant called Changwon. "One of you must yield to the other," he said to me. "So let's first have Kim Young-sam choose between being the presidential candidate and the party president."

It seemed that Mr. Kim Byung-kwan had discussed this plan with Mr. Kim Young-sam before meeting with me. I gladly agreed on the spot because I thought we had to achieve a power change, no matter what. However, a few days later, Mr. Kim Byung-kwan contacted me again and said that I should forget about our previous discussion. This meant that Kim Young-sam wanted to take both the candidacy and the party presidency.

One day, three assemblymen belonging to my Donggyo-dong faction, Yang Soon-jik, Choe Yeong-geun, and Lee Choong-jae, came to me after meeting with Mr. Kim Young-sam and his followers. They told me he said that the military would kill me right away if I were to become the president, and that I must not become the presidential candidate because of the military's veto based on their accusation that I was "a commie."

I was extremely surprised to hear this. Did Mr. Kim Young-sam mean to say that he had been working for the democratization of our country with a commie? A democratization movement comrade using the backbiting logic of the dictators—*how could this be?* After fighting to end the military dictatorship, he now wanted to cater to the military again. How absurd and grotesque! Out-of-office democratization movement leaders like Ahn Byung Mu, Ham Sok-hon, Moon Ik-hwan, and Moon Dong-hwan were all enraged at this news, and believed that I must run for the presidency.

Mr. Kim Young-sam and I met at the Diplomatic Club for two hours on September 29 in what would be our last negotiation for the unification of presidential candidacy. I sincerely tried to persuade Mr. Kim Young-sam to yield because it would be hard for me to refuse the Korean people's wishes after seeing their unimaginable support of me and demand for my presidential candidacy. Mr. Kim Young-sam brought up the matter of a so-called veto group. I refuted his logic, arguing, "How could we, who have fought to end military regimes and bring democracy, say such a thing? Look at the cases of Argentina and Brazil. After ending the military dictatorship, Argentinian President Raul Alfonsin settled democracy and embraced the military despite their faults, didn't he? In contrast, look at Brazilian President Tancredo Neves, who vaguely reconciled with the military! The political situation declined and the military interfered with it."

Mr. Kim Young-sam said that my candidacy could cause acute regional conflict between Gyeongsang-do and Jeolla-do. I refuted that, too. "You know well where that regional conflict originated from, don't you? As those who suffered from regional antagonism, don't we have to help each other? If you help me this time, this election can serve as a golden opportunity to stamp out regional antagonism."

In the end, we could not agree. Shortly after, Mr. Kim Young-sam announced that he would accept my request for the authority to appoint chief organizers for the thirty-six yet-to-be-founded district party chapters, but it was too late, given the election timetable.

Both individual and organizational support of me increased every day. The cradle of the Korean out-of-office democracy movement, the NCDR, invited both Mr. Kim Young-sam and me to a debate in order to assess our qualifications as presidential candidate. Following the debate, I was overwhelmingly recommended as the unified opposition party candidate by a vote of twenty-nine to two. The NCDR issued a precious statement in support of me on October 13, in which they said, "We recommend Advisor Kim Dae-jung as *the* national candidate."

I far surpassed Mr. Kim Young-sam at a nationwide student council straw poll and the opinion polls at major newspapers. Catholic priests, Protestant pastors, Jogye order Buddhist monks, 350 college professors, and 200 writers all issued statements in support of my candidacy. They generously evaluated my qualities as future president, my contribution to the democratization struggle, and my support on the national level. However, the candidacy unification negotiation wasn't making any progress. Out-of-office leaders who supported me gathered at Dr. Ahn Byung Mu's house in Suyuri and, after a lengthy discussion, decided to found a new political party.

On October 30, we declared both the establishment of a new political party and my candidacy. We left the Democratic Party and founded the Pyeonghwa Minju (Peace and Democracy) Party (also known as the Pyeongmin Party). I silently wrote that party name, composed of my two favorite words—peace and democracy—on my heart. On November 12, we held a party foundation ceremony and held the national convention, during which I was nominated for presidential candidacy. This also marked the first time I was nominated as a party president. After the nomination, I gave an acceptance speech in front of 3300 delegates and guests. "Although I am not a unified candidate for the opposition parties," I spoke, "I am the only candidate supported by the out-of-office democratization movement forces. The significance of the upcoming December election lies in the complete ending of the military regime and the recovery of a true civilian government. I promise to forever cease the bad custom of a small minority of the political military's interference with politics through this election and to re-establish the millennial Korean tradition of civilian government."

We elected seven party vice presidents during this convention: Lee Choong-jae, Yang Soon-jik, Lee Yong-hee, Roh Sung-hwan, Choe Yeong-geun, Yoo Jei-yeun, and Park Young-rok. Mr. Kim Jong-wan was elected as the convention chair. As we worked and debated, between 20,000 and 30,000 people gathered outside of the building to express their support. After the convention, a car parade traveled from Seoul City Hall to the Sinchon Rotary.

Presidential candidates for the thirteenth term presidency included Roh Tae-woo (Minjeong Party), Kim Young-sam (Democratic Party), me (Pyeongmin Party), Kim Jong-pil (Republican Party), and Baek Gi-wan (independent). As the media put it, it was competition between one Roh and three Kims.

With only twenty-five days to go until the election, we were short on everything, including time, organization, and funds. Everything was rushed. I wore traditional Korean clothes throughout my canvassing tour; I wanted to talk about our nation while wearing our national clothes. When the Philippines overthrew the dictatorship, they waved yellow flags, and so the color yellow also symbolized the Pyeongmin Party. Our canvassing sites overflowed with waves of yellow.

The regime and ruling party provoked regional antagonism once again. They also carried out an operation to divide Mr. Kim Young-sam and me, sending people to chant Mr. Kim Young-sam's name at my stump speeches and vice versa. They also staged organized heckling incidents everywhere.

On November 1, while I was staying in Busan following a stump event, more than 300 mobsters suddenly raided my hotel, breaking glass and wielding steel pipes and thin square wooden bars. "Send Kim Young-sam to the Blue House!" they shouted.

My secretaries and bodyguards used their bare, bloodied fists to defend us against them. All told, about fifteen people, including my bodyguards, were severely injured, and ten cars were damaged. Although we called the police at 8:20 p.m., they didn't arrive until nearly an hour later. Not only was their delay incredible, but so too was the fact that they neglected to guard the hotel where a presidential candidate was staying in the first place.

A similar incident occurred at my canvassing stop in Duryu Park in Daegu, where we were holding a special event titled "Pledge Event to End Military Dictatorship and Regional Antagonism by Yeongnam and Honam

Citizens." During Reverend Moon Ik-hwan's address, curses and shouts suddenly erupted among the crowd. Then, rocks, glasses, and eggs were ruthlessly thrown toward the podium, threatening to end the event. While the rocks continued to fly toward the podium, I stepped forward to stand on the podium despite my secretaries' and bodyguards' pleas not to. "I will be hit by the rocks," I said. "I will fight against those evil forces that encourage regional antagonism. Throw rocks at me."

Still, the disturbance continued. Suspicious fellows pushed the crowd aside and rushed toward the podium. "Don't look at them," I demanded. "Look at me. I came to Daegu sixteen years after the 1971 presidential election. Aren't you curious how my face and voice have changed?" The audience turned their attention back toward me. I raised my voice again. "If we lose here, there is no democracy for us! I won't go down, even if my head is shattered. I will stay here even if I die." Incredibly, the event site where 70,000 people were gathered instantly fell into silence. No more rocks were thrown. I finished my speech without any further incident. The audience clapped and cheered when I finished.

It was later confirmed that, as we had guessed, all of these incidents were the result of the Chun regime's elaborate scheme to encourage regional antagonism. Candidate Roh Tae-woo's stump speech in Gwangju was also brought to a halt because of thin wooden square bars and mobsters' attack on the podium. Similar incidents happened all over the country. These thugs moved around systematically. The media labeled it as regional antagonism and television stations broadcasted the incidents straight into the homes of people across the country in an effort to provoke anti-Honam sentiments. The intentional distortion of events by television news was truly detestable. They used only images that showed me frowning or using large gestures. Although I thought I performed better than any other candidate at the Kwanhun Club debate, they used only the footage that showed me pausing before moving on to smooth answers.

Television programs were edited to cater to the regime's needs. As Election Day approached, they broadcast programs that focused on communism in Vietnam and Cambodia, and showed confusion in the Philippines. With its focus on ideology and regional antagonism, television served as the surest election tool for Candidate Roh Tae-woo—one that I was, frankly, completely helpless in the face of. Although I tried to win the favor of the media, it was of no use. The biggest beneficiary of the media was Roh Tae-woo; I was its greatest victim.

Nevertheless, the last large-scale stump rally before Election Day (held at Boramae Park in Daebang-dong, Seoul) was unforgettable. I was surprised at the size of the crowds. Altogether 2.5 million passionate and excited people gathered together. From the podium, I couldn't see where the crowd ended. About 100,000 people marched 15 kilometers to Seoul City Hall. The marchers seemed to anticipate our upcoming victory. I, too, did not doubt my overwhelming victory. Not only democracy movement forces, but also students, young people, and white-collar workers all supported me.

My camp was very encouraged. But, on November 29, as the campaign heated to a boil, Korean Air flight 858 exploded in midair over the sea near Myanmar. More than one hundred passengers were killed, most of whom were Korean workers on their way home from working in Bagdad, Iraq. This turned out to be a critical blow to me.

Kim Hyon-hui, who perpetrated the Korean Air flight bombing, was arrested and taken to Korea the day before Election Day. The investigators said that this disaster was the work of a North Korean operation, and concluded that North Korea, isolated internationally after the Soviet Union and China decided to participate in the Seoul Olympics, executed this crime to shift the political climate.

The media turned its attention from the election to Kim Hyon-hui. The public's attention also shifted to the absolute benefit to Candidate Roh Tae-woo. National security became everyone's foremost concern. Additionally, Candidate Roh Tae-woo's camp waged the "color" war, goading people by chanting slogans such as "Security or chaos?" They didn't hesitate to threaten Koreans, saying: "If the opposition party takes power, our country will drift."

In fact, I had to suffer from this ideological attack throughout the entire campaign. The political soldiers who participated in the December 12 Coup d'État poured out dangerous ideological accusations against me to the media, among which was the threat that if I were to be elected, there was no telling what the military would do. "There are people who declared that they'd jump at his car, holding a bomb," they said.

Threatening phone calls continued coming in to my campaign headquarters. "There's a plan to assassinate Kim Dae-jung," the caller would speak. Or, "We'll shoot you." Former Army Chief of Staff Park Hee-do issued a statement saying that he was against my candidacy, making it sound as if that was the opinion of the entire military.

In the end, I lost the election. Roh Tae-woo garnered 36.6 percent of the votes (8.28 million votes), Kim Young-sam 28 percent (6.33 million votes), and I 27.1 percent (6.11 million votes). Election fraud was rampant and obvious. Demonstrations protested the fraud and demanded the results of the election be nullified.

The fraud in this election took many forms. On December 7, a pro-government newspaper extra was distributed in the Jamsil neighborhood of Seoul, with a headline that blared: "Roh Tae-woo President Elect." This extra, distributed at 7:00 a.m., carried the percentage of votes obtained by that point in the day, which was completely absurd. Interestingly, the percentages included in the paper coincided almost exactly with those shown on TV. It was later discovered that the newspaper extra was printed at dawn to be distributed that afternoon; it was mistakenly distributed earlier.

A suspicious event occurred in Guro-dong, Seoul, as well. On Election Day, the fair election observation mission members caught a person attempting to carry an unsealed absentee ballot box outside of the building. Not only that, but nine police officers in charge of accompanying and guarding the ballot boxes to the ballot-counting office had disappeared with suspicious men. The attempt to remove the absentee ballot box before voting was over was a clear act of fraud.

Inside of this unsealed ballot box, a pile of ballots, all with the same vote, was found. It was very likely that the person fraudulently substituted the ballot box. Not only this, but stamps and ink that appeared to have been used to manufacture fraudulent ballots were also found. In protest, the watchdog members and citizens waged a sit-down strike at the Guro-gu office. The police poured teargas bombs into the office building and sent armed plainclothes police officers to raid it and disperse the protestors. This was not limited to only the Guro-gu ballot-counting office. I could not accept the result of this election no matter how hard I tried. The Pyeongmin Party issued a statement that read: "We cannot acknowledge the election of Mr. Roh Tae-woo, and urge Mr. Roh to apologize to the Korean people and step down."

Mr. Kim Young-sam and the Democratic Party also defined the election as "fundamentally fraudulent," and declared their intention to fight to overthrow the regime. NCDR Chairman Moon Ik-hwan began a fasting strike, demanding the nullification of the presidential election and the investigation of the Guro-gu Office Violence Incident.

The Pyeongmin Party published the *White Book of Presidential Election Frauds*, in which we listed all of the incidents of ballot-counting fraud, together with evidence supporting our claims. We distributed this book among civilian organizations, including the Catholic Priests' Association for Justice.

Catholic Priests' Association for Justice president Father Kim Seung-hoon and the Fair Election Observation Mission president Father Oh Tae-sun revealed in a press conference at the Myeongdong Cathedral on February 16, 1988, that they too believed the December 16 election was fraudulent. They showed examples of the prior manipulation of election results according to region and candidate.

In retrospect, it is telling that on the day before the election, Candidate Roh Tae-woo emphasized that everyone should accept the election result unconditionally. Unfortunately, as time passed, the opposition parties' condemnation of election fraud dampened. Everything tends to be buried under the bright light that shines upon the winner. It was hard for the opposition parties alone to remain obsessed with this problem alone. The general election, scheduled for April, was rapidly approaching.

The Korean people suffered from a tremendous sense of loss after the presidential election—it felt much like there had been a bombing. The streets were extremely quiet. The democratization camp was particularly at a loss with the realization that our country's worst possible scenario had come to fruition. I was truly sorry that I had failed to unify opposition party candidates. We lost in the election acquired only after so many democratization movement activists' sacrifices and the June 10 Uprising; the first direct presidential election in sixteen years, after finally overthrowing the dictatorship. The Korean people's grief was so high that it seemed to touch the sky. I should have yielded the candidacy. I still regret that. Of course, even with a unified opposition candidate, there is still no guarantee that we would have won the election. We could not have prevented election fraud. Nevertheless, it was clearly wrong for us to be divided in the face of our people. The media analysis determined that the opposition parties lost because of our failure to nominate a single candidate, and that became the general consensus.

My supporters in particular felt a great sense of loss. Because we believed that the world had changed, we could not believe that we had lost. The Republic of Korea sank hard in the aftermath of the election.

Asking My Way to the Korean People (1988)

After my defeat in the presidential election, the Pyeongmin Party fell into a deep shock and depression. The opposition parties and I, in particular, were under heavy attack. Public opinion began to support the merger of opposition parties. Reverend Moon Ik-hwan visited the Pyeongmin Party headquarters and yelled at us to urge the merger of opposition parties. Madam Lee Tai-young sat down in front of me crying—almost to the point of a tantrum—and said, "We are all ruined!"

On December 30, 1987, Democratic Party president Kim Young-sam began his attack at the year-end gathering. "The opposition forces should unite under the roof of the Democratic Party, the headquarters of democratic forces," he spoke. "This unity of democratic forces is historically reasonable. I hope that the Pyeongmin Party will wisely decide what they have to do for election revolution in the upcoming general election. As this is quite urgent, we cannot take complicated merger measures. Those who left the Democratic Party can just return to our party."

This proposal suggested that the Democratic Party would simply absorb our party members. It was a very rude suggestion. The Democratic Party itself suggested that the Pyeongmin Party should be dissolved. They also suggested that a significant number of Pyeongmin Party members, including national assemblymen, return to Democratic Party.

While putting pressure on the Pyeongmin Party, Democratic Party president Kim Young-sam met with president-elect Roh Tae-woo and approved the election result. The Democratic Party had condemned election fraud most strongly after the election was over, and had declared the overthrow of the regime, saying: "At a minimum, more than two million ballots were stolen [from Candidate Kim Young-sam]. Therefore we declare this election null and void." After all those condemnations, Democratic Party president Kim Young-sam met President-Elect Roh Tae-woo ahead of anyone else and pledged cooperation with the Minjeong Party's plan to pursue medium-sized electoral districts for the National Assembly.

Our party immediately counterattacked. "President Kim Young-sam and the Democratic Party revealed that they are jealous of the clearest opposition party. Considering they begged for an interview with Mr. Roh Tae-woo, who won the election through fraud, and thereby accepted his victory, we cannot find any other explanation than that the Democratic Party is a government-controlled opposition party."

Mr. Kim Young-sam appeared to think that the Pyeongmin Party would crumble immediately. However, our party members were not grains of sand, and our party was not a sand castle. What the Democratic Party and President Kim Young-sam meant by a "merger" was, in fact, the dissolution of the Pyeongmin Party. It was exactly the same attitude that he demonstrated during the negotiation for the unification of two party candidates, where he insisted that I should just accept that he would be the unified candidate. They also argued that the two opposition parties should take gradated responsibility for the loss of the presidential election. I could not agree with them. As expected, a few National Assembly members who belonged to the Pyeongmin Party switched their affiliation as a result of the persistent operation.

I could not simply give up. On February 3, 1988, the Pyeongmin Party invited in ninety-one out-of-office leaders from various fields, including academia, civil rights, law, religion, and literature. The leaders included Park Young-sook, Lee Kil-jae, Moon Dong-hwan, Seong Nae-un, Lim Chae-jung, Jeong Dong-nyeon, Lee Hae-chan, Lee Sang-soo, Ko Yong-gun, and Yang Sung-woo. This was a historical event that signified the entrance of out-of-office leaders into the political arena.

Even with all of this, the people's demand for the union of opposition parties did not subside. Also, the Democratic Party's attack was persistent. While the Pyeongmin Party remained unfazed in our preparation for the general election, Mr. Kim Young-sam took the extreme measure of resigning from his position as party president on February 8, saying, "I will not seek a title for the quick merger of the opposition forces."

I did not have any reason to oppose the merger itself. I demanded that the Democratic Party stop collaborating with the Minjeong Party to introduce medium-sized electoral districts. We pursued the merger to become the majority party in the Assembly, and medium-sized electoral districts would not be helpful in achieving this goal. We had to fight the ruling party members head-on in the single-member electorate system.

I had always been a supporter of the single-member electorate system, which is what most advanced democratic countries utilized. I also thought that the single-member electorate system was better suited to settling the two-party system. Additionally, voter polls showed that the Korean people overwhelmingly supported the single-member electorate system.

Although I urged the Democratic Party to scrap its pursuit of medium-sized electoral districts, it rejected my proposal and insisted that I step down from my position as Pyeongmin Party president. The media, and especially newspapers, urged my resignation, reporting as if all of the country's problems would go away as soon as I stepped down. They also published creative articles predicting that the Pyeongmin Party would crumble based on inner conflicts that were the result of my refusal to resign. I couldn't help commenting, "As professional mourners cry more sorrowfully than real mourners, the newspapers are making more noise than the [Pyeongmin Party]."

Mr. Kim Young-sam devoted all of his energy to the dissolution of the Pyeongmin Party, rather than strategizing to win against the ruling party. Even the Minjeong Party offered to accept our election law amendment proposal if the opposition parties built a consensus, but the Democratic Party was obsessed with the system of medium-sized electoral districts, a legacy of the Yusin regime. In the end, I decided to personally try to persuade Mr. Kim Young-sam of my stance. When we met, I proposed that both parties share the presidency of the merged party. "In order to overwhelmingly win the general election, both of us should go to Busan and Gwangju together," I urged him.

Still, the Democratic Party did not budge, and I had to yield again. I officially scrapped the co-presidency proposal on March 3, but I could not give up the single-member electorate system. "I believe that both Mr. Kim Young-sam and I should lead the party in order to win the general election," I said. "But I do not want this to stand in the way of a single-member electorate system, so I hereby declare that I am willing to sacrifice myself and change my party position in order to achieve the single-member electorate system."

Nevertheless, the Democratic Party rejected any preconditions, insisting that I unconditionally withdraw. Democratic Party spokesperson Kim Tae-ryong went even further. "The leadership system of the new, merged party should be a single leadership system and the Democratic Party should provide the president as it is stronger [than the Pyeongmin Party]," he commented.

The Democratic Party would not relent on its stance for medium-sized electoral districts. The party was not able to control a considerable number of its candidates, who wanted to be elected jointly with the ruling party candidate as their inferior partner in the medium-sized electoral districts. At this point, even the Minjeong Party argued that we should adopt the single-member electorate system, according to the people's wish. They read the public sentiment and were trying to capture constituents first. On March 8, the National Assembly Election Law Amendment, based on the single-member electorate system, was passed in the plenary session at the National Assembly.

On March 17, I stepped down from the party presidency and urged the renewed discussion of an opposition party merger. Finally, I had yielded completely to the Democratic Party's demand. Now, however, the Democratic Party argued for a partial merger first, and a merger with the entire Pyeongmin Party later on down the line. Although both party leaders met for negotiations, we could not make any progress. Then, one day, students and some party members came to the negotiation location and demonstrated, demanding the Democratic Party's sincere effort in negotiations. As soon as this happened, the Democratic Party unilaterally declared that they would stop negotiations. In retrospect, the Democratic Party didn't really want to pursue a merger. They simply wanted to get national assemblymen from the Pyeongmin Party, bring about the collapse of our party, and bury their responsibility for the presidential election defeat with me as the sacrificial lamb.

The Pyeongmin Party prepared for the general election with Ms. Park Young-sook at the helm as acting party president. I decided that I would humbly accept the situation and wait for Korean people's judgment. The general election was imminent.

The general election for the thirteenth term national assembly was held less than five months before the Olympics, the ruling party's trump card. The April 26 general election was crucial to both the Pyeongmin Party and me. If we failed again in this election, it was clear that we would be irrevocably hurt—not to mention the fact that our party would be perceived as a temporary stopgap party. We also had to win for the sake of the out-of-office movement leaders who had thrown themselves into an institutional political party simply because they trusted me.

I requested that I be registered as number eleven on our party's national constituency member list. Although everyone argued against it, I insisted. It was like burning the bridge against general speculation that the Pyeongmin Party would win a maximum of thirty seats. It was my declaration that I would retire from politics if people decided to discard me. I felt that I did not deserve to become the national assemblyman if our party could not acquire enough seats to guarantee eleven assemblymen from the national constituency.

I went on a canvassing tour as the Pyeongmin Party's standing advisor. In comparison to the Minjeong and Democratic Parties, the Pyeongmin Party lacked both funding and organization. In every way, we were inferior. But what we did have on our side was passionate voters, which had been confirmed during the presidential election. I thought we had a sufficient chance of winning the election if we could channel that passion into votes. I went everywhere there was a party candidate, even if that meant I lost sleep. I threw myself into the campaign. Again, people paid attention to me and to the Pyeongmin Party. I had a good feeling about the election results.

Compared to previous elections, fraud was reduced in this first single-member electorate general election in seventeen years. The Pyeongmin Party won seventy seats—fifty-four from electorates and sixteen from the national constituency. I enjoyed the thrill of winning. Even more significant was the fact that people chose to give me another chance. The Minjeong Party won 125 seats, the Democratic Party 59 seats, and the Republican Party 35 seats. The ruling party failed to win the majority for the first time in history. The ratio between the ruling and the opposition parties was 34 percent versus 66 percent.

As a result of this election, the Pyeongmin Party became the largest opposition party. Many out-of-office movement leaders in our party won the election as well, including Moon Dong-hwan, Park Young-sook, Lee Hae-chan, Lee Sang-soo, Chung Sang-yong, Park Seok-moo, Lee Chul-yong, and Yang Sung-woo. Their congressional activities were of a different style than those of professional politicians and breathed new vitality into the National Assembly. By transfusing new blood into the system, the National Assembly's Constitution improved.

Reporters asked me what our party would do as the largest opposition party. I answered: "Through this general election, the Korean people asked for the military regime to be checked and for the pursuit of democratization. The Pyeongmin Party, in collaboration with out-of-office movement organizations, will play a major role in accomplishing these two wishes. We are willing to cooperate with the Roh Tae-woo regime if it means sincerely working to pursue democratization."

President Roh said that he humbly accepted the Minjeong Party's defeat in the general election and, significantly, added that "through the election, the people of Korea ordered us to lead the governance not through the number of assembly seats, but through dialogue and compromise, and through political ability. We will firmly respond to people's new demand and lead this new era. Now no politician, no political faction can reject the collaborative politics of dialogue and compromise."

Perhaps he really meant it at the time. However, his promise began to deteriorate in the middle of his term. I was again selected as party president at the temporary party convention on May 7. About 2000 party members gathered at the Sejong Center Annex to celebrate our party's miraculous victory at the general election. I appointed Mr. Moon Dong-hwan as the first vice president, and Ms. Park Young-sook, Mr. Choe Yeong-geun, Mr. Chough Yoon-hyung, Mr. Son Joo-hang, and Mr. Park Young-rok as vice presidents. Soon, I reshuffled the party officials by appointing Mr. Lee Jae-keun as the Secretary General, Mr. Kim Won-ki as the leader of the house, Mr. Chung Dai-chul as the policy committee chair, and Mr. Lee Sang-soo as the spokesperson.

On May 30, the National Assembly opened with opposition parties outnumbering the ruling party. With the assemblyman badge pinned on my suit my heart was too full for words. This marked the first time I had entered the National Assembly building since I was expelled because of the October Yusin sixteen years ago. How moving it was to be raised again by the Korean people and to reenter the National Assembly building as the president of the largest opposition party! That morning, I returned to the palace of people's will after ordeals of imprisonment, exile, house imprisonment, and many life-or-death crises. It was my first entrance to the National Assembly building in Yeouido as a national assemblyman. I began that day by paying reverence at the National Cemetery and the April 19 Graveyard with my party assemblymen and leaders. We then crossed the Han River. The wind was refreshing and fragrant and the May sun was gentle on my way to the National Assembly.

On June 29, I gave my first speech at the National Assembly as the president of the largest opposition party. I worked hard on the script, making sure to address the many important tasks and difficult problems we were sure to encounter as a nation on our way to a new society. Within this speech, I tried to present the roadmap to the true democratization of our country:

"Now, when we're working toward democratization, the most pressing problem that lies on our way and that we cannot avoid is that of clearing the legacy of the fifth republic. It is only when we solve this problem that we can proceed toward democracy. The tasks in front of us are the clarification of the truth of the Gwangju Uprising, the scraping out of the power-based corruption under the fifth republic, including: Mr. Chun Doo-hwan's family's accumulation of wealth by illicit means; the investigation of fraud in the two recent elections; alteration or abolition of all anti-democratic laws; and the cleanup of regional antagonism, which is the cause of national ruin. Among them, the Gwangju problem and the problem of scraping out corruption contain the most sensitive and dangerous elements that will sway the future of our political situation.

"We should solve these problems as soon as possible and in the way the Korean people can accept. For this purpose, first, I strongly argue that, since Mr. Chun Doo-hwan was most greatly related to the 1980 Gwangju Righteous Uprising as someone who assumed the reign of the government at that time, the quickest and surest way to solve the problem is for him to disclose the full truth about the suppression of the Gwangju Righteous Uprising and to apologize to and ask for the forgiveness of the citizens of Gwangju and the Korean people if he thinks that he was responsible for the unjust suppression and bloodshed of Gwangju citizens.

"Second, Mr. Chun Doo-hwan and his family's enormous accumulation of wealth through illicit means has now become a matter of common-sense knowledge that nobody can deny. The only unclear element is its specific size and contents. Mr. Chun Doo-hwan should openly reveal to the Korean people the domestic and overseas wealth his family accumulated by illicit means and sincerely try to clear his wrongdoing by returning it to our people.

"Third, President Roh Tae-woo should reveal the truth about the Gwangju Righteous Uprising and the power-based corrupt accumulation of wealth by the fifth republic. The government should publish white books about these two matters and have the parties responsible for the Gwangju situation apologize to the Korean people; further, the parties that accumulated wealth by illicit means should return their wealth to our nation. This is the way for the Roh Tae-woo regime to quickly and satisfactorily resolve the problems that have resulted from the Gwangju Righteous Uprising and the fifth republic's corruption, and to achieve a stable and more advanced political situation.

"As our party principles clearly state, the Pyeonghwa Minju Party and I are firmly against any political retaliation. All we demand is self-reflection and apologies from those involved. We will try our best to prevent their criminal prosecution and punishment."

I tried very hard to contain my solution for the pressing issues in my speech. For the sake of the common good, we could not move forward without finding out the truth about the Gwangju Uprising and clearing up the corruption of the Chun Doo-hwan regime during the fifth republic.

Mr. Chun Doo-hwan, who had been the ringleader of the coup d'état and the head of the state, was now looking at an uncertain future. It was the opposite of my fate.

On June 27, the National Assembly established seven special committees to handle the injustices, corruption, and misgovernment of the fifth republic. These included the Special Committee for the Investigation of the Truth of the May 18 Gwangju Democratization Movement (Special Committee for Gwangju), Special Committee for Amendment of Laws for the Development of Democracy, Special Committee for Reunification Policies, Special Committee for the Dissolution of Regional Antagonism, Special Committee for the Investigation of the Fifth Republic's Corruption from Political Power (Special Committee for the Fifth Republic), Special Committee for the Investigation of Frauds in the Two Recent Elections, and Special Committee for the Release of Political Prisoners and Discharge of the Wanted for Political Reasons. This was the beginning of the dissolution of the fifth republic at the National Assembly.

I visited military bases for the first time since the declaration of the Yusin Constitution sixteen years ago. On August 1, I visited the Baekgol [skeleton] Unit in Cheorwon in Gangwon-do province. In my speech I said, "I hope that we build 'Nation Park' and 'Unification Stadium' in fierce battlegrounds like Cheorwon and contribute to increased peace between the South and the North."

On August 19, I left for a four-night, five-day visit to the Philippines. I paid a courtesy visit to President Corazon Aquino and was awarded the Philippine Freedom and Democracy Medal. I paid reverence at late Senator Aquino's grave at Memorial Park in suburban Manila. In my memorial address for the former comrade of the democratization movement who I befriended in exile, I said: "While Marcos, who murdered Senator Aquino, became an eternal loser, Senator Aquino, who was murdered, became an eternal winner. Senator Aquino's death taught us how to acquire eternal life."

The 24th Seoul Olympics began on September 17. More than 13,000 athletes from 160 countries—the maximum number of athletes in the history of the Olympics—participated. For the first time in twelve years, all countries from both the Western and Eastern Blocs participated. It was a festival of harmony, where we all finally left ideological strife and racial discrimination behind. I was truly happy to witness this moment; however, I was sad to see North Korea's absence.

The Seoul Olympics were excellent. Both the games and safety measures were thoroughly managed. Korea won twelve gold, ten silver, and eleven bronze medals, proving its standing as a strong, athletic country. Interestingly, the US had the third-highest medal count after the Soviet

Union and East Germany. I think we showed our cultural heritage and tradition quite well throughout the Olympic Games. It felt like a blessing from God to enjoy such clear, early fall weather throughout the Olympic Games. At the successful conclusion of the Olympics, I commented, "The biggest winner of the Olympics is the Korean people." For the Roh Tae-woo government, the Seoul Olympics provided self-confidence in governance.

The people's attention turned toward the activities of the Special Committee for Gwangju and the Special Committee for the fifth republic. After acquiring the blessing of the Pyeongmin Party leadership, I appointed First Vice President Moon Dong-hwan as the chair of the Special Committee for Gwangju and suggested that they call me as their first witness. Since I had been sentenced to capital punishment as the wirepuller of the uprising, my testimony could draw both domestic and international attention. I also wanted my testimony to contribute to the clarification of the truth. I frequently attended the preparatory meetings with other committee members and urged their thorough preparation.

For the first time in National Assembly history, the hearings were reported live in the media. All eyes and ears were on the matter of clearing the fifth republic, to the point that viewer ratings reached around 60 percent. I attended the Special Committee for Gwangju hearing on November 18. During my testimony, I said: "It is difficult to forgive soldiers for firing at unarmed civilians during the Gwangju Uprising. It was violence and massacre. The biggest question is who ordered this firing. Former President Chun Doo-hwan is responsible for ordering this, as the Joint Investigation Headquarters Chief who had life-or-death authority over all Koreans."

Numerous witnesses testified. The most disappointing of them all were President Choi Kyu-ha and Minister of Education Kim Ok-kil. president Choi Kyu-ha did not attend the hearing with the excuse that, as a former president, he could not set a precedent for revealing secrets about national affairs. I don't know what he meant by "secrets about national affairs." Could there be anything more important than revealing the truth in front of the Korean people and for history? Former Minister of Education Kim also exercised the right of silence. As someone who attended the cabinet meeting that decided on the expansion of emergency martial law, she decided not to stand on the side of truth until the very end.

As the Special Committee for the Fifth Republic began to fully operate, the full scale of their corruption began to reveal itself. The media called the former president simply "Mr. Chun," instead of "Former President Chun." The astronomical scale of Mr. Chun and his family's accumulation of wealth by illicit means was exposed. His family members and relatives went to prison in droves. Mr. Chun had no way out. On November 23, he issued a statement of apology and went into voluntary exile at Baekdamsa Temple.

President Roh Tae-woo issued a statement three days after Mr. Chun's departure for Baekdamsa Temple and requested that the Korean people grant him amnesty. He also promised redemption and compensation for the Gwangju Uprising victims and clarified his intention to release all political prisoners, to amend National Security Law, and to clean up both the government and the ruling party. I accepted his declaration and emphasized that, although I did not wish for the punishment of former president Chun, his responsibility for the Gwangju Uprising should be clarified.

Although the activities of the Special Committee for Gwangju began solemnly, they began to dwindle as time went on. Witnesses were insincere and politicians pursued personal interests rather than the truth during most of the year-long investigation. In the end, the presidents of four political parties gathered and decided that we should end the committee activities by summoning former president Chun for testimony. He stood on the witness stand of the Gwangju hearing on December 30, 1989. As expected, he spat out endless lies. Assemblyman Roh Moo-hyun threw a nameplate at him, and Assemblyman Lee Chul-yong ran toward the witness stand, yelling, "You homicidal maniac! Do your testimony right!"

Although the end of the Gwangju hearing was very weak, the Korean people knew who was lying and who was guilty.

Spector of Public Security State (1989)

As 1989 began, Democratic Party President Kim Young-sam abruptly brought up the issue of a midterm referendum for President Roh Tae-woo, which President Roh had promised toward the end of his election campaign when the campaign was in crisis. This promise proved to be a trap and shackle he had placed upon himself—which the Democratic Party persistently chased down. During the New Year press conference on January 5, President Kim Young-sam said: "President Roh promised a mid-term referendum during his campaign, and he should follow through on his promise. That is the ethical and commonsensical thing to do. The time and method of it is not a matter of negotiation with the opposition parties. The referendum should be about scraping out the fifth republic's corruption and the achievement of democratization measures."

The midterm referendum shouldn't have been rushed. I was of the opinion that we should hold the midterm referendum after observing how thoroughly President Roh worked for the liquidation of the fifth republic's corruption and his progress in democratization measures. The three opposition parties had already agreed that we would delay the midterm referendum for a year since it could be abused and might poison the Korean people.

In my opinion, the extreme right wing could gain power within the ruling party if President Roh received popular confidence through an early midterm referendum. It also appeared to me that if the referendum were to be held then, President Roh didn't have a real chance of receiving non-confidence votes from people. After all, the president was popular in the wake of the successful Seoul Olympics, and the Korean people didn't appear to want disorder.

There were two midterm referendum currents within the government and ruling party. The majority of the Minjeong Party actually wanted an early midterm referendum in order to get out of the defensive phase caused by their inferior numbers in the National Assembly. In contrast, those close to President Roh opposed it because they were worried about the slim chance he would get non-confidence votes. Even within the ruling party, only a small minority of people argued to withhold or dissipate the referendum.

The Minjeong Party officially recommended that, to instill confidence, President Roh hold a midterm referendum on February 8. Minjeong Party President Park Jyun-kyu said, "If President Roh receives confidence votes in the mid-term referendum, the opposition parties will not be able to sway the political situation like they do now." The ruling party wanted to break through their defensive position by way of the midterm referendum and to reshuffle the political situation. The Minjeong Party was moving in exactly the direction I was worried about.

On February 25, I expressed my concern about this hardliner trend. "The Minjeong Party's enforcement of the mid-term referendum on presidential confidence does not show their willingness to be judged by Korean people," I spoke. "It is a threat to them. Their real intention is to abuse the mid-term referendum. How can the Korean people judge their performance when solving the problems of liquidating the fifth republic's corruption, democratization, and the livelihood of the people has yet to be completed? It is more reasonable to hold the mid-term referendum only after the above-mentioned problems have been completely handled, regardless of the timing."

The Democratic Party continued to argue for immediate referendum and declared their intention to carry out a movement for non-confidence in President Roh by saying, "Although it is not right to hold a mid-term referendum when the fifth republic's corruption has not been completely liquidated, we will fight the matter of confidence in President Roh because the Minjeong Party expressed its will to hold the referendum." Something seemed strange about this attitude of President Kim Young-sam and the Democratic Party. It was unclear why they insisted on the referendum, even while acknowledging that it was not right to hold the midterm referendum before the fifth republic's corruption had been completely liquidated. They were being voluntarily implicated in the ruling party's scheme to reshuffle the political field post-referendum.

The referendum heated up the political arena. President Roh's term was only one-fifth of the way complete; it was very premature to discuss the achievements and failures of the Roh government. During the first year of its term, the Roh regime focused on the Seoul Olympics, and the political arena focused on the matter of fifth republic—there really were no grounds upon which to evaluate President Roh.

I decided that I should do something to end this factional strife about the midterm referendum, and set up a three-hour conference with President Roh at the Blue House. We agreed that the referendum should be tied not to the matter of confidence in the president, but to the matter of policies. We also agreed on a radical deal for Mr. Chun Doo-hwan's testimony at the National Assembly, the solution to the Gwangju problems, and the local autonomy system. To me, this seemed like the most reasonable solution.

Then, President Kim Young-sam and the Democratic Party declared that they would continue their movement for the non-confidence and resignation of President Roh, even if the referendum were only about the policies.

One day a foreign reporter came to me. "The Democratic Party said that they'd like to hold a new election once President Roh steps down after the referendum," he said. "What do you think about that?" I answered that we should ask for the Korean people's opinion again, should such a situation happen. The ruling party must have wanted to reverse their politically defensive stance through midterm referendum, and Mr. Kim Young-sam, who lost the largest opposition party to the Pyeongmin Party, must have wanted to shake up the situation—a dangerous thing to do. The Roh regime was born of direct presidential election, despite the fact that they won through a fraudulent election and were a remnant of the military. If the midterm referendum turned into a struggle to over-throw the current regime, disorder would reign whether or not the president received a vote of confidence. Ultimately, it was the Korean people who would suffer from this chaos.

In the end, Mr. Kim Young-sam and I had to ask the Korean people. The Pyeongmin and Democratic Parties held open-air rallies about the midterm referendum. The Pyeongmin Party was of the opinion that it was premature, while the Democratic Party thought it had to be enforced. On March 18, the Pyeongmin Party held a rally in Bucheon, Gyeonggi-do, and the Democratic Party in Onyang, Chungcheongnam-do. All eyes were on these two rallies.

Before the overflowing audience at Bucheon Civic Stadium, I argued, "Recently within the ruling party there is a very foul movement trying to connect the mid-term referendum with the matter of confidence in the president. Additionally, they want to shake up the current minority ruling and majority opposition party situation through a premature mid-term referendum. If that happens, the Pyeongmin Party will fight with all dem-ocratic forces for the conclusion of the present regime. Mid-term referen-dum is premature now. It should be held after we have seen more of the Roh regime's measures for democratization, when people can give a true opinion about the result of those measures. We have not yet reached 'mid-term.' If we push it through, we are handing over an excuse for the anti-democratic forces within the ruling party to stage a comeback and oppress democratic forces."

More than 10,000 people responded with cheers and applause. The enthusiasm I witnessed during this rally confirmed that the Korean people agreed with our party's solution to the midterm referendum. In contrast, only about 1000 people gathered at the Democratic Party's rally in Onyang, despite the party's concerted effort. Even those who gathered left the rally early, causing it to dissipate willy-nilly.

After these rallies, the desires of the Korean people became clearer. On March 20, President Roh issued a statement that he would delay the midterm referendum, and this political phase came to an end. In the Pyeongmin Party leader meeting that day I declared that our party won this phase.

The ruling and opposition parties gathered often to manage the National Assembly. In this minority ruling and majority opposition party situation, compromise was the best policy. This meant negotiation and yielding. Unilateralism and self-righteousness had no place in our work. Occasionally, the ruling party tried to railroad a matter through without asking for the opposition parties' cooperation, and collided with us head-on. In June 1988, junior judges at the Seoul District Court and the Family Court appealed for renovation of the administration's personnel management. Junior judges argued for "the recovery of people's trust in the judicial branch of the government." Chief Justice of the Supreme Court Kim Yong-cheol resigned because of this appeal.

President Roh tentatively decided that Justice of the Supreme Court Chung Ki-Seung would be his successor and requested the National Assembly's approval. The opposition parties decided to reject this appointment because we did not think Mr. Jeong's character was suited to the independent nature of the judiciary branch. The fact that all three opposition parties agreed to reject him illustrated that it was clearly a problematic appointment. President Roh then recommended Mr. Lee Il-kyu, whom the opposition parties gladly approved. Even though the opposition was the majority, we could not make decisions unilaterally. We had to faithfully follow the people's opinion because we shared responsibility for the country's governance.

As all the laws were handled according to the agreement between the ruling and opposition parties, our term's National Assembly made mostly unanimous decisions. Both the ruling and the opposition parties frequently held a five-man conference (including the president and party president of the ruling party and three opposition party presidents) to ensure the smooth management of the National Assembly.

The Pyeongmin Party laid out the Family Law Reform Bill. I had long argued that family law should be reformed to improve women's rights. According to the existing law, wives didn't have the right to inherit their husbands' property. Daughters were discriminated against as well. Although the Constitution guaranteed equality between the sexes, in reality women were discriminated against—both at home and in society. Family law reform was a long-cherished wish of Korean women's organizations. In particular, Madam Lee Tai-young was very passionate about this matter, but the reform bill had been repeatedly repealed or postponed.

I believe I was unusually interested in gender equality. My wife and I installed a nameplate inscribed with both of our names onto the entrance column of our house, not because my wife wanted to, but because *I* wanted to. Of course, my women's movement activist wife influenced me. In some sense, I probably should have felt pressure from it. However, my belief in gender equality originated from my nature, as I believed God's will was a society without discrimination.

In the spring of 1989, I argued for the necessity of family law reform and requested other parties' cooperation. I persuaded each party president, listing the wrongs against women that had continued even after the liberation of our country. "Nowhere in the world do you see this kind of discrimination," I argued. "We should be ashamed of Korea's current family law and the elements of it that violate the Constitution."

Only Park Jyun-kyu, the president of the ruling party, nodded. President Roh and Presidents Kim Young-sam and Kim Jong-pil disagreed. Family law reform was postponed again, pushed aside in favor of other pressing matters.

However, I didn't forget about it. I brought it up again in the five-man conference on December 15. The Pyeongmin Party demanded the revival of a local autonomy system and family law reform in exchange for the ruling party's closure of the fifth republic's corruption cleanup within the year. Surprisingly, President Roh responded positively, suggesting his willingness to consider negotiating. Since the president agreed to the largest opposition party's proposal, nobody dared disagree. We established a subcommittee in the National Assembly and began investigation.

Because the Pyeongmin Party proposed it, our party member chaired the subcommittee. However, subcommittee chair Assemblyman Hong Young-gi was against the reform, so the subcommittee activities did not make any progress. I called him and, smiling, asked, "How about changing the subcommittee chair to another assemblyman?"

"Please do," he responded. "I really don't like working on this matter."

I asked my chief of staff Assemblyman Cho Seung-hyeong to take on the role, but he was also reluctant. "Although I am against the family law reform, I will try because you want it," he said.

I was surprised to hear this. Many assemblymen were against family law reform. The bill never would have passed if it were voted on through secret ballots. We ran into a wall on the last day of the ordinary session of the National Assembly. Breaking the agreement, the ruling party members refused to vote. I called the Blue House and protested to the president. "I don't know what to do because the ruling party members refused to vote after we pursued the bill together, based on the agreement with you," I said.

President Roh immediately ordered the ruling party leaders to cooperate on voting, and the reform bill barely managed to pass. I felt moved. After congratulating House Leader Kim Young-bae, I said, "Mr. Kim, let's have our party members, if not the other party members, applaud when the passing of the bill is announced."

After going around the Assembly seats, House Leader Kim returned and told me, "They say, 'What is there to applaud for after losing all the rights of men?'"

Nevertheless, passing the Family Law Reform Bill was a new milestone in the history of women's rights expansion. A new world opened up for women, in which mothers were allowed to enjoy the same rights as fathers, and daughters the same as sons.

I cannot help but mention the public security phase under the Roh regime. During his presidential election campaign, President Roh declared, "I'll open up the era of great ordinary men." After his inauguration, he used this as his government's slogan and listed democratic harmony, balanced development, and unification and prosperity as policy themes. The Roh government had to carry out the so-called June 29 spirit. However, realistically, this was impossible. Although the president was elected through direct election, he was rooted in the military. Additionally, when the general election brought about the minority ruling party and the majority opposition parties, the regime must have thought of taking control of the situation by fostering a public security phase. It targeted me, the president of the largest opposition party.

In the spring of 1989, Reverend Moon Ik-hwan visited Pyongyang by way of Tokyo, Japan. This incident caused a fuss, and the public security phase followed. This turn of events began on March 25 with Reverend Moon's visit to the North with Democratic Party member Yu Won-ho and Korean Japanese journalist Cheong Kyong-mo. In the North, he met with President Kim Il-sung and Peaceful Reunification of Fatherland Committee Chairman Ho Dam. On April 2, he held a press conference at the People's Palace of Culture.

Reverend Moon met with me before his visit to the North on March 16. Reverend Moon, who came with his younger brother senior vice president of the Pyeongmin Party Moon Dong-hwan, abruptly told me that he was visiting North Korea. He said that there was no reason why he could not go after President Roh's July 7 Declaration. The Special Presidential Declaration for the Self-respect and Prosperity of the Korean Nation essentially regarded North Korea not as an antagonistic enemy for competition and confrontation, but as a partner in reunification. He presented six practical plans for the execution of this declaration. The first of these plans was "Interchange between South and North Koreans and free visit to both Koreas by Koreans abroad." Reverend Moon used this as the reason why there should not be a problem with his visit to North Korea.

"Did you get permission from the government?" I asked him.
"No," he answered.
"Then, it will be illegal," I pointed out. "What are you thinking, sir?"
"After the July 7 Declaration, what would they do to me?"

I realized this was a grave situation. I sat up straight and responded, "If you don't get permission from the authorities, three problems will occur. First, you'll be arrested as soon as you return. Second, the democratic forces will be oppressed. Third, the democratization movement will be dampened. You cannot successfully go to the North without the people's support. If you visit without permission, if other people all do the same thing, what will happen in this country? How will you handle the chaos? And, what will people think?"

Nevertheless, Reverend Moon insisted that he had to visit the North. He was a truly innocent person, courageous and never afraid of hardship. However, he was such an idealist that he sometimes couldn't see reality. I could not categorically condemn his decision. He was probably able to put what he believed to be right into action only because he had such a pure soul. Assemblyman Moon Dong-hwan and I were of the same opinion; however, Reverend Moon did not listen to us. I suggested an alternative. "Since you're planning to go via Japan, why don't you request permission at the Korean Embassy in Tokyo?" I said. "I think it would be wise for Assemblymen Moon Dong-hwan to go and see Minister of the Board of National Unification Lee Hong-koo for permission."

Reverend Moon agreed, but we could all clearly foresee that the Korean government would not give him permission. What should he do then? We could not reach a conclusion.

The Sunday after our talk, I heard on the news that Reverend Moon had visited the North and met with President Kim Il-sung. Unaware of what I was doing, I moaned. I rushed to check and found out that Reverend Moon hadn't even let the Korean Embassy in Japan know. The government immediately established the National Security Joint Investigation Headquarters as if it had been waiting for this moment, and arrested Reverend Moon as soon as he returned. I issued a statement that read: "It is not right to arrest a democracy movement leader. This is the result of the government not following through with its declaration that the North was not our enemy, but our partner."

Reverend Moon's visit to the North wrought an enormous storm in its aftermath. As I expected, the investigation included civic organizations like the Nationwide Association for Nationalism and Democracy. Its leaders, including Poet Ko Un, were arrested.

The north wind of national security began to blow. The regime abused Reverend Moon's pure passion by coloring it with ideology. Reverend Moon was not a politician, so he could dream a different dream than that of a politician. Although idealists like him can shift the direction of history, they can also create difficult situations. Reverend Moon himself suffered greatly because of the prison sentence, but the democratization movement forces also suffered considerable oppression for a while.

Before long, the Suh Kyung-won Illegal Visit to the North Incident occurred. One day in June, House leader Kim Won-ki reported, "A strange rumor is circulating, sir. They say that Assemblyman Suh Kyung-won has been to North Korea."

"No way," I told him. "Did you hear anything from Assemblyman Suh beforehand?"

"Never, sir," he replied. "This is the first time I've heard of it."

"Then, it's probably not true."

Although I couldn't be sure, I thought this must have been a groundless rumor, and ignored it. A few days later, a white-faced House Leader Kim exclaimed, "What a disaster, sir! I met Assemblyman Suh Kyung-won and he told me he has been to North Korea."

Utterly taken aback, I just stared at House Leader Kim's face. I could not believe that Mr. Suh had been to North Korea without discussing it with party leaders. I told House Leader Kim to report this to the authorities and discuss measures to save the situation. Our party leaders took

Assemblyman Suh to ANSP Director Park Seh-jik and had him confess his visit to North Korea. He also confessed that he had received money from North Korea. Director Pak thanked our party leaders for the voluntary confession, and said that he would handle it without arresting Assemblyman Suh since he was serving a term as national assemblyman. He also sent his thanks to me.

A few days later, the incident was revealed. The national security authorities held a press conference for Assemblyman Suh Kyung-won's Illicit Visit to the North Incident on June 27. Assemblyman Suh was immediately arrested. Mr. Park Seh-jik was dismissed from his directorship of ANSP and Seo Dong-kwon took the helm. Director Seo seized the incident as a national security issue. Assemblyman Suh was tortured ruthlessly at the ANSP; he was refused sleep and made to stand day and night.

They tortured him so that they could fabricate my connection to his actions. On July 25, the prosecution and ANSP publicized groundless, fabricated accusations about me to the media. They claimed that I ordered Assemblyman Suh to go, offered to pay a portion of his travel costs, and received about $10,000 from the North. They meant to kill off my political career.

On August 3, the national security prosecution declared that they would take me into custody, and an unprecedented operation to take the president of the opposition party into custody followed. I was dragged out of my office in Yeouido by force. Many citizens and party members tried to stop my arrest, but I told them not to. I decided to go in a dignified manner and scold them for their base actions. On my way from Yeouido, party members and my supporters laid down on the street to block my car from advancing. I got down from the car and pleaded with them to open the road, telling them that I was on my way to tell the truth.

I was questioned overnight at the Downtown Seoul Police Station. Although they had loudly advertised the "delivery of my autographed letter," they didn't even ask me about it. The accusation against me was just "non-notification." They accused me of knowing about Assemblyman Suh's visit to North Korea for two months without notifying the authorities. However, even this proved groundless, as Assemblyman Suh stated in court that he had confessed under duress following severe torture. Besides, where else on earth but Korea is "non-notification" a crime? It was truly shameful.

Investigators could not present any evidence. All of them simply asked me, "Assemblyman Suh said so-and-so. Is this true?" So I demanded a face-to-face questioning with Assemblyman Suh. "Let me see him. You'll know everything then," I promised.

My demand was not accepted. The investigation dragged on with no substance whatsoever. After questioning, I was allowed to leave the police station at 3:00 a.m. the next morning. The Pyeongmin Party leaders, members, and citizens were outside the police station, surrounding the building. They cheered and applauded. It was a cry of condemnation of the national security state.

Although they charged me, they could not try me because they didn't have a single shred of evidence. The prosecution then pleaded with me to handle their plight generously. They asked me to cooperate with them to nullify their charge. It was truly laughable. In the end, the Suh Kyung-won Illicit Visit to North Korea Incident dissipated without any clear closure.

I thought about President Roh again at this juncture. After the Pyeongmin Party and I had cooperated with him during the difficult mid-term referendum phase, he had stabbed us in the back. The national security phase originated from their ridiculous intention to oppress democratic forces and destroy both the Pyeongmin Party and myself. Additionally, President Roh revealed the false nature of his July 7 Declaration by blocking various unification discussions that came about during that time.

Three days after the Assemblyman Suh Kyung-won Incident, Hankuk University of Foreign Studies student Lim Su-kyung attended the World Festival of Youth and Students in Pyongyang on behalf of the Jeondaehyeop (Nationwide University Student Representative Council). This was an incident of enormous significance that drew attention from not only domestic but also foreign media. Soon after, the people allegedly involved in this incident were arrested. The political world froze. The Pyeongmin Party held the National Rally for the Crushing of the National Security Governance in Boramae Park in Seoul on August 8. More than 300,000 people from all over the country gathered despite the midsummer heat.

While the Korean regime was turning the clock back, the rest of the world was changing rapidly. On November 9, 1989, the Berlin Wall finally collapsed, and German reunification was historically achieved. On December 3, US President Bush and USSR General Secretary Gorbachev held a summit and officially declared the end of the Cold War. The world was overflowing with waves of reconciliation, but the straw mat of a national security state was spread in Korea again and the regime was dancing on it.

As the president of the largest opposition party, the year 1989 brought me a series of hardships; however, precious opportunities came my way, too. I went on a six-country tour on January 31, 1989, visiting Sweden, Italy, the Vatican, Norway, the Netherlands, and Hungary. Many party colleagues accompanied me on the trip, including Pyeongmin Party Direction Committee Chairman Lee Yong-hee; Assemblymen Heo Gyeong-nam, Kim Bong-wook, Lee Young-kwon, Kim Deuk-soo, Kwon Rho-kap, Yu In-hak, Lee Chan-koo, and Suh Kyung-won; Special Aid for Foreign Affairs Choe Un-sang; Foreign Relations Committee Chairman Lee Kil-jae; Vice Spokesperson Kim Su-il; Assistant Chief of Staff Namkung Jin; Aid Choe Jae-seung; and Central Political Training Institute Vice President Park Moon-soo.

We landed in Stockholm, the capital of Sweden and our first destination, around noon on February 1. The schedule officially began with a dinner hosted by Minister of Foreign Affairs Sten Andersson. I still vividly remember what I said during my dinner speech: "Sweden might not be the strongest country in the world, but it is a great country morally. I would like to learn from the Swedish national treasures like its democratic system."

On the morning of February 2, we visited the grave of late Prime Minister Olof Palme, who was often called the conscience of the world. His grave was located in an ordinary cemetery in Stockholm, and was marked only with a natural stone with his name inscribed on it. It was a very modest monument. His widow Mrs. Lisbet Palme came to the grave and welcomed us. She teared up when she saw me. Prime Minister Palme had tried very hard to save my life. During my exile at Harvard, I met with him often and we talked a lot. I remembered his smile so vividly, and yet here he was lying in a grave.

I then met current Prime Minister Ingvar Carlsson to talk about current affairs. Prime Minister Carlsson was also the president of the ruling Social Democratic Party. I told him that the Pyeongmin Party would like to attend the Socialist International (SI), scheduled in June that year, as an observer. Prime Minister Carlsson was glad and promised me that he would immediately let SI Chairman Willy Brandt know.

That afternoon, I gave a lecture about Korean democratization at the renowned International Institute in Sweden. About 300 people attended the lecture, all of whom appeared to know quite a bit about me. Among the attendees was a student wearing a kimono. "There are many Korean adoptees in Sweden," she said. "What's your opinion about adoption?"

I thought she was Japanese, but it turns out she was a Korean orphan who had been adopted when she was two years old. She was currently a student at Stockholm University.

"As a Korean political leader, I feel very sad about the 8,000 orphans who were adopted in Sweden," I replied. "But, since there are two sides to everything in this world, I hope that you will turn it into an opportunity and embrace two homelands."

I invited about 200 Koreans and Korean adoptees for dinner with me while I was there. All of the adoptees seemed to have grown up well, which made me even more emotional. I talked with them late into the night.

The next day, I visited Uppsala, one of the oldest university towns in the world. The university president acted as my tour guide. The university looked very old and was so enormous that we felt overwhelmed. We then had a luncheon with thirty other guests, including university professors. During this lunch, an announcement was made that twenty-seven Swedish leaders had recommended me for the Nobel Peace Prize. Many leaders involved in this recommendation were at the luncheon, including political, religious, and academic field leaders like Uppsala Governor Hans Allen and Archbishop Trem.

Although I felt a bit awkward to hear the news directly from those who recommended me, I was deeply moved. They believed that I deserved this honor because I had "dedicated [my] life to democratization with unyielding will and passion." Everyone there cheered and congratulated me.

My next destination was Italy. In Rome, I met Minister of Foreign Affairs and five-time Former Prime Minister Giulio Andreotti. The elderly statesman confided in me, "We're considering establishing a trade representative in North Korea. What do you think of that as president of the opposition party in South Korea?"

"I am for it, of course," I responded. "A trade representative will be very useful for inducing change in North Korea. Please do. But it would be good to pursue it after discussing it with the South Korean government."

"All right. You're a politician," he responded, smiling.

I visited the Vatican and was granted an audience with Pope John Paul II. While my wife and I waited for him in the reception room, the pope asked us to come to his office, which was apparently a special consideration for us. I still cannot forget the moment when I first saw his face. *To think that a human being's face could look that clear!* I thought.

In Catholicism, the pope is the agent of God. Pope John Paul II looked the role. In a low voice, the pope said to me, "I know very well how much you sacrificed for your country's democracy. I'm honored to meet with you today. I am also happy that the Korean church has been growing so exemplarily."

The pope was humble and kind. As a Catholic named Thomas More, I felt extremely honored. The pope gave me a cross. I thanked him for that and for the signed letter that he had sent to me following my death sentence.

The pope smiled gently again. When the new military junta had sentenced me to capital punishment, the pope sent the Vatican's ambassador to the Blue House three times to deliver the message that he was against the execution. After the confirmation of my death sentence, the pope sent a letter to President Chun Doo-hwan, wherein he requested I receive a commuted sentence. "I appeal to you on purely humanitarian grounds for an act of clemency," he wrote.

When my sentence was commuted to a life sentence, the pope sent another letter to President Chun to thank him for commuting the sentence. "I wish to assure you of my warm appreciation for the promptness with which the case was given consideration," he wrote. I was deeply indebted to this great man.

I then met Italian Acting President Giovanni Spadolini. Surprisingly, he belonged to the Republican Party, a minority party. Italy had nine parties in its assembly, five of which formed a coalition cabinet around the largest party, the Christian Democratic Party. I learned a lot of lessons from Italian politics, where conservatives and progressives coexisted and assimilated each other's arguments. I also thought that we should learn from the Italian economy, where they protect and nurture small- and mid-sized businesses.

My schedule in the Netherlands was very tight. I met and talked with Prime Minister R. Lubbers, Speaker of the House of Representatives Doman, and Minister of Foreign Affairs Hans Vandenbroke. We also visited Anne Frank's house. On the second floor was the attic behind the bookcase where Anne hid from the Nazis. I read *Anne Frank's Diary* in prison and marveled at all of the human emotions that she experienced in that small space and, also, how the war pervaded everything in it.

My visit to Hungary was the first by a South Korean politician. About ten days before my visit, Korea and Hungary had forged a friendly relationship. I was surprised to see Korean-speaking merchants downtown. I visited President Bruno Straub and the two of us had a pleasant chat. As the first non-Communist party member to be elected in a communist country, he was a symbolic figure of the Hungarian open-door policy. I could feel the dynamic movement of a small but strong country, a country that was leaping forward after shrugging off the heavy coat of communism.

On the day I returned to Korea after my seventeen-day trip to Europe, I went to human rights activist and thinker Mr. Ham Sok-hon's mortuary. Mr. Ham used to come to demonstrations, white hair and whiskers fluttering, gracefully wearing his traditional coat and shoes. He was the co-chair of the 1974 National Congress for the Recovery of Democracy with me and also participated in the 1976 March 1 Declaration for Democracy and National Salvation Event. He was a thinker in action who fought injustices like the three-term constitutional amendment head-on. He founded the magazine *Sound of a Seed* to inspire national consciousness. His passion for peace never cooled until the day he died. He was also a historian who understood ordinary people—whom he called seeds—to be the agents and protagonists of Korean history. I can still see him, an all-white presence from head to toe.

The high-principled Former West German Chancellor Willy Brandt visited Korea at the end of October. Germans revere him as the father of German unification. I held a dinner reception for him at Walker Hill on November 9. He had passionately tried to save me, both when I was kidnapped by the Park Chung-hee regime and when I was sentenced to capital punishment by the new junta. I continued to be indebted to him. I wondered how we could sympathize with one other so naturally from so far away.

When I asked him when he expected the reunification of Germany would occur, the former chancellor said that it would take time. It was then that we suddenly received the news of the fall of the Berlin Wall. It all happened so abruptly and unexpectedly that even the seasoned statesman Willy Brandt could not predict it. He rushed back to Germany.

A Three-party Merger, Coup d'État Against the Korean People (1990–1992)

At 10:00 a.m. on January 22, 1990, President Roh Tae-woo and two opposition party presidents, Mr. Kim Young-sam and Mr. Kim Jong-pil, held an urgent press conference at the Blue House. With the two party presidents on either side of him, President Roh read a joint declaration. "The Minjeong, Democratic, and Republican Parties have tried to make their best efforts for our country. However, today's reality demands a more solid leading political force and the unification of the people's power. All nationalist and democratic forces in our country should now be united. In order to respond to this reality, we have decided to give birth to a grand national political party through the unity of middle-of-the-road democratic forces and to establish a new political order on the foundation of political stability."

After this declaration of a three-party merger, the new political party Minja (Democratic Freedom) Party held a convention on February 9. At the convention, President Roh Tae-woo was elected the president, Mr. Kim Young-sam was elected the supreme council president, and Mr. Kim Jong-pil and Mr. Park Tae-joon were elected supreme council members. As a result, the minority ruling party and majority opposition parties phase evaporated and the ruling party became a dinosaur party, with 221 of the 299 National Assembly seats. The only opposition parties were the Pyeongmin and Democratic Parties, composed of only eight remaining assemblymen. The remaining Democratic Party members who refused to join the merger included Lee Ki-taek, Kim Jung-kil, Roh Moo-hyun, and Kim Gwang-il.

The Blue House called this merger a "glorious revolution for the first time in constitutional history." Roh Tae-woo mentioned a "historical mission," Kim Young-sam "God's will," and Kim Jong-pil "resolution for national salvation." However, this was in fact a coup d'état that betrayed the people's will. A few leaders artificially reversed the political topography that the Korean people had determined through their votes. This merger was immoral because it was done behind closed doors without any procedure to ask for the people's opinion. It seemed to me that this was the worst result of the vague compromise of Roh Tae-woo's June 29 Declaration.

I was shocked to learn that Mr. Kim Young-sam had played a central role in this coup d'état, this illicit union. I guess he had his own reasons, but, as one-time comrades in the democracy movement, I still feel sad about this choice of his and how he will be remembered in history. There is no other explanation but that his desire for power was bigger than his desire for democracy. In retrospect, Mr. Kim's situation was very sad. On April 13, 1989, the Democratic Party bribed and bought a candidate during the special election in Donghae. As a result, Democratic Party Secretary General Seo Seok-jai was arrested; rumors that President Kim Young-sam was involved circulated. The public perception of President

Kim Young-sam's ethics was critically damaged, and his political future was threatened.

Now vulnerable to the Roh regime, President Kim Young-sam sent an open signal of courtship toward the regime. During a debate at the Kwanhun Club, President Kim Young-sam, the person who had most strongly condemned election fraud and pressured the midterm referendum, defended the Roh regime without batting an eye. "People elected the president through election, so we have to acknowledge the authenticity of the current government," he said. And, "We cannot unilaterally say whether the presidential system of government or the parliamentary system of government is better." President Kim Young-sam also favored the national security phase in the period that followed the successive visits of Moon Ik-hwan, Suh Kyung-won, and Lim Su-kyung to North Korea.

The Democratic Party continued to struggle. During the special election at the Yeodeungpo-eul electorate on August 18, the Democratic Party candidate won only 18.8 percent of the vote, while Pyeongmin Party candidate Lee Yong-hee won 30 percent. The Democratic Party lost disastrously even in an election where the Pyeongmin Party was still under the negative influence of the national security phase. President Kim Young-sam must have thought that he could not survive in the political arena if he didn't do something drastic, and thus decided to join forces with the ruling party's conspiracy to overthrow the minority ruling and majority opposition parties situation. This is how democracy fighter Kim Young-sam disappeared.

The three-party merger was clearly an illicit union that happened behind closed doors. Although the parties involved wanted to argue that it was a grand association of conservative forces, history will not record it that way. It was an illicit union of anti-democracy and anti-Honam forces.

In fact, President Roh had proposed the merger of our parties to me. Toward the end of 1989, President Roh requested that I remain after a five-man conference at the Blue House to have a word with him. With just the two of us there, he said to me, "President Kim, please stop your suffering. Come with me. You should live more comfortably."

Not understanding, I asked what he meant.

"Let's join our parties together," he answered. "And let's enjoy the good and the bad together. Haven't you had enough hard times?"

I could say nothing at that moment. I just stared at him. I had to think it through. Then I answered, "I opposed the military regime. I opposed the May 17 Coup D'état. How can I join our parties together? We have walked different roads, and we have different political views."

"President Kim, don't be so particular. Please join me to save our country."

"The minority ruling majority opposition parties situation was chosen by the people. Didn't you yourself say that it was God's and the people's will, sir? Merging the Minjeong and Pyeongmin Parties together would be a grave betrayal of the people's will."

President Roh said nothing.

I also pointed out the injustice of merging the ruling and opposition parties together. "I heard a rumor that the three parties were going to merge. That should never happen. Nothing is currently inconvenient within the governance, is it? The Pyeongmin Party has been collaborating across the aisle for the benefit of the nation. Mr. President must know that we have never interfered with the administration. Although the ruling party is the minority, we have been handling everything through consensus. Look at the United States! Even when the opposition party is in majority, there hasn't been a problem in years. In fact, our current situation will be helpful in developing democracy. The Korean people will never support politics without opposition parties. If the Pyeongmin Party unites with the Minjeong Party, a party of completely different character, we'll become trash to Korean people. If the Korean people consider the merger to be a sin and shameful, that will become a lifelong yoke to you, too."

Still, the Roh regime did not cease their efforts for a merger. One day, House Leader Kim Won-ki reported to me after his meeting with the First Minister of State for Political Affairs Pak Chor-eon, then the actual power-holder behind the scenes. "The ruling party said that they would negotiate only with the Pyeongmin Party if we were willing to merge with them," he told me.

"Please say no more. You're soiling my ears," I responded.

Mr. Pak Chor-eon had, in fact, worked hard to improve the relationship between North Korea and the Soviet Union. He visited me multiple times to seek my advice. I thought highly of his efforts to open up a new road. However, in the end, he promoted the worst regional antagonism by isolating the Jeollado region. I suppose Mr. Kim Young-sam wanted to be President Roh's successor and Mr. Kim Jong-pil wanted constitutional amendment incorporating the parliamentary government system. Mr. Kim Young-sam threw away his principles and beliefs, essential virtues of an opposition party leader. By throwing them away, he wanted to assume the position of successor and, in the end, take power. With the three-party merger, the Roh Tae-woo regime threw away the June 29 spirit. It represented a fall into an anti-ethical, anti-democratic, anti-historic, and anti-unification government.

Although the three parties merged, the Minja Party internally collided on just about every issue at hand. Before the merger, Roh Tae-woo, Kim Young-sam, and Kim Jong-pil signed a memorandum that stated: "We will amend the Constitution for the implementation of a parliamentary government system." After this memorandum was leaked, the factions within the Minja Party were bogged down in a whirlpool of power struggles. The former Minjeong and Republican Party factions intended to grab power through the parliamentary government system, while the former Democratic Party faction preferred the current presidential government system and wanted Mr. Kim Young-sam to succeed President Roh Tae-woo.

After the merger the Minja Party began to handle everything unilaterally. First, the Minja Party passed the Bill of Compensation related to the Gwangju Democratization Movement alone, for the first time since the Roh Tae-woo regime came into power. In protest, eighty assemblymen from the Pyeongmin and Democratic Parties (in addition to some independents) submitted their resignation letters to the Speaker of the Assembly. While the National Assembly went into a skid, it was revealed that the ANSP had spied on civilians and national assemblymen from both the ruling and opposition parties. The Minja Party also tried to delay the implementation of a local autonomy system, despite the fact that the bill had passed with the votes of both the ruling and opposition parties. Based on their numbers, the Minja Party began to enforce everything.

I began an indefinite hunger strike at my party building on October 8, 1990, demanding the implementation of a local autonomy system, abandonment of the parliamentary government system scheme, a halt on the ANSP's political spying, and the solution of the people's economic plight. I could no longer passively allow their fraudulent tactics to go on.

I believe that a local autonomy system is essential to democracy and I fought hard for its implementation throughout my entire political career. The local autonomy system was introduced partially during the Rhee Syngman government and fully during the Chang Myon government. It was only after Park Chung-hee took power through the coup d'état that it was abolished. When we met right after the assassination of President Park, Harvard's Professor Reischauer told me: "The foremost task is the implementation of a local autonomy system. Democratization begins with the local autonomy system." I still remember it vividly.

My hunger strike became the eye of the typhoon as opposition party assemblymen resigned. I only drank water, read, and meditated. On the eighth day of my hunger strike, my health deteriorated because of dehydration. I was taken to Severance Hospital, but I refused to eat there too.

Mr. Kim Young-sam came to visit me in the hospital. While there, he said that he had merged with the ruling party for the sake of democracy. It was so preposterous that I could not help retorting, "What democracy do you mean to enact with the people the farthest removed from democracy?"

I tried to persuade him that the local autonomy system was imperative. "You and I both fought for democracy," I reminded him. "So what is democracy? Aren't parliamentary and local autonomy systems the essence of democracy? How can you ignore that just because you merged with the ruling party and became part of a majority party?" Mr. Kim Young-sam agreed with me. He knew well why the local autonomy system is necessary, as he had suffered from election fraud during his long opposition party life.

Finally, the Roh government promised to implement a local autonomy system and the age of local autonomy resumed after a thirty-six-year absence. The local assembly election was scheduled for early 1991, and the election for the local government was set for June 1994, according to the Local Autonomy Law. I ceased my thirteen-day hunger strike upon receiving this news on October 20. A hunger strike is a scary thing, and I suffered physically for some time in its aftermath.

Our society changed greatly following the introduction of a local autonomy system. Above all, residents became the owners of their own locality. The provision of grassroots democracy helped nurture their sense of sovereignty. The central government could no longer plot unilateral election fraud, and the local government could pursue its own agenda without worrying about the central government. It is thanks to the local autonomy system that local events like the Bull Fight in Cheongdo and the Butterfly Festival in Hampyeong became world-famous and contributed to the local economy. Now the public servants whose terms were guaranteed only through local votes were forced to work in their constituents' best interests.

A little before the local assembly election on April 9, 1991, the Pyeongmin Party welcomed out-of-office leaders and former opposition party members into its fold and was reborn as the Sinmin (Sinminju yeon-hap; New Democratic Association) Party.

On April 26, Myongji University student Kang Gyeong-dae was murdered by the Skeleton Unit, a plainclothes police unit. The police wielded steel pipes at random during a demonstration for democracy. As I see it, once they began murdering students, the police were no longer the police. I attended the funeral service for Mr. Kang on May 24, and during my memorial address declared that I would continue to fight against anti-democratic dictatorship. After the three-party merger, the Sinmin Party was the only political force resisting the brutal atrocities of the regime. After the funeral ceremony, I marched at the forefront of the mourners and pallbearers. The police blocked the funeral procession as we headed to the Sinchon rotary at the Namgajwa-dong intersection. During our confrontation, a teargas bomb exploded right above my head. It was so painful that I could not even breathe for a while and had to be carried to my house in Donggyo-dong.

On August 17, I proposed a merger with the Democratic Party. Although our two parties' Assembly seat numbers were radically different (the Sinmin Party held sixty-seven, while the Democratic Party held eight), I proposed an equal merger that included co-presidency. Thanks to our radical concession, the merger came to fruition on September 16, with the Sinmin and Democratic Parties being reborn as the Democratic Party. Mr. Lee Ki-taek and I became co-presidents. The supreme committee members included Lee Oo-chung, Park Young-sook, Park Young-rok, and Huh Kyung-man from the former Sinmin Party, and Chough Soon-hyung, Kim Hyeon-gyu, Lee Bu-young, and Mok Yo-sang from the former Democratic Party. Mr. Kim Won-ki was selected as Secretary General, Mr. Kim Jung-kil house leader, Mr. Yoo Joon-sang policy committee president, and Mr. Roh Moo-hyun spokesperson.

Early the morning of September 17, the UN General Assembly admitted both South and North Korea for membership. North Korea became the 160th and South Korea the 161st member countries.

With the opposition party merger process complete, I decided to visit the Soviet Union and attend the UN General Assembly on a diplomatic visit. I also planned to visit Poland and Germany.

The Soviet Union was in the midst of being divided when I arrived on September 17. The three Baltic states (Lithuania, Latvia, and Estonia) had just become independent. Every day was a historic day.

I met with the former Soviet minister of foreign affairs and the main player in Perestroika, Eduard Shevardnadze, and we exchanged our thoughts on international affairs, including the future of the Soviet Union and the change in the Eastern Bloc. Upon invitation, I delivered a lecture at Moscow State University. In summary, I said: "For the 150 years since the publication of Karl Marx's 'Communist Manifesto' in 1848, the world has been a place of fierce competition and struggle between capitalism and socialism. Now, that history of struggle is over. The old Soviet Union, the suzerain state of socialism, and the Eastern Bloc have collapsed and the few remaining communist countries are on the road away from it.

"Many people want to say that capitalism won and socialism lost. My thoughts are different, though. I think that the communist countries collapsed not because they adopted socialism, but because they did not adopt democracy. It is not socialism, but the *dictatorial* socialism that did not adopt democracy that failed.

"Many capitalist countries collapsed—Nazi Germany and militarist Japan are good examples. They were also countries that did not adopt democracy, but held onto dictatorial capitalism.

"What matters is democracy. The countries that adopted democracy are all successful, whether they subscribe to capitalism or socialism. Countries in the Western Bloc adopted either capitalism or democratic socialism and they are both successful. So, why do countries with democracy succeed while those without it fail? The reason is clear. With democracy, people's criticisms and demands are delivered to the government. If that criticism is not accepted or if their demands are not met, then people change the government through election. Political feedback systems work smoothly. However, under dictatorship, the will comes from the top down only—it never goes back up. And there is no way to change the regime.

"Therefore, people will develop the habit of obedience in front of the regime and defiance behind it. After cheering for the communist party and its leaders to their faces, they don't really work hard or manufacture good products behind the scenes. These countries cannot help but fail in international competition. This vicious cycle brings about the collapse of the economy. In the end, the omnipotent communist regime collapsed without even firing a shot, despite its powerful military and secret police.

"The twentieth century saw not capitalist victory over socialism, but democratic victory over dictatorship."

My lecture seemed to move the Russian audience. Perhaps those who accepted the collapse of the communist party simply as the decline of socialism were shocked. Moscow State University president Dr. Anatoli Logunov told me that he was stirred by my insight. He awarded me with an honorary professorship at Moscow State University and frequently asked me to come give lectures. Later, I received an official invitation from the university to lecture for a month every year while residing at its guesthouse. Three months after my visit, the Soviet Union disappeared into history.

On September 22, I flew to New York. As I had argued for the joint membership of South and North Korea in the UN during the 1971 presidential election campaign, I was deeply moved by the recent realization of my proposal. I stopped for a while and watched the South and North Korean flags fluttering side by side in front of the UN Headquarters. As a member of the celebratory diplomatic mission, I happily attended and watched President Roh Tae-woo's keynote address at the General Assembly.

After a stop in Poland, I visited Germany. I fell speechless in front of the Berlin Wall, now nothing more than a relic from the division era. I saw "Our Hope is Reunification" written in Korean on a corner of the Berlin Wall. It must have been written by a Korean either living or traveling in Germany. The idea that we were the final remaining divided country made my chest feel hot and painful.

I met two men who I will never forget: Former Chancellor Willy Brandt and the first unified German President Von Weizsäcker. Knowing that I suffered from a leg injury, Mr. Brandt prepared a high and hard chair instead of a sofa for me. After being criticized for being authoritarian in Korea because I sat on a higher chair due to my leg injury, I was deeply moved by this careful consideration abroad. This would be my last meeting with Mr. Brandt, who passed away a year later. I sent my wife and second son to attend the funeral. I can still see his intellectual appearance in my mind.

I met Mr. Von Weizsäcker, the hero of German unification, at the presidential palace. He brought in teacups and a coffee pot, and poured my coffee himself. Although he was an aristocratic descendent and the current president, he was humble in every way, which I envied. I asked him about the details of the German unification process. In particular, I asked how hard it was to get foreign governments on board with German unification. He said it was not easy, but also said: "We have to decide our fate. Who can interfere with that?" He also remarked that unification should be achieved through the nation's independent abilities. He showed interest in my three-step reunification plan and said he fully supported it.

I also met Minister of Foreign Affairs Hans-Dietrich Genscher, and asked him about the problems Germany was facing now that it was unified. "The difference in living standards between the two Germanys was remarkable," he answered. "Also, both Germanys had been different countries in every aspect of life—politics, economy, society, and culture. In fact, two systems are currently coexisting, and the biggest challenge is to overcome this difference."

While divided, West and East Germany had various interchanges for seventeen years. Also, West Germany spent a long time preparing for the unification. Still, there was an enormous difference to be bridged. As the communist country thoroughly closed off their society and gave false information to the outside world, the free world did not know their reality. I wondered how we could reunite with North Korea, a society even more closed than East Germany.

The fourteenth general election was set for March 24, 1992. It was supposed to be a confrontation between the ruling Minja Party and the opposition Democratic Party. As soon as the New Year began, however, Mr. Chung Ju-yung, the Hyundai Corporation founder and financial field elder, organized the Tongil Kukmin Party (also known as the Kukmin Party), thus throwing down a gauntlet. At the beginning-of-the-year press conference, President Roh Tae-woo declared that the Minja Party would fight for the general election under the leadership of Supreme Committee President Kim Young-sam. This remark signaled that President Roh would nominate Mr. Kim Young-sam as the Minja Party presidential candidate.

The Minja Party solidly lost the March 24 general election, reducing their number of seats from 219 to 149 (116 from local electorates and 33 from national constituents). In contrast, the Democratic Party increased its number of assembly seats from sixty-three to ninety-seven (seventy-five from local electorates and twenty-two from national constituents). The newly minted Kukmin Party won thirty-one seats. The Korean people punished the Minja Party for their three-party merger by delivering this crushing defeat.

I don't think that the late Mr. Chung Ju-yung should have attempted to enter the political arena. I met and spoke with him many times, and I got the impression that he took politics too lightly. On his canvassing tour, he showered all kinds of promises on voters, not to mention spending an enormous sum of money to support the funding of his party. Although it may appear that money can buy everything, there are, in fact, many things that can't be bought. In the end, he failed as a politician.

On May 5, I went to Los Angeles to console those Koreans in America who had suffered greatly during the Los Angeles riots. Although the riots were provoked by racial conflicts between whites and African-Americans, the Koreans still suffered from it. Together with the Investigation Mission—consisting of twelve people, including Assemblymen Chung Dai-chul and Lee Bu-young—I looked around Koreatown and other places. We met Los Angeles Mayor Tom Bradley and urged active measures. I met Democratic Party presidential candidate Bill Clinton for the first time at LA City Hall and asked him to show interest in the Koreans. We visited the mortuary of Mr. Lee Jae Sung, who died in his efforts to defend Koreatown.

During my exile in the US, I had taken every opportunity I could to urge Korean-Americans to live harmoniously with other Americans. In particular, I mentioned that Koreans who sold merchandise in black communities should not socialize only with whites. I also pointed out that, as conscientious members of a minority that was discriminated against, we should not discriminate against African-Americans. My biggest worry became reality in the LA riots. I knew, of course, that many respectable Koreans did not discriminate against African-Americans. It was truly unfortunate that Koreatown became another minority's target.

On May 25, the Democratic Party held its first annual national convention and nomination event at the Second Gymnasium in Seoul Olympic Park. Following a free competition, I was nominated as the presidential candidate for the third time in my career. In my acceptance speech, I presented my vision for our country, such as politics of grand harmony, economic justice, the achievement of the first step of reunification according to my federation of republic system proposal, and our continued evolution into an ethically advanced country. I pledged victory for our party.

President Roh Tae-woo stepped down as Minja Party president on August 25, saying that he wanted to manage the presidential election from a neutral position. Mr. Kim Young-sam became president and was nominated as their presidential candidate. Thus, the age of Roh Tae-woo came to a close and all of the power in the ruling party was handed over to Mr. Kim Young-sam.

As the successor of the military regime, President Roh Tae-woo's achievements included hosting a successful Olympics and normalizing South Korean relations with communist countries like the Soviet Union and China. The so-called Northern Diplomacy was clearly his achievement. I also think that he deserves credit for attempting to improve our relationship with North Korea through the July 7 Declaration. However, it is truly regrettable that he tried to follow in the footsteps of the military regime after the initial stage of his regime. If he had continued to take care of our country as modestly as he did in the beginning, Korean politics would have advanced and he would have been deeply appreciated by later generations. His plot to reintroduce majority-power-based politics through a three-party merger was his biggest mistake.

On September 6, I visited Russia, rather than the Soviet Union. There I gave a lecture entitled "The New World Order and the Relationship Between Korea and Russia" at Moscow State University. The next day, I received a Ph.D. from the Diplomatic Academy of Russia under the Ministry of Foreign Affairs; my dissertation was entitled "On the Principles of Birth and Development of Democracy in Korean Society." As I was the first Korean Ph.D. recipient at the Diplomatic Academy of Russia, it became a news item both domestically and abroad.

Receiving a Ph.D. meant a lot to me since I had a sort of "university complex." I believe I overcame this complex to a degree during the sixth term National Assembly. I belonged to the Finance and Economy Committee, which was composed of prominent personalities, all of whom had Ph.D.s or were former cabinet members. I worried about whether or not I could do a proper job as a member of that committee. I studied and prepared hard. If I felt I was not ready or confident about my ability to handle a matter, I did not attend or speak at the meeting. When criticized, I always tried to get to the core of the matter and present clear alternatives. This was, indeed, the principle that governed my entire political life.

Not only Finance and Economy Committee members, but also the Korean people and media paid attention to how hard I studied. I ended up chairing the committee for a while. Nobody thought that I was unfit for the job. I was recognized not because of my education, but because of my ability. When I was the chair of that committee, Dr. Yu Chin-o, whom people often called the most outstanding genius Seoul National University ever produced, was our party president. Upon watching me work to establish our party policies, President Yu praised and encouraged me many times. His encouragement was a great help for me in overcoming my "university complex."

Instead of being depressed because I did not go to college, I tried to transcend it through self-development. I still wanted to get a Ph.D. In the end, I succeeded in achieving my dream by receiving not an honorary Ph.D. but a *real* Ph.D. after submitting a written dissertation and passing an oral examination at the Diplomatic Academy of Russia.

REGIONAL ANTAGONISM AND MEDIA PREJUDICE
(1990–1992)

I have suffered from—and struggled to overcome—regional antagonism and media prejudice all my life. Regional antagonism held me down, and the media blocked my way forward. Let me turn back the clock a little to demonstrate some examples of this.

On March 3, 1989, a fight dubbed the Cho-Pyeong Incident broke out between the Pyeongmin Party and *Chosun Ilbo* newspaper. It began with an article entitled "A Report on the Pyeongmin Party President Kim Dae-jung's European Tour" in the *Weekly Chosun*.

Its subtitle, "Nods to Both Leftists and Rightists, Accompanying Assemblymen Full of Unseemly Sights," was inauspicious. This kind of fabricated story can only result from a hidden agenda. Although it's unpleasant to even think about it, let's take a closer look at this incident.

The reporter's prejudice was prominent throughout the entire article, but the most problematic parts were the following:

> President Kim insisted on not taking the first class seat reserved for him, but sat in an economy seat with the accompanying reporters. After witnessing this, a reporter murmured, "President Kim's endless political gesture ..."
>
> He tried not to miss anti-Japanese martyrs' and Korean War veterans' memorials and ferociously scolded the spokesperson if a TV camera did not follow him ...

He also reported that assemblymen showed disgraceful conduct by "walking around the airplane barefoot, addressing the pope by saying 'Hey,' and asking a foreigner's wife, 'Do you like so-and-so?'" The reporter even turned a very insulting personal opinion—that he felt a "sense of shame for electing characters of such poor quality as assemblymen"—into an article.

At the party leadership meeting on March 3, I suggested that we confront the *Weekly Chosun* article. A sham of an article destroying the people's trust in politicians had been building up for decades. I found it regrettable that no one dared punish a malicious medium that fabricated such a slanderous article, although we knew well that the *Chosun Ilbo* was behind it all.

As I was resolute in taking the responsibility for this fight, the Pyeongmin Party established the Committee to Fight the False and Distorted Reporting by the *Chosun Ilbo*. We published "A Statement Addressed to Journalists."

We are not a nonsensical group that finds fault with journalists' sentences and expressions or violates editorial rights. We suspect that you journalists know better than anybody else that Kim Dae-jung and the Pyeongmin Party have suffered the pain from and endured without complaint persistent and cruel blades from the *Chosun Ilbo*.

We intend to fight resolutely and with dignity against the *Chosun Ilbo* on behalf of the Korean people. Who called citizens of Gwangju "mobsters" and who called Mr. Chun Doo-hwan "the great leader of our fatherland?" As clouds can hide the sun briefly, yet cannot hide it forever, it is our firm belief that historical truth takes up the space between the lines of the newspaper, breathes, and is alive.

We immediately lodged a complaint against five people, including the publisher of the *Chosun Ilbo*, for defamation by way of publication at the Seoul District Public Prosecutor's Office. We also ran an ad in daily newspapers with the headline "Dear Korean People! We Can No Longer Tolerate the Tyranny of the *Chosun Ilbo*." The advertisement expressed my most sincere feelings.

Although the *Chosun Ilbo*, condemned for its active role as the "trumpet of dictatorship" during the fifth republic, has run innumerable articles slandering President Kim Dae-jung and the Pyeongmin Party, we have endured with patience and tolerance, and without complaint. During the National Assembly Culture and Communication Committee hearing, Assemblyman Park Seok-moo asked the CEO of the *Chosun Ilbo*, who participated in the National Security Legislative Committee, about his responsibility for the merger and abolition of the media and mass purge of journalists.

At that time, the *Chosun Ilbo* accused Assemblyman Pak of being "a contractor" and its random calumny of our party has been escalating ever since. However, it is not because of a simple defensive instinct that we condemn the *Chosun Ilbo*. It is because the *Chosun Ilbo* serves a small minority of people with vested interests rather than the marginalized and suffering people, and because it has endlessly continued to create theories similar to those of dictatorial forces that we condemn its mass manipulation and journalistic violence at the risk of enormous damages. We lay a complaint against this period of distorted reporting … so that this period of shameful media will not be repeated in our country again.

The *Chosun Ilbo*'s evil effect was serious and ran deep. First, the *Chosun Ilbo* kicked numerous journalists and reporters out onto the street during not only the Yusin period, but also the fifth republic era, and played the role of the trumpet in dictatorship, deceiving the Korean people with crafty theories. Second, the *Chosun Ilbo* served the interests of dictators and *chaebols* rather than those of ordinary people. Third, despite all of these actions, the *Chosun Ilbo* has never expressed regret for its actions, nor has it apologized to Korean people.

The *Chosun Ilbo* fought against us tooth and nail. It ran articles criticizing and denouncing the Pyeongmin Party and myself. After holding an editorial department assembly, they issued the so-called Declaration for the Protection of Freedom of the Press, wherein they claimed: "Having just been reborn out of the oppression of the press during the Yusin and the fifth republic periods, we consider the series of aggressive behaviors the Pyeongmin Party shows toward the *Chosun Ilbo* as a new form of oppression of the press, not unlike that of the dictatorial power of the old age."

This was yet another deceptive action on the part of the *Chosun Ilbo* as their logic hid the fact that the newspaper essentially served as a spokesperson for the government during the Yusin and the fifth republic periods. Many organizations issued statements and comments in support of our party. Journalists who had been fired from the *Chosun Ilbo* scolded them. Following is a passage from the statement issued by the Chosun Free Press Protection Struggle Committee:

> We would like to ask what the *Chosun Ilbo* wrote and said while the Korean nation was suffering under the boots of foreign powers and as democracy was stifled and human rights were violated. "Declaration for the Protection of Freedom of the Press" is not some accessory that a newspaper company can wear for its private interest whenever it's convenient. If the newspaper, which did not write even a line of truthful article when it should have, soils the pages, which should be a public medium for its private interest under the excuse of the protection of freedom of the press, it cannot avoid the Korean people's condemnation.

The National Union of Media Workers' *Eollon nobo* (National Union of Media Workers Newsletter) also scolded the *Chosun Ilbo* in an opinion piece entitled "The *Chosun Ilbo* Should be Reborn." *Gijahyeophoebo* (Korea Journalists Association Newsletter) also ran an article based on their interviews with other reporters who accompanied me on my trip to Europe along with the *Chosun Ilbo* reporters, and confirmed that the *Weekly Chosun* article distorted the facts. Also, representatives from sixteen nationwide college newspapers staged a demonstration in front of the *Chosun Ilbo* building. The Democratization Practice Family Movement Council, National Parents of Arrested Students Council, Democratic Media Movement Council, and *Workers Newspaper* all joined forces in condemning the *Chosun Ilbo*.

This sharp confrontation ended seven months later when the Pyeongmin Party withdrew our complaint on October 17. However, the Cho-Pyeong Incident did not end with this. Although the *Chosun Ilbo* promised to change, they didn't at all. The Pyeongmin Party and I confronted the *Chosun Ilbo* at the risk of their retaliation because we felt that we would forever regret it if we stood idly by in the face of their injustice. When I later became president, I led tax investigations on all of the newspaper companies without exception, and an indictment of corrupt company owners for the same reason. As someone who had worked for justice and conscience all my life, I simply could not stand by and allow injustice to reign.

All regimes want to control the media. The less authentic a regime is, the more dependent it is on propaganda. The Media Guidelines created under the fifth republic are an example of this. The military junta that took power through a coup d'état merged and abolished media organizations in November 1980, and legislated the Basic Press Law in order to control the media. Accustomed to the everyday censorship they had enjoyed under martial law, they created a new organization to control the media. They accomplished this through a newly minted organization known as the Propaganda Control Office under the Ministry of Culture and Public Relations, which created daily media control guidelines and sent them to media companies. The Propaganda Control Office did not have the real power, however—the Blue House Secretary Office for State Affairs made all of the decisions.

These media guidelines determined whether or not certain matters should be reported on. They arranged categories for reporting allowances, which included "absolutely not allowed," "not allowed," and "allowed." The established media faithfully followed these guidelines. The size and weight of articles was also decided at the Blue House, rather than at newspaper editorial desks. The Blue House even went so far as to designate which page an article should go on. Furthermore, the guidelines determined the direction and emphasis of an article. Not a single media company or journalist ever revealed or protested these guidelines while it was happening.

Later on, though, several courageous reporters eventually reported these media guidelines. Reporters Kim Tae-hong, Shin hong-bum, and Kim Joo-eun published an article in the monthly magazine *Mal* (Words), where they revealed the media guidelines from October 1985 to August 1986, arranged by date. Although this practice had been vaguely presumed over the years, people were still extremely shocked by the thoroughness of the government's control of the media and found it absurd that other journalists had kept silent about this atrocious operation.

The media guidelines continued as long as they did because journalists actively cooperated with it. Their prejudicial, slanderous reporting of me was another offshoot of this. The powers that be fabricated my image as they pleased and delivered it to the media. I suspect that their customary practice of "Kill Kim Dae-jung" could have congealed into the practice of the media's voluntary antagonism of me. I believe that, even now, it is not too late for the media to apologize to the Korean people and their readers for cooperating with Japan and the dictatorial regimes, for hiding the truth through their distorted reporting.

The *Hangyoreh* newspaper was founded on May 15, 1988. Journalists fired during the dictatorial period led this foundation, and it depended entirely on public funding. I participated in it, too, as a stockholder. For the first time, a major daily newspaper adopted horizontal typesetting. I was able to trust *Hangyoreh* because conscientious journalists professed its mission to be truthful reporting in pursuit of democracy and reunification. I deeply inhaled the smell of fresh ink when I opened the first newspaper off of the rotary press along with founding president Mr. Song Kun-ho. The launch of this people's newspaper was a marker event in media history.

I'd also like to mention the matter of regional antagonism. Whenever the opportunity presented itself, I argued that we had to wipe out regional antagonism as it could be the ruin of our country. I was the biggest victim of regional antagonism in modern Korean history; this is a fact that I do not believe anybody can deny. Although I continued to denounce those who provoked regional antagonism, the situation did not improve ... it just got worse. I tried to find various ways to fight it.

In the fall of 1990, there was a special election in the Yeonggwang and Hampyeong electorate in the Jeolla region, arrested assemblyman Suh Kyung-won's electorate. I wanted to nominate a candidate from the Gyeongsang region in order to show my will to dissolve regional antagonism. I felt that this could be a meaningful experiment, even if our party ended up losing a seat. I met General Director of YMCA Kang Moon-kyu, a Gyeongsang native, and urged for his candidacy. He responded by laughing, believing that it was an absurd idea. In the end, we nominated Yeungnam University Professor Lee Soo-in. Professor Lee was a righteous character with strong ties with out-of-office movement leaders. Unfortunately, people in the electorate resisted more strongly than I had anticipated. Despite the fact that I had not quite recovered from the aftereffect of my hunger strike at that point, I went to the electorate to stump for Candidate Lee. The ruling party candidate attacked our party every day, asking, "Why send a Gyeongsang person to Jeolla-do? Do they mean that we don't have a person in Yeonggwang and Hampyeong?"

When I met twenty pastors at a coffee shop in downtown Hampyeong, they also complained about the nomination. "How could you bring someone we don't know at all?" they asked incredulously. "What do you think of us?"

After listening to their complaints, I responded: "God considers everyone in the world to be His children. How could you who spread the word of God say something like this, dividing the people from Gyeongsang and Jeolla? I can, of course, understand your concerns because this is the Jeolla electorate, but please keep an eye on the stump speech I'm giving today in Yeonggwang, not here in Hampyeong. Why don't you make a decision after watching the audience's response there? If the audience supports me, you support me too. If they are not excited, then I'll withdraw our nomination."

About 20,000 people were waiting to enthusiastically welcome us in Yeonggwang. I explained why we nominated a candidate from Gyeongsang. "We dream of accomplishing a democratic society," I spoke. "But the biggest hurdle on our way to democracy is none other than regional antagonism. We're squabbling in a small area while neglecting a great cause. We have to stop it. It is not a big deal for the Pyeongmin Party to lose or win a seat here. If you elect a candidate from Gyeongsang, even if it's someone you don't know and who hasn't been here before, the Gyeongsang people will understand your true feelings and sincerity. That will be many more times beneficial to our politics than gaining scores of Assembly seats. I know that this nomination is against common sense. However, I believe that we should defy even common sense if it's what is necessary for the achievement of a great cause."

The audience clapped and cheered. After the rally, I looked for the pastors but they had disappeared. Although I haven't seen them since the election, I believe they, too, voted for Candidate Lee.

Our party overwhelmingly won that election, with Candidate Lee winning even more votes than Mr. Suh Kyung-won had won the previous election. However, I was a little saddened that Assemblyman Lee did not demonstrate an enthusiastic effort to dissolve regional antagonism. Of course I realized that only a few people had the power and strength to accomplish this, but I also expected a lot from him. I had particularly hoped that he would deliver the Jeolla people's sincere will to the Gyeongsang people.

Despite all of our efforts, the reaction from the Gyeongsang province was cold. "Kim Dae-jung uses Lee Soo-in to deceive us," they said.

It was really hopeless. Although the Jeolla people were thirsty for the dissolution of regional antagonism and the abolishment of regional discrimination, the people of Gyeongsang were suspicious of our intentions and considered our sincere desire to be a political tactic.

After the 1992 presidential election, a Gwangju newspaper wrote, "If Mr. Kim Dae-jung was born in Gangwon-do, he should have already become the president." I couldn't help but cry when I read that remark because it made me think of the Jeolla people's sadness. *I'm fine if I don't become the president*, I thought. *I am proud to be a Jeolla native. I am only sorry that I made the Jeolla people sad.*

How unjust it is to be discriminated against simply because one is born in the Jeolla region! Looking back over history, Honam (i.e., the Jeolla region) was a region that elevated the national spirit and saved our nation. When the entire nation was trampled during the Japanese Invasion (1592–1598), Admiral Yi Sun-sin and General Kwon Yul made their headquarters in Honam and vanquished the Japanese invaders. Admiral Yi Sun-sin said, "Without Honam, we don't have our country." Although the Japanese occupied even the northernmost Hamgyeong and Pyeonngan provinces, Honam withstood them. What would have happened to our country without Honam?

How about the second phase of the Japanese Invasion in 1597? After the crushing defeat of the navy, led by Admiral Won Gyun, Admiral Yi Sun-sin defeated a Japanese Navy consisting of 133 battleships with only 12 battleships in the Myeongryang Sea. Without this victory, the Japanese would have trampled the capital city of Hanyang (Seoul) via Incheon. It was the people of Honam who enabled this victory.

Jeon Bong-jun and the people of Honam also led the Kabo Peasant Uprising in 1894, as believers of Donghak that had begun in Yeongnam (i.e., Gyeongsang region). During the Jinju Uprising (1862), the people of Honam rose up in consort with the Jinju people of Yeongnam. Both the Donghak Peasant Uprising and the Jinju Uprising were jointly achieved by the people of both Honam and Yeongnam. Under Rhee Syngman's Liberal Party regime, the strongest anti-dictatorship struggle was waged in both Gyeongsang-do and Jeolla-do. In the face of an effort for democracy, how is there any difference between Gyeongsang-do and Jeolla-do? During those times, Honam natives not only from big Yeongnam cities like Busan and Daegu, but also from remote Yeongnam regions like Sangju, were elected to the National Assembly. I once supported a Gyeongsang native candidate from Mokpo.

As I mentioned earlier, it was the operation politics of the Park Chung-hee military regime that changed this universal sentiment. They tried to isolate Honam in every election, and thoroughly excluded the Honam people from public office. Being born in Honam became a sort of divine punishment. Did Gyeongsang natives benefit from this discrimination? The answer is a resounding *no*.

Although many high officials have been Gyeongsang natives, not all Gyeongsang natives have benefited from preferential treatment. How well do the people of Daegu and Gyeongsangbuk-do, the headquarters of the TK regime, live? How well do the people of Busan and Gyeongsangnam-do, the cradle of the PK regime, live? Ordinary people are still living difficult lives, not so different from the people of the Jeolla and Chungcheong regions. Houses in farming areas are empty, young men cannot marry, and babies continue to cry.

If a Gyeongsang native president adopted the policy of regional discrimination, the result is not that *only* people from Gyeongsang live well, but that *even* people from Gyeongsang *cannot* live well. Regional discrimination ruins everyone. It is only a small minority of the privileged class that benefits from it; the majority of people are left unhappy. People are divided, our ability to unite weakens, and our national ideal drifts.

I am proud to be a Honam native, and I have never felt differently. I have always been sad that I could not work more for the people of Honam. That's why I feel I deserve to share their pain—in fact, it is truly my honor. Nevertheless, I often refrained from visiting my home region of Jeolla in order to avoid the misunderstanding that I was trying to provoke regional antagonism. I wanted to go, but I intentionally avoided it.

I missed my hometown. I often looked at the southern sky and pictured its landscape. Many times, I wanted to cry in its embrace; however, I had no choice because those who provoked regional antagonism watched me closely after putting the bridle of regional antagonism over me. Although I knew the sadness of the Jeolla people, I could not comfort them as I wanted to.

It is only now that I express my gratitude to the Honam people and my great debt to them. The media's slanderous reporting and regional antagonism still follow me, even after my retirement from politics. Perhaps I will become free of it after I die. But even after I die I won't forget the people of Honam's love of our country and of me.

Making the Korean People Cry Once Again (1992)

The whirlwind of the presidential election began once again. I believed that I would definitely win this time. The Pyeongmin Party and I prepared dutifully, and professionals positively evaluated our policy changes. The foreign media also reported that there was a very high chance I would win. They also commented that I was the right person to end the military regime and achieve regime change in the true sense of the word.

On October 6, 1992, immediately before the full-scale campaign season began, the Yi Seon-sil Spy Ring Incident shook up the election topography. According to the ANSP, members of Workers' Party of Korea, a spy organization under the direct control of North Korea, were active behind the scenes. Yi Seon-sil, a big shot spy, ranked number twenty-two in North Korea and an alternate politburo member in the Workers' Party of Korea, infiltrated South Korea three times and established operational leadership. They infiltrated out-of-office organizations, political, labor, and academic fields, and established a local chapter of the Workers' Party of Korea. They sent more than ten spies, including big shots along the lines of a cabinet minister, all of whom were active behind the scenes for more than ten years. They won over more than 400 Koreans from all walks of life, and together worked for the communization of South Korea. This was the largest spy incident in Korean history and the authorities arrested sixty-two spies in all, including former president of the Minjung (People's) Party, Kim Nak-jung. Yi Seon-sil is believed to have gone north to Ganghwado Island in October 1990, immediately before the spy ring was discovered.

A great fuss erupted in the wake of this announcement. The media reported as if South Korea would collapse at any moment. This was the same northern wind that the ruling party had consistently used to attack me in every election season. It reminded me of the Kim Hyon-hui Incident, which erupted immediately before the 1987 presidential election. The ANSP claimed that one of my staff members, Yi Geun-hui, had handed over materials related to the Ministry of National Defense budget, making the most of it. However, Mr. Yi had no knowledge of the other person's identity as a spy. Also, there was a strong chance that it was a part of the ANSP operation. ANSP even spread the rumor that the spy Yi Seon-sil visited my wife at our home and took a photograph with her.

Minja Party Spokesperson Park Hee-tae issued a weird comment: "According to the directive that the spy ring received, they were to unite their support for the Democratic Party candidate so that the candidate would become elected. The authorities should find out whether this directive has anything to do with the handover of military secrets through the secretary of President Kim Dae-jung."

ANSP confirmed in the National Assembly that North Korea sent such a directive to the spy ring. The ruling party attacked me over this spy ring incident throughout the entire election campaign period. Both party leaders and campaign headquarter leaders launched a series of attacks on me.

I tackled this head-on in my speech at the National Assembly on October 14. "What has ANSP been doing for more than ten years, letting spies be active with impunity while spending 500 billion *won* budget every year?" I asked.

Nevertheless, the spy ring incident continued to rear its head throughout the election. Interestingly, the incident simply vanished from the investigative authorities, political arenas, and media as soon as the election was over. Later, after an investigation by the National Intelligence Service Committee for Development through Truth Examination of Past Incidents, the NIS concluded that "this incident was exaggerated or inaccurately presented." It also declared, "This incident created innocent victims by publicizing various unconfirmed allegations of implication. It is also suspected that this incident was fabricated for political purpose because the authorities not only revealed but also actively spread unconfirmed intelligence."

Despite all of the fuss, I led all candidates during the early and middle stages of election season. Top Korean corporations' intelligence analysis teams predicted my victory. Foreign media outlets preemptively requested interviews with me after the inauguration to hear about my policies. Some sent teams of reporters to my hometowns, Mokpo and Hauido Island. I was confident about my victory, as was everyone else in my party.

At this juncture, the ANSP again leaked false information: "North Korean President Kim Il-sung is encouraging South Koreans to vote for Candidate Kim Dae-jung through broadcasting to the South." The media blared this misinformation in their headlines. The ruling party openly attacked me, saying, "Kim Il-sung supports Kim Dae-jung and opposes Kim Young-sam. Can we elect Kim Dae-jung, who Kim Il-sung supports?"

Minja Party Election Polling Committee Chairman Jeong Won-sik also said, "North Korea expressed through Minminjeon (National Democracy Front) Broadcasting that they welcomed South Korean democratic forces' decision to support Candidate Kim Dae-jung as the only candidate of all democratization forces."

I immediately pointed out the falsehood of these claims. "If the ANSP's claim about North Korean broadcasting is true, then Kim Il-sung must definitely not want my election. Why else would they do that, when it's perfectly clear that a connection to Kim Il-sung would be disadvantageous to me? If North Korea said such a thing, then that is because they do not want me to be elected."

Nevertheless, my refutation was not effective. Although I appealed to the Korean people to please not associate me with pro-communism, I was no match for the mainstream media that manipulated public opinion at their will. As expected, this intelligence was also fabricated information. In an assembly hearing after the election, Assemblyman Namkung Jin asked, "Is it true that North Korea expressed its support for Candidate Kim Dae-jung through broadcasting or other media?" The answer from the prime minister and the ANSP director was, "No." Minja Party Representative of Supreme Council Kim Jong-pil officially apologized for the government's fabrication of pro-communism. It was, of course, too late.

Toward the end of the election campaign, something even scarier happened. Just six days before the election, Candidate Kim Young-sam, my one-time comrade in the democratization movement, began to utilize a full-blown red scare. He did not hesitate to attack me, using the same age-old malicious propaganda that had been enacted since the Park Chung-hee military regime. "Recently, North Korea issued a directive through Pyongyang Broadcasting that you should defeat me, Kim Young-sam, and elect the Democratic Party candidate," he shouted. "What are you going to do by giving power to the party whose color is unclear? Are you going to elect the candidate North Korea wants, or are you going to elect the candidate you want?"

He also said that "a candidate whose ideology is suspicious should not become president" and "a responsible presidential candidate should sever all ties from forces siding with the Kim Il-sung line." The media delivered all of these malicious propaganda messages straight to people's homes without any filtration. Such words should not have come from the mouth of a thirty-year comrade of the democratization movement. It was really depressing. Although this was the first election in which civilians confronted each other since the May 16 Military Coup d'État, my opponent's election campaign style was not at all different from the election fraud tactics utilized by the military regime. I couldn't even imagine how someone could use a red-scare tactic against a comrade for the sake of winning an election.

I was angry, but also sad about Mr. Kim Young-sam's transformation. I almost felt pity for his greed and desire to become the president even by way of such a base tactic. The only tactic that the Minja Party utilized against me—through stump speeches, millions of leaflets circulating on a daily basis, and the party spokesperson's comments and statements—was this red-scare tactic.

Unable to simply sit by and watch, our party election polling headquarters proposed an extreme tactic to me. They believed that we should fight fire with fire by bringing up the matter of Candidate Kim Young-sam's character and womanizing tendencies. I strongly dissuaded them, saying, "I cannot go as low as them. I want to take the high road even if I lose this election."

The Minja Party's election fraud did not stop there. Election Polling Committee Chair Kim Dong-gil for Candidate Chung Ju-yung revealed the Chowon Bokjip Incident at a press conference on December 15. He presented a transcript that clearly showed that the ruling party had mobilized the entire public office network. On December 11, less than a week before Election Day, high officials in the Busan area gathered at the Chowon Bokjip Restaurant, where they were invited by former Minister of Law Kim Ki-choon. They decided to utilize regional antagonism to guarantee Candidate Kim Young-sam's victory. The gathering was named the Busan Area High Officials' Polling Meeting to Make Kim Young-sam President.

The former minister of law, who was supposed to defend the law, a soldier who was meant to defend the country, a prosecutor who was relied upon to eradicate corruption, the ANSP branch director who managed national intelligence, the police chief who was tasked with public order and safety, the mayor who was in charge of city administration, and the superintendent of education who supervised just education shouted, "Are we strangers [to Kim Young-sam, a Yeongnam native]?" Those who shouted about overthrowing regional antagonism during the day gathered to discuss how to encourage it at night.

They also discussed how to bribe and win over journalists. Recklessly, they claimed that the country would face revolution if Candidate Kim Dae-jung won the election. They disturbed the national foundation and flatly denied democracy. With the revelation of this transcript, President Roh's declaration of neutrality was proven to be a simple disguise tactic. Similar meetings were held in other major cities like Gwangju, Daejeon, and Daegu.

The Blue House and Office of the Prime Minister talked themselves out of this situation by claiming: "This incident was committed by government officials in no relation to the will for neutrality of President Roh and Prime Minister Hyeon Seung-jong." The Minja Party also said that it had nothing to do with them. Candidate Kim Young-sam went even further, saying: "The Busan Incident has nothing to do with the Minja Party, and I am the biggest victim of this incident. I am the victim of the operation politics and the recording of the conversation itself is part of operation politics. We must root out illegal wiretapping." It was like a thief audaciously calling a victim the thief. Essentially, he was bullying those who revealed the crime committed by high government officials, by saying, "Why did you eavesdrop?"

The media also accused the Kukmin Party of eavesdropping. The newly born, inexperienced Kukmin Party was flustered and did not know how to properly respond to this kind of preposterous attack. If the Kukmin Party had revealed the transcript while saying that they would take responsibility for eavesdropping, the situation could have turned out quite differently.

I felt that the Chowon Bokjip Incident was encouraging for my campaign. I thought that Candidate Kim Young-sam could not survive such corruption, even though he was the ruling party candidate. I also thought this incident would help stamp out regional antagonism. I expected that the people of Gyeongsang-do would change their minds now that it was revealed that government officials had fanned regional antagonism. I thought that the voters of Gyeongsang-do must be angry with the ruling party and the government, but I was naïve to think that.

I openly proposed a television debate to Candidate Kim Young-sam, hoping that we could openly debate matters following his accusation of me being pro-communist and provoking regional antagonism. In fact, in the early stages of the campaign, Candidate Kim Young-sam had expressed a strong desire to participate in a televised debate. On October 21, I said at a meeting with the foreign press that "I am planning to propose a televised debate among presidential candidates after the presidential election is officially announced. We can now do a televised debate like in America."

At the Kwanhun Club debate on December 2, Candidate Kim Young-sam said that he would not avoid a televised debate. However, as the days went by, he came up with more and more conditions, eventually rejecting the debate proposal altogether. This rejection had been somewhat anticipated. Although the Korean people had the right to check Candidate Kim Young-sam's qualifications as president, he simply denied them the opportunity. The media remained silent on this matter.

When Election Day was only a few days away, leaflets provoking regional antagonism began to spread throughout the entire Gyeongsang region. They read: "Do you know that a vote for Chung Ju-yung will become a vote for Kim Dae-jung?" "If Kim Dae-jung is elected, there will be bloody revenge for the Gyeongsang-do region." "Let's revive the pride of the Gyeongsang-do people by electing Kim Young-sam."

I was short of funding, oppressed by the power, and marginalized by the media. Add regional antagonism to the mix, and I had no chance.

Just like that, the election campaign was over. After casting my vote on December 18, I went to Reunification Hill in Imjingak Pavilion. Looking north, I remembered the more passionate moments of the election campaign. If I won the election, the first thing I wanted to do was to visit my mother's grave in Pocheon and cry there.

Ballot counting showed regional antagonism from the beginning. The Chowon Bokjip Incident brought about a huge reaction. The bump turned into a red carpet, and votes for Candidate Kim Young-sam flooded in from the Gyeongsang region. Regional antagonism and the red scare swallowed up all reasonable judgment. The anti-Jeolla sentiment spread to other regions besides Gyeongsang-do. I lost in regions besides Seoul and Jeolla-do. The end result was about 9.97 million votes (41.4 percent) for Kim Young-sam, 8.04 million (33.4 percent) for me, 3.88 million (16.1 percent) for Chung Ju-yung, and 1.51 million (6.3 percent) for Park Chan-jong. Candidate Kim Young-sam beat me by 1.3 million votes in the Yeongnam and Honam regions. Their abuse of regional antagonism succeeded.

I lost again in a defeat that was really hard for me to accept. I stood up from my seat around 3:00 a.m. on the silent night of December 19. I prayed to God, who had constantly given me strength and courage. *What should I do at this point?* I wondered. My wife watched me. My voice rang loudly throughout the room as I spoke to her in the quiet of that early hour. "I failed to become president again," I said to her. "The past forty years feel far away. I have not avoided death for democracy during those years … I devoted all I had to democracy, justice, and reunification. Other people may not know my efforts, but you do. Still, I could not gain the Korean people's trust. This seems to be all I could do. I'd like to finish my career. I hope you agree."

My wife slowly nodded her head. Teardrops ran from her eyes. As we hugged, I felt a renewed sense of love and admiration for her. Lee Hee-ho was my constant comrade, friend, and life partner. Thanks to her, I didn't feel cold that morning. As my wife wrote while I dictated, her small shoulders shook. I went to her, held her hands and said, "Darling, if we think back to the time when I was sentenced to capital punishment, isn't this an occasion for laughing?"

Nonetheless, my wife continued to cry as she composed my retirement statement. This single statement marked the end of my eventful thirty-eight-year political career. At 8:30 a.m. on December 19, 1992, I entered the Democratic Party office building only to be greeted by the tears of the party members. I had to be strong in front of them. When I said that I'd like to give up my party membership too, Secretary General Hahn Gwang-ok, Assemblyman Kwon Rho-kap, and Chief of Staff Cho Seung-hyeong burst into tears, protesting, "That won't do." I had to yield to them. I did not cry when I shook hands with party members. I went straight to the pressroom and read my prepared retirement statement.

My Dear Fellow Koreans!
I failed to win your trust again. I humbly accept my defeat, and will consider it due to my deficiency.
I sincerely congratulate Candidate Kim Young-sam on his victory. I hope that President Kim will succeed as the president of our country in every field, including politics, economy, and society, and contribute to the democratic development and the reunification of our country.
My Dear Fellow Koreans!
I decided to resign from my position as assemblyman today and become an ordinary citizen. I feel overwhelmed to think that I will finish my eventful

political career of forty years. I have received enormous love and support from you. I thank you sincerely. I am saddened and sorry that I will retire without repaying you for your generous support.

Also, all of my party comrades from Representative Supreme Council Member Lee Ki-taek on down have not spared any of their incredible collaboration and support for me. I don't have words to express what a colossal blessing your support has been to me. I promise that I will devote my remaining life to our party's development and cooperate with you as best as I can as an ordinary party member. Again, I am overwhelmed with gratitude to you and pray for the Korean people's and your good health.

Now I return to life as an ordinary citizen, leaving all evaluations of me to history. I wish you and my party comrades the very best of luck.

Memories of Cambridge (1993)

After I declared retirement from politics, the media was flooded with articles of praise for me. Articles, opinion pieces, and columns ran headlines like "Political Giant," "Political Big Tree," "Politician of Principles," and "Forty Years of Straight Road to Democratization." The media, which had handled me so brutally during the election campaign, changed their tune overnight and transformed me into a hero.

Phone calls flooded my house, too. Some people just cried on the phone. Some said they were grateful that I made my supporters proud, though they were extremely sad that I had retired. Others said they were proud of their votes for me. Some people said they finally realized they had misunderstood me. Some were sorrowful, others were angry, and still others regretful. After the election, I had to comfort many people's sorrows. Although it was me who lost the election, they were hurt even more than I was. I realized again how much I was loved by the Korean people. Perhaps the most beautiful scenes in my life unfolded after that loss. I said good-bye to various civic organizations—literary, women's, and journalists.' I will never forget how sad they were.

Since there were people who were sadder about my retirement than I was, I could not indulge in my own sorrow. There were people who shut their stores, who gave up eating and drinking, who drank day and night, who broke their televisions. A lot of snow fell after the election. I was worried about people, and hoped that the white snow covered their wounded hearts. It was a melancholy end to the year.

On January 2, Cardinal Kim Sou-hwan visited me at my house. He comforted me deeply. He said that when he visited President-Elect Kim Young-sam after the election victory he said, "I guess you may be sorry about this, but I voted for another candidate." He also told the media that he had voted for me, reasoning, "I thought that if he was elected president, the regional antagonism problem could be greatly diminished."

On January 4, my wife and I were invited to a lunch at the Blue House with President Roh. During lunch, I recommended a large-scale amnesty and reinstatement for prisoners of conscience. It was my last request to him during his presidency. President Roh said to me, "The Korean people will remember your contribution to our country's democracy for a long time."

Foreigners also said they were moved by my retirement. The Japanese station NHK proposed making a documentary about my life. At first, I refused, but they were persistent. They later came to England, where I was studying, and continued with their request. Finally, I agreed. I felt it could be a good opportunity for the Japanese to get to know Korea better and more truthfully. It was a four-segment miniseries entitled *Kim Dae-jung, An Autobiography in Japan*. The producer of this program was Mr. Hotta Kingo. After the documentary was finished, the two of us often met to chat about world affairs. He was a small man, but his passion was bigger than a mountain. When I later heard the news of his untimely death, I thought maybe he worked so hard and so much because he had to leave early.

My sixty-eighth birthday was on January 6. I attended my birthday party, which had been prepared by Democratic Party officials, assemblymen, and constituent officers. I talked frankly about my feelings. "It was more painful to be falsely charged than to go to prison and be oppressed," I told them. "The operation politics falsely charged me as being ideologically suspicious and accused me of making lots of money. Whenever the Korean people condemned me because they were deceived by false allegations, I shed tears. That was the most scary and painful thing."

President-Elect Kim Young-sam proposed a meeting with me. He probably found it burdensome to neglect the encouragement and praise I received after my retirement. He sent me many messages; however, I had no particular reason to meet him. At first, I refused. Then, the Democratic Party demanded an official apology for all of President-Elect Kim's false accusations about my pro-communist stance, essentially presenting it as a prerequisite for my meeting with him. As a retired politician, I could not neglect the Democratic Party's opinion. Mr. Kim Young-sam did not apologize, so we never met. He called me right before I left Korea. We talked for just one minute. In retrospect, I did not envy Mr. Kim Young-sam for achieving his goal by fair means or foul.

After living life as a politician for forty years, I didn't know what to do post-retirement. Whenever I ran into a difficult situation, I always checked my problems and possibilities. I would draw a line down a piece of paper and write my problems on the right side of the line and my possibilities on the left side, then compare them. I did the same upon my retirement and found there were many things written on the left side. First of all, I had the support of 8 million Korean people. I also had my wife, with whom I shared constant love and care, and my children, as well as numerous comrades who did not spare their lives for me. I also had health. I was healthy after three rough elections and forty years spent walking along a thorny path. I was also full of passion.

I realized that I had no reason to be disappointed. I decided to stand up again and find work for my country and people. I decided to first leave Korea and concentrate on studying. I chose to do so in England. It was a new, exciting, and interesting challenge.

Upon receiving an invitation from Cambridge University, I left to study abroad as a visiting scholar on January 26, 1993. I planned to study and give lectures for between six months and a year. I wanted to study the process of German reunification and think about a desirable model for Korean reunification. About 2000 party officials and supporters waited at the airport to see me off. They hung a large placard that read, "Dear Indongcho (a kind of honeysuckle; the name means enduring winter), bloom in the hearts of 70 million people!" Although it was supposed to be a farewell party, everyone's faces looked gloomy. "I am sorry and I have mixed feelings about leaving Korea, leaving many troubled hearts behind because of my unworthiness," I spoke. "Although I leave politics, I don't leave Koreans. I will serve you until the end of my life. I will study harder and make more efforts, and I am determined to serve the Korean people with all of my heart in areas other than politics. There may be temporary setbacks in history, but there is no regression. There is no defeat to people who do not despair. I sincerely hope that you keep progressing without being frustrated, firmly believing that the country of freedom, prosperity, and welfare, as well as our dream of a unified fatherland, will be achieved. I promise to meet you again with renewed hopes."

In the airplane to Cambridge, I closed my eyes, deep in thought. Was my life a failure? I had failed again in achieving my dream of forty years and acquiring the opportunity to work for the Korean people and nation. My biggest sadness was not my election defeat, but my disappointment that the Korean people were swayed by regional antagonism and the red scare, and held on to selfish safety rather than choosing change.

Even though the Korean people discarded me, I could not discard them. They were the source of my life and my reason for living. I had believed that God would set things straight this time. He wouldn't accept this kind of result, would he? I could not pray well after the election. I wasn't like this even during the desperate times in 1980. The party most responsible for ruining Korean politics and state affairs was the media. But they were so powerful. There was no way for me to change or correct them. I could neither die nor give up like this. I should still believe in God, trust history, people, and myself, and proceed, fighting to the finish for history. I should maintain my belief that how we live is more important than what we become. I should encourage myself and try to live my best for a new reward. I should live conscientiously, significantly, and rewardingly as conscience in action—just like my nickname suggested.

I chose to study in England instead of America in order to be as far from Korean politics as possible. The US was too close to Korean politics. I took into account the fact that I could communicate in English in England, too. I, of course, knew of Cambridge University's fame and that it was located in a nice campus town. I landed in England with Assemblymen Namkung Jin, Choe Jae-seung, and Hong Sa-duk, as well as my son Hong Up. My wife and Assemblyman Kim Ok-du and Secretary Park Keum-ok, who arrived there ahead of me, welcomed us at the airport.

Cambridge was a college town. First established during the Roman period, it was made up of altogether thirty-one colleges, including three women's colleges and two graduate schools. The colleges were located along river Cam, which ran through the town, and with the exception of the main library, all of the buildings were less than five stories tall. The old buildings were surrounded by lawns and the forests were old-fashioned. Although the entire town felt solemn, it was comfortable to me.

I lived in Pine Hurst Lodge, a three-bedroom brick building within a townhouse, located in a forest a little ways outside of downtown. I lived in the eastern part on the first floor, and Dr. Kim Sang-u (who studied international politics and was of great help to me) and his family lived in the western part.

I began my lectures and study as a visiting scholar of Clare Hall, one of the thirty-one colleges of Cambridge University. At Clare Hall, they offered graduate studies in natural and social sciences and history, and supported the research of visiting scholars from all over the world. Photographs of visiting scholars lined the halls. My study was a small room next to the corridor that overlooked the courtyard. The bookshelves were filled with books from all over the world, but there were only a few Korean books. Probably because of my position as professor emeritus at Moscow State University, everyone called me Professor Kim Dae-jung. The vice president of Cambridge University welcomed me with excessive praise. "While Bill Clinton studied at Oxford, Mr. Kim Dae-jung came to Cambridge," he remarked.

It felt like a dream that I had left my country to study. My past stay abroad as an exile had been troubled and tricky, like walking on a thin sheet of ice. But my life in England was relaxed. I read books, took walks in the forest, and meditated. I went to the study in the morning and stayed there all day long. It took me ten minutes to walk from my residence to the school.

While in Cambridge, I met world-renowned scholars, such as physicist and cosmologist Stephen Hawking, sociologist Anthony Giddens, and democracy scholar John Dunn. Meeting with Dr. Hawking was particularly moving. During my time in Cambridge, he was across the wall from me, and served as a kind and warm-hearted neighbor. He was completely disabled, with the exception of his eyes, ears, and brain. He barely managed to eat food with his mouth, and communicated only through sound mechanisms within his computer. His misfortunes were not limited to his body—he also suffered from the fact that his wife left him and his two sons. Nonetheless, Dr. Hawking overcame his misfortune and became a scientist on the level of Newton and Einstein. I was even more moved by his positive attitude toward life than his academic achievements. It was miraculous.

When I left England, Dr. Hawking was sadder than anyone. He and I had known each other before I came to Cambridge. When he visited Korea in 1991, I had dinner with him at the British Embassy. Guests asked him many questions, but they all expressed curiosity about his enduring spirit. I asked him about the birth and future of the universe, and its relationship with humanity. They were things I had always been curious about. Dr. Hawking seemed to be impressed by my questions.

It was interesting karma that we met again in England. Dr. Hawking remembered me immediately and treated me like an old friend. He even remembered our conversation in Korea. We visited each other's houses and talked. Sometimes, when I tried to leave because I didn't want to tire him with a long conversation, he detained me. Often, I found him waiting for me in front of my house. I didn't know how long he waited because he couldn't speak. When I greeted him, he smiled and then went back into his house. Once I asked him, "Where do your passion and power come from when your health is in such poor condition?"

"Because I have a wife and children, I have to sustain them," he responded. "In order to do that, I have to live hard."

Although it might sound trite, Dr. Hawking touched my heart. He asked me about Korean reunification and North Korea's nuclear capability; sometimes, he offered his opinion about these issues, too. He showed a deep interest in my future. Despite his own disabilities, he cared about the well-being of others; in fact, his own adversity might have made his own life even more dynamic and fulfilling. I felt humbled in front of the greatness of this man who challenged the very notion of infinity with his genius. Dr. Hawking was intensely intellectually curious, and he was always smiling. His eyes were bright and displayed a happiness that only someone who had overcome adversity could experience. He seemed truly happy and comfortable.

I had in-depth discussions about democracy with Professors Anthony Giddens and John Dunn. We talked about how there had been unhappy incidents in which democratic countries had invaded other countries in their interest. We agreed that we should develop democracy beyond the national level. Everyone in the world, especially those in pain, had the right to live in a world with freedom and justice. Furthermore, as brethren, all living beings deserved peace. I discussed how I hoped to accomplish global democracy where all beings—including not just humans, but also trees, grass, soil, land animals, fish, birds, and the air—were guaranteed the right to live. Professor Giddens said that this kind of democracy should be named "cosmopolitan democracy." I proposed calling it "global democracy."

I gave lectures not only at Cambridge University, but also at Oxford and London Universities as well as at Chatham House, the Royal Institute of International Affairs. The audience asked questions freely and I gave my sincere answers. After my lectures, the Korean students frequently told me that they were proud of their heritage.

During my lecture at Oxford, a Japanese student asked, "Before the Second World War, many countries were colonies of Britain and France. But these former colonies are now enjoying a friendly relationship with their former colonizers. Why is Korea still holding onto the past and failing to reconcile with Japan?"

The room fell into complete silence as all eyes turned toward me. "I'd like to ask you the same question," I answered. "While Britain and France are on friendly terms with their former colonies, why isn't Japan on friendly terms with their former colony, Korea? Who is more responsible for it— Korea or Japan?

"Let's compare Britain and France with Japan," I continued. "That will clarify the answer. Japan forced Koreans to change their last names to Japanese names, which the Korean people considered to be on par with giving up their lives. They also forbade Koreans from using the Korean language and learning Korean history. They forced Koreans to bow toward the emperor in the east. France and Britain, on the other hand, did not trample on the pride of their colonies.

"Now, let's compare Germany and Japan. Both countries committed war crimes during World War II. Germany apologized for its past actions and offered billions of dollars in restitution to Jews and Israel. But what did Japan do? Japan gave only $300 million to Korea. While Germany teaches their past crimes to its children, Japan covers up its past crimes and pretends to apologize. You ask this question because you don't understand the atrocities the Japanese committed toward Koreans.

"Furthermore, while Germany acknowledges its defeat in the war, Japan calls it 'the end of war.' While Germany calls the allied forces the 'occupying troops,' Japan calls them the 'stationary troops.' From the way Japan tells it, we don't know who won the war and who surrendered. How could we forgive Japan when it holds this attitude? Japan has grown into a superpower without reflecting on its past faults; how can its neighbor Korea not worry about this? It is natural that Korea is suspicious of Japan and wonders about its former colonizer's true intentions. How can Korea move on from the past when Japan's attitude is so different from Germany's?"

The audience applauded loudly. After the lecture, the Japanese student came up to me and apologized. "I really did not know," he said. "I will try to make an effort to change Japanese policies."

When I left Korea, I had no specific plans for the future. I had a vague plan to look around Europe and unified Germany, and to study them. It was jarring to see the now-unified Germany suffer greatly following the "unification through absorption." It was from seeing this that I realized what I should be doing.

It is true that the German reunification occurred abruptly. Chancellor Helmut Kohl was not very positive about unification through absorption. Neues Forum, the group that led the democratic revolution in East Germany, also wanted gradual unification. However, the people of East Germany yearned for an affluent West German lifestyle and, gradually, more of them demanded unification through absorption. Chancellor Helmut Kohl overwhelmingly won the election against the Social Democratic Party (which advocated for equal unification) by advocating unification through absorption.

East Germans had a sort of materialistic illusion. They thought West Germany's affluence would automatically transfer to East Germany as soon as the two countries were united. Unfortunately, the rushed unification in September 1990 proved to be very costly. Enormous unexpected costs grew larger and larger. Most East German companies were closed down because they couldn't survive on their own. The East German economy faced irrevocable collapse. Unemployed citizens overflowed the streets. When we met in September 1991, Minister of Foreign Affairs Genscher told me that there was not a single usable factory in East Germany. I looked around East German factories myself and was surprised to hear that there used to be 9000 workers in the factory where only 800 were now working.

As a matter of fact, East Germans didn't have economic worries prior to the unification. The state took care of housing, work, and education. Once you gave up your freedom and human rights, the government gave you the rest for free. In some sense, they enjoyed a comfortable life. Now that they were driven to free market competition, they found it difficult and scary. Individuals had to take responsibility for what the government used to take care of. It proved really dangerous for a communist system to be incorporated into capitalism overnight.

During my stay in England, I visited Germany three times. I looked around various places and met with people from all walks of life. The forty-year division between the East and West had scary consequences. Although it was ideology that divided them, it was their cultures and lifestyles that collided when they met again. Wherever you turned, there were conflicts and oppositions. Although political division was cleared away, economic and social division remained. East Germany and West Germany may have disappeared, but East Germans and West Germans still existed. Before, it was one nation, two states; now it was one state, two societies. They spoke the same language, but their lifestyles and thoughts could not communicate with one another.

President Von Weizsäcker said to me, "Although the Berlin Wall collapsed, there remains a wall in our hearts." He sighed, explaining that it would take at least thirty years to overcome this heterogeneity. It was clear that hasty unification by absorption brought about problems of almost disastrous proportions. German reunification offered us much to learn from.

From the German experience, I concluded that we must not rush to reunify, and we must not attempt unification by absorption. Reunification in and of itself was not a trump card. What was more important was *how* the reunification occurred. Looking at the Berlin Wall, I realized again that it was not an easy task for divided countries to overcome systemic and ideological differences. When I met with him in Berlin, the final East German Chancellor Lothar de Maiziere expressed his deep regrets. "We made a mistake," he said. "We never should have reunited by absorption. It should have been done in stages."

The two Koreas have waged war against each other. We have lived, hating each other, despite the fact that we are the same nation. It was more than obvious that we would encounter serious confusion and conflict if we were to reunite overnight. Our burden would be even heavier than that of West Germany. As communism disappeared along with the Cold War, reunification was the obvious next step. However, we should find wiser and more appropriate ways of doing it.

My observations of post-reunification Germany confirmed to me that the three-step reunification plan I had first presented in 1971 was a good plan.

North Korea withdrew from the Treaty on the Non-proliferation of Nuclear Weapons (NPT) in March 1993. As I was visiting Berlin in the early summer that year, the world was nervous and suspicious that North Korea was developing nuclear weapons. The world media was flooded with predictions that the North Korean economy might collapse at any moment. When I met with North Korean specialist Professor Aidan Foster-Carter of Leeds University, he made the shocking diagnosis that "North Korea already seems to be in a very desperate situation. Still, they have lost the will to change."

I was most worried that North Korea would start a war out of economic desperation; that they could invade South Korea as suddenly as they had in the Korean War. In order to eliminate this possibility, we should not give the hardliners in North Korea any excuse to invade us, while simultaneously helping their moderates bolster their position. However, finding this solution was the most difficult of work. Since then, North Korea's development of nuclear weapons had an enormous effect not only on the Korean Peninsula, but on the entire world.

Thanks to my days in Cambridge, I felt better, but I could not help missing my friends and my homeland. I missed the flowers and plants in my garden. I remembered the swarms of sparrows that flew in my yard and ate the food I gave them. I grew flowers in England too. I would take my flowerpots outside when they bloomed, and pedestrians would stop to look at them. I also fed the birds as I had in Seoul. The sparrows in England were about a third larger than Korean sparrows, but they were still as nimble as their Korean counterparts. Life was the same everywhere.

One day, I noticed a strange-looking bird within the group of sparrows. It was a little larger than a sparrow and had reddish feathers around its chest. It flew alone and ate freely. It was not scared of human beings. Not only did it look beautiful, but it acted dignified.

Although I didn't know its name or its sex, this bird fascinated me. Some time later, I visited a friend in Geneva, and his wife told me that this mystery bird was a robin. She told me that a robin watched Jesus' death and the feathers on its chest turned red because of Jesus' blood. Of course it was only a legend, but upon hearing this story I found the bird even more lovable and worthy of respect.

Because I was so in love with the robin, my friends suggested that I take it to Korea. I could not do that to the robin to satisfy my own selfish wishes but I often thought of that robin when I returned to Korea and promised myself I would visit Cambridge again to see that robin. I wonder if that robin is still in Cambridge … or in this world.

I visited the Hague, the Netherlands, to visit Korean patriot Yi Jun's grave, on my way to Germany. Along with two other patriots, Yi Jun was a secret delegate to the Second Peace Conference in the Hague. Yi Jun died in protest of Japan's unlawful invasion of Korea, maintaining that the 1905 Eulsa Protectorate Treaty was null and void. Yi Jun was frustrated with Japan's successful intervention and prevention of Korean delegates at the conference. Ultimately, he was found dead in his hotel room. Although we don't know exactly how Yi Jun died, a press conference about his death received worldwide attention.

After the Eulsa Protectorate Treaty, independence armies arose both within and outside of Korea. Their struggle to regain Korea continued until liberation day in 1945. Although there were many colonies in the world, it seems that Korea was the only country to establish a temporary government overseas and fight against a colonizing country with armed forces.

In China, for example, the Mongolians who established the Yuan Dynasty were completely assimilated into China. The Manchus who founded the Qing Dynasty also didn't leave much of a trace, and were completely absorbed into China. The force of China's cultural absorption was mighty. Despite this, although Korea had been politically, economically, socially, culturally, and religiously under the influence of China for two millennia, the Korean nation continued to maintain its independence. Both Buddhism and Confucianism bloomed even more splendidly and profoundly in Korea than in China. It was no wonder that Korea gave birth to a patriot like Yi Jun.

When I went to Yi Jun's grave, fresh flowers and a burning cigarette were placed atop it, probably because Koreans living and traveling in Europe continued to pay homage to him. His bust was next to the grave and below that was a stone with an inscription of his achievements. With my eyes closed, I remembered him.

I attended a world leaders' conference in Lisbon, the capital of Portugal. Leaders from twenty-four countries gathered together to discuss welfare, the environment, and society. Current and former heads of state and CEOs of world-class corporations welcomed me enthusiastically. During this visit, I met and talked with Portuguese President Mario Suares, who had been imprisoned twelve times and was in exile in France for some time. As our lives were similar in many ways, it felt as if we were old friends.

My research life at Clare Hall came to a close as the semester ended in late June 1993. I had hoped to stay longer, but the black cloud of North Korea's nuclear capability darkened the Korean sky. After North Korea's withdrawal from the NPT, tension escalated in the Korean Peninsula. The Kim Young-sam regime's hardliner policy quickly worsened the situation, and the opposition Democratic Party did not seem to have any alternatives to offer. While Korean politicians stood idly by, the relationship between North Korea and the US was deteriorating to the point of the threat of war. I felt the situation was urgent and wanted to contribute to its improvement. I also hoped to help ease the tension of the South-North relationship through a plan for reunification that I had studied and thought about during my time in England. I had to return to Seoul and try to contribute to the situation in my own small way.

My farewell dinner was held at the university on June 22. I expressed my gratitude, saying, "Half a year ago, I came to Cambridge with no specific hope for my future. Now I have peace and new hope in my heart. They were the best gifts that Cambridge gave me. Thanks to those gifts, I return to my country reborn. And thanks to Cambridge, I return not as a politician, but as a scholar who has studied the problem of reunification."

Professors, students, and many fellow researchers solemnly listened to me, probably because they knew my political career well. To lighten up the atmosphere, I ended my speech by saying, "I came here to stay for a year, but I leave after only half a year because I want to contribute to England in my own small way. I want to lower the unemployment rate in England, which is currently suffering from a high unemployment rate." The audience burst into laughter.

Cambridge University treated me like a VIP guest until the very end of my stay. Upon my departure from Cambridge I was selected as a life member of the Clare Hall College Faculty. They also changed the name of the apartment complex from Pine Hurst Lodge to Kim's Lodge.

I saw and experienced a lot in Cambridge. It was here that I outlined my autobiographical essay book, *For a New Beginning*. In these pages I looked back on my life and reflected on moments that could be helpful to young men and women. This book was published after my return to Korea and remained on the bestseller list for a while.

There was an episode during my stay in Cambridge that I still remember. Many supporters and national assemblymen visited me there. They brought me many gifts, including juice from pickled seafood, fish, and thornbacks. We also cooked *kimchi* stew and *doenjang* stew often. Unfortunately, this food did not smell good to the English people. Although we tried very hard to reduce the odor, it inevitably drifted out of our apartment. Once, the apartment superintendent warned us about the smell; however, my neighbors knew that I was a retired politician and democratization fighter, so they didn't complain. I was grateful for their kind consideration.

Many guests brought me hope and encouragement, as well as news from Korea. To meet them was always a joyful occasion. I feel happy whenever I think back on the times I spent in Cambridge. I acquired a lot there, and I left a lot there too. I felt I could always feel leisurely in its embrace again. However, that time never came.

THE NEST OF REUNIFICATION AND PEACE: KIM DAE-JUNG PEACE FOUNDATION (1993–1995)

When I landed in Seoul on July 4, 1993, a few thousand people were gathered at the airport to welcome me. I hadn't expected such a warm welcome, and felt surprised and uncomfortable. It was difficult to leave the airport gate and make my way to the podium. While being pushed around, I was more worried about my wife, whose arthritis had worsened in England, than myself. I couldn't even help her because of the crowd. People chanted my name and I gave an impromptu speech. "When I left this airport six months ago, I felt I was going into exile, but I no longer feel that kind of pain," I spoke. "I came back with a firm plan, hope, and confidence about the remainder of my life."

After the welcome event, reporters asked me if I had any ideas about the South-North relationship after my sojourn to England. "The South and the North should meet," I responded. "Combining the North's rich and low-cost labor with the South's investment is a win-win situation for both. North Korea will be different from East Germany, which only became a burden to West Germany."

About a week after my return, we moved to an apartment in Ilsan. I completely cut off contact with the media and spent all of my time on reunification.

A twenty-year anniversary celebration of my safe return from kidnapping was held on August 13. I gave a lecture entitled "Lessons from the German Reunification and the Direction and Prospect of Korean Reunification." On the previous day, the Korean government had abruptly declared the implementation of the real-name financial transaction system. The Korean Peninsula situation was extremely sensitive because of North Korea's withdrawal from the NPT. It was almost impossible to see even an inch ahead because both the South and the North had adopted hardline tactics. In my speech, I presented a package plan to solve the North Korean nuclear crisis. I argued that North Korea should give up nuclear capability and the US should try to improve its relationship with North Korea. Many people, both domestically and abroad, agreed with me.

On September 8, I gave a special lecture entitled "The Current of World History and the Political Situation in Northeast Asia" at Seoul National University Graduate School of Public Administration. On September 16, I delivered the lecture "The Possibilities and Necessities of Korean Reunification" at Yonsei University Institute of East and West Studies.

Beginning on September 21, I embarked on a twenty-two-day tour of Germany, Russia, and the US. I wanted to discuss peace in Asia and the Korean reunification with renowned leaders and to get their cooperation for the Peace Foundation that I was considering to establish. I also wanted to establish a network with outstanding overseas foundations. I talked about the ideas I had brought to maturation during my stay in Cambridge. The Nauman Foundation in Germany, Gorbachev Foundation in Russia, Carter Foundation, and Brookings Institute in the US all agreed to collaborate with me. Although I had just begun to draft it, I felt confident that I could grow the Peace Foundation into a world-class organization.

I also met with German President Von Weizsäcker, former Minister of Foreign Affairs Genscher, former East German Chancellor de Maiziere, former Soviet President Gorbachev, former US President Jimmy Carter, and former US Secretary of State Kissinger. They were all enthusiastic about and supportive of my plan for the Peace Foundation.

I will never forget my meeting with former Russian President Gorbachev. When I visited him in Moscow, I was surprised to see how humble his office and environment were. I had heard that President Yeltsin had treated him harshly—almost oppressively. But Gorbachev himself was lively, cheerful, and dignified.

"You have contributed most greatly to the people of the twentieth century—no, perhaps the entirety of human history—all over the world, regardless of your political success in Russia," I said to him. "You saved humanity from the fear of nuclear war by ending the Cold War. Through the policies of Glasnost and Perestroika, you offered freedom to the people of the Soviet Union and Eastern Europe, which played a decisive role in ending communism and universalizing democracy all over the world. You opened the road for freedom and independence for sixteen federation and satellite communist countries through a policy of reform and openness. You also greatly changed the power dynamic of European leaders by deciding to cooperate with German reunification."

I thought that the world needed to appreciate his role more and to express the gratitude and respect he deserved.

At the request of its East Asian Studies faculty I gave a lecture at Columbia University on October 1. Once again, I emphasized that the reunification between the South and the North should not happen by absorption, but in stages.

That evening during a dinner held by the Human Rights Institute's New York branch, I answered a question about reform policies under the Kim Young-sam government. "I think the cleansing of factions in the military and the real-name financial transaction system stand out among President Kim's reform achievements," I replied. "President Kim Young-sam should do well so that we can show those people who argued for 'the retirement of both Kims.' I really hope President Kim succeeds."

The dinner guests all laughed, but I really meant what I said—I hoped that President Kim would succeed. However, there were dark nuclear clouds hanging over the sky of the Korean Peninsula.

I continued my lectures in major US cities, including New York, Atlanta, Washington, DC, Pittsburg, and Los Angeles. The Carter Center, the Korea-America Association, the US Congress, the LA Human Rights Institute, and Korean-Americans all wanted to hear from me. During this period, the North Korean nuclear capability crisis escalated. The atmosphere in the US Congress was extremely tense. In Korea, people were stocking up so much ramen and rice that they were hard to come by.

During my lecture trips to the US, I strongly urged a package deal for the North Korean nuclear crisis. In other words, the US needed to economically and diplomatically cooperate with North Korea in exchange for North Korea's abandonment of nuclear development. I also urged that the Korea-US joint military training exercise Team Spirit be brought to an end. To me, this kind of package deal seemed to be the most effective and persuasive alternative.

On December 10, an international conference for Asian democracy and human rights was founded in Bangkok, Thailand. I delivered the keynote address and attended as a Korean representative. I also met the mayor of Bangkok, Chamlong Srimuang. His humble house and thrifty lifestyle were was deeply impressive.

I often went to the flower market in the Gupabal area of Seoul with my wife. We bought plants and transplanted them in our garden. The fun we had doing this was beyond imagination. We had a persimmon tree in our garden, and every year it bore large and delicious fruit. I loved looking at them and counting the fruit as I strolled through my garden. One day, I noticed that the number of persimmons was greatly reduced. I asked my wife what had happened. "I asked people to pick some so that we can taste them," she answered.

"If you wanted to eat persimmons so much, you should have bought them," I muttered to myself.

"Why should we give all those persimmons to the magpies?" she asked.

My retirement allowed me to enjoy some other leisurely activities, too. I frequented the cultural scene and watched movies like *Blue in You*, *Sopyonje*, *I'd Like to Visit That Island*, *Hwimori*, *Schindler's List*, and *Vanished*; the newly created *pansori Rice*; the opera *River Geumgang*; and the musical *Guys and Dolls*. Interestingly, after I watched or attended a show, audiences flooded it—perhaps because of that, I received a lot of invitations to performances and exhibitions. I was grateful, but sorry that I couldn't go to all of them.

After watching *Sopyonje*, I told the actors and staff, "I think the sorrow in the movie is neither a grudge nor despair, but the people's will not to give up and try to make the best of their situation." Upon hearing this, Korea University Professor Suh Ji-moon wrote a newspaper column entitled "*Sopyonje* and DJ's Sorrow." She wrote:

> Is there anyone who has more reasons for sorrow than DJ? However, the more reasons he had for sorrow and the more he represented groups of people with great sorrow, the more Korean people—more than half of Koreans—have distrusted and guarded against him. Regardless of my feelings about the movie *Sopyonje*, I find it significant that after watching it DJ said that sorrow is not for revenge, but for endurance, overcoming, and achievement. The timid Korean people who feared the sorrows of DJ, the victim of Korean political history, while they themselves condemned the very history that brought sorrow to him, are now not just moved by but also feel sorry for the resolute attitude that DJ showed while finishing his eventful political life with a defeat.

Later, actress Oh Jung-hae, who played the main character in *Sopyonje*, requested that I officiate her wedding. I witnessed a brilliant young couple during this wedding and said, "Love is completed through patience."

On January 18, 1994, Reverend Moon Ik-hwan suddenly passed away from cardiac arrest. I didn't even dream of him leaving us so suddenly. As a theologian, a pastor, a poet, and a reunification activist, Reverend Moon had lived a clear and upright life. He was one of the most representative people of conscience and intelligence in our divided country, and had lived fiercely and passionately in its midst. I sometimes agreed passionately with him and at other times our opinions differed. However, we fundamentally agreed about wanting and working to bring about a world where all people were their own masters.

Reverend Moon always said emphatically, "Democracy is the Korean people's resurrection and reunification is our nation's resurrection." I can still hear him speaking these words. Although he was a stern fighter against the dictatorial regime, he was a sensitive person who could not fall asleep easily on autumn nights when the leaves were falling. He was a true scholar who had devoted his energy and time entirely to lecturing and translating the Bible until he participated in the Declaration for Democracy and National Salvation on March 1, 1976. Ever since then, he was always on the scene where people's rights were being trampled. We lost the reunification worker of our time, and his death was a blow to the reunification movement. As soon as I heard the news of his death, I rushed to his mortuary. Looking at his photograph, I could not help but shed tears. I took the role of advisor for his funeral committee and gave a memorial address at his funeral. During that address, I said, "Reverend Moon felt the kind of pain one would feel when his body is cut down the middle about our nation's division. He symbolized the purest national spirit of our times."

After a lot of hard work, I launched the Kim Dae-jung Peace Foundation on January 27, 1994. I was hoping that this foundation would become the cradle for working toward peace in the Korean Peninsula and for the prosperity of our nation, the development of democracy in Asia, and world peace. Former Soviet Union President Gorbachev, former president of the Philippines Corazon Aquino, and former German Minister of Foreign Affairs Genscher accepted offices as overseas counselors. Within Korea, Cardinal Kim Sou-hwan, Reverend Kang Won-yong, Jogye Order of Korean Buddhism Director Seo Eui-hyun, and President of Korea Legal Aid Center for Family Relations Lee Tai-young accepted the office of counselors. Advisory committee members included Kim Chong-un, Kim Hui-jip, Song Ja, Park Hong, Chang Eul-byeong, Kim Min-ha, Cho Wan-gyu, Ahn Byung Moo, Lee Don-myung, O Gi-pyeong, Byeon Hyeong-yun, Lee Sae-joong, Cho Sun, Kang Moon-kyu, Ko Un, Kim Chum-kon, Kwon Ho-kyung, Suh Young-hoon, Shin Nak-kyun, Chang Gi-cheon, and Hahn Seung-hun. Overseas advisory committee members included president of Moscow State University Victor Sadovnici, Dr. Selig Harrison of the Carnegie Foundation, and Assistant Director of Harvard-Yenching Institute Edward Baker.

The Kim Dae-jung Peace Foundation built its nest in the Aryung Building in Changcheon-dong, Seoul. About 200 guests, including Mrs. Aquino and former East German Chancellor de Maiziere, attended its opening ceremony. I was deeply moved as I looked at the Peace Foundation sign.

We held a celebration event with more than 2000 guests at the 63 Building in Yeouido, Seoul. Cardinal Kim Sou-hwan blessed the occasion by saying, "If we have to point to a Korean politician who suffered the most pain and experienced the most danger, it must be president of the Peace Foundation Kim Dae-jung. I hope that the Peace Foundation will accomplish its mission and contribute greatly to the reunification of Korea as well as democracy and peace in Asia and in the world."

Former President of the Philippines Corazon Aquino also said in her congratulatory remarks, "President Kim and I are comrades who share religious and democratic values. I wish for the Peace Foundation's success for the sake of world peace."

People were passionately interested in our foundation. When we accepted applications for five research scholars, more than one hundred Ph.D.-holders applied. I went to the foundation office every day. For the first time since my defeat in the presidential election a year ago, I had a job. I appointed Mr. Cho Young-hwan as Secretary General and Mr. Chung Dong-chea as chief secretary.

The central research subjects of the foundation were peace in and the reunification of Korea, Asian democracy, and world peace. The first international scholarly seminar was held on March 16. It was titled "The Relationship Between the Collision of Civilizations and Asia." Director of Peace Research Institute Oslo (PRIO) Dan Smith and Hanyang University Professor Gong Sung-jin presented their papers.

A little before this seminar, on February 13, I heard the news of poet Kim Nam-joo's death and visited his mortuary. Kim Nam-joo was one of the most representative resistance poets of our times.

On March 17, I received an honorary Ph.D. in political science from Wonkwang University; this was my first honorary Ph.D. in Korea. President Kim Sam-ryong and Graduate Dean Han Jong-man warmly welcomed me.

June 1994 was like a nightmare for South and North Korea and the US. After the failure of a package deal for the North Korean nuclear capability issue, North Korea ignored the US warning and removed nuclear fuel rods. When their diplomatic efforts failed, the Pentagon began considering an attack on North Korean nuclear facilities. Although it was supposed to be a precision attack with the specific target of Yongbyon, it was sure to expand to a full-scale war. If war broke out on the Korean Peninsula again, the Pentagon predicted that the casualties would number 52,000 US military troops, 490,000 Korean troops, and more than a million civilians. It was also obvious that most industrial facilities would be destroyed.

US Secretary of State William Perry concluded that nuclear development beyond the red line in North Korea should be immediately stopped through an attack of the nuclear facilities in Yongbyon. He presented a three-step strategic plan at the National Security Council, presided over by President Clinton. The war looked inevitable.

At this juncture, former president Carter brought miraculously hopeful news during a trip to North Korea. President Kim Il-sung and former president Carter reached a remarkable agreement: If the US removed its threat of nuclear attack on North Korea, then North Korea would freeze its nuclear development. The US accepted this agreement.

Former President Carter's visit to North Korea was possible because of my recommendation. On May 12, 1994, I presented a proposal about North Korean nuclear development during a speech at the National Press Club in Washington, DC. It had been more than a year since North Korea's withdrawal from NPT and the situation was bogged down in a bottomless swamp. In my keynote address, I presented a concrete plan for the package deal, arguing that "North Korea and the US should yield two things to each other. North Korea should give up its ambition for nuclear capability and guarantee South Korea's safety. The US should pursue economic cooperation through diplomacy and guarantee North Korean security by methods such as ending the Team Spirit exercise."

I then proposed sending someone in for a dialogue with President Kim Il-sung. "I'd like to recommend that the US send an elder politician who is internationally respected, trusted in China and North Korea, and who has a similar position to President Clinton," I said. "I believe that a special envoy from President Clinton could play a significant role in US relations with China and North Korea."

After the keynote address, I was asked for my recommendation on a candidate for special envoy. "I think that would be former President Jimmy Carter," I responded.

Because I expected this question, I had called former president Carter the day before to let him know I was planning to mention his name during my address. He gladly agreed and he said that if he ended up going to North Korea, he would need my advice.

After this news reached Korea, one after another, the ruling Minja Party officials stepped forward and condemned or ridiculed my proposal. They called former president Carter's visit to North Korea unrealistic and said that my idea was ridiculous. However, my speech at the National Press Club moved the US and was repeatedly broadcast. The US seriously considered my proposal while carefully watching North Korea. In the end, former president Carter visited North Korea for three days upon President Kim Il-sung's invitation. He successfully reached an agreement with President Kim Il-sung, thus removing the danger of war.

As I mentioned earlier, former president Carter wanted to seek out my advice while he was in Seoul, but President Kim Young-sam opposed his visit to North Korea. Senior Secretary for Foreign Affairs and National Security to the President openly ridiculed former president Carter. "I wonder why an elderly man like Carter wants to go to North Korea without any guarantee of success. Perhaps he covets the Nobel Peace Prize," he mused.

Upon former president Carter's arrival in Seoul, President Kim Young-sam attempted to dissuade him from visiting North Korea. Because of this, former president Carter was unable to visit me. US Ambassador to Korea James T. Laney visited my house in Donggyo-dong instead. He told me that Mr. Carter was very worried about his visit. I told him that the former president should not worry. "I know a little bit about President Kim Il-sung. He wouldn't have invited former president Carter if he didn't mean to offer some gifts," I assured the ambassador. "His visit will definitely be a success."

My package deal proposal and suggestion that former president Carter visit North Korea played a decisive role in shifting the political situation from confrontation to dialogue. Former president Carter crossed Panmunjeom with the unexpected gift of the South-North Summit. I am truly grateful for his courage and wisdom, for clearing the dark clouds of war from our sky.

President Kim Il-sung suddenly died right before the South-North Summit, on July 8. It was such a pity that this unexpected incident happened right at the cusp of solid progress toward the peace and reunification of the Korean Peninsula for the first time in fifty years. Many were also concerned that his death would cause the South-North relationship to deteriorate.

Kim Il-sung's death left behind a feeling of emptiness. During my imprisonment, I had played a checkers game with President Kim Il-sung in my mind. If I ever met him, I wanted to openly discuss with and propose to him the best way for our two lands to live and let live. Although he had contributed to the Korean independence fight during the Japanese colonial period and was quite successful in uniting his people, he was ruthless in cleansing his opponents in order to seize power, and he governed North Korea with the most vicious dictatorship of any communist country.

I heard that President Kim Il-sung knew a lot about me and wanted to have a conversation. In fact, I was politically damaged by this rumor. I even sent a letter to President Kim Il-sung through Japanese Representative Utsunomiya Tokuma, in which I requested that he not say anything like that about me. At any rate, the absence of Kim Il-sung meant the arrival of a new wind in the Korean Peninsula.

In South Korea, people overwhelmingly predicted that North Korea would collapse at any moment. Kim Young-sam's government immediately put the entire military on alert. The preparation for the summit dissipated and they seemed to be planning for what they saw as North Korea's imminent collapse.

Things were thrown into turmoil three days after the death of President Kim Il-sung. At the National Assembly Foreign Affairs and Reunification Committee, Democratic Party Assemblyman Lee Bu-young carefully asked, "Does our government have any intention of making a condolence call?" Immediately, the conservative media took his words out of context and went on the attack. "How could he suggest that our government make a condolence call for the war criminal who caused the Korean War?" they asked. This was the beginning of the Condolence Call Crisis. Soon, ultra-right-wing characters added their voices to the condemnation. The South-North relationship froze immediately. I was very sorry to see this development.

A condolence visit can be executed for various reasons. Sometimes you go to cry with principal mourners, but other times you make a condolence call for diplomatic reasons. If we had acted more wisely then the South-North relationship could have improved. Many countries, including the US, Japan, China, and Russia, were sorry about the South Korean government's ungenerous behavior during the Condolence Call Crisis. In contrast, North Korea exercised extraordinary diplomacy and succeeded in drawing the four countries into their camp. South Korea's position weakened in comparison. North Korea demonstrated an arrogant attitude toward South Korea, even going so far as to ask for an apology from the president.

The Condolence Call Crisis made me realize once again how important diplomacy was. The Cold War era was clearly going away. Other countries were also no longer blindly following the US. It was a time when Korea should have reinforced its diplomatic capabilities and engaged in multifaceted diplomatic activities with various countries, while continuing to strengthen ties with the US.

Instead, South and North Korea became enemies again. The South Korean government announced a whole host of national security breach incidents, thus creating the national security situation. North Korea also rushed to resume its slanderous broadcasts about South Korea.

I flew to the US on September 17, hoping to resolve the hardened relationship between the South and the North, as well as to draw the North and the US back into the reconciliation phase. I met former president Jimmy Carter in Atlanta and thanked him for his efforts to bring peace to the Korean Peninsula. He told me, "I wouldn't have visited North Korea if you hadn't encouraged me to go. What would have happened if President Kim Il-sung died and I hadn't visited? The Korean Peninsula would be incredibly tense right now—some crisis could have already happened. So, I'd like to thank you and let you know that I appreciate what you've done." His words made me feel that we had achieved a great deal.

I hoped that former president Carter would visit North Korea again. But he said that although the US Department of State would welcome a visit to North Korea, the current situation could not be resolved without the cooperation of the South Korean government. He also said that although he had been criticized in the US for negotiating with a dictator, he always thought of and was encouraged by what I said about the Sunshine Policy—the policy symbolic of reconciliation and cooperation between the South and the North. The former president Carter did not visit North Korea again.

I met Assistant Secretary of State for East Asian and Pacific Affairs Winston Lord, Senator Edward M. Kennedy, Senate leader and Republican Party member Bob Dole, former White House National Security Advisor Zbigniew Brzezinski, and former Ambassador to Korea Donald Gregg. I maintained that the improvement of North Korean and US relations would be an essential prerequisite to peace in the Korean Peninsula. I also warned against North Korean attempts to alienate South Korea and the US. Since the Condolence Call Crisis, North Korea tried to completely exclude South Korea from the discussions they were having with the US. This became known as the Communication with the US and Blocking South Korea Policy.

I actively warned against this movement and argued that all relevant parties should be involved in the resolution of the Korean Peninsula situation, that the US should not give North Korea any excuses. Although many people agreed with me, South Korea could not actively participate in the North Korea-US conference in Geneva shortly thereafter.

American and North Korean delegates held talks in Geneva from September 23 to October 21, 1994, during which they negotiated a resolution for the nuclear issue on the Korean Peninsula. Both sides agreed on actions for this resolution, including US arrangement to provide the DPRK with a Light Water Reactor (LWR) Project; US arrangement to offset the energy forgone due to the freeze of the DPRK's graphite-moderated reactors and related facilities; the DPRK freeze of its graphite-moderated reactors and related facilities and eventual dismantling of these reactors and related facilities; and expert discussion of issues related to alternative energy and the replacement of the graphite-moderated reactor program with the LWR Project. In essence, the US guaranteed the North Korean regime in exchange for the freeze of all nuclear development. Thanks to this, the dark cloud of war began to clear from the Korean Peninsula. Unfortunately, the Kim Young-sam regime did not participate in this agreement due to its declaration following North Korea's withdrawal from NPT in 1993. It did not accept the package deal the US was pursuing, either. In the end, South Korea was thoroughly excluded from negotiation and ended up paying 70 percent of the costs to support the North Korean LWR project.

Around that time, President Kim Young-sam invited me to the Blue House. He showed me a satellite photograph of the Korean Peninsula taken at night, where the South was bright while the North was dark.

"Look at this," President Kim said. "This is how North Korea is. We have nothing to worry about if North Korea collapses tomorrow."

Since I had no information, I said nothing. However, I knew that, at the very least, North Korea wasn't going to collapse that easily. President Kim's thought that Korea would reunite now that Kim Il-sung had died was both very naïve and dangerous. President Kim Il-sung had already handed over the power to his son. President Kim Young-sam made a critical mistake by ignoring North Korea after acknowledging it by preparing for the summit. North Koreans were very upset and instantly united.

Upon the invitation of the Chinese People's Institute of Foreign Affairs, I visited China for the first time on November 1, 1994. Because there wasn't a direct flight between Seoul and Beijing then, I traveled from Tianjin Airport to Beijing by car. During my visit, I also gave a lecture at the Chinese Academy of Social Sciences titled "The Age of Northeast Asia and the Direction of Korea-China Cooperation." I was awarded an honorary professorship at the Chinese Academy of Social Sciences, Nankai University, and Fudan University.

I also met with Chinese officials at the Ministry of Foreign Affairs and discussed current affairs in Northeast Asia and the Korean Peninsula. When I met Chairman of the National Committee of the Chinese People's Political Consultative Conference Li Ruihuan, I thanked him for the contribution China had made in easing tension in the Korean Peninsula. He appreciated my role in enabling Carter's visit to North Korea. I emphasized two things about the North Korea issue: First, that although China and North Korea shared the same ideology, China should remain fair in matters related to both of the Koreas' national interests so that it could play the role of arbiter between the two and lead three-way cooperation among the three countries. Second, I emphasized that this was the way to peace and co-prosperity in Northeast Asia and the Korean Peninsula. Chairman Li readily agreed with me. In Beijing, I visited Zǐjìnchéng and the Great Wall of China; in Xian, I looked around Qin Shi Huang Mausoleum and Terracotta Army. Envoy Kim Ha-joong took special care of me.

During my ten-day visit to China, I got the impression that China was dynamic. I could feel the power of a great continent. I also felt a renewed pride that Korea had maintained the nation and its culture for so long despite the repeated invasions and pacifications from this grand country. In Shanghai, I gathered with reporters and reflected on my visit to China and how optimistic I felt about its future. "In China, they will maintain the collective leadership system after the death of Deng Xiao Ping, so there won't be a power struggle."

I founded the Asia and Pacific Democratic Leaders Council at the Hilton Hotel in Seoul on December 1. Former president of the Philippines Corazon Aquino and I were elected co-presidents. Attendees included former government heads such as former Costa Rican president Oscar Arias Sanchez and former president of the Myanmar government in exile Sein Win. Additionally included were twenty-six scholars like Professor Bruce Cumings and forty-four congressmen from various countries.

In my opening remarks, I said: "Today is the day when Asians found an organization for Asian democratization for the first time. An Asian tradition of democracy will revive and deeply root itself by the early twenty-first century."

In 1994, I refuted former prime minister of Singapore Li Quan Yu in an article published in the November–December issue of *Foreign Affairs*, a renowned scholarly journal on international politics published in the US Prime Minister Li Quan Yu argued that Asian countries did not have a tradition of democratic philosophy, and that it was unreasonable to demand democracy from them. This logic could be used to defend developmentalist dictatorship in Asian countries.

In my opinion, there was a rich tradition of democratic philosophy in Asia, despite the fact that the West created democratic institutions and mechanisms first. If we install a hydro-generator in an Asian river, it will still generate electricity. Water flows downward everywhere.

In my article "Is Culture Destiny?" I set forth the following argument about democratic philosophy in Asia.

It is widely accepted that English political philosopher John Locke laid the foundation for modern democracy. According to Locke, sovereign rights reside with the people and, based on a contract with the people, leaders are given a mandate to govern, which the people can withdraw. But almost two millennia before Locke, Chinese philosopher Meng-tzu preached similar ideas. According to his "Politics of Royal Ways," the king is the "Son of Heaven," and heaven bestowed on its son a mandate to provide good government, that is, to provide good for the people. If he did not govern righteously, the people had the right to rise up and overthrow his government in the name of heaven. Meng-tzu even justified regicide, saying that once a king loses the mandate of heaven he is no longer worthy of his subjects' loyalty. The people came first, Meng-tzu said, the country second, and the king third. The ancient Chinese philosophy of Minben Zhengchi, or "people-based politics," teaches that "the will of the people is the will of heaven" and that one should "respect the people as heaven" itself.

A native religion of Korea, Donghak, went even further, advocating that "man is heaven" and that one must serve man as one does heaven. In 1894, these ideas inspired and motivated nearly half a million peasants to revolt against exploitation by feudalistic government internally and imperialistic forces externally. There are no ideas more fundamental to democracy than the teachings of Confucianism, Buddhism, and Donghak. Clearly, Asia has democratic philosophies as profound as those of the West.

This article drew international attention. In my debate with Prime Minister Li Quan Yu, world-class scholars and leaders agreed with me—at first cautiously, and later openly.

I used the term Sunshine Policy for the first time during my 1994 talk at America's Heritage Foundation, a powerful conservative think tank. The title of my talk was "The Sunshine Policy Based on Strong Will." Within this, I explained the power of the sun: "An interesting phenomenon is that America has, on the one hand, triumphed brilliantly where it has applied the Sunshine Policy; it has failed miserably where it has stuck to the strong-wind policy. For example, the Sunshine Policy toward the former Soviet Union and Eastern European countries resulted in their disintegration, without a single bullet being fired from outside. This was truly a brilliant achievement on the part of America's sunshine diplomacy. Similarly, the Sunshine Policy has pushed China to the point where one can no longer entertain the possibility of reverting to the old regime. On the other hand, in spite of its all-out effort to subjugate a nation, America was humiliated by Vietnam, and a similar effort against Cuba has produced nothing but headaches for the US.

"In this context, the latest success of the Sunshine Policy has been the Geneva agreement between the United States and North Korea … South Koreans do not wish any harm to, nor do they want confrontation with, their compatriots in the North. South Korea sincerely places hope in the stability of the Kim Jong Il government and its quick recovery from economic crisis, because South Koreans seek to coexist peacefully and march together toward prosperity and reunification in the warmth of the sunshine.

"In conclusion, I would like to emphasize that it is important for the US to stay with the Sunshine Policy in order to bring the North out of international isolation, and to maintain its forces on the Korean Peninsula for the benefit of the region as a whole as well as for its own strategic interest."

Along with the Sunshine Policy, the book *Kim Dae-jung's Three-step Reunification Plan* was completed based on our passionate work at the Peace Foundation. Behind this hard work was a remarkable person named Lim Dong-won, who had enabled the July 7 Declaration and the South-North Basic Agreement under the Roh Tae-woo government. As he had rich experience and outstanding ability in negotiations with and strategies for North Korea, I wanted to invite him to the Peace Foundation. He was in between jobs after serving as the deputy minister of the Board of National Unification, so I sent a messenger to invite him to work at the Peace Foundation. Utterly surprised, he refused, saying that he had no qualifications to work there. I sent another messenger to persuade him. Mr. Lim refused again, this time with the excuse that he was in poor health. I sent a third messenger and, finally, he responded affirmatively.

Over lunch, I proposed that Mr. Lim work at the Peace Foundation. For two hours, we talked about current affairs, including the South-North problem and North Korea's nuclear capability. As I expected, he had outstanding knowledge and insight. He sympathized with me and accepted my offer. I appointed him as Secretary General of the Peace Foundation. Mr. Lim had no interest in politics. To borrow a vulgar expression, what I did was like a cattle thief stealing a lady.

Secretary General Lim and I passionately debated. Neither of us gave in easily when we thought we were right. The hours passed quickly during our discussions and debates. Once we spent the entire night talking about the three-step unification plan in a hotel room. Upon much discussion, we drafted a manuscript based on my previous work. The end result of this was *Kim Dae-jung's Three-step Reunification Plan.*

Many people contributed to making of this book. Kim Nam-sik, Kim Sung-hoon, Ra Jong-il, Park Chong-hwa, Baek Gyeong-nam, and Han Sang-jin participated in the steering committee. Park Kun-young, Pak Pyeong-seok, Lee Kang Rae, Lee Seok-soo, Lee Sung-bong, Choe Seong, Ha Sang-sik, Ham In-hui, and Hwang Ju-hong participated in the research committee.

The book was published in August 1995, and was the result of more than three decades of work and the sweat of more than a hundred specialists from all fields. In the preface I wrote:

Presenting this Three-Step Reunification Plan to the Korean people at this juncture where the happiness from five decades of liberation intersects with the regret about five decades of division, I feel a flood of emotions. I feel that I'm finally beginning to repay my debt to our people. This is an important fruit of the unification picture that I have been painting without taking the brush out of my hand for a moment over the past twenty-five years. Now we have the blueprint for reunification in our hands.

INTO THE SEA OF THE PEOPLE'S WILL (1995–1997)

Kim Young-sam government's catchphrase was "The Creation of a New Korea." In the beginning, it implemented reform policies, such as the high officials' asset disclosure, the implementation of a real-name financial transaction system, and a law reform bill. They also disbanded the Hanahoe Society, a military political force. The Korean people welcomed them, thinking that a civilian government was different from the previous military ones. In the early honeymoon period, President Kim Young-sam's popularity soared.

However, beginning in the second year of his presidency, serious problems began to emerge. The side effects of his dogmatic governance appeared everywhere as he simply ignored the will of both the people and democratic forces. He also failed to acknowledge the opposition party as a partner in governance.

Large-scale disasters began to occur, one after another. Among them were a train overturning at Gupo Station on the Gyeongbu line; a ferry sinking in the Western Sea; the collapse of the Grand Seongsu Bridge over the Han River; a fire on a cruise ship in Chungju; an Asiana airplane crash; a gas explosion in Ahyeon-dong, Seoul; an explosion at the Daegu subway construction site; and the collapse of the Sampoong department store building. Additionally, a cluster of corrupt tax officials was arrested for intercepting people's tax money.

Despite all these problems, the government officials worried only about their own safety and interests. The Kim Young-sam government could not control them. Although the president shouted, "Reform Without Pause!" the Korean people's expectations continued to be neglected, until they finally turned their backs against the government. President Kim was like the captain waving a flag in a ship with a dead motor.

Because the Kim Young-sam government was born from an illicit merger with the fifth and sixth republic military governments, its power was limited. Although it could push some reform through in the beginning, it lost its grip as time went by. Although the flag of reform and inspection was fluttering, corrupt incidents like the Tonghwa Bank

Incident, the Slot Machine and Casino Incident, and the Sangmudae Army Training Facilities Corruption Incident continued to occur. People also began to notice that the authorities picked and chose to punish only those criminals who belonged to the ruling power's political opponents. People openly talked about "target inspections."

Although President Kim shouted, "Personnel matters are everything!" his government appointed only those officials who had connections. People ridiculed this policy and twisted President Kim's catchphrase into "Personnel matters are the ruin." Discipline among government officials and employees collapsed because they were too busy trying to find connections.

On May 19, 1995, President Kim said something unbelievable—a remark nobody expected to come from the mouth of the head of a civilian government—at a luncheon with the board of directors of the International Press Institute (IPI) Korea branch. Speaking about the year-long labor-management dispute at Korea Telecommunication (KT), President Kim said, "The Korea Telecommunication Labor Union has interfered with information and communication by taking illegal actions such as waging a struggle against the Korean government's communication policies. This means that they have the intention of subverting our government."

I was extremely surprised to hear this news. President Kim's perspective on labor relations was not different from that of the dictatorial regime at all.

The core leadership of the KT Labor Union escaped to the Myeongdong Cathedral and Jogyesa Temple when the police raid was imminent. They waged a strike and the union members waged a legal struggle. The police suddenly raided the Myeongdong Cathedral and Jogyesa Temple on June 6 and arrested all of the union leaders. The Myeongdong Cathedral and Jogyesa Temple were both extremely indignant and out-of-office democratic forces condemned the police action.

The Myeongdong Cathedral protested particularly vehemently, issuing a statement that read:

> The present government violated the laws of the church that have been kept for two millennia. The illegal power abuse committed during the 5th and 6th Republics and condemned by the people has not changed with the current government. The government is responsible for any incidents that happen from now on.

Every day, Catholic priests, nuns, and believers staged rallies condemning the current government's abuse of power. This marked the end of the Kim Young-sam government's reform. Instead of managing the country in collaboration with the people and democratic forces, it aligned itself with reactionary conservative forces.

Even harder to understand was the government's excessive check and oppression of me. People found it hard to believe that the civilian government ran a "Unit Solely in Charge of Kim Dae-jung" in collaboration with the police, ANSP, and Blue House. But it was true. They monitored my every movement and reported it to the president. The existence of this unit was revealed in the October 1995 issue of the monthly journal *Shindonga*. When my book was scheduled for release, they went to the publisher to block it. They also applied pressure to stop production on a movie about me, as well as attempted to put a stop to my lectures at universities. The media further revealed that there were four safe houses around my house in Donggyo-dong. President Kim did not consider me to be his collaborator in building a democratic society in Korea. He did not want to accept the fact that I had risen again.

President Kim Young-sam kicked Minja Party president Kim Jong-pil out as well. President Kim Young-sam and the Sangdo-dong faction were busy shouting about globalization without thinking about what that word meant. And then they claimed that Minja Party president Kim Jong-pil did not suit the image of globalization. There was a rumor that President Kim Jong-pil was prevented from attending events that he should have as the party president. It was not just neglect, but an insult.

Even Mr. Kim Jong-pil, famous for his knack for living as the second-best man, could not endure it. After a meeting with President Kim Young-sam, he left the Minja Party on February 9, 1995. He criticized President Kim Young-sam and his followers for being "people who dump their promises like trash." On March 30, he established a new party called Jayuminju yeonhap (Freedom and Democracy Alliance; abbreviated as Jaminryeon) and adopted constitutional amendment for the parliamentary government system as its main principle.

The local election was approaching. On June 27, 1995, the four local elections—for heads and assembly members of large local administration units, as well as heads and assembly members of basic local administration units—were held at the same time. People were very interested in this election. Mr. Lee Ki-taek was leading the Democratic Party, after being elected at the party convention during my stay in England. I had expressed my sincerest support for him then.

Although I was an ordinary member of the party, I tried my best to add my power to the election campaign. In contrast, the Minja Party promoted "generation change" and tried their best to drag me down politically. Our party president Lee Ki-taek behaved rather strangely. He spoke about generation change sympathetically and led out-of-parliament struggles every time. Although I urged him to stay in the parliament, he ignored my point of view as the opinion of just one party member.

President Lee nominated unlikely characters to local posts, which caused popular ridicule. He ignored party and public opinion, choosing only his followers. Although this election was critical to the future of the party, he wouldn't budge. His nomination of Mr. Chang Gyeong-u as the governor of the Gyeonggi-do province was a good example. I invited Mr. Lee to my house and said, "I would be greatly indebted to you if you yield the nomination of Gyeonggi-do governor to Mr. Lee Chong-chan. I'll fully support your party presidency for the next term."

I tried to persuade him by sharing the poll numbers, which indicated that our party could win the Gyeonggi-do governor election with Mr. Lee Chong-chan as a candidate. Of course, President Lee should have known this, too. "I'll respect your opinion in my decision," he replied.

Unfortunately, he did not change his position at all. I was very disappointed in his self-complacency. Not knowing what else to do, I invited Mr. Chang Gyeong-u to my house. "In my opinion, it would be hard for you to win the Gyeonggi-do election," I attempted to persuade him. "Please yield this time. I'm sure you'll be elected in the next National Assembly election."

Mr. Chang also avoided an affirmative answer. The problems didn't stop there. During the Gyeonggi-do branch convention where they were going to elect party candidates, it was discovered that Candidate Chang was distributing money to voters. The vote counting had to stop! Candidate An Dong-seon's camp presented the actual envelope with money in it as evidence and declared that they would not accept the result of the voting. This internal struggle occurred at the party's historic first candidate nomination through election. In the end, Candidate An Dong-seon stepped down from candidacy. President Lee visited me and said that he would take all responsibility if Candidate Chang lost the election.

There really was nothing more for me to do at that point. I couldn't keep on arguing with him when the election was fast approaching. The commotion surrounding the nomination of the Gyeonggi-do gubernatorial candidacy made the headlines every day. Neither party members nor the Korean people liked the way President Lee handled the matter. Although it was initially presumed that the Democratic Party would easily win the election, the results were now unpredictable. My fantastic plan involving Seoul's Mayor Cho Sun and Gyeonggi-do Governor Lee Chong-chan collapsed. After all of the hard work involved in bringing Candidate Cho to our party, now we couldn't be sure of his victory. The poll results indicated that the Democratic Party's election prognosis was not good.

At this juncture, party members and individual candidates both strongly urged me to embark on a stump tour to enhance our chances in the election. Candidates included mention of their "special" relationship with me in their pamphlets. In the end, President Lee and the party leadership officially asked me to do a stump tour for the candidates. Even Candidate Chang Gyeong-u requested that I give a stump speech. I finally officially registered as the speaker of our party.

Once again, I set out on a nationwide campaign tour. Unexpectedly large crowds were waiting for me at the rally sites. Wherever I went in the greater Seoul area, scores of thousands gathered. When I finished my speech and left one rally to go to the next, people surrounded me and chanted my name. I lived on *kimbop* and tried to go as many as eleven rallies a day. Wherever I went, I saw placards that read: "We are waiting for Kim Dae-jung."

During my speeches, I condemned the Kim Young-sam government's hypocrisy. "The so-called civilian government of Kim Young-sam called the labor-management dispute at KT a subversive activity and exaggerated its danger," I spoke. "I deplore the police raiding the Myeongdong Cathedral and Jogyesa Temple. Not even the Japanese colonizers and military dictators violated those sacred places. It is hateful that they place the epithet 'civilian' in front of their name."

I also argued for "equal rights" among regions as an alternative for regional hegemony and antagonism. I was of the opinion that only regions with equal rights could collaborate horizontally. I said, "We have so far lived under the TK hegemony and PK hegemony. A specific region monopolized all rights and privileges, while other regions were marginalized. Unequal and aberrant development among regions has blocked the progress of our country. However, we'll deal a fatal blow to this regional hegemony in the June 27 local election. This election will open up the road to the age of localism, where regions enjoy not vertically but horizontally equal rights."

The media made an issue of my proposition. "The upcoming local election will serve as the arena of judgment for Mr. Kim Dae-jung's return to politics and his argument for equal regional rights," they claimed. This subtle agitation aimed to induce anti-Kim Dae-jung and anti-Democratic Party sentiments. My return to politics and argument for equal regional rights became the biggest election issues. The wind was changing in the greater Seoul area.

At this juncture, President Kim Young-sam, who was also the Minja Party president, proposed the generational shift. In an interview published in the June 26 issue of *Time* magazine, he said, "When my term is over, I am certain that more than 90 percent of the Korean people will want a generational shift in the political arena. I can confidently say that a candidate from the next generation will be elected in the next presidential election." Despite the fact that anybody could see this remark was aimed at me, our party president Lee Ki-taek welcomed it. "His remark reflects the current of the times," he commented. Nonetheless, it is the people who elect the president. Politicians should follow the people's will. President Kim Young-sam was rude in randomly predicting the people's will.

The Minja Party mobilized all of its leadership to attack my argument for equal regional rights. Again, they plotted to abuse regional antagonism between Honam and Yeongnam. Although the people abandoned their support of the Minja Party, it continued to operate. What was interesting, though, was our party president Lee Ki-taek's actions: He met with Minister of Government Administration Seo Seok-jai, thereby creating all kinds of conjecture.

The day before the election, I performed stump speeches at seven locations throughout Seoul: Tapgol Park, Seoul Station Square, Myeong-dong, Sinchon, Dongnimmun Park, Marronnier Park in Hyehwa-dong, and Yeongdeungpo. I tried my best.

In the end, the result was our party's overwhelming victory and the Minja Party was completely crushed. Of fifteen gubernatorial positions, the Minja Party won only five. Even in the Kangwon and Chungbuk regions, which traditionally voted on the side of the ruling party, Minja Party candidates lost. The Democratic Party lost by only a narrow margin in Gyeonggi-do. If President Lee had followed my advice, our party could have swept the entire greater Seoul area.

In terms of the election of basic local administration heads, the Minja Party won less than a third of the seats—only 71 out of 230. In particular, they won only two seats out of twenty-five in Seoul. Our party won all twenty-three of the remaining seats. The Democratic Party held the most seats, winning eighty-four districts nationwide. My return to politics, which the media and ruling party made an issue of in order to block my return, was essentially approved by the people.

Even after the election, President Lee Ki-taek's movements were suspicious. Naturally, his responsibility for the mistaken nomination of the Gyeonggi-do gubernatorial candidate and self-complacent management of the party became an issue. He had promised to take responsibility, but he did not show any intention to follow through with that. Ridiculously, he claimed that because our party won the election, he didn't have to take responsibility. He then brought up the issue of a generational shift again. It seemed impossible for the Democratic Party to be reborn as a strong opposition party with solid leadership.

On July 13, 1995, fifty-one national assemblymen officially requested that I resume my political career. They argued that the opposition party should be reestablished and our country righted after Kim Young-sam's misgoverning. I decided to accept this request. I could not ignore the Korean people's suffering, even though I might be criticized.

In addition, the election campaign proved that people still wanted me. Our party members said that I was the only person who could prop up the opposition party and gather supporters. Someone told me about former French President Francois Mitterrand. "He lost three times and then won the fourth time. You should try one more time," I was urged. Frankly, that gave me courage. Besides, my three losses were all the result of unfair fights, red-scare fabrication, and other election fraud tactics.

The most fundamental reason why I decided to return to politics was because I wanted to accomplish my two lifelong dreams: to establish Korea as a democratic country and to contribute to our nation's reunification. I could not give up without accomplishing even one of them. I had thought deeply about my future in front of the collapsed Berlin Wall, the scene of German reunification. I wanted to change the world by becoming the president. I wanted to repay the people's support for me. I was equipped with policies that I had taken a long time to polish. I had passion. I decided to request that the Korean people give me another chance.

On July 18, I issued a statement wherein I declared the establishment of a new party and my return to politics after two years and seven months of retirement. The statement read:

My Dearest and Most Respected Fellow Koreans,

For forty years I have worked hard for our country's democratization and peaceful reunification, despite many hardships. I have now decided that I'd like to establish a new political party to finish those efforts of mine and to serve you for the last time. I will do my best in order to turn your criticism of me into your universal acceptance of and support for me. I hope that you will generously watch me and support us without reservation if we meet your expectations.

I'm now again apologizing to you most humbly. At the same time, I promise you that I will try my best to develop this new party into a party that will responsibly accomplish your wishes. I hope to have your understanding of and support for my resolution.

Before making the decision to establish a new party, I had tried my best to reform the Democratic Party, but its leadership didn't listen to me at all. I had no choice but to build a new home for a true opposition party. I wanted to build a party that served the Korean people, a party that worked for the reunification of our country. I believed that this would be my last opportunity.

Although I was attached to the five-story Democratic Party office building in Mapo (the acquisition of which had been painstaking), I had to give it up because Democratic Party leadership would not budge. Some people suggested that I remain in the Democratic Party and take away the building by winning the party presidential election. I resolutely rejected the idea because I did not want to stage an ugly internal struggle in front of the Korean people.

We got a new party building at the Taeha building in Yeouido and held a house-warming party on July 20, 1995. I became the standing advisor of the new party establishment preparation committee. On this occasion I declared that we would invite many new leaders into our party. "Many upright leaders are joining our party," I spoke. "As you'll soon understand, we're very hopeful about this development."

On the morning of July 22, sixty-five assemblymen who had decided to join the new party gathered at the National Assembly building for our party's first general assembly. It was the first time I had entered the Assembly building in three years. I encouraged the new party members to become the kind of assemblymen who studied hard and engaged in transparent activities.

As the new party foundation event approached, leaders who were to participate in it were arrested and investigated. It smacked of targeted prosecution. Even their donations to the Peace Foundation were made into an issue. Media headlines blared out these accusations. It was part of an operation to hurt me and to block the establishment of the new party. In response, we organized the Emergency Committee for Measures Against the Opposition Party Oppression. I strongly urged the Kim Young-sam government to cease their operation to destroy the opposition party. "The present government is engaged in immoral activities because they are afraid of the emergence of an opposition party in the true sense of the word," I said. "This is an unforgivable, shameless act."

Despite these interferences, we continued establishing the new party. Before its founding, we welcomed about 250 leaders from all walks of life into our fold. We adopted a two-tier party leadership: the presidential group and the leadership committee. Although we subscribed to a one-man leadership system under the president, the leadership was shared. We named the party National Congress for New Politics (abbreviated to: National Congress), inspired by the National Congress led by Jawaharlal Nehru, the Indian prime minister who led the Indian independence movement through non-violent struggle.

On September 5, 1995, we held the party inauguration ceremony at Seoul's Olympic Park. The sky was clear as approximately 10,000 party members and domestic and foreign guests gathered on the fencing court. People were enthusiastic and the party members' faces looked bright. I was elected president, and our vice presidents were Assemblymen Cho Se-hyung, Lee Chong-chan, Chung Dai-chul, and Kim Young-bae, former Democratic Party Vice President Kim Geun-tae, and leaders newly welcomed into politics, including Park Sang-kyu, Shin Nak-kyun, and Yoo Jay-kun. Assemblyman Kim Sang-hyun was elected as chairman of the leadership committee, which consisted of Assemblymen Kwon Rho-kap, Hahn Gwang-ok, Shin Soon-bum, and Yoo Joon-sang, as well as Heo Jae-yeong, Kil Soong-hoom, Ra Jong-il, and Chung Hee-kyung.

The party inauguration ceremony lasted for seven hours, all of which were filled with cheers and applauding. At our party members' request, I stepped down from the podium to the floor and beat a gong. It was a happy day.

The Korean people congratulated us and were encouraged by the appearance of a strong opposition party that could achieve horizontal regime change, our people's most cherished wish. I proposed a summit for ruling and opposition party heads to usher in smooth governance during the latter half of the President's term. I also issued a warning that President Kim could no longer unilaterally railroad the government, ignoring both the Korean people and the opposition party.

The National Congress adopted the party foundation's declaration and platform for a middle-of-the-road party that defended the middle-class and ordinary people, and that improved people's welfare based on participatory democracy. We also declared that we were the party that succeeded the independence movement and led the democratization movement, a party where legitimate national and democratic forces gathered. The "new politics" in our party name referred to politics of participation, politics led by the goal of reunification, and politics that prepared our nation for the radical changes to come in the twenty-first century. Witnessing the successful completion of the difficult task of founding a party made me realize anew that politics is a living organism. I was overwhelmed by my fear of the future and my resolution to serve the Korean people well.

Former president Roh Tae-woo's Slush Fund Scandal erupted shortly after our party founding. In early October, Democratic Party Assemblyman Park Kye-dong presented account statements at the National Assembly plenary session as proof that President Roh's slush fund was divided up and deposited into various bank accounts using borrowed names. The Korean people were all surprised at the enormous amount of slush funds that, until then, had been known only through rumors. The authorities immediately began an investigation. Before long, it was reported that part of this slush fund had flowed to me, too. I heard this news during a visit to China.

I had, in fact, received a donation from President Roh during my last presidential campaign. When First Secretary for State Affairs Kim Joong-kwon offered the money I was, frankly, surprised. Mr. Kim told me that the president donated funds to all of the candidates. Honestly, I believed what Mr. Kim said and it was hard for me to reject a gift from the president. Also, it was not illegal to receive that money since there wasn't a Political Fund Law that forbade it then. As this became an issue, I was honest with the Korean people about how the whole situation had unfolded. Regardless, I should not have taken the money. I am glad that I confessed to the Korean people, but I am ashamed of my involvement in the scandal.

On December 15, 1995, we moved to a two-story house in Ilsan, Gyeonggi-do. We invited Priest Kim Jong-guk from Seogyo Catholic

Church and a pastor from the church my wife attended for a house-warming prayer gathering. A part of me was sad to leave the house in Donggyo-dong where our family had gone through so many joys and sorrows, but I was glad to leave the house to my eldest son, Hong Il.

A general election was held on April 11, 1996. The ruling New Korea Party (formerly the Minja Party, which had changed its name in 1995 in an effort to win back the people) earned 139 seats (121 from local constituents and 18 from national constituents); our National Congress Party won seventy-nine seats (sixty-six from local constituents and thirteen from the national constituents); and the Jaminryeon fifty seats (forty-one from local constituents and nine from national constituents). We were underwhelmed by these results, but it was true that we lost by the skin of our teeth (less than 3000 votes in fifty-eight electorates). It was a comfort to know that we were still strongly supported by the people.

When the election was over, the New Korea Party secured the majority by having independents join it. The ruling party tried to have Jaminryeon members join it too, threatening Jaminryeon's existence. National Congress and Jaminryeon strongly condemned this tyranny and, as a result, it became natural and necessary that the National Congress and Jaminryeon collaborated.

Toward the end of 1996, the Kim Young-sam government fell vertically once again. At dawn on December 26, 1996, 155 out of 157 New Korea Party members gathered together at the National Assembly and rushed the ANSP and labor-related bills through by surprise. The Korean people did not approve of this. Labor organizations declared an indefinite general strike, calling it fundamentally null and void. Our party and Jaminryeon called it the Kim Young-sam Coup d'État. Laborers continued to strike and hundreds of thousands of workers flooded the streets. Because of this turmoil, the ruling party had to try to amend the bills they had just rushed through.

The ANSP bill was an amendment to their own amendment in the early stage of the Kim Young-sam government—the very one that they had taken so much pride in. The ANSP regained investigative authority for crimes of encouragement, praise, and non-notification under the National Security Law four years after they had handed it over to prosecutors in order to prevent the ANSP's abuse of power, to stamp out human rights abuse, and to block political surveillance. It was a symbolic incident that showed the Kim Young-sam government's will to reform had faded in the meantime.

Soon afterward, a bomb in the form of the Hanbo Scandal fell on the Kim Young-sam government, which had already lost a significant amount of its control. On January 23, 1997, Hanbo Steel (under the Hanbo Group) filed for bankruptcy. During the investigation, prosecutors uncovered an enormous amount of bribery involved in the process of bank loan lending and business licensing. Together with this, many politicians—leaders from both ruling and opposition parties—and finance company officials were summoned. A hearing was held at the National Assembly, and President Kim Young-sam's second son, nicknamed Sosan (which means "small mountain") in relation to his father's nickname Geosan (which means "big mountain"), was summoned for testimony.

The declaration of conscience was made by a doctor who was close to the president's son. A videotape was disclosed, proving Sosan's corrupt activities in conjunction with this scandal, which served to tie the scandal to the president. As soon as the investigation of the president's second son began, incidents of corrupt activities by the people close to the president were revealed. It was a very unhappy event, not only for President Kim and his civilian government, but also for the future of Korean politics.

A funny episode also occurred around that time. Early the morning of July 3, 1996, I went out to exercise with my wife, as usual. But that morning, a TV crew was waiting for us; it was a surprise filming of an MBC program called *On Sunday, Sunday Night*. My wife and I were unexpectedly featured on a TV entertainment program. We went to the lake at our neighborhood park, did some stretching, and looked around at the flowers as usual, all while the TV crew filmed us. I briefly talked about professional baseball, *dongpyonje*, and *sopyonje* with MC Lee Kyung-kyu, a very polite and witty man. It was an unexpected, but pleasant surprise.

We never skipped our morning exercise once we moved to Ilsan. We walked in the park and hiked Mt. Jeongbalsan, which was not too high for me to hike with my uncomfortable legs. My staff members, Chang Hong-ho, Kim Jeong-seon, Bang Gi-seop, and Lee Jae-man, built a staircase on a slope especially for me, and I was very grateful for their caring thoughts and actions. I often enjoyed driving on the Jayuro (Freedom Way) while thinking about our reunification, since North Korea was not too far from there.

PRESIDENT KIM DAE-JUNG (1997)

On May 19, 1997, the National Congress Presidential Nomination Convention was held at the Olympic Gymnastics Arena. About 10,000 people, including delegates, witnesses, and ordinary party members, attended. I was elected our party nominee by 77.5 percent of votes, defeating Candidate Chung Dai-chul. I also won the party president election, beating Candidate Kim Sang-hyun by a large margin.

Our party's convention was broadcast live on TV for the first time in opposition party nomination convention history. During my acceptance speech, I promised, "If I am elected to be president, I will not engage in political retaliation. If Mr. Chun Doo-hwan and Mr. Roh Tae-woo apologize, I will pardon them. I will also help President Kim finish his term without any incidents."

Many foreign guests attended this convention, including South African President Nelson Mandela's daughter, who gifted me the watch that President Mandela had worn in prison for twenty-seven years. The watch, which had a faded black leather strap, still worked fine. I gave her the old brown briefcase that I had carried during my exile. I had translated President Mandela's autobiography *Long Walk to Freedom* into Korean and published it in Korea. Looking at the watch, I remembered the dark days he spent on Robben Island and felt overwhelmed and moved by his life. I drew hope from the fact that he overcame all that suffering and eventually became the president of South Africa.

President Kim Jong-pil was nominated as the Jaminryeon Party's presidential candidate. Meanwhile, in the New Korea Party, President Lee Hoi-chang had appeared to be the invincible nominee, but Gyeonggi-do Governor Rhee In-je was rising as an alternative. At the July 21 national convention, President Lee Hoi-chang was confirmed as the nominee with 60 percent of the votes. However, even after the convention, an internal struggle continued within the party between Candidate Lee Hoi-chang and the former Democratic Party faction—this was, in fact, a struggle between Candidate Lee and President Kim Young-sam.

Candidate Lee Hoi-chang's poll numbers plummeted in the wake of the nomination, whereas defeated candidate Governor Rhee In-je's poll numbers rose. After openly arguing for the change of party nominee based on the poll numbers, Governor Rhee In-je left the New Korea Party. Immediately after his departure, Governor Rhee In-je declared his presidential candidacy and founded a new party. Mr. Lee Man-sup was elected as the new party's president.

I continued to lead the poll numbers. According to the *Kyunghyang Sinmun* opinion poll on October 6, I won 35.8 percent, Rhee In-je 24.2 percent, Lee Hoi-chang 20.3 percent, Cho Sun 7.2 percent, and Kim Jong-pil 4.4 percent. The New Korea Party's Candidate Lee Hoi-chang was supported even less than Rhee In-je. More than 61 percent of those polled predicted my overwhelming victory in the election.

The next day, the ruling party broke the so-called Kim Dae-jung Slush Fund Incident in an attempt to revive Candidate Lee Hoi-chang's numbers. Although Secretary General Kang Sam-jae came forward with the accusation, it was clear that Candidate Lee Hoi-chang was behind it. At a press conference, Secretary General Kang Sam-jae argued that I had been managing the 67 billion *won* slush fund, and my wife's nephew Lee Hyung-tack was managing a portion of it through bank accounts under faked, borrowed, and stolen names. He also argued that I had received 600 million *won* more than the already acknowledged 2 billion *won* from President Roh. Although I clarified that I hadn't received a single penny more than the 2 billion *won*, they spread the rumor and soiled my name. Candidate Kim Young-sam had received an astronomical amount of election funding from him, but it wasn't even an issue.

I heard this slush fund revelation news in a car as I headed to an event. I had, of course, assumed the ruling party would cook up something to check me; however, I did not anticipate this kind of malicious propaganda at that early stage of the election campaign. At the time I was working on a collaboration with Jaminryeon, which was about to come to fruition. The ruling party clearly intended to interfere with this progress.

The New Korea Party's smear campaign did not stop there. Their spokesperson Lee Sa-churl said that I had received 13.4 billion *won* from ten corporations before the 1992 presidential election, and demanded that the authorities investigate this allegation. "As opposition party candidate, I received donations from acquaintances and corporations, but I never received any illegal funds or bribery," I responded.

These irresponsible "disclosures" caused protest from corporations. As a whole, the economic sector condemned these groundless claims. The ruling party leaders were also concerned about the reversal of public opinion. However, Candidate Lee Hoi-chang came forward more actively and encouraged this kind of smear tactic.

Four days later, the New Korea Party again disclosed additional "slush funds." Assemblymen Chung Hyung-gun and Hong Joon-pyo argued that I had been managing a 37.8 billion *won* slush fund through 342 bank accounts under the names of families, relatives, and Peace Foundation officers for the past ten years. The New Korea Party lodged a complaint against me at the Supreme Public Prosecutors Office, accusing me of bribery, tax evasion, and false accusation under the Additional Punishment Law on Specific Crimes.

It was really base and ridiculous to argue that people I didn't know at all hid my slush funds in their bank accounts. Suspicion immediately grew as the ruling party's Secretary General made a fuss and lodged a complaint and the sensational media exaggerated the accusation. It was the worst bump along my campaign road.

I could not just sit still and suffer. As it was the period of parliamentary inspection of the administration, I proposed that we investigate the matter at the Assembly. The ruling party avoided this parliamentary investigation, urging prosecutorial investigation instead, and thus putting pressure on the prosecutorial office.

Prosecutor General Kim Tae-joung must have thought long and hard about this matter. If prosecutors began an investigation, I would be critically hurt regardless of the truthfulness of the allegations. If prosecutors raided my home and summoned people around me, if they leaked rumors to the media, then, no matter how fabricated the accusations were, I would be crippled in terms of public opinion. After the election, the incident would no doubt vanish.

A truly righteous thing happened at this juncture. The wise and courageous Prosecutor General Kim Tae-joung officially announced that prosecutors would delay the investigation of my alleged slush fund activities until after the fifteenth-term presidential election. "When most politicians wouldn't be free from past political fund matters, I judge that the investigation of this incident only two months before the presidential election would clearly cause an extreme split in public opinion, difficulty in the national economy, and chaos in the nation as a whole," he stated. Of his decision, Prosecutor General Kim said, "As a lawyer, I could not begin the investigation with a clean conscience. How can you investigate something without any ground?"

The public welcomed this decision. The prosecutors also welcomed it, saying that "Today is the day the prosecutors are reborn." In fact, it was thanks to public opinion that the prosecutors chose not to investigate the incident. An opinion poll among ordinary prosecutors showed that more than 90 percent of them thought the investigation should not be carried out at that time. Even Assemblyman Kang Sam-jae, who was in charge of this alleged disclosure, resigned as the New Korea Party Secretary General, revealing, "I received the material regarding President Kim Dae-jung's slush fund incident from President Lee Hoi-chang." Seventeen days after the "disclosure" and three days after Prosecutor General Kim's announcement of the investigation delay, the alleged slush fund incident subsided.

In fact, there were rumors that an uprising could erupt if I was investigated. I was very upset about Assemblyman Kang Sam-jae. I even felt that I should ask him to take responsibility for this incident should I be elected President. However, once I was elected, I felt I could forgive him, though I requested an investigation of this incident in order to clarify the truth. According to the investigation, this slush fund incident was a complete fabrication. They simply collected lists of inactive bank accounts.

As I mentioned earlier, I was in the midst of negotiating a unified candidacy with Jaminryeon. The party members who joined our party as out-of-office democratization movement leaders, like Assemblyman Kim Geun-tae, opposed it. Outside the party, religious leaders opposed it too. I persuaded them that we needed an alliance with Jaminryeon to overcome the red-scare tactic and the Honam isolation that had been reinforced since the three-party merger. In particular, I reminded them that the anti-dictatorship and democratization front had relaxed since the June Uprising, and the anti-Honam structure that had been established after the three-party merger had begun to collapse following the establishment of Jaminryeon. I told them that I understood their antipathy toward the forces they had fought in the past, but realistic choices were as important as causes in politics. Above all, we needed a regime change.

Young party members who had been democratization activists, like Lee Hae-chan and Sul Hoon, accepted my sincerity. Based on their scholarly work on the Honam isolation, young scholars like Hwang Tae-yeon, Kang Joon-mann, Kim Man-heum, and Chun In-kwon presented "resistant regionalism alliance" as a means of opposing the Yeongnam hegemony. They greatly contributed to people's understanding of the justice of horizontal regime change.

I had to quickly finish the unified candidacy negotiation with the Jaminryeon. Our party's Vice President Hahn Gwang-ok and Jaminryeon's Vice President Kim Yong-hwan met time and time again. Mr. Kim wanted to get as much as possible in exchange for their party handing over the presidential candidacy to ours. Inevitably, Mr. Han was on the defensive.

Mr. Kim did not seem to want to break up the negotiation. He tried very hard to accomplish negotiations while insisting on constitutional amendment for the parliamentary government system. In the end, the National Congress and I yielded a lot. We agreed that we would consider the constitutional amendment if the Korean people wanted it. After coming to an agreement, I visited President Kim Jong-pil's house in Cheonggu-dong. Our agreement was that I would be the unified presidential candidate, and the prime minister would be appointed from Jaminryeon and have the substantial power of appointing cabinet members and the right to recommend their firing.

This was the birth of the DJP alliance, so named by combining the initials of our first names, DJ and JP. This alliance had been in the making for a year and half. As President Kim Jong-pil was closer to the ruling party in political credo, up until the New Korea Party's national convention, there was the possibility of him reuniting with the ruling party. It was then that our party actively sought alliance with Jaminryeon. I was confident that our party's identity wouldn't be hurt by the alliance. Also, it was essential for our party to win the presidential election.

Although some people considered the DJP alliance an illicit union, I disagree. In Germany, the Social Democratic Party is allied with the Christian Democratic Party, and the Christian Democratic Party is allied with the Christian Socialist Party. I knew I could succeed in running an alliance government.

On November 3, the National Congress and Jaminryeon held the Unified Presidential Candidate Agreement Signing Ceremony. Former POSCO CEO Park Tae-joon, a very trustworthy general who had just won the special election for the National Assembly in July, joined the presidential candidate alliance. A mythical character who had built POSCO from scratch, Assemblyman Park was a leader the Korean people trusted deeply.

I met Assemblyman Park Tae-joon in Tokyo, Japan, during the World Cup Soccer qualifier between Japan and Korea. Korea came back from behind to win a dramatic victory just seven minutes before the game ended. Korea Football Association President Chung Mong-joon and I stood up and cheered from the VIP seats. I met Assemblyman Park at the celebratory reception that evening and proposed that we have breakfast the following morning.

During breakfast, Assemblyman Park asked me frankly, "People say that if you become president, the people of Honam will take everything. Is that true? Also, what's your ideological belief?" My answer was also frank. Assemblyman Park and I were of the same mind and he was a man of outstanding intellect. We immediately recognized and trusted each other. He said that he would like to actively support me. He joined the Jaminryeon and was elected president. This is how the DJT (Kim Dae-jung—Kim Jong-pil—Park Tae-joon) alliance was formed.

The extremely shrunken Democratic Party had offered Mayor of Seoul Cho Sun the party presidency and the presidential candidate nomination. As his poll numbers failed to improve and he began to be drawn toward political strife, he resigned the candidacy. The New Korea Party then snatched up Mr. Cho Sun. Mr. Lee Hoi-chang and Mr. Cho Sun agreed on a merger of the New Korea Party and the Democratic Party, and thus the Grand National Party was born. The Democratic Party sank into the heavy seas of the presidential election.

Just two years before, during the summer of 1995, I had tried my best to help Mr. Cho Sun be elected mayor of Seoul. The whole world knew I had worked for him day and night, stumping everywhere in Seoul. Nevertheless, Mr. Cho Sun claimed, "It was Mr. Kim Dae-jung who I helped, not he who helped me." It was hard to believe. I had to give up on him.

On November 13, National Unity Promotion Council President Kim Won-ki and its eight standing executive committee members, including Roh Moo-hyun and Kim Jung-kil, joined the National Congress in a signing ceremony. I was really happy to welcome them into our party. I had trusted their righteous actions in remaining independent from the Democratic Party. If the National Congress won the right wing through its alliance with the Jaminryeon, it won the left wing through this alliance.

The presidential election became a competition among three candidates: Lee Hoi-chang, Rhee In-je, and myself. My catchphrase was "Horizontal Regime Change," Lee Hoi-chang's was "Liquidation of Three Kims," and Rhee In-je's was "Generational Change."

Korea faced the very humiliating situation of economic trusteeship toward the last stage of the election. The Korean government requested an IMF bailout program for its financial crisis. It was the worst disaster since the Korean War, a disaster in which Koreans lost our economic sovereignty in a truly ridiculous turn of events. Less than a year ago, the

Korean government had been boasting about joining the OECD, but this crisis revealed that was just a false show of power. Through this, Korea became a troublemaker in the eyes of the world.

In fact, there had been warning signs about the financial crisis for more than a year. Nonetheless, Korean high officials claimed, "This is not a crisis because the Korean economy has a strong foundation."

The Korean people trusted what they said; however, this thirty-year myth collapsed in an instant toward the end of 1997. At 10:00 p.m. on November 21, 1997, Deputy Prime Minister for the Economy Lim Chang-ryul announced that the Korean government was requesting a $20 billion bailout from the IMF. The IMF working group flew to Korea and the negotiation ended on December 3. Afterward, IMF Director Michel Camdessus went directly to the Blue House for an unscheduled visit. He demanded that all presidential candidates sign a memorandum stating that they would carry out the Korean government's agreement with the IMF. Although I found it humiliating, I had no other choice but to sign.

I strongly criticized the Kim Young-sam government for the financial mess it had created and demanded a renegotiation with the IMF. Candidate Lee Hoi-chang attacked me for making the foreign currency crisis worse, but no matter how you looked at the government's agreement with the IMF it was very unfair. We had to increase the upper limit of foreign stock investments by 50 percent and open our financial market, including banks and the stock market. Although this was considered an economic trustee-ship, the IMF demanded too much. Of course, behind the IMF was pressure from the US and Japan; however, the price Korean people had to pay was very high. I was worried about mass unemployment. I also believed that we should turn this crisis into an opportunity.

The day after the IMF agreement had been finalized, I spoke in front of 300 European businessmen, including 15 EU envoys. "In order to over-come the IMF system quickly," I said, "we have to break the close ties between business and government. Although we were forced to accept the IMF's demands, we can turn this crisis into opportunity that can be of great help to our future development if we actively accept the IMF's demands and apply them to the reinforcement of our economic constitu-tion. Because the Korean people have strong patriotism and a firm resolu-tion to revive our country, we will definitely succeed."

On the televised debate, I said that although I would faithfully keep our promise to the IMF, I would try to renegotiate. I also said, "Demands like increased foreign participation in domestic financial markets and liberalization of capital markets weren't made to Mexico or Indonesia. Accepting these demands was a mistake. These should be discussed again."

The financial crisis worsened and Candidate Lee Hoi-chang's camp attacked me for arguing for renegotiation. Even IMF Director Michel Camdessus said that the IMF was willing to renegotiate on a few articles that could cause mass unemployment. Still, the Lee Hoi-chang camp did not hesitate to abuse this national crisis for their benefit. It is actions like this that drove our country into crisis.

As expected, the northern wind also blew down on me. The government and opposition party began to adopt red-scare tactics again. The media reported a quote from the government authorities that read: "Former Cheondogyo high priest O Ik-je, who went to the North last August, said on Pyongyang broadcasting that he had discussed the reunification with me immediately before going north." They had a Korean-American pastor, who had recently visited North Korea, hold a press conference in Japan where he showed reporters copies of three letters from North Korean Vice President Kim Byong Sik to me. The letters included a message along the lines of "Now is the time when an independent democratic government should be established in the South. I sincerely wish for your victory in the election."

It was a daring and shameless operation. As soon as this report was published, Grand National Party president Lee Han-dong and the party spokesperson, as well as Election Polling Committee Co-chair Choe Byung-yul, attacked me. Only, this time, red-scare tactics did not work. The Korean voters knew very well that such red scares appeared during election season and disappeared right after it.

They also made an issue of my health. Rumors, the sources of which were unclear, circulated. They were along the lines of "Kim Dae-jung suddenly collapsed on the street in Busan" or "I called late Assemblyman Shin Gi-ha at a meeting." There was even a rumor that my wife was suffering from dementia.

On December 1, I publicized the results of my comprehensive physical from Severance Hospital through Chief of Staff Yoo Jay-kun. The results showed that I had normal blood pressure, blood sugar, cholesterol, and liver levels. The doctor's opinion was "He has no geriatric diseases like hypertension and diabetes. As he is healthy physically and mentally, there will not be any problem with his conducting presidential obligations." Even after this publication, the Lee Hoi-chang camp continued to spread rumors about my ill health.

They also revived the specter of regional antagonism, one of my worries every election. They also used the third candidate to isolate me. The Grand National Party spread the rumor that "Support for Rhee In-je is Kim Dae-jung's victory." This was exactly the same tactic that they used five years ago, when they said "Support for Chung Ju-yung is Kim Dae-jung's victory."

The media's unfair reporting was also at its height. Candidate Rhee In-je's camp fought against this tooth and nail, but they could not erase false reports that were already out there. It was truly unjust tyranny. The conservative media must have believed that it had the power to create a regime.

This fifteenth presidential election was the first in Korea to hold a televised debate between candidates. As this happened, the power of rallies began to decrease since voters could examine the qualities and policies of each candidate through their own TVs. It was a great event that transformed the campaign culture.

Whenever there was a televised debate, I prepared for it at my sister-in-law's house in Mok-dong. It was a place I used whenever I needed to work on important manuscripts or meet someone. Our house in Donggyo-dong was too crowded to allow me to have my own time. My sister-in-law was always kind to me. She prepared good food and made sure that I had alone time. Whenever I left her house, she encouraged me with remarks like "Brother, your tie looks wonderful" or "I have a feeling you'll have a good day today."

People generally responded positively to my television debate performance. During the last debate, I appealed to the Korean people: "Unfortunately, I failed in my three previous attempts. It seems that Korean people saved me for this time. I will become the bridge that helps you cross over the river of crisis. Please mount my back and cross the river. I do not have any more opportunities. The other two candidates will have other opportunities. Please give me a chance."

As we neared the finish line, the election results became unpredictable. I emphasized that I would be a well-prepared president and promised that I would lead the country out of the IMF system within the first year and half of my presidency. The poll numbers predicted my victory by a paper-thin margin. I could not feel reassured. I went on a stump tour at twelve locations in Seoul the day before Election Day.

The last rally was held in front of the Commercial Bank building in Myeong-dong. It was dark when I arrived, but thousands of people were waiting for me. I got on the podium a little past 6:00 p.m. This was my last election rally as a presidential candidate and as politician. No, it was the last rally in my life. When I was about to begin my speech, the audience started chanting my name. Their chants seemed to turn into bright lights falling from the sky. I almost lost my voice. I began to speak with all my might. "I have wisdom and experience that I have accumulated as I trained for forty years to become the president. I prepared for this job in prison and in the US. Nobody else in the world has prepared so much to become president. Please give me a chance. I can do well."

When I finished my speech and came down from the podium, the audience gathered around me. The tearful voice of Assemblyman Kim Min-seok filled the streets of Myeong-dong. "Tomorrow is the day when the regime will be changed in our country," he spoke. "Tomorrow is the day when President Kim Dae-jung will be born. Tomorrow is the day when the age of suffering will be over and the age of hope will begin."

After finishing the election campaign, I felt anxious. Although I had been through numerous elections and I continued to lead the election polls, feeling nervous was inevitable on the eve of Election Day.

On December 18, the election was over and I won by about 400,000 votes. According to the National Election Commission, 10,326,275 voters chose me; 80.7 percent of voters cast their votes, and I won 40.3 percent of them. For the first time in Korean history, a regime change between the ruling and opposition parties occurred. My victory was an honor dedicated to Korean political party history, and to numerous opposition party politicians. It was the glory of the Korean people and a victory for Korean democracy.

People called me Indongcho. *Indongcho* bear red fruits in the fall and they look even redder in the winter snow. The fragile *indongcho* must endure winter because of its belief that spring will surely come soon. However, we cannot help but feel a bit sad when we look at them. There are tears in *indongcho*, in their sorrowful beauty. That's right. The tears that my supporters had shed for me gathered to form a river and this river finally carried me to the presidency.

In retrospect, I was the cause of many people's tears. I also shed a lot of tears myself. Now that I was president, I had to dry their tears. For as harsh as the past winter was, the spring of tomorrow had to be even more beautiful.

The horizontal regime change between the ruling and the opposition parties meant that the Korean people had decided on their fate on their own for the first time. The Korean people had never before determined their destiny and regime of their own will—not during the Goryeo or Joseon dynasties. Many peasant revolts and the Donghak Revolution failed. Finally, toward the end of 1997, the Korean people succeeded in a people's revolution through election. The Korean people protected me despite financial, political, and even red-scare schemes. It was the great victory of the people.

As the night deepened, the broadcasting companies confirmed my victory. I went to bed. It felt like a dream.

I woke up around dawn. A new day began. I could hear the anthem and songs like "Our Wish is Re-unification" and "Mokpo's Tears" from over the wall of my house in Ilsan. People chanted my name: "President Kim Dae-jung!"

The day was breaking.

PART II

Life Is Beautiful and History Progresses

CHAPTER 7

December 1997–May 1998

THE LONG AND HEAVY WINTER (DECEMBER 17, 1997– JANUARY 1998)

At dawn on December 17, 1997, I received a phone call from my eldest son, Hong Il. I could hear the sadness in his voice as he told me that my beloved younger brother Dae-ui had died. How many people had to live in pain for so many years just because of their connection to me? All three of my sons had been dragged to Korean Central Intelligence Administration (KCIA) safe houses and tortured just because they were my offspring. Hong Il even had to live with a limp in the aftermath of the torture. I feel so sorry for them.

Dae-ui died the day before the presidential election. We had nurtured our dreams while running around the beaches of Hauido Island and looking at the sea together. We had come to the brink of death and survived together in Mokpo Prison during the Korean War. He gladly accepted my suffering as his own, and had lived as my shadow. On his deathbed, he told people not to let his death be known to the outside world. He must have done so because he didn't want voters to associate his death with my age and health. How could I ever forget his love for me, so great that it made him feel sorry for dying before me?

President Kim Young-sam called to congratulate me on winning the election and invited me to meet with him as soon as possible. The chief of staff for state affairs visited me in Ilsan early in the morning, bringing with him a potted plant. I called Candidates Lee Hoi-chang and Rhee In-je to

© The Author(s) 2019
Kim Dae-jung, *Conscience in Action*,
https://doi.org/10.1007/978-981-10-7623-7_7

comfort them on their defeat, which both of them seemed to calmly accept. I politely requested their future cooperation in state affairs.

I stood in my garden with my wife. Citizens surrounded our house. Cameras continued to flash and people cheered. In my first greeting to the Korean people as president-elect I said, "I sincerely thank the Korean people. A new history began today through the first turnover of power from the ruling to an opposition party since the founding of our nation."

I held a press conference at the National Assembly Members' Hall at 9:00 a.m. I emphasized the importance of our international credit rating in overcoming the financial crisis, and promised to fully support the current government's agreement with the IMF. I appealed to the Korean people for reconciliation and solidarity. I also emphasized the parallel development of democracy and the market economy. "December 18, 1997 will be remembered as the historical turning point when our people achieved solidarity and unity," I spoke. "We should never have political retaliation or regional and class discrimination. I respect and love all regions and classes. As president, I will sweep away all discrimination and guarantee the equal rights of all members of our nation to make sure that confrontation based on discrimination never sets foot on this land.

"We will completely liberate all businesses from both the chains and the patronage of the power. From now on, only businesses that can adapt to the world market and overcome worldwide competition will survive. This is the reality of a globalized world. The purpose of economy is the people's happiness. Therefore, I will open the age when we develop a democratic market economy by thoroughly protecting ordinary people's rights. Our new government will manage our country through effective strategies and policies."

After the press conference, I paid my respects at the Seoul National Cemetery. Upon returning to the National Assembly Hall, I received a call from President Bill Clinton. "I send congratulations and respect to you, President-Elect Kim, for your great victory," he said. "You have devoted your entire life to democracy and political progress."

Although this message was moving, things were difficult as Korea was on the verge of collapsing. President Clinton urged me to carry out the Korean government's agreement with the IMF. He said that the Korean economy was in critical condition and he would send American negotiators quickly. Frankly speaking, I felt that it was a little impolite for him to mention them in his first call after my election victory, but what he said was not an exaggeration.

After this phone conversation with President Clinton, I talked with Japanese Prime Minister Hashimoto Ryutaro, who had been waiting on hold. I asked him to help Korea through its greatest crisis since our founding. Prime Minister Hashimoto said that he would do his best.

That afternoon I visited and paid my respects at the April 19th National Cemetery. Mothers who were members of the Minkahyup Human Rights Group and the National Council for Families of Perished National and Democratic Movement Activists were also there. They continued to hold my hand. How could I not know that the democracy of this land grew from their tears? Through their tears, the mothers said that once democracy was achieved they would dance on behalf of their children. I silently resolved to devote myself to the creation of a new world. I went home to Ilsan, where US Ambassador to Korea Stephen W. Bosworth visited me. We discussed the Korean economy.

I had dinner with Mr. Kim Jong-pil and Mr. Park Tae-joon at my house. During the election campaign period, the three of us had been united in our fight. I thanked them for their collaboration. As they say, victory was sweet and heroic episodes were splendid. Despite the fact that it was a dinner among victors, the atmosphere was somewhat oppressive. Something heavy was pressing down on part of our hearts. The financial crisis was indeed a national crisis.

It wasn't until after 11:00 p.m. that the managing director of the IMF, Michel Camdessus, called me. Soon afterward, World Bank President James Wolfensohn also called. I asked both of them to help us. Their promises to help Korea were sweeter to my ears than their congratulations on my victory.

I didn't go to bed until after midnight, but I still could not sleep. I had hoped that I could sleep to my heart's content after the election. I had planned to go somewhere remote after my election victory and calmly plan state affairs. However, as soon as I was elected, everyone sought me out. Numerous pending issues were waiting for me. I had to make decisions and statements.

Foreign media paid an unusual amount of attention to my victory, treating it as a very significant event. My victory made the headlines in major media outlets in Japan, Europe, and the US, including the *New York Times* and *Washington Post*. They ran articles detailing my long and hard political career, and all of its ups and downs. They called my victory a "historic victory of the eternal opponent" and "the victory of Korean democracy," emphasizing that I was the first opposition party leader elected to the presidency in Korean history. The Chinese newspaper *People's Daily* reported on my projected victory unusually quickly considering the fact that the election results weren't issued until 1:00 a.m. The Chinese Ministry of Foreign Affairs officially commented that it "enthusiastically welcomed" my victory, testifying to the fact that the Chinese government had been paying attention to me.

The *Wall Street Journal* compared my election victory to those of Lech Walesa and Nelson Mandela. The German *Süddeutsche Zeitung* reported that many Koreans believed President-Elect Kim Dae-jung would contribute to the end of the Cold War in East Asia by blazing the road to reconciliation between South and North Korea, just as former Chancellor Willy Brandt had laid the foundation for the end of the Cold War in Europe through his New Eastern Policy.

At the same time, the foreign media expressed concern about the enormous challenges associated with the foreign currency crisis. Some even said it was as if I had received a poison cup, given that we were on the brink of national bankruptcy.

I began checking on pending matters for the transition. Above all, I decided to check on the state of national housekeeping. I met with Vice Prime Minister and Minister of Finance and Economy Lim Chang-ryul at the National Congress building at 10:00 a.m. on December 20. I wondered about the foreign currency situation, and was shocked to hear his answer. "The foreign currency reserve on December 18 was a meager $3870 million," he told me. "Even with immediate support from the IMF, it will be hard to repay the foreign debts due next January."

The national financial situation was dire beyond belief. I did not expect it would be this serious. Regardless of all the big talk by government officials, the vice prime minister sat helplessly in front of me. If the IMF bailout program could not solve the crisis of national bankruptcy, what on earth would we do? "What has the government done to make our economy end up in this plight?" I asked him.

Vice Prime Minister Lim acknowledged the government's failures. "The main reason for this financial difficulty is our government's lack of an adequate response to the matter," he said. Mr. Lim told me that the government grew the currency crisis by focusing only on the foreign exchange rate and neglecting short-term foreign loans and the foreign currency reserve. I told him that we should turn this national bankruptcy crisis into an opportunity. "Under the new government the economic policy will be managed entirely according to the market economy principle," I told him. "We will thoroughly exclude political logic from economic policies. We will follow only economic logic."

I had a luncheon with President Kim Young-sam at the Blue House that same day. President Kim greeted me at the entrance. I led our meeting and we agreed that we would form a twelve-member Emergency Economic Committee, comprising six current government members and six transition team members. We appointed Vice President Kim Yong-hwan of the Liberal Democratic Alliance (LDA) as committee chair. Former Minister of Finance Kim Yong-hwan had a talent for political negotiations, which he had demonstrated during the DJP alliance negotiations. The members of the Emergency Economic Committee were National Congress Policy Committee Chair Kim Won-gil, National Assemblyman Chang Jae-sik, and Governor of Jeollabuk-do You Jong-keun from the National Congress; LDA Policy Committee Chair Lee Tae-sup and National Assemblyman Huh Nam-hoon from LDA. Included from the current government were Vice Prime Minister of Economy Lim Chang-ryul, Minister of Foreign Affairs Yoo Chong-ha, Minister of Trade and Industry Chung Hae-joo, Chief Economic Secretary to President Kim Yong-sup, Chief of Administrative Management to Prime Minister Lee Young-tak, and president of the Bank of Korea Lee Kyung-shik.

This Emergency Economic Committee played the role of an emergency cabinet. Although the current government had to manage national matters until the next term began, the new government had to intervene in matters related to economy. Above all, the Korean people and international society did not trust the current government. If economic bankruptcy occurred, it would be a national calamity that would cause the Korean people to suffer. The new government had to take on the burden.

I decided to pardon and rehabilitate former Presidents Chun and Roh, although I expected there would be enormous resistance from Korean people. I made this decision based on my belief that true reconciliation is possible only when victims forgive their perpetrators. It was a symbolic measure embodying my wish to eliminate any further political retaliation or regional antagonism.

This was in part inspired by the politics of forgiveness, the undercurrent of English democracy. In England, King Charles I was executed during the Puritan Revolution in 1649. This retaliation brought confusion and internal division, which was responsible for an even harsher dictatorship by Cromwell. During the Glorious Revolution that followed, King James II was allowed to escape to France, where he established a government in exile and plagued the English government for three generations. Despite these aftereffects, which the revolutionary forces should have fully expected, they chose not to execute the king in order to avoid larger consequences from political retaliation. It is thanks to this spirit of forgiveness and reconciliation that parliamentary democracy flourished in England.

I believe that this decision of England's was wiser and better than the execution of King Louis XVI in France or the execution of the entire family of King Nicolai II in Russia. England has enjoyed the blessings of this spirit of tolerance for more than three centuries, maintaining democratic and peaceful prosperity. It was because of my belief in this spirit of reconciliation and tolerance that I decided to forgive the two former presidents, although it certainly was not easy.

The two former presidents were released on December 22. During former president Chun's statement he said, "I am happy that President-Elect Kim Dae-jung, a man of dignity and trustworthiness, won the election."

US Under Secretary of the Treasury for International Affairs David Lipton visited Korea on December 22. President Clinton urgently dispatched him only a few days before perhaps the biggest holiday in America. Before this visit, I had a discussion with the governor of Jeollabuk-do, You Jong-keun, who had a Ph.D. in economics from the State University of New York and was a former and long-time chief economic advisor to the governor of New Jersey. He was well versed in the American economy and his advice always proved useful.

When I asked him what he expected Lipton to demand of us, he replied, "He will probably mention the matter of layoffs. The US will want to know what you think. They are coming to test you."

That night I thought about what I should emphasize to them and how I could win them over. On the morning of December 22, Special Envoy for Foreign Collaboration Kim Ki-hwan came to my house after meeting with a wide range of American political and economic leaders. He reported on the Korean foreign currency crisis and the atmosphere of the US government. Mr. Kim showed me some materials from the Bank of Korea, which predicted that the foreign currency reserve could range from negative $600 million to a surplus of $900 million by the end of the year. I could not believe it. The end of the year was less than ten days away. "Is this correct?" I asked.

Mr. Kim explained the situation in detail. I asked him how we could induce US assistance. "The United States demands reforms in addition to those that the IMF does," he responded.

When I queried him further about the gist of this demand, he explained they also wanted: acceptance of layoffs, the full-scale amendment of the Foreign Exchange Control Law, permission for an antagonistic merger and annexation, and the introduction of a class action law suit. These had not been included in the agreement with the IMF reached on December 3. The US demanded many more reform measures than the IMF negotiators had. I could not easily accept any of them. In particular, during my election campaign I had promised to delay layoffs for two years. If I accepted this condition, laborers would surely condemn it. However, it was also clear that I could not drive my entire country of 40 million people into bankruptcy in an effort to prevent several hundreds of thousands being unemployed. I made up my mind.

I met Under Secretary of the Treasury for International Affairs David Lipton, US Ambassador to Korea Bosworth, and their party at the National Congress building in Yeouido at 11:30 a.m. I was accompanied by National Congress Policy Committee Chair Kim Won-gil, National Assemblyman Chang Jae-sik, Vice President Kim Yong-hwan of the LDA, and Jeollabuk-do Governor You Jong-keun. The US representatives proceeded to interview my new government and me.

As expected, Mr. Lipton mentioned the matter of labor flexibility. I told him, "The revival of both public and private businesses is impossible without restructuring and personnel cutback. The Korean people know this very well. Therefore, we will carry out layoffs if necessary. If a business goes bankrupt because we hesitate to fire 10 to 20 percent of its personnel, then 100 percent of its employees will lose their jobs. If a business revives and becomes competitive after layoffs, it can offer those laid-off workers the chance to be re-hired. I am planning to pursue an economic policy based on democracy and market economy."

The US envoys' faces brightened. They could trust me. Lipton and his party smiled. On Christmas Eve, we received an announcement from thirteen advanced countries and the IMF that they would send additional support of $10 billion. Thus, we overcame the crisis of national bankruptcy.

If there is only one road that leads to your destination, you should not hesitate to take it. I believe that my decisive position moved the leaders of advanced countries, including President Clinton. At that time, there was a movement among some financial specialists in advanced countries to leave Korea alone and make an example of it. Foreign media analyses pointed to the fact that this decision of early, additional support would not have been easy if I had not shown a clear intention to accept layoffs. The *Wall Street Journal* wrote that my close relationship with labor forces could be advantageous for the implementation of painful policies, such as business insolvency and layoffs.

Whether or not laborers would willingly accept these changes was still seriously questionable. Although they might not be entirely free from blame in the financial crisis, the real culprits were the cozy relationship between politics and economics and government-directed financing. Most businesses simply increased their size through loans, hanging on to the illusion of "too big to fail." Governments and financial institutions stood by. Disputes over preferential financing never stopped.

Korean *chaebols* did not hesitate to make excessive and repetitive investments. Because they did not pay close attention to competitiveness and profitability, sometimes the president of the *chaebol* made an investment decision based simply on his personal preference. They used funds from financial institutions as if they were their private funds, with the attitude that they would make a profit if it was successful and the government would take the loss if they failed. The result was the loss of business' competitive ability and the financial institutions' insolvency.

The Asian financial crisis began in July 1997, when the Thai *baht* collapsed and spread financial crises through Indonesia, the Philippines, and Malaysia. Even international financial markets like Hong Kong and Singapore became tight, making it difficult for Korean financial institutions to borrow money. If the Korean government and financial authorities had taken effective measures, they could have prevented IMF intervention. If the Korean government hadn't simplemindedly focused on the exchange rate and spent all of its foreign exchange holdings, the liquidity crisis wouldn't have come so quickly.

At any rate, the foreign currency crisis put an end to the Park Chung-hee-style developmentalism model that focused solely on development. The insolvent cozy relationship between politics and economics, founded on the sacrifice of workers and medium- and small-sized businesses, began to collapse. To a degree, this disaster was expected because Korean society was not run democratically. If we had developed the economy together with democracy, we would not have allowed large-scale corruption that welcomed cozy relationships between politics, economics, and government-directed financing. It's inevitable that a country with a market economy will decline without democracy—history has proven it. As I mentioned earlier, the Eastern Bloc collapsed not because of socialism, but because of its lack of democracy.

On December 24, I met with the heads of economic organizations, including the Federation of Korean Industries, and clarified my policy principles regarding business. The backbone of my policy was the liquidation of businesses without competitiveness, the reduction of government intervention, the establishment of a collaboration system between big and small- and medium-sized businesses, and the eradication of the cozy relationship between politics, economics, and government-directed financing. I still remember how President Choi Jong-hyun of the Federation of Korean Industries responded. "As a businessman, I find your remarks refreshing," he said. "These days, businessmen have nothing to say. It is due to our errors that things have turned out this way. We're the worst among sinners."

On December 25, I announced the twenty-four-member transition committee and its chair. I appointed Vice President of National Congress Lee Chong-chan as chair, in addition to twelve members each from the National Congress and the LDA. During the signboard hanging ceremony the following day, all of the members looked quite anxious, aware of their historic task in transferring power from the ruling to the opposition party. Committee Chair Lee Chong-chan said, "The committee will examine the past, present, and future of the current government." Committee member Lee Hae-chan said, "I feel a heavy sense of responsibility for this task." I encouraged every member individually.

At first, this committee came off as a powerful institution due to the great enthusiasm of its members, who wanted to present the blueprint for a new government based on a thorough examination of the current government's faults, which had led the country to the brink of bankruptcy. Although I knew they were sincere and enthusiastic, I urged the committee members to be careful not to come across as an overbearing institution that considered itself above the past government and Korean people.

During this transition process there was a report that the Blue House and a few government offices were shredding documents. In particular, the information agencies, including the Agency for National Security

Planning, began systematically shredding all sorts of secret documents as soon as the presidential election was over. The transition committee requested that Prime Minister Goh Kun stop this document shredding immediately. However, the practice continued at both the Blue House and other major government offices. They must have had a lot to hide. How many illegal actions must have been carried out because there had never been a regime transition between ruling and opposition parties! How many fraudulent customary practices must have been buried in the dark!

After two months, the transition committee chose one hundred tasks for the government to work on, which included forty economic tasks; twenty unification-related, diplomatic, and national security tasks; twenty tasks related to education, culture, social welfare, and environment; and twenty state, legal, and administrative affairs. Although there was confusion and some trial and error in the beginning, the committee members worked very hard day and night. I greatly appreciated their hard work, and I asked them to create a white paper that laid out everything they had done. I believe this book was very beneficial during the next transition.

To everyone's surprise, I appointed Mr. Kim Chung-gwon, a Gyeongsangbuk-do native and former senior political affairs secretary to President Roh Tae-woo, as the chief of staff. Through this appointment, I wanted to clearly announce to the Korean people that I would keep my campaign promise to hire talented people, regardless of their regional and political background. I had noticed Mr. Kim's talents and character for a while.

On December 29, I visited a military base. I emphasized that the major agents for security are human beings, and that high morale among soldiers is therefore the most important element of national security. As there was only one Jeollado native who ranked above lieutenant general at that time, I requested fair personnel management. "Only when fair personnel management is in place—regardless of one's native region or school—will the military concentrate on the North, rather than looking at Seoul."

The next day, I visited the Gyeryongdae in Daejeon, where the Army headquarters was located, in the presidential helicopter. This was the heart of the military, which my political opponents had claimed to be my greatest "veto group." When I arrived at the steps of the main building, about seventy generals stood in line and saluted me. I heard that the number of stars on their shoulders was 120 altogether. I promised that, as their commander-in-chief, I would protect the military and become their comrade. The generals applauded loudly. I had a luncheon with them, and the three chiefs of staff each made a toast and promised their loyalty to me as their commander-in-chief.

Although we put out the fire of immediate financial crisis, the financial market remained uncertain. International society looked coldly at Korea. A more flexible labor market was inevitable; however, the Korean labor world was strongly against it. We needed a social consensus. During my campaign, I had already promised to establish the labor-employer-government tripartite commission to discuss and arbitrate all pending labor issues. The establishment of this organization for mutual prosperity was a historical event. We could not overcome the financial crisis without sacrifice and collaboration from both labor and business.

The establishment of the labor-employer-government tripartite commission was not an easy task. I met President Park In-sang of the Federation of Korean Trade Unions (FKTU) and urged him to participate in the tripartite commission. He was noncommittal and urged the *chaebols* and government officials to take the lead. I then met Acting Secretary of Korean Confederation of Trade Unions (KCTU) Bae Suk-bom, who was even more adamant. He presented conditions for his organization's participation in the tripartite commission, such as a National Assembly hearing on the economy; the punishment of those responsible for the financial crisis; and apologies from the *chaebol* presidents as well as a donation of their private wealth to society. He was also firmly against the layoffs.

I tried to persuade him about its inevitability, as its legislation had already been agreed upon with the IMF. Layoffs were also necessary for restructuring businesses and financial institutions. Still, the labor leadership remained staunchly against it. It was a truly difficult situation. Nevertheless, I did not give up. I continued trying to persuade them, trusting that they would understand if they were informed about the true reality of our economy. It was not easy for me to get them to understand and trust my fair approach. Although I felt misunderstood, I also understood their suspicions since no former regime had ever been on their side.

In the end, the FKTU agreed to participate in the tripartite commission on the night of January 13; the KCTU agreed early the morning of January 14. I encouraged a ceremony celebrating the establishment of the tripartite commission be held at the Korea Federation of SMEs Building in Yeouido on January 15. The commission would become the central axis for overcoming the financial crisis and establishing a new framework for the twenty-first-century Korean economy. I assured them that this financial crisis could also be an opportunity, depending upon how we responded to it.

The tripartite commission agreed on ten agenda items, including guidelines for how the three parties would share pains. The businesses promised to come up with a plan for reforming the *chaebol* system and selling non-business-purpose real estate. The government promised to discuss plans for price stabilization and the expansion of social welfare. Labor promised to discuss reforming the system as it related to job cuts, the last stumbling block. The labor union was opposed to including a clear statement about the legislation of job cuts in the statement. In the end, we agreed on an indirect phrase, which read: "We will do a package settlement on the agreed-upon agenda in the near future before the extraordinary session of the National Assembly, scheduled for February." Although this was not entirely satisfactory, we were still showing both domestically and abroad that we could work together through dialogue and compromise.

The legislation of job cuts continued to hit the skids. Although the labor leadership understood it was necessary, it wasn't easy for them to persuade field workers. We had to come up with something substantial in exchange for their sacrifice. The government promised that it would allow labor unions' political activities and legalize a teachers' union beginning in July 1999. We also yielded to the long-standing wishes of labor unions by greatly expanding basic labor rights. Government employees were allowed to form a workplace council, beginning in January 1999. We increased funds for unemployment support from 44,000 billion to 50,000 billion won. In exchange, job cuts and the worker dispatch system would be introduced immediately. This was a great compromise among the three parties—laborer, employer, and the government.

The tripartite commission announced that they had reached a package deal on ten agendas and ninety tasks. It showed the Korean society's ability to achieve mutual prosperity through grand reconciliation between labor and businesses. I am proud of the tripartite commission's achievement. Given the relationship between labor and businesses at that time, this achievement was close to a miracle. The new laws passed through the National Assembly on February 14.

The year 1998 dawned. It was one of the most depressing years for Koreans. The media poured out gloomy prospects for the New Year. I was entirely devoted to finding ways to revive the Korean economy. During the New Year holiday, it snowed a lot. It was beautiful outside the hotel where I was staying. I thought how nice it would be if the white snow could cover up the Korean people's worries as well.

On January 4, I met international financier and the president of the Quantum Group of Funds, George Soros. Believing that the international society should support a country led by a democratic leader with a humanitarian governing philosophy, Mr. Soros told me that he was deeply moved by my struggle for human rights and democracy. He had advised me through videoconference immediately before the presidential election. Although some viewed him negatively for his foreign exchange speculation, since the dissolution of the USSR he had invested in and donated enormous sums of money to Eastern European countries and Russia as they made their way toward democracy.

I met Mr. Soros early in the New Year because I wanted to attract overseas capital. He met with me despite the fact that he was on vacation. President Soros promised to actively invest in Korea since the IMF bailout money was not enough to properly deal with our foreign currency crisis. I continued to meet numerous individual and institutional investors and plead for their investment. I tried to mobilize any means possible. I wished that I could turn whatever international reputation I might have into dollars. If I had acquired some trust from international society, I hoped to use it as collateral for loans.

On January 5, I attended the opening ceremony of the New Year at the National Congress building in Yeouido. At the ceremony, I emphasized that we should not demand suffering only from workers, but that government and businesses should also make reciprocal efforts. Although it was a celebratory event, the atmosphere was somber. I shook hands with party officials and National Assembly members, saying, "I'm sorry that it continues to be hard even after our party has come into power. But, let us bear this fate together."

January 6 was my birthday, but I ordered that there not be any sort of event for the occasion. I did not schedule a dinner with my family, and celebrated my birthday only with traditionally served seaweed soup. I was particularly busy that day. I had a regular meeting with President Kim Young-sam at the Blue House and received a report from the minister of labor in the morning. After attending the New Year opening ceremony for civic social organizations that afternoon, I met with former Japanese Prime Minister Nakasone Yasuhiro. After that, I went to the transition committee's office and received a report from them. I also appointed National Congress Special Assistant to the President Park Jie-won as my spokesperson because I admired both his sincerity and his ability to understand the essence of affairs.

In the meantime, Koreans were moving the world with their gold collection campaign. They brought their cherished gold possessions to banks and waited in line to sell them. Newlyweds brought their wedding rings, young parents brought the customary rings people had given their babies to celebrate their first birthdays, and old couples took the rings their children had bought them to express their love. Sportsmen brought their hard-won gold medals and Cardinal Kim Sou-hwan brought the gold cross he had received when he was appointed cardinal. When people tried to dissuade him from parting with the cross, he responded, "This is nothing compared to what Jesus did. He gave his body." My wife collected about 450 grams and I about 375 grams of gold.

In fact, it was I who had proposed this gold collection campaign at the end of the previous year during my meeting with consumer protection agency leaders. "Our country annually imports $60 billion in gold," I mused, "but a lot of it remains in people's safes. If we wage a gold collection campaign and sell the collected gold, we can get a substantial amount of dollars."

I was just sharing my thoughts with them because I remembered the campaign to repay our national debt to Japan during the Korean Empire period. I proposed that the banks could use the money they would get from selling the gold to repay foreign debts, and then pay back those who brought their gold with interest three years later.

The Korean people responded enthusiastically to this campaign, which lasted until March 1998. Altogether 3.5 million people collected 226 tons of gold, worth $2.15 billion. Thanks to the export of this gold, the national export rapidly increased by 21 percent in February 1998 and there was a trade surplus of $3.2 billion. The amount of gold export that month was $1.05 billion. The Korean people transfused blood into their country as it laid on the brink of death.

This campaign's effect was not just monetary. The world was moved and wanted to help Korea, believing in our future. Chinese president Jiang Zemin, US president Bill Clinton, and Canadian prime minister Jean Chretien all told me later how moved they were by this campaign. I was so proud of Korean people. I felt confident that we could overcome our difficulties.

On January 18, I held a televised town hall-style meeting. Since my return to the political world in 1995, I had always maintained that we should engage in a new kind of politics, where people directly participated in the policy decision making. During my presidential campaign, I also said that in a truly democratic society, people should be able to express their opinions for or against policies through a simple button in their own living rooms.

Personally, I'm not very good with computers, as is perhaps the case with many people of my generation. I tried to learn, but it took a long time for me to get the hang of it; however, you don't need to be a computer whiz to know that you should use such technology in your communication with people. What I needed was not necessarily personal competency, but, rather, the ability to see its function in future society.

During the town hall meeting, people wanted to know about the economic crisis. I answered frankly, "I participated in politics, but I did not imagine that the state of affairs would be this dire. When I learned of the reality of our financial situation after my election victory, I felt as if I opened a safe and did not find so much as a single 1000 won bill. Instead, there were piles of IOUs. When the present government began its term, the national debt was $40 billion. I wonder how it grew to $150 billion … It turned out that we lived off of debts. Now that the creditor countries want their money back, our country is on the brink of bankruptcy. We have $25.1 billion short-term debts that should be repaid before the end of March. I heard from today's report that we have only $12 billion in the foreign currency reserves. In order to solve this problem, we have to extend some of the debts, change short-term debts to long-term ones, and invite foreign investments. We have to increase our exports as well. Although the reality is grave, Korea's international credit rating is improving and we are moving the world through our collaborations, including the gold collection campaign. We're beginning to overcome the crisis, but we are not yet at the stage where we can feel at ease."

I listed the three advantages of foreign investment: First, we can get foreign currency; second, we can learn excellent foreign management skills and strengthen Korean businesses; and third, we can create jobs.

Another participant said, "I hope that you make visible reforms in the government and *chaebols* in order to overcome the national bankruptcy crisis. Please also break the cozy ties between politics and economics." "I have a long-standing interest in workers since my contribution of an article about labor issues to *Sasanggye* magazine in 1955," I responded. "My heart aches when I think of the current labor situation. First, let me tell you that the age of the cozy relations between politics and economics is over. Businesses gave 140 billion won to the ruling party during the Kim Young-sam regime, while giving not even 1400 won to my party. As my party does not owe anything to businesses, we have no reason to please them. I like businessmen who make lots of dollars in the international market, who create jobs for Korean people, and who manufacture the best products in the world at the lowest prices.

"I will do my best to solve the problem of unemployment. I will demand from the *chaebols* things that were unimaginable in the past, and make them change their practices. They will have to present combined financial statements that include all their subsidiaries, and the subsidiaries will not be able to guarantee each other under the roof of the same *chaebol*. They will be required to liquidate subsidiaries other than the major ones. The presidents of the *chaebols* should invest their personal assets and take responsibility for their mismanagement. I will not be unfairly cruel to workers. We will reduce the Blue House staff, and the government will boldly reduce its size."

After this frank revelation, I appealed to the Korean people to share in our collective pain. "I feel two feelings now. My heart aches to think of the Korean people's suffering and anxiety. At the same time, I feel that we are agents in Korea's history. This is an opportunity to display our internal strength. I promise that the government will make a life-or-death effort to overcome the current crisis. I will report accurate facts to you. Inevitably, this will be a difficult year. Through every possible means, I will make an effort to overcome these hardships so that we can have hope from around mid-year next year on."

"Please Don't Call Me 'Your Excellency'" (February 25, 1998–May 12, 1998)

On February 25, the day of my inauguration, my wife Lee Hee-ho congratulated me. How could the glory that day be only mine? "Congratulations to you, too!" I told her.

After paying my respects at the Seoul National Cemetery, I entered the Blue House with my wife at around 9:00 a.m., the time when government officials are supposed to begin their day's work. In the office, I signed my name in Hangeul on the application for parliamentary approval of the appointment of Kim Jong-pil as prime minister and Han Sung-hon as the chairman of the Board of Audit and Inspection. This marked my first official work and exercise of power.

I went to the National Assembly building for the inauguration ceremony. It was a clear and warm day, with sunlight pouring softly through the windows. All of the previous presidents—Kim Young-sam, Roh Tae-woo, Chun Doo-hwan, and Choi Kyu-ha—attended the ceremony. I also invited various leaders who had offered essential help saving my life and ensuring my safety during the periods when I was a condemned criminal, under house arrest, kidnapped, and in exile, such as former German president von Weizsäcker, former president Corazon Aquino of the Philippines, and former US Congressman Michael Foglietta. Also in attendance were former Japanese prime ministers Nakasone and Takeshita, former Japanese foreign minister Kono Yohei, Japanese Lower House Speaker Doi Takako, President Samaranch of IOC, Vice President of International Relations at the Russian Foreign Ministry Evgeny P. Bazhanov, former Chinese Vice Minister of Foreign Affairs Liu Shu Qing, and pop singer Michael Jackson. Forty thousand people gathered and were waiting for me at the square in front of the National Assembly building.

I took the oath. "I do solemnly swear that I will preserve the Constitution, protect the Republic of Korea, make efforts to increase the Korean people's freedom and wellbeing, as well as to advance national culture, and to faithfully execute the Office of President."

A salute was fired and doves flew into the sky. I became the president of the new government dubbed the "People's Government." World-renowned soprano Jo Sumi sang "Oh, the Country of Morning in the East." Then I read my inauguration speech entitled "Let's Open a New Age of Overcoming National Crisis and Re-Take-Off."

I began my speech by sharing my feelings about launching the People's Government. "Today's inauguration ceremony is of truly great historical significance. Today is a day when we can all be proud because democratic regime change occurred for the first time in our history. It is also finally the day when the government that intends to develop democracy and economy is born. The current government is the People's Government in the true sense of the word because it was created thanks to the power of the people. I offer all glory and blessings to the Korean people and firmly promise you that I will devote all I have to serve you."

I also emphasized that we needed to change the Constitution of our country through society-wide reform and appealed that all people share in the pain of our nation. "We're now facing the crisis of national bankruptcy. Under the burden of enormous debts, we're busy defending ourselves from foreign debts that demand to be repaid everyday. This is truly an absurd situation. We are now avoiding catastrophe only thanks to your patriotic collaboration and the help from IMF, World Bank, Asian Development Bank, and such friendly countries as the US, Japan, Canada, Australia, and the European Union. We will experience rising prices and increasing unemployment this year. Our income will decrease and businesses will go bankrupt. Sweat and tears are now demanded from all of us." I could not help choking up because of the fact that I, a newly inaugurated president, had to make such a request from the Korean people, who were suffering from the fault of the elite.

I declared that the People's Government would not exercise any sort of political retaliation or discrimination. I also expressed my desire to establish Korea as a powerful information country, despite our foreign currency crisis. "The Korean people are highly educated and equipped with a brilliant cultural tradition. The Korean people are excellent people who have the potential to lead the information age of the twenty-first century. The new government will make an effort to nurture new generations to become the leaders of knowledge- and information-based society. We will teach computer from elementary school onward, and make sure that students can choose computers as a subject on their college entrance examinations. By turning our country into a nation that knows how to use computers the best, we will lay ourselves a strong foundation as an information powerhouse."

In terms of the division, I declared three basic principles in our relationship with the North: "First, we will not allow any form of armed invasion; second, we have no intention of harming or absorbing North Korea; and, third, we will actively pursue reconciliation and collaboration with North Korea from the most practicable field. I hope that the South-North interchange will be carried out according to the South-North Basic Agreement. I propose that we exchange special envoys for the implementation of the South-North Basic Agreement. I am willing to meet for a summit if North Korea agrees."

Finally, I appealed to the Korean people to participate in the work of opening up a new age by overcoming national crisis, while emphasizing that we were at a crossroads of advance and retreat: "Our history of five millennia is watching us. The souls of our ancestors are encouraging us. Like our admirable ancestors, who saved our nation from crisis at every turn with their unyielding will, let's become the creators of a history that overcomes today's crisis and leaps forward into tomorrow. Let us turn today's crisis into tomorrow's blessing. The Korean people can do this. Our history of rising up from the ruins of the Korean War proves it. I will be at the front of the line. Let us elevate the glory of the Republic of Korea again!"

Citizens cheered and applauded on both sides of the square as I walked through it after my inauguration speech. Although I was happy, I felt oppressed by the heavy sense of responsibility to meet the Korean people's expectation.

After returning to the Blue House, I inquired about the National Assembly. I was told that the application for parliamentary approval of the appointment of prime minister could not be laid before the Assembly because all of the assembly members from the Grand National Party were absent. The absolute majority opposition party was showing its muscles to the new president, claiming that Mr. Kim Jong-pil was not an appropriate person for the office.

Worried about this possibility, I had even appealed in my inaugural address, "A sincere request to the national assemblymen from the majority opposition party: We cannot overcome today's crisis without your collaboration. I will discuss everything with you. Please help me, if only during this first year, as our country is on the brink of a precipice."

Despite this desperate open appeal, the national assemblymen from the Grand National Party did not attend not only the inauguration ceremony, but also the plenary session of the National Assembly that afternoon. This resulted in an unprecedented state where the government consisted only of a president, without a prime minister or cabinet members. It was a preview of the five difficult years ahead of me as the president of a minority ruling party.

I appointed senior secretaries to the president including Chief of Staff Kim Chung-kwon, Senior Secretary for Foreign Affairs and National Security Lim Dong-won, Senior Secretary for Social Welfare Cho Kyu-hyang, and Senior Secretary for Public Relations and Spokesperson Park Jie-won. Although the previous civilian government had eleven senior secretaries and fifty-one secretaries, my government began with six senior secretaries and thirty-five secretaries.

An inaugural reception was held at Sejong Hall in the Sejong Center, with about a thousand guests in attendance. Here also, I urged the majority opposition party to cooperate with the government in affairs of the state. "The affairs of the state are drifting because the ruling party is a minority at this critical moment in our country's destiny. Please confirm the appointment of prime minister."

Night settled over the Blue House, where previous presidents had oppressed me for so long. *What were they thinking when they were here?* I wondered. I could still see the people cheering and applauding during the inauguration ceremony that day. Despite the grave situation Korea was in, it was still a hopeful event. I could not understand why the majority opposition party would not even hold a hearing for the prime minister's appointment. I felt sorry for the Korean people. I could not fall asleep; my wife couldn't either. She seemed surprised and uncomfortable about how large our bedroom was. It was indeed too large a room for a couple in their seventies to live in. It even felt cold.

I spent all of next day greeting foreign dignitaries. All told, I met seventy-nine guests from twelve countries in eighteen fifteen- to twenty-minute meetings. My first guest was former German president von Weizsäcker. I thanked him for Germany's active collaboration in the resolution of Korea's foreign currency crisis. Then I met Japanese leaders, including former prime ministers Nakasone and Takeshita. I reminded them of the superficiality of the past friendly relationship between Korea and Japan and urged them to work toward a real improvement in the relationship between our two countries. After this meeting, I met Mr. James Rainey and former US Ambassador to Korea Donald Gregg. French Premier Pierre Mauroy brought a handwritten letter from President Jacques Chirac, and former president of the Philippines Corazon Aquino brought a handwritten letter from President Fidel Ramos. I asked all of the foreign guests for their help in the Korean effort to overcome the recent financial crisis. I also asked pop singer Michael Jackson to invest in Korea.

The protocol secretary's office was worried about my forced march. My voice grew huskier by afternoon. Nevertheless, I had to meet all of the guests. My secretaries urged me to listen rather than speaking; however, it was I who needed to talk. I had to appeal for their help with the urgent economic and political situations.

On March 1, the first national holiday since my inauguration, I again urged North Korea to exchange special envoys for the implementation of the Basic Agreement. "Both South and North Korea should respect each other's system and refrain from any action to harm the other party," I said. "We are willing to respond to any level of dialogue for the sake of peaceful co-existence, peaceful exchange, and peaceful reunification."

I also said that we had to speed up the process of family reunions and the confirmation of separated family members' whereabouts, although immediate reunification would be difficult. I made it clear that I was willing to respond to any level of dialogue with them. I didn't receive a reply from North Korea.

That year March 1 landed on a Sunday, the day when I customarily went to church and had lunch with my children and grandchildren. But that day I stayed home. I did not want to ruin the atmosphere at the church and inconvenience other Catholics because of measures that would have to be taken for my protection.

Although I had slept only four nights at the Blue House by that point, I felt as if I had been there for a year. My wife went to the Special Concert to Collect Dollars at the Seoul Arts Center. It was moving to see musicians make such an effort, although it didn't feel right to have a word like "dollars" in the title of a music concert where beautiful tunes were played.

Grand National Party president Cho Sun and I agreed on the prime minister confirmation during our lunch meeting on February 27. The application was laid before the National Assembly on March 2. During our meeting, President Cho requested that I withdraw Mr. Kim Jong-pil's appointment, but I firmly rejected his request. "My coalition with the LDA was my promise to the Korean people. It is an act of betrayal if I break my promise to the LDA. If you object to Mr. Kim Jong-pil as prime minister, then you should participate by voting against it."

I paid close attention to the National Assembly as they voted. Although assemblymen from the Grand National Party participated, they cast blank votes. When the ruling party assemblymen found this out and protested, the voting came to a halt. I was very disappointed. This was a political statement that they could not accept the result of the presidential election.

In the end, I had to make a difficult decision. I could not just drift along, being pushed by the majority opposition party. I launched the Acting Prime Minister Kim Jong-pil cabinet on March 3. I was able to do so thanks to the recommendation of outgoing Prime Minister Goh Kun. In order to create a small but effective government, I abolished the two vice prime ministers' positions for economy and reunification, and reduced the number of ministries from twenty-three to seventeen. I appointed ministers from members of National Congress and seven ministers upon the recommendation of the Liberal Democracy Alliance. In addition, I appointed two ministers unaffiliated with either party.

The next morning, I also appointed Mr. Lee Chong-chan to the head of the ANSP and president of Kia Group Jin Nyum to the chair of the Planning and Budget Committee. On March 6, I appointed Mr. Chung Hae-joo to the head of the Office for Government Policy Coordination, Professor Jeon Cheol-hwan to president of the Bank of Korea, Mr. Lee Hun-jai to governor of Financial Supervisory Service, and Dr. Yoon Hoo-jung to the Special Committee for Women. I also had Chairman of the Fair Trade Commission Jeon Yun Churl remain in the office. I issued a statement to the Korean people explaining why I had to appoint the acting prime minister, and reiterating the reasons I mentioned above.

On March 13, I carried out the largest-ever pardon and reinstatement to celebrate the new government's inauguration. Altogether, it consisted of 5.52 million people, including many businessmen, workers, government officials, and prisoners of conscience. Although many politicians were included, I had to exclude former Assemblyman Kwon Rho-kap, who had been involved in the Hanbo Incident. People who knew us both appealed to me and told me that he was unjustly involved in the incident, but I could not ignore public opinion. Although Mr. Kwon accepted this decision, I felt sorry to him.

The night before my move to the Blue House, my former secretaries visited me. Very moved, they congratulated me on my presidential election. Although they went through so many difficult times with me, we did not often see each other from thereon out. Former secretaries like Hahn Hwa-kap, Kim Ok-doo, Namkung Jin, and Yoon Chul-sang openly declared that they would not participate in the next government if I won the election. After my victory, I confirmed the exclusion of close associates, saying, "I have comrades from the democracy movement, but I don't have retainers." My former secretaries again repeated their intention not to participate in official positions appointed by the president and government.

The so-called Donggyo-dong faction did exist in Korean political history. I know very well that some people view us negatively, based on the evils of factional politics. However, what would our country have been like without them during those dark age of dictatorship? Also, what would have happened to me? Unity with comrades was my and our power. I feel infinitely grateful to them.

The Asia-Europe Meeting (ASEM) began in London, England, on April 2. Unlike in the past, I ordered a simple send-off ceremony—no arch, banner, or national flag were hung. We did not hold an inspection of the tri-service honor guard or sound a fanfare. Live broadcasting, which was customary in the past, was not done, either. Only ten people came to the airport, and I also cut the presidential entourage in half.

Although ASEM was my first summit diplomacy event, I did not want to step on a red carpet to fanfare while the Korean people were suffering. The only goal I had in attending this meeting was to exercise my ability as a president who believed in the philosophy of "seeking truth, founded on concrete evidence." As soon as I arrived in London, I openly said, "I came to England to do sales." *The Times*, a renowned daily newspaper in England, ran a special three-page article on me, the Korean economy, national security, society, and culture.

I met with many people in London, aware that this was an opportunity to meet the heads of many major countries. It was a great blessing and fortune, and I continued to persuade them. I might have begun each conversation differently, but the conclusion was always the same: "Please trust me and lend us money. Please trust the Korean people and invest." Heads of major countries, including Chinese Premier Zhu Rongji, Japanese prime minister Hashimoto Ryutaro, British prime minister Tony Blair, and French president Jacques Chirac, listened to me carefully and appreciated my will and courage for reform.

I had an unexpected summit with French president Chirac upon his cordial request. I asked that he make a decision about the return of Oegyujanggak books, historical relics that had been illegally taken out of Korea. I also asked Chinese Premier Zhu Rongji for help, saying: "A friend in need is a friend, indeed."

The greatest achievement of the ASEM was the decision to send an investment promotion team from European countries to Asia in order to solve the financial crisis. I proposed and successfully pushed this through, although the process was not easy. I made this abrupt motion in the second summit meeting, but they did not seem to seriously consider it. Prime Minister Tony Blair, who was the chairman of the ASEM, tried to gloss over it, saying: "Let's consider it later." I decided to push it at the reception offered by Queen Elizabeth II, where I made the rounds and visited each head of country. To Prime Minister Blair, I said, "If you don't help us with this crisis, Asian countries might say there is no use for ASEM. This could be the last ASEM." It was almost a threat.

At the third meeting the following day, we focused on my motion while mostly ignoring the original agenda item, the future of ASEM. Chairman Tony Blair, French president Chirac, and Japanese prime minister Hashimoto Ryutaro actively supported me. Soon, German chancellor Helmut Kohl and Italian prime minister Romano Prodi joined in. A stronger form of my proposal was included in the chairman's final statement. It read that we "adopted a Trade Facilitation Action Plan (TFAP) and an Investment Promotion Action Plan (IPAP), including the establishment of an Investment Experts Group (IEG)." I received big congratulations from the heads of participating countries. I believe that this achievement was possible only because they appreciated my passion and sincerity. It was a breathtaking five nights and six days. Through this meeting I acquired self-confidence.

After my inauguration, I ordered the abolishment of a few customary practices. First of all, I banned the title "Your Excellency." "The title 'president' is enough to express respect," I said. "We call a teacher 'Teacher so-and-so' and a chairman 'Chairman so-and-so' to pay respect. To call me 'president' is enough."

To me, the title "Your Excellency" sounded almost scary and had authoritarian connotations. Although I emphasized the abolition of this title many times during both my president-elect days and my presidency, it took some time to eliminate the title entirely.

I also demanded that my photographs not be hung in government offices. It seemed like a meaningless thing to do when Korean people already knew who their president was, and when I was featured on TV and in the newspapers every day. In the past, the president's photographs were hung everywhere—not only in government office buildings, but also in *dong*-offices and police boxes. It was also wasteful to distribute tens of thousands of new photographs when the entire country was suffering.

I also refused to honor requests for my handwriting for signboards or stones. Of course, I received numerous requests as this had previously been the practice. However, I refused, first because I wasn't confident about my handwriting, and, second, because I knew they would fade and be erased with time, no matter how meaningful they were.

The only exception to this practice was the code of conduct for the National Intelligence Service (NIS) when the National Security Planning Agency was reborn as NIS, a pure intelligence service agency, after obliterating its negative past as an agency for political and civilian surveillance. The phrase "Intelligence is the Strength of a Nation" was inscribed in a stone, which was erected in the yard of the NIS. Although they inscribed my name on the back of the stone, I ordered them to erase it. I did not want to leave my name there because the NIS would continue to exist after my five-year term.

Ten years after this code of conduct was created, the NIS code of conduct changed. I wonder what happened to that stone. We do our best, but there is nothing that does not change in this world. Seeing how I wonder about this one piece of handwriting, how glad I am that I refused all of the other requests!

I appointed President Ahn Chu-sop of the Republic of Korea Army College to the chief of the Office of the Presidential Security. Chief Ahn was a reserved person who did not make a single mistake during my five-year tenure. I urged that he do his work "democratically." I did not want the office to become another overbearing authoritarian institution, pulling its weight around other governmental offices and civilian organizations like it had in the past. As they had to conduct their tasks more openly and democratically, their work became even harder and heavier, but they did not complain. People called them gentlemanly. Foreigners admired their calm and invisible presence.

I also ordered that the Office of the Presidential Security open the Blue House to everyone, regardless of age, gender, or nationality. We hosted 250,000 visitors annually, and about 1.27 million visitors during my five-year term. Occasionally, I would shake hands or pose for pictures with visitors on my way to and from the main office building. During those times, my security officers were busy, but they were never authoritarian. I am very grateful to them.

A little more than a month after my inauguration, I received reports from each ministry. Getting reports from the Ministry of Justice and the ANSP was special because they were the same agencies that inflicted unjustifiable suffering on me.

After listening to a report on the year's plans, I asked Minister of Justice Kim Tae-joung, "The Korean people criticized the past investigation of the Hanbo Group, saying that only a feather was caught and the body escaped once the person in charge of the investigation was replaced. Do you think the investigation was fairly carried out?"

Minister Kim didn't seem to expect that question. After a long pause, he replied, "The prosecutors did their best. I feel sorry that people mistrusted their work. I will do my best to make sure all investigations receive people's support and trust during my tenure."

I wanted to believe what he was saying. I hoped that I could trust him to create this sort of spirit in his department. At the end of discussion, I said, "It's impossible to express how important the role public prosecutors play. Although we cannot blame them for our current economic crisis, it is also true that the Ministry of Justice could have prevented it by being faithful to its mission. The Hanbo Incident happened because of the cozy relationship between politics and economics, because the powerful people controlled bank loans and the appointment of bank presidents. If the prosecutors had guarded the law well, banks would not have become what they did and businesses would still be competitive.

"The prosecutors can investigate even the president and arrest powerful politicians. Look at how the Japanese prosecutors arrested Prime Minister Tanaka. When you stand straight, nobody will dare commit corruption. In the past, the prosecutors were controlled by the power, and engaged in targeted investigations according to the power's direction. I know because I am a victim. In 1989, during the fabricated incident of my pro-communism, the prosecutors tortured Suh Kyung-won and did not let him sleep for three days to get to him falsely confess that he handed me $10,000.

"A country can stand tall only when the prosecutors stand straight. This is what I really want to tell you. I'm telling you that my government will hire and fire people regardless of their school and regional backgrounds. I will not request you exercise your power to serve my purposes."

In addition to this request for a radical change in legal administration, I also urged that he thoroughly revamp the prison administration. Based on my observations in prison, imprisoning ten people in a room together could *encourage* rather than *discourage* their evil qualities.

On May 12, I visited the Agency for National Security Planning (ANSP) to receive their report. Its predecessor, the KCIA, was the den of shady political operations and its name alone evoked terror in people's minds. Although it changed its name to ANSP, its practices did not change. The organization still did not hesitate to commit bribery, intimidation, and illegal wiretapping and surveillance, as well as to arrest, torture, and kidnap. I was one of its biggest victims. It was the KCIA that staged my kidnapping in Tokyo in 1973 and bought a house next to mine in Donggyo-dong in order to put me under surveillance during my house imprisonment. The current Kim Dae-jung Presidential Library and Museum building site was one of the KCIA safe houses. The KCIA and

ANSP also fabricated North Korean spy incidents during every election campaign in order to turn the tide of the election in the direction most favorable to the ruling party. They also created and distributed materials that falsely accused me of being a commie and a liar. Considering the history between the agency and me, this visit was an unusual event.

I told the ANSP officials: "I am the example of the unhappy history of ANSP. I suffered from all kinds of operations against me, including kidnapping, a death sentence, and pro-communist fabrications. The ANSP should never repeat these practices. You should start anew. You should respect the president as the head of the country and administrative branch, but not politically. You should not listen to any unjust demands from the president. My government will not abuse the ANSP or use it as our political tool. I believe you don't want this either."

ANSP Chief Lee Chong-chan told me that he changed the name of the agency to the NIS and decided its code of conduct would be "Intelligence is the strength of a nation." I liked this code of conduct. Its past code of conduct—"We work in the shade while facing the sun"—was vague in meaning and felt somewhat shady.

Toward the end of our discussion, I said: "The ANSP worried and concerned the Korean people. It's true that it was viewed negatively for its political role. Now, the ANSP is reborn as the National Intelligence Service. Please work hard to strengthen your intelligence abilities; make them as strong as economic research institutes. You must be able to help with important decision in economic wars. You must study hard to explore ways to make North Korea open its doors. The NIS should not stand over the Korean people. It has to share information with other government institutions and thoroughly manage potential causes of national crisis. The NIS should now talk straight and warn the people of impending danger. As president, I urge you one last time: Please stay completely neutral."

On a slow Sunday, an unexpected accident happened out of the blue. My wife fell on the hard surface of the *ondol* floor in the library because the chair in front of her desk—which had wheels on it—moved as she was about to sit down on it. Although she called for help, nobody heard her because of the heavy library door. She was alone for twenty minutes before she got help.

She was hospitalized at the Armed Forces Capital Hospital for a fracture in her femoral area. She had never once been hurt or hospitalized in the time since we'd been married, even while going through such difficult times. Perhaps she had not had the time or the space to be hospitalized even when she *was* sick. How ironic that she was hurt in the library of the Blue House! I visited her every night after work—it felt so cold in the Blue House without her.

Reform in the Four Major Areas (1998)

My favorite spring flowers are forsythias and azaleas, and my favorite fall flowers are cosmoses. In the spring, the flowers always looked glorious on my drive through Bugak Skyway and the roads of Mt. Namsan in Seoul. The spring mountains full of azaleas were heaven on earth. One day in the spring of 1998, I took some time to drive through the roads of Mt. Namsan with my wife. The flowers were beautiful as always, but there was something strange about them. Normally, forsythias bloom before azaleas, but this spring they were blooming at the same time. Nature seemed to be mistaken about the season.

On April 10, during the report from the Ministry of Environment, I said: "We talk about environmental preservation, but this expression is very arrogant. After ruining the environment, we say we'd like to 'preserve' it, as if we're doing nature a favor. No animal has harmed the environment as much as human beings have.

"When we look at human history, our ancestors were very friendly to the environment. For example, there's the spirit of 'peace under heaven' in Asia. It is a spirit of respecting peace for all things under heaven.

"Buddha said, 'Earth, water, and air are all Buddha.' He equally cherished nature and human beings. In the Bible, God first created the Earth, and then each animal and plant. He then created human beings so that we could take care of them. As you know, it is the government's job to make people happy and it is up to us human beings to make nature comfortable. I hope you incorporate these ideas into your work.

"Human beings have never destroyed the environment like they do today, and we don't know what punishments are in store for us. Look at El Niño, for example."

Unfortunately, the environment was an "ideal" and the economy was "reality." Although I hoped that the ministries would come up with a plan to respect both, they did not follow my wishes. How easy it is to destroy, but how hard it is to restore!

The economic crisis continued to be a very difficult situation. We all shed a lot of sweat and tears to reform the economy that we had enjoyed based on borrowed money. But how could the president look the other way when his people were suffering? In order to recover the economy, we had to coldly and ruthlessly reform, which inevitably meant large-scale layoffs. The flowers were blooming, but the spring of 1998 was, nonetheless, a long stretch of heartbreaking days.

Although we had made it through the most urgent phase of the financial crisis, the flame of crisis still remained. If the world decided not to trust and help us, the crisis could blow up at any moment. A strong Korea that could withstand any flame or gust of crisis would be possible only when we liquidated the government-directed economy and moved to a market economy. Without reform, we could not raise our credit rating. Without reform, we could not expect the extension of loans, foreign investment, or aid from international organizations like IMF. There was no other choice.

The basic principle of market economy is free competition and responsible management. Businesses and financial institutions that had been under the control and protection of the government should have entered the market governed by these principles. We had to apply principles of a market economy to both government organizations and public sector industries. We also had to introduce flexibility into the labor market to bring it in step with international trends. I decided that we should reform all four areas of economy—business, finance, the public sector, and labor.

Among those four areas, I focused the most on financial reform with a particular emphasis on bank reform. The recovery of banks' competitiveness was where all reform should begin. Only then could businesses feel the pressure. The source of our foreign currency crisis was that the banks had lent enormous sums of money to *chaebols* without evaluating the value of their businesses properly.

In the past, bank officials were like financial bureaucrats. Ordinary customers who entrusted the banks with their money could not act as owners. Big businesses monopolized loans. After I became president, I ordered that the government, including myself, should not interfere in any way with the personnel matters of banks.

Insolvent banks had to be liquidated as soon as possible. If we left them alone, we would end up managing funds conservatively to protect them from bankruptcy. This would intensify the credit crunch, which would result in insolvent businesses, and this, in turn, would make financial assets insolvent. It was a vicious cycle. The size of insolvent loans at the time was about 120 trillion won. It was no wonder that the entire country was insolvent.

I ordered transparent bank reform. The Financial Supervisory Committee formed the Committee for the Evaluation of Bank Reform Plans and began their evaluation on May 20, 1998. As it became clearer which banks should be liquidated, fierce lobbying for survival ensued. The entire country was boiling. I told the committee chair to continue working based on principle alone.

On June 29, Governor of Financial Supervisory Service Lee Hun-jai officially announced the liquidation of five banks: Tonghwa, Tongnam, Taedong, Gyeonggi, and Chungcheong. Reform plans for seven banks— Korea Exchange Bank, Chohung Bank, Hanil Bank, Commerce Bank, Peace Bank, Gangwon Bank, and Chung Buk Bank—were approved on the condition of fundamental management personnel reform and by issuing new shares to be purchased.

As expected, the labor unions of banks that were to be liquidated strongly protested. Both the FKTU and KCTU demanded job security for employees of liquidated banks. They refused to participate in the tripartite commission and declared their intension for a solidarity strike. However, the banks that were taking over liquidated ones refused to guarantee jobs to the employees of the banks they were taking over. The government could not force them to do this, while also asking for their reform. Senior Secretary for Policy Planning Kang Bong-kyun proposed requesting that all takeover banks reemploy any employees under the fourth level (senior assistant). I issued a special order that the employees of liquidated banks were not to be disadvantaged. Nevertheless, 5000 out of the 8000 employees from liquidated banks lost their jobs.

The seven banks that survived were given a month to plan their management normalization, including foreign investment invitations and mergers. Mergers between big banks happened unexpectedly quickly. Hanil Bank and Commerce Bank merged to become Hanbit Bank, a large bank with assets worth 100 trillion won, and ranked within the ninety largest banks in the world.

Chohung Bank merged with Gang'won and Chung Buk Banks in February 1999. Korea Exchange Bank came up with a plan to normalize on its own after accepting 3.5 billion won from German Commerzbank. Of the already proficient banks, Kookmin Bank and Korea Long-term Credit Bank merged on January 5, 1999. The next day, Hana Bank and Boram Bank announced their merger. This was the end of the first phase of restructuring, and an enormous event that changed the topography of the Korean financial world.

Of the 2101 financial institutions in 1997, 659 insolvent institutions were liquidated. In addition, the debt-to-equity ratio of financial institutions was raised to the international level, and the bad loan ratio was reduced from 12.9 to 3.4 percent. This reform improved Korea's credit rating, and banks' net profit for the term of 2002 was 5.9 trillion won, even after allotting for bad debt reserve.

We needed an enormous sum of public funding in order to buy bad loans from banks, which was necessary for financial restructuring. But it was difficult to know exactly how much public funding was necessary. At the Economic Measure Coordination meeting, we decided to provide financial institutions with 50 trillion won, based on Minister of Finance and Economy Lee Kyu-sung's recommendation. Altogether, we created 64 trillion won in public funding, including the 14 trillion won provided to Korea First Bank and other financial institutions prior to my inauguration.

Although this first stage of financial restructuring was successfully completed toward the end of 1998, the situation became unstable again after the Daewoo Group went bankrupt in 1999 and the Hyundai Group faced a crisis in 2000. Once more, we had to stabilize the financial field by again injecting public funding. This was the second stage of financial restructuring. The newly appointed Minister of Finance and Economy Jin Nyum reported that we urgently needed an additional 40 trillion won in public funding. The opposition party protested strongly, demanding an apology from me and that responsible parties be reprimanded for wasting public funding.

In order to secure the transparency demanded by the opposition party, I demanded that the officials whose morals had slackened during the creation and implementation of public funding be strictly reprimanded. About 1400 people from 464 financial institutions were prosecuted. In the end, I called Grand National Party president Lee Hoi-chang to discuss this matter, and was able to have this bill passed in early December 2000. Total public funding amounted to 104 trillion won and to 159.6 trillion won if we add the amount that was collected and reinjected to it. Fortunately, the collection ratio gradually increased and exceeded 50 percent as of 2006. It was a very encouraging result, even in comparison with foreign examples.

For the reform of business, I had to shatter the popular belief of any business being "too big to fail." I met with the presidents of four *chaebols*—Lee Kun-hee of Samsung, Chung Mong-koo of Hyundai, Koo Bon Moo of LG, and Choi Jong-hyun of SK—and reached a five-article agreement. The five articles were heightened transparency; eliminating subsidiary mutual payment guarantees; radical improvement of financial structures; focusing on essential main business and strengthening collaborations with small- and medium-sized businesses; and strengthening the responsibility of majority shareholders and management.

After much thought, I also requested that the presidents inject their private money into their businesses. This request was contradictory to the market economy principle, but social criticism of them could not be ignored. In particular, the laborers demanded that the government collect *chaebol* management's private assets, accusing them of accumulating wealth by illicit means. That is why I made this suggestion, although the *chaebols* strongly resisted it.

After the agreement, the *chaebols* announced their very disappointing plans for restructuring. They tried to simply liquidate subsidiary companies in the red. I ordered the Emergency Economic Committee to obtain specific restructure plans from thirty *chaebols*, and had their main creditor banks evaluate their plans. This way we restructured through banks, rather than through direct intervention by the government.

Nevertheless, the *chaebols* seemed to simply wait it out until the government lost its momentum for reform. I ordered the Financial Supervisory Committee to liquidate insolvent companies by the end of May. I was disappointed with the list of liquidated companies Governor of Financial Supervisory Committee Lee Hun-jai gave me on June 3. Out of 313 companies belonging to sixty-four *chaebol* groups, the list included only twenty-one companies, which did not include a single company affiliated with the five big *chaebols*. I urged him to review it again and mentioned my position at the cabinet meeting on June 16. The list given to me the next day included fifty-five companies, twenty of which were affiliated with the five big *chaebols*. Although this was not entirely satisfactory, it was a meaningful event because it marked the first occasion when banks liquidated insolvent companies all at once. However, the *chaebols* were still very passive about restructuring, which ultimately resulted in the collapse of the Daewoo Group and the division of the Hyundai Group.

The collapse of the Daewoo Group is worth mentioning. On January 24, 1998, President Kim Woo-jung proposed that companies dramatically increase their exports to instantly fill up the national storeroom. He also argued that we could immediately overcome the financial crisis by dramatically cutting back on unnecessary imports, which would result in a $500 billion trade surplus. He also promised to set the restructuring example. I was very grateful for what he said he meant to do. I was hopeful because I appreciated his business acumen and upright character. He also helped the opposition party and me during our difficult times.

However, he changed his tune completely in the World Economic Forum meeting in Davos at the end of the same month. He blamed financial institutions for the financial crisis and denied companies' responsibility. I wondered why he changed his position. Perhaps he hoped he could get an enormous foreign investment. Daewoo announced a $70 billion joint venture with GM on February 2. The president of GM visited the Blue House to explain his company's plan for the joint venture with Daewoo. This ultimately fell through because of the general strike at the GM Headquarters in the US. Although Daewoo belatedly tried to take over Kia, it lost its bid to Hyundai. In the end, the Japanese firm Nomura Securities issued a report on Daewoo entitled "Emergency Bell at Daewoo," which resulted in the market's cold response to Daewoo.

President Kim wished to see me, so I met with him at the Blue House. During our meeting, he was hopeful. He said he would actively restructure Daewoo by engaging in a "big deal" with Samsung, taking over Samsung Automobile, the symbol of an insolvent company, and handing Daewoo Electronics over to Samsung. This was a radical plan that was in step with the government's recommendation. In order to prevent redundant investments and inefficacy, the government recommended this sort of big deal. The government, of course, could not force these kinds of deals on to *chaebols*, but a voluntary deal was certainly welcome.

Unfortunately, Daewoo's plan for a big deal came too late. The market had already lost their trust in Daewoo. In addition, its finances were seriously strained as Daewoo depended heavily on export and because of government restrictions on trade financing. During this crunch, President Kim flew to Hanoi, where I was attending the APEC summit, to see me. During a lunch meeting with me and Senior Secretary for Policy Planning Kang Bong-kyun he pled that I lift the restrictions on Daewoo. Although I ordered Mr. Kang to review the matter, the Financial Supervisory Committee concluded that they could not support Daewoo because the prospects of its overseas businesses were unclear.

Daewoo demanded 2 trillion won in cash from Samsung in exchange for taking over Samsung Automobile. Although I called President Kim to the Blue House and urged him to show visible achievements, the situation didn't change much for Daewoo. After the government's open declaration about intervening in the restructuring of *chaebols* that did not show active efforts, Daewoo announced more plans for restructuring: the sale of eleven companies affiliated with Daewoo, including Daewoo Heavy Industry's shipbuilding department and the Hilton Hotel. In a conference between politicians and businessmen held on April 27, President Kim again promised to carry out the company's restructure within the year.

Unfortunately, the market did not respond positively, and Daewoo's finances became more and more strained. After a tedious nerve war with Samsung, Samsung declared that it was giving up on the big deal, requesting the legal management of Samsung Automobile. Although Daewoo announced additional plans to rescue its companies—including President Kim offering all of his assets (worth 10 trillion won) as security for loans—the market had already frozen for Daewoo. On August 26, twelve companies affiliated with Daewoo were liquidated.

This is how Daewoo, the third largest group in Korea, was completely liquidated, shattering the folk belief that a business could be "too big to fail." President Kim resigned as president of the Federation of Korean Industries and went abroad in October of that year. It was a very unfortunate turn of events that I certainly did not hope for. I trusted him and believed in the future of Daewoo. However, he ignored my will and underestimated the market movement. I still don't know why he delayed restructuring his group. Daewoo's liquidation ushered in the arrival of a new age where growth based only on loans and insolvency hidden behind creative accounting no longer worked. I believed that President Kim Woo-jung would return and begin anew.

Government organizations also could not avoid reform. I had decided this was necessary before the new government was even inaugurated. I wanted to come up with a structure that would use less tax money and work more efficiently. The Presidential Commission on Government Innovation was launched on January 6, 1998, under the leadership of Chairman Park Kwonsang.

In order to make a small but efficient government, I wanted to put the functions of budgeting and personnel management under the immediate control of the president. Accordingly, a plan was made to establish the Office of Planning and Budget, which took charge of the work of the Budget Office under the Ministry of Finance and Economy, and the Office of Central Personnel Committee, putting both offices under the immediate control of the president. However, the Grand National Party protested this plan, accusing me of intending to arbitrarily control personnel matters; this was, however, a complete misunderstanding. By establishing the

Office of Central Personnel Committee, I intended to effectively control the personnel management rights exercised by the president and cabinet members. The result was disappointing. The Office of Planning and Budget was divided up into the Committee for the Planning and Budget (under the control of the president) and the Office of Budget (under the Ministry of Finance and Economy), making the matter unnecessarily complicated. The Office of Central Personnel Committee wasn't adopted at all.

We also divided up the enormous dinosaur institution of Ministry of Finance and Economy (under the control of a vice prime minister) into the smaller Ministry of Finance and Economy, Office of Budget, and Finance Supervising Committee. The work of trade was also handed over to the Ministry of Foreign Affairs and Trade. We reduced the size and work of the Ministry of Finance and Economy because the previous institution monopolized power over all aspects of national finance and economy, and was never checked on its defective policies. The government-restructuring bill passed through the National Assembly on February 17, 1998.

The government restructure became inevitable after my inauguration. Chair of the Planning and Budget Committee Jin Nyum proposed that the government be evaluated by civilian consulting firms. This was a radical proposal, but it made sense. Civilian consulting firms could be more objective than government officials, who were not free from organizational self-interests. We divided the government into nine areas and a total of nineteen civilian consulting firms evaluated its structure.

After a four-month evaluation, the second phase restructuring plan was prepared. This plan, announced on March 4, 1999, was quite drastic. It included the establishment of the Ministry of Planning and Budget (which merged together the functions of the Planning and Budget Committee and the Budget Office) and the Central Personnel Committee, which had been given up. The Ministry of Industry and Resources, the Ministry of Science and Technology, and the Ministry of Information and Communication would merge into the Ministry of Industry and Technology. The Ministry of Labor and Ministry of Welfare would merge into the Ministry of Labor and Welfare. The Ministry of Oceans and Fisheries would be abolished. According to Chairman Chin, most cabinet members responded positively to this plan.

However, this plan also ran into fierce opposition. Not only with the related offices, but also with the Liberal Democracy Alliance, our coalition partner, which condemned it harshly. Because the LDA was in favor of a parliamentary government system, its members condemned this plan for concentrating power in the president. I asked Chairman Chin to have Prime Minister Kim Jong-pil participate in our discussion.

The result was again disappointing, and we practically scrapped all of the plans to merge ministries. The Ministry of Planning and Budget (under the direct control of the president) changed to the Ministry of Planning and Budget, and was now under the control of the prime minister. The only plan that survived was the establishment of the Central Personnel Committee. The second government-restructuring plan also ended anticlimactically. My dream of a small but efficient government remained an incomplete reform. I hope that someone will refer to it later.

In the age of borderless, infinite competition, deregulation was inevitable for our survival. Although I raised this issue at my inauguration, bureaucrats came up with trite plans, as expected. I brought the topic up again during the cabinet meeting on April 14, 1998. Two weeks later, on April 28, the head of the Office for Government Policy Coordination laid out the Comprehensive Guideline for Deregulation before the cabinet council. The gist of this plan was to reduce governmental regulation to two-thirds of its current level; however, there were no clear criteria for this two-thirds.

I again ordered an evaluation of all regulations and the elimination of all unnecessary regulations. On May 1, the head of the Office for Government Policy Coordination reported that about 7000 regulations of more than 10,000 were under review. By June, there still wasn't any progress.

This lack of progress had a lot to do with opposition from politicians and interest groups. Some bills were delayed or completely transmuted in the process of discussion in the National Assembly. Permission for multiple organizations for professionals such as doctors, pharmacists, tax accountants, CPAs, and customhouse brokers could not even be discussed in the National Assembly standing committee.

Due to desperate lobbying activities by interest groups, 50 out of 268 deregulation bills were weakened during the National Assembly discussion. The government glossed them over as "realistic difficulties." I wanted to veto these weakened bills, but it was too politically burdensome. In the end, I signed all of the bills, but requested that eighteen be reverted to the original bills and resubmitted at the extraordinary session of the National Assembly in February 1999. The fight continued between interest groups and their allies in the National Assembly and the government.

Despite enormous resistance, 5430 (48.4 percent) out of 11,125 government regulations were abolished and 2411 (21.7 percent) were improved in 1998. The next year, we reviewed the remaining 6811 regulations (including the new regulations introduced in 1998) and abolished 503 (7.4 percent) and improved 570 (8.4 percent).

Public companies also had to be reformed. Despite staunch resistance from labor unions, I did not abstain from this task. We selected eleven public companies for privatization, which had been attempted many times by previous governments to no avail. This was because there had not been a social consensus regarding a concrete program for privatization.

In order to clearly express my will for the privatization of public companies, I thought the most representative public company, POSCO, needed to be privatized. I discussed this matter with the founder of POSCO and president of the Liberal Democracy Alliance Park Tae-joon, who readily agreed with me, confirming my view of him as a person of farsightedness.

I urged Chairman of the Office for Government Policy Coordination Chin to pursue this matter thoroughly, but progress was delayed. Even POSCO was included in the second phase sale list due to opposition from the relevant offices that were concerned about its hostile takeover by foreign capital. The management of the Korea Electric Power Corporation also openly opposed its sale. I could not sit still and leave it alone as it was clear that the whole matter would end up in smoke. I rebuked Chairman Jin in order to support his effort during the cabinet meeting on June 16, 1998.

The Planning and Budget Committee announced the first Public Corporation Privatization Plan on July 3. It selected eleven out of twenty-six public corporations. Five of them—POSCO, Korea Heavy Industry, Korea Integrated Chemical Inc., Korea Technology Finance, and State Textbook Company—were to be immediately put up for sale. The remaining six—Korea Telecom, Korea Tobacco and Ginseng, Korea Electric Power Corporation, Daehan Oil Pipeline Corporation, Korea Gas Corporation, and Korea District Heating Corporation—would be privatized in stages. Despite many difficulties, I was able to privatize eight public corporations during my term. I could not finish the privatization of three energy-related public corporations: Korea Electric Power Corporation, Korea Gas Corporation, and Korea District Heating Corporation.

I have already mentioned implementing job cuts and launching the tripartite commission. The flexible labor market and expansion of basic labor rights are two sides of the same coin. In the past, the government had given only limited rights to workers, while guaranteeing employment and wages at a certain level. The government legalized the teachers' union and the KCTU, and guaranteed the political activity of labor unions.

The Korean Teachers Union (KTU) launched and began its official activities in May 1989. The Roh Tae-woo government then declared it illegal and fired about 1500 of its members. The term "fired teacher" was born at that point. Although they rehired about 1200 previously fired teachers during the Kim Young-sam government's reign, the KTU remained illegal. The union continued to carry out its activities and demanded legalization.

I thought that we had to legalize the KTU because it already existed, although there were strong objections, especially from the Korean Federation of Teachers' Associations (KFTA). The KFTA argued that legalizing the KTU would create opposition and antagonism among teachers; however, I thought that it could help reform the world of teachers through competition in good faith.

There were also debates about KTU's name. Some people argued that teachers weren't laborers; teachers considered themselves laborers, though, so I didn't think it should matter. A unified teachers' voice could be helpful in eliminating long-standing problems in the field. I also thought, though, that, as teachers taking care of our children, the KTU had to withhold their right for collective action.

I had acknowledged the KCTU even before my inauguration, as we desperately needed their cooperation to solve our national economic crisis. On November 23, 1999, the Ministry of Labor finally issued a registration certificate to KCTU, four years after it had launched.

During this period of four-area reform, every day was like a war. I had to criticize and condemn many things. I am very grateful to my cabinet members and the government workers who trusted me and followed my leadership. Through this reform, we were able to change the character of our country in many ways and to enter the new millennium with hope.

Still, unemployment remained a big problem. Ten thousand people per day lost their jobs. One thousand businesses per day closed their doors for good. Although the financial crisis abroad began to look hopeful, domestic unemployment did not ease up. On March 26, during the third Emergency Economic Committee meeting, relevant offices predicted that the number of unemployed would reach 1.5 million. When we included their family members, we had to worry about several million people's livelihoods. I urged cabinet members to come up with ways to solve this problem. I was so worried about their livelihood that I couldn't fall asleep at night. One April night, I even had to take a sleeping pill. The next morning, I asked all of the offices to create diagrams demonstrating what they were doing for unemployment in order to encourage them to think about the matter.

Dr. Alvin Toffler was visiting Seoul around that time, so I invited him to the Blue House and asked for his advice on solving the unemployment problem. He told me that emphasizing and nurturing small- and medium-sized companies was on the right track, citing America as a successful example of this. According to him, although big companies in the US had been significantly reducing their employment for the past decade, small- and medium-sized companies hired more workers than the big companies laid off. I was very encouraged by his remarks about my government's plan to nurture small- and medium-sized businesses as well as venture companies.

As far as unemployment goes, I continued to emphasize the following four points: first, to encourage companies to delay layoffs in exchange for government compensation; second, to create jobs by nurturing venture companies; third, to train workers for new jobs; and fourth, for government to take responsibility for the minimum livelihood through a social safety net.

I should not forget to mention that the generals of economic war during the early phase of the People's Government were all leaders the LDA recommended. Minister of Finance and Economy Lee Kyu-sung and Finance Supervising Committee Chair Lee Hun-jai demonstrated excellent leadership as we worked to overcome the financial crisis and reform the economy. I also cannot forget the vice president of the LDA, Kim Yong-hwan, who helped Korea regain market trust at every corner, despite the fact that he continually refused my offer of a cabinet position. It was also he who recommended Minister Lee Kyu-sung and Chairman Lee Hun-jai. Other cabinet members recommended by the LDA also worked hard. I never discriminated against them. I favored only those who did excellent work. I trusted them and they proved they deserved my trust.

EIGHT NIGHTS AND NINE DAYS IN AMERICA
(MARCH 1998–JUNE 1998)

From the time of my election victory until my inauguration, North Korea did not mention my name or the People's Government at all. However, there was no doubt that North Korean authorities were examining and exploring inter-Korean relations very carefully during that period. At the fifth inter-Korean Red Cross talk in March 1998, North Korean representatives requested that the South Korean Red Cross support the North by providing 200,000 tons of fertilizer. Given the size of this request, South Korean Red Cross representatives proposed a government-level conference, and North Korean representatives officially proposed a talk on the deputy minister level.

I had clarified three principles when it came to North Korea in my inauguration speech: that we would not accept any violent provocation; that we would not harm or absorb North Korea; and that we would actively pursue reconciliation and collaboration. All countries, including America, China, Russia, and Japan, supported these three principles. I also presented three principles for concrete cooperation: humanitarian support, separation of politics and economy, and reciprocity.

There were three choices for North Korea. First, they could provoke South Korea by force, which would be an act of desperation. Although we could not entirely discount this possibility, there was only a very slim chance it would happen because it was the worst choice, and both Koreas might end up collapsing. Second, they could seek isolation by rejecting an interchange and opening of the country. This choice would have damaged their economy, eventually leading them to collapse. As the cases of the Soviet Union and Eastern European countries had shown, isolation ultimately meant collapse. Third, they could adopt an open-door policy as China and Vietnam had done. I thought that North Korea would choose this third alternative for its survival. They would maintain their authoritarian regime, but they would also try to develop their economy. I thought they had no other choice than this third one, if not immediately, then definitely in the long run. Renowned Norwegian scholar Professor Johan Galtung, who visited Korea, agreed with me.

Our government pursued a North Korean policy that would induce their choice of the third alternative. The proposal made at the inter-Korean Red Cross talk meant that North Korea was sending us a meaningful signal. It might not have been a wink exactly, but it was still a significant gesture. They must have known that I was actively pursuing reconciliation and reunification.

The deputy minister-level inter-Korea talk occurred at the China World Hotel in Beijing, China, for a week beginning on April 11. Authorities from both Koreas sat face to face for the first time since the preliminary meeting for the summit between Kim Young-sam and Kim Il-sung in June 1994. It had been nearly four years. The head of the delegation from the South was Deputy Minister of Foreign Affairs Jeong Se Hyun. The North requested that we offer them 200,000 tons of fertilizer as humanitarian aid. South Korea promised to send the aid that spring in exchange for another humanitarian measure, such as the reunion of dispersed family members that fall. The North Korean delegation responded with a proposal that we should discuss the fertilizer matter first and other matters later, claiming, "It is un-humanitarian to apply the principle of reciprocity in humanitarian matters." After a tedious investigative skirmish, we failed to come to an agreement.

This was the first inter-Korean war of nerves since the launch of my People's Government. My approach to the inter-Korean problem was neither forcing nor begging for dialogue, and neither pausing nor hurrying efforts. Before this talk, I had expected that North Korea would accept our proposal for the reunion of dispersed family members. More than 60 percent of displaced North Koreans in South Korea had died by then. What could have been more important and urgent than having them meet their family members—if not, at the least, just letting them know whether they were alive or not?

Nonetheless, North Korea fiercely criticized this principle of reciprocity. About ten days after the Beijing talks, they criticized our government through Pyongyang Broadcasting, claiming that we were continuing the confrontational anti-North policy of past regimes. They broke their silence about the Sunshine Policy as well, by criticizing it. Both domestically and abroad, people were deeply disappointed about this failed talk. Some criticized us for bringing up the reunion of dispersed families. Others in the media sneered at the Sunshine Policy for its inability to solve such a basic problem as the reunion of dispersed families. There were also some conservative media and majority opposition party types that demanded a stronger implementation of the principle of reciprocity toward inter-Korean relations. I personally realized that North Korea was a very proud country, and that we had to be careful in approaching the matter of giving, because we had more.

In the early stage of my presidency, I renewed the function and operation of the National Security Council (NSC). It had previously belonged to the Emergency Planning Committee, probably based on the understanding that presidents who had been soldiers knew well about national security matters. However, that kind of structure made it a name-only institution. The Emergency Planning Committee was the institution in charge of various wartime mobilization plans and government action plans in the early stage of the war, and, therefore, was not an institution for handling national security. When inter-Korea relations issues emerged during previous governments, ministers related to the matter gathered to exchange opinions. There wasn't a specific organization that dealt with it, and there weren't any records of their meetings. Although they discussed foreign policies, national security, and policies about North Korea, their decisions did not have any legally binding power since the gatherings were arbitrary.

I decided to turn the NSC into the supreme institution where we would make decisions about foreign policies and matters related to national security. I transformed the NSC into a council where the president was the chairman, and of which the prime minister; ministers of unification, foreign affairs, and defense; ANSP director; and NSC general secretary (cum senior secretary for foreign affairs and national security for president) were members. We established a six-member standing committee and an office for this supreme policy organization that made decisions about matters of unification, foreign policy, and national security. The standing committee was composed of the above-mentioned five members and the director of the office for government policy coordination.

We called for a president-chaired NSC meeting whenever we had to make important decisions about inter-Korean relations. The weekly standing committee meeting assisted me in gathering and summarizing opinions in the fields of foreign affairs, national security, and reunification. I trusted and respected the committee decision, accepting most of their recommendations during my five-year presidency term. The Korean people gradually came to trust the NSC's quick but careful ability to handle situations.

The NSC standing committee, led by Senior Secretary for Foreign Affairs and National Security Lim Dong-won, presented six basic themes for the three principles for the inter-Korean relations to be officially adopted at the cabinet meeting on March 19. The six themes were the simultaneous pursuit of national security and cooperation; prioritization of peaceful coexistence, interchange, and cooperation; creation of conditions for change in North Korea through more contact, dialogue, and cooperation; pursuit of mutual benefit for the South and the North; securing international support for the decision made between parties concerned; and the transparent and steady pursuit of inter-Korean policies.

Toward the end of April, we announced the South-North Economic Cooperation Stimulation Measures. According to the principle of separation between politics and economy, we removed restrictions against all businessmen's visits to North Korea and allowed them to take or rent production facilities to the North, both free and for a fee. South Korean businessmen could now freely decide on joint economic enterprises with North Korea.

Around this time, US Secretary of State Madeleine Albright visited Korea to discuss mutual interests ahead of the Korea-US summit scheduled for the following month. Mrs. Albright was a Czechoslovakia-born politician and diplomat, who had become an American citizen when she was young. She came to America with her father, a diplomat who was exiled to the US. On May 1, I welcomed her to the Blue House by saying, "I welcome you not only as the secretary of state of a friendly nation, but also as an admired human rights movement leader and true friend of Koreans. I am grateful for your persistent help during my fight for democracy."

Mrs. Albright showed me my calligraphy piece that read, "Seeking Truth Grounded on Concrete Evidence," and said "I still have this calligraphy you gave me in the summer of 1986." It was the calligraphy I had written for her when she visited me at my house while I was imprisoned there. Back then, she was a professor at Georgetown University.

After serving successfully as US ambassador to the UN, she was now traveling all over the world as one of the key members of President Clinton's cabinet. "I think that if we live justly, sometimes we see a day of success like this," I told her.

"I can't express how happy I am to see you here. I am speechless," she responded.

We talked for an hour and twenty minutes, far exceeding our scheduled thirty minutes. I didn't even realize how much time had passed. She was a constant comrade. When I explained the Sunshine Policy, she said, "I believe that your excellent approach will result in establishing trust between South and North Korea. I fully support the South Korean effort for an inter-Korean dialogue."

There was a local election on June 4. It was the first nationwide election since my inauguration and, therefore, a sort of people's judgment on the coalition government. The result was the coalition ruling parties' overwhelming victory. Out of sixteen governor-level elections, National Congress won six, LDA won four, and the opposition Grand National Party won six. The ruling parties particularly swept the greater Seoul area including Seoul, Gyeonggi-do, and Incheon, which was an encouraging sign that my government's reforms were working.

National Congress's candidate Goh Kun was elected as the mayor of Seoul. I had invited him into our party despite opposition from some party leaders and members. Those in our party who opposed his candidacy were concerned about the fact that he was the prime minister of the previous regime. It was a reasonable concern, but I thought we needed a candidate with administrative experience. I explained my reasoning at the luncheon for the Honorees of the Day of Law. "I believe a true identity comes from doing what people want," I said. "Our identity comes from respecting people's will. It is not essential whether our party has other members who have worked hard and suffered in the past. Our identity as the People's Government is based on the fact that we are a government that solves all problems according to the people's will and that honors the people like heaven."

This day of election victory by the coalition government happened to coincide with my hundredth day as president. After confirming the Korean people's support of me, I went on to my visit as a state guest of the US at the invitation of President Bill Clinton. I was very excited about this visit because America was a very special place for me—it was the country that saved my life twice. I had an interview with the *New York Times* reporter Nicholas Christopher, who was based in Tokyo. He asked me an interesting question. "During your past stay in Washington, it was hard for you to enter the White House and you had a very difficult time," he commented. "Now you are going to make a speech at the US Congress and have a meeting at the White House. Are you personally excited?"

"I feel two things about your question," I said in answer. "First, you have to live long, and second, you have to live justly. I believe that then you'll eventually be recognized."

I received similar questions many times. Observers must have found my return to the US as the president of South Korea interesting. Indeed, my two-and-a-half-year exile in the US during the Chun Doo-hwan regime had been a very difficult and sad time. There were state department officials in charge of Northeast Asia on the right who were on friendly terms with the Chun Doo-hwan regime. On the left, however, was the assistant secretary of state for East Asian and Pacific Affairs and for human rights, who boldly adopted the human rights report about Korea like Amnesty International. I told my friends then that I didn't know if I should be angry at or thankful to America. During an interview on the airplane, I frankly said, "My friends in America found this visit strange and special."

As a president visiting a friendly nation it was my duty to prepare as best as I could. All of my major speeches were prepared in English. Although my English was less than perfect, I thought it better to speak English in order to persuade the American people. My visit was a great opportunity for Korea to get out of our economic plight. Since I learned English on my own, I felt confident about my grammar, but my pronunciation left something to be desired. I heard that I spoke English with my Jeolla region accent. I had a secretary with good English pronunciation record my speech and tried to improve my pronunciation by listening to and repeating after the tape.

More than seventy events, including fifteen speeches, awaited me in America. Although the people around me called the schedule murderous and worried about my health, I happily looked forward to it. I arrived at the John F. Kennedy International Airport in New York City on the afternoon of June 6. US Ambassador to Korea Stephen W. Bosworth flew to New York from Washington, DC, to greet me. About thirty reporters approached my plane when I arrived.

My first event was a visit to UN Secretary General Kofi Annan at the UN Headquarters. When I gave him my book *Kim Dae-jung's Three-stage Approach to Korean Reunification*, he generously responded, "Although you wrote the book, I will execute it." I received the Human Rights of the Year Award from the International Federation for Human Rights at the Waldorf Astoria Hotel, where I was staying. I dedicated it to the Korean people. In my award speech, I said, "This is the result of the Korean people's persistent effort toward democracy and human rights throughout long periods of suffering and pain. I believe that the honor of this award should be returned to the Korean people, who achieved democracy by struggling with me."

The International Federation for Human Rights was the same organization that had protested to the Korean regime about my capital sentence and worked to save me. The organization's Human Rights Award had been given to Dr. Andrei Sakharov of the Soviet Union and the Polish independent trade union, Solidarity. South African president Nelson Mandela received it the next year. In my speech, I announced the legislation of the Human Rights Law and establishment of the National Human Rights Commission in Korea.

The next morning, I visited the New York Stock Exchange. Before my speech, Chairman Richard Grasso made the audience laugh with his opening remark. "When President Kim visited us three years ago, the Dow Jones index was about 4300, but it is now above 9000. I hope that number will double when he visits us three years from now."

In my speech entitled "Challenges and Vision of Korean Economy" I urged American financial leaders to trust Korean potential and to invest in Korea. The New York Stock Exchange was a symbolic place where leaders of various countries, including Chinese president Jiang Zemin and Israeli Prime Minister Benyamin Netanyahu, visited to explain their economic policies. I officially declared the Korean economy's opening to the American financial world with the key phrase: "The companion development of democracy and market economy."

After the speech, I moved to the second floor with high officials of the New York Stock Exchange and President Grasso. At 9:30 a.m., I pressed the bell to signal the opening of the stock market. I walked around the floor and stockbrokers applauded and cheered. I felt like they were cheering for the Korean economy. Reporters gathered in the distance, and I gave them a thumbs up.

I went to Washington, DC, on June 8. I first attended a reception for Korean-Americans at the official residence of the Korean Ambassador to the US. The house was overflowing with people. I was delighted by this opportunity to make a speech in Korean in a foreign country. "I am truly moved," I spoke. "The days when I was busying myself with you in this country for the democratization of Korea feel like just yesterday. And, ladies and gentlemen, our country has now been democratized. I who fought against dictatorship have returned here as the Korean president, chosen by the Korean people's support, and supported by your encouragement.

"We had such a difficult fight then. How embarrassing it was to have to say that we were fighting for the democratization of our country in another country! How dearly we wanted to say that our country was a democratic country like America or England! I know you all felt the same way.

"Now, although our economy is going through a little bit of a rough patch, we have proudly achieved democracy for the first time in fifty years through the people's free will, through secret voting, and by the people. I thank you deeply and say that this was the Korean people's victory as well as the victory of those who are gathered here and who have supported both the Korean democracy movement and me."

I met South Korean professional golfer Miss Pak Se-ri at the reception. She had brought joy to the Korean people by winning the McDonald's LPGA Championship as the youngest champion ever. She said that she was wearing high heels for the first time that night, and shyly smiled when I said, "You worked hard."

Miss Pak Se-ri gave the Korean people an unforgettably moving scene with her victory at the US Open a month later. When her ball fell into a pond, she took off her socks and jumped into the water to retrieve it. Her hard work, symbolized in the contrast between her tanned calves and white feet, moved the Korean people, who were still struggling in the midst of economic hardship. When she returned home after winning the championship, I awarded her the Maengho Medal, the Order of Sports Merit, and called her a "hero." Some people in the media made an issue of the term hero, arguing that it applied only to men. But I retorted, "There is no gender difference in a hero." By the time she was twenty, she had won three LPGA Championships.

June 9 was a very important day, the day of the Korea-US summit. I arrived at the entrance for the heads of state with my wife. We were led through the southwestern gate of the White House to meet the president and Mrs. Clinton while the military band played music. We were also introduced to other high officials, including the vice president and Mrs. Al Gore, Secretary of State Albright, and the Chairman of the Joint Chiefs of Staff and his wife. I stood on the stand with President Clinton as the national anthems of Korea and America played while a twenty-one-gun salute was fired. I reviewed the honor guard with President Clinton before he made his welcoming remarks. "We live in remarkable times," he said. "In the 1980s, some of the greatest heroes of freedom were the political prisoners of repressive regimes: Lech Walesa in Poland, Vaclav Havel in Czechoslovakia, Nelson Mandela in South Africa, and Kim Dae-jung, who faced a death sentence in South Korea after years of unjust and brutal treatment by the government.

"How very different things are now. Lech Walesa was elected Poland's president; Vaclav Havel and Nelson Mandela are the presidents of their countries; and Kim Dae-jung is here today as president, after the first-ever democratic change of power from the governing party to the opposition in the 50-year history of the Republic of Korea ...

"Let me conclude by saying something to men and women all around the world who work to protect human rights: Your work matters. You help transforms nations and ends tyranny. You save lives. Standing with me today is living proof—Kim Dae-jung, a human rights pioneer, a courageous survivor, and America's partner in building a better future for the world."

I spoke next. "The Korean people achieved an historic victory of democracy through a peaceful regime change between the ruling and opposition parties after a persistent 50-year effort for democracy," I began. "The message of hope for freedom and democracy that the American people delivered to us was behind this brilliant victory of the Korean people.

"Now, Koreans begin a new struggle. We began the struggle to cleanse the legacy of dictatorship that had oppressed democracy and a market economy, not only to overcome today's national crisis, but also to join with advanced nations in the twenty-first century through the implementation of both democracy and a market economy. Together with the Korean people, I will definitely achieve victory in this struggle as well."

I had a one-on-one meeting with President Clinton in the Oval Office for about sixty-five minutes, twenty-five minutes more than scheduled. I was accompanied by a few Korean officials, including Minister of Foreign Affairs and Trade Park Chung-soo, Senior Secretary of Foreign Affairs and National Security Lim Dong-won, and Korean Ambassador to the US Lee Hong-koo. From the American side, Vice President Gore, Secretary of State Albright, and National Security Advisor Samuel Berger accompanied President Clinton. As expected, President Clinton asked me to explain my North Korean policies. I spent about thirty minutes explaining the Sunshine Policy and its background.

"I actually learned from the United States' success when it came to developing the Sunshine Policy," I told him. "The extreme Cold War system against the Soviet Union after World War II meant only an arms race, which heightened the sense of crisis and of mutual destruction. As a result, America changed its policy to focus on détente and pursued economic cooperation and interchange. Fifteen years after this change, the Soviet Bloc that had controlled half of the world simply collapsed. It collapsed without a single outside gunshot or internal rebellion. This was an unprecedented event in human history.

"America at first defined China as a war criminal because of its participation in the Korean War. Condemning China as evil and consistently
applying the blockade policy, however, resulted in Chinese development
of nuclear weapons and extreme resistance. After this, President Nixon
encouraged China to participate in the United Nations and visited China
to persuade Mao Zedong to open the country in exchange for American
help. As China accepted this reconciliation gesture and opened up the
country, the Chinese middle class developed and civilians led the
economy.

"Also, look at Vietnam. America considered Vietnam an enemy and
waged war against it, but lost. Afterward, when the two countries normalized their relationship and America offered economic aid, Vietnam became
pro-American. Although the Vietnam War was a war to defend the southern part of the country, America has now penetrated the northern part as
well. The American reconciliation policy succeeded.

"On the contrary, the United States has sanctioned and pressured Cuba
for forty years, but failed in getting it to surrender. If America normalized
its relationship and interchange with Cuba, Cuba might have already
opened up. Communism becomes stronger if its door is closed, and it collapses if its door is open. We learned this lesson through the examples of
the Soviet Union, China, and Vietnam. The same is true of North Korea.
When dealing with communism, we have to apply some military pressure
so that they will not invade while we induce economic opening. Our
Sunshine Policy has already been tested through American foreign
policies."

Everyone listened to me very carefully. President Clinton said,
"Considering President Kim's importance and experience, please lead the
Korean Peninsula matter from now on. President Kim will take the wheel
and drive, and I will assist you from the passenger seat."

I was very happy to hear this response because it indicated we would
take charge of the inter-Korean policy for the first time since the division
of the country. We finally opened the new age of independent diplomacy
that would take Korean-American relations to a higher level of partnership
for the twenty-first century. This agreement that our two countries would
work closely together to improve the relationship with North Korea
through the Sunshine Policy and American policy of tolerance was included
in the joint summit statement.

Apart from this agreement, President Clinton also asked me to actively
persuade Congress. He told me that there were many congressmen who

praised me and who mistrusted North Korea, but that no congressman had my kind of vision about policy as it pertained to North Korea.

President Clinton then unexpectedly asked me about an issue unrelated to Korea–US relations. "I'd like to seek your advice regarding a matter," he said. "Human rights activists in America do not want me to visit China. According to today's *New York Times*, the Chinese government has oppressed its people even more to prevent them from demonstrating during my visit. Some argue that I should talk about human rights at the welcome event in Tiananmen Square, while others argue that I should not even visit the country."

It was a question that showed President Clinton's personal view of me. I, of course, did not have an answer prepared for this question, but I told him my honest opinion. "In China, pride is very important. For pride, they will sacrifice anything. I hope you go to China, but say the things you have to say. It will be helpful in the pursuit of strategic cooperation between the two countries. While pursuing a strategic relationship, you can cooperate and criticize at the same time. If you respect their pride while demanding what's necessary, you can make human rights achievements. Other Asian countries will get the impression that the US sticks to its principles even while pursuing its interests."

President Clinton later visited China and made a speech at Tiananmen Square. I don't know how much his decision was influenced by my advice, but he certainly listened to what I said very carefully.

We next had an extended summit meeting and agreed that the US would send an investment team to Korea and that the two countries would pursue a bilateral investment treaty soon. "The United States will continue our strong support for Korea's economic reform efforts," President Clinton said. "In this context, I reaffirm our commitment to provide bilateral finance under appropriate conditions if needed."

I attended a state reception held by President Clinton that evening. The East Room in the White House felt cozy. Perhaps because there were many people that I had invited and knew well, I felt as if I had been there for a long time. President Clinton wished for the revival of the Korean economy and my success in his welcoming remarks, quoting the Korean saying I had written in my *Prison Writings* and that means: "Every cloud has a silver lining."

Soon, Korean-American operatic lyric soprano Ms. Hong Hei-Kyung appeared. Before she began singing she said, "My mother has a passionate crush on President Kim, so we call President Kim her boyfriend." People laughed out loud, and then Ms. Hong sang "Oh Let the Sun of God Enfold You" in honor of my life and "How I Miss Mt. Kumgang," a wish for reunification. Before the latter song, she said, "Mt. Kumgang is a beautiful mountain in North Korea. South Koreans have been unable to visit it and missing it for almost fifty years. We sing this song like a second anthem with all of our heart, wishing for reunification." Indeed, she sang it with all of her heart. We could all feel the passionate yearning in her voice. After her performance, President Clinton, clearly moved, said, "We're all Koreans in this moment."

Among the guests there that night was world-renowned Korean-American video artist Mr. Paik Nam-june. He appeared in a wheelchair while President Clinton and First Lady Hilary Clinton and my wife and I were standing at the entrance welcoming guests. Mr. Paik didn't look very healthy. When he got out of his wheelchair to approach President Clinton, his pants suddenly dropped. He wasn't wearing anything under them. Surprised, officers ran to him and took care of the situation. President Clinton and I just laughed it off, considering it a harmless artistic performance by a genius. As his life was itself surreal art, this might have been an unconventional performance he had planned. Above all, I was worried about his health.

On the morning of June 10, I gave a speech at the joint congressional session. As the ruling party was the minority in the US Congress, President Clinton asked me to persuade Congress through my speech. I worked hard on the speech and was able to finish it after repeated revisions just the night before. When I entered the main hall, I received a standing ovation from all members of the Congress. I spoke: "To lead North Korea toward reconciliation, the Republic of Korea and the United States should promote the Sunshine Policy, which offers inducements against the backdrop of strong security measures. And we should extend to North Korea both goodwill and sincerity so that suspicion dissolves and openness emerges.

"Above all, we need a flexible policy. To get a passerby to take off his coat, so the fable goes, sunshine is more effective than a strong wind.

"We are going to promote cooperation in a wide range of areas, under the principle of separation of politics and economics. We want America's support in this effort. Both our nations need to be more confident, coordinated, and composed in our relations with North Korea."

The Congress members listened attentively to my speech. It seemed that they were particularly impressed by the fact that a South Korean president who had achieved a peaceful regime change had had a special relationship with the US.

It was a hectic visit. I could not accept all of the interview requests I received. For a long time, I felt bad about the fact that former President Jimmy Carter wanted to meet with me, but I couldn't find the time. I met Korean journalists at the official residence of the Korean ambassador to the US. During this meeting with the media a journalist asked a mischievous question: "I heard that you read *I ching*. President Clinton is a good politician, but he is plagued by scandals, too. You met President Clinton on this trip. Please tell us what you think of his fortune in terms of phrenology."

"I looked at his face, but I don't think he looked like he was ruined because of the scandals," I responded. "Because his face has an innocent, childlike look, bad luck would run away from it even if it came." Everybody laughed in response.

I met president of IMF Michel Camdessus and president of the World Bank James Wolfensohn at the guesthouse where I stayed. I thanked them for their advice about the financial crisis. President Wolfensohn expressed concern about mass unemployment and told me to take care of the Korean welfare system.

After Washington, I flew to San Francisco. The city declared June 11, the day of my visit, Kim Dae-jung Day. A Korean-American reception was held at the San Francisco Asian Art Museum. Mayor Willie Brown attended and officially declared it Kim Dae-jung Day. As he gave me a good luck key, he said, "This key is the symbol of unity and gratitude toward you from the citizens of San Francisco. This key is actually very heavy. It fits the gate of San Francisco, so you can always come here. Now San Francisco is your home."

When I stood on the podium, Korean-Americans cheered and applauded. In retrospect, San Francisco was the place that had supported and encouraged me more than any city during my exile.

I next visited Stanford University and toured the Silicon Valley. The Silicon Valley drew talent from prestigious universities nearby, including Stanford, Berkeley, and Santa Clara. Regardless of race, age, and origin, talent gathered there and concentrated on research without constraint. Free souls were creating the world of the Internet. This outpost of the hi-tech industry was responsible for the future of the global village. It was moving to witness this scene where the brains of the world gathered to open up a new chapter of future industry. To experience the real scene of hi-tech industry, I visited Hewlett Packard and Intel.

While interviewing major industry leaders in Silicon Valley, I appealed for the venture industry's entrance into Korea. "Our goal is to become the country where people use computers best. Please invest in Korea's possibility," I implored them.

Los Angeles also declared the day I visited it, June 12, to be Kim Dae-jung Day. On behalf of the Los Angeles City Council, Senator Holt delivered a memorial tablet to me. I also received an honorary citizenship certificate. Famous Los Angeles Dodger pitcher, Park Chan Ho, attended the Korean-American reception at the Omni Hotel. He gave me a Dodger's jacket with "DJ Kim" inscribed on it. A star of American professional baseball, he looked reliable and brave. He visited me often after I finished my term. Once he came with his fiancée, and I congratulated them and asked them not to forget their country.

I also visited with former First Lady Nancy Davis Reagan. I asked her about her ailing husband's health, and we reminisced about President Reagan's effort to save me when I was sentenced to death in 1980.

During my visit to the US, I received an unforgettable welcome. The American media called me a "returned hero." Major newspapers like the *New York Times* and the *Washington Post* and major broadcasting stations like CBS, NBC, ABC, and CNN ran in-depth coverage about my life of suffering and reversal. The media continued to shadow me throughout the duration of my visit.

Commenting on my sales diplomacy, a newspaper article read: "It was a new form of economic diplomacy where the government raised the credit rating of the country while civilians pursued material gains below the water." It estimated the overall gain of the Korean economy to be $16.797 billion. This was the equivalent of half of the Korean foreign currency reserve at the time, which was $35 billion. Newspaper headlines termed it as "Injection of 'Gas' to the Reform Train," "Acquisition of 'Seed Money' for Economic Revival," and "Heavy 'Return Baggage' is Fund for Reform."

CHAPTER 8

June 1998–December 1999

A Herd of Cows Across Panmunjeom
(June 1998–September 1998)

Two days after my return from America, a herd of cows crossed Panmunjeom and went north. Hyundai president Chung Ju-yung, accompanied by his brothers and sons, drove 500 cows across the truce line to his hometown in North Korea. On his way north, Mr. Chung said to the Korean people, "I am happy to visit my hometown via Panmunjeom for the first time since my reckless rush to Seoul as a young man. Born as the son of a poor farmer in Tongcheon, Gangwon-do, I sold my father's cow for won 70 and left home at eighteen years old. Now that single cow has become one thousand cows. I am visiting my hometown, which I have been seeing in my dreams, in order to repay my debt."

Mr. Chung was a man of incredible audacity and a drive that was as enormous as his audacity. At age eighty-three, he was still holding on to his imagination and his dreams. I wished him the best on his return to his hometown as a world-famous businessman. Mr. Chung looked like a cowboy in a children's folktale as he crossed Panmunjeom on trucks loaded with 50,000 tons of corn and 500 cows.

An art critic said that Mr. Chung's visit to North Korea was a piece of performance art that he produced, directed, and starred in. The world was moved as Mr. Chung and his cows crossed over Panmunjeom, the symbol of Korean division. Major American stations, including CNN, reported it live as a headline news item.

© The Author(s) 2019
Kim Dae-jung, *Conscience in Action*,
https://doi.org/10.1007/978-981-10-7623-7_8

Koreans who had come south from the northern region went to Imjingak near the border and shed tears as they watched Mr. Chung and his cows cross the border so easily. Their words filtered through the air: "I'd like to hide in a corner of that truck and visit my hometown." "Cows, please plow the field for reunification." "Cows, please carry my heart with you."

Their tears stirred my heart. We had a cabinet meeting that morning and Minister of Reunification Kang In-duk reported, "The cows crossed left here at 9:00 a.m. I believe that Mr. Chung Ju-yung and his entourage are all now in North Korea, in the conference room of the Neutral Nations Supervisory Commission in Panmunjeom. Out of 1001 total cows, 500 were taken to North Korea this time. Originally, it was supposed to be one thousand. However, Mr. Chung asked for 1001 because a number that ends in zero symbolizes the end, whereas a number that ends in a one symbolizes the beginning. There are 287 adult cows and 213 calves, worth a total of 870 million won. These cows were donated to Tongcheon-gun, Mr. Chung's hometown, as well as South Hamgyong Province, Ryanggang Province, and Chagang Province."

I was very happy to hear Minister Kang say that Mr. Chung was planning to discuss a Mt. Kumgang tour and the establishment of an automobile factory during this trip. This represented the first product of the principle of separation between politics and economy. It also seemed as if North Korea had taken off their gloves as a result of our Sunshine Policy. Cabinet members' face brightened when I said, "I heard that 150 of the five hundred cows are pregnant, so it's more like we're sending 650 cows."

Mr. Chung returned with a big bundle on June 23. He had drawn up a contract with North Korea for the development of tourism in Mt. Kumgang. His remarks at a press conference excited the Korean people. "As soon as we get approval from the government, more than a thousand tourists will be able to tour Mt. Kumgang on cruise ships."

Known to Koreans as the most beautiful mountain, Mt. Kumgang remained a mystery that had existed only in songs, art, and literature for the past half-century. I myself had never been to Mt. Kumgang. What did its 12,000 peaks and all of the legends that existed within the mountain look like? I was excited too. It was a small reunification, but I was deeply moved.

Despite this warm breeze, the Sunshine Policy encountered trouble. The day before Mr. Chung's return, a North Korean submarine was found in the sea near Sokcho. The combat submarine was adrift after being caught in the net of a fishing boat. This incident was a big test of the Sunshine Policy—South Koreans were not happy that North Korea returned our gift of cows with a combat submarine.

However, North Korea responded to this incident unusually quickly. Before twenty-four hours had passed, the Pyongyang Broadcasting Station reported that communication with the small submarine was abruptly cut off during a training. They said that it appeared to be wrecked from currents and storms, and that the authorities were searching for it. The content of the report was carefully presented. Clearly, North Korea did not want the incident to be overblown.

I declared that I would maintain the Sunshine Policy despite the submarine incident. I called the National Security Council (NSC) and presided over the meeting. The NSC issued a statement saying that we would not allow provocation, and that we would maintain the basic principle of the Sunshine Policy. "Considering the current situation, the government will continue to maintain a two-pronged strategy of acquiring firm security and pursuing interchange and cooperation. We reaffirm that strong security will enable reconciliation and cooperation, and that the improvement in inter-Korean relations will reduce national security threats."

The debate about the submarine incident tediously continued on. The opposition party and some media outlets attacked the government every day. I believed that we shouldn't be disturbed by every single movement North Korea made. I reminded people that the North Koreans had provoked us before we had adopted the Sunshine Policy too.

The Sunshine Policy was not an appeasement policy. In fact, it could not be pursued without power, confidence, and firmness. The North Korean leaders criticized our Sunshine Policy. It was not a policy that flattered them, as it was intended to take off their coat like in an Aesop's fable.

During the Asia-Europe Meeting (ASEM) in England, Asian and European countries had all actively expressed support for the Sunshine Policy. Powerful neighboring countries supported it too. In particular, President Clinton openly supported it. In this sense, the policy was internationally tested. I felt resolute and confident about our security, which is why I declared that we would maintain the Sunshine Policy. We did not have to be disturbed because of North Korea's attitude.

Even after the submarine incident, 86.6 percent of South Koreans supported the Sunshine Policy. I was grateful for our people's resoluteness. Around this time, military talks between UN Command and North Korea took place in Panmunjeom after a seven-year gap. North Korea accepted the submarine incident as an agenda item, which was unusually flexible of them. I could see hope despite the disputes that were being waged about the Sunshine Policy.

On July 21, there was a special National Assembly election. The ruling National Congress won two seats—acting president Cho Se-hyung for the Gwangmyeong-eul district in Gyeonggi-do and vice president of the party Roh Moo-hyun for the Jongno district in Seoul. Although opinion polls predicted our party would win by a landslide, we won only two out of seven seats. The margin was extremely slim in the Gwangmyeong-eul and Paldal districts in Suwon. Liberal Democratic Alliance (LDA) won one seat and the Grand National Party won four.

Although I emphasized clean elections, illegal and abusive campaign activities still ran rampant. I was worried that our political and election reform efforts would prove futile. This situation resulted in a heap of legal actions and suits.

The two winners from the ruling party were talents that our government and I needed. Before Mr. Cho Se-hyung was a National Assembly member, he had been a competent president of the ruling party. He was bright and rational. With him as a member of the National Assembly, the National Congress could work more organically.

I thought very highly of Mr. Roh Moo-hyun's beliefs and persistence. He rejected the illicit merger among the three parties led by Mr. Kim Young-sam. He had continued to fail in elections in Busan—a stronghold for Mr. Kim Young-sam's party—where he ran both for the National Assembly and for mayor. The results were predictable, but he did not avoid the fight. After the People's Government launched, he said to me, "I will work in whatever position you need, whether it's a clerk or a department chief." He was that kind of person. His image and beliefs as a reformer were a great asset to Korean politics.

On July 25, I left for Cheongnamdae for a week's vacation. I had run non-stop since becoming president, so I decided to do nothing but rest while I was there. The passage into Cheongnamdae was beautiful, and the graceful *bansong* pine tree on the way to the main building was spectacular.

While I was there, I took walks and did some fishing, too. It had been a long time, probably more than twenty years, since I last went fishing, which I believe was with some friends, including Assemblyman Ye Choon-ho. I did some leisurely reading as well, including *Segye gyeongje jeonmang* (World Economic Forecast), *Jisik chabonjueui hyeongmyeong* (Intellectual Capitalism Revolution), and *Mensius.*

My wife went to the pool every day. Since breaking her hip joint, she had begun swimming upon her doctor's instruction. She really liked swimming and stayed in the pool for a long time once she got there. It was probably her first time getting in an outdoor pool since we had been married. In fact, it might have been the first time she was able to enjoy such leisurely time since our marriage. I was so very happy to see her like that.

It was really quiet around Cheongnamdae, but I could not help occasionally taking care of urgent matters. I called senior secretaries to Cheongnamdae or talked with them over the phone. The president could never be an ordinary person. I could not rest comfortably in the bosom of nature.

I invited previous presidents and first ladies to the Blue House for a dinner on July 31. All of the living former presidents—Choi Kyu-ha, Chun Doo-hwan, Roh Tae-woo, and Kim Young-sam—and first ladies attended. This was the first time in modern Korean history such an event had happened. I wanted to deliver a message of unity to the Korean people, and it also gave me the opportunity to learn how previous presidents had overcome difficult times.

"Please be persistent and overcome this crisis," President Choi Kyu-ha urged me.

"I was amazed to see your leadership in overcoming economic crisis," President Chun Doo-hwan said.

"I am relieved to hear what you say," President Roh Tae-woo told me.

"Although people praise only Mt. Kumgang these days, the scenery at Haegeumgang near Geojedo Island is beautiful, too," President Kim Young-sam remarked.

Their comments were wide-ranging and their later attitudes would come to reflect what they said that day.

A spy scandal between Moscow and Seoul erupted when a South Korean diplomat was accused of illegal espionage activities and ordered to leave Russia within three days. A councilor, who also worked for our intelligence officer at the South Korean Embassy in Moscow, was arrested on the night of July 3, reportedly because he met with a Russian Foreign

Ministry official who was accused of "regularly passing confidential information to the South Korean intelligence services." This was a very rude, unilateral action that ignored international custom seeing as how our councilor had diplomatic immunity. In response, our Ministry of Foreign Affairs and Trade expelled a Russian diplomat. Thus began the diplomatic conflict and crisis.

While both governments were trying to stop the situation from getting worse by facilitating a meeting between the foreign ministers of Korea and Russia, suspicion was raised about our foreign minister. It was alleged that he agreed to allow the Russian councilor to reenter South Korea through a backdoor deal. Allowing an expelled councilor's reentrance was a disgrace. Although I ordered a quick response to the situation, it was unfortunate that our foreign minister was being viewed with such suspicion. Not only this, but the Ministry of Foreign Affairs and Trade was arguing with the National Intelligence Service (NIS). In the middle of all this, the Ministry of Foreign Affairs and Trade made conflicting statements about the readmittance of a Russian diplomat. In the end, Foreign Minister Park resigned on August 4, and I decided to respect his decision, despite my appreciation of his hard work as a messenger and sales diplomat. I appointed Mr. Hong Soon-young, who had worked as professional diplomat for a long time, to his post.

That August, the entire country drowned. Heavy rain fell around Mt. Jirisan beginning on the night of July 31. Ninety-five people, including many who were enjoying vacations, went missing or died. This was a completely unexpected natural disaster because the Korea Meteorological Administration declared the rainy season to be over on July 28. For the next twenty days, heavy rain flooded our country.

I could not sleep that night. Early the next morning, I called relevant ministers, heads of local administrative districts, and the head of the Korea Meteorological Administration. I was frustrated that there was nothing more I could do. The weather forecast proved wrong every day, but we couldn't lay the blame on the meteorologists—it seemed that these kinds of microbursts were hard to predict.

In fact, the entire earth was suffering from flooding that summer. The Chinese river Yangtze was on the verge of overflowing, and the flood damage was enormous in Thailand and Bangladesh. It was truly mysterious—even countries like Iran and Yemen were suffering from massive damages from landslides due to heavy rain.

I visited cruel flood scenes and refugee camps. Unlike scenes of a fire, where there are at least ashes remaining, nothing was left in the wake of the flood. I tried to encourage refugees and asked officers to make their best disaster relief and reconstruction efforts. "It is heaven that brings us disaster, but it is human beings that can heal the damage," I said. The rain continued to pour, even as I was still seeing the images of weeping and suffering disaster victims. By the time the rain stopped the number of causalities, including the dead and missing, was 322; the damage amounted to 1300 billion won.

That summer's microburst was truly unpredictable. I wondered if nature was beginning to wreak its revenge on human beings. What was happening to the earth? Have we been too rude to nature, forgetting that we are, in fact, helpless in front of it? Koreans lined up to donate for the flood victims, and I couldn't help thinking that it hadn't been that long since we had lined up to collect gold. My heart felt heavy.

We celebrated the fiftieth anniversary of our independence on August 15. In a statement delivered on that Independence Day, I advocated for the second foundation of our country. "All sectors of our society, including the economy, are deficient, and our international competitive ability is weak. The restructuring of our society for the enhancement of our national productivity and competitiveness is inevitable."

In order to fulfill this goal, I also presented six tasks for the administration: the execution of participative democracy; the structural reform for the liberation of the economy from government-directed economy; the establishment of the value of universalist globalism; the establishment of a country of creative knowledge; the creation of a new employer-labor relation culture; and the opening of the cooperative era between South and North Korea.

In particular, I proposed to North Korea that we found a standing inter-Korean dialogue institution at the minister and deputy minister level. I also said that I was willing to send a special envoy to Pyongyang to discuss these matters if North Korea agreed.

I appealed to the Korean people to actively participate in these efforts. "The second nation-building will rescue our country from crisis and explore its fate anew. It is the people's movement and all-out reform of our government that will complete democracy and the market economy, based on industrialization and democratization. The People's Government honors freedom, justice, and efficiency as its practical principles. The second nation-building is possible not through unilateral government leadership, but also by the gathering of people's real-life wisdom. That's the only way to succeed."

Sadly, this second nation-building movement failed. I expected that civil society would actively support it, and that people would enthusiastically participate in it. Unfortunately, the support and participation were not as enthusiastic as I had hoped. In the end, it became a government-led movement; I must have failed in making the Korean people understand what we were trying to accomplish.

Acting Prime Minister Kim Jong-pil finally lost the "acting" prefix from his title on August 17; that is the afternoon the motion to appoint him passed. This served as great encouragement for Prime Minister Kim. When I awarded him the appointment certificate the following morning, he broke into a bright smile and said, "Since you gave me certificates twice, it is like you appointed me twice."

On August 25, I visited Mokpo for the first time since my inauguration. For me, it was really *geumuihwanhyang*, or "returning to one's old home in glory." After attending an opening ceremony for the highway between Mokpo and Muan, my car entered downtown and was greeted by tens of thousands of citizens lining the streets. My passage was transformed into an unexpected car-parade event. I decided to stay the night in Mokpo. I could see the sea from where I stayed, and memories of my days in Mokpo and Hauido passed through my mind. My family and relatives visited me; it was a happy and warm night there in the arms of Mt. Yudal.

The next day, I paid my respects at the May 18 graveyard in Gwangju. In the guestbook, I simply wrote: "President Kim Dae-jung on August 26, 1998." I had attended the completion ceremony for the graveyard consecration work the previous year as the president of the opposition party. Then, I had written: "Eternal Victory." I hoped that I could dedicate my successful presidency to the spirits of the May 18 fighters by the time I finished my term.

I visited the Jeollanam-do province administration building to receive administrative reports. While sitting in that building that the citizen fighters risked their lives to defend, I thought about the democracy that they wanted to protect. "This was a people's struggle that we should be proud of," I said. "Once again, I would like to express my admiration and respect for the Gwangju citizens who waged a great fight for democracy here. From the bottom of my heart, I grieve and pray for the happiness of those martyrs for democracy now in the other world. I express my sincerest condolences to their families. A long time has passed since the Gwangju Uprising. Having finally fulfilled the task that followed in the spirit of Gwangju, a peaceful regime change and the birth of a democratic government are ours. I will always perform my work as president in honor of the Gwangju spirit. I will try my best not to waste the sacrifice of the deceased, and to be worthy of the struggle of the Gwangju citizens who rose up to demand my release."

I invited officials of the Board of Audit and Inspection, led by Chairman Han Sung-hon, to Seoul. They were trying to be reborn as an organization that honored its original function as the watchman of the government. When I had visited the Board of Audit and Inspection building four months previously, the media focused on the fact that my visit was the first by a president in a quarter century. They also highlighted my special relationship with Chairman Han.

Having defended numerous democracy fighters, Chairman Han was one of the most representative human rights lawyers in Korea. He was a man of integrity, intellect, and humor. He was also a great writer. He left his post after a year due to the age limit, which was sixty-five. He changed this limit to seventy during his term, but did not apply it to himself. I was truly sorry to let him go.

I participated in an advertisement for Korean tourism at the invitation of Minister of Culture and Tourism Shin Nak-Kyun. After filming at the Gimpo Airport and Nokjiwon in the Blue House, I invited the celebrities, artists, and sportsmen who participated in the production with me to a luncheon on August 29.

That same day, New People's Party president Lee Man-sup and I announced the merger of National Congress and the New People's Party (Kungminsindang). National Congress absorbed the New People's Party and seven assemblymen, including Rhee In-je, joined our party. The Grand National Party held a national convention on August 31 and elected Mr. Lee Hoi-chang president. Eight months after his defeat in the presidential election, Mr. Lee returned to the front line of politics. He proposed the interparty summit in his acceptance speech.

That day, North Korea test-fired a two-stage ballistic missile named Taepodong, part of which flew over Japan, landing in the Pacific Ocean. The US and Japan were extremely alarmed. The South Korean government had caught on to signs of this test fire, which was being prepared at the Taepodong Missile Test Site in North Hamgyong Province, in early August. Because we received a report about the installation of the missile in mid-August, we were observing it attentively.

North Korea officially confirmed this test fire, which they called Kwangmyongsong-1, on September 4, and declared it to be a success. The

North Korean media reported that the satellite carried transmitters that broadcast the "Song of General Kim Il-sung," the "Song of General Kim Jong-il," and "Juche Korea" in Morse code. Although this experiment turned out to be failure, North Korea alarmed the entire world with its potential to develop ballistic missiles that could be aimed not only at Japan, but also at Hawaii.

Our government very carefully examined North Korea's intentions. Given that the test fire was announced the day before the Supreme People's Assembly amended the DPRK Constitution to usher in the Kim Jong-il era, it was clear that this was meant to celebrate the new era with the image of *gangseongdaeguk* (national strength and prosperity).

Due to this event, the Sunshine Policy fell into crisis again. Fear about a North Korean missile attack spread quickly in Japan. Japan stopped its ongoing negotiation for amity with North Korea, as well as its food aid. Japan brought the issue to the UN Security Council and indefinitely postponed signing the bill for its $1 billion support of the North Korean light water reactor according to the Agreed Framework in Geneva.

The US also responded swiftly. Republican hardliners raised their voices and cut the budget to fund the purchase of 150,000 tons of heavy fuel oil for North Korea. They also urged the American government to stop its dialogue with North Korea.

I discussed this situation with former US Secretary of State Henry Kissinger, who was visiting Korea at the time. He had played an important role in establishing an amicable relationship between China and the US, as well as fostering a détente between the Soviet Union and the US. Mr. Kissinger told me that Chinese leadership was also concerned about this event and urged me to respond carefully.

On September 5, the day after the North Korean authorities officially acknowledged the test fire of the ballistic missile, the Supreme People's Assembly was held in North Korea. In this assembly, they wrote the president's post out of their Constitution and reelected Kim Jong-il as chairman of the National Defense Commission, the highest post of the state. Four years after the death of Kim Il-sung in 1994, North Korea announced that the Kim Jong-il era had finally arrived.

Despite the world's prediction to the contrary, I had already predicted that Kim Jong-il would not succeed in the post of president. I could see that heading the administration while the North Korean people starved could be burdensome to Kim Jong-il. He chose instead to take real power while diffusing responsibility. At any rate, the amendment of the constitution represented a serious change in North Korea, and I ordered our senior secretary of foreign affairs and national security to pay close attention to North Korea.

A Miracle Does Not Happen Miraculously (September 1998–October 1998)

President of Germany Roman Herzog visited Korea on September 15 as the first state guest since my inauguration. He quoted the article I had published in *Foreign Affairs* and said that the Korean government was taking the correct road. In his words:

> The Korean government chose to open Korea to the world to overcome crisis. I firmly believe that this was the correct choice. President Kim emphasized that democracy and a market economy are two sides of the same coin.
>
> In his 1994 article in *Foreign Affairs*, President Kim convincingly argued that the road to democracy was prepared in Asia as it had been in Europe, and that Asians have always believed in democracy as firmly as Europeans have. In particular, he showed that there was a philosophical movement with strong democratic orientation in Korea during the nineteenth century. I think that everyone should read this article. I think it particularly important now, since some people still think that democracy is not suitable for Asians or that democracy will not work well in Asia.
>
> Only democracy and a market economy can naturally fulfill all people's yearning for a creative life and economic welfare.

He also enthusiastically supported the Sunshine Policy. "I hope that the sunshine sent from the South will reach the head and heart of the policy decision-makers in the North. And I believe that this policy is the only reasonable policy in the long run," President Herzog advocated.

October 1 marked the first Armed Forces Day since my inauguration. It was also the fiftieth anniversary of the establishment of the Korean armed forces. I was looking forward to the day, but the fall typhoon that had hit the southern region hard had us all worried about the weather.

The southern region was flooded again. I was concerned that if it rained the troops who had prepared for the event all summer long would be discouraged. Fortunately, the typhoon did not head north. It was sunny and clear when the day of the celebration arrived. We held a celebration event at the Seoul airport. The media reported that as the commander-in-chief

I made eighty-nine hand salutes during my march-past and inspection of the troops. The media must have made a big deal out of all the details of this event because certain political soldiers and politicians had distorted my relationship with the military in the past and spread rumors that the military would veto me under any circumstance. That day, it was clear that the rumors were groundless. During my speech, I promised that I would not allow war in Korea, and I urged North Korea to cooperate with us. "I hope that the new leadership in North Korea will work together with us for the new age of reconciliation and cooperation," I spoke.

On October 7, I went to Japan for a state visit. I wanted it to be an opportunity for the two countries to settle the past and to begin again as true partners. We should not drag the rancor and wounds of the twentieth century into the twenty-first century. I had to recover the relationship that had taken a hit during the Kim Young-sam government. President Kim Young-sam had not hesitated to use extreme expressions like, "I'll teach them their manners." This hardline tactic naturally brought a hardline response from Japan. The diplomatic channel between the two countries had broken down and all trust disappeared, which created a very unhappy and unfortunate situation for both countries. Naturally, Japan was very interested in my visit and the fact that a person who had been kidnapped and almost died in Japan was returning as president. Leading up to my visit, the Japanese media heavily reported on my life and career.

On my first night in Tokyo, I visited Emperor Akihito and his empress, attending a dinner he had set up at the Homeiden Hall. While there, Crown Princess Masako said that she had heard my speech at Harvard University. She and I must have studied there at the same time in 1983. I told the emperor, "Your Majesty, the crown prince and princess are a beautiful couple."

I addressed him as "your majesty" according to his status as emperor. Before my visit, there had been disputes in Korea about the title I should use to address him. Some people argued that I should call him "Japanese king" rather than "emperor." I, of course, understood why some Koreans felt that way, but I felt that for diplomatic reasons we should use the same title Japanese people used out of respect for their people.

The emperor mentioned the history between Korea and Japan during his speech at dinner and apologized for his country's colonial rule of Korea. "Your culture had influenced greatly Japan. We can find traces of mutual interchange in *Nihon Shoki*, compiled during the eighth century. The book includes records indicating classics scholar Dr. Wang In came to

Japan during the period of King Ahwa in Baekje and of Emperor Ojin in Japan and taught Crown Prince Uji no Wakiiratsuko. As a result, the crown prince mastered the classics.

"Later, scholars of five classics, medicine, and astrology took turns visiting Japan from Baekje, and Buddhism also came through the same route. Many people from your country contributed greatly to the improvement of our culture.

"While there was this history of close interchange, there was also a time when our country brought great pain to you in the Korean Peninsula. Great sadness about this time always remains in my memory."

During our conversation after dinner, Emperor Akihito quoted an old Chinese phrase, saying that Korea and Japan were as close as across a stream. He was a modest man with great knowledge about history. Surprisingly, he also said, "I heard that the mother of Emperor Kanmu in Tokyo was an immigrant from Baekje."

Empress Michiko commented to me, "Despite many years of suffering, you seem to have a very moderate philosophy, strong beliefs, and a hopeful attitude."

"You're too kind," I responded. "Rather than being brave, I am easily scared. Funny to say, but I am scared of goblins in the dark. However, I get courage from two things. One of them is my Christian belief. A true disciple fights social injustice and corruption like Jesus, who died on the cross after fighting oppressors. The second is my belief in history. When you look at history, those who committed evil might not be punished for it during their times, but they are sure to be punished later. On the other hand, those who lived justly and were not rewarded during their times are sure to be justly appreciated later. In Japanese history, for example, there was Sakamoto Ryoma. As you know well, he died without worldly success. But as someone who contributed most greatly to the Meiji Restoration, he is now respected more than anyone who became an aristocrat or prime minister. We can learn from lessons like this in Japanese history that those who live justly never fail."

The conversation was pleasant. We exchanged opinions about both countries' histories. The empress had read my wife's book and remembered it very well. Princess Kuroda Sayako also knew that I like television programs about animals.

Out of respect for the Japanese people who loved their emperor, I did not mention our shared sad history at all during the dinner. The Japanese press reported that my attitude was exceptional. The *Asahi Shimbun* commented: "President Kim has shown a strong will to settle the past since before his visit, but he showed his sincere desire to build a friendship between the two countries by being considerate of the symbolic status of the emperor."

The next day, I had a summit with Prime Minister Obuchi Keizo. It was here that I mentioned our history and the fundamental stumbling block in the relationship between our two countries. "Historically, after a Japanese prime minister apologizes for the past, other cabinet members or ruling party leaders abruptly made a contradictory remark. From the Korean point of view, it can thus be interpreted that the prime minister has apologized for the sake of appearance, while the Japanese people did not actually share the sentiment. I understand that there might be various opinions among Japanese people, as they are due through freedom of speech. However, at least members of the cabinet and ruling party should refrain from making such remarks." Prime Minister Obuchi agreed that we should break this vicious cycle of misunderstanding.

After the summit, we issued the Japan-Republic of Korea Joint Declaration under the title "A New Japan-Republic of Korea Partnership Toward the Twenty-first Century." It included many principles and concrete action plans. The most important among them was the Japanese prime minister's apology for the colonial past. "Looking back on the relations between Japan and the Republic of Korea during this century, Prime Minister Obuchi regarded in a spirit of humility the fact of history that Japan caused, during a certain period in the past, tremendous damage and suffering to the people of the Republic of Korea through its colonial rule, and expressed his deep remorse and heartfelt apology for this fact."

This was a significant event because it was the first time the Japanese government explicitly expressed "deep remorse and heartfelt apology" to Koreans. Before this apology, Prime Minister Murayama Tomiichi of the Socialist Party also had expressed remorse and apology in 1995, but it was to many countries in Asia, rather than to Korea specifically.

This statement also importantly included the decision to open Korea to Japanese culture. Most people believed that this was premature and were concerned that Korea might become a cultural colony of Japan. I did not agree because I trusted the power of both the Korean people and its culture.

Korea has always been a cultural nation. Although we had lived under the strong influence of the Chinese culture until the nineteenth century, we firmly stood our ground. Chinese culture had been assimilated in neighboring cultures, such as the Mongolian culture of the Yuan Dynasty and the Manchurian culture of the Qing Dynasty. Conversely, it is difficult to find traces of their cultures in contemporary China. However, Korea still maintains our identity, territory, and culture after two millennia of Chinese influence. Miraculously, 70 million people live in Korea, making it the twelfth largest country in terms of population.

Why haven't we been assimilated by China? Because of the originality of our cultural identity. We absorbed Chinese culture and created our own culture. After Sung Confucianism was imported to Korea during the late Goryeo period, scholars like Jeong Mong-ju, Jo Jun, Yi Saek, Seo Hwa-dam, and Gi Dae-seung refined it, and, in the end, Yi Toegye and Yi Yulgok created a branch of Confucianism specific to Joseon. Renowned scholars from twenty countries have now formed a society to study Toegye's Confucianism.

Koreans have the ability to absorb advanced culture and create something new. Although many heterogeneous cultures flowed into Korea following its liberation in 1945, Korean culture is only stronger because of it. I believed that we would have no problem if we opened our country to Japanese culture. In fact, if we continued to block it, only low-quality culture focusing on sex and violence would enter through the backdoor.

I do not believe that we should pick and choose when to interchange cultures. A culture is formed through a continuous learning from the past and future. Cultural interchange is a process of learning about one another. It was shameful to close our door to Japanese culture. My judgment ultimately proved to be correct. Wasn't it after the opening of Korea to Japanese culture that the Hallyu (Korean Wave) rose in Japan?

The statement also included an agreement about fisheries according to the new fishing order based on the UN Convention on the Law of the Sea that went into effect in 1994. After this, Japan declared the 200 nautical miles to be an exclusive economic zone (EEZ), causing confusion in the fishing industries of the East Sea. This agreement between Prime Minister Obuchi and me addressed this confusion.

The Korea-Japan agreement on fisheries applies only to EEZs of the two countries, so it does not apply to each country's territory and territorial waters. Therefore, Dokdo Island and our territorial waters within 12 nautical miles of it had nothing to do with this agreement and could not be influenced by it.

This new agreement was a choice I made in consideration of both the international law and our national interest. Although Korean fishermen were dissatisfied in the beginning, their loss was less than Japanese fishermen's. We increased the fishery area by accepting the 200 nautical miles of the EEZ, while avoiding the effect of this by maintaining Dokdo Island as our territory. I want to repeat here that we should not be involved in international disputes about Dokdo Island because we are practically controlling it as our territory. Creating disputes is exactly what Japan wants.

After the summit, I gave a speech at the main hall of the House of Councilors, which the Japanese media and congress showed great interest in. Apparently the maximum number of congressional members ever— 527 out of about 730—attended the event. I also heard that, quite exceptionally, the wife of the current prime minister and five former prime ministers' wives, as well as cabinet members and congressmen all listened to my speech at the hall. My speech was broadcast live on NHK.

I first thanked the Japanese government and people. "As I—who almost lost my life in my struggle for democracy during the kidnapping incident in Tokyo twenty-five years ago and again after my capital sentence in 1980—stand here as the president of the Republic of Korea, I am deeply moved. I have not forgotten how hard the Japanese people, media, and government tried to protect my life and safety for such a long time."

I also promised that I would cherish and protect the human rights and peace that the Korean people finally acquired after our fifty-year struggle against dictatorship. "A miracle does not happen miraculously. Korean democracy—and, in particular, the first peaceful regime change in the history of the Republic of Korea—is a miracle that was made possible only through the Korean people's sweat and blood. The Korean people and I will firmly protect this preciously acquired democracy."

I advised Japan that it should look toward the future instead of holding on to the past, and that this would be possible only when they could clearly view their past. "Korea and Japan now face a time when we should see our past clearly, and build a future-oriented relationship. To see the past clearly means acknowledging historical facts for what they really are; to build a future-oriented relationship means joining hands together in exploring a better future after learning lessons from the past. Japan needs true courage to see its past clearly and to fear history, while Korea needs to appreciate a changed Japan and hope for future possibilities."

Japanese congressmen applauded often during my speech. Many people later told me how well they remembered that speech of mine. Some said that it demonstrated how heavy and powerful a politician's words could be.

I attended a dinner reception held by Prime Minister Obuchi. He outlined my life in his welcoming remarks, saying: "During the 1965 Japan-Korea normalization, you courageously argued *for* it and the necessity for friendship and understanding between our two peoples when the majority of Korean national assemblymen were against it. We cannot talk about the present and future Japan-Korea relationship without mentioning that historical decision of yours.

"I would like to express my sincerest admiration for your infinite courage and firm belief with which you, as literally 'the conscience in action,' have overcome numerous sufferings and adversities for the advancement of human rights and democracy throughout your dramatic and stormy political career.

"The late Shiba Ryotaro, an author I admire greatly, sent a letter to Prime Minister Suzuki Zenko and Minister of Foreign Affairs Masayoshi in 1980 during the time when you were still on your hard road of struggle. It contained just one sentence: 'I am praying for the life of Mr. Kim Dae-jung as a human being.' You have undergone a lot more suffering since then, until you finally became the leader of Korea. Your footsteps were the Korean history of democratization and economic development."

Prime Minister Obuchi emphasized the cultural interchange between Japan and Korea, mentioning and praising professional Korean baseball player Sun Dong-yeol, who was playing for the Chunichi Dragons team in Japan, as well as Korean singer Kye Eun-suk. He also showed my calligraphy "Gyeongcheon aein (敬天愛人—respect for heaven, love for people)" and said that he considered it his motto.

On the morning of October 9, I invited about seventy Japanese comrades who had helped me during my difficult years to a tea reception at the Guest House. House of Councilors member Den Hideo was the chairman of the truth-finding committee of the Kim Dae-jung Kidnapping Incident. Representative Sasaki Hidenori was in charge of the administrative affairs of the same committee. Cho Hwal-jun was my secretary at the time of the kidnapping, and my elementary school friend Kim Jong-chung offered his house as refuge during my exile. The wife of the late Yasue Ryosuke, the president of Iwanami Publishing Company (which published the monthly magazine *Sekai*), also attended, as well as the magazine's editor-in-chief Okamoto Atsushi. The late Mr. Yasue published a special interview with me in *Sekai* and we had developed a special friendship in the course of that. President of the Socialist Democratic Party Doi Takako and former prime minister Murayama Tomiichi were politicians who supported me.

Former Liberal Democratic Party president Kono Yohei and I had been friends for thirty years. Among the guests were also writer and Nobel Laureate Oe Kenzaburo and Reverend Lee In-ha, who had led the anti-fingerprinting movement.

They had all worried about me and tried very hard to save my life. As I finally stood in front of them alive as president of Korea, I was deeply grateful and moved; they seemed to be moved too. We had all aged. I said that I'd cherish their friendship forever. We met for just an hour in the morning, but how nice it would have been if we could have eaten and drank together at night and held hands for a long time! It was my last meeting in this world with some of them.

The emperor and empress came to visit me at the Guest House to say goodbye. I officially invited them to Korea, which the emperor said he was deeply grateful for. I hoped that his visit would help the relationship between our two countries mature. This visit has yet to happen.

I invited Japanese political leaders to a luncheon. The guests included six former prime ministers—Nakasone Yasuhiro, Takesita Noboru, Hashimoto Ryutaro, Murayama Tomiichi, Hata Tsutomu, and Kaifu Toshiki—and five party leaders, including Democratic Party president Kan Naoto and Liberal Party president Ozawa Ichiro. From Korea, president of LDA Park Tae-joon, former prime minister Shin Hyun-hwak, and former Speaker of National Assembly Kim Soo-han joined the luncheon.

I vividly remember Social Democratic Party president Doi Takako's words: "It has been twenty-five years since August 1973, when the Kim Dae-jung Kidnapping Incident occurred. When we think of those twenty-five years, I am deeply moved by President Kim's visit to Japan. I believe that it was President Kim Dae-jung who continued to encourage me whenever I ran into difficulties during the past twenty-five years.

"In addition, he said yesterday, 'A miracle does not happen miraculously.' I think that, out of all speeches at the Japanese congress, that sentence will be remembered. I believe that he has taught us for the past twenty-five years that we should all try our best, no matter what happens. It is an attitude we politicians should always remember."

Former Prime Minister and the Chairman of the Korea-Japan Cooperation Committee Shin Hyun-hwak said, "Korean presidents have visited Japan many times, but I believe this is the first time a Korean president has been appreciated like this. Looking back at the past, I myself came to believe only this time that the building of a partnership between the two countries for the twenty-first century is possible."

For me, this meeting with political leaders was the most impressive during my visit to Japan. The elders were polite and warm. Everyone was optimistic about the future of Korea and Japan as true partners.

On the afternoon of October 9, I left for Osaka from the Haneda Airport. Mrs. Obuchi Chizuko, the wife of the prime minister, came to see us off. On our way from Kansai Airport to the Teikoku Hotel, citizens and students lined the street and waved both countries' flags. There were not only Koreans, but also Japanese people. Although the security team tried to dissuade me, I got off the car to shake hands with them.

Osaka was a special place for Koreans. Many Koreans who were either dragged or went to Japan during the colonial period settled there. Osaka is the city where the majority of Koreans in Japan live. I hear that Japanese people living in Osaka are temperamentally similar to Koreans.

On the morning of October 10, I had a meeting with Japanese cultural leaders. Novelist Sono Ayako said: "There was a period between Japan and Korea, for which I feel sorry. When the war broke out, I was thirteen and the emperor was eleven. We were both children. I believe that, if there has been an unhappy history between the two countries, it would be a new step between the two countries to maintain a happy relationship that far surpasses it. As a novelist, I think that interest is the beginning of love and that sometimes it appears as hatred, but it can eventually become love."

I responded: "I was already a young man during the colonial period, so I know the periods both before and after the war. In retrospect, things like economic exploitation rarely remain as wounds, but cultural matters still remain as deep wounds. Koreans consider their last name more important than their lives. Nevertheless, Japan forced Koreans to change their names to Japanese ones and banned the use of the Korean language. Also, Japan forced us not to learn Korean history, abolished Korean-language newspapers, and forbade Korean-language literature. And, toward the end, they dragged innocent young girls to work as 'comfort women' in the military. These cultural matters and human rights violations still remain as wounds. Most Japanese don't know about these things. Because they don't know about them, they don't reflect on them. Because they don't reflect on them, they can't truly apologize for the past. As you work in the cultural area, I believe you can understand that these cultural wounds are far deeper and more fundamental problems than economic wounds."

I returned to Korea after a successful state visit to Japan. At a press conference back home, I listed two things as major achievements: first, Japan apologized for the past in clear language and in a document; second, we received a $3 billion loan to use freely at an annual interest rate of 2 percent. There were many invisible achievements too.

Some people argue that we could call the relationship between Korea and Japan after the 1965 normalization treaty the 1965 System, and the Korea-Japan relationship crafted by Prime Minister Obuchi and me with "A New Japan-Republic of Korea Partnership Towards the Twenty-first Century," the 1998 System. I believe the true success of this declaration will be proven in the future. I just want to say that we made very elaborate efforts to achieve this result.

I believe I was able to achieve as much as I did during my visit to Japan because of the Korean government's peaceful regime change. I don't think anything could have been more persuasive to the Japanese people, press, and political parties than the horizontal regime change in Korea. Since the Japanese could *not* achieve this, its people admired and envied us.

UN Secretary General Kofi Annan came to Korea to accept the Seoul Peace Prize. I asked him about many things during his visit. Since he was from Ghana, an African country, I asked which country among all African countries he thought had the most positive prospect in terms of joint development of democracy and a market economy.

Mr. Kofi Annan responded, "I believe South Africa has the most potential. Its economy is advanced, and the foundation for its finance, engineering, and mining industries are firm. As for democracy and human rights, President Mandela's personal leadership and high moral reputation have great influence in the country."

I also inquired specifically about the situation in East Timor. "Indonesian authorities are ready to allow a considerable level of autonomy in areas such as society, education, politics, and economy, except for national security, finance, and foreign affairs," Mr. Kofi Annan responded. "We're demanding Indonesia withdraw its troops and free political prisoners."

"I'm personally very interested in the human rights situation in Myanmar," I told him. "Korean national assemblymen sent a letter of protest with one hundred signatures to the government. I also sent two letters. I'm in contact with Madame Aung San Suu Kyi. I think we should not tolerate Myanmar's military government. I hope that the United Nations get more actively involved."

"Although we wanted to urge Myanmar authorities not to oppress Madame Aung San Suu Kyi by sending an envoy, the authorities did not even meet with our envoy," Mr. Annan answered. "Their reason was that they were not ready."

"There were two cases where the military rejected the results of an election and took power—one was Haiti and the other was Myanmar," I commented. "The United States sent troops to Haiti to help the elected president establish his government. However, it seems that the United States does not make enough of an effort in Myanmar."

I have continued to watch these countries very carefully.

That afternoon, I met Korean native overseas adoptees who were visiting their homeland as members of the home country cultural experience group. There was a special guest among them: Lina Kim, the young female student who had asked me about my thoughts on Korean overseas adoptees during my lecture at the International Research Institute in Sweden in February 1989. She had interviewed me as a reporter a few years later during my visit to Sweden. This was our third meeting, and Lina was now a thirty-three-year-old legal consultant.

"Mr. President," she said, "I'm happy to see you again. When you first visited Sweden, you were a democracy fighter. Our meeting then changed me greatly. Now I've come to Korea and witnessed it changing into a country honoring democracy and equality. I am so moved that I am speechless." Lina was on the verge of tears, and participants here and there sobbed. Their tears flowed into my heart. How lonely and sad they must have been in a foreign country as young children! How desperate they must have felt knowing that their home country was so far away! I apologized again. "As the president of Korea, I am sincerely sorry and feel that we did such a great wrong to you."

Honorary president of Hyundai Chung Ju-yung returned to Seoul on October 31 following his second visit to North Korea, during which he had ushered 501 cows over the border. A photo of him standing in between Chairman Kim Jong-il and his own son, President Chung Mong-hun, was circulating through the media. It was an impressive photo, indeed. For a long time, I stared at this photo in which Chairman Kim Jong-il yielded the center spot to Mr. Chung.

The two sides agreed that they would jointly pursue the development of Mt. Kumgang and oil fields, an interchange of sports, and economic cooperation. What stood out most was the Mt. Kumgang cruise, which would be launched on November 18. Mr. Chung wanted to explain the results of this meeting to me directly.

On Monday, I met the Hyundai team that had visited North Korea, including honorary president Chung Ju-yung, president of Hyundai engineering and construction Chung Mong-hun, and president of Hyundai securities Yi Ik-chi. The father and son Chungs gave me a detailed round-up of their discussions. They seemed very encouraged and told me that they would develop oil fields near Pyongyang and supply oil to the South.

"Please be sure that the media doesn't exaggerate this enterprise," I warned them. "It is best that we progress one step at a time. In the past, many enterprises were loudly publicized, but few achievements were made. People's sentiments will remain most positive if we work one step at a time."

I, of course, hoped their enterprise was successful. If we built an industrial complex, it would be mutually beneficial. North Korean labor could offer inexpensive but well-educated and high-quality labor, and it would benefit South Korean businesses greatly. Citing the example of Taiwanese businesses' successful advances in China, I encouraged their pursuit of industrial complex construction.

They told me that North Koreans said that Changjon port was not a North Korean naval port, but a South Korean Hyundai port. The Mt. Kumgang tour was changing many things.

Chairman Kim Jong-il's participation in all of this represented a very significant change. I thought that *finally* a door had opened in North Korea after we had been knocking on it for eight months. It appeared to me that there had been an internal change in North Korea since Chairman Kim's inauguration. It seemed that the pragmatist force had gained more of a voice. Our constant pursuit of separation of politics and economy, as well as dialogue between authorities after civilian economic cooperation, began to change North Korea. I expected that there would be an opportunity to meet Chairman Kim Jong-il during my presidential term.

On October 10, I had an interparty summit with Grand National Party President Lee Hoi-chang in the midst of political scandals related to the Kim Young-sam regime and the last presidential election. The most shocking revelation was that the Grand National Party mobilized the National Tax Service to create their election fund and requested North Korean authorities stage a shooting incident near Panmunjeom. The media called them *sepung* (tax storm) and *chongpung* (gun storm). The former was an attempt to completely overturn the national tax administration while the latter was an unforgivable crime, an attempt to take power in collusion with communists. It was a grave crime that shook the foundation of South Korea.

Desperately cornered, the Grand National Party claimed that the regime was oppressing the opposition party. We demanded an apology from the Grand National Party as a precondition for the interparty summit. President Lee offered an apology only for the election fund incident. After a few crises, we were able to hold the summit a day before my visit to China, because I did not want a national division hanging over our heads during our national economic crisis. We agreed to overcome national crisis and recover mature politics through interparty dialogue and reconciliation, based on mutual understanding and cooperation.

Mt. Kumgang Tourism (November 1998–September 1999)

November 1998 was a month of diplomacy. I went on a nine-night, ten-day overseas tour beginning on November 11. After visiting China, I attended the Asia-Pacific Economic Cooperation (APEC) summit meeting in Malaysia, and then visited Hong Kong on my way back. On November 20, the day of my return, President Clinton came to visit Korea for a summit.

China felt different every time I visited. The Chinese leaders and people were very friendly toward me. In the past, the Chinese media had provided relatively detailed reports about my activities against dictatorship. My books had been translated into Chinese and received well. Upon the invitation of the Chinese People's Institute of Foreign Affairs—a governmental institution under the Ministry of Foreign Affairs—I had visited China three times before my presidency.

My first visit was in November 1994, when I was a retired politician and the president of the Asia Pacific Peace Foundation. Despite my retired status, the Chinese government still sent security details to the building where I was staying. I gave a speech, entitled "Reunification in the Korean Peninsula and China."

I visited China again in October 1995 and 1996. In 1996, my visit followed soon after the North Korean submarine incident, so the Chinese government had me stay at the state guest house Diao yu tai, and again sent a special security detail to protect me. While there, I met with Foreign Minister Tang Jiaxuan and Vice Premier Zhu Rongji. When I first requested a meeting with Vice Premier Zhu Rongji, he replied that it would be difficult because he had previous engagements. In the end, he actually flew on a helicopter from Dalian to Diao yu tai to meet me.

Mr. Zhu said that he hadn't met any Korean politicians before me. "I came to meet you because of my admiration for your life devoted to Korean democracy. I have twenty minutes," he told me. I talked for ten minutes, and then he for twenty-five—mostly about the Chinese economy.

This time, I visited China as a state guest upon President Jiang Zemin's invitation. Korea and China had enjoyed a friendly relationship since the establishment of our diplomatic relationship in 1992. We decided to elevate our existing relationship to a partnership. China had established a five-step foreign relationship structure that graduated from simple diplomatic relation to friendly relation to partnership to traditional friendly cooperation to blood alliance. China's relationship with North Korea had downgraded from blood alliance to traditional friendly cooperation. China's relationship with the US and Russia was that of strategic partnership. In building their relationship with South Korea, China remained strongly aware of North Korea.

As soon as I arrived at Beijing Airport on the afternoon of November 11, I went straight to Diao yu tai, where I had a meeting with Koreans in China. I talked about the importance of Korea's relationship with the four powerful countries, and, in particular, with China. "China is currently the seventh economic power in the world, but, potentially, it could easily be the first or the second soon," I said during the meeting. "You're now living in this important country. When it comes to China, we have not only a geographic advantage, but also an historical and cultural advantage. Because Korea is in the middle of four powerful countries, we are always in danger of being split and preyed upon, but we can also induce their cooperation, depending upon how we approach them. Metaphorically, we can let four young men compete for a single bride. That is diplomacy. One of the most important of these countries is China. China is important today, but it could be even more important tomorrow."

On November 12, I had a summit with President Jiang Zemin at the Renmin Dahuitang (National People's Congress). He and I were the same age. He began by commenting on my appearance. "President Kim, you are eight months older than me, but you look younger than me," he commented. "I know very well that you have led a very extraordinary life. Looking at you, I am reminded of two proverbs. One is: 'There is a way where there is a will.' You have been through storms to become president. The other is: 'The person who survives great catastrophe is sure to be rewarded with fortune later.' We can say that you were rewarded with good fortune after risking many dangers."

"When I go abroad, people often tell me that I look younger than my age and ask what my secret is," I responded. "Because I lived under the persecution of military dictatorship, my life almost stopped. I often explain that my aging had to stop too."

President Jiang laughed out loud. I explained the Sunshine Policy to him, as well as the recent signs of changes in North Korea. "North Korea amended its Constitution in the recent Supreme People's Assembly," I told President Jiang. "Their new Constitution contains articles for the early stage of a market economy. Another important change is that Chairman Kim Jong-il showed a more positive attitude toward cooperating with the Hyundai Group. Because of these changes, we are planning to patiently and gradually pursue an interchange with North Korea."

"We have supported the principle of an independent Korean solution," President Jiang said. "I think the South Korean policy of engagement toward North Korea is a correct one. As North Korea is now facing the issue of its survival due to the deterioration of economic conditions, it responds more sensitively to outside movements. If cold winds rather than warm winds blow, it will hold on to its clothes more tightly. It is most important for you to be patient and to not hurt their pride, not to provoke but to create a tolerant environment. Peaceful stability in the Korean Peninsula is China's basic position. I hope that your two countries gradually recover trust and improve your relationship."

Although our meeting was scheduled for forty minutes, it ended up lasting for an hour longer than that. We then held the expanded summit, which all of our official entourages participated in. For the sake of both countries' national interests and peace and stability in Northeast Asia, we agreed to elevate our countries' relationship to a full-scale cooperative partnership.

President Jiang held a dinner reception that evening. We talked about a lot of things, and it turned out that he knew a lot about me. During the dinner the military band alternately played both countries' folk music. When a Chinese singer sang "Evening Song," President Jiang sang along. After thanking the workers following the dinner, he sadly said, "I couldn't sing the last line of 'Evening Song' because the tune was too high."

"Then, please sing the song again," I cajoled him.

President Jiang requested that the military band play the music, and he began singing. He was a great singer. He asked me to sing, too. Together with my wife, I sang the Korean folksong "Doraji taryeong" (Song of a Broad Bellflower).

President Jiang was a great, very frank man. We got along very well, and spoke in English without interpreters. We could talk about both personal and diplomatic matters on a person-to-person level. We could trust each other.

About ten days later, while he was flying through the Korean skies on his way to Japan, President Jiang sent me a message from the airplane. "After a visit to Russia, I'm passing through the sky of Korea on my way to Japan," he wrote. "I send my regards to President Kim Dae-jung and the friendly Korean people. I wish for your country's prosperity and a cooperative partnership between China and Korea for the twenty-first century."

I was deeply moved by this letter from the sky. President Jiang also sent Maotai liquor to the official twelve-member entourage of my state visit to China through the Chinese Embassy in Korea.

I gave my third speech at Beijing University. In honor of the one hundredth anniversary of the university's founding, I gave them a calligraphy print of a phrase written in Chinese that translates to "seeking truth grounded on concrete evidence." There were more than 1000 people in the lecture hall—the passages were invisible due to all of the professors and students filling the hall.

"I enthusiastically wish that the young people of both of our countries will rise up as heroes of the twenty-first century, stepping on the bridge of the comprehensive partnership between Korea and China," I spoke. "The young people of Korea and China both have sufficient potential for it. Advance hand-in-hand. Your country's leaders and I will gladly lay that bridge."

I met Premier Zhu Rongji, Chairman of the Standing Committee of the National People's Congress Li Peng, Vice President Hu Jintao, and Vice Premier Qian Qichen on November 13. I heard that this kind of consecutive and comprehensive meeting with Chinese leaders was unprecedented.

After meeting with Premier Zhu Rongji at the Diao yu tai, we had dinner. While requesting the delay in depreciation of the Chinese *yuan*, I presented five economic cooperation measures: Korean business participation in Chinese nuclear power plants; permission to build automobile assembly plants in China; the advancement of the Korean telecommunication business in China, based on uniquely Korean CDMA technology;

permission for Korean financial institutions in China to handle *yuan*; and Korean business participation in a high-speed railway construction between Beijing and Shanghai.

Premier Zhu said that he would accept or examine all of my requests. After responding in detail to all five items in my proposal, he said, "This is not a simple diplomatic rhetoric. I am earnest because I admire you."

I thanked him in a roundabout way. "I'm glad I was elected president. It is only because I am president that I can meet and ask you these things."

I specifically emphasized the adoption of our CDMA telecommunication system because I had heard that China intended to adopt the European GSM system. In the time since then I am happy to say that Korean cell phones have sold like hot cakes in China.

Premier Zhu also gladly accepted my invitation to Korea. "When you visited China in 1996, I flew in a helicopter to meet you at Diao yu tai. I met you then not because of your position but because I admired your remarkable character. You're the first Korean politician I ever met," he told me. "There are many mysteries about you," Premier Zhu continued. "I talked about your physical discomfort with President Jiang today. I thought it was a result of being tortured by the military dictatorial regime, but President Jiang thought it was because of an attack disguised as a traffic accident. Who is correct?"

"During the stump speech tour for the 1971 National Assembly election, a large truck drove into my car head on," I explained to him. "Two people died on the spot, and my leg was badly injured. I can walk downstairs okay, but going upstairs is still very painful."

Premier Zhu and I share a history of hardship. He had lived apart from his family for twenty years during the Cultural Revolution, and experienced all kinds of difficulties in the countryside. We comforted one another about our past hardships. I told him about how I learned to catch a fly without killing it in prison; the fly would just pass out in the process. I joked that it was a hi-tech skill to hang an unconscious fly in a spider web. "I'll teach you this skill when you visit Korea early next year," I joked. "You should bring a CC TV reporter for special coverage."

"If your two skills were included in the Olympics, you'd easily win two gold medals," Premier Zhu responded.

I also separately invited Chinese leaders who had helped me during my difficult opposition party years. The invitees included the former chairman of the Chinese People's Institute of Foreign Affairs Liu Shu Qing and Deputy Chief of the National People's Congress Committee for Foreign Affairs Li Shu Zheng.

During my visit, Chinese leaders were extremely respectful toward me. I heard that there had been fierce debate about whether or not to raise China's relationship with South Korea to partnership, given that they also had to consider their relationship with North Korea. In the end, China accepted almost all of our requests.

After Beijing, I went to Shanghai. I first toured the Pudong development zone and then visited the former Korean Provisional Government building. The building where the dream of Korean independence and national soul had once resided was shabby—it looked as if it had been abandoned in a back alley. I felt ashamed. Where else in the world had a nation established a provisional government and waged an armed struggle during a period of colonization?

On the first March 1st Independence Movement anniversary since my inauguration, I declared, "The People's Government is a legitimate government that succeeded the Korean Provisional Government." Although Korean leaders had established the Provisional Government only nine years after the collapse of the Joseon Dynasty, they did not pursue the restoration of monarchy. They established a people's republic. They made the right choice, and my People's Government succeeded this legitimate government line.

I looked at the Provisional Government's bust of President Kim Koo for a long time. In the guest book, I wrote: *What our patriotic ancestors wanted to achieve with all their might will remain forever as fragrance among us.*

I said to my entourage, "In his diaries, Master Baekbom (Kim Koo) advocated for a society of economic justice and fairness. We should not hesitate to revive the spirit of democracy, independent economy, and the just society of the provisional government."

As I returned home from my visit, I did not feel very comfortable about the fact that our precious and just history was neglected in a back alley of Shanghai, a prosperous developing city. I felt that Master Kim Koo also compelled me to think about this building. I ordered my entourage to explore options available to us for the improvement of the building.

On November 15, I flew to Kuala Lumpur in Malaysia to attend the APEC summit and to work on four-day summit diplomacy. I met Prime Minister Mahathir the next morning. This meeting attracted serious media attention for a few reasons.

I had prepared common measures for the Asian economic crisis to discuss at this summit. Prime Minister Mahathir drew attention because he was the chair of this meeting. The prime minister and I held different opinions about both the diagnoses and prescription for this crisis. Whereas I considered it a general economic crisis, Prime Minister Mahathir considered it a limited financial crisis.

I also considered the widespread corrupt systems throughout Asia to be a very important factor in the crisis, and proposed the parallel development of democracy and a market economy. Blaming hedge funds for robbing money, Prime Minister Mahathir declared, "We'd rather starve to death than become the colony of IMF."

We had already collided in the April ASEM meeting. Prime Minister Mahathir repeated his position during the keynote speech. "The main culprit of the Asian financial crisis is international hedge funds," he opined. "We need to create a system to supervise international finance and the exchange rate in order to prevent exchange speculation."

In contrast, I acknowledged our faults first. "In Korea, the financial system was ruined and businesses lost their competitive ability due to the cozy relations between politics and economics," I spoke. "We will reform our system in order to carry out democracy according to the market economy principle. The method of reform might be different in each country, but all Asian countries should make an effort to reform according to their situations."

I met Prime Minister Mahathir again, this time at the Kuala Lumpur Fog Hotel. Again, our opinions were quite different.

Prime Minister Mahathir said, "In Malaysia, we at first opened our market and welcomed foreign investment. However, we suffered greatly from market manipulation by short-term international speculative capitalists who abused the free market system. Although it is inevitable that Malaysia depends heavily on foreign capital because we do not have enough capital, technology, and market, we are planning to control capital movement by encouraging the introduction of foreign capital to only the productive fields."

I, on the other hand, said, "Although I agree with you about the short-term capital problem, I believe we should not enforce excessive restrictions on the movement of capital, which we need to overcome the international financial crisis. Instead of fundamental restrictions, I believe that we have to strengthen international cooperation by creating an information interchange system for short-term capital movement. I think that we need support from G7, including Japan, in order to minimize the damage from short-term capital movement."

I emphasized the necessity of reform and opening to build a free market system that would help Asia overcome the financial crisis. I wrote about the necessity of reform and opening in terms of universal globalism in a special article published in the *Korea Times* on November 5: "Recent revolutionary changes in world civilization dictate that mankind move even more rapidly toward universal globalism, embracing the Earth as one community ... Amid such rapid changes, no single nation, wherever it is in the world, can develop and run its own economy without being inextricably linked with the other countries of the world ... Both competition and cooperation will take place simultaneously ... I believe that the spirit and moral norms of humanity and benevolence of Confucianism and Buddhism as it has developed in Asia will give us the impetus and vitality to deepen the freedom and human rights that have made big strides under democracy."

Although Malaysia and Korea had different approaches for overcoming the economic crisis, we both ultimately succeeded. I don't know whose approach was better. Although there wasn't a correct answer to the economic problem, it is true that many specialists paid attention to my argument.

I attended a summit with the heads of New Zealand, Singapore, Australia, Canada, and Chile. I also met American Vice President Al Gore. During our visit I confirmed that our administrative policy of parallel development of democracy and a market economy was supported internationally.

On November 18, the Mt. Kumgang Tour Cruise set sail from Donghae port. Honorary president of Hyundai Chung Ju-yung was on board the cruise ship with his sons. At 5:45 p.m., a historic whistle rang out from the Hyundai ship Kumgangsan, which carried 1418 passengers on it. This South Korean tour of Mt. Kumgang—which allowed the average South Korean tourist to venture on a trip to North Korea—represented an extraordinary event in our history. Tourists and those who saw them off all waved their hands as the cruise ship disappeared over the Northern Limit Line (NLL). I happily watched this scene on the news from the airplane as I returned from my trip.

The Mt. Kumgang tour was a precious child of the Sunshine Policy and the symbol of Korean détente. North Korea opened its front and Changjon, a place of strategic importance. This reconciliation current was also going to be helpful in overcoming of our financial crisis by raising Korea's credit rating. The effect was truly enormous, and cannot be quantified by any sort of numeric figure.

Of course, there were bumps along the road of this historic development. At exactly the same time as South Korean tourists were climbing Mt. Kumgang, US Special Envoy for the Korean Peace Talks Charles Kartman said to reporters, "We [The United States and South Korea] have information that has led us to believe that the site in Kumchangri is related to nuclear development."

Mr. Kartman returned to Seoul after exchanging opinions with North Korean officials during his visit to Pyongyang. I received a report about all of this while I was in Hong Kong. I ordered senior secretaries to find out the truth behind this allegation. This development seemed related to President Clinton's visit to Korea.

Although it looked suspicious, there was no confirmed proof. The US claimed that there was "strong evidence," but Korean authorities concluded that there was no "decisive evidence." I ordered this situation to be actively handled. In the end, Mr. Kartman reversed his own claim. "There is no decisive evidence of nuclear facilities," he announced.

Early the morning of November 20, a spy ship appeared in front of Ganghwado Island. Our military and police surrounded and chased the ship, but it fled to the North. While the tour cruise was heading north in the East Sea, a spy ship came southward in the West Sea. I could not accept this kind of behavior from North Korea. However, I thought it would be most effective for us to form a "Sunshine Front" with the US through an engagement policy.

On November 21, I met with President Clinton at the Blue House. Public opinion in the US was not too favorable of North Korea because of the recent Kumchangri nuclear facility allegation and the September ballistic missile incident. In addition, President Clinton was going through a difficult time because of the Monica Lewinsky scandal. In our one-on-one talk, I explained the result of the APEC meeting and my visit to China to President Clinton, and he explained the result of his visit to Japan to me.

"I strongly support President Kim's policy of gradual engagement with North Korea," President Clinton began. "I have appointed Dr. Perry as our special coordinator for Korean policy to intensify our efforts and to make sure that we have the best possible policy. We have to make sure to carry out the Geneva Agreed Framework."

"We need to continue our engagement policy," I told him. "We should patiently and consistently handle them without creating unnecessary tension."

"We should continue to support a diplomatic approach through the 4-party talks and President Kim's engagement policy," President Clinton said. "We should also get international support and, in particular, that of China and Japan. It would be effective if we engaged North Korea as one voice in close cooperation. I saw the news about Mt. Kumgang tourism on TV last night. It was very beautiful. This enterprise means that your policy of engagement has been successful."

Our summit meeting exceeded the scheduled time by more than thirty minutes. President Clinton said that he felt at home. In the expanded summit, I requested that the US actively help Myanmar and Madame Aung San Suu kyi.

At the press conference, President Clinton said: "First, with regard to security, our goal is what it has always been: a peaceful Korea that is part of a prosperous Asia. America stands by its unshakable alliance with the Republic of Korea ...

"I support President Kim's policy of gradual engagement with North Korea. The 4-party peace talks offer the best avenue to lasting settlement, but they demand tremendous patience and perseverance. Both President Kim and I, as you heard him say, are convinced that the agreed framework is the best way to prevent North Korea from developing nuclear weapons, provided Pyongyang abides by its commitments."

At this press conference we announced that our two countries had engaged in a strong cooperative system for our policy toward North Korea. President Clinton and I got along very well. During the Q & A session, a reporter asked a question about impeachment because of the Lewinsky scandal. A serious expression crossed President Clinton's face as he answered, "There has been a lot of suffering."

I had never seen a person who spoke as well as President Clinton. He was simultaneously logical and flexible, and extremely effective at persuading others. Despite his exceptional ability, even away from home he faced a plight because of the scandal.

After the dinner, President Clinton watched his younger brother rocker Roger Clinton perform in Korea. He even unexpectedly joined his brother on the stage. His unreserved behavior was enviable.

President Clinton left Korea on November 23. That day, I was interviewed live on CNN. I said that I would continue to pursue the Sunshine Policy with North Korea, as well as send humanitarian food aid.

Choi Myung-hee, the author of the saga *Honbul*, died toward the end of the year. I sent a staff member to her bed when I heard that the author was in critical condition. Despite our wishes for her recovery, she passed away. I very much admired her unique style. I sent my staff member again to express my condolences.

US Special Coordinator for Korea Policy and former Minister of Defense William Perry visited Korea on December 6. The Clinton administration was in a difficult spot with the engagement policy because of North Korean nuclear development allegations and the ballistic missile incident. Congress was applying pressure for the administration to overhaul its North Korea policy. Mr. Perry was a well-known hardliner.

Mr. Perry was the minister of defense during the first North Korea Nuclear Crisis in 1994. At that time, he argued for the bombing of North Korea, as well as preparation for an all-out war. It was only thanks to the miraculous agreement between President Carter and President Kim Il-sung during the national security meeting that the crisis ended peacefully.

Mr. Perry began his official investigation with the goal of submitting a report to the US. Congress within five months. Senior Secretary of Foreign Affairs Lim Dong-won presented me with a comprehensive approach strategy. The general outline of its content was as follows:

North Korean nuclear and ballistic missile development originates from the Cold War system in the Korean Peninsula. Therefore, we cannot solve this situation by responding to individual incidents. A fundamental solution to North Korean nuclear development is dismantling the Cold War system in the Korean Peninsula.

There are six factors in the Cold War system in the Korean Peninsula: mistrust and confrontation between South and North Koreas; North Korean society's closed-ness and rigidity; an antagonistic relationship between the United States and North Korea; weapons of mass destruction; military confrontation and arms race; and the armistice system.

In order to dismantle this system, it is necessary that South and North Koreas reconcile with each other, overcoming their half-century of mistrust and confrontation. We have to gradually build mutual trust through various interchanges and cooperation and peaceful coexistence. Also, the United States and Japan should dissolve their antagonistic relationship with North Korea and achieve normalization. However, the United States and Japan do not currently recognize North Korea. As long as the United States antagonizes North Korea, North Korea cannot help feeling threatened and cannot avoid the temptation to develop weapons of mass destruction.

The South Korean government's basic position is that North Korean nuclear development should not be tolerated and the Korean Peninsula should be free from nuclear weapons. However, military measures cannot be a solution. No war can be allowed. Our basic position should be anti-nuclear, anti-war, and peace. According to this basic principle, we have to recognize North Korea and pursue dialogue and negotiation with the North Korean regime, based on engagement policy according to the policy of gradual change rather than unrealistic collapse pressure theory.

In addition, we have to try to remove mutual threats after acknowledging the North Korean threat that we feel, and the US and South Korean threat that North Korea feels. For this purpose, we should build trust by comprehensively settling all problems through exchanges and by gradually and simultaneously carrying them all out.

In this work, the cooperation among the US, Japan—a country that can help economically rebuild North Korea—and Korea is necessary, and we need to secure support and cooperation from China and Russia. Also, the negotiation with North Korea should be based on a powerful US-Korean ability to restrain North Korea. In handling North Korea, we need confidence, patience, consistency, and flexibility.

Senior Secretary Lim's strategy was almost perfect. It almost felt like he had read my mind. In early December, the cabinet passed this Comprehensive Approach Strategy for the Dismantling of Korean Peninsula Cold War Structure after consideration at the NSC standing committee. I met and talked with Mr. Perry at the Blue House for more than an hour on December 7. I told him that pending issues between North Korea and the US should be solved through a package settlement. I said, "With the understanding that we help North Korea if they cooperate with us and we firmly punish them if they provoke us, we should give what is necessary to North Korea and demand what we need. I hope that the relationship between North Korea and the United States normalizes; it is now time for the US to consider lifting its sanction against North Korea."

I then explained to him the process of ending the Cold War through an engagement policy in Europe. I also told him how, during the 1994 crisis, I gave a speech at the US National Press Club and encouraged former president Carter's visit to North Korea for a peaceful solution while Mr. Perry was considering a military solution. It was a useful conversation. I explained, and he listened attentively. He later remembered how extremely surprised he was when he had listened to me then, as he was a hardliner.

USFK Commander John Tillelli told Mr. Perry that the situation in the Korean Peninsula had fundamentally changed since 1994. Commander Tillelli supported an engagement policy toward North Korea.

When Mr. Perry returned it was impossible to know what he was thinking. We had to persuade him no matter what, so I decided to send Senior Secretary of Foreign Affairs Lim Dong-won to Washington as a special envoy. Although Mr. Lim was at first hesitant to take the job, I persuaded him by saying that he should go because he was the person who had planned the comprehensive approach strategy.

When Mr. Lim met Mr. Perry in Washington and explained the plan in detail—the engagement policy and comprehensive approach strategy, as well as gradual steps to be taken by Korea, the US, and Japan—Mr. Perry finally responded positively. "That is a creative and bold plan," he said.

Mr. Perry was considering a visit to North Korea and asked Mr. Lim if South Korea would agree. Mr. Lim told him that I would gladly encourage him to do so. Mr. Lim returned to Seoul and told me about this meeting in detail. I was glad that I had sent him to Washington.

Mr. Perry visited Korea again in early March 1999. We met at the Blue House, along with US Ambassador to Korea Bosworth, Professor Ashton Carter, and Mr. Phillip Yoon. Holding a chart of his plan for the North Korean policy, he said, "I showed President Clinton this plan. President Clinton said that our policy toward North Korea should be harmonious with the South Korean policy. He asked me to report this to you and get your opinion."

He opened his chart, entitled "Comprehensive Approach Plan for an Engagement Policy." As soon as I saw the title, I was relieved. Mr. Perry first presented his analysis of the current situation in the Korean Peninsula compared to that of 1994. He considered how North Korean military power has reduced since 1994, at the same time as the South Korean and the US power of preventing war has increased. He also noticed that South Korea was confidently pursuing an engagement policy, although the North Korean response was still limited. He also pointed out that despite famine and the dire situation, North Korea was developing underground nuclear facilities and threatening the 1994 Agreed Framework.

After this analysis, Mr. Perry presented five possible alternatives for the US: status quo, undermining the DPRK, reforming the DPRK, "buying" our objectives, and negotiating for mutual threat reduction. He chose the fifth alternative. His report says the following about this alternative:

A better alternative, and the one this review has recommended, is a 2-path strategy focused on our priority concerns about the DPRK's nuclear weapons and missile-related activities ...

The first path involves a new, comprehensive, and integrated approach to our negotiations with the DPRK. We will seek complete and verifiable assurances that the DPRK does not have a nuclear weapons program. We will also seek the complete and verifiable cessation of testing, production, and deployment of missiles exceeding the parameters of the Missile Technology Control Regime, and the complete cessation of export sales of such missiles and the equipment and technology associated with them ...

On this path the United States and its allies will, in a step-by-step and reciprocal fashion, move to reduce pressures on the DPRK that it perceives as threatening. The reduction of perceived threat would in turn give the DPRK regime the confidence that it could coexist peacefully with us and its neighbors and pursue its own economic and social development. If the DPRK moved to eliminate its nuclear and long-range missile threats, the United States would normalize relations with the DPRK, relax sanctions that have long constrained trade with the DPRK, and take other positive steps that would provide opportunities for the DPRK.

If the DPRK were prepared to move down this path, the ROK and Japan have indicated that they would also be prepared, in coordinated but parallel tracks, to improve relations with the DPRK.

The report also laid out the steps that should be taken to pursue this policy:

If North Korea rejects the first path, it will not be possible for the United States to pursue a new relationship with the DPRK. In that case, the United States and its allies will have to take other steps to assure their security and contain the threat. The US and allied countries should seek to keep the Agreed Framework intact and avoid, if possible, direct conflict. But they will also have to take firm but measured steps to persuade the DPRK that it should return to the first path and avoid destabilizing the security situation in the region.

I was very satisfied with this report. It was almost hard to believe that Mr. Perry symbolized the hardline policy toward North Korea. "This is incredible because your plan is exactly what I want," I told him. "I think North Korea will find this to be an attractive proposal."

Modestly, Mr. Perry said, "This is really your idea. I heard great ideas from Mr. Lim Dong-won. I'm embarrassed to say it, but we just stole, plagiarized, and repackaged the strategic plan Mr. Lim presented."

We laughed together. How wonderful it was to have that moment of agreement! Nobody is a born hardliner. Mr. Perry changed because he learned more. The sun was shining over South-North relations. Again, I urged him: "We should not worry about potential bad consequences. What we need is confidence that we can persuade North Korea. Only then we can have good results. International support and cooperation for this policy is very important. South Korea, the United States, and Japan should put a coordinated system in place and work closely with China, Russia, and the EU."

I urged Mr. Perry to visit Pyongyang in person to explain this plan. I also told him that, in order to persuade North Korea, a very proud country, a sincere and polite persuasion effort was very important. Mr. Perry gladly agreed.

A week later, welcome news reached us. On March 16, 1999, the US and North Korea reached an agreement to solve the alleged Kumchangri nuclear site. The agreement included the US donation of food through the UN World Food Program, institutional bilateral food programs, and steps toward improving political and economic relations with North Korea; North Korea would permit multiple site visits to the entire Kumchangri site by a US team (which were carried out later—the US State Department spokesperson issued a statement that the basement tunnel was an empty tunnel) and both countries would reaffirm their commitment to the 1994 US-North Korean Agreed Framework in its entirety, and to the principles of US-North Korean bilateral relations as expressed in the June 11, 1993 US-DPRK Joint Communiqué. Finally, they would agree to meet again on March 29 to discuss North Korea's missile export and development programs.

As promised, Mr. Perry visited Pyongyang toward the end of May. He met Kim Yong-nam, head of the Supreme People's Assembly, and delivered a letter from President Clinton to Chairman Kim Jong-Il. He also met North Korean high officials and explained US policy toward North Korea.

In early September 1999, a crucial round of talks was held in Berlin between US negotiator Ambassador Charles Kartman and DPRK Vice Foreign Minister Kim Gye Gwan. When the talks concluded on September 12, the two sides released a short statement saying they had agreed to "preserve a positive atmosphere" in anticipation of further talks about missiles and easing US economic sanctions. Subsequently, President Clinton's National Security Advisor Samuel Berger announced that North Korea had agreed to "freeze" its long-range missile program for an extended period while talks continued. North Korean Minister of Foreign Affairs Paek Nam-sun confirmed this in his UN keynote address. Thus ended the Cold War system in the Korean Peninsula.

On September 15, Mr. Perry released the "Review of United States Policy Toward North Korea: Findings and Recommendations," which included the contents from "A Comprehensive and Integrated Approach" I quoted previously. It also included five key policy recommendations to the Clinton administration. That it should adopt a comprehensive and integrated approach to the DPRK's nuclear weapons and ballistic missile-related programs; create a strengthened mechanism within the US government for carrying out North Korean policy; continue the new mechanism established last March to ensure close coordination with the ROK and Japan; take steps to create a sustainable, bipartisan, long-term outlook toward North Korea; and approve a plan of action for dealing with the contingency of DPRK provocations in the near term, including the launch of a long-range missile.

With this report, the comprehensive and integrated approach that our government had been consistently pursuing became a consensus among all relevant parties. This report was an unprecedented historic event and an example of our independent diplomacy. Although the report called the roadmap it included the "Perry Process," I feel that it should more accurately be called the "Lim Dong-won Process" since it reflected Mr. Lim's entire proposal.

WHOSE 21ST CENTURY? (DECEMBER 1998–MARCH 1999)

In early December 1998, I visited Vietnam to attend the Association of Southeast Asian Nations (ASEAN) and Korea-China-Japan summit in Hanoi. Like Korea, Vietnam is a proud nation. When the Vietnamese Speaker visited me on March 10, 1998, I said to him, "Vietnam is located outside the southwestern border of China, and Korea is outside of its northeastern border. Despite our locations, neither country has been assimilated with China. I hope that we can cooperate in various areas based on this proud common history of overcoming the pressure of a powerful country."

Like Korea, although Vietnam has been invaded many times throughout its long history, it has never surrendered. They also share with Koreans a passion for education, diligence, and strong patriotism.

Altogether 320,000 Korean troops participated in the Vietnam War between 1964 and 1973. More than 5000 soldiers died and 16,000 were wounded. The war's aftereffect still remains in Korean society. Many veterans, including victims of defoliants, are living an unhappy evening of life. The blood that our youth shed in a foreign land contributed to the Korean economy. In this way, Vietnam is deeply embedded in modern Korean history. It is also a country that we cannot simply judge, one way or another.

During my opposition party assemblyman year in 1966, I visited Korean soldiers in Vietnam to comfort them, despite my opposition to Korean participation in the war. I did not expect that Vietnam would win the war against the US. No, it might be more accurate to say that I did not even dream that the US would lose the war. It is true that Koreans did not know much about Vietnam then.

The Vietnamese people were full of pride for being a nation that had not been assimilated into China; the nation that vanquished the Mongolian invasion; the nation that drove out France on their own; and the only nation that won against the US.

We had to address the issue of Korean participation in the Vietnam War. Vietnam did not demand any apology from us for it. Maybe it was because of their pride as the winner. However, I brought up the issue of our unfortunate past because I wanted to comfort and help heal the wounds of the Vietnamese people.

As soon as I arrived in Vietnam, I had a summit with President Tran Duc Luong. For the first time as the president of South Korea, I mentioned our countries' unfortunate past. "Since the establishment of a diplomatic relationship between Korea and Vietnam in December 1992, our relationship has achieved remarkable developments. Although there was once an unfortunate period, I am truly glad that we have tried to overcome it and develop a relationship of future-oriented friendly cooperation."

President Tran responded, "I listened carefully to your remark about our unfortunate past. I would like to emphasize once again here that the Vietnamese people and leaders want a solid, friendly, and cooperative relationship with Korea, and to work toward it based on our peaceful and friendly tradition."

I visited the Communist Party headquarters and met with Communist Party Secretary Le Kha Phieu. Everyone, both domestically and internationally, called this a very exceptional action. I mentioned our unfortunate past once again during my meeting with Mr. Le. His response was the same as President Tran's. "The Vietnamese government and people look at the future rather than the past in terms of our relationship with Korea," he said. "Considering what we have achieved so far, we believe that the past has been overcome. I believe we have no need to dwell on it any longer."

His words were an official acknowledgment that the past really had been overcome. As the perpetrator apologized and the victim accepted the apology, everything felt easy and comfortable. I paid my respects at the grave of former president Ho Chi Minh, whom the Vietnamese people revere as the father of their nation.

Vietnam did not demand any apology or reparation from *any* country, not just from Korea. Despite their enormous suffering and sacrifice, they simply focused on the future only. When Prime Minister Phan Van Khai visited the US and met with President Bush in June 2005, he also did not mention a single word about the past. He discussed only economic matters. I learned a lot from their attitude, and I came to admire Vietnam.

At the ASEAN and Korea-China-Japan summit (9+3), I proposed the establishment of the East Asian Vision Group (EAVG) to discuss matters of active trade and investment within East Asia, and to support cooperation in both industry and resources. East Asia was the only area that did not have a regional economic cooperative organization. This was partially responsible for their inadequate response to the 1997 East Asian financial crisis. Also, trade and investment within the region were rapidly increasing, intensifying the level of mutual dependency. The need for an economic cooperation organization was gradually increasing.

The vision group that I was imagining was not the kind of government-led, exclusive, and firm organization characteristic of other regional economic blocks, but a civilian-led organization where scholars and businessmen participated. There are organizations of a similar nature in ASEM and APEC. My idea was to form an intellectual group where government officials on the level of aide to the deputy minister would participate as observers and reflect what was discussed in government policies.

At first, Southeast Asian countries were wary of my proposal. Malaysian Prime Minister Mahathir did not hide his suspicion when he asked, "President Kim today proposed the establishment of EAVG. You mentioned that both civilians and governments should participate in it. Could you please elaborate on it more specifically?"

"I hope that various professionals such as scholars, businessmen, and cultural leaders can gather and exchange ideas for mutual development and interests among East Asian countries," I responded. "The participants can make recommendations through the free and broad exchange of ideas to the 9+3 summit or their cabinet meetings. I hope that this will be an organization in which civilians take the initiative and discuss broad subjects like youth, women, and the environment."

Prime Minister Mahathir still wasn't convinced. "Considering your explanation of the EAVG, I think that the East Asian Business Council (EABC) that we're talking about establishing could serve the same purpose. Could you explain what the difference would be between the EABC and EAVG?"

Prime Minister Mahathir had already proposed the establishment of the EABC in the early 1990s. Ultimately, no progress was made because the US opposed it on the grounds that they considered it to have a political purpose.

Rather at length, I answered: "I mean the EAVG to work for comprehensive development in the twenty-first century in a variety of directions, including culture and youth interchange and not just limited to economy. The twentieth century was a period of industrialization, when we manufactured visible objects and mobilized capital and technology for them. The twenty-first century will be the time when industry based on knowledge and culture will be prevalent.

"This phenomenon is already clear. For example, the United States made the same amount of money from exporting just two movies—*Titanic* and *Jurassic Park*—that the four Korean automobile companies made through automobile export over the course of a year. The age of completely different industry from that of the present will come in the twenty-first century. It will be the age of culture and professionals. College diplomas will not be important in the twenty-first century. It will be a time when anyone, whether a farmer or a mail carrier, who improves productivity in his field can increase the productivity of the entire nation.

"Nationalism had controlled the world since the Industrial Revolution and, spreading like a fever, it gave birth to colonialism. Democracy developed in the process of the independence movement against colonial rule. Nationalism developed because the unit of economic development fit well with a nation. However, due to developments in transportation, knowledge, and telecommunications, the nation-state is losing its desirability as an economic unit. In particular, since the emergence of the WTO system, the world economy has been unified as one economy across national borders.

"There are still nationalist elements in East Asia, and we have to consider mutual sentiments and national interests. However, we are now facing an inevitable march toward globalism. We are advancing toward a relationship between competition and cooperation whereby the entire world becomes a single market.

"We are in serious need of responding to this situation in the East Asian region. Looking ahead to the twenty-first century, we need to gather wisdom and present vision not only about economy, but also about information, culture, youth, and scholarship. This is the background of my proposal for the establishment of the EAVG."

In the end, my proposal to consider the EAVG was accepted by Southeast Asian countries. In the course of five meetings within two years, this group completed a report about the basic direction and mid- to long-term vision for East Asian cooperation in six areas—economy; finance; politics and security; environment and energy; society, culture, and education; and institution. This report includes plans for the establishment of the East Asian Free Trade Area (EAFTA) and the East Asian Investment Area (EAIA). In particular, it also proposes transforming the ASEAN+3 summit into the East Asian Summit (EAS) and establishing the East Asian Forum for this purpose.

In November 2000, I proposed establishing the East Asia Study Group (EASG) at the fourth ASEAN+3 summit in Singapore. This was to be a governmental organization that would replace the work of the EAVG and materialize the EABC. The EASG studied and examined pending Asian economic issues for the next two years, and selected a total of twenty-six projects—seventeen short-term projects, including the establishment of the East Asian Forum, and nine long-term projects, including the EAS. They were adopted at the sixth ASEAN+3 summit in Cambodia in November 2002.

The East Asia Forum launched in Seoul in December 2003. Although my presidential term was already over, I was invited to give a speech. In my speech, I said: "Today is a significant day, a day when we launch our work for regional cooperation and the East Asian community. The East Asia Forum should actively examine issues that EAVG and EASG have raised for the past five years. The East Asia Forum should strengthen agreements on various fields, including balanced development and cultural exchange in East Asia, eradication of social poverty, and development of education. Considering the experience of foreign currency crisis, regional trade rate amounting to 32.4 percent, and the importance of regional security, it is now meaningless to distinguish Northeast Asia and Southeast Asia. I look forward to the establishment of an EAS and the expression of strong political will for the development of a regional community there.

"In East Asia, a hopeful rainbow for the future of the twenty-first century is now emerging. We hope for the arrival of a peaceful, abundant, and just East Asia. It is desirable to establish this kind of East Asian community. We can do it. For it, we need resolution. I hope that today's gathering will promote that resolution of the thirteen East Asian countries."

The second East Asia Forum was held in Kuala Lumpur in Malaysia in December 2004. Again, I was invited. Former Malaysian Prime Minister Mahathir and former Japanese Prime Minister Hata Tsutomu also attended. During my keynote address, I listed six short-term tasks: cooperation in politics and security; economic cooperation; establishment of the EAFTA and EAIA; financial cooperation; energy cooperation; and interest in anti-poverty programs. I also welcomed the fact that the EAS had been agreed upon at the historic ASEAN+3 summit a month ago.

Former Japanese Prime Minister Hata Tsutomu said nice things about me in his address. "The EAS is what former President Kim Dae-jung proposed. The project of EAFTA also began through former President Kim's initiative. He proposed the EAVG and EASG, and successfully led the first East Asia Forum in Seoul last year. I admire former President Kim's ideas and his foresight, which contributed greatly to building the East Asian community."

If the East Asian community is built, I guess my name will be recorded in some corner of it.

I believe that the twenty-first century is the Asian century, just as Arnold Toynbee predicted. In the twenty-first century, Asia will surpass Europe in democracy, economic development, and cultural creation. Asia is rising again. Past economic powers, like China and India, are rising. Asia has a profound spiritual tradition and rich intellectual resources, and it is currently achieving rapid technological revolution. Diversity in religion and culture does not cause conflict, but works as a positive stimulus and creates mutual cooperation.

I hope that we will have many leaders who have foresight for the future and for the East Asian community. I am waiting for them.

I received news that the US invaded Iraq while I was at the Daewoo Hotel in Hanoi on December 17. The Korean government issued a statement that said: "We hope the United States' military measures would end soon." It was worrisome and unpredictable.

As soon as I returned home later that day, I got news of the passing of honorary president of the Korea Legal Aid Center for Family Relations, Lee Tai-young. I visited the funeral home with my wife the next day. I was as sad as I would have been if I'd lost my own parents or sister. Lee Tai-young always cared about my wife and me, and sincerely hoped that I would become president. My wife teared up while burning incense.

Madam Lee's life epitomized the modern Korean women's history. Her name was always accompanied with the modifier "first woman." She did not hesitate to criticize me when she found it necessary. When I was elected president, my wife went to see her first to deliver the news; however, Madam Lee was already too sick to recognize my wife. She used to say that she would build the Korea Legal Aid Center for Family Relations for dispersed families when the day of reunification came. Unfortunately, she died without ever revisiting her home in the North. Her grand life's traces will not be erased from this land. I think she is now happy in heaven and reunited with her husband Dr. Jeong Il-hyeong.

On December 21, I met the famous actor Anthony Quinn, who was holding an exhibition of sculptures, prints, and paintings with his sculptor son in Seoul. He looked very young. "You mainly played strong characters," I mused. "Was that your choice? Or were you given only those roles?"

"I was born during the Mexican Revolution," he told me. "I cannot help displaying my strong character. Although I do not agree with the revolution, I sympathize with the revolutionary spirit that we should live for all people."

"Do you love Mexico?" I asked him.

"Yes," he responded. "I want to die in Mexico. In Mexico, when a person dies, people leave him or her on a windy mountaintop. It's an aerial burial. I like that custom. It's dark under the ground."

His thoughts were unusual. He told me that he had been devoted to various religions, like Buddhism, Christianity, and Islam. He also said something interesting about art: "I realized that I was a part of this world and I felt we needed a way to share our thoughts. I believe art is one way."

On December 21, I appointed president of Samsung SDS Namgoong Suek to the minister of information and communication. I had never met him face to face, and did not know him personally, but I appointed him because he was a professional businessman, well-versed in the fields of information and communication. As I handed him the appointment certificate, I said, "Ministry of Information and Communication is a very important department that will decide our national fortune in the twenty-first century. Please take charge of your ministry and lift our country."

Ever since I read Alvin Toffler's *The Third Wave* in prison, it had been my dream to make Korea a powerful country of knowledge and information. I was very shocked and moved by what I read in that book. I thought over and over again about this new world, and began reading other books about relevant topics. Peter Drucker's books were interesting too. The more I read, the more I was amazed by the topic. Prison was a good place to dream.

When I finally became president, I had the opportunity to turn this dream into a reality. I emphasized this in my inauguration speech even in the midst of our financial crisis.

As far as I understand, human beings have undergone five revolutions. The first revolution was the birth of human beings. The second was the introduction of farming about 10,000 years ago. The third was the city civilization that occurred along the Tigris and Euphrates Rivers, the Indus River, and the Yellow River between about 5000 and 6000 years ago. The fourth was the philosophical revolution that occurred in India, Greece, Israel, and China around 2500 years ago around the ideas of scholars like Confucius, Lao Tzu, Mozi, and Xun Kuang in China; religious leaders like Sakyamuni and the Brahman monks in India; philosophers like Thales, Aristotle, Socrates, and Plato in Greece; and prophets like Isaiah, Amos, Haggai, and Jeremiah in Israel. Most modern thoughts originated from them. And the fifth was the Industrial Revolution in the eighteenth century.

The twentieth century was the height of this industrial revolution, but we are now entering an entirely different era. The era where material—money, labor, resources, and land—were at the center of economy is receding. Now we are entering an era where knowledge and information will be at the center of our economy. This is the sixth revolution of the twenty-first century—the revolution of knowledge and information. This is both an enormous challenge and an enormous opportunity for us.

In a society based on knowledge and information, knowledge and information are the source of national wealth. Creative knowledge creates high added value. It is the essence of a nation's competitive ability, and can lift its economy to the top of the heap with a single stroke. Since the 1980s, advanced countries have been rapidly transforming from industrial societies to societies of knowledge, culture, and information. They have controlled the world market with their superior knowledge and technology. A futurologist once warned that "a country without knowledge will disappear." That futurologist is still right. Countries that own creative knowledge and can harness it effectively will lead the twenty-first century. Without this, a country will end up on the road to decline and collapse.

It was with this thought in mind that I advocated for the establishment of a nation based on creative knowledge, during the Independence Day ceremony on August 15, 1998. I wanted to reform Korea and turn it into a country where creativity overflows and information flows freely. For this goal, we selected industries of culture, tourism, information and communication, and design as the first knowledge-intensive industries to be supported and nurtured by the government.

This new era of knowledge and information revolution is a great opportunity for South Korea. Throughout human history, a new winner has been born during every transitional period. The Industrial Revolution in the late eighteenth century gave birth to England as the world superpower. The second Industrial Revolution around heavy industry in the late nineteenth century made Germany and America the superpowers of the world market. It is now time for a new superpower to appear in the twenty-first century.

I believed that Korea had the foundation to lead the new age of knowledge and information. We have excellent human resources based on a high education level, as well as an independent culture that we have maintained for thousands of years. This is why, when I visited America in June the previous year, I made sure to visit Silicon Valley. A professor at Stanford whom I met during my visit said something interesting. "Although the Japanese economy is enormous, the information industry takes up only 15 percent of it. This is the biggest problem in the Japanese economy in the twenty-first century."

That remark provided me with the conviction that Korea should be the powerful country of knowledge and information in the twenty-first century. Where else could you find people as highly educated, cultured, and patriotic as Korea? We fell behind in our participation in the Industrial Revolution because of delays in modernization during the late nineteenth century. That's why we had a very difficult hundred years. We should not have this kind of history ever again. Although we were late to the Industrial Revolution, we can be ahead of the game in the information industry.

I urged Minister Namgoong Suek to lead this new age, and told him that we must set along a path to be *the* information powerhouse, no matter what. Fortunately, he had both capability and drive. I was not disappointed.

The extremely tense year of 1998 was drawing to a close. I couldn't believe that I had made it through what had seemed to be a very long year. I had devoted my entire heart and soul to overcoming the financial crisis. The Korean economy was beginning to recover, though it was far from being secure. Above all, unemployment was now a serious problem. Unresolved political issues, including the constitutional amendment for the parliamentary system, was waiting for me. The next year promised to be very hectic and difficult. I prayed to God that the Korean people and I might overcome this crisis.

On the afternoon of February 5, 1999, I met a master ceramic artist who was active in Japan, Shim Soo-kwan. I awarded him the Silver Crown Culture Medal for his contribution to the cultural interchange between Korea and Japan. I wished that I could have also awarded medals to the souls of Master Shim's ancestors, and the many other ceramic artists who had been kidnapped and taken to Japan 400 years ago. Although Korea had a great tradition of Goryeo celadon porcelains and Joseon white porcelains, we could not successfully develop this tradition in our native land. The Shim Soo-kwan family continued to develop the Korean ceramic art tradition in Japan. Not only this, but they also maintained their Korean name for four centuries so as not to forget their family's roots. As I awarded the medal, I said, "I award this medal in the name of the Korean people. This is not just for you, but for all fourteen generations of your ancestors." Master Shim replied, "I am greatly honored to receive this medal directly from you, Mr. President. I am deeply moved and speechless. I will report to my ancestors upon my return."

I asked Master Shim something I had always wondered about. "What is your opinion about Korean ceramic art and its future?"

"I think the skill level is very high," Master Shim answered. "But people seem to be confused about what they want to make. The reality is that people are making copies of porcelains from the Goryeo and Joseon periods. Korea is the only country in the world where the color of porcelain changed when the dynasty changed. Once the Joseon dynasty ended, it was time to create something new, but that did not happen. I think that this is a task not only for ceramic artists, but also for intellectuals."

"How do you compare the skill level of ceramic art between Japan and Korea?" I queried him further. "Koreans show outstanding manual skills," Master Shim observed. "But Japan is more advanced in using machines and science to complement weaknesses in manual skills."

"How do you see the contemporary skill level in Japan and Korea in comparison to that in Goryeo and Joseon?" I asked. Master Shim answered, "We cannot judge ceramic art according to the skill of making forms. Without the rich mind of an artist who understands his times, the work has no artistic value. Even in Japan, contemporary ceramic art shows great technique, but lacks the ability to sing of his or her times with a rich mind."

"Perhaps the commercialization of ceramic art makes it lose its purity," I mused. Master Shim agreed. "That's right. People are too obsessed with money. I heard that the carpet in front of the Korean porcelains at the Louvre wore out more quickly than the carpet of any other display in the museum. Three times more people gather there than any other exhibit in the museum. They see the work over and over again. Although their skill level might not be very high, the freedom from desire and greed that is embodied in the work fascinates Europeans. I think that's the ultimate level we should strive to achieve."

My conversation with Master Shim made me simultaneously happy and sad. I wondered where the spirit of the ceramic artists of our land had gone while the Korean ceramicists who had been kidnapped and taken to Japan maintained our artistic tradition.

On March 11, 1989, I welcomed 206 graduates from 141 universities nationwide. In the past, this event had been reserved for valedictorians, but I invited students who had overcome difficulties—both physical and financial. This included a blind graduate who came with his guide dog, a seventy-eight-year-old graduate who studied preschool education, and a disabled graduate who passed the state examination for a pharmacist certificate. Their stories were all so moving. Minister of Education Lee Hae-chan told me that he had a hard time fighting back his tears. I told the graduates about my meetings with the indomitable Dr. Stephen Hawking. I also shared with them my thoughts about what constituted a truly successful life. "In our lives," I said, "the goddess of fortune sometimes smiles upon us, but other times she is angry. We should not be scared or give up in the latter case. Only when we overcome such an occasion can we succeed. In the business of our life, we cannot always succeed. We cannot achieve all of our goals or all of our hopes. However, we can all succeed in life. We succeed when we live honestly and for our neighbors. My neighbors are my wife, my parents, my siblings, and the people who live in society together with me. If we serve them and live honestly while cherishing our own lives, then we live a successful life."

On March 17, I held an interparty summit with Grand National Party president Lee Hoi-chang. We agreed on six matters: the materialization of grand politics; the elimination of an artificial reshuffling of the political world and mutual respect between all parties; the quick handling of a political reform act based on agreement between parties; the instatement and operation of an interparty council for overcoming the economic crisis; a transparty discussion on the inter-Korean matter; and an ad hoc interparty summit.

On March 18, I met with representative Confucian scholars of Korea. I thought about the Confucian Joseon society. The Joseon Dynasty was based on loyalty and filial piety; the people shared these values and their society gave birth to competent scholars. These beliefs were overturned when King Sejo usurped power from King Danjong, effectively nullifying the value of loyalty. This was also a great betrayal of filial piety because King Sejong asked his son, Prince Suyang (later King Sejo), to take good care of his nephew King Danjong.

This usurpation of the kingship by King Sejo destroyed both spiritual foundations of the Joseon Dynasty with a single stroke. As soon as King Sejo took power, the elite was divided into two groups—for and against the king. Those who held on to the two basic virtues were all murdered or expelled. Unjust people became powerful and wielded their power arbitrarily. This destruction of Confucian ethics stifled the Joseon court for its remaining 450 years.

As the royalty lost its legitimacy, officials and scholars could not argue about fundamental questions. Instead, they fought over trivial issues like how long one should wear mourning attire following the death of Queen Dowager. These debates had nothing to do with the national fortune or the people's well-being. As their minds were unhealthy, their bodies, too, were weak. Joseon rapidly declined, but it still demanded loyalty and filial piety from its people.

I talked about this incident of power usurpation and the harm it had wrought upon our history with the Confucian scholars. I told them my modern interpretation of the Confucian values of loyalty and filial piety in the hope that Confucianism was open to the modern world. "What is loyalty for?" I pondered. "Often, we think of the state. However, if we think of the state as the object of our loyalty, we could end up like Hitler's Nazis or Japan's militarism. I believe the object of loyalty should be people. In our Constitution, the people hold sovereignty. Therefore, the object of our loyalty should be our wives, our husbands, our children, and our neighbors. All of the people around me are the objects of my loyalty, and they are my king. In the past, the king held the sovereignty, but now the people are the king and the owner. If we want to do loyalty well, we have to do democracy thoroughly.

"Who are the objects of filial piety? Of course, there is no doubt that it is our parents. However, the time when respect is required only of children is gone. It is the relic of the time of agricultural society, the time of the extended family system. For children to behave like children, it is necessary for parents to behave like parents. The relationship between parents and children should be mutually respectful.

"In this era, it is not easy for children to take care of their parents all of the time. Therefore, the state should display filial piety. As a sign of respect for the spirit of filial piety, the state should protect the elderly. It is now time to take care of the elderly through a combination of children's filial piety and the state's social filial piety. It is from this perspective that the People's Government will establish policies and reflect them in the budget."

I, of course, knew that the Confucian scholars who visited me were far more learned about Confucianism than me—to a level that was actually beyond comparison. But I hoped to let them know what I thought about traditional Confucian virtues, and that they would try to keep an open mind about modern interpretations of Confucianism so that Confucian scholars who could lead our people into the future would continue to be born.

Although many religions have developed in Korean society, Confucianism is still the most powerful religion, and the one that fundamentally governs the Korean people's mentality. Basic Confucian ethics are still the foundation of our society. I just hope that this traditional philosophy will intersect with the modern worldview on a higher plane.

Knotting Diplomacy Through the Four Most Powerful Countries of the World (February 1999– June 1999)

It had been a year since my inauguration and Korea's economic index had improved a lot. Our foreign exchange holding, which had been only $3.8 billion, increased to $52 billion—indeed, the largest in our history. The trade deficit, which had been $8.7 billion, turned around to a trade surplus of $39.9 billion. Thanks to the four reforms, banks and corporations regained their competitive ability, and the cozy relationship between politics and economy, government-directed financing, and corruption dwindled considerably. However, business recovery was slow, and there was still quite a way to go to resolve unemployment, reform politics, and stabilize the labor market.

On the evening of February 21, I had a conversation with the people on TV. I explained the government's achievements and shortcomings over the past year, as well as our plans for the future. A female university student in the audience asked me what I would take to a deserted island in the Pacific if I could choose only three things. I told her that I would take "unemployment, corruption, and regional antagonism."

The Korean people's household incomes worried me greatly, indeed. I devoted myself to the creation of jobs, but the unemployment number was not easily reduced. Public officials still took bribes. Some continued to provoke regional antagonism and divided the people.

An electronics storeowner in the audience told me that he still could not feel the effects of economic recovery. I explained to him, "Our economic reality is like an *ondol* (hypocaust) room, where the part of the room near the fuel hole is a little warm, but the part farthest away from it is still cold. When the economy fully improves, the warmth will be felt everywhere." This metaphor of different parts of the room was often used whenever economic recovery was discussed from thereon out.

On March 30, a recall and special election was held for assemblymen and local government heads in the greater Seoul area. Hahn Gwang-ok of the National Congress was elected assemblyman in Guro-eul; Kim Eui-jae of LDA in Siheung, Gyeonggi-do; and Shin Jung-dae of the Grand National Party was elected mayor of Anyang. It so happened that the three major parties won one seat each, and the ruling parties' seats increased to 159. Disputes about election fraud continued for a while. I found it deplorable that our election culture was still in that state. I ordered our party to hurry political reform legislation.

On April 7, a motion to arrest Assemblyman Suh Sang-mok, who had collected illegal election funds for Grand National Party (GNP) candidate Lee Hoi-chang during the 1997 presidential election season, was voted down in the assembly. There were dissident votes within the ruling parties. I was deeply shocked because I wasn't expecting this result, even though my government was a coalition government between two parties. After the public prosecutor's investigation, Assemblyman Suh Sang-mok's central role in the scandal (alongside with Mr. Lee's brother and officials in the National Tax Service) was crystal clear and unforgivable. Nevertheless, the GNP continued to prevent his arrest. People called it the "bulletproof assembly."

According to media analysis, about twenty assemblymen participated in dissident votes. The coalition between the National Congress and LDA revealed a serious crack. Both ruling and opposition parties were afraid of political reform. To me, this incident was a clear statement against political reform, as we could not begin political reform without punishing such a blatant election-related incident of corruption.

I immediately fired the acting president of the National Congress Cho Se-hyung and the leader of the Assembly Hahn Hwa-kap, and appointed vice president of National Congress Kim Young-bae as the new acting president. Our party's assemblymen elected Sonn Se-il as the Assembly leader.

On April 7, the city of Philadelphia announced that they had selected me as the recipient of their Liberty Medal. It was a high honor to receive this medal, which was nicknamed "the second Nobel Prize," and that had been bestowed upon renowned world human rights leaders such as Lech Walesa, Vaclav Havel, and Jimmy Carter. They compared me to Nelson Mandela, and said, "During almost half a century, Kim Dae Jung [*sic*] has been not only a symbol of democratic values in the Republic of Korea, but also a heroic figure in its progress toward democracy. He has won the admiration of his people and of the leaders of all continents."

Egyptian president Muhammad Hosni Mubarak visited Korea for a summit with me on April 9. This marked the first visit of an Egyptian president to South Korea because the nation had maintained a friendly relationship with North Korea. President Mubarak had already visited Pyongyang four times. When Supreme Leader Kim Il-sung was alive the two leaders had considered one another a friend. I asked him to arbiter our relationship with the North, including a possible summit. "We do not have any ill will toward the North," I told him. "We only want reconciliation and cooperation. We are willing to begin a dialogue with the North whenever they want. Please tell them that we want peace." President Mubarak replied that he was actively in favor of our policy of tolerance toward North Korea and that he would deliver our sincere wishes to them.

I had great expectations from President Mubarak's arbitration as he was an influential Middle Eastern leader. As promised, he delivered our wishes to the North. When I think of him, I will always remember his large build and his even larger-mindedness. During an official welcome event in the main yard of the Blue House, the stool for the ceremonial car cracked and broke because of his weight. Although bodyguards rushed to him, alarmed and embarrassed, he simply laughed it off.

Speaking of foreign dignitaries' visits to Korea, Queen Elizabeth II of Britain visited Korea with her husband Prince Philip on March 19, a little before President Mubarak's visit. This was the first English head-of-the-state visit to Korea since the establishment of a diplomatic relationship between the two countries in 1883. I had invited her during the ASEM conference in April the previous year. During the state dinner, I remembered the precious relationship between the two countries. "As the first European country with which Korea established a diplomatic relationship, Great Britain has always extended help and encouragement as a friend and partner at every critical moment in modern Korean history. Ernest T. Bethell, who founded *Taehan maeil sinbo*, spoke for Korean independence in the late nineteenth century; numerous young British men participated in the Korean War; and British technicians sweated alongside the Korean people for the success of Korean economy during the 1970s and 80s. All of these people were benefactors who built the foundation for a friendly relationship between our two countries. I express my sincerest thanks to and admiration for all of them on this occasion.

"The good relationship between the two countries continues. Shakespeare and the Beatles have enriched the intellect and emotions of Korean youth. The first Korean satellite Uribyeol #1 is a symbol of scientific cooperation between Korea and Britain."

I ended my remarks with my wish for the queen and her husband to deeply enjoy Korean culture and the spring in Korea. "Korea is a country that has maintained a history of dignity and pride," I said. "We have developed an independent and creative culture, and overcome numerous national crises. Under the warm April Korean sun, you will meet energetic and proud Koreans. And wherever you go, you will feel our people's love for you."

I still remember Queen Elizabeth II's silvery hair and horn-rimmed glasses. She had a serene and warm smile. Befitting her status as a descendent of the Great British Empire, she was dignified and graceful. In her remarks, she said: "The Korea that I saw today was very different from what English people thought in 1952, when I ascended to the throne. When the Korean War broke out, my father King George VI held the throne. The Armistice Agreement was signed in 1953, six weeks after my coronation. I vividly remember the photos portraying the painful experiences of Koreans.

"As the fiftieth anniversary of the Korean War approaches, we are thinking of the resolute and energetic process with which Koreans have reestablished their shattered country, and developed it into one of the main industrialized countries of the world. Trade between Britain and Korea has increased both ways, and the names of Korean corporations like Hyundai, Samsung, and LG have become household names everywhere in Britain."

The queen visited a venture business that introduced British animation technology. Her business-savvy tour was admirable and enlightening. She also visited Insa-dong, Ewha Womans University, and Midong Elementary School. She visited Hahoe village in Andong on her seventy-third birthday, and had her birthday meal at the Chunghyodang House, the old house of Prime Minister Yu Seong-ryong during the Japanese Invasion (1592–1598). Wherever she went, the Korean people welcomed her. I believe she must have felt the Korean people's warmth toward her. Prince Phillip was full of curiosity, and asked many questions about Korean culture. He had attended the ceremony when Cambridge University changed the name of the building I stayed at during my time there from Pinehurst Lodge to Kim's House.

The media often reported about alleged discrimination in personnel matters and budget concentration under my government. Ignoring my efforts and will, their reports were inaccurate and distorted. When I was briefed about the Busan and Gyeongsang-do area administration, I emphasized that there would not be any discrimination against their regions. "I am not the president of any one region, but of all 48 million Koreans. As president, I think about the fate of the entire nation. I have done nothing under the sun to feel ashamed of. Nevertheless, there are people who are suspicious of my practices.

"I maintain thorough fairness in personnel matters. If you find any discrimination based on region, please do point it out to me and I will right it. But, recently, a newspaper reported that there are currently 152 civil servants in the government above the third rank from the Yeongnam region and 120 from the Honam region. Demonstrated by these numbers, my government is trying very hard to maintain regional balance among important government posts.

"This is true of the budget as well. I gathered all sixteen governors and metropolitan-area mayors in Seoul. Together with the head of the National Budget Administration and the chair of the Planning and Budget Committee, we divided the budget in the way that all governors and mayors could agree on. The result was that 2.6 trillion won was assigned to the Gyeongsang-do province and 1.5 trillion won went to the Jeolla-do province. This was distributed as such because the Gyeongsang-do region was building more new harbors.

"Despite this reality, some people try to stir up regional antagonism. You know very well that I suffered greatly from regional antagonism for many decades. How could I, of all people, do anything that contributes to regional antagonism? If I did, history will punish me.

"Now is time to harmonize. Even after I finish my term and leave this world, I will continue to fight for regional harmony. I will no longer run for the office. I will have nothing to do with presidential or assembly elections. From now on, only history, and not votes, will judge me.

"President Lincoln opposed the Northerners' plight for revenge against Southerners after the American Civil War ended. As a result, Northerners criticized him even more than Southerners. Nevertheless, he embraced the South. He was assassinated after his re-election; however, President Lincoln is still alive in the hearts of Americans. Without his spirit of harmony, America might have been divided into two countries. As the greatest power in the world, the United States we know today would not have existed. A leader's resolute and self-sacrificing decision rescued a country.

"We have to end the evil legacy of regional antagonism during our generation. We have to let future generations live free from the curse of regional antagonism."

People listened carefully to my words, but there were some who would not hesitate to aggravate regional antagonism for their political and personal gains, regardless of how ruinous it was for our country.

After receiving a report on the Gyeongsangbuk-do administration on May 13, I had dinner with leaders of the region, including Governor Lee Eui-geun and former prime minister Shin Hyun-hwak. The dinner was meant to be an opportunity for me to hear about their plan for commemorating President Park Chung-hee's achievements. I promised to support it fully, and the media dubbed it a "historical reconciliation."

On May 24, I launched the second phase of the cabinet under my administration through a sweeping reshuffle that changed eleven cabinet members. This included the appointment of Mr. Kang Bong-kyun to minister of finance and economy, Mr. Lim Dong-won to minister of unification, and Mr. Park Jie-won to minister of culture and tourism. In addition, I appointed heads to three newly established ministry-level offices: the Ministry of Planning and Budget, the Civil Service Commission, and the Government Information Agency. The next day, I appointed new heads to theNIS, National Tax Service, and Special Commission of SMEs as well as new prosecutor general. The same day I also appointed three new chief secretaries to the president in the fields of economy, foreign relations and national defense, and public relations.

I urged the new cabinet members to accomplish a thorough economic reform and build a strong foundation for our economy. I also asked them to take care of the weak. "During the first phase, the cabinet had to take on the rather tough task of focusing on security and reform. During this second phase, we are facing the important task of completing reform by ensuring sustainability. If the first phase was the hardware, the second phase is the software. At the same time, we have to make it our task to build a productive welfare system that will prevent those people in the lower- and middle-class brackets who are currently suffering from the reform from collapsing."

As I had already visited America, China, and Japan—three out of the four great powers—I next made a state visit to Russia toward the end of May. I had had a strong relationship with Russia, having visited it four times as an opposition party politician and as the president of the Asia Pacific Peace Foundation. It was also in Russia that I received a regular doctorate degree—not an honorary one—as a mere high school graduate.

I landed in the Vnukovo International Airport in Moscow, the official airport for state visitors, on May 27. Prime Minister Sergei Stepashin and his entourage welcomed us at the airport and I went to the Kremlin to settle in. It just so happened that I was there for the bicentennial commemoration of Russian poet Alexander Pushkin's birth.

I first met with Koreans in Russia, who were known as Goryeoin. Koreans began migrating to Russia in 1863 (during the fourteenth year of King Cheoljong's reign). In the early stages of this migration, most

Koreans went to Russia to farm, but during the colonial period many inde-pendence fighters had fled to Russia for exile. In 1937, they were all forced to move to Central Asia. About 100,000 Koreans lost their lives in this process, and those who survived it had to go through indescribable pain. Although they suffered through difficult and sorrowful lives, they over-came adversities like the descendants of independence fighters they were. Today there are about 500,000 Koreans living in Russia and the CIS (Commonwealth of Independent States). I wanted to visit them to com-fort them.

Korean Association President Cho Wasily said in his welcoming remarks: "We third- and fourth-generation Koreans in Russia think of Korea as our homeland. Our ancestors—our grandfathers who fought against Japanese oppression and brutality, while living in the Far East—handed down their love for Korea to us so that we would not forget it. But it breaks our heart that Korea is divided into two countries."

While living in hardship in a faraway land, Koreans were worried about their divided homeland and scolded us for this endless state of division. The spirit of the independence fighters remained in their hearts. I felt very sorry about this. When would we dance together in a unified country?

I had a summit meeting with President Boris Yeltsin. President Yeltsin gladly supported our tolerance policy toward North Korea; this support was evident in our joint statement: "We appreciate the South Korean gov-ernment's effort to ease tension and build permanent peace in the Korean Peninsula through positive measures, and support Kim Dae-jung govern-ment's policy of promoting inter-Korean contact and productive dialogue, which will solidify peace and stability in the entire region."

With this, the sun shone on the formerly cloudy relationship between South Korea and Russia. The damage from the mutual expulsion of diplo-mats from Russia and South Korea was resolved as well. During the state dinner at St. Catherine Hall in the Kremlin, President Yeltsin said: "I wel-come you to the Kremlin in Moscow, the heart of Russia. There is a Korean saying, 'A good neighbor is better than a distant relative.' Korea and Russia are not only geographically close and have a shared historical fate, but we are also related through our will to secure democratic values, uni-versal peace, and prosperity."

I knew very well about President Yeltsin's passion and courage for democracy. In 1991, when the conservative hardliners staged a coup d'état because they were dissatisfied with the democratization of the country, he immediately came forward to fight against them, appealing to the people for their participation in resistance. He climbed the coup d'état troops' tank and used his body to block its progress. The image of him waving his fist from atop a tank was deeply etched in the brains of people all over the world. I remembered this image of him as the hero of the democratization movement in my remarks: "I still vividly remember President Yeltsin's image as he stood up against the reactionary forces who were trying to turn the tide of change in 1991. He looked like a guardian angel for democracy in the image of him making a speech from the top of a tank. As someone who has devoted his entire life to the achievement of democracy against the oppression of freedom and human rights and had survived many life-or-death moments, I am deeply moved by his actions and feel a comradely love toward him."

I visited President Yeltsin during the time when the world news media was reporting their theories about the leader's poor health. When I saw him, I found him to be a man of broad-mindedness—as broad as his large-framed body. Although his choice of words sometimes sounded rather exaggerated, they also conveyed sincerity. He was also a very affectionate person. He did not eat much, perhaps because he wasn't feeling too well, but he held his seat at dinner. I was worried about his health. When we parted, he gave me a big hug and said, "Let's meet in Korea again."

I gave a lecture at Moscow State University. When I entered the hall, the voices of the university choir rang resoundingly throughout the room. They were singing the World Students Song. Although I had always been welcomed at Moscow State University, this was on quite a different scale. The moderator introduced me as the honorary professor of Moscow State University and president of Korea Kim Dae-jung.

In my remarks I said, "I admire and love Russia a great deal. I am deeply impressed by the remarkable reform Peter the Great achieved during the seventeenth and eighteenth centuries. I believe there are not too many examples of leaders like him, who overcame all obstacles through bold reform.

"During my long stay in prison, I had a chance to read Russian literature broadly. I read many Russian classics, including Pushkin, Lermontov, Tolstoy, Dostoevsky, and Turgenev. I also enjoyed reading Solzhenitsyn and Sakharov. Reading their works, I could not help but admire the power and creativity of those Russian people, who produced such great literature. Russian literature's influence on me is immeasurable. I even think that it was worth spending time in prison because I was able to read them.

"I am also deeply moved by the courage and spirit of sacrifice that we see in modern Russian history. When Napoleon conquered Europe, Russia defeated him. Without the sacrifice of the Russian people who waged an indomitable fight against Hitler, the course of world history might have been different. In this respect, I believe all the people of the world are indebted greatly to Russia.

"Russia is great not just because of its past. In the present, as well, Russia is one of the most influential countries in the world. Russia is a country that owns outstanding science and technology, as well as the richest resources in the world. Supported by them, Russia has infinite potential that guarantees its bright future."

When my speech was over, the university choir gave me the gift of singing "Seonguja." This Korean song is widely loved and associated with our people's resistance against Japanese colonialism and the democratization movement of the 1970s and 1980s.

I watched a spectacular ballet performance at the Bolshoi Theatre. I was even more impressed by the audience's response than by the performance itself. It seemed that their enthusiasm enabled the best performance imaginable. Art is not just about the performers, but also about those who appreciate it.

After the four-day visit to Russia, I set off for Mongolia. My visit was Korea's first state visit to Mongolia. I landed at the Chinggis Khaan International Airport in Ulaanbaatar on May 30. The afternoon sun was clear and the wind was rather gusty. Although the wind was cold, it did not feel chilling—rather, it was soft and clean. On my way to the Genghis Khan Hotel, I saw endless plains with the light green colors of spring scattered here and there.

After looking at the man-made beauty of Russia like the Kremlin Palace and various cathedrals, the endlessly extending plains of Mongolia made me feel as if I had traveled through time. The country appeared mysterious to me. I had always wanted to visit Mongolia and meet the people who looked the most like Koreans. It would be wonderful to confirm the sense of historical and racial closeness between Mongolians and Koreans. I also wanted to tread upon the land of the nomads who had built a great empire. I felt as if I might hear the sound of racing horse hooves. As I looked at the streets of Mongolia, I saw that these people did, indeed, look exactly like Koreans.

I had a summit meeting with President Natsagiin Bagabandi during which I explained my tolerance policy toward North Korea and President

Natsagiin Bagabandi expressed his warm support of it. Mongolia had continued to maintain a very close diplomatic relationship with North Korea since their establishment of a diplomatic relationship in 1948. I hoped that Mongolia would exert its influence on North Korea as a friend nation of half a century. President Natsagiin Bagabandi seemed to immediately understand my intentions.

During the state dinner, I enjoyed a prolonged conversation with President Natsagiin Bagabandi and the first lady. Both of them knew a lot about Korea, and their daughter had obtained a master's degree in international economics at a Korean university. There was so much I wanted to know about Mongolia, so I asked many questions of President Natsagiin Bagabandi.

"I know that there have been interchanges between Mongolia and Korea on the elite level," I began. "The queen of the last emperor of the Yuan dynasty was a Korean prince, and five or six Korean kings married Mongolian princesses. Also, the Yuan-Korean coalition troops attempted to conquer Japan twice."

"The conquest failed both times due to storms," President Natsagiin Bagabandi told me. "The Japanese call that storm *kamikaze*, or 'divine wind.'"

"You have great knowledge of history," I said to him. "The Mongolian troops were strong on land, but weak in the sea. For example, when Mongolians invaded Korea, the Korean king and his retainers evacuated to the Island Ganghwado, which was only a few thousand kilometers away from land."

In response, President Natsagiin Bagabandi said, "I heard that when the Mongolian troops conquered Europe and reached the sea during Genghis Khan's time, they could not go any further. So, they said that they had arrived at the end of the world and returned. Mongolian troops were, indeed, strong on land, but weak on the sea."

"How many Mongolian troops were there then?" I asked.

"Historians argue that they were about five million," President Natsagiin Bagabandi replied.

"At any rate," I continued, "it was because of the Mongolian Invasion that the *Palman Daejanggyeong* (Tripitaka Koreana), which was designated as a UNESCO Memory of the World, was created in Korea. Also, after the failed attempt to conquer Japan, the Yuan dynasty created a large-scale pastureland in Jejudo Island to prepare for Japanese retaliation. Jejudo Island has now become a world famous tourist destination."

I made a speech at the Mongolian National Assembly—this marked a first for the head of a foreign nation. "You and I and all Mongolians and

Koreans were born with a Mongolian spot. Mongolian children's games like *jeginori* (a kicking shuttlecock game), *gongginori* (a game of picking up five stones), and cat's cradle are all Korean children's traditional games as well. Also, your Alan Gua myth (a foundation myth very similar to the Goguryeo foundation myth in Korea) and your ability to sing the Korean traditional folksong "Arirang" just as tastefully as Koreans indicates a close affinity between us. How can all Koreans, including myself, not feel a strong sense of solidarity toward Mongolians? I visit Mongolia for the first time as the president of Korea in order to enhance our two nations' cooperation, based on the historical and emotional sense of solidarity.

"I firmly believe that Mongolia is on its way to prosperity and development. Some say that world history exists only thanks to Mongolians. Mongolian strength and mobility created the Age of Genghis Khan. Some also recognize that Mongolians founded the first international communication network no less than seven hundred years before the internet. This means that Mongolians are equipped with a sense of communication that is primed for the information age of the twenty-first century. I know very well that Mongolia has been continuously exploring ways to change and develop. Mongolia has responded excellently to the historical challenges of a rapidly-changing world."

A day before my return home, I had a gathering with reporters who accompanied me on my trip. I told them my evaluation of my visit's achievements as follows: "This trip concludes my tour of four powerful countries—America, Japan, China, and Russia—that I began in June last year. A very close partnership with all four neighboring countries has been formed. This visit created friendship and amity, which official documents confirm. Also, all four countries expressed their support for our tolerance policy toward North Korea. During this trip, we confirmed that Russia also very strongly supports it. I believe this successful completion of diplomacy with four powerful countries greatly enhanced our international stature, and it contributed greatly to national security as well. At the same time, we gained great power in the advancement of our relationship with North Korea. All this is our national fortune, and I believe that I could achieve these results thanks to the support of the Korean people."

It took me a year and four months as the president of South Korea to accomplish this diplomatic task. However, to me, who had argued for guaranteeing peace in the Korean Peninsula by establishing a diplomatic relationship with the four powerful countries during my 1971 presidential election campaign, this was the first substantial step toward a goal I had set twenty-eight years ago.

Meanwhile, Korean society was in turmoil due to the Clothing Lobby Scandal. While I was working hard to enhance the international status of Korea abroad, the domestic media was busy digging up and reporting all kinds of allegations against my administration. Articles about my diplomatic efforts were confined to a tiny corner of the newspapers.

It was a very weird incident. When a certain *chaebol* group president was arrested for investigation about a year ago, his wife allegedly gave clothes to high government officials' wives as a way of lobbying for her husband. I had been briefed about it, but the investigation did not turn up any evidence. It seemed like nothing more than a rumor.

However, according to the allegations, many wives of high officials, including the wife of Minister of Justice Kim Tae-joung (who had served as prosecutor general the previous year), were involved in it. While I was still on my trip, I had to think long and hard about how to handle this matter of one of my cabinet members being morally injured. During the press conference after my return, I was, as expected, asked about this incident. I began by apologizing for the first scandal my administration had faced. "I sincerely apologize that one of the leaders of our government caused the Korean people concern," I said. "In order to prevent an incident like this from happening again, I had newly appointed high officials' wives attend the appointment ceremony and cautioned them myself. Nevertheless, one or two of them might not have been thoughtful enough, and I am very pained and would like to say I'm sorry to the Korean people.

"However, I am firm in my approach about this matter. I will handle it transparently, as though Koreans were watching it happen through a window. I will take action against the people responsible, regardless of their status or closeness to me. The matter of the Ministry of Justice will be decided according to the results of an investigation. If his wife did wrong, then he will have to take responsibility."

In the end, this matter became politicized and a special prosecutor had to be introduced. Even after this, the tedious process of accusation and response continued, and my administration received a thousand cuts.

A very weird incident occurred once again on June 7, when the drunken chief of the Department of Public Security at the Supreme Prosecutor's Office talked to journalists at random in his office. He said that the Prosecutor General's Office had instigated the 1998 strike at the Korean Mint Corporation. Although he later retracted this statement explaining that it had been a confused drunken remark, it was of no use. The incident instantly became a scandal. I was extremely surprised by this turn of events, and ordered a thorough investigation of the matter.

I believe people became extremely angry about these incidents because of the sense of deprivation and loss that the Korean middle class had been feeling since the Asian financial crisis. To think that the wives of high officials were receiving dresses as bribes while the people were suffering from the restructuring of the Korean economy, or that the public security office was instigating a strike while workers were being driven out of their workplaces!

I fired Minister of Justice Kim Tae-joung for his irresponsibility the next day and appointed Attorney Kim Jung-kil to the post.

Not a Naïve and Weak Government (June 1999–September 1999)

On June 9, I attended the Toji Cultural Center opening ceremony in honor of novelist Park Kyung-Ree's epic novel *Toji* (The Land) with my wife. Although I hadn't met the author many times, I read the novel and was deeply moved by the superb depiction of the vitality and persistence of our ancestors and, specifically, her portrayal of the Korean emotion of *han*.

Madam Park's opening remarks were significant. "Science is accompanied by disasters, and nature has its own disasters," she spoke. "I believe that it is culture that finds the balance between the two, builds the best road, and creates the framework and basis for our lives. These days, however, the essence of that culture has disappeared, and 'culture' remains only as a word and serves as the maid of consumer goods. How can we bring culture back to its essential and proper place? This cannot be done without the awareness and devotion of intellectuals. Mr. President and the First Lady are visiting us today. This is a very significant and encouraging occasion."

The old novelist's sincere concern was clear.

I hoped that the Toji Cultural Center would become a place where the future of humanity was created at the turn of the century, during a time when people were worried about all of the crises in life. I said in my congratulatory remarks: "Madam Park Kyung-Ree established an indelible monument by writing *Toji*, a novel of eight million characters that was written between 1969 and 1994.

"I still vividly remember how I cried over the beautiful love scene where the character Yong-yi helplessly witnesses his lover Wol-seon die on his lap. I also thought about the essence of Korean *han* in the dialogue between them, when Yong-yi asks Wol-seon, 'You don't have remaining *han*?' and Wol-seon answers, 'No, I don't.' Wol-seon felt happiness because of her union with her lover Yong-yi, rather than feeling sadness because of her own impending death.

"Like in this story, *han* does not allow us to give up until we achieve our goal. We can also understand the Korean people's *han* about Korean independence in *Toji* in the same way.

"I am particularly impressed by the passion and persistence it took Madam Park to devote twenty-five long years to writing only one novel. I feel her *han* here as well."

Madam Park exited this world in May 2008, leaving her novel *Toji* and the Toji Cultural Center behind. I visited the mortuary, burned incense, and dedicated flowers to her. I expressed my condolences to Madam Park's daughter and the Director of the Toji Cultural Center Kim Yeong-ju and her husband and poet Kim Chi-ha. "The deceased was Korean people's pride," I said. "As one of her readers, I am deeply saddened by this loss."

A battle broke out in the West Sea on the morning of June 15 when there was a shootout between our Navy warships and a North Korean coastal patrol boat. The North attacked first, and the South responded with gunfire. A North Korean torpedo boat sank and a coastal patrol boat was greatly damaged. Four other patrol boats were damaged and retreated as well.

Scores of North Koreans died or were wounded, but the damage to our side was minimal. On that day, our Navy executed one of my government's three principles toward North Korea: We will not allow any sort of armed provocation from the North.

Before this shootout, suspicious actions had been occurring on the sea in front of Yeonpyeongdo Island. Every year, North Korean fishing boats would come below the NLL to catch blue crabs; South Korea's high-speed navy speed boats would drive them back out. However, that year, about five or six North Korean coastal patrol boats came down to protect their fishing boats. They continued to come down every day since June 4, and did not budge even when our coastal patrol boats approached.

All attention was drawn to the sea in front of Yeonpyeongdo Island. It was hard to understand why North Koreans continued to provoke us after we had spent so much time explaining our engagement policy, and when a deputy minister-level inter-Korean talk was scheduled for June 21 in Beijing. My concern over the matter kept me awake at night. *What is the goal of this reckless demonstration?* I wondered. *Are there perhaps some internal struggles between the hardliners and the moderates?*

It was on one of those sleepless nights that I got a phone call from Minister of National Defense Cho Seong-tae. He reported that he was going to forcefully respond to their provocation. I gave him four strategic guidelines. "First, be sure to secure the NLL; second, do not attack first; third, if they attack first, punish them forcefully; and, fourth, even if there is a shootout, make sure not to expand it."

I ordered the NSC to fine-tune our response to North Korean provocation. Minister Cho proposed that we use large warships to push North Korean vessels out of the NLL, and the NSC standing committee agreed. After I had provided the guidelines, I left concrete decisions to the military. I knew that I was not very knowledgeable about military strategy, and I did not want to ruin what had to be an airtight military operation with my ignorant meddling. I was worried.

Ignoring our continued warnings, the North Korean vessels and fishing boats invaded the NLL again on June 15. Around 9:30 a.m., our vessels began to push North Korean vessels and boats north of the NLL. As North Koreans were being pushed back in this competition of physical strength, they began to shoot. Our vessels immediately responded with shots, and a fierce battle broke out. The shooting stopped fourteen minutes later, but more than thirty people from the North died.

South Korean soldiers stood firm. The media dubbed it the Yeonpyeong Naval Battle. Despite our victory, the incident was truly regrettable. Unfortunately, another battle broke out again on the same sea in 2002. After this, the battle in June 1999 began to be called the first Yeonpyeong Naval Battle and the 2002 battle the Second Yeonpyeong Naval Battle. Former US Ambassador to Korea Donald Gregg later commented that no previous Korean regime had responded to North Korean provocations with military force like my administration had.

This first Yeonpyeong Naval Battle showed both domestically and abroad that the Sunshine Policy was neither a naïve idea nor an appeasement policy. As I had often emphasized, the Sunshine Policy could be successful only when it was supported by strong power. As this battle was going on, South Korean tourists were climbing Mt. Kumgang in the North. I was worried about their safety.

Minister of Unification Lim Dong-won called me and said, "I will allow the cruise to Mt. Kumgang today. As Minister of Unification, I will take full responsibility for the result." I was relieved to hear his opinion, which meant that North Korea did not mean to worsen the situation. The Mt. Kumgang cruise left as planned, and all passengers got on board without showing any signs of worry. The Korean people trusted my administration and me, and assumed the role of sunshine for the tolerance policy toward North Korea. North Korea did not continue its provocation, and I was relieved.

The day after the battle, I called an emergency presidential meeting between the ruling and opposition parties. I felt that, in order to reassure the Korean people, both parties should form a united front during this national emergency. Speaker of the Assembly Pak Chun-gyu, President of the Grand National Party Lee Hoi-chang, Acting President of the Democratic Party Kim Young-bae, President of LDA Park Tae-joon, and Minister of National Defense Cho Seong-tae attended the meeting. Mr. Lee Hoi-chang argued that we should reconsider the Sunshine Policy. I explained again why it was necessary in this situation. "The tolerance policy toward North Korea should be based on a firm security system," I replied. "The four powerful countries, as well as the entire world, support it. Although the North Korean government is now hesitating, worried that we're trying to take off their coat, our position is that the sunshine should be sent mutually.

"There are both positive and negative elements to the process of pursuing the Sunshine Policy. Negative circumstances include the mystery over North Korea's nuclear missile development, their missile tests, and the recent incident in the Western Sea. Positive circumstances include the inter-Korean military talks and the Mt. Kumgang tour that began last year. We have to appreciate these positive changes."

On June 21, North Koreans detained a South Korean Mt. Kumgang tourist. They accused her of being a spy for speaking to a North Korean guide. It was a serious situation. I ordered that the tour be stopped so that we could properly handle the incident. I decided that we would send them neither the cruise ship nor money unless they quickly returned the detained tourist. Fortunately, they released her four days later. I ordered that the relevant office establish measures to prevent such an incident from happening again. Although North Korean authorities urged us to resume the tour quickly, it had to stop until we could come up with suitable measures. In the end, the cruise ship had to moor in the harbor for forty-five days.

Honoring the demands from civic organizations, we established the Office of Chief Secretary for Civil Affairs at the Blue House. I appointed Professor Kim Sung-jae as chief secretary. "Please be among people, listen to their voices, and discuss matters with them," I urged him.

On the early morning of June 30, twenty-three people, including nineteen children, died in a fire at the Sea Land Youth Training Camp in Hwaseong, Gyeonggi-do. It was a disaster that should have never happened. There were many problems with both the facility and its operation. I visited the joint memorial altar, established inside of the Gangdong Education Office, with my wife. Families were sobbing. I looked at the children's pictures for a long time and held the families' hands one after another. My wife hugged them and wiped tears from her eyes. I was so utterly appalled at this death of innocent children, who must have trusted the adults who were in charge of the camp. As their president, I felt responsible. "I cannot express how appalling I find this tragedy," I said sorrowfully. "This was a manmade disaster. The building, fire station, and kindergarten management were all responsible. I will make sure that a disaster like this never happens again." I could not find any words to alleviate the families' pain. What words can soothe the pain of a parent who has lost their child?

On July 2, I went on a five-night, six-day tour of America and Canada. I was going to the US upon President Bill Clinton's invitation, and to Canada upon Governor General Romeo LeBlanc's invitation. My tight schedule included the Liberty Medal award ceremony in Philadelphia.

Just three hours after my arrival in America, I met President Clinton at the White House for the third time since my inauguration. Although this was a working visit, the US offered the official guesthouse for accommodations. In the meeting, President Clinton and I agreed that we would consistently pursue the engagement policy with North Korea based on firm national security. We also agreed that we would jointly and firmly respond to North Korean provocation, as we had during the recent incident in the West Sea. President Clinton congratulated me on the recovery of the Korean economy, saying that he sincerely admired my leadership. I felt very flattered, especially because he said it was not diplomatic rhetoric.

President Clinton often held my hands. He also complimented my receipt of the Liberty Medal. "President Kim deserves the medal more than anybody else, and we're very happy for you," he said.

I went to Philadelphia to receive the medal. When I landed, I found that US Ambassador to Italy Thomas M. Foglietta was included in the welcoming party. We hugged each other warmly. He had been my comrade during my struggle for Korean democracy during my exile in America in the 1980s. When I returned home in 1985, the then-assemblyman accompanied me to act as a human shield, despite the Chun Doo-hwan regime's opposition. He had flown in from Italy just to see me.

I first visited the Philip Jaisohn Memorial House, where Dr. Seo Jae-pil had lived while working for Korean independence in the US. It was a two-story wooden house in a secluded forest area. His personal effects were on display. I wrote "A pioneer lives forever" in the guest book, and signed my name and title. When I raised my head, I saw that Dr. Seo was looking out at me from a picture hanging in the room. I bowed to the hero of my youth.

The medal ceremony was held in the outdoor yard at Independence Hall on July 4. It was the same day that the Declaration of Independence was adopted, and at the same sacred place where it was declared and the Liberty Bell is kept. The State of Pennsylvania declared July 3 Kim Dae-jung Day, and the City of Philadelphia declared July 4 the same.

Despite the fact that it was a very hot day, more than 3000 people attended the ceremony. It began with a celebratory march by the Pennsylvania Honor Guard. After the opening remarks, our two countries' national anthems were played. Three Korean students sang the Korean anthem, which was followed by a celebratory Air Force fly-over. The mayor of Philadelphia Edward Rendell hung the medal, upon which the Liberty Bell was carved, around my neck. During the ceremony, Korean students from America sang "Geuriun Kumgangsansan" (How I Miss Mt. Kumgang), and I felt hot tears under my eyelids.

I prefaced my acceptance speech by saying that I would only speak briefly because of the heat. "It gives me profound honor and joy to be awarded the prestige and distinction of the Liberty Medal on this day, the 223rd anniversary of Independence Day, in this city, the place where the Declaration of Independence and the Constitution of the United States were written ...

"I have had a life-long pilgrimage toward freedom. Along the journey, certain forces have sustained me.

"The first is Christ, whom I believe in. He gave his life upon the Holy Cross for the rights of the oppressed people of Israel. He taught us how to be free in spirit.

"He also told us to bear the cross as he had, if we wished to be his disciples. The cross was my training toward freedom.

"The second is my understanding of history. Throughout history, wherever in the world, those who fought for liberty and justice ultimately prevailed. Too many times, the reality was grim. But I was always certain that history would make me a winner.

"The third is my view of life. I have believed that success and happiness in life lie not in what one becomes, but in how one lives. I believe in living forthright according to my conscience. 'Conscience in action' is my motto in life.

"The fourth has been the support of my wife and children. They have been my companions in the pilgrimage toward freedom.

"I still remember an experience I had in 1980. I had been sentenced to death. I was waiting in the army prison for execution day. My wife and children came to visit me. We all prayed to God in tears. We cried together.

"But no one in my family told me to compromise with the military dictatorship. They all encouraged me to keep my faith in God, and in freedom."

At this point I introduced my wife and my son Hong Gul to the audience as they applauded. Despite the extremely hot weather, they listened to my speech attentively; I could not keep my promise to make only a brief speech. I was sorry, but I also wanted to talk about my passion for liberty.

"I know that there is no such thing as perfect liberty," I continued. "I know that our mission as humankind lies in the constant endeavor toward the perfection of liberty.

"The history of the human race is evolving in the direction of greater liberty. The future of mankind belongs to liberty. When we side with liberty, we are with God, who implanted the love of liberty in all of us. When we side with liberty, we enhance our own dignity.

"Freedom is like air—difficult to appreciate when you are living in it. I am one of those people who well appreciate the value of freedom. And so, today, I am awarded the Liberty Medal.

"As I accept the honor, I am determined to become an honoree you can be proud of for a long time to come. I wish to be remembered as 'a man dedicated to liberty.'"

My speech was followed by a blessing from the cardinal, a gospel choir, and a military band.

When the ceremony was over, we moved to the Carpenter's Hall at the Four Seasons Hotel, where I stayed for a reception. There, I said, "I hope that, together with my receipt of the Liberty Medal, today's American Independence celebration is also a celebration of the victory of human rights in Asian countries like Korea. I believe that selecting me as the Liberty Medal winner in this last year of the twentieth century indicates your appreciation of the growth of Korean liberty and human rights, as well as your expectation that all regions of the world will be filled with liberty and human rights in the twenty-first century."

I flew to Ottawa, Canada, on July 4 for a two-night, three-day state visit. After checking in at the Governor General's residence, I attended a reception for Korean Canadians at the Chateau Laurier Hotel.

The next day, I met with Prime Minister Jean Chrétien and we agreed that we would expand the special partnership between our two countries that had been agreed upon at a summit meeting in 1993. I also explained the Sunshine Policy to him in the context of the state of affairs around the Korean Peninsula. He readily agreed with me.

I interviewed Dr. Frank W. Schofield's descendants at the state dinner. Dr. Schofield was a Canadian who supported Korea's March 1 Anti-Japanese Movement in 1919, and let the international society know about the atrocities the Japanese colonial government had committed in Je-am-ri and other places at that time. He was expelled from Korea by the Japanese governor general and returned to Korea again in 1955 to teach at Severance Medical School. He also established an orphanage to take care of the Korean War orphans. Dr. Schofield died in Seoul at the age of 81 in 1970. He was one of the rare foreigners who were buried in the Korean National Cemetery. I remembered his special love for Korea and my relationship with him with his daughter-in-law Catherine and his granddaughter and grandson. "Dr. Schofield condemned military dictatorship in Korea even while he was living in a small apartment and suffering from illness," I told them. "I still vividly remember my visit with him while he supported the democracy movement in Korea."

On July 7, I disembarked the plane in Seoul with the Liberty Medal around my neck. I greeted the Korean people by saying, "I received this medal not just because of my efforts for human rights and democracy, but also on behalf of the Korean people, who have fought for human rights and democracy in our nation."

Another problem erupted in the coalition government. While I was in Canada, Prime Minister Kim Jong-pil and National Congress Acting

President Kim Young-bae disagreed about appointing a special prosecutor to deal with the Clothing Lobby Scandal and the Strike Instigation Allegation. Before my trip, I had left the matter entirely up to Prime Minister Kim. Prime Minister Kim wanted to accept the special prosecutor appointment, but Mr. Kim Young-bae disagreed, arguing that his party would not support it. Prime Minister Kim was very angry about this, and suggested that he would break up the coalition. He also pressured me to replace the National Congress acting president because of this matter.

After a lot of thought, I realized that I had no choice but to change the National Congress party leadership because I could not break up the coalition government. I read in the news that former acting president Kim Young-bae was completely distraught. I felt very sorry for him and the fact that he served as acting president for only three months. He had taken the straight road of the opposition for the forty years since the May 16 military coup d'état, despite the incredible hardships he had endured because of it. For such a democracy fighter to be driven out by the prime minister who led the May 16 coup d'état! He must have been so frustrated, but I really had no other choice.

I thought hard about the appointment for the new party leadership during my vacation at Cheongnamdae. After spending an extra day there to finalize my decision, I announced the new party leadership members, which included Mr. Lee Man-sup for acting president and Mr. Hahn Hwa-kap for Secretary General.

On August 2, I invited 190 members of the Indonghoe who had worked with me throughout my long and difficult political career to express my thanks to them. I did not do anything for them personally, but they had, nonetheless, continued to support me. That day too, I also did not have any special gifts to give to them; instead, I decided to repay their support by working hard myself. In my speech I said: "My dear comrades who shared hardships with me in the past! Some of you became national assemblymen, others work in my government, and still others do not work in any of those capacities. It's not my prerogative to offer you some sort of official position, and the Korean people will not forgive us if we do such a thing. However, we all own the precious treasure of pride that we have overcome dictatorship through persistent fights and that we successfully established a democratic government. We all have this pride without exception. What other more honorable asset could there be?

"I hope that you'll cherish this pride. I will never forget you, who were beside me when I shed tears, although I can't see you often. I hope that you will continue to do your best to bless this country with freedom, justice, prosperity, and peace until the day you die. Our task is not over just because we established a democratic government. It is over only when this democratic government can establish Korea as a world-class country during the twenty-first century.

"Even if the sky breaks in half, I still will not repeat our past leaders' wrongs, such as acting anti- or semi-democratically, committing corruption and injustice, concentrating wealth to a small minority, and taking advantage of inter-Korean conflict for political gain. I will become a president who lays down the foundation for a world-class country."

On August 6, I first expressed my personal objection to building the Donggang Dam in Yeongwol during an interview with broadcasting stations in the Gangwon-do province. "I think that the government should not do what many environmental protectionists worry about," I said.

There had been a lot of debates about this dam. The Donggang River begins in Jeongseon, Gangwon-do, and flows down to Yeongwol for 51 kilometers around precipitous cliffs. It is a habitat that hosts rare species of animals and plants, so there was a need to protect the natural environment. However, it was also true that people around Seoul were suffering from a water shortage. There were pros and cons for both arguments. However, since the primary purpose of the proposed dam was to supply drinking water to the Seoul area, I believed that we could find another solution.

The Ministry of Construction and Transportation reached a similar conclusion. However, the government could not simply accept the civic organizations' demands without scientifically verifying the validity of their argument. I ordered that the officers start again from scratch, after organizing a joint civilian and governmental inspection team. The officers who had pursued this project must have felt frustrated, but I thought it was time to reset the government's attitude toward nature.

We human beings have committed too many crimes against all things on earth. If we open our eyes, we cannot avoid seeing the tears of nature and hearing the painful screams of all natural beings. All of this is our doing. I had emphasized this very point at cabinet meetings many times. It is a shame that "the lord of all creation" brings such a scourge to nature.

For example, we are now consuming water too haphazardly. Perhaps because I grew up on an island where water was a rare commodity, it pains me to see water wasted. Although the UN had already designated Korea as having a water shortage, Koreans did not take the problem seriously.

Relevant government offices hadn't come up with specific plans to cope with the situation. No matter how many large dams we would build, the water produced could not meet the desires of an increasing population.

It is said that we just borrow the earth for a while, and then hand it down to our descendants. It is really dangerous for our generation to decide on a large-scale development with long-lasting repercussions. The Ministry of Construction and Transportation concluded that we would have a water shortage of about 2 billion tons by 2011. Nonetheless, continuing to drain underground water without making an effort to save it means that our generation will squander the asset handed down to us from our ancestors.

In our land, the rivers are as deep as the mountains are high. The rivers are our life source, and this is a great blessing. How many countries have a capital like Seoul, with a river as big as the Han River flowing right through it? Whenever I look at the Han River, I marvel and feel grateful. The river is a treasure and water is the source of life. When I look at the powerful river flowing downstream, I feel like being carried away, too.

I am also reminded of Israel, where there was neither a river nor a mountain. When I visited Israel during my stay in England in 1993, I was struck by the barrenness of the land, which was completely different from the Bible's description of it as "the land of milk and honey."

The time when development was the supreme good and talk of environmental matters was considered to be a luxury has passed. We have to realize that the cost of post-development recovery is much higher and that, even then, a complete recovery is impossible. What's more important is reducing the quantity of trash in half, and to double the size of recycling. I hoped that Korea would be on its way to becoming one of the environmental greats, a civilized and advanced country. Regrettably, I still could not completely ignore the voices of the developers. Thankfully, though, the Dongang Dam construction plan was scraped in June 2000.

On August 15, I pardoned and reinstated 2864 people in an effort to open the road to the unity of our nation on the day of liberation. Because former president Kim Young-sam's son was included on the list of those released and his sentence was suspended, the public criticized this as a political decision. People called even the Blue House to protest.

In my statement in honor of the fifty-fourth anniversary of Korean Independence Day, I included many promises: that we would focus on the reform of the *chaebols* and establish the Special Committee for Anti-corruption directly under the president; and that we would adopt a productive welfare policy in order to improve the lives of the middle and lower classes, and enrich the four basic insurances. I also announced my plan to found a new political party. This plan was due to a party discussion that we should be reborn by inviting new talent in order to become a new nationwide party. I said: "I feel deeply about the ruling party's responsibility for our politics' lack of playing a proper role in our society. National Congress, the ruling party, will be reborn to become the party that will instill trust and hope in the Korean people. The new party will emerge as the national party of reform, focusing on the middle and lower class. We'll become the party that focuses on human rights and welfare. We will become a national party that ends regional division. We will become a party that leads the Information Age of the twenty-first century.

"We will invite trustworthy social leaders, professionals from various fields, and energetic young members. By embracing reform-oriented conservative powers and healthy reform powers, we will build a wide-ranging and solid political party. We will actively recruit female leaders and assign 30 percent of the national assembly seats, chosen according to the system of proportional representation, to women."

The opposition parties and some media presented my strong argument for the reform of *chaebols* as being ideologically against a market economy. They also objected to the amendment of National Security Law, although crimes such as non-notification and praise and encouragement were too vaguely defined and could be abused. The conservatives argued that not even a single word of those laws could be changed. The aftereffects of this argument lasted for some time.

On September 1, I invited both second-term Chair Kim Won-ki and third-term Chair Kim Ho-jinof the labor-employer-government tripartite commission and both term members to the Blue House for a dinner to celebrate the launch of the commission's third term. As a president who emphasized the vital role this commission played in our country's fate, I was happy to see the new labor-employer culture settling in in Korea. I expressed my gratitude for their hard work: "The freedom of demonstration, assembly, and strike, which was illegal in the past, is now fully guaranteed. Whoever follows legal procedure can exercise it. While 134,400 teargases were used in 1997, only 3400 were used last year on two occasions. Not a single teargas has been used this year so far.

"Demonstrations and assemblies continue to occur, but they are very orderly. We will guarantee all legal strikes because that is democracy. In the past, because they were all blocked, resistance was illegal. But now, because strikes are all legally guaranteed, people who wage demonstrations and assemblies should perform them in a legal manner.

"The new labor-employer culture should be able to survive global competition in the twenty-first century, a time of the fiercest transformation. This new culture is not beneficial to only one side, but to both sides. Only that kind of culture can last. That is the way to serve both employers and workers."

On the afternoon of September 9, I visited the Yongsan Branch of the National Agricultural Cooperative Federation and Namdaemun Market to look at scenes from ordinary people's everyday lives and to learn how consumer prices were faring in the season of the *chuseok* harvest festival. Both merchants and consumers said that the economy had improved. My wife and I had *sundae* and *tteobokki* in the Meokja *golmok* (eatery alley) of the Namdaemun Market. It had been a long time since we last had street food. My wife, who loves *sundae*, relished the food. Even nicer than the food were the bright faces of the spectators around us. Someone in the crowd shouted, "Be healthy! Hurray for our president!"

"Things are better this year than last year," I shouted back. "It will be even better next year. Please have hope! And have a wonderful *Chuseok*!"

"WITHOUT PRESIDENT KIM, 100,000 MORE WOULD HAVE DIED" (NOVEMBER 1999–DECEMBER 1999)

On September 11, I left Korea for the APEC summit meeting and a state visit to New Zealand. Prime Minister of New Zealand Jenny Shipley welcomed me at the Auckland International Airport. I checked in at the Carleton Hotel and immediately had a summit meeting with Chinese president Jiang Zemin. I congratulated him on the impending transfer of sovereignty of Macau from Portugal. Since the sovereignty of Hong Kong had been transferred to China two years ago, this Macau transfer would mark the complete disappearance of Western colonies from Asia. This was a good thing for both China and Asia.

I also confirmed Chinese cooperation for our tolerance policy with North Korea. I urged China to play an active role in preventing North Korea from shooting missiles. "I thank you for Chinese support of peace in the Korean Peninsula," I told him. "I thank you for encouraging President Kim Yong-nam of the Presidium of the Supreme People's Assembly of North Korea to participate in an inter-Korean dialogue during his visit to China. Since my inauguration, I have continued to maintain the three principles with North Korea. North Korea should engage in neither armed provocation nor missile blasts."

"I will do everything possible to help secure and maintain peace in the Korean Peninsula," President Jiang promised. "I will deter anything that might be harmful to them. I was honest with President Kim Yong-nam about this."

I proposed to President Jiang that we adopt measures in response to the recent bloody incident in East Timor. Although this was not a prearranged agenda item, I felt that Asian leaders should not ignore the atrocious incident. The fact that the Indonesian military broke its government's promise to grant independence to East Timor and massacred a third of the East Timorese population caused me a lot of pain. How could such barbaric brutalities happen at the threshold of the twenty-first century? It was for the sake of peace and democracy in Asia that I had established the Asia Pacific Peace Foundation in 1994. I did not feel that we could simply ignore such an abuse of human rights—my conscience wouldn't allow it.

Before coming to the APEC summit meeting, I had interviewed young Asians who attended the Asia Pacific Democratic Youth Workshop, which the Forum of Democratic Leaders in the Asia-Pacific held annually. There, I told them optimistically, "When we held the first workshop, regime change had not happened in Korea and democracy had not spread throughout Asia. I said then that the power of the Korean people would enable regime change in Korea, and that democracy would spread in Asia as well.

"I believe that those Asian countries that have not yet been democratized will be on the road to democracy soon. In particular, I firmly believe that democratization will progress throughout all of Asia in the early twenty-first century. Democracy is a universal value that humanity craves, it is the road to economic development, and the way to materialize social justice."

That was what I believed. I believed that Asia would become the continent of hope that would assume the task of leading humanity toward the future as it completed the process of democratization.

Sadly, my optimistic vision was betrayed by an incredible tragedy in East Timor right at the turn of the century. I thought that we Asian leaders who gathered for the APEC summit should not ignore this trampling of democratic principle and the dignity of life. The bloody atrocities that occurred in East Timor should have been stopped in the name of humanity's conscience. This is why I said to President Jiang, "I believe we should express our concern in whatever form we can."

Although rather passive in his response at first, after listening to my clear position President Jiang also expressed his wish for a peaceful resolution. Before this meeting with President Jiang, I had a similar conversation about East Timor with Prime Minister of New Zealand Jenny Shipley. In fact, I tried to persuade all of the heads of Asian countries gathered at the meeting, by saying: "People are dying even at this moment. Although APEC is an organization that handles economic cooperation, there will be no point for the APEC if we ignore this problem."

I also discussed this matter with President Clinton and prime minister of Japan Keizo Obuchi at our three-country summit. I told them: "I discussed this matter with the presidents of China and Chile yesterday, and with the King of Brunei and Prime Minister of Singapore today. Although they may have different opinions about how to approach it, they agreed that this was a serious problem that needs to be addressed. If leaders of the Asia Pacific region leave without discussing this situation, then not only we, but also the APEC, cannot avoid becoming a target of condemnation and doubt. I propose that the heads of all countries participating in the APEC meeting request that the Indonesian government takes responsibility for ending these bloody atrocities and ratifying the independence of East Timor, and that UN steps in as necessary."

Prime Minister Obuchi and President Clinton immediately agreed that my proposal was worth considering, and that we discuss the matter in a separate meeting the next day.

Before the close of the APEC summit, the heads of Korea, the US, and Japan issued a statement urging the active involvement of the UN and Indonesian government in establishing independence in East Timor. Indonesian president B. J. Habibie did not participate in this APEC summit meeting, but the Indonesian minister of finance did. I urged him to convince the Indonesian government to come up with a solution for East Timor. Without it, I told him, the APEC itself would issue a statement. He called President Habibie a few times and told him about the atmosphere at the summit. At midnight that night, the Indonesian military ordered the East Timorese militia to check its oppression of residents. They also announced that they would accept UN multinational forces. The light of peace began to shine on an explosive situation. It was a very meaningful and rewarding day.

A few weeks later, Jose Ramos Horta, the exiled spokesman for the East Timorese resistance, visited me at the Blue House. He had explained the urgent crisis a few weeks before. "Two hundred thousand people lost their lives during the three years Indonesia occupied East Timor," he said. "Without you, 100,000 more would have died. When I met President Clinton during the APEC summit, I thanked him for his leadership in resolving the East Timor situation, but he told me to thank you. That is when I heard about your leadership."

In the twenty-five years since the Indonesian occupation of East Timor in 1975, Mr. Jose Ramos Horta had been touring the world to appeal for help in establishing independence. He won the Nobel Peace Prize with Bishop Carlos Belo in 1996 and was later elected president of East Timor.

After the APEC summit meeting, UN multinational forces entered East Timor. The Korean government also decided to send troops to help maintain public safety and to assist with residents. The opposition party fiercely opposed this troop dispatch, citing concerns about the Indonesian government's potential retaliation against Koreans in Indonesia. I remained firm about this matter. As a country that respects human rights and loves peace, Korea had to send our troops to East Timor. It could also be our way of repaying the UN for the support it had provided us during the Korean War, when tens of thousands of UN troops lost their lives while helping us defend our people against communist aggression. Assembly woman Lee Mi-Kyung was the only GNP member who voted for troop dispatch against her party platform.

I continued to mention the East Timor situation at summit meetings with America, Japan, China, and Russia. I also requested other countries' support at international meetings, such as ASEM and APEC.

Finally, in August 2001, East Timor administered an election for a constituent assembly, where the Revolutionary Front for an Independent East Timor, led by Xanana Gusmao, won an overwhelming victory. East Timor achieved complete independence in May 2002, and Gusmao became president. Ramos Horta became Minister of Foreign Affairs. Korea immediately acknowledged its sovereignty, established a diplomatic relationship, and exchanged ambassadors.

Korean Sangnoksu (evergreen) troops changed to peacekeeping forces after a four-month stay as UN multinational forces. They were praised as apostles of peace until their withdrawal in October 2003. In fact, East Timor named the biggest street downtown Korean Friends Street. I am very proud of my people for preventing any further sacrifice in East Timor and for helping the country establish independence.

After the APEC summit meeting, I immediately flew to Wellington, the capital of New Zealand, on an Air Force plane provided by the New Zealand government. I had a summit meeting with the Prime Minister Jenny Shipley on September 15. In this meeting, we agreed to expand the relationship between our two countries to that of partnership. Before the meeting, Prime Minister Jenny Shipley and I exchanged our pride about our countries' respective signature fruits. I told her, "I gave two boxes of Korean pears to Asian country heads at the APEC. Please take interest in Korean pears." She responded by saying, "I enjoy Korean pears. I would like to introduce New Zealand peaches to Korea. We will send you our peaches."

The previous day, we agreed on the Kiwi Alliance. Kiwi is not only a fruit, but also the name of a bird native to New Zealand and considered holy by the indigenous New Zealand tribe, Maori. With this alliance, we could export to the same countries in different seasons and secure common interests.

New Zealand sent troops during the Korean War, and I mentioned my gratitude for this to the prime minister. "While dedicating flowers at the Great War Museum, I remembered the past. New Zealand and Korea are blood alliances."

After my visit to New Zealand, I headed to Australia for a state visit. I had visited Sydney three years before to receive an honorary doctorate from the University of Sydney. Revisiting Australia, I found it as beautiful and bright as ever. On September 16, I attended a dinner with the business community, held by Premier of New South Wales Robert John Carr at the Sidney Convention Center. Premier Carr said in his welcoming remarks: "As President Kim said, we think that knowledge-based enterprise will be the main industry in the twenty-first century, and we are making efforts accordingly. I heard President Kim address the APEC CEO meeting on September 11, and he mentioned that we have to pay attention to the development of new intellectuals in order to nurture new knowledge workers. Invisible knowledge and information have gradually become more important at the threshold of the twenty-first century. Large Korean enterprises like Samsung, Hyundai, and LG are very present in South Wales. While preparing for the next Olympics, we think that we have a lot to learn from Korea, which successfully held the 1988 Seoul Olympics."

I traveled to the nation's capital Canberra and had a summit meeting with Prime Minister John Howard. We agreed to cooperate so that North Korea could advance in the international community through improved relationships with countries in Asia and the Pacific. Prime Minister Howard said that Australia would be contacting North Korea to renew their diplomatic relationship—which had been unilaterally discontinued in 1975—since North Korea had expressed its intention to do so. I responded positively to this move.

I attended the groundbreaking ceremony of the Korean War Memorial in honor of the 17,000 troops Australia had sent to the war. After the first shovel, I said, "This monument is the historical symbol of Australia's friendship with Korea, as well as the blood alliance between the two countries. Koreans will never forget how Australians helped us during the war."

I announced the new appointees for the Chief Justice of the Supreme Court and Chair of the Board of Audit and Inspection positions: Mr. Choi Jong-young and Mr. Lee Jung-nam. My spokesperson Park Joon-Yung said that people would find it interesting that both of them were graduates of commercial high schools, but I had had no idea that was the case. Spokesperson Park also said, "The prime minister is from the Chungcheong province, Chief Justice is from the Gangwon province, the speaker of the Assembly is from Daegu, and the Chair of the Board of Audit and Inspection is from the Gyeonggi province. All regions of our country are represented."

"Well, Honam is the only one missing," my wife commented.

"The president is from Honam, you know," I reminded her with a smile.

Two days after my return home, I invited the former presidents and first ladies to the Blue House and explained the tour results, our troop dispatch to East Timor, and the agreement on the US–North Korea talk in Berlin. Former President Kim Young-sam did not join.

Toward the end of September, the Associated Press published an exposé about the Nogeunri civilian massacre allegation. The AP called it the Korean version of the killing field, and argued that the person in charge of the decision to fire should take responsibility for the massacre.

On July 26, 1950, in the early days of the Korean War, the Nogeunri massacre originated from a US military order to consider refugees as enemies. The US military gathered 500 residents, including women and children, from Jugok-ri and Imgye-ri in Yeongdong-eup on the railroad tracks of the Seoul-Busan line, telling the refugees they would help them evacuate. Once there, they simply killed them with machine guns. When the refugees ran inside the tunnel under the railroad tracks, they installed machine guns on the hill right in front of it and shot them all. The AP reported that they confirmed these allegations as fact through official US government documents and testimonies by US Army veterans.

I immediately ordered that relevant offices investigate this allegation and take appropriate measures, including reparations. President Clinton did the same thing and expressed his regrets to our government.

After a three-month investigation of his holdings at Bogwang Group, the CEO of *JoongAng ilbo* Hong Seok-hyun was arrested for tax evasion and dereliction of duty on October 2. Some people tried to call this out as a gag on freedom of the press, but the charges against him had nothing to do with such matters and were of a very serious nature. I ordered a strict and transparent investigation, but the opposition party and some media outlets continued to argue against it.

The 1999 Seoul International Conference of NGOs was held on October 11. About 7600 people from more than one thousand domestic and overseas organizations participated. Many world leaders, including former and current heads of countries, foreign dignitaries, and UN diplomats, participated in the opening ceremony. I attended to congratulate the meaningful activities of people who were exploring the roles of NGOs in the twenty-first century.

The president of the Conference of Non-governmental Organizations in Consultative Relationship with the UN (CONGO) Afaf Mahfouz's opening remarks were passionate and impressive. She began with a quote from Alfred Tennyson's poem, "Ring Out, Wild Bells." "Ring out old shapes of foul disease / Ring out the narrowing lust of gold / Ring out the thousand wars of old / Ring in the thousand years of peace."

She continued, "We are not gathered here to enjoy the Korean people's warm welcome and glory. We are gathered here on behalf of changes that will transform a century of violence into a century characterized by respect for humanity. That is why the global community will pay attention to us. This is a blessing and an enormous opportunity. People say that there will be an age when the power of a country will be measured no longer by GNP or military power, but by its ability to take care of its own and world citizens with respect and passion. That age is now, and we are holding that great possibility within our arms."

The sincere and passionate atmosphere created by the NGO activists reminded me of my old days. I said in my congratulatory remarks: "Before becoming president, I dedicated forty years of my life to being the leader of an opposition party and a human rights activist. I had to endure a 6-year imprisonment and forty years of oppression. Throughout this process, numerous domestic and overseas human rights organizations staged unwavering movements to save my life. In 1994, I founded the Forum of Democratic Leaders in the Asia-Pacific, an international NGO, in order to repay my debt to them a little bit. Together with world human rights advocates like Mrs. Corazon Aquino of the Philippines, Ms. Aung San Suu Kyi of Myanmar, and Mr. Nelson Mandela of South Africa, we have been making efforts for democracy and human rights. Therefore, I am pleased and moved to attend this event not only as president of Korea, but also as an NGO activist.

"In retrospect, international NGO movements have made remarkable progress in various areas, such as human rights, the environment, social development, and peacekeeping, for the past several decades. These efforts are now becoming powerful enough to open the twenty-first century as one of hope. Thanks to these efforts, I firmly believe that the twenty-first century will effectively become the age of NGOs. As all people point out, the twenty-first century will be the age when democratic government, market, and civil society will become the three axes of national and world development."

On October 16, I attended the opening ceremony of Democracy Park in Busan. I heard that Father Song Gi-in and attorney Moon Jae-in worked to get the budget from the Ministry of Culture and Tourism. Former president Kim Young-sam attended the event too. He criticized both my administration and me in his congratulatory remarks. "Democracy in our country is in crisis," he spoke. "According to the way things go these days, the general election next year will be an unprecedentedly corrupt and unjust election, and the specter of dictatorship will come back alive. The Korean national community will be divided into regions, and we will return to a state similar to that of the 1970s, the times of division and antagonism between dictatorship and anti-dictatorship. They will try a long-term hold of power through the constitutional amendment introducing a parliamentary government system."

I later heard that he prepared even harsher script, but somehow the wind took that particular script away. I wonder why the wind interfered with him.

In my address, I said: "My most respected President Kim Young-sam, and my most respected and dearest citizens of Busan. Today, as we celebrate the twentieth anniversary of the Busan-Masan Democratic Movement, I am deeply appreciative of Democracy Park, which commemorates the passion for and devotion to democracy that the citizens of Busan have shown.

"At the same time, I offer my infinite admiration for all the spirits of those who did not hesitate to sacrifice themselves for the achievement of democracy, and look back upon their memory with respect and affection. Together with you, I would also like to laud the achievements of former president Kim Young-sam, who led a brave struggle as the president of an opposition party in 1979, despite all kinds of oppression, and contributed to the rise of the citizens of Busan and Masan, as well as the entire country."

I performed the tape-cutting ceremony standing next to Mr. Kim Young-sam. I held his arm when he was about to turn around without exchanging a greeting. When I offered my hand, he responded to a handshake. Still, his face remained frozen and we didn't exchange a single word. I dropped by the Jagalchi Market in Busan. Many people cheered me; their passionate welcome made me feel better.

According to my pledge during my election campaign, for the first time in our country's history, my government assigned 1 percent of the total government budget to the cultural sector. While the entire budget increased only by 5 percent, the budget for the cultural sector increased no less than 40 percent. It was a reflection of my administration's and my strong will to promote culture and tourism.

I encouraged officials to also maintain this principle. "We actively support cultural activities, but do not interfere with them," I told them. This consistent policy changed the atmosphere of our culture in general. For example, we established the Korean Film Council to support the film industry, but abolished pre-censorship in order to not interfere with it. The result was films like *Shiri* and *Joint Security Area*—films that fully represented our ideological reality. Finally, democracy and freedom began to penetrate cultural products.

I attended a ceremony to celebrate Culture Day on October 20. This event was a very meaningful one because Minister of Culture and Tourism Park Jie-won invited both Yechong (Federation of Artistic and Cultural Organizations of Korea) and Minyechong (National Federation of Artistic and Cultural Organizations)—rival organizations that had never gotten along very well—to prepare it together. I encouraged them, saying, "With the beginning of the new millennium, we face great opportunities to display our true identity as a culturally refined country to the world: The 2000 ASEM meeting, the 2001 Visit Korea Year, and the 2002 World Cup and Asian Games. We will have to show the great cultural heritage of our nation and the outstanding creative ability of cultural workers to the people of the world.

"Culture is now the central axis that will lead a country's development. You cultural workers are the protagonists who will lead this new millennium, the age of culture. Please feel pride and a sense of mission for your leadership in the national development in the twenty-first century."

Former Prime Minister of Singapore Lee Kuan Yew visited Seoul. When I invited him to the Blue House on October 22, the media published articles anticipating our debate about Asian values. It referenced the written debate we had in *Foreign Affairs* in 1994, and they provocatively titled their stories "The Second Round of Asian Value Debate" and "Clash After Dinner."

Neither Prime Minister Lee nor I had any interest in this, though. We simply had different opinions about the matter, and it was up to others which of our opinions to accept. We also did not doubt the depth of one another's thought. Although he had a different opinion, Prime Minister Lee was still an outstanding leader and thinker. He did not mention Asian values at all during his visit.

As Prime Minister Lee had years of experience in governance, I asked him some serious questions. "Please tell me what you think of North Korea and the Korean Peninsula problem from a neutral perspective," I requested.

"I believe it is important to focus on policies changing North Korea," he answered. "If you skillfully aid them with capital and technology, I believe you might solve the problem in your generation. Communist thought in North Korea is even more rigid than in Mao Zedong's China. You have to take a risk, you just have to reduce the danger. An increase in economic, academic, and human interchange is the way to go. If you expand interchanges in all sectors, you can reduce danger. Within a decade or two, the internet will fully penetrate North Korea, too. Then their way of thinking and looking at matters can change, too."

"Mutual assistance among Korea, America, and Japan is important in preventing North Korean aggression or missile launches," I mused. "But, we believe that China is in a position to influence North Korea. How much influence do you think China has on North Korea?"

"China has the influence," Prime Minister Lee concurred. "China provides food and crude oil to North Korea, and it shares a border with North Korea. If North Korea opens up, there will be a great migration, like that of East Germans to West Germany. North Korea is disappointed in China for befriending South Korea for its economic development. They are disappointed that China put its economic interest before socialist fraternity. China has changed its position.

"On another level, after the death of Deng Xiao Ping and Kim Il-sung, the personal friendship between the North Korean and Chinese leaders disappeared. There is no longer the kind of relationship between the two that enabled Chinese participation in the Korean War. There is no relationship like that between China and Kim Jong-il. Things are different now."

"We take the influence that the relationship between America and China will have on East Asia very seriously. What's your view about it?" I questioned further.

"The relationship between America and China will become the most important one in the next half a century," Prime Minister Lee predicted. "People think that it will take about thirty to fifty years for China to catch up with America. They also think that there will not be any clash or conflict during that period."

"America defends as well as checks Japan. What are your thoughts about that?" I asked.

"Basically, as long as Japan is under the umbrella of US military protection, you don't have to worry too much about it," he answered. "However, without the nuclear umbrella, Japan would not sit still."

On October 25, 1999, an opposition party member revealed a document entitled "Plans to Improve Environment for a Successful Reform" during a government questioning session. This was dubbed the Media Control Document Allegation Incident. The document contained a plan to change public opinion and control media through shock therapy. I, of course, had no idea about it. Nevertheless, the opposition party claimed that the plan in that document had been put in place, and that it was proof of a government conspiracy to control the media.

I ordered a transparent investigation, and, through the investigation, it was revealed that a certain newspaper reporter personally wrote and delivered the article to the former chief of the NIS, Lee Chong-chan, and that a broadcasting company reporter stole and delivered it to an opposition party assemblyman. Nevertheless, the opposition party continued to make an issue of it and Assemblyman Chung Hyung-gun even alleged that I introduced a communist guerrilla-like tactic to control the media. I wonder whether he thought about what it meant to call me a communist to the very Korean people who had elected me. At any rate, while the opposition party politicized groundless allegations, political reform acts, including the amendment to the election law, drifted.

On October 30, fifty-six people, including some students, perished in a fire in a building that housed a bar and billiard room in Incheon. It turned out that there weren't any emergency exits or fire escapes in the building. Even more shocking, the storeowners were in consort with regulators and engaged in illegal practices. They also bribed various levels of police officers. It was a man-made disaster, caused by the combination of our society's insensitivity to safety and the corruption of public servants. The police tried to cover it up to protect their own, which angered the public even more. I fired the National Police Agency chief and appointed Seoul police agency head Mr. Lee Moo-Young to the post.

My wife and I met with Reverend Pak Dae-in (who was originally named Edward Poitras) and his wife. They had greatly helped my wife and me during my fight for democracy. They also let the outside world know about the reality of Korean dictatorship. The couple was working on translating Korean poet Park Tu-jin's poems. Mr. Park Tu-jin had passed away the year before, and I sent flowers to his funeral. I was happy to hear that they were translating his poems, as I know that both the poet and his poems were honest.

"Mr. Park Tu-jin lived a life that corresponded with his poems," I told Reverend Pak and his wife.

The reverend, too, remembered his pure poetic spirit in his incredibly fluent Korean. "He did not compromise with forces oppressing democracy at all."

"We need to live well because we have only one life," I mused. "In the past, military regimes manipulated good poets, writers, and scholars, and ruined their honor."

Reverend Pak told me that he would do whatever he could to be helpful to Korea until the day he died. I asked him if there was anything that I could do to help him, and he responded, "We live a simple life. I am grandfather who needs nothing."

On November 24, I made some personnel changes in the Blue House. Two days later, on November 26, I accepted the resignation of Secretary for Legal Affairs Park Joo-Sun, who was involved in the Clothing Lobby Allegation Incident.

The ASEAN+3 conference was held in Manila, Philippines. After landing at the Ninoy Aquino International Airport during the day on November 27, I began a three-night, four-day official schedule. I had a Korea-Indonesia summit meeting with President Abdurrahman Wahid at the Manila Hotel. President Abdurrahman had been elected a month before, and Madam Megawati Sukamoputri was elected vice president. President Abdurrahman Wahid was called a religious leader in action for his fight against Suharto's dictatorship. He was the first democratically elected president in Indonesia. He had visited Korea a few years before to attend the Forum of Democratic Leaders at the Asia-Pacific meeting. I heartily congratulated him on winning the election. I admired him for his struggle for democracy and efforts for harmony among religions, despite his poor health.

I also brought up the matter of South Korean troop dispatch to East Timor. "Some in Korea were worried that our participation in East Timor multinational forces could cause friction in Korea's relationship with Indonesia," I said. "But our government made the decision after a full discussion with the Indonesian government, and according to Indonesia's request. We also decided to send our troops because we believed that our contribution to security and peace in East Timor could contribute to peace in Indonesia in the long run."

"There is no reason why Korean participation in the multinational forces in East Timor would be harmful to Indonesia," President Abdurrahman Wahid responded. "I am scheduled to meet East Timor's leader Gusmao in Jakarta on December 13. I hope that he will be elected president of East Timor. I will allow the establishment of the East Timorese Resistance Council's office in Jakarta." His words clearly showed that the worries some Korean media outlets had expressed were groundless.

On the morning of November 28, a Korea-China-Japan summit breakfast was held in the Coconut Palace in Manila, according to Japanese Prime Minister Obuchi's proposal. This was the first time the three countries' heads of the state sat down together for a meeting. Premier of China Zhu Rongji and Prime Minister of Japan Obuchi actively supported my proposal that the three countries have our research institutes conduct common studies, establishing the first step toward an economic cooperation system among three East Asian countries.

I then had a summit meeting with Japanese Prime Minister Obuchi. I proposed that we advance to third-country markets through a partnership between Korean technology and Japanese capital, and I invited Japanese investment in Korean parts and materials industries. Prime Minister Obuchi agreed to actively examine my proposals.

Although it had not been scheduled previously, I proposed a summit meeting to Burmese Head of State Than Shwe. We met in a conference room in the early evening. While discussing ways for the two countries to cooperate economically, I also urged him to engage in a dialogue with Madam Aung San Suu Kyi, saying that it would help him secure political stability and support from the world. He answered that the government was protecting Madam Aung San Suu Kyi, and that people in Myanmar firmly supported the military government. He also added that he hoped his would be the last military regime. I was surprised at how similar his logic was to that of Korean military dictators of the past.

"I am deeply impressed to hear that you hope your government will be the last military government," I responded. "If your government is firmly supported by the people as you mentioned, then you can confidently resume a dialogue with opposition forces.

"If your country achieves political harmony through patience, tolerance, and dialogue with opposition parties, the world will offer great support, and it will be helpful to your country's future."

"Frankly speaking," Mr. Than Shwe said, "Myanmar is not yet a democratic country." Listening to his staunch disagreement, I worried about the future of Madam Aung San Suu Kyi.

On December 15, we held the Scientists and Technologists Conference to Open the New Millennium at the Blue House. About 160 scientists and technologists attended the event. I announced there that my administration would actively support Korean scientists' plans to build a satellite launch station with solely Korean equipment and materials.

On December 22, I met with Prime Minister Kim Jong-pil and we concluded that we would not merge our parties. Although we negotiated many times over the course of a year, we could not agree on terms. Considering that Prime Minister Kim changed his position many times, I believe he had spent many hours of difficult thinking too. I decided to respect his opinion. We did not have time to drag negotiations on, either, because the general election was approaching.

At a dinner with both parties' assemblymen that evening, Prime Minister Kim praised my achievements. "Our country, which was on the verge of bankruptcy and required emergency help from the IMF, achieved 9 percent growth and became a creditor country," he said. "This is like a dream. As the lines of unemployed on the streets decrease, we can feel our people's energy everywhere as they regain will for their lives.

"Thanks to the consistent engagement policy toward the North that Mr. President has been pursuing, it appears that a common ground for both the South and the North is gradually being built. I returned yesterday from my trip to South America and the United States. Wherever I went, foreign leaders and Koreans abroad did not spare praise for Korea and how it rose up again forcefully. I believe all these are results of the collaboration between the leadership of Mr. President, who has taken great care running this country day and night, and the Korean people's wholehearted efforts to follow his lead."

His praise for me sounded like his closing remark as he planned to finish his service as prime minister and to return to his party. Because I wanted to lighten his burden about the merger decision, I frankly disclosed the result of our discussion earlier that day to the assemblymen gathered for dinner: "I met Prime Minister Kim today and told him, 'I read your words in the newspaper. I think there is some truth to what you said. If that is what you think, then, let us conclude our discussion.' So we decided that we would stop negotiating the merger of our two parties. Prime Minister Kim said, 'Let us, both parties, continue to cooperate in the election and until the end of this administration.' I agreed with him.

"We do not have to take one single road to cooperate. However, all of you should not forget one absolute condition. That is the fact that we promised the Korean people that we would cooperate in taking responsibility for governing our country for five years. That was an absolute promise."

CHAPTER 9

January–June 2000

INTO THE NEW MILLENNIUM (JANUARY–MARCH 2000)

The new millennium was dawning. How would the last millennium be remembered, and what would the new one usher in? What would humanity do in the new millennium? At what point are we in the vast expanse of history and grand evolution of civilization? The world, Korea, and I, Kim Dae-jung were standing in between the past and the future. I was one of 6 billion members of the human race. I was the last Korean president of the last millennium and the first president of the new millennium.

Many thoughts swarmed my mind. I was anxious and almost scared. It was certainly good fortune to observe and be a part of the moment when we entered a new millennium. But it also felt foolish to measure time in such a way. Regardless of how we felt, we all had to enter the new millennium. Time was fair and drew us all into the new century together.

We were entering into the knowledge and information-centric society that I had so emphasized, but would it really bring us happiness? Could the oppression and subjugation that existed between human beings and nature, between the West and the non-Western world, between advanced countries and developing countries, and between the haves and the have-nots be eliminated? Would a world without discrimination come? Would we experience a global village where universal human values thrive? If families and hometowns changed, as they inevitably would, what would that look like?

© The Author(s) 2019
Kim Dae-jung, *Conscience in Action*,
https://doi.org/10.1007/978-981-10-7623-7_9

Would the millennium bug really happen? Would the fields of finance, transportation, communication, national security, and medicine—where computers played an essential role—be okay? Would there be disruptions to industry? Although we tried very hard to prevent them from happening, we could never be sure. Also, would our society be sustainable? While we were destroying the environment and so many species of animals and plants were disappearing, would only human beings survive? Sometimes, it was indeed scary. However, God was always with us. I continued to pray to God to bless us human beings, Korea, and Koreans.

Korean society was not quiet during this period of transition to the new millennium. My days were hectic, and I felt hurt about many things. I woke up early in the morning while it was still dark outside, and the Blue House felt like an island in that darkness. I meditated deeply and alone.

At the close of the twentieth century, I issued a special year-end statement. In it, I said: "My dear fellow Koreans, whom I respect and love. The twentieth century is now setting and the new millennium is dawning. At this historical juncture, I would like to talk about our resolutions, to reflect on the lessons we learned during the last century, and to greet the new millennium.

"The twentieth century was a truly eventful era in Korean history when shame and glory, and frustration and achievement intersected. Although we underwent shame from the loss of our sovereignty, we achieved independence through our indomitable struggles. Even in the midst of the pain of the division of our country and fratricidal war, we defended South Korea from Communist invasion and developed into an economically powerful country. Today, we are the eleventh-largest economy in the world.

"During the lengthy period of military dictatorial regimes and an authoritarian system, we continued to willingly sacrifice our lives for our passionate dream of achieving democracy. We finally achieved a peaceful regime change between the ruling and opposition forces after a 50-year struggle. This was a great victory for our democracy.

"We faced the IMF foreign currency crisis. It destroyed the economic achievements Korean people had worked so hard for over the course of decades overnight. But we also overcame it, and are ready for the new challenges of the new millennium.

"But, in order to achieve a world-class country in the twenty-first century, we also have to look at other aspects of our society at this final stop of the twentieth century. Deeply rooted regional antagonism, injustice and corruption, egotism, and political confrontation and chaos are shackles on the ankles of our society.

"Nobody living in our land is free from these mistaken practices. Before entering into the new millennium, we should all atone for those mistakes and bravely bid them goodbye. This is also a declaration of our freedom, the declaration of our rebirth. At the same time, we should begin a history of grand harmony. In it all of us will forgive and embrace one another. Reconciliation and harmony among regions, classes, generations, genders, and ruling and opposition powers are prerequisites to a new millennium of hope.

"My dear fellow Koreans whom I respect and love. If we have lingering resentments toward our spouses, our siblings, our friends, our neighbors, and our colleagues or superiors, let us shake them all off while sending off the twentieth century. And let's transform confrontations and conflicts into reconciliation and harmony.

"To the Korean people who have continued our 5000-year history while fighting high seas during the last century, this beginning of a new millennium is an opportunity that we should not miss. I hope you will participate in my sincere effort to finish off the last century with pride and self-reflection and to greet the twenty-first century with hope."

On the verge of the new millennium, I pardoned 1 million people; 3501 prisoners were released on parole and many financial criminals were legally relieved. In particular, I ordered the release of two long-term prisoners who were North Korean spies, and Korea became a country where there were no long-term prisoners for an ideological cause.

The Grand National Festival celebrating the new millennium was held in the Gwanghwamun Crossroads area of Seoul. Although the weather was cold, an enormous crowd gathered. Finally, January 1, 2000 arrived. I pulled the 2000 Lever of the large Universe Pendulum that counted down to the New Year. Light poured over the crowd and the New Year began as the Bosingak Bell rang.

I returned to the Blue House. Fortunately, the millennium disaster that so many had feared did not happen. Man-made computers did what they had always done. Airplanes flew fine and cellphones showed the correct numbers. I was relieved.

On New Year's Day morning, I declared that we would create an advanced welfare state and Internet powerhouse in Korea. I believed that we had to open a new era by taking advantage of our assets—that is, our cultural creativity and passion for education. As is customary in celebration of the New Year, in calligraphy I wrote a message on a piece of paper. The phrase I chose was "New Millennium, New Hope."

On January 5, I presided over the National Security Council meeting. The basic guiding principle this year was improvement of the inter-Korean relationship. For this purpose, we set four essential tasks: unconditional conferences between officials of both the South and the North; diversification of inter-Korean interchanges; pursuit of inter-Korean economic community building; and active support for the reunion of dispersed families. Asking all council members to try their best to lead North Korea toward the road of peace, I said, "We will make this year the first year of the settlement of secure peace by fully pursuing the process of dismantling the Cold War system in the Korean Peninsula."

Prime Minister Kim Jong-pil resigned from his post, and I nominated Liberal Democratic Alliance (LDA) president Park Tae-joon to succeed him on January 11. Prime Minister Kim attended a cabinet meeting for the last time that day. I thanked him for his dedicated service during his term, and he responded by saying, "It was most rewarding to wisely overcome the IMF crisis under your leadership." I watched him from the front of the main building of the Blue House until his car disappeared.

On January 12, I appointed Mr. Kim Sung-jae to senior secretary for policy and planning and Mr. Shin Kwang-ok to senior secretary for civil affairs. I also eliminated the secretary for legal affairs under the immediate control of chief of staff, and, instead, installed the secretary for audit and inspection and the secretary for public office discipline under the control of senior secretary for civil affairs. I trusted the newly appointed Senior Secretary for Policy and Planning Kim Sung-jae greatly. I asked him to actively pursue policies that would be helpful to the information age and to discover new talent.

On January 13, I reshuffled the cabinet, changing seven ministers and two cabinet officials. The media called this cabinet the Park Tae-joon Cabinet, and I called it the Millennium Cabinet. During the first meeting of the new cabinet, I said to its members, "We should try our best to accomplish our mission as those in charge of a community with a shared destiny. At this greatest revolutionary phase in our history, let us find the right road and hand down our great fatherland to our descendants."

I appeared with my wife on an MBC TV entertainment program, called *21st Century Committee*, the theme of which was "21st Century with the President." This was yet another way of communicating with the Korean people.

During the program, I was asked a wide variety of questions. One university student, for example, asked me to recommend a good place for a date. "It's winter now, so put on a thick parka, bring coffee in a thermos, and take your date to the Han River bank," I advised. "Since it's cold, you can naturally cover her with your parka and drink warm coffee with her. Then, it will be warm and you'll get closer. If you watch the river and talk, it will be romantic. If there's moonlight, it will be even better."

On a more serious note, someone asked me to come up with three qualities required of the youth of the twenty-first century. I said that he or she needs to have an adventurous spirit, be a "new intellectual," and think of neighbors. A new intellectual is an intellectual who competes, based not on his or her academic background, but on his or her ability and talents. In the past, to be a leader of a group was important, but now society recognizes those individuals who stand out for their abilities. Those individuals who add their values to the highest goals and compete by developing their abilities and talents are new intellectuals. "You should study hard, but studying hard is not the only thing that matters," I advised. "Create more value and be more efficient than others by utilizing knowledge. You were born in a better time than in the past, when academic background and scholarly abilities were everything."

Someone in the audience asked me if I had ever been upset with my wife. "When I was in prison and condemned to death in the 1980s, my wife prayed to God in front of me. Rather than praying to God to save me, she said, 'God's will be done.' That's when I was most upset with her." The audience burst into laughter.

Another person asked my wife what from my prison letters was the most memorable to her. "The most memorable phrase was his address to me: 'My dearest whom I respect and love,'" she replied. "There is nothing better than being respected and loved by your husband." This was the first time I had ever heard her say this.

I also gave advice to young couples. "The most important thing between husband and wife or between girlfriend and boyfriend is to find the other person's merits. Everybody's face has some handsome features. Everybody has some merits. Your partner might be kind, quick, or humorous. You have to praise those merits. When I am with my wife, we always laugh. It is me who is funny, and it is she who laughs. I sometimes tell her, 'You became healthy while living with me because you laugh a lot. You have to acknowledge it.' It is good to laugh often, to share happy stories or jokes. It is not just the relationship, but also your life that becomes bright."

On January 20, the New Millennium Democratic Party (a.k.a., Democratic Party) foundation convention was held at the Olympic Gymnastics Arena in Seoul. I was elected party president. When the president of the convention declared my election, party members cheered and waved both Korean national flags and our party flags. I received a giant-sized party flag. Chairman Suh Young-hoon and Central Election Polling Committee Chair Rhee In-je were also ratified. The Democratic Party officially launched as the National Congress that had made me president of Korea disappeared into history. We built the Democratic Party with our dreams of and will for rebuilding our country. Reform could be completed only when we won the general election.

In retrospect, I could not carry out state affairs because of the majority opposition party's tyranny. Reform policies drifted because of majority power, and the idea of a horizontal power shift was lost. In the beginning, the majority opposition party did not even approve the prime minister appointment; they fettered each and every state affair. Although I was busy trying to overcome the foreign currency crisis, those who brought about the crisis did not cooperate on reform policies. I could not understand their behavior and sometimes felt very angry. In the end, the only solution was to create a majority ruling party. The goal of founding a new party was to achieve the majority in the National Assembly.

The National Congress had officially declared its intention to found a new party on July 23 the previous year. During my Independence Day address, I said that the new party would be a reform party that represented the middle and working classes.

Many men of renown joined our party, including an elder of the Red Cross and civic movements, Mr. Suh Young-hoon; a leading business-woman and the president of Aekyung Group, Chang Young-shin; president of SungKongHoe University Lee Jae-joung, who had devoted his life to the democratization movement; and renowned conductor Mr. Chung Myung-Whun. Madam Chang Young-shin worked particularly passionately and energetically as the party founding preparation committee chair.

There were many opinions about the name of the new party. I was fond of the name Democratic Party. Established in 1955, the Democratic Party was at the root of the traditional democratic forces in our country, and I hoped to regain that name. Although it had been inevitable that I leave the Democratic Party and found the National Congress, which brought me victory in the presidential election, my political roots were in the Democratic Party. Perhaps honoring my wish, the preparation committee chose the name New Millennium Democratic Party. I was very happy about that decision.

Leaders from all areas, including the economic, academic, military, and women's sectors, participated in our new party. In the speech I delivered after being elected president, I declared that I would propose an inter-Korean summit to North Korea after the general election. I appealed to the Korean people for their support of our party during the general election.

"It has been almost two years since the people's government was born," I spoke. "We have done a lot of things in the meantime. We revived an economy on the verge of bankruptcy. We stabilized a society where teargas bombs and Molotov cocktails had been flying around. We greatly enhanced the rights of workers, women, people who contributed to the democratization of our country, and journalists. The labor world is unprecedentedly stable. Our Sunshine Policy is being supported by the entire world, while reducing the threat of war and encouraging inter-Korean interchanges. By winning the Yeonpyeong Naval Battle, for the first time we punished North Korean armed provocation with force. As shown in these examples, in all areas other than politics we have accomplished achievements previously unimaginable. However, in the field of politics, confrontation and extreme conflict have continued for two years without any pause, damaging the great achievements of state affairs and driving our country to crisis and frustration.

"Why do we need the New Millennium Democratic Party? We can easily answer this question by only looking at the present state of our politics. Politics today are excessively unproductive and neglectful of the people's wishes; they are the object of the wholesale mistrust and condemnation of the Korean people. The ruling party, of course, also holds its share of the responsibility. However, the National Congress for New Politics has continued to try hard to achieve political stability and reform in order to complete its obligations as the ruling party. Unfortunately, our party has only one-third of the Assembly seats and is regionally limited. Additionally, it was not easy for us to recruit new talent. Therefore, we finally came to the conclusion that, in order to achieve political stability and reform, it was inevitable that we would have to burn ourselves and create a new party that brings together new talent from all walks of our society. Finally, today we founded the New Millennium Democratic Party together with many reform-oriented and professional people of renown who the Korean people trust.

"The New Millennium Democratic Party is a party that will survive politics. It is a new party that will revive our country. Let us rise up and act together in order to meet our national mission, knowing that the future of our nation and people rests on our shoulders.

"The New Millennium Democratic Party is a party that succeeds the tradition of the Democratic Party that was founded during the Liberal Party government and governed after the April 19 Revolution. I firmly believe that the New Millennium Democratic Party is an orthodox party that continues the 50-year tradition of the democratization movement, which persistently fought for democracy during military dictatorships and finally achieved a power shift from ruling to opposition party for the first time in Korean history. Ideologically, the New Millennium Democratic Party is a reform party that pursues democracy, market economy, and productive welfare. The New Millennium Democratic Party is the only party that represents the interests of the middle and working classes in Korea. I declare in front of history that the New Millennium Democratic Party is the only proud national reform party in terms of its democratic legitimacy and ideology, and its class representation.

"The election this year will be the crossroads that will determine our country's fate. If today's political instability continues, we cannot avoid frustration and bankruptcy. The achievements of the past two years could all come to nothing. I cannot help but become extremely anxious when I think of that possibility. The Korean people entrusted me with our country for three more years according to our Constitution. Fellow Koreans, please give me strength so that I can work to my full capacity. Please help the New Millennium Democratic Party. Our party and I will repay your grace by becoming the most successful ruling party and the most successful president. We will achieve the five great tasks: political reform, an economic leap, productive welfare, national harmony, and the end of the Cold War in the Korean Peninsula."

On February 2, I sent my first email order to all of the cabinet members. The subject was Quick Execution of Electronic Government. In this email, I wrote: "The number of domestic internet users exceeded 10 million, and our economic and social structures are changing as the role played by information and knowledge in our society rapidly increases. Our government should take the initiative in carrying out electronic democracy through interactive communication with the Korean people by gathering public opinion and actively announcing government policies through the Internet. Please make an effort to clearly understand what people want from our government by actively utilizing the homepage of each ministry."

The prime minister and cabinet members sent me electronic replies. Some of them included unique ideas such as "I will encourage all government departments to actively use email in their operations," "I delivered your order to all heads of local governments and agencies through an email," "Your email will encourage all high officials," "I will establish a cyber environment education institution," "I will replace face-to-face monthly meetings with email meetings," and "I will establish a cyber direct transaction shopping mall."

It was so refreshing and rewarding to receive those emails! I read them slowly and repeatedly. I was a happy president, exchanging emails with cabinet members. I renewed my resolution to build an electronic country.

On February 9, I had an interview with Tokyo Broadcasting in Japan during which I evaluated Chairman of the Central Military Commission Kim Jong-il. "I believe that he is equipped with judgment and insight as a leader. There is no other way besides dialogue with him to solve inter-Korean issues."

The Grand National and Liberal Democratic Parties criticized my remark; however, insofar as we had already acknowledged North Korea as our dialogue partner, we could not expect any result by condemning or slandering its supreme leader. Around that time, a meaningful signal was sent from the North. Around the end of January, Minister of Culture and Tourism Park Jie-won came to visit me at the Blue House. Unexpectedly, he said, "A Hyundai official contacted an important figure in the North, and his impression is that the inter-Korean summit is possible."

I thought for a while before speaking, and then said, "Since Hyundai has been interacting with the North about the Mt. Kumgang tour and sending cows, they could play a role in this. Please ask them about it."

I had a good feeling about our chances. While getting a report from the National Intelligence Service (NIS), I told Chief Lim Dong-won, "Minister Park Jie-won heard from the president of Hyundai Chung Mong-hun that North Korea is willing to pursue the summit. Please inquire about it and explore the possibility."

Therefore, my remark about Chairman Kim Jong-il was a sort of multipurpose test. The media presented an analysis that it was like "opening a sluice gate." I did not deny it. Something was happening in the North.

In early March, I left for state visits to Italy, the Vatican, France, and Germany. I arrived in the Leonardo Da Vinci International Airport in Rome on the afternoon of March 2. This was the first Korean presidential visit since our establishment of a diplomatic relationship with Italy 116 years before. I had a summit with President Carlo Azeglio Ciampi in the Presidential Palace. We agreed on a strategic partnership in mid-sized enterprises. The next day, after meeting with Senate and House speakers, I had a meeting and lunch with Prime Minister Massimo D'Alema. Italy was anticipating the establishment of a diplomatic relationship with North Korea. I told Prime Minister D'Alema, "The South Korean government wishes that more countries would contact and establish a diplomatic relationship with North Korea. Opening North Korea means maintaining peace."

Afterward, my wife and I went to the Vatican for a state visit. I entered the pope's residence, Pope Sixtus V Palace, and met with Pope John Paul II in the Tronetto Room. Pope John Paul II greeted us in Korean, saying, "*Chanmi yesu, gamsahamnida* (Praise the Lord, thank you)." The last time I visited the Pope was eleven years before, while I was an opposition party president. He still looked the same. "I always consider you as my teacher," I told him. "I wish you God's blessing and constant health."

"I am happy that you are visiting me for the first time as a Korean president—in particular, a Catholic Korean president," he replied.

"My baptism name is Thomas More," I shared with the Pope.

"I think your life is similar to his," Pope John Paul II mused. "I had the honor of canonizing 103 Koreans in Yeouido Square in 1984. I still remember how moving the canonization ceremony was. I cannot forget my visit to Korea during the Eucharistic Congress in 1989."

I asked the Pope to visit North Korea, hoping that he would bless the last frozen land on earth with his love. "North Korea is still under communism, and their church activities are very limited. I wonder if you have any plans to visit North Korea? If not, I hope you will consider it."

"I do not have a plan to yet," he replied.

"If you visit North Korea, it will greatly contribute to peace in the Korean Peninsula and in East Asia," I encouraged him.

"If I can visit North Korea, it will be miracle. I will always pray and hold a mass for Korea."

Although I could not measure the pope's spirituality, I felt he was an incredibly clear person. The Vatican gave me special treatment, breaking its custom of not holding any state visits during the Great Jubilee year. They also allowed me to enter through St. Peter's Basilica, which is reserved for the Pope. After the meeting, they made sure that I stepped through the Pope-only passage while heading to St. Peter's Basilica, which they then gave us a personal tour of.

The Pope gave me a commemorative medal with his face etched on it, and he gave my wife a rosary. I gave him a metal model of the Turtle Ship and a white porcelain vase with the phrase "respect heaven, love people" written on it. When I explained the meaning of the phrase, the Pope stared at it for a while, and then said, "It's beautiful."

After looking around the Coliseum and Galleria Borghese the next day, I headed to Milan where the mayor of Daegu Moon Hee-gap and the heads of textile-related organizations were waiting for me. They were going to explain the Milano Project to economists in Milan and invite their investment. The Milano Project was being pursued to revive the textile industry in Daegu through the introduction of advanced technology. I appealed for their active investment at a meeting with both countries' economists. I then briefly visited the Santa Maria Delle Grazie Convent and saw Leonardo Da Vinci's masterpiece, "Last Supper." It was extremely well preserved and incredibly vibrant, despite the fact that it was painted 500 years ago.

I headed to France that afternoon. After arriving at Paris' Orly Airport and checking in at a guesthouse, I immediately visited Élysée Palace and had a summit with President Jacques Chirac. I proposed that we build a Trans-Eurasia Network that would connect Asia and the EU through a high-speed telecommunications network that could be used for electronic commerce and trade. With this, Asia and Europe could become cyber neighbors; therefore, we might call it Light-speed Silk Road. President Chirac welcomed my idea and agreed to my proposal to present it as a main agenda item at the Asia-Europe Meeting (ASEM) summit to be held in Seoul that October. I also urged him to pursue the return of books stolen from the royal Korean library Oegyujanggak. Although it was decided at the 1998 ASEM meeting that Korea and France would each nominate a representative to discuss the matter, the negotiation was not progressing.

"It looks like the French representative has little authority," I said to President Chirac. "Please cooperate so that representatives from both countries have substantial authority and can quickly conclude the negotiation."

President Chirac seemed frustrated about the slow speed of the negotiation, too. "How about we lock them up until they conclude the negotiation?" he suggested.

Although we laughed together, it was a unique opportunity to observe the French manner of handling cultural heritage. The negotiation continued to move sluggishly.

The spokesperson for the French Ministry of Foreign Relations made a surprise announcement that "the Renault Group could conclude its acquisition of Samsung Automobile during President Kim's visit to France." The announcement implied that it was being offered as a gift on the occasion of my state visit. In fact, Renault Group offered $450 million (504 billion won) for their acquisition of Samsung Automobile just in time for my visit.

I tried to persuade Premier Lionel Jospin that the Renault Group should acquire Samsung Automobile when we met. "The creditors of Samsung Automobile want to sell the company to the Renault Group. The question is how much the Renault Group should pay for it. Although the Korean government cannot be too greedy about selling an insolvent enterprise, it would not be good to give the Korean people the impression that we sold the company too cheaply."

Frankfurt, Germany, was the last stop on my European tour. It was in Frankfurt that most Korean migrant workers—miners and nurses—settled in the 1960s. I delivered a speech to 250 German economists. "I will tell you two personal stories," I began. "Citizens of Frankfurt and media outlets like *Allgemeiner Zeitung* supported Korean democratic forces and condemned dictatorial regimes. It is thanks to your support that I can be here as president of the Republic of Korea, a democratic country.

"Also, Cha Bum-kun, the soccer player whom you call 'Cha Bum,' played on the Frankfurt soccer team. Whenever I read articles about him, I was proud and it made me feel close to Frankfurt, like you are a good neighbor."

Korea and Germany share the very precious experience of achieving the miracle of economic revival from the ruins of war. I stressed the fact that our two countries would remain partners, united in reliable economic cooperation with one another.

I also said, "German poet Friedrich Schiller said, 'Happiness shared doubles and sadness shared is halved.' I sincerely hope that Korea and Germany will develop our friendship further to become closer."

I had a summit with President Johannes Rau and we agreed that our two countries would strengthen our interchange and cooperation with one another. Germany was a country to which I felt deeply grateful. When I was kidnapped in Tokyo in 1973 and when I was sentenced to death in 1980, Germany served as the base camp for the international movement to save my life. During the foreign currency crisis after my inauguration, Germany was the only country that did not collect their investment money from Korea. I expressed my thanks during the state dinner. "For more than a century since the establishment of our diplomatic relationship, Germany has always sent both Koreans and myself great courage and generous support at every difficult valley on our road to democracy. The relationship between our two countries is exactly like that described in a German proverb: 'True friendship does not freeze in the winter.'"

President Johannes Rau called me "the father of Korean democracy." He also expressed his active support for the Sunshine Policy toward North Korea, saying, "It is our experience that sunshine eventually thaws the ice."

I gave a speech in front of 900 professors and students and 300 reporters at the Free University of Berlin. Before my speech, the president of the university Peter Gaehtgens presented me with the Free University Medal. My speech included the so-called Berlin Declaration, upon which I worked with all of my soul, will, and sincerity, revising it even during my European tour. I thought about it over and over again, while keeping the North Korean position in mind. I thought that both sides should be frank with each other. While I had supported civilian economic cooperation according to the principle of separation between politics and economics, I decided that it was now time for the government to actively explore an inter-Korean relationship. I made the following four suggestions: "On this significant day of my visit to the Free University of Berlin, I appeal to all concerned to help bring down the Cold War structure on the Korean Peninsula. I make the following suggestions in an effort to establish permanent peace and realize reconciliation and cooperation with North Korea.

"First, the government of the Republic of Korea is ready to help tide North Korea over as the country gets through its economic difficulties. Presently, private-sector economic cooperation is underway based on the principle of separating the economy and politics. However, to realize meaningful economic collaboration, the social infrastructure, including highways, harbors, railroads, and electric and communications facilities, must be expanded. The governments of the two Koreas have important roles to play, including instating bilateral agreements for investment guarantees and preventing double taxation, so that private businesses will be able to invest in a secure environment. The severe food shortage that North Korea now faces cannot be solved merely by supplying food. A fundamental solution requires comprehensive reforms in the delivery of quality fertilizers, agricultural equipment, irrigation systems, and other elements of a structural nature. Private businesses can do only so much in terms of expanding the social infrastructure, promoting a favorable investment environment, and reforming the overall agricultural setup. The time is ripe for government-to-government cooperation. The government of the Republic is ready to respond positively to any North Korean requests in this regard.

"Second, at the present stage, our immediate objective is to put an end to the Cold War confrontation and settle peace, rather than attempting to accomplish reunification. The government of the Republic intends to do its best to lend assistance to North Korea in the spirit of genuine reconciliation and cooperation. We urge the Pyongyang authorities to accept our goodwill without reservation, to come forward and respond to our offer for cooperation and reconciliation.

"Third, North Korea should respond to our call for arranging reunions for relatives separated in different parts of the divided land. We cannot afford to lose precious time any longer, considering the fact that many elderly family members are passing away.

"Fourth, to effectively deal with various pending issues, the government authorities of the two Koreas should open a dialogue without delay. In my inaugural speech, I proposed to the North that Seoul and Pyongyang exchange special envoys to implement the Basic South-North Agreement concluded in 1991. I reiterate that North Korea should respond positively to this proposal.

"We believe that, ultimately, the issues involving the Korean Peninsula should be solved by governmental authorities of the two Koreas. The government of the Republic will adhere to this principle with consistency and patience ...

"There is a saying in Korea that 'those who suffer from the same illness understand each other the best.' Korea and Germany have suffered the same kind of pain—the division of the land. Our two peoples have empathy for each other. Koreans have tremendous respect for the Germans, who overcame the pain and achieved the great task of reunification first. You are our role model."

Before this address, I sent an outline of this declaration to North Korea through Panmunjeom. This kind of direct communication was unprecedented. I also let the US and Japanese ambassadors know about the declaration. How would North Korea respond? I anxiously anticipated their response as I returned home.

During my trip to Europe, I attained more than $10 billion in foreign investments from Italy, France, and Germany.

AT MIDNIGHT, WAITING FOR THE SPECIAL ENVOY TO THE NORTH (FEBRUARY–JUNE 2000)

The North wanted a summit with the South. The signs had been visible through various channels. Director of NIS Lim Dong-won and Minister of Culture and Tourism Park Jie-won reported frequently on the movements of the North. One day in February, Director Lim said to me, "The North chose Vice Chair of the Asia Pacific Peace Committee Song Ho-gyong as their negotiation leader and proposed a meeting with our team in Singapore."

A little before my European tour, on February 27, I called both Director Lim and Minister Park to the Blue House. "The North proposed a secret meeting in Singapore," I told them. "I will appoint Minister Park as my special envoy. The North also wanted you. Director Lim, please choose people who specialize in negotiations with the North from the NIS and support Minister Park. From now on, Director Lim should specially assist me with the inter-Korean summit."

Minister Park said that the minister of unification would be more appropriate for the job of a special envoy. "It is difficult for him to do the work because his movement is exposed," I explained. "Security is essential in this kind of meeting. I trust that you will do a good job. Please discuss everything with Director Lim."

Director Lim reported that he chose two specialists: Kim Bo-hyun and Suh Hun. I told Minister Park that he should let them know that I was willing to visit Pyongyang and that the inter-Korean summit would make inter-Korean economic cooperation easier. I also asked him to treat North Koreans with both sincerity and pride.

On March 8, 2000, Minister Park secretly met with Vice Chair of the Asia Pacific Peace Committee Song Ho-gyong. The next day, I announced the Berlin Declaration at the Free University in Berlin, Germany. I later heard from Minister Park that North Korea wanted to know the intentions of the highest authority in the South.

Minister Park told Mr. Song about my career in the democratization struggle and the oppression I faced due to my activities. He also explained my arguments for the Guaranteeing of Peace by the Four Powerful Countries and the Three-Step Reunification Plan during my election campaign in 1971. He showed him the Berlin Declaration, as well. Of course, I did not write this declaration for that particular secret meeting. Minister Park also delivered the message that we hoped for the summit in May or June and that I was willing to visit Pyongyang.

Vice Chair Song Ho-gyong proposed that this meeting remain secret, and that was the end of exploration between the South and the North. In this preliminary meeting, both sides confirmed each other's will to have the summit; however, no agreement was made other than to meet again.

Upon his return, Minister Park reported, "When I spoke about you and your plan to Vice Chair Song Ho-gyong he said, 'I feel as if I am listening to President Kim Dae-jung's voice.' That remark somehow gave me the feeling that this summit could happen."

I encouraged Minister Park and told him that we should wait and see.

On March 17, the first special envoy meeting occurred in Shanghai. Again, both Mr. Park Jie-won and Mr. Song Ho-gyong met. Before the meeting I told Minister Park, "Do not decide anything on the spot. When explaining the advantages of establishing a relationship with us to the North, speak to them in terms of advantages and disadvantages. For example, tell them what they would lose were there a war, and what they would gain if there is not a war. Let them see the concrete benefits of economic cooperation and peaceful interchange."

I also told him what not to omit in the agreement, should that happen. "The agreement should include three things: first, Chairman Kim Jong-il should invite me; second, the counterpart for the summit should be Chairman Kim Jong-il; and third, they should respond to our invitation as well."

Unfortunately, there was no visible progress during this meeting. Minister Park reported, "Although there was interest in the summit, we could not reach an agreement regarding concrete details, such as the inviting party; the time and schedule of the summit; and the agreement document following the summit."

This is what I expected. Chairman Kim Jong-il still remained in the background. Again, I ordered him, "Please work out every detail clearly."

There was the second special envoy meeting on March 23. I waited for Minister Park to bring good news as if I were a folktale character eagerly waiting for a swallow to return with a calabash seed in its mouth in the spring. The South and the North were gradually approaching the summit. Our side proposed again that the agreement should clearly state that it would be Chairman Kim Jong-il who would invite me, and that the summit would be held between June 12 and 14. The North agreed with the mid-June timeframe, but there was no progress in clearly stating who would invite whom. The North's argument was that, although Chairman Kim Jong-il would be a partner at the summit, there was not a diplomatic precedent for including him in the agreement document.

After receiving this report, I determined that the North was changing. I again ordered Minister Park to include the inviting party in the agreement, and advised him to also include the matter of dispersed families.

The third meeting was held in Beijing. The North sent a message requesting a meeting through Hyundai president Chung Mong-hun. My staff had already prepared an outline of a compromise agreement while working with their North Korean counterparts in Beijing. Before leaving for Beijing, Minister Park said to me: "I believe there is a very strong possibility of an agreement this time, sir."

Again, I urged him, "Please work out a clear agreement. I have great expectations."

Minister Park finally returned with a calabash seed in the form of the April 8 Agreement. It read:

> The South and the North agree to the following in order to advance national reconciliation and union, interchange and cooperation, and peace and reunification, while re-affirming the three principles for reunification, declared in the historic July 4 South–North Joint Communique. President Kim Dae-jung will visit Pyongyang from June 12 to June 14, 2000, according to Chairman Kim Jong-il's invitation. During this visit to Pyongyang, there will be an historic meeting and a summit between President Kim Dae-jung and Chairman Kim Jong-il. Both parties will meet preliminarily in April to discuss procedural matters.

North Korea wanted to publicize this agreement on April 10. The South proposed announcing it in Beijing on April 9, as it was difficult to maintain secrecy. However, the North insisted, saying that they had to announce it on April 10, the day the April Spring Friendship Art Festival in honor of the late president Kim Il-sung's birthday. We had to yield.

I was deeply moved by the news of this agreement. The Sunshine Policy that we had promoted for two years finally succeeded in thawing North Korea's suspicions. It was all thanks to the Korean people's support of the Sunshine Policy. The Korean people had continued to support it despite the propaganda against it. *Finally the opportunity to materialize my lifelong reunification dream has come*, I thought; I promised myself that although I could not immediately achieve reunification, I would solve the issue of dispersed families no matter what.

I let the US and Japan know about the status of inter-Korean dialogue, which had been conducted in secrecy for a month. I sent Director Lim Dong-won to visit ambassadors from the US and Japan. American Ambassador Bosworth wanted to hear directly from Minister Park Jie-won. "Tell him every single detail, without omitting even the sound of a breath," I ordered Minister Park.

At 10:00 a.m. on April 10, Minister of Unification Park Jae Kyu and Minister of Culture and Tourism Park Jie-won announced the agreement for the inter-Korean summit. The same announcement was simultaneously made in the North. The media poured out analyses and prospects in response to the news. Civic and economic organizations, like the Nationwide Council for National Reconciliation and Cooperation and the Federation of Korean Industries, issued welcoming statements. They read:

> This is an epoch-making historical event in the history of Korean division. We expect that it will provide the momentum for ending the Cold War, as well as the impetus for reconciliation and cooperation.
>
> The inter-Korean summit provides a new turning point in inter-Korean economic cooperation. We also expect that foreign investment in Korea will become livelier.

All of the countries that had been supporting our Sunshine Policy also welcomed the news. President Clinton issued a special statement, saying:

> I welcome the announcement that the Republic of Korea and the Democratic People's Republic of Korea will hold an historic first summit in June. Direct dialog between the two Koreas is something we have long advocated and is fundamental to solving the problems of the Korean Peninsula. This announcement is testimony to the wisdom and long-term vision of President Kim Dae-jung's engagement policy. I congratulate both leaders on their decision to meet.

Japanese Minister of Foreign Affairs Kono Yohei issued a statement, and the Ministry of Foreign Affairs in Russia, China, Germany, France, and Italy also issued statements in support of the agreement. President of Egypt Mubarak and president of IOC Samaranch sent letters of congratulation. Ninety percent of South Koreans supported this meeting. The stock price soared too. Former presidents also did not spare encouragement. Even Mr. Kim Young-sam, who had so condemned me, told the Senior Secretary for Foreign Affairs and National Security to "Please send President Kim my congratulations."

Nonetheless, the opposition party criticized it as sensationalism. Of course, their argument was understandable since the general election was at hand. Of course, I could not know what effect this agreement would have on the general election; if anything, it was burdensome to have this kind of event immediately before the general election. In fact, before the announcement, the NIS submitted a report predicting public sentiment about this agreement to me that read:

> The opposition party's criticism and fierce protest about the agreement, claiming that it is a political tactic for the general election, as well as spreading theories of suspicion about the agreement and [the President's] obsession with the Nobel Peace Prize could have a negative influence on the general election. It would be advantageous for the government to delay announcing the agreement until after the election.

I made the decision to announce it at the time we had agreed upon with North Korea despite this recommendation. The relevant offices and I immediately began preparing for the summit. We had very little time since the summit was only two months away. I had Director of NIS Lim Dong-won take charge of the entire process. Both the NIS and the Ministry of Reunification worked feverishly.

We formed the Inter-Korean Summit Promotion Committee, led by Minister of Reunification Park Jae-gyu. Senior Secretary of Economy Lee Ki-ho participated in it, in addition to the standing committee members of the National Security Council. We also formed the Preparation and Planning Committee, led by Vice Minister of Reunification Yang Young-shik. The Preparation and Planning Committee was in charge of planning and negotiations regarding all practical affairs for the summit, as well as inter-Korean communications.

There were five inter-Korean summit-planning meetings in Panmunjeom between April 22 and May 18. The officials went back and forth between the House of Peace in the South and the Palace of Reunification in the North in order to create and sign off on the Agreement on Practical Procedures to Carry Out the Inter-Korean Agreement. According to this agreement, the number of delegates from the South would be 130, with an additional 50 reporters present. The agreement included fourteen items altogether, including the format and number of meetings, the schedule, the dispatch of the advance party, security for personal protection, recording and reporting of the summit, and live reporting. I received a report that everything was going smoothly.

I had a lot to prepare, too. First of all, I wanted to know exactly what kind of person Kim Jong-il was. I read many books about North Korea and Kim Jong-il, including *I Saw the Truth of History*, written by the former president of Kim Il-sung University, Hwang Jang-yop, who chose exile in 1997. The NIS also sent me various books, images, photos, and videos. All of them were unilaterally negative. I called Director Lim and asked him to gather objective and concrete information. "If all of this is true, then, how can I sit with someone like that face-to-face and engage in a meeting?" I asked. "I need accurate information."

I also needed to have a concrete idea about what intentions the North was bringing to the summit. I realized that this kind of information could not be gathered through the officials in charge of practical procedural affairs, so I asked Director Lim to visit Pyongyang. I said, "It is inevitable that you visit Pyongyang as my special envoy. Please meet Chairman Kim Jong-il and do three things. First, please find out what kind of person he is. Second, please fully explain the agenda items for the summit and find out about their positions. Third, please bring back a draft for the joint statement that will be issued after the summit. Your task is to do a preliminary meeting for the summit."

At dawn on Saturday, May 27, Director Lim went north through Panmunjeom with four attendants. I was anxious all day long. Just after 7:00 p.m. I received a phone call from Director Lim, his voice so clear it was as if I was talking to someone in Seoul. He told me that he was still in Pyongyang, but it was impossible to meet Chairman Kim. I told him to come right back. The result was disappointing.

Time moved slowly as I waited for Director Lim at the official residence. He finally entered my office at 11:20 p.m. and explained what happened during the twelve hours he had stayed in Pyongyang.

"I met Chief of the 1st Division of the United Front Department of the Workers' Party of Korea Lim Tong-ok. He told me that if you don't visit the Kumsusan Palace of the Sun, you can't meet Chairman Kim." The body of President Kim Il-sung was enshrined in the Kumsusan Palace of the Sun. We'd struck a wall, just as we'd been worried we would.

"I said that it was impossible because of the special nature of inter-Korean relationship," Director Lim continued, "but they would not budge. He said to me, 'When you visited Hanoi, you paid your respects at the tomb of President Ho Chi Min, so how does it make sense not to visit a Korean's?' I could not even meet Secretary Kim Yong-sun."

Director Lim's voice was low, but clear. The earnest expression on his face told me how hard he had tried on his visit to Pyongyang. Even his hair looked whiter. "Director Lim," I said, "you worked very hard today. Let us discuss how to handle this situation tomorrow afternoon."

Director Lim later wrote about that day's disappointment and sadness in his memoir, *Peace Maker*.

That night, I flew in a helicopter at a low altitude through the rainy pitch-black night sky of the "dark republic," along the Pyongyang-Kaesong Highway. North Koreans, including Choi Song-chul and Kwon Ho-ung, were on board too. No one on board could hide their anxiety about this dangerous flight through the torrential rain. In the helicopter, I remembered Isaiah 43:1–2, which my wife had read to me before I left the house earlier that morning: "Do not fear, for I have redeemed you; I have summoned you by name; you are mine … When you walk through the fire, you will not be burned; the flames will not set you ablaze."

After about seventy minutes, we could see the torch indicating our landing point. After we landed near Kaesong around 9:30 p.m., I finally breathed a sigh of relief. About thirty minutes later, I safely crossed the DMZ and returned to the brightly lit land of freedom. Although I returned without much achievement, the joy I felt upon returning is indescribable. It was only then that I felt hunger—I had been so anxious that I skipped dinner. Although it was very late at night, President Kim was waiting for me in his office.

He did not tell me about these moments of despair and crisis then. Reading his memoir, I fully understood what an unusual experience he underwent during his transformation from a peacekeeper, that is, a person who guards peace, to a peacemaker, that is, a person who creates peace. I am grateful to him.

He left the Blue House around midnight. I felt sorry for him as the back of his small-framed body walked away.

On June 3, Director Lim crossed the Demilitarized Zone (DMZ). There were less than ten days left until the summit. The summit *had* to happen. If it didn't happen after all of the Korean people's cheers and the world's support, both the South and the North would become the laughing stalk of the world. If we missed this opportunity, we couldn't even talk about the summit again.

I sent a signed letter to Chairman Kim Jong-il through Director Lim, presenting four agenda items that I hoped to discuss at the summit: the improvement of the inter-Korean relationship and reunification; the relaxation of tensions and instatement of peace; interchange and cooperation for coexistence and co-prosperity; and dispersed families. I also proposed issuing a joint statement with practical measures for the new inter-Korean relationship. Finally, I added that I could consider visiting the Kumsusan Palace of the Sun after successful completion of the summit.

I waited again. This time, Director Lim sent me a midterm report stating that he had met Chairman Kim Jong-il. Director Lim spent the night in the North before returning to Seoul very late the next night. We sat together again at midnight. I asked a lot of questions and he gave a lot of answers. Director Lim said that Chairman Kim Jong-il had a favorable view of me. "Chairman Kim knew about your life of hardship throughout the democracy struggle. He said that you have performed very well as president. He said that he personally admires you, and I felt that he really did. He also said that if you visit Pyongyang he will treat you respectfully, as a venerable elder. Chairman Kim Jong-il said that you should not worry because he is planning to treat you more magnificently than any other foreign heads."

I was quite relieved to hear that. I was curious about Chairman Kim Jong-il as a person. Director Lim said that he did not get the impression that he was "shady," "cranky," or a "screwball," as some seemed to believe.

"He listened to me very carefully and enjoyed talking, too," Director Lim reported. "I got the impression that he was bright and very quick. He was cheerful and had a great sense of humor. He appeared to have an open-minded and practical approach. Although he did not speak logically, he did not lose sight of the topic at hand. I got the impression that he is a good conversationalist. He particularly seemed to treat elders courteously."

Director Lim's face was bright as he explained all of this. I felt very relieved. However, the question of visiting the Kumsusan Palace of the

Sun remained unresolved. Director Lim said that Chairman Kim had stated that he could not yield on this matter, and that he seemed very resolute. I could almost hear Chairman Kim's voice through Director Lim's words. According to Director Lim, when he asked Chairman Kim to consider the South Korean sentiment, Chairman Kim told him, "Why do you think only of the South Korean sentiment? Is the North Korean sentiment not important? Isn't it an old Korean custom to pay respect when you visit a house of mourning, and, therefore, isn't it natural?"

On the other hand, Chairman Kim showed an active interest in the matter of dispersed families, to which I was also devoted. He had said that he was willing to take active and positive measures for their meeting. I spoke with Director Lim for about an hour; I wished to talk with him more, but it was very late.

The general election was on April 13. Although the exit polls predicted the Democratic Party would win in an overwhelming victory, we were defeated. By winning 115 seats, the Democratic Party yielded the position of majority party to the Grand National Party, which won 133 seats. The LDA won seventeen seats, the Minguk Party two seats, the Hanguksin Party one seat, and the independents five seats. The Democratic Party was supported evenly in regions other than the Gyeongsang area, where we could not win the people's hearts. We became a national party and increased our seats by thirty, though.

I had high hopes for this election, but all of our party candidates who I trusted would win in the Gyeongsang area were defeated, including Kim Chung-gwon, Roh Moo-hyun, and Kim Jung-kil. My party and I had all done our best over the past two years to overcome the foreign currency crisis and revive the economy. I had trusted that the Korean people would appreciate that. The results, however, were different from my expectations; I had failed at reading people's minds again. When I thought of the difficult road ahead, I felt very discouraged. The LDA failed to even form a negotiation body.

On April 17, I issued a special statement. I congratulated the Grand National Party and comforted the LDA. I also clearly stated my will to continue our party's collaboration with the LDA. I emphasized the grand politics of dialogue and compromise, and reform without interruption. "I will try my best to carry out the grave heavy task of the presidency for the next three years of my term," I said. "I will lead state affairs modestly and sincerely, as well as resolutely and strongly. I will decide everything according to the people's will."

I then had an interparty summit with president of the GNP Lee Hoi-chang. We agreed to practice mutually beneficial politics through cooperation between the ruling and opposition parties, and to cooperate on the inter-Korean summit regardless of party politics. Unfortunately, we collided on just about every matter since then. True politics were lost in what turned into a contest of strength, and my fears came true. Although I hoped for stability, I had to captain a boat that was continuously rocking.

Candidate Putin won the Russian presidential election. I called President Elect Putin on April 28. After congratulating him, I asked for his interest in and support for the inter-Korean summit. President Elect Putin congratulated me on the summit and promised to support our efforts. "Nothing has changed in Russia between yesterday and today," he assured me. "We will continue to support the inter-Korean dialogue and try our best to support the success of the inter-Korean summit."

On May 9, I handed the appointment certificate to Chairman of the Presidential Commission on Women's Affairs Baek Kyung-nam and urged her, "Please arbitrate well among the women's rights tasks that are dispersed throughout different offices and cooperate with them for the real benefit of women."

I invited 171 foreign diplomats in Korea to a garden party at the Nokjiwon in the Blue House on May 12. The sunlight rolling across the grass was soft and the sky was transparent. Even the breeze felt green. The *bansong* pine in the corner of Nokjiwon was beautiful. This pine tree was 150 years old, and its beauty stood out. It looked pretty and elegant, whenever you saw it. I often meditated in front of it. Foreigners loved the open and quiet landscape of Nokjiwon. I thanked them for helping Korea during the financial crisis, and asked them to support the inter-Korean summit.

"A month from today," I said, "I will meet and talk with the North Korean leader in Pyongyang. Although I am over seventy years old, I have never been to Mt. Kumgang or Pyongyang. I sometimes sadly thought that I would never visit them in my lifetime, but I am about to visit Pyongyang now, and I am deeply moved.

"In February 1972, President of the United States Richard Nixon visited China and met Chairman Mao Zedong. The meeting itself was more important than any agreement, and it became a historical turning point.

"If I visit Pyongyang, shake hands with the North Korean leader in front of the world, and declare reconciliation, I believe it would be a great event and a great success."

Former Prime Minister of Japan Obuchi Keizo passed away on May 14. After hearing about his cerebral infarction, I had been worried about him. He had a very informal and ordinary demeanor, and made those around him comfortable. Whenever we met, he welcomed me with a gentle and benevolent smile. He cherished my opinion in international conferences and spared words, always considerate of others. I sent my condolences via telegram and wrote: "Former Prime Minister Obuchi contributed greatly to opening a new era of friendship and cooperation between Korea and Japan. The deceased was my friend who I respected most and who was closest to me. I cannot help feeling empty and sad that I have lost such a friend."

On May 18, I attended the twentieth anniversary ceremony of the Gwangju Democracy Movement. On a brilliant May day in this new millennium, I stood at the May 18 Cemetery once again. Whenever I visited it, I was overwhelmed by sadness. I said in my address: "Whenever I think of the numerous heroes of democracy who fell without any glory on the roads of Chungjang-no and Geumnam-no and inside the Jeollanam-do provincial government building … I feel immeasurably sad and moved, and I renew my resolutions again and again.

"It has been twenty years. Their noble sacrifices were not at all in vain. The flames of democracy that they burned with their own bodies did not die, but rose even in the pitch-dark times of dictatorship.

"The citizens of Gwangju, who were falsely accused of being 'mobs,' are now revered by people around the world as great defenders of democracy. Also, Gwangju, the city trampled upon under the evil firearms and swords, is now standing tall as the holy ground of democracy in history.

"Who among those who live in this land is not indebted to the Gwangju of that day? Now is the time when we should do our best to fulfill our duty as survivors."

I was deeply overwhelmed, and citizens of Gwangju were sobbing. When will they stop shedding tears? I promised to treat all May 18 victims with respect as "contributors to democracy" and to elevate the status of the May 18 Cemetery to a national cemetery. I promised to do my best to have the spirit and sacrifice of the May 18 Struggle remembered forever and enhanced by history.

Prime Minister Park Tae-joon was involved in the real estate title trusting allegation. He resigned abruptly on May 19, just twenty days or so before the inter-Korean summit. Yet, I had no choice but to accept his resignation. I asked the LDA to recommend his replacement. This recommendation became the test board for the coalition between the Democratic Party and LDA.

I sent Chief of Staff Hahn Gwang-ok to honorary president of LDA Kim Jong-pil to discuss the matter. Mr. Kim Jong-pil recommended president of LDA Lee Han-dong. With this recommendation, the coalition between the Democratic Party and LDA—which the LDA had unilaterally discarded before the April 13 general election—was practically restored. On May 23, Assemblyman Chung Kyun-hwan was elected as minority leader. The sixteenth-term National Assembly opened on June 5. Assemblyman Lee Man-sup was elected as the speaker of the Assembly. In my Assembly address, I requested their cooperation in the inter-Korean summit regardless of party affiliation.

Before the summit, I gathered people's opinions both domestically and abroad. I met many people and listened to their thoughts. I met former presidents, high officials in three government branches, and the leaders of both ruling and opposition parties. I invited specialists in inter-Korean matters, such as Sejong Institute senior researcher and, later, Minister of Reunification Lee Jong-seok, Professors Ahn Byung-joon and Moon Chung-in, and Director of the Social Science Institute Kim Kyung-won, and participated in discussions about the significance and tasks of the summit. I also gathered with about forty people who were engaged in inter-Korean cooperation businesses, including president of the Kohap Group Chang Chi-hyuk, CEO of Hyundai Asan Kim Yoon-kyu, president of Pyeonghwa Motors Park Sang-kwon, president of Korean Good Neighbors Yi Il-ha, Eugene Bell Foundation Chair John Linton, and Secretary General of the Korean National Welfare Foundation Kim Hyung-seok. I heard about their experiences and advice.

On Memorial Day, I visited the Seoul Bohun Hospital and comforted patients. They said, almost in chorus, "We wish you success at the inter-Korean summit!"

That afternoon, I held two model summits in the Chungmu Room of the Blue House. Former Executive Director of Inter-Korean Dialogue Kim Dal-sool played the role of Chairman Kim Jong-il and former Vice Minister of Reunification Jeong Se Hyun took the role of secretary-in-charge of Anti-ROK Operations Kim Yong-sun. From our side, Director of NIS Lim Dong-won, Senior Secretary of Foreign Affairs and Security Hwang Won-tak, and Senior Secretary of Economy Lee Ki-ho participated. Those who played the role of North Koreans asked sharp questions about the confederation system and US armed forces in Korea, imitating even their dialects and accents. The rehearsal took five hours. Most of the questions and answers we practiced came up during the real summit in Pyongyang.

I finalized ten official attendants and twenty-four special attendants. The special attendants included chief vice president of the National Unification Advisory Council Kim Min-ha; chairperson of the Policy Committee of the Democratic Party Lee Hae-chan; LDA executive member Lee One-koo; president of Ewha Womans University Chang Sang; chairperson of the Korean Council for Reconciliation and Cooperation Kang Man-gil; president of the National Academy of Arts of the Republic of Korea Cha Bum-suk; president of the Korean Olympic Committee Kim Un-yong; president of the Korea Football Association Chung Mong-joon; president of the Korean Broadcasters Association Park Kwon-sang; president of the Korea Association of Newspapers Choi Hak-rae; secretary general of the Korean Red Cross Park Ki-ryun; advisor of the Association of Writers for National Literature Ko Un; president of Korea International Trade Association Kim Jae-chul; vice president of the Federation of Korean Industries Sohn Byung-doo; vice president of Korea Federation of SMEs Lee Won-ho; director of Hyundai Asan Chung Mong-hun; vice president of Samsung Yun Jong-yong; president of LG Koo Bon-moo; president of SK Son Kil-seung; chair of the Inter-Korean Economic Cooperation Committee Chang Chi-hyeok; president of Rinnai Korea Kang Song-mo; president of the Board of Directors of the Inje Educational Foundation Paik Nak-Whan; director of Yonsei University Reunification Studies Institute and Professor Moon Chung-in; and director of Inter-Korean Relationship at the Sejong Institute Lee Chong-sok. Presidential physician Dr. Huh Kap-bum accompanied us as well.

I landed in Tokyo with my wife on the morning of June 8 to attend the funeral of former prime minister of Japan Obuchi Keizo. I had successive summit meetings with Japanese Prime Minister Mori Yoshiro and US president Bill Clinton. Despite rejecting all other summit requests, President Clinton met with me. It had been nine months since we last met at the Asia-Pacific Economic Cooperation (APEC) summit meeting, where our summit included the late Prime Minister Obuchi Keizo. He was now lying silently while the two of us brought flowers to lay before his spirit. In consideration of my special relationship with the deceased, President Clinton let me pay my respects before he did. The more I got to know President Clinton, the more I liked him. He congratulated me on the summit and said, "I hope you will succeed in this important summit. You are the person best suited to persuade and help North Korea's development. I will be greatly honored to play any small role in this historic event."

"It will be an historical turning point for me just to cross the barbed wires to North Korea for the first time in fifty-five years," I replied.

President Clinton then made a very significant, if rather premature, remark. "We will meet again at the APEC meeting in November. If you come with Chairman Kim Jong-il then, it will be great news."

I had a summit with Prime Minister Mori Yoshiro as well. Afterward, President Clinton and Prime Minister Yoshiro also had a summit and issued a joint statement, saying: "We support the inter-Korean summit and, at the same time, we hope for a change in North Korea." Through summits, the three heads of state from Korea, the US, and Japan officially confirmed our three-way cooperation. "The parties concerned should take the initiative in the inter-Korean matter, and the inter-Korean summit will be helpful to the United States and Japan as well."

In the end, my condolence diplomacy prior to my trip to Pyongyang contributed to spreading the historic news of the inter-Korean summit to the world.

During the cabinet meeting on June 9, I thanked the Korean people for their support of the inter-Korean summit. "I visit North Korea next Monday. What and how much we agree on will be important, but what is more important is to meet, and to exchange our thoughts and know eath other's thoughts.

"When we look at historic summits of the past like the inter-German summit, China-Japan summit following the Sino-Japanese War, or President Nixon's visit to China, they were not all immediately successful. However, those meetings had an enormous historical impact in the long run.

"I know very well and I am thankful that all Koreans are interested in and support this meeting. The world's attention is unusually focused on one place in the Korean Peninsula."

All of the assemblymen adopted a written resolution that expressed the National Assembly's support for the summit. Pope John Paul II issued a statement wishing for a successful summit. Many countries and international organizations (including the UN) from all over the world successively issued statements of support.

Suddenly, through a written message, the North requested that I delay my visit by a day. "We request that President Kim Dae-jung postpone his visit for a day and visit Pyongyang for two nights and three days from June 13 to 17, due to technical preparation matters."

This sudden notice puzzled me. The media wrote many speculative articles. I ordered my secretaries not to be disturbed. Although a little ominous, I also trusted that North Korea would not be so irresponsible as to break an international promise. "If we have waited for fifty-five years, we can wait one more day," I said.

The road to the North was uneasy until the very last moment. I did not have an official schedule on June 12. That morning, I took a walk with my wife in Nokjiwon. Thinking about how I would walk on the land of North Korea the next day, I fed fish in the pond and sat on the bench under the *bansong* pine, feeling the warmth of the June sun on me for a long time. I felt a lot more relaxed than before. I returned to the residence and fed and patted Cheoyong and Nari, our Jindo dogs. Netizens left an enormous number of messages on the Blue House website sending wishes for a successful summit. I heard that there was a rain shower and double rainbow in the northern area of Seoul that afternoon. The media reported it as an auspicious sign for the inter-Korean summit.

A very special morning broke on June 13. It was the tensest morning of my entire Blue House life. The weather was fair and clear. I prayed and said to myself, "The noble moment that will open a new chapter for Korean history is approaching. I'll do my best so that today's visit can greatly contribute to leading our nation to reunification and a peaceful future. I will not disappoint the wishes of 70 million Koreans and the expectations and will of world citizens."

My wife and I ate bean sprout soup and half-cooked eggs for breakfast. Her face displayed excitement and anxiety.

When I left the residence for the office building, all of the secretaries were waiting for me. I ordered Senior Secretary of Policy and Planning Kim Sung-jae to take charge of the Blue House, before I left at 8:15 a.m. The Blue House staff members stood in a line and waved their hands; citizens gathered on Hyoja-ro Street in front of the Blue House. I got out of the car and shook their hands. An elderly man showed me a black and white family photo and said, "This is a picture of my parents and siblings in the North. Please have a successful meeting and help me meet them."

The people in the photo all looked very young. I held the man's hand tightly. At Seoul Airport in Seongnam, about 1000 people were waiting for me, including the Speaker of the National Assembly Lee Man-sup, Chief Justice of the Supreme Court Choi Jong-young, Sohn Byung-doo Acting Prime Minister Lee Han-dong, cabinet members, and evacuees from the North. We held a send-off ceremony where I read my departure statement.

"Fellow Koreans Whom I Respect and Love: Today I embark on a trip to Pyongyang for two days and three nights. I would like to visit with passionate love for our people and a calm, realistic mind. In Pyongyang, I will have the historic inter-Korean summit with Chairman Kim Jong-il. The road to the summit that has appeared to be forever blocked for the past fifty-five years is now opening in front of us. It is thanks to the Korean people's constant wishes and support for the inter-Korean reconciliation and cooperation and peaceful reunification of our country that this road is opening up. I sincerely thank you for your support.

"I sincerely hope that my visit to Pyongyang will become the road to peace and reconciliation. I hope that it will become the momentum for the elimination of the threat of war and the end of the Cold War so that all 70 million Koreans can live peacefully.

"I hope that my visit to Pyongyang will bring about great advancement in inter-Korean interchanges and cooperation in all fields, including politics, economy, culture, tourism, and the environment. I am also firmly resolved that my visit will enable dispersed families to reunite and share their familial affections. This visit to Pyongyang should not end with mine, but be the road to continuous and ordinary dialogue. We will also have to achieve Chairman Kim Jong-il's visit to Seoul.

"Now I leave for the North, carrying with me the Korean people's wishes. I urge your special support for this visit so that I can achieve my historical mission for our nation."

I later realized that I had omitted the customary Korean greeting "I will be back soon." I must have been really anxious.

In fact, there were a few matters that had not been agreed upon, such as the content of the joint statement and the matter of visiting the Kumsusan Palace of the Sun. Also, North Korea did not allow reporters from the *Chosun ilbo* newspaper and KBS broadcasting station to visit. I ordered those reporters to be on board the plane. It was a matter of the values of our system. I resolutely said, "South Korea is a democratic country. It does not make sense to limit the freedom of the press in a democratic country. To hold a summit means to recognize each other's system. It is we who decide which reporters will accompany the visit. There is no need for the summit if we have to yield on the matter of accompanying reporters."

All of these issues were, indeed, worrisome. We got on the plane, as children sang "Missing Hometown" and "Our Wish is Reunification." The plane took off from the Seoul Airport at 9:15 a.m.

"You Came to a Scary, Frightening Place" (June 13–14, 2000)

Our plane flew toward the north as if nothing unusual was happening. The sky was so clear that there wasn't a single cloud. The sunrays were bright on the skyway that had not been opened once in fifty-five years.

Then an announcement came on. "My name is Lieutenant Colonel Park Yeong-seop. I will escort Mr. President to Pyongyang. I earnestly hope that the historic summit will be successful. The weather in Pyongyang now is clear with a few clouds."

Pyongyang. That's right, I was going to Pyongyang. Why was I so anxious to go to a land where my own people lived? Nobody talked on the plane. Again, an announcement broke the silence. "Air Force Flight #1 will soon cross the thirty-eighth parallel. To the right, you can see Cape Changsangot in the Ongjin Peninsula in North Korea. The temperature in Pyongyang is 23 degrees."

I entered my office on the airplane alone, where I continued to look out of the window. Northern mountains and rivers caught my eyes. The mountains were naked and dark red. The mountains, fields, and roads felt as familiar as those in the South; however, the people working in the rice paddies and fields and the passersby on the road looked shabby. Although the scenery passed by quickly, I was left with clear afterimages.

We arrived at the Sunan Airport around 10:30 a.m. It had only taken about an hour to connect what was broken for half a century. Protocol Secretary Kim Ha-joong came to me and said, "Chairman Kim Jong-il came to greet you."

The door opened and I stood on top of the trap. I looked up at the sky and then around me. I was deeply moved to see North Korean land for the first time. I couldn't find words to express my feelings. Momentarily, I was swarmed with numerous thoughts. I was there, between the sky and the land of the North. I could feel something hot in my heart. I could see crowds waving flowers and chanting something. A large portrait of President Kim Il-sung hung on the airport building. I could see Chairman Kim Jong-il below, wearing a Maoist suit. I stepped down the trap and landed on northern soil. I wished I could kneel and kiss the soil, but I could not because of my stiff leg.

Chairman Kim approached me and we held hands. Almost in unison, we said, "I'm glad to meet you."

Chairman Kim then said the same to my wife. He looked warm and cheerful. I inspected the North Korean Honor Guard. When I approached it, the Honor Guard chief resoundingly reported, "General Secretary of the Workers' Party of Korea, Chairman of the Central Military Commission of Korea, and Korean People's Army Commander-in-Chief, the Army, Navy, and Air Force Honor Guards lined up to greet President Kim Dae-jung with dear comrade and Commander-in-Chief."

After the inspection, Chairman Kim introduced the North Korean leaders to me. They included President of the Presidium of the Supreme People's Assembly (SPA) of North Korea Kim Yong-nam, First Vice Chairman of the National Defense Commission Jo Myong-rok, Premier Hong Song-nam, Chairman of the Deputies' Credential Screening Committee of the SPA Kim Kuk-tae, Secretary of the Workers' Party of Korea Kim Yong-sun, Chairman of the SPA Choe Thae-bok, First Vice Foreign Minister Kang Sok-ju, Vice Chairman of Asia Pacific Peace Committee of Korea Song Ho-gyong, and Chief Director of the Committee for the Peaceful Reunification of the Fatherland An Kyong-ho.

I issued a written statement upon my arrival. If Chairman Kim had not come to the airport, I would have read it at the airport.

"Citizens of Pyongyang Whom I Respect and Love, and Fellow Koreans in the North: I am really glad to be here. I came here because I want to see you. I came because I want to see the northern mountains and rivers that I have seen only in my dreams. It has been too long. I am finally here after a long period of twists and turns.

"It has not been just once or twice that I felt despairing, worrying that I would never step on the northern land. But, I have now accomplished my lifelong dream. I sincerely hope that 70 million Koreans in both the South and the North can accomplish their wishes, too.

"We cannot materialize the desire of our hearts, which has accumulated for half a century, all at once. However, beginning is half the work. I sincerely hope that my visit to Pyongyang will encourage reconciliation and cooperation, and the hope for peaceful reunification for all Koreans.

"We are one nation. We are a community of the same destiny. Let us all firmly hold hands. I love you."

As I walked to the black car that was waiting for us with Chairman Kim, the welcoming crowd waved flowers. Their cheers were so loud that they seemed to bury the airport. Chairman Kim escorted me to the back right seat, then walked around the car and got into the back left seat. Nobody expected that. Although he took my wife's seat, I was happy. My wife got in a car with Director of Asia Pacific Peace Committee of Korea Park Seon-ok.

Many people wonder what I talked about with Chairman Kim in the car. In fact, we could not talk much. As hundreds of thousands of people enthusiastically cheered outside, I was, frankly, overwhelmed. Chairman Kim told me to relax. "Were you not scared to come to the North?" he asked. "How could you come to such a frightening place? All of those people voluntarily came out to welcome you. We'll take good care of you during your stay here. Do take it easy."

"All Koreans and the world are looking at us. I hope we will have good results from this meeting," I said to him. "Results that will give our nation hope."

We held hands in the car as the citizens of Pyongyang chanted outside. "Hurrah!" "*Gyeolsaongwi!*" (We will guard you to death!) Most of the women wore colorful traditional Korean attire and the female students wore white tops and black skirts. North Koreans seemed to love those traditional Korean clothes that people in the South wore only on festive days.

We stopped the car briefly at the entrance of downtown Pyongyang, which had the pretty name, Yonmot-dong (pond village). A student gave me flowers. I got out of the car and shook hands with citizens. The marching band's music was cheerful.

Our car passed Chollima Street, the Korean Revolution Museum, the Mansudae Hill where the statue of Kim Il-sung stood, the Chollima Statue in Moranbong, the Arch of Triumph, Kim Il-sung University, and the Kumsusan Palace of the Sun. Throughout this journey, the flowery waves continued on the street. All of the monuments were enormous and, in comparison, the citizens standing under them looked very small. The Arch of Triumph, for example, looked a few times larger than its French equivalent.

We arrived at the Paekhwawon State Guesthouse, which means "a place where hundreds of flowers bloom." I heard that President Kim Il-sung had named it. A large mural depicting Haegeumgang, washed by waves, hung in the lobby of the first building of the guesthouse. Chairman Kim Jong-il and I took a picture in front of the mural. We took another picture with Chairman Kim Jong-il on the left of me and my wife on the right. Chairman Kim Jong-il also posed for a photo with South Korean delegates.

Chairman Kim Jong-il and I went to the reception room and chatted. This first summit was televised live. Chairman Kim said more than I did. It marked the moment when his unreserved and dignified voice was first known to the world.

"We told people about your course two nights ago," he said. "We let them know which course you would be taking from the airport to Paekhwawon State Guesthouse. The foreign media said that we delayed a day because we were not ready, but that was not true. The people are very glad we did this."

"I was surprised to see so many people come out to welcome me, and I am grateful," I responded. "I thought I would never tread on northern land, and I am overwhelmed by and thankful for your enthusiastic welcome. The weather in Seoul and Pyongyang are clear and beautiful to celebrate the dialogue for 70 million Koreans. It seems like it is congratulating us on this happy national occasion and to predict our success."

"I watched TV before I went to the airport this morning," Chairman Kim told me. "I saw you leave the airport and your plane connect with the Daegu control center before I headed to the airport. I heard that you ate only half of your half-cooked eggs this morning. Why did you eat so little when you were on your way to a tour?"

"I thought that I would be fed well in Pyongyang," I replied. Everyone around us, from both the North and the South, laughed.

"We will not brag about ourselves, but will treat you well," Chairman Kim told me. "We have an ethical code of 'the country of courteous people in the East.' We welcome foreign heads of the state, and there is no reason why we would not welcome you. People bravely ran out to see your brave visit to the North. We will show you clearly how we support and welcome your visit. The ministers who accompanied you also came to a scary, frightening place. However, communists have ethical codes too, and we're the same Korean people as you are."

I made a joke about my fearlessness and everyone laughed again. When our audience settled, I thanked Chairman Kim once more.

"June 13 will be proudly recorded in history," Chairman Kim declared.

"Let us make such history," I responded.

"If the late president was alive, he would have welcomed you," Chairman Kim told me. "It was what he wished for until his demise. I heard that when he was planning the summit with President Kim Young-sam, he was asked a lot of questions. President Kim Young-sam requested data about us through the UN. If President Kim Young-sam had been more sympathetic, we could have handed him everything in a direct phone call. We have a good precedent this time. I am confident that we will handle all relationship matters accordingly."

"I agree. From now on, we should directly communicate."

"The world is paying attention to us now," Chairman Kim said. "They are wondering why President Kim is visiting the North and why Chairman Kim accepted this summit. We have to offer the answer over the course of the next two nights and three days. I ask not only President Kim, but also the ministers to contribute to offering the answer."

After finishing this first summit, Chairman Kim shook hands with every attending person. To Chief of the Office of the Presidential Security An Joo-seob, he said, "Don't worry." People from both the South and North broke into bright smiles.

The drawing room of the guesthouse was about 30 *pyeong* (just under 120 square yards). We could watch all of the South Korean TV stations, each of which repeatedly looped my meeting with Chairman Kim at the Sunan Airport. I had lunch, my first meal in the North. Pyongyang's *onban*, rice in chicken stock, tasted unique—refreshing and simple, with a fresh aftertaste. My wife liked it too. Because I enjoyed it greatly, they later cooked *onban* at the Blue House, but it tasted different. I still can't forget how the *onban* tasted in Pyongyang.

I made a courtesy visit to President of the Presidium of the SPA of North Korea Kim Yong-nam at the Mansudae Assembly Hall that afternoon. From the North Korean side, Vice Presidents of the Presidium of the SPA Yang Hyong-sop and Ryo Won-gu, Chairman of the Central Committee of the Korean Social Democratic Party Kim Yong-dae, Vice Chairman of the Social Democratic Party Kim Yun-hyok, Minister of Culture Kang Rung-su, and Chief Director of the Committee for the Peaceful Reunification of the Fatherland An Kyong-ho attended this meeting. All official attendants from our side accompanied me.

After congratulating me on my visit, President Kim Yong-nam mentioned my democracy movement career. "I know very well about President Kim's career in the democratization struggle," he said. "We discontinued our relationship with Japan when you were kidnapped in Tokyo. Objectively viewing the situation as a Korean, I thought that you definitely should have been rescued. Our people began to know about you then."

This was the first time I had heard this, and I was rather surprised. I thanked him and said: "Our people should reconcile and unify. I've lived all my life wishing for reunification. We only live once, and I will also serve as president only once. I am past seventy now. Therefore, meeting with Chairman Kim Jong-il and beginning with all things possible, I would like to serve our people and contribute to reunification by giving 70 million Koreans hope and avoiding war.

"It has been twenty-eight years since the July 4 Joint Statement was announced and eight years since the Agreement on Reconciliation, Non-aggression, and Exchanges and Cooperation Between South and North was adopted," I continued. "However, nothing from those agreements has been executed. That's why this meeting is significant, and we should make an effort for eventual reconciliation by agreeing on and executing simple things that will benefit both the North and the South."

President Kim Yong-nam guided us to the Mansudae Art Theater—a performance hall for the exclusive use of the Mansudae Art Troup, a group of artists of the highest caliber—where we watched a performance entitled "People at Pyongyang Fortress." Their dance was lively and dynamic. Unlike dance performances in the South, its content felt exceedingly realistic. After the performance was over, we all went up on the stage and had a photo taken with the performers.

After taking a rest at the guesthouse, I attended dinner hosted by President Kim Yong-nam at the People's Culture Palace. About 300 guests attended it. There was a *ryuk-ryuk nalgaetang* made of six quail eggs among the dishes. Chairman Kim Jong-il named it to commemorate the date, the twelfth of June (6+6 *ryuk-ryuk*). Unfortunately, the dinner was also shifted to the thirteenth, so the name lost its shine a little. However, it was surprising to know that Chairman Kim paid attention to such a minute detail.

I went back to the guesthouse. Although a lot had happened that day, the next day was even more important. I reviewed the day with Chief of Staff Hahn Gwang-ok, Director Lim Dong-won, and Senior Press Secretary Park Joon-young. Electronic waves from Seoul poured the televised news from Pyongyang into my room.

I went to bed with my wife under a stiffly starched comforter. I could smell the starch, a scent I hadn't smelled in a long time. I felt warmed by the smell, which reminded me of my childhood on Hauido Island.

The live news of my visit to Pyongyang spread throughout the global village. A press center was installed in the Lotte Hotel in Sogong-dong, Seoul, and 1257 reporters (including 503 foreign journalists) from 289 media outlets (including 173 foreign outlets) registered. This was the largest press center registration since the founding of our country. I heard that about 1000 reporters in the press center stood up and applauded when Chairman Kim and I held hands at the Sunan Airport. I also heard that many of the reporters wiped their eyes. The global village was focused on the Korean Peninsula.

The North Korean media was filled with articles on the inter-Korean summit, too. The gist of all of them was the same: "The first reunion and meeting since the division of our country is being held according to the April 8 Agreement. It is an important incident wherein our people proudly display their firm will to achieve the holy task of reunification through independent national effort."

The second morning in Pyongyang broke. First, I met President Kim Yong-nam at the Mansudae Assembly Hall. I wrote in the guest book, "We are the same body that share a common fate as the same nation and as blood relations. Let us steadily advance toward peaceful interchange and cooperation, and the reunification of our nation. President of the Republic of Korea Kim Dae-jung, June 14, 2000."

President Kim Yong-nam emphasized the principle of independence when he said, "Foreign powers do not want the Korean nation to be reunited and become a powerful country." He was a very fluent speaker.

"In the twenty-first century, any nation or state will be miserable if it does not overcome the challenges of globalization and become a knowledge-and information-based society," I responded. "Our nation inherited from our ancestors the foundation of knowledge and education, as well as cultural creativity. If both the South and the North cooperate and utilize our legacy competently, we will become an advanced nation. But if not, we will waste our nation's energy and regress.

"We should not fear foreign powers, but utilize them. Although the Korean Peninsula used to be the plundering ground of the imperialists, we are now in the position to utilize the four powerful countries to our advantage. It is desirable for North Korea to establish a diplomatic relationship with the United States and Japan. Just as the South has a friendly relationship with China and Russia, it is important that the North has a friendly relationship with the United States and Japan. If we unite, we can move our neighboring countries.

"In terms of reunification, we should study and examine proposals from both sides. To be realistic is best; not being realistic is a waste of time. It is necessary to respect one another's system and confirm our intention to not attempt armed conquest. We also need to examine both Koreas' emergency military communication systems. Let us operate a common economic committee and have it examine works that can be beneficial to both sides and methods to cooperate in the fields of agriculture, electricity, railways, harbors and bays, and roads. Let us hurry to solve the problem of dispersed families. First-generation dispersed family members are dying in sorrow because they cannot see their blood relations. It is our duty to reunite them today."

After my speech, President Kim Yong-nam asked me three things. "You say independence at the same time as you mention the '3-way South Korea-United States-Japan cooperation.' What are your thoughts about this?"

"The 3-way cooperation is not a policy of blockade against the North, but based on the Sunshine Policy that South Korea presented," I explained. "The gist of it is that the three countries should give what can be given to North Korea and receive what can be received from you, too. We are absolutely against the use of armed forces in the Korean Peninsula, and hope to cooperate together to guarantee security for North Korea, lift the economic embargo against North Korea, and help you participate in the international community. US armed forces in Korea are necessary not for aggression, but for peace in East Asia."

President Kim Yong-nam asked me again, "What do you think of the National Security Law, which prevents visits, contacts, and interchanges between the North and the South?"

"It should be amended," I answered. "We already agreed to discuss the matter in 1992. Although we submitted the amended bill to the National Assembly, we have not been able to pass it through."

President Kim Yong-nam asked, "Although I understand very well that you think we should unite our power and achieve reunification independently, why do you not guarantee freedom of activities that encourage reunification capabilities and arrest and imprison patriotic reunification leaders, accusing them of violating the National Security Law?"

"Both the South and the North have a positive law and both systems cannot ignore it until our relationship improves," I said to him. "If the inter-Korean relationship changes, matters like those will improve as well."

After this conversation, I understood their position. It was greatly helpful to my summit with Chairman Kim Jong-il later that afternoon. I also hoped that my answers about our position would be delivered to Chairman Kim in detail.

We visited the famous Okryugwan Restaurant. It was enormous, capable of accommodating more than 1000 people. The *naengmyon* tasted simple and clean. "I thought I would never taste Pyongyang *naengmyon* in Pyongyang," I said, "but now I am enjoying it here."

That afternoon, my wife met Mr. Kim Ji-han, her teacher during her Ewha High School days. He was eighty-five years old.

At 3:00 p.m. I had the second summit with Chairman Kim Jong-il at the Paekhwawon State Guesthouse. Unlike the previous day, he was wearing a light gray suit with a Chinese-style collar and a Kim Il-sung badge on his left chest. Director of NIS Lim Dong-won, Senior Secretary for Foreign Affairs and National Security Hwang Won-tak, and Senior Secretary for Economy Lee Ki-ho accompanied me. From the North, only Secretary of the Workers' Party of Korea Kim Yong-sun attended the meeting, although we had agreed on three attendants each.

We chatted a little before getting down to business. "Your schedule has been intensive since this morning," Chairman Kim Jong-il said.

"I went to various places," I agreed.

"Was your bed comfortable?" he inquired.

"I slept well, and I had *naengmyon* at Okryugwan Restaurant, where I have always wanted to have it."

"I hope your lunch wasn't rushed because of our meeting this afternoon," Chairman Kim said. "And I hope you'll enjoy it again more leisurely. I watched South Korean TV broadcasting until late last night, including MBC. It seems that the people in the South also welcome this event. I also watched programs about displaced families and defectors. They were anxious to hear news from their home. I saw them actually crying."

"I heard that when we shook hands at the airport, about a thousand reporters, including foreign ones, all stood up and applauded," I said.

"Am I really such a big shot?" Chairman Kim asked. "I went to the airport to greet you. Westerners often say that I live in seclusion, and some have even said that this is the first time I appeared out in the open. But I have been to China and Indonesia and often other foreign countries privately. But, nonetheless, they say that I was released because of your visit. Well, it does not matter what they say, because I often do private visits."

We all laughed cheerfully when he spoke frankly about his private trips.

We then asked all of the reporters to leave and had a closed meeting. "Nobody lives forever, and nobody holds the same position," I began. "Now we are representing the South and the North. If we make one mistake, all our people could die. But, if we, solemnly in front of our ancestors and our nation, look for a way to let our nation live, we can bless our people with peaceful reunification. In order to do that, let's not rush. Let's first peacefully co-exist, interchange, and cooperate, and then, maybe ten or twenty years later, we can achieve reunification peacefully."

Chairman Kim completely agreed with me. The real meeting followed, and suddenly, the smile disappeared from Chairman Kim's face. "If the NIS initiated your visit, I would not have agreed to it because our impression of the NIS is really bad," he said. "Fortunately, the civilian economic enterprises run by the Asia Pacific Peace Committee of Korea and Hyundai have been going well and are lively. Also, because Minister Park Jie-won contacted us, we thought that you pursued this visit directly through a channel other than the NIS. But, in reality, it turns out that the NIS was behind it and Mr. Lim Dong-won was pulling the strings behind the scenes. Still, since the regime changed, we decided to respond."

"The government and NIS are quite different now than they were in the past," I replied simply.

Chairman Kim also said that he was upset about something he had seen the night before. "Because of the presence of North Korean flags in South Korean university campuses, the authorities are accusing them of violating the National Security Law and saying that they would arrest those responsible for it," he said. "Isn't this dumping cold water over this summit? How could you do that? I was really saddened. I saw yesterday at the airport that you came with South Korean flags on the airplane. Also, your attendants are all wearing South Korean flag badges, but we did not bother. So, I thought a lot about it. I thought that we could just part ways, since you had a meeting with President Kim Yong-nam and we had dinner yesterday. I came today only because the people around me dissuaded me from canceling."

It was an unexpected attack, but I replied calmly. "I have not heard about this. I will investigate when I return. There are many sorts of people in the South. Please don't bother with that." I later found out that about ten universities in the South had hung both South and North Korean flags in celebration of the inter-Korean summit, and that the public prosecutor made an issue out of it. Chairman Kim also mentioned the matter of amending the National Security Law.

About thirty minutes passed in this way. I mostly listened. Then, Chairman Kim asked me to speak first. I began by thanking him for the warm welcome, and then said, "I am deeply impressed by your filial piety, observing the 3-year mourning period after President Kim's demise, and embodying the nickname of our country: 'the country of courteous people in the East.' Let's talk frankly about our thoughts and agree on those things we can agree on."

I presented four agendas that had already been delivered by Special Envoy Lim Dong-won. I calmly explained what I was thinking while looking at the prepared material.

"The international Cold War is over, and the world is being transformed from an industrial society to a knowledge-and information-based society. The era of unlimited competition has arrived. It is time now to reconcile and end the Cold War for the survival and prosperity of our nation. We cannot delay it any longer. As a nation with a strong foundation in education and information, as well as cultural creativity, we are in the right position to achieve the highest level of development and prosperity in this era of knowledge and information. It is now important for us to reconcile and cooperate for our common development and prosperity. Let us lead the way forward.

"We should pursue reunification gradually, one step at a time. We should also cooperate in managing the process of reunification. I would like to propose the union of the two states. The 1992 Agreement reflected this same spirit.

"The South is worried about Communist reunification and being invaded by the North, and the North is worried about reunification by absorption and being invaded by the South," I continued. "Both are, in fact, impossible options, because a war will cause the mutual destruction and obliteration of our nation. Our position is firm. We promise that we will never pursue reunification by absorption and invasion of the North, so your people should not worry. As we agreed at the 1992 Agreement, let's establish a South-North Joint Military Commission, discuss problems, and carry out steps to build up military confidence and realize arms reduction, including measures to prevent accidental armed conflicts. In order to solve inter-Korean problems, we should solve our problems with neighboring countries together. When I visited the United States in 1998, I recommended that they lift economic sanctions against the North. I also urged Japanese Prime Minister Mori to normalize Japan's relationship with the North, and we discussed ways to promote this relationship in-depth. We will fully support you in establishing friendly relationships with the United States, Japan, and European countries. I hope you observe the 1994 Geneva Agreed Framework Between the United States of America and the Democratic People's Republic of Korea and carry out the US-DPRK missile negotiations carefully. In this way, we will gradually build peace in the Korean Peninsula. And, let us try to form and run an East Asian security cooperation organization that includes both the South and the North, the United States, Japan, China, and Russia for the sake of peace and stability in the Korean Peninsula and Northeast Asia."

I next discussed inter-Korean interchange and cooperation. This was an agenda item that required substantial help to the North. "In order to solve the inter-Korean relationship, it is important to pursue economic cooperation," I said. "Although our government is based on the principle of separation between politics and economics, we are willing to actively pursue inter-governmental cooperation in various fields, such as railways, communication, harbors and bays, electricity, and agriculture, for the sake of inter-Korean cooperation, considering the unique nature of inter-Korean matters. Let's connect broken railways and roads, and build an industrial complex on the west coast together. Let's expand our tourism industry to include not only the Mt. Kumgang tour, but also tours of Mt. Paektusan and Pyongyang. We will actively support your effort to become a member of and get support from international financial organizations. In order to pursue inter-Korean economic cooperation smoothly, we will have to quickly make agreements and create economic cooperation agreement documents, which include guaranteeing investments.

"Why don't you participate in the 2002 World Cup, and let's revive the regular Seoul-Pyongyang Soccer Match? Let's enter the opening ceremony together at the Sydney Olympics. Let's actively pursue interchange and cooperation in all areas, including society, culture, scholarship, public health, and environment."

From a humanitarian perspective, the reunion of dispersed families was a very urgent issue. I presented concrete measures, such as confirming the addresses of lost family members and whether or not they were alive, exchanging letters, running a reunion station, and reunion, based on the people's free will. I also proposed that we help dispersed families meet in honor of the August 15 Liberation Day. I told Chairman Kim that I wanted to pursue this purely, without any political calculations. "It has already been twenty-eight years since the July 4 North-South Joint Statement, where the principles of independence, peace, and national unity were presented," I said. "It has been eight years since the adoption of the 1992 Agreement, where the methods of advancing inter-Korean relations were perfectly presented. However, nothing from them was carried out. Now, all we have to do is put the agreement into practice according to established principles and methods. Let's gather our hearts and give our nation hope and trust through carrying them out. Let's instate South-North High-Level Negotiations, the South-North Economic Cooperation Commission, and the South-North Joint Military Commission, and cooperatively carry out the reunion of dispersed families and various interchanges.

"I also officially invite you to Seoul. Polls in the South show that 81 percent of people want you to visit Seoul. Please make sure to visit soon—I am already seventy-six years old. My presidential term lasts for only two years and eight more months. I have lived my entire life trying my best to make the reconciliation and reunification of our nation a reality, while being imprisoned many times and surviving the life-or-death crises. I would like to accomplish my dream with you in the remaining two years and eight months. I would like to build a firm foundation so that no later government can change the path we've set. That is my wish."

It took me a full thirty minutes to explain all four agenda items. I handed a document that summarized everything I'd said to Chairman Kim. He had listened carefully to my words. When he spoke, he said politely, "I thank you for your excellent remarks. It was very helpful of you to have Special Envoy Lim Dong-won deliver your signed letter so that he could explain your intentions. Now that I've heard about them in detail from you directly, I feel that I know your plans very well. I agree that nothing has been carried out, despite many agreements between the North and the South."

Chairman Kim proposed that we include only big picture negotiations in the accord. In other words, his proposal was to include large questions like the principle of internal solution and the methods of reunification, and to leave the rest, like interchange and cooperation between the South and the North and the matter of dispersed families, to ministerial-level negotiations.

I had a different opinion. Because the principles for reunification and inter-Korean relationship development methods were already included in the July 4 Statement and the 1992 Agreement, we could give hope to the Korean people and build trust with each other only when we agreed on immediate practical tasks. Therefore, I argued that we should include the matters of the reunion of the dispersed families, interchanges in economy, society, and culture, and Chairman Kim Jong-il's visit to Seoul in the accord. Otherwise, it was like my returning empty-handed, I told him.

"Since people mistrust us in the South, calling us 'main enemy' and 'puppet,' would the opposition party be satisfied even if I yield to a few big items to save your face?" Chairman Kim asked. "While the people in the South still call us puppets, even while chanting for co-existence, we in the North no longer call the South the 'South Korean puppet gang.' What matters are people's thoughts. We have to enlighten them. We should be aware that we are brothers and sisters. Didn't people in the South call us a 'puppet regime' in the sense that we are a 'puppet of the USSR,' and argue that we will soon collapse now that the USSR had collapsed? In fact, unlike South Korea, we had the Soviet troops withdraw immediately after the liberation. There is no foreign military troop in the North. We have maintained independence."

I actively explained: "What matters now is not the opposition party. It is important to show the world that the South and the North are a nation with the ability to solve our problems internally and to continue to do so. By the way, people in the South do not use the expression 'puppet' these days, either."

Secretary Kim Yong-sun said, "On May 24, Minister of Defense Cho Sung-tae said, 'North Korea is our main enemy; it's a puppet,' didn't he? Also, aren't people openly calling us names like that?"

"Neighboring powerful countries are still trying to solidify division in the Korean Peninsula and to control us by dividing us," Chairman Kim said. "But you tell me to go to this and that country, ask for their cooperation, and seek balance. I would like to avoid such an approach and to solve our problem internally among ourselves."

"We have a security alliance with the United States and are friendly with Japan," I explained, "but at the same time, we maintain a good relationship with China and Russia. Of course, I know that the North is close to China and Russia. It is only when both the South and the North have good relationship with all four countries that it will help foster peace and reunification in the Korean Peninsula. However, as long as the North maintains an antagonistic relationship with the United States, it is difficult to expect peace in the Korean Peninsula. Security and economic recovery are your goals, right? The United States can help you achieve this. Therefore, you should improve your relationship with the United States soon by observing the 1993 US-DPRK Joint Communiqué in Geneva and carrying out missile negotiations with the US. I will fully support your friendly relationship with the US, Japan, and European countries. Their cooperation is essential to bringing about peace in the Korean Peninsula. I do think 'independence' is an important prerequisite to solving our nation's problem. But, I think it should not be 'exclusive independence,' but 'open independence.'"

"Your words are not wrong, but the South and the North should unite our power to solve the matter of reunification," Chairman Kim said. "I am saying that only the relevant parties should solve the problem."

We continued to argue about the method for reunification. Chairman Kim proposed that we, first, declare our national will for an internal solution; second, agree on beginning with a lower-level federation system; and, third, immediately resume an inter-Korean dialogue to solve the political, economic, and social problems. I said that we could not accept the reunification plan, based on the "two systems, one federation" approach. I explained to him that the South-North confederation system we proposed was a system of cooperation between two systems and two governments before the reunification stage. However, Chairman Kim insisted on the word "federation," while arguing that "confederation" was, indeed, a lower-level federation system.

Director Lim asked me permission to speak and explained the difference between the confederation and federation systems. "A confederation system and a federation system are different concepts. The federation system is a system wherein a unified federal government exercises military and diplomatic authority, while regional governments exercise internal affairs only. In the confederation system, multiple sovereign states with respective military and diplomatic rights cooperate. A Commonwealth of Independent States (CIS), established after the dissolution of the USSR, would be a form of this. The confederation of the South and the North that we argue for is not to form a unified government, but a pre-unification stage in which both the South and North governments cooperate for reunification. Please understand that it is different from a federation, a unified state."

Chairman Kim then said, "I know that President Kim said it would take ten to twenty years to complete reunification. But I think it would take forty to fifty years to complete reunification. I am not arguing that we should immediately reunite through the federation system; that was the logic during the Cold War era. The lower-level federation system that I speak of is a system where both governments maintain respective authority for military and diplomacy, and gradually pursue reunification, like the confederation system the South argues for."

"The reunification plan cannot be agreed upon here and now," I said. "We can agree on a continuing discussion about our confederation system and your lower-level federation system."

"Then, let's agree on this," Chairman Kim said. "Because the confederation system and lower-level federation system mean the same thing, let's say that we would cooperate on a lower-level federation." He insisted on their term.

I proposed a compromise. "We say that the North has proposed a lower-level federation system and the South proposed a confederation system, that they share many common ideas, and that we will discuss this matter together from now on."

"That's fine, then. Let's agree on that," Chairman Kim said.

We then discussed economic cooperation between the South and the North. I began, "According to what I've heard, Hyundai prefers places close to the South, like Haeju, rather than Sinuiju, for an industrial complex. Please make a decision soon. Also, if we connect the Seoul-Sinuiju train line and build a 2-track line, it will benefit both sides, as the North will profit and the South will save logistic costs. Not only is there the symbolic value of re-connecting the broken main artery, but also it could turn the Korean Peninsula into a logistic hub."

Chairman Kim said, "We will pursue economic cooperation through building an industrial complex and reconnecting the Seoul-Sinuiju train line, and we will proceed according to the agreement with Hyundai."

It had been two hours since we began the meeting. Chairman Kim suggested we take a break.

"Before taking a break," I said, "how about going over the things we agree on, and having Director Lim Dong-won and Secretary Kim Yong-sun write a draft for the agreement?"

Chairman Kim gladly agreed with me. "As I told Special Envoy Lim Dong-won last time, we have no objection to the reunion of dispersed families. After exchanging one hundred visitors each between Seoul and Pyongyang on Liberation Day, I think that it would be great for us to accumulate experience like that and expand in stages. But there *is* something I want to mention before we conclude this matter. Why do the NIS and Ministry of Unification in the South continue to bring up defectors from the North? You are protecting criminals who escaped from here and are taking advantage of them in propaganda, defaming and slandering us."

"Our government never entices defectors," Director Lim responded. "But, isn't it natural to accept defectors who want to come to Seoul? As director of the NIS, I am telling you that we never take advantage of defectors to use them in broadcasting. In addition, we should not defame or slander each other as determined in the 1992 Agreement. I believe that it would be meaningful if you two heads of the state agree on halting any defamation and slander."

Chairman Kim immediately agreed. "All right," he said. "Let's say that we will not defame or slander each other. Let's stop the military broadcasting against each other too."

I summarized what we discussed and agreed on the following: first, the South and North, as the masters of national unification, will join hands in an effort to resolve the issue of national unification independently; second, acknowledging that the different formulas that the North and South favor for reunification have common factors, they will strive to work together to achieve this goal; third, the South and North will exchange groups of dispersed family members around August 15 and resolve humanitarian issues as soon as possible, including the repatriation of communist prisoners who have completed their jail terms; fourth, the South and North will pursue a balanced development of their national economies and build mutual trust by accelerating exchange in the social, cultural, sports, health, and environmental sectors; and, fifth, in order to put these agreements into practice, the South and North will hold a dialogue between government authorities at an early date.

I also proposed that we include a clear statement about Chairman Kim's visit to Seoul and the second summit meeting; however, he didn't agree to this. His face froze again, and it appeared there was no persuading him. I fell into despair. I decided to try one last pitch by appealing to his humanity. "Everybody knows that Chairman Kim treats seniors with respect as the leader of 'the country of courteous people in the East.' And I am older than you. When I, the senior, have visited Pyongyang first, what will it look like if you don't visit Seoul? You must visit Seoul. We will welcome you and treat you with respect."

Chairman Kim remained silent for a while. It was obvious that he was hesitating. I could not know what was preventing him from coming to Seoul. "How about this?" Director Lim said. "'President Kim Dae-jung cordially invited National Defense Commission Chairman Kim Jong Il to visit Seoul, and he agreed to do that at a convenient time.' After this level of agreement, we can discuss the date of visit later."

Chairman Kim was deep in thought again. Finally, he gestured that he accepted it. Moments like this were truly critical, and I was relieved when they passed. Ultimately, we changed the phrase "a convenient time" to "an appropriate time."

Chairman Kim relaxed again, and the atmosphere became lighter than before. He said to me, "If there is a problem carrying out our agreements, please send Special Envoy Lim Dong-won to Pyongyang as frequently as necessary."

"I hope you don't pay too much attention to speculative articles or abrupt political remarks," I said. "If there is any important problem, let's directly communicate with each other. How about installing an emergency hot line between us?"

"That's a great idea," Chairman Kim responded. "Let's do that."

We installed an emergency hot line and have solved sensitive inter-Korean issues through that hot line since then. It was a precious result of the summit.

We took a break at 5:22 p.m. It had taken us no longer than two and a half hours to make all of this progress. Outside of the meeting room, the June 14 morning newspapers were exhibited. A photograph showing Chairman Kim Jong-il and me holding hands decorated the front page. The *Kyunghyang Sinmun* included only that photo and nothing else—not an article or an advertisement.

"This is the first time I've seen a front page like this," I said. "How symbolic it is!"

Chairman Kim also looked at it carefully. In fact, that single photo said everything. How could anyone convey the overwhelmingly important significance of this first summit in half a century in writing or titles?

THE BEST DAY IN A CENTURY OF MODERN HISTORY (JUNE 14–15, 2000)

When the meeting resumed Chairman Kim asked me rather aggressively, "What is the opposition party's position on the reunification plan? Why does the Grand National Party quarrel and create friction about each and every matter involved in improving the inter-Korean relations? Why didn't they send a single party member on this visit to Pyongyang?"

"Our reunification plan was created according to an agreement between the ruling and opposition parties in 1989, when the current opposition party was the ruling party," I told Chairman Kim. "So they don't fundamentally oppose it. The Grand National Party simply emphasizes that an improved inter-Korean relationship should not hurt the Republic of Korea's sovereignty and security. Of course, that is an unfounded fear. In addition, they argue for 'strict reciprocity' in our aid to the North, but people do not support it. In fact, there were many opposition party members who personally wanted to accompany me on this visit to Pyongyang. Assemblywoman Park Geun-hye, the late president Park Chung-Hee's daughter, announced that she would accompany us on this visit, but Grand National Party leadership did not allow it."

"No matter how good an agreement we make and how well we improve the inter-Korean relationship now, we will all have to go back to the starting line again if the Grand National Party assumes the reins of the government in the next election, won't we?" Chairman Kim asked. "If GNP assumes the reins of the government, what do you think will happen?"

"GNP does what they do now politically because they are the opposition party," I responded. "But if they assume the power, I don't think the policy direction that we are pursuing now will be too different from theirs. They also argued for the confederation system and they would not object to a peaceful coexistence between the South and the North. Of course, there might be some differences in the concrete methods of carrying out the policies."

"I will officially tell you one secret," Chairman Kim said unexpectedly. "This concerns the US armed forces in Korea. We sent Secretary Kim Yong-sun to the United States as a special envoy in 1992 during the Republican government period and delivered the message that the South and the North had decided not to fight. We also requested that US armed forces continued to remain in Korea to prevent war between the South and the North. Citing the history of neighboring powerful countries' numerous invasions due to their interest in the strategic geopolitical value of the location of the Korean Peninsula, you said that it was better for US armed forces to remain in Korea to maintain peace here. I know that you said, 'Even if Korea is reunited, US armed forces should be in Korea,' and I agree with you. Although the presence of US armed forces in Korea could be burdensome to the South Korean government, wouldn't it be something you could overcome in the end?"

"Then, why do you continue to argue for the withdrawal of US armed forces from Korea in the media?" I asked Chairman Kim.

"That's to comfort our people's sentiment," he replied. "I hope you understand that."

"When I heard your views about the US armed forces in Korea from Special Envoy Lim Dong-won, I was really surprised," I told Chairman Kim. "I did not know that you had such outstanding knowledge about our national situation. Yes. If neighboring powerful countries fight for their hegemony, it would cause pain to our nation, but the presence of the US armed forces in Korea maintains the power balance and secures the safety of our nation."

"Although our places of origin are different, I'm telling you this because I think we could understand each other very well ... perhaps because we are the same Kims," Chairman Kim said. We all laughed out loud at his joke.

"Where is your place of origin?" I asked.

"I am Kim from Jeonju."

"Jeonju? Then, you're really a Jeolla-do person. I am Kim from Kimhae, so I'm originally a Gyeongsang-do person." At my joke, the atmosphere significantly improved. We were full of happiness. Chairman Kim returned to the subject that we had been discussing previously and emphasized that we should not depend on foreign powers to solve our problems.

"I fundamentally agree with you about that," I said. "Isn't this summit not what others told us to do, but what we decided on, thus surprising the world? As you said, we should unite to lead the solution to the Korean Peninsula question, but we should also gather support and cooperation from neighboring countries. I want to stress again that 'independence' should not be 'exclusive independence,' but 'open independence.' Our decisions in this meeting decide our nation's fate. If we make a mistake, we may cause war, which would be a disaster. But if we do well, we can open the road to peace and reunification. Nobody lives forever, and nobody holds the same position forever. Let's unite our strengths and do well while we are in charge of our nation."

The summit was winding down. We had to decide whose names should be on the statement and when to announce it. Chairman Kim seemed to want to conclude around that point. "We've discussed enough," he said. "Since we negotiated most of the things, let's bring the joint statement draft tomorrow morning, reach a final agreement, and announce it at noon."

I asked him to let us announce it earlier. "Let's agree on the final version this evening so that it will be published in tomorrow morning's newspaper," I urged him. "We can publish it with tomorrow's date. If we announce it at noon tomorrow, it will be published the day after tomorrow. It will be very delayed. Let's conclude the agreement this evening."

"Then, regarding the signature, let's have Secretary of the Workers' Party of Korea Kim Yong-sun and Director of NIS Lim Dong-won sign, 'by the wish of our respective superiors.'"

I firmly objected to this. "Chairman Kim and I should sign. If not, it is like omitting the eyes on a painting of a dragon."

"I don't mean to lower the level of the accord," Chairman Kim said. "As we have the President of the Presidium of the Supreme People's Assembly of North Korea Kim Yong-nam in the North, it would be better if I don't sign it. Let's have you and President of the Presidium of the Supreme People's Assembly of North Korea Kim Yong-nam sign and I'll guarantee it."

Again, I firmly rejected this proposal. Chairman Kim did not appear to back down either. Secretary Kim Yong-sun came up with another compromise "What if we just write your names?" he proposed.

I rejected this right away too. "If we omit our titles, it could cause a lot of misunderstanding."

Chairman Kim tried to persuade me. "There is the precedent of the July 4 Joint Statement, where it was signed: '*By the wish of our respective superiors,* Lee Hu Rak/Kim Young Ju.' Let's write: 'By the wish of President Kim Dae-jung, Lim Dong-won and by the wish of Chairman Kim Jong-il, Kim Yong-sun.'"

"At that time, it was Mr. Lee Hu-rak who visited Pyongyang, but this time, I, the president, visited in person and had the summit," I replied. "Please, let's do things clearly."

Director Lim then chimed in. "Shouldn't the beginning of the accord include something along the lines of, 'President Kim Dae-jung of the Republic of Korea and Kim Jong Il, chairman of the National Defense Commission of the Democratic Peoples' Republic of Korea met in Pyongyang, had a summit, and agreed as follows at so-and-so time'? Therefore, it is very natural to write your names and add your signatures. This accord is a monumental document that represents a turning point in our national history. Shouldn't you, who worked to bring it about, sign it in person and hand it down through history forever? How historic and proud an event this is!"

Suddenly Chairman Kim Jong-il said, "President Kim is very obstinate, perhaps because he is from the Jeolla-do province." This joke immediately broke the sense of desperation.

"Aren't you a Kim from Jeonju, Jeolla-do? Let's do as I propose," I joked right back.

"It looks like you want to called a triumphal general," Chairman Kim said.

"Why not make me a triumphal general?" I responded. "I came all the way here, so let me get some benefit."

Finally, Chairman Kim laughed and the summit ended at 7:00 p.m. We decided to call the document the South and North Korean Accord. We delivered the draft that the staff members and Director Lim wrote to the North.

That evening, I held a dinner at the Mokrangwan. Chairman Kim suggested that we take the same car to dinner. I met him in the lobby of the Paekhwawon. "It's 99 percent perfect. I mean the joint statement!" he called out from the other side of the room. He was clearly satisfied with the draft our side had prepared.

In the car, Chairman Kim said to me privately: "You don't have to go to the Kumsusan Palace of the Sun."

The solution of this sticking point was thanks to our attendants' devoted efforts. Director Lim Dong-won and Minister Park Jie-won sincerely conveyed the reason that I could not pay respect at the Kumsusan Palace. Minister Park met with and persuaded his secret negotiation partner Vice Chairman of Asia Pacific Peace Committee of Korea Song Ho-gyong. Minister Park said to him, "President Kim's visit to the Kumsusan Palace will not do. If you continue to insist on it, then, Chief of Staff Hahn Gwang-ok and I will visit on his behalf and return to Beijing first. Then, we will return to Seoul to be arrested." Minister Park told me about this meeting, but we could not be sure how the North would respond.

Director Lim also delivered the message that we had prepared in Seoul before our trip to Chairman Kim. "More than 70 percent of South Koreans oppose President Kim's visit to the Kumsusan Palace. If President Kim's leadership is hurt, then the meaning of this summit will also fade and it may become difficult to carry out our agreement. We should pursue this in a direction that is beneficial to both parties." Thanks to these efforts, a North Korean official delivered the good news to Minister Park the next morning. "This time, you don't have to pay respect at the Kumsusan Palace, per the order of the superior," he said.

I heard this news during my tour of the Mangyongdae Children's Palace. I was relieved. It seemed that the decision had already been made before Chairman Kim's private announcement to me in the car.

The dinner was held at 8:00 p.m., an hour after the originally scheduled time. About 150 North Korean and 50 South Korean delegation members attended. Before the dinner began, Chairman Kim and I chatted in the lobby. On the wall of the lobby was a large picture of Heaven Lake on top of Mt. Paektusan. Naturally, we talked about mountains. Chairman Kim proudly talked about Mt. Paektusan, Mt. Kumgang, and Mt. Chilbosan. Then, he talked about the conflict between the tourist industry and environmental preservation. "Although we gain a lot from the tourist industry, we also lose a lot," he said. "Italians and Yugoslavians say that tourism is helpful to make money, but their land is devastated and polluted as a result. So, it is necessary to think about which is more important— money or environmental protection. Although I don't unconditionally revere their words, I think they are worth considering."

"The environment is a really difficult conundrum," I replied. "Both development and environment are important. We need to sustainably develop."

"I've seen South Korean TV programs where reporters said that downtown Pyongyang is quiet. But being quiet means that it lacks something, doesn't it? Washington DC is much quieter than New York City. But being 'quiet' is our policy. New York City is a gutter and sewage, while Washington DC is clean. Why does Seoul want to become like New York instead of Washington DC?"

"In the United States, while Washington DC is clean, New York is crowded and messy," I replied. "Canberra and Sydney in Australia are in a similar situation. When they said Pyongyang was quiet, they didn't mean that it lacked anything, but that it was clean. The population in Seoul, which was 400,000, is now 10 million. We in the South should also think seriously about ecological environment destruction and air pollution."

"I must have spoken too rashly."

"No. What you said is important. Environment is an important issue. After reading the news article about fish-kill in the Jungrangcheon Stream a few days ago, I was reminded again of the seriousness of this issue."

"It's the result of focusing too intensively on urban development," Chairman Kim said. "We are not planning on increasing the population of Pyongyang. For Seoul, take Washington DC rather than New York as a model."

I responded with a smile, and we entered the dining room. Perhaps because the summit went well, it felt like a festival night. People were somewhat relaxed. I read my dinner remarks: "Even at this moment, 70 million Korean hearts are concentrated on Pyongyang. I report that Chairman Kim Jong-il and I successfully finished our meeting. Finally, we are looking at a bright future for our nation. Hope for reconciliation, cooperation, and reunification has risen. When you think about it, we have truly waited a long time for this day. Until very recently, we could not think about this day even in our dreams.

"For me, it has not been just once or twice that I have felt sad, wondering if I would ever step on the northern land. To what can I compare this overwhelming feeling today?

"Now, finally, the time has come to stop shedding the tears that we have been shedding for one hundred years. It is now time for us to cover the wounds that we have inflicted on each other. We must walk the road to peace, cooperation, and reunification. That is why the heads of the state from both sides met in the first year of the twenty-first century. These are missions that history has entrusted us with, and we should not fail to carry them out.

"I have been oppressed a lot over the past forty years. However, no oppression could break my will to devote my life to inter-Korean reconciliation, cooperation, and unification. I have cherished the passionate desire to dedicate my life to a peaceful reunification of our fatherland, which is also the sincere wish of 70 million Koreans. For this task, Chairman Kim and I would like to unite our hearts in laying the foundation for mutual trust and peaceful co-existence and co-prosperity of the South and North. Let us all gather our strength and wisdom to drive out the fear of war from our land and open the new age of interchange and cooperation.

"Now, June should be recorded in history as the month not of national tragedy, but of hope. Thus, our descendants who will live in this land eternally will remember June as the proudest month.

"Chairman Kim Jong-il, and leaders of the North, let's meet in Seoul!"

President Kim Yong-nam also made a remark. "The greatest reward to Korean politicians lies in their devotion to the nation. The historical opportunity is not always given to us, and our time is not eternal. We politicians should gather all of our wisdom and strength together in order to turn reunification from the future tense to the present tense. In the faraway future, history will not forget patriots who contributed to the reunification of our fatherland, but remember them forever. I firmly believe that President Kim Dae-jung's visit to Pyongyang will continue us along the road to reunification, all Koreans' long-standing desire."

I was struck by his urge to turn reunification from the future tense to the present tense. We prepared a royal court cuisine for the dinner because that is what Chairman Kim wanted. All ingredients were brought from the South. My wife sat not at the head table, but at the delegates' table. Almost yelling, Chairman Kim said, "Madam Lee, please come join us. You should not be a dispersed family. While President Kim insists on the reunion of dispersed families, it won't do if you become one in Pyongyang, will it?"

The dinner guests burst into laughter. Chairman Kim talked a lot. I was happy too. The sound of glasses clinking one another echoed endlessly throughout the room. Everyone was drinking a toast to the South and the North.

Director Lim brought the draft of the joint statement with him. Chairman Kim had already examined it, and I didn't have any complaints either. Finally, we had agreed on a joint statement.

I could not sit still. I proposed to Chairman Kim that we go to the podium together to celebrate this momentous event. When we both stood up, the room fell into complete silence. Attendants from both sides looked at us attentively.

"Ladies and gentlemen, please let us celebrate," I spoke. "We have completely agreed on the South and North Korean Accord!" My voice sounded excited even to my own ears. I held and raised Chairman Kim's hand. Everyone stood up and applauded for what seemed to be an endless amount of time. It was a climactic moment.

But this moment of a climax would have to be performed once more. There was not a cameraman in the room at that critical moment. Senior Press Secretary Park Joon-young approached me with an embarrassed expression and said, "I'm really sorry, sir. But the scene at the podium was not captured, because there wasn't a cameraman in the room. Because it is such an important scene, please do it again. I'm so sorry."

It was a very impolite request, but Mr. Pak did not have any alternative since it was such an important moment. He could not hold his head high. I was embarrassed too, but I had to tell Chairman Kim.

Chairman Kim gladly said, "Then, let's act today. It's a great day, so why not?"

Chairman Kim and I went to the podium again, held hands, and raised them high. The cameras flashed brightly. I said, "We are announcing this again because they could not take a picture before. We finally and completely agreed on the South and North Korean Accord! Please let us celebrate!"

The response was enthusiastic again. Everyone stood up and applauded thunderously. The historic photo that drew the world's attention was actually a second take.

The room was then engulfed in uncontrollable enthusiasm and excitement. The room itself seemed to be moving up and down.

Chairman Kim said loudly, "Hello, where are the members of the National Defense Commission? Why don't you all come here and offer President Kim a glass each?"

The generals of the People's Army came up to the head table and greeted me. Six generals, including General Park Jae-kyong, stood in line before me and poured me wine. I also poured wine for each of them. Chairman Kim cheered and joked with the Chief of Staff Hahn Gwang-ok and Ministers Lee Hun-jai, Park Jae-gyu, and Park Jie-won. "Since I went to the podium twice, I should get an actor's fee," he told them.

Everyone's face was flushed. Although I couldn't drink, I felt like drinking too. My face was flushed, just like all of the other bright faces in the room.

Poet Ko Un, our special delegate, went up to the podium. The elderly poet overwhelmed the room with his dignity and passion. He said, "I wrote this poem in my room this morning, thinking about our nation." He then recited "In Front of the Taedong River."

> To what purpose did I come here?
> The sleepless night recedes,
> And Taedong River
> Was yesterday
> Is today
> And will be tomorrow's waves.
>
> The time is coming like this
> The time of change is coming
> Along the road that nobody can block.
> Change *is* truth ...
>
> To what purpose am I here?
> One nation
> That we should achieve
> Is not a nostalgic return to the past;
> But burying all mistakes of the past,
> All barbaric actions,
> All shames,
> And gather to rebuild.

Thus, unification is not reunification,
But new unification.
Unification must be an eye-tingling creation
Not of the past
But of the future.

To what purpose am I here?
To what purpose have I made this trip here?
To our nation, there must be tomorrow.
Standing in front of Taedong River in the morning
I look at the tomorrows of successive generations and mine.
Oh, isn't this very meeting
The best face of a century of our modern history
That has come here for this meeting?
I'm returning now,
I'm returning, holding a flower.

The poet shouted and the poem was alive and fluttering. Watching his passionate gestures and listening to his resounding voice gave everyone in attendance a frighteningly moving sensation.

The dinner lasted until very late that night. We all returned to the Paekhwawon Guesthouse. Around midnight, we held the signing ceremony for the June 15 South and North Korean Accord. Director Lim Dong-won stood next to me and Secretary Kim Yong-sun stood next to Chairman Kim. Delegates from both the South and the North held their breath while Chairman Kim and I signed. Then, Chairman Kim and I held and raised hands. The camera flashes were bright. Champagne glasses were delivered to us, and we cheered, raising our glasses. Chairman Kim downed his glass immediately. It took me a few gulps to finish mine. Champagne-filled glasses were then distributed to the delegates and we cheered together. Chairman Kim went up to each and every South Korean delegate to cheer, and said, "Now that we have finished national business, let's have a commemorative photo taken."

We all had a picture taken together, and all of our scheduled events were over. We must not have grown tired of each other after such a long day because we were of the same land. We saw Chairman Kim off when he left the building.

"Now that everything has gone so well, please take a good rest," Chairman Kim said to me. "I'll treat you to lunch tomorrow. I'll invite all of the delegates from both the South and the North."

"Thank you," I replied. "You have worked very hard today."

While walking down the corridor together, Chairman Kim stopped as if he had remembered something. He turned around and said, "While President Kim is taking a rest tomorrow, please have the delegates visit our chicken factory. We recently finished building a chicken factory with German support. Please visit it and give us an objective evaluation."

All our official attendants congratulated me. I thanked them for their hard work. An indescribable feeling overwhelmed me.

After everyone returned to their room, I was left with just my wife. As soon as I laid down, exhaustion washed over me … the drinks had their effect too. The entire day, from beginning to end, felt distant. While imprisoned by the dictatorial regime in the past, I had often imagined myself at a summit with President Kim Il-sung. Although imaginary, I had tried to negotiate with him for our nation's sake. But time passed by and I ultimately had a summit with his son. I finally achieved what I had dreamed about for so long.

Of course, there were many crises during the meeting. Every time I felt tempted to give up, I thought of our nation. I had poured out all of my might and tried my best. It was the longest day of my life, a day when I had the heaviest burden on my shoulders, and a day when I felt most rewarded. I fell into sleep.

The morning of June 15 broke. The delegates all went to tour the chicken factory that Chairman Kim was so proud of. I rested with my wife at the guesthouse, while thinking about the speech I would make to report back. The farewell lunch reception occurred at the Yongbingwan at Paekhwawon at noon. Fifty delegates each from the South and the North attended. First Vice Chairman of the National Defense Commission Jo Myong-rok made the opening remark, declaring his support for the June 15 Accord on behalf of the North Korean military. It was a sort of military pledge. From our side, Director Lim made a remark.

Chairman Kim led the conversation again. He was openhearted. "I was deeply moved when President Kim said yesterday to remember June not as a month of national tragedy, but of the hope for the future," he said. "So, I ordered members of the National Defense Commission not to celebrate June 25, which will come in ten days, the way we used to. Besides, this year is the fiftieth anniversary of the war, isn't it? But, the members of the National Defense Commission protested, 'Why should we do that, while they don't change in the South?' You'd think that you'd get tired of

a 50-year enmity, but soldiers always think of the other party as their enemies. It is important to dissolve their hatred."

Chairman Kim also announced the first positive result of the June 15
Accord. "As the Commander-in-Chief of the People's Army, I ordered the
military to stop all slanderous broadcasting about the South on the frontline at noon today."

We also took the same measure the next day. The mutual slanderous
broadcasting finally stopped.

The lunch reception felt like a festival. People moved around to clink
their glasses. It was like meeting neighbors from your old hometown for
the first time in a long while. Chairman Kim called the generals and party
officials and had them offer me a drink. Vice Chairman of the National
Defense Commission Yon Hyong-muk, First Vice Chairman of the
National Defense Commission Jo Myong-rok, General Hyon Chol-hae,
General Pak Jae-gyong, Chairman of the Deputies' Credential Screening
Committee of the SPA Kim Kuk-tae, Secretary of the Workers' Party of
Korea Kim Yong-sun, Vice Chairman of the National Defense Commission
Jang Sung-taek, and First Vice Foreign Minister Kang Sok-ju clinked their
glasses with mine.

Our delegates offered wine to Chairman Kim too. When Minister Park
Jie-won requested inviting media company chairmen to the North,
Chairman Kim gladly accepted. "All right," he said. "I'll invite them in the
capacity of chairman of the National Defense Commission or just as
myself. I hope that they will visit us before August 15 and that singers, Lee
Mi-ja and the Eunbangul Sisters, will visit us too. I hope that not only
journalists and businessmen, but also politicians will visit us."

Chairman Kim Jong-il made a farewell remark. "Let us now make previous politicians sigh and regret. Let us have President Kim recorded in
history as the president who opened a new chapter in inter-Korean history.
Let us have him remembered. I look forward to the roles that will be played
by all secretaries and ministers."

While everyone was excited, Minister Park Jie-won proposed that we
sing, "Our Wish is Unification" together. Everyone stood up, held hands,
and sang together. Chairman Kim and I held hands and waved them to
and fro. After the song, Minister of Culture Park sang a couple of songs
upon request.

After the lunch was over, we said our goodbyes. Officials from the North
said goodbye to me, and officials from the South said goodbye to Chairman
Kim. Sad to leave, delegates from the South lingered around Chairman

Kim and me. Finally, Chairman Kim looked around them and said, "Let's carry out our agreement. Let's make an effort together. I cannot tell the people about everything I spoke with President Kim about. There are some things we'll let others know about and there are other things that we shared between ourselves. Please work hard in the South, President Kim. I'll work hard in the North. We should borrow each other's strength. I'll make sure that the reunion through the Red Cross happens."

As the time when we had arrived, Chairman Kim got in the car with me on the seat my wife usually sat in. Hundreds of thousands of Pyongyang citizens came out to the streets to see us off, waving flowers as we drove by. A brief farewell ceremony was held in front of Kim Il-sung University. When I got out of the car with Chairman Kim, citizens cheered. A female marching band played cheerful music. Two girls gave my wife and me flowers.

When we arrived at the Sunan Airport a little past 4:00 p.m. the marching band was playing a resounding song, and a crowd lined the street to bid us farewell. I inspected the Honor Guards with Chairman Kim. I said goodbye to high officials of the North one after another: Kim Yong-nam, Jo Myong-rok, Kim Kuk-tae, Choe Thae-bok, Yon Hyong-muk, and Kim Yong-sun. The last was Chairman Kim. We shook hands and then Chairman Kim gave me a hug (Fig. 9.1). We hugged three times. I thought I would meet him again soon, but that would be our last hug.

After climbing the trap, I turned around to see Chairman Kim waving his hand. My wife and I waved too. He stood in the same spot until our airplane entered the runway. The leader in the Maoist suit, Kim Jong-il—his image lingered in my mind for a long time.

When I departed Pyongyang, I left a letter for my fellow Koreans in the North. I wrote: "We surprised the world by successfully finishing the summit by working passionately and sincerely together. The entire world is blessing our new beginning as we move toward reconciliation and cooperation. Because we achieved the summit that seemed impossible, I firmly believe that the day of reunification will also come if both the South and the North work together with all our hearts and minds."

I had spent fifty-four hours in Pyongyang, and eleven hours with Chairman Kim. We also had conversations in the car. During those times, I got to know him better. My impression of Chairman Kim coincided with Director Lim's impression of him.

Fig. 9.1   Kim Dae-jung being seen off by Kim Jong-il after the first inter-Korean summit in June 2000

Chairman Kim was a polite person. After President Kim Il-sung's death, he observed three years' mourning, according to our custom. He was very polite to me as his senior. Breaking the custom of summit diplomacy, he came to welcome me at the airport. He rode in the car with me, carefully escorting me so that I got in the car first. He prepared an armchair for me at the farewell lunch, after finding out that I used one.

Chairman Kim was a man of understanding, judgment, and resolution. Although he had the capacity to become insistent about a particular argument, he changed his stance if my explanation made sense. He showed this kind of attitude during our discussion on the matters of US armed forces in Korea, internal national decisions, and reunification methods. He immediately changed even long-standing North Korean arguments if what I said made sense.

Other people who met him after me agreed about these impressions. US Secretary of State Madeleine Albright, Swedish Prime Minister Göran Persson, and Japanese Prime Minister Koizumi all shared the same impression. Madam Albright wrote in her memoir, *Madam Secretary*: "I can confirm Kim Dae-jung's view that his DPRK counterpart was an intelligent man who knew what he wanted. He was isolated, not uninformed."

The October 26, 2000, *Washington Post* article covering Secretary Albright's visit to North Korea was similar to it:

> This scary image of a lunatic with his finger on a button that could launch missiles and perhaps a nuclear bomb or two was a nightmare that drove US policy. For years, Washington tried to keep North Korea isolated as a dangerous "rogue" state and has used Kim's unpredictability to justify a need for a hugely expensive missile defense system.
>
> But, in American eyes, the specter is rapidly dissolving. With the US anti-missile system on hold, Kim is being recast as a leader who could be dealt with and could be seen shaking Clinton's hand, who might be persuaded—with some wheat and maybe some money—to hand over the key to his missiles.

As shown in these examples, Chairman Kim showed his lesser-known characteristics during the South-North Summit.

Many people welcomed us at the airport in Seoul. I was finally able to say to Koreans that I had a good trip. "Fellow Koreans whom I respect and love, I have just returned from accomplishing my task during my historic visit to the North," I spoke. "I am sincerely grateful to you who cheered me day and night so that I could accomplish my tasks.

"It seems that a new day has finally dawned upon us. We seemed to arrive at the point where we could finish the 55-year division and antagonism and open up a new turning point in our national history. If my visit was the first step on the road to inter-Korean interchange, cooperation, and national reunification, I could not be happier.

"What is important is that we met. Pyongyang was our land, too. People living in Pyongyang are our blood relations and fellow Koreans. Whatever they have said outwardly, I could feel after only a few words that they have a deep love for their fellow Koreans and they have missed us. And that is very natural. Our people had lived as a single nation for five thousand years. It had been 1300 years since Korea achieved unification. It is natural that such people cannot forever turn their backs on each other and become strangers after fifty-five years of forced division. I confirmed this during my visit."

I also explained the South and North Korean Accord in detail, emphasizing that this was not a conclusion, but a beginning. "We should progress from the easiest and the most possible, trusting that we should try doing things that will benefit both sides. While working together, we can gradually build trust and common interests. If I leave after building that foundation, I trust that my successors will follow through well.

"I am confident that we can hand down the entire Korean Peninsula as a proud and prosperous fatherland to our descendants. I thank you again for your support and I promise that I will serve you with all my might."

Songs like "Our Wish is Unification" and "To the Country of Hope" resounded throughout the airport. People who had been displaced from the North came in droves and cheered. On the road to the Blue House, many citizens waved pickets and Korean flags. "Thank you, President, for comforting the sadness of dispersed families," "Unification grandfather, you did great," and "The Republic of Korea is united."

In a poll, the percentage of people who answered that they were satisfied or supported the summit was between 93 and 98 percent. The support for Chairman Kim Jong-il's return visit was around 70 percent.

President Clinton issued a statement in support of the Accord:

The historic summit between President Kim Dae-jung and Chairman Kim Jong-il marks an initial, hopeful step toward peace and reconciliation on the Korean Peninsula. I welcome the agreements the two leaders reached on humanitarian and economic cooperation and on a future summit in Seoul, and hope that both sides will continue down this promising path. I applaud

Kim Dae-jung's persistence and wisdom as he has moved, soberly and real-istically, to improve relations with the North. President Kim and I have consulted very closely on this issue, and I look forward to supporting his future initiatives toward lasting peace and full reconciliation.

UN Secretary General Kofi Annan also sent a congratulatory message: "As UN secretary general, I will actively support international society's effort to support the inter-Korean trust-building process."

There were many evaluations about the summit, but I was particularly impressed by Professor Don Oberdorfer's in his 2002 edition of *The Two Koreas*. The gist of what he wrote was this: With this South-North summit as the starting point, South and North Korea took the opportunity to decide on the future of the entire Korean nation for the first time in history.

The support for the summit from international society continued. Special statements in support of the summit and accord were issued at many international meetings: the G-8 Summit in Okinawa; the ASEAN Ministerial Meeting at the ASEAN+3 and the ASEAN Regional Forum; the UN Millennium Summit and the fifty-fifth UN Plenary Session; the ASEM Summit in Seoul; and the APEC Meeting in Brunei.

The June 15 North and South Korean Accord was a grand drama with-out a script. All participants tried their best to play their roles. The peo-ple's will prevailed. I served the people's will, and, therefore, the real protagonists of this drama were the Korean people.

CHAPTER 10

June–December 2000

FLOWERS BLOOMING UNDER THE SUNSHINE
(JUNE–SEPTEMBER 2000)

I had a few principles for the summit meetings. First, to never say "no," no matter what. Second, to listen to what the other side has to say as much as possible. Third, to always clearly say that I agree when I have the same opinion about something. Fourth, to insert what I have to say throughout our conversation, and to not omit anything on my agenda. Fifth, to give my partner the impression that the success of the summit is thanks to him or her. Sixth, and most important, to treat the other party with sincerity.

During the inter-Korean summit, some Koreans might have wondered why I didn't talk much and Chairman Kim Jong-il talked so much. They might have wondered if I was nervous or had other issues. But I had intended our conversation to go exactly as it had. I had to spare my words until I knew who he was and what his ideas were. Although I did not talk much, the accord included more of my arguments.

I consider it is a success if I say one thing while my partner says three things during a summit. And it's a failure if the other party wants me to leave when I stand up to go. I have to leave when the other party wants me to stay a little longer. I must spare my words if I want the other party to want me to linger.

I called President Clinton the day after I returned from Pyongyang and explained how the summit went. I first told him that I strongly urged the North to strictly observe the 1992 Agreed Framework and the

© The Author(s) 2019
Kim Dae-jung, *Conscience in Action*,
https://doi.org/10.1007/978-981-10-7623-7_10

1993 US-DPRK Joint Communiqué. I also let him know that, although Chairman Kim silently listened to my words during our meeting, he later told my Senior Secretary for Foreign Relations and National Security that everything would be fine as far as the missile question goes.

I also told President Clinton that Chairman Kim was of the opinion that US armed forces in Korea should remain in the Korean Peninsula as long as they could guarantee they wouldn't attack North Korea. I also let President Clinton know that I had delivered his remark from Japanese Prime Minister Obuchi's funeral that it would be great if Chairman Kim came to the next APEC meeting. In conclusion, I told him that I had learned that North Korea really wanted to improve its relationship with the US. I advised President Clinton that if someone from the US came to meet Chairman Kim in North Korea, a frank dialogue and good results were possible.

After listening to my explanations, President Clinton congratulated me on the successful summit and thanked me for raising the issues of nuclear and missile development. "From this point," he said, "it is important to decide what our next measure should be. I will have a conversation with you before I make a decision." I could tell that the US would take some measures soon.

Three days after our phone conversation, President Clinton made a statement about easing sanctions against North Korea. The US had agreed to partially lift economic sanctions on North Korea in September 1999, and this June 2000 statement materialized the agreement.

Thanks to this statement, trade and financial transactions that had been banned for fifty years resumed. North Korea could export raw materials and other merchandise to the US, and both countries could open their territorial air and steamship routes to one another.

US businesses were also allowed to invest in certain areas, such as agriculture, mining, roads, harbors and bays, travel, and tourism. However, international financial institutions' aid to North Korea through loans and claims on frozen North Korean assets remained frozen under the Trading with the Enemy Act.

Chairman Kim gifted me with two Pungsangae dogs that I named Uri and Duri. We gave a couple of Jindogae dogs to him. Uri and Duri ran around the Blue House residence and grounds, quickly making friends with our old family Jindogae dog. When I left office, I gave Uri and Duri to Seoul Grand Park. I also planted an eighteen-year-old rose of Sharon in the front garden of the Blue House Yeongbingwan guesthouse in honor of the inter-Korean summit.

On June 23, US Secretary of the State Albright visited Seoul. She wanted to hear about my visit to the North. She wore a yellow suit and a sunshine broach to symbolize the Sunshine Policy. Minister of Foreign Affairs Lee Joung-Binn, Senior Secretaries Hwang Won-tak and Park Joon-young, and North American Bureau Chief of the Ministry of Foreign Affairs Song Min-soon attended with me. From the US side, US Ambassador to Korea Stephen W. Bosworth, Counselor of the US Department of State Wendy Sherman, and Assistant Secretary of State Harold Hongju Koh accompanied Secretary of State Albright.

I expressed my gratitude for the US' consistent support of my Sunshine Policy. "You exercised strong leadership during a difficult time," Secretary Albright praised me. "I admire your persistence in pursuing an idea to success. I personally admire you, but now the whole world admires you."

I said that easing the US sanctions against North Korea would contribute greatly to leading North Korea into the international community. Also, citing the example of the 1994 visit to North Korea by former president Carter, I said, "I believe that it would be effective for the US secretary of state or the president to directly meet with Chairman Kim Jong-il. I enjoyed these achievements because I met with him face-to-face, and direct meetings are the way to solve problems."

"What measures should South Korea and the US take now?" Secretary Albright asked me.

"The inter-Korean relationship should be steadily developed by carrying out agreements," I replied. "The DPRK-US relationship and the DPRK-Japan relationship should be developed in parallel. Cooperation among Korea, the United States, and Japan is important. It is essential for the leaders of the United States and Japan to engage in direct dialogue with North Korean leaders."

"I will visit North Korea," Secretary Albright promised.

I attended the Kim Koo Museum and Library groundbreaking ceremony on June 26. Master Baekbom Kim Koo once said, "What is important is not whether something is realistic or not, but whether it is right or wrong. We chose to live in exile for thirty years because it was the overriding wish of the Korean nation, although it might have been the most unrealistic."

This was his answer to many who were criticizing his effort for reunification, both inside and outside of Korea. Although there were many voices talking about my summit, my answer was similar to his. I could feel Master Baekbom's loneliness deep in my heart. Many people left the Provisional Government under severe oppression and atrocious violence, but he did not give up the title of Provisional Government until the very end. He moved around from Shanghai to Hangzhou, from there to Nanjing, and from there to Chongqing. He led the heroic deeds of martyrs like Lee Bong-chang and Yun Bong-gil as the entire Chinese continent held its breath.

After returning home post-liberation, he devoted his life to reunification. "I will fall on the 38th Parallel if for the sake of reunification," he said. He worked like a tiger in a strange, cold land. Japan did not dare to hurt him. In the end, he fell to a fellow Korean's bullet, a victim of assassination in his beloved fatherland. How shameful! We built a museum for him—a space to honor his love for the nation, activities for his country's independence, and footsteps toward the reunification of the nation. As the first president of the country who had succeeded the legitimacy of Provisional Government, I took the first shovel, and then bowed.

On June 28, I met world-famous tenor Luciano Pavarotti for the second time. We had met briefly before during a lunch with Andrea Bocelli on my visit to Italy in March. He was visiting Korea to perform in a concert celebrating the inter-Korean summit and promoting peace in the Korean Peninsula. I requested two things of him: to perform at a charity concert for North Korean children, and to sing at the 2002 World Cup. Mr. Pavarotti gladly accepted my requests. In fact, he said he would perform together with Placido Domingo and Jose Carreras at the World Cup. He kept this promise.

On July 6, the first APEC Tourism Ministerial Meeting was held at the COEX building in Seoul. It was the meeting I had proposed at the APEC Summit meeting in Kuala Lumpur, Malaysia, in November 1998. At that time, I argued that developing the tourism industry would contribute to development and peace in the Asia Pacific region in the twenty-first century. I thought that we could gather wisdom for the activation of the tourism industry in Asia at the APEC Tourism Ministerial Meeting. Ministers and vice ministers, as well as high officials and international tourism organization leaders, gathered in Seoul from twenty-one member countries.

I made an opening remark: "Tourism is an industry based on human interchange. Both tourists and hosts should understand and respect one another. Tourism should be more than just entertainment, but cultural activity that respects various cultures and histories. At the same time, tourism should increase local residents' income, rather than creating a larger gap between the rich and poor. Also, national resources like nature, culture, and history are not limited to the country only. They are precious assets not only to tourists but also to our descendants."

The meeting participants created and issued the Seoul declaration on an APEC tourism charter.

From July 29 through 31, an inter-Korean ministerial-level talk was held in Seoul for the first time since the summit. The South and North agreed on five matters, including: to resume affairs at the liaison office in Panmunjeom; to hold events in support of the June 2000 accord in the South, the North, and overseas; to cooperate in hometown visit by Koreans in Japan belonging to the Pro-North Korean Residents' League; to connect the disconnected section of the Seoul-Sinuiju Line; and to hold the second ministerial-level talk in Pyongyang between August 29 and 31.

I met the North Korean delegates, including their leader and Senior Cabinet Counselor Jon Kum-jin. I congratulated them on their hard work and wished for even better results at the Pyongyang talk. "What is important is that we are one nation and one community with one destiny," I said to them. "We should work to accomplish peaceful reunification and live with smiles and happily as one nation in the twenty-first century by carrying out agreements, one after another."

The head of the delegates, Jon, said, "I noticed an important change during this visit to Seoul: People's sentiments have changed, and their enthusiasm for reunification is enhanced."

On August 5, media company presidents visited North Korea. Fifty-six members toured North Korean attractions for seven nights and eight days. Chairman Kim Jong-il kept his promise. This was the first civilian interchange since the summit. Chairman Kim was chatty during lunch with the visiting team. The visitors asked him when he would visit Seoul.

He said, "I owe my visit to Seoul to President Kim Dae-jung. The National Defense Commission and the Ministry of Foreign Affairs are discussing the matter now, but I haven't received their report yet."

They also asked him about when the North would establish a diplomatic relationship with the US and Japan. Chairman Kim said frankly and significantly, "As soon as I give the green light, we can establish a diplomatic relationship with the United States—even tomorrow. As soon as the United States clears our false classification as a terrorist country, then we will establish a diplomatic relationship with them. However, establishing a diplomatic relationship with Japan is a little more complicated. There are problems from the past, and things to settle. Japan should compensate us for thirty-six years. I will never establish a diplomatic relationship with Japan if it means hurting our pride. The smaller a country, the prouder it should be."

When Minister Park Jie-won went to the North with media company presidents I ordered him to have Chairman Kim Jong-il invite the president of the Grand National Party to meet with him. There could not be distinctions between ruling and opposition parties in national discussions. We also needed the opposition party's cooperation to use organizations like the South-North Cooperation Fund for various kinds of economic cooperation with the North.

When Minister Park explained this to Chairman Kim during his visit and requested his invitation of the opposition party president, Chairman Kim expressed extreme anger with the opposition party for calling his government "fascist." According to Minister Park, Chairman Kim said, "Six hundred thousand people welcomed President Kim when he visited Pyongyang. Most of them came out voluntarily. How can the opposition party call this fascist?" Minister Park persuaded him how essential it was for him to meet the opposition party. In the end, Chairman Kim accepted the suggestion.

I ordered Minister Park to create a document about Chairman Kim's invitation and to send it to the Grand National Party. However, the opposition party president's visit to the North did not happen.

During a lunch with some academics in mid-August, a professor asked me, "If you want to pursue an improved inter-Korean relationship, won't you need to actively support the opposition party president's and members' visits to the North?"

"I believe that the opposition party is working on a visit to the North," I replied. When this was reported in the media through Senior Press Secretary Park Joon-young's briefing, the Grand National Party immediately denied it. "[We] have not received any notice from the government," they said. "The Blue House is distorting the truth as if the opposition party is attempting contact with the North."

Days after the delivery of the North's invitation intention, they feigned ignorance. Even GNP president Lee Hoi-chang's close associates denied it, which is why we kept silent about the fact. We hoped President Lee would visit the North in order to build a national consensus for the reconciliation and cooperation with the North. If his visit had gone through, the inter-Korean relationship would have become closer. It is very regrettable that it did not.

On August 7, I reshuffled the cabinet, changing eleven ministerial-level officials. I gave five tasks to the new cabinet and urged them to work hard. The five tasks were the establishment of democracy, human rights, and law and order; the completion of reforms in four areas, including finance; implementation of productive welfare; regional harmony; and improvement, reconciliation, and cooperation in the inter-Korean relationship.

Unfortunately, Minister of Education Song Ja resigned from his post within twenty-three days for alleged plagiarism. I appointed Mr. Lee Donhee to the post. Soon afterward, I also reshuffled three senior secretaries—those for foreign affairs and national security, education and culture, and welfare and labor.

On August 15, our liberation day, the reunion of dispersed families occurred in Seoul and Pyongyang for the first time since the first reunion event fifteen years ago. One hundred and two people from the South were selected from 76,793 applicants to visit with 218 family members in Pyongyang. One hundred and one people from the North met 750 family members in the South in Seoul. I had invited South Koreans on their way to Pyongyang to stop by the Blue House for lunch the day before their trip. One elderly gentleman thanked me, saying he felt as if he were in a dream. "It has been fifty years since I left my family there and came south," he said. "There is not a single moment that I don't think of my children. I grew old and became white-haired. I'd like to run there and hug them. But, there are so many people who want to visit their families that I could not tell my friends that I am visiting my family members in the North."

Even before they met their family members, the visitors were choking with emotion. Many people were sobbing. They had grown old while missing their hometowns. How could we turn our eyes from them? The lunch event became a lunch of tears.

I attempted to comfort them, saying: "Even I, who am not from the North, felt sad when I turned seventy, wondering if I would die without ever visiting the North. So how sad you must be! This time, only one hundred go there. But, as they say, the beginning is half of the work. So I will keep on trying to make it possible for dispersed families to live wherever they want to live with their families."

They prepared heartfelt gifts for their family members: photos, gold rings, family genealogies, necklaces, and food. They included gifts from a deceased mother for her family members in the North.

I saw the scenes of reunion on TV the next day. Very old people were hugging each other and crying. My wife and I could not help crying, either. I felt lucky to have become president and rewarded for my difficult effort to visit North Korea. The TV screen showed dispersed families who could not visit this time, crying and calling their family members' names. These scenes made the entire world cry. I heard that people in Lebanon, a country with a lot of dispersed families, cried while watching them too.

We really had to at least give them the opportunity to be united, because the first generation of dispersed families was dying out. How deeply sad would it be for them not to be able to see their families before they died? We were all sinners for neglecting them. That is why I had appealed to Chairman Kim Jong-il for the reunion of dispersed families as the top priority issue.

On August 31, Dr. Stephen Hawking gave a lecture to the members of the Blue House staff, including the Office of Presidential Security. He came to Korea to attend the COSMO-2000 conference, sponsored by Seoul National University and the Samsung Electronics Company. Upon hearing this news, I invited him to the Blue House in the hopes that my staff members' perspective would open to the universe after hearing Dr. Hawking speak.

Although I did not attend the lecture, I heard that the attendants could feel Dr. Hawking's pride and humor during his introduction of himself. As I heard it, he said, "In 1963, I was diagnosed with Lou Gehrig's disease, which you're supposed to live with for only two or three years. My greatest achievement is that I'm still alive. Before I became ill, on a whim, I thought of becoming a politician. But, looking at Tony Blair, I am glad that I yielded the job of prime minister to him. I am much more satisfied with my work than his, and I think my work will be remembered in history for much longer."

Before the lecture, I met with Dr. Hawking. "I am very honored to have lived as your neighbor," I said. "There is an expression in Korean, which is a 'neighbor-cousin.' Since our time together in Cambridge, you have continued to accomplish great scholarly achievements and publish books. I admire it. Your scholarship is the pride of humanity."

"I'm glad to see you again," Dr. Hawking said. "I think very highly of your constant efforts for peace."

"Do you think there are other living organisms in the universe?" I asked him.

"I think that there could be primitive organisms, but I'm not sure about organisms with intelligence," he replied.

"Out of a world population of 6.5 billion, there is nobody who knows about you and doesn't admire you."

"I'm honored," he said. "Please visit Cambridge again."

He then gave me his most recent book, *The Brief History of Time*. Inside was his fingerprint, rather than his signature. It looked like the last trace of his writing, fighting his disability.

Toward the end of August 2000, our house in Donggyo-dong was demolished. I had moved there from a small rental room in 1963 and lived there for the next thirty-three years until I moved to Ilsan in 1995. Even when bombs were thrown into it and I was imprisoned there, my house in Donggyo-dong was a place where I could lie down and stand up again. It was surrounded by the police all the time and suffered whenever there was a coup d'état. It was often wiretapped and searched for seizure. Donggyo-dong was the symbol of the opposition party and resistance against the dictatorial regime.

It was there where the political soldiers of the new junta dragged me out and it was there where I failed in three presidential elections. Still, my wife and children waited for me there. Even in the midst of hardship, we were full of energy for democracy and never stopped praying for democracy. It was a place where my suffering and tears seeped into every corner and where my love and passion pervaded. I was very sad to see it demolished. I hesitated a lot at first, but there was no doubt that it was necessary for my own safety once my term was over. I considered moving to Paju, Gyeonggi-do, briefly, but, in the end, I decided to return to my old house in Donggyo-dong.

On September 2, I returned sixty-three long-term prisoners from North Korea who had not denounced communism back to their homeland. North Korea greeted them in Panmunjeom. They held a grand welcome event and poets wrote poems for them. These long-term prisoners had lived as strangers in South Korea because they refused to denounce communism. Most of them were elderly—in their seventies—and had spent more than thirty years on average in prison. I decided that they needed to spend their remaining few years with their families in the bosom of their hometowns. In some sense, wasn't ideology fading over time? Isn't it somewhat like a slogan that can be shaken by a small wind? There were long-term prisoners who chose to remain in the South for various reasons. It must have been a heavy day for both those who chose to go and those who chose to remain. How could they be entirely happy to part with the South after all these years? That's what karma is like. I hoped that North Korea would reciprocate our goodwill by allowing kidnapped South Koreans or prisoners of war to reunite with their families or to return. There were between 700 and 800 South Korean prisoners in the North, but the North Korean authorities had been denying their existence. As the reunion of dispersed families continued, they could meet their family members as a member of a dispersed family.

There was a UN Millennium Summit at the UN Headquarters in New York from September 6 to 8. I was going to have a meeting with North Korean president of the Presidium of the Supreme People's Assembly Kim Yong-nam. The world was paying attention to this event.

An unexpected incident happened, though. As President Kim Yong-nam was checking in to board an American Airlines flight in Frankfurt, airline security attempted a rather rude body search on him. Although the North Korean delegates explained who he was and protested, the security personnel insisted on a body search and argued that they must perform them on anybody from eight rogue states, regardless of their position. To protest this incident, North Korean delegates suddenly canceled their visit to the US. The North Korean vice minister of foreign relations held a press conference in Germany and said, "We cannot consider the rude body search by airline security as nothing other than an intentional provocation by the United States. We return because we cannot accept this duplicity of the United States in ignoring the president of a sovereign country."

North Korean delegates returned home via China. The US learned of this incident through the South Korean NIS. Although they urgently expressed their regrets to North Koreans through the American Embassy in China and urged their participation in the UN plenary session, it was in vain. I heard about all of this on the airplane on my way to the US. I was at a loss. I was also upset about the way the US handled the situation. It was impossible to accept their insulting attempt at body searches of the diplomatic delegates who were invited by their government. The US government announced that this incident had nothing to do with the government, and that it was the civilian airline's mistake.

I was disappointed at the arrogance of the US. My ambitious dream of inducing the world's support for peace in the Korean Peninsula on the international stage dissipated. If President Kim Yong-nam had gone to New York and met President Clinton through my mediation, history would have turned out differently. It was truly regrettable.

The UN Millennium Summit was held to gather wisdom for solving problems that we, humanity as a whole, were facing, such as civil wars, poverty, disease, environmental destruction, terror, and drugs. One hundred sixty-four out of 189 heads of state of UN member countries gathered, making it the most heads of state and government representatives who had ever attended. In my keynote address, I confirmed the Korean will for peaceful co-existence with one another, while remembering the significance of the inter-Korean summit. I said, "The new millennium is beginning with a miracle on the Korean Peninsula. Warm sunshine has begun to melt down the wall of ice that has stood between the South and North during the past fifty-five years of Cold War division.

"You must have seen some of the televised scenes of the South-North Korean Summit in June, as well as of the separated families reuniting on August 15 for the first time in all these years of national division. They were miraculous, and they were brought about not only through the efforts of South and North Korea, the principal parties, but also through the steadfast support and encouragement of the United Nations and the leaders of the world. I thank you wholeheartedly.

"Unification is the ultimate goal of the Korean people. However, unification must be achieved peacefully, no matter how long it takes. Unification must be a success for both sides. This was the agreement of the South-North Korean Summit."

The UN issued a statement under the names of the co-chairperson of the UN Millennium Summit that they welcomed the inter-Korean summit meeting held in June.

I had summit meetings with other countries' heads. I met with President Jiang Zemin at the Waldorf Astoria Hotel, where I stayed. He welcomed and congratulated me on the progress in the inter-Korean relationship. "There is a Chinese proverb: 'Where there is a will there is a way,'" he said. "I am carefully observing the progress in the inter-Korean relationship. I'm interested in stability and peace in the Korean Peninsula. I have also been very carefully watching reports on the progress in the relationship, such as the moving reunion of the dispersed families."

When I expressed my regrets about the incident that led to North Korean President Kim Yong-nam's absence in the UN plenary session, he comforted me and said warmly, "I heard the news. Sometimes there are twists and turns. I hope that this incident will not have any influence on the inter-Korean relationship."

I met President Clinton the next day. He expressed his regrets about President Kim Yong-nam's cancellation. "I sincerely regret the incident in Frankfurt. I hoped that North Korean delegates would change their minds and come to New York. I regret that their visit did not happen in the end. We will try our best to mend their hurt feelings. Please help us in our efforts."

I raised the issue of the US-South Korea Status of Forces Agreement revision and said, "In Korea, there is strong demand that this agreement be revised so that the relationship between Korea and the US is on the same level as the US is with Japan and Germany. Since both sides are earnestly negotiating now, it is necessary that both sides try their best to resolve this issue as amicably as possible."

I attended a closed-door roundtable in which about fifty heads of state participated. I urged the active resolution of the Myanmar situation. "The UN has passed a resolution about the Myanmar situation many times, and Korea actively participated in it. However, the UN resolution that urged the Myanmar government to resolve the situation through dialogue with Madam Aung San Suu Kyi has not been carried out yet. I believe that the UN should make an active effort to enable this resolution."

British Prime Minister Tony Blair, who was sitting next to me at the roundtable, requested a summit with me. We met in another room during a break. It was a seventeen-minute "mini-summit." I congratulated him on his new baby.

During my meeting with Russian President Putin, we agreed to pursue economic cooperation among South and North Korea and Russia, such as the connection of the Seoul-Wonsan train line and the Trans-Siberian Railway. President Putin was very astute about North Korea. "I visited North Korea recently," he said. "During my meeting with Chairman Kim Jong-il, I got the impression that North Korea was enthusiastic about the improvement of the inter-Korean relationship. I also recently met with heads of Japanese and Chinese states, and they were both supportive of reconciliation and cooperation between the two Koreas.

"As you have always emphasized, it is correct not to isolate North Korea, to find areas for cooperation, and to connect with them through the overall development of a relationship. I got the impression that Chairman Kim was a young leader who was thinking hard about the future of North Korea.

"We should never isolate North Korea. By developing a relationship with North Korea, we have to help them shake off their fear of the outside world. We have to help them not feel cornered and threatened. Once they realize that neighboring countries are friendly, they will no longer develop weapons. In the end, military confrontation will be relaxed and there will no longer be human sacrifices originating from antagonism."

Despite his rather negative background as an intelligence officer, President Putin saw the essence of the problem. He was also very positive about my proposal for the railway connection. "Common projects like the inter-Korean railway connection are very important in terms of relaxing the tension in the Korean Peninsula," he said. "I think it could become a large-scale project in which all neighboring countries participate. If the inter-Korean railways are connected, we may be able to connect fiber optic cable, which will expand the regional communication network. You can pursue cooperation in the field of energy, such as gas and electricity, together with neighboring countries. I hope that an inter-Korean economic community committee will discuss 3-way economic cooperation projects in which both Koreas and Russia will participate. Thanks to your will and effort, we are beginning to find clues to solve problems that have been accumulating for a long time."

During the summit, my wife received an honorary Ph.D. in humanities from Drew University in New Jersey. I couldn't be happier for her.

From the North, Special Envoy Kim Yong-sun flew to Seoul on an Air Koryo plane through a direct route between the two Koreas. He brought 300 ten-gram button mushrooms boxes from Mt. Chilbosan as Chairman Kim Jong-il's *Chuseok* (harvest festival) gift to us. They also provided a list of gift recipients, including former presidents, the heads of the three branches of the government, presidents of political parties, the June summit delegates, and the media company presidents who had visited Pyongyang in August. I appreciated Chairman Kim's generosity, but I did not feel comfortable accepting goods from them, knowing how poverty-stricken the North Korean people were. The ministry of unification took charge of distribution. I tried the mushrooms on *Chuseok*. They were very flavorful.

Special Envoy Kim's group traveled through tourist destinations, such as Jejudo Island, Pohang, and Gyeongju, as well as industrial facilities like POSCO. NIS Director Lim Dong-won and Secretary of the Workers' Party of Korea Kim Yong-sun had a high official-level special envoy meeting and issued a seven-point joint press release. The seven points were:

1. Chairman Kim Jong-il will visit Seoul in the near future and president of the Presidium of the Supreme People's Assembly of North Korea Kim Yong-nam will visit ahead of this summit.

2. Both parties welcome a discussion about holding a meeting between the ministers of defense of the South and the North.

3. To solve the problem of dispersed families, we decided to begin the quick work of confirming the life and death of dispersed families in September. We will first pursue the exchange of letters between people who are confirmed to be alive. Also, we agree to hold the South-North Red Cross conference at Mt. Kumgang on September 20 and discuss two more additional visits of dispersed families within this year, as well as the institution and operation of a family reunion center.

4. We agree to hold a working-level meeting for the Constitution of protection of investments and prevention of double taxation in order to promote inter-Korean economic cooperation in Seoul on September 25, and to resolve these issues quickly.

5. Both the South and the North will hold a groundbreaking ceremony in the near future for the connection of a railway and road between Seoul and Sinuiju.

6. The North will send a fifteen-member economic inspection team to the South in October.

7. Both the South and the North will carry out a joint investigation and prepare a concrete plan within the year for flood control in the Imjingang River Valley.

I had lunch with Special Envoy Kim Yong-sun and his delegate team. He delivered an oral message from Chairman Kim Jong-il. "I send my regards to President Kim. I believe that the June 15 Accord created during the historic Pyongyang summit contains excellent contents, and I am satisfied that they are being carried out. The accord was made in the spirit that President Kim expressed in Pyongyang when he said that he did not like empty formalities and vanity. We should now carefully carry it out and see it through. The signatures in the accord are surely drying and firming. As there are excellent contents in the accord, we should not return to past practices again. We should firmly execute and carry out the accord no matter what. I am full of resolution."

I also sent him a reply message. "I thank you for sending heartfelt gifts for *Chuseok*. The June 15 Accord should be fully carried out. As I said in

Pyongyang, our life is not eternal. What we do while we live in this world is most important. It is truly meaningful to be in a position to decide our nation's fate at this time. Although we wish for national reunification, we should not rush it. It is important to build a firm foundation. I will make an effort during my term, and I think that my successor will follow through with this work."

Special Envoy Kim Yong-sun and his team returned to the North through Panmunjeom that day.

On September 15, the Olympics opened in Sydney, Australia. For the first time in history, the South and North Korean athletes entered the opening ceremony together carrying a Korean Peninsula flag. The song "Arirang" spread throughout the stadium during the opening ceremony. In that moment, 110,000 people stood up at the same time and cheered. It was a beautiful sight and a great march. The Olympics are always a festival of humanity, but that day, they were a special blessing to the Korean Peninsula. The joint entrance of the last divided country in the world was the most moving moment of the entire opening ceremony. Throughout the Olympic Games, both sides united and continued to praise and root for each other. The world media reported that a new century was dawning in the Korean Peninsula. President of International Olympic Committee Samaranch sent a letter of congratulations.

The groundbreaking ceremony for the connection of the Seoul-Sinuiju Railway was held in front of the Bridge of Freedom on September 18. The Seoul-Sinuiju Railway opened in April 1906, but the train stopped running immediately after the liberation in September 1945; the 24-kilometer section between Munsan and Kaesong was discontinued. This groundbreaking ceremony was a historic event that reconnected the railway and land road, an event that connected the nation's artery.

The joint South and North Korean military landmine removal project would happen in the near future to erase the trauma of the fratricidal war. It would also serve as a promise that there would be no war in this land. Young sprouts would grow in the place of the landmines, and those sprouts would bloom as the flowers of peaceful reunification.

This inter-Korean railway connection establishes the "iron silk road," which will take us across the entire Eurasian continent. It is exciting to think that a train that leaves from Busan will reach Paris and London.

On September 20, the Presidential Commission on Sustainable Development launched. I believe that while the twentieth century was the age of development and utilization, the twenty-first century is the age in which development and preservation exist in harmony. My government simultaneously pursued environmental preservation and economic development. I had dreamed of a community where human beings and nature could live together for a long time; however, I could not prioritize it due to the economic crisis that I had had to face. Still, I could establish comprehensive measures for the Hangang and Nakdonggang Rivers and scrap the Yeongwol Dam Plan. In addition, my government legislated the Wetland Preservation Law and transferred the management of national parks to the Ministry of Environment. We also introduced urban buses that used natural gas.

The flip side of the word "sustainable" is that our society could cease existing at any moment. It contains the scary warning of cultural discontinuation. The Presidential Commission on Sustainable Development was installed so that it could mediate different opinions about pending issues, such as large-scale government-run projects, reckless land development, agreements related to climate change, and energy-related issues. I appointed Mr. Kang Moon-kyu as its inaugural president.

I left for a two-night, three-day visit to Japan on September 22. There, I met Korean and Japanese cultural agents at the New Otani Hotel in Tokyo. I emphasized that a new era of cultural exchange was opening between Korea and Japan. "Recently, the latest fashions on Ginza Street show up in Seoul a few days later," I said. "Also, the fashions from Seoul's Dongdaemun Market are directly exported to Japan everyday. The Korean film *Shiri* is garnering an audience of millions in Japan, and Korean youths are enthusiastic during the performance of the popular Japanese music duo Chage and Aska in Seoul.

"The closer the cultures of Korea and Japan get, the more expansive the exchanges and friendship between the two people, and the deeper the trust will be. Professionals say this expansion of mutual trust is what will promote the destined community at low cost and high efficiency."

The next day, I had a summit meeting with Prime Minister Mori Yoshiro at Hotel Hyakumangoku in Itami, a hot spring vacation spot near Tokyo. When I arrived in Itami, I was surprised to see that about 4000 citizens waving both Korean and Japanese national flags had come out to welcome me in the rain. Prime Minister Mori was staying overnight in the same hotel I was, and was waiting for me in the meeting room.

I attended a dinner reception held by Prime Minister Mori that evening. A beautiful thirty-minute firework show brilliantly decorated the night sky in front of the hotel. Prime Minister Mori told me that the city had prepared it to welcome me. I had never seen such splendid fireworks.

On September 24, the defense minister of North Korea visited the South for the first South–North Defense Ministers' Meeting as a member of a thirteen-delegate team. This was the first time North Korean military leaders had come south of the DMZ since the Korean War. After crossing Panmunjeom, the delegates flew to Jejudo Island on a South Korean military plane. At the meeting, Defense Minister of the South Cho Sung-tae and Defense Minister of the North Kim Il-chol agreed that soldiers from both sides would guarantee each other's safety at DMZ for the road and railway connection construction.

North Korean Defense Minister Kim Il-chol visited me at the Blue House. His team members saluted me. It was also the first time the highest North Korean defense leader had visited the Blue House in the fifty-five years since the division. It was an event previously unimaginable.

"We should never aim our guns at each other again," I said. "Since we have maintained an antagonistic relationship for a long time, our relationship is very sensitive now. If we neither hurry nor take a break in our effort to build trust, we will be able to achieve peaceful reunification."

The delegates listened to my words attentively. I was overwhelmed by many thoughts as I looked at them. The June 15 Accord changed all inter-Korean relationships both qualitatively and quantitatively. Economic cooperation and social and cultural interchange began to flow as though a dam had been broken. Even more importantly, each of us came to understand the other party in a new light, as partners rather than enemies in co-existence and co-prosperity. North Korean residents' view of the South completely changed, and South Korean residents could now be entirely devoted to their calling, entrusting their security to their government's policy of peace. How fortunate that we could wash away the mistrust of half a century and build trust! The salute of North Korean high military officials signified all of this.

On September 28, the RAFTO Foundation for Human Rights, head-quartered in Bergen, Norway, chose me as the winner of the RAFTO Prize for Human Rights. They announced that they appreciated that my "policy of engagement and reconciliation toward North Korea, better known as the Sunshine Policy, rendered hope for peaceful and democratic development, with respect for fundamental human rights." It was a prize established to commemorate Professor Thorolf Rafto—who taught economic history at the Norwegian School of Economics in Bergen—and who had devoted his life to promoting democracy and respect for human rights, especially in Eastern Europe. My son Hong Up and his wife attended the award ceremony on my behalf.

WELFARE IS NOT ALMSGIVING, BUT HUMAN RIGHTS (1998–OCTOBER 2000)

On January 4, 2000, I declared the governing policy of "productive welfare" in my New Year's address. This clarified that the three governing policies of my government were the parallel development of democracy and market economy as well as productive welfare. In fact, my idea of productive welfare dated back to before my inauguration, but I had not had room for the issue amid the urgency of financial crisis at the beginning of my presidential term. However, the economy improved in 1999 with increased tax revenue and a surplus of 3800 billion won, so we had funds to use for lower- and lower-middle-class welfare. The Committee for Policy and Planning had already begun studying ways to implement productive welfare.

I explained what I had always believed to the members of the Committee for Policy and Planning during my lunch with them in June 1999. "I talked about 'productive welfare' during my election campaign," I said. "I believe that we should pursue it not in the sense of almsgiving, but in the sense of providing people with retraining so that they can produce added value and high efficiency, which will be helpful both to themselves and to the national economy. We should open the road to work for those who are capable and willing, while strengthening protection for the seriously disabled, elderly, and weak."

From that point on, the government studied productive welfare and I received the results of their studies as they came in. The shape of productive welfare was becoming clearer. It was different from the welfare of almsgiving in Europe. There were three things that the government should do for the kind of productive welfare I had in mind:

- First, the government should provide protection for the weak who were incapable of working through the National Basic Livelihood Security Act.
- Second, we would orient toward "welfare through work"—in other words, the government should provide more and better work

opportunities for the capable and willing. For this purpose, the government should carry out active policies to help people's reentry into the labor market by providing job search information, helping them find jobs, training them for jobs, and supporting the establishment of new businesses.

- Third, the government should provide an environment where everyone in our country could enjoy their right to happiness. In the old days, people considered a perfect state a state where food, clothing, and shelter were provided. However, we are living in a time when those basic needs alone cannot make us happy. It is a time when our need for culture, leisure, sports, and environment are necessary for satisfaction. For this, we needed education and accomplishment. Accordingly, during my government, we legislated the Continuing Education Law, which enabled people to study whenever they wanted.

The Committee for Policy and Planning and other relevant governmental offices worked to embody my ideas. I know some people criticize me as a neoliberal. I guess my emphasis on the principle of a thorough market economy during the financial crisis was the root of such criticism. However, there was really no other alternative than that to the 1997 IMF system. I tried to correct the side effects and harmful results of the market economy and to complement it through my idea of productive welfare, which was the result of learning from the failures of European-style, excessive welfare.

We began operating the National Basic Livelihood Security system in October 2000. Through this system, the government provided livelihood for the lower-class people who earned wages below the minimum living cost, regardless of their abilities. The Livelihood Protection Law, legislated in 1961, was not working as a social safety net for the poor class created after the mass layoffs of the financial crisis.

The difference between the National Basic Livelihood Security system and the livelihood protection system lay in the paradigm shift in the concept of welfare. The National Basic Livelihood Security Law clarified a minimum standard of living to be a guaranteed constitutional right. It was a departure from the previous concept of welfare as a simple, almsgiving-level protection, and clarified that welfare was everyone's right and the state's duty. The terms for welfare changed from "protection target" to "recipient by right," from "livelihood protection" to "livelihood allowance," and from "protection agency" to "security agency."

Also, we included everyone who made below the minimum living cost, unlike the old law, which did not provide living costs for those who were capable of working.

At the same time, we introduced a comprehensive support program for financial independence so that the poor could escape social alienation and poverty. This would be helpful not only to the individual pursuit of happiness, but also for social unity through their contribution to neighbors, society, and the nation.

This institution of the National Basic Livelihood Security system had a huge impact on our society. The number of livelihood allowance recipients quadrupled from 370,000 in 1997 to 1,550,000 in 2002. It also guaranteed real security by increasing the monthly allowance for a family of four from 330,000 won in 1997 to 870,000 won in 2002.

Later, people commented that this system elevated the welfare of Korean citizens to another level. When I signed this law, I said, "I am happy to know that now nobody in Korea will die of hunger or forgo their studies due to a lack of money."

I checked how this system was operating whenever I went to the countryside or joined in cabinet meetings.

There had been strong opposition to this law. A small minority of conservatives attacked it as a socialist approach. There were some in the cabinet who thought that its introduction was premature. However, I did not hesitate to implement it. It is too cruel and sad to do nothing when people who live in the same place and time as you are starving.

There is an old saying that "Even a king cannot save those living in poverty." These days, the state has to solve the problem of poverty. In the past, communities embraced and took care of poor people, but these days when communities based on villages and blood are rapidly dissolving, poverty means illnesses and starvation.

Minister of Welfare Choi Sun-jung later remembered how I did not yield to the opposition on the implementation of the National Basic Livelihood Security, saying, "This system that people in the field of welfare would call the system of dreams, this system that was of the world's highest caliber, was possible entirely thanks to President Kim's resolution."

After leaving office, I have sometimes seen people on TV say that the basic livelihood allowance was their only recourse. Whenever I saw them, I felt rewarded.

In my inauguration address I said: "We should offer jobs to the elderly and the disabled with some ability to work, while embracing those who

don't have the capability to work. I will become the President of the people who will wipe away the tears of the alienated and encourage those who
sigh."

In a way, I became president as a disabled elderly man. Maybe that is
why I paid special attention to the elderly and disabled. However, in retrospect, I could not know then whether I would have the kind of success
that I hoped to achieve. I often checked the progress of elderly welfare
projects. In fact, I issued a special statement in 1999, the year the UN
designated as the "international year of old persons." In October 1999, I
said at the Elderly Welfare Project Briefing session: "I believe that we
should spend our late years happy; that is the only way we will end our
lives happily. Society and the state have the duty to do that for our elderly,
as a way of repaying their hard lives. As I always say, we should practice
filial piety by the state and by the society. As long as their children pay
taxes, the state should help parents whose children cannot take care of
them themselves. I believe that is an advanced concept of filial piety."

The Government of the People introduced a respect-for-the-elderly
pension plan and subsidies for the employment of the elderly. We also
legislated a law that promoted the employment and vocational rehabilita-
tion of the disabled. We implemented benefits for the disabled and support for medical and educational costs. We also gave preferential treatment
to the disabled for the installation of kiosks and vending machines. We
expanded exemptions for a special excise tax for the disabled when they
purchased automobiles. However, society's views of and prejudices against
the disabled were not easily changed. It made me sad.

I completed the four basic social insurances in order to protect the
Korean people from the dangers of old age, disease, accidents, and unemployment. A state pension, health insurance, employment insurance, and
workers' compensation insurance were social safety nets. Together with
the National Basic Livelihood Security system, they were the essence of a
productive welfare policy.

By expanding the requirement for employment insurance and workers'
compensation insurance to workplaces that hired one or more employees,
we made sure that all Korean people would be free of the dangers of
unemployment and industrial accidents. In particular, employment insurance played an essential role during the unemployment crisis that resulted
from the Asian financial crisis. It helped the unemployed retain their
livelihood and help themselves. We also unified the health insurance management system, which had been a topic of debate for a long time. By

raising the quality of medical service for all Koreans, we thus secured the foundation of a communal society.

There were a lot of twists and turns in the expansion of the state pension system. We might consider state pension as one of two important axes of the social welfare system (with the other being health insurance). Nine million new people, including the urban self-employed, needed to register for state pension. First, we had to make sure we had the financial ability to expand state pension to the urban self-employed sector. We made the decision to pursue it in the first year of my term. I thought that we needed to hurry its implementation through because our society was rapidly aging. Also, I thought that if we delayed it to be cautious, it could come to nothing due to opposition. I thought it would be better to pursue it while my early term momentum was still fresh.

The Ministry of Health and Welfare and National Pension Service, which worked on the introduction of this institution, estimated the average income of the urban self-employed, asked them to report their income, and to sign up for state pension. People did not quite understand what this new institution was all about because the government hadn't done enough work to enlighten them. In addition, the income estimation was not very competently done. In some cases, the sign-up sheet was delivered to another person. It was revealed that government organizations were not well prepared to introduce this new system. The individual income report filing that began in February 1999 did not progress very well, with less than a quarter of individuals filing. Korean people resisted the introduction of this new institution, and this issue was fodder for the opposition party to attack during the special election. Even now, my face feels hot when I think back on that time.

The expansion of the state pension system should have been received as the best of the best governance. The Korean people should have been happy and cheered for it. Instead, they criticized us. It was all because we failed to properly inform the Korean people about it and because we did not prepare it well enough. I was very upset about this, and I reprimanded both the Ministry of Health and Welfare and the National Pension Service. Unfortunately, it was already spilt milk. I engaged in a dialogue with the Korean people and apologized to them. Even while apologizing, I could not help sighing. "This is really absurd," I said. "I began this work in order to do a really good thing for the Korean people. I feel a great responsibility for the technical and management mistakes made by those who executed it. I am extremely disappointed."

The public opinion called for delaying the system's implementation, which had been scheduled for April. Even the ruling party urged me to delay it because they were afraid it would become a bump in the general election. I rejected those pressures. Despite all of the twists and turns, the state pension system was expanded to urban residents, finally opening the era of the universal state pension system. It was a great achievement that was possible for the first time since its introduction eleven years before. Minister Kim Mo-im underwent great pains and suffering during this time. I felt so sorry for her, but, in the end, we achieved it.

The state pension system needed reform because of its continued unreasonable structure of low contribution and high yield. The task was to secure financial health. Although ten children might be assisting an elderly relative now, pretty soon only several children would be able to support that individual. Reform was necessary to establish a balanced structure between contribution and yield.

Also, the necessary enormous fund management size was a problem. Although we established a headquarters made up of professionals within the agency, the situation did not improve very much. The Government of the People made various efforts, but it was not enough. It was necessary to gather wisdom so that the national pension would become the modern version of a filial child.

There had also been labor pains in the unification of health insurance, including the financial crisis. Health insurance had been based on cooperatives (regional, workplace-based, teachers' union, etc.) since its introduction in 1977. However, it was necessary to unify them due to the difference in co-pays according to financial ability gaps; the difference in the quality of medical service; and inefficiency in management and operation. I believed that health was everyone's basic right, so health care should be distributed evenly to all people according to the principles of social welfare and social solidarity. Naturally, I hoped to unify various cooperatives. It was one of my campaign pledges, and the transition committee also included it as one of one hundred tasks for the government. The National Assembly had already passed resolutions for health insurance unification many times.

However, in practice, there were many difficult problems in unifying health care. The methods of co-pay calculation were different according to each cooperative, and the estimation of individual income was very difficult. It was impossible to satisfy every party involved. It was natural that people were dissatisfied. In addition, the restructuring of cooperative employees became a difficult issue, and we anticipated labor-employer conflicts.

However, we had to march on since we were moving along the right road. In October 1998, we unified 227 regional health insurance cooperatives and health insurance services for government and private school employees. We also unified 145 workplace health insurance cooperatives in July 2000, although they opposed it by waging a strike. The twenty-year debate was finally over. The new health insurance system launched.

However, a crisis occurred in financing the National Health Insurance Service. In March 2001, the National Health Insurance Service announced that there would be a deficit of approximately 4 trillion won. Both the Korean people and I were very surprised. It was the result of inaccurately predicting many factors: the raises in medical charges due to the separation of pharmacies and clinics; the rapid increase of expensive drug usage; the increase in use of medical services; and the rapid increase in medical costs for the elderly due to an aging society. I was greatly disappointed with how incompetently relevant agencies handled the matter. That day, Minister of Health and Welfare Choi Sun-jung resigned.

The government established an emergency headquarters and made its daily financial report public. We also implemented comprehensive measures including 50 percent government support for regional insurances, a gradual raise of the co-payment, and borrowing the deficit amount from banks for gradual repayment. The unification of health insurance was one of the most significant reforms the Government of the People achieved. We finally solved a twenty-year-old problem. However, it is also true that the significance of this accomplishment faded because many old problems resurfaced. The complete unification of finance had to be handed over to later governments.

During my term, the separation of pharmacy and clinic caused the biggest social conflict. This separation meant that doctors took charge of diagnosing and prescribing, and pharmacists took charge of filling the prescriptions and medication. We introduced this system to prevent the abuse and waste of drugs, and eventually to better manage the Korean people's health and enhance the quality of our medical services. Although it is rather inconvenient for a patient to visit a pharmacy after visiting a clinic, most advanced countries already adopted this system a while ago.

The separation of pharmacy and clinic was a sort of cultural revolution in Korea, where pharmacies and clinics had not been separated for thousands of years. Since the liberation, each regime tried it in vain (eight times altogether!), and was ultimately stymied in its efforts due to the opposition of interest groups. When the government came up against group oppositions, it simply handed the matter over to the next government.

The opposition was fierce during my government as well. As the amended Pharmaceutical Law should have been carried out before July 7, 1999, my government began working on it in 1998. The Council for the Promotion of Separation of Pharmacy and Clinic, composed of people from the medical, pharmaceutical, and academic fields, presented basic principles for the implementation of this separation. But the Korean Medical Association, the Korean Pharmaceutical Association, and the Korean Hospital Association presented a petition to the National Assembly for the postponement of its implementation with the excuse that they were not well prepared. As a result, the implementation was delayed for a year.

On May 10, 1999, the Korean Medical Association, the Korean Pharmaceutical Association, and the Citizens' Committee submitted a so-called May 10 Agreement to the government. The government created the Committee for the Implementation of the Separation of Pharmacy and Clinic and finalized the government plan based on this agreement. The government also amended the Pharmaceutical Law. As the concrete schedule of implementation was finalized, however, an unprecedented medical strike occurred, bringing the medical system to a grinding halt with one stroke. The media called this medical upheaval. There were disasters in which patients died due to the strike. Despite the Korean people's condemnation, the medical field did not stop the strike.

The government had some responsibility for this turn of events. The relevant offices worked in such a way that the three interested parties—the Korean Medical Association, the Korean Pharmaceutical Association, and the Citizens' Committee—agreed on a plan and then recommended it to the government. I reproached them for this approach, since the government did not take charge of the execution. "Don't leave the matter only with the interest groups," I said. "The government should come up with an acceptable alternative."

The separation of pharmacy and clinic became a matter of national importance. I listened to various opinions from all walks of life. Many people argued for delaying its implementation.

On March 29, 2000, I met with representatives from the medical field. I tried to persuade them to come around. "Doctors are the highest intellectuals," I said. "You're also people with a conscience. Please, doctors are people who work to save lives. Please solve this problem through dialogue.

This government is a democratic government. We legalized the Korean Teachers Union, and the Korean Confederation of Trade Unions created the Labor Party and sent candidates to elections. You can wage demonstrations legally."

The chair of the Committee for the Winning of Medical Rights said, "The separation of pharmacies and clinics is scheduled to begin on July 1. There are a lot of problems to be solved. The government says 'improvement after the fact,' but we say 'improvement before the fact.'"

He even gave me a big bow. It was a truly difficult situation. I hoped that the repercussions from the separation between pharmacy and clinic would be solved through dialogue. However, I thought that it was most important to maintain the principle. By principle, I meant protecting the Korean people's health through the prevention of abuse and wasting drugs. For this purpose, this matter should not be regressed. In fact, the government did everything that we could. We could not yield to groups that tried to protect only their interests by taking people's lives hostage. Once that happened, how could I govern the country?

I made up my mind to think about the future, even if it was hard at the moment. I decided to continue to pursue it. To protect the people's health was a basic duty of the state.

The medical field waged a nationwide strike on June 20, soon after my return from Pyongyang following the June 15 Accord. Most clinics closed their doors. The entire medical field pressured the government with all their might. President of the Grand National Party Lee Hoi-chang proposed a meeting with me on June 24. I immediately accepted it. President Lee proposed a model separation of pharmacy and clinic instead of the all-out execution of it. I rejected this proposal, but I agreed to amend the Pharmaceutical Law to ban pharmacists' preparation of medicine without a doctor's prescription. If I yielded completely, the separation of pharmacy and clinic would not have happened. It would have been swept under the carpet of group egotism and political logic.

Still, resistance from the medical field continued. Even residents in hospitals and professors participated in the strike. I did not budge. In the cabinet meeting on August 21, I said emphatically, "The separation of pharmacy and clinic was produced through agreement among doctors, pharmacists, and civilian organizations. We also recently amended the Pharmaceutical Law, after gathering opinions from doctors and pharmacists. In addition, we also raised medical fees and improved treatment for residents. The government did what we could, as best we could. Therefore, we cannot yield to an attempt to achieve group egotism while taking people's lives hostage. If we do, we cannot govern our country. It is important to resolve this matter soon, but it is more important to resolve it according to our principles."

Despite all the difficulties along the way, my intention was accomplished in the end. I was, of course, responsible for the event to a degree. Our preparation was less than thorough. I trusted the relevant officers too easily. Despite all of the labor pains, the system began to settle in the end. People took it for granted that they could get a prescription from their doctor and get it filled by their pharmacist. The use of antibiotics, which had been abused and wasted in the past, was greatly reduced. This trend continued even after my term was over. I believe that Korean people's health improved as a result.

I often heard that the separation of pharmacy and clinic was a failed and very exhausting reform. Some people said that the government pursued it only because it didn't know what it would entail, and that we would not have pursued it had we known. Nevertheless, my government and I persisted.

The Ministers of Health, in particular, were frequently replaced under my government. That was the reflection of the size of their difficulties. Ministers Kim Mo-im, Cha Hong-bong, Choi Sun-jung, Kim Won-gil, Lee Tae-bok, and Kim Sung-ho worked with me on the front lines to reform the field of welfare. No other ministries were plagued as much as the Ministry of Health and Welfare; however, they worked hard. Despite trial and error, and despite inconveniences and splits in national opinion, we truly tried our best. I said to the ministers, "We have to take care of the Korean people's livelihood, but it is also important to help them feel rewarded in their lives. We have to have them feel that the government and society care about them—that there are places that take care of them beside themselves. They should feel that they are contributing members of our society and that they *want* to contribute to the society."

In fact, welfare policies are so immediately related to people's individual everyday lives that they cannot help but be sensitive. How hard it is to raise the quality of life and to take care of the poor! Welfare involves looking into the pockets of the haves and taking care of the have-nots.

The frequent replacement of Ministers of Health and Welfare does not necessarily indicate an inability on their part but, rather, my great interest in the people's welfare. Although welfare policies were troublesome throughout my term, I feel rewarded in retrospect. I believe all the ministers who worked with me must feel similarly.

Brilliant Days in the Fall of 2000 (October 2000)

On October 9, First Vice Chairman Jo Myong-rok of the North Korean National Defense Commission visited the US. He issued a very meaningful statement upon arrival, saying: "I came to Washington to discuss important current issues with President Clinton as a special envoy of the great Chairman of the National Defense Commission of the Democratic Peoples' Republic of (North) Korea. I am planning to hold talks with other officials, including the secretary of the state and the minister of national defense. To enhance the DPRK-US relationship to a new level corresponding with the environment of peace and reconciliation spreading in the Korean Peninsula in the beginning of the new century is an important task for our two governments. We will try our best to have honest talks with the US leadership in order to effect an epoch-making change that eliminates deep-seated mistrust and advances the relationship between the two countries to a new level during our visit."

Vice Marshall Jo visited President Clinton in his military attire and delivered Chairman Kim Jong-il's handwritten letter. He also had talks with Secretary of State Albright, Defense Minister William Cohen, and Counselor of the US Department of State Wendy Sherman. The US government offered Vice Marshall Jo's group a limousine and car escort. Before the visit, the US and the DPRK issued the "Joint US-DPRK Statement on International Terrorism" on October 6, 2000. They stated:

> During the talks, the DPRK side affirmed that, as a matter of official policy and as its government has stated previously, it opposes all forms of terrorism against any country or individual. The DPRK noted that it was the responsibility of every UN member state to refrain from organizing, instigating, facilitating, financing, encouraging, or tolerating terrorist activities.

The relationship between the two countries changed radically. The speed with which they moved into the reconciliation phase seemed almost too rapid. President Clinton said in a White House press conference that President Kim Dae-jung had asked him to have any form of contact with North Korea that it found appropriate.

Vice Marshall Jo and Secretary of the State Albright issued a "Joint Communiqué" after the talk. Its last sentence particularly stood out: "It was agreed that Secretary of State Madeleine Albright will visit the DPRK in the near future to convey the views of US president William Clinton directly to Chairman Kim Jong-il of the DPRK National Defense Commission, and to prepare for a possible visit by the President of the United States."

The statement also said: "The two sides agreed there are a variety of available means, including Four Party talks, to reduce tension on the Korean Peninsula and formally end the Korean War by replacing the 1953 Armistice Agreement with permanent peace arrangements." It was news that Koreans had wanted to hear for a long time. When asked in a press conference if Secretary of State Albright meant President Clinton when she said "the president of the United States," she responded: "I don't make commitments on behalf of the next president of the United States ... so, yes. And, you know, I will be going very soon—by the end of the month probably—and then President Clinton, I think he hopes to go. We're going to work very hard to make it possible. And if we assess that we can make some serious progress on our key issues, this will proceed... it's important that I go. I'm very pleased that the vice marshal proffered an invitation, and I will, as I said, try to go by the end of the month."

It was very symbolic to mention "replacing the 1953 Armistice Agreement with permanent peace arrangements." Finally, the dark clouds of war were receding from the Korean Peninsula. Unfortunately, President Clinton's term would be over in about one hundred days, which worried me.

In October, foreign news media reported that I would win the Nobel Peace Prize. The AP and AFP were particularly positive about this prediction. As the day of the prizewinner announcement approached, the foreign media began reporting more. Korean journalists were sent to Norway to await the announcement. Since 1987, when German Chancellor Willy Brandt had first recommended me, I had been on the nominee list every year.

The nominee field was very crowded in 2000 because it was the centennial of the Nobel Peace Prize and the year that began the new millennium. Altogether, 35 organizations and 115 candidates were recommended, including the Salvation Army, President Bill Clinton (who worked hard on the Middle Eastern Peace Process), former US Senator George Mitchell (who mediated the Northern Ireland Peace Process), and former prime minister of Russia Viktor Chernomyrdin (who contributed to the peace in the Balkans).

At 6:00 p.m. on October 13, 2000, the day the Nobel Peace Prize winner was announced, I watched TV with my wife. It seems that many other Koreans were also sitting in front of their TVs in anticipation. When Chairman of the Norwegian Nobel Committee Gunnar Berge called my name, I hugged my wife. It felt like dream.

Upon my selection, Chairman Berge read the following:

The Norwegian Nobel Committee has decided to award the Nobel Peace Prize for 2000 to Kim Dae-jung for his work for democracy and human rights in South Korea and in East Asia in general, and for peace and reconciliation with North Korea, in particular.

In the course of South Korea's decades of authoritarian rule, despite repeated threats to his life and long periods in exile, Kim Dae-jung gradually emerged as his country's leading spokesman for democracy. His election as the republic's president in 1997 marked South Korea's definitive entry among the world's democracies. As president, Kim Dae-jung has sought to consolidate democratic government and to promote internal reconciliation within South Korea.

With great moral strength, Kim Dae-jung has stood out in East Asia as a leading defender of universal human rights against attempts to limit the relevance of those rights in Asia. His commitment in favor of democracy in Myanmar and against repression in East Timor has been considerable.

Through his Sunshine Policy, Kim Dae-jung has attempted to overcome more than fifty years of war and hostility between North and South Korea. His visit to North Korea was the impetus for a process that has reduced tension between the two countries. There may now be hope that the Cold War will also come to an end in Korea. Kim Dae-jung has worked for South Korea's reconciliation with other neighboring countries, especially Japan.

The Norwegian Nobel Committee wishes to express its recognition of the contributions made by North Korea's and other countries' leaders to advance reconciliation and possible reunification on the Korean Peninsula.

My secretaries and cabinet members were in the living room waiting to congratulate me. I dictated my feelings about this honor to Blue House Spokesperson Park Joon-young: "I am extremely honored. I attribute this honor to all Korean people, who have continued to support democracy, human rights, and inter-Korean peace and reconciliation. I thank all citizens of the world who love democracy and human rights. I also would like to share this honor with my family, comrades, friends, and the many people who sacrificed and devoted their lives for democracy and peace in this land. I would like to continue to devote myself to human rights, democracy, and peace in the Korean Peninsula, and democracy and peace in Asia and around the world."

The Blue House website crashed due to the number of congratulatory messages. I had dinner with my eldest son Hong Il's and second eldest son Hong Up's families. Around 9:40 p.m. I had a telephone interview with the Norwegian national broadcasting station as all Nobel Peace Prize win-ners did. I said: "I consider this award as encouragement to me to con-tinue to work hard for human rights, democracy, and peace. I have lived my entire life with the belief that justice will always prevail—if not in my lifetime, then in history. Now that I have received this award, I feel I am perhaps receiving more than I deserve in this world."

It was an overwhelmingly beautiful fall night. After all of the visitors left, my mind raced in the darkness. I felt very grateful to be awarded this precious honor in my lifetime, because I had simply lived with faith in God and a belief in history, a belief that justice would eventually prevail although it might not be during my lifetime. Winning the Nobel Peace Prize was the world's recognition of the blood and sweat of the Korean people who had suffered under the dictatorship, and of all the pioneers of the reunifi-cation movement. I have come to this moment today only because of the Korean people's trust in and protection of me. Therefore, the true recipi-ent of the Nobel Peace Prize were the Korean people.

Although other awards were *fruits*, the Nobel Peace Prize—at least the Nobel Peace Prize that I received—was the *beginning*. I would go down to even lower places than until then and continue to work for human rights and peace. My wife couldn't fall asleep either. I held her hand.

The Norwegian media reported: "Although there have been debates about the qualifications of past recipients, there wasn't a single objection about the selection of President Kim Dae-jung." However, in Korea (and this was perhaps unique in the world), there were people who cynically regarded my winning the prize.

The world media paid tribute to my receipt of this award, which was truly flattering. The Japanese newspaper *Yomiuri* published and distrib-uted an extra edition, just to report on my receipt of the Nobel Peace Prize. It reflected their great interest in the event.

An October 14 opinion piece in the *Washington Post* read:

People who have yet to win their freedom in places such as Malaysia and Hong Kong look to Mr. Kim for inspiration … And those who still argue, like the gerontocrats in China, that democracy is unsuited to Asia are embar-rassed and shamed by the story of his life.

Or, the opinion piece in *The Times* the same day that read:

Gloom enfolds world news. War threatens the Middle East; floods engulf southern England. But the award of the Nobel Peace Prize yesterday to

South Korea's President Kim Dae Jung [*sic*], for patient work promoting reconciliation on his ideologically divided peninsula, is a gleam of hope in the unremitting darkness.

The Japanese newspaper *Asahi* wrote in its opinion piece:

This is a well-deserved selection. We would like to sincerely congratulate him. His achievements in advocating for universal human rights, demanding democratization in Myanmar, working against the oppression of the residents in East Timor, and ending the conflict with Japan are all highly appreciated.

The next day, all of the Blue House staff members stood in line to congratulate me. I entered the office amid cheers and applause. I immediately received a congratulatory phone call from President Clinton. I felt sorry for him, so I offered comfort: "In fact, you have worked more than me for human rights and peace. You have consistently and carefully supported our effort in North Korea. Without your support, we would not have the changes we are seeing today. The good results during North Korean Special Envoy Jo Myong-rok's visit to the United States will contribute greatly to peace and stability in the Korean Peninsula, and the future inter-Korean relationship. The small advance in peace in the Korean Peninsula will become the greatest diplomatic achievement during your 8-year term. I hope that negotiations with North Korea will progress smoothly, and that if you visit Pyongyang it will bring good results."

President Clinton congratulated me very humbly and sincerely, saying, "I can think of few leaders who have done so much over so many years to earn this honor. All I did was to help you. How hard it is to move people's minds and hearts in the Korean Peninsula! You have achieved it. Depending upon the results of Secretary of State Albright's visit to Pyongyang, I hope to visit North Korea. I also hope that Palestine and Israel can achieve peace in the Middle East, following in your footsteps of reconciliation and cooperation."

Secretary of State Albright also called me immediately after the announcement, sincere happiness dripping off of her voice. "I could not help calling you right away because I am so excited to hear that the leader I so admire has received the Nobel Peace Prize," she said. "After my visit to Pyongyang, I will visit and discuss the results in detail."

Many countries all over the world either issued a congratulatory state-ment or sent a message to me.

On October 16, I ordered the elimination of the National Police Agency's Department of Investigation (the so-called Sajik-dong team), which had been established according to the Ministry of Home Affairs' order twenty-eight years ago. The Sajik-dong team had worked to gather intelligence and investigate corruption of high officials and their families and relatives. Although it was meaningful work in theory, in reality it had been a tool for government abuse of power. Some people within the rul-ing party worried about the lame duck, and a few media outlets reported that the Blue House gave up its clubs of power.

The third Asia-Europe Meeting (ASEM) summit was held at the COEX ASEM Tower building in Samseong-dong, Seoul on October 20. It was the largest event of its nature since the foundation of our country; twenty-six heads of state from Asia and Europe attended. I gave the opening address as the chairman of the meeting. "We are now living in the midst of an information revolution and in a society of knowledge-based industries.

"However, there are gray areas as well. The phenomenon of the digital divide is emerging as a new obstacle to the balanced development of the global village. It is becoming a task that has to be resolved by Asia and Europe together. The problem of poverty and the gap between the rich and the poor that are a cause of conflict and disputes both within nations and between nations can be resolved through the development of human resources. I hope that there will be active cooperation between Asia and Europe to open a new era when all humankind will benefit from the enhancement of information capabilities and higher standards of living."

Then, French president Jacques Chirac, Thai prime minister Chuan Leekpai, president of the EU Romano Prodi, and British prime minister Tony Blair gave addresses. They all began by congratulating me on receiv-ing the Nobel Peace Prize. I was particularly struck by British Prime Minister Tony Blair's congratulatory remark: "President Kim Dae-jung's winning of the Nobel Peace Prize is due to his lifelong will and dedication for democracy, human rights, and peace. We wish his attempt at reconcili-ation with North Korea a success. He is a true leader of Asia and a source of inspiration for us all.

"I am an optimist. One of the most important facts about this meeting is of course optimism. Last night, I read President Kim Dae-jung's *Prison Writings*. In it, he wrote, 'Although the world looks fragile, why does it never collapse? It is because there is desire for truth and justice, whether consciously or unconsciously, in everyone's mind.' I think he is right about it. That very internal desire explodes and is sublimated to become uncontrollable desire to respond to the opportunities of an age, a desire that becomes power to conquer evil."

During this summit, large-scale NGO demonstrations protested globalization outside of the building. I took measures to prevent an incident where radical demonstrators successfully shut down or prevented meetings, as had happened due to large-scale anti-globalization protests against the WTO (1999) and IMF (2000) meetings in Seattle and Prague. I let domestic and international organizations know that we would allow legal and orderly demonstrations. The demonstrators indeed held peaceful protests, and I was very grateful for their maturity. In fact, their arguments included many points that were worth listening to. Toward the end of the summit, I argued: "In fact, as in Seattle and Prague, Korean and foreign organizations held rallies and waged demonstrations against our meeting and globalization. Our government allowed them on the condition that they observe the law, remain orderly, and do not become violent. I just heard the report that, although about 10,000 people participated in the rallies and demonstrations, they have ended peacefully.

"I think that there is something to their argument that today's globalization makes the poor people and poor countries poorer. Nevertheless, stopping globalization is now neither possible nor right. Globalization happens not because we want it or someone orders it, but because it is necessary. In other words, it is a result of humanity's development. However, I believe that we should prevent it from increasing the wealth gap, as some people worry and reality demonstrates, and that we should make an effort to enable poorer people and countries to participate in the creation of wealth through the enhancement of information technology."

The summit adopted the Seoul Declaration for Peace on the Korean Peninsula. This declaration was the first ASEM declaration to extend its area of activity by taking a position regarding a nation's politics and stability, thereby breaking its custom of not discussing a specific country's affairs. The declaration expressed that the leaders of ASEM "shared the view that peace and stability on the Korean Peninsula were closely linked to those both of the Asia-Pacific region and of the world as a whole."

That day, October 20, 2000, was probably one of the busiest days of my life. I was at the center of the entire ASEM summit schedule. I had to moderate two summit meetings in the morning and act as chairman in the afternoon. Afterward, I also had successive summits scheduled with heads of state from many countries. That evening, I held a dinner reception with the heads of state and their spouses at the Blue House. The media commented that this was the most "brilliant" day of my life. Heads of state from twenty-six Asian and European countries cheered at the Blue House Guesthouse. It was quite moving. During the welcoming address, I said: "The world is now undergoing an era of rapid change. After we sent away the twentieth century and greet the twenty-first century, we are now experiencing great change that is unprecedented in the history of human civilization. History quickly advances from being material-driven to human- and knowledge-driven, from an industrial society to a society of intelligence and life, and from the age of territorial and national disputes to the age of harmony and cooperation. In particular, as a result of the information revolution, the geographical distinction between Asia and Europe is now becoming obsolete.

"In order to achieve co-prosperity in the world in this new era, respect for diversity is most important. The effort to understand and respect other countries, other nations, and other cultures is more urgent than in any other period throughout history. Fortunately, this respect for diversity is one of the most important values shared by Europe and Asia."

During the ASEM summit, I also had individual summits with fourteen heads of state from countries such as Denmark, Finland, China, France, the UK, Malaysia, Germany, Spain, the Netherlands, Brunei, Portugal, Luxemburg, and Ireland. The original plan was to have individual summit meetings with four country heads, but requests had come pouring in since the news of my receipt of the Nobel Peace Prize. It was hard for me to refuse requests from guests who had come all the way to Korea. I had to take ten-minute rests between meetings. Out of about eighty meetings at the APEC summit altogether, I was in charge of twenty-six—a third of all of the meetings.

As the inter-Korean relationship moved toward reconciliation, most heads of state expressed their intention to establish a diplomatic relationship with the North. I welcomed and actively supported this movement. After his visit to Panmunjeom, Prime Minister of Luxembourg Jean Claude Juncker said, "I hope that this is my first and last time visiting Panmunjeom. Thanks to your brave policy, Panmunjeom will disappear."

French president Jacques Chirac said that France would also establish a diplomatic relationship with North Korea. He handed me a document on which he had written: "Bravo! Great success! Thank you, DJ Kim!" I saw it in the middle of the meeting and nodded at him.

It was a hectic three days and two nights. On October 21, the Seoul ASEM summit meeting ended after adopting the Final Chair Statement. Participants said that we had better results than any previous ASEM meeting. As chairman, I felt that the relationship between Asia and Europe had advanced to another level and that we had begun a solid partnership.

First, this summit presented a new direction for ASEM in the new millennium. Leaders adopted the Asia-Europe Cooperation Framework 2000. This was the basic document that dictated the direction for mid- to long-term cooperation between Asia and Europe, as well as the direction for development of the ASEM.

Second, the summit adopted the Seoul Declaration for Peace on the Korean Peninsula. This meant the ASEM supported reconciliation and cooperation in the Korean Peninsula.

Third, we agreed to establish a high-speed trans-Eurasia Information Network in order to meet the needs of an information and knowledge-based society. Korea took the initiative in proposing this agenda item.

Fourth, leaders also agreed that human cooperation and interchange should increase in the fields of society and culture. We agreed to expand interchange among students and educators.

Fifth, we adopted new projects in various fields. Leaders endorsed many new ASEM initiatives, including the Initiative to Address the Digital Divide; the Anti-corruption Initiative; the Anti-money Laundering Initiative; the Initiative to Combat Trafficking of Women and Children; the Symposium on Law Enforcement Organs' Cooperation in Combating Transnational Crimes; the Environment Ministers' Meeting; the Initiative on HIV/AIDS; the Ministerial Conference on Cooperation for the Management of Migratory Flows in Europe-Asia; Science and Technology Cooperation on Forestry Conservation and Sustainable Development; and Project for a Euro-Asian Network for the Monitoring and Control of Communicable Diseases.

Although my primary care physician and secretaries tried to talk me out of my hectic schedule, calling it "murderous," I was just happy to have that kind of opportunity to work for my country and humanity. It was a great blessing, for which I thanked the Korean people and God.

After the closing ceremony, I stood at the entrance with my wife and saw off the heads of state whom I had become friends with. They left with good wishes for the future of both Korea and me.

Secretary of State Madeleine Albright visited Pyongyang, North Korea, on October 23. Her party included all of the policy planners and professionals who were involved with the Korean Peninsula: Counselor of the US Department of State Wendy Sherman, Assistant Secretary of State for Asian and Pacific Affairs Stanley Roth, Assistant Secretary of State for Nonproliferation Robert Einhorn, and Assistant Secretary of State Harold Hongju Koh, Special Envoy for the Korean Peace Talks Charles Kartman, and Director of the National Security Council's Asia Desk Charles Pritchard. About sixty reporters accompanied them from major news outlets such as the three largest communication companies—AP, AFP, and Reuters—broadcasting stations such as CNN and NBC, major newspapers like the *New York Times* and the *Washington Post*, weekly magazines, including *Time* and *Newsweek*, and the Korean company Yonhap News.

Secretary Albright stayed at the Paekhwawon Guesthouse where I had stayed. She first visited Kumsusan Palace of the Sun, the mausoleum where President Kim Il-sung was laid to rest. It was evidence of the strong dedication of the US government to the improvement of its relationship with the North.

Secretary Albright met Chairman Kim Jong-il that afternoon. Although she was scheduled to meet him on the twenty-fourth, Chairman Kim—in his typical way—abruptly visited her at the guesthouse. He welcomed and shook hands with all of Secretary Albright's attendants. Chairman Kim and Secretary Albright had two meetings that day, the first for two hours and the second for an hour. Secretary Albright delivered a letter from President Clinton to Chairman Kim.

After their meeting, Chairman Kim escorted the American delegation to the Rungrado 1st of May Stadium in Pyongyang, where they watched mass callisthenic and artistic performances by 100,000 performers. They also attended a dinner reception held by Chairman Kim at Paekhwawon.

The next day, the third meeting lasted for more than three hours. After the meeting there was a press conference and, in answer to a question about what would be necessary to warrant a presidential trip, Secretary Albright replied: "This [a change in terms of our own relationship] has been going on for at least a year and a half in a variety of venues and on a variety of subjects—a whole range of subjects. And we are taking a very step-by-step approach and doing everything that we are doing in terms of the United States' national interests.

"I will report to the president the results of this trip and the results of what I have described, characterized as constructive talks and the value, frankly, of face-to-face discussions ... It's always useful to have these kinds of discussions, but I will be reporting to the president and he will make the decisions about future steps."

About her personal impression of North Korea and Chairman Kim Jong-il, she answered: "We haven't exactly seen a lot of this country ... Quite beautiful, I think, with its landscape and heroic monuments, and I was obviously interested in seeing that. I found the performance last night ... I must say that I thought it was ... quite spectacular and amazing ... As far as the Chairman himself ... I spent, as I said, not only the six hours at meetings together, but also dinner last night and the performance. And we're going to be having dinner tonight. So there have been informal times, too. I think I would describe him as a very good listener and a good interlocutor. He strikes me as very decisive and practical and serious."

After finishing her visit to North Korea, Secretary Albright came to Seoul. She immediately visited me and spent an hour telling me about her visit in detail. I said, "Congratulations on your successful visit. How did you feel during your visit to North Korea? I still wonder whether it was real or I dreamt it."

"I felt the same way," Secretary Albright responded. "This was possible thanks to you. We could not have done it without you persistently pushing it."

"I thought you might encounter a surprise like I did," I said. "I was surprised when the schedule abruptly changed."

"I expected that I would meet Chairman Kim on the second day, but I met him on the first," Secretary Albright recounted. "It was a great help because we could take our time to discuss specifics. We discussed many matters for a long time, including history and geography. Chairman Kim was polite, listened to me carefully, and answered my questions immediately. As you told me last time, Chairman Kim was not a strange person, but, rather, seemed intelligent and quite knowledgeable about regional matters. Your evaluation was accurate."

Secretary Albright told me about the mass calisthenics. There was a scene where a missile fired in this performance, and Chairman Kim explained to her and Counselor Sherman that this would be the first and last firing. Listening to her experience, I felt that North Korea was desperately courting US. Secretary Albright also said that Chairman Kim especially liked and respected me for all of the hardship I'd overcome in my life. She also told me that Chairman Kim thought my life would make a good movie.

Secretary Albright shared her uneasiness, as well. "Although Chairman Kim is the supreme leader, do you think that he could change his stance?"

"That is possible," I responded. "But I think he is a pragmatic person. He would not change unless his interests change. He knows very well about the interests of the four powerful neighboring countries as well. Chairman Kim is aware of the importance that the US has on the stability and economic recovery of North Korea. Therefore, it is important that the United States confidently and firmly approach North Korea according to its interests."

In her book *Madam Secretary*, Secretary Albright wrote that she had three impressions from her visit to Pyongyang:

> The first concerned the prospects for a summit. Certainly North Korea's response to my visit showed its leader was serious. The DPRK seemed willing to accept more significant restraints on its missile programs than we had expected. I had avoided any specific discussion of compensation, but the costs of what the North Koreans were seeking in food, fertilizer, and help in launching satellites would be minimal compared to the expense of defending against the threats its missile programs posed.
>
> My second impression was of Kim Jong Il himself. I could confirm Kim Dae-jung's view that his DPRK counterpart was an intelligent man who knew what he wanted. He was isolated, not uninformed … He seemed confident. What did he want? Above all, normal relations with the United States; that would shield his country from the threat he saw posed by American power and help him to be taken seriously in the eyes of the world … My conclusion was that we should approach Kim in a businesslike way, not hesitate to engage in direct talks, and take advantage of North Korea's economic plight to drive a bargain that would make the region and world safer.
>
> Finally, I had tried to form an overall impression of North Korea itself … North Korea's entire political, economic, and social life continued to revolve around the teachings of a single human being, Kim Il Sung … It was clear they [most North Koreans] had little accurate knowledge of the outside world.
>
> Back in Washington we had to decide whether President Clinton should go to Pyongyang. Sandy Berger and I both felt that he should if it would lead to an acceptable deal on missiles.

Secretary Albright left early the next morning after sharing many stories. The *Washington Post* quoted Secretary Albright as describing Chairman Kim Jong-il as "very engaged." It also helped him shed the image of a mad man that had taken root in the outside world in the past decades.

Around this period, the ministers of foreign affairs in Korea, the US, and Japan met in Seoul. The three countries had cooperated closely in our policy toward North Korea. They shared information about the historical changes in the Korean situation and explored new directions for cooperation.

I met with Japanese Minister of Foreign Affairs Kono Yohei, a very old friend of mine. He brought a picture of two magpies watching one spot as a gift to celebrate my Nobel Peace Prize. I said, "My honor is all thanks to the Korean people's encouragement and my many friends for democracy in the world, friends who did not hesitate to support me during my exile as comrades around the 1973 Kidnapping Incident. I believe that I received this prize because of the support of friends like Mr. Utsunomiya Tokuma and Mr. Shiomiya Kazuo."

Both Mr. Utsunomiya Tokuma and Mr. Shiomiya Kazuo had since passed away. Minister Kono Yohei also delivered Prime Minister Mori's congratulations on the success of the ASEM summit. I said that Asia and Europe should collaborate for the future of humanity. "In everything, it is desirable for Asia and Europe to be connected. Originally, Europe and Asia belonged to a single continent. During the period of Alexander the Great, the region east of the Bosporus Straits was called 'Asia Minor.' I believe we should look at both continents from the perspective of one continent, called Eurasia."

On October 30, I received a phone call from former president of South Africa Nelson Mandela. He congratulated me on the Nobel Peace Prize. "I believe the prize went to the person who deserves it," he said. "I was deeply moved by your achievements and activities. I am deeply moved and admire your efforts for democracy and peace, and for overcoming hardships with an indomitable spirit."

I also praised his active career, including his presidency. "Please do more great works for humanity," I told him.

BILL CLINTON, GEORGE BUSH, AND THE KOREAN PENINSULA (NOVEMBER–DECEMBER 2000)

The Office of Presidential Security was in charge of security inside the Blue House. When I first entered the Blue House, I had the impression that the atmosphere was somewhat rigid and dry. The barricade in front of the Blue House reminded me of military camp. Chief Ahn Chu-sop of the

Office of Presidential Security reported that he would try to change this atmosphere into one that was more friendly and bright. I gladly agreed.

First, we redecorated the garden in front of the guesthouse. We moved the Office of Presidential Security building that stood right in front of the guesthouse to near the Office of Secretary building. We also flattened the garden, which sloped a little. In the process, we removed all of the trash buried under the soil. It was surprising to see all of this garbage under the ground of the Blue House. Although we could not change the shape of the guesthouse, the cultural identity of which was ambiguous, we could clean it up. We had the dinner reception in this building during the ASEM summit. We also cleaned up the Chilgung (shrine for seven queens) in Gungjeong-dong. The Chilgung is a simple place, but has a dignified garden.

The entire shape of the Blue House changed gradually. In particular, we moved the military base behind the Blue House on top of Mt. Bugaksan and planted trees instead. We also tore down the military facilities on the nearby Mt. Inwangsan and Mt. Bugaksan. We removed weapons installed for the purpose of "protecting" the Blue House, because, in reality, they stifled it. We also tore down the three-story building next to the guesthouse where the security guards, killed in association with the October 26, 1979 Assassination Incident, used to live. One day, I suddenly realized the Blue House looked much brighter than before.

For the fifth year in a row, we had an abundant harvest in the fall of 2000. Despite frequent typhoons, farmers worked hard and harvested 37 million *seok* (about 189 million US bushels) of rice. However, this was not necessarily a good thing for the farmers. This year again, farmers waged demonstrations, demanding that the government purchase more rice from them at a higher price. Unlike the old saying, farmers were not winter hermits, but winter fighters. How could we turn them away? But, I was also helpless in the face of market and consumer trends.

Although we had a surplus of rice in the South, people in the North were suffering from a rice shortage. Their farming technology was backward and they rarely used chemical fertilizers. During our summit, Chairman Kim Jong-il thanked me profusely for the fertilizer we had sent them as aid. By helping them with the fertilizer, we helped them radically increase production. It was much more helpful than direct crop aid. During my term, our government sent 200,000 tons of rice and 400,000 tons of fertilizer to the North every year.

The Government of the People reformed farmers' cooperative, which was overdue by half a century, and unified institutions that managed water. In order to preserve farmers' income, we introduced the direct payment system for rice farming and crop disaster insurance. We also made efforts to write off debts that farmers had accumulated over decades. In particular, my government radically increased investment in the farming produce circulation sector to improve the structure from the beginning of the process. We tried to improve the situation so that farmers wouldn't always selling their produce cheaply and consumers wouldn't always end up paying high prices. We continued to expand the direct transaction and electronic commerce between farmers and consumers through facilities like a comprehensive circulation center. Nevertheless, we could not make farmers entirely happy.

Although the government tried to increase and develop demand for rice through campaigns, rice consumption decreased every year. Rice was no longer farmers' pride, and the fields were no longer objects of their trust. The rice paddies were no longer the source of their livelihood. We had to find ways to help farmers love and work energetically in their fields, but we could not. Nobody could think of a good solution. It was sad.

On November 13, I arrived in Bandar Seri Begawan, the capital of Brunei, to attend an APEC summit and make a state visit to Brunei. I had a meeting with King Hassanal Bolkiah during which we agreed to collaborate to promote investment and trade between our two countries. I also requested that he soon pay Hyundai Construction the $38 million construction fee he owed them for the Jerudong Theme Park. Fortunately, he said he would make a particular effort. Although it was a civilian matter, I had to intervene, so I explained to him the background of my request. "I am sorry to demand the payment of debt as a guest, but Hyundai, the largest cooperation in Korea, is in critical condition. Although I know this is impolite, I say this only because I hope that Hyundai will revive."

This debt occurred because the king's brother's company had gone bankrupt. He was friendly to me, and did not reject my request. He ordered his cabinet to resolve the matter as soon as possible.

I had a relay meeting with the heads of state of many countries. On November 15, I met the heads of state of four neighboring powerful countries—the US, Japan, China, and Russia—for a summit for the first time in the history of Korean diplomacy.

I visited President Clinton at Edinburgh Palace, where he stayed. This was, in fact, his farewell summit as president. He again congratulated me on winning the Nobel Peace Prize and I congratulated him on his wife Hilary Clinton winning a Senate seat.

I asked President Clinton to visit North Korea, and he said, "[A] decision will be made on the matter after taking into consideration all relevant factors, including North Korea's attitude toward its missile development program."

As I said before, President Clinton was a very charming person. I liked him a lot and I was sad to see him leave the international stage. Only two months of his term were left. We reminisced about our meetings and I thanked him for supporting my policy. "You made remarkable contributions to regional peace and prosperity by supporting my tolerance policy toward the North," I told him. "Together with President Truman, who stopped the Communist advance into the entire Korean Peninsula, the Korean people will remember you forever. I hope that we will remain good friends after you leave office."

For his part, President Clinton expressed satisfaction and gratitude for my contribution to the improved inter-Korean relationship and peace in the Korean Peninsula, attributing it to my leadership and resolution. He also said he was honored to have worked with me.

He saw me off, walking with me along the long corridor to where my car was waiting for me. As I left him, I suddenly felt his loneliness. Would my friend President Clinton visit North Korea? Could he visit North Korea at the very end of his term, despite all the difficult circumstances? Although he was the president of the most powerful country in the world, he acted very carefully.

On a personal level, President Clinton was a very good-natured person. While the leaders of all of the countries were chatting before the last session, he was busily making rounds with a paper and pen. It turned out that he was asking for signatures from each leader, just like a child would ask for a signature from a celebrity. He was so free-spirited as to request other country leaders' signatures at his last international stage. The mighty US and President Clinton's liveliness went together well, despite their contradictory appearances.

The APEC summit ended after we adopted the Leaders' Declaration. The declaration included three tasks that I had been emphasizing domestically and internationally: even distribution of information and communication technology revolution; prevention of financial crises and strengthening of the international financial system; and reform based on the market principle. Our proposed action plans included building high-speed information and communication networks; establishing networks among developing countries; vitalization of economy based on knowledge; expansion of cyber education; founding of a social safety net; establishment of a hedge fund monitoring system; and promoting dialogue for reform policies according to issues.

I also persuaded APEC leaders to give North Korea the opportunity to enjoy the benefits of globalization and information technology as a member of international society. Accordingly, we decided to invite North Korea to the next APEC meeting as a guest.

I attended a party to celebrate the publication of the book *Truth of the Kim Dae-jung Rebellion Incident Conspiracy* at the Hyatt Hotel on November 21. The book chronicled the process by which the military junta had detained twenty-five social leaders and fabricated a rebellion incident through torture during the Seoul Spring in 1980. Professor Lee Moon-young of Korea University was the chief editor of the book.

My old comrades, who had not hesitated to fight bravely against the dictatorial forces, could not resist time. Their hair was white and their fearless expressions were hidden under wrinkles. In what was a very moving moment, Professor Lee gave me a book. How many people had to sacrifice to bring about this day of democracy! I felt indebted to them. I urged all of us who had survived the severe dictatorial years, including myself, to continue to lead an upright life. "We stood in front of the Korean people," I said. "I believe that, as leaders, we have the responsibility to try our best to work for freedom, human rights, justice, and the happiness of our people until the day we leave this world."

On November 23, I left for Singapore to attend the ASEAN+3 Summit. I stayed at the Shangri-La Hotel. The next day, I attended the Korea-China-Japan summit. At the ASEAN+3 Summit, I proposed that we form an economic consulting body as a stepping stone to an East Asian economic bloc. The leaders included this proposal in the Chairman's Statement.

I met with Singaporean Prime Minister Goh Chok Tong for a summit meeting, where we agreed to hold minister-level meetings on a regular basis in order to discuss the establishment of a free trade agreement, step up cooperation on two major information technology infrastructure projects, and other issues of mutual concern. The North Korean chargé d'affaires participated in the official welcoming reception and politely bowed to me. I was happy to see him, shaking his hand.

I met Singaporean Senior Minister Lee Kuan Yew. It had been a year since I last saw him. "Could you tell me what you thought of the inter-Korean summit in June—whether you see it as signifying a fundamental or temporary change?" I asked him.

"I don't know if it signifies a tactical, strategic, or fundamental change," he replied, "but I think it is a change that even North Korean authorities cannot control. If technology enters North Korea every year and both human contact between the South and the North and investment increase, North Korea will become a different society than it is today."

When I met President Jiang Zemin in Beijing on June 13, he was very pleased with the inter-Korean summit, which we discussed for ten minutes. He said it represented very significant progress. Although there is no proof of it, Chairman Kim Jong-il must have discussed the summit with Chinese leaders. North Korea must have tried very hard to understand the Chinese situation, and China must have confirmed that it would not accept unification through absorption to give confidence to Chairman Kim.

"China would not want North Korea to reunite with South Korea in the near future," President Jiang Zemin speculated. "Reunification would mean the loss of a buffer state for China. As a country that experienced enormous sacrifice and learned its lesson during the Korean War in 1950, China would not want North Korea to be absorbed by South Korea. Although the inter-Korean summit was not great progress in terms of reunification, it was great progress in the sense that it brought about a change that no country—not South Korea, North Korea, nor the United States—can control.

"The US armed forces in Korea are necessary for the Korean Peninsula. No matter how the domestic situation develops, they should remain there. Unless they remain, the South Korean position will weaken against North Korea, China, and Japan."

His analysis was outstanding. I shared with him my dialogue with Chairman Kim. "I told Chairman Kim that US armed forces should remain in Korea not simply to check North Korea, but even after reunification," I explained. "I mentioned Korean history in which Korea, as the only country surrounded by four powerful countries, was embroiled in the Sino-Japanese War and the Russo-Japanese War and eventually annexed by Japan. I told him that was why the power balance was dependent upon having US armed forces in Korea, and that it was essential to the stability not only of the Korean Peninsula, but also to all of East Asia. I also referenced the example of NATO in Europe, which was created to check Communist advance, but remained even after the collapse of the Eastern Bloc.

"Although I thought Chairman Kim might strongly oppose my remark, he actually said he was surprised that I thought exactly like him. He believed that the US armed forces should remain in Korea to check powerful countries like Russia, China, and Japan. When Secretary of State Albright visited North Korea, he said to her that he did not object to US armed forces in Korea as long as they did not hurt North Korea."

From November 27 to 29, I went to Indonesia for a state visit. President Abdurrahman Wahid came to the airport to greet me in person. I heard that they even had a rehearsal for my welcome event at the airport the day before. Everywhere on the streets, there were large portraits of my wife, me, and President Abdurrahman Wahid. We had a summit meeting the next day. After a one-on-one meeting, we met with all of the Indonesian cabinet members according to President Abdurrahman Wahid's special order. He said, "I've told you many times how much I admire you, but you really are my teacher. In order to welcome my teacher, I took the unprecedented move of inviting all the cabinet members. This is like a cabinet meeting with you."

Indeed, it looked like a joint cabinet meeting. President Abdurrahman Wahid tried his best to help Korea. He promised to securely provide Korea with crude oil and natural gas. He also said that he would partially guarantee Korean business participation in an Indonesian apartment construction project.

On November 30, I met US Congressman Tony Hall on his way back from a visit to North Korea. As he had visited mostly the countryside outside of Pyongyang, he told me how the North Korean people were really living. According to him, they depended mainly on just 200 to 250 grams of rationed food a day and, in addition, ate leaves and branches from trees. He also said that the water was so dirty that people suffered from indigestion. There was a shortage of painkillers and antibiotics, and most factories had ceased operation.

He said that North Koreans were eagerly awaiting President Clinton's visit. It seemed apparent that the people wanted change. I felt sad because the change they wanted was to relieve themselves of immediate hunger, the most basic need. Human beings cannot help getting angry when they are hungry and smiling when they are eating well. Making the people smile—wouldn't that bring peace to Korea?

The US presidential election was in turmoil. The election between Democratic candidate Al Gore and Republican candidate George Bush was very close, as expected. Eventually Bush won Florida, the final battleground state. A few news outlets hastily reported that Bush won, which was a mistake because a rule required a mandatory recount when the results were within less than 0.5 percent of one another. In addition, there were claims of voting fraud. In the end, the Supreme Court intervened; it took this conservative-leaning Supreme Court more than five weeks to decide on Bush's victory.

It was regrettable to see the presidential election, the greatest festival of a democratic country, mired in controversy. The fact that the Supreme Court had to make a decision hurt American democracy. Not only that, but sensationalist media coverage scandalized the presidential election. The pride of the US was hurt. It was a demoralizing event and other countries openly made fun of America.

I paid unusual attention to this election. I hoped Al Gore would win because he would succeed the Clinton administration's policies. However, I was generally optimistic and thought that, even if Bush won, he could not easily abolish the policy of tolerance toward North Korea that had been progressing steadily.

I was anxious and hoped that President Clinton's visit to North Korea would materialize soon. Unfortunately, his position was clearly weakened after the election. Middle East peace talks also resumed around that time, and President Clinton made a special effort to settle peace in the Middle East during his term. Naturally, he looked at the Middle East more often than North Korea.

In the end, Bush was elected president of the US. I talked with him on the telephone on December 16. "I hope to work closely with you for peace in the Korean Peninsula, East Asia, and in the world," he said.

On December 21, President Clinton called me. "I would like to discuss North Korea with you," he said. "As you know, we have wasted precious time because I could not discuss the matter with my successor due to the ambiguous election results. At the same time, Middle East peace talks resumed and this time they appear to be concluding successfully. I would like to take this opportunity for success before I leave office. Therefore, it is almost impossible for me to visit North Korea. I would like to discuss alternatives with you.

"The change you brought about in the Korean Peninsula is very important. I would like to help you maintain the momentum so that the next US administration will continue to support it. Because I cannot visit North Korea, I am considering inviting Chairman Kim Jong-il to Washington in

January next year. This will show them our intentions and enable us to resolve missile issues. It will also alleviate the aftereffect of my inability to visit Pyongyang. However, I will not pursue it unless you agree. I would like to hear your opinion."

My worries had become a reality. However, I had to remain calm. "First of all," I politely said, "I deeply appreciate this effort at the end of your term. But I am not sure how North Korea will respond to your invitation. It would be difficult for Chairman Kim Jong-il to return from Washington without any results. Therefore, success should be guaranteed beforehand, and your successor should be on board, too."

"I completely agree with you," President Clinton responded. "If they agree to stop selling missiles and developing long-range missiles, we will provide them with food. I talked with my successor and understand that the next administration will honor this."

I asked him to be sure to improve the US' relationship with North Korea. I even advised him about how to negotiate. "In my opinion," I told him, "it would be best to officially invite Chairman Kim after fine-tuning preliminary negotiations. I believe that North Korea is clearly feeling the absolute necessity to improve its relationship with the United States, and that they want to resolve this issue during your term. If this matter is handed over to the next administration, it is inevitable that it will be delayed. We welcome the resolution of the North Korean missile issue, and it will also contribute to peace in the Korean Peninsula.

"You have to clearly and simply state what you will give and what you expect in return. In doing this, you'll reassure Chairman Kim that he can visit Washington without worrying about the possibility of failure. As I told you before, Chairman Kim is resolute and boldly accepts what he can understand. You have to negotiate directly with him by clearly articulating what you will give and what you will take."

"It's a great idea," President Clinton said. "I will keep all of this in mind and keep you posted."

"Thank you for working hard on this issue until the very end. I appreciate your contribution to the United States economy and Korean nuclear and missile issues. Also, you have tried hard to reduce the threat of weapons of mass destruction in international society and made great strides in peace in the Middle East."

President Clinton asked me to keep this phone call a secret. He said that since he had called me without discussing it with anyone, I should make sure that our conversation did not leak to the press. I reassured him and kept my promise.

President Clinton wrote about the reason why his visit to North Korea did not happen in his autobiography *My Life*: "Madeleine Albright had made a trip to North Korea and was convinced that if I went, we could make the missile agreement. Although I wanted to take the next step, I simply couldn't risk being halfway around the world when we were so close to peace in the Middle East, especially after Arafat had assured me that he was eager for an agreement and had implored me not to go."

In the end, President Clinton issued a statement on December 28, in which he said: "I believe new opportunities are opening for progress toward greater stability and peace on the Korean Peninsula. However, I have determined that there is not enough time while I am president to prepare the way for an agreement with North Korea that advances our national interest and provides the basis for a trip by me to Pyongyang. Let me emphasize that I believe this process of engagement with North Korea, in coordination with South Korea and Japan, holds great promise and that the United States should continue to build on the progress we have made."

President Clinton sent a letter inviting Chairman Kim Jong-il to visit the US, but he refused. It was the response everyone had anticipated given North Korea's style of diplomacy, which placed pride above all else. In addition, it must have been burdensome to accept the invitation from President Clinton at the very end of his term. At any rate, the US violated the agreement made in the Joint US-DPRK Statement. Secretary of State Albright had visited North Korea on the condition that a visit by the president of the US would follow hers.

Nevertheless, I felt that Chairman Kim should have accepted President Clinton's invitation. It really was a rare golden opportunity. If he had visited the US, the relationship between the two countries would have normalized, and the Bush administration would have acknowledged it. There would have been no longer confrontation between the two countries and the inter-Korean relationship would have undergone unimaginable changes.

I was very sorry that President Clinton had to cancel his visit to North Korea. Had he visited, I believe it would have changed history in the Korean Peninsula. It was a deeply regrettable turn of events. I was very sad as the president of South Korea—half of Korea, the only remaining divided country in the world.

If only Democratic candidate Gore won the election, if President Bush's victory was confirmed earlier, if the Middle East peace talks did not happen at the same time, a different history might have evolved in the Korean Peninsula.

I met President Clinton again in November 2003, when he visited the Kim Dae-jung Presidential Library and Museum. At that time, my health was not in good condition. Former President Clinton worried about my health. Still sad about the missed chance, I said to him, "Your administration made great achievements in your country's relationship with North Korea. If the agreements made then were carried out, there would already be stability in the Korean Peninsula. I am really sad."

"I wonder if you remember what I said during the APEC summit in Brunei," former president Clinton responded. "If my term lasted just one more year, we could have resolved the North Korean crisis."

Since his term ended, the world had become mired in terror and war. President Bush was in the middle of it all. The 9/11 terrorist attack—where the World Trade Center Twin Towers collapsed and the Pentagon was set on fire—occurred during his first year in office. During the State of the Union address in 2002, President Bush attacked North Korea as one of the axis of evil countries. The US-DPRK relationship had grown worse. The Bush administration invaded Iraq, which the president had included together with North Korea in the axes of evil. The US forced all countries to choose sides. They divided the world into friends and enemies. President Bush's hawkish policy threw the world into fear. I could not understand his dogmatism, no matter how hard I tried.

President Clinton was also sad about his failure to visit North Korea. However, our wishes could not change the cold reality. In 2003, both of us were former Presidents. We did not have power, only worries. Regardless, President Bush continued to surround himself with neocons and did not give up his hawkish policies. The distance between the US and North Korea grew larger and larger.

On December 17, Democratic Party Supreme Council member Kwon Rho-kap stepped down. He issued a statement saying that this "was his fate." He had been suffering from arguments within the party that he should retreat from the front lines. Another member of the Democratic Party Supreme Council even argued in front of me that Council Member Kwon should resign. His argument did not come across as genuine. However, I had to respect council member Kwon's choice. I heard that he had a tearful meeting with his colleagues. Politics is a very cold business. I called him to express my sympathy and, after waiting for people's interest in him to dwindle, I had breakfast with him. I comforted him again about his "fate."

THE FIRST DROP IS THE BRAVEST (DECEMBER 2000)

On December 8, 2000, I left for Oslo, Norway, to attend the Nobel Peace Prize award ceremony. The plane ride was more than ten hours long, and during the flight I exchanged greetings with all of the invited guests.

I invited fifty-four people altogether, all of whom had helped me through my years of hardship. They included leaders of the democratization movement, religious leaders, leaders of non-governmental organizations, and a few politicians, business leaders, and leaders in the fields of culture, journalism, and academia. In addition, I also invited Security Department Chief Kang Bok-gi of Hongsong Prison, who had been the guard while I was imprisoned. My family members, including my sons, daughters-in-law, and grandchildren, also accompanied me. Among foreign guests, US Ambassador to Italy Thomas Foglietta and Vice Chairman José Ramos-Horta of the Revolutionary Front for an Independent East Timor (a 1996 Nobel Peace Prize co-winner) flew directly to Oslo to attend the ceremony.

Upon arriving, I attended a dinner reception with invited guests. "Today, I accepted the high honor that is the Nobel Peace Prize," I spoke. "However, I don't think the prize is given to me alone. I believe that it is a recognition of all the Korean people who have dedicated themselves to freedom and peace, at times making great personal sacrifices, and the encouragement of the international community, which has been unsparing in its support for democratization in Korea and peace on the Korean Peninsula."

I had an interview with *BBC World*. Reporter Nik Gowing was very knowledgeable about Korea, and, in particular, my policy and determination. His questions were very sensitive and sharp.

"While you were suffering from hardships, including house arrests, did you not think of quitting this road?" he asked.

"Although my road was accompanied with many pains, I have always maintained my belief that what is important is living a meaningful life," I responded. "'Conscience in action' is the motto of my life."

"You're known to be a devout Catholic," the reporter observed. "Why did you forgive former President Chun Doo-hwan? Didn't he sentence you to death?"

"Although I did not forgive his sin, I forgave him as a human being."

"You decided to support a museum that commemorates President Park Chung-Hee. Didn't he try to kill you three times?" Mr. Gowing asked.

"I think that the museum could evidence not only his good sides, but also his wrongs."

"Aren't there still political prisoners in Korea?"

"There were a small minority of prisoners who violated the law by spying for North Korea," I replied. "But they were released and allowed to return to North Korea. My government guarantees all rights to people. Recent permission to establish a teachers' union is a good example."

The next day, I visited the Nobel Institute bringing my own lunch, according to custom. It was an old, small five-story building. I met and chatted with the Nobel Committee members and wrote the phrase "Gyeongcheon aein" (respect for heaven and love for people) in their guestbook.

The wall of the committee office was decorated with portraits of previous winners of the Nobel Peace Prize including Willy Brandt, Henry Kissinger, Lech Walesa, the Dalai Lama, Oscar Arias Sanchez, Mikhail Gorbachev, Aung San Suu Kyi, Nelson Mandela, and Ramos Orta. These people to whom I was now related were looking over me. They were true heroes who safeguarded the peace of the global village. They seemed to be asking me why I had come so late. My picture was the last.

I signed a document that said I entrusted the loyalty of my award speech with the Nobel Committee. I got on the elevator as committee members saw me off. The elevator was old and small like the building. Only five of us—my wife and me, Secretary of the Norwegian Nobel Committee Geir Lundestad, Chief of Staff Kim Hanjung, and Chief of the Execution Department Kim Jeong Kee—filled it tight. The elevator stopped abruptly between floors. Everyone was at a loss. I tried to joke to alleviate the tension and said, "You should be alone with a woman in an elevator like this." My joke fell flat because everyone was panicked.

My guards who were waiting for me downstairs must have been very alarmed too. Fortunately, about five minutes later, the elevator began to work again. I heard later that the Nobel Committee replaced the elevator with a brand new one after that incident.

I had a press conference with foreign reporters. The third question was from a female reporter with Asian features. Surprisingly, she said in Korean, "Congratulations on winning the Nobel Peace Prize!"

Although I could detect a foreign accent in her Korean, I was very happy. She was a Korean adoptee who had been sent away from Seoul when she was only one year old, and grew up as a member of a middle-class family in Norway. She switched to English for her question, but I felt really happy for her. Although there were fewer than 300 Koreans living in Norway, there were more than 6000 Korean adoptees that had been raised in Norwegian families. How scared those young children must have been during their long, long trip to a faraway country! I hoped that my winning the prize could be a small comfort to them. Once again, I was moved by Norwegian generosity.

On the day of the ceremony, thousands of people were lined up on the streets for the kilometer between the hotel and city hall, waving Korean and Norwegian flags. When I arrived at the square in front of the back entrance of Oslo City Hall around 11:40 a.m., 2000 children were waiting for me. I went up to the podium with my wife and cheers burst out. A girl handed me the Torch of Peace, and I lit the peace monument with it. The monument was surrounded by twenty-two rocks, which symbolized the number of countries suffering from civil and other wars.

The peace flame blazed, and boys and girls sang "Save the Children" in clear, heavenly voices. I made an impromptu speech for the children: "Boys and girls, I'm really happy to meet you all here today. I see the Torch of Peace you just handed me as a symbol of love and peace for people all around the world. This is because children are our hope for the future. We have hope in this world because of you, boys and girls. Your smiles brighten the world. I am sure that this Torch of Peace will burn forever, filling up the world with the light of love and hope. Thank you." After my remarks, the children cheered and surrounded me. It was a truly moving prologue to the ceremony.

Next was the award ceremony. Secretary of the Norwegian Nobel Committee Geir Lundestad and Vice Chairman of the Nobel Committee Gunnar Johan Stalsett guided me to the main hall of City Hall. As soon as I entered, a military band sounded a fanfare and 1100 guests, including Prime Minister of Norway Jens Stoltenberg, ambassadors from all over the world, and guests from Korea, stood up and applauded. After my entrance, King Harald V entered.

The main hall of Oslo City Hall was decorated with yellow flowers to symbolize the Sunshine Policy, breaking the long tradition of decorating the space with red roses. Thousands of oranges, yellow roses, and sunflowers decorated the front of seats and the columns and walls behind the podium.

Chairman Gunnar Berge of the Norwegian Nobel Committee stood on the podium and declared, "The Norwegian Nobel Committee has decided to award the Nobel Peace Prize for the year 2000 to Kim Dae-jung." The audience applauded again.

Chairman Berge continued to explain the reason for their selection. Although rather long, I quote parts of his presentation speech here: "The question of whether it is too early to award the prize for a process of reconciliation that has only just begun has been raised," he spoke. "It would suffice to say in reply that Kim Dae-jung's work for human rights made him a worthy candidate irrespective of the recent developments in relations between the two Korean states. It is also clear, however, that his strong commitment to reconciliation with North Korea, and the results that have been achieved—especially in the past year—added a new and important dimension to Kim Dae-jung's candidacy.

"While recognizing that reversals in international peace work are something one has to be prepared for, the Nobel Committee nevertheless adheres to the principle: nothing ventured, nothing gained. The Peace Prize is a reward for the steps that have been taken so far. However, as so often before in the history of the Nobel Peace Prize, it is intended this year, too, as an encouragement to advance still further along the long road to peace and reconciliation.

"This is, to a large extent, a matter of courage: Kim Dae-jung has had the will to break with fifty years of ingrained hostility, and to reach out a cooperative hand across what has probably been the world's most heavily guarded frontier. His has been the kind of personal and political courage that, regrettably, is all too often missing in other conflict-ridden regions.

"The same applies to peace work as to life in general when you set out to cross the highest mountains: the first steps are the hardest. But you can count on plenty of company along the glamorous finishing stretch.

"Gunnar Roaldkvam, a writer from Stavanger, puts this so simply and so aptly in his poem 'The Last Drop':

Once upon a time
there were two drops of water;
one was the first,
the other the last.
The first drop
was the bravest.
I could quite fancy
being the last drop,
the one that makes everything
run over,
so that we get
our freedom back.
But who wants to be
the first
drop?

"Today, Kim Dae-jung is the president of a democratic South Korea. His path to power has been long—extremely long. For decades he fought a seemingly hopeless fight against an authoritarian regime. One may well ask where he found the strength. His own answer is: 'I used all my strength to resist the dictatorial regime, because there was no other way to defend the people and promote democracy. I felt like a homeowner whose house was invaded by a robber. I had to fight the intruder with my bare hands to protect my family and property without thinking of my own safety.'

"Kim Dae-jung's story has a lot in common with the experience of several other Peace Prize Laureates, especially Nelson Mandela and Andrei Sakharov. And with that of Mahatma Gandhi, who did not receive the prize but would have deserved it. To outsiders, Kim's invincible spirit may appear almost superhuman. On this point, too, the Laureate takes a more sober view ....

"But in 1997 Kim Dae-jung saw a new opportunity. Incredibly enough, with his political enemies divided amongst themselves, the military regime's leading opponent was elected president. That was the definitive proof that South Korea had at long last found a place among the world's democracies. The idea of revenge must have occurred to the new president. Instead, as with Nelson Mandela, forgiveness and reconciliation became the main planks in Kim's political platform and guided the steps he took. Kim Dae-jung forgave most things—including the unforgivable ....

"The same way of thinking led the Nobel Committee, in its grounds for this year's award, to draw particular attention to the important role

Kim has played in the development of human rights throughout East Asia. As José Ramos Horta, Peace Prize Laureate in 1996 and with us here today, has stated, Kim also vigorously took up the cause of East Timor. There was great symbolic force in the decision to place the South Korean army, used only a few years previously to suppress political opposition in its own country, at the disposal of the global community in defense of human rights in East Timor. Kim Dae-jung has also actively supported Aung San Suu Kyi, Peace Prize Laureate in 1991, in her heroic struggle against the dictatorship in Burma ....

"The dialogue between Kim Dae-jung and Kim Jong II at the Pyongyang summit last June led to more than loose declarations and airy rhetoric. The pictures of family members meeting after five decades of separation made a deep impression all over the world. However restricted and controlled these contacts may be, the tears of joy are a stark contrast to the cold, hatred, and discouragement felt so strongly by all visitors to the border at Panmunjom ....

"In most of the world, the Cold War ice age is over. The world may see the Sunshine Policy thawing the last remnants of the Cold War on the Korean Peninsula. It may take time. But the process has begun, and no one has contributed more than today's Laureate, Kim Dae-jung. In the poet's words, 'The first drop was the bravest.'"

After this speech, he awarded me with the Nobel Peace Prize Medal and Certificate. I posed for a photograph, holding the medal in my left hand and the certificate in my right. Cameras flashed and applause burst out again. Soprano Jo Sumi sang Luigi Arditi's "Il Bacio" and Korean folksongs, including "Arirang." (Photo 10.1)

Then it was my turn to give the acceptance address. The hall was full. I looked out at my wife and daughters-in-law, wearing their traditional Korean attire. The award ceremony was broadcast live around the world, on stations like CNN and Norway National TV. I shared my feelings and resolutions in front of the citizens of the world. I began by saying: "Human rights and peace have a sacred ground in Norway. The Nobel Peace Prize is a solemn message that inspires all of humanity to dedicate ourselves to peace. I am infinitely grateful to be given the honor. But I think of my countless people and colleagues in Korea who have given themselves willingly to democracy and human rights and the dream of national unification. And I must conclude that the honor should go to them. I also think of the many countries and my friends around the world who have gener-

Photo 10.1   Kim Dae-jung after receiving Nobel Peace Prize in December 2000

ously supported the efforts of my people to achieve democratization and inter-Korean reconciliation. I thank them very sincerely."

I then proceeded to talk about the process and results of the inter-Korean summit and recent development in the inter-Korean relationship. I also talked about the deep Asian roots of the idea of human rights that went back further than Western ideas. I mentioned my administration's pursuit of the parallel development of democracy and a market economy, as well as the productive welfare policy.

After that, I talked about my life. While preparing for this address, my secretaries did not like the text that I dictated, the text that emphasized my personal life. Although they did not express their reluctance to my face, I could sense it from their faces. My secretaries wanted to emphasize my dignity as the winner of the Nobel Peace Prize rather than my life of "challenges and responses," already quite well known to the world. However, I had a different opinion. I wanted to tell people about myself—my life and my beliefs—even if many people already know of them. I hope my readers will also indulge me here. "Allow me to say a few words on a personal note. Five times I faced death at the hands of dictators, six years I spent in prison, and forty years I lived under house arrest or in exile and under constant surveillance. I could not have endured that hardship without the support of my people and the encouragement of fellow democrats around the world.

"My strength also came from deep personal beliefs.

"I have lived, and continue to live, with the belief that God is always with me. I know this from experience. In August of 1973, while exiled in Japan, I was kidnapped from my hotel room in Tokyo by intelligence agents of the then-military government of South Korea. The news of the incident startled the world. The agents took me to their boat, which was anchored along the seashore. They tied me up, blinded me, and stuffed my mouth. Just when they were about to throw me overboard, Jesus Christ appeared before me with such clarity. I clung to him and begged him to save me. At that very moment, an airplane came down from the sky to rescue me from the moment of death.

"Another source of faith is my belief in the justice of history. In 1980, I was sentenced to death by the military regime. For six months in prison, I awaited execution day. Often, I shuddered with fear of death. But I would find calm in the fact of history that justice ultimately prevails. I was then, and am still, an avid reader of history. And I knew that in all ages, in all places, he who lives a righteous life dedicated to his people and humanity may not be victorious, may meet a gruesome end in his lifetime, but will be triumphant and honored in history; he who wins by injustice may dominate the present day, but history will always judge him to be a shameful loser. There can be no exception.

"Your Majesty, Your Royal Highnesses, ladies and gentlemen, accepting the Nobel Peace Prize, the honoree is committed to an endless duty. I humbly pledge before you that, as the great heroes of history have taught us, as Alfred Nobel would expect of us, I shall give the rest of my life to human rights and peace in my country and the world, and to the reconciliation and cooperation of my people. I ask for your encouragement and the abiding support of all who are committed to advancing democracy and peace around the world."

After I finished my speech, the audience, which had already indulged me with applause five times during my speech, were all on their feet again to applaud. The sound of applause was particularly long and loud while I talked about my personal life. The ceremony was solemn and elegant.

After the ceremony, we headed to the palace. On our way, thousands of citizens again waved Korean and Norwegian flags. Some of them were carrying their Korean adopted children on their shoulders, clad in traditional Korean attire, and cheering. It was deeply moving. I got down from the car and held their hands. One mother had her son, adopted from Korea, shake hands with me. Among the crowd, there were many children wearing traditional Korean clothes. I murmured: "Although your own country could not take care of you, you are growing well here."

King Harald V held a luncheon reception in my honor. I heard that this was the first time he had offered this for a Nobel Peace Award winner. Officers of the Swedish Nobel Foundation and Norwegian Nobel Foundation attended.

The daytime was very short in Norway in the winter; the sun set around 3:00 p.m. Citizens and Koreans marched through Oslo holding torches. The torches, after gracing the streets of Oslo, stopped in front of the Grand Hotel, where I was staying. I could hear their cheers and gong sounds. They felt quite similar to the crowds who had come to my house in Ilsan after I won the presidential election. As it had been very cold that dawn in Ilsan, it was also quite cold in Oslo that night. I went out to the second floor balcony and waved at the crowd. Hundreds of torches waved in response and their cheers soared up to me. Koreans repeated: *Manse!* (Hurrah!); some of them sang the Korean anthem.

Committee Chair Berge and other committee members warmly welcomed me at the reception. In my remarks, I said: "I place special importance on this visit to Norway, a country of human rights and peace.

"I am told of a saying among the Vikings that goes something like this: 'A bad friend may live close by, but he seems distant; a good friend may live far away, but he feels close.' It took me more than eleven hours to fly from Seoul to Oslo. But I came in great comfort, thinking that I was visiting the home of a close friend ….

"Standing here in this honored setting that you have so generously granted me, I am overcome less with joy than with a sense of duty.

"Our efforts to settle peace on the Korean Peninsula have barely began. Furthermore, there is much work that remains for us to advance human rights and democracy in many corners of the world ….

"Recalling the noble ideals of Alfred Nobel, I rededicate myself to the elevation of democracy and peace on the Korean Peninsula and around the world."

The next day, I visited the Norwegian Parliament and Oslo City Hall. At city hall, Mayor Per Ditlev-Simonsen guided me to an exhibition of works by winners of Oslo students' writing and art contests, as well as students' performances of songs and dances built around the theme of peace.

Mayor Per Ditlev-Simonsen proudly told me that the city was given about 2000 paintings that Edvard Munch had painted over the course of twenty years, and that the city had sold only a few of them when it was necessary for tax reasons. With its rich cultural legacy, Oslo seemed like a solid city.

That evening, a concert was televised live throughout the world in celebration of the award ceremony. About 5500 people gathered in the audience at Oslo Spektrum. The event was emceed by British actress, Jane Seymour. Norwegian singer Sissel got on stage and said, "I'm probably the most blessed person in the Northern hemisphere, as I am standing here with singers from all over the world to celebrate President Kim's award. I have nothing more to wish for. I am proud of myself and I sincerely congratulate President Kim Dae-jung on behalf of the Norwegian people for winning the Nobel Peace Prize."

She then said congratulations in Korean. After Sissel finished singing, they showed a documentary about my life and the inter-Korean summit. Then, soprano Jo Sumi went onstage and sang two songs, which overwhelmed the audience. The hall was buried in applause. I gave an address, in which I said: "Although I have been honored on many occasions in the past, this is the first time I have been congratulated with a concert. Could there be any more moving occasion or greater happiness for an individual than this? We are now communicating in the universal language of music. We are sending a message of love and peace to all people around the world.

"This concert is also an occasion to renew our pledge to forge a world where everyone is blessed with peace. I believe that the event here today is a memorable occasion to express our wishes and desires for peace and prosperity in the world."

After my speech, Ms. Jo Sumi sang again—this time, my favorite, "How I Miss Mt. Kumgang." During breakfast with my wife and me that morning, she had told us that she was planning to sing "Seonguja" (Pioneer), but she must have changed her plan after asking me what songs I liked. She explained what the song was about before she began to sing. "I'll sing a Korean song," she said. "It is a song about the beautiful Mt. Kumgang in North Korea that all the South Koreans want to visit. It is a song that expresses all Koreans' wish for peace and reconciliation to settle in our country. I dedicate this song to President Kim Dae-jung and the Korean people."

She sang the song truly elegantly and earnestly. South Korean tourists must have been climbing Mt. Kumgang at that very moment. I choked up as I listened to her sing that song so beautifully. After the song, she ran toward me and gave me a hug. The audience was on its feet applauding.

Ms. Jo Sumi had sung at my inauguration too. As a daughter of Korea, she made Koreans all over the world proud. Although she must be happy to be welcomed everywhere, I also felt sorry for her for having to travel so much.

The last singer, Nathalie Cole, made a dedication to me before singing "Angel on My Shoulder." She said, "I would like to dedicate this song specially to President Kim Dae-jung. Like the title of this song, I believe that there is a guardian angel on his shoulder. God bless you!"

In the middle of the performance, they also screened congratulatory video messages from President Bill Clinton, Russian President Vladimir Putin, and German Chancellor Gerhard Schröder.

President Clinton's message reflected his warm character and in-depth knowledge of my life. He said: "There might not have been any winner of this prize who had to overcome so many hardships for such a long time as he did before receiving this prize. As he has fought for freedom all his life, his winning this prize is natural. Like other, past winners, he was arrested and imprisoned, and almost lost his life. Nevertheless, he never gave up on his principles, did not choose easy roads, and did not respond to violence and deception in kind. He only took the road he had to, and finally reaped the fruits of his courage, endurance, and resolution. The Republic of Korea became a country of true freedom, and the guardian of human rights in Asia, no, in the world.

"Also, by transforming from an out-of-office moral leader to a political leader, he overcame difficult economic crises with tenacity and wisdom, proving that democracy is not a luxury item that can be enjoyed only during good times, but a necessity that should be more firmly defended the more difficult a situation is. However, above all, we cannot omit mentioning his extraordinary vision and courage, and his achievement in inducing peace and harmony from North Korea. Thanks to him, tension will ease, dispersed families will meet, and inter-Korean problems will be resolved not through destruction but through dialogue in the Korean Peninsula."

After it was announced that I won the Nobel Peace Prize, opposition party politicians pledged that they would fight against my receipt of the award. Even more seriously, some members of the Korean Confederation of Trade Unions also came forward to stop me from receiving the award. They were dissatisfied with my government because we did not release its president and used governmental authority to disperse bank strikes. Delegates from the Korean Confederation of Trade Unions first visited the ILO office in Geneva and then Oslo. They demanded an interview with the Nobel Committee.

Secretary Geir Lundestad told me about this turn of events. The labor union, which was powerful in Norway, expressed concern. Without my convincing explanation, they would have also participated in the movement to boycott the award ceremony and rally in protest together with Korean workers. I decided to meet the president of the Norwegian Confederation of Trade Unions, although my schedule was extremely tight.

I asked calmly, but firmly, "Whose government is it to legalize the Korean Confederation of Trade Unions and open the road for their participation in politics? Which government in the world allows an illegal strike, a violent one at that?"

After the meeting, the president of the Norwegian Confederation of Trade Unions thanked me for my explanation and said they had misunderstood me. He asked me to pose for a photograph with him.

On December 12, I officially visited Sweden for the first time as president of my country. As a member country of the Neutral Nations Supervisory Commission, Sweden has a five-member delegate in Panmunjeom, in addition to embassies in both Seoul and Pyongyang. As a result, Sweden has three official offices in the Korean Peninsula. I had visited Sweden twice before—in 1989 and 1994. Former Prime Minister Carlsson welcomed me at the Stockholm Arlanda Airport. I visited the Swedish Parliament upon Speaker Birgitta Dahl's invitation. About 300 members were waiting for me. I asked that Sweden made an effort to support the inter-Korean reconciliation and cooperation as well as the opening of North Korea.

I said in my speech: "Sweden, as the most experienced and informed of all the Western countries about North Korea, has much to contribute to peace on the Korean Peninsula.

"The 3rd ASEM Leaders' Meeting in Seoul in October adopted a statement welcoming the peace process on the Korean Peninsula and underscoring the importance of building better ties between ASEM member countries and North Korea. Taking a step further, many EU countries have recently come up with concrete action plans vis-à-vis the North."

I also had a summit meeting with Prime Minister Göran Persson and asked him, as the leader of the country that North Korea respected and trusted the most, to meet with Chairman Kim Jong-il.

The next day, I visited the Nobel Foundation and had a pleasant chat with twelve winners of the Nobel Prize in literature, medicine, and economy, and had a photograph taken. I also delivered a few personal items for the Nobel Prize Centennial Exhibition: postcards I wrote in prison; a note I wrote with a nail during my forced stay in Seoul National University Hospital in the late 1970s; the copy of the Bible and Alvin Toffler's *The Third Wave* I read in prison; and the prison uniform I wore.

On December 25, Pearl S. Buck International selected my wife for the Woman of the Year Award. They said she had been selected because "We highly appreciate her leadership role in the democratization movement and movement for children's and women's rights, and her excellent role in her partnership with President Kim Dae-jung." It was a great Christmas gift to us.

CHAPTER 11

December 2000–February 2003

Belated Birth of the Ministry of Women (December 2000–March 2001)

Three Democratic Party members left to join the Liberal Democratic Alliance (LDA) toward the year's end, which meant that the LDA could form a negotiating body. The opposition party became very upset, and some media called it "renting" or "leasing" assemblymen. It did not look good, but it was our only choice to restore the coalition government. While there were mountains of work to do, the majority-opposition party was determined not to work with us at all. We explained to the Korean people that it was not a desirable choice, but it was an inevitable one.

On January 8, 2001, I had dinner with the honorary President of LDA Kim Jong-pil, and we agreed that we would fully restore our coalition.

I received a phone call from President Clinton—the last one during his term. "I have a few things to tell you," he said. "The first concerns the result of our governments' parallel investigations into the Nogeunri Incident and our common interests. I expressed my regrets about the tragedy through a statement, and I would like to take this opportunity to personally express my deep regret for those Koreans who lost loved ones at Nogeunri."

"I understand how you feel," I replied. "Thank you for expressing your regret and condolences. I believe that the Korean people will understand your sincerity. I am very happy that I could work with you for the past three years as your friend. I sincerely hope that our friendship continues. I

© The Author(s) 2019
Kim Dae-jung, *Conscience in Action*,
https://doi.org/10.1007/978-981-10-7623-7_11

wish Senator Hillary Clinton great achievements and all your family members the very best of luck!"

"I believe you know how deeply I admire you," President Clinton said. "You cannot imagine how much I treasure your friendship, advice, and encouragement during my hard times. You have achieved a breakthrough in the inter-Korean relationship and peace and security in the area that nobody could have dreamed of.

"I had a long conversation with President-Elect Bush about North Korea. I told him about the importance and strength of our relationship and cooperation, and urged him to continue to engage in a dialogue with North Korea. Although I could have done more, I feel positively about where we stand with North Korea as I leave office. I hope that I can be of help after my retirement."

"I am moved by your effort for Korea and the friendship with me that you have extended through the very end of your term," I replied. "What you said to President-Elect Bush is very helpful to us. I have been a very happy man in the three years we have worked together. I hope that your cooperation and friendship continue." I was sad that it was my last conversation with President Clinton during his term.

On January 16, I attended an environmentalists' New Year's celebration event. Dr. Kang Won-yong, the director and president of the Korean Christian Academy, said in his toast: "We are at a crossroads in the twenty-first century. The lives on this earth could all be exterminated at the hands of greedy human beings or we can embark upon a great new world that will launch us into a grand new era, opened up at the hands of people who respect and save lives."

It was quite a serious remark. I remembered how we scrapped the Donggang Dam construction plan in June last year and completed comprehensive measures for the management of water in the four big rivers, a focal project of the Government of the People. It was true that we could face the complete destruction of humanity if we continued to waste environmental resources because of greed. It was now time for the water management policy to change its focus from supply to demand. We had to try to control the production of trash through reduction and recycling rather than focusing on its burial and burning. We had abolished the semi-farmland and semi-forest systems, which had been the cause of random development of national land, and reinforced the building-to-land ratio and floor area ratio in order to encourage environmentally friendly remodeling and urban development. We had to use water sparingly before we experienced a water shortage, and to reduce trash before it overflowed.

I emphasized my environment-friendly position during my remark. "The state of our economy makes people's everyday lives very difficult now. But we should not make the silly mistake of neglecting environmental protection. Now we have to boldly denounce the kind of thinking that views environmental protection as simply raising costs and interfering with economic development. Rather, we should acknowledge that protecting and managing the environment could enable sustainable development.

"We have been given the mission to build a world-class country in the twenty-first century. We should nurture an advanced country where the economy is strong, the environment is comfortable, and the culture is thriving. We should consider the earth our mother and everything on the earth as our siblings. We should treasure, prosper along with, and take care of it."

A few days later, during a report on operations in the Ministry of Environment, I praised their introduction of a national park sabbatical system. I also suggested we introduce reserved hiking and eco-guide systems. Our mountains had suffered from development and the rapid explosion of the hiking population. I also asked questions about the existing environmental impact assessment system, as there had been controversies despite the system.

"According to my experience, despite prior environmental impact assessments, both Sihwaho Lake and the Saemangeum developments ran into problems," I said. "From now on, we have to make sure we conduct an environmental impact assessment that people can trust and professionals can all agree to. Once an assessment is complete, there should no longer be any controversies. We should secure fairness and improve technology in order to achieve trustworthiness."

On January 18, I ordered the expansion of compulsory middle school education, which had been carried out only partially, to the entire country. As a result, the compulsory education period increased from six to nine years. In my administration, there were three goals in education: the democratization of education; education in IT; and education welfare.

To democratize education, we legalized the teachers' union, which had existed illegally for the past ten years. Initially established under President Roh Tae-woo's government, it had been oppressed as an illegal organization. Despite this oppression, the union had continued to fight. No less than 1800 teachers had been fired for union activities. We passed a law in January 1999 to legalize the Korean Teachers Union. Most of the teachers who had been fired for union activities could now return to their schools to teach.

I had hoped the Korean Teachers Union would contribute to the improved quality of public education. However, it did not meet my expectations. Perhaps my expectations were too high.

My government also pursued field-based education reform from below by forming an educational community in which parents, educators, civic organizations, and local leaders participated. For this project, we founded the Presidential Commission on Education and Human Resources, the control tower and birthplace of educational reform, in July 1998.

Schools should be managed more democratically and independently than any other sector. Therefore, we established a school steering committee, a self-governing body, in every school. Parents, teachers, and local leaders participated, discussed, and decided on matters related to the management of the school, such as the principal's recommendation for college applications, the management of school athletic teams, the election of superintendents and school board members, and school lunches. This school steering committee served as the essence of the educational self-government.

We also accepted a system whereby university presidents were directly elected. We did not arbitrarily select the second choice from graded multiple candidates in public universities. However, self-government of universities did not make great strides. Although we knew what the problem was, it was not clear whether our solution was the correct one for the problem.

I also focused on the introduction of IT to education. We wired all schools and classrooms with the Internet. This project began in Finland, but Korea finished it first. During my inauguration, I emphasized the importance of this task in making Koreans the most computer-literate people in the world. With the exception of Singapore, Korea was the first country in the world where all classrooms were equipped with the Internet, and all elementary and middle school level teachers were provided with a PC. In April 2001, I participated in a ceremony celebrating the completion of the Internet launch at all schools. I said, "We should complement public education by introducing new pedagogy and an educational system that utilizes information technology and networks."

The curriculum at schools has changed greatly since then. Classes that utilized the Internet spread widely. Cyber universities, where students learn through the Internet, spouted like new leaves after a rain.

In addition to expanding compulsory education, we also radically increased scholarships. I always told the officers at the Ministry of Education: "Nobody who wants to study should have to stop their studies due to costs."

The economic crisis that had overwhelmed our country at the time of my inauguration brought enormous pain to the lives of the middle and lower classes. In particular, university tuition was a great burden to Korean households. Students rushed to take leaves of absence and male students chose to go to the military to speed along their compulsory military service. My government radically increased student loans for middle- and lower-class families. In 2003, 300,000 students borrowed money for tuition.

We also introduced school lunches at elementary and middle schools. The government offered free lunches for students from poor families. Also, by increasing special education schools and classes, we expanded educational opportunities to disabled children.

In order to meet the challenges of the information age, it was most important to nurture talents of creativity and character. I thought that education was the foundation of our future and that without education there would be no future for us. I had a strong belief in the Korean people's excellent tradition of and passion for education. I firmly believed that we could succeed if we continued to reform education.

However, this will for reform did not reach the schools as I had imagined. In September 1999, I spoke about the current status of our educational system at the Report-back Event of the Educational Reform Toward the New Millennium. "Korean education has failed to prepare students for the new age of knowledge, information technology, and globalization. By single-mindedly focusing on subjects like Korean, English, and mathematics, rote memorization, and entrance to renowned universities, we are not nurturing precious creativity during our children's adolescence. Now is the time to change our education."

What seemed most serious to me was the fact that the level of students' academic achievements decreased as they advanced to higher grades. While Korean elementary school children's academic level was at the top level in the world, middle and high school children ranked in about the middle, and university students ranked low. I pointed this out many times. I encouraged universities to change the current system, wherein it was hard to gain entrance, but easy to graduate. "Although the state has the duty to offer educational opportunities, it does not have the duty to graduate those who do not qualify," I said.

I argued that universities should compete against each other and that incompetent professors should be weeded out. I also criticized the customary practice of giving preferential treatment to alumni when hiring. At that time, the percentage of alumni professors in universities in Seoul ranged from 60 to 90 percent.

I had learned a lesson from my year-long stay at Harvard during the 1980s. There, for a Harvard graduate to become a Harvard professor, he or she was required to have worked at and been recognized at other universities. I believe that the US became the greatest country in the world thanks to the power of its university education. In universities in the US, a faculty applicant's institution of education does not matter—what matters are their academic achievements. Jean-Jacques Servan-Schreiber, a writer and politician during the De Gaulle government, wrote in his book titled *The American Challenge*: "The biggest challenge is that America is taking outstanding professors from European universities. In France, one has to graduate from Sorbonne and in England, you have to graduate from either Cambridge or Oxford, but in America, all you need is your ability. Those who did not go to renowned universities, but have excellent abilities go to America."

Only when academic ability becomes the most important standard in university communities can their members exercise creativity and imagination. In order to nurture the talents required by a knowledge- and information-based society, we had to overthrow the educational environment where network rather than ability, and educational background rather than academic ability, prevailed.

We introduced the Brain Korea 21 project in order to grow the talents required by the twenty-first-century knowledge-based society. This project had two branches: the development of graduate-school-centered universities and the development of specialized local universities. Instead of random universal support, we chose to selectively support specialized universities.

The Brain Korea 21 project radically changed the scholarly environment. The government supported creative projects. We also made sure that young scholars had sufficient funds to conduct research. We changed our support focus from professors and their research projects to students and their scholarship. We put 1.4 trillion won into the system for a seven-year period beginning in 1999. Seventy percent of these funds went toward supporting young scholars who were pursuing master's and doctoral degrees.

The effect of this project gradually became visible. Publication of Korean scholars' articles in internationally renowned journals increased. We established an institutional foundation for developing regional universities into research-based universities. The Brain Korea 21 project was known internationally, as well. Japan and China studied it to learn from it.

The educational world was in turmoil throughout my presidential term. Every new educational policy had to contend with counter-currents. The more ambitious a policy was, the stronger the counter-current. Our ministers of education had to be changed seven times. The world of education was quite conservative, and the ministers of education could not withstand the attacks from the opposition party and the media. Nevertheless, the first Minister of Education Lee Hae-chan pushed through many reform measures. He laid down a university application reform including various admission systems, such as admission without examination and rolling admission. He also introduced a reduced professor retirement age and a contract professor system. The education world was at first nervous about and then opposed successive reform measures by this politician-minister.

What I regret most is my government's failure to improve conditions for adjunct professors. Although I ordered that this matter be handled many times, it did not happen. I was very angry about the neglect, exploitation, and general mistreatment of intellectuals. How does it make sense to study so hard to get a Ph.D. and then become a peddling professor!

On January 22, I held a cabinet meeting and we passed a resolution for an amended bill of government organization, which included the elevation of ministers of finance and economy as well as education to the status of vice prime minister and the establishment of the Ministry of Women. On January 29, I appointed Mr. Jin Nyum to vice prime minister and minister of finance and economy, Professor Han Wan-sang to vice prime minister and minister of education, and Assemblywoman Han Myeong-sook to minister of women.

The launch of the Ministry of Women was an especially happy event. Women had spent so many difficult years in a patriarchal system, both in agricultural society and in industrial society. During the time when power governed everything, they lived a life of oppression. However, during the information age, one's brain was more important than his or her physical power. Therefore, the information age was also the age of women.

Women had gradually been breaking into the male-dominated world. Scores of female students entered the military academy every year, and a female student even graduated from it as valedictorian—this would have been unimaginable in the past. The walls against women were still high in various areas in society, and women continued to be discriminated against.

I believed that in order to save our nation, we had to encourage women. Women's refined sensibilities and meticulous approach were resources that the state needed to take advantage of. During the information age, the development of female manpower was a national task. We also had to appreciate the full-time work of housewives. We needed a special ministry to handle all of these issues. Ironically, the Ministry of Women worked toward a day when the ministry would no longer be necessary.

In the Government of the People, we legislated various laws to enhance women's position in society and gender equality. In order to eradicate domestic violence, in July 1998 we introduced the Special Act on Domestic Violence Crime Punishment and Law on Prevention of Domestic Violence and Protection of Victims. Also, the Law on the Ban on Gender Discrimination and Relief was a legal relief instrument for gender discrimination. This provided an institutional tool to correct gender-discriminatory practices, prevent sexual harassment in workplaces, and ban indirect discrimination.

The Ministry of Women was born through an elevation by the Presidential Commission on Women's Affairs. This ministry was not only the first of its kind in our country, but it was also a rarity in the world. I had no doubt that women would be major players in the twenty-first century. I said to the first Minister of Women Han Myeong-sook, "We are now finally witnessing signs of gender equality in the twenty-first century. I hope that women will participate more actively in our society from now on and use their own power to play an active role in achieving an equal society."

Interestingly, Minister Han requested that I appoint a male vice minister to her ministry. Surprised, I expressed my concern about women's objection to this decision, but Minister Han said confidently, "I will take responsibility. Please appoint women to vice ministers of other ministries instead."

I accepted her request and appointed Mr. Hyun Jung-taik to vice minister of women, and Ms. Kim Song-ja to vice minister of labor. She was the first female vice minister in our government. I paid special attention to women-related issues, as other ministry officials tended to ignore the Ministry of Women. The Ministry of Women felt like my youngest child.

On February 26, Russian President Vladimir Putin made a state visit to Korea upon my invitation. We had a summit the next day and adopted a joint statement that included seven key points. President Putin made his intention to support our policy toward North Korea clear and promised that he would try to contribute to the establishment of peace in the Korean Peninsula.

President Putin seemed quite confident about his governance. After his inauguration, he had argued for the Construction of Great Russia, and I could sense his strong will and passion. He was very eager about our economic cooperation; for example, connecting the Trans-Siberian Railway and Korean railways. I could tell just by looking at him that Russia was wriggling to rise up again as *the* giant Eurasian country.

After his visit, however, our joint statement caused problems. Now under the leadership of President Bush, the White House protested the two countries' support of the 1972 Anti-ballistic Missile (ABM) Treaty. This was the result of a very unfortunate oversight by our Ministry of Foreign Affairs and Trade. The staff in charge thought that it wouldn't be a problem because the US had supported the ABM Treaty at the 2000 G-8 Summit in Okinawa. It turned out that he was not up to date with the change of position that had come with the Bush administration; the Bush administration wanted to abolish the ABM Treaty in order to develop the Missile Defense (MD) system.

Not knowing about this unintentional mistake, both the American and the Russian media highlighted it as an intentional challenge to the US policy. It gave the appearance that my government was challenging the new Bush administration. Not only that, but this happened about a week before my visit to the US for my first summit with President Bush. Domestically, also, I was subject to fierce attack by the opposition party. But, more importantly, I felt a heavy burden on my shoulders because I was leaving for a summit in the US.

On March 6, I went to the US for an official visit. After his inauguration, I was the first head of state from Asia that President Bush invited to the US. I was more anxious than I had ever been before. I did not know how the Republican government would greet me. I prepared for the summit in the guesthouse all day long.

Meanwhile, there was news about Secretary of State Colin Powell's remark at a press conference. He said that the administration "plan[s] to engage with North Korea to pick up where President Clinton left off. Some promising elements were left on the table and we will be examining those elements."

On March 8, I had a breakfast meeting with Secretary of State Colin Powell, during which I explained the basic principles of the Sunshine Policy. He said that it was an excellent idea and he supported it. The atmosphere was quite nice and I felt relieved.

Then, the summit with President Bush followed. Before the meeting began, he said that it was his honor to meet a Nobel Peace Prize winner. I began by clarifying that our government did not oppose US Missile Defense system and expressed my regrets for the unnecessary misunderstanding. President Bush said he understood fully.

The meeting went smoothly. I explained the Sunshine Policy in detail and how North Korea had been changing due to this engagement policy. Citing the fact that Chairman Kim Jong-il proposed "New Thinking" that year and visited China, I said that North Korea appeared to be exploring reform and an open-door route. President Bush said he appreciated my government's and my contribution. He even said, "I very much appreciate the progress you have made in the inter-Korean relationship. I recognize your initiative. Our government actively supports an engagement policy toward North Korea."

I emphasized again that North Korea was changing, and that Korea and the US should cooperate to ensure the success of our policy toward North Korea. But President Bush's response to this remark of mine was rather strange. He said, "North Korea is a secretive country. I look at the nature of the North Korean regime rather suspiciously. So, I hope that North Korea will take more visible measures."

Nevertheless, this first meeting was relatively satisfactory. President Bush even showed interest in Chairman Kim's projected visit to South Korea. There was a press conference after our summit, during which President Bush gave rather unrefined comments, like: "I do have some skepticism about the leader of North Korea," "I am concerned about the fact that the North Koreans are shipping weapons around the world," and "We're not certain as to whether or not they're keeping all terms of all agreements."

President Bush even interfered with my answers and called me "this man." Although some argue that he was just being friendly, I found it very unpleasant. I was the president of Korea and he had to respect our cultural sentiment. I usually don't care much about people's age and seniority, but at that moment I could not help remembering that he was my children's age. I realized that our future relationship with the American government would not be smooth.

As the tone of President Bush's comments about North Korea clearly contradicted Secretary of State Powell's remarks the previous day, Secretary Powell did not stay until the end of the press conference. It was unusual. He also held a press conference and changed his earlier remarks.

After the second meeting, which was also a lunch meeting, we issued a joint statement. Its major points were, first, reaffirmation of "the fundamental importance and strength of the US-ROK security alliance;" second, recognition of the Sunshine Policy's achievements; third, recognition of the South Korean government's leadership in the inter-Korean relationship; fourth, support for the second inter-Korean summit; and fifth, reaffirmation of our "commitment to continue the 1994 Agreed Framework."

I had no problem with this joint statement. But, President Bush's unexpected (and perhaps previously calculated) remarks were worrisome. In particular, I was alarmed and discouraged to witness Secretary Powell's change of position. After returning to the guesthouse, I thought about what I should do next. I had to meet influential characters to change the public opinion.

Together with the American Enterprise Institute and Council on Foreign Relations, the next day I hosted a luncheon and invited specialists for conversation. The conference room was filled with Korea-issue specialists and veteran reporters from major media outlets. Major American media outlets had already published negative articles about the previous day's summit. Sharp questions were directed at me and I answered frankly. After the Q&A session, about 200 participants gave me a standing ovation, expressing their sympathy toward me.

I attended a meeting with members of the Senate Foreign Relations Committee and the House Foreign Affairs Committee and had an interview with the *Washington Post*. That evening—my last night in Washington, DC—I had an informal dinner with conservative leaders in the Republican Party, the Bush administration's think tank. President Bush came to mind again as I sat in my room at the guesthouse later that night. He was rude to me, which also meant that he was ignoring the Korean people. Frankly speaking, I felt insulted. "The right road will definitely prevail. I'll turn everything back to the right place," I resolved.

I arrived in Chicago on March 9. After my scheduled events, I called former president George H.W. Bush. He was home and accepted my phone call, sounding surprised at its abruptness. I hoped to get through to President George W. Bush through his father. "I had a valuable conversation with your son in Washington DC," I told the former president. "He understands the situation in the Korean Peninsula, and I was very encouraged by his positive support for my Sunshine Policy. I expect that we will closely cooperate in our future relationship with North Korea based on the trust formed during this summit."

"I am glad that you think the meeting was successful," the former president said. "I am sure he appreciates your achievements. I hope that you will achieve many successes, and please do not hesitate to let me know if there is anything that I can do to help. I think you have been doing excellent work."

The next morning I called former president Bill Clinton. I asked for his help more frankly and sincerely. "Although the new government is in a transitional stage now in terms of their examination of North Korean policies, I expect that in the end the Korean situation will develop the way you planned. Although you did not complete all that you wanted to achieve about North Korea, it is true that you opened a new road. I heard that *The New York Times* and *Washington Post* ran articles predicting that the new government would eventually succeed your policy for the Korean Peninsula. After this transitional period, what you began will revive."

"I hope so too," former president Clinton responded. "I am sure you gave useful advice to President Bush."

"I believe our friendship will last forever," I told former president Clinton. "Please send my regards to Senator Clinton and tell her that I expect she will say many good things about Korea in the Senate."

"She will definitely do that," Clinton promised. "Thank you for calling me and for your friendship."

As Secretary Powell's reversal demonstrated, the Bush administration's policy was not yet settled at that point. All the brouhaha was symbolic of neocons led by Vice President Dick Cheney trying to take initiative over Korean affairs. The hawkish branch of the Bush administration, which included Vice President Cheney and Defense Minister Donald Rumsfeld, wanted to use the threat of North Korean missile development as an excuse for MD system development. It was therefore impossible for them to engage North Korea. Neocons must have been considering the use of weapons against North Korea. However, it was a wild fantasy.

I also wonder if President Bush's hawkish position about North Korea originated from his ABC (Anything But Clinton) position. Although their MD system development policy targeted China, they had to aim at North Korea, as they could not provoke China. That's the thought that came to my mind.

On March 12, former president of South Africa Nelson Mandela visited Seoul and met with me at the Blue House. Although this was our first meeting, we had many indirect conversations and were friends even before meeting face to face. The thought of someone in a faraway country who had lived a life similar to mine gave me strength and courage. We were both fighters against injustice and missionaries of peace. We both received the Nobel Peace Prize when we were seventy-five years old. He supported our Sunshine Policy. "The Sunshine Policy is a policy for the whole world," former president Mandela said. "I admire and respect it. Regardless of the Nobel Peace Prize, it will be recorded in history. I would like to hear your thoughts about the proposal for the establishment of DMZ Peace Park."

"I agree in principle," I said. "Our government also feels the need to preserve the DMZ area. There are two stages to do it: first, it can be designated as an environmental protection area by UNESCO; and second, both South and North Korea can establish a peace park."

We held a joint press conference during which former president Mandela expressed infinite trust in our government. "Mankind's greatest weapon against major international crises is peace," he said. "The policy of reconciliation and cooperation will appeal to everybody since it is based on peace."

I thanked him for his support during dinner. I also celebrated his admirable life. "Despite a lengthy time of suffering, you did not lose your gentleness," I remarked. "You reminded the entire world of the greatness of courage and tolerance, which can melt even antagonism and grudges. You taught Koreans, who are pursuing inter-Korean reconciliation and cooperation, a precious lesson."

We published the "Message for World Peace and Prosperity," which we created together, making sure that we agreed on every single letter. We pledged to work together for world peace, democracy, and human rights, as well as the elimination of poverty.

On March 21, former honorary president of Hyundai Chung Ju-yung passed away. I sent my Chief of Staff to the mortuary with my condolences. "Former Honorary President Chung Ju-yung contributed greatly to the development of the Korean economy by growing his enterprise during the industrialization period. Koreans will remember his achievements for a long time," I said. I remembered him crossing Panmunjeom with cows. He was a special person who prepared the entire nation for post-unification. North Koreans also sent messengers of condolence.

On March 26, I reshuffled the cabinet, changing twelve minister-level officials. The cabinet included Minister of Unification Mr. Lim Dong-won and Minister of Foreign Affairs and Trade Han Seung-soo. I also appointed Shin Kuhn as the Director of the National Intelligence Service (NIS).

I attended the opening ceremony of the Incheon International Airport on March 21. It was the result of eight years of long, hard work. There had been some controversies about its safety but, in the end, it was completed beautifully and grandly. Everything worked smoothly and there have been no accidents whatsoever. To me, Incheon International Airport was one of the few centers that would connect Korea to the world. Together with the Seoul-Sinuiju Railway (which would complete the Iron Silk Road that connected Eurasia with the Pacific Ocean) and Busan port (the third-largest container port in the world), Incheon would turn Korea into a distribution center for the global village by connecting us with the rest of the world through sky, land, and sea.

I said in my congratulatory remarks, "If the opening of the Jemulpo port, forced by imperialist powers a hundred years ago, was our shame, today's opening of the Incheon International Airport will become the glory of the Republic of Korea and will advance us into the world with vision and will."

The first airplane took off from the runway. I was happy to watch it.

New Light on the Country of Human Rights (May–September 2001)

I took notes about laws to be legislated and often examined them. They were laws that I had envisioned for decades. We had to protect democracy through laws and institutions and recover the honor of those who were sacrificed during the fight for democracy. We had to alleviate their sadness. Even though our party was the minority, I did not give up on these measures. I frequently encouraged ministers and discussed such legislation with leaders of political parties and non-governmental organizations.

My to-do list included many things, such as just appreciation of and compensation for those who had suffered in the democracy movement;

truth-finding about the Jeju April 3 Incident, as well as the restoration of honor for its victims; truth-finding about suspicious deaths during the military regimes; the establishment of a national human rights commission; revision and abolishment of National Security Law; and revision of the election law.

First on my list was the Law for the National Human Rights Commission. This law symbolized Korea's respect for human rights. However, it could be legislated only in May 2001. There had been the opposition from the opposition party, but, more importantly, there had also been differences of opinion between the government and civic organizations.

The UN Human Rights Council urged all countries in the world to establish a human rights organization in 1993. During my election campaign I pledged to establish one if I were to be elected. In February 1998, the transition committee included "the legislation of a human rights law and the establishment of a national human rights organization" in the one hundred tasks for the new government. When I received the Human Rights Award from the International League for Human Rights in New York in June 1998, I promised the same things to international society in my acceptance speech.

I expected that the cabinet would quickly pursue this matter, given my background. I was wrong, though. Judging that their authority and positions would change once the governmental human rights organization launched, the Ministry of Justice and the Public Prosecutors Office were negative about the legislation. They delayed it with various excuses. It also took time for civic organizations to fine-tune their own different opinions. Once the draft bill was completed, relevant offices argued about the legal status and authority of the chairman and standing committee members of the human rights organization.

I urged both sides. The governmental offices and civic organizations gradually approached each other and eventually came up with a unified draft. When I examined this draft bill, I found that it guaranteed an independent governmental organization. Although the process was torturous, the result was great. The National Human Rights Commission Law was legislated in May 2001, and the commission itself launched in November the same year. The commission independently worked on the tasks assigned to it by law. It was the organization that protected all individuals and enabled their dignity and values. It played a substantial role in promoting the human rights of all Koreans through researching actual human rights conditions, providing relief for various human rights violation practices, and offering education about human rights.

After signing the law in May 2001, I said, "Today is a significant day in our democratic history. We have tried to build a democratic country that respects human rights. Today's achievement is the result of the Korean people's sacrifice, and we achieved it only gradually. Since launching the Government of the People, we have been acknowledged as a democratic country that respects human rights of the world and many human rights organizations. However, blind spots still remain, and there is room to improve. Our law is equal to international standards required by the UN and other international organizations. By using this law well, the commission should function as the most useful and valuable organization for substantially protecting human rights."

I appointed Attorney Kang Chang-kuk as the first chair of the commission. The commission worked very hard and became reliable watchmen for human rights. The commission went to the Cheongsong Protective Custody Office for its first site visit. It often pointed out examples of human rights violations by the government and ordered corrections. Although their scolding was often sharp and sometimes difficult, I did not dislike it. In April 2002, the commission made its first decision that the government should rectify its decision not to hire someone as the director of a health center because he was disabled. We followed the order.

In their February 2001 Human Rights Briefing, the US Department of State called Korea one of the shining lights of Asia in the areas of democracy and human rights.

The Republic of Korea is the only country in Asia where people won democracy through their fight. China still has not adopted democracy, India learned it from Britain, and Japan was forced by General MacArthur to adopt it. To win democracy, many Koreans had to make a lot of sacrifices. As the president of a country where a peaceful power shift happened for the first time, I had to reward the people who had made those noble sacrifices. I had to appease their sadness. Isn't politics about appeasing people's sadness? Isn't it true that we can do nothing when people are sad?

In January 2000, I had had the official signing ceremony for the Special Law for the Truth-finding of Suspicious Deaths, the Law for the Restoration of Honor and Compensation for People Related to the Democratization Movement, and the Special Law for the Truth-finding and Recovery of Honor for Victims of the Jeju April 3 Incident. Representatives of relevant organizations and other leaders attended the ceremony. There had been truths in the past, but there had not been laws. How much people sighed and cried! I gave the pen I used to sign the law into effect to the relevant organization. In comparison to the enormous sacrifice, it was too small a token of recognition. However, with that pen, I wanted to deliver my will to inscribe the truths of the national tragedies that colored our history.

The Special Law for the Truth-finding of Suspicious Deaths did exactly what its name implied, examining the suspicious deaths of democratization activists. Many democracy movement leaders, citizens, and students had "suddenly" died. Their dead bodies told us nothing, and we were left with questions. Despite suspicious circumstances, the authorities usually did not fully investigate the circumstances of their deaths. As the authorities neglected those deaths, these victims were essentially killed twice. I believed that it was our duty as survivors to find out the truth about their deaths and to let them be remembered in history. If their deaths were buried like their bodies, how could we say that there was justice in our land? It was a matter of conscience and obligation as fellow citizens to find out the truth about their deaths, not only for those who were gone, but also for their families and loved ones. The Presidential Commission on Suspicious Death launched in October 2000. Among the deaths examined was that of Professor of Seoul National University Choi Jong-gil, who had returned dead after being dragged to the Korean Central Intelligence Administration (KCIA).

The Law for the Restoration of Honor and Compensation for People Related to the Democratization Movement was legislated so that the state could restore honor to those who were sacrificed during the democratization movement and to compensate them. It covered those who were involved in the Jeon Tae-il Self-immolation Incident, the YH Labor Union Incident, the People's Revolutionary Party Incident, the March 1 Democratic National Salvation Declaration Incident, the Three-term Constitutional Amendment Opposition Struggle, the Democratic Youth and Student Association Incident, and the Busan-Masan Rebellion Incident.

The Special Law for the Truth-finding and Restoration of Honor for Victims of the Jeju April 3 Incident was an epoch-making legislation. The April 3 Incident involved the civilian massacres that occurred on Jeju Island around the time of the Korean War. I thought that the state should restore the honor of and apologize to the victims, whom the authorities had condemned as "rebels" and "commies." This incident was a disgrace in our modern history. Our government launched the truth-finding mission according to the law and adopted a report in 2003. Although there had been arguments about the true identity of the perpetuators of this incident, the committee accomplished the work of truth-finding, and clearly stated: "The April 3 Incident originated from an armed rebellion staged by the Workers' Party of Korea Jeju Branch, but violent suppression resulted in enormous casualties, which mostly included civilians."

Thanks to this truth-finding mission, Jeju Island could free itself from the fetters of ideology. I believe that the fifty-year sorrow of Jeju Islanders was appeased a little. But this did not apply to only Jeju Island. There are sad stories everywhere in our country. Our modern history turned all our land into graves and dyed it with blood. How many people died for no reason during the Donghak Revolution and the Korean War when people killed one another without feeling guilty?

Bloody incidents continued throughout the course of modern Korean history. How could we move forward without appeasing the sad spirits and their loved ones' cries? How could we reconcile while neglecting their deaths? Taking care of history was necessary for the reconciliation of those of us who survived too.

I made a special effort to improve the prison environment so that the human rights of prisoners would be respected. In the past, prisoners tended not to prepare for a better life in prison, but instead learned new criminal tricks to commit worse crimes. Without changing the correctional administration, there could not be real correction; I had realized this much during my long prison life. When I looked at the prison system as president, things hadn't changed much. They lacked everything necessary to perform the work of correcting the prisoners: facilities, budget, and personnel. In the beginning of my term, I promised three things to prison wardens during our conversation: first, we would better the poor facilities; second, we would improve the treatment of correctional officers; third, we would establish measures to help released prisoners. Since then, the correctional administration had changed a lot. We reformed the youth correctional facilities' education system as well. We introduced the education of practical foreign languages and computer skills. For this, we provided multimedia language labs and computer labs in all youth correctional facilities throughout the country.

We also amended the Criminal Administration Act to enhance prisoners' human rights: they were now able to petition, and we improved the punishment system, and banned the random use of correctional instruments. We allowed them to read newspapers and gave them the right to wear the hairstyle of their choice. Unconvicted prisoners were allowed to wear private clothes. These were changes that I couldn't have even dreamed of while I was in prison. Our most important task was to help released prisoners successfully be rehabilitated into society. For this purpose, we established councils to facilitate job searches and job information centers in prisons. We also offered them support for their livelihood according to the Basic Livelihood Act.

The director of correction was a post under the Ministry of Law, and was in charge of all prison officers, 25 prisons, and between 40,000 and 50,000 prisoners. When I received the first report from the minister of law after becoming president, I asked him, "Why is the director of correction always appointed from prosecutors rather than prison wardens?" Since then, the director of correction has been appointed from those who have had experience as a warden.

International society, including the UN, urged us to abolish the National Security Law in the 1990s. In 1992, for example, the UN Council called it a major obstacle to the complete materialization of rights guaranteed in UN human rights agreements, and urged us to gradually abolish it. The US Department of State urged the same steps through its human rights report.

Domestically as well, many civic organizations and scholars were of the opinion that the law should be either amended or abolished because of the various abuses of power and human rights violations that had resulted from this law. I pledged to amend the law and legislate alternative laws during my election campaign at the urging of both international society and domestic public opinion. Since my inauguration, I had tried to follow through with this promise.

The administration and the ruling party prepared a bill to amend articles regarding the non-notification crime and the crime of praising and inciting North Korea. The LDA agreed to this bill, albeit reluctantly; however, the opposition party and conservative organizations vehemently protested the amended bill. Civic and religious organizations argued for the complete abolishment of the law. Due to these two extreme oppositions, the bill drifted.

After the June 2000 inter-Korean summit, the opposition party protested even more fiercely, attacking our government for trying to abolish the law to enable Chairman Kim Jong-il's visit to Seoul. During an interview with Internet news media site Ohmynews in February 2001, I said, "Although public opinion is considerably in favor of the amendment, national consensus has not been fully achieved. Also, the ruling and opposition parties cannot yet agree on it. We need to take the time to discuss it fully. We do not need to amend it before Chairman Kim Jong-il's visit. Chairman Kim also said when he met our newspaper company presidents that it was up to us."

In the end, I could not accomplish the amendment and abolishment of the National Security Law during my term. I feel that I failed to keep my promise to the Korean people. However, I emphasized that the law should be cautiously applied and that human rights violations could not be accepted. During my term, National Security Law violation offenses were greatly reduced.

During an interview with press from the Gwangju area at the beginning of my term, I said that we should be proud of Gwangju and view it as a symbol of the democratization movement. I promised fair national measures to make Gwangju the pride of both Koreans and the world. According to this promise, my government amended the law to additionally examine and compensate the people involved in the democratization movement in Gwangju. We also elevated the May 18 Cemetery in Gwangju to a national cemetery, together with Masan March 15 Park, and as we had done with the April 19 Cemetery. The May 18 Cemetery is now holy ground for all Koreans. Many Asians visit to remember the spirit of Gwangju—it is now the cradle of Asian democracy.

I also released many prisoners of conscience who had been serving terms since the military dictatorship era. Some had been in prison for decades. Although domestic and overseas human rights organizations had strongly advocated for their release for a long time, previous governments had reluctantly released only a small minority of them according to the political situation at hand. I had very firm beliefs on this matter and, from my own experience, I knew that I had to release a great many of them.

Afghanistan's Taliban government carried out a massive destruction campaign of Buddhist statues, which were world cultural heritages. Their supreme leader ordered all Buddhist statues be destroyed according to Islamic law, which banned idolatry. To destroy Buddhist heritage and 1500-year-old Buddhist Gandhara art was really deplorable! If a religion does not acknowledge another religion, how can we call it the most important teaching? I sent urgent messages to Speaker of the UN General Assembly Member Harri Holkeri and UN Secretary General Kofi Annan on March 3 imploring them to stop this destruction immediately. In the message I wrote, "I must convey to you my grave concern upon learning the news of the Taliban decree ordering the destruction of all Buddha statues within the Afghanistan territory.

"Buddha statues in Afghanistan, including the great Bhamiyan Buddha statue, must be preserved as an irreplaceable cultural heritage of mankind. The Taliban leadership must immediately put an end to its systematic acts of destruction and take the necessary measures to protect this cultural heritage. As confirmed by the resolutions of the United Nations General Assembly and the Security Council, Afghanistan's cultural and historical heritage must be respected.

"I call on you to take all measures within the competence of the United Nations to keep Afghanistan's cultural relics, which constitute a common cultural heritage of mankind, from being devastated. My government and I will fully participate in the efforts of the international community to protect the common heritage of mankind."

On May 3, 2001, the DPRK and EU summit was held in Pyongyang for the first time in history. At a press conference in Pyongyang, an EU delegation headed by Swedish Prime Minister Göran Persson reported that Kim Jong-il pledged that he would extend Pyongyang's moratorium on missile testing until 2003, and that Kim was "committed" to a second inter-Korean summit.

That afternoon, Prime Minister Göran Persson flew from Pyongyang to Seoul on a special plane. I was truly grateful for his efforts in inter-Korean reconciliation. I met his party at the Blue House. During the dinner reception, I expressed my gratitude to members of the EU delegation, including Secretary General of the Council of the EU Javier Solana. I said, "'We must always stand on the side of those who yearn for peace.' This is a remark from one of His Excellency Prime Minister Persson's books, *Ideology and Speech*. You are such people, standing on the side of the 70 million Koreans in the South and North and all those in the world who love peace and play a role as a messenger of peace. I am most grateful to you."

Prime Minister Persson delivered a message from Chairman Kim Jong-il to me, explaining the results of the summit in Pyongyang. "Chairman Kim Jong-il sent his warm regards to you and said he looked forward to seeing you again," he said. "We received the impression that he had the firm will to carry out the accord that he created with you last year."

I had urged Prime Minister Persson to visit North Korea during my visit to Sweden the previous year. Sweden was the country that would provide the next EU Secretary General. His simultaneous visit to North and South Korea on behalf of fifteen EU countries was the result of this talk with me. In January 2003, when North Korean nuclear development became an issue, he also sent a signed letter to Chairman Kim, urging him to abolish the nuclear program and to suspend missile development. My friendship with him continued even after he left office. I treated him to breakfast when he visited me at my house in Donggyo-dong in March 2004. We talked a lot about the future of the Korean Peninsula.

On May 15, I met Prime Minister of New Zealand Helen Clark during her official visit to Korea. She had asked to meet me when I visited New Zealand in 1999, saying that she had admired me from her days as a student. She was the president of the opposition party then. I felt very happy to know that my fight for democratization had planted courage and a sense of justice in the heart of a student in a faraway country. How blessed I was to be able to warm someone's heart with my life! She told me that she led the movement to save my life when I was sentenced to death by the new military government. She had already worked as the first female vice prime minister in New Zealand. She visited and paid reverence at the Gwangju May 18 Cemetery for the first time as foreign head of the state during her visit to Korea.

On May 21, I changed the minister of justice and prosecutor general positions, appointing Attorney Ahn Dong-su to the former position. Unfortunately, as soon as Minister Ahn took office, he was engulfed in a "loyalty document" scandal. The media publicized a document he wrote in which he professed excessive loyalty to the person who had appointment power. As a result, I had to change the minister again only two days after appointing Minister Ahn. This time, I appointed Mr. Choi Kyung-won to the post. That was the same day I signed the National Human Rights Commission Law, the day when I declared to the world that Korea was a country that respected human rights. This was the precious fruit of our democratization struggle. Although there were a few comrades of the democratization movement, I could not have the minister of justice next to me during this signing.

On June 28, the Prevention of Corruption Law passed through Assembly. Its main contents included job restriction for corrupt government officials, protection of whistle-blowers, and the introduction of a direct prosecution appeal system for high officials. According to this law, we established the Presidential Commission for Anti-corruption, which was in charge of establishing policies to prevent officials' corruption, as well as accepting complaints about corrupt activities. Civic organizations had argued for this legislation since 1995. On this occasion, in order to ensure that my government embodied a clean government, I held a cabinet-level meeting for measures to prevent corruption. I had each office present their plan for preventing corruption in order to build the infrastructure for scraping out corruption. I expressed my firm resolution: "Since my inauguration, I have tried my best to cut off the cozy relationship between politics and economics, to keep my relatives under control, to be uninvolved in personnel affairs and in loan matters with financial institutions in order to set a good example for all government officials and the Korean people. As you have observed me from various angles so far, you know what I am talking about. We should eradicate corruption from our land."

On June 29, the National Tax Service announced the results of their tax probe of media companies. They investigated twenty-three companies nationwide for more than four months. This investigation exposed the widespread customary practice of tax evasion by media companies and the acquisition of wealth by company owners through illegal means and abusing loopholes. The National Tax Service filed complaints with the Public Prosecutors Office about six media companies and twelve people, including three owners. It was shocking news that the owners' families abused their companies as a means of private wealth acquisition. Although some media outlets strongly protested, we did not back down, and handled the matter strictly legally. In the end, the owners of the *Chosun Ilbo* and the *DongA Ilbo* newspapers were arrested.

This tax investigation was a great burden to my government and me. I thought long and hard when I received the report that the National Tax Service was planning on investigating media companies. In the past, regimes did not publish the results of tax investigation into media companies and were subject to suspicion that there were political trades between the power and the media. However, even media companies should not be taboo. It was an inevitable choice to do the tax evasion investigation fairly in relation to other companies and in order to practice tax justice. I also felt that I would regret my choice if I avoided it and history would judge me as a coward. I did not want to make a choice that I would not be proud of in the long run. I did not want to live as a president with regrets. I made a decision and ordered that they should carry it out transparently and according to principles.

Although there had been controversies regarding this tax evasion investigation both domestically and even internationally, it provided the momentum necessary to break off the cozy relationship between the power and the media. I could not avoid it as a responsible president. Although the media companies that had been charged with tax evasion later fiercely attacked my government and me, I do not regret my choice. I would do the same faced with the same situation again.

On the forty-second Day of the Newspaper, I said to the media: "I have both received help from the media and been hurt by it. Whenever I got hurt, I was angry and wondered if there was any way of getting back at you. However, I believe that it is due to the existence of such media that I can be here today and that our democracy could reach this point. I hope for friendly criticism rather than uncritical reverence."

In fact, I have been thirsty for friendly criticism all my life. Nevertheless, I could not engage in shady negotiations and trades with the media. The media had to change voluntarily. They had to be honorable before their readers and dignified as public social media. The result of this media tax investigation was evidence of past illicit liaisons between the media and the power. When our media becomes straighter at some later point in time, I believe that they will reevaluate my difficult decision. If I wanted an illicit liaison with the media, I would not have taken such a risk during the later years of my term.

I saw the Chancellor of the London School of Economics Anthony Giddens at the Blue House on July 4. He was the author of *The Third Way* and his theories influenced many European leaders. I had become friends with him in 1993 while staying at Cambridge University. He said that the European economy had raised its first wave in the 1960s economic boom, and was now raising the second wave. I asked him to explain this in more detail.

"In the forty years since World War II ended, the world economy has been governed by traditional industries and, as a result, a traditional life-style has continued," Mr. Giddens said. "This has some limits, however. We need a second wave of renovation. For this second leap, state institutions are actively incorporating the second wave into their systems in Europe. Denmark and the Netherlands are successful examples. Although they did not succeed in the first renovation wave, they are now developing. In contrast, Germany was successful in the first wave, but is reluctant to accept the second wave. That is why they are having difficulty now."

I thought that what he called the first wave in the 1960s in Europe was the last flash of industrial society and we were now entering the age of IT. I said, "I read in some reports that countries that have not stood out in the past, like Finland, Sweden, Ireland, and Denmark, will become leaders in the future."

"I agree," Mr. Giddens replied. "Countries that were successful during the first wave are slow to ride the second wave. They are slow to accept the changes occurring in the twenty-first century. This is the dilemma of a political leader. You did what you had to do, but you became less popular as a result. It seems that the situation has worsened since I visited Korea last year."

"You're right," I said. "They say that reform is harder than revolution."

"I have been watching carefully, and that seems true," he responded. He then emphasized that the only road leaders could take was that of the third wave. He reminded me of the fact that neither traditional Keynesian economics nor a completely liberal economy had succeeded.

August 23 was a meaningful day: We repaid the final balance of $140 million out of the $19.5 billion IMF loan. We were able to repay the entire balance three years ahead of 2004, as had been originally planned, and could be released from the humiliating state of economic trusteeship. In the early days of my term, I could not sleep because of my worries about the financial situation of our country. All of the news was so gloomy as we were perched on the brink of national bankruptcy. I had to run to wherever we could go to acquire dollars, even if that search led me to the ends of the earth. At that time, I really regretted my disabled body. Nevertheless, I had to chase dollars anywhere and everywhere, and met any and everybody. Thankfully, we were able to repay all of our debts during my term.

President of the IMF Horst Köhler sent me a letter of congratulations upon our debt repayment. In his memoir, former Minister of Finance of the US Robert Rubin called my and my government's effort "a heroic act." Also, the former president of the IMF Michel Camdessus and Secretary General of the OECD Donald Johnston highly praised Korea's process for overcoming the foreign currency crisis as an unprecedented and exemplary model for the world.

We held two events in celebration of our early graduation from the IMF system. I visited Kia Automobile's Soha-ri plant on the morning of August 22. Kia was one of the exemplary models of successful restructuring. In 1997, Kia represented the foreign currency crisis, but the origin of this disaster transformed it into the outpost of export. After looking around the plant, I talked about *chaebol* reform.

"Out of thirty *chaebols*, sixteen either shut down or changed owners," I said. "Kia is one of them. You have all witnessed our country's foremost *chaebols* dissolving despite the myth of 'too big to fail.' Although we know our reform was not perfect, the world appreciates Korea as the country that carried out the most exemplary reform of all the newly emerging countries. Michigan University Graduate School's evaluation of economic reform in emerging countries ranked Korea as second only to Singapore in terms of competitive reform."

That evening, I invited the leaders who had worked so hard to overcome this national disaster to dinner. Looking at their faces, I remembered the way they had run around to rescue our country. They were outstanding generals. I had pushed them hard, and we worked tirelessly. How nice that we could overcome the disaster and laugh together!

Former Minister of Finance and Economy Lee Kyu-sung said, "It was your high statesmanship that united all Koreans, and it was thanks to your summit diplomacy that we could gain trust from international financial institutions and friendly countries."

Former Emergency Economy Committee Chair Kim Yong-hwan, former Chair of the Labor-Employer-Government Tripartite Commission Kim Won-ki, former Minister of Finance and Economy Lee Hun-jai, and president of the Korean Confederation of Trade Unions Lee Nam-Sun attended, too. I shared my feelings with them when I said: "In my view, two things we Koreans did moved the world most: one was our gold collection campaign, and the other was the Labor-Employer-Government Tripartite Commission. Koreans was not afraid of making sacrifices to rise up together from our disastrous situation. I am infinitely grateful to the Korean people. I know that numerous corporations underwent a painful restructuring process. I am also grateful for the labor world, which cooperated even while workers suffered. I believe that historians will definitely remember these sacrifices and the cooperation of our businessmen and workers when they write about the relationship between the IMF and Korea, and the process by which we overcame the foreign currency crisis.

"The Korean people, businesses, and laborers supported our government, and we in the government also worked tirelessly to complete our tasks. Despite internal conflicts, we treasured one another. We are comrades who did our best for our country and people. How can we forget that precious time?"

As of September 15, Korea's foreign currency reserve surpassed $100 billion, making ours the fifth-largest foreign currency reserve after countries like Japan and China. The world was surprised and called this "unprecedented."

The Mangyongdae Guestbook Incident occurred when Professor Kang Jeong-koo of Dongguk University, who had visited President Kim Il-sung's birthplace Mangyongdae, wrote in the guestbook: "Let us succeed the spirit of Mangyongdae and accomplish the great task of reunification." The media made an issue out of it and the opposition party fiercely attacked the government. They demanded that I fire Minister of Unification Lim Dong-won for his responsibility in allowing Professor Kang to visit North Korea. The opposition party presented the motion for his dismissal and the LDA supported it.

Although the opposition party fiercely attacked us, I could not fire Minister Lim, a veteran unification worker. He was deeply trusted by leaders of North Korea and China. If I dismissed him, it could give the impression both domestically and internationally that the basic principle of the Sunshine Policy was shaken. People could interpret it as a retreat on our reunification policy. I could not yield the inter-Korean relationship to political considerations. Minister Lim was the talent that we needed for the future of the Korean Peninsula. In addition, critically important events like Chinese president Jiang Zemin's visit to North Korea and President Bush's visit to South Korea were scheduled for the second half of 2001. I needed to have him beside me.

I sent Chief of Staff Hahn Gwang-ok to urge honorary president of LDA Kim Jong-pil for his support. However, President Kim openly urged Minister Lim to resign, arguing that his dismissal and the coalition were separate matters. He made it clear that his party would support the dismissal during the vote at the National Assembly.

On September 3, the motion to dismiss Minister Lim passed the Assembly due to the LDA's support. The coalition government naturally dissolved after three years and eight months. The political landscape changed to one ruling party and two opposition parties. A difficult road of a minority ruling party-based government lay ahead of us.

Ministers who were recommended by the LDA stepped down too and I changed five ministers. Although Prime Minister Yi Han-dong had to step down as well, I asked him not to. He issued a statement saying that he would follow my will.

On September 11, I changed Blue House staff members. In particular, I appointed former Minister of Unification Lim Dong-won to special advisor to the president for foreign affairs and national security. Although I could anticipate the opposition parties' fierce opposition to it, I wanted to send a clear message about my intention to continue the Sunshine Policy.

IT Powerhouse: From Dream to Reality (September–November 2001)

In my inauguration speech I said: "We, as a people, have a high level of education and a brilliant cultural tradition. We are a superior people who have enormous potential in the age of information of the twenty-first century.

"The new administration will make efforts so that the young generations will be able to become main players in the knowledge and information society. We will teach computers in primary schools and let high school graduates have the option for computer science on university entrance examinations. We will lay a firm foundation for a leading nation in the information age by training the most skilled computer users in the world."

Because of the imminent foreign currency crisis, the Korean people and media did not pay much attention to my remark at that time, though. However, I achieved my dream of building a leading nation in the information age by doing my best to materialize this vision.

I did not doubt that Koreans were the people most fit to adjust to the twenty-first century, when knowledge, information, and cultural creativity would take the center stage. Around the late Joseon dynasty, Korea, surrounded by four powerful countries, was in the most disadvantageous geopolitical situation. This led to Korea's annexation by Japan after the Sino-Japanese War. Now, however, the imperialist period was over. We were living in an era when software was important. Accordingly, our geopolitical location now became an advantage. A vast market for goods and investment, including the four powerful countries of the US, Japan, China, and Russia, as well as Mongolia, were right next to us. If we built a leading nation in the information age, we could become a high tower in the center of powerful countries.

President of GE Jack Welch said to me, "An adventurous spirit is in the blood of Koreans."

Alvin Toffler, Bill Gates, and Masayoshi Son (Son Jeong-ui) were advisors and teachers who showed me the road to becoming a leading nation in the information age. As I have already mentioned, Dr. Toffler taught me about the arrival of the information age and inspired me with the dream of achieving it in Korea. He also showed special affection to Korea and me. Before I was inaugurated as president in January 1998, he volunteered to advise me on the IT field of the new government. I met him in the Blue House on April 7. Like a curious child, I asked him many questions. His advice was very useful. "There are not too many leaders around the world who have an accurate understanding of the importance of the information technology in our age," Dr. Toffler said to me. "I think very highly of the fact that you understand it fully and have a vision for it."

In fact, I became more confident hearing his acknowledgment. Since then, he has given us a lot of help in businesses related to IT. I still remember his words when he visited Korea in June 2001. He said, "While IT has influenced BT (bio-technology) in the past, BT will influence IT now. From now on, bio-information technology that combines both fields will flourish."

When I met the CEO of Microsoft Bill Gates and CEO of Softbank Son Jeong-ui on June 18, 1998, they gave me concrete and clear advice. I asked them about the best way forward for the Korean economy.

Mr. Son immediately said, "It is broadband, broadband, and broadband. Korea should become the world's best broadband country." Mr. Gates agreed. At that time, broadband was an unfamiliar term. I ordered the Ministry of Information and Communication to explore ways to quickly build a high-speed communication network. This is how the history of high-speed Internet in Korea began.

High-speed Internet served as the infrastructure for IT. Beginning in 1999, when the economic crisis was settled to a degree, we began to fully invest in high-speed Internet. In January 1999, Minister of Information and Communication Namgoong Suek chose the early construction of high-speed Internet and securing 10 million Internet users as the major tasks for the year. The Ministry of Information and Communication refined this plan and pursued the Cyber-Korea 21 project. The Cyber-Korea 21 project had four goals: first, early building of the IT infrastructure; second, using the IT infrastructure to heighten the productivity and transparency of government, businesses, and individuals; third, job creation, using the IT infrastructure; and, fourth, intensive nurturing of IT items as strategic export merchandise.

Among them, we pursued early building of the IT infrastructure as our most important task. Out of the 2.8 trillion won that we budgeted to invest in this project, we decided to invest 1.2 trillion won in the early building of the IT infrastructure.

I pushed this project so hard that some officials considered it reckless. I thought that once we fell behind we would not be able to catch up in this digital age that was supposed to change at light-speed. I encouraged all

Koreans to learn IT, and used any chance I had to emphasize that knowledge and information were the best sources of competitiveness we had. Some officials complained about my passion for this project and pushy monitoring of its progress. Nevertheless, I did not stop.

During the strategic meeting for electronic business transaction promotion on February 15, 2000, I appealed to officials, saying, "I also feel tired. I don't handle the computer well. My old age could also be a factor for this weariness. However, our times demand that we know about computers. The future develops at light-speed. We are living in a time when we cannot rest even if we want to, a time when it is not easy to live in a sense.

"I read an article that says 650 workers at the company Amazon.com produce output equal to those produced by 200,000 workers at the Ford Company. We must prepare for the age of electronic business transactions. If we do not win in the age of global competition, we do not have future."

Intensive investment got us results quickly. In December 2000, we opened the information highway. We connected 144 major areas of our country with fiber-optic cable high-speed Internet. It was a distance forty-four times longer than the length (19,988 km) of the Seoul-Busan Highway.

On February 25, 2001, we held the first "video cabinet meeting" by connecting the Central Government Building in Seoul and the Government Complex in Gwacheon in celebration of the third anniversary of my inauguration. I hoped that it would provide more inspiration for the cabinet members to actively work on the introduction of IT.

As soon as the information highway opened, everyone drove on it. The number of high-speed Internet users increased rapidly. The number of households subscribing to the service increased from 370,000 in 1999 to more than 10 million in October 2002. All of this change happened in the four years since the Internet service launched in June 1998. The number of Internet users increased from 1.63 million at the end of 1997 to 27 million at the end of 2002. The OECD reported that Korea was the number one country among member countries in high-speed Internet distribution, with a rate of 17.16 per 100. Our Internet user population was four times that of the US (the country with the most powerful economy) where the high-speed Internet distribution rate was 4.47.

On November 6, 2002, we held a ceremony to celebrate a historic 10 million-household users of high-speed Internet at the Government Complex. I was truly overjoyed. "We now have the opportunity to leap forward as an advanced country for the first time in our 5000-year history," I said. "If we continue to make an effort based on our achievements so far, our dream of achieving a world-class country will definitely come true. Let us all believe in ourselves. Let us all go forward in achieving the foremost knowledge-based economy in the world."

At the same time as the Internet infrastructure was being built, I emphasized IT education. In the information age, knowledge of the Internet was our best weapon. As the entire country entered the Internet age, we needed talents who could move around stealthily in this cyber world. In particular, IT offered poor people the opportunity to enter the middle class.

When Japanese Softbank CEO Son Jeong-ui visited Korea at the end of 1999, he said, "The internet is about speed. Investing in students will be most effective. If you pursue 'a PC a student' under your leadership, the contents of education will change too. Until now, we had to memorize a lot, but from now on we will have to think about and apply knowledge from the internet creatively. We will use our brain to solve problems. Therefore, the contents of education will become more advanced, and Korean students will become adults who can use the internet most proficiently. It will be the investment that will bring the most profit."

I agreed with him and followed his advice on investing in education. In December 2000, Korean elementary, middle, and high schools became the first in the world to be connected to high-speed Internet. We provided PCs to 330,000 teachers. We also taught computer for free to 500,000 students from poor households.

I emphasized that nobody should fall behind in the IT society. We provided ways for those classes of society less exposed to IT—such as housewives, the elderly, and the disabled, as well as those who lived in remote places and the countryside—to become computer-proficient. We taught computer in the military and in prisons. We pursued projects to dissolve the digital divide across the entire government. We introduced the Information Technology Education for 10 Million People project. It sounded like dream when we launched it, but by March 2001, we had officially taught 10 million people. As a result, we raised workers who could fly through the vast territory of the Internet on their computers. I believed that they would enlighten the twenty-first century through their creativity and adventurous spirit.

On February 14, 2000, I sent a video message to the Cyber Jeumeuni (Millennium) Launching Ceremony. I said in my message, "Governed by knowledge, information, and cultural creativity, the twenty-first century is an opportunity for our nation's great leap forward and development. There are not many nations that possess high education levels and a tradition of cultural creation like our nation. Our future depends on you. I hope that you will accomplish your dreams and hopes on the unknown continent of information with your infinite creativity and adventurous spirit."

At the Asia-Europe Meeting (ASEM) summit in October 2000, leaders of France and England boasted that their Internet populations were 6 or 7 million. By then, the Korean Internet population was no less than 17 million, but I could not boast about it in front of them.

The connection of 144 areas nationwide through the high-speed Internet network by late 2000 proved very useful in many ways. I also pursued a completely electronic government. I formed the Special Commission for Electronic Government with both government officials and civilian leaders on January 29, 2001. I appointed Professor of Korea University Ahn Moon-suk as its chair. Establishing an electronic government was a strategic tool for everyday government reform in the wake of restructuring the four areas of our society. We could form a transparent and competitive government and expand this spirit to the entire society. Once completed, the electronic government could reduce the volume of traffic, save oil, and reduce environmental impact. Above all, our entire country would not waste time and, as a result, we could secure more time. At that time, the US, the UK, and Singapore were also actively pursuing an electronic government.

We built a basic database for each governmental department and legislated relevant laws, such as the Basic Act for the Promotion of Information Technology, the Act on Electronic Signature, and the Act of Electronic Government. However, it was not easy to destroy the walls between different governmental offices for information sharing. They did not want to disclose their information. It was the residue of the closed-door administration. I requested the Special Commission for Electronic Government to closely check each office's progress in this matter and to advise me if there was a problem.

The first fruit of the electronic government was the establishment of an electronic procurement system, which held its opening ceremony in September 2002. As a result, businesses could get information for procurement and participate in bidding for the government's and public institution's procurement through the Internet. In November 2002, we established an innovative customer service system. The Korean people could be guided to learn about 4000 government services and handle 393 major applications. This was the beginning of the living room government service system. Also, government offices could share all information owned by the government.

Three months before my term was over, on November 13, 2002, we held the Electronic Government Foundation Completion Report Event at the Blue House after finishing the electronic government establishment project in two years. We accomplished our slogan: "Government in Your Palm!" Minister of Information and Communication Lee Sang-chul handed me my certificate of digital signature, the ID of the electronic era.

I expressed my gratitude to the Special Commission members, including its Chairman Ahn Moon-suk. I said: "When the electronic government operates well, the efficiency of our country will reach the highest level, corruption will disappear, and everything will be done transparently and be trusted by the Korean people. Korea will become the country where doing business is good, and Korea will boast the highest competitiveness in the world. The importance of electronic government cannot be overemphasized. Let us develop it and create the world's best government."

This effort and achievement of ours were internationally recognized. German Chancellor Schröder said in March 2002 that Korea was the country where the IT industry developed most rapidly in the world, and Germany was trying to catch up with Korea. In May 2002, the US magazine *Business Week* reported that the Korean dream of becoming the center of Northeast Asia could be realized with our 25 million Internet users and 30 million mobile phone users.

In 2003, the city of Seoul ranked number one in electronic government assessment among one hundred cities throughout the world. The City of Seoul signed a memorandum of understanding with Moscow, Hanoi, and Ulaanbaatar, and exported its model of electronic government.

We had built the IT infrastructure passionately and sometimes tearfully. We built an IT powerhouse and nurtured IT talents. But we had to turn this foundation into industry. I requested that traditional businesses graft IT into them. IT penetrated the shipbuilding, automobile, and steel industries. Europe and the US brought a case against the Korean steel and shipbuilding industries before the WTO for dumping practices. An international investigation team visited Korea and performed a site inspection. After finding out that all companies had reduced their production costs by introducing IT, they returned to their home countries in admiration.

This was behind the retreat of the traditional shipbuilding powerhouse Norway. When I went to Norway to receive the Nobel Peace Prize, Chairman of the Nobel Committee Gunnar Berge surprisingly praised Korean IT to the utmost degree. He said that he was originally a shipbuilder, and had been very surprised after looking around Korean shipbuilding companies. He said to me, "While we're still hammering nails in Norway, IT was commanding production lines in Korea. I thought that our shipbuilding industry was over."

Prime Minister of Japan Koizumi Junichiro expressed his envy of the Korean IT industry when he visited on October 15, 2001. Noticing the general use of the T-card, a rechargeable smart card used for public transportation, he said admiringly that they did not have such a system in Japan.

I ordered the development of new knowledge-based industries such as biotechnology, cultural technology, environmental technology, and space technology. On November 30, 2001, we announced a project that would develop these sectors into major export industries by investing 10 trillion won through 2005.

Despite this progress, the Korean IT industry was weak in the software field. Although we built the infrastructure in a short time, we would become a true knowledge and information powerhouse only when we developed software. I argued for it, but my government did not have time to follow through with this plan.

I requested Indian cooperation in the software field when I met Indian Minister of Communication and Information Technology P. Mahajan in September 2001. "It is marvelous to watch software development in India," I said. "While we focused on hardware, India focused on software. I hope that our two countries can complement each other in development."

On October 17, 2001, Microsoft CEO Bill Gates advised me, "Korean IT industry hardware has grown remarkably. In some areas, Korea has the most advanced hardware in the world. High-speed internet, in particular, and wiring schools will reap great benefits. But, you have to work harder on software."

His remark was on point. As I worked hard to build the hardware for the construction of an IT powerhouse and finished the electronic government project right before the end of my term, unfortunately the task of building software to the world's highest standards had to be handed over to the next government.

While I was taking a rest in my residence after dinner on September 11, 2001, I got a call from Protocol Secretary Choi Jong-il. He said that according to CNN breaking news, airplanes had flown into the World Trade Center buildings in New York City. I turned on the TV and watched CNN. The World Trade Center buildings were in flames. It continued to loop footage of the airplanes flying into the Twin Towers. I could not believe my eyes—it did not seem real.

The US was helpless in the face of simultaneous suicide terrorist attacks, despite its state-of-the-art equipment and missile defense system. The Twin Towers—the symbol of American wealth—collapsed. The Pentagon building, which symbolized American power, was burned.

Senior Secretary for Foreign Affairs and National Security Kim Ha-joong briefed me about the incident. I immediately placed our military and police on alert and called an Emergency National Security meeting and cabinet meeting for the next day. As time passed, the outline of the incident became clearer. Terrorists had taken civilian airplanes and used them for suicide terrorist attacks. The casualties were estimated to be in the thousands.

I could not fall asleep. We were living in a world where terror groups could attack a country—the heart of the national defense of the mightiest country in the world, at that—so there was no country that was perfectly safe. Battle lines, wartime, and war zones did not exist separately. There was no doubt that America would punish those behind the attack strongly, but then, what would happen to the Korean Peninsula? In the end, I was worried about our nation.

On September 12, I presided over the national security and cabinet meetings. I also canceled all scheduled events for that day, and issued a special statement: "We are witnessing a truly sad and tragic reality … Terrorism is the enemy of all peace-loving people around the world. Whatever the reason for and whatever the target of the attack, terrorism is a most heinous crime that should not be allowed. I strongly denounce terrorism that threatens the life and safety of the people. I will take part in the efforts to free humanity from terrorism."

Koreans trusted their government. Despite this attack on US soil, they did not rush out to stock up on daily necessities. This was a product of the inter-Korean reconciliation. The power of peace in the Korean Peninsula could not be shaken for any reason.

On September 15, the fifth ministerial-level inter-Korean talk was held in Seoul, despite the attack a few days earlier. Thirteen items were agreed upon, including a land route for the Mt. Kumgang tour; to hold working-level talks for the establishment of the Kaesong Industrial Complex; and the fourth dispersed families visit group exchange.

Finally, the US began its revenge attacks. On October 7, it attacked the Taliban regime in Afghanistan, accusing the group of protecting Osama Bin Laden, who was the mastermind behind the September 11 Attack. President Bush declared this to be the War on Terror and urged other countries to participate.

With its pride hurt, the US was seized by hatred and forced other countries to choose between being a friend or an enemy. This extreme approach represented America's needy condition. The Korean government placed our military and police on alert to protect strategic facilities, including US bases.

North Korea, however, was very upset about this measure. They considered this to be an antagonistic action on our part. They notified us that they could not send the dispersed families to Seoul, arguing that our government brought another country's problems upon ourselves and promoted tension and antagonism. They also demanded that we change the location of various talks to Mt. Kumgang, instead of alternating between Seoul and Pyongyang as we had done up to this point. Our government proposed that we hold the sixth ministerial inter-Korean talk in Pyongyang as planned.

Both sides went into a tedious back-and-forth about the location for the talk. In the end, we yielded to the North and the talk occurred in Mt. Kumgang on November 8. They agreed on the working-level meeting schedule and on holding the ministerial-level meeting in Seoul. However, the head delegate from our side abruptly walked out of the room during an open meeting to work on the agreement. This happened as we were negotiating the date for the next meeting. I was extremely disappointed and angry that he did this—the minister was obligated to work according to my orders in matters involving unification and national security. Despite this, he committed an egregious action against my order.

The Appeal of Conscience Foundation, a major New York-based organization, announced that it had officially decided to confer the 2001 World Statesman Award to me on September 20. The foundation's honorary award committee was chaired by President George W. Bush and co-chaired by Vice President Dick Cheney and all living former US presidents.

On October 8, I nominated Democratic Party Standing Advisor Roh Moo-hyun to its Supreme Committee member. As he was a very strong presidential candidate, I felt I should give him opportunities equal to those of other party members. The competition for the presidential candidate nomination was rearing its head at the time. I listened as they criticized me from time to time.

On October 15, Prime Minister of Japan Koizumi Junichiro visited Seoul's Seodaemun Independence Park (the site of the prison during the colonial period), and looked around the history museum. After dedicating flowers to the monument, he mentioned Japanese colonial rule. "I sincerely apologize for the pain and sorrow Japan inflicted on the Korean people under Japanese colonial rule," he said.

At that time, there were three pending issues between Korea and Japan: Japan's understanding of its recent history and distorted description in history textbooks; Prime Minister Koizumi's Shinto shrine worship; and Japan's ban of the Korean fishing of mackerels in the South Kuril Islands. Due to these matters, the South Korean sentiment toward Japan was very negative. Koreans were particularly concerned about Prime Minister Koizumi's right-wing actions. During our summit, I mentioned these worries. I said that, although history was a matter of the past, understanding history was a matter of the present and future, and that I would like Japan to handle the matter of distorted history textbooks like Germany. "Although Germany inflicted aggression, they apologized and compensated for it after the war, and thoroughly educate Germans about what happened. They preserved historical relics in order to show the various atrocities committed under Hitler. Germany itself has benefitted most from this thorough reflection on its past."

I also pointed out that Prime Minister Koizumi worshipping at the Yasukuni Shrine was unjustified. I reminded him of the fact that A-level war criminals, who had inflicted pain even on the Japanese people, were enshrined there. I also asked him not to hurt our traditional fishing practices, reminding him that fishing in the South Kuril Islands area was a commercial activity unrelated to territorial sovereignty. Unfortunately, Prime Minister Koizumi responded very passively.

At our lunch after the meeting, I said to him, "Let me tell you a joke. If you solve the three problems—that is, the problems of the textbook, the Yasukuni Shrine worship, and fishing in the South Kuril Islands area—I will respect and consider you to be my greatest friend. If not, I will not even so much as greet you when we meet from now on."

It was not really a joke, but my last entreaty. We laughed together. His reply was funny too. Referencing my kidnapping in Japan, he said, "Wouldn't I be bound and thrown into the sea afterward?"

He left after his seven-hour visit to Seoul.

I arrived in Shanghai to attend the ninth Asia-Pacific Economic Cooperation (APEC) summit on the afternoon of October 18. The next day, I had successive summit meetings with eight heads of state, including American president George Bush, Chinese president Jiang Zemin, Russian president Vladimir Putin, and Japanese prime minister Koizumi Junichiro.

President Bush confirmed that he supported the Sunshine Policy strongly and was willing to engage with North Korea. During my summit with Japanese Prime Minister Koizumi, he showed a positive attitude about the three pending issues we had discussed a few days before, laying the groundwork for Japan and Korea possibly co-hosting the World Cup.

In the special election on October 25, the Democratic Party suffered a serious defeat in all three districts: Dongdaemun-eul and Guro-eul in Seoul and Gangneung in Gangwondo. The Democratic Party was thrown into internal turmoil as a result.

On November 16, my old friend, former US Secretary of State Henry Kissinger, visited Seoul. We discussed the inter-Korean relationship, which was not showing any signs of improvement. As I was clearly troubled about it, Secretary Kissinger made an optimistic remark about the inter-Korean relationship and encouraged our current policy toward North Korea. "You'll be the person in history to bring fundamental change," Secretary Kissinger said. "Although there might be occasional setbacks in the South's relationship with the North, you have set a clear basic direction. It is similar to what Willy Brandt in Germany did, although the situation was different. You should take the initiative in matters of the Korean Peninsula. US foreign policy should follow your lead, two steps behind. It should not go two steps ahead."

"The Sunshine Policy succeeded in drawing North Korea into international society," I mused. "However, it cannot end there. I don't mean to achieve this during my term, though."

"North Korea must be hesitating because they are not sure which way they should go," Secretary Kissinger speculated. "More opening might mean their collapse. They are afraid of the success of your policy, in a sense."

Mr. Kissinger thought that the Bush government's policy toward North Korea would eventually become more flexible. I asked him to lend his experience and wisdom regarding the Korean Peninsula to the current US government. He gladly accepted my request.

Resignation from the Democratic Party Presidency (November 2001–February 2002)

I attended the ASEAN (Association of Southeast Asian Nations)+3 summit in Brunei early November. On November 5, Chinese Prime Minister Zhu Rongji, Japanese Prime Minister Koizumi Junichiro, and I had a three-way summit. We agreed on five points during this meeting, including the establishment and operation of a three-way economic ministers' meeting and a Korea-China-Japan Business Forum. Next, I had a summit with Chinese Prime Minister Zhu Ruogji. At the beginning of our meeting, I told him that Shanghai should yield the 2010 World Trade Fair to Yeosu, Korea.

"I am glad to see my friend whom I have always admired," I said to Prime Minister Zhu. "Above all, I congratulate you on holding the last very successful APEC meeting, your upcoming membership in WTO, and the Chinese soccer team's advance to the final round. They say that happiness shared is doubled. As you're blessed with many auspicious occasions, I hope you'll yield the 2010 World Trade Fair to Yeosu."

"I consider you to be like an elder brother," the prime minister responded. "Frankly, I tried my best because you mentioned the CDMA matter. Since I made this effort, I hope that you will address the trade imbalance between Korea and China. Also, Korean culture and art haven't just attacked Singapore. China is also under attack from what is no longer a 'Korean Wave,' but a 'Korean Current.' Chinese actors are imitating Korean actors."

Although Prime Minister Zhu was complaining, I was happy. Mobile phones made with our technology were connecting Chinese voices, and the Korean Wave was soaking Chinese hearts.

"China's openness to Korean pop culture means that your country has a large cultural tolerance," I responded. "It means that you have a calm mind, and that you feel confident about your ability to digest it. China has exported its culture to Korea for 1500 years, and Korea has balanced its culture through this interchange. In this sense, I think it is okay if China is influenced by Korean culture for at least one hundred years, if not 1500."

We laughed together. Prime Minister Zhu continued to call me "older brother" and persisted in his request for our additional openness to Chinese agricultural products. I continued asking him to consider the fact that Korean farmers were in serious crisis.

I gave the first keynote address at the ASEAN+3 summit. I proposed that we better systemize our summit meeting by transforming the ASEAN+3 summit into the East Asian Summit. I pointed out that with the current trend of region-based reshuffling of global economic order into NAFTA, EU, and the South American Trade Bloc MERCOSUR, the loose form of the ASEAN+3 summit could not help being alienated from the center of the world. I also proposed the creation of the East Asian Forum as a successor of the East Asian Vision Group, based on cooperation between civilians and governments.

I also urged that we begin exploring the creation of an East Asian Free Trade Area and proposed that the East Asian Research Group and East Asian Forum explore concrete approaches to this. Participating heads of state agreed and supported my proposals.

The internal division within the ruling party became deeper after the special election defeat. Some people again attacked former Supreme Council Member Kwon Rho-kap, saying that he was someone who needed to be cleaned up. Sensational remarks poured out of presidential candidates at random. On November 2, all of the Supreme Council members decided to step down. The Supreme Council had been created based on my proposal, so this was a great blow to me. The so-called Donggyo-dong faction council members were also involved in this decision.

I felt very uncomfortable as I left for Brunei to attend the ASEAN+3 summit. Even as I spoke with heads of state, I could not shake the internal division of the Democratic Party from my mind. I was being attacked not only by the opposition party, but also by my own party. I felt awkward rather than happy when other country heads said that they should learn from Korea. *Would they say this if they knew what was going on domestically right now?* I thought. *If they knew our political situation, how would they look at me? Would they still understand me?*

After returning from Brunei, I met with Democratic Party leadership. Since they had already resigned from the Supreme Council, our meeting was termed a "Leadership Conference." They were busy proposing strategies for settling the situation. They all said things could not go on as they were. But their strategies were all very abstract and vacant.

I had already made up my mind in Brunei. It was clear that the party leadership would drag me into their fights for party leadership and presidential candidacy if I retained my post as party president. I thought it would be very sad if I were in the center of political strife, so I decided to resign from the party presidency. My turn to speak came last. When it did,

I said, "As the president of both our country and our party, I feel painfully responsible for this situation. I am thinking about what I should do to take responsibility for this situation. I will state my thoughts at the party meeting tomorrow after mulling over your thoughts and proposals."

It seemed to me that former Supreme Council member Kwon Rho-kap should retire from the political front lines. I delivered my recommendation to him through Senior Secretary of Policy and Planning Park Jie-won. Mr. Kwon rejected my recommendation, perhaps feeling that it was unjust and oppressive. However, politics was a living organism. I was sad when Mr. Park delivered his response to me: "I'm now seventy years old. I want my children to be proud of me. If I retreat now, I will be blamed for everything. I cannot do that."

There was nothing I could do. How miserable to have to question one another's intentions in such an unfortunate circumstance! Fate can be so cruel.

I wrote a statement giving my resignation from the party presidency and sent the statement to the party administrative meeting through the Blue House senior secretary for political affairs on November 8. My statement read: "I am very sad and sorry about the October 25 special election defeat, and the subsequently unstable situation within our party. I am sorry that the Korean people have to worry about it too. After a lot of thought, I would like to let you know that I have decided to resign from the party presidency.

"I decided to resign, first, because I feel painfully responsible for lowering the Korean people's trust in our party and for disappointing my party comrades and supporters through the defeat in the special election. Second, I believe that I, as the highest leader, should take responsibility for the situation that led to the Supreme Council members' intention to resign from party leadership. Third, I would like to devote myself to the effort to cope with the extremely tense international situation and deterioration of the economy since the September 11 terrorist attacks.

"At the same time, I would like to devote my efforts to next year's World Cup and Busan Asian Games, and the successful administration of important national business, like local autonomous elections and the presidential election. I am now going to work as an ordinary member of the party, but, my love and loyalty for our party has not changed a bit."

On December 2, I left to visit the UK, Norway, Hungary, and the European Parliament. I had three goals for this visit to Europe: to jumpstart the halted inter-Korean reconciliation; to attract foreign currency through sales diplomacy; and to publicize World Cup in Europe.

I had a summit meeting at the 10 Downing Street Prime Minister's Office. Prime Minister Tony Blair and I expressed our concerns about terrorism and agreed to urge international society to punish such acts.

Prime Minister Blair pointed out two bumps that had resulted from the War on Terrorism: the breakdown of Middle Eastern Peace negotiations and various conflicts and disputes in many countries in Africa. He said that if religious fundamentalists abused the anti-American and anti-West sentiment in the Middle East and Africa, the world could become very dangerous. His analysis was accurate. Our meeting was too short to fully discuss the terrorist threats to humanity and the state of international affairs.

On December 5, Queen Elizabeth II and her husband the Duke of Edinburgh warmly welcomed my wife and me to Buckingham Palace. She awarded me with the Knight Grand Cross (GCMG). It was the highest medal given to foreign heads of state. The Queen escorted us to the Picture Gallery and explained the art pieces exhibited.

I then visited Cambridge. As we drove from London, I watched in silence the hills rise and fall through the window on the same road I had travelled eight years before. Studying abroad at the age of seventy had been lonely and sad, but now I was traveling the same road with many guard cars.

The house I used to live in remained the same. Although I referred to this period as "studying abroad," it felt more like an exile at the time. I was very sad then, but I was also very encouraged by the environment here. My old neighbors still welcomed me warmly. "Now that I see you again, I am reminded of my life here eight years ago," I said to them. "I will never forget growing plants and feeding a robin here." As if they had read my mind, a representative for the residents gave me a bronze robin as a gift. There was also a plaque with my name on it on the house where I used to live. "Here lived Kim Dae-jung, defender of democracy and human rights, the 15th President of Korea, and the Nobel Peace Prize winner," it read.

I looked at the plaque for a while, then visited my good neighbor Dr. Stephen Hawking. He smiled like a child when he saw me. I thanked him for sending me a congratulatory letter when I won the Nobel Peace Prize. "I haven't forgotten what you wrote in your letter: 'It is easy to raise war, but it takes courage to achieve peace.'"

Through the electronic voice mixer attached to his wheelchair, Dr. Hawking said, "I congratulate you for winning the Nobel Peace Prize. Please continue to make an effort to bring peace to the world."

As I was watching the sentences being slowly written, I suddenly felt as if Dr. Hawking was an alien visiting from a faraway star. His wife told us that she still used the teaspoons I had given them eight years before.

I went to Cambridge University to receive an honorary Doctorate in Law. The Korean national flag was hanging on the campus. Altogether 250 people, including President Alec Broers and thirty-one deans, attended the ceremony. The atmosphere and ceremony were solemn. Everything was carried out in Latin.

On December 6, I arrived in Oslo, Norway, for a two-night, three-day official visit. That afternoon, I attended the Nobel Peace Prize Centennial Symposium, with eighteen former recipients, including Lech Walesa, Desmond Tutu, and the Dalai Lama, as well as fifteen representatives from organizations that had received the prize. I gave the first keynote address, and said: "In the age of knowledge-based economy, the gap in information capabilities among nations has rapidly created a widening gulf between the rich and the poor. If we ignore this phenomenon, the gap between the advanced and developing nations will be further widened. Behind the destructive fundamentalism that is occurring in various places in the world today and the anti-globalization movement, there is people's anger about the gap between the rich and the poor. Moreover, worldwide environmental degradation will be accelerated if the digital gap triggers indiscriminate development by developing nations as a means of survival.

"Whenever there have been international conferences of various kinds, we have encountered violent demonstrations by those who were angered by the gap between the rich and poor and social inequality, which is a side effect of globalization.

"We cannot guarantee world peace in the twenty-first century unless the gap between the rich and poor is resolved. Nuclear weapons or missiles will not be completely effective because the nature of war is changing. The issue is now War Against Terrorism.

"The terrorist attacks on the United States last September have fundamentally changed the concept of war. Terrorism is war without declaration. We do not know when or where it will occur. We do not know what kind of weapons will be used. Terrorism kills civilians indiscriminately. International law and treaties are useless. Private life cannot be maintained.

We cannot travel on airplanes with peace of mind. We cannot go into a building or open our mail without anxiety.

"We must root out such cowardly, cruel and barbaric terrorist acts. But we must solve the root cause of terrorism in the long run while imposing immediate punishment against terrorists. The gap between the rich and poor is the foundation of religious, cultural, racial, and ideological conflicts.

"All of humanity must share the benefits of enhanced information capabilities and globalization. The interests and diversity of all nations and all people must be respected. We must not expect poor nations and poor people to be patient forever. I urge the international community to hold serious and active discussions about these issues."

The world media picked up my opinion that "the gap between the rich and poor is the root of religious, cultural, racial and ideological conflicts" as a headline.

Afterward, I had a summit with Prime Minister of Norway Kjell Magne Bondevik. He and I were old friends. He knew that I was going through a difficult time because of the current political situation in Korea, and he offered me encouraging words. We agreed on a strategic alliance in the fields of information and communication.

On December 7, I flew to Budapest, Hungary, for a three-night, four-day visit. I had summit meetings with President Ferenc Madl and Prime Minister Viktor Orvan. We agreed to seek ways to help our respective businesses jointly participate in the reconstruction of the war-torn Balkan area. We also signed bilateral agreements to cooperate in telecommunications, precision chemical industries, and electronic parts development.

During my visit to the UK, Norway, and Hungary, I focused on sales diplomacy. Lee Ki-ho, my senior secretary for economic affairs, said, "Korea has received orders, drawn foreign investments, and cut joint business ventures totaling $10.4 billion," as a result of my sales diplomacy.

On December 11, I visited the European Parliament in Strasburg, France. It was a peaceful city where only the Parliament building stood out. I became the first Asian leader to address the European Parliament. My address was translated into eleven different European languages and broadcast live. I met EU Commission president Romano Prodi, with whom I had worked to realize a closer Korea-EU partnership by holding summits on an annual basis. Accordingly, Korea became the seventh country to hold annual summits with the EU, following in the footsteps of the US, Canada, Russia, Japan, China, and India.

The Asia Pacific Peace Foundation building, which was to be my work-place after I retired, was built next to my house in Donggyo-dong. It was the location from which the police had always monitored me. How unpredictable life was to build the Asia Pacific Peace Foundation building on that very spot! I heard from my secretaries that it would be an eight-story building (five stories above the ground and three stories underground). Although it was a happy development, I did not feel entirely settled about the fact that they had to borrow some of the construction costs.

The opening ceremony of the West Coast Highway was held on December 21. The time that it would take to travel between Incheon and Mokpo was reduced in half from eight hours to four. I went to Gimje on this highway. If you traveled to Mokpo early in the morning, you could take care of your business, have lunch, and come back before sundown. It would be the artery of the West Coast Era.

The first snow of the year came down during the opening ceremony. As I watched the snow fall, I remembered how I had opposed the construction of the Seoul-Busan Highway as an opposition party member during the Park Chung-hee era. The Park regime began highway construction in February 1968. I argued that we should pave the existing roads before launching the Seoul-Busan Highway construction; that we should build a highway only after carefully researching the quantity of goods transported. Building a highway between Seoul and Busan meant that we would build another road in a section of the country where road conditions were already the best, which would result in unbalanced national land development. Once the highway construction was complete, goods and industrial development would concentrate around the area next to the highway.

The ill-advised construction of this Seoul-Busan Highway turned out to be slipshod. Pretty quickly, the highway became like rags due to frequent repair work. In a speech around that time, I said: "That highway would have collapsed a long time ago if it was standing vertically instead of lying down horizontally." Some people criticized me for my "short-sightedness" at the time, but I still believe my argument was right.

I hoped that the West Coast Highway would stimulate development in the west coast area, which had fallen behind. I had emphasized perfect construction work in the hopes that it would turn out to be a safe and solid industrial artery.

I met with my senior advisors on January 2, 2002. As we were looking at only a year or so left of my term, they talked mostly about my achievements. "A year is not such a short time," I told them. I had to finish up all the things I had begun. The World Cup, the Asian Games in Busan, the local autonomous government election, and the Presidential election were still ahead of us. "It is not important that one is in this position for a long time, but what one does while in the position," I said. "Let us work hard so that we can look back happily at what we did in the Blue House."

That afternoon, I met with major Korean leaders, including the heads of the three governmental branches, for New Year's greetings. At the Blue House New Year's celebration I said that I would focus on governance, leaving politics completely behind. "Although I am a member of the Democratic Party and wish the best for it, I promise you that I will not interfere with party affairs or be involved in the creation of a new party as some rumors say."

On January 3, the first Korean female general was born. I gave Brigadier General Yang Sung-sook a *samjeongdo* sword, the symbol of Korean generals. She looked dignified.

On January 9, I had a signing ceremony for the Special Act on Three Large Rivers (which actually included four rivers: Nakdonggang, Geumgang, Yeongsangang, and Seomjingang) to protect the rivers. We had a difficult time drafting this law due to conflicting interests between residents of the upper and lower reaches of rivers. Through this law, we switched the focus of water management from pollution cleanup to the prevention of pollution. This was unprecedented legislation and a glorious event. I called it "historic." Minister of Environment Kim Myung-ja worked really hard, meeting with residents in person. I heard that she talked with them over *maggeolli* even though she could not drink. Ceremony attendees, including the leaders of environmental groups, praised her hard work.

Toward the end of 2001, there had been many power-related corruption incidents, and their aftereffects continued into the New Year. I can assert that the government itself was never involved in corruption, but I could not control all government officials, some of whom committed personally corrupt acts. In fact, I could not even catch on to the corruption some officials committed as they took advantage of the "venture boom."

Many secretaries in the Blue House left due to their involvement in various incidents. Although I initially trusted them completely, in some cases I ended up being disappointed. During the New Year's press conference on January 14, 2002, I had to begin my remarks with an apology. The media reported that I looked down frequently and repeated the words "sorry" and "regrets" six times altogether. The Blue House received many phone calls from citizens who were worried about my health.

The next day I held a cabinet meeting focusing on anti-corruption. I scolded the Public Prosecutors Office; there were many incidents in which the Public Prosecutors Office did not do their work well, ultimately causing my government trouble.

President George Bush's visit to Korea—which had originally been scheduled for October the previous year, but was postponed due to September 11—was rescheduled for the end of February. I met former Ambassador to Korea Gregg on January 17 and discussed the inter-Korean relationship and the Bush administration's policy toward North Korea. I told him that I had emphasized the necessity of engaging North Korea when I met President Bush in Shanghai. I said to him, "I told President Bush, 'We sometimes have to engage with those whom we do not trust for the sake of our interests and peace. If the other party keeps their promise, then we can accumulate trust bit by bit.'"

Former Ambassador Gregg said that President Bush was only aware of North Korean threats, but was ignoring the country's fear of the US. He said: "North Korea's fear of the United States has deepened since the Afghanistan War. In particular, they are afraid of US air power. President Bush does not understand this well."

He told me to have an informal "Texas-style conversation" with President Bush in order to persuade him. He also advised me to guide President Bush to the DMZ and have him look around the construction site of the railway connection between the South and the North. His advice was quite detailed.

On January 29, I reshuffled the cabinet, changing nine ministerial-level officials. Through this reshuffling, I returned ministers who were also assemblymen to the National Assembly. I also reshuffled the office of the president at the Blue House. This included the appointment of Ms. Park Sun Sook to senior press secretary to the president and presidential spokesperson and Mr. Park Jie-won to special advisor to the president for policy. The media spotlighted Ms. Park Sun Sook, the first female presidential spokesperson. Although gentle, she was a woman of iron will. On February 3, I ordered the abolishment of the public prosecutor dispatch system (the system of dispatching public prosecutors to the Blue House) in order to eliminate disputes about the neutrality of the Public Prosecutors Office.

President George Bush arrived in Korea on February 20. I poured all my energy into preparing for this summit. I wonder if there has been any other instance when the Korean people have been so interested in a Korea-US summit. Since President Bush called North Korea one of the axes of evil (along with Iran and Iraq) in his State of the Union address, tension had mounted between North Korea and the US. Some people in the international circle were even talking about the possibility of a preemptive US attack on North Korea. Naturally, our Sunshine Policy was under threat as well. The distance between the Sunshine Policy and the axis of evil was too far to broach.

We had our summit the morning of February 20. President Bush said, "I know that your government is embarrassed because of my recent tough remarks. I did not mean to cause you problems and I support the Sunshine Policy." He then said that he was not a belligerent person, but argued that we needed to send a clear message to North Korea that we would not tolerate evil actions. I explained the Sunshine Policy again in detail. I argued that only an engagement policy could lead to openness and change in North Korea. I emphasized that North Korea also wanted to normalize its relationship with the US for its survival and economic recovery.

Nonetheless, President Bush did not hesitate to share with me his negative opinions about North Korea. "Chairman Kim Jong-il is an evil dictator who starves his people and tramples on their human rights," he said. "We should send winds of freedom into North Korea and let them collapse. Also, why has Chairman Kim not kept his promise to visit Seoul?"

I used President Bush's aggressive question as an opportunity to persuade him to my point of view. "Although President Reagan called Russia an evil empire, he engaged in dialogue with Secretary Gorbachev and pursued a détente, and, in the end, achieved a change in and the end of the communist system," I replied. "President Nixon condemned China as a war criminal, but he visited China, which resulted in an improved relationship, openness, and reform. Although it is difficult to have dialogue with someone you dislike, sometimes we need to engage with them for the sake of the country when necessary. The United States even had a dialogue with communists during the Korean War.

"If we guarantee the security of North Korea and open a way for their survival, North Korea will definitely give up nuclear weapons and weapons of mass destruction. Please give North Korea a chance. It won't be too late to sanction them if such an effort doesn't work."

I tried with all my might to persuade President Bush. His face brightened after listening to me, and he said that I had provided good analogies while wearing a characteristically innocent expression on his face. I proceeded to list all of the good effects of the Sunshine Policy: the easing of inter-Korean tension, the reunion of dispersed families, and human interchanges. I also pointed out that the Sunshine Policy was an aggressive policy, possible only when our side was stronger. I told him about the Battle of Yeonpyeong as an example of the first punishment for North Korean military provocation since the Korean War.

President Bush repeated phrases like "I see" and "That's a great idea," after almost every sentence I spoke. He then expressed his interest in the matter of dispersed families and the food shortage in North Korea. Our one-on-one summit lasted for an hour and half, forty minutes longer than our originally planned time. As a result, we had to skip the expanded summit. As he left, President Bush looked satisfied and brightly said, "That was a very frank and useful talk."

We held a joint press conference during which we received a question about whether or not the gap between the Sunshine Policy and the axis of evil had narrowed. I spoke first, saying: "In my view, I believe that the US policy and the Korean policy are fundamentally similar; there are no major differences. We both believe in democracy and a market economy. Furthermore, we are allies. Korea and the US are strong allies, and I believe that this is important and vital for the national interests of both our countries. And so that's our top priority."

President Bush also answered: "I will not change my opinion on the man, on Kim Chong-il [sic], until he frees his people and accepts genuine proposals from countries such as South Korea or the United States to dialogue, until he proves to the world that he's got a good heart, that he cares about the people who live in his country ... We're peaceful people. We have no intention of invading North Korea. South Korea has no intention of attacking North Korea, nor does America. We're purely defensive ... And so, obviously, my comments about evil were toward a regime, toward a government, not toward the North Korean people."

President Bush clarified his support of the Sunshine Policy. He also clearly said that the US wanted a peaceful resolution. "That was the purpose of our summit today, to reconfirm that our nation—my nation—is interested in a peaceful resolution ... here on the Korean Peninsula." He also declared that his government would continue to send food to North Korea. I felt rewarded for my sincere effort to persuade him and that this was our diplomatic achievement.

I met President Bush again at the Dorasan Train Station, the northernmost station of the Seoul-Sinuiju Line in South Korea. I arrived in Dorasan

Station via train, while President Bush arrived in a van after visiting a nearby US military base.

President Bush's visit to Dorasan Station was a sort of "peace event." It was customary for a visiting US president to visit the DMZ in order the look around the scene of division and confrontation. However, this time, we wanted to show him the reconnection of disconnected railways and roads. It could be a good opportunity to reassure the Korean people and North Korea. I also hoped that President Bush would send a message of peace rather than confrontation while he was at the scene of reconciliation.

The railway was disconnected at Jangdan-myeon, Paju-si, Gyeonggi-do. The milepost there read "Seoul 56 kilometers—Pyongyang 205 kilometers." We took a commemorative photograph in front of it, and President Bush wrote on a crosstie: "May this railroad unite Korean families!"

At the construction site of the Seoul-Sinuiju Railway, the past, present, and future of the Korean Peninsula melted into one. The past was the war, the present was division, and the future was reunification. I made a speech with the milepost behind me. "Right now, we are witnessing the last remnant of the Cold War," I spoke. "The stalled train engine as well as the cut and badly rusted rails symbolize the half-century of division of Korea into South and North. The sorrow of the Korean people permeates the air in this spot ... There is a bright side to the Dorasan Station, however. If this railway is extended northward by only fourteen kilometers, the two Koreas will be reconnected by a land route ... With the deep interest and cooperation of President Bush, the Korean nation expects to realize its wishes in the near future."

President Bush also made a remark. "[As] I stated before the American Congress just a few weeks ago, we must not permit the world's most dangerous regimes to threaten us with the world's most dangerous weapons.

"I speak for these convictions even as we hope for dialogue with the North. America provides humanitarian food assistance to the people of North Korea, despite our concerns about the regime. We're prepared to talk with the North about steps that would lead to a better future, a future that is more hopeful and less threatening. But like this road left unbuilt, our offer has gone unanswered ... People on both sides of this border want to live in freedom and want to live in dignity, without the threat of violence and famine and war. I hope that one day soon this hope will be realized."

The visit to Dorasan Station was successful. President Bush stared at the land in the north for a while, and then at the railway stretching toward the North. The railway itself was the best persuasion for an engagement policy with the North.

That evening, we held a dinner reception for President Bush and First Lady Laura. It was an informal dinner as the US had requested. From the US side, Secretary of State Colin Powell, National Security Advisor Condoleezza Rice, Ambassador and Mrs. Thomas Hubbard, and Senior Director at the National Security Council James F. Moriarty attended. From our side, attendees included Minister of Foreign Affairs and Trade Choi Sung-hong, Special Advisor Lim Dong-won, Ambassador and Mrs. Yang Sung-chul, and Senior Secretary to the President for Foreign Policy and National Security Yim Sung Joon.

President Bush mentioned his visit to Dorasan Station a few times, perhaps because he was still moved by it. During dinner, he poked at my side and said with an impish smile, "I used what you told me about President Reagan during the press conference this afternoon."

President Bush understood the truth about the Sunshine Policy and my sincerity on the matter. Finally, he began to hear me. During my visit to Washington, DC, in 2001, he might have ignored Korea and me, considering Korea a marginal country and me a country bumpkin, but his attitude had changed remarkably. I heard that he said about me, "I re-discovered President Kim. I admire him."

When I asked what religion he was, President Bush replied that he was a Methodist. He then talked frankly about his past, saying that he had been an alcoholic and his wife had led him to church; now he was a devout Christian. President Bush did not touch alcohol at all—he drank non-alcoholic beer that his staff had brought with them. He asked me about my religion in turn. I told him that I was a Catholic and my wife was a Methodist. President Bush said that he was happy he and my wife belonged to the same denomination. I discussed the role of Methodists since the Industrial Revolution in England, saying: "England won the Napoleon War in 1815, but the domestic situation in England was at its worst. Farmers who had lost their land after the Industrial Revolution came to cities and became paupers. Workers were upset about poor working conditions. England was on the verge of rebellion. There were three elements that rescued England from this crisis and enabled the brilliant Victorian era of the nineteenth century: media, the court, and Methodism.

"The media reflected and supported the just demands of the bourgeois and working classes. This made it possible for citizens to have outlets for their thoughts without using violence. The court maintained fairness in their trials, serving as the last resort for people suffering from unfairness. Methodism offered people spiritual comfort and security. At that time, the Anglican Church became like a private religion for royal families and aristocrats, and neglected the ordinary people's suffering. It was John Wesley who founded Methodism and embraced those who were neglected by the Anglican Church. By comforting and protecting those who were abandoned and thus dissatisfied and angry, Methodism led them to hope. Methodism contributed greatly to saving English society. That is why your belief is great."

After this, President Bush's eyes grew brighter and he was very friendly to me. I tried my best for the remainder of his stay in Korea.

Nevertheless, North Korea did not budge. At the time, I was upset and sometimes really angry at North Korea. But, then again, I also felt very sorry for them. The entire situation was disappointing.

Spring Days in Physical Pain (March–June 2002)

On March 21, 2002, Japanese Prime Minister Koizumi Junichiro visited Korea. We had to restore our relationship, especially in relation to the joint World Cup events. We held a summit.

Prime Minister Koizumi visited the National Gugak Center, where he tried the Korean traditional twelve-string instrument *gayageum* and received the gift of a *danso* (short bamboo flute). He ate traditional Korean food and bought CDs, including one with the theme song from the popular Korean TV drama, *Winter Sonata*, and by singers like Jo Young-pil and Kye Eun-suk. Widely popular in Japan, *Winter Sonata* was the origin of the Korean Wave in Prime Minister Koizumi's country. The prime minister noticed that Korean and Japanese traditional instruments were similar and said that was probably because Japanese musical instruments originated in Korea. We also visited the Seoul World Cup Stadium in Sangam-dong, Seoul. We autographed several footballs and the official uniforms of our respective national players, then exchanged them with each other.

Around that time, as I gave an appointment certificate to the newly appointed president of the Bank of Korea Park Seung, I said to him, "You should be free from interference from government and public opinion.

You should work according to your beliefs without being at the beck and call of public opinion."

President of Indonesia Megawati Sukarnoputri visited Seoul after finishing her visit to North Korea. She left Pyongyang on the morning of March 30 and arrived in Seoul via the direct West Coast route. She had urged Chairman Kim Jong-il to resume an inter-Korean dialogue and to speak with the US immediately, per my request. During our summit, President Megawati Sukarnoputri told me that Chairman Kim wanted to see me and hoped to resume the inter-Korean dialogue.

The North sent a message that they would accept my special envoy. I hoped that my successful summit with President Bush would create new momentum for the inter-Korean relationship. I appointed Special Advisor Lim Dong-won as special envoy and discussed the matter for hours with him. I dictated my oral message for Chairman Kim to him. "First," I said, "please tell him to improve North Korea's relationship with the United States. He should acknowledge that the world has changed. Even powerful countries like China and Russia are cooperating with the United States for their countries' interests. That is the reality. He should also acknowledge the fact that the Bush administration is completely different from the Clinton administration. He should not try to get everything that the Clinton administration agreed to give. Also, President Bush said that they would engage in dialogue with North Korea rather than war. I confirmed it. Please tell him how hard and anxiously I worked to get that promise for him. Chairman Kim should not miss this chance to improve North Korea's relationship with the United States for the interest of his country. He should make a give-and-take package deal. It's time to make a decision.

"Second, I spoke with Prime Minister Koizumi about improving Japan's relationship with North Korea, and he is willing to do so. But the stumbling block is the kidnapped Japanese. However, this is a past incident. In my opinion, if Chairman Kim approaches this matter with a broad view, he can solve it. I don't think it is desirable for past problems to become a chain for the present and the future. Also, it is essential that North Korea receive compensation from Japan for their colonial rule. There is a strong possibility that Japanese economic aid could generate more international support. The current North Korean situation is like starving when there is a lot of food in the warehouse. Now is not the time for ideology, but for practical benefit. You should solve this problem when there is a popular prime minister like Koizumi at the helm. Please make sure to let him know that now is the best time.

"Third, regarding the inter-Korean relationship, please tell him that we should end the era of adverse winds and open the era of a fair wind. Only then will there be a fair wind in North Korea's relationship with the United States and Japan. It is now impossible to reunite our country through war. Peaceful reunification is the only way to live. We will help North Korea. North Korea should keep all agreements, no matter what. If North Korea does not keep its promises, even the South Korean government suffers from opposition. The inter-Korean relationship wasted an entire year last year. If Chairman Kim had visited South Korea as promised, the United States could not have called North Korea an axis of evil. Also, I would like North Korea to send people to the World Cup—whether that means performing troupes, tourists, or President Kim Yong-Nam. Only when we establish a strong foundation in the inter-Korean relationship this year can everything be continued in the next government."

On April 3, special envoy Lim Dong-won went to the North. He landed at the Sunan Airport on the presidential plane. His group included several essentially relevant government officials. Special Envoy Lim carried my signed letter.

I waited anxiously for their return. Special Envoy Lim did not return on the scheduled day, although he did let me know that he had met with Chairman Kim. Every time Mr. Lim had made me wait in the past, he had brought me good news. I felt good about the results this time as well. The morning after he was originally scheduled to return, Mr. Lim came across Panmunjeom. We were in the midst of a severe drought at the time, but it rained that morning. His bundle was thick and his report made me feel good. It was like a rain had also fallen upon the inter-Korean relationship after a period of drought. However, Chairman Kim still did not confirm his return visit to Seoul, which made me sad.

Special Envoy Lim said: "Chairman Kim wanted to visit Seoul last year. He said that he actually wanted to see you again as soon as possible. But the situation has changed with the Bush administration, which has antagonized North Korea. He also felt uncomfortable about Southern conservatives' demonstration against his visit. He said that his advisors dissuaded him from visiting Seoul. Chairman Kim was sincerely wishing for the normalization of the North Korean relationship with United States, although he fears and distrusts them."

Chairman Kim proposed through Mr. Lim that we met in Irkutsk, Russia, saying that we could have a three-way summit with President Putin if necessary. I rejected this plan. His promise should be kept. Even if it wasn't in Seoul, Chairman Kim should meet me in South Korea.

Special Envoy Lim explained the results of his visit to the North at a press conference. He announced the following in a joint press statement.

> South and North Korea agreed to the following major points: first, mutual respect and restoration of the frozen inter-Korean relationship; second, new railways and roads along the east coast and reconnection of the Sinuiju-Seoul Railways and the Kaesong-Munsan road on the west coast; third, the second meeting of the South-North Committee for the Promotion of Economic Cooperation in in Seoul from May 7 to 10; fourth, construction of the Kaesong industrial complex, and Imjin River flood damage control project; fifth, the second round of the Mt. Kumgang tour talks at Mt. Kumgang on June 11; sixth, the fourth round of the separated family reunions at Mt. Kumgang on April 28; seventh, North Korean economic study group's visit to South Korea in May; eighth, the seventh round of the inter-Korean ministerial talks in the future; and ninth, the resumption of the inter-Korean military talks.

On May 11, Assemblywoman Park Geun-hye visited North Korea and met with Chairman Kim Jong-il as the director of the Europe-Korea Foundation. I hoped that many people would visit North Korea. I heard about Assemblywoman Park's thoughts after this visit from Minister of Unification Jeong Se Hyun. She said: "I am conservative. But there cannot be a difference between conservatives and progressives in solving inter-Korean problems. Reconciliation and cooperation are the only ways. The inter-Korean policy should continue in the current direction."

Moody's Investors Service upgraded Korea's sovereign debt rating two notches, from Baa2 to A3. It listed five reasons for this upgrade: stable economic growth, a healthy level of foreign debts and a sufficient foreign currency reserve, the capability to absorb outside shock based on a diversified economic structure, the maintenance of financial health despite the influx of a 150 trillion won public fund, and the achievement of financial and corporational restructuring. We recovered from "unfit" to an A rating in just four years, the shortest time in history. Korea was the only A-rated country among all of the Asian and South American countries that had undergone a foreign currency crisis. The Fitch Group also upgraded our sovereign credit rating two notches to A. Many countries in the world were surprised and congratulated us. As a point of reference, it took Israel, which underwent a foreign currency crisis in 1983, twelve years to recover an A rating.

There was a reception to celebrate our A-level sovereign debt rating in early April. American Chamber of Commerce Head Jeffrey Jones's congratulatory remarks made me happy. He said: "For the past four years, Korean people, corporations, and, especially, government officials have worked tirelessly because of the difficult financial crisis. I am so surprised to have this opportunity to congratulate you so soon. You have made Korea a truly transparent and honest country. People can trust you because all government policies and guidelines are very clear."

I also made congratulatory remarks. "We have many happy things these days. Of course, the happiest event is the recovery of our sovereign credit rating to A. Also, we had a very welcome rain the day before yesterday. In addition, Mr. Kim Dong-sung swept six gold medals in all six men's events of the World Short Track Speed Skating Championships in Montreal, Canada. Our beloved Miss Park Se-ri won the LPGA. Furthermore, Special Envoy Lim Dong-won brought back good results from North Korea. It looks like this will be a happy year. I hope that only happy events happen during this last year of my term and that I can finish my term successfully."

Although there were happy events in Korea, my body was in pain. I had pulled the muscle inside of my left thigh while getting up one morning. Although my doctor said that nothing was wrong with my bones, I experienced severe pain and felt weak. On the morning of April 9, I did not feel well. Although my wife woke me up, I was very sleepy and felt like lying down. In the past three days I hadn't been able to eat well, either—I did not have any appetite. My leg felt heavy and I felt weak, but I still had to get up. There was a summit scheduled with Finnish president Tarja Halonen and I had to drag my heavy body to the room. Fortunately, I was able to finish the summit successfully. I also attended and made congratulatory remarks at the Grand Buddhist Service, where we prayed for success in the World Cup games. I felt unusually exhausted.

That afternoon, my body felt even heavier. My secretaries called the medical team. My physician Huh Kap-bum, the medical treatment room chief Chang Seog-il, and Yonsei University Professors Jung Nam-Sik and Kim Sung-soon rushed to assist me. The medical team found an arrhythmia and advised that I be hospitalized right away so that I could prevent the condition from worsening. However, there was a dinner reception scheduled with Finnish president Halonen that evening. After finishing the dinner an hour earlier than planned, I was hospitalized at the Armed Forces Capital Hospital. After treatment, the arrhythmia was immediately cured, but the doctors recommended that I rest, saying that I was suffering from accumulated exhaustion, gastroenteric trouble, and malnutrition. My wife stayed in the hospital room with me, where I remained for six days.

Vice Prime Minister of Finance and Economy Chin Nyum resigned in order to run for the governor of Gyeonggi-do. On April 15, I appointed Mr. Jeon Yun Churl to his post, Mr. Park Jie-won to chief of staff, and Mr. Lee Ki-ho to special advisor for economy, welfare, and labor.

The public primary for the Democratic Party presidential candidate nomination was interesting. The Korean people participated in the nationwide primary every weekend according to their region. Regardless of the result, the public primary system that the Korean people participated in and celebrated was a people's festival. It was clear that it would make various official elections dynamic in the future. It also offered a precious opportunity to liquidate closed-door and top-down politics. During the appointment certificate awarding ceremony, I praised the system highly. I said, "Politics began to change. The election for the nomination of presidential candidate is going on amidst the people's excitement and interest. I believe that our politics have made a leap. It is very fortunate."

Standing Advisor Roh Moo-hyun was elected as the Democratic Party presidential candidate. Candidate Roh raised a storm in Gwangju and had swept the rest of the country since then. He traveled north like a typhoon, fiercely capturing people's minds and hearts. His ratings surpassed 50 percent in various polls. Some candidates spread rumors about a secret deal between him and myself, which raised suspicion. This was not true—I was not involved in the candidate nomination process at all.

On April 29, I met with Candidate Roh. "When I resigned as president of the Democratic Party," I told him, "I promised not to be involved in politics. The Korean people have supported my decision. I am planning to focus on wrapping up my governance tasks."

"I regret that the Government of the People is not fully appreciated," Mr. Roh said. "I have openly appreciated it and I feel proud of the fact that I won a nomination while openly stating what I believed."

I decided to leave the Democratic Party in order to maintain neutrality in the election and focus entirely on governance. I issued a statement to that effect through Chief of Staff Park Jie-won.

Spring 2002 was cruel to me. My sons were publicly condemned for their alleged involvement in corruption incidents. Also, the Asia Pacific Peace Foundation that I had founded was subject to a media trial. Every day media coverage treated this foundation, established for peace, as if it were a hotbed of corruption. An executive officer was arrested. In addition, the media ran daily coverage of an alleged corruption incident involving my second son, Hong Up, and youngest son, Hong Gul. Still, I believed they were innocent, even as allegations about my son Hong Gul, who was living in the US, mounted. I was afraid of reading the newspaper in the morning. My son Hong Gul who I knew was such a good person! I could not believe the report. I sent Chief of the Office of the President Kim Hanjung to the US to speak with my son directly. Chief Kim returned and stuttered as he reported back, "Mr. Hong Gul did not ask a favor directly, but it seems that he has been taken advantage of."

I was greatly disappointed. I ordered Chief Kim, "Please tell him to respond to the investigation truthfully. Tell him he should be punished if he committed a crime." I also ordered Chief Kim to tell Hong Gul to return home immediately. Although I could not express it, I felt the earth collapsing under my feet. I felt as if I were falling from a precipice many times a day.

My wife prayed day and night. I saw her vomit, as she occasionally did when she was shocked. My healthy wife, who did not usually so much as catch a cold, collapsed too. Hong Gul returned home on May 16 and was arrested two days later.

I wanted to be alone. Although flowers bloomed and green leaves sprouted, only silence gathered in the garden of the Blue House. My wife was anxious not only about our son, but about me, which made me even sadder. We sometimes sat together in silence for hours. After Hong Gul was arrested, the media aimed at Hong Up. For more than a month, his name was mentioned and, in the end, he was arrested on June 21. What father has ever sent two sons to prison at the same time? I was very embarrassed to see the Korean people. I had promised the Korean people they shouldn't worry about my children many times, but I could not keep my promise. I decided to leave them to the law and focus on government affairs. That afternoon, I issued a statement of apology to the Korean people. "Over the past few months, I have felt thoroughly responsible for not taking proper care of my sons. I have lived in shame and apologize for hurting the hearts of the people who supported me. Although I have experienced many difficulties in my life, I never dreamt of such a miserable incident. Again, I express my sincerest apology."

I would not allow Hong Up and Hong Gul to come to the Blue House after that. Hong Up visited me at my private home in Donggyo-dong after my retirement. I scolded him and asked, "How could you be so greedy?"

Hong Up cried as he answered, "I am sorry, Father, but I was accused unjustly."

I later found out that he was, indeed, unjustly accused. As a father, I would like to defend my two sons. Under the firm belief that the regime would change, the Public Prosecutors Office intentionally aimed a sharp knife at the lame duck. The aim was my two sons. They investigated 580 people close to Hong Up. Among them, they targeted Hong Up's old friend and tried to dig up dirt. After searching and seizing his company office and documents, they forced a false confession from him by threatening to expose his private affairs. Unable to resist this threat, he acknowledged the allegation as the prosecutor demanded. Suffering from guilt, that friend apologized to my son after my son was released. Two days before his death in February 2008, he left a recorded will, where he stated, "All of my statements at the Public Prosecutors Office were false."

My youngest son, Hong Gul, trusted people too easily. As he had studied abroad for a long time, he did not understand domestic politics and opened his heart to a businessman who approached him. Knowing Hong Gul was naive, I always told him to be careful, that he was too trusting. I regret that I could not do better.

In May, my medical team dissuaded me from taking a long-distance trip so I could not attend the UN Special Session on Children as planned. Instead, my wife attended on my behalf. She presided over the meeting as acting president. She was the first woman to the meeting and to declare the opening of the meeting. She also gave the keynote address for the UN Special Session on Children at the UN headquarters. She received the first Vanderbilt University Award for Moral Leadership in appreciation of her "gifted leadership in advancing the cause of individual human rights" and "unfaltering dedication to the disadvantaged around the globe."

On June 13, we held an election for local autonomous governments. The Grand National Party won eleven out of sixteen mayoral and gubernatorial seats. The Democratic Party won four posts in the Honam and Jeju areas, and the LDA won one post in Chungcheongnam-do. The GNP swept the election in Seoul. Although I did not belong to any party, I was worried about the results of this election. It appeared that the theory that Lee Hoi-chang should be the party presidential nominee according to the grand trend would prevail in the Grand National Party (GNP), while there might be internal strife within the Democratic Party because of the election defeat.

During my term, people very positively evaluated my government's overall economic policy. However, I did feel sorry for two things that happened under my government's watch: creating a bad credit standing for many people due to poor supervision of credit card over-issuing and an intensified wealth gap due to a wider divide between the haves and the have-nots. Also, although I made a concerted effort to promote SMEs by going so far as to create the Presidential Commission on Small and Medium Businesses, my government did not succeed in this effort.

There were two reasons why our government encouraged credit cards. First, we wanted to reactivate our economy, which went into a recession as a result of the foreign currency crisis. Second, we wanted to prevent tax evasion by making all transactions transparent. When the cold wind of the foreign currency crisis swept through businesses, their production activities shrunk significantly. Even pouring money into the economy did not revive them. The problem was consumption.

In an economic measures meeting in September 1998, we decided to promote domestic consumption. Many plans were proposed, one of which was encouraging credit card use. Accordingly, the National Tax Service drafted policies to expand credit card use. Businesses were required to always get credit card receipts and to report on them when they carried out transactions with independent businessmen. Establishments with cash income, such as hospitals, clinics, restaurants, hotels, and other service industries, were required to accept credit cards. I also proposed a lottery of credit card receipts to encourage consumer credit card use. In addition, some tax deductions were given for the use of credit cards. As a result, credit card usage increased greatly.

As usage increased, it was natural that the number of people with a poor credit standing increased. By February 2003, toward the end of my term, 2.8 million people had a bad credit standing. About half of these bad ratings were due to people's inability to pay their credit card balance. In the end, it was my government's credit card usage expansion policy that brought about this result. Credit card companies issued cards without asking and credit card users used them without thinking about their income. Although financial institutions and card users held the primary responsibility, the government was ultimately responsible for the lack of control and supervision. I feel I should acknowledge this responsibility. Although the use of credit cards contributed to our society's road to becoming a transparent society, we had to pay too high a cost on our way to becoming a trust-based society.

Often, things we use for convenience become a cause of disaster. Everyone who uses credit cards can end up being caught in the spider web of debt, which is hung everywhere in our society. My government's credit card policy appeared to be an example of this. It represented hope for economic recovery in the beginning, but became the root of concern.

Also, although my government tried to solve the problem of unemployment—so much so that some called it the "unemployment cabinet"—we could not stop the collapse of the middle class. The middle class in Korea was mostly composed of white-collar workers and independent businessmen. Layoffs and business abolishment meant that they collapsed into the poorest class. Because the social safety net did not solidly support them, we had a hard time controlling it. Although we tried to create many measures for the unemployed, they merely helped them to survive, rather than giving them their lost work back.

The collapse of the middle class brought about the polarization of income. It was extremely hard for those who entered the poor class to get back to the middle class. High interest rates made the wealthy wealthier and the poor poorer. Some called it the 20 versus 80 society.

In fact, this structure was probably an inevitable trend worldwide, originating from globalization. However, I felt very sad that this polarization of income happened during my term. Some people even said that the wealthy were enjoying the IMF system. The relative sense of being deprived that the middle and lower classes felt must have become more intense when they observed the consumption behavior of the upper 20 percent of people. I knew it and I tried hard to rectify the problem, but I could find no better way.

RED DEVILS AND CANDLELIGHT (JUNE–OCTOBER 2002)

"Today, we begin the first FIFA World Cup of the twenty-first century, which is being cohosted by Korea and Japan." I made this declaration at the opening of the 2002 FIFA World Cup. On May 31, 60,000 people filled the Seoul World Cup Stadium in Sangam-dong. Japanese prime minister Koizumi Junichiro, Polish president Aleksander Kwasniewski, East Timorese president Xanana Gusmao, Palauan president Tommy Remengesau, and prime minister of the Dominican Republic Pierre Charles participated in this ceremony as well. I greeted the cheering audience holding hands with FIFA president Sepp Blatter and Prime Minister Koizumi. I sincerely wished that this would be a festival of peace in which humanity became united beyond differences in race, ideology, and religion.

We combined our traditional culture and cutting-edge IT for the opening ceremony. We delivered the message of peace through our unique grace and refinement. I urged the preparation team to turn the World Cup into an IT World Cup and to thus spread the image of Korea as an IT powerhouse to the entire world. During the World Cup, we were the first in the world to operate a full HD TV broadcasting system.

We created symbols of peace with a laser video, a piece of art created by cutting-edge technology. The light poured out of the work of the master of video art, Paik Nam-june, and was united with the sound of a Silla bell from a Buddhist temple. It was a fitting show for this global festival.

I watched the entire opening match between France and Senegal. Senegal, a first-time World Cup team, won 1:0 against France, the winner of the last World Cup. It was the prelude to the extraordinary twists and turns that would happen in the course of the games.

The night of June 4, there was a match between Korea and Poland in Busan. I had a summit with Polish president Aleksander Kwasniewski at the Lotte Hotel before the match. The meeting ended with us rooting for our respective teams.

"I am worried that you rooting for your team will encourage the Polish players too much," I joked.

"Regardless of today's results, both teams will have more opportunities to advance to the next round," he responded.

"I think you mean the Polish team intends to yield this game to Korea."

"We will never yield," he replied.

When we entered the stadium together, 50,000 people gave us a standing ovation. Asiad Main Stadium in Busan was a sea of red waves. I wore a red tie, red muffler, and red hat. Our supporters all became "red devils."

Mr. Hwang Sun-hong scored a goal in the first half. I took off my red hat and waved it around. In the second half, Mr. Yoo Sang-chul scored a goal. Unconsciously, I stood up and waved my hat around again. I forgot that President Aleksander Kwasniewski was sitting next to me.

That night the Korean soccer team won its first World Cup game ever, with a score of 2:0. It was a moving moment. President Aleksander Kwasniewski raised my hand high in congratulations. It was a beautiful and ecstatic night. I visited the locker room and shook hands with Coach Hiddink and all the players. "I thank and congratulate you on behalf of the Korean people who won't be able to fall asleep tonight. We now feel confident that our team will make the final sixteen."

I hugged Coach Hiddink, who had confidently declared that he would surprise the world prior to the beginning of the World Cup. He did not seem like a foreigner, but a neighbor who had been around us for a long time.

When I left the stadium, the citizens of Busan recognized me and cheered. Hundreds of thousands of people were rooting for our team on the streets of Seoul and in major cities throughout the provinces. Everyone was wearing red. This was the beginning of the "red legend."

The preliminary match between Korea and the US was held in Daegu on June 10. I decided not to attend this match. Korean sentiment toward the US was very negative then due to various incidents, including President Bush's rude handling of the Korean Peninsula issue. Some were worried that the two sides of the audience would collide during the game.

I watched the game on TV with the Blue House staff. This time too, I wore a red T-shirt. We yielded a goal during the first half, but a goal did not happen for us in the second half for a while despite our predominance. Then, Mr. Ahn Jung-hwan scored! The game ended in a 1:1 draw.

The match between Korea and Portugal occurred in the Incheon Munhak Stadium. We beat Portugal 1:0. Mr. Park Ji-sung scored a great goal. The Korean team made it to the second round with two wins and one draw, thus moving Asian soccer from the margins of the game to center stage. It was a signal that announced that soccer was no longer owned only by Europe and South America. I visited the locker room again after the match and said, "Right now, 40 million, no, 70 million Koreans, are cheering. I sincerely thank you as a Korean myself."

Despite all of this victory and achievement, I was sad about my children's situations throughout the entire World Cup. Frankly, I was ashamed to stand in front of the Korean people, and constantly wondered what they thought about me.

I watched the second round match with Italy with cabinet members in the Blue House. People advised me that it would not be fair for me to watch it in person while my Italian counterpart was not in attendance.

When it was a 1:1 draw, Mr. Ahn Jung-hwan scored the winning golden goal during overtime. All the cabinet members and I cried, "Long Live Korea!"

The quarterfinal occurred in Gwangju on June 22. It was a bloody fight against Spain that went into extended time. I was worried about the players' physical condition. The game ended without either side scoring a goal. A penalty kick would decide the semifinal. The fourth Spanish kicker made a mistake. Mr. Hong Myung-bo aimed at the goal and Korea, no, the *world* held its breath. The net shook. It was a very accurate corner goal. Everyone in the VIP seats stood up and shouted: "Korea!" Korea became the first Asian country to advance to the semifinal. I could not help crying. "Today is the happiest day in our country since the days of our founding father, Dangun," I said. "We have opened the road to national prosperity."

Another victory during the World Cup was the audiences who rooted for our team. The world was particularly surprised by the crowds on the streets that rooted for our team. Our red devils planted into the hearts of the Korean people the message that dreams can come true. Altogether, 23 million people took to the streets to cheer for our team. During our game against Spain, 5 million people gathered on the streets and cheered for our team. The foreign media reported not only about the great achievements of the Korean team, but also about the audiences cheering on the streets. The street cheering scenes were the opposite of what foreigners were used to seeing on European streets, where hooligan demonstrations, drunken scuffles, and group fights were quite common.

The red devils of our nation were good devils who drove away evil spirits. The passion was explosive, but there was no hatred in it. No violent incidents happened. The crowds were just festive. They took care of their trash and shouted "Safety!" whenever well-being seemed endangered. After they left, the street was clean and there were no accidents, despite hundreds of thousands of people in the crowds. I was truly proud of our young people. No, I was awestruck. I felt that with these young people, we didn't have to worry about the future of our country. This street cheering inspired the next World Cup in Germany. It called all youths in the world to the public square.

Foreign media praised it too. The Canadian newspaper, the *Toronto Sun*, wrote:

> A foreigner could sit alone without any worries among the crowds of red devils. Such a frictionless peaceful atmosphere is not so easily found in any other country. Of course, Korea had worked as hard as any other country in world to win these moments of victory, which therefore they well deserved.

What's more amazing is that Koreans want to share the moments of their victory with others.

The Japanese newspaper *Nikkei* wrote:

The subtle difference in generational perception of the symbolic cheering color "red" was completely engulfed in the heat of the World Cup. In Korea, red was the symbol of communism for a long time.

I think that somebody should do research on the phenomenon of concentrated pure and explosive energy in the future.

I don't know how accurate this estimation was, but some people said that 70 percent of the people cheering on the streets were women. It was an unprecedented phenomenon. Although I had said that the twenty-first century was the age of women, I did not know it would arrive so soon.

Korea lost 1:0 to Germany, and 3:2 to Turkey in the match that decided third place. But, this time also, Koreans showed encouragement and consideration rather than disappointment from the defeat. Since its participation in the Korean War, Koreans had considered Turkey a brother country. The world praised Korea's attitude. I was proud to be the president of this country.

After the World Cup was over, Spanish Prime Minister Jose Maria Aznar said to me at the ASEM summit in Copenhagen, Denmark, "Didn't Korea advance to the semi-final thanks to the home field advantage?"

Although I could just smile about it, I did not want to hurt the Korean people's pride. I ordered the senior secretary of foreign affairs to deliver the following formal message: "Korea did not defeat only Spain in the World Cup. We defeated Poland, Portugal, and Italy as well. Do you think all of those victories were due to home field advantage? Also, there seems to be some sort of misunderstanding that Koreans chose the referees, but FIFA did."

I learned a lot from Coach Hiddink. In the beginning he faced a lot of criticism because the results of the exhibition games did not seem auspicious. But he never compromised his beliefs. He was free from cliques based on schools, regions, or other relations. He evaluated players based only on their capabilities. We could not have done such a thing in the past. Coach Hiddink armed our players with steely physical and mental capabilities. He eliminated their fear of European players. He was a true hero who showed how much a good leader can do. I awarded him with a medal and honorary Korean citizenship at the Grand Festival in celebration of the World Cup success.

My government gave the benefit of exemption from military service to national team players based on the soccer world's recommendation. Our team players signed the official match ball of the 2002 FIFA World Cup and gave it to me. I pictured the faces of all the players as I looked at each signature.

I had had three concerns about the FIFA World Cup: first, security, including terror; second, whether the Korean team would make it to the second round; and, third, whether we could run this historic joint game with Japan smoothly despite differences in history, culture, and technology. However, my concerns proved unwarranted. We ran the best World Cup games in history.

Another battle broke out in the Western Sea—near the Yeonpyeongdo Island on the morning of June 29, the day before the World Cup closing ceremony. When two North Korean patrol boats crossed the border, our patrol boats approached to stop them. The North Korean boats tried to attack, and, although South Korean soldiers tried their best to counterattack, they were helpless because of the suddenness of the situation. Six of our navy soldiers died; I heard later through a report that they bravely fought until the moment of their death.

This battle exposed many problems. There were no guard ships to protect the patrol boats within rifle range. Although warships should have supported the patrol boats during their operation, this was not the case. It was a serious breach.

The media later called it the Second Battle of Yeonpyeong. I could not understand why North Korea provoked us while the entire Korean Peninsula was in a celebratory World Cup festival mood. The prevalent analysis was that it was an attack based on North Korea's plan to avenge itself after the first battle. However, we could not be sure whether or not North Korean leadership was involved in it. I immediately summoned the National Security Council. I began by expressing my sincerest condolences to the sacrificed soldiers' families and ordered our government to do everything possible for them. Then I issued a strong condemnation of North Korea and ordered a cool response by establishing measures to prevent expansion or a recurrence of the battle.

The minister of national defense then issued a statement, saying: "Our government stringently protests this armed provocation that cannot be ignored. We strongly urge an apology, the punishment of responsible parties, and prevention of a recurrence from North Korea."

North Korea quickly responded. Early the next morning, they sent an urgent notice through the hotline that was established following the inter-Korean summit. "We confirmed that this incident happened not according to a plan or intentionally, but as an accident between inferiors. We regret that this happened and let us make an effort to ensure this kind of accident does not recur."

The North Korean message meant that they did not want the situation to worsen. However, we could not publicize their message of apology at that time. We therefore demanded a public apology, punishment of responsible parties, and a guarantee that such an event would not occur again. About four weeks later, on July 25, North Korea sent an electronic notice expressing regret to the minister of unification. This was the first letter of regret that the South Korean government had ever received from North Korea. Prior to this, I went to Yokohama, Japan, to attend the closing ceremony of the World Cup. I sent Park Jie-won, the Blue House chief of staff, to visit and console the families of the sailors who were killed or injured.

With this incident as their excuse, some media outlets and the opposition party continued to attack the Sunshine Policy, arguing that it was the cause of our defeat in the battle.

Although the opposition party presidential candidate urged us to put a stop to the Mt. Kumgang tour, the Korean people did not budge. That was the power of the Sunshine Policy. That night when the match against Turkey was held to determine the third-place team, millions of people poured out into the streets. Tourists continued to visit Mt. Kumgang, and North Korean light water reactor safety guards came to study and train at Daedeok Science Town in the South.

After my summit with Prime Minister Koizumi at his official residence, I stated that I would continue to pursue the Sunshine Policy. Prime Minister Koizumi also reaffirmed his full support of my engagement policy with North Korea. Once again, we let it be known both domestically and internationally that the Sunshine Policy was possible only when we had power.

On July 2, I returned home and immediately visited the Armed Forces Capital Hospital to comfort soldiers who had been wounded during the Western Sea Battle. A family member burst into tears, saying: "Please help him!" I comforted her and said, "Please do not lose hope." That night I attended the Grand National Festival to celebrate the World Cup's success. I embraced the pain of my divided country during the day and watched dynamic Korea at night.

While our attention was entirely on the World Cup games, a US Army armored vehicle struck and killed two fourteen-year-old middle school-girls, Shin Hyo-sun and Shim Mi-son. The vehicles were returning to their base in Uijeongbu on a public road after completing training maneuvers in the countryside. At the time they were struck, the girls were on their way to their friend's house for a birthday party. The American soldiers involved were quickly found not guilty of negligent homicide by the court martial. After the trial, about one hundred people gathered in Jongno, Seoul, for a candlelight vigil protest.

Once this news spread across the Internet, citizens gathered for candle-light vigils every night. They demanded punishment of the American sol-diers who murdered the girls and the revision of the SOFA (Status of Forces Agreement). By December 14, more than 50,000 citizens had gathered around the US Embassy in Seoul.

At the cabinet meeting I gave orders to discuss the SOFA revision at the annual Korea–US Security Consultative Meeting. I also made a state-ment cautioning people against developing the candlelight vigil into an anti-American demonstration. "I offer my deepest condolences and mourning to families," I said. "I know that the Korean people are all deeply shocked. I feel the same way. However, we can direct sound criti-cism to United States policies, but an unconditional anti-American senti-ment is not helpful to our national interests."

Unfortunately, we could not reach an agreement on the Korea-US Security Consultative Meeting that would put out the candles in the streets. Meanwhile, US Chairman of the House Committee on International Relations Henry Hyde abruptly canceled his visit to Korea. Deputy Secretary of State Richard Armitage immediately came to Seoul to visit me. He told me that President Bush asked him to send his sincerest regrets to the Korean people and that they understood that this was a mat-ter of national pride.

I emphasized to him that a substantial measure, including the revision of SOFA, must be taken soon. I also told him that civic organizations demanded President Bush's direct apology.

On December 13, President Bush called me to apologize in person. He expressed his sincere regrets in that phone call and had his press secretary say in a press briefing: "The President conveyed his deep, personal sadness and regret over the deaths of two South Korean girls who were acciden-tally killed during a training exercise by a United States military vehicle, and he pledged to closely work with South Korean government officials to prevent such accidents in the future."

After the largest candlelight vigil on December 14, the gatherings began to decrease in size. I did not order any physical restraint or violent control of the candlelight vigils. The Government of the People should do everything legally. We allowed freedom of assembly. As the US acknowledged, the incident was a matter of pride to Koreans. The US might not have liked my approach, but any other alternative would have been shortsighted. The good neighbor relationship is based on fairness. Where else in the world was there such a solid alliance as that between Korea and the US? The US should treasure it too.

On January 6, 2003, the *Washington Post* ran a column by Robert Novak titled "Perhaps It's Time South Korea Tried Its Wings," where he argued that I "proved to be the most anti-American president in the Republic's history. Roh was the idolizing protégé of Kim, but he has gone well beyond his patron in pulling Uncle Sam's whiskers."

I had a Korean diplomatic representative in the US deliver a letter of protest to the *Washington Post*. The Korean people opposed not the US, but its policy. Demanding a revision of SOFA meant that we were *not* anti-American. If we had been anti-American, we would have demanded the troops to withdraw, rather than revising an unequal agreement. I later said at a Japanese broadcasting station NHK program: "There are many people who are against American policies. However, there is nobody who demands the abolishment of our alliance with the United States. There are people against US policies in the United Kingdom and Japan. President Eisenhower could not visit Japan because of Japanese demonstrators. We should distinguish between opposition to policies and opposition to the country."

As a democratic citizen, I trusted the Korean people's mature civic sensibility. Anti-Americanism was an unnecessary concern, but the SOFA revision remained a real problem as a matter of national pride.

To me, the candlelight vigils on the same streets and squares where the red devils had roared were significant. If someone proposed a candlelight vigil on the Internet, people covered the squares in an instant, and the flame spread all across the country. It appeared that public opinion would be formed on the Internet from now on. Comments about incidents and expressing various opinions were very interesting. A short sentence could be quite powerful. An incident could expand into an international conflict.

The IT powerhouse that I had promoted—how would that cyber space evolve? I felt that people no longer neglected injustice. It appeared that social evils, like structural corruption and group egotism, would not have a place in society. The candlelight vigil that embodied the people's wish to burn down the unequal agreement between Korea and the US greatly influenced the sixteenth presidential election, both directly and indirectly.

On July 11, I reshuffled the cabinet for the last time during my term. Prime Minister Lee Han-dong returned to his political career after securely leading the government for two years and two months. He assisted me without fail, even while the alliance between the Democratic Party and LDA was collapsing. I thanked him sincerely.

I nominated the president of Ewha Womans University Chang Sang to prime minister. She was the first woman to be nominated to the position. I worked hard to invite Madam Chang Sang to the cabinet, as I knew her character, abilities, and achievements. I sent the chief of staff to persuade her and even mobilized my wife. I was grateful that she accepted the invitation. During the appointment certificate award ceremony, I asked her to let us make the remaining seven-month term a time of crowning achievement. "The Government of the People has done many things for women," I said. "We legislated many laws and founded the Ministry of Women. We gave birth to a female general and chief of staff. Finally, we have a female prime minister, so all we need now is a female president."

Prime Minister nominee Chang Sang attended the confirmation hearing for the first time according to the Confirmation Hearing Act, legislated in June 2000. However, the appointment motion was voted down in the National Assembly. The media reported that even Democratic Party members voted against her appointment. I was very sad, but there was nowhere for me to appeal in the political arena. I had to accept Madame Chang's resignation. I presided over the cabinet meeting without a prime minister. I said, "I nominated Madame Chang because she was clearly politically neutral and the most fit person for the elevation of women's position in the government. Although we are working toward becoming a world-class country, that goal is impossible to achieve in the current environment of weak female leadership. I accept the National Assembly's decision, but history will appreciate my action."

On August 9, I nominated Mr. Chang Dae-Whan, the president of the *Maeil Business Newspaper*, to prime minister and awarded him the appointment certificate. I thought that he, who had just turned fifty, was a leader and driving power fit for our information-based society. However, the

National Assembly voted him down, too. He resigned and left. I had to choose *another* person. On September 10, I nominated Mr. Kim Suk-soo to prime minister. He won the National Assembly confirmation.

I felt sick again. I coughed severely for a few days and could not perform my official duties. The medical team diagnosed me with pneumonia. I was hospitalized for two days and then took rest at the official residence. I could not attend the Liberation Day celebration event. The media began publishing speculative articles about my health. Phone calls and messages wishing for my quick recovery flooded the Blue House phones and homepage. President Bush sent me a letter with well wishes. I presided over the cabinet meeting at the Government Complex in Sejongno, Seoul, on August 19. It was the first official event I had attended since becoming ill.

My primary care physician Huh Kap-bum retired from his university position and, thus, my primary care physician post. He had been my doctor since 1990 and he took care of my health during my hunger strike for the local autonomous government system. He was a gentle doctor who tended to his patients' minds as well as their bodies. He visited me often, even after retirement. I trusted him a lot. I commissioned Dr. Chang Suk-il with the position of my primary care physician.

Despite the Western Sea Battle, the inter-Korean relationship was relatively smooth during the summer of 2002. In August, Minister of Unification Jeong Se Hyun and North Korean Team Leader Kim Ryong-song had the seventh ministerial-level conference. An inter-Korean sports conference, the second inter-Korean Economic Cooperation Promotion Committee meeting, and the civilian-level August 15 National Unification Assembly were also held. For the first time since the division of our country, 115 North Koreans visited Seoul for the Nation Unification Assembly.

At the second inter-Korean Economic Cooperation Promotion Committee meeting in Seoul, both parties agreed to launch railway and road construction on the east and west of the peninsula at the same time on September 18. It was a historic event that reconnected national arteries and would lay the groundwork for reunification. Also, South and North Korea agreed to have players and cheerleaders participate in the Asian Games in Busan together. One after another, our efforts at reconciliation and cooperation were coming to fruition.

Around this time, Japanese Prime Minister Koizumi made a surprise visit to North Korea. On September 17, he had a summit meeting with Chairman Kim Jong-il and adopted the Pyongyang Declaration. The international community was surprised. As someone who had actively urged Prime Minister Koizumi to visit North Korea, I watched the turn of events carefully. In the letter I had sent via special envoy Lim Dong-won in April, I advised Chairman Kim that the improvement of the North Korean relationship with Japan was necessary for economic development to be possible. The Japanese media reported on my hidden role.

During this summit, North Korea and Japan agreed to resume their negotiations for normalizing their relationship in October. Also, Japan agreed to cooperate in North Korea's economy through free funding and low-interest long-term loans as a way of compensating and apologizing for its past colonial rule. Prime Minister Koizumi called me to recap the summit. He said that they agreed it was important to follow through with the inter-Korean dialogue and the South and North Korean Accord to ease tension. Prime Minister Koizumi and I agreed that it was important to develop inter-Korean, DPRK-Japan and DPRK-US relations together. However, the relationship between North Korea and Japan has faltered due to many unfortunate circumstances since then. The rightist trend in Japan delayed the progress of the North Korea–Japan relationship at every turn.

I left Korea on September 20 to attend the fourth ASEM summit in Copenhagen, Denmark. As the chairman of previous ASEM summit meeting, I made a speech at the opening ceremony. "Please allow me to touch on the dramatic changes that are taking place on the Korean Peninsula at the moment. South and North Korea have finally entered the stage of actually implementing the agreements contained in their historic South–North Joint Declaration of June 15, 2000.

"The restoration work on the inter-Korea railroads and highways that began last week has many important ramifications. The most significant of all is that the reconnection of the railways will substantially reduce military tension.

"Parts of the barbed-wire fence along the DMZ have started coming down. The two sides began to engage in substantive economic cooperation in tandem with cultural and other exchanges. These drastic changes point toward a unified Korea.

"The effects of the inter-Korean railways will go beyond the Korean Peninsula; they will constitute an Iron Silk Road that will directly link Korea to Europe over land.

"The railroad will provide ASEM with a means to realize its ideal of creating a viable Eurasian community. When it opens, trains leaving various European cities will travel through the two continents all the way to Seoul and the southernmost harbor of Busan. This also means that cargo originating in Europe will be able to reach Busan, the third-largest container port in the world, in a matter of days. There it will be unloaded and shipped to all Pacific locations. Likewise, trains departing from Korea will travel to Western Europe and Atlantic Coast cities with the same advantage. The savings realized in transport time and costs will be enormous.

"ASEM has been pushing another Eurasian link in the form of a Digital Silk Road, which is nearing completion. The backbone of the Trans-Eurasia Information Network between Korea and France, the major gateways at either end, opened last December. When the Iron Silk Road is completed, Europe and Asia will have taken a giant step toward forming a cooperative Eurasian community."

The heads of state from Asia and Europe did not spare praise for the successful World Cup games and the launch of the inter-Korean railway construction. The Korean Peninsula and the Republic of Korea were at the center of their conversation. The heads of state unanimously adopted the "Political Declaration for Peace on the Korean Peninsula." This declaration included five main points: first, a renewed commitment to peace and stability on the Korean Peninsula and reaffirmation of their support for the process of inter-Korean reconciliation and cooperation; second, emphasis on the need to prevent the recurrence of the unfortunate recent naval clash, and the underlying importance of observing the 1953 Armistice Agreement and promoting confidence building measures; third, encouragement to carry out good faith measures for the implementation of the Joint Declaration and follow-up agreements, and the shared view that holding a second inter-Korean summit would be of great value in sustaining the momentum of the peace process on the Korean Peninsula; fourth, hope that all outstanding issues, including nuclear- and missile-related matters, should be resolved through dialogue in a timely manner; and, fifth, hope that the prospects for the US and the DPRK resuming a dialogue would continue to improve. This declaration absorbed the outline of the engagement policy our government had been pursuing. It was deeply significant that they expressed full-scale trust in our diplomatic policy and urged dialogue between the US and the DPRK.

Nonetheless, once again, the inter-Korean relationship ran into a stumbling block. I received a phone call from President Bush toward the end of September. He announced that he would send a high-level special envoy to North Korea in the near future. He also told me that North Korea and Iraq were different, and asked me to let the Korean people know his opinion on this matter. President Bush and I both appreciated the progress that had been made both between South and North Korea, and between North Korea and Japan.

President Bush sent Assistant Secretary of State for East Asian and Pacific Affairs James Kelly to Pyongyang in early October. I believed that President Bush was actively exploring the possibility of engagement with North Korea, but this was a misunderstanding on my part. After his visit to North Korea, Special Envoy Kelly gave us a briefing. According to him, when he presented North Koreans with evidence of their high-enriched uranium program, North Korean First Vice Foreign Minister Kang Sok-ju confirmed the allegation. This was news that would surprise the entire world.

North Korea expressed their willingness to resolve the situation through dialogue, but they also presented three preconditions: first, recognition and respect for the regime; second, a non-aggression pact; and, third, lifting of economic sanctions. This was a package deal that was proposed through a top-level conference.

I was extremely discouraged by this report. It was clear that North Korea's confirmation of the high-enriched uranium would derail the progress in their relationship with the US. As a result, the inter-Korean relationship would also deteriorate. In my opinion, North Korean leadership was played by the US neocons' persistent shakedown of their country. As expected, a US media attack on North Korea began, and domestic media began to exaggerate the allegations even more. The conclusion of such reports always called for the delay or abandonment of the Sunshine Policy.

I decided first to persuade North Korea. I sent a message to Chairman Kim Jong-il through Minister of Unification Jeong Se Hyun, who was on his way to Pyongyang to attend the eighth ministerial-level conference. I wrote: "Development and possession of weapons of mass destruction cannot be accepted. Please propose a dialogue and send a special envoy to the United States. On no occasion should you break the Geneva Agreed Framework. It is important to clarify your position before the APEC+3 Summit in Los Cabos, Mexico."

North Korea issued a statement before the Korea-US-Japan summit. Although it showed North Korea's sincere wish for improving its relationship with the US, its tone was aggressive and rude, condemning the US for being "one-sided," "arrogant," and "brazen." It concluded with the demand for the above-mentioned three conditions.

I decided to persuade President Bush again at the Korea-US-Japan summit, scheduled during the APEC summit in Los Cabos, Mexico. Special Advisor Lim Dong-won, Minister of Foreign Affairs and Trade Choi Sung-hong, and Senior Secretary of Foreign Affairs and National Security Yim Sung Joon accompanied me, while Secretary of State Powell, National Security Advisor Condoleezza Rice, and Chief of Staff Andrew Card accompanied President Bush. On Japan's side, Vice Chief Cabinet Secretary Abe Shinzo and Ambassador to Korea Takano Toshiyuki accompanied Prime Minister Koizumi. I argued that although I could not accept nuclear development by North Korea, we should resolve the issue peacefully in consideration of the specific circumstance of the Korean Peninsula.

"During the recent South-North Ministerial Meeting held in Pyongyang, the South strongly urged North Korea to take immediate action for prompt and peaceful resolution of the nuclear issue," I said. "North Korea then expressed their wish to reach a package deal with the United States, covering both the non-aggression treaty and the abandonment of nuclear development. We can solve these problems through diplomatic negotiations. Considering the danger of failing to carry out the Geneva Agreed Framework, this must be decided upon very carefully. We should not offer North Korea the excuse to resume nuclear facilities' operation or to develop nuclear weapons."

President Bush reiterated his February statement that the US had no intention of invading North Korea, and that he had been prepared to pursue a bold approach to transforming USDPRK relations.

The three countries issued a "Joint United States-Japan-Republic of Korea Trilateral Statement," declaring our will to peacefully resolve the North Korean nuclear issue. However, I failed to include the continuation of the Geneva Agreed Framework in the trilateral statement. Neocons in the US did not change their position. The US would engage with North Korea only after North Korea gave up nuclear development, and not until the nuclear test by North Korea in October 2006. Although I tried my best to prevent this situation from deteriorating, my term was almost over. I was extremely sad about all of the lost chances to better the inter-Korean relationship. I always seemed to be the only one anxious to resolve the situation.

LEAVING THE BLUE HOUSE (OCTOBER 2002–FEBRUARY 2003)

Although I left my party, the media still reported that I fell into a lame duck period. This was not the case. I did not neglect my responsibilities as the head of state. I worked hard for the future of our country and the Korean people. I ordered all government offices and the Blue House staff to summarize tasks that we should devote ourselves to for the last year of my term. We selected eighty tasks in six areas in January 2002, including strengthening our economic competitiveness, creating economic stability in the middle and lower classes, cleansing corruption, improving the inter-Korean relationship, a clean election, and successfully hosting an international sports events.

I took care of these tasks meticulously. Privatization of Korea Telecom and the pursuit of an electronic government could drift, as it was the end of my term. However, we continued to try our best until the very end. The Presidential Commission on Government Innovation, led by Chairman Ahn Moon-suk, completed its mission two months before the promised date. When we began the work two years earlier, many had doubted the commission. But, the commission members did their best. One member had to undergo a big operation due to accumulated stress, and Chairman Ahn was battling with his hypertension. The commission, mostly composed of civilians, successfully persuaded administrative officials and finished this great project.

Many people trusted and assisted me until the very end. Although there had been many difficulties, I was lucky enough to have many talents working next to me. My government finished seventy of the eighty tasks we set out to complete. We did not have a "lame duck" in the Government of the People—there was no time for that.

The Asian Games were held in Busan, beginning with the opening ceremony in Busan Asiad Main Stadium on September 29. South and North Korea repeated the moving scene from the Sydney Olympics, entering together, led by the Korean Peninsula flag, wearing the same uniform, and holding hands. The audience gave a standing ovation as the sacred flame soared, fueled from the flames that the North and the South had lit in Mt. Paektusan and Mt. Hallasan, respectively, and united in Imjingak.

Players from countries that had been suffering from war—like Afghanistan, Palestine, and East Timor—also entered in a dignified manner, headed by their national flags. All forty-three OCA (Olympic Council of Asia) member countries participated; East Timor did too, as an observer.

North Korea sent not only players, but also cheerleaders. Out of 376 North Korean participants, 288 traveled on the ship Mangyongbong to Dadaepo Harbor in Busan. The media covered this event with the headline: "Mangyongbong, the Symbol of a Spy Ship in the Past, Brought Envoys of Reconciliation." North Korean media reported on the opening ceremony in detail. The North Korean female cheerleaders were very popular; they immediately grabbed the audience's attention with their beauty and measured routines. The media called them the "Beauty Cheerleaders." There were many warm moments of the South and North cheering together.

Citizens gathered at Dadaepo Harbor to watch the cheerleaders every day. If the audience cheered, the cheerleaders sometimes delivered an impromptu performance. Tickets for the games where they were scheduled to appear sold out. A North Korean brass band performed on the street too. More than 10,000 people watched their performance at the Haeundae Square.

Although Busan was a rather conservative region, its citizens welcomed the North Korean cheerleaders warmly. Busan drew the attention of the world as the space for inter-Korean reconciliation. Although the North Korean anthem played and its flag fluttered in the stadiums, the event was incident-free. Concerns about the inter-Korean conflict proved groundless, and Koreans throughout the entire peninsula confirmed that we were the same people.

During the live broadcast farewell ceremony, the North Korean head cheerleader said, "Warm affection of our blood relatives will be inscribed in our hearts as eternally unforgettable memories." Some cheerleaders wiped their eyes as she spoke.

North Korea's participation invigorated the entire Asian Games, which could have easily been buried under the heat of the World Cup. I was truly happy. In fact, when the mayor of Busan Ahn Sang-young asked us to request that North Korea join in the games, we did not know that they would send cheerleaders too. After delivering the message to Chairman Kim Jong-il via special envoy Lim Dong-won in April, we simply waited. Unexpectedly, we received a reply that they would send not only players, but also cheerleaders.

We ran the Asian Game flawlessly. Everything—including the facilities, media center, athletes' village management, volunteer activities, and the results of the games—was satisfactory. We won 260 medals altogether—96 gold medals, 80 silver medals, and 84 bronze medals—and ranked second, which was the best result we had ever achieved. North Korea ranked ninth, winning nine gold medals, eleven silver medals, and thirteen bronze medals. However, the greatest achievement, of course, was the inter-Korean reconciliation.

North Korea also sent their economic inspection group to visit us. On October 26, the North Korean economic inspection group came with one hundred boxes of pine mushrooms as a gift from Chairman Kim Jong-il. Despite nuclear conflict with the US, the group included five top North Korean officials, such as Director of the Planning and Finance Department Pak Nam-gi and Chairman Kim Jong-il's brother-in-law and Vice Chairman of the National Defense Commission Jang Sung-taek. The inspection team toured and learned about the South Korean economy for eight nights and nine days.

Every day, the inspection group requested adding other, unscheduled visits. Although the eighteen members were mostly elders, they were all anxious to learn more and to learn everything in-depth. They were often heard to say, "We want to see more, but we don't have enough time!" When the high-speed train ran at 300 kilometers per hour, they all stood up and cheered. When they saw citizens use credit cards or cell phones to get on the subway, they appeared very surprised. I read a newspaper article that mentioned the head of the inspection group, Mr. Pak Nam-gi, wrote in the guestbook of a large cooperation: "Our nation is the best." I understood how he felt.

Former president Jimmy Carter was chosen as the 2002 Nobel Peace Prize winner. After his retirement, former president Carter had become a missionary for human rights. His activities were brilliant. The Korean Peninsula had been included in his stops. In 1994, he visited North Korea during the nuclear crisis between North Korea and the US and removed the threat of war from the Korean Peninsula. He also actively participated in the international Habitat for Humanity movement. I had met him at the building site in Dogo-myeon, Asan-si, Chungcheongnam-do, to volunteer for Habitat for Humanity Korea when he visited in August 2001. Former president and Mrs. Carter and former president Corazon Aquino were building a house together with Assemblymen Kim Young-jin and Kim Geun-tae under the hot August sun. It was beautiful to watch. He deserved the Nobel Peace Prize more than anybody. I was sorry that I won it before him, and relieved when I heard the news that he was a Nobel Prize recipient. I sent him a congratulatory message.

I left Korea on the afternoon of October 24 to attend the APEC summit in Los Cabos, Mexico. This was my last overseas diplomacy mission. After the tripartite summit with the president of the US and Japanese prime minister, I met Chinese president Jiang Zemin at Royal Solaris Hotel, where I was staying. President Jiang expressed his wishes for my good health. "Our common duty is to take care of each other's health," he said.

"I am grateful for your concern as a friend," I responded. "Thank you for coming here to meet me."

"It is natural that I visit you as you are my elder brother."

When we parted, I did not know when we would meet again, but I wished for his good health.

President Bush proposed we go on a fishing trip together in Los Cabos, but my health was not very good. I had to use a cane during the summit. Although it was my last meeting with the heads of state, I could not bid a proper goodbye.

I stopped by Seattle on my way back home. After meeting Koreans in the area at the Four Seasons Hotel, I received Microsoft CEO Bill Gates. He had contributed greatly to the rise of IT in Korea. Recently, he had also supported the Seoul National University International Vaccine Institute, so I thanked him for that. He told me that he would cherish the memory of discussing the future of IT industries with me. Although he was the grand master of the IT industry, Mr. Gates was a very modest person. He autographed the newest cell phone made by a Korean company and gave it to me. I used that cell phone after my retirement. I could even take photographs with it! The phone was my friend, and represented the cyber world I had dreamt of.

A terrible incident happened at the Seoul branch building of the Public Prosecutors Office when a murder suspect died from a beating. I was completely surprised. An incident like this should have never happened—and it particularly shouldn't have happened under my government of human rights. It was unforgivable that a public prosecutor, who should *defend* human rights, beat a suspect to death. I accepted the resignations of the minister of justice and prosecutor general. I appointed Mr. Shim Sang-myung to minister of justice and nominated Mr. Kim Kak-young as prosecutor general.

On November 15, I awarded the Maengho Medal in the Order of Sports Merit to professional golfer Choi Kyoung-Ju in honor of his win at the PGA tour in America. He was the first Korean winner of the PGA tour in its more than hundred-year history. I heard about how he would practice in the sand of his hometown in Wando Island. One could tell at a glance that he was a very hard-working sportsman.

On that same day, Korean marathon hero Mr. Sohn Kee-chung passed away. He had won the marathon in the Berlin Olympics during the Japanese colonial period, awarding Koreans with the most dramatic and moving sports moment of the twentieth century. He was a hero to me too. I sent the chief of staff to the funeral and made sure the event was taken care of. I conferred a posthumous medal to him and delivered a message of condolence through the presidential spokesperson. "I mourn the loss of Mr. Sohn's great footprints, which awakened our national soul, with my fellow Koreans."

The presidential election approached. In the beginning, the election was a triangular fight between Candidates Roh Moo-hyun, Lee Hoi-chang, and Chung Mong-joon. Candidate Chung Mong-joon was the president of the South Korean soccer association and ran for the election with the previous summer's historic South Korean soccer achievement under his belt. However, his support fizzled as time went by, and he and Candidate Roh Moo-hyun decided to unite under Mr. Roh Moo-hyun's candidacy, based on the poll numbers. The election between Roh Moo-hyun and Lee Hoi-chang was a very close one.

The day before the election, a strange incident happened: Mr. Chung Mong-joon revoked his support of Candidate Roh Moo-hyun. His reason was that Candidate Roh mentioned someone other than Mr. Chung as a candidate for the next presidential election. It was really outrageous, but, in the end, Candidate Roh won, earning 12.01 million votes (48.9 percent) to defeat Candidate Lee, who won 11.44 million votes (46.6 percent). Candidate Roh's election victory was very dramatic.

I was very happy about his victory. A current president's biggest dream is to have his party succeed his government. Although I left the Democratic Party, its victory was the ruling party's victory. That must be why the opposition party continued to obsessively attack me, even when I was no longer a member of the Democratic Party.

President-Elect Roh Moo-hyun visited me at the Blue House on December 23. I waited for him at the front entrance, in the very same spot where former president Kim Young-sam had waited for me five years before. We made a toast during lunch. He was the rising sun and I was the setting sun. I eagerly explained many pending subjects, including North Korea's nuclear issues. He pledged to continue the Sunshine Policy.

In 2003, I declared the disbanding of the Donggyo-dong faction. I asked the media and political world to never use that name again. I also stated my position to the Democratic Party through Chief of Staff Park Jie-won. I wanted to become an ordinary citizen, without being involved in domestic politics. I also did not want to burden the new Roh Moo-hyun government with my political presence. I did not want to belong to an independent political faction, and I hoped that everyone would become part of a new political order. It was my duty to help my successor succeed. My comrades all agreed to follow my wishes.

At the same time, I decided to donate the Asia Pacific Peace Foundation to Yonsei University. The foundation was the nest of my thoughts and philosophy, a place my wish for peace permeated. When it launched in 1994, many democratic leaders of the world participated in it. We had been actively engaged in various research activities for the development of unification and democracy in the Korean Peninsula. We accomplished many great achievements in collaboration with other world-class institutes.

The Asia Pacific Peace Foundation chose East Timor and Myanmar as strategic support countries in Southeast Asia. We supported national reconstruction in East Timor and the democratization movement in Myanmar. I had hoped to spend the remaining years of my life after retirement working for the peace and reunification of the Korean Peninsula and the enhancement of human rights throughout the world. But that became an impossible dream because the foundation was engulfed in disputes regarding renovation and management, and its officials were arrested.

Before the decision to donate the Asia Pacific Peace Foundation to Yonsei University, Chief of Staff Park Jie-won and Chief of the Office of the President Kim Hanjung discussed the matter in detail with Yonsei University president Kim Woo-sik and Professor Moon Chung-in. On January 17, 2003, President Kim Woo-sik announced that the university had decided to open the Kim Dae-jung Presidential Library and Museum by taking over the Asia Pacific Peace Foundation. I donated 16,000 books and materials from the library of my official residence to the university as well. The Asia Pacific Peace Foundation disappeared like that and was reborn as the first presidential library in Asia.

North Korea announced that it was withdrawing from the nuclear non-proliferation treaty (NPT) on January 10, 2003. Their announcement read:

A dangerous situation where our nation's sovereignty and our state's security are being seriously violated prevails on the Korean Peninsula due to the United States' vicious hostile policy toward the DPRK.

This hardliner response from North Korea was expected because the US had stopped their supply of crude petroleum in December 2002, the provision of which was a prerequisite for North Korea freezing their nuclear development according to the Geneva Agreed Framework. Although North Korea had tried to continue its efforts to improve its relationship with the US, it proved ineffectual. North Korea could expect nothing more from the US. As a result, North Korea chose this strategy.

Soon afterward, on January 12, 2003, US Senator Edward M. Kennedy slammed the Bush administration's foreign policy. He said in a speech delivered to the National Press Club: "Surely, we can have effective relationships with other nations without adopting a chip-on-the-shoulder foreign policy, a my-way-or-the-highway policy that makes all our goals in the world more difficult to achieve." He also said: "The sudden emergence and escalation of the crisis with North Korea is the result of a US foreign policy that was AWOL on that issue for the first twenty-one months of the Bush administration. Then the administration lurched into an unsustainable over-reaction when it initially refused to even talk unless the North Koreans backed down. Even as our ally South Korea sought to engage the North, the US rebuffed any dialogue at all, leading to an embarrassing deterioration in our relations with South Korea."

Senator Kennedy was an astute politician who knew the Korean Peninsula situation in-depth. His remarks sounded to me like he was cheering for the Koreans.

Although my retirement was imminent, I hoped to resolve the North Korean nuclear issue as best as I could. I decided to send Mr. Lim Dong-won as my special envoy, accompanied by Senior Secretary of Foreign Affairs Yim Sung Joon and a transition committee member of President-Elect Roh Moo-hyun, Lee Jong-seok. They flew to Pyongyang on January 27 via the direct West Coast route. It was a snowy day. I hoped that special envoy Lim would return safely and with good news. However, our prospects were bleak. I sent a letter to Chairman Kim Jong-il offering my advice about the North Korean nuclear matter, inter-Korean relationship, and their relationship with the new government. As the international situation was very complicated, I sincerely requested that he improve North Korea's relationship with the world's superpower, the US, and resolve their suspicions about nuclear development and, in particular, their high-enriched uranium plan. At the end of my last letter to him during my term I wrote:

> I sincerely wish that the inter-Korean reconciliation and cooperation will continue to develop in whatever situation. My successor President-Elect Roh Moo-hyun has also publicly pledged that he actively supports the June 15 Accord and the development of a reconciliation and cooperation policy.
>
> I will not stop my wholehearted effort for our nation's peace, reconciliation, cooperation, and peaceful reunification until the day I retire and even after my retirement.
>
> Since my meeting with Chairman Kim, the current of inter-Korean understanding and cooperation has grown. I would like to prove this historic national current by connecting the Seoul-Sinuiju Railway during my term. It will be more than material evidence that records our time by becoming a way to dramatically advance reconciliation and cooperation and a shield to defend against counter-currents.
>
> However, I am extremely sad that this important business has not been completed yet. As we still have time, I firmly believe that we can accomplish the connection of the Seoul-Sinuiju Railway if Chairman Kim decides to do so.
>
> As the president who worked with Chairman Kim to begin the work of collapsing the wall created by a half a century of division, I hope more than anything that the day when both Koreas coexist peacefully and enjoy prosperity together will come soon.

Special Envoy Lim's team stayed in Pyongyang for two nights and three days, but they could not meet Chairman Kim. They were told that Chairman Kim was teaching important lessons in a field in the countryside. Special Envoy Lim read for me the message that Secretary Kim Yong-sun had delivered from Chairman Kim. It read:

> I learned that you sent your special envoy to me and I thank you for your signed letter and warm advice. I will examine your advice in detail and contact you later.

I was greatly disappointed. I was also angry that he did not even meet my special envoy, who visited him on my behalf at the end of my term. Perhaps understanding my feelings, Special Envoy Lim told me that the North Koreans had offered them a nice dinner reception in return for our welcome of the North Korean Economy Inspection Team. Special Envoy

Lim told me that all of the inspection team members who had attended the reception emphasized the necessity for inter-Korean economic cooperation.

The confrontation between the neoconservative Bush administration and the North Korean regime, which responded with nuclear development, was truly dangerous. However, it was not easy to persuade either America or North Korea. Also, the Cold War era, brought on by domestic conservatives, was a barrier that I found very difficult to overcome. I was upset about both the US and North Korea. I was also very worried about the hardline tactics of the Bush administration, which broke the agreement first. In the end, it resulted in nuclear development in North Korea.

Mr. Lee Jong-wook, who had worked for the Global Programme for Vaccines and Immunizations and Stop Tuberculosis, was elected as director-general of the World Health Organization (WHO). This was the first time a Korean was elected to an international organization. Minister of Health and Welfare Kim Sung-ho had contributed greatly to Dr. Lee's election. He had requested to meet with me alone and recommended that we send Dr. Lee to the election. I gladly agreed and wrote a letter to the heads of state of seven countries, including Russia, Saudi Arabia, Jordan, Kuwait, Colombia, the UK, and Lithuania. Minister Kim went on a tour to elect Dr. Lee Jong-wook as the director-general of the WHO with my signed letters in his pocket. The vote was so close that they had to vote seven times. Thirty-two countries that were members of the executive committee participated in the voting, and Dr. Lee won the election with seventeen votes.

When I met Dr. Lee on February 7, 2003, I said, "I once said that terror fundamentally originated from poverty. Please make an effort to appease the despair and anger of people who suffer from disease because of poverty."

He told me that he would work hard.

About ten days before my term was over, we completed the Korea-Chile Free Trade Agreement (FTA). Ministers of foreign affairs from both countries signed the agreement at the Blue House while President Ricardo Lagos and I watched. This FTA was the first between countries on opposite sides of the Pacific. There had been many twists and turns for four years before this was materialized.

In its first meeting after my inauguration in November 1998, the Fair Trade Commission made a very important policy decision that harkened the great transformation of trade policies. The commission decided to make a FTA with four countries—Australia, South Africa, Chile, and Turkey—and expand it to America, Japan, and ASEAN. The four countries that the commission selected for the FTA belonged to Central and South America, Africa, the Middle East, and Oceania, respectively. Through this FTA, we wanted to secure a foothold in each continent; however, it was not easy to decide which country we should select for the first FTA. If we received something, we had to give other things in return. This meant that some domestic sectors would be disadvantaged as a result of FTA. In particular, free trade in agriculture was sure to meet farmers' fierce opposition.

Our government chose Chile as the first country to have the FTA with because each country was strong in other industries and the trade quantity was not very large. This meant that we would not risk much, and the opposite season in each country meant reduced risk to farmers. We also thought that, as a democratic country, Chile was a good counterpart for us.

When I met Chilean president Eduardo Frei in Kuala Lumpur, Malaysia, at the APEC summit, I officially proposed that we begin a working-level discussion for a FTA. Our two countries began negotiating, but, as expected, farmers objected to it. Grape growers in particular were fiercely against it because of Chilean wine. The negotiation had to stop.

However, we could not discontinue this approach. As the world economy was gradually grouped into blocks, the only way to break through was an FTA. In October 2001, I met President Lagos at the APEC summit in Shanghai and we agreed to resume the negotiation. Farmers' opposition did not weaken. In the end, in exchange for the exclusion of rice, apples, and pears from the FTA, Chile also excluded our refrigerators and washers from custom-free items. That is how we reached the Korea-Chile FTA on October 25, 2002.

I do understand why people are against FTAs. But the only way Koreans can make money from a country with a shortage of resources is by selling what we make. We need markets and the only way to open them up is through an FTA. If we cannot avoid an FTA, then we should approach it wisely through an accurate prediction of the impact of the FTA on our domestic industries.

People often say that Korea is "sandwiched" between China and Japan, but I do not agree with this. I have thought for a long time that Korea is like a cow in a drain—a cow that can graze for grass on both sides of the drain. An FTA essentially gives us the right to graze freely from the fields on both sides. We should pursue FTAs actively, while working hard to find the best way to help those who will be disadvantaged from it. The "productive welfare" that my government pursued could be a solution.

An incident involving a money transfer to North Korea occurred when an opposition party assemblyman alleged that Hyundai Merchant Marine Company borrowed $400 million and sent it to North Korea as a reward for Mt. Kumgang tourism. The incident quickly snowballed. The opposition party alleged that the Blue House was involved in this incident and that it was a reward for the inter-Korean summit. Later, they even argued that we bought the summit with money.

Because this incident occurred at the very end of my term, it was difficult for me to handle it properly. Not only the public, but also President-Elect Roh Moo-hyun, pressured the Public Prosecutors Office to investigate the situation. The Chief of Staff for President-Elect Roh said openly: "The Kim Dae-jung government should leave after solving it." Although President-Elect Roh must have known how hard we had worked to improve the inter-Korean relationship, he prioritized politics over the inter-Korean relationship. At the end of my term, my government was really helpless. I decided to come forward directly and tell the Korean people the truth. On February 14, I read a statement, which was broadcast live. I stayed up overnight to write it.

"The dispute about Hyundai Merchant Marine Company's money transfer to North Korea has recently worried you greatly," I said in my statement. "I am very sorry for that. Personally, I feel very sad and miserable about it.

"Our government received a lot of cooperation from Hyundai, which contacted the North Korean authorities a lot in the process of pursuing the inter-Korean summit. In return for the money transfer, Hyundai received rights to seven enterprises in North Korea, including railway, electricity, communication, tourism, and the Kaesong Industrial Complex. As our government judged that this would be very beneficial to peace and our national interests, we accepted the situation despite its potential to violate current law. However, as this has become a public problem, our government should clarify the situation and, as President, I should take full responsibility for it. Therefore, I will do exactly that.

"The North Korean government is legally an anti-government organization and an object for serious punishment according to National Security Law. However, according to national consensus, we are pursuing reconciliation and cooperation even while strengthening national security. Due to the dual nature of the inter-Korean relationship and the North Korean regime's exclusivity, there are occasions that should be handled secretly and outside of the legal boundary of the inter-Korean relationship.

"Similar examples can be found in the inter-German relationship. This incident also originated from our sincere desire to block war in the Korean Peninsula and to enjoy peace and prosperity together, to nurture the hope for reunification while living without worry.

"I will take responsibility for this event. I just hope that you will understand my sincere wish for peace and our best national interests. I also hope that you will not spare generosity and cooperation in order to preserve the let-up of tension that we have finally achieved and the opportunity to develop national interests."

Despite my earnest appeal, the opposition party continued to attack and argue the appointment of a special prosecutor. On the very day when I read my statement at the press conference, the Mt. Kumgang tourism via land route test began. The truce line opened and a bus from the South crossed to the North.

The time to leave the Blue House was approaching. My wife was busy packing up, despite the fact that there were few things to take with us. She must have been uncomfortable; when we were alone together, she did not say much. However, during dinner with the Democratic Party and LDA leaders who had served under the coalition government, she said something she couldn't have said had it been just the two of us. "I regret many things that happened during the past five years," she said. "My husband tried his best for the nation and people. I would like to praise him, despite the fact that he is my husband. From what I have seen, it is true that he has worked for the love of our nation and people, not even sparing time for his sleep."

Indeed, I often could not fall asleep during my term. I spent many nights tossing and turning. Five years in the Blue House—it felt as vivid as if it were yesterday one moment, but the in the next moment it all felt long ago and far away.

As my wife said, I really worked hard. How surprised I was when I heard that the national storeroom was empty right after I was elected! I ran everywhere there might be dollars. Although we had had only $3.9 billion then, we now had more than $120 billion—the world's fourth-largest foreign currency reserve.

Although we had had exported a lot in the past fifty years, the accumulated deficit amounted to $90 billion when I took office; we now had

$5 billion, even after offsetting it. While foreign investment totaled $24.6 billion in the past fifty years, more than $60 billion had been invested over the past five years. This increase was thanks to foreign investors' trust in our government and their firm belief that there would not be war in the Korean Peninsula.

Through the reform of finance, cooperation, the public sector, and employer-employee relations, Korea was praised as an economically honorable country. We became an IT powerhouse with an Internet population of 27 million. We also completed the four basic insurances: health insurance, unemployment insurance, industrial accident insurance, and a national pension system. By legislating the National Basic Livelihood Security Act, we banished the sorrow of hunger and lack of education from our land. Although we could not complete the social safety net, foreign countries were now visiting us to learn from our system. For the past five years, Korea had also stood tall as a country that valued human rights. Teargas disappeared from demonstration scenes, and violent suppression did, too. Although arguments about the Sunshine Policy continued, what better alternative did we have? With it, we melted inter-Korean tension and contributed to foreign investment and change in North Korean society.

In retrospect, none of this was easy. However, once I believed something was right, I did not hesitate. I persuaded people over and over again, and completed one task after another. All of this served as the foundation for building Korea into a world-class country. It was hard, but truly rewarding.

I read reports alone at night at the official residence, often well past midnight. My wife used to tell me, "Go to bed today." Since she never went to bed before me, I felt sorry for her. When I found passion and wisdom for our country in those reports, I was excited and experienced an incomparable joy. Who else but me could recognize all the effort and hard work of our national talents!

Before retirement, my anxiety grew. In retrospect, some of the policies my administration had pursued required a lot of difficult labor, beginning with the planning stage and going from there. They required courage and decisiveness, and I remembered all of those moments.

How will the new government handle the incident of money transfer to North Korea? I wondered. *How will the North Korean nuclear crisis be resolved? What will happen to human rights in Korea? Will Koreans remember my government and me?*

But I immediately decided that I should not be too greedy about any of this. *If I did my best, that should be all that matters,* I thought. *What more could I want? President Roh Moo-hyun's government will carry on with those things that I could not finish. Isn't he the president the Democratic Party selected?*

Japanese economic critic and UCLA Professor Ohmae Kenichi contributed an article about my achievements to the biweekly *Sapio*. He had contributed a very critical article entitled "Reasons Why Korea Cannot Rise Again Under President Kim Dae-jung's Leadership" to the same magazine in 1999. In that 1999 article, he wrote: "He is dissolving his country just as the United States orders. Historians will condemn it as his worst failure." That article had created controversy because of its direct attack of my administration and me, even as we were working hard to reform the country. This time, though, Professor Ohmae praised me very highly. I was grateful for his scholarly conscience and courage, which made him frankly acknowledge his mistake. He wrote:

> As no president has ever contributed as much to the Korean economy as President Kim, the Korean people should be grateful to him from the bottom of their hearts as he transitions into retirement. It is hard to find a president who has transformed his country in a single 5-year term as much as he did. He is a rare, distinguished president who recovered the Korean economy in a V-shape in five years. Although I criticized him harshly once, I sincerely apologize for it here.

Eighty-five Blue House journalists sent me a memorial tablet with an inscription that read: "For Mr. President." I kept it in my bedroom and looked at it often after my retirement. They wrote:

> You worked tirelessly for the past five years. You have rescued the Republic of Korea from the desperate IMF foreign currency crisis. The Pyongyang inter-Korean summit was joy itself. Your acceptance of the Nobel Peace Prize was moving. The World Cup united the Korean people. We all love you, President who will be remembered in history.

I was surprised to know that the journalists who had criticized me sharply for the past five years supported me and appreciated my achievements so much. The faces of journalists who had visited from all over the world and observed so many historic scenes with me came to mind.

I took time for a farewell with the Blue House staff and took a commemorative photograph with them: Director Mun Mun-sul, who cooked for me, and the kitchen staff; my barber Mr. Park Sung-bae; Coordinator Cho Hyo-jeong; and staff members who worked under the title of *jeong-niwon*. I ran into them every day and how I appreciated their hard work! I said goodbye to each of them individually.

Finally, the day of my departure came. On the morning of February 24, I paid reverence at the Seoul National Cemetery and presided over the last cabinet meeting. Before the meeting, I made a farewell remark to the Korean people, entitled "Dedication to Great Koreans." "Dear fellow Koreans whom I respect and love, today is the last day I will work for you as your president," I said. "I respectfully say good-bye to you. Above all, I bow to you and thank you for your mountainous grace in encouraging and helping me for the past five years. I have dedicated my entire life to the work of serving you and participating in the exploration of the fate of our nation and people with you, as I believed that would be my greatest reward.

"However, there were many things I lacked and for which I regret. But, I believe that you and my administration have, together, spent the past five years doing our best to establish a grand foundation for the prosperity of our nation.

"I have run without taking a break all my life, and, in particular, during the past five years. I need some rest now. But, I will, until the day my life is over, cherish my loyalty to our people and nation.

"Dear fellow Koreans, please actively support President Roh Moo-hyun. The inter-Korean reconciliation and cooperation, as well as the participative reform that the new government will pursue, should succeed. I have no doubt that President Roh Moo-hyun will accomplish his mission.

"I have great hope for our people's future. The Republic of Korea will grow to become a great nation that the whole world will admire. The Korean people deserve it. We can also accomplish the dream of becoming an economic powerhouse. We will accomplish the dream of peaceful reunification some day.

"I am now stepping down from the scene of governance. I would like to extend my sincerest apologies and words of reconciliation to those who might have been hurt or been sad because of me during my difficult political career.

"Dear fellow Koreans whom I respect and love! Let us all unite. Let us work hard to proceed with hope for tomorrow. Let us cooperate for the grand cause. Thank you."

I then watched them hang my portrait on the wall of the Sejong Room, where the portraits of former presidents were hung. Regardless of their successes and failures, they all worked to lead the Republic of Korea. I stared at them for a long time with my wife. After having lunch with the last cabinet members of my Government of the People, I had a photograph taken with the cabinet in the main building lobby. I then posed for a photograph with senior secretaries and special aids: Park Jie-won, Lim Dong-won, Lee Ki-ho, Choi Jong-chan, Cho Soon Yong, Lee Jae-Sin, Hyun Jung-taik, Yim Sung Joon, Cho YoungDal, Kim Sang-nam, Park Sun Sook, Cho Young-jai, and Park Keum-ok. Wasn't it beautiful to share that last moment together?

I left the Blue House at 5:00 p.m. All of the staff members stood in a line and said goodbye. I wonder how they knew, but citizens also came to the streets and applauded and waved Korean national flags. Many people gathered in the alley leading up to my house in Donggyo-dong. In particular, young people chanted my name and greeted me. I was grateful and made an impromptu speech.

I entered my private home, the newly constructed house that some media had called "Afang Palace" and "a mansion." This was the first time I had entered the house, so it was strange. I looked around, but no matter how hard I looked, it was no Afang Palace. The bedroom was full with only a single bed. I sat on that bed and looked out the darkening window for a long time. The past five years felt like a dream. Sleep overtook me.

CHAPTER 12

February 2003–2009

EMBRACING THE WORLD ALONE
(FEBRUARY 2003–DECEMBER 2005)

I attended the inauguration ceremony for the fifteenth president of our country, President Roh Moo-hyun, on February 25, 2003. Many congratulatory guests, including former presidents, gathered. I hadn't felt well since the moment I left home that day. Although I could manage as president, I was not sure whether I could manage my body any more. It was lucky that people were all looking at the new president. I barely managed to focus and support myself … but I had to be there for the occasion no matter what.

My health had deteriorated over the past five years, and my time in the Blue House wore my body out. My hip joint, in particular, hurt a lot, and I was afraid that I would fall while walking, although I did not mention it then. I tried my best not to fall during national events or diplomatic ceremonies, thinking that my fall would be my country's fall. Even in pain, I smiled and succeeded in not falling even once. In fact, out of grades one through six, I was grade three disabled.

On March 15, President Roh Moo-hyun announced a special bill for the Money Transfer to North Korea Incident. All of the cabinet members except for one opposed it, but President Roh ignored it. Minister of Unification Jeong Se Hyun opposed it and said, "The disclosure of the process of the inter-Korean relationship pursuit could result in halting the inter-Korean dialogue and civilian interchange." I was shocked. Only ten

© The Author(s) 2019
Kim Dae-jung, *Conscience in Action*,
https://doi.org/10.1007/978-981-10-7623-7_12

days before my retirement I had sincerely appealed that this should not become a matter of legal judgment. I took responsibility for it, admitting that I pursued it knowing that it was illegal, but, nonetheless, thought it would be helpful in bringing peace to the Korean Peninsula and for the improvement of national interests.

It was true that my administration wanted to send $100 million in support to North Korea. What wealthy elder brother visits his poor younger brother empty-handed? But we supported it through Hyundai because of the legal issue. Hyundai also received rewards from North Korea for its contribution of $100 million.

Although I was at first angry to hear that Hyundai agreed to send $400 million to North Korea, I found that it made sense once I saw the concrete benefits for seven business ventures that Hyundai received in return. I remembered British Prime Minister Benjamin Disraeli, who secured the Eastern route by secretly buying all of the Suez Canal stocks. He decided to do this in extreme secrecy after learning that Egypt was planning to sell them because they needed cash. It was clear that French control of the Suez Canal would be a great blow to Great Britain—the problem was the enormous sum of money necessary for the purchase. Prime Minister Disraeli had to secure a budget through Parliament, but that meant that France would obtain the information, which could lead to an international conflict. So, he secretly borrowed money from the biggest funder, Rothschild, and secured control of the Suez Canal. I made my decision, as well, for the sake of our national interests and for the purpose of opening the way to inter-Korean reconciliation and cooperation.

It was not clear to where President Roh wanted to drag this matter. He should have known well that the inter-Korean relationship could not be a matter of political strife. If the head of our country handled a top national secret so lightly, what other nation would trust our government from thereon out? Although President Roh said that my government's and my policy direction was correct, he chose a different route, thus beginning his term on the wrong foot. He did not even try to ask the people's opinion about it. The inter-Korean relationship would freeze again and public opinion would be divided. The side effect was crystal clear. However, I said nothing.

On April 22, my wife and I had dinner with President Roh and the first lady. President Roh asked me about the Hyundai money transfer to North Korea as soon as we sat down together. It was really hard to understand his intentions and quite unpleasant, but I told him calmly, "I still firmly believe that Hyundai's transfer of money to North Korea should not be legally judged."

President Roh viewed the workers of the Government of the People and me suspiciously. At that time, I found it hard to understand him. I also could not understand the Democratic Party leadership's silence about the special prosecutor appointment. In particular, I was extremely disappointed at President Hahn Hwa-kap's passive stance.

The special prosecutor's investigation progressed ruthlessly. He summoned all relevant parties from banks, businesses, and government offices, and investigated them thoroughly. Sensitive matters were exposed and created awkward situations for the people involved. In the end, former Financial Supervisory Commission Chair Lee Keun-young, former Senior Secretary of Economy Lee Ki-ho, and former Chief of Staff Park Jie-won were arrested. They were not criminals, but workers who fought for reunification. The incident expanded to the Hyundai slush fund allegation, which speculated that former Chief of Staff Park Jie-won received 15 billion won from Hyundai as a bribe. Mr. Park Jie-won was found innocent of this charge at the Supreme Court much later. During this trial, the tragic incident of President Chung Mong-hun's suicide occurred. He threw himself out of his office window. The money transfer to North Korea had a huge impact on our society. I was extremely sad as I watched it evolve. However, late president Chung Mong-hun's widow Hyun Jeong-Eun's courage in succeeding her late husband—as had been his dying wish—was admirable. After her inauguration as the president of Hyundai Asan, she calmly managed the company even while the inter-Korean relationship faced this difficult situation. Because she managed her company well and acquired respect from her company employees, she appears to have emerged as a great leader for the future.

The US finally invaded Iraq on March 20, 2003. Even while claiming that they wanted to maintain peace, the Bush administration made war. How stupid it is to think that one can bring peace through war! President Bush invaded Iraq under the pretext that Iraq owned Weapons of Mass Destruction (WMDs)—however, no WMDs were found there. It appeared that he took the daring step of invading Iraq to change the political phase that had arisen due to the American people's disappointment about the recession and anxiety in the wake of the September 11 terrorist attack.

I expected the US would face an adverse wind as a result. In fact, the world condemned the US. People from traditionally friendly countries turned their backs on the US. The war dragged on and the US became bogged down in it. The US waged war in many places, so it spent an enormous amount of money on the military and the manufacturing of weapons. The US ended up having a hard time because of snowballing national debts.

The Pax Americana, during which the US has controlled the world for almost a century since the end of World War I, is declining. The US was the most powerful nation in economic, military, and scientific technologies. However, gradually, domestic public opinion has cooled and the world has lost interest in the US. Moving forward, the global economy, too, will undergo a great change as a result of the decline of the era of American leadership. The Bush government precipitated the downward spiraling status of the US. Arrogance is poison not only to individuals, but also to countries. President Bush's administration was a disaster not only for the US, but also for the world.

I was hospitalized due to symptoms of angina pectoris. I received an angioplasty and kidney hemodialysis for the first time on May 12. I was told the very distressing news that I would need kidney hemodialysis for the rest of my life. I had not expected this kind of difficulty, and it was very hard to accept. The medical staff and my secretaries tried to comfort me, saying that I could still travel, even overseas.

In fact, I found out during the 1997 election campaign that I had a little problem with my kidneys, although my health was fine. The medical team told me then that I might need dialysis in three years; however, I refused to get dialysis during my presidency. In December 2002, Doctor Han Dae-seok urged me not to delay angioplasty and dialysis. I thought hard about it, but I did not feel that I could take care of governing a nation from bed. The dialysis itself would take more than four hours, and I could not work normally immediately after the treatment. I had to delay it until after my retirement.

President Bush sent me a letter through the US Embassy in Korea wishing for my speedy recovery: "I am delighted to hear that you were discharged and are recovering your health. I trust that you will overcome the current difficulty as you did during decades of fighting for democracy and human rights."

I felt heavy whenever I thought about President Bush. He was very rude during our first summit in 2001. He reversed our agreement and spoke ill of Chairman Kim Jong-il during the press conference. He surrounded himself with neocons and handled his policy toward North Korea according to their will. However, he changed his way of thinking after my earnest and persistent persuasion. He also treated me with respect. In the end, President Bush apologized to me. When he visited the Kim Dae-jung Presidential Library and Museum in 2004, Minister of Foreign Affairs Ban Ki-moon said to me, "President Bush feels very sorry for what happened during the 2001 summit. He asked me to deliver this message to you."

That May, the Reverend Moon Ik-hwan Commemorative Foundation announced that it was giving me the eighth Nutbom Unification Award for my contribution to peace and reunification in the Korean Peninsula. My wife attended the award ceremony and received the award on my behalf at the Kim Koo Museum and Library. In August, I won the seventh Manhae Grand Prize for Peace.

On August 27, the Six-party Talks were held in Beijing, China. In order to solve the North Korean nuclear problem, six countries—South and North Korea, the US, China, Japan, and Russia—attended the meeting. It happened only after North Korea withdrew from the Nuclear Nonproliferation Treaty (NPT) and the International Atomic Energy Agency (IAEA) special board of directors' meeting passed a resolution to report to the UN Security Council.

When North Korea declared its withdrawal from NPT and full intention to develop nuclear weapons, the US rushed to turn the North Korean nuclear crisis into an international problem. The Bush government wanted to form a five-country anti-North Korea alliance, and to sanction and destroy North Korea. However, the five other countries were not on board with this strategy. Nevertheless, the US continued to argue that North Korea should give up nuclear development first, while North Korea continued to argue for a package deal in connection with economic support. The Six-party Talks resulted in a stalemate, and North Korea continued its nuclear development. The Bush administration's hardline tactic drove the situation to the worst possible scenario.

I had already argued for a peace guarantee in the Korean Peninsula with four neighboring countries during the 1971 presidential election campaign. The Six-party Talks basically added the two Koreas into the mix. I had since used every opportunity possible to argue that the North Korean nuclear problem should be peacefully resolved in Six-party Talks, while criticizing the US' hardline tactic. North Korea continued to want a dialogue with the US. The neocons in the US kept the flame of war alive by manipulating public opinion and breaking its promise to North Korea every time.

The Democratic Party was divided into two after a long internal conflict between its mainstreamers and non-mainstreamers. On September 20, new mainstreamers followed President Roh to form a negotiating body in the National Assembly named the People's Participation Unified New Party (PPUNP). That day, President Roh left the party, the nest that raised him to become president. In November, the PPUNP declared that it had formed the Yeollin Uri Party (abbreviated as Uri Party). The Democratic Party condemned it, calling it an "unprecedented act of betrayal." I could not understand why President Roh was rushing so much, why he was creating enemies. A political party cannot exist while neglecting its supporter base. His action was like kicking out his own in order to invite a guest. It was extremely unfortunate.

On November 3, 2003, the Kim Dae-jung Presidential Library and Museum opened. About 300 guests, including President Roh, the presidents of political parties, and foreign diplomatic envoys in Korea, attended. About twenty former and current world leaders, including former American presidents Bill Clinton and Jimmy Carter, former Soviet Union president Mikhail Gorbachev, Japanese prime minister Koizumi Junichiro, British Prime Minister Tony Blair, French President Jacques Chirac, Swedish Prime Minister Göran Persson, German Chancellor Gerhardt Schröder, and former president of the Philippines Corazon Aquino, sent congratulatory messages. President Roh made a congratulatory remark, citing overcoming the foreign currency crisis, establishing the foundation for an information- and knowledge-based society, and facilitating the inter-Korean summit as my achievements. He said, "History will forever remember former President Kim's passion for and dedication to democracy, peace, and reunification."

I believe that the Yonsei University Kim Dae-jung Presidential Library and Museum will become an international research center for peace and reunification in the Korean Peninsula and will play an important role in building peace in the world. Professor Shin Dongcheon was appointed as its first director.

Toward the end of 2003, I received an unexpected award—the Merit Award at the Chunsa Art Film Festival. They decided to give me the award because: "He gave firm support for the long-term development of Korean film by protecting the screen quarter system, guaranteeing freedom of creation, and founding the 150 billion won film promotion fund."

The Government of the People felt proud of bringing about the Korean film renaissance. We got rid of previous regulation- and restriction-based film policies by changing the film industry from a permission system to registration system. However, the screen quarter system, through which Korean films were guaranteed a certain proportion of screen time, was a difficult problem because of US pressure. I met with American delegates directly and persuaded them for the sake of protecting our domestic film industry and cultural diversity.

However, we could not forever protect our film industry through the screen quarter system. We needed to develop our films' competitiveness in the international film market. We therefore offered various types of governmental support to the Korean film industry. In May 2002, Lim Kwon-taek won the Best Director Award at the Cannes Film Festival for his film *Painted Fire*. This was the first time a Korean film director had won this honor. He was the first filmmaker to receive the Gold Crown Cultural Medal from our government. Since then, Korean films have grabbed global attention at various major film festivals. Although the market share of Korean films began at 25.1 percent in the early stage of my term, it grew to 50 percent in 2001, 48.3 percent in 2002, and 53.5 percent in 2003. I was very happy about this development. As I believed, Korea was a cultural powerhouse.

Another interesting development in film during my term was that the material our films could deal with was no longer restricted, thanks to the inter-Korean reconciliation. Many films about the division of the country were produced. People enjoyed films like *Shiri*, *J.S.A: Joint Security Area*, *Tae Guk Gi: The Brotherhood of War*, and *Silmido*.

I gladly attended the award ceremony with my wife. Many people in the film industry flattered me. Someone said, "Human beings are animals of forgetfulness. However, there are things we should not forget. The Government of the People offered decisive momentum for today's Korean film renaissance by greatly expanding the film industry's infrastructure through its policy."

Another person said, "There are only a few people who we can call 'teacher' in our times. Mr. Na Woon-gyu is one, and Mr. Kim Dae-jung, who devoted his entire life to the democratization of our society, is another."

I felt hot tears in my eyes as I listened to their speeches. I was embarrassed to be so moved by such recognition, but I also realized that I felt proud of my work as president.

Of course, governmental support could not entirely account for the growth of the Korean film industry. Above all, artists in the film industry worked painstakingly hard and exhibited extraordinary artistic talent. I am proud of the incredible potential that the Korean people exhibited through their achievements. I thanked the committee for giving me the award for my small contribution and said, "I find it very meaningful to receive this award in honor of Mr. Na Woon-gyu, a patriot and great forefather of Korean film."

I met singer Seo Taiji as a fan at the Kim Dae-jung Library and Museum. I had listened to his music for about ten years. During the election campaign tour, I listened to it in the car. Although I tried to sing along, I found it too hard—in the end, I had to settle for just listening. I appreciated the social messages he included in his songs. I said to him, "You stand out for combining traditional Korean music and rock music. You'll be remembered in the history of popular music for a long time."

Speaking of musicians, I remember a few more encounters with Korean singers. I had been to the complete performance of "Sugungga" by mastersinger of traditional Korean song An Sook-sun at the National Theatre of Korea in July 1994. It was a very hot day, but they did not turn on the air conditioner in order to protect the sound of the song. The singer and the audience all endured the heat with their individual fans for three hours. The incredible voice that came out of An Sook-sun's small-framed body gave me goose bumps. The three hours passed very quickly, while the audience responded with *chuimsae*. My wife and I invited the singer to our house for a dinner. I said, "I thank you for so superbly maintaining the tradition of the music that contains our national soul." Looking at her small body, I was amazed again as I remembered her thunderous sounds.

Singer Lee Mi-ja also visited our house in the fall of 1994, the thirtieth anniversary year of her debut as singer. She began singing songs about the sorrow and regret of the Korean people during the most difficult post-Korean War period. She was a very simple and modest person. I went to see her thirtieth anniversary performance. Singers Shin Hyung-won and Lee Sun-hee visited my house occasionally, too. Both of their charms were as refreshing as their songs.

On January 29, 2004, I attended the new trial for the Kim Dae-jung Conspiracy of Rebellion Incident. I was given the verdict of "not guilty" twenty-three years after the first guilty verdict. After the trial, I said, "The new military junta was judged by the law. I realize again that people and history will always prevail."

I sought this retrial because I believed that legal judgment about the new military's destruction of the Constitution was necessary for our descendants and our history. However, I did not seek it during my term as president because I did not want to burden the judiciary branch. I hoped that the day of the retrial decision would become a day when justice and history proved they were alive through nullification of the lawless judgment in the new military's court in 1980. Attorney Choi Jae-cheon worked hard for this retrial. His legal argument was clear and compelling.

On March 12, assemblymen who belonged to the Grand National and Democratic Parties abruptly laid a motion for the impeachment of President Roh Moo-hyun before the Assembly, arguing that he had violated the neutrality requirement. It passed through the National Assembly in a secret vote, and President Roh became the first Korean president to be impeached. Before the seventeenth general election, President Roh Moo-hyun said, "I hope the Korean people overwhelmingly support the Uri Party."

It was truly outrageous. The National Assembly should not have impeached a president that the Korean people had elected for such a small offense. I could not believe that party presidents like Choe Byung-yul and Chough Soon-hyung led this impeachment. The National Assembly immediately sent the impeachment decision to the constitutional court. It was tyranny by the majority. I thought that public opinion would not forgive it.

As I expected, a nationwide movement condemning the National Assembly rose. Candlelight vigils against the impeachment were held every day. Civic organizations considered it a practical coup d'état. Popular wrath exploded. This popular sentiment expanded to the seventeenth general election on April 15. The Uri Party was rising rapidly.

The Democratic Party members who remained in the party, refusing to join the Uri Party, were all looking at me to help them. The party was in critical condition, much more so than the Grand National Party. The Democratic Party claimed that they were the true successors of my ideology, policies, and philosophy. Assemblywoman Choo Mi-ae went to the Honam area with my son Hong Il in a wheelchair and appealed for the people's support, doing three-step-one-bow tours. They appealed to people to rescue the Democratic Party. How could I not know that this was a call for me? However, I decided not to come forward.

The Uri Party won the majority in the election, as expected. The Democratic Party collapsed, winning only nine seats. After the election, seven Democratic Party winners visited me. I tried to comfort them, saying, "Although you must be in pain now, take this as the momentum to begin again."

On April 22, 2004, a train disaster occurred in the town of Ryongchon, North Korea, near Sinuiju. Flammable cargo exploded at the station and about 3000 people either died or were hurt. It was a truly tragic incident. I sent a letter of condolence to Chairman Kim Jong-il.

Although I was retired, I received many invitations to international events. I was grateful and wanted to attend all of them to discuss lofty matters with world-class intellectuals, but I could not attend most of them due to my poor health. On May 10, 2004, I went on a trip to France, Norway, and Switzerland for the first time since my retirement, upon invitations from the OECD, Prime Minister of Norway Kjell Magne Bondevik, and the WHO. At the OECD Forum 2004, I gave the keynote speech, entitled "The 21st Century and East Asia." At the Nobel Institute in Norway, I gave an address, titled "The Sunshine Policy: Past, Present, and Future." At the fifty-seventh World Health Assembly in Geneva, Switzerland, I gave a special lecture, called "Health Care and Poverty Reduction as the Starting Point for the Happiness of Mankind."

After the lecture, I met and thanked Director-General Lee Jong-wook for WHO's support of North Korea. I also asked him to see to it that WHO became actively involved in improving the poor health care condition in North Korea. Director-General Lee promised to continue to pay attention to the matter, but he suddenly passed away of a cerebral infraction two years later. Since becoming the first Korean head of the international organization, he had devoted all of his passion and energy to eradicating illnesses and protecting the health of mankind. I was really sad.

On the fourth anniversary of the June 15 Joint Accord, both Koreas held various events, including an international conference and a Korean national festival. In particular, the Kim Dae-jung Presidential Library and Museum from the South and the Unification Research Institute from the North jointly held an international conference at the Grand Hilton Hotel in Seoul for four days, starting on June 14. Seven people from North Korea attended, including Vice Chairman of the Asia Pacific Peace Committee of Korea Lee Jong-hyok. I held the welcoming dinner for the attendees and gave a special address. Unfortunately, we could not hold a joint event commemorating the June 15 Joint Accord since then.

On June 29, I visited China upon the invitation of the Chinese People's Institute of Foreign Affairs. I met and talked to President Jiang Zemin. Former Chinese foreign minister Tang Jiaxuan and president of the Chinese People's Institute of Foreign Affairs Lu Qiutian joined the meeting from the Chinese side, and Korean Ambassador to China Kim Ha-joong and former Special Aid for Foreign Affairs and National Security Lim Dong-won attended from the Korean side. Although I was retired, President Jiang showed the same respect to me as before. I explained to him my thoughts about the Six-party Talks and China's role in it. "I believe that the North Korean nuclear problem will be resolved through Six-party Talks," I said. "However, even after you resolve the matter, I recommend that you not disband the 6-party talk, but expand it to a common cooperation body. I think it's desirable for it to continue to exist as a permanent establishment that would guarantee peace in the Korean Peninsula and Northeast Asia."

That night, he sent me a message through former Foreign Minister Tang. "I agree with your opinion that we should not settle, but elevate the Six-party Talks to a new peace establishment," he wrote. "A new mechanism is required in the Korean Peninsula, one that can protect the mutual interests of both Koreas."

I asked my secretaries to officially publicize this message in the hopes that all relevant countries in the Six-party Talks would carefully consider the idea.

I left Korea again on November 6, 2004, this time to visit Sweden and Rome, Italy, upon the invitation of Swedish Prime Minister Göran Persson, Mayor of Rome Walter Veltroni, and the Gorbachev Foundation. I gave an address at the Palmer Center in Sweden titled "Peace in the Korean Peninsula and Expectation for Sweden." At the fifth World Summit of Nobel Peace Laureates in Rome, I gave a keynote address. Former president Gorbachev, former president Lech Walesa, former president of Pubwash Joseph Rotblat, East Timorese Minister of Foreign Affairs Jose Ramos-Horta, Madam Betty Williams, and I adopted a joint declaration, wherein we urged the peaceful resolution of the North Korean nuclear issue and the Middle East crisis, and the preservation and strengthening of the Nuclear Non-proliferation Treaty.

On January 6, 2005, I celebrated my eighty-first birthday. President Roh Moo-hyun sent me a congratulatory message and orchid through Senior Secretary of Public Relations Lee Byung-wan. I sent a message to President Roh to urge the government's active role in advancing the inter-Korean relationship. "President Roh attended the June 15 event last year and thanked me for 'planting many seeds.' I said then, 'It is important to plant seeds, but it is more important to water and fertilize them to bear many fruits and to make sure that the Korean people can enjoy the fruits.'"

Yonsei University president Chung Chang-Young visited me that afternoon. I said to him, "I hope that the Kim Dae-jung Presidential Library and Museum will become the center of peace study that will contribute to peace in the Korean Peninsula, East Asia, and the world, in the spirit of the Nobel Peace Prize." I donated 300 million won from the award money I received with the 2000 Nobel Peace Prize to the presidential library.

Secretary Kim Hanjung, who had worked for me for a long time, went to study in the US. I wished for his success. Mr. Yang Bong-Ryull, a former Consul-General in Houston, was appointed to the post.

On February 10, 2005, North Korea's Foreign Ministry announced that Pyongyang had "produced nuclear weapons." They also withdrew the postponement of nuclear missile tests. This was immediately after President Bush's second term began. In early May that same year, North Korea's Foreign Ministry announced that it had "successfully finished unloading 8000 spent fuel rods" from its Yongbyon reactor. As the situation deteriorated, the US again tried to contact North Korea. As a result, the Six-party Talks resumed and the participants created a joint statement of principles to guide future negotiations. This statement showed that North Korea and the US had agreed to a package deal principle similar to that of the 1994 Geneva Agreed Framework. They agreed, first, that North Korea would abandon all nuclear weapons and existing nuclear programs; second, that North Korea and the US would respect each other's sovereignty, exist peacefully together, and take steps to normalize their relationship subject to their respective bilateral policies; third, that the Six Parties would undertake to promote economic cooperation in the fields of energy, trade and investment, bilaterally and/or multilaterally; fourth, that the Six Parties were committed to joint efforts for lasting peace and stability in Northeast Asia; and, fifth, that the Six Parties agreed to take coordinated steps to implement the aforementioned consensus in a phased manner in line with the principle of "commitment for commitment, action for action."

However, the US did not observe this agreement, either. Neocons continued to harass North Korea by exercising economic sanctions, such as freezing North Korean bank accounts in Banco Delta Asia in Macau.

North Korea strongly objected to this. The DPRK-US relationship was moving at a snail's pace and no solution could be found.

On March 15, I met Madam Yun Yun-jeong, the daughter of musician Yun I-sang, and reminisced about Mr. Yun I-sang together at the Kim Dae-jung Presidential Library and Museum. Mr. Yun had flown to Tokyo and held a press conference when I was kidnapped in 1973, and had worked with religious and democracy leaders in Germany in 1980 to save my life when I received the capital sentence. How could I ever forget him? Sadly, he passed away in 1995, before witnessing the peaceful regime change.

As the ideology of communism was painted over him, a great musician's patriotism and clean soul were wounded. In the end, he could not return to his home country. Only his music returned. It was such a sad incident. I celebrated the launch of the Yun I-sang Peace Foundation through a video message. "Master Yun I-sang was a world-renowned musician and the symbol of patriotism. We did not pay him the respect that he deserved while he was alive. Instead, we humiliated and pained him. It was a truly shameful past."

I went to the US with my wife upon the invitation of the Asia Foundation. In celebration of the fiftieth anniversary of the foundation, I gave a lecture on Korea's strategic role in the peace, security, and prosperity of Korea and Northeast Asia. I received an honorary doctorate in humanities from the University of San Francisco, and gave a lecture on human rights and the pursuit of social justice in Asia. I also gave a lecture on the inter-Korean relationship and the future of the Korean Peninsula at Stanford University.

The NIS announced that they had practiced illegal wiretapping under my government. This information came out during the investigation of the "Mirim Team," which had illegally wiretapped important people within the Korean Central Intelligence Administration (KCIA) under the Kim Young-sam government. It was absurd, and I could not believe that NIS officers ignored my stern order to eradicate illegal wiretapping. There was no doubt that I had been the greatest victim of the illegal wiretapping practice. It was not possible for me to order—or even *allow*—such a practice during my presidency. I had Secretary Choi Kyung-hwan announce my position on this scandal. He expressed my thoughts accurately, saying: "As the greatest victim of the KCIA and the Agency for National Security Planning, I ordered all NIS directors to abolish illegal wiretapping, political investigation, shadowing and surveillance, and torture. I also

banned all illegal information-gathering activities. I ordered the disband-
ment of the illegal wiretapping team as soon as I was elected. I also emphasized this during the NIS director's reporting, and I never received a
report about those illegal activities."

The Public Prosecutors Office sought arrest warrants for former directors of the NIS Lim Dong-won and Shin Kuhn for their violation of the
National Communication Privacy Protection Law. I refuted it through my
secretary again. He said: "The Government of the People eliminated the
illegal wiretapping team through restructuring and destroyed the illegal
wiretapping instruments. How could anyone do such an evil act to those
leaders?"

After seeing my sons go to prison, I thought that my suffering was over,
but I could not help being worried for the accused victims. It was truly
difficult for me to endure.

On August 10, I was hospitalized at Severance Hospital for a slight
fever and inflammation. The media reported that I was very unhappy
about the investigation into my government's "illegal wiretapping." The
implication was that I was suffering not only physically but also psychologically. That might have been true. After being tested, I was diagnosed
with bacillary pneumonia. Many people came to see me to the hospital.
North Korean leaders who had come to the South to attend the Korean
Nation Festival also visited me. I was discharged on August 21.

It was a difficult summer. I felt very weak. I was hospitalized again
because of difficulty in breathing and exhaustion on September 22. After
being tested, I was diagnosed with pulmonary edema. My wife stayed in
the hospital room with me. Although I felt weak, I could not eat well.
Even my voice failed me. My wife brought me dog soup and said that she
heard it was good for recovering energy. Usually, she abhorred even the
idea of dog soup, and always said she didn't understand how any human
being could do such a cruel thing. But she got even dog soup for me.
I had hoped that we could travel leisurely together after my retirement.
I had hoped to travel to Africa, where I had never been, and to tour all
over South America. Instead, my wife had to take care of me in a hospital
bed. I was discharged two weeks later.

On the fifth anniversary of my Nobel Peace Prize, I invited former
German president Von Weizsäcker and his wife to participate in a special
interview on "The Experience of German Reunification and the Korean
Peninsula." Seoul National University Professor Han Sang-jin moderated
the interview, which was broadcast on KBS TV at the end of the year.

Professor Han asked me about my method for building a system of peace in the Korean Peninsula, which was the dream of all Korean people.

"The North Korean nuclear issue should be resolved through the Six-party Talks," I said. "I expect that the missile and various chemical weapons issues could also be resolved after the resolution of the North Korean nuclear issue. After the North Korean nuclear issue is resolved, the Six-party Talks should become a permanent establishment that takes charge of security in the Korean Peninsula and Northeast Asia. In addition, Korea should end war by making a Korean Peninsula peace agreement and contribute to peace in the world by working together with other countries. For peace, we should become a country that gives hope to poor people in both the South and the North, and supports the poor, ill, and suffering people in the world."

Former president Von Weizsäcker also responded. "Do not hurry. Please do not repeat our mistake. We rushed to unify the currency, but it was a mistake economically, although there were political reasons for it. Also, you have to prepare thoroughly for unpredictable situations. I confess here that we were not fully prepared for unification."

Moderator Professor Han Sang-jin was a true and sincere scholar. He took charge of the Academy of Korean Studies and Presidential Commission on Policy Planning during my government. Although he did not want to become a government official, he could not reject the positions I entrusted him with. Whenever we met, we talked about Korean reunification procedures and the future of our nation. After my retirement, he visited me at my house and held my hand tightly, saying, "You have a lot more to do. You should stay healthy." However, I knew that my time was coming to a close.

YOU SHOULD WALK JUST HALF A STEP AHEAD OF YOUR PEOPLE (JANUARY 2006–MAY 2008)

Many politicians visited me for the New Year's celebration in 2006. I asked them to always pay attention to public opinion. I met the Uri Party leadership, including former Minister of Health and Welfare Kim Geun-tae and Speaker Kim Han-gill. "Who are your supporters who gave you majority seats and the presidency?" I asked. "The Uri Party should focus on reconnecting lost families. Please walk just half a step ahead, holding hands with the Korean people."

Although I appreciated the current government's series of democratic measures, it appeared to me that they were not doing too well in listening to public opinion. In modern politics, you can't succeed while ignoring the people. You should run neither too far ahead of nor too far behind them. Running apart from the people is like rushing toward failure. Politicians should always keep in mind the solemn principle of "with people," in whatever form. The more just and noble your goals are, the more strictly you should observe democratic principles.

I told the government and the Uri Party to be humble, to learn from and go with the people. I advised them that only then would runaways return home and bring their friends with them.

On February 11, 2006, we renamed the Forum of Democratic Leaders in the Asia-Pacific the Kim Dae-jung Peace Center. Former Ministers Kim Sung-jae, Lim Dong-won, and Kim Jung-kil had served as board presidents for the forum. Together with the renaming, I was inaugurated as the center's new board president. I appointed former Minister of Unification Jeong Se Hyun as board vice president. We decided on tasks such as inter-Korean reconciliation and cooperation; increasing peace in the Korean Peninsula, Northeast Asia, and the world; and reduction of poverty.

On March 21, I received an honorary doctorate in political science from Yeungnam University, the founder of which was the late president Park Chung-hee. At first I hesitated a little about the proposal, but I decided that there was no reason why I should, particularly if it would be helpful to the harmony between the East and the West. I hoped that we could leave the unhappy past behind.

After planting a tree in celebration of the event, I gave a "Seeking Truth Grounded on Concrete Evidence" calligraphy piece to the school. After my lecture, a female student said: "Please give advice to young people like me who want to become politicians."

"To succeed as a politician," I answered, "I believe that you should have the mind of a student and the sensibility of a merchant. With the firm foundation of a student's mind, based on principles and philosophy, you have to execute quick, merchant-like decisions."

I also repeated what I had said to the Uri Party leaders: "Walk only half a step ahead of the people, holding their hands." I also discussed leadership that serves and respects the people several times since I talked about it with Professor of University of Tokyo Kang Sang-jung.

Concrete discussions about my visit to North Korea were under way. This was first mentioned in late 2004, when Uri Party president Lee Bu-young asked me to visit as a special envoy for peace in the Korean Peninsula during his visit with me. I indirectly refused because North Korea needed to work not with me, but with President Roh Moo-hyun. I said, "The current government is important—not a former president. North Korea cannot be responsible for an agreement with me. They can take responsibility only when they make agreements with the current president."

There was another reason why I could not readily accept this proposal. Although we had an agreement for Chairman Kim Jong-il's return visit in the 2000 Accord, he had not yet kept his promise.

Meanwhile, in June 2005, Chairman Kim Jong-il said to Minister of Unification Chung Dong-young that he would like to invite former president Kim when the weather was nice. When I was hospitalized for pneumonia in August, Secretary of the Workers' Party of Korea Kim Ki-nam and Vice Chairman of the Committee for the Peaceful Reunification of Fatherland Lim Dong-ok visited me at the hospital and delivered Chairman Kim's invitation again. They paid reverence at the Seoul National Cemetery for the first time since the division of the country.

I thought a lot about this invitation and came to the conclusion that I should do any little thing possible if it would be helpful to establishing peace in the Korean Peninsula. I replied that I would contact them at an appropriate time, practically accepting their invitation.

In 2006, the prospect of my visit to Pyongyang drew attention both domestically and internationally. I said that I would visit North Korea not as special envoy, but as an individual. On April 25, Minister of Unification Lee Jong-seok visited me and explained the result of the ministerial-level inter-Korean meeting. He said that they discussed the organization of a working-level team for my visit to North Korea. I urged him to prepare it quietly and said, "As this is going to be a personal visit, it is not desirable for my visit to become a big issue."

Former Minister of Unification Jeong Se Hyun and my secretary Mr. Choi Kyung-hwan met with North Korean delegates at Mt. Kumgang on May 16 and 17. They comprehensively discussed my visit to the North and agreed that I would visit for three nights and four days in late June. However, they could not agree on my mode of transport, because our side wanted to use the train, while they insisted that I travel by air through the direct West Coast route.

I wanted to observe North Korea in detail, which traveling by train would allow me to do. There would not have been a technical problem with it. Also, if my visit by train happened, the inter-Korean train connection project might become livelier. However, in the end, I could not revisit North Korea. Late June came and went, but we did not hear from the North.

Then, on July 5, North Korea test-fired six missiles. International society condemned North Korea extremely severely. Because the US rejected North Korea's demand to lift the financial sanction and drove North Korea into a dire situation, North Korea once again chose an extreme response. However, this tactic would only offer the hardliners an excuse to attack North Korea harder. I was really disappointed with North Korea's shortsightedness. It became more difficult for me to visit North Korea. I could understand why North Korea did not invite me in the end. They clearly *could not* invite me.

On June 14, I attended the opening ceremony of the National Unification Grand Festival at World Cup Stadium in Gwangju. The next day, I attended the World Summit of Nobel Peace Laureates in Gwangju. The World Summit of Nobel Peace Laureates, which had begun in 1999 in order to discuss pressing issues threatening world peace, had been held in Rome six times previously. Gwangju was the first host city other than Rome. Seven individual winners, including Mikhail Gorbachev, Shirin Ebadi, Rigoberta Menchu, and representatives from seven group winners, such as Amnesty International, Red Cross, and International Physicians for the Prevention of Nuclear War International, attended the event. It was so meaningful for the missionaries of peace and human rights to gather in Gwangju, the holy city of the democratization movement. We had symposiums for two days on topics such as "Spirit of May 18 and Korean Democratization," "Spreading of Democracy and Growth in Human Rights in East Asia," "International Cooperation for the Spreading of Peace in East Asia," and "The June 16 Accord and Peace in the Korean Peninsula."

On June 18, I had a talk with former president of the Soviet Union Gorbachev at the KBS Special program. He clearly agreed with my idea of turning the Six-party Talks into a permanent institution. We agreed on pretty much everything. Moderator of the talk Professor Moon Chung-in summarized it well when he said, "The lesson is clear. Only when we pursue reconciliation and cooperation rather than coercion and antagonism, gradual change rather than radical change, multilateral cooperation rather than unilateralism, and mutual understanding and security, will peace and prosperity come to the Korean Peninsula."

On July 27, I began dictating for this autobiography. I also participated in the Kim Dae-jung Presidential Library and Museum Oral History

Project. Mr. Kim Taek-Geun, senior editorial writer for *Kyunghyang Shinmun*, library director Rhyu Sang-young, secretary Choi Kyung-hwan, director Chang Ok-chu, and research fellow Chang Sin-gi participated in the project.

Reverend Kang Won-yong passed away. He was my comrade in the democratization movement and a shepherd of our times. He worked a lot for interfaith harmony. Many religious leaders, including Buddhist master monks, brought flowers to him at the mortuary. His life was a truly beautiful one. I paid reverence at the mortuary on August 18 and talked about his incredible life. "Reverend Kang showed outstanding leadership for democratization and social justice in our land and in inter-Korean reconciliation and cooperation. He will be remembered in the Korean people's hearts forever."

Two months later, Attorney Hong Nam-sun passed away in Gwangju. He left behind his example of a righteous life as a human rights lawyer. A period seemed to be drawing to a close. Many comrades were leaving this world, leaving behind the legacy of many passionate moments of collaborative work to create a new world. Thinking about these things, I think of my death too.

On September 15, I did an interview for the inaugural issue of the Korean edition of the French magazine, *Le Monde Diplomatique*. I argued that neocons in the US were abusing North Korea, and urged the Bush administration to immediately resume a dialogue with North Korea. "The current deterioration in the relationship between North Korea and the United States is due to hurdles appearing everywhere," I said. "Although North Korea sincerely wishes to have a dialogue with the United States, neocons in the US are pushing North Korea up against a wall, much like Israel building walls in Palestine. Neocons should not interfere with the North Korean nuclear issue, and the Bush administration should respect the Korean opinion."

On September 24, I invited specialists in inter-Korean issues, including Lim Dong-won, Lee Jang-Hie, Paik Haksoon, Moon Chung-in, Kim Geun-sik, and Koh Yu-hwan to a lunch at the Korean restaurant Sujeong. We discussed what North Korean reaction would be to the US' coercion. Almost all attendees predicted that North Korea would perform nuclear tests. Their analysis was that the Korean Peninsula would be thrown into turmoil. It was very serious.

Fifteen days after this lunch, on October 9, the North Korean Central Broadcasting Station announced that North Korea had successfully conducted an underground nuclear test near the village of Punggye. The seismic wave was felt in South Korea too. It was truly reckless. President Roh Moo-hyun said, "We lost ground for an emphasis on dialogue." The next day, I had lunch with former presidents upon President Roh's invitation. At this lunch, which former Presidents Chun Doo-hwan and Kim Young-sam attended, Mr. Kim Young-sam abruptly began to attack the Sunshine Policy. He said to President Roh, "You got us into this situation because you succeeded former President Kim Dae-jung's policy and adopted the engagement policy." He then demanded that President Roh and I apologize to the Korean people. His malicious remarks continued for a while. He was truly rude.

"The inter-Korean relationship has progressed steadily and made achievements through the Sunshine Policy," I said. "The problem is the lack of progress in the relationship between North Korea and the United States. Whichever stage North Korean nuclear development has reached, we should dismantle it and prepare measures to prevent further North Korean aggression. We can think of three alternatives.

"First, we can engage in war. But the United States does not have the ability to do that while they are bogged down in Iraq. Besides, there is absolutely no place for war from the Korean people's point of view. Second, we can apply economic sanctions to North Korea. Although it will surely be painful for North Korea, it can offer an excuse for North Korean aggression near the truce line or NNL. Also, this will not have any effect unless China also participates. Third, North Korea and the United States can engage in a dialogue. Democratic Party and former Secretary of State James Baker, who is from the United States, also thinks there should be engagement between the two countries.

"Don't we all know which of these three is the wisest approach? We should calmly handle the situation. The UN resolution is important, and we should discuss it with the four powerful countries. Before the nuclear test, we had to work to prevent it. But now that it's done, we don't have to lead the sanction."

President Roh clarified that he would prudently manage the situation to prevent anxiety and disturbance among the Korean people.

The next day, while I was staying at a hotel in Gwangju for a lecture at Chonnam National University, I received a phone call from President Roh. He said to me, "I am sorry I made you uncomfortable yesterday." He sounded as if he thought that I was unilaterally attacked. I pointed out that whether or not I was insulted was not as important as his problematic understanding of the situation. I mentioned the problems with his remark that acknowledged the limits of the engagement policy and the debate on the Sunshine Policy.

"What is wrong with the engagement policy?" I asked him. "Why did you say that about the engagement policy when it has always eased tension in the inter-Korean relationship? I cannot agree with you that North Korean nuclear testing is connected to the innocent Sunshine Policy. The Sunshine Policy is not such an easy target."

President Roh responded that he completely agreed with me. Since then, his government has gradually distanced itself from hardliner tactics against North Korea.

I received an honorary doctorate in literature from Chonnam National University. Since I was given the opportunity to give a lecture, I scolded North Korea and the US at the same time. I said: "North Korea should abandon nuclear armament. They should stop this tactic that does not accomplish any purpose in front of the vast nuclear strategy of the United States, but only encourages hardliner policies in the United States and Japan. Instead, it is desirable for them to demand a direct dialogue with the United States.

"The nuclear test by North Korea means the failure of the United States' policy for the North Korean nuclear issue. This is combined with North Korea's withdrawal from NPT, expelling International Atomic Energy Agency agents, and abandoning the 1994 Agreed Framework. Since 1994, we have argued for a package deal. However, the Bush administration has continued to ignore this and brought about today's failure."

Many media outlets requested interviews with me, including *Newsweek*, Reuters, CBS, AP, and the French newspaper *Liberation*. In interviews, I said: "North Korean nuclear tests prove the failure of the Bush administration's hardliner policy for the past six years. The United States should make a sharp turn and engage North Korea right now."

That November, the Democratic Party won the majority at the US midterm election, which weakened President Bush's position. In the end, the US began a bilateral dialogue with North Korea, and the Six-party Talks in February 2007 agreed upon and adopted an "action plan" of initial steps to implement the September 19, 2005, joint statement on North Korea's denuclearization. Since then, both North Korea and the US have steadily and quickly followed up on their agreements. North Koreans handed over their 18,000-page nuclear development documents and blew up the cooling tower in Yongbyon.

On October 28, I visited Mokpo for the first time since my retirement. It had been eight years since my last visit. Citizens were overflowing the Mokpo Station Square to welcome me.

I sang "Spring in My Hometown" and "Tears of Mokpo" along with Mokpo citizens. I slowly looked around downtown Mokpo through the car window. Citizens gathered everywhere, waved their hands, and shouted, "Please be healthy!" Their faces were bright and happy. Although it was fall, my hometown was warm. The next day, I visited the Jeollanam-do gubernatorial office in Muan. The building, which was completed a year before, was grand and clean. From the observation deck of the building, I looked out at the areas near Mokpo and Muan. I wrote in the guestbook: "No Honam, No Korea."

On November 2, the exhibition hall of the Kim Dae-jung Presidential Library and Museum opened. Many guests, including President Roh Moo-hyun, attended the opening ceremony. That night, an event to support the library was held at Yonsei University Auditorium. I presented three agenda: democracy, peace, and elimination of poverty.

President Roh visited me at my home two days later. As far as I can remember, that was the first time a current president visited a former president at his home. President Roh looked around the living room and said, "I waited here for you in the old days. I visited you to learn, and sometimes to borrow money."

I remembered the old days too. President Roh expressed much interest in the presidential library. He said it would not be easy for other presidents to build a presidential library and museum, including himself. "Some presidents have too many things to hide, so they will not have many things to exhibit," he observed. "As for me, I do not have many things to exhibit and I have not kept many things, either."

That frankness and simplicity were characteristics that made him charming. First Lady Kwon Yang-sook said, "He does not have a single photograph wearing a judge's robe from his judge days." I treated them to lunch. President Roh's expression made it clear that he still felt awkward about the uncomfortable lunch at the Blue House following the North Korean nuclear test. We exchanged a silent dialogue.

On November 12, I was selected to receive the 2007 Van Fleet Award that is annually given by the Korea Society. Van Fleet was a general who served as the commander of the US Eighth Army. The Korea Society has given this award to people who contributed to the relationship between Korea and the US annually since 1992.

My son Hong Up was elected to the National Assembly at the special election on April 23, 2007. He had restored his honor. I was overjoyed. I urged him to work hard without losing sight of his principles.

On May 12, 2007, I left for Germany to receive the first Freedom Award from Free University of Berlin. After the award ceremony on May 16, I made a speech on the Berlin Declaration and peace in the Korean Peninsula. I remembered when I had issued the Berlin Declaration seven years before. Germany had developed a lot in the meantime. It appeared that the economic gap between East and West Germany had reduced considerably. When shall we achieve reunification? I felt sad.

I met a very special person during this visit to Germany. Mrs. Renate Hong had been living alone for forty-six years, raising two sons on her own after she sent her husband to study abroad in North Korea just one year after their marriage. He never returned. She asked me to help her reunite with her husband before they died. It was such a sad and moving story. In July 2008, she met her husband with the help of the Red Cross and the North Korean Embassy. There were dispersed families in places other than the Korean Peninsula.

I also visited the Jewish Museum in front of the Federal Convention Building. I was very surprised at the scale and size of this museum. There were hundreds of caskets in a room the size of two soccer fields. Reading the stories of numerous victims, I wondered how human beings could be so cruel. There is no other country in the world that so thoroughly regrets its past and educates people so much about it as Germany does.

On June 19, futurist scholar Dr. Alvin Toffler visited me at my house. Together with Microsoft CEO Bill Gates and the CEO of Softbank Son Jeong-ui, Dr. Toffler had been the most influential figure in Korea's IT project. He predicted that humanity would suffer from "future shock," that is, a personal perception of "too much change in too short a period of time," more often in the future. However, he also speculated that our brains would change due to developments in neurology and genetics, which would help us to overcome this limit thirty to fifty years later. He was predicting the emergence of a new humanity.

Although interesting, I also got goose bumps listening to his prediction. What would the future be like? How will the new humanity live? Although enormous waves are overtaking us, we're having trouble perceiving them. According to Dr. Toffler's predictions, the next half-century will be the most difficult and confusing period in humanity. I thought that people who could not adjust to new waves and fell into panic could resist the change altogether, arguing for the return to a primitive society. Dr. Toffler also agreed with my concern.

On September 17, I visited Washington, DC and New York upon the invitation of former president Bill Clinton, the National Press Club, and the Korea Society. I met president of the Korea Economic Institute (KEI) Jack Pritchard, Professor Don Oberdorfer, former Secretary of State Colin Powell, president of the Heritage Foundation Edwin Feulner, former Secretary of State Madeleine Albright, former Counselor of the US Department of State Wendy Sherman, former Minister of Finance Robert Rubin, former Deputy Secretary of Finance David Lipton, and former Secretary of State Henry Kissinger. I was very glad to see these people who had been my partners in political, economic, and diplomatic fields during my presidency. I also met former Senior Secretary of Economy Lee Ki-ho, UN Secretary General Ban Ki-moon, and Minister of Foreign Affairs and Trade Song Min-soon.

I tried to appeal to and persuade them about the peaceful resolution of the North Korean nuclear issue, mobilizing all my common sense and logic. Everyone agreed with and encouraged me.

As usual, I found my conversation with former Secretary of State Henry Kissinger useful. I asked him about the future of China and the relationship between Korea and China. He said: "China will, of course, become stronger. It is important to have China as a partner. Also, the stronger the Chinese economic and military power becomes, the more important it is for the United States and Korea to continue to have a close relationship. It is dangerous if Korea neglects either one of the powers or oscillates between China and the United States."

Mr. Kissinger asked me about Japan. "Its current trend of swinging to the right is worrisome," I replied. "And the young people's and young congressmen's trend of swinging to the right is even more worrisome. They deny past Japanese aggression and those Koreans and Chinese who were victims of Japanese aggression respond sensitively to such denials. The fundamental reason why Japanese people swing to the right is because they were not taught about their past aggressions. Unlike Germans, 90 percent of Japanese under the age of sixty-five do not know what the Japanese did, which is why they do not regret their past. Recently, Francis Fukuyama expressed worries about Japanese international isolation."

Mr. Kissinger showed much interest in and support of me. As I thanked him, he said, "It is because you have a wonderful vision and imagination."

"It is my great honor to hear you, a world-renowned scholar, say that about me," I thanked him. "I will definitely mention this remark by you in my autobiography."

Former Minister of Finance Robert Rubin and former Deputy Secretary of Finance David Lipton had watched the Korean foreign currency crisis and actively helped my government; they appreciated my philosophy of parallel development of democracy and market economy. Former Minster Rubin voiced his concerns about the US economy: "The US economy needs restructuring in all areas, including finance and education, like the Korean economy did in 1998. For that, we need a leader like you. If you'll run in the US presidential election, I know Lipton here will help you run the campaign."

"I'm so flattered that I probably will not be able to fall asleep tonight," I responded.

We had a good laugh. During the foreign currency crisis, we established good policies and did not doubt one another's intentions. In retrospect, how many critical moments there were! I worked really hard. I was happy that I was able to laugh today.

My secretary Yang Bong-Ryull returned to the Ministry of Foreign Affairs and started his new post as Ambassador to Malaysia. Home-based Ambassador Ha Tae-yun was appointed as my secretary.

On October 2, President Roh left for the inter-Korean summit in Pyongyang. I watched him walk across the DMZ live on TV. Chairman Kim Jong-il did not look as energetic as he had looked in 2000. In the end, Chairman Kim Jong-il's promised return trip did not happen until a second visit to Pyongyang by the South Korean president. How fortunate it was to have this summit, belated as it was! Until the day we achieved reunification, the inter-Korean summits should keep happening.

I had urged and appealed many times for the inter-Korean summit. However, it happened only toward the end of President Roh's term. The summit concluded with an eight-point joint declaration in which both sides agreed to take steps toward reunification, ease military tensions, expand meetings of separated families, and engage in social and cultural interchanges. The declaration also expressed a "shared understanding" by the two countries "on the need to end the current armistice mechanism and build a permanent peace mechanism." It was quite a lot of progress. The agreement to create a "special peace and cooperation zone in the West Sea" was particularly noteworthy because the Yeonpyeong Battles occurred in the West Sea, and there was always the danger that warfare might break out in the area again.

However, the opposition party attacked this agreement, again accusing it of being a *peojugi* (free giving), while claiming that we wouldn't have the funding for what was promised. To this criticism, I loudly claimed that this *peojugi* would soon turn out to be *peo-ogi* (free taking). North Koreans speak the same language as us and we share the same culture. They live nearby and offer the most economical but highest-quality labor. There are also an enormous amount of underground resources in North Korea. According to a report by the Korean Chamber of Commerce and Industry, these underground resources are worth $2 trillion. If we create a common profit with North Korea from these resources, we can enter an era of *peo-ogi*.

The Kaesong Industrial Complex had been the foremost frontline base for an attack on Seoul. We built an industrial complex after pushing away three brigades and long-range missiles from the North. If we gave away Munsan to North Korea, what would the South Koreans think? As for Mt. Kumgang, North Korea gave us Changjin Port, which had been a place of strategic importance for their navy. North Korea gave up their pride in order to eat and survive. Our engagement policy is now shaking down North Korean society in its entirety.

In addition, there are bonanzas north of North Korea in Central Asia and Siberia. There are rich minerals, oil, and gas. If the inter-Korean relationship improves and we open the Iron Silk Road, we can export our excellent merchandise and import rich resources directly. As in the legendary story of Heungbu, who takes care of a swallow with a broken leg only to be rewarded with treasures from the swallow the next year, taking care of North Korea will eventually bring us great fortune. It is clear that we will give a peck and get a bushel.

In fact, there are a lot of misunderstandings in this *peojugi* controversy. Before the reunification, West Germany sent $3.2 billion to East Germany every year for twenty years. We have sent $150 million annually for thirteen years. On average, this means that South Korea sent 5000 won ($4–5) per person per year to help North Korea. As a reward, we ended the Cold War system and opened an era of reconciliation and cooperation. The tension in the peninsula abruptly eased and we have lived for the past ten years without worrying about security. Considering the enormous amount of national defense costs, the *peojugi* controversy is completely off the mark.

Also, there are people who accuse us of ignoring the issue of human rights in North Korea. I do not think that is an accurate assessment of the situation. There are layers to human rights. In the modern period, political rights—such as freedom of the press, assembly, and association—are important, but there are social rights too, such as the right not to starve, to live a healthy life, and to live safely. Supporting North Korea with food, fertilizer, medical supplies, and daily necessities is helping them with basic social human rights. When hundreds of thousands of North Koreans are starving and dying, how much are we helping them? Also, there are thousands of North Korean escapees. We protect them by offering living expenses. No other country that raises North Korean human rights issues accepts these escapees. We *are* contributing to their human rights by accepting them. If we really care about their human rights, we should push the inter-Korean interchange and cooperation and help North Korea stand alone. Then they can take care of their human rights problem themselves.

On November 23, I received a certificate of appreciation from the chief of the Korea branch of Amnesty International, Go Eun Tae, for my efforts to abolish capital punishment. During my five-year term, not a single person was executed. I believe we should never take away God-given life at our will. In Buddhism, there is a saying, *manyubulseong*, which means "There is Buddha in every life." Life is a God-given human right and the very essence of democratic rights. Even under the name of the law, killing another human being is a great sin. There are frequently examples of misjudgment and intentional political abuse of capital punishment. In particular, there have been many examples of the latter in Korea. I am an example of someone who barely escaped capital punishment; the People's Revolutionary Party Incident, which I discussed previously, is another good example.

Capital punishment was devised to prevent and reduce atrocious crimes. But there is no evidence that capital punishment actually accomplishes this. Conversely, violent crimes seem to have increased. Capital punishment destroys a person's life in vain and does not contribute to the stability and peace of our society. Rather, we can expect to reduce violent crimes by abolishing capital punishment and refining our social environment. There are many examples of changes of heart by condemned criminals. There are both angels and devils in the human heart. Defeating evil depends on environment, education, faith, and personal effort. We should not deprive anybody of an opportunity for such personal transformation.

One hundred and thirty-one countries in the world have already either abolished capital punishment or not executed condemned criminals in the past ten years. To become a member country of the EU, a nation is required to abolish capital punishment. My faith and belief in human rights has led me to the conclusion that capital punishment should be replaced by life sentences. Although I wanted to reduce all condemned criminals' sentences to life sentences, I could not ultimately coordinate different departments' needs in such a way that this was possible to accomplish. At least I was able to reduce some condemned criminals' sentences. I still regret that I could not accomplish what I believed to be right. By abolishing capital punishment, we can join the group of civilized countries. I also believe that is what God wants. Under my government, Korea became a country that *practically* abolished capital punishment. I hope that we will *legally* abolish it soon.

In celebration of the seventh anniversary of my Nobel Peace Prize, we held the Burma (Myanmar) Democratization Night event. A few months before, the Saffron Revolution, an anti-military dictatorship and pro-democracy demonstration, occurred in Myanmar. In the course of this, thousands of monks and citizens were either killed or arrested. The name "saffron" came from the color of the robes that the monks wear. Madam Aung Saan Sui Kyi, who spent more than twelve years under house arrest during the eighteen-year military dictatorship, was imprisoned again.

The history of Myanmar is similar to ours. They were colonized by England and Japan for sixty years, and the military took power through coup d'état in 1962. Thousands of people were either killed or wounded during the struggle for democracy in 1988. This historical similarity made me sad. Whenever I met leaders of the Myanmar democracy movement, I encouraged them by saying that democracy requires blood and tears; that, unfortunately, true democracy cannot be achieved without this, although outside support is important too. I really hoped that they would end the long-term military dictatorship and achieve democracy with the recent Saffron Revolution. We collected $40,000 through the event and delivered it to the movement activists through the appropriate channels.

The Democratic Party candidate was dealt a crushing defeat at the December 19 presidential election. Throughout my entire political career, I had never seen this kind of defeat happen. The prospect for next year's general election was also very grim. There was a danger of one-party rule and the subsequent collapse of the long tradition of the two-party system. But, even worse, there did not seem to be any ingenious plan to break through this situation. During President Roh Moo-hyun's five-year term, the foundation of the Democratic Party collapsed. The special prosecutor appointment regarding the financial aid to North Korea and breaking up the ruling party had been mistakes. In addition, President Roh had disappointed

Honam natives and the youth, his greatest support base, by violating a very fundamental principle and proposing a coalition government to the Grand National Party.

In addition to regional cliquism, there was another bad legacy that had to be eliminated from Korean politics: school cliquism. Although I tried very hard to reform high school- and college-based cliquism during my term, I could not root it out. I often saw people who did not appear to subscribe to school cliquism but were indeed mired in it. I also tried to guard myself. I found it fortunate that I had graduated from a commercial high school and was, therefore, relatively free from such cliquism.

I was worried about President-Elect Lee Myung-bak's governance. He revealed an autocratic tendency, which he was known to have wielded during his years as the president of a construction company. His government reform plan was like a bulldozer, crushing everything in front of it, proposing to either abolish or reduce the Ministry of Unification, Ministry of Science and Technology, Ministry of Information and Communication, and Ministry of Women. In my opinion, these were offices that would feed us in both the present and the future. His shortsightedness seemed very dangerous. In particular, he came up with the policy of "abandonment of nuclear development before cooperation," a policy that even the Bush administration had already abandoned. When he had visited me as a presidential candidate, he said many times that he sympathized with the Sunshine Policy. I had expected him to be practical as he claimed and to not go against the current, but I seem to have misjudged him. Being practical means finding the most universally agreed-upon road for the country and the people, but he seemed to misunderstand the concept of practicality.

His inauguration speech was disappointing too. It included neither philosophy nor vision. It was just a list of policies without any plans. Of the inter-Korean relationship, he said that he would respond to the inter-Korean summit any time, but his words did not carry any sincerity. In particular, he did not mention at all how he would carry through with the agreements made in the first and second summits.

On January 28, I watched the epic TV drama *Yi San*. Watching the fate of Crown Prince Sado and King Jeongjo, I learned again how cruel factional strife was during the Joseon period. However, I was also proud of King Jeongjo, who, after surviving it, made great achievements in governance during his twenty-year reign.

After my retirement, I enjoyed dramas and, in particular, historical dramas. During my presidency, I suggested to president of KBS Park Kwonsang that it would be great to make historical dramas about three great men in Korean history: Yi Sun-sin, Jeon Bong-jun, and Chang Bo-go. This was, of course, the opinion of a private individual. I think that Jeon Bong-jun was a great man who we should be proud of. The anti-feudal ideas that Jeon Bong-jun and Donghak peasants advocated for were the most advanced ideas of their time. It is remarkable that a teacher at a traditional school in the countryside had a sense of mission that included the liberation of slaves, permission for widows' remarriage, domestic tax administration reform, and anti-imperialism. He put his beliefs into action and rose up as the leader of millions of peasants. "Sea King" Chang Bo-go was also a great man who made Koreans proud by traveling across oceans and continents.

In connection with their historical backgrounds, their lives appeared to yield most dramatic television. If I had been a program director, I would have wanted to depict them. After my retirement, the lives of Yi Sun-sin and Chang Bo-go were made into TV dramas. *Immortal Admiral Yi Sun-sin* was truly excellent, but *Haesin* (Emperor of the Sea), which was modeled after the life of Chang Bo-go, was disappointing. Rather than depicting a hero of the sea, it highlighted domestic political strife.

On February 11, president of the Daetonghap Minjusindang Party Sohn Hak-kyu and president of the Democratic Party Park Sang-chun announced that they would unite their parties and form the Tonghap Minjudang Party (abbreviated as Democratic Party). Although President Roh Moo-hyun broke up the Democratic Party and created the Uri Party, his party lost the local election, special election, and then the presidential election. The party was full of wounds. I had always argued for the grand unification of the parties, and I was happy to see it happen.

I went to Mokpo on February 15. Governor of Jeollanam-do Park Joon-young and mayor of Mokpo Jeong Jong-deuk came out to welcome me. My visits to my hometown were always warm. I visited the sites of the Decisive Victory of Myeongnyang. In the Decisive Victory of Myeongnyang, Admiral Yi Sun-sin and a Joseon Navy of twelve ships defeated a Japanese Navy of 133 ships with courage and ingenuity, reversing the tide of the war. It was indeed the place where our country was saved. The Jeolla people and their ancestors, who never stopped working to defeat the enemy during the first and second Japanese invasions, deserved our praise. I saw the strong currents of Uldolmok from a restaurant on the side of Usuyeong. The strength of those currents was so powerful that they seemed to have come directly out of history. I felt so moved that I would never forget that feeling.

In Jindo, I visited the old site where Sambyeolcho resisted the Goryeo dynasty that had yielded to Mongol for nine months. To resist the foreign influence, they even founded an independent kingdom. Although they could not hold out for long, their spirit of independence deserves our appreciation. Jindo residents welcomed me, with people everywhere waving their hands.

The Korean Wave is sweeping the world. According to media reports, the Korean Wave reached even the faraway continent of Africa. The movies, dramas, songs, and music that we make are grabbing the attention of the world. The Korean Wave is probably the most successful software product that we could draw from our old cultural heritage.

There is no doubt that our culture is very elegant. Nothing is vulgar. Although many foreign cultures have flowed into our country, we haven't entirely assimilated with them. We've filtered them and incorporated them into ours. Although we mixed with them, we didn't disappear into them. We have the ability to create the best by mixing the past and the present, and our own and the foreign.

Once I went to the National Museum of Korea and saw the traditional *bojagi* exhibition. Ordinary women—our mothers and sisters—made them. People from all around the world came to see them and were amazed at these handcrafted products that were made under traditional lamps. The artistic sensibilities of the mostly illiterate women during the Joseon period were just amazing. These elegant genes run through our bodies.

I trusted our culture and the underlying abilities of the Korean people who created it. When we decided to open our door to Japanese culture, some people were worried about our cultural subjection to Japan. But I truly believed in our culture. No thought or philosophy withered in our country. They took root in Korea in our own way. That is because the Korean people have the ability and room to absorb other cultures.

On March 18, Han Bi-ya, a World Vision Korea emergency relief team leader, visited me. She is a remarkable person who travels all around the world on foot and offers support to disaster zones. She adopted three children of different races. As someone who practices love of humanity with courage and conscience all over the world, she is another kind of Korean Wave.

In April, I visited Portland, Oregon and Boston, Massachusetts, in the US. It was a sort of speech tour. I received an honorary doctorate from the president of University of Portland William Beauchamp, and gave a lecture, titled "Challenges and Responses, and God." After my speech, people gave me a standing ovation. President Beauchamp said to me, "I have listened to many lectures in my life, but I am most moved by your lecture." I was happy and grateful to still be able to move someone, even in my old age.

I arrived in Boston and visited Harvard University on April 20. It had been twenty-four years since I studied at the Harvard University Center for International Affairs. I was very moved. I met President Drew Gilpin Faust and gave a lecture at the Kennedy School titled: "The Sunshine Policy is the Way to Success." It was a very important address for me. I revised the manuscript many times. I had lunch with old friends at the Harvard Faculty Club, where I'd had lunch many times with friends like Professors James Leach and Ezra Vogel. I walked around the campus and reminisced about the old days. The souvenir shop, which I had often visited, was still there. I bought gifts for my grandchildren.

Since the beginning of my political career, I have always worked hard writing the manuscripts for my addresses. I always wanted to include many things. Whenever there were rallies, I was always worried about my speech. But I enjoyed writing, too. It was exciting to address other people with my ideas. I have made innumerable public speeches over the course of my career. There were times when I even thought that politics was nothing more than speeches. That's why I wrote my manuscripts earnestly, pouring all of my spirit and effort into them. The "labor pains" were tremendous for important speeches. I moved from one hotel room to the next hotel room, thinking and polishing.

Audiences sometimes cheered at my speeches, and other times they became angry about what I said. Although all of these are now long-ago memories, I cannot forget those moments. More than a million people gathered to hear my serious speeches at Jangchungdan Park, Yeouido Square, and Boramae Park. Speeches were also the most useful instruments to spread my thoughts. My every word had to enter deeply into the audience's heart.

I tried to write speeches that anybody could understand, with clear sentences and easy examples. I was careful not to fall into the trap of flowery prose, and excluded sentences that could be misunderstood. I also repeated important ideas almost to the point of tiring the audience. Only then could they recognize what I was saying.

During my presidency, secretaries in charge drafted my speeches, but I polished them myself. Although they tried their best, sometimes my secretaries did not understand me accurately. Other times, they were not as clear as I wanted them to be. I had to write and polish at midnight and during rests. Secretary Lee Hoon read my thoughts most accurately.

In order to persuade others, I had to know what I was saying very well. For me, writing speeches was a sort of study and an opportunity to sum up my ideas. Also, a speech had to be sincere. If you fall into the trap of word-play or rhetoric, your values, philosophy, and will simply disappear. I thought of my speeches as historical documents.

During my presidency, the most memorable speeches were my addresses at the joint congressional session in the US (June 1998), the Japanese Parliament (October 1998), the Berlin Declaration (March 2000), and the Nobel Peace Prize Acceptance Speech (December 2000). As I mentioned before, I continued to polish my speech for the joint congressional session in the US even after I arrived at my hotel room. I finished the manuscript right before my speech. I was happy to receive a standing ovation after that speech. For the speech at Japanese Parliament, I focused on the plan for the future of the Korea-Japan relationship. I used the Berlin Declaration to let the important change in Korean policy toward North Korea be known to the world. I honestly reflected on my life in my Nobel Peace Prize Acceptance Speech.

I did not write any of my speeches randomly. I took care and tried my best. In this autobiography, I have included considerable excerpts from my speeches because they were very often more accurate than any explanation or rhetoric could be. Also, because they contain my philosophy, vision, passion, and values as they were.

During summits, I also tried to open my counterpart's heart by using clear logic and easy language. I tried to speak reasonably. I also made sure to include some nugget that my counterpart could take away from our conversation. That's why I had to prepare so much. I also needed an interpreter who could accurately translate my style. I trusted interpreters Kang Kyung-Wha and Kim Il-beom. I took note of interpreter Kang Kyung-Hwa when I was an assemblyman and she was working for a foreign dignitary at the National Assembly, and picked her as my interpreter during my presidency.

SOME THINGS ARE ETERNAL (MAY 2008–JUNE 2009)

Citizens held candlelight vigils every day. Koreans were entirely outraged by the excessive yielding on beef import in the Korea-US Free Trade Agreement (FTA). In particular, our government's approach to mad cow disease appeared too naïve. The Korean government should have listened to the people's cries to regain their healthy sovereignty.

The candlelight vigils were not about the beef import alone, though. They appeared to originate also from people's accumulated frustration with the government about various issues: the Grand Canal project; the attempt to introduce an English immersion program into early education; rapid increase in education costs; excessive inflation; preferential treatment in government personnel hiring; random layoffs of civil servants with guaranteed terms; and the worsening inter-Korean relationship. I had the impression that President Lee Myung-bak treated the Korean people with the mentality and sensibility of the Yusin period, without clearly understanding the enormous change that had been under way in our society for the past decade.

Candlelight vigils were evolving unusually. Koreans carried out direct democracy—made possible by the Internet and text messages—for the first time since its equivalent, the *agora* (marketplaces and civic centers), in ancient Athens. The Korean people's wisdom and power were truly remarkable. The foundation of this was the IT society that the Government of the People had worked so hard on.

When citizens uploaded their opinions online or communicated them via text messages, they spread instantly all across the country. After planning discussions in cyberspace, people gathered in public squares. They held festive cultural events. Unlike rallies in the past, these rallies didn't have sponsors or directors. Neither PR nor mobilization was necessary. And, of course, it cost nothing. The impact on the people was enormous.

People in President Lee's government arrogantly believed they could just turn back the clock to the previous decade. They recognized neither that the information- and knowledge-based era was upon us, nor that this great revolution had already happened in the past decade. In fact, even I, who had argued for the great transformation of our times, did not realize how much society had evolved.

On the eighth anniversary of the June 15 Summit, held at the 63 Building, I made the opening remarks entitled "I Think of the Korean People." I said, "Through the recent candlelight vigils, we're experiencing direct democracy in Korea for the first time since it began in Athens, Greece, two thousand years ago. This democracy is carried out through alliances between online communities who gather through the internet and text messages and offline, through street rallies and candlelight festivals. We should recognize that these people who gather peacefully are becoming an important part of direct democracy, and we must find ways to accept their demands."

I thought of many things as I observed the candlelight vigils. I thought that human history was not determined by economy, as Marx had theorized, but by the intellectuals who play such a major role. During the feudal period, peasants were ignorant, and the king and a small number of aristocrats and officials alone owned knowledge and governed the country. However, during the capitalist period, the bourgeoisie class that owned both knowledge and money held hegemony, and controlled workers and farmers. Nowadays, with the advancements in industrial society, workers are educated, so the alliance of workers and intellectuals hold power. Finally, everyone participates in governance. I saw the beginning of a new form of direct democracy in the candlelight vigils.

Utterly alarmed, the Lee Myung-bak government blocked Seoul Square in front of Seoul City Hall. They blocked events not only of a political nature, but of any nature. I had many expectations for Seoul Square, after it was established in 2004. As it was the birthplace of street cheering during the World Cup Games and a dynamic tourist destination, I did not doubt that it would be reborn as the public square of communication. I believed that it would become the open space where musicians played, orators spoke about current affairs, and acrobats displayed their skills.

I thought that the more expanded cyberspace became, the more we needed this kind of real space. Although I had never deeply engaged in cyberspace, I knew that it was possible for our descendants to suffer from the solitude of the Internet. It is true that the street culture in our nation has not flourished much. However, it will be different from now on. In a democratic society, we need an open space. In the participative, direct democracy of the Internet, we also need an open space where we can gather offline to communicate with our eyes and mouths, where speeches can be given. During my presidency, I expressed strong regrets to the Seoul City administration for turning Yeouido Square into a park. This project had already begun before I became president. In April 1998, I said to acting Mayor Kang Deock-ki during a report on the operation of Seoul, "The City of Seoul eliminated Yeouido Square. There is no public square to speak of now in Seoul. Where in the world do you find a capital city like that? The park could have been created in places other than Yeouido. Why on earth did you eliminate the public square and turn the city of Seoul, with 11 million people, into a city without a single public square?"

It was a deploration rather than a reproach. Yeouido Square was equivalent in size to Tiananmen Square in China or the Red Square in Russia. An island in the middle of the city, Yeouido was, indeed, a godsend. If the street cheering for the 2002 World Cup Games had occurred in the Yeouido Square, it would have been another kind of spectacle.

Although I did not like them planting grass in the newly created Seoul Square, I still did not doubt that it would become a space for the citizens. Unfortunately, Seoul Square was becoming more and more isolated. After the candlelight vigil, the government thoroughly blocked citizens' approach to it. Why should the authorities be so afraid of an open space? Why do they fear public opinion? It is only when the public square is alive and the citizens' speeches are vibrant that the country and its people are comfortable. This is proven by the histories of countries that have had public squares.

On July 11, a female tourist at Mt. Kumgang was shot to death during an early morning walk. She appeared to have strayed into a restricted area. It was a very sensitive, ominous, and unfortunate accident. Our government immediately demanded a site investigation by our investigation team and temporarily stopped the Mt. Kumgang tour. Although North Korean authorities expressed "regrets," they rejected the demand for investigation, saying that the South was responsible for this accident. I hoped that they would resolve this dispute through dialogue, and that this incident would not serve as momentum to entirely cease the Mt. Kumgang tour and other projects in the Kaesong Industrial Complex and other places. However, the situation continued to deteriorate.

Soon afterward, the newly appointed Blue House Chief of Staff Chung Jung-gil and Senior Secretary of Political Affairs Maeng Hyung-gyu visited me to give their regards. I gave them advice about the recent Mt. Kumgang Incident and the Dokdo issue that was also in dispute then. I said to them that they should look at these problems not with a microscope, but with a telescope. When new Speaker of the Assembly Kim Hyong-o visited me to pay his respects, I said the same thing.

Amnesty International East Asia Team researcher Norma Kang Muico visited me when she traveled to Seoul to investigate the candlelight vigils and human rights violations. She said that, although people working at the

Amnesty International Korea branch had tried to dissuade her from visiting me so as not to offend the Korean government, she had insisted. "Mr. Kim Dae-jung is my hero," she said simply. She teared up in front of me. I was moved, too.

I received an honorary doctorate from the University of Malaysia. As I did not feel well, my wife attended the ceremony on my behalf. The award statement was very special—they knew about my life very well and their expression was very elegant. The statement ended with the words: "We would not be able to capture the entire drama of his life and its greatness through these episodes. We just would like to look back on his life that captured so many people and reflect on the essence of his life."

On August 13, the anniversary of my safe return from kidnapping, my family members gathered at Hong Il's house in Seogyo-dong to celebrate the occasion. My children are all good-hearted and bright. My greatest fortune is that I have a harmonious family in which everyone loves and cares about each other. My family members were oppressed in innumerable ways because of me. However, even in the midst of this suffering, we loved one another and gathered our strength. We became one in our efforts to serve our neighbors and to bring about a just society.

Before I became president, all of our family members—my three sons, three daughters-in-law, and seven grandchildren—gathered together every weekend to eat lunch. These were the happiest moments for me. What more could one wish for than good, healthy children who care about and love one another? However, I have moments like that less often these days. In particular, Hong Il is too sick to get out of bed. I wish I were in his place! It would be less painful.

My wife and I went to the Byeonsan Peninsula for a summer vacation. While we were there, we visited Seonunsa Temple in Gochang. I had visited it during my high school days, and decided to revisit it now, as I missed those times. Giant trees shaded the way to Seonunsa Temple, just as they had during my youth. The quiet and profound atmosphere led my wandering mind to quiet recollection and meditation. After paying reverence at the main temple, I made a donation. I drank some tea and had a conversation with the chief priest, then returned with my wife to where we were staying. The sun was setting. The shore scenery and sea landscape were spectacular. No words could describe the beauty of that setting sun.

I attended the World Summit of Nobel Peace Laureates in Stavanger, Norway, in early September. Stavanger was a small port city in southwest Norway, dominated by oil refineries and oil-related industry. I was glad to see former Nobel Committee Chair Gunnar Berge again. About 500 people, including the Crown Prince of Norway, Nobel Committee members, environmental organization members, scholars, journalists, and businessmen, attended the event. During the three-day conference, we discussed global issues such as global warming; post-9/11 security; communication with the masses; and UN millennium development goals. I gave an address on "Power of Dialogue: Dialogue Based on the Principle of Reciprocity for the Goal of Achieving Mutual Interests." I proposed that, for the sake of mutual interests, we solve today's problems through peaceful dialogue, a method that was historically proven. Many participants expressed their sympathy for my proposal. It was a very physically challenging trip.

The Korean-American media in Washington, DC, New York, and Los Angeles published articles saying that I had hidden an enormous sum of money in the US. It was so absurd and outrageous that these so-called journalists wrote such groundless articles. In the National Assembly, a Grand National Party (GNP) assemblyman, who was formerly a prosecutor, maintained that I had a 10 billion won Certificate of Deposit (CD). He presented this as a rumor as a cunning way of avoiding legal consequences. In a radio interview, he went further to say that my wife had withdrawn 6 trillion won from a bank. Although we lodged a complaint, as of now the Public Prosecutors Office has postponed the investigation.

I have been enormously abused by regionally biased groups and rightist forces. I do not care, though, because God and many Korean people have trusted and supported me. I also firmly believe that those who misunderstand me now will eventually regret their mistakes after my death. There is no defeat for those who have lived justly. It is my dream to live a righteous life and to win after death.

I appeared on MBC Radio's "Kim Mi-hui's World and Us." I urged the inter-Korean summit and said that President Lee Myung-bak and Chairman Kim Jong-il could have a good dialogue. I thought highly of Ms. Kim Mi-hui as a comedian, but I was pleasantly surprised to find that she was also a very talented emcee of current affairs.

On October 26, I attended and gave a keynote address at the Forum on Northeast Asian Regional Development and Cooperation, co-sponsored by the Chinese People's Institute of Foreign Affairs and Shenyang city. After the event, we went straight to Dandong and the Amnok River, which I had always wanted to visit before I die. I saw Sinuiju far away from the riverbank, and I looked around the railway bridge that had been destroyed during the Korean War. The Amnok River was tragic and majestic. I have lived imagining it. It seemed as if Amnok River would say something to me if I visited it. However, when I got there, the river flowed absentmindedly and did not tell me anything. There was no tension in this river that had become the national border. I could not even feel the difficult thoughts and ambitions of Yi Seong-gye, the Goryeo general who had turned the military around and founded Joseon.

Dandong was the Chinese city where Korean envoys, merchants, and study-abroad students had gone by foot or on horseback in the old days. I was deeply moved to visit. They said that 80 percent of materials entering North Korea passed through from Dandong to Sinuiju. In this sense, Dandong is North Korea's lifeline. If we open up the Iron Silk Road that would begin in South Korea and go through North Korea and Eurasia, North Korea will change greatly. Although South Korea is located in a peninsula, we are like an island because the land road is blocked. If we can transport our merchandise through land on iron horses to Paris and London, we will probably enjoy the "Miracle of the Amnok River." I prayed that such a day would come soon and that North Koreans would live as affluently as those living in Dandong.

The national border along the Amnok River was peaceful. Although hundreds of thousands of soldiers confronted each other along the DMZ, both the people and landscape along the area near the Amnok River were relaxed. It was not our people that divided the Korean Peninsula. The division is the traces of violent confrontations between powerful countries and bitterly painful wound for us. Nevertheless, we have not yet erased that wound. We are the last divided country in the world. North Korea looked poor even from afar. It was so sad. The Amnok River flowed alone, leaving North Korean residents behind.

As I hoped for, Candidate Barack Obama won the US presidential election. It seemed like an auspicious event, not only for the US but also for the Korean Peninsula. How much the world had suffered from the wrong choices America made for the past eight years! With the election of President Obama, the US boasted its greatness again. Sometimes I find America hateful, but I still think it is amazing. The victory of Obama was an event as great as the liberation of the slaves by President Lincoln. With his election, the US shifted from the age of white-centered governance to multiethnic governance. I expect that a new era of reconciliation and cooperation with other countries will open up. A spirit of peace that includes even North Korea, Syria, and Iran will begin to rise. The Six-party Talks will sail smoothly, and Northeast Asia will be able to enter a new age of peace and security. I hope that President-Elect Obama will be neither arrogant nor muscling. His predecessor ruined himself, the US, and the world with arrogance and might. I hope that President-Elect Obama will bring peace with modesty and dialogue. I believe that he can. It is my prayer.

I know Obama's running mate Joseph Biden well. He has an excellent knowledge of international relations and actively supported the Sunshine Policy. During my presidency, he visited me at the Blue House and we exchanged neckties. Although my necktie happened to be stained that day, he did not mind. He said he would keep my necktie as a sign of good fortune. I was happy about his success.

On November 11, we held a celebration for the publication of my wife's autobiography *Donghaeng: Gonangwa yeonggwang-ui hoejeonmudae* (Traveling Together: A Turning Stage of Suffering and Glory). Her book will be translated into various languages and remembered forever. I was happier for and prouder of her than I ever was of my own accomplishments.

On November 27, Democratic Labor Party president Kang Ki Kab and Supreme Council Member Lee Young-sun came to see me after their visit to Pyongyang. They said that the inter-Korean relationship felt like walking into pitch darkness. I could feel their enormous frustration as they asked for my advice.

I said to them that people were worried about opposition parties, so they should gather their power together, breathe deeply, and look far. I said, "If you bear today, you can win tomorrow. Then people will take courage and help you. We are people who walk the road of history, the right road. It is just a matter of time. We will eventually succeed."

On December 16, we held the Grand Lecture for Peace in the Korean Peninsula in celebration of the eighth anniversary of my Nobel Peace Prize. We invited renowned scholars from Korea, America, and Japan and heard from them about the possibility of policy change after the launch of the new US government. Former US Ambassador to Korea James T. Laney gave a talk about "New US Government and Peace in the Korean Peninsula," Professor Don Oberdorfer about "Prospect of Inter-Korean Relationship Seen From the USA," Honorary Professor Ito Narihiko of Chuo University in Japan about "North Korea-Japan Relation Normalization Plan for the Establishment of Peace and Friendly Relationship in Northeast Asia," and former Minister of Unification Lim Dong-won about "Current Status and Prospect of Inter-Korean

Relationship." I gave a lecture entitled "Let Us Restore Inter-Korean Dialogue and Cooperation." I believed that since President Lee Myung-bak's government Korean society was now facing three crises: democracy, the market economy (for ordinary people), and the inter-Korean relationship had all retreated.

Professor Paik Nak-chung served as the preparation committee chair for this event. He is also a "conscience in action" of our time. Because he does not avoid chores and difficult tasks, people look to him when they cannot find a reliable worker. You don't realize how precious he is when he is nearby, but you realize how big a role he plays when he is absent.

The year 2009 dawned. I received visits to celebrate the New Year and made plans for the year ahead. I played the board game *Yunnori* with my wife. I lost three times in a row, losing a total of 300,000 won. I had led such a busy life that I didn't even know how our days had passed by. I went out with just my wife for the first time in a long while. Although it was very cold, the sun shone. We had lunch and drove along the Hangang River. Our relationship had always been the best, ever since we got married. I love and admire her. Without her, I probably could not have overcome those difficult, desperate years of suffering. Without her, it would probably be hard for me to live now.

We always pray to God to let us live long and healthy lives together. For more than a year now, we have sung together every night before going to bed—mostly, we sing "Spring in My Hometown." We feel happy, singing together. Last New Year, I took her to a dress shop for the first time since we were married and bought her a suit. I regretted that I had never done it before, realizing that it was not such a difficult thing to do, after all. I bought just one suit for my wife, who had lived a life of sacrifice for me—and, at that, I bought it only in our old age. I felt very sorry about that as I saw how happy she was. I cannot even imagine life without her. I hope that she does not leave this world before me. Nowadays, we sometimes spend the entire day together, but I always enjoy time with her.

On January 21, the police commando unit raided the residents who were waging strikes against the demolition of their houses. As a result, five residents and one police officer died, and about fifteen people were wounded. As they were not given any alternative moving arrangements, the residents fought a life-or-death struggle. It was a truly atrocious action on the part of the police. I could not help but feel angry. I felt so sorry for the residents who were driven out of their homes in the middle of the freezing cold winter. The current government considered the Korean people to be their enemy, and served only the powerful and wealthy. It is so deplorable for the police to take human lives lightly and to serve only the powerful. It was so painful that there was nothing I could do for those who suffered.

A year after President Lee's inauguration, too many problems appeared. The Lee government forced, above all, the Non-nuclear Opening 3000 Policy on the inter-Korean relationship. It was a throwback to the Cold War mentality. There was no way that proud North Korea would accept this proposal. Accepting it meant that South Korea would help North Korea by providing $3000 per capita income if North Korea gave up nuclear development and opened its doors. As expected, North Korea rejected the proposal and, as a result, the inter-Korean relationship remained blocked. It was worrisome that North Korea would now communicate with the US, but not with South Korea. The Lee government's policy reminded me of the 1994 nightmare situation wherein the Kim Young-sam government was excluded from the Geneva talks as a result of their hardliner tactics that involved refusing to negotiate with North Korea based on their motto: "No handshake with one with nuclear weapons." According to the Geneva DPRK-US Agreed Framework, it was South Korea that paid 70 percent of the $4.6 billion construction costs for North Korea's light water reactor, but South Korea did this under the name of the US. It appeared that President Lee's government was on the road to repeating this shameful diplomatic failure.

The Lee government switched its minister of unification from Mr. Kim Ha-joong to Professor Hyun In-taek, the leader of the Non-nuclear Opening 3000 Policy. I wondered if all of the efforts of the two previous governments would come to nothing. If they wanted to return to such an antagonistic policy, I wondered why we even needed the Ministry of Unification. President Lee had no philosophy about the inter-Korean relationship.

On February 1, I drove around downtown Incheon and had lunch in Chinatown. Although it looked quite different than it used to, it was great to see the revival. After South Korea was liberated, we had practically driven the Chinese living in Korea out of our country. By giving them all kinds of disadvantages, we made it almost impossible for them to make a living here. As a result, the Chinese in Korea dispersed into Japan and the US. It's a shameful history. Now, we have massive migrant populations, including Koreans from China and people from other Asian countries, like

China, Vietnam, Indonesia, and the Philippines. The age of multicultural-ism is here. This might be a fortunate turn of events.

Historically, countries that have tolerated and recognized multiple val-ues have prospered. By offering opportunities and motivation to other peoples, the host country has benefited from passion, energy, and growth. Countries like Persia, Tang dynasty China, Rome, and the US are good examples. Conversely, countries like Spain, Nazi Germany, and militarist period Japan all collapsed due to their exclusion of other peoples.

If we want Korea to prosper, we should not fall into pure-blood-ism of race, culture, and ideology. When we look at past dynasties like Silla, Goryeo, and Joseon, we notice that the emphasis on purity in ideology and religion was prominent during the Joseon dynasty. That is why the Joseon society could not actively handle the changing times and had to suffer the decline of national strength.

Today, migrants are coming to Korea from many countries. They will work very hard to accomplish their dreams in our country. We should boldly accept talented and ambitious workers from foreign countries and take care to encourage them so that they do not lose hope.

After I retired, I received a plaque of appreciation from foreign workers and Koreans from China. The plaque reads:

> You lay the foundation of legislation for foreign workers and Koreans from China who are working in Korea. You led us, who had been living alienated and hard, to live proudly as workers. Remembering your care and love, we deliver you our appreciation in this plaque.

I did not feel entirely happy because I knew that they were still suffer-ing from discrimination in our society. I felt sorry for their difficult lives. We should not delay improving the rights of these foreign workers.

Director of the Kim Dae-jung Presidential Library and Museum Rhyu Sang-young took a sabbatical. On February 3, I expressed my thanks to him for his hard work. Chair-Professor of Yonsei University Kim Sung-jae was appointed to the position.

Cardinal Kim Sou-hwan passed away. He lived a great life. As a priest, human rights guardian, and defender of the poor, he had earned true admiration and love from the people. During my imprisonment, he visited me at prisons in Jinju and Cheongju. He was a thoughtful and warm-hearted person. On February 17, I visited Myeongdong Cathedral to pay my reverence. I prayed for his eternal life in Heaven. From the photograph of him that hung, his face looked clear and pure. The lines of mourners were looped endlessly around Myeongdong Cathedral. This great priest was well appreciated, even after his death.

I was surprised to receive a call from Secretary of State Hillary Clinton as she was on her airplane returning from a visit to Seoul. "My husband wanted me to send his regards to you," she said. "He has good and warm memories of the times you worked together. He remembers your leadership during the financial crisis of the 1990s and in the inter-Korean relationship."

She also said that he hoped to meet me again.

President Obama chose Senator Hillary Clinton, his powerful rival during the Democratic Party election campaign, to be his secretary of state. His skill for finding talent was surprising. I welcomed her appointment more than anyone else's. I hoped that the DPRK-US normalization that had stopped when President Clinton left office in 2000 would resume. In a sense, her phone call to me was more meaningful than just sending regards.

Secretary of State Hillary Clinton named former Ambassador Bosworth as Special Representative for North Korea Policy. He was an old friend of mine who had worked as the Executive Director of the Korean Peninsula Energy Development Organization (KEDO) and as Ambassador to Korea. He had visited North Korea many times. When I visited Boston in the previous year, he was the Dean of Tufts University Fletcher School. I met him and we talked about the essence of and solution for the North Korean nuclear issue.

When Special Representative Bosworth visited Korea a little while later, he called me. I told him that, although North Korea was doing unreasonable things, a patient and wise response by the US could create the kind of success that had been possible during the Clinton administration. He said he completely agreed with me and that he would do his best. We said that we would definitely meet in person the next time he visited. I felt hopeful that the inter-Korean relationship could improve through DPRK–US normalization, despite the fact that it had been worsening lately.

On March 13, my secretary, Mr. Ha Tae-yun, was appointed Ambassador to Iraq. Although I congratulated him on this promotion, I was worried about him because the situation in Iraq was unstable. Former Consul-General to Qingdao, China Kim Seon-hong was appointed as my secretary.

I am worried about Korea. Dictatorial forces, disguising themselves as the right wing, are rearing their heads. The right wing originated from pro-Japanese collaborators. They chose two things to maintain their wealth and power after the liberation of Korea. First, they approached

Dr. Rhee Syngman, who immediately embraced them since his position was inferior to that of Master Kim Koo. Second, they adopted "anti-communism" as their cause in order to acquit themselves of their anti-national past.

The pro-Japanese forces overturned the Chang Myon government within a year in the May 16 military coup d'état. Park Chung-hee's eighteen-year military government ended in tragedy, but another military government succeeded it. Thanks to fierce resistance by the democratic forces, at last, we could peacefully accomplish a power shift and the decade of democracy that unfolded during my and President Roh Moo-hyun's governments. As the saying goes: A decade is a long enough time to change mountains and rivers. So it appeared that democracy was standing on firm ground after a decade of democratic government. The Korean people also did not doubt this. However, nowadays, unbelievable things are happening. The specter of military dictatorship is returning.

When we look back on Korea's ten years of democratic government, the state of things today seems especially absurd. It is hard to believe it—I feel as if I am in a dream. Although I retired from politics for a long time, I cannot just sit around when our society is rushing toward anti-democracy, an anti-people economy, and anti-unification. How many people suffered from capital punishment, massacres, imprisonment, and torture during the half-century anti-dictatorship struggle? How did we achieve freedom and inter-Korean reconciliation? Those hard-won freedoms and the inter-Korean reconciliation are collapsing. I resolved to do what I could, although my body was old and weak.

The media and people around me told me to rest. I really wanted to rest, too. But the situation was serious and our country was facing a crisis, so I had to step forward. As an elder of the country, I could not just *say* abstract truisms. That was not how I had lived. If democracy slipped away, my life was meaningless. I could not consider myself alive even if I was alive. And even if I died, how could I close my eyes comfortably? What would those righteous fighters who are underground say if democracy retreated? It really pained me. I prayed every night as I held hands with my wife: "Lord, we are facing crisis in democracy, in the economy for the people, and in the inter-Korean relationship. I am old now. I have no strength. I have no power, either. Although I worry a lot, I don't know what I can do. Lord, please give us our last strength. Please give us our last wisdom. Please take care of our country and people."

As I get older, I cry more often. In fact, I tended to cry even when I was a child. I cried, worrying that goblins would appear and worrying that my mother would die. I feel it was thanks to those tears that I had the strength to fight against the dictatorial regimes. What is as clean and clear as tears? Young people who were sacrificed during their fights against the dictatorial regimes were weak and gentle. It was because they were clear and pure that they sacrificed their lives to fight against injustice. Thinking of them, I could not check my tears from flowing. I will not stop my fight against injustice until the day I die. How can I be respectfully treated as an elder and play someone noble and do nothing? I have to wipe my tears and shout again.

I have supported the presidential system for a long time. I risked my life to defend it. I won the direct presidential election system with the Korean people and served as president for a term. However, what I really wanted was a presidential system that was supported by a vice president. We need a vice president. If there is a president-vice president pairing, they can complement one another. One can be reformist while the other is conservative. Or, one can be from the east while the other is from the west. Also, the president will be less burdened with ceremonial needs, and a gap in the government can be prevented if anything happens to the head of state. If the opposing sides can share the leadership, we can also overcome ideological strife and regional antagonism, which are the ruin of our country. This was why I argued for the president-vice president pairing system and the two four-year term system after the 1987 Revolution. However, as it is well known, the ruling party fought tooth and nail against this, as they were afraid of an alliance between Mr. Kim Young-sam and myself.

Although I still think the president-vice president pairing system is a good system, my thoughts have changed a lot over time. We have experienced ten presidents under the presidential system. Although dictatorships like those of Rhee Syngman, Park Chung-hee, and Chun Doo-hwan ended tragically, dictatorial presidents have appeared since then. To prevent this, it is worth considering alternatives to the presidential system. There is no way to have the president account for his government under one five-year term system. It is now time for people to drive a dictator who does not respect the public opinion out of the office. I think that a dual-executive system and a parliamentary government system are worth considering. A decade of democratic government changed a lot of things in our society and, in particular, the Korean people's democratic awareness is very mature.

The same is true of the US. Although it was once the model country for a successful presidential system, we cannot say the same thing after an eight-year Bush administration. The harm it inflicted on the global village and on humanity is enormous. It failed both domestically and internationally. Nevertheless, there was no way to check it. We had to helplessly live through it. I am very sad that we cannot correct a leader's failure and wrongdoing even with our advanced civilization and reason. If that is the eternal nature of power, then we should try to find institutions to prevent it.

I visited my hometown on Hauido Island. This might have been my last visit there. I attended the opening ceremony of the Three Hauido Islands Museum of Farmers Movement. I gave an address to commemorate farmers' movement activists on the three Hauido islands. I also paid my reverence at my ancestral burial ground. I visited the Deokbong School in Dae-ri. I dropped by Haui Elementary School. I was moved watching the lively and joyful children. There was a light rain and my secretaries tried to dissuade me from visiting various places. But I insisted on my visits as planned, including the Great Stone Face. The beach where I used to catch octopuses looked much smaller than I remembered. I wondered if it was always that small or if it had grown smaller over the years. It might be just because memories grow bigger as one gets older, although your size gets smaller. Despite the rain, residents of Hauido Island enthusiastically welcomed me. It was a happy visit, but I didn't know if I would ever be able to revisit again.

On May 4, I visited China upon the invitation of the Chinese People's Institute of Foreign Affairs. I met Vice President Xi Jinping at the Great Hall of the People in Beijing. He was going to be the next leader of China and had been selected as one of *Time*'s 100 Most Influential People. He welcomed me warmly. "During your term, Korea and China established a cooperation-based partnership for the twenty-first century," he said. "We cannot think of the current good relationship between Korea and China without also thinking of your efforts."

"China is now one of two most powerful countries in the world," I said. "These two countries are taking charge of the fate of the world. I hope that you will cooperate to contribute to the peace, development, and justice in the world today. In the past, powerful countries controlled and exploited other countries, but the world today does not accept that. Through cooperation and yielding, we should write a new history for humanity."

I also asked that, as the chairperson country, China would play a more active role in the Six-party Talks. Toward the end of Bush administration, North Korea expressed a strong will to abolish nuclear development through various measures, including blowing up a cooling tower. When Obama's government launched, we had all high hopes for the resolution of the North Korean nuclear issue. However, unbelievably, in early April North Korea launched long-range missiles again. This was an unfortunate incident during the period in which a policy toward North Korea was being established by the Obama administration. North Korea's action was absurd.

However, these kinds of incidents continued to happen. It is North Korea's way of expressing its wish to have a package deal with the US, which includes normalization of the DPRK-US relationship and the abolishment of nuclear development. Therefore, I expressed my wish that China would take initiative to resume the Six-party Talks and resolve the issue. Vice President Xi Jinping said that China's position on denuclearization in the Korean Peninsula remained firm, and that it would continue to actively work toward the goal.

On May 18, I had dinner with former president Clinton at his invitation. We went to a Western restaurant in the Hyatt Hotel while he was visiting Korea to attend the C40 Global Climate Summit. We had in-depth discussion about the North Korean nuclear issue and the Six-party Talks. It was very cold in the restaurant, and I was shaking. I asked if they could turn off the air conditioner, but they could not because it was centrally controlled.

I tend to feel cold more easily these days. As I got weaker, the cold air became harmful to me. However, there was no way President Clinton could have known this. When I had lunch with President Clinton at the White House in 1998, I also had a hard time. Although there was a feast in front of me, I could not eat it. It was so cold that I felt nauseous. What if I vomited up what I had eaten? In retrospect, it was a very dangerous moment.

Whenever I attended international events, I always wore thick underclothes underneath my suit because it tended to be well air-conditioned in conference rooms. However, that day, I forgot to put on thick underclothes. Although my teeth were almost chattering and I was shaking, I smiled and tried not to show it.

"President Obama said during his presidential campaign that he would meet with Chairman Kim Jong-il and that he would adopt your government's policy rather than the Bush administration's policy toward North Korea," I said to Mr. Clinton. "North Korea had high hopes about Obama's government, but is now very anxious because the United States appears to focus only on Afghanistan and Pakistan. If President Obama declares he will carry out the September 19 Joint Declaration, it will solve the North Korean nuclear issue."

"That is a correct approach," Mr. Clinton said. "After I return home, I will explain this to Secretary Hillary Clinton so that the matter progresses well."

That was what I had hoped to hear from him. I handed the former president a document that I had prepared and asked him to deliver it to his wife. I hoped that Secretary Clinton would examine and deliver it to President Obama. It included the progression of the North Korean nuclear issue from the 1994 nuclear crisis to the present; the example of the Eastern Bloc collapse; the true intention behind the recent North Korean hardliner approach; the Chinese position toward the North Korean nuclear issue; and the example of success in the Clinton administration. The document ends with:

> Before his election, presidential candidate Obama expressed his willingness to meet with North Korean leaders. After his election, President Obama said that he would pursue President Clinton's North Korean policy, rather than President Bush's. State Secretary Clinton said in her speech at the Asia Society, "if North Korea is genuinely prepared to completely and verifiably eliminate their nuclear weapons program, the Obama administration will be willing to normalize bilateral relations and replace the peninsula's long-standing armistice agreements with a permanent peace treaty."
>
> It is true that these encouraging remarks of two top US leaders certainly gave great hope and expectations to North Korean leadership. But as time lapses, North Korea conceived doubt and suspicion over the intentions of the US. This state of mind has led Pyongyang to turn to harsh rhetoric and aggressive behavior.
>
> Under these circumstances, I believe it is crucial for President Obama and Secretary Clinton to make bold proposals to North Korea as soon as possible based on the terms of September 19 Joint Statement, rather than keeping North Korean issues on the back burner. I am sure that the United States' bold and decisive initiatives will pave the road to success and keep the situation from deterorating.

The corruption investigation of former president Roh Moo-hyun's relatives and close associates headlined the newspapers every day. There were even allegations involving his son. A whole host of people was investigated every day. The Public Prosecutors Office leaked allegations to the media, and the media was in a frenzy to report them. It was trial by public opinion. This was a very unhappy turn of events, not only for President Roh, but also for me (because I was from the same progressive political camp), as well as for the Democratic Party and the Korean people.

On the morning of Saturday, May 23, just after I finished my interview with the German weekly *Der Spiegel*, my secretary told me that former president Roh Moo-hyun had passed away. Utterly shocked, I felt momentarily blank. As someone who shared ten years of democratic government, I felt as if half of my body had collapsed.

President Roh threw himself to his death from a mountain in his hometown. Every day of his life must have been too painful. The Public Prosecutors Office was performing an unreasonable investigation—summoning all of his family members, including his wife, son, daughter, elder brother, and niece's husband—as if they were doing some sort of a sweep. Every day, they illegally leaked allegations and engaged in media play. They also spread rumors about committing President Roh for trial. In the end, the Lee Myung-bak government drove President Roh to suicide.

The funeral committee for President Roh asked me to make a memorial address, and I accepted. But, the committee ultimately revoked their invitation, saying that the current government was opposed to it. In the end, I could not read the memorial address I had prepared. Now, finally, I dedicate this memorial address to his spirit.

Dear President Roh Moo-hyun, whom I admire and respect. How incredible it is that I, who am more than twenty years older than you, should make this memorial address for you! I cannot believe this astonishing reality.

When I heard the news of your demise, I said that I felt as if half of my body collapsed. I wonder why I used such an expression. It was not just about the past we had lived together. Witnessing the crisis of democracy, I thought while you were still with us that we should probably come forward to fight again soon. It is because you passed away while I was thinking about it that I felt that way.

President Roh Moo-hyun, please do not die even in death. We need you. Please live on in our hearts and give us strength in our fight during this period of three crises—crisis in democracy, crisis in economy, and crisis in the inter-Korean relationship. Let us gather our strength—you from the other world and me from this world—and guard democracy. Only then will we feel rewarded for our lives. I feel very honored to have shared time with a leader like you, a cheerful, courageous, and extremely intelligent leader. I don't know if there is another world, but, if there is, let us meet there and share the stories that we could not share here. In the meantime, please protect the Korean people, even in the other world. Please protect this country and our people in crisis.

The Korean people were all thunderstruck at the sudden demise of President Roh.

More than 5 million people paid reverence at incense-burner stands all across the country in honor of him.

I attended his funeral, which was held in front of Gyeongbokgung Palace, with my wife on May 29. The sun was pouring down on me as if it wanted to collapse me entirely. It was almost scary. I could not help crying as I looked at First Lady Kwon Yang-sook.

The Public Prosecutors Office was the biggest cancer of our country. Its members were spiteful, political, and regionally cliquish. It was deplorable. They were submissive to the powerful and bit hard at the weak. I was worried—Korea seemed to be deteriorating into a republic of the Public Prosecutors.

June 11 was a very important day. I was scheduled to make an address at the ninth commemorative event of the June 15 Inter-Korean Accord. However, I did not feel well that morning. Although medical staff tried various treatments, I could not find energy. I asked chief nurse Kim Jeon-u many times to please take good care of me. I finally arrived at the event later than promised, and entered amid enthusiastic applause. Summoning up all of my energy, I said: "I tell you sincerely, with a bleeding heart: Please let us become 'conscience in action.' Conscience in inaction is on the side of evil. How many people has the dictatorial regime murdered in the past? In order to reward their deaths, in order to protect the democracy that the Korean people have built with their blood and sweat, we should do our part. All human beings have a conscience. Although we know what is right, we sometimes avoid doing it because of fear, because of trouble, because of disadvantages that may result from it. Many just, innocent people have to suffer and leave this world because of such an attitude. At the same time, we are enjoying the democracy that those just fighters have achieved. Is this really conscientious?

"President Roh Moo-hyun recently passed away. If, during the time when he was suffering so much, a tenth of the 5 million condolence callers had come forward to protest the investigators who were doing such a thing to a former president—leaking groundless allegations every day and shocking and giving him such psychological stress—then President Roh would not have died. How shameful, how regretful, and how sorry we are!

"I tell you: please abide by your conscience if you want a free country. Please become conscience in action if you want a truly peaceful and just country. To do nothing is to be on the side of the evil. There is no need to even talk about people who kowtow, flatter, and serve dictators. All we need to do to accomplish a liberal democracy, just economy, and inter-Korean reconciliation and cooperation is to obey the voice of the conscience in our hearts and to express and act on it. During the election, we have to vote for the good, rather than the bad, political party. This is also true of expressing our opinions in polls. So, if all 47 million Koreans obey their conscience, advise, criticize, and encourage one another accordingly, how can dictatorship rear its head again? How can Korea become a society where only a small minority of people enjoy luxury, while the majority have a hard time?

"Let us all become conscience in action, protect everyone's economy, come forward to protect a peaceful inter-Korean relationship, and build a country where we can all live without worrying, a country with hope!"

The More I Think About Life, The More Beautiful It Is

The Korean Peninsula touches Manchuria in China and the Maritime Province of Siberia in Russia. On the east, it faces Japan across the sea, and China across the sea in the west. The Korean Peninsula is located in the middle of three military powerhouses—China, Japan, and Russia. It is a place of strategic importance. That is why the Korean Peninsula has always been an arena of competition among powerful countries. Also, because it is a peninsula that can reach the continent from the Pacific Ocean, Western countries and the US have also wanted to have a foot in it. Now, we have the US military stationed in it. There is no other country surrounded by four powerful countries like Korea. Therefore, Korea is the country that needs the highest level of diplomatic skills. It is no exaggeration to say that diplomacy decides our fate. We might be able to correct domestic mistakes, but diplomatic mistakes cannot be corrected or revoked. Our history proves this well.

In the recent past, China, Russia, and Japan have all fought for control of the Korean Peninsula during the 1894 Sino-Japanese War and the 1904 Russo-Japanese War. After Japan won both wars, the US approved Japanese annexation of Korea through the secret Katsura-Taft Agreement. They did not care about Korea or the Korean people at all. Not knowing this, Koreans tried to drive out foreign powers by relying on the power of the US. We had the opportunity to maintain our independence around the end of the nineteenth century by taking advantage of the competition among the four powerful countries, but we did not seize it. Regent Daewongun was competent in domestic government, but he failed in foreign affairs. Failing to read the global currents, he caused the collapse of our country by insisting on seclusionism.

In contrast, Thailand is an example of a country that competently took advantage of the power dynamics between competing powerful countries. In a crisis of national fate, wedged between Britain—which had advanced through India, Myanmar, and Malaysia—and France, which had occupied three Indo-China countries—the Thai people exercised their wisdom and national unity and successfully persuaded the two powerful countries that they needed a buffer state between them.

As shown in these examples, diplomacy is directly connected to a country's fate. For Korea, the four powerful countries around us can be either a medicine or a poison. If we are weak and divided, they will completely control us. But if we are strong and united, they will try to cooperate with us. All of this is up to us.

Although small, Korea is a very important country geopolitically. Our diplomatic principle toward the four powerful countries should maintain the system of one alliance and three friendships: a solid military alliance with the US and friendly relationships with China, Japan, and Russia. As we expected, China has rapidly emerged as an economic and military superpower. During my presidency, I tried my best to elevate the diplomatic relationship with China and expand interchange. China is a large market and a close neighbor; we cannot avoid breathing its yellow sand. In addition, it is close to North Korea, part of our nation. China has already become one of the two superpowers of the world, and our economy cannot avoid Chinese influence. China has the impression that Korea is a unilateral follower of the US. We should make an effort to erase this understanding. I hope that my successors will consider why I paid so much attention to Korea's relationship with these four powerful countries. I repeat: *To us, diplomacy is like a lifeline.* The Korean Peninsula is the land of opportunity and crisis, where the interests of the four powerful countries are closely intertwined. Whether we will be like a cow in a drain that leisurely enjoys grazing grass on both sides, or like the prey behind iron bars—it entirely depends on us. Those who take charge of our country and our diplomats should be more awake than anybody else.

The Korean people have finally achieved a peaceful regime change after a long, hard century of Japanese colonization, liberation, the Korean War, and military dictatorship. Throughout this period of hardship and suffering, Korean people's lives were devastated. But the Korean people always overcame and rose up again. We showed our indomitable spirit.

When our country was divided, we established a government even within the southern half. Although we were pushed back down to the Busan area because of communist invasion, we fought and pushed them back. When dictators emerged, we did not yield, but fought against them until, finally, we achieved democracy and a peaceful regime change. Out of the 150 countries that acquired independence after World War II, Korea is the only country that has accomplished both democracy and a market economy.

Koreans are passionate about learning and education. We are the people who are most fit for the age of knowledge and information. Although we stood at the end of the line and declined during the age of industrialization, we will emerge as a powerful country during the age of knowledge and information. The world will pay attention to our culture, which is the product of our passionate interest in learning and education and democracy. The first revelation of this is the Korean Wave.

French critic of civilization, Jacques Attali, said that Korea would become a geographical "core city" within the next three decades. The US investment bank Goldman Sachs predicted that Korea would develop into a country where the average individual income would be $81,000 annually by the mid-twenty-first century, a country second only to the US in its economic power. The German newspaper *Die Welt* reported that Korea had the potential to overtake Germany in the next three decades.

The world pays attention to Korea and the future is open to Koreans. But there are prerequisites for the kind of future that many predict for us. We need to secure democracy on firm ground and Korea should be united. Even if the unification itself can be delayed, both Koreas should reconcile and cooperate so that the Korean Peninsula can become the bridge of peace that connects the continent with the ocean. Our most important partner for this task is North Korea. If we set back the clock of democracy, become antagonistic toward North Korea, and lose this great opportunity for national prosperity, we will be forever regretful. If we invite in dictatorship and the Cold War again, we should be sorry to our ancestors and descendants.

North Korea is where our people live. Although the division has lasted for more than half a century, that is only an instant in comparison to our long history. We will definitely reunite. If we live better, we should help them. It is natural for an elder brother to bring rice to his starving younger brother's house. The North Korean hardline tactic is the product of the pride of the weak. We should persuade, pat, and stroke them. We should not hurt their sense of pride. Even if they are kicking and screaming, we should soothe them gently. At least, there should never be war again in our land. We should never become poor again. Even if we should wait for reunification, we should connect the broken middle of our body and let the blood circulate in this land. We should give peace to the lives of all in the Korean Peninsula. There is nothing greater in this world than life.

At any rate, I am optimistic, because history never retreats if you look at it from a large view. Although it can retract momentarily, it will take the right direction in the end. That is because it is people who move history. Our modern history proves this.

Like clockwork, I have been getting dialysis three times a week (Monday, Wednesday, and Friday). I must lie in my bed in the living room for four and a half hours every time. All my blood comes out of and reenters my body through a machine. It has become harder every time. When I take a rest after breakfast, my secretary comes to me and says quietly, "It's ready, sir." Although I am thankful for their care, they feel sorry for me. I sometimes feel upset about the fact that I must continue this regimen until the day I die. Nobody told me, but I *know* that most people cannot survive on dialysis for five years. It has been more than five years for me, but I am still alive and in this world. I am blessed. I am thankful to so many people and to Jesus for giving me life every day.

Dialysis begins at 9:00 a.m. and ends around 1:30 p.m. From my bed, I can see pictures of me on the wall that capture those many moments when I worked so energetically; I see all of the books that I devoured with such great attention, resting in the bookcases. Sometimes, the light on the ceiling seems to look down on me. I can hear the sound of the dialysis machine whirring. Sometimes, I fall asleep while listening to the radio. When I wake up and look at the clock on the wall, all too often there's a lot of time left before the dialysis is over.

After dialysis, I feel weak and faint. Even to my eyes, I look too pale. I can do nothing. In fact, although dialysis has been a part of my everyday life since retirement, I have always been worried about and sometimes afraid of it. Doctors Chang Suk-il, Han Dae-seok, and Jung Nam-sik have been taking turns caring for me.

On the days when I do not get dialysis, I feel leisurely in the morning. I feel happy. If I do not have any other engagements, I have lunch with my wife and look at the garden from the window. Sparrows come and sing, and the flowers smile. The coffee tastes delicious and everything is fragrant; time feels sweet. I can remember where all of the trees and plants are in the garden. When the roses bloom, I ask my wife to pay me for the roses because I take care of them. She replies that she does not have money and writes me an IOU. Sometimes, she writes a million won IOU, and other times a hundred thousand won IOU. She probably does not know that I keep them all. Our happiness stays in that small garden. After enjoying that happiness for a half an hour, I take a nap.

It is getting harder to walk, so I have to use a wheelchair. I am still happy. My lovely, healthy wife is still next to me, and my secretaries take such good care of me. I am really a lucky person to have them all: Secretaries Kim Seon-hong, Yun Cheol-gu, and Choi Kyung-hwan; Chiefs Park Han Soo, Chang Ok-chu, and Pak Jun-hui; Chief Guard Cho Yeong-min; Chief Nurse Kang Chwon-woo; and personal Secretaries Pak Sun-nam, Yi Yeong-gil, Yi Seung-hyeon, Kim Seon-gi, Byeon Ju-gyeong, and Kim Jin-ho.

My favorite Bible phrase is Matthew 25:40. Jesus says, "Truly I say to you, to the extent that you did it to one of these brothers of Mine, even the least of them, you did it to Me."

After coming to this world, Jesus continued to live on the side of the suffering and the marginalized. He was always with those people who were deserted and condemned, like lepers, tenant farmers, day laborers, and beggars. While fighting against the hypocrisy and tyranny of the ruling class like Pharisees and Sadducees, he was killed as a political prisoner.

If we want to be a true student of Jesus, we have to bear the cross. Bearing the cross means fighting against injustice for the marginalized and the suffering, and resisting the powerful. Then, naturally, the haves and the powerful hate and persecute you. Jesus was also falsely accused of plotting for Jewish independence and to become a Jewish king.

Although Mahatma Gandhi was a Hindi, he was one of Jesus' best students in the twentieth century. His life was the life of a sacred person—he practiced a life of disinterested love for neighbors, led the thrifty life of a poor person, and was tolerant toward his enemies. Gandhi considered seeing and not acting against evil to be a sin even worse than violence. This is not because he approved of violence, but because he considered fighting against evil to be the most important thing. He argued that we have to fight against evil, but not violently. His life inspired me with belief and vision during my youth.

When I was falsely incriminated, unjustly accused, and harshly persecuted, I thought of Jesus's life. I believed that we can eventually teach the evil people through non-violent resistance and thus change the world. The powerful unconditionally persecuted and condemned me. They did not even want to know who I was. It was blind condemnation. Every time, I thought of Jesus' last moment: The crowd spat on, cursed, and threw stones at Him. To be on His side meant risking your own life. I dared to be on His side. True courage does not come from your character, but from your dedication to the truth.

True religion requires risking your life, and true life requires you to side with the weak, no matter what difficulties come to you as a result. I have lived without forgetting Father Kim Cheol-gyu's remark when he gave me the baptismal name Thomas More: "You should do politics at the risk of dying a martyr for your faith." Thomas More was a politician too.

I met Jesus when my death was imminent in 1973. I have always discussed difficult and painful things with God and asked for His forgiveness when I made mistakes. All human beings have both goodness and evil in their minds. You can reduce sins and increase goodness through religion. God, who I believe gave me a lot of goodness, cleansed me.

I sometimes tell my grandchildren about my life. I tell them that love of your neighbor is the essence of life. I hope that they will be happy in love that they will receive in return for their love. They are my eternal love. I am grateful for God for giving them to me.

Although my life stretched from the twentieth century into the twenty-first, in retrospect, it was like a flash. Where are all the things that I dreamt and loved now? Where are the people who chanted my name and where are those who threatened and cursed at me now? I would like to meet them in the world where there is no longer falsehood and hatred.

I have floated down a long way and I am now about to enter the sea. Born on a small island in the southern sea of the Korean Peninsula, I travelled all around the world. Although all kinds of times were given to me, the great God also gave me courage and wisdom. And He also finally gave me the blessed time to work, too.

I have tried to live for democracy, justice, peace, and the Korean people. I always told myself that I should live a consistent life, based on the philosophy of *jungyong* (the golden mean). I overcame five life-or-death moments, six years of prison life, decades of surveillance and house arrest, and years of exile. I found meaning in every moment of suffering. I confirmed that I was alive through it all. Nevertheless, how could I not be shaky at times? I could overcome all those difficulties only thanks to those people who shared my suffering with me and helped me to rise up. I am truly grateful to them.

I often stood on the blade of a knife from which you could lose your life from just a moment of absentmindedness. Sometimes, I was tempted by a life of wealth and power. Still, I believe that I made the right choice every time. In retrospect, they seem far away, but they were passionate moments. My life has been an adventurous life with many turns and twists. I fought for democracy with my life and I worked with all my might to revive our economy and open the road for inter-Korean reconciliation. Although there are things that I could have done better, I have no regrets. I fear the judgment of history most. Although we can deceive people for a brief period of time, we cannot deceive history. History is on the side of justice.

I trust history and people until the very end.

CHAPTER 13

Afterword to the Korean Edition

The late president Kim Dae-jung began planning his autobiography in 2004, when he returned home to Donggyo-dong after leaving the Blue House in February 2003. He started dictating his autobiography in July 2006. This biography covers his entire life, from his birth through his presidency and after. The participants in this dictation were Rhyu Sang-young (Second Director of Yonsei University Kim Dae-jung Presidential Library and Museum), Park Jie-won (Secretary General of Kim Dae-jung Peace Center), Kim Taek-Geun (senior editorial writer of *Kyunghyang Shinmun*), Choi Kyung-hwan (secretary), Chang Ok-chu (Director of the Kim Dae-jung Peace Center), and Chang Sin-gi (Kim Dae-jung Presidential Library and Museum Research Fellow). This work took forty-one sittings and two years to complete.

Kim Taek-Geun wrote this autobiography, based on dictation and referring to various books and essays by President Kim Dae-jung, as well as other reference materials. In particular, he referred to the draft written by Choi Kyung-hwan, Rhyu See-choon (novelist), and Joung Suk-ku (senior editorial writer of the *Hangyoreh* newspaper) for the period of his presidency. Also referenced were the diaries the president kept in 2006, 2008, and 2009, which cover the period after his retirement.

In April 2006, President Kim Dae-jung also formed an advisory committee for his autobiography to cover the period of his presidency. The committee was headed by former Vice Prime Minister Lee Sang-Joo, and its members included thirty-four former ministers and senior secretaries

© The Author(s) 2019
Kim Dae-jung, *Conscience in Action*,
https://doi.org/10.1007/978-981-10-7623-7_13

in the fields of politics; foreign affairs, national security, and unification; economy; education and culture; and society and welfare. In March 2007, a publication committee was formed and headed by attorney Han Sung-hon. Director of Yonsei University Kim Dae-jung Presidential Library and Museum Kim Sung-jae and research fellows worked on fact-checking and document-finding.

President Kim Dae-jung read and revised the manuscript in 2008 and 2009. He also completed additional dictation when necessary.

Four days before his hospitalization at Severance Hospital, on July 9, 2009, President Kim Dae-jung awarded the certificate of editor-in-chief for his autobiography to Kim Taek-geun, and the certificate of assistant editor-in-chief to Chang Ok-chu. He charged them with finishing his autobiography.

After President Kim's death, First Lady Lee Hee-ho examined the final manuscript.

Kim Dae-jung Chronology: 1924–2009

1924	Jan. 6	Born in Hugwang-ri, Haui-myeon, Muan-gun (now known as Sinan-gun), Jeollanam do to father Kim Un-sik and mother Chang Su-geum. In order to avoid compulsory military conscription by the Japanese in 1943, his parents modified his birthdate to December 3, 1925.
1933		Studied traditional Chinese classics under Master Choam Kim Yeon at Deokbong Seodang.
1934	May 12	Transferred to the four-year Ha'ui Elementary School and began the second grade.
1936	Sept. 2	Transferred to Mokpo Public First Normal School after moving to Mokpo for education.
1939	Apr. 5	Entered Mokpo Commercial High School (five-year course; currently, Moksang High School) at the top of his class.
1943	Dec. 23	Graduated from Mokpo Commercial High School in an expedited wartime graduation.
1944	May	Entered Jeonnam Steamship Company, and was soon promoted to a management position.
1945	Apr. 9	Married Cha Yong-ae, with whom he would have two sons, Hong Il and Hong Up.
	Aug. 19	Participated in the Preparatory Committee for National Construction, led by Yeo Un-hyeong.
1946	Feb.	Joined the Sinmin Party, but left after discovering its leftist propensity.
1947	Feb.	Bought a 50-ton boat and established the Mokpo Marine Transport Company.
1948		Changed the name of his company to the Dongyang Marine Transport Company. As the company flourished, he owned two 70-ton ships in addition to a 50-ton ship.
1950	June 25	The Korean War broke out during a business trip in Seoul. Returned on foot to Mokpo around August 10.
	Sept. 28	Escaped execution by the communists in Mokpo Prison.
	Oct.	Repaired two ships to resume his business. Took over the Mokpo Newspaper Company, where he would work as the CEO until March 1952.
	Nov.	Appointed Vice Captain of the Coast Guard Jeonnam Headquarters and worked in the same capacity until October 1951, mostly in charge of the marine transportation of South Korean military supplies.
1951	Mar.	Changed the name of his company from the Dongyang Marine Transport Company to the Mokpo Merchant Ship Company.
1952	May 25	The Busan Political Crisis occurred. After witnessing this incident, he decided to enter the political arena.
	July	Moved his company to Busan and changed its name to the Heungguk Marine Transport Company. Expanded the business by purchasing three used ships from Japan.

(continued)

(continued)

1954	Apr. 21	Revised the Chinese character of the last syllable of his first name from 中 to 仲 in the official registration after finding out that it had been misspelled when it was originally entered. However, he later switched it back to 中.
	May 20	Ran as an independent for the third House of Representative election in Mokpo, but lost.
1955	Apr.	Moved to Seoul and engaged in various social activities, including working as the editor-in-chief at the Korea Labor Issue Research Institute.
	Oct. 1	Contributed a lead article, "Korean Labor Movement's Path," to the October issue of *Sasanggye*.
1956	June 2	Baptized Catholic by Father Kim Cheol-gyu in Archbishop Ro Paul-M's office at Myeongdong Cathedral. His baptismal name was Thomas More.
	Sept. 25	Joined the Democratic Party and worked as a member of the New Faction, led by Dr. Chang Myon.
1958	Apr. 8	Registered as the Democratic Party candidate for the House of Representatives election in Inje, Gangwondo, but this registration was canceled due to fraudulent interference by the Liberal Party.
1959	Mar. 11	According to the Supreme Court's decision, the previous year's cancellation of registration was invalid, and the previous election result was nullified.
	June 5	Ran for the fourth House of Representative special election in Inje, Gangwondo, but lost.
	Aug. 28	Madam Cha Yong-ae died of an acute illness.
1960	Sept.	Appointed and worked for eight months as the spokesman of the Democratic Party.
1961	May 13	Ran for the fifth House of Representative special election and won. Despite this success, he could not be sworn in due to the May 16 Coup d'État.
1962	May 10	Married Lee Hee-ho, with whom he would have a son, Hong Gul.
1963	July 18	Participated in the reconstruction of the Democratic Party and became spokesman.
	Nov. 26	Ran for the sixth Representative election in Mokpo and won.
1964	Apr. 20	Made a five-hour, nineteen-minute speech at the National Assembly in order to delay the ratification of a bill allowing the arrest of Assemblyman Kim Jun-yeon.
1965	May 3	After the establishment of the Minjung Party, he worked as its spokesman and the chair of its policy deliberative committee.
1967	Feb. 2	After the establishment of the Sinmin Party, he worked as its spokesman.
	May 15	His first book, *Echoes of Wrath*, was published.
	June 8	Won the seventh National Assembly election in Mokpo despite the Park Chung-hee regime's Operation Defeat Kim Dae-jung.

(*continued*)

(continued)

1969	July 19	Made a speech titled "The Three-Term Presidency Constitutional Amendment Is a National Polity Reform" at the rally at the Hyochang Field, organized by the Nationwide Struggle Committee Against Three-term Presidency Constitutional Amendment.
1970	Sept. 18	His second book, *The 1970s That I Am Walking*, was published.
	Sept. 29	Nominated as the seventh presidential candidate at the Sinmin Party national convention.
	Oct. 16	Proposed policies at the first press conference as a presidential candidate. The policies included abolishing the Homeland Reserve Army; securing war deterrence by allying with the four powers of the US, China, the USSR, and Japan (Security by Four Powerful Countries); and reconciling and pursuing free exchange between the South and the North.
1971	Feb. 3	Laid out the three-step reunification proposal in a speech at the National Press Club in Washington, DC
	Mar. 13	*Mr. Kim Dae-jung's Mass-participatory Economy Policy: 100 Questions and 100 Answers* was published.
	Apr. 18	Held a campaign rally at Jangchungdan Park, which drew a record audience of a million.
	Apr. 27	Lost the presidential election (earning 46 percent of the votes).
	May 24	His car was hit by a truck in a suspicious traffic accident in Muan during his election campaign tour in support of other Sinmin Party candidates for the National Assembly.
	May 25	Won the eighth National Assembly election (national constituency).
1972	May 10	Mother Madam Chang Su-geum passed away.
	July 13	Proposed at a press conference after the South-North Joint Communiqué on July 4 that both the South and the North simultaneously join the UN.
	Oct. 18	Began political exile after publishing a statement in opposition of the October Yusin, the news of which reached him during his medical visit to Japan.
1972 Oct. to 1973 Aug.		Engaged in activities against the Yusin regime in Japan and the US.
	June 28	*Dictatorship and My Fight* (in Japanese) was published in Japan.
	Aug. 8	The Kim Dae-jung Kidnapping and Attempted Murder Incident occurred. Korean CIA agents kidnapped him from Grand Hotel in Tokyo and attempted to drown him.
	Aug. 13	Brought back to his house in Donggyo-dong, Seoul, by the kidnappers. Imprisoned in his house and banned from all political activities.
1974	Feb. 25	His father, Kim Un-sik, passed away.
	Nov. 27	Participated in the National Congress for the Recovery of Democracy, an organization led by the union of out-of-office politicians and civilian movement leaders.
1976	Mar. 1	Led the March 1st Democratic National Salvation Declaration with democratic leaders such as Yun Po-sun, Jeong Il-hyeong, Ham Sok-hon, and Moon Ik-hwan.

(*continued*)

(continued)

	Mar. 10	Arrested and detained in Seoul Prison with other leaders who signed the March 1st Democratic National Salvation Declaration.
1977	Mar. 22	The Supreme Court confirmed his five-year sentence by dismissing the appeal.
	Apr. 14	Transferred to Jinju Prison.
	May 7	Began a six-day hunger strike in protest of the prison interview ban.
	Dec. 19	Transferred to Seoul National University Hospital, where he soon waged a hunger strike in protest of severe human rights violations, including interview, letter, and exercise ban, and window blocking.
1978	Dec. 27	Released after a ten-month term on a stay of execution of the sentence, only to immediately be put under a long-term house arrest.
1979	Mar. 1	Led the establishment of the National Coalition for Democracy and Reunification with democracy movement leaders, such as Yun Po-sun, Ham Sok-hon, and Moon Ik-hwan. Detained three times as its co-president.
	Dec. 8	Released from his 226-day house imprisonment when Emergency Measure #9 was lifted after President Park's October 26 assassination.
1980	Mar. 1	Received a special pardon and restoration of civil rights.
	Mar. 26	Gave a public speech for the first time in nine years at the YWCA.
	May 13	Appealed for the self-control of student demonstrators when the protest intensified.
	May 16	Presented six articles on the state of affairs control (including the immediate lifting of martial law; release, pardon, and restitution of all political prisoners; and the abandonment of the government-led constitutional amendment) at a joint press conference with Sinmin Party president Kim Young-sam.
	May 17	Detained in his house in Donggyo-dong after the expansion of the Emergency Martial Law.
	Aug. 9	Imprisoned in the army prison.
	Sept. 11	The prosecutor demanded capital punishment for him for violation of the National Security Law, martial law, the Anti-communism Law, and Foreign Exchange Management Law, arguing that he organized the anti-national Korean Democracy Restoration and Unification Promotion National Congress and acted as its ringleader.
	Sept. 13	Gave an hour-and-forty-eight-minute final statement at the eighteenth session of the Kim Dae-jung Conspiracy of Rebellion Incident trial.
	Sept. 17	Sentenced to capital punishment.
	Nov. 3	The capital punishment sentence was confirmed at the review trial, which occurred at the Army Grand Bench of the High Court.
	Nov. 6	Appealed to the Army Grand Branch of the Supreme Court together with eleven other defendants in the Kim Dae-jung Conspiracy of Rebellion Incident.
1981	Jan. 23	An hour after the Supreme Court confirmed his capital punishment, his sentence was reduced to life imprisonment in the cabinet meeting "in consideration of the appeal by friendly countries and himself and for the sake of national harmony."

(*continued*)

(continued)

	Jan. 31	Transferred from the army prison to Cheongju Prison.
	Nov. 3	Awarded the Bruno Kreisky Peace Prize in prison.
1982	Mar. 2	Received sentence reduction from life imprisonment to twenty years.
	Dec. 23	Left for America with family to take care of his medical condition, after being released on suspension of execution of prison term.
1983	Jan. 31	Made a public statement about the status of democracy and human rights in Korea during an interview with *Newsweek*.
	May 16	Awarded an honorary doctorate in law from Emory University in America.
	July	Established the Korean Human Rights Research Institute.
	July	Participated in demonstrations with Korean-Americans on the streets of Washington, DC, and New York City in support of Mr. Kim Young-sam's hunger strike.
	Sept.	Served as a visiting scholar at Harvard University's Center for International Affairs. Submitted a thesis on the Korean economy, which was later published as a book, *Mass-participatory Economy: A Democratic Alternative for Korea*, at the end of the year-long visiting scholarship.
	Dec. 23	*Kim Dae-jung's Prison Writings* was published.
1985	Feb. 8	Returned home despite Korean authorities' objection and friendly worries about the possibility of his assassination after his twenty-six-month exile. Separated from other people upon arrival at the airport and imprisoned at home.
1985	Feb.–June 1987	Imprisoned at home altogether fifty-five times.
1985	Mar. 6	Although the political activities ban on him was finally lifted, he was still excluded from amnesty and reinstatement and therefore banned from political activities.
	Mar. 18	Accepted the position of the Council for the Promotion of Democratization (CPD) co-chairmanship with Kim Young-sam.
	Nov.	*Mass-participatory Economy: A Democratic Alternative* (in English) and *Conscience in Action* were published.
1986	Feb. 12	Led the 10 million signature-gathering campaign, urging a constitutional amendment in favor of a direct presidential election with the Sinmin Party and the CPD.
	Nov. 5	Declared his intention not to run for the presidential election if the military regime voluntarily accepts the direct presidential election system.
1987	Apr. 6	Declared the founding of a new party with Kim Young-sam.
	Apr. 8–June 25	House imprisonment for seventy-eight days.
	July 10	Received amnesty and reinstatement together with 2300 other activists, including those involved in the Kim Dae-jung Conspiracy of Rebellion Incident and the Gwangju Uprising after the June 29 Declaration by Minjeong Party president Roh Tae-woo.

(*continued*)

(continued)

	Sept. 8	Visited Gwangju for the first time in sixteen years and paid his respects at the Mangwoldong graveyard. Visited Mokpo and Hauido Island for the first time in twenty-eight years.
	Oct. 27	Awarded the George Meany Human Rights Award from the American Federation of Labor and Congress of Industrial Organizations (AFL-CIO) in America.
	Nov. 12	Founded the Pyeonghwa Minju (Peace and Democracy) Party. Nominated for presidential candidacy at the party convention.
	Dec. 16	Lost the thirteenth presidential election.
1988	Apr. 26	Won the thirteenth term National Assembly election (national constituency).
	May 18	Reached an agreement on five items, including the Investigation of the Truth of the May 18 Gwangju Democratization Movement and the Investigation of the Fifth Republic's Corruption from Political Power at the three opposition party presidents' conference.
	Nov. 18	Testified as a witness at the May 18 Gwangju Democratization Movement Committee at the National Assembly that the Kim Dae-jung Conspiracy of Rebellion Incident was a fabrication by the new junta, led by General Chun Doo-hwan, who used it to justify his coup d'état.
1989	Aug. 12	Arrested, interrogated overnight, and indicted in relation to the Suh Kyung-won Illegal Visit to the North Incident.
1990	Jan. 22	Began the struggle against the illicit three-party merger by Roh Tae-woo, Kim Young-sam, and Kim Jong-pil.
	July 27	Reelected as the party president at the Pyeongmin Party convention.
	Oct. 8	Waged a thirteen-day hunger strike, demanding the implementation of a local autonomy system, abandonment of the parliamentary government system scheme, the halt on the Agency for National Security Planning's (ANSP) political spying, and the solution of the people's economic plight.
1991	Apr. 9	Established the Sinmin (Sinminju yeonhap) Party by welcoming out-of-office leaders and former opposition party members, including Lee Oo-chung, into the Pyeongmin Party's fold.
	Sept. 10	Reestablished the Democratic Party by merging with the Democratic Party, led by Mr. Lee Ki-taek.
1992	Mar. 24	Elected to the fourteenth National Assembly term (national constituency).
	May 26	Nominated to the fourteenth presidential candidacy at the Democratic Party convention.
	Sept. 7	Received a Ph.D. from the Diplomatic Academy of Russia under the Ministry of Foreign Affairs with a dissertation entitled "On the Principles of Birth and Development of Democracy in Korean Society."
	Dec. 18	Lost the fourteenth presidential election.
	Dec. 19	Declared retirement from his political career.
1993	Jan. 26	Left for England and began a visiting scholarship at Cambridge University.
	July 4	Returned home from England.
	Dec. 10	His book *For a New Beginning* was published.

(continued)

(continued)

1994	Jan. 27	Established the Asia Pacific Peace Foundation in order to study Asian democratization and Korean reunification.
	May 12	Proposed a package deal between North Korea and the US and President Carter's visit to North Korea during a US National Press Club address.
	Sept. 20	Gave an address titled "The Sunshine Policy Based on Strong Will" at America's Heritage Foundation to ease the intensified tension between South and North Korea and between North Korea and America since the death of Kim Il-sung on July 8.
	Dec. 2	Founded the Asia and Pacific Democratic Leaders Council and became its co-chairman.
1995	July 13	Publicly accepted fifty-one national assemblymen's request that he resume his political career.
	Sept. 5	Established the National Congress for New Politics party.
1997	May 19	Nominated to the fifteenth presidential candidacy at the party convention.
	Oct. 27	Agreed with Jaminryeon president Kim Jong-pil for his unified presidential candidacy.
	Dec. 18	Won the fifteenth presidential election.
	Dec. 20	Agreed to pardon and rehabilitate former Presidents Chun and Roh in the conference with President Kim Young-sam, as well as to form the Emergency Economic Committee, a temporary organization to handle the foreign currency crisis until the new government was launched.
1998	Jan. 15	Attended the launch ceremony of the labor-employer-government tripartite commission at the Labor Research Institute.
	Feb. 25	Inaugurated as the fifteenth president.
	Mar. 1	Proposed the inter-Korean exchange of special envoys in the special address in honor of the March 1 Movement anniversary.
	Oct. 8	Agreed on "A New Japan-Republic of Korea Partnership Toward the Twenty-first Century" at the Korea-Japan summit.
	Dec. 15	Agreed to overcome an unfortunate period between Vietnam and Korea and develop a relationship of future-oriented friendly cooperation at a Korea-Vietnam summit.
	Dec. 16	Proposed the establishment of the East Asian Vision Group (EAVG) at the Association of Southeast Asian Nations (ASEAN) and Korea-China-Japan summit (9+3).
	Dec. 29	The Korean Teachers Union (KTU) was legalized.
1999	July 4	Selected as the recipient of the Liberty Medal by the city of Philadelphia.
	Sept. 7	The National Basic Livelihood Security Act was legislated.
	Nov. 23	The Korean Confederation of Trade Unions was legalized.
2000	Jan. 12	The Law Regarding the Compensation for the People Related to the Gwangju Democratization Movement was legislated.
	Jan. 15	The three Democratic Reform Laws—the Special Law for the Truth-finding of Suspicious Deaths, the Law for the Restoration of Honor and Compensation for People Related to the Democratization Movement, and the Special Law for the Truth-finding and Recovery of Honor for Victims of the Jeju April 3 Incident—were legislated.

(*continued*)

(continued)

	Jan. 20	Established the New Millennium Democratic Party and was inaugurated as the party president.
	Mar. 9	Published the Berlin Declaration for the dissolution of the Cold War system in the Korean Peninsula and the establishment of permanent peace and inter-Korean reconciliation and cooperation during a speech at the Free University of Berlin.
	June 13–15	Held the historic inter-Korean summit in Pyongyang for the first time in fifty-five years since the national division, and published the June 15 joint statement, titled the North and South Korean Accord.
	June 26	The first nomination hearing was held at the National Assembly.
	Aug. 1	The separation of pharmacy and clinic was implemented.
	Sept. 2	Sixty-three long-term prisoners from North Korea were returned.
	Sept. 18	Attended the groundbreaking ceremony for the connection of the Seoul-Sinuiju Railway.
	Dec. 10	Won the Nobel Peace Prize.
2001	Jan. 29	The Ministry of Women was launched.
	May	The Law for the National Human Rights Commission was legislated.
	June 29	The National Tax Service lodged complaints against *Chosun Ilbo*, the *DongA Ilbo*, and the *Kukmin Ilbo* newspapers and their owners as well as previous owners and the companies of the *Joongang Ilbo*, *Hankook Ilbo*, and *Daehan Maeil* newspapers.
	July	Legislated the Anti-corruption Law.
	Aug. 23	Released from the state of IMF economic trusteeship three years ahead of schedule.
	Nov. 5	Proposed to establish the East Asian Free Trade Agreement (FTA) and the East Asian Forum, based on cooperation between civilians and governments, at the fifth ASEAN+3 summit.
2002	Jan. 14	The Special Act on Three Large Rivers (Nakdonggang, Geumgang, and Yeongsangang) was legislated.
	Feb. 20	Visited the Dorasan Train Station, the northernmost station on the Seoul-Sinuiju Railway in South Korea, with President Bush.
	July 11	Nominated a woman, Madam Chang Sang, to prime minister for the first time since the establishment of the Republic of Korea.
	July 27	The May 18 Cemetery in Gwangju was elevated to a national cemetery.
	Sept. 14	South and North Korean military authorities agreed to jointly remove landmines from the DMZ for the construction of the Seoul-Sinuiju Railway and the East Coast Railway in the working level conference in Panmunjeom. This was the first occasion of DMZ opening since the cease-fire in 1953.
	Nov. 6	Attended a ceremony to celebrate a historic 10 million household users of high-speed Internet.
	Dec. 13	Received a phone call from President Bush, during which he expressed his sincere regrets over the deaths of two South Korean girls who were accidentally killed during a training exercise by a US military vehicle.
2003	Feb. 15	Attended the signing ceremony of the Korea-Chile FTA.
	Feb. 24	Returned home to Donggyo-dong after leaving the presidential office.

(*continued*)

(continued)

	May 10	Hospitalized at Yonsei University Severance Hospital and received coronary artery bypass surgery.
	May 12	Began dialysis during hospitalization at Severance Hospital.
	May 27	Selected as the eighth Nutbom Unification Award recipient.
	June 12	For the first time criticized the appointment of a special prosecutor to investigate money transfer to North Korea during a media interview in honor of the third anniversary of the inter-Korean summit.
	Aug. 8	Received the seventh Manhae Grand Prize for Peace.
	Oct. 23	Petitioned for a retrial of the Kim Dae-jung Conspiracy of Rebellion Incident.
	Nov. 3	The Kim Dae-jung Presidential Library and Museum opened.
	Dec. 9	Awarded the Grand Cross of the Order of Merit from the Chilean government.
	Dec. 15	Awarded the Merit Award at the Chunsa Art Film Festival.
2004	Jan. 29	Attended the retrial for the Kim Dae-jung Conspiracy of Rebellion Incident and was given the verdict of "not guilty" twenty-three years after the first guilty verdict.
	May 10–19	Toured three European countries (France, Norway, and Switzerland) and gave lectures at the OECD, the Nobel Committee, and the WHO.
	June 15	Urged Chairman Kim Jong-il's return visit during a special address at the international conference in Seoul jointly held by the Kim Dae-jung Presidential Library and Museum from the South and the Unification Research Institute from the North.
	June 29	Visited China and met Chinese leaders, including President Jiang Zemin.
	Nov. 6	Visited Europe upon the invitation of Swedish Prime Minister Göran Persson, Mayor of Rome Walter Veltroni, and the Gorbachev Foundation. Delivered a keynote address at the fifth World Summit of Nobel Peace Laureates in Rome.
	Dec. 6	Gave a special address at the plenary session of the second East Asia Forum in Kuala Lumpur, Malaysia.
	Dec. 22	*The Twenty-first Century and the Korean Nation*, a collection of his major addresses and interviews, was published.
2005	June 12	Awarded the Grand Cross 1st Class of the Order of Merit of the Federal Republic of Germany from the German government.
	Aug. 10	Hospitalized at Severance Hospital for a slight fever and inflammation and discharged on August 21.
	Aug. 16	Received Chairman Kim's invitation to visit the North from North Korean delegates who visited him at the hospital.
2006	Mar. 21	Received an honorary doctorate in political science from Yeungnam University.
	Nov. 4	Showed the exhibit hall of the Kim Dae-jung Presidential Library and Museum to President Roh Moo-hyun and First Lady Kwon Yang-sook and had lunch with them in his private home.
	Dec. 7	Awarded the 2007 Van Fleet Award from Korea Society.
2007	May 16	Awarded the first Freedom Award from Free University of Berlin.

(*continued*)

(continued)

	Sept. 17–29	Visited New York and Washington, DC. Met with former president Clinton, Henry Kissinger, and Madeline Albright and discussed the North Korean nuclear crisis.
	Oct. 9	Met with President Roh Moo-hyun at the Blue House and listened to his explanation about the results of the recent second inter-Korean summit.
	Oct. 30	Awarded an honorary doctorate in law from Ritsumeikan University in Kyoto, Japan.
2008	Apr. 22	Visited Harvard University and gave a lecture at the Kennedy School on "The Sunshine Policy is the Way to Success."
	Sept. 11	Attended the World Summit of Nobel Peace Laureates in Stavanger, Norway.
	Oct. 27	Attended and gave a keynote address at the Forum on Northeast Asian Regional Development and Cooperation. Went to Dandong afterward and looked around the Amnok River on the border between North Korea and China.
2009	May 5	Visited China and met Vice President Xi Jinping.
	May 29	Attended the late president Roh Moo-hyun's funeral and expressed his sympathy to First Lady Kwon Yang-sook.
	June 11	Attended and gave an address on "Let us all become conscience in action" at the ninth commemorative event of the June 15 Inter-Korean Accord.
	July 13	Hospitalized at Severance Hospital for pneumonic symptoms.
	Aug. 18	Passed away.

Index[1]

---

[1]Note: Page numbers followed by 'n' denote notes.

© The Author(s) 2019
Kim Dae-jung, *Conscience in Action*,
https://doi.org/10.1007/978-981-10-7623-7

Milton Keynes UK
Ingram Content Group UK Ltd.
UKHW021414060923
428074UK00028B/447